# Short-Term Financial Management

THIRD EDITION

# Short-Term Financial Management


TERRY S. MANESS
*Baylor University*

JOHN T. ZIETLOW
*Lee University*



THOMSON
SOUTH-WESTERN

Australia · Canada · Mexico · Singapore · Spain · United Kingdom · United States

THOMSON
SOUTH-WESTERN

**Short-Term Financial Management**
**Third Edition**

Terry S. Maness
John T. Zietlow

**VP/Editorial Director:**
Jack W. Calhoun

**VP/Editor-in-Chief:**
Dave Schaut

**Acquisitions Editor:**
Mike Reynolds

**Senior Developmental Editor:**
Elizabeth Thomson

**Marketing Manager:**
Heather MacMaster

**Production Editor:**
Cliff Kallemeyn

**Technology Project Manager:**
John Barans

**Manufacturing Coordinator:**
Sandee Milewski

**Senior Designer:**
Anne Marie Reckow

**Production House:**
Litten Editing and Production, Inc.

**Compositor:**
GGS Information Services, Inc.

**Printer:**
Courier
Kendallville, IN



Printed in the United States of America
3 4 5 07 06 05

ISBN: 0-324-20293-8

Library of Congress Control Number:
2004104842



For more information contact South-Western,
5191 Natorp Boulevard,
Mason, Ohio 45040.
Or you can visit our Internet site at:
http://www.swlearning.com

This Book is Dedicated to

*My wife Nancy, son David, daughter-in-law Stacy, daughter Amy, and son-in-law Matt*

*T.S.M*

*My wife Kathy, and daughters Julie and Christy*

*J.T.Z*

# Preface

As we continue to teach and learn more about the area of short-term financial management, we are more convinced than ever about the importance of this area of financial management for our students. These beliefs are confirmed by the increasing number of business schools offering course work in this area, by continued discussions with corporate practitioners, and by surveys indicating the amount of time that financial managers spend in this area. Widely publicized accounting scandals and earnings manipulation have refocused financial managers and investors on cash flows.

Over the years, we have taught short-term financial management as a separate course or as a topic within other finance courses and have found that both undergraduate and MBA interest in this subject continues to grow. Numerous colleges and universities, including our own, have split either the introductory corporate finance or the upper-level financial management curriculum into two courses, one of which is titled Working Capital Management, Short-Term Financial Management, Treasury Management, Operational Financial Management, or Financial Management II. Topics covered in these courses typically include many or all of the following treasury management topics: liquidity analysis; inventory, credit, and payables management; cash collection, concentration, and disbursement systems; cash forecasting; short-term investing, borrowing, and risk management; bank relationship management; international cash management; financial risk management; and finally, electronic commerce and treasury information systems. We strongly believe that many important corporate decisions relate specifically to these short-term topics and that many of these topics are likely to grow in importance as we navigate through the twenty-first century. Already, as one widely publicized study found, financial managers spend over one-half of each day managing current assets and liabilities.

Although several other fine textbooks include limited coverage of the topic of short-term finance, we have not found any of them to be satisfactory across the board. Most courses currently require additional coverage of treasury and working capital management. Several key topics that need to be addressed more thoroughly include bank selection and relationship management, credit management, short-term investing and borrowing, and treasury management information systems. Several texts include spotty coverage of the core cash management topics, and in our view, none have adequately utilized the cash flow timeline as an integrating focus. Others fail to incorporate shareholder value maximization as an overriding decision criterion. Finally, we have found that the books were either written at too high a level, making them difficult to use in an MBA-level course—and especially an undergraduate course—or, are oriented too much toward practitioners. Practical aspects are important, but so is an analytical approach to the subject. Practice, informed by theory, is our goal. We cannot improve on René Stulz's comment in receiving an award at the 1999 Eastern Finance Association annual meeting: ". . . everything that makes finance interesting has to do with what happens in the presence of frictions. It is time to reverse the order of things and focus on the real world first."

## Coverage

This textbook is appropriate for the second undergraduate finance course in Financial Management, Short-Term Financial Management, Working Capital Management, Treasury Management, Operational Financial Management, and Cash Management. It is also addressed to MBA-level Financial Management, Treasury Management, and Short-Term Financial Management courses, and we have included several cases and appendices that are especially attractive to upper-level undergraduate and MBA courses. Students should have completed an introductory corporate finance course as a prerequisite.

We have titled the book *Short-Term Financial Management* for two reasons. First, although we cover most of the topics of treasury management, we do not address long-term financing and pension issues that are part of that field. Second, we include current liability management, bank relationship management, and risk management issues, implying that much more than working capital management or cash management is included here. Nevertheless, we are confident that treasury department practitioners and those preparing for the Certified Treasury Professional (CTP; formerly the Certified Cash Manager, or CCM) exam will find much of the material they need within our presentation. We are both certified—Terry as a permanently certified CCM; John's CCM converted over to the new designation of CTP—and we continue to stay alert to new developments in the treasury management field.

We believe that the following strengths characterize our book:

- Broader and better integrated coverage of treasury and working capital management. Not only are core cash management concepts covered with adequate detail, but the text also uses valuation and the cash flow timeline as integrating themes. In-depth coverage is provided for credit management, bank selection and relationship management, and interest rate risk management. Furthermore, we provide coverage of inventory management, treasury information systems, and international treasury management. Two chapters on short-term investments and one chapter each on cash forecasting and short-term borrowing fill out the topical coverage.
- Reader interest is captured by using a lucid writing style with a decision-making emphasis including numerous real-world examples and management decision dilemmas, which are solved later in the chapter. Text-integrating cases help the student put seemingly unrelated topics together. We also provide a special chapter on short-term financial modeling in order that interrelationships in cash, inventory, credit, payables, investments, and borrowing will be driven home. Reader interest and retention is also aided by chapter-beginning objectives. Survey evidence of state-of-the-art financial management practices is included throughout the text, along with footnote or end-of-chapter citations for readers wishing to review the empirical findings in greater detail. Also in this edition, we offer additional Web sites at the end of each chapter that may be used to supplement chapter material or as a basis for Web-based homework assignments.
- Up-to-date presentations with the most recent developments in treasury management, banking deregulation, globalization of financial services delivery, and electronic ordering and payment. The reader will also find carefully incorporated sections on recent developments, such as electronic commerce and international cash management. We note, with interest, the recent observation by a Bank of America officer that Enterprise Resource Planning (ERP) integration with treasury systems is moving working capital management closer to real time—a development we try to capture in the numerous Focus on Practice boxes throughout the text. We also offer integrated sections in almost every chapter focusing on the international aspects of that topic, and for those desiring more, we have included an entire chapter on international cash management with a heavy focus on managing foreign exchange risk.
- Cohesive organization is used throughout the text. Part I includes an introduction, valuation concepts, and liquidity analysis and management. Part II focuses on working capital management including credit and receivables, inventory, payables, and ac-

cruals. We provide thorough coverage of the payment system in Part III, which provides the infrastructure for developing cash collection, concentration, and disbursement systems. Part IV includes two chapters focusing on cash forecasting and financial modeling. Part V provides coverage of the short-term financial market environment along with the development of short-term investment and borrowing strategies. This part also includes a chapter on managing multinational cash flows. Part VI concludes with discussions of managing financial risk with futures, options, and swaps; utilizing electronic business methods; and managing treasury information.

- Problem-solving skill enhancement is provided through the numerous end-of-chapter questions and problems, as well as the cases. The questions enable students to test their understanding of chapter concepts and relationships, and the problems require students to demonstrate understanding of each chapter's decision-making approach. Each formula is illustrated with an example to assist students in how to apply the formula.
- End-of-text appendix on the basic time value of money calculations. This assists the students who may not have received a strong presentation on time value computations, or who may have forgotten how to make the computations.

## Changes to This Edition

The following highlights comprise the major changes found in this edition:

- "Useful Web Sites" appearing at the end of each chapter are updated and expanded.
- A new section on the "Cash Conversion Efficiency" metric has been added to the liquidity analysis chapter.
- A new section on the NPV of changes in the cash conversion period has been added to the valuation chapter.
- A number of new research findings have been added to the chapters on liquidity analysis, credit management, cash collections, cash position, cash disbursements, short-term investments, short-term borrowing, and electronic commerce and information management.
- A key piece of legislation passed in 2003, Check 21, was incorporated into the payments and disbursements chapters. This will greatly reduce check float in future years. Accordingly, we placed less emphasis on check float in the disbursements chapter.
- Many statistics were updated in the payments and banking systems chapter. New versions of the availability analysis statement and availability schedule are included.
- The redesigned Dun & Bradstreet Business Information Report, now Web-based, is presented in Chapter 5.
- More international payment system information appears throughout, including the euro, globalization, and outsourcing.
- Coverage of information-based products, including ERP systems and treasury workstations, has been greatly expanded in Chapter 19.
- Revised PowerPoint presentation outlines are available to adopters.
- Many of the Focus on Practice boxes were updated, and new ones were added.
- End-of-chapter questions and problems have been modified in many chapters, and new problems have been added in several chapters.

- Important pedagogical items such as Chapter Objectives that begin each chapter, the Financial Dilemma vignettes highlighting the key issue in the chapter, Focus on Practice boxes that present actual business practices related to the material discussed in the chapters, and Focused Cases and Integrative Cases were maintained in this edition.

### Course Supplements

The course supplements have been designed to provide flexibility to instructors teaching the course at either the undergraduate or MBA level. Emphasis can be placed where the instructor wishes and can be varied depending on the background of the students. The following supplements are available:

*INSTRUCTOR'S MANUAL* A very complete instructor's manual is available on the text's Web site, **http://maness.swlearning.com**, and in print. The Instructor's Manual includes notes regarding the best approach for undergraduate or MBA-level coverage, and solutions for all questions and problems. We also include an array of test questions, both objective and essay, for those professors wishing to use them. This edition's supplement was developed by Dev Prasad, at the University of Massachusetts-Lowell.

*SPREADSHEET SOLUTIONS* Found on the text's Web site, **http://maness.swlearning.com**, all adopters will have access to worksheets for all end-of-chapter problems, financial spreadsheet solutions, and models for cases. The instructor may provide copies of these spreadsheets for student use, or they can be loaded on the host institution's network for more convenient student access. Several instructors have commented on how much they appreciate the flexibility of doing "what-if" analysis of key inputs when covering homework problems.

*POWERPOINT SLIDES* Found on the text's Web site, **http://maness.swlearning.com**, all adopters will have access to the lecture presentation notes in the form of Microsoft PowerPoint slides.

## ACKNOWLEDGMENTS AND CREDITS

Many people made significant and helpful contributions to this book. Without the classroom experience, guidance, and practical advice of these individuals, this book could not have been written. We welcome any constructive criticism any reader might have in order to further improve the presentation.

We were blessed with the assistance of an excellent group of reviewers who helped guide the development of the first edition of this text, and we wish to continue to acknowledge their contributions. We very much appreciate their helpful assistance and ideas for improved presentation. The following individuals provided valuable input:

William Beranek
University of Georgia

David A. Burnie
Western Michigan University

Michael D. Carpenter
University of Kentucky

C. Steven Cole
University of North Texas

Stephen Dukas
Kansas State University

Joseph E. Finnerty
University of Illinois

Alan W. Frankle
Boise State University

Erika W. Gilbert
Illinois State University

James B. Kehr
Miami University of Ohio

Yong H. Kim
University of Cincinnati

Edgar Norton
Illinois State University

Gabriel Ramirez
SUNY-Binghamton

Frederick W. Siegel
University of Louisville

Robert J. Sweeney
Wright State University

David J. Wright
Notre Dame University

To aid in the development of the second edition, South-Western obtained the assistance of the following professors. We very much appreciate their helpful suggestions and ideas.

Brian Belt
University of Missouri at Kansas City

Steven A. Carvell
Cornell University

Richard Edelman
The American University

Joseph Finnerty
University of Illinois at Urbana-Champaign

James A. Gentry
University of Illinois

Erika W. Gilbert
Illinois State University

Preston Gilson
Fort Hays State University

Waldemar M. Goulet
Wright State University

Bernie J. Grablowsky
United Property Associates

Yong H. Kim
University of Cincinnati

Duncan J. Kretovich
Portland State University

Surendra K. Mansinghka
San Francisco State University

D. J. Masson
The Resource Alliance

Graham R. Mitenko
University of Nebraska at Omaha

Donald A. Nast
Florida State University

Edgar Norton
Illinois State University

Josee St. Pierre
Universite du Quebec a Trois-Rivieres

Paul Ruggeri
Siena College

Daniel L. Schneid
Central Michigan University

Michael D. Sherman
University of Toledo

Luc Soenen
California Polytechnic University

John D. Stowe
University of Missouri

Antoinette C. Tessmer
University of Illinois at Urbana-Champaign

Alan Wong
Indiana University Southeast

In the present edition, South-Western obtained the assistance of the following professors, whose suggestions were very helpful in improving and updating the text:

Dorla Evans
University of Alabama, Huntsville

Erika W. Gilbert
Illinois State University

Glenn Pettengill
Emporia State University

Sorin A. Tuluca
Fairleigh Dickinson University

We are especially indebted to the following treasury management, consulting, and bank personnel who provided the cutting-edge information we believe sets our book apart: Dennis Aron, David Bochnovic, Terry Callahan, Kathy Carr, Peter Crane, Kim Finley, Debbie Gorman, Bob Gray, William Kiesel, Coleen Knerr, Maryann Kriner, J. R. Lawhead, Everett Likens, Jeff Love, Eric Pierce, Davis Smith, Deborah Smith, Karen Thor, Bob Wiese, and Mike Wright.

We thank Steven Lay of Lee University and David Skinner of Mount Vernon Nazarene University for their assistance in checking the calculus derivation for the net present value of cash conversion period section in Chapter 3.

The following individuals provided invaluable help in assembling background materials and providing clerical assistance: Anna Ellis and Amberly Noble at Lee University. The support of each of our institutions was also instrumental in allowing time for writing this edition.

We would like to thank the staff at South-Western, particularly Cliff Kallemeyn, and Malvine Litten and Denise Morton, of LEAP, Inc., for the outstanding editorial and production support that helped us complete the revision process. James Reidel did a great job tracking necessary copyright permissions. Thanks also go to Elizabeth Thomson and Mike Reynolds, Senior Developmental Editor and Executive Editor, respectively, at Thomson Business and Professional Publishing.

We are deeply grateful to Dev Prasad at the University of Massachusetts-Lowell, for updating the Instructor's Manual and Test Bank.

Finally, we deeply appreciate the two professors who introduced us to a lifelong love of working capital and treasury management: Ken Burns of the University of Memphis and Ned Hill at Brigham Young University (formerly at Indiana University).

*Terry S. Maness*
Terry_Maness@baylor.edu

*John T. Zietlow*
jzietlow@leeuniversity.edu

# Brief Contents

# Contents

## PART II Management of Working Capital 96

### CHAPTER 4 Inventory Management 98



### CHAPTER 5 Accounts Receivable Management 126



### CHAPTER 6 Credit Policy and Collections 192



### CHAPTER 7 Managing Payables and Accruals 234

## PART V Short-Term Investment and Financing 478

### CHAPTER 14 The Money Market 480



### CHAPTER 15 Short-Term Investment Management 528



### CHAPTER 16 Short-Term Financing 568



### CHAPTER 17 Managing Multinational Cash Flows 592

## PART VI Special Topics 610

PART 1

# Introduction to Liquidity

Part I introduces the concept of liquidity. In Chapter 1, the management of the various working capital accounts such as inventory, receivables, payables, and accruals is linked to the impact each area has on cash flow and how these areas cause cash flow and profit to diverge. This chapter also introduces the key pedagogical tool used throughout the text, the cash flow timeline diagram, which is in each chapter to link the current decision-making area to the overall cash flow timeline. Chapter 2 introduces the reader to measurement issues of liquidity. Many traditional liquidity indicators are shown to measure other aspects of the firm such as solvency rather than liquidity. The chapter differentiates between solvency measures, liquidity measures, and financial flexibility measures. Part I concludes with a chapter focused on the valuation of cash flows. Strategic financial decisions such as capital budgeting and tactical financial decisions such as working capital management must consider the value impact of changing the pattern and amount of cash flows.

CHAPTER

1

# The Role of Working Capital

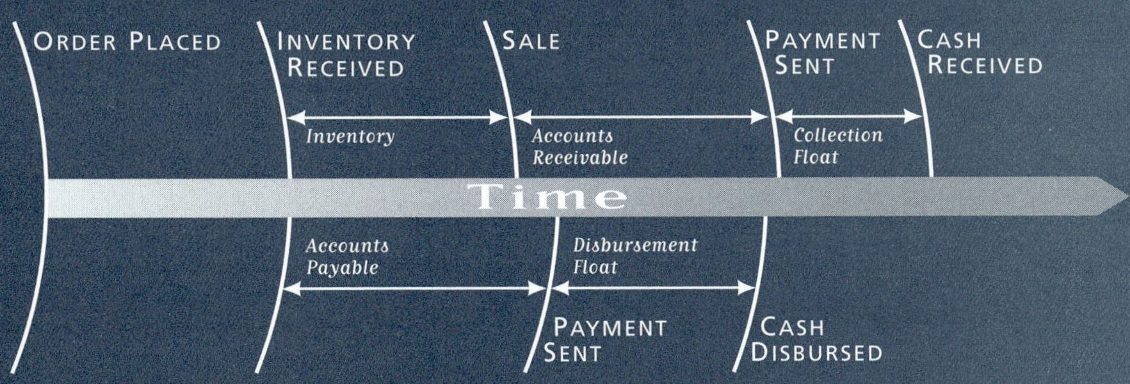

## OBJECTIVES

*After studying this chapter, you should be able to:*

- view a firm as a system of cash flows as represented by a timeline.
- understand how depreciation charges and working capital flows create a disparity between profit and cash flow.
- appreciate the basic issues involved in managing working capital.

It may be apparent that an unprofitable firm will experience financial difficulties that can lead to bankruptcy. It is less obvious how seemingly profitable firms may also experience financial strains and end up bankrupt. This will be the case if operating cash flows are not managed properly. If too many resources are tied up in inventory or if accounts receivable are not collected in a timely fashion, then even a profitable company may not be able to pay its bills. A successful firm manages its operations from both a profit perspective as well as from a cash flow perspective.

In this chapter we will discuss the role that working capital plays in management of the operations of a firm. We begin by presenting the firm as a system of cash flows and discuss how operating activities impact cash flow and the various accounts that make up the financial statements of the firm. We clarify how the different working capital accounts depicted on the balance sheet reflect a disparity between profit and cash flow. A cash flow timeline structure is introduced, which serves as the main pedagogical tool used throughout the textbook.

We then conclude with an introductory discussion focusing on the management aspects of the various working capital accounts followed by a discussion of the appropriate or optimal level of working capital.

### FINANCIAL DILEMMA

How Does Profit Differ from Cash Flow?

Sports Junction, Inc., a retail sporting goods corporation, just hired a new treasurer. The prime selling season is just beginning, and the company's management is looking forward to a record level of sales. The company is very profitable, with a gross profit margin of 40 percent. Customers pay on time, averaging 30 days. The company doesn't use trade credit but instead pays for all inventory when purchased. The company's policy is to keep one month's sales on hand in inventory. Although the company is profitable, the new treasurer is wondering whether the investment in inventory and receivables, during a brisk period of business, may eventually cause cash flow problems.

## INTRODUCING THE CASH FLOW TIMELINE

Manufacturers purchase raw materials for production purposes, while retailers purchase inventory from wholesalers to satisfy their customers' demand. The inventory is converted into accounts receivable as customers make purchases on credit. Receivables are then collected by customers remitting payment to the company. Cash is received when the payment medium, such as a check, is collected through the banking system. Delay in collecting payment on the check on behalf of the seller is known as **collection float**.

The initial purchase of inventory creates an accounts payable owed to suppliers. The actual disbursement of cash occurs when the payment medium used to pay for the purchase, such as a check, is collected by the banking system. Delays created in the collection of payment on behalf of the supplier is referred to as **disbursement float**. The relationships between these various working capital accounts along with collection and disbursement delays are depicted on a timeline as shown in Exhibit 1–1.

Exhibit 1–1

*A Cash Flow Timeline Diagram*

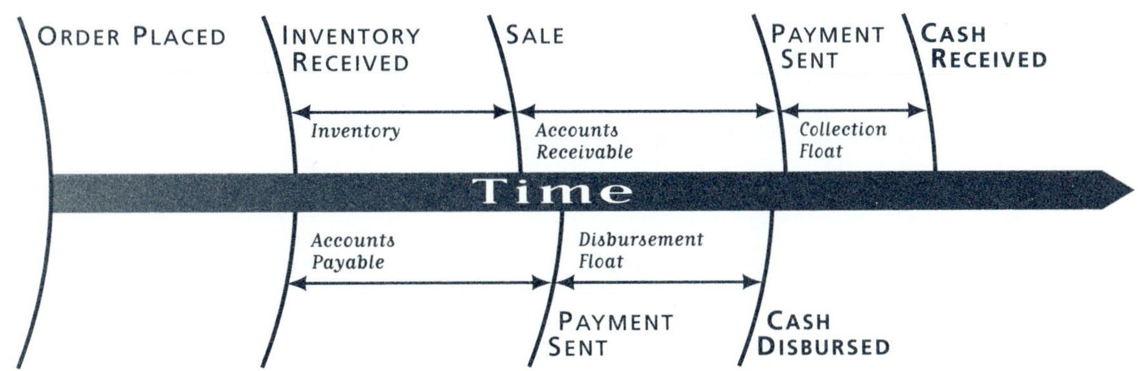


The **cash flow timeline** diagram relates the various working capital accounts on a time dimension scale. Indeed, it is this time dimension on which working capital management must focus. The longer that resources remain idle in inventory, receivables, or collection float, the more value is lost. The longer that resources can be conserved through reasonable delay of cash payment of payables and accruals, the more value is gained. A long lag time between the date that cash is received and the date that cash is paid, referred to as the **cash conversion period**, creates a financing problem for the firm. In general, firms must pay for resources received, such as inventory, before cash is received from its manufacturing and selling process. The shorter this cash conversion period, the more efficient are the working capital policies and the less value lost due to working capital management activities.

We will develop a numerical example using the simple case of a firm just beginning operations in order to fully understand the intricacies of managing the cash flow timeline as represented in Exhibit 1–1. By working through the numbers in this example, we will learn how the various balance sheet and income statement items relate to the operations of the firm. In addition, we will be able to better understand the very important relationship between profit and cash flow.

Consider the initial balance sheet for the newly formed company San Juan Anglers, Inc. Assuming that the owners put in $500 and borrow $500 from a bank, the accounts on the balance sheet will have the following balances:

Balance Sheet—June 1

| | | | |
|---|---|---|---|
| Cash | $1,000 | Debt | $ 500 |
| | | Equity | 500 |
| Total | $1,000 | Total | $1,000 |

The next day, the owner spends a portion of the initial funds to purchase operating facilities ($600) and an initial supply of inventory ($300). In purchasing the inventory, the firm's suppliers allow it to purchase the goods on credit ($300). The firm does not have any initial cash outlay for inventory. The total payment is due, say, in 45 days, or by July 15.

Balance Sheet—June 2

| | | | |
|---|---|---|---|
| Cash | $ 400 | Accounts payable | $ 300 |
| Inventory | 300 | Debt | 500 |
| Fixed assets | 600 | Equity | 500 |
| Total | $1,300 | Total | $1,300 |

Notice how total assets increased by $300, the dollar amount of the inventory purchased. This purchase is funded not out of cash (cash dropped only to $400, reflecting the purchase of the fixed assets) but out of suppliers' funds. This transaction is evidenced by the creation of the liability account, Accounts Payable, in the amount of the inventory purchase, $300.

When the firm begins to produce and sell its products, it generates operating expenses such as salaries, utilities, advertising, and depreciation of its fixed assets. When it sells its products on credit, accounts receivable are generated, giving its customers, say, two months to pay for their purchases. The firm's balance sheet as of the last day of the month, June 30, and the income statement for the month of June are shown below. The balance sheet shows the $200 of operating expenses (salaries, advertising, utilities, etc.) on the income statement as an accrued operating expense on the balance sheet. This practice is caused by charging off these expenses on the income statement even though they have not yet been paid in cash. The firm intends to pay these expenses on the first day of July.

Balance Sheet—June 30

| | | | |
|---|---|---|---|
| Cash | $ 325 | Accounts payable | $ 300 |
| Accounts receivable | 700 | Operating accruals | 200 |
| Inventory | 0 | Debt | 500 |
| Fixed assets | 600 | Common stock | 500 |
| (Accumulated depr.) | 100 | Retained earnings | 25 |
| Total | $1,525 | Total | $1,525 |

Income Statement—June 1–June 30

| | |
|---|---|
| Sales | $700 |
| Cost of goods sold | 300 |
| **Gross profit** | $400 |
| Operating expenses: | |
| Salaries, advertising, etc. | 200 |
| Depreciation | 100 |
| **Operating profit** | $100 |
| Interest | 50 |
| Taxes | 25 |
| **Net profit** | $ 25 |
| Dividends | 0 |
| Addition to retained earnings | $ 25 |

The balance sheet as of July 1 is shown below. Note how operating accruals are zero and the cash balance has been reduced by $200. The changes in these balance sheet accounts reflect the cash payment for the accrued expenses.

Balance Sheet—July 1

| | | | |
|---|---|---|---|
| Cash | $ 125 | Accounts payable | $ 300 |
| Accounts receivable | 700 | Operating accruals | 0 |
| Inventory | 0 | Debt | 500 |
| Fixed assets | 600 | Common stock | 500 |
| (Accumulated depr.) | 100 | Retained earnings | 25 |
| Total | $1,325 | Total | $1,325 |

Move forward in time to July 15. Consider the situation where no new business transactions occurred during July. The firm owes its suppliers $300 for the inventory purchased during June. The new balance sheet that follows reflects the payment of this debt. Note that the reduction of accounts payable by $300 reflects the payment made, and the cash balance is likewise reduced by the $300 payment. The resulting cash balance is negative, ($175). In actual practice, this would result in some problems for the firm. It is spending cash it doesn't have. But how can the firm be short of cash when the income statement reported a profit? The answer is that management paid cash for most, if not all, of the expenses but has yet to collect any cash from sales.

Balance Sheet—July 15

| | | | |
|---|---|---|---|
| Cash | $ (175) | Accounts payable | $ 0 |
| Accounts receivable | 700 | Operating accruals | 0 |
| Inventory | 0 | Debt | 500 |
| Fixed assets | 600 | Common stock | 500 |
| (Accumulated depr.) | 100 | Retained earnings | 25 |
| Total | $1,025 | Total | $1,025 |

Finally, assume that all the firm's customers pay for their June purchases by July 31. The following balance sheet reflects the cash receipts of $700 and the corresponding reduction of accounts receivable by $700. The firm completes its first cash cycle with a profit of $25 reflected in the retained earnings account and a cash balance of $525, which is $125 more than it had in cash on June 2, following its purchase of fixed assets.

Balance Sheet—July 31

| | | | |
|---|---|---|---|
| Cash | $ 525 | Accounts payable | $ 0 |
| Accounts receivable | 0 | Operating accruals | 0 |
| Inventory | 0 | Debt | 500 |
| Fixed assets | 600 | Common stock | 500 |
| (Accumulated depr.) | 100 | Retained earnings | 25 |
| Total | $1,025 | Total | $1,025 |

## THE RELATIONSHIP BETWEEN PROFIT AND CASH FLOW

The example in the previous section should have raised two questions in your mind. First, why did the firm end up with an extra $125 in its cash balance when it earned a profit of only $25? Second, why did the firm run out of cash during its operating cycle?

The first question can be addressed by recognizing that some of the firm's expenses result in a cash disbursement while others do not. For example, wages and utility expenses result in actual cash disbursements to employees and to the utility companies, respectively. In contrast, depreciation is simply an accounting entry to record the utilization of capital or fixed assets. Depreciation expense is not paid to anyone. Thus, while the $100 depreciation expense charged off on the income statement reduces profit, it does not reduce cash flow.

The second question can be explained by the existence of receivables, payables, and accruals. Receivables represent the dollar amount of sales that have yet to be collected. Thus, the $700 of receivables on the balance sheet reflects $700 of sales that remain uncollected from customers. The customers actually pay for the goods on July 31. Payables reflect resources the firm has the use of but for which it has not yet paid. Recall that the firm purchased $300 of inventory on June 2, which it could then sell, but payment for the goods was not required until 45 days later or on July 15. By July 15, the firm has had to pay $200 (paid on June 30) for operating expenses and $300 for its inventory purchases. But it had yet to receive any cash receipts from sales. While its operations were profitable, as shown by its income statement, the firm still was experiencing a cash flow problem due to the difference in timing of cash disbursements and cash receipts.

From this discussion we can learn that there are two basic aspects of managing the operations of the firm. First, the firm must manage a cost structure so that it can generate a profit. As we saw, after the accrued expenses and payables were finally paid and receivables collected, cash flow equaled net income plus depreciation expense. Secondly, the firm must manage its accruals, payables, receivables, and inventory (usually referred to as the working capital accounts) so that an adequate amount of liquidity is maintained and its interim cash flow position does not force the firm into bankruptcy or unplanned financial distress. Until all the accruals, payables, receivables, and inventory had worked themselves through their complete cycle, the firm experienced a wide range of cash flow from a deficit of $575 to a surplus of $125.

As shown in Exhibit 1–2, changes in the receivables, inventory, payables, and accrual accounts on the balance sheet, as well as the depreciation expense account on the income statement, can be used to adjust the income statement to reflect the true operating cash flow position of the firm. To arrive at cash receipts from sales, subtract an increase in the accounts receivable balance or add a decrease in accounts receivable. A short-hand way to express this type of adjustment is to subtract the change in the accounts receivable balance (where the change can either be positive, an increase, or negative, a decrease) from sales revenue. Cash disbursed for cost of goods sold is calculated by subtracting the change in accounts payable and adding the change in the inventory account from the income statement item cost of goods sold. Cash operating expenses are calculated by subtracting the change in operating expense accruals from operating expenses on the income statement. Although, in our example, interest and taxes are assumed to be paid in cash, both of these income statement items could also be adjusted by their respective accrual accounts and the deferred tax account, if these accounts exist on the balance sheet. Cash flow from operations is then calculated by subtracting all cash operating expenses from cash receipts, as shown in Exhibit 1–2.

Exhibits 1–3, 1–4, and 1–5 show how the June income statement is adjusted as the various expenses are paid and as customers pay off the accounts receivable. Exhibit 1–3 shows the difference between profit and cash flow as of the end of June 30. Cash flow is −$75 because no sales have been collected and the only expenses paid are interest and taxes.

**Exhibit 1–2**

*Adjustments to Convert the Accrual-Based Income Statement to a Cash Basis*

| Income Statement Account | Adjustment Account | Cash Flow Account |
|---|---|---|
| Sales | − Change in accounts receivable | = Cash collected from customers |
| Cost of goods sold | − Change in accounts payable<br>+ Change in inventory | = Cash paid to suppliers |
| Operating expenses | − Change in operating accruals<br>− Depreciation | = Cash paid for operating expenses |
| Interest | − Change in accrued interest | = Cash paid to creditors |
| Taxes | − Change in accrued taxes<br>− Change in deferred taxes | = Cash paid for taxes |

Cash Flow from Operations:
Cash collected from customers
minus cash paid to suppliers
minus cash paid for operations
minus cash paid to creditors
minus cash paid for taxes
Equals cash flow from operations

**Exhibit 1–3**

*June 1–June 30*

| Income Statement Account | Adjustment Account | Cash Flow Account |
|---|---|---|
| Sales<br>$700 | – Change in accounts receivable<br>$700 | = Cash collected from customers<br>$0 |
| Cost of goods sold<br>$300 | – Change in accounts payable<br>$300<br>+ Change in inventory<br>$0 | = Cash paid to suppliers<br>$0 |
| Operating expenses<br>$300 | – Change in operating accruals<br>$200<br>– Depreciation<br>$100 | = Cash paid for operating expenses<br>$0 |
| Interest<br>$50 | – Change in accrued interest<br>$0 | = Cash paid to creditors<br>$50 |
| Taxes<br>$25 | – Change in accrued taxes<br>$0<br>– Change in deferred taxes<br>$0 | = Cash paid for taxes<br>$25 |
| Net profit<br>$25 | | Cash profit<br>($75) |

**Exhibit 1–4**

*June 1–July 15*

| Income Statement Account | Adjustment Account | Cash Flow Account |
|---|---|---|
| Sales<br>$700 | – Change in accounts receivable<br>$700 | = Cash collected from customers<br>$0 |
| Cost of goods sold<br>$300 | – Change in accounts payable<br>$0<br>+ Change in inventory<br>$0 | = Cash paid to suppliers<br>$300 |
| Operating expenses<br>$300 | – Change in operating accruals<br>$0<br>– Depreciation<br>$100 | = Cash paid for operating expenses<br>$200 |
| Interest<br>$50 | – Change in accrued interest<br>$0 | = Cash paid to creditors<br>$50 |
| Taxes<br>$25 | – Change in accrued taxes<br>$0<br>– Change in deferred taxes<br>$0 | = Cash paid for taxes<br>$25 |
| Net profit<br>$25 | | Cash profit<br>($575) |

**Exhibit 1–5**

*June 1–July 31*

| Income Statement Account | Adjustment Account | Cash Flow Account |
|---|---|---|
| Sales<br>$700 | − Change in accounts receivable<br>$0 | = Cash collected from customers<br>$700 |
| Cost of goods sold<br>$300 | − Change in accounts payable<br>$0<br>+ Change in inventory<br>$0 | = Cash paid to suppliers<br>$300 |
| Operating expenses<br>$300 | − Change in operating accruals<br>$0<br>− Depreciation<br>$100 | = Cash paid for operating expenses<br>$200 |
| Interest<br>$50 | − Change in accrued interest<br>$0 | = Cash paid to creditors<br>$50 |
| Taxes<br>$25 | − Change in accrued taxes<br>$0<br>− Change in deferred taxes<br>$0 | = Cash paid for taxes<br>$25 |
| Net profit<br>$25 | | Cash profit<br>$125 |

Exhibit 1–4 shows a cash flow of −$575 by July 15. At this point suppliers have been paid $300, operating expenses of $200 have been paid, and the $75 of interest and taxes have also been paid. Still, no cash receipts have been collected to offset these cash disbursements. Finally, Exhibit 1–5 shows a cash flow of $125 reflecting the cash collections of $700 from customers offsetting the $575 of cash disbursements.

## FINANCIAL DILEMMA REVISITED

Before turning to the next section, which explores the management of a firm's working capital accounts, let's see if what we have learned can be applied to the dilemma facing the newly hired treasurer of Sports Junction, Inc., the sporting goods corporation introduced at the beginning of the chapter. First, she had the staff gather historical balance sheet data for the month of January, just ended, and make income projections for the months of February, March, and April.

Balance Sheet, January

| **Assets** | | **Liabilities and Net Worth** | |
|---|---|---|---|
| Cash | $ 70,000 | Payables | $ 0 |
| Receivables | 50,000 | Common stock | 150,000 |
| Inventory | 30,000 | Retained earnings | 0 |
| Total assets | $150,000 | Total liabilities/net worth | $150,000 |

| Projected Income Statement | February | March | April |
|---|---|---|---|
| Sales | $50,000 | $100,000 | $150,000 |
| Cost of sales | 30,000 | 60,000 | 90,000 |
| Gross profit | $20,000 | $ 40,000 | $ 60,000 |
| Fixed costs | 10,000 | 10,000 | 10,000 |
| Net profit | $10,000 | $ 30,000 | $ 50,000 |

The staff used the following purchasing schedule and cash budget to help forecast the income statement and balance sheet. The purchasing schedule is developed from the basic accounting relationship that ending inventory (EI) is equal to beginning inventory (BI) plus purchases (PUR) less cost of goods sold (COGS), shown in Equation 1.1.

$$EI = BI + PUR - COGS \tag{1.1}$$

Management's policy is to maintain ending inventory, for any given month, equal to that month's cost of goods sold. A purchasing schedule can be developed by taking Equation 1.1 and solving it for the dollar amount of purchases as shown in Equation 1.2.

$$PUR = EI - BI + COGS \tag{1.2}$$

For example, management's desired ending inventory for February is $30,000, based on February's estimated COGS of $30,000. February's beginning inventory is equal to $30,000, which is January's ending inventory. Plugging these values in for the variables shown in Equation 1.2 results in the projected dollar amount of purchases required to maintain the target ending inventory levels. The purchasing schedule for the three projected months is shown below.

| Purchasing Schedule | February | March | April |
|---|---|---|---|
| Desired ending inventory | $30,000 | $60,000 | $ 90,000 |
| Less: Beginning inventory | 30,000 | 30,000 | 60,000 |
| Plus: Cost of goods sold | 30,000 | 60,000 | 90,000 |
| Equals: Purchases | $30,000 | $90,000 | $120,000 |

The company's receivables are outstanding an average of one month. So, collections in one month are equal to the previous month's credit sales. Purchases are paid for in the month the purchase is made. These policies result in the following cash budget for the projected three months. In the cash budget, net cash flow is equal to cash collections, line 2, less cash disbursements, lines 5 and 6.

| Cash Budget | February | March | April |
|---|---|---|---|
| 1. Credit sales | $50,000 | $100,000 | $150,000 |
| 2. Cash collections | 50,000 | 50,000 | 100,000 |
| 3. Purchases | 30,000 | 90,000 | 120,000 |
| 4. Cash disbursed for: | | | |
| 5. Purchases | 30,000 | 90,000 | 120,000 |
| 6. Fixed costs | 10,000 | 10,000 | 10,000 |
| 7. Net cash flow (lines 2 − 5 − 6) | $10,000 | $ (50,000) | $ (30,000) |
| 8. Plus: Beginning cash | 70,000 | 80,000 | 30,000 |
| 9. Equals: Ending cash | $80,000 | $ 30,000 | $ 0 |

The projected balance sheet follows from the income statement and the cash budget. Cash is taken directly from the last line of the cash budget. Receivables equal last month's receivables balance plus credit sales for the new month less cash receipts from receivables. Inventory is taken from the top line of the purchasing schedule. Accounts payable equals zero, since the firm pays for all purchases with cash. Common stock is assumed to remain constant, and retained earnings grow by the amount of net profit retained each month.

| Projected Balance Sheet | February | March | April |
|---|---|---|---|
| **Assets** | | | |
| Cash | $ 80,000 | $ 30,000 | $ 0 |
| Accounts receivable | 50,000 | 100,000 | 150,000 |
| Inventory | 30,000 | 60,000 | 90,000 |
| **Liabilities & Net Worth** | | | |
| Accounts payable | $ 0 | $ 0 | $ 0 |
| Common stock | 150,000 | 150,000 | 150,000 |
| Retained earnings | 10,000 | 40,000 | 90,000 |

It's not hard to see that the treasurer does indeed have a dilemma. Her company is expected to earn a very reasonable rate of profit over the coming three months, as evidenced by the income statement, but will run out of cash by the end of April. Cash is being drained by the ever-increasing investment in receivables and inventory. This simply emphasizes the importance of managing the working capital relationships to ensure that an adequate level of liquidity is maintained. The relationship between the income statement and the statement of cash flows is shown below.

FEBRUARY

| Income Statement Account | Adjustment Account | Cash Flow Account |
|---|---|---|
| Sales<br>$50,000 | − Change in accounts receivable<br>$0 | = Cash collected from customers<br>$50,000 |
| Cost of goods sold<br>$30,000 | − Change in accounts payable<br>$0<br>+ Change in inventory<br>$0 | = Cash paid to suppliers<br>$30,000 |
| Gross margin<br>$20,000 | | Gross cash margin<br>$20,000 |
| Operating expenses<br>$10,000 | − Change in operating accruals<br>$0<br>− Depreciation<br>$0 | = Cash paid for operating expenses<br>$10,000 |
| Operating profit<br>$10,000 | | Operating cash margin<br>$10,000 |

MARCH

| Income Statement Account | Adjustment Account | Cash Flow Account |
|---|---|---|
| Sales<br>$100,000 | − Change in accounts receivable<br>$50,000 | = Cash collected from customers<br>$50,000 |
| Cost of goods sold<br>$60,000 | − Change in accounts payable<br>$0<br>+ Change in inventory<br>$30,000 | = Cash paid to suppliers<br>$90,000 |

*continued*

| | | |
|---|---|---|
| Gross margin<br>$40,000 | | Gross cash margin<br>($40,000) |
| Operating expenses<br>$10,000 | − Change in operating accruals<br>$0<br>− Depreciation<br>$0 | = Cash paid for operating expenses<br>$10,000 |
| Operating profit<br>$30,000 | | Operating cash margin<br>($50,000) |

APRIL

| Income Statement Account | Adjustment Account | Cash Flow Account |
|---|---|---|
| Sales<br>$150,000 | − Change in accounts receivable<br>$50,000 | = Cash collected from customers<br>$100,000 |
| Cost of goods sold<br>$90,000 | − Change in accounts payable<br>$0<br>+ Change in inventory<br>$30,000 | = Cash paid to suppliers<br>$120,000 |
| Gross margin<br>$60,000 | | Gross cash margin<br>($20,000) |
| Operating expenses<br>$10,000 | − Change in operating accruals<br>$0<br>− Depreciation<br>$0 | = Cash paid for operating expenses<br>$10,000 |
| Operating profit<br>$50,000 | | Operating cash margin<br>($30,000) |

The adjustments to the income statement clearly show that the growth in receivables and inventory are soaking up cash flow resources. During growth periods, firms with mismatched working capital accounts (where resources are held in inventory and receivables longer than in payables), such as Sports Junction, Inc., can expect to experience cash flow problems. Growth causes a greater spontaneous investment in working capital accounts, which slows down the flow of cash. This dilemma could be resolved by slowing down the outflow of cash, such as finding suppliers offering longer payment terms. Other alternatives would be to reduce the investment in inventory by developing better supply channels or collecting receivables more quickly. Finally, if these are not feasible alternatives, then the treasurer needs to establish a credit facility at a local bank so that funds could readily be borrowed during upswings in the firm's seasonal business cycle and the borrowings paid down on the back side of the seasonal cycle.

The next chapter will present ways to analyze the cash flow timeline, and Chapter 3 will discuss how to value the cash flows using basic time value of money techniques. But before we leave this chapter, let's briefly discuss the role that working capital plays in the management of a firm's operations and consider why working capital is needed and how much is enough.

## MANAGING THE CASH CYCLE

Even profitable firms can experience cash flow difficulties due to timing differences of cash receipts and cash disbursements. The **cash cycle** refers to the continual flow of resources through the various working capital accounts, such as cash, accounts receivables, inventory, payables, and accruals. Expansion of the working capital asset accounts absorbs resources, while expansion of working capital liability accounts provides resources. This continual transformation of resources over the production cycle results in periods of cash flow surpluses and deficits. The manner in which these working capital accounts are managed can ameliorate or accentuate cash flow difficulties.

It seems apparent that over the last decade, measures of working capital such as the current ratio and working capital as a percent of sales have generally been trending downward. Companies ranging from Dell Computer and General Electric to Quaker Oats and Campbell Soup are moving in the direction of zero net working capital. Reducing net working capital yields two benefits. First, reductions in net working capital flow straight to cash flow. Second, the journey leading to reduced net working capital leads to an increased efficiency in operations resulting in a permanent increase in earnings. Working capital costs money. Therefore, less of it increases earnings.

## Managing Receivables

Accounts receivable is created when customers purchase goods on credit. This credit must be properly managed in order to generate a timely receipt of cash. First, the financial manager must decide which customers should be allowed to buy on credit. A general framework for this kind of analysis is the five C's of credit. The financial manager must ascertain the customer's **C**haracter, **C**apacity to pay, **C**ollateral, and **C**apital. After these aspects have been analyzed, the credit decision must be put in context of current business **C**onditions.

Second, the financial manager must decide on a set of credit terms to offer. Typical terms might be net 30 days, or 2/10, net 30. The first set of terms simply instructs the customer to pay the invoice amount 30 days from the invoice date. The second set of terms allows for a 2 percent discount if paid within 10 days from the invoice date, or otherwise, the total invoice amount is due in 30 days. Obviously, the longer the allowed period to pay, the longer the customer will take to pay, which stretches out the receipt of cash. In most cases, a firm cannot set its credit terms independently. The terms offered must be competitive with terms offered by other firms in the industry.

Once credit is given, the outstanding balance must be monitored to ensure that outstanding credit balances are not growing faster than sales. The company should have a well-developed set of procedures to follow when a customer's account becomes past due. Immediate attention to past-due accounts is necessary and will increase the odds of collection. Chapters 5 and 6 provide discussion and decision models related to the management of receivables.

Finally, once the customer remits payment, management must create an effective collection system to reduce collection float, the time that is spent converting the payment medium into cash. Chapter 9 will focus on a variety of collection systems that can effectively manage collection float.

## Managing Inventory

In general, inventory balances act as shock absorbers between the production process and an uncertain consumer demand, between two production processes that are interdependent, or between the supplier and the production process. The more inventory stored, the less concern there is about product shortages at the retail level or about shutting down a production line due to a shortage of work-in-process or raw material inventory that feeds it.

However, increases in inventory balances absorb financial resources. So, it is imperative that inventory balances be managed in order to reduce financial requirements without excessively increasing stock-out risk. Excess inventory, while costly, does not impinge on sales. Inventory stock-outs are potentially more costly in that they create lost sales.

There have been many advances in the area of inventory management. Perhaps the most noteworthy is the **just-in-time** system popularized by the Japanese and, more recently, a system known as **demand flow**, which builds on just-in-time management concepts but is broader. These inventory management systems are designed to reduce the levels of inventory kept at the manufacturing site while still meeting production demands. They do this by redesigning the operations process and by shifting inventory burdens to suppliers. Chapter 4 will focus on the cash flow implications of managing inventory.

### Managing Payables

The vast majority of purchases made by one corporation from another are done on credit. In making the purchase decision, the buying firm should seek to purchase using the most favorable or longest terms possible. Then, payment should be made at the latest date possible so that payment arrives when due and not before. Payables should be viewed as interest-free financing and should be utilized until the last date possible. The manager should seriously consider the pros and cons of taking a cash discount if offered. Although taking a cash discount speeds up the disbursal of cash, the reduction in the amount paid may be more advantageous to the purchaser than foregoing the cash discount and paying at the end of the credit terms. Managerial issues of managing payables are discussed in Chapter 7.

Once payment is initiated, management must have an effective disbursement system in order to efficiently control the actual outflow of cash. Chapter 11 will discuss how to design an effective disbursement system.

A well-managed cash cycle results from aggressively monitoring the receivables balance, from reducing idle inventory, stretching payables to the last day possible given the terms of purchase, and implementation of an effective cash collection and disbursement system. An excessively long cash cycle puts added financial pressure on the firm and can generate liquidity crises.

### The Cash Cycle and Electronic Commerce

Electronic commerce is revolutionizing the way that the various components of the cash cycle are being managed. Initially, individual companies developed proprietary systems to conduct electronic commerce that in many ways slowed the growth of the potential for electronic commerce. The advent of the Internet changed the rules of the game.

The Internet is supporting an explosion in the development of systems with the ability to impact all aspects of the cash cycle, including product catalog and product ordering (sales), credit checking, product delivery, invoicing, and finally payment. While the investment in the needed technology is large and many issues (such as security) still remain, the ultimate cost savings and the increase in the efficiency of the cash cycle are significant. The following chapters highlight specific applications of electronic commerce to the various components of the cash cycle, and Chapter 19 provides an overview and a strategic look at the potential for electronic commerce and its impact on the cash cycle.

## HOW MUCH WORKING CAPITAL IS ENOUGH?

The growing debate over the role of working capital focuses on why working capital exists and what its appropriate level is. One extreme point of view is that the optimal level of net working capital is zero. This point of view sees working capital as an idle resource providing little or no value. Value is created by the fixed assets of the firm that produce the product, demanded by consumers, from raw materials. Thus, the production process creates something that did not exist before. Inventory and receivables are assets representing that

## FOCUS ON PRACTICE

### *How Management of Working Capital Is Changing*

Historically, since accounts such as inventory and receivables are assets, the more of them on the balance sheet, the better. After all, can a firm operate without working capital? Today, more and more firms appear to be setting a level of zero or very low net working capital as an operating goal. Exhibit 1–6 shows the trend of working capital requirements as a percentage of sales for four well-known computer companies—Dell, Compaq, Apple, and Gateway—from 1994 to 2002. Working capital requirements is defined as the sum of receivables and inventory less accounts payable. As you can see, the trend is distinctly down with some of the companies actually experiencing a working capital requirements level that is negative (payables exceed receivables and inventory) for the more recent years.

*Source:* For additional discussion, see Shawn Tully, "Raiding a Company's Hidden Cash," *Fortune* (August 22, 1994).

**Exhibit 1–6**

*Working Capital Requirements as a Percentage of Sales*

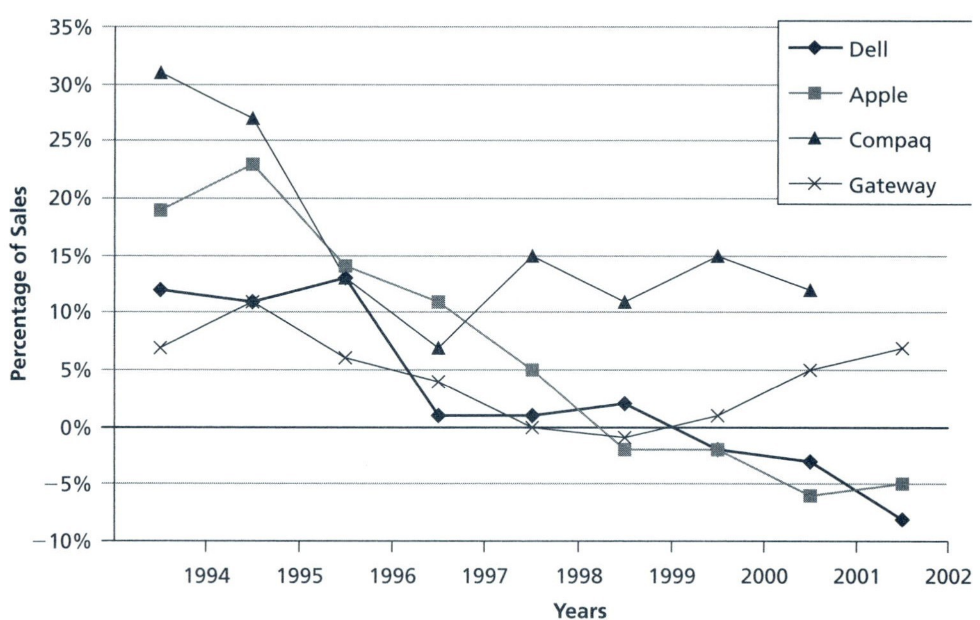


same product but are created primarily in getting that product to the ultimate consumer. How much of their assets should firms commit to this working capital management phase?[1] The following discussion will examine each of the working capital areas and look at why each may exist.

[1] A rough estimate is that in the United States working capital includes between 40 and 50 percent of total assets.

## Inventory

As we have seen, inventory is created by inefficiencies between the production cycle and the selling function. The greater the time delays and waste in the production process, the greater the need for inventory. Inventory is generally viewed as a type of shock absorber providing a cushion for work-in-process inventory between two contingent production processes or between production of finished goods and the selling function. Work-in-process inventory could be eliminated with increased efficiencies in the production process. This increased efficiency would also reduce the need for finished goods inventory, though forecasting uncertainties may prohibit it from being completely eliminated. For example, Dell has moved to a build-to-order production system that minimizes inventory at all levels (raw materials, work in process, and finished goods).

## Trade Credit: Receivables and Accounts Payable

Trade credit can be viewed as existing because of inefficiencies in the financing market. After all, why should a manufacturing firm that produces the product also provide the short-term financing for the purchase of the product when well-developed financial markets could be used to reduce the need for this activity on the part of nonfinancial firms? Why can't the customer make purchases with cash or financing obtained through traditional financial market channels such as commercial paper or bank lines of credit? If trade credit were eliminated, about half of a firm's working capital could be eliminated, thus improving the return on assets of all businesses.

It would seem that many parties share in the responsibility for reducing resources tied up in trade credit. The Federal Reserve and Banking System must continue to take steps to encourage the use of electronic forms of payment over the traditional paper-based system. Although tremendous strides have been taken during the decade of the 1980s and 1990s, much still remains to be done as we move into the twenty-first century. On the manufacturing side, as production processes become more efficient and just-in-time inventory techniques applied universally, delays that create the need for inventory can be eliminated, reducing the need for extended credit terms.

## Short-Term Investments

Why do firms hold funds in cash and short-term investments? Possible rationales include:

- cash for day-to-day operations
- cash as a marketing tool—strength of balance sheet in comparison to competitors
- cash as a buffer for corporate shocks such as bankruptcy or litigation
- cash for strategic purposes such as acquisitions

Most recently, and especially during the weak economic conditions that existed from 2000 through 2003, the focus has tended to be on the latter two reasons. For example, Microsoft's treasury had a $50 billion cushion in cash and short-term investments in 2003, with annual cash flow exceeding $12 billion. Why should the company maintain such a large liquidity reserve when its operations are generating such healthy cash flows? Microsoft said that such a reserve was needed to ensure coverage of potential litigation from a variety of antitrust suits in the United States as well as in Europe. In addition, the company also faced costs as it transitioned its compensation system away from stock options to stock grants, which could consume as much as $9 billion of its annual cash flow. But this would be a one-time transition cost. Many analysts and institutional investors assert that Microsoft could reduce its liquidity reserve to $30 billion without impairing its financial flexibility. As a response, Microsoft doubled its dividend from $0.08 per share to

$0.16 per share and did not rule out a possible stock buyback to return more money to shareholders.[2]

At the other extreme, the CFO of Bell Atlantic Corporation declared that the appropriate level of cash for a firm to hold is zero.[3] Firms that maintain low cash balances by design must rely on the credit markets to provide them liquidity—a strategy that works great in a perfect world but runs the risk of liquidity crises when credit gets tight.

There may also be managerial motives for holding large liquidity reserves. Having a pool of ready resources that can be deployed for discretionary investment purposes enhances managerial power and prestige. The decade of the 1980s witnessed a new constraint on this type of activity in the form of the corporate raider. The existence of excessive free cash flow or large pools of liquid resources instigated many raids.

Thus, it would seem that reductions in resources in cash and short-term investments could be accomplished through increased efficiencies in the financial markets, legal environment, and institutional structures.

## SUMMARY

There are two critical aspects to managing the cash cycle of a firm. First, the firm must operate at a profitable level. All firms incur certain levels of overhead or fixed costs. The firm must operate at a level such that the relationship between the fixed and variable costs results in operating profits.

Secondly, a profitable firm may still run into financial difficulties if operating cash flow is not managed properly. A profitable firm may still not be able to pay its bills if too many resources are tied up in inventory or if credit sales are not collected in a timely manner. A successful firm is one whose operations are managed from both a profit perspective as well as a cash flow perspective.

## USEFUL WEB SITES

Association for Financial Professionals: **http://www.afponline.org**

*CFO* Magazine: **http://www.cfo.com**

A great Web site for treasury information: **http://www.gtnews.com**

*Treasury and Risk* Magazine: **http://www.treasuryandrisk.com**

## QUESTIONS

1. Discuss the sequence of resource conversions generally referred to as the cash cycle.
2. What causes cash flow and net profit to diverge? When will they be the same?
3. Discuss the two basic aspects of managing the operations of the firm.
4. What role do the five C's of credit play in managing the receivables area?
5. How does collection float impact the cash cycle? Give an example.
6. How do inventory balances act as shock absorbers?

---

[2] Steve Lohr, "Microsoft Says It Is Planning to Double Its Dividend," *The New York Times* (September 13, 2003).

[3] S. L. Mintz, "Lean Green Machines," *CFOnet* (July 2000), p. 1.

7. How does a disbursement float impact the cash cycle? Give an example.
8. When the date that cash is disbursed comes before the date that cash is received on the cash flow timeline, what are some of the options available to the financial manager as to funding the disbursements?
9. Why do firms have working capital?
10. How can a profitable firm go bankrupt?

## PROBLEMS

1. For each part below, calculate the amount of cash received by a company from its customers using the following data:

| | Beginning Receivables | Ending Receivables | Sales |
|---|---|---|---|
| a. | $ 0 | $ 500 | $2,000 |
| b. | 900 | 1,500 | 5,000 |
| c. | 1,000 | 750 | 2,500 |

2. For each part below, first calculate the dollar amount of purchases, and then using that result, calculate the dollar amount of cash paid to suppliers using the following data:

| | Beginning Accounts Payable | Ending Accounts Payable | Beginning Inventory | Ending Inventory | Cost of Goods Sold |
|---|---|---|---|---|---|
| a. | $ 0 | $600 | $ 0 | $1,200 | $2,000 |
| b. | 0 | 600 | 300 | 1,500 | 3,000 |
| c. | 500 | 300 | 800 | 500 | 5,000 |

3. Consider the following balance sheet and income statement data for Rockwall Enterprises, Inc.
   **a.** Develop a statement of cash flows similar to Exhibit 1–2.
   **b.** Discuss why the cash position of the company is different from the profit of the company. Specifically, note that net profit was $425 yet the cash account stayed the same.

Rockwall Enterprises, Inc.
Balance Sheet
12/31/03 (000's)

| | | | |
|---|---|---|---|
| Cash | $ 500 | Accounts payable | $ 200 |
| Accounts receivable | 750 | Operating accruals | 300 |
| Inventory | 400 | Debt | 1,000 |
| Fixed assets | 1,000 | Common stock | 500 |
| (Accumulated depr.) | 400 | Retained earnings | 250 |
| Total | $2,250 | Total | $2,250 |

Rockwall Enterprises, Inc.
Balance Sheet
12/31/04 (000's)

| | | | |
|---|---|---|---|
| Cash | $ 500 | Accounts payable | $ 950 |
| Accounts receivable | 2,000 | Operating accruals | 275 |
| Inventory | 600 | Debt | 1,000 |
| Fixed assets | 1,000 | Common stock | 500 |
| (Accumulated depr.) | 700 | Retained earnings | 675 |
| Total | $3,400 | Total | $3,400 |

Rockwall Enterprises, Inc.
Income Statement
For the Year Ended 12/31/04 (000's)

| | |
|---|---|
| Sales | $9,000 |
| Cost of goods sold | 4,500 |
| **Gross profit** | $4,500 |
| Operating expenses: | |
| Salaries, advertising, etc. | 3,500 |
| Depreciation | 300 |
| **Operating profit** | $ 700 |
| Interest | 100 |
| Taxes | 175 |
| **Net profit** | $ 425 |
| Dividends | 0 |
| Addition to retained earnings | $ 425 |

**4.** Consider the following balance sheet and income statement data for Landmark International.

**a.** Develop a statement of cash flows similar to Exhibit 1–2.

**b.** Explain why the cash balance increased by $350 when the company generated a net profit of $405.

Landmark International, Inc.
Balance Sheet
12/31/03 (000's)

| | | | |
|---|---|---|---|
| Cash | $ 200 | Accounts payable | $ 200 |
| Accounts receivable | 800 | Operating accruals | 300 |
| Inventory | 250 | Debt | 750 |
| Fixed assets | 1,000 | Common stock | 400 |
| (Accumulated depr.) | 400 | Retained earnings | 200 |
| Total | $1,850 | Total | $1,850 |

Landmark International, Inc.
Balance Sheet
12/31/04 (000's)

| | | | |
|---|---|---|---|
| Cash | $ 550 | Accounts payable | $ 250 |
| Accounts receivable | 700 | Operating accruals | 150 |
| Inventory | 150 | Debt | 395 |
| Fixed assets | 1,000 | Common stock | 400 |
| (Accumulated depr.) | 600 | Retained earnings | 605 |
| Total | $1,800 | Total | $1,800 |

Landmark International, Inc.
Income Statement
For the Year Ended 12/31/04 (000's)

| | |
|---|---|
| Sales | $4,500 |
| Cost of goods sold | 2,200 |
| **Gross profit** | $2,300 |
| Operating expenses: | |
| Salaries, advertising, etc. | 1,300 |
| Depreciation | 200 |
| **Operating profit** | $ 800 |
| Interest | 75 |
| Taxes | 320 |
| **Net profit** | $ 405 |
| Dividends | 0 |
| Addition to retained earnings | $ 405 |

**5.** Consider the following balance sheet and income statement data for Brothers, Inc.
  **a.** Develop a cash flow statement similar to Exhibit 1–2.
  **b.** Why is the company able to make a profit when its cash account has gone to a deficit position?

Brothers, Inc.
Balance Sheet
12/31/03 (000's)

| | | | |
|---|---|---|---|
| Cash | $1,000 | Accounts payable | $1,250 |
| Accounts receivable | 1,500 | Operating accruals | 450 |
| Inventory | 1,750 | Accrued interest | 0 |
| | | Deferred taxes | 0 |
| | | Debt | 2,750 |
| Fixed assets | 3,000 | Common stock | 1,000 |
| (Accumulated depr.) | 800 | Retained earnings | 1,000 |
| Total | $6,450 | Total | $6,450 |

Brothers, Inc.
Balance Sheet
12/31/04 (000's)

| | | | |
|---|---|---|---|
| Cash | $ (100) | Accounts payable | $ 800 |
| Accounts receivable | 1,850 | Operating accruals | 500 |
| Inventory | 2,100 | Accrued interest | 50 |
| | | Deferred taxes | 100 |
| | | Debt | 2,000 |
| Fixed assets | 3,500 | Common stock | 1,000 |
| (Accumulated depr.) | 900 | Retained earnings | 2,000 |
| Total | $6,450 | Total | $6,450 |

Brothers, Inc.
Income Statement
For the Year Ended 12/31/04 (000's)

| | |
|---|---|
| Sales | $9,000 |
| Cost of goods sold | 4,000 |
| **Gross profit** | $5,000 |
| Operating expenses: | |
| Salaries, advertising, etc. | 2,900 |
| Depreciation | 100 |
| **Operating profit** | $2,000 |
| Interest | 200 |
| Taxes | 800 |
| **Net profit** | $1,000 |
| Dividends | 0 |
| Addition to retained earnings | $1,000 |

**6.** Return to the Sports Junction, Inc., example in the Financial Dilemma. Assume that sales for May, June, and July are forecasted to be $125,000, $90,000, and $75,000, respectively.
  **a.** Construct the monthly income statement, purchasing schedule, cash budget, and balance sheet for the three months.
  **b.** Explain why the cash balance increased over these three months.

**7.** Returning to the Sports Junction dilemma, assume that the treasurer decided to change policies starting in February and have customers pay during the month of the sale. Assume, too, that new supplier terms allow the company to pay for purchases during the month of the purchase.

**a.** Create a monthly income statement, purchasing schedule, cash budget, and balance sheet for February through July assuming that sales for May, June, and July are forecasted to be $125,000, $90,000, and $75,000, respectively.

**b.** Discuss the impact these changes have on the liquidity position of the firm.

## REFERENCES

Richard H. Gamble, "Working Capital: Key to Cash Flow that Treasury Rarely Manages," *Corporate Cash Flow*, 17 (4) (1996), pp. 20–26.

John J. Goetz, "Ten Ways to Conserve Working Capital," *Journal of Working Capital Management* (Fall 1995), pp. 27–31.

Chris Hall, "Total Working Capital Management," *AFP Exchange* (November/December 2002), pp. 26–32.

L. C. Heath, "Is Working Capital Really Working?" *Journal of Accountancy* (August 1989), pp. 55–62.

Chang-Soo Kim, David C. Mauer, and Ann E. Sherman, "The Determinants of Corporate Liquidity: Theory and Evidence," *Journal of Financial and Quantitative Analysis*, 33 (3) (1998), pp. 335–359.

Raghuram G. Rajan and Stewart Myers, "The Paradox of Liquidity," *Quarterly Journal of Economics* (August 1998).

Cecilia Wagner Ricci and Gail Morrison, "International Working Capital Practices of the *Fortune* 200," *Financial Practice and Education* (Fall 1996), pp. 7–20.

George Schilling, "Working Capital's Role in Maintaining Corporate Liquidity," *TMA Journal*, 16 (5) (1996), p. 4.

Hyun-Han Shin and Luc Soenen, "Efficiency of Working Capital Management and Corporate Profitability," *Financial Practice and Education* (Fall/Winter 1998), pp. 37–45.

K. V. Smith, "State of the Art of Working Capital Management," *Financial Management* (Autumn 1973), pp. 50–55.

Bernell K. Stone, "Liquidity Assessment and the Formulation of Corporate Liquidity Policy," *Readings in Short-Term Financial Management, Third Edition* (St. Paul, MN: West Publishing Company, 1988), pp. 32–41.

Shawn Tully, "Raiding a Company's Hidden Cash," *Fortune* (August 22, 1994).

CHAPTER

2

# Analysis of Solvency, Liquidity, and Financial Flexibility

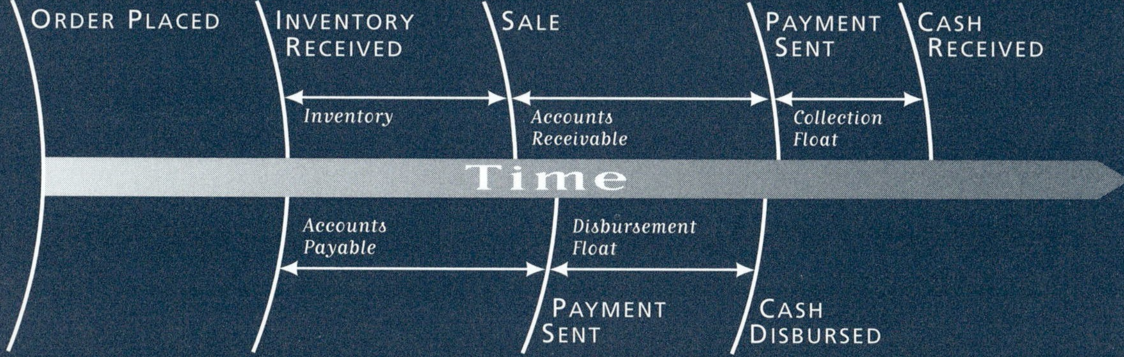

## OBJECTIVES

*After studying this chapter, you should be able to:*

- differentiate between solvency and liquidity ratios.
- conduct a liquidity analysis of a company's financial position.
- assess a firm's financial flexibility position.

Chapter 1 identified the importance working capital management plays in impacting the operating cash flow of the company. Once the firm's working capital management policies have been determined, it is then important to monitor the impact that these policies have on the **solvency**, **liquidity**, and **financial flexibility** of the firm. A firm is solvent when its assets exceed its total liabilities. It is liquid when it can pay its bills on time without undue cost. Finally, it has financial flexibility when its financial policies including financial leverage, dividend policy, profitability, and asset efficiency are consistent with its projected growth in sales.

### FINANCIAL DILEMMA

What Happened?

Back in 1993 things looked pretty bleak for Dell Computer Corporation. The company was growing too fast, inventories were ballooning, cash reserves were low, and receivables were growing faster than revenue growth rates. The company posted a loss for the most recent fiscal year and came under attack by securities analysts for its speculative use of derivatives. Dell's stock price plummeted from $49 to $16 per share. Stepping up to the plate, the company's new CFO, Tom Meredith, saw an opportunity to turn the company around by bringing the "Golden Triangle" formed by the three key variables of growth, profitability, and liquidity back into balance.[1]

[1] Stephen Barr, "The Best of 1998: Thomas Meredith," *CFO Magazine* (September 1998), pp. 42–43.

Exhibit 2–1 presents five years of balance sheet data and five years of profit and loss statements for Dell Computer Corporation. We will use these financial statements to demonstrate the calculation and interpretation of the solvency, liquidity, and financial flexibility ratios that will be presented.

## SOLVENCY MEASURES

Although the ratios presented in this section are generally referred to as liquidity ratios, they each essentially measure the solvency of the firm. As discussed earlier, a firm is considered solvent when its assets exceed its liabilities. The solvency ratios presented in this section are based on balance sheet accounts and measure the relationship between current assets and current liabilities. In some respects, these solvency ratios demonstrate the degree to which current liabilities are covered in the event of liquidation.

### Current Ratio

One of the first financial ratios ever developed was the ratio of current assets to current liabilities, commonly referred to as the **current ratio**. This ratio's origin can be traced back to the early 1900s. Although it has always been viewed as a liquidity measure, its approach to liquidity ignores the "going concern" aspect of the firm. Rather, it indicates the degree of coverage that short-term creditors have if current assets were to be liquidated to pay off current liabilities. Liquidating current assets in order to pay off current maturing liabilities would obviously disrupt the operating cycle of the firm and is clearly not an option unless the firm is being liquidated.

**Exhibit 2–1**

*Balance Sheets and Income Statements for Dell Computer Corporation*

Dell Computer Corporation Annual Balance Sheet ($Millions)

| | 1999 | 2000 | 2001 | 2002 | 2003 |
|---|---|---|---|---|---|
| ASSETS | | | | | |
| Cash & Equivalents | $3,181.00 | $ 4,132.00 | $ 5,438.00 | $ 3,914.00 | $ 4,638.00 |
| Net Receivables | 2,481.00 | 2,678.00 | 2,895.00 | 2,269.00 | 2,586.00 |
| Inventories | 273.00 | 391.00 | 400.00 | 278.00 | 306.00 |
| Prepaid Expenses | 0.00 | 0.00 | 0.00 | 0.00 | 0.00 |
| Other Current Assets | 404.00 | 480.00 | 758.00 | 1,416.00 | 1,394.00 |
| Total Current Assets | $6,339.00 | $ 7,681.00 | $ 9,491.00 | $ 7,877.00 | $ 8,924.00 |
| Gross Plant, Property & Equipment | 775.00 | 1,140.00 | 1,534.00 | 1,438.00 | 1,662.00 |
| Accumulated Depreciation | 252.00 | 375.00 | 538.00 | 612.00 | 749.00 |
| Net Plant, Property & Equipment | 523.00 | 765.00 | 996.00 | 826.00 | 913.00 |
| Other Assets | 15.00 | 3,025.00 | 2,948.00 | 4,832.00 | 5,633.00 |
| TOTAL ASSETS | $6,877.00 | $11,471.00 | $13,435.00 | $13,535.00 | $15,470.00 |
| LIABILITIES | | | | | |
| Long-Term Debt Due in One Year | $ 0.00 | $ 0.00 | $ 0.00 | $ 0.00 | $ 0.00 |
| Notes Payable | 0.00 | 0.00 | 0.00 | 0.00 | 0.00 |
| Accounts Payable | 2,397.00 | 3,538.00 | 4,286.00 | 5,075.00 | 5,989.00 |
| Taxes Payable | 0.00 | 0.00 | 0.00 | 5.00 | 54.00 |
| Accrued Expenses | 355.00 | 337.00 | 428.00 | 1,127.00 | 1,458.00 |
| Other Current Liabilities | 943.00 | 1,317.00 | 1,829.00 | 1,312.00 | 1,432.00 |
| Total Current Liabilities | $3,695.00 | $ 5,192.00 | $ 6,543.00 | $ 7,519.00 | $ 8,933.00 |
| Long-Term Debt | 512.00 | 508.00 | 509.00 | 520.00 | 506.00 |
| Other Liabilities | 349.00 | 463.00 | 761.00 | 802.00 | 1,158.00 |
| EQUITY | | | | | |
| Preferred Stock | 0.00 | 0.00 | 0.00 | 0.00 | 0.00 |
| Common Stock | 12.72 | 25.75 | 26.01 | 26.54 | 26.80 |
| Capital Surplus | 1,768.29 | 3,557.25 | 4,768.99 | 5,578.46 | 5,991.20 |
| Retained Earnings | 540.00 | 1,725.00 | 827.00 | 1,338.00 | 3,394.00 |
| Less: Treasury Stock | 0.00 | 0.00 | 0.00 | 2,249.00 | 4,539.00 |
| TOTAL EQUITY | $2,321.00 | $ 5,308.00 | $ 5,622.00 | $ 4,694.00 | $ 4,873.00 |
| TOTAL LIABILITIES & EQUITY | $6,877.00 | $11,471.00 | $13,435.00 | $13,535.00 | $15,470.00 |
| COMMON SHARES OUTSTANDING | 2,543.00 | 2,575.00 | 2,601.00 | 2,602.00 | 2,579.00 |

Source: Thomson Analytics

## Exhibit 2-1

*continued*

Dell Computer Corporation Annual Income Statements ($Millions)

| | 1999 | 2000 | 2001 | 2002 | 2003 |
|---|---|---|---|---|---|
| Sales | $18,243.00 | $25,265.00 | $31,888.00 | $31,168.00 | $35,404.00 |
| Cost of Goods Sold | 14,034.00 | 19,891.00 | 25,205.00 | 25,422.00 | 28,844.00 |
| Gross Profit | 4,209.00 | 5,374.00 | 6,683.00 | 5,746.00 | 6,560.00 |
| Selling, General, & Administrative Expense | 2,060.00 | 2,761.00 | 3,675.00 | 3,236.00 | 3,505.00 |
| Operating Income Before Depreciation | 2,149.00 | 2,613.00 | 3,008.00 | 2,510.00 | 3,055.00 |
| Depreciation, Depletion, & Amortization | 103.00 | 156.00 | 240.00 | 239.00 | 211.00 |
| Operating Profit | 2,046.00 | 2,457.00 | 2,768.00 | 2,271.00 | 2,844.00 |
| Interest Expense | 26.00 | 34.00 | 47.00 | 29.00 | 17.00 |
| Non-Operating Income/ Expense | 64.00 | 222.00 | 578.00 | 231.00 | 200.00 |
| Special Items | 0.00 | −194.00 | −105.00 | −742.00 | 0.00 |
| Pretax Income | 2,084.00 | 2,451.00 | 3,194.00 | 1,731.00 | 3,027.00 |
| Total Income Taxes | 624.00 | 785.00 | 958.00 | 485.00 | 905.00 |
| Income Before Extraordinary Items & Discontinued Operations | 1,460.00 | 1,666.00 | 2,236.00 | 1,246.00 | 2,122.00 |
| Preferred Dividends | 0.00 | 0.00 | 0.00 | 0.00 | 0.00 |
| Available for Common | 1,460.00 | 1,666.00 | 2,236.00 | 1,246.00 | 2,122.00 |
| Extraordinary Items | 0.00 | 0.00 | −59.00 | 0.00 | 0.00 |
| Adjusted Net Income | $ 1,460.00 | $ 1,666.00 | $ 2,177.00 | $ 1,246.00 | $ 2,122.00 |

Source: Thomson Banker ONE, **http://banker.analytics.thomsonib.com.**

The calculation of the 2003 current ratio for Dell is shown below. Dell has approximately $1.00 of current assets for every dollar of current liabilities.

$$\text{Current ratio} = \frac{\text{Current assets}}{\text{Current liabilities}}$$

$$\text{Current ratio} = \frac{\$8,924}{\$8,933} = 1.00$$

The 5-year trend for this ratio follows. There has been a definite downward trend for this ratio over this 5-year time horizon. Historically, analysts have regarded a current ratio of 2.00 to be the norm. However, over the past ten years, companies have begun to find ways to economize on the level of current assets needed to support operations. As a result, current ratio levels have tended to be lower than historical norms. In fact, Dell's ratio has fallen from a level of 1.72 in 1999 to a value of 1.00 in 2003. A review of Dell's balance sheet indicates that while cash and equivalents have increased, the level of receivables and inventories have remained relatively constant, even though revenues have almost doubled. In addition, Dell's management has relied more and more on short-term funding from suppliers, resulting in a significant increase in accounts payable and accruals. Thus, while a declining current ratio would have been of concern historically, Dell's ratio has declined for all the right reasons: efficient current asset management and increased reliance on spontaneous financing from suppliers and operations.

| | 1999 | 2000 | 2001 | 2002 | 2003 |
|---|---|---|---|---|---|
| Current ratio | 1.72 | 1.48 | 1.45 | 1.05 | 1.00 |

## Quick Ratio

A variation of the current ratio is the **quick ratio**, also referred to as the **acid-test ratio.** The only difference here is that the quick ratio ignores inventory in the numerator on the basis that inventory is the current asset that is the furthest removed from cash.

$$\text{Quick ratio} = \frac{\text{Current assets} - \text{Inventories}}{\text{Current liabilities}}$$

$$\text{Quick ratio} = \frac{\$8{,}924 - \$306}{\$8{,}933} = 0.96$$

The 5-year trend for this ratio is shown below. Like the current ratio, Dell's quick ratio demonstrates a definite downward trend over the 5-year period. This ratio indicates that Dell has about $0.96 of cash, receivables, and other current assets, exclusive of inventories, covering a dollar of current liabilities.

| | 1999 | 2000 | 2001 | 2002 | 2003 |
|---|---|---|---|---|---|
| Quick ratio | 1.64 | 1.40 | 1.39 | 1.01 | 0.96 |

## Net Working Capital

Another common solvency measure is **net working capital**. Net working capital is the difference between current assets and current liabilities. This measure reports the dollar amount of long-term funds used to finance current assets if net working capital is positive or the dollar amount of current liabilities financing fixed or long-term assets if net working capital is negative. While it is generally agreed that a company is more solvent the greater the current assets are relative to the level of current liabilities, recently net working capital has been shrinking as more firms have become more efficient in the management of receivables and inventory. Dell's 2003 net working capital calculation follows:

$$\begin{aligned}\text{Net working capital} &= \text{Current assets} - \text{Current liabilities}\\ \text{Net working capital} &= \$8{,}924 - \$8{,}933\\ &= (\$9)\end{aligned}$$

The 5-year trend for net working capital is shown below. The level of net working capital has generally fallen over the last five years, from a level of $2.6 billion in 1999 to approximately zero in 2003.

| (Millions of dollars) | 1999 | 2000 | 2001 | 2002 | 2003 |
|---|---|---|---|---|---|
| Net working capital | $2,644 | $2,489 | $2,948 | $358 | ($9) |

One problem with net working capital is that it is an absolute measure rather than a relative measure. Generally, the dollar amount of net working capital will be larger the larger the firm's assets, thus making it difficult to make comparisons across firms.

## A Variation on Net Working Capital

Shulman and Cox[2] refined the concept of net working capital by adding new interpretations to various working capital relationships. First, they observed that the traditional definition of net working capital, or NWC (i.e., current assets minus current liabilities) does not reflect its real impact on liquidity. They offered an alternative interpretation that equated NWC to the difference between permanent capital (long-term liabilities and net worth) and net fixed assets. From this perspective, the dollar amount of positive net working capital measures that portion of current assets financed with permanent funds. In such a case, management is using long-term funds to finance current assets, which is a relatively safe strategy. A negative level of net working capital indicates that portion of current liabilities financing net fixed assets, which is a relatively risky strategy.

However, even with these interpretations, Shulman and Cox felt that net working capital was not a very useful measure because it combined in one measure operating strategies (strategies involving receivables, inventory, and payables) and financing strategies (strategies involving short-term investments and short-term debt). So, to refine their analysis, they created two new definitions. First, they defined **working capital requirements**, or WCR, as the difference between current operating assets (such as receivables, inventory, prepaids, and other current assets) and current operating liabilities (such as accounts payable, operating accruals, and other current liabilities). These accounts represent spontaneous uses and sources of funds over the firm's operating cycle.

They then defined **net liquid balance**, or NLB, as the difference between current financial assets such as cash and marketable securities and current discretionary or nonspontaneous financial liabilities such as notes payable and current maturities or long-term debt. One should note the relationship between WCR, NLB, and NWC, specifically, NWC = WCR + NLB. Exhibit 2–2 may help the reader visualize the connection between these three balance sheet measures.

*NET LIQUID BALANCE* NLB serves as a measure of liquidity rather than solvency, as proposed by Shulman and Cox. To see how NLB measures liquidity, remember the interpretation of a positive level of net working capital (NWC): the dollar amount of current assets financed by permanent capital. Over the operating cycle of the firm, the dollar amount of positive working capital requirements, which is a component of NWC, will generally expand as sales expand (increasing receivables and inventory) and contract as sales contract (selling off of inventory and collection of receivables). During the upswing, the expanding dollar amount of WCR must either be financed by drawing down the net liquid balance (NLB), adding to permanent capital by acquiring new long-term debt or equity financing, or both. Therefore, the more positive the net liquid balance, the greater the amount of liquid resources the firm has to finance its working capital requirements. If the increase in WCR is seasonal, then drawing down the net liquid balance is appropriate. However, if the increase in WCR is permanent because of a new higher level of operations, then the increase in WCR should be financed with a permanent source of funds in order to maintain the firm's level of liquidity. Dell's 2003 level of net liquid balance follows:

Net liquid balance = Cash and equivalents − Notes payable and Current maturities of long-term debt or leases

Net liquid balance = \$4,638 − (\$0)
= \$4,638

The 5-year trend for Dell's net liquid balance follows. This liquidity measure has demonstrated little trend over the 5-year period, rising from 1999 to 2001 and then dropping

[2] "An Integrative Approach to Working Capital Management" (full citation in the end-of-chapter references).

**Exhibit 2–2**

*The Relationship between Net Working Capital, Net Liquid Balance, and Working Capital Requirements*

Net Working Capital (NWC) = Current Assets (CA) − Current Liabilities (CL)

| Current Assets | Current Liabilities |
|---|---|
| Cash | |
| Marketable securities | Accounts payable |
| Accounts receivable | Notes payable |
| Inventory | Current maturities |
| Prepaids & other CA | Accruals & other CL |

Working Capital Requirements (WCR) = A/R + Inv. + Prepaids & Other CA − N/P − Accruals & other CL

| Current Assets | Current Liabilities |
|---|---|
| Cash | |
| Marketable securities | Accounts payable |
| Accounts receivable | Notes payable |
| Inventory | Current maturities |
| Prepaids & other CA | Accruals & other CL |

Net Liquid Balance (NLB) = Cash + Mkt. Sec. − N/P − Current Maturities of Long-Term Debt (CMLTD)

| Current Assets | Current Liabilities |
|---|---|
| Cash | |
| Marketable securities | Accounts payable |
| Accounts receivable | Notes payable |
| Inventory | Current maturities |
| Prepaids & other CA | Accruals & other CL |

NWC = WCR + NLB

from 2001 to 2002, and then increasing again in 2003. Dell has significantly increased its stock of cash and cash equivalents relative to its use of short-term debt.

| (Millions of dollars) | 1999 | 2000 | 2001 | 2002 | 2003 |
|---|---|---|---|---|---|
| Net liquid balance | $3,181 | $4,132 | $5,438 | $3,914 | $4,638 |

The absolute dollar NLB balance may be used as a measure of a firm's liquidity. A negative measure signifies dependence on outside financing and is indicative of the minimum borrowing line required. While a negative NLB does not by itself suggest that the firm is going to default on its debt obligations, it does imply that the firm has reduced financial flexibility.

**WORKING CAPITAL REQUIREMENTS** Using working capital requirements as an index of working capital needs, Hawawini, Viallet, and Vora[3] performed a comparison of the

[3] "Industrial Influence on Corporate Working Capital Decisions" (full citation in the end-of-chapter references).

working capital policies across industries. The working capital requirements approach is useful because the traditional net working capital figure includes accounts that are not directly related to the operating cycle.

For example, the cash account, the marketable securities account, and the notes payable balance should be viewed as balances that result from internal financial decisions or policies, not balances directly impacted by the cash cycle of the firm. They should therefore be excluded from consideration. This approach is consistent with the decomposition of net working capital into net liquid balance and working capital requirements developed by authors Shulman and Cox discussed earlier.

The authors then standardized working capital requirements by dividing it by sales, developing a working capital requirements to sales ratio, **WCR/S**. They found that this ratio was statistically different across industry categories, indicating that industries have significantly different working capital needs. All other factors being constant, the greater this ratio, the greater the reliance a company will have on external funds given a change in sales. Thus, the larger the WCR/S ratio, the less financial flexibility and less liquidity the firm will have, because its operating cycle will require significant investment of funds. In those cases where WCR is negative, the firm's cash cycle becomes a permanent source of financing and the positive impact on liquidity will be significant. The 2003 ratio value for Dell is:

$$\text{WCR/S} = \frac{(\$2{,}586 + \$306 + \$1{,}394) - (\$5{,}989 + \$54 + \$1{,}458 + \$1{,}432)}{\$35{,}404}$$

$$= \frac{(\$4{,}647)}{\$35{,}404} = -0.1313$$

The 5-year trend for the working capital requirements to sales ratio is shown below. This ratio generally dropped over the 5-year period and remained at a negative level the entire time. This indicates that the firm has more funds available in payables and accruals than it requires for its receivables and inventory needs.

| | 1999 | 2000 | 2001 | 2002 | 2003 |
|---|---|---|---|---|---|
| WCR/S | −0.029 | −0.065 | −0.078 | −0.114 | −0.131 |

## WHAT IS LIQUIDITY?

Liquidity has three basic ingredients: time, amount, and cost. The first essential ingredient of liquidity is the time it takes to convert an asset into cash or to pay a current liability. Simply put, the quicker that an asset can be converted into cash, the more liquid it is. A second ingredient of liquidity is amount. Does a firm have enough liquid resources to cover its financial obligations coming due? Cost is the third ingredient. An asset is thought to be liquid if it can be quickly converted into cash with little cost. Summarizing, a firm is considered to be liquid if it has enough financial resources to cover its financial obligations in a timely manner with minimal cost. This approach to liquidity analysis takes a flow (of resources) as well as a stock (of resources) perspective and is very short-run in nature in relation to the firm's cash cycle, as discussed in Chapter 1.

Liquidity may also be viewed as the ability of a firm to augment its future cash flows to cover any unforeseen needs or to take advantage of any unexpected opportunities. This concept of liquidity has been referred to as financial flexibility by Campbell, Johnson, and Savoie[4]. This viewpoint is much broader and would consider such things as the firm's sta-

[4] "Cash Flow, Liquidity, and Financial Flexibility" (full citation in the end-of-chapter references).

bility of earnings, its relative debt/equity position (which may affect its access to external financing sources), and the availability of credit lines. We will study the concept of financial flexibility in more detail later in the chapter.

It is interesting to study management's attitude and perception of liquidity. Campbell, Johnson, and Savoie surveyed the Fortune 1000 companies with a resulting 30 percent response rate. The purpose of the survey was to summarize management's perceptions of the importance of various factors on the internal monitoring of liquidity. They found that the traditional monitoring of accounts receivable and inventory, as well as short-term cash flow projections and good bank relationships, are viewed as extremely valuable tools in the management and planning of corporate liquidity. Perhaps the most important finding of this study is that a traditional method of analyzing financial statements—ratio analysis—is considered a weak tool for monitoring liquidity. It may be safe to say that it is not ratio analysis itself that is a weak tool but rather that ratios have yet to be developed that are effective at measuring the liquidity aspect of a business operation.

To measure and monitor liquidity properly, the standards and approaches used in the past must be discarded and a new framework developed. Ludeman[5] was one of the first proponents of developing a new perspective on liquidity analysis. He suggested that liquidity analysis should include the following:

- Amount and trend of internal cash flow
- The aggregate lines of credit and degree of line usage
- The attractiveness to investors of the firm's commercial paper, long-term bonds, and common equity
- Overall expertise of management

From this discussion, it should be obvious that liquidity is a complex issue and the analysis of liquidity should consider the firm's ability to generate the necessary levels of operating cash flow and the availability of a stock of liquid resources.

## THE STATEMENT OF CASH FLOWS

Exhibit 2–3 presents the statement of cash flows for Dell Computer Corporation for five years.

### Purpose of the Cash Flow Statement

The primary purpose of the **statement of cash flows** is to provide information as to the cash receipts and cash disbursements of a business operation during a specified time period, which really gets at the heart of measuring liquidity. The statement presents cash flow data organized into three areas: operating, investing, and financing. Those who use financial information, such as investors, creditors, and financial analysts, will find the cash flow data helpful in assessing future cash flows, determining the relationship between net income and cash flow, and evaluating the ability of a firm to pay dividends, service its debt, and finance growth from internal operations.

### Statement Structure

The statement of cash flows is divided into the three categories of operating activities, investing activities, and financing activities. Cash flow information grouped by activity is

[5] "Corporate Liquidity in Perspective" (full citation in the end-of-chapter references).

**Exhibit 2-3**

*Statement of Cash Flows*

Dell Computer Corporation Annual Statements of Cash Flows ($Millions)

| | 1999 | 2000 | 2001 | 2002 | 2003 |
|---|---|---|---|---|---|
| INDIRECT OPERATING ACTIVITIES | | | | | |
| Income Before Extraordinary Items | $1,460.00 | $1,666.00 | $2,236.00 | $1,246.00 | $2,122.00 |
| Depreciation and Amortization | 103.00 | 156.00 | 240.00 | 239.00 | 211.00 |
| Extraordinary Items, Discontinued Operations | 0.00 | 0.00 | −59.00 | 0.00 | 0.00 |
| Sale of Property, Plant, Equipment | 0.00 | 0.00 | −307.00 | 17.00 | −67.00 |
| Funds from Operations—Other | 455.00 | 1,210.00 | 1,143.00 | 1,407.00 | −150.00 |
| Receivables—Decrease (Increase) | −598.00 | −394.00 | −346.00 | 222.00 | 190.00 |
| Inventory—Decrease (Increase) | −41.00 | −123.00 | −7.00 | 111.00 | −21.00 |
| Accts Pay & Accrued Liabilities—Increase (Decrease) | 0.00 | 0.00 | 0.00 | 0.00 | 0.00 |
| Other Assets and Liabilities—Net Change | 1,057.00 | 1,411.00 | 1,295.00 | 555.00 | 1,253.00 |
| Operating Activities—Net Cash Flow | $2,436.00 | $3,926.00 | $4,195.00 | $3,797.00 | $3,538.00 |
| INVESTING ACTIVITIES | | | | | |
| Investments—Increase | 0.00 | 3,101.00 | 2,606.00 | 5,382.00 | 8,736.00 |
| Sale of Investments | 0.00 | 2,319.00 | 2,331.00 | 3,425.00 | 7,660.00 |
| Short-Term Investments—Change | −1,118.00 | 0.00 | 0.00 | 0.00 | 0.00 |
| Capital Expenditures | 296.00 | 397.00 | 482.00 | 303.00 | 305.00 |
| Acquisitions | 0.00 | 4.00 | 0.00 | 0.00 | 0.00 |
| Investing Activities—Net Cash Flow | −$1,414.00 | −$1,183.00 | −$ 757.00 | −$2,260.00 | −$1,381.00 |
| FINANCING ACTIVITIES | | | | | |
| Sale of Common and Preferred Stock | 212.00 | 289.00 | 404.00 | 295.00 | 0.00 |
| Purchase of Common and Preferred | 1,518.00 | 1,061.00 | 2,700.00 | 3,000.00 | 2,290.00 |
| Cash Dividends | 0.00 | 0.00 | 0.00 | 0.00 | 0.00 |
| Long-Term Debt—Issuance | 494.00 | 20.00 | 0.00 | 0.00 | 0.00 |
| Long-Term Debt—Reduction | 0.00 | 6.00 | 0.00 | 0.00 | 0.00 |
| Financing Activities—Other | 0.00 | 63.00 | −9.00 | 3.00 | 265.00 |
| Financing Activities—Net Cash Flow | −$ 812.00 | −$ 695.00 | −$2,305.00 | −$2,702.00 | −$2,025.00 |
| Exchange Rate Effect | −10.00 | 35.00 | −32.00 | −104.00 | 459.00 |
| Cash and Equivalents—Change | $ 200.00 | $2,083.00 | $1,101.00 | −$1,269.00 | $ 591.00 |

Source: Thomson Financial, Thomson ONE Banker, **http://banker.thomsonib.com**.

**Exhibit 2–4**

*Classification Scheme for Identifying Cash Flow Activities*

**Operating Activities**
- Inflows of Cash
  - Receipts from customers for the sale of goods
  - Receipts from customers for the provision of services
  - Interest receipts on loans
  - Dividend receipts on equity securities
- Outflows of Cash
  - Payments to suppliers
  - Payments to employees
  - Payments of interest to lenders
  - Payments to government

**Investing Activities**
- Inflows of Cash
  - Receipts from loans
  - Receipts from the sale of loans to another entity
  - Receipts from the sale of debt or equity securities of other business entities, other than cash equivalents
  - Receipts from the sale of property, plant, and equipment and other productive assets
- Outflows of Cash
  - Loans made to other business entities
  - Loans purchased from other business entities
  - Payments to acquire debt or equity securities of other business entities, other than cash equivalents
  - Payments to acquire property, plant, and equipment and other assets

**Financing Activities**
- Inflows of Cash
  - Proceeds from the issuance of equity securities
  - Proceeds from the issuance of debt
- Outflows of Cash
  - Payments of dividends or other distributions to shareholders
  - Payments to repurchase stock of the entity
  - Payments of debt principal

valuable to internal management and the external analyst because it matches inflows and outflows within each activity and makes it easier to identify related transactions within each category.

The **FASB Statement 95** provides a set of guidelines to help classify cash receipts and disbursements according to type of activity. Using these guidelines, **operating activities** is a residual category encompassing everything that is not classified as **investing activities** or **financing activities**. Exhibit 2–4 presents the general guidelines for the suggested classification scheme. The purpose of this classification scheme is to combine transactions with similar characteristics and to separate transactions with dissimilar characteristics. Grouping activities in this way enables analysts to identify significant relationships within each category and evaluate an entity's ability to meet its financial obligations. At the bottom of the statement, the net increase (decrease) in cash and cash equivalents is equal to cash flow from operating activities plus net cash flow from investing activities plus net cash provided from financing activities.

## LIQUIDITY MEASURES

Liquidity tied up in the current assets of a firm is continuously changing form within the total category of current assets. Indeed, this must be the case if the firm's current assets are truly liquid. For example, funds are originally invested in inventory. After a period of time, the inventory is sold. If the sale is a cash sale, the transaction is reflected in an increase in the firm's cash balance. Similarly, a credit sale results in an increase in the receivables balance. The eventual collection of accounts receivable results in an increase in the cash balance. During this cycle, various payments must be made to employees, suppliers, creditors, and the government. Funds owed to these groups are reflected in accounts payable and accruals. As funds become owed, these accounts increase, and as payments are made, these accounts decrease. There have been many measures designed to analyze the component parts of the cash cycle. The following sections present several of the more notable measures.

### Cash Flow from Operations

One of the most direct flow measures of liquidity is **cash flow from operations.** Until FASB Statement 95, this number was not generally available from a firm's financial reports but could be estimated by taking reported profit after tax and adjusting for changes in the working capital accounts and adding back depreciation, amortization, and long-term deferrals.

In 1980, Largay and Stickney reported that the then recent bankruptcy of W. T. Grant, a nationwide chain of department stores, should have been anticipated, since the corporation had been running a deficit cash flow from operations for eight out of its last ten years of corporate life.[6] This meant that every day the company's stores were open, more cash went out the doors than came in. While this can certainly happen for short periods of time, and indeed is characteristic of firms going through a start-up or high-growth period, it certainly shouldn't be a long-term trend as in the Grant case. Over a long period of time, a company must generate a positive flow of cash from operations. A positive operating cash flow provides resources to invest in fixed assets and/or use to service creditors' and owners' invested funds. A deficit operating cash flow forces the firm to delay investment in fixed assets or to obtain external funds. The 5-year trend for operating cash flow for Dell Computer Corporation is very strong and is shown below ranging from a low of $2.4 billion to a high of $4.1 billion.

| (Millions of dollars) | 1999 | 2000 | 2001 | 2002 | 2003 |
|---|---|---|---|---|---|
| Cash flow from operations | $2,436 | $3,926 | $4,195 | $3,797 | $3,538 |

### Cash Conversion Efficiency

Knowing the dollar amount of cash flow from operations that is being generated is certainly an important piece of information. However, the information content of the level of cash flow becomes even more apparent when it is measured in relation to the level of

[6] "Cash Flow Ratio Analysis and the W. T. Grant Company Bankruptcy" (cited in the end-of-chapter references).

revenues generated by the company's operations. Generating revenues is one thing, but what is even more important is the ability to convert revenues into cash flow from operations. Calculated below is a cash conversion measure referred to as cash conversion efficiency (CCE), which is cash flow from operations divided by sales. Dell's cash conversion efficiency is compared to two traditional profitability measures: operating profit margin and net profit margin. Data for these two measures are taken from the balance sheet and income statement presented in Exhibit 2–1, while operating cash flow data are taken from the statement of cash flows (Exhibit 2–3).

| (Millions of dollars) | 1999 | 2000 | 2001 | 2002 | 2003 |
|---|---|---|---|---|---|
| Cash flow from operations | $ 2,436 | $ 3,926 | $ 4,195 | $ 3,797 | $ 3,538 |
| Revenues | 18,243 | 25,265 | 31,888 | 31,168 | 35,404 |
| Operating profit | 2,046 | 2,457 | 2,768 | 2,271 | 2,844 |
| Net profit | 1,460 | 1,666 | 2,177 | 1,246 | 2,122 |
| (Percentage of sales) | | | | | |
| Operating profit margin | 11.21% | 9.72% | 8.68% | 7.28% | 8.03% |
| Net profit margin | 8.00% | 6.59% | 6.82% | 3.99% | 5.99% |
| Cash conversion efficiency | 13.35% | 15.54% | 13.15% | 12.18% | 9.99% |

Cash conversion efficiency indicates the degree of efficiency of a firm's financial supply chain, including cost efficiency and the management of its receivables, payables, and inventory. As you may note, Dell's management is able to generate a higher efficiency converting revenues into cash compared to its profit margins. According to REL Consultancy Group, the technology industry in general had a CCE of 11 percent. Note, too, the general decline over the 5-year time period in Dell's cash conversion efficiency. Interestingly, this tracks rather well the overall general decline in Dell's profit margins. Obviously, the level of profitability impacts the amount of cash flow that can be generated. But how has Dell's management been able to generate a higher cash conversion efficiency than its profit margins? To answer this question, we turn our attention to the management of the **working capital cycle**, also known as the financial supply chain.

## Cash Conversion Period

Richards and Laughlin developed the concept "cash conversion period" as a useful framework for the analysis of the cash cycle.[7] Their approach, which measures liquidity from the perspective of a "going-concern," differs from the traditional liquidation value approach, which uses standard accrual-based solvency measures such as the current ratio. Their flow approach to liquidity analysis actually blends operating balance sheet accounts with the related income statement items at a firm's given level of operations. Calculation of the cash conversion period relies on three accrual-based measures of activity, specifically:

- Days inventory held, DIH
- Days sales outstanding, DSO
- Days payables outstanding, DPO

These measures focus on the cash cycle of the firm, as shown in Exhibit 2–5.

The first step in calculating the cash conversion period is to estimate the efficiency of inventory management, as measured by the average length of time that an inventory item is in stock before it is sold. This is referred to as days cost of goods sold in inventory, or simply **days inventory held (DIH)**. Conceptually, the ratio measures the number of days

[7] "A Cash Conversion Cycle Approach to Liquidity Analysis" (cited in the end-of-chapter references).

**Exhibit 2-5**

*The Cash Conversion Period*

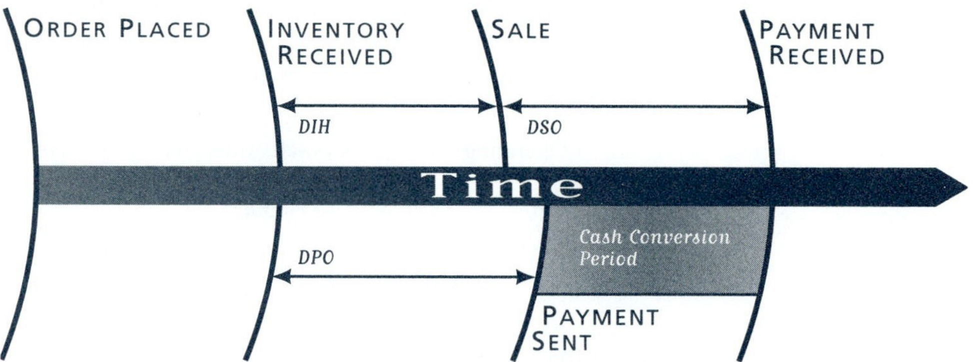


between the receipt of an item until it is actually sold to a customer, or the average number of days inventory sits idle. It is calculated by dividing ending inventory (or an average inventory balance may be used) by average daily cost of goods sold. The calculation of Dell's 2003 days inventory held is:

$$\text{Days inventory held} = \frac{\text{Inventory}}{\text{Cost of Sales/365}}$$

$$\text{Days inventory held} = \frac{\$306}{\$28{,}844/365} = 3.87 \text{ days}$$

The second step is to measure the efficiency of the credit and collections aspect of an operation by calculating the average collection period or **days sales outstanding (DSO)**. This ratio is a measure of the average number of days that it takes for customers to pay for merchandise. DSO is calculated by dividing end-of-period receivables (or an average of beginning and ending receivables may be used) by average daily sales. Dell's 2003 DSO is calculated using data from Exhibit 2–1.

$$\text{Days sales outstanding} = \frac{\text{Receivables}}{\text{Sales/365}}$$

$$\text{Days sales outstanding} = \frac{\$2{,}586}{\$35{,}404/365} = 26.66 \text{ days}$$

The third component in the analysis is an estimate of the efficiency of the accounts payable management, as measured by **days payable outstanding (DPO)**. Days payable outstanding is the elapsed time between the day that inventories are received and the day when payments are made for those inventories. This ratio can be calculated by dividing the ending accounts payable balance (or an average payables balance may be used) by average daily cost of goods sold.[8] The calculation for Dell's 2003 days payable outstanding measure follows:

[8] Instead of using cost of goods sold, purchases can be used. Purchases can be estimated using the following accounting relationship: ending inventory equals beginning inventory plus purchases less cost of goods sold. While the use of purchases is really more correct, we are using cost of goods sold in the chapter because that tends to be the approach used when calculating industry averages for benchmarking purposes.

$$\text{Days payable outstanding} = \frac{\text{Payables}}{\text{Cost of goods sold/365}}$$

$$\text{Days payable outstanding} = \frac{\$5{,}989}{\$28{,}844/365} = 75.79 \text{ days}$$

The cash conversion period is calculated by adding days sales outstanding to days inventory held (a concept referred to as the **operating cycle**) and then subtracting days payable outstanding.

$$\begin{aligned} \text{Operating cycle} &= \text{Days sales outstanding} + \text{Days inventory held} \\ &= 26.66 + 3.87 \\ &= 30.53 \end{aligned}$$

$$\begin{aligned} \text{Cash conversion period} &= \text{Operating cycle} - \text{Days payable outstanding} \\ &= 30.53 - 75.79 \\ &= -45.26 \end{aligned}$$

The 5-year trend for Dell's cash conversion period is shown below.

| (Days) | 1999 | 2000 | 2001 | 2002 | 2003 |
|---|---|---|---|---|---|
| DIH | 7.10 | 7.17 | 5.79 | 3.99 | 3.87 |
| DSO | 49.64 | 38.69 | 33.14 | 26.57 | 26.66 |
| Operating cycle | 56.74 | 45.86 | 38.93 | 30.56 | 30.53 |
| DPO | 62.34 | 64.92 | 62.07 | 72.87 | 75.79 |
| Cash conversion period | −5.60 | −19.06 | −23.14 | −42.31 | −45.26 |

Dell's cash conversion period declined dramatically from the range of approximately −5.60 days in 1999 to −45.26 days in 2003, with the majority of the change resulting from a 23-day improvement in collections and a 13-day lengthening of the disbursement period. An analyst must be careful when interpreting changes in the length of the cash conversion period. For example, the cash conversion period can be reduced even if the operating cycle expands by stretching payables by a greater number of days than the operating cycle expands. This is clearly not a signal of increased liquidity if the stretching of payables violates supplier credit terms. Thus, any changes in the length of the cash cycle must be analyzed according to its cause.

To review the cash conversion period concept, refer to Exhibit 2–5. The cash conversion period is a measure of the elapsed time between the firm's payment for inventories and its customers' payment for finished products. Note that this measure ignores the collection and disbursement float associated with the payment medium.

The concept of the cash conversion period provides useful information for the manager responsible for managing and forecasting cash. In practice, it becomes a measure of the time interval during which the financial manager must arrange for nonspontaneous financing. The greater the cash conversion period, the greater the financial strain on the firm and the less liquid it is. A long cash conversion period can absorb a significant amount of liquidity during a period of growing sales and therefore must be managed very carefully.

Quicker turnover of the various current asset accounts, including accounts receivable and inventory, tends to indicate increased efficiency and enhanced cash flow. An analyst must determine the reason for the increased asset turnover to determine whether efficiency has changed or whether management policies have changed. Slower turnover in the liability accounts, including accounts payable and accruals, will also improve the cash cycle. Again, the analyst must make sure that the slower turnover is not affecting relations with suppliers.

In the case of Dell, its CFO at the time, Tom Meredith, identified the cash conversion period as a key performance indicator and spent his first couple of years focusing Dell's employees on how they could influence this metric. As a result, Dell continued to

## FOCUS ON PRACTICE

### *Increasing the Efficiency of the Financial Supply Chain*

Financial managers historically seemed to be mainly concerned with generating profits. More recently, though, cash or liquidity has become king and financial managers are spending much more time analyzing their companies' overall liquidity position by reviewing all components of their financial supply chain. Financial managers charged with this responsibility review the rate of cash turnover generated by their working capital cycle, also known as the financial supply chain.

As discussed in the chapter, one method for measuring the turnover of cash is the cash conversion period. By increasing the efficiency of the financial supply chain, the financial manager at Apply Computer was able to shift $6 billion out of working capital and into the investment portfolio. This was accomplished through a multifaceted approach analyzing all components in their financial supply chain. One might be tempted to focus simply on slowing payments. At Apple, however, they chose to follow the rules and not pay late. They pay when due, but consider paying early when discounts offered make economic sense.

As a result of focusing on the efficiency of the financial supply chain, cash has become Apple's single largest asset with cash and short-term investments totaling $4.5 billion out of total assets of less than $7 billion.

*Source:* Anne Bacher, "Cashing In On Control—How Apple Maximizes Treasury Efficiency," Apple Computer, October 16, 2003. **http://www.gtnews.com/article/5205.cfm.**

grow rapidly but no longer at the expense of liquidity and profitability. Meredith's new performance metrics, of which the cash conversion period was one, helped the company hone its direct-sales operations and build-to-order strategy, enabling Dell to generate a multi-billion-dollar portfolio of cash resources and become one of Wall Street's top performers.[9]

## HOW MUCH LIQUIDITY IS ENOUGH?

Thus far we have discussed solvency from a balance or stock perspective and liquidity from a flow perspective. In reality, liquidity is a function of both a flow of cash resources, which can be used to cover currently due obligations, and a stock of resources, which can be drawn down if the current cash flow is not sufficient. This section presents two measures that account for the combination of the stocks of liquid assets and the flow of cash through the cash cycle. These two measures focus management's attention on the appropriate level of liquidity that should be maintained.

### Current Liquidity Index

Fraser developed a type of liquidity flow index by combining cash assets (cash plus marketable securities) and cash flow from operations in the numerator divided by current li-

[9] An article that looks at the importance of analyzing days sales outstanding and days inventory held for Dell can be found in, "How Efficient Is that Company?" *Business Week* (December 23, 2002), pp. 94–96.

abilities.[10] Such a ratio, when it decreases over time, signals potential liquidity problems. We have chosen to modify her ratio slightly and call the modified liquidity measure the **current liquidity index**. The interpretation remains the same. Dell's 2003 current liquidity index is:

$$\text{Current Liquidity Index}_t = \frac{\text{Cash assets}_{t-1} + \text{Cash flow from operations}_t}{\text{Notes payable}_{t-1} + \text{Current maturing debt}_{t-1}}$$

$$\text{CLI}_{2003} = \frac{\text{Cash assets}_{2002} + \text{Cash flow from operations}_{2003}}{\text{Notes payable}_{2002} + \text{Current maturing debt}_{2002}}$$

$$\text{CLI} = \frac{\$4{,}638 + \$3{,}538}{\$0 + \$0} = \text{infinite}$$

The figures for cash assets, notes payable, and current maturing debt are taken from the 2002 balance sheet (Exhibit 2–1), and the figure for cash flow from operations is taken from the 2003 statement of cash flows (Exhibit 2–3). Dell's CLI is infinite in a mathematical sense in that it has no short-term bank debt that must be repaid. This holds true for the entire time period of 1999 through 2003. Dell's management was able to fund operations from internal cash flow and did not rely on short-term bank debt.

## Lambda

Emery developed a liquidity measure from a function of the likelihood that a firm will exhaust its liquid reserve.[11] The measure consists of three parts. First, firms rely on a stock of liquid resources. These are resources that can be quickly converted into cash without impairing the operations of the firm. Examples of such liquid resources include cash, marketable securities, and lines of credit. The second component of the liquidity measure is the level of cash flow from operations expected over the planning horizon. The final component is a measure of the variability of the expected cash flow. These three components taken together form a liquidity index he refers to as **lambda**, as shown below:

$$\text{Lambda} = \frac{\text{Initial Liquid Reserve} + \text{Total anticipated net cash flow during the analysis horizon}}{\text{Uncertainty about the net cash flow during the analysis horizon}}$$

The denominator of the above ratio is the standard deviation of the distribution of the firm's expected net cash flow from operations. It can be approximated by finding the range of the distribution and dividing it by six (i.e., optimistic cash flow minus pessimistic cash flow divided by six). If future cash flows are expected to be similar to past cash flows, then historical data can be used to assess the future cash flow.

Lambda can be used like a *z* value from the standard normal distribution table. For example, a lambda of 3 means that there is only about one chance in a thousand that cash needs will exceed available cash resources, while a lambda of 1.65 signals a 5 percent chance of running out of cash. Exhibit 2–6 presents a table of lambda values from 1.645 to 3.291 and their associated probability values. Thus, the lambda value gives an approximation of the probability of a firm running into a liquidity problem.

This measure represents the first attempt at incorporating information about the distribution of cash flow into a liquidity measure. It is very appealing because a firm with a

[10] "Cash Flow from Operations and Liquidity Analysis" (cited in the end-of-chapter references).

[11] "Measuring Short-Term Liquidity" (cited in the end-of-chapter references).

## FOCUS ON PRACTICE

### A Cash-Flow Based Rating System

Fitch Investors Service, Inc., a New York based credit-rating agency, recently unveiled a new cash-flow based rating system. The rating system compares net free cash flow, defined as earnings available to pay debt after interest costs, taxes, and capital expenditures have been considered, to the average amount of debt maturing over the next five years. This rating system is thought to provide a useful early warning system for corporate bond investors. A high rating indicates the company should have continuing liquidity, while a low rating generally indicates that the company may have to raise additional financing.

*Source:* "Investors Have a New Tool for Judging Issuers' Health: Cash-Flow Adequacy," *The Wall Street Journal* (January 10, 1994).

**Exhibit 2–6**

*Lambda Values and Their Related Probability Values*

| Lambda | Probability in Left Tail | Lambda | Probability in Left Tail |
|---|---|---|---|
| 1.645 | 5.00% | 2.108 | 1.75% |
| 1.670 | 4.75 | 2.170 | 1.50 |
| 1.695 | 4.50 | 2.241 | 1.25 |
| 1.722 | 4.25 | 2.326 | 1.00 |
| 1.751 | 4.00 | 2.432 | 0.75 |
| 1.780 | 3.75 | 2.576 | 0.50 |
| 1.812 | 3.50 | 2.808 | 0.25 |
| 1.845 | 3.25 | 2.879 | 0.20 |
| 1.881 | 3.00 | 2.969 | 0.15 |
| 1.919 | 2.75 | 3.090 | 0.10 |
| 1.960 | 2.50 | 3.291 | 0.05 |
| 2.004 | 2.25 | | |
| 2.053 | 2.00 | | |

relatively low liquid balance and a moderate level of cash flows may be just as liquid as a firm with a large liquid reserve and above average positive cash flows if the cash flows of the firm with the low liquid reserves are much more certain. In other words, liquid reserves are needed only to meet unforeseen circumstances that come about when there is a high degree of uncertainty regarding future cash flow. If the future is relatively stable, then there is less of a need for a significant level of liquid reserves.

## FINANCIAL FLEXIBILITY

Although not yet considered, the role of sales growth is important because cash flow can be adversely affected by the growth rate of the company even though the company may be very profitable. For example, rapid growth puts a strain on the liquidity of those companies with large working capital requirements per dollar of sales. Management's response to that type of liquidity problem should be different than liquidity problems resulting from a lack of profitability or some other reason. Firms with a large market share in a slow-growth industry tend to have very strong cash flows (such companies are often referred to as cash cows), while firms with a small market share in a rapidly growing industry tend to have very poor operating cash flows.

Determining the rate of sales growth that is compatible with a firm's established financial policies is a key element in understanding financial flexibility. The concept of sustainable growth developed by Robert C. Higgins provides a framework to test whether a firm's growth objectives are contributing to its liquidity problems.[12]

Analysis of financial flexibility starts with the premise that there is a certain sales growth rate, referred to as the **sustainable growth rate**, that can be supported by the firm's current financial policies (including asset turnover, net profit margin, dividend payout, and debt-to-equity ratio) without having to issue new external equity. Firms with growth rates that exceed this level will experience difficulties adhering to their target financial policies.

As a company experiences a growth in sales, it must finance the purchase of additional assets to support the higher level of sales. If a firm is not generating sufficient cash flow from operations to support the addition of new debt consistent with its debt-to-equity ratio so that new assets can be acquired, then the firm's target financial policies will need to be altered. Firms that grow faster than the sustainable rate must support that growth through cash generated from investing or financing activities (i.e., selling fixed assets, acquiring new debt in excess of the desired debt ratio, or selling additional equity shares). Firms growing at rates below the sustainable rate will have surplus cash to build an asset base, pay off debt, or possibly increase the dividend payout.

A firm's future growth potential is dependent on its total asset base. In other words, total assets must increase more or less proportionately with sales or the firm's long-term ability to grow will be diminished. In addition, creditors often impose external restrictions on an operation in the form of financial covenants in loan contracts, and shareholders place a high value on the payment of dividends. These restrictions will dictate certain target values for various ratios (e.g., sales to total assets, debt to equity, and dividends to earnings).

When policy dictates certain values for these three ratios, sales growth is an interdependent variable in the operating system. If the firm has the ability to grow at a rate faster than its sustainable growth rate and management desires to achieve that higher rate of growth, then management should formulate a new set of financial policies that will guide the sustainable growth rate toward the desired growth rate.

Following Higgins' approach, sustainable growth can be estimated by equating annual sources of capital to annual uses. First, define the following parameters:

S = prior-year sales
gS = change in sales during the planning year where g is the growth rate for sales and S is defined above
A/S = target ratio of total assets to total sales
m = projected after-tax profit margin
d = target dividend payout ratio (i.e., ratio of dividends to earnings)
D/E = target debt-to-equity ratio

If sales are to increase by gS, then assets must grow proportionately to keep A/S constant. In other words, sales growth of gS will require an addition to the asset base of gS(A/S), which represents a use of capital.

---

[12] "How Much Growth Can a Firm Afford?" (cited in the end-of-chapter references).

Sources of capital originate from the liability and equity side of the balance sheet. Additions to retained earnings equal net profit minus dividends paid. This is depicted by the expression $[m \times (S + gS) \times (1 - d)]$. As equity increases by this amount, liabilities can increase proportionately and still maintain a constant value for D/E. The expression for the increase in liabilities is $[m \times (S + gS) \times (1 - d) \times (D/E)]$.

Total uses must equal total sources. Equating the two results in the following expression:

$$gS \times (A/S) = m \times (S + gS) \times (1 - d) + m \times (S + gS) \times (1 - d) \times (D/E).$$

The growth rate for sales, g, that satisfies the above equality is defined as the sustainable growth rate and presented below.

$$g = \frac{m \times (1 - d) \times [1 + (D/E)]}{A/S - \{m \times (1 - d) \times [1 + (D/E)]\}}$$

The critical operating variable in the equation is the addition to retained earnings, the major spontaneous source of cash in this framework. One could argue that in order to support the growth objectives of the firm, new external equity could be issued if earnings retention is insufficient in maintaining the desired debt-to-equity mix. However, this ignores the nonspontaneous aspect of new equity issues, and future conditions in equity markets may not be conducive to new issues when funds are needed. The sustainable growth rate for Dell using end-of-year 2002 data is calculated below. We used 2002 data in order to calculate a sustainable growth rate for 2003 sales. Actual 2003 sales grew 13.59 percent, versus a calculated sustainable growth of 36.14 percent.

$$g = \frac{0.039977 \times (1 - .00) \times (1 + 1.8834)}{0.43426 - [0.039977 \times (1 - .00) \times (1 + 1.8834)]}$$

$$= \frac{0.11527}{0.31899} = 0.3614, \text{ or } 36.14 \text{ percent}$$

Dell grew at a slower pace than its sustainable growth.

The 4-year trend for Dell's sustainable growth rate is shown below. Dell's strategies contributed to an increasing degree of financial flexibility as its assets-to-sales ratio fell (resulting from improved working capital management) and its profit margin improved. As a result, the firm was able to grow at annual revenue growth rates up to almost 40 percent between the period 1999 to 2003 without straining the firm's financial resources.

| (Percent) | 2000 | 2001 | 2002 | 2003 |
|---|---|---|---|---|
| Sustainable growth | 169.57% | 45.74% | 66.04% | 36.14% |
| Actual growth | 38.49% | 26.21% | −2.26% | 13.59% |

## FINANCIAL DILEMMA REVISITED

So what have we learned from the Dell experience? When management brings into harmony the three key variables of growth, profitability, and liquidity, the value created can be significant. Dell was able to sustain a strong growth rate without straining its resources because, in part, it restructured its working capital policies so that its financial supply chain was able to not only become self-financing but also become a significant net supplier of funds for the firm. With the cash conversion period decreasing from (5.60) days in 1999 to (45.25) days in 2003, cash flow from operations increased by a factor of 1.45 times, from $2.4 billion in 1999 to $3.5 billion in 2003. Thus, the firm was able to fund its growth with internally generated funds.

## FOCUS ON PRACTICE

### *How Long Can a Firm Survive Without Profit or Cash Flow?*

So what could be wrong with having an impressive customer base, $1 billion in cash, and expanding sales? After hitting a peak of 106 11/16 on December 10, 1999, and trending downward until mid-June, Amazon.com, Inc.'s stock price settled into a trading range between the mid-40s and the mid-50s.

The company's balance sheet negatives could be easily overlooked. Why? Because management was willing to go into the red to build up a dominant position in e-commerce, and as triple-digit growth rates and expansion into new product lines led to far heftier sales, Amazon would eventually cross over into profitability.

However, in June of 2000 it became evident that debt analysts and equity analysts were looking at the company through very different lenses. Debt analyst Ravi Suria, with Lehman Brothers, released a very negative report on the company's deteriorating credit situation. He, in essence, questioned the business model on which Amazon and most e-tailers were based. He argued that the excessive debt and poor inventory management at Amazon would make the company's operating cash flow worse the more it grows. However, the company's founder, Jeffrey P. Bezos, was quick to counter saying the company would have positive operating cash flow over the last three quarters of 2000 and was on the road to profitability. He did concede, however, that inventory control could be improved.

Because the company had some significant inventory missteps during the 1999 Christmas season, its cash flow nose-dived from a positive $31.5 million to a negative $320.5 million during the first quarter following the all-important Christmas season. By adding product lines such as electronics and toys and building distribution centers all over the country, the job of policing its inventories became much more difficult. Amazon's ability to turn over its inventory has declined since the end of 1998, falling from 8.5 times to just 2.9 times for the first quarter of 2000. In fact, inventory has been growing faster than sales.

Equity analysts have generally sided with Bezos and believe the debt analysts focused too heavily on the one year of Amazon's greatest expansion and then projected those costs forward. For Amazon, the costs came up front, but now, they argue, the company will exploit its ability to handle a far higher volume. Suria's critics claim he was looking at these one-time capital costs assuming that Amazon would have to keep spending at those levels. However, now that the distribution centers are built, the company can work to make them more efficient. In fact, as Amazon's sales grow, some analysts estimate that it will require no more than a third of the investment of a brick-and-mortar retailer for the same amount of sales. By the third quarter of 2003, Amazon reported a positive net income, on sales of $1.13 billion, for the third time in its history. While not out of the woods yet, the company is beginning to reap benefits from its enormous investment in infrastructure.

*Source:* Adapted from "Can Amazon Make It?" *Business Week* (July 10, 2000), pp. 38–43.

The importance of financial flexibility and liquidity did not go unnoticed at another company, AT&T. "The most important job I can do for AT&T, given the uncertainty [in the telecom sector and the economy], is to ensure that we have financial flexibility so we don't have to make sub-optimal decision," the treasurer says. "The credo around here is liquidity and financial flexibility. Without it, you are at the mercy of the market."[13]

[13] "Honey, I Shrunk the Company," *Treasury & Risk Management* (July/August 2003), pp. 28–29.

## SUMMARY

This chapter introduced the basic concepts of solvency, liquidity, and financial flexibility. All three concepts are valid, and all three are important. The issue for the manager, analyst, investor, or lender is to match the question being asked with the appropriate concept.

Solvency is an accounting concept comparing assets to liabilities. It is an appropriate measure addressing the degree of coverage of liabilities by assets in the event of liquidation.

Liquidity is more of a tactical concept related to the firm's ability to pay for its current obligations in a timely fashion at minimal cost. Payment can be made either through current-period cash flow or by drawing down a stock of liquid resources. The question here is whether the firm has the cash resources to cover its debt service or other significant payment obligations on an *ongoing* basis.

Financial flexibility, as measured by the sustainable growth rate, is a more strategic concept related to the firm's overall financial structure and whether its financial policies allow the firm enough flexibility to take advantage of unforeseen opportunities.

## USEFUL WEB SITES

Source for corporate financial statements: **http://www.sec.gov/edgar.shtml**

## QUESTIONS

1. What is liquidity, and how does it differ from solvency?
2. How is liquidity related to financial flexibility?
3. How does the sustainable growth rate concept relate to the concept of financial flexibility?
4. How might a balance sheet measure of solvency be converted into a liquidity measure?
5. What new information is contributed by lambda that is not provided by the current liquidity index?
6. What useful information does the statement of cash flows provide?
7. What is your interpretation if a company's current ratio is 2.00? What is your interpretation of a company's current liquidity index value if it is 2.00? Does this help you understand the difference between solvency and liquidity?
8. In your own words, describe why the cash conversion period is listed as a measure of liquidity.
9. How are the current liquidity index and lambda like the flow measures of liquidity (such as cash conversion cycle and cash flow from operations) and the solvency ratios (such as current ratio)? How are they different?
10. Is it possible for a firm to have high (low) solvency ratios but low (high) flow measures of liquidity? Explain.
11. In your own words, what information does the rate of sustainable growth provide?

## PROBLEMS

1. Compute the lambda value from the following financial data. To calculate the cash flow uncertainty number, use a range of three years of cash flow, find the difference between the high and low values, and divide by 6. Calculate lambda for 1997 using end-of-year 1996 cash assets

and the 3-year range of cash flow starting in 1994. Then calculate the value for lambda for each succeeding year, and discuss the appropriateness of the firm's management of its liquid resources.

| Year | Cash Flow | End-of-Year Cash Assets |
|---|---|---|
| 1994 | 15 | |
| 1995 | 0 | |
| 1996 | −1 | 3 |
| 1997 | 2 | 0 |
| 1998 | 4 | 5 |
| 1999 | 8 | 2 |
| 2000 | 0 | 0 |
| 2001 | 2 | 5 |
| 2002 | −1 | 4 |
| 2003 | 5 | 1 |
| 2004 | 8 | |

2. Presented below are three different liquidity positions for a firm. Which position provides the greatest amount of liquidity based on the calculated lambda value? Use the probability values provided in Exhibit 2–6 and explain your result.

| | Liquidity Scenario | | |
|---|---|---|---|
| | A | B | C |
| Initial liquid reserve | $ 500 | $1,000 | $ 100 |
| Anticipated net cash flow | 3,000 | 200 | 1,500 |
| Standard deviation of net cash flow | 2,127 | 729 | 972 |

## The following financial data are to be used for problems 3 and 4.

| | 2000 | 2001 | 2002 | 2003 | 2004 |
|---|---|---|---|---|---|
| Cash & equivalents | $ 75 | $ 75 | $ 90 | $ 100 | $ 100 |
| Accounts receivable | 300 | 400 | 600 | 550 | 500 |
| Inventory | 150 | 250 | 350 | 250 | 250 |
| Gross fixed assets | 700 | 800 | 900 | 900 | 900 |
| (Accumulated depr.) | (75) | (125) | (190) | (260) | (335) |
| Total assets | $1,150 | $1,400 | $1,750 | $1,540 | $1,415 |
| Accounts payable | $ 125 | $ 175 | $ 250 | $ 225 | $ 200 |
| Notes payable | 165 | 162 | 178 | 136 | 99 |
| Accrued operating exp. | 10 | 63 | 65 | 49 | 36 |
| Current maturities | 50 | 98 | 100 | 40 | 40 |
| Long-term debt | 600 | 500 | 400 | 200 | 150 |
| Shareholders' equity | 200 | 402 | 757 | 890 | 890 |

| | 2000 | 2001 | 2002 | 2003 | 2004 |
|---|---|---|---|---|---|
| Revenues | $1,500 | $2,250 | $3,000 | $2,000 | $1,500 |
| Cost of goods sold | 600 | 900 | 1,200 | 800 | 600 |
| Operating expenses | 600 | 700 | 800 | 750 | 725 |
| Depreciation | 35 | 50 | 65 | 70 | 75 |
| Interest | 30 | 33 | 28 | 25 | 10 |
| Taxes | 94 | 285 | 420 | 142 | 36 |
| Net profit | $ 141 | $ 282 | $ 487 | $ 213 | $ 54 |
| Dividends | 40 | 80 | 132 | 80 | 54 |

**3.** Use the information contained in the above financial statements to perform the following:
   **a.** Calculate the solvency ratios, current ratio, quick ratio, net working capital, and working capital requirements for each of the five years. Discuss and interpret the trends you see.
   **b.** Calculate cash flow from operations for 2001 through 2004 and the cash conversion efficiency and interpret the 4-year trend.
   **c.** Calculate the cash conversion period for each of the five years and interpret the trend.
   **d.** Assuming cash flow from operations to be the following, calculate the current liquidity index and interpret the 4-year trend.

| | |
|---|---|
| 2001 | $250 |
| 2002 | 400 |
| 2003 | 350 |
| 2004 | 130 |

   **e.** Compare and contrast your interpretation of the current ratio trend with your interpretation of the current liquidity index.
   **f.** What is your opinion of the firm's liquidity position and why?

**4.** Using the financial statements above, calculate the sustainable growth rate for each year of the 4-year period 2001 through 2004 and compare it with the actual sales growth rate. Interpret and discuss disparities between the two growth rates.

## The following financial data are to be used for problems 5 and 6.

| | 2000 | 2001 | 2002 | 2003 | 2004 |
|---|---|---|---|---|---|
| Cash & equivalents | $ 25 | $ 75 | $ 100 | $ 50 | $ 25 |
| Accounts receivable | 450 | 700 | 1,200 | 2,000 | 3,000 |
| Inventory | 400 | 500 | 800 | 1,400 | 2,500 |
| Gross fixed assets | 1,000 | 1,000 | 1,500 | 1,500 | 2,500 |
| (Accumulated depr.) | (200) | (250) | (350) | (400) | (550) |
| Total assets | $1,675 | $2,025 | $3,250 | $4,550 | $7,475 |
| Accounts payable | $ 100 | $ 200 | $ 400 | $ 700 | $1,226 |
| Notes payable | 50 | 275 | 1,092 | 598 | 1,550 |
| Accrued operating exp. | 60 | 55 | 60 | 70 | 80 |
| Current maturities | 50 | 50 | 50 | 50 | 200 |
| Long-term debt | 400 | 382 | 330 | 1,508 | 2,315 |
| Shareholders' equity | 1,015 | 1,063 | 1,318 | 1,624 | 2,104 |

| | 2000 | 2001 | 2002 | 2003 | 2004 |
|---|---|---|---|---|---|
| Revenues | $1,500 | $2,250 | $3,750 | $5,500 | $9,000 |
| Cost of goods sold | 750 | 1,125 | 1,875 | 2,750 | 4,500 |
| Operating expenses | 700 | 750 | 900 | 1,600 | 2,500 |
| Depreciation | 100 | 50 | 100 | 50 | 150 |
| Interest | 40 | 45 | 100 | 200 | 400 |
| Taxes | (36) | 112 | 310 | 360 | 580 |
| Net profit | $ (54) | $ 168 | $ 465 | $ 540 | $ 870 |
| Dividends | 45 | 120 | 210 | 234 | 390 |

**5.** Use the information contained in the above financial statements to perform the following:
   **a.** Calculate the solvency ratios, current ratio, quick ratio, net working capital, and working capital requirements for each of the five years. Discuss and interpret the trends you see.
   **b.** Calculate cash flow from operations for 2001 through 2004 and the cash conversion efficiency and interpret the 4-year trend.
   **c.** Calculate the cash conversion period for each of the five years and interpret the trend.

**d.** Assuming cash flow from operations to be the following, calculate the current liquidity index and interpret the 4-year trend.

| | |
|---|---|
| 2001 | $ 40 |
| 2002 | −75 |
| 2003 | −550 |
| 2004 | −650 |

**e.** Compare and contrast your interpretation of the current ratio trend with your interpretation of the current liquidity index.

**f.** What is your opinion of the firm's liquidity position and why?

**6.** Using the financial statements above, calculate the sustainable growth rate for each year of the 4-year period 2001 through 2004 and compare it with the actual sales growth rate. Interpret and discuss disparities between the two growth rates.

## The following financial data are to be used for problems 7 and 8.

| | 2000 | 2001 | 2002 | 2003 | 2004 |
|---|---|---|---|---|---|
| Cash & equivalents | $ 25 | $ 75 | $ 100 | $ 50 | $ 25 |
| Accounts receivable | 750 | 534 | 416 | 312 | 243 |
| Inventory | 125 | 157 | 160 | 138 | 121 |
| Gross fixed assets | 1,000 | 1,000 | 1,000 | 1,000 | 1,000 |
| (Accumulated depr.) | (200) | (300) | (400) | (500) | (600) |
| Total assets | $1,700 | $1,466 | $1,276 | $1,000 | $ 789 |
| Accounts payable | $ 125 | $ 163 | $ 160 | $ 138 | $ 121 |
| Notes payable | 850 | 300 | 141 | 47 | 0 |
| Accrued operating exp. | 100 | 75 | 50 | 40 | 30 |
| Current maturities | 50 | 50 | 50 | 50 | 50 |
| Long-term debt | 0 | 303 | 300 | 150 | 88 |
| Shareholders' equity | 575 | 575 | 575 | 575 | 500 |

| | 2000 | 2001 | 2002 | 2003 | 2004 |
|---|---|---|---|---|---|
| Revenues | $9,000 | $5,500 | $3,750 | $2,500 | $1,750 |
| Cost of goods sold | 4,500 | 2,750 | 1,875 | 1,250 | 875 |
| Operating expenses | 3,000 | 1,600 | 1,065 | 925 | 888 |
| Depreciation | 100 | 100 | 100 | 100 | 100 |
| Interest | 40 | 45 | 35 | 25 | 12 |
| Taxes | 544 | 402 | 270 | 80 | (50) |
| Net profit | $ 816 | $ 603 | $ 405 | $ 120 | $ (75) |
| Dividends | 816 | 603 | 405 | 120 | 0 |

**7.** Use the information contained in the above financial statements to perform the following:

**a.** Calculate the solvency ratios, current ratio, quick ratio, net working capital, and working capital requirements for each of the five years. Discuss and interpret the trends you see.

**b.** Calculate cash flow from operations for 2001 through 2004 and the cash conversion efficiency and interpret the 4-year trend.

**c.** Calculate the cash conversion period for each of the five years and interpret the trend.

**d.** Assuming cash flow from operations to be the following, calculate the current liquidity index and interpret the 4-year trend.

| | |
|---|---|
| 2001 | $910 |
| 2002 | 600 |
| 2003 | 300 |
| 2004 | 100 |

**e.** Compare and contrast your interpretation of the current ratio trend with your interpretation of the current liquidity index.

**f.** What is your opinion of the firm's liquidity position and why?

**8.** Using the financial statements above, calculate the sustainable growth rate for each year of the 4-year period 2001 through 2004 and compare it with the actual sales growth rate. Interpret and discuss disparities between the two growth rates.

## REFERENCES

David R. Campbell, James M. Johnson, and Leonard M. Savoie, "Cash Flow, Liquidity, and Financial Flexibility," *Financial Executive*, 52 (8) (1984), pp. 14–17.

Gary Emery, "Measuring Short-Term Liquidity," *Journal of Cash Management*, 3 (9) (1984), pp. 25–32.

Lynn M. Fraser, "Cash Flow from Operations and Liquidity Analysis: A New Financial Ratio for Commercial Lending Decisions," *The Journal of Commercial Bank Lending*, 66 (3) (1983), pp. 45–52.

Gabriel Hawawini, Claude Viallet, and Ashok Vora, "Industrial Influence on Corporate Working Capital Decisions," *Sloan Management Review*, 27 (4) (1986), pp. 15–24.

R. C. Higgins, "How Much Growth Can a Firm Afford?" *Financial Management* (Fall 1977), pp. 7–16.

J. A. Largay and C. P. Stickney, "Cash Flows Ratio Analysis and the W. T. Grant Company Bankruptcy," *Financial Analyst Journal* (July–August 1980), pp. 51–54.

K. W. Lemke, "The Evaluation of Liquidity: An Empirical Study," *Journal of Accounting Research* (Spring 1970), pp. 47–77.

Douglas H. Ludeman, "Corporate Liquidity in Perspective," *Financial Executive*, 42 (10) (1974), pp. 18–22.

V. D. Richards and E. J. Laughlin, "A Cash Conversion Cycle Approach to Liquidity Analysis," *Financial Management* (Spring 1980), pp. 32–38.

Joel M. Shulman and Raymond A. K. Cox, "An Integrative Approach to Working Capital Management," *Journal of Cash Management*, 5 (6) (1985), pp. 64–67.

Bernell K. Stone, "Liquidity Assessment and the Formulation of Corporate Liquidity Policy," *Readings in Short-Term Financial Management, Third Edition* (West Publishing Company, 1988), pp. 32–41.

G. P. Tsetsekos, "Liquidity Balances and Agency Considerations," *Readings in Short-Term Financial Management, Third Edition* (West Publishing Company, 1988), pp. 17–22.

FOCUSED CASE

# Just for Feet, Inc.

Just For Feet, Inc. operates retail stores in the brand-name athletic and outdoor footwear and apparel market. Just For Feet was founded in 1977 with the opening of a small mall-based store, and opened its first superstore in Birmingham, Alabama, in 1988. As a result of the success and high sales volume generated by the larger store format, the Company has focused primarily on developing and refining its superstore concept. In addition to the prototype superstore, the Company operates high visibility, high profile "flagship" superstores in select markets, which provide added entertainment.

As of January 30, 1999, there were 120 Just For Feet superstores operating in 23 states and Puerto Rico. Of the 120 Company operated superstores, 23 superstores were opened in fiscal 1997 and 26 superstores were opened in fiscal 1998, along with 21 converted Sneaker Stadium superstores. The Company plans to open approximately 25 superstores each during fiscal 1999 and 2000.

As part of its long-term growth strategy, the Company entered the smaller specialty store market of the athletic and outdoor footwear and apparel industry in 1997 through the acquisitions of Athletic Attic and Imperial Sports, which are now operated as the specialty store division of the Company. As of January 30, 1999, the Company operated 141 company-owned specialty stores in 18 states. The Company opened 51 new specialty stores in fiscal 1998 and plans to open approximately 60 new specialty stores in fiscal 1999 and approximately 50 to 100 in fiscal 2000.

The Companyís financial statements are presented below. Assess the solvency, liquidity, and financial flexibility position of the company. Specifically address the following questions:

1. Why did the current ratio go up and the quick ratio go down?
2. Discuss the working capital cycle position of the Company.
3. Discuss the ability of the Company to pay its current obligations.
4. Compare and contrast the solvency position of the Company with its liquidity position.
5. Discuss the impact of the Company growing faster than its sustainable growth rate.
6. What conclusion might you draw about the liquidity management of the Company and its future?

| BALANCE SHEET | JANUARY 30, 1999 | JANUARY 31, 1998 |
|---|---|---|
| ASSETS | | |
| Current assets | | |
| Cash and equivalents | $12,412 | $82,490 |
| Accounts receivable | $18,875 | $15,840 |
| Merchandise inventory | $399,901 | $206,128 |
| Other | $18,302 | $6,709 |
| Total | $449,490 | $311,167 |
| Property and equipment, net | $160,592 | $94,529 |
| Goodwill, net | $71,084 | $36,106 |
| Other | $8,230 | $6,550 |
| Total assets | $689,396 | $448,352 |
| LIABILITIES AND EQUITY | | |
| Liabilities and net worth | | |
| Current liabilities | | |
| Short-term borrowings | | $90,667 |
| Accounts payable | $100,322 | $51,162 |
| Accrued expenses | $24,829 | $9,292 |

| | | |
|---|---|---|
| Income taxes | | $1,363 |
| Deferred income taxes | $902 | |
| Current maturities | $6,639 | $3,222 |
| Total current liabilities | $132,692 | $155,706 |
| Long-term obligations | $216,203 | $16,646 |
| Deferred lease rentals | $13,162 | $7,212 |
| Deferred income taxes | $1,633 | $704 |
| Total | $363,690 | $180,268 |
| Shareholders' equity | | |
| Common stock | $3 | $3 |
| Paid-in capital | $249,590 | $218,616 |
| Retained earnings | $76,113 | $49,465 |
| Total shareholders' equity | $325,706 | $269,084 |
| Total liabilities and equity | $689,396 | $448,352 |

| STATEMENT OF EARNINGS | FISCAL 1998 | FISCAL 1997 |
|---|---|---|
| Net sales | $774,863 | $478,638 |
| Cost of sales | $452,330 | $279,816 |
| Gross profit | $322,533 | $198,822 |
| Franchise fees, royalties, etc. | $1,299 | $1,101 |
| Operating expenses: | | |
| Store operating costs | $232,505 | $139,659 |
| Store opening costs | $13,669 | $6,728 |
| Amortization of intangibles | $2,072 | $1,200 |
| General and administrative | $24,341 | $18,040 |
| Total operating expenses | $272,587 | $165,627 |
| Operating income | $51,245 | $34,296 |
| Interest expense | ($8,059) | ($1,446) |
| Interest income | $143 | $1,370 |
| Earnings before income taxes | $43,329 | $34,220 |
| Provision for income tax | $16,681 | $12,817 |
| Net earnings | $26,648 | $21,403 |
| Shares outstanding | 30,737 | 29,615 |
| Diluted | 31,852 | 30,410 |

| STATEMENT OF CASH FLOWS | FISCAL 1998 | FISCAL 1997 |
|---|---|---|
| Net earnings | $26,648 | $21,403 |
| Adjustments to reconcile net earnings to net cash used by operating activities: | | |
| Depreciation and amortization | $16,129 | $8,783 |
| Deferred income taxes | $12,100 | $2,194 |
| Deferred lease rentals | $2,655 | $2,111 |
| Change in assets and liabilities: | | |
| Accounts receivable | ($2,795) | ($8,918) |
| Merchandise inventory | ($170,169) | ($56,616) |
| Other assets | ($8,228) | ($5,643) |
| Accounts payable | $34,638 | $7,495 |
| Accrued expenses | $7,133 | $2,264 |
| Income taxes | ($181) | $543 |
| Net cash used by operating activities | ($82,070 | ($26,384) |
| Net cash used for investing activities | ($79,183 | ($32,067) |
| Net cash provided by financing activities | $91,175 | $2,156 |
| Net (decrease) increase in cash and cash equivalents | ($70,078) | ($56,295) |

CHAPTER 3

# Valuation

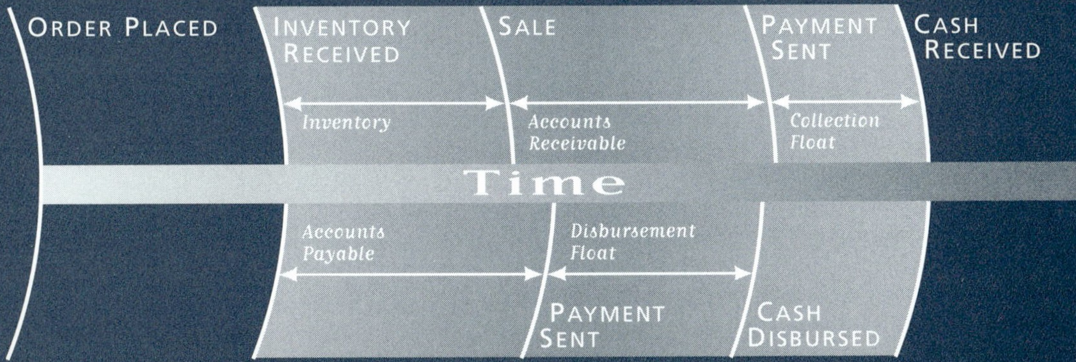

# OBJECTIVES

## *After studying this chapter, you should be able to:*

- use the cash flow timeline and discounting techniques to value future cash flows.
- explain the importance of the time value of money for short-term financial decisions.
- apply the net present value technique to select proposals that should enhance shareholder value.
- explain how short-term financial decisions fit into the economic value added (EVA™) framework.
- apply the net present value technique to value changes in the cash conversion period.
- recognize the difficulties involved in selecting an appropriate discount rate.

Capital budgeting is the process of generating, selecting, implementing, and controlling long-term investments in working capital and fixed assets. Because the primary objective of a publicly held company is to maximize shareholder wealth, this process should be carried out to balance risk and return appropriately within the context of the company's strategic plan. For consistency, multiyear working capital decisions should be made at the same time and in basically the same way as fixed asset decisions. Ongoing allocation of funds to inventories or receivables might be done in the context of an Economic Value Added (EVA™) framework, discussed later, or not reevaluated because the strategy of which they are part is projected to maximize shareholder wealth. Changes in working capital policy, however, should be subjected to capital budgeting evaluation using the Net Present Value (NPV) method that is utilized for long-term capital asset selection. Companies reporting the most satisfaction with their capital planning processes are those that evaluate all their capital spending proposals consistently.[1]

The process of short-term financial decision making is often less complex than that of making long-term investment and financing decisions. The time value of money only slightly affects decisions for which financial impacts are limited to the present year's cash flow; so, they do not require extensive analysis. Although important, the timing of the associated cash flows is rarely the deciding factor in the "go/no-go" decision. Deciding which bank to use for a nonrenewable credit line would be an example of this type of decision. Many other decisions, such as permanent reductions of receivables or inventory, would change the firm's financial position for a period of years, however, and in those cases, the time value of money becomes vital.

In this chapter, we learn two approaches to short-term financial decision making: the valuation approach and the financial statement approach. We then examine why a valuation approach is superior when the project's cash flows can be quantified. **Valuation** is the determination of the present dollar value of a series of cash flows. When deciding whether to adopt a policy, we take into account all cash flows and the time value of money. In Chapter 1, we focused on the unsynchronized nature of cash flows. In Chapter 2, we saw how this led to the maintenance of liquidity and some of the ways of measuring liquidity. In this chapter, we turn our attention to the dollar amounts that occur on the cash flow timeline and how they affect shareholder value.

Throughout this and the following chapters, we assume that the manager's objective is to **maximize shareholder value**, which simplifies to maximizing the common stock price. The implication for managers is that those policies and projects that should increase the company's stock price are to be favored. Short-term financial policies and decisions have a significant effect on shareholder value, as we

[1] Neely, et al., "A New View of Capital Planning," *The CFO Project*, Vol. 2 (October 1, 2003). Accessed online 11/19/2003 at www.cfoproject.com.

see in Exhibit 3–1. Inventory, payables, receivables, cash management, and short-term investing and borrowing decisions alter the firm's cash flows, cash conversion period, risk posture, net interest revenue, and information accuracy and timeliness. These, in turn, increase or decrease shareholder value.

The following hypothetical situation illustrates the type of issues that financial managers deal with, and it helps frame our suggested approach for determining the value effects of short-term financial decisions.

### FINANCIAL DILEMMA

Evaluating the Financial Impact of a Change in Credit Terms

DigiView, a maker of DVD players, is considering changing its credit terms from "net 30" to "net 60," allowing 30 more days for consumer electronics retailers to pay for merchandise. DigiView believes the relaxing of terms would stimulate sales, particularly at the present time when many electronics retailers are facing intense competition and financially strapped. The DigiView credit analyst is wondering how to evaluate the financial impact this alternative would have on the company.

## TWO APPROACHES TO FINANCIAL DECISION MAKING

Two approaches may be used for making short-term financial decisions: the **financial statement approach** and the **valuation approach**. Their treatment of the (1) advisability, (2) timing, and (3) risk of proposed decisions is contrasted. We then demonstrate how economic value added systems attempt to incorporate aspects of both approaches.

### Financial Statement Approach

The traditional approach to making working capital decisions, and the approach often taken in an introductory finance course, is to estimate the incremental revenue and expense effects of the proposal and then calculate the anticipated profit effect. If the effect is positive, the proposal would increase profits and it should be implemented. In the case of our Financial Dilemma, the DigiView manager would follow these steps:

1. Estimate the additional unit sales expected, and multiply this by the profit contributed per unit.
2. Estimate the capital cost of the additional investment in receivables by subtracting the present average receivables balance from the balance expected under the new terms and then multiplying that difference by the annual cost of capital.
3. Determine the additional bad debt loss under the new terms.
4. Calculate the overall profit effect by subtracting the expenses in steps 2 and 3 from the revenue estimate made in step 1.

*PROJECT ADVISABILITY IN THE FINANCIAL STATEMENT APPROACH* The advisability of the project is based on the projected incremental profit: if the profit effect is

Exhibit 3–1

*Value Creation from Short-Term Financial Management Activities*

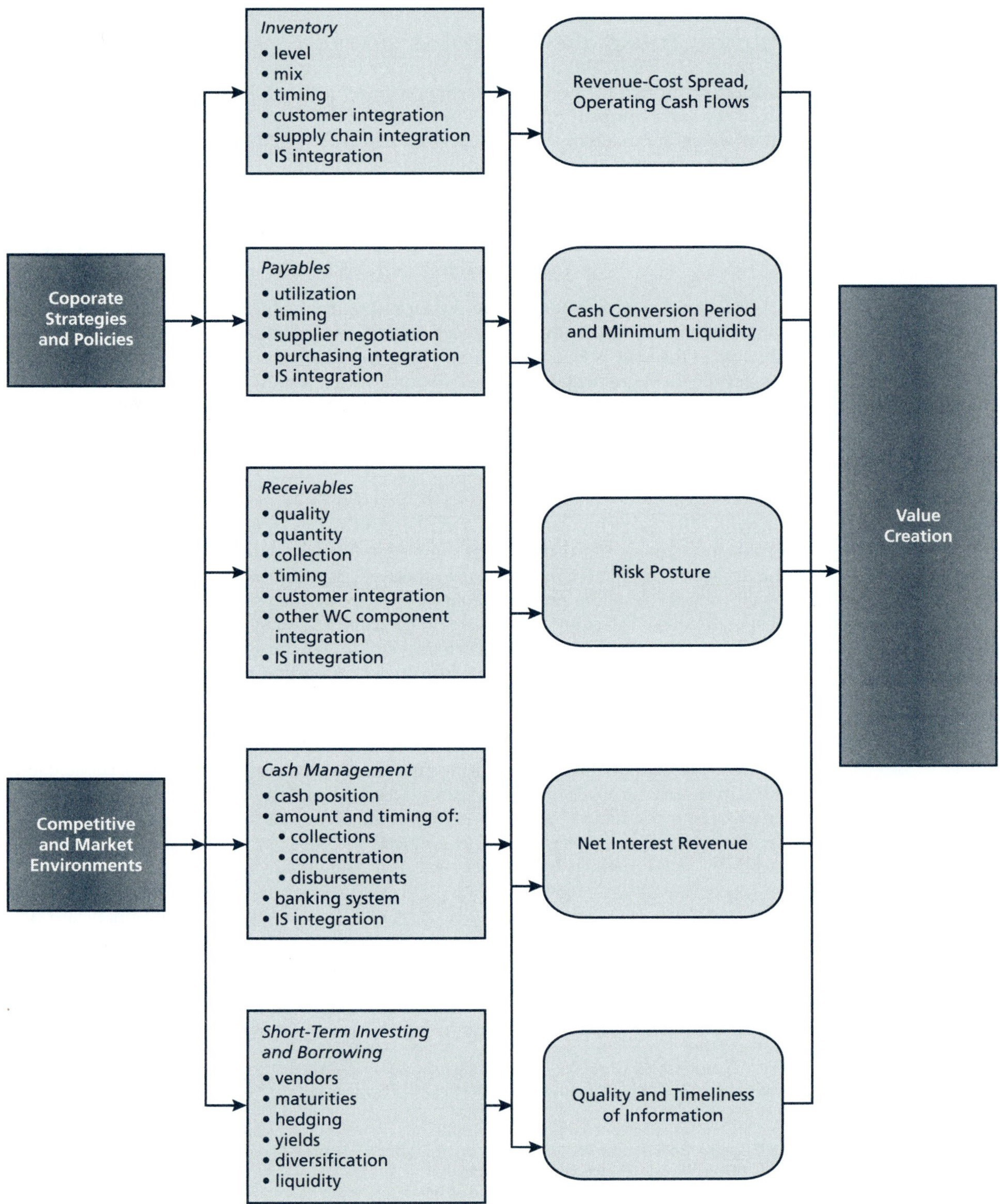

positive, the analyst would recommend that the new credit terms be adopted.[2] The financial manager might slightly modify the traditional approach by dividing the profit effect by the change in receivables investment that was calculated in step 2. This modification would provide a rate of return on investment.

*PROJECT TIMING CONSIDERATIONS IN THE FINANCIAL STATEMENT APPROACH* How does this approach account for the time value of money? It does so only indirectly, through the capital cost estimate made in step 2. How this occurs is not obvious. Let's say a company anticipates payment in 60 days on annual sales of $100 million, all of which are made on credit. Recognize that daily credit sales multiplied by the payment date gives the average accounts receivable balance.

$$\text{Average receivables} = (\$100{,}000{,}000/365) \times 60$$

$$\text{Average receivables} = \$273{,}972.60 \times 60$$

$$\text{Average receivables} = \$16{,}438{,}356.16$$

This average receivables balance is then multiplied by the annual cost of capital to estimate the financing cost of the ongoing investment. If that rate is 10 percent, the financing cost in this case is $1,643,836. This amount is then subtracted from the sales revenue (as part of the incremental profit calculation); we get almost the same result as if the entire sales amount is received in 60 days and we discount the revenue for 60 days at a 10 percent discount rate (assuming daily compounding, the present value is $100 million less $1,630,176.90, or $98,369,823.10). Some inaccuracy is introduced because the revenue and expense amounts are spread throughout the year.

*PROJECT RISK TREATMENT IN THE FINANCIAL STATEMENT APPROACH* In the financial statement approach, risk of short-term financial decisions is often overlooked. If the decision should have major balance sheet effects, the risk might be crudely measured by showing the resultant projected balance sheets. The analyst is interested in what effect a proposed course of action would have on the company's liquidity and cash position. Approximate *timing* of financial effects can be seen through the use of pro forma, or projected, balance sheets. A more complete analysis might tie together projected income statements (based on the above incremental profit determination), projected balance sheets, and projected statements of cash flow. Proposal *risk* assessment is limited to whether the company's ability to pay near-term obligations would be impaired if the proposal were to be implemented. Traditional ratio analysis, using ratios such as the current ratio, quick (or acid test) ratio, inventory turnover ratio, average collection period, and the ratio of current assets to total assets, is conducted.[3] The analyst studies the changes in ratio values to establish when the financial effects might be most pronounced and what risks this poses to the company. Implicitly, risk is defined as a project's effect on liquidity or financial requirements.

*ASSESSMENT OF THE FINANCIAL STATEMENT APPROACH* The financial statement approach, although popular, has two major shortcomings. First, it implicitly defines

---

[2] In equation form, using $\Delta$ to denote an incremental change, the evaluation of a change in credit policy would be:

$$\Delta \text{ profit} = (\Delta \text{ revenue} - \Delta \text{ operating expenses} - \Delta \text{ financing costs} - \Delta \text{ cost of bad debts})$$

If the analyst is careful to compute the incremental revenues and costs on a cash basis, this technique may provide the same accept/reject signals as present value analysis according to Sachdeva and Gitman (see the end-of-chapter references). We emphasize the present value approach because it is more exact, its linkage to shareholder wealth maximization is widely accepted, and it is consistent with the way in which long-life capital projects are evaluated.

[3] These and other liquidity measures are developed in Chapters 2 and 5.

project riskiness as the project's effect on the company's liquidity. Whereas this may be valid for a struggling company, it is too limited for most companies. Ideally, risk analysis should encompass the variability of the project's cash flows and the effect of the proposal on the company's existing cash flow distribution. Second, this approach is flawed with respect to the evaluation of timing effects. Cash flows may occur anytime within a month or quarter, and quarterly or annual pro forma statements may not capture the true liquidity strain of a proposed course of action. More importantly, the exact timing of cash inflows and outflows and the time value of money are overlooked. The analysis does not take account of the preference for cash available today instead of at some point in the future. Cash available today has greater value because it can be invested to earn interest income or used to pay down short-term borrowings, thus reducing interest expense. The financial statement approach is appropriate for decisions whose financial impacts are limited to the present year's cash flow because their desirability is only slightly affected by the time value of money.

### Valuation Approach

The second, and preferred, way of evaluating financial decisions is to calculate the **net present value (NPV)**. This approach accounts for the exact timing of cash flows and their present values and results in making decisions that tie directly to maximizing shareholder wealth. The Focus on Practice box argues that NPV should be applied to many short-term financial decisions. When calculating the NPV of the proposed course of action, we net cash expenses against cash revenues, and we also account for the timing of cash inflows and outflows. A project with a positive NPV is considered acceptable to invest in because

## FOCUS ON PRACTICE

### *Applying Present Value Analysis to Short-Term Financial Decisions*

Financial analysts are generally more comfortable applying NPV analysis to long-term capital projects than to short-term financial decisions. However, the criteria companies use in determining which projects merit NPV analysis indicate that even short-term financial decisions having multiyear impacts should be included. One company's criteria for whether to apply time value calculations when there might be some doubt regarding applicability are as follows:*

1. Does the expenditure have long-run consequences?
2. Is the decision outside the ordinary course of business?
3. Does the unit proposing the investment put special emphasis on it?
4. Does the unit proposing the investment request top management deliberation?

Clearly, items 1 and 3 (and possibly 2 and 4) argue for NPV analysis of credit policy changes, inventory policy changes, information system investments, and banking relationship changes. Failure to subject these decisions to capital budgeting evaluation may result in misguided decisions, lowering profitability and cash flows and eroding shareholder wealth.

* Richard J. Marshuetz, "How American Can Allocates Capital," *Harvard Business Review* (January–February 1985), pp. 82–91.

its net cash flow more than covers the cost of capital needed to fund it; a negative NPV implies unacceptability. Computing the NPV involves four steps:

1. Determining the relevant cash flows
2. Determining the timing of those cash flows
3. Determining the appropriate discount rate
4. Discounting the cash flows

The decision criteria are as follows:

If calculated NPV is positive, invest in the project.

If calculated NPV is zero, probably invest in the project.

If calculated NPV is negative, do not invest in the project.

Financial managers need to understand that money has a time value, so that they can determine the impact of short-term financial decisions on shareholder value. Specifically, it is necessary to incorporate the *risk* and *timing* of cash flows correctly when making financial decisions.

*Assessment of the Valuation Approach* We have already seen that the financial statement approach is deficient in incorporating cash flow timing and risk. *Only the valuation approach accurately represents the time value effect of cash flows and allows for an objective appraisal of cash flow risk.* We therefore advocate its use. However, the valuation approach is difficult to implement in some cases, as we see in Exhibit 3–2. Financial managers have been able to address difficulties 2 and 3 to a degree through the use of a planning framework known as "Economic Value Added," in which one gains an overall view of the company's financial position.

## Economic Value Added: An Attempt at Synthesis

Although we are oversimplifying, we may view the use of Economic Value Added (EVA) models as an attempt to incorporate elements from both the financial statement approach and the valuation approach. Copeland, Koller, and Murrin, affiliated with management consultant McKinsey & Company, argue that value creation necessitates adopting a long-run viewpoint, managing all cash flows on both the income statement and balance sheet, and properly risk-adjusting cash flows from different time periods.[4]

Many companies are now linking major financial decisions to EVA. Essentially, this is net operating profit minus a charge for the opportunity cost of capital. It gives a one-period addition to value from a company's operations. Using EVA™ allows the financial manager to integrate short-term decisions having both revenues and costs into the company's capital budgeting process, for those companies not using NPV or which prefer to merge all decisions into one decision-making framework. Equation 3.1 gives the formula for calculating EVA™, followed by an illustrative example. The tax rate, T, is the company's marginal tax rate. "Capital Employed" refers to long-term debt plus equity, in most economic value added models.

$$\text{EVA}^{\text{TM}} = \text{Operating Profit}(1 - T) - (\text{Cost of Capital})(\text{Capital Employed}) \qquad (3.1)$$

*Example of EVA™ Calculation* Dwenger & Associates, a medical care practice, has a weighted-average cost of capital of 10 percent. It has employed $30,000,000 of mostly

[4] Tom Copeland, Tim Koller, and Jack Murrin, *Valuation: Measuring and Managing the Value of Companies, Third Edition* (New York: John Wiley & Sons, 2000).

long-term capital to run the practice, according to its most recent balance sheet. Its marginal tax rate is 40 percent. The most recent income statement shows the following:

| | |
|---|---|
| Revenues | $40,000,000 |
| − COGS | 24,000,000 |
| Gross profit | $16,000,000 |
| − Operating expenses | 7,500,000 |
| Operating profit | $ 8,500,000 |

If the company's marginal tax rate is 40 percent, the Economic Value Added for this period would be $2,100,000, calculated as follows:

$$\begin{aligned} \text{EVA} &= \text{Operating Profit}(1 - \text{T}) - (\text{Cost of Capital})(\text{Capital Employed}) \\ &= \$8{,}500{,}000(1 - 0.4) - (0.10)(\$30{,}000{,}000) \\ &= \underline{\underline{\$2{,}100{,}000}} \end{aligned}$$

Dwenger's management team added value during this period.

## Exhibit 3–2

*Practical Difficulties in Conducting NPV Analysis*

1. The value effect of a proposal is tied directly to the difference of the present value of cash inflows and outflows. This implies that **valuation is predicated on the analyst's forecasting ability**. Although it is true that short-term projects with a "one-shot" payoff might be accurately evaluated, other projects have longer-term horizons (e.g., a permanent change in credit terms), and their cash flows are much more problematic. Furthermore, the very financial or product market inefficiencies that make short-term financial management valuable to the firm make the accurate projection of cash flows challenging. It is exceedingly difficult to project the degree of inefficiency and how long it might persist.
2. Although the project's risk is captured in the discount rate, **the effect the project has on the corporation's overall business or financial risk is overlooked**. We assume, in other words, that the overall business and financial risk are unaffected by changes in working capital accounts.
3. **It is very difficult to value the effect of a project on the company's liquidity**, because there is neither a theory of liquidity nor a "real-world" knowledge of what liquidity is worth. (Although, in a later section, we report on a very recent study that contributes an estimate of this value.) Yet, it is clear that liquidity is valuable, particularly in the case of companies that have a clear edge in this regard relative to their competitors. This difficulty exists whether we define liquidity as cash plus marketable securities or expand the definition to include short-term borrowing capacity (the latter, more inclusive definition is sometimes labeled the "liquid reserve").
4. Related to the valuation of liquidity, **we lack a well-developed understanding of the value of unused short-term debt capacity**. Especially perplexing is the value effect of a change in the maturity structure of debt, in which short-term debt is substituted for longer-term debt, or vice versa.
5. Finally, how does one handle the interactions between short-term changes to working capital accounts and long-term investment, financing, and dividend decisions? **Simultaneous effects on the magnitude of a corporation's cash flows and risk are difficult to pinpoint.**
6. Analysis of present value is not possible for some projects having permanent impacts, such as whether to upgrade the company's treasury information system. **Projects may not even have a quantifiable financial impact.**

*Advantage of Using EVA™* By emphasizing EVA™ as a planning framework throughout the organization, executives are gaining a better company-wide understanding of the importance of improved working capital management. The CFO of one of the divisions at AT&T reports that EVA™ makes financial performance relevant to all company areas, from plant managers to payables clerks, as they see how their decisions and activities relate to EVA™. Using a customized form of EVA™, Valmont Industries, Inc., found that its best route to improvement in a French division was to reduce investment in receivables. Although division personnel had a culture-related objection to reducing credit to customers, top management was able to demonstrate through case study success stories what could be done. The cultural barrier was overcome, and downward spiraling EVA™ reversed as receivables were slashed. The Focus on Practice box provides more examples of economic value added applications.

*Caution in Using EVA™* If not coupled with individual project NPV evaluation and future years' company-wide cash flow projections and risk analysis, EVA™ is justifiably criticized as a framework that focuses only on a single period and that does not properly account for risk. McKinsey's "value based management" framework joins EVA™ with "market value added" (amount by which stock market capitalization increases in a period) and an emphasis on individual project discounted cash flow analysis to attempt to gain the benefit of both the financial statement approach and the valuation approach. The key issue for a company is not whether it uses EVA™, but whether it is conducted within a framework of net present value. One breakdown that has been noted is the way taking an early payment discount is handled in EVA™: payables are typically subtracted from "capital employed," with no adjustment for the cost savings of taking the discount. See the Focus on Practice box for more on EVA™, which is now used by about one-half of U.S. Fortune 1000 companies.

To calculate NPV, it is essential that the analyst understand the time value of money. The necessary background is provided in Appendix A at the end of the book, for those students who are not familiar with time value concepts and calculations. The following discussion applies a basic valuation model to short-term financial decision making.

## NPV CALCULATIONS

The valuation approach to financial decision making requires that the analyst incorporate the time value of money and the riskiness of the cash flows. We begin our presentation with the time value of money and later add the complexity of risk analysis. The principles of valuation are carried out in financial management choices by calculating the NPV of each alternative and selecting the alternative with the highest NPV. To compute NPV, each cash inflow and outflow must be converted to its dollar value at a standard point in time. The point in time chosen is usually the present, which is labeled time period zero. Our calculations will involve discounting all cash flows to the beginning of the timeline and then subtracting the present value of the outflows from the present value of the inflows.

### Valuation: Simple Interest Case

We turn now to a simple way of finding the present value of short-term flows that typically show up on a corporation's cash flow timeline. Ignoring compounding, we can use a **simple interest formula** to "discount" the future cash flow(s) to approximate the present value effect of a financial decision. This formula assumes that interest is only added to or charged to the account at the end of the period, eliminating the possibility of earning "interest on interest."

## FOCUS ON PRACTICE

### EVA™ and Short-Term Financial Decisions

Numerous companies have benefited from applying economic value added analysis. Ryan and Ryan (2002) find that one-half of the Fortune 1000 companies in the U.S. now use some form of economic value added analysis, and about one-third use a measure of how much value is created by a company in a period, called market value added (MVA). A U.S. telecommunications company began including capital costs in customer contract bids, eliminating some deals that were value-destroying. Prior to incorporating economic value added, salespersons were compensated based on a customer's revenue stream, and so the salesforce would freely extend credit and payment terms to "book the deal." Middle managers were misled by the greater apparent operating profit margin of some of the deals. Now, credit-related costs and payment timing issues are included in contract approval decisions.

Dell Corporation, profiled in Chapter 2, links its working capital investment to its stock price through EVA™. Internationally, a growing number of companies, which have already reengineered processes and cut costs, are finding that internal cash can be freed up by applying economic value added techniques. A Finnish consultant recommends that capital costs attributable to receivables, raw materials and work-in-process inventories, and finished good inventories be shown individually, along with a "credit" for payables and accruals. These can then be summed to get an annual "cost of working capital." The three main drivers of the capital charge of EVA™ are then highlighted: net working capital, fixed asset investment, and weighted average cost of capital. Managers are much more aware of working capital management and its ability to create shareholder value when using this framework.

*Sources:* Lee Mergy, "Overcoming Value Barriers," *Financial Executive* (June 2002); Elizabeth Fry, "Working Harder," *CFO* (Australia) (October 1998); and Richard Ketchen, "Selling Treasury as a Strategic Corporate Function," *TreasuryPoint.com Knowledge Center* (Accessed online 11/19/2003).

*Simple Interest Using an Annual Interest Rate* We begin our discounting calculation with an annual interest rate. The following example introduces the formula and illustrates its application.

**Example.** Mary has a $5,000 tuition payment due in six months, and she is wondering how much she must invest today to have the necessary funds at the end of six months. She plans to invest in a six-month certificate of deposit (CD), which pays the interest in a lump sum at maturity at an annual interest rate of 7.5 percent. Mary's bank is unique in that it will tailor the CD size to the investor's requirements.

**Solution.** We use the symbol $k$ to denote the interest rate on an annualized basis. Investors often use this annualized rate, sometimes called the nominal interest rate. Equation 3.2 is the simple interest formula that we can use to discount the future cash flow to determine its present dollar equivalent, $PV$.

$$PV = \frac{FV_n}{1 + (k \times n/365)} \tag{3.2}$$

Where: $FV_n$ = Future Value received in period $n$
$k$ = the interest rate earned per year (the nominal rate)
$n$ = number of time periods from now

Mary equates six months to 182.5 days, which is the value we will use for *n*. Substituting the other values from the problem, we find that the present value, or the amount Mary must invest today in the CD, to be

$$PV = \frac{\$5{,}000}{1 + (0.075 \times 182.5/365)}$$

$$PV = \$4{,}819.28$$

*Simple Interest Using a Daily Interest Rate* An even simpler formula can be used if one has already converted the interest rate *k* to a daily rate *i*. This formula (Equation 3.3) requires that the interest rate and the number of periods be stated in the same units, which in our example is days. We demonstrate the formula by returning to our example. If the 7.5 percent nominal annual rate is expressed as a daily interest rate (we use seven decimal places to avoid significant rounding errors, so we get 0.075/365 = 0.0002055), we can determine the present value with a simpler equation.

$$PV = \frac{FV}{1 + (i \times n)} \tag{3.3}$$

Substituting the values for Mary's upcoming tuition payment into Equation 3.3, we determine the amount that must be invested today to be worth $5,000 in six months (182.5 days).

$$PV = \frac{\$5{,}000}{1 + (0.0002055 \times 182.5)}$$

$$PV = \$4{,}819.26$$

Again, we emphasize that this formula assumes interest is added to the account only at the end of the six months. Notice that the result differs very slightly from that found using an annual rate, due to the rounding off of the daily interest rate. Both simple interest formulas, Equations 3.2 and 3.3, give the same result.[5]

### Valuation: Compound Interest Case

Notice that the simple interest formulas overlook the fact that interest can be earned on freed-up funds. For example, consider an investment with a stated, or nominal, interest rate of 8 percent but with a maturity of six months. The **effective annual rate** that the investor earns on two subsequent six-month investments (which would yield 8 percent / 2, or 4 percent, per six-month period) cannot be determined by multiplying the six-month rate by 2. The effective rate would be higher than 8 percent because in the final six months we will earn interest on the original principal invested and also on the interest earned during the first six months. Accordingly, a slightly more accurate evaluation of financial decisions incorporates this "compounding" of interest through time. Whenever the interest is compounded semiannually (as with the consecutive six-month maturities), monthly, or daily, the effective annual rate will exceed the nominal rate.

*Compound Interest Using an Annual Interest Rate* We can see what happens when we account for "interest on interest" by redoing our earlier example. Continuing with Mary's investment decision, we introduce Equation 3.4, which reflects daily compounding.

[5] Technically, dividing a nominal annual interest rate by 365 does not give an equivalent daily rate when compound interest is earned. One assumes, when doing this, that the annual rate is compounded continuously, if the daily rate is termed an "equivalent daily rate" with daily compounding.

$$PV = \frac{FV}{[1 + k/365]^n} \tag{3.4}$$

Where: $FV$ = future value
$k$ = annual nominal interest rate
$n$ = number of days until amount is received

Substituting, we find that the present value is $4,815.99.

$$PV = \frac{\$5{,}000}{[1 + 0.075/365]^{182.5}}$$

$$PV = \$4{,}815.99$$

The keystrokes for doing this calculation using a popular financial calculator are shown in a footnote.[6] Notice that Mary can start with slightly less today and still reach her target because of the "interest on interest" that her account is earning. Notice that the present value using this simple interest approximation ($4,819.26) is almost identical to that found when accounting for compound interest ($4,815.99). Also, because Mary is getting the interest compounded daily, the effective annual rate she is earning (7.79 percent)[7] is higher than the 7.5 percent nominal, or stated, rate.

*JUSTIFICATION FOR USING SIMPLE INTEREST* Because the results are so similar, we use the simple interest formula for most of our calculations in the remainder of the book. Another justification for using simple interest is its widespread use in calculating money market yields and short-term borrowing rates. Further, simple interest calculations are easily done on a standard four function calculator.[8] We use simple interest while cautioning that the result may differ markedly when the investment has one or more of these characteristics: (1) frequent compounding, in which interest is added to the account daily or continuously, (2) a substantial amount of principal invested, and (3) long time horizons.

Having established the desirability and mechanics of the valuation approach to decision making, we are now ready to apply our knowledge of discounting to short-term financial decisions.

## BASIC VALUATION MODEL

Earlier, we suggested that businesses should make financial decisions that add value to the corporation. The NPV rule simply compares the benefits of a proposed project with the costs, including funding costs, and recommends implementation of those projects whose

---

[6] The keystrokes for doing this computation on a Hewlett-Packard 10-BII financial calculator are as follows:
5000 [FV]
365 ■ P/YR
7.5 [I/YR]
182.5[N]
Press [PV] to get $4,815.99.

[7] The keystrokes for doing the effective annual rate computation on a Hewlett-Packard 10-BII financial calculator are as follows (for precision, make sure you are showing nine decimal places in your display):
365 ■ P/YR
7.5 ■ NOM%
Press ■ EFF% to get 7.787584644%. Then, use this rate as [I/YR] with 1 ■ P/YR and 0.5 [N].
Enter 5000 [FV] and press [PV] to get $4,815.99.

[8] For readers using this material to help prepare for the Certified Treasury Professional (CTP) examination, we note that only a basic nonfinancial calculator is allowable.

benefits at least offset the costs. *Determining the NPV of a proposed course of action applies the valuation approach to financial decision making.* After presenting the NPV model, illustrating its use, and identifying some of its weaknesses, we will be equipped to resolve our chapter-opening financial dilemma.

We start by recognizing that NPV is the difference between the present value of all cash inflows (or cash receipts) and all cash outflows (cash disbursements) attributable to the proposal:

$$NPV = (\textit{present value of all cash inflows} - \textit{present value of all cash outflows})$$

Expressing all cash inflows with positive signs, all cash outflows with negative signs, and with $n$ being an integer representing the period in which we will receive the final cash flow, we can express the NPV in symbol form:

$$NPV = (CF_0 + PV\ of\ CF_1 + PV\ of\ CF_2 + \cdots + PV\ of\ CF_n)$$

Time period 0 represents the beginning of the cash flow stream, which generally is the time at which the initial outlay for the project is made. We calculate the NPV by discounting the actual cash flows, as shown in the general formula for annual future cash flows in Equation 3.5:

$$NPV = CF_0 + \frac{CF_1}{(1+k)^1} + \frac{CF_2}{(1+k)^2} + \cdots + \frac{CF_n}{(1+k)^n} \tag{3.5}$$

When making the transition to daily interest, it is logical to use a daily compounding process to reflect the fact that firms will invest more in overnight investments or pay down daily credit line borrowing if funds are released from working capital investments. However, as noted earlier, a simple interest formula can serve about as well for short-term financial decisions and is computationally much quicker. We can revise our simple interest formula (Equation 3.3) for the NPV context quite easily. Allow N to be a counter for the number of cash flows occurring; $n$ continues to be the number of periods (days) until the cash flow is received, and $i$ represents the approximate daily interest rate:

$$NPV = CF_0 + \frac{CF_1}{(1 + i \times n_1)} + \frac{CF_2}{(1 + i \times n_2)} + \frac{CF_n}{(1 + i \times n_N)} \tag{3.6}$$

Notice that Equation 3.6 is just an expanded version of our earlier simple interest formula (Equation 3.3), with the ability to handle more than one cash flow. Because of their simplicity, we will attempt to use one of the simple interest formulas whenever possible.

There is one other simplification of which you should be aware. Even though they are not "one-shot deals," many short-term financial decisions can be handled as if they were, to make accept-reject decisions. This means that Equation 3.3 can be applied even in some cases in which there is a series of cash flows and the decision has multiyear financial effects. Evaluating the first sale occurring under new credit terms, for example, is sufficient to determine whether the new terms are beneficial to our company. In other cases, the more general formula in Equation 3.6 must be applied.

## Applying the Model

The steps we follow in the remainder of the chapter in making decisions with the NPV model are listed below.

1. Lay out the relevant cash flows on a cash flow timeline.
2. Determine whether the cash flows can be represented by a single sum, meaning we ignore all cash flows except those linked to the first sale under the new policy and

discount with a simple interest formula (Equation 3.3), or whether the cash flows must be handled as a "mixed stream" of differing dollar amounts (Equation 3.6).

3. Select an appropriate discount rate, which necessitates considering the riskiness of the proposal and what interest rate projects in that risk class must earn.
4. Discount future cash flows, subtract any initial outlays necessary for the project, and determine if the NPV is positive (accept), zero (probably accept), or negative (reject).

The calculated NPV and the resulting accept-reject recommendation depend greatly on the accuracy of the inputs—estimates of the relevant cash inflows, estimates of the relevant cash outflows (including the initial investment required, if any), and the choice of the discount rate. Our next section deals with the cash flows, and in later sections, we illustrate the discounting process and address the discount rate.

## Cash Flow Estimation

There are three distinct types of cash flows to be considered in most financial decisions. First, the relevant cash inflows are the cash benefits arising from sources of cash increases. We must ask ourselves what would be the net increase from these cash-producing sources, being careful *to include only those that change due to the proposed course of action.* If we initiate a new product line or expand an existing line of business, the dollar amounts related to the new business are used as the cash inflows. When we are considering two alternative ways of doing something, however, we must be careful to compute the change in inflows based on the difference between the two alternatives. Second, as we look at the cash outflows, we must again be careful to include only those cash flows affected by implementing the proposal. For example, **fixed costs** that do not increase with sales volume, unless changed by the proposal adoption, are ignored in computing the cash flows associated with a change in sales. Many working capital policy decisions affecting the company's sales level do not change such fixed costs as salaries, utility expenses, and insurance. The *relevant* costs to consider are those that would be altered by the decision. Almost always the decision will alter total **variable costs**, which are those costs that *are* expected to vary with sales.

Third, the **initial investment** necessary to implement the proposal must be determined. This investment may include setup costs, physical asset acquisition or disposition costs, permanent increases in the company's investment in cash balances necessary for additional transactions, and other cash outflows incurred at the time the project is initiated. At this point, we have completed the task of laying out the relevant cash flows.

Our discussion of relevant cash flows has been necessarily brief.[9] We discuss more complex NPV modeling in the appendix to this chapter, and we tailor the model to decisions on inventory policy (in Chapter 4) and accounts receivable policy (in Chapter 6). Before concluding our valuation section, we remind you to refer back to Exhibit 3–2 for several practical difficulties that the financial analyst might face in applying the NPV model to short-term decisions.

## Valuation Using the NPV Model

We are ready to return to our financial dilemma and consider how to frame DigiView's dilemma in the context of the cash flow timeline and our NPV model. Our approach will

---

[9] Expanded discussion of cash flow estimation is available in any managerial finance textbook. Our recommended sources: Chapter 7 of Scott Besley and Eugene F. Brigham, *Essentials of Managerial Finance, 13th ed.* (Cincinnati: South-Western, 2005) or Chapter 8 of Lawrence J. Gitman, *Principles of Managerial Finance, 10th ed.* (Reading, MA: Addison-Wesley Longman, 2003). Advanced material, including tax and inflation adjustments, is found in Chapters 8–10 of Neil Seitz and Mitch Ellison, *Capital Budgeting and Long-Term Financing Decisions, 5th ed.* (Cincinnati: South-Western, 2005).

be to first draw a cash flow timeline and then calculate the daily NPVs of present and proposed credit policies to provide a recommendation to the company. The cash flow timeline is a helpful tool for visualizing the timing of a decision alternative's cash flows. We will show cash inflows as vertical bars above the horizontal axis and cash outflows as bars extending below that axis.

## FINANCIAL DILEMMA REVISITED

The DigiView decision is a financial decision in which sales would change, and yet the consideration of one sales transaction provides all the necessary information to determine whether DigiView would benefit from the new terms.[10] We can ignore the cash outflows associated with each sale because neither their amount nor timing changes. For simplicity, assume DigiView's sales are \$36,500,000 per year. This implies daily sales of \$100,000 = \$36,500,000/365. For each day's sales, the cash flow timeline for DigiView's credit terms at present (net 30) would appear as shown in Exhibit 3–3.

Using Equation 3.2, we can determine the present value of one day's sales. We use a discount rate of 10 percent, assuming that this is DigiView's short-term borrowing rate.

$$PV = \frac{\$100{,}000}{1 + (0.10 \times 30/365)}$$

$$PV = \$99{,}184.78$$

For the proposed credit terms of net 60 days, we have only a minor modification of the cash flow timeline, as shown in Exhibit 3–4.

The present value of the proposed terms would be found using the same formula, Equation 3.2. We use the same discount rate, although one might argue for a slightly higher rate due to the greater risk for partial, late, or nonpayment when extending the credit period.

$$PV = \frac{\$100{,}000}{1 + (0.10 \times 60/365)}$$

$$PV = \$98{,}382.75$$

**Exhibit 3–3**

*DigiView's Present Credit Terms Cash Flow Timeline*

[10] The value effect can be determined by evaluating one sale as long as two conditions are met: (1) the policy change does not change the growth rate of cash sales revenues or cash expenses and (2) the policy change does not alter fixed costs subsequent to the time of the initial investment. The mathematical demonstration is given in Sartoris and Hill (1983).

**Exhibit 3–4**

*DigiView's Proposed Credit Terms Cash Flow Timeline*

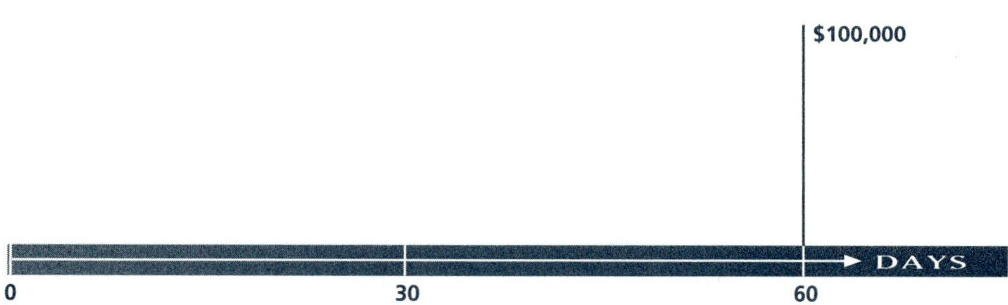


Note that if sales do not change at all with the proposed lengthening of credit terms, which is a very conservative assumption, DigiView would be losing $802.03 per day, in present dollars ($98,382.75 versus the $99,184.78 formerly received). We could multiply this $802.03 difference by 365 to arrive at an approximate annual effect. In this case, the policy change would cause an annual value erosion of $292,740.95.[11] The proper analysis of the time value of money enables the analyst to make the value-enhancing, short-term finance decision. Before making a final decision, the analyst would want to consider risk factors that could call into question the original projections. These risks could arise externally in the industry's environment, within the consumer electronics industry, or they may arise from some company-specific factor such as an interruption in production capability or a material sourcing problem.

*EXTENDED ANALYSIS* Our analysis becomes more realistic if we allow for the positive effect on sales that we would expect to result from easier credit terms. The following table indicates the projected figures for our modified analysis.

EXTENDED NPV ANALYSIS OF CREDIT PERIOD LENGTHENING

| VARIABLE | PROJECTED VALUE |
|---|---|
| Initial investment | $0 |
| Sales increase | + 3% |
| Cost of goods sold (inventory, labor, other related production costs) | 65% of sales revenue |
| Payment terms | Net 30 |
| Inventory Conversion Period components: | |
| Inventory-to-production lag | 30 days |
| Production-to-sale lag | 10 days |

[11] This approximation ignores the compounding to year-end of the intrayear daily flows. The NPV of the proposal, assuming the daily effects persist indefinitely and, therefore, constitute a perpetuity, would be $802.03/(0.10/365) = $2,927,409.50.

Exhibit 3–5

*DigiView's Cash Flow Timeline, Present Credit Terms, Extended Analysis*

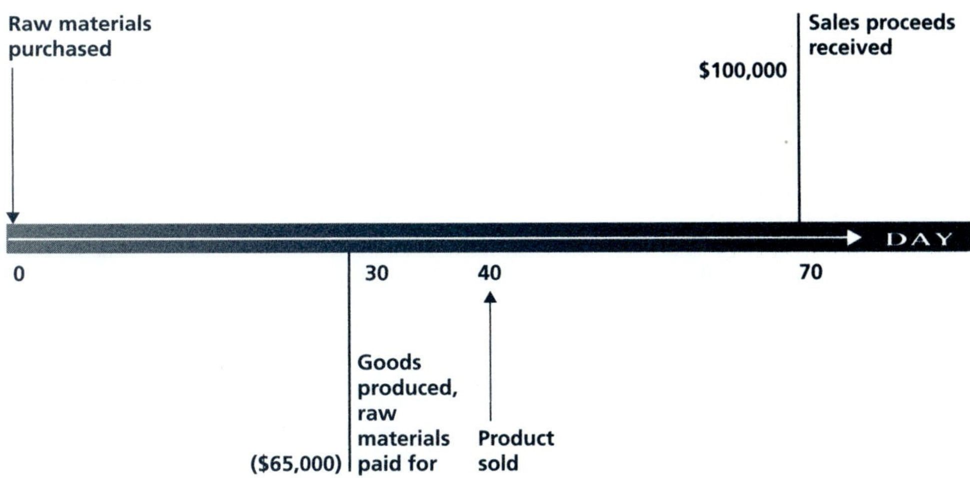


*Extended NPV Analysis* The daily selling rate will be assumed to increase by 3 percent under the 60-day terms (see previous table) and to be even throughout the year.[12] Exhibit 3–5 shows the cash flow timeline for the extended analysis of the present 30-day credit period. The day 30 outflow of $65,000 represents 65 percent of the sales revenue amount.

We compute the NPVs of the present terms and proposed terms and recommend the alternative with the largest NPV.

1. **Present terms.** First, we calculate the present value of the cash inflows. DigiView receives $100,000 in 70 days. The present value of the cash inflow would be:

$$PV_{cash\ inflow} = \frac{\$100{,}000}{1 + (0.10 \times 70/365)}$$

$$PV_{cash\ inflow} = \$98{,}118.28$$

We next calculate the present value of the cash outflows:

$$PV_{cash\ outflow} = \frac{\$65{,}000}{1 + (0.10 \times 30/365)}$$

$$PV_{cash\ outflow} = \$64{,}470.11$$

[12] If we were working with uneven or lumpy sales, we would have to first compound the intrayear flows to their year-end values. This step is necessary to use the formula for determining the present value of an annual perpetuity accurately, which assumes a series of end-of-year cash flows. Illustrating, with a day 70 cash flow, we would first calculate the year-end value of each of the cash flows ($CF$) using this formula:

$$\text{Future Value } (FV) \text{ at end of year } 1 = CF(1 + k)^{(365-70)/365}$$

After individually compounding all intrayear flows to year-end, we would sum them and then insert the end-of-year sum into the annual perpetuity formula:

$$\text{Present Value } (PV) \text{ of annual perpetuity} = CF \text{ per year/discount rate}$$

The general approach to discounting perpetuities is covered in the appendix at the end of the chapter (see the Linke and Zumwalt article, listed in the end-of-chapter references, for more information on using the intrayear compounding formula).

The **daily NPV** is then the difference between the present value of the daily inflows and the present value of the daily outflows:

$$\begin{aligned} \textit{Daily NPV} &= \textit{PV of inflows} - \textit{PV of outflows} \\ &= \$98{,}118.28 - \$64{,}470.11 \\ &= \$33{,}648.17 \end{aligned}$$

We can calculate the NPV for the present credit period by using a perpetuity formula to turn the daily NPV into an aggregate NPV. The implicit assumption here is that the daily NPV would persist indefinitely. We provide a perpetuity present value formula as Equation 3.7.

$$NPV = \frac{\textit{Cash flow per period}}{\textit{Interest rate per period}} = \frac{CF}{i} \tag{3.7}$$

We have seen that the daily NPV is $33,648.17. The daily interest rate would be 0.10/365 = 0.0002740. Substituting, we get an NPV for the present credit period of $122,803,540.15:

$$NPV = \frac{\$33{,}648.17}{0.0002740}$$

$$NPV = \$122{,}803{,}540.15$$

We now compare these results with the NPV of the proposed change in terms.

2. **Proposed terms.** Exhibit 3–6 shows the cash flows for the proposed credit terms, assuming that sales volume would increase by 3 percent. The new level of daily sales is thus $100,000 + (0.03 × $100,000) = $103,000. Note on the cash inflow timeline the extra 30 days related to the longer credit period (70 + 30 = 100 days). Because cost of goods sold is 65 percent of sales revenue, daily cost rises to 0.65 × $103,000 = $66,950.

   We follow the same approach in arriving at the NPV of the proposed terms, by first calculating the present value of the perpetuity of daily cash inflows and then that of the daily cash outflows:

Exhibit 3–6

*DigiView's Cash Flow Timeline, Proposed Credit Terms, Assuming Sales Increase*

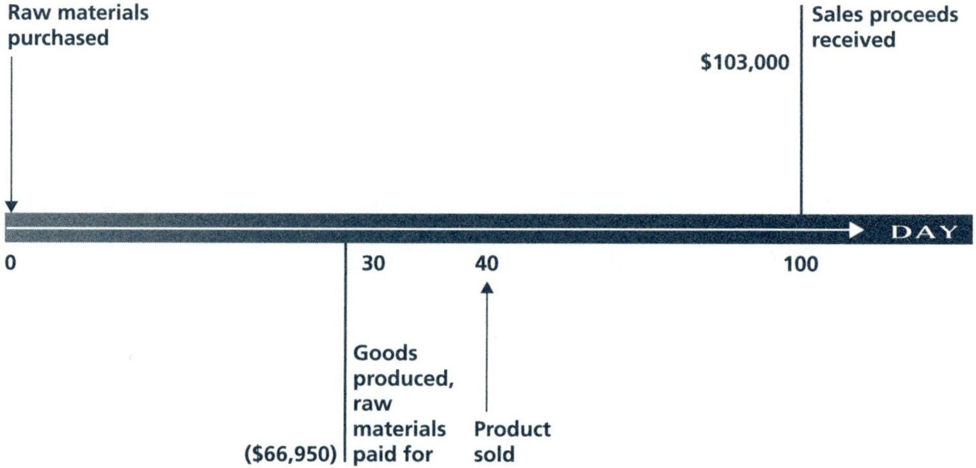

$$PV_{cash\ inflow} = \frac{\$103{,}000}{1 + (0.10 \times 100/365)}$$

$$PV_{cash\ inflow} = \$100{,}253.33$$

We next calculate the present value of the cash outflows, based on 65 percent of $103,000:

$$PV_{cash\ outflow} = \frac{\$66{,}950}{1 + (0.10 \times 30/365)}$$

$$PV_{cash\ outflow} = \$66{,}404.21$$

The **daily NPV** is then the difference between the present value of the daily inflows and the present value of the daily outflows:

$$\begin{aligned} Daily\ NPV &= PV\ of\ inflows - PV\ of\ outflows \\ &= \$100{,}253.33 - \$66{,}404.21 \\ &= \$33{,}849.12 \end{aligned}$$

We see that the daily NPV is $33,849.12. Dividing by the daily interest rate, we get an NPV for the proposed credit period of $123,536,934.31:

$$NPV = \frac{\$33{,}849.12}{0.0002740}$$

$$NPV = \$123{,}536{,}934.31$$

3. **Decision rule.** As with any capital budgeting problem having mutually exclusive alternatives, the decision rule is to select the alternative with the highest NPV. Because the proposed terms give a higher NPV, the credit period extension is recommended. One caution is appropriate: If the analyst thinks that the cash flow effect will last only several years, an annuity formula should be used to estimate NPV instead of a perpetuity formula.
4. **Risk factors.** The key risk factor in this discussion is the amount and duration of the positive sales effect. The opportunity cost of funding, captured in the discount rate, is 10 percent. As noted earlier, this represents DigiView's short-term borrowing rate. This rate is linked to the business and financial risk *before* the change in credit terms. If that risk increases (decreases) due to the change in terms, the discount rate should be increased (decreased). In a later section, "Risk and the Discount Rate," we provide guidance on that adjustment.

   In practice, because that risk is hard to estimate, analysts could use sensitivity analysis as a decision aid. Might the sales increase only 2.5 percent instead of 3 percent and still add value (have a higher NPV than the present terms)? If so, the analyst becomes more confident in the recommendation to adopt the new terms. Or, more formally, one could employ simulation, in which probability distributions for revenues and expenses are combined in a quantitative model to determine a whole distribution of NPVs for a proposed financial change. The probability of having an NPV in excess of the present terms' NPV can be assessed. The reader may refer back to Exhibit 3–2 to review the difficulties in conducting NPV analysis.

## Valuing Changes in the Cash Conversion Period

Financial managers and investments analysts increasingly use the cash conversion period, introduced in Chapter 2, to manage or evaluate a company's finances. The cash conversion period (CCP) reveals how efficient the company's working capital management is.

Changes in any of the components, such as days inventory held (DIH), days sales outstanding (DSO), or days payables outstanding (DPO), can signal developing problem areas. We now apply the NPV model to valuing changes in the cash period. Recalling that we prefer the cycle time—the time elapsing from when a company pays its payables until it receives payment for its receivables—to be shorter, we expect longer periods to reduce value and shorter periods to increase value.

Let's show a company's sales and purchases on a cash flow timeline. This could represent daily purchases and sales, or purchase and sale amounts for a single transaction. For illustration purposes, let's assume that our company (which we will call Beacon Enterprises) has a cost of funds of 10 percent and cycle times of:

$$\text{DIH} = 30 \text{ days}$$

$$\text{DSO} = 30 \text{ days}$$

$$\text{DPO} = 45 \text{ days}$$

Let's further assume the following relationships for Beacon:

$$\text{Purchase amount} = 70\% \text{ of Cost of Goods Sold amount}$$

$$\text{Cost of Goods Sold amount} = 70\% \text{ of Sales amount}$$

$$\text{Sales amount} = \$1$$

The sale amount of $1 will simplify our illustration, and we can adjust sales to the actual rate later. Since the purchase amount is 70 percent of Cost of Goods Sold (COGS) and COGS is 70 percent of the sales amount, purchases are $0.49 ($0.49 = 0.7 \times 0.7 \times \$1$), or 49 percent of the sales amount. The company disburses $0.49 on day 45 and receives $1 on day 60 (60 days = Operating Cycle = DIH of 30 days + DSO of 30 days). The company's operating cycle of 60 days, less the DPO of 45 days, gives a CCP of 15 days. (Refer to Exhibit 2–5 in Chapter 2 for a review of the operating cycle and CCP.) Our cash flow timeline is shown in Exhibit 3–7.

Notice that this framework fits a nonmerchandising firm, as Beacon processes and adds value to the purchased amounts, giving a COGS greater than the purchased amount. As a result, we must calculate DPO using purchases, not COGS, in the denominator (unlike the example in Chapter 2). This more general approach may be used for any type of firm.

Equation 3.8 shows us the per-transaction NPV of the company's cash conversion period ($NPV_{CCP}$).

**Exhibit 3–7**

*Cash Conversion Period Cash Flow Timeline*

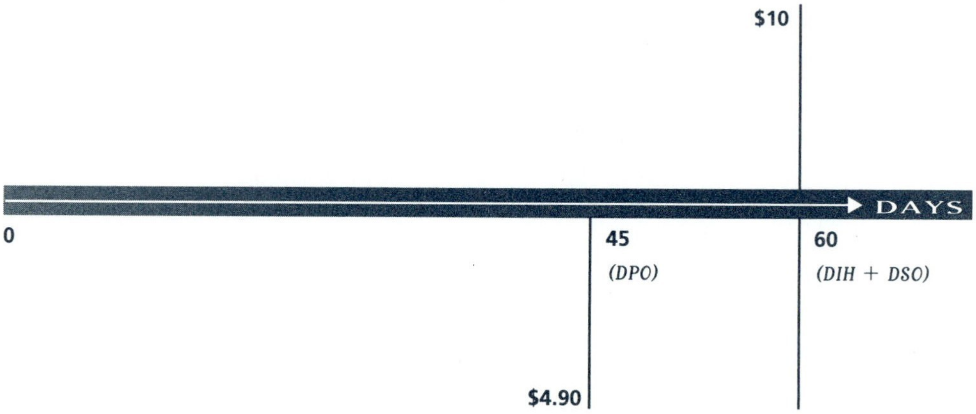

$10

DAYS

0

45

*(DPO)*

60

*(DIH + DSO)*

$4.90

$$NPV_{CCP} = \frac{-PURCHASE}{(1+i)^{DPO}} + \frac{SALE}{(1+i)^{DIH+DSO}} \tag{3.8}$$

In which:

PURCHASE = purchase amount
SALE = sales amount
$i$ = daily interest rate ($k$/365)
DPO = days payable outstanding
DIH = days inventory held
DSO = days sales outstanding

Using Beacon's data, we get an NPV per dollar of sales of \$0.4997, as shown below.

$$NPV_{CCP} = \frac{-0.49}{(1+0.10/365)^{45}} + \frac{1.00}{(1+0.10/365)^{30+30}}$$

$$NPV_{CCP} = \frac{-0.49}{(1+0.0002740)^{45}} + \frac{1.00}{(1+0.0002740)^{60}}$$

$$NPV_{CCP} = \frac{-0.49}{1.012404618} + \frac{1.00}{1.016573591}$$

$$NPV_{CCP} = -0.483996212 + 0.983696614$$

$$NPV_{CCP} = \$0.499700402 \textit{ or } \underline{\underline{\$0.4997}}$$

Recognize that we calculated the NPV for each dollar of sales. If we now view this as each dollar of daily sales, and we believe that this will last indefinitely, we may multiply this NPV by daily sales (annual sales divided by 365) and then divide by the daily interest rate to get the overall NPV effect, which we will label $NPV_{CCP\text{-}Aggregate}$. If the company is selling \$10 million of products annually, and sales and purchases are stable and not seasonal, the NPV of the company's CCP is:

$$NPV_{CCP\text{-}Aggregate} = NPV_{CCP} \times \text{Daily Sales/daily interest rate}$$

$$NPV_{CCP\text{-}Aggregate} = \frac{\$0.4997 \times (\$10{,}000{,}000/365)}{0.0002740}$$

$$NPV_{CCP\text{-}Aggregate} = \underline{\underline{\$49{,}965{,}043.70}}$$

Beacon's CCP is creating about \$50 million in shareholder value for the company.

Unfortunately, this formula does not provide a multiplier to use in determining the NPV effect of a one-day change in the CCP. Using calculus,[13] we may devise a formula that allows us to put in various interest rates, purchase and sale amounts, and then change DPO, DIH, or DSO by one day and see how NPV changes. This formula separates the CCP changes into two parts. We label $CCP_P$ as a change up or down in DPO: if DPO increases by one day, $CCP_P$ decreases by one day. We label $CCP_O$ as a change, up or down, in the operating cycle (either due to a change in DIH or in DSO). Equation 3.9 gives us the approximate value effect ($\Delta NPV_{CCP}$) of a one-day decrease in DPO (resulting in $CCP_P$ changing) or either DIH and DSO (resulting in $CCP_O$ changing).

$$\Delta NPV_{CCP} = \left[\frac{-PURCHASE}{(1+i)^{OC-CCP_P}} - \frac{SALE}{(1+i)^{CCP_O+DPO}}\right]\ln(1+i) \tag{3.9}$$

[13] The derivation of this formula is beyond the scope of our presentation. It is available, as part of a working paper, upon request from the authors.

In which:

$$\text{PURCHASE} = \text{purchase amount}$$
$$\text{SALE} = \text{sales amount}$$
$$i = \text{daily interest rate } (k/365)$$
$$OC - CCP_P = \text{DPO (days payable outstanding)}$$
$$CCP_O + DPO = \text{DIH} + \text{DSO (or, days in operating cycle)}$$

Recognize that this formula gives the change in NPV for *increases* in the CCP—the signs would be reversed for CCP decreases. The key in using this formula is to keep separate changes in DPO and either DIH or DSO. Changes in DPO affect only the first term, even though you see the DPO symbol in the second term. Changes in either DIH or DSO affect only the second term, even though you see the operating symbol, OC, in the first term. (The reason for this oddity is that this expression is the only way we may incorporate CCP effects in both terms, when the dollar amounts are different for purchases and sales.) *Only a one-day increase in both* $CCP_P$ *and* $CCP_O$ *would allow us to use all of the terms to do the NPV effect in one calculation.*

Let's consider the interpretation of the formula. Any lengthening of the CCP, whether due to a decrease in DPO (causing an increase in $CCP_P$) or an increase in DIH or DSO (an increase in $CCP_O$), reduces value. Therefore, both terms in our formula have negative signs. This formula could be used for a one-time, purchase-and-sale analysis and for daily purchases and daily sales streams. Recapping, NPV declines due to an increase in CCP caused by a decrease in DPO as the company must pay for its purchases sooner ($CCP_P$ increases) or due to an increase in the operating cycle as it takes longer before the company gets paid for its products ($CCP_O$ increases). Notice that a decrease in CCP due to an increased DPO or reduced DIH or DSO will result in a positive change in NPV. Since the formula is set up for an increase in CCP, we must change the sign in order to use Equation 3.9 for a CCP decrease. Returning to our example will help clarify.

***CCP Change Example*** Recall that Beacon Enterprises formerly had DPO of 45 days, DIH of 30 days, and DSO of 30 days. Its purchases are 49 percent of sales amounts. Its cost of capital is 10 percent. Let's say that its suppliers have given it and other firms in its industry a 46-day credit period, as an inducement for each buyer to accept electronic billing. Recognize that DPO is now one day longer, so $CCP_P$ is one day less. Use $CCP_P$ in Equation 3.9 to determine the change in NPV that would result in either a shortened or lengthened DPO. Since the operating cycle would not change for Beacon, we will ignore the second term. The $CCP_P$ is decreasing, so we insert a minus sign in front of Equation 3.9.

$$\Delta NPV_{CCP} = -\left[\frac{-0.49}{(1 + 0.0002740)^{46}}\right] \ln(1 + 0.0002740)$$

$$\Delta NPV_{CCP} = -\left[\frac{-0.49}{1.012682017}\right] 0.00027396$$

$$\Delta NPV_{CCP} = -[-0.483863633]\ 0.00027396$$

The minus signs cancel out leaving:

$$\Delta NPV_{CCP} = \underline{\underline{\$0.0001325605}}$$

This is the daily change in NPV associated with a one-day decrease in CCP (corresponding to a one-day increase in DPO). By contrast, if DPO decreases, we would see a decrease in NPV. Now we may use this daily change in NPV to determine the aggregate change in NPV effect. To do so, multiply this change in NPV by daily purchases (annual purchases divided by 365), and then divide by the daily interest rate to get the overall change in NPV effect, which we will label $\Delta NPV_{CCP\text{-}Aggregate}$. Since the company is purchasing $4.9

million of products annually and sales and purchases are stable and not seasonal, the NPV of the company's CCP is:

$$\Delta NPV_{CCP-Aggregate} = (\Delta NPV_{CCP} \times \text{Daily Purchases})/\text{daily interest rate}$$

$$\Delta NPV_{CCP-Aggregate} = \frac{\$0.0001325605 \times (\$4{,}900{,}000/365)}{0.0002740}$$

$$\Delta NPV_{CCP-Aggregate} = \$6{,}494.82$$

The one-day lengthening of DPO increases Beacon's value by $6,494.82. Generalizing, for each one-day change in DPO, Beacon's value would change by roughly $6,494. This is a significant value effect, and it underscores the importance of cycle time and a company's reduction in CCP. Wal-Mart has as one of its objectives "to sell merchandise before we pay for it" and has increased the percentage of its inventory sold before bills are paid from 55 percent to 63 percent over the past four years.[14] Increases in CCP, due to a shorter DPO, would have similar effects. The effect would be larger for a change in DIH or DSO, because we are now working with the sales amount, which is larger than the purchase amount. If DIH or DSO change, we can still use Equation 3.9, but now we must ignore the first term in Equation 3.9 and calculate the NPV effect by changing the second term. Also, we must use daily sales, not daily purchases, in getting the aggregate NPV effect of a change in DSO or DIH.

## Corporate Cash Holdings and Value

We noted in Chapter 1 that, even though many firms are striving to minimize their investment in net working capital, a number hold significant amounts of cash and short-term investments. We do not have an NPV approach to valuing those holdings—EVA models usually subtract their amount from capital before doing the capital charge calculation and then add them back in, dollar for dollar. We address here the possibility that investors perceive added value in a company's cash holdings.

A decade ago, companies were being advised to keep cash holdings to a minimum. First, the long-term cost of funds far exceeds the small return on short-term investments (at the time of this writing, the Treasury bill rate is 1 percent). Second, these cash holdings were viewed as "negative debt," and it was thought better to hold more debt and less cash to get the tax deduction on interest that comes with debt. So, the idea went, hold more debt relative to equity, and do not add equity to fund increased cash holdings. The double taxation of retained earnings to add to cash holdings seems to support this argument: corporate profits are taxed and then used to invest in cash holdings, on which interest earned is taxed a second time.

A strong counter-trend developed in the late 90s and early in the new millennium. Bond rating agencies started conducting "liquidity risk assessments" and indicated that many firms had too little in cash holdings. This was based on the possibility that external financing via the capital markets would cease to be available (or would be available only at unattractive terms). Pinkowitz and Williamson (2002) studied cash holdings and their relationship to companies' market-to-book ratios (the ratio of stock price to book value per share) and found that investors marked up stock value about $1.26 per $1 of cash held, on average. The strategic value of cash holdings may underlie this finding. Clearly, one premise of the "old school" of thought, that markets are so efficient that companies can costlessly raise funds at their normal cost of capital at any time, has been found to be invalid. The implication is that companies may wish to hold significant levels of cash and short-term investments.

---

[14] *The Wall Street Journal* (November 10, 1999).

### Concluding Comments on Valuation

The NPV model, used in conjunction with the cash flow timeline, is a powerful method for evaluating the financial dimensions of project proposals. We summarize with three pointers about using the NPV model in short-term financial decision making. First, we can often use a simple interest formula, which ignores compounding, to value short-term financial decisions. Second, we must remember that nonfinancial considerations at times predominate in working capital decisions. For example, the parts subsidiaries of domestic automakers have had to stock a large inventory of exhaust system parts due to a government regulation stipulating that specific levels of inventory be available for recent model-year cars and trucks. The impact on and reactions of stakeholder groups other than common stockholders must also be taken into account in decision making. Practitioners report that a major stride they are making in improving capital allocation decisions is the application of nonfinancial measures to supplement financial estimates. Third, unless fixed assets or future-period fixed costs change because of the proposal, there will rarely be an initial investment to consider in the project evaluation. We recap our discussion to this point in Exhibit 3–8.

We have purposefully left a very important topic to last: selection of the appropriate **discount rate**. This subject can quickly become complex, and we postponed until the chapter appendix some of the advanced considerations.

## CHOOSING THE DISCOUNT RATE

In all our calculations, we have been supplied with a discount rate. How do we determine the discount rate, $k$, used to determine the present values of cash flows? The appropriate discount rate is based on the riskiness of the cash flows. Conceptually, the rate chosen should reflect **opportunity cost**, or the interest rate one could earn on the next-best investment opportunity of equal risk. While asset risk ("standalone risk") is usually defined as the variability of the asset's cash flows, for the company as a whole, risk is a function of the variability of the average project undertaken. This heavily influences the required returns on the company's equity and debt securities. Correspondingly, the discount rate used for making long-lived capital budgeting decisions is the company's **weighted-average cost of capital**,[15] in which the funding sources generally included are long-term ones.

### Discount Rate Selection and Project Lifespan

Three unique problems face the analyst trying to determine a discount rate for short-term decisions. First, corporations rarely raise funds specifically to finance the types of projects considered in short-term finance. This handicap is not present when making capital budgeting decisions, such as building a new plant or buying a major piece of machinery. The analyst is without the luxury of having market signals of funding cost such as those available for fixed-asset decisions. Second, the short time horizon of many decisions (other than those with multiyear effects) implies that we cannot use the long-term cost of funds and will, instead, have to tie the discount rate to a short-term interest rate. Third, risk should be incorporated into the discount rate, but how do we do it? The riskiness of many short-term projects is negligible, ambiguous, or both. For example, changing the number and location of collection points for mailed customer checks would not be very risky. As a banker making a loan to a corporation implementing a new collection system, what

---

[15] Calculation of the weighted-average cost of capital using actual company data is presented in George E. Pinches, *Essentials of Financial Management, 4th ed.* (New York: HarperCollins, 1992).

**Exhibit 3–8**

*Using the NPV Model for STFM Decision-Making*

| Principle/Concept | Explanation | Implications and Cautions |
|---|---|---|
| 1. Use simple interest instead of having to utilize compound interest to discount future cash flows. | Time frame is too short to cause major difference in investment desirability, so simple interest calculations are usually adequate. | 1. Calculations are easier, able to be performed by those not trained in finance.<br>2. Be cautious: multiyear cash flows and large dollar amounts argue for compound interest formulas and use of a financial calculator or computer spreadsheet. |
| 2. Capture nonfinancial aspects of short-term finance decisions. | Along with an alternative's NPV, consider political/legal, ethical, and stakeholder ramifications before making a decision. | 1. Get input from legal department and other areas such as purchasing, accounting, production, and marketing to bring various perspectives into decision.<br>2. Consider ethical dimensions of decisions.<br>3. Incorporate external stakeholder views, where possible. |
| 3. Unlike long-term capital projects, most short-term decisions have no initial investment other than variable cost(s). | Make decisions by laying out operating cash outflows (from variable costs such as labor and materials) and operating cash inflows (from sale), then discounting future flows, and netting to get NPV. | 1. Short-term financial decisions are typically simpler than long-term decisions.<br>2. At times, fixed costs must also be included at the time of the decision, or in a later period.<br>3. Fixed asset increases are sometimes necessitated by short-term decisions. This results in an initial investment amount. It also results in noncash depreciation charges, which affect future cash tax payments. |

interest rate would you charge for the loan? What risk adjustment, if any, would you make to reflect the differential risk of this or other related short-term decisions? Or, as the financial analyst making the "go or no-go" recommendation on this proposal, what discount rate would you use? Finance theorists recommend choosing a discount rate that reflects the opportunity cost of deploying funds in this particular project, which in turn is determined by both the project's risk and lifespan. Further guidance is provided in the chapter appendix.

*Use of the Weighted Average Cost of Capital* Some might argue for using the company's weighted-average cost of capital as a discount rate for all short-term as well as long-term investment decisions. Calculated using only long-term funds, typically, this benchmark works well for long-term decisions. The short-term financial context is more complex. First, current asset allocations are seldom, if ever, financed solely with long-term capital. This argues against simplistic use of the weighted-average cost of capital based only on long-term funding sources. Second, the average cost of short-term funds is very difficult to estimate. For example, how does one put a cost on accruals or accounts payable financing? Even on bank borrowing, the bank may disguise its loan pricing by adjusting it upward or downward based on the volume of cash management or other nonlending services the company uses. The interest rate that a company pays may also be artificially high due to imperfect competition in the local lending market for companies of its size. To help resolve the dilemma of what rate to use, we will distinguish between "one-shot" and multiyear projects.

## One-Shot versus Enduring or Multiyear Projects

Other than the distinction between risky and risk-free projects, the most important guide to the appropriate discount rate is whether the decision involves a one-shot intrayear cash impact proposal or enduring multiyear effects.

*One-Shot Projects* One-shot decisions, such as whether to take a cash discount on a one-time purchase, whether to enter into a one-year contract with a treasury service provider, or which bank to use for a one-time working capital loan, are much like other operational purchasing decisions. When buying office supplies, typically you shop around until you find the best price. No calculating is done to compute the present value effect of these items. The corporate financial analyst will probably not do an NPV analysis of one-shot financial decisions either. Exceptions might occur when the dollar amounts are very large and/or when the flows occur at various points within the next year (especially when they are staggered toward year-end); two alternatives may be compared based on the net present values. When money has a very high time value, such as in an economy experiencing hyperinflation, present value analysis is also warranted. Finally, whenever there are follow-on effects, such as the linkage of a loan with reduced rates on future buys of cash management or loan products, one should try to integrate these with NPV analysis, as demonstrated in the multiyear project approach that follows.

The appropriate discount rate for one-shot projects is usually the firm's short-term borrowing or investing interest rate. This follows the opportunity cost concept, in that investors can make approximately that interest rate if their funds are not used by the firm. Cash flows are going to be tied up (or freed up) for less than a year, and the rate of return that could be earned on those flows is a short-term rate. Note that this might entail using a discount rate in excess of the company's average capital cost when the organization is illiquid and borrowing at very high interest rates. Furthermore, if the proposal is more risky than the typical near-term project, one could apply a higher rate, such as that paid on short-term notes by speculative-grade ("junk") issuers. Examples of such projects might be those located in less-developed countries, in which there is a great deal of near-term uncertainty.

*Recap for One-Shot Projects* The implication of all this is that (1) one-shot projects may not be subjected to NPV analysis if the cash flows are not significant and (2) the analyst may be forced to use considerable judgment in applying the opportunity cost concept when determining a discount rate. At the margin, if the company is consistently cash poor (illiquid) and must fund temporary outlays with borrowing, the borrowing rate may serve as the discount rate. If the company has excess cash, the investing rate may be used because dollars diverted to a project will come from the liquidation of investments. The forgone interest, then, is the true opportunity cost attributable to the project. Risk adjustment, due to project cash flows that are either less risky or more risky than the company's typical project, results in using a lower or higher discount rate than the short-term borrowing or investing rate.

*Multiyear Projects* When policies or projects have multiyear effects, it is important to conduct NPV analysis to maximize shareholder wealth. Short-term financial decisions, particularly those involving a payables, receivables, or inventory policy change, often have long-term cash flow effects. Thus, they should compete for capital along with all other multiyear capital budgeting proposals. Assuming they have cash flows associated with them that are no more or less variable than those of capital projects normally undertaken, use the weighted-average cost of capital as the discount rate.

## Risk and the Discount Rate

The general principle followed in financial decision making is "the greater the risk, the greater the **required rate of return**." Because bondholders and stockholders require compensation for risk in the form of higher required returns, the discount rate should be higher if the riskiness of the project's cash flows is greater. Generally, projects having greater variability in their cash flow distributions should have those flows discounted at a higher rate than projects characterized by less variability.

*Risk-Free versus Risky Projects* Some short-term decisions are practically risk-free, such as whether to take a cash discount on a one-time buy. We could use a short-term, risk-free rate, generally the three-month Treasury bill rate, to discount cash flows related to such decisions. For risk-free projects with multiyear cash flows (e.g., switching from biweekly to monthly payroll disbursement system, establishing a lockbox network for collections, or implementing a new computerized treasury management information system leased at a contracted price), the Treasury bond rate could be used as the discount rate. Although some analysts would prefer to again use the Treasury bill rate, the Treasury bond rate can be thought of as a composite of a sequence of the present and future Treasury bill rates and, therefore, is preferable.[16]

For decisions that affect the company's cash flows in a significant and unpredictable manner (e.g., a change in credit terms), we must include some type of risk premium to account for the greater risk. The simplest approach is to start with the cost of funds that are borrowed for short-term purposes. This cost might be the prime lending rate for some middle-sized companies, a certain amount above the prime rate for smaller companies, and a certain amount below the prime rate for larger companies. Companies with very large marketable securities portfolios, such as Microsoft, would prefer to use the interest rate being earned on those securities, because the opportunity loss when financing short-term projects is the interest given up when they sell off some of the investments. Depending on how risky the project is perceived to be, a risk premium might be added to that short-term rate. We now turn to a more formal discussion of the risk premium.

## Project Life and the Risk-Adjusted Discount Rate

For decisions whose effects stretch beyond one year, it is essential that the analyst consider making a risk adjustment when determining the appropriate discount rate. Modeling the

---

[16] A lucid and persuasive argument for discounting multiyear, risk-free project cash flows with the Treasury bond rate to match holding period interest rates to the periods in which cash flows are received is found in Neil Seitz and Mitch Ellison, *Capital Budgeting and Long-Term Financing Decisions, 5th ed.* (Cincinnati: South-Western, 2005).

discount rate as the sum of the risk-free rate of return investors can earn, a risk premium reflecting the risk of the company's typical projects, and an adjustment for whether a project possesses greater or lesser risk as compared with a normal project, we have the following equation:[17]

$$k_{adj} = k_{rf} + k_{avg} + k_{\Delta} \tag{3.10}$$

Where:
$k_{adj}$ = risk-adjusted discount rate
$k_{rf}$ = risk-free rate
$k_{avg}$ = risk premium for company's typical project
$k_{\Delta}$ = risk adjustment for specific project

Notice that the sum of the second and third terms in Equation 3.10 ($k_{rf} + k_{avg}$), equates to the company's cost of capital. The fourth term, $k_{\Delta}$, gives the modification to the cost of capital necessary to arrive at $k_{adj}$, a **risk-adjusted discount rate**. Furthermore, the project risk adjustment $k_{\Delta}$ will be positive if the project under consideration is riskier than the company's typical project, but negative if the project is less risky than those normally considered. There are two main approaches to determining the amount of risk adjustment, $k_{\Delta}$. The analyst may either use the capital asset pricing model (CAPM) or the company's cost of capital as modified by subjective risk classes.

*Capital Asset Pricing Model* The **capital asset pricing model (CAPM)** is a mathematical representation of the relationship between risk and return, which gives the analyst an estimate for $k_{adj}$; this model is covered in Appendix 3A. We simply note here that for the analyst trying to pinpoint the effect of risk on a project's required rate of return, using the CAPM can provide an estimate of the necessary adjustment consistent with the shareholder's view of risk.

*Subjective Risk Class Adjustment* Analysts uncomfortable with the assumptions underlying the CAPM, or who are unable to generate the necessary informational inputs for the model, might prefer to develop discount rates based on **risk classes**. Proposals having multiyear effects on the firm's cash flows would be assigned a higher discount rate if they have longer time horizons, or a very large range (or standard deviation) of cash flow outcomes. The riskier the project, the higher the discount rate, as Exhibit 3–9 illustrates.

Assigning discount rates based on risk classes is considered to be overly subjective by finance theorists, but it might be used by managers who have had difficulty in generating precise, risk-adjusted discount rates.[18] Additionally, we should recognize that any approach to project risk adjustment ignores the effect of a proposed project on the overall liquidity of the company—which might be the most attractive or unattractive aspect of the project. Accept/reject decisions should not be based solely on the outcome of an appraisal of project risk.

---

[17] This equation is adapted from one developed and discussed in John J. Clark, Thomas J. Hindelang, and Robert E. Pritchard, *Capital Budgeting: Planning and Control of Capital Expenditures, 3rd ed.* (Englewood Cliffs, NJ: Prentice-Hall, 1989), pp. 219–222. Also, see that presentation for an example of how risk classes map into risk-adjusted discount rates.

[18] For a classic practitioner's perspective on why formal risk analysis has failed, see K. Larry Hastie, "One Businessman's View of Capital Budgeting," *Financial Management* (Winter 1974), pp. 36–44. Hastie makes a strong case for the use of sensitivity analysis in which the key inputs are identified for further study. Their values can be varied up or down 5, 10, or 25 percent and the resulting NPV observed.

**Exhibit 3–9**

*Risk Classes and Risk-Adjusted Discount Rates*

| RISK CLASS | EXAMPLES | DISCOUNT RATE |
|---|---|---|
| Low Risk | 1. Change in lead concentration bank<br>2. Adoption of lockbox network<br>3. Automation of treasury information system | Significantly less than company's weighted-average cost of capital ($k_\Delta$ negative) |
| Moderate Risk | 1. Change in cash discount<br>2. Switch to "just-in-time" inventory system | Slightly less than weighted-average cost of capital ($k_\Delta$ negative but small) |
| High Risk | 1. Shortening of credit terms below industry standard<br>2. Decision to pay vendor invoices late | Above weighted-average cost of capital ($k_\Delta$ positive) |

## CAPITAL ALLOCATION DECISION MAKING IN PRACTICE

In this chapter we have presented several approaches to short-term financial decision making and argued for a valuation approach that is consistent with "best practices" in capital budgeting. In this final section, we review recent studies of capital allocation decision making. Although not specifically addressed in many of the studies, anecdotal evidence suggests that the key driver for integrating working capital management into capital budgeting practices is the adoption of EVA™ or a similar framework such as "cash flow return on investment" (CFROI). The surveys we profile do not offer much evidence of working capital allocation inclusion in capital allocation practices, but they do provide evidence as to the degree of risk adjustment.

The Gilbert & Reichert (1995) study, especially valuable because of its scope and longitudinal insights, provides some useful insights into capital budgeting practices. Their 1991 survey of Fortune 500 CFOs found that 85 percent of companies calculated NPV in their capital budgeting and 91 percent calculated either NPV or IRR, another discounted cash flow evaluation technique. This was a marked increase from 1980 and 1985. Models for managing accounts receivable are used by 59 percent of the companies, and inventory management models by 60 percent of companies, but it is not clear whether allocations were considered alongside long-term projects with NPVs calculated.

Farragher, Kleiman, and Sahu (1999) conducted a mail survey of U.S.-based companies included in the S&P Industrial Index. They found, like Gilbert & Reichert, that companies are using sophisticated capital evaluation tools and they make strategic analysis a cornerstone of their capital investment process. Sixty-two percent of respondents indicated that corporate strategy was more important than individual project return/risk factors in searching for investment opportunities. Unfortunately, 15 percent do not evaluate working capital changes that might arise from capital projects. Slightly over one-half of respondents (55 percent) do require a quantitative risk assessment of *cash flows*, a significant increase from numbers reported in earlier studies. Mostly, this risk assessment was made with sensitivity analysis or scenarios (high-average-low outcomes), not with simulation models or capital market risk analysis (using beta). While risk factors are often nonquantifiable, about two-thirds require a formal, written assessment of those factors. When evaluating *capital projects*, 47 percent of the companies required a quantitative risk-adjusted evaluation (the majority of those, about three in five, doing so with the capital asset pricing model), with the adjustment made on the required rate of return by about three of five of those companies and two in five adjusting the cash flows (mostly subjectively).

Three recent studies find an increasing usage of NPV. Graham and Harvey (2001) surveyed CFOs of firms in various industries and of different size and found that 74.9 percent of CFOs always or almost always used NPV and 75.7 percent always or almost always used IRR. Companies using relatively high levels of debt financing are more likely to use NPV and IRR, relative to payback and other techniques, and they are also more likely to use sensitivity and simulation analysis of projected capital allocation cash inflows and outflows. Ryan and Ryan (2002) surveyed the Fortune 1000 and determined that NPV usage has finally surpassed IRR in the United States as the primary capital project evaluation technique. Their survey finds 85.1 percent of respondents "always or often" using NPV, versus 76.7 percent for IRR and 52.6 percent for payback (many firms use multiple evaluation techniques, so these numbers total more than 100 percent).

In the manufacturing sector, Chadwell-Hatfield, Goitein, Horvath, and Webster (1996–1997) found that companies use more than one evaluation technique for capital budgeting (and favor IRR and payback over NPV) and that sophisticated risk analysis is not emphasized even though managers appear to be concerned with risk. Undiversifiable (market) risk is not a significant factor in their capital budgeting analysis. Most companies operated with constraints on the total capital budget, turning down some attractive projects as a result ("capital rationing"). Of significance to our topic of relatively smaller working capital allocations, surveyed manufacturers often exempted projects with relatively low cost from formal financial analysis.

Block's (1997) study of 232 small businesses with less than $5 million and fewer than 1,000 employees indicated that nondiscounted techniques such as payback still dominated for evaluation but that NPV and IRR usage as the primary evaluation technique had increased from 14 percent in 1983 to 28 percent in 1995. Almost 70 percent of firms specifically consider risk in doing their capital budgeting analysis, mostly by increasing the rate of return. For payback users, this means shortening the allowable payback period, and for NPV or IRR users, this implies using a higher discount or hurdle rate. Graham and Harvey (2001) also found that small firms were significantly less likely to use NPV than were large firms. They found that small firms were prone to using payback almost as commonly as NPV or IRR.

Whether cash holdings policy, credit policy, payables policy, or inventory policy decisions are subjected to NPV or other explicit capital budgeting analysis in practice is still unknown. Clearly, though, the EVA™ methodology subjects operating-related cash flows and associated capital requirements to a similar evaluation. This brings continuity to company-wide resource allocation, as working capital must be scrutinized in the same way as all other capital requests. It also incorporates elements of both the financial statement approach and the valuation approach that we presented at the beginning of the chapter.

## SUMMARY

Short-term financial decisions offer the potential to create value for the firm. They do so by affecting the spread between revenues and expenses and altering operating cash flows, by changing the length of the cash conversion period, by changing the risk posture of the firm, by increasing or decreasing net interest revenue, and by changing the accuracy and timeliness of critical information.

Both the financial statement approach and the valuation approach offer insight into working capital management decisions. The financial statement approach is helpful for seeing the effect of proposed courses of action on the company's overall liquidity, but it suffers from a too-limited view of risk and it ignores the time value of money. The valuation approach recommends computing the present value of cash flows to make appropriate decisions. EVA™ models attempt to draw from both approaches to guide corporate financial policy making and analysis. The NPV calculation is central to making value-maximizing financial decisions. The tools necessary to assess the time value of money for financial decision making were introduced and illustrated in this chapter. For most decisions, we can overlook the compounding of interest through time and can calculate value effects using a simple interest equation.

We also saw how companies could apply valuation tools to maximize the value of the cash flow timeline. We concluded the presentation by surveying several of the practical difficulties the analyst must overcome in arriving at value estimates. The key problem here is selecting the appropriate discount rate to use. If a working capital venture would have a multiyear impact on cash flows, the company's weighted-average cost of long-term funds should be appropriate, as the project is competing with other capital projects for the firm's funds. For shorter-lived ventures, a different opportunity cost approach might be followed. In such cases, the company's short-term borrowing rate or short-term investing rate are the logical candidates. At times, the analyst may decide to average these rates or, if the policy decision involves more or less risk than the normal company project, develop a risk-class approach to discount rate determination.

Compared with capital budgeting and capital structure decisions, the time value of money is of less importance in short-term financial decision making. This is due partly to the low risk of most such projects and partly to their short lifespans. Some decisions regarding the management of cash and other working capital accounts do have lasting effects, however, necessitating our coverage of valuation theory and NPV. Financial managers wish to maximize the discounted net cash flows arising from financial decisions. They are aware that valuation concepts are sometimes inapplicable, perhaps because a project does not have identifiable cash inflows. Regardless, the choice of a discount rate is less critical in the short-term setting, and the decision on which is the "best" course of action from among several alternatives is therefore less sensitive to the discount rate chosen.

Surveys of capital allocation practices in U.S. firms indicate that formal models are used for receivables and inventory management by large firms and that risk analysis is usually accomplished with risk-adjusted discount rates or sensitivity analysis. While many firms do include working capital changes linked to capital projects, we remain unclear about how many firms conduct NPV analysis on strictly short-term financial decisions.

## USEFUL WEB SITES

| | |
|---|---|
| Association for Financial Professionals | **http://www.afponline.org** |
| CFO Magazine | **http://www.cfonet.com** |
| Stern Stewart & Co. | **http://www.eva.com/evaabout/whatis.php** |
| Stern Stewart & Co. | **http://www.eva.com/evaluation/overview.php** |
| Stern Stewart & Co. | **http://www.sternstewart.com/advisory/overview.php** |
| Global Treasury News | **http://www.gtnews.com** |

## QUESTIONS

1. Is the time value of money as important in short-term financial decisions as in capital project decisions? Why or why not?

**2.** Distinguish between the financial statement approach and the valuation approach to making short-term financial decisions. Which approach is superior for making short-term financial decisions? Why?

**3.** Use your understanding of long-term capital sources and the calculated cost of capital to indicate why economic value added would typically be different from net income.

**4.** When given data on daily sales, it would seem that one would have to work with at least 365 days on a cash flow timeline to properly assess short-term financial policy decisions. Why is this generally not the case? When should you consider the actual cash flow pattern in its entirety?

**5.** In what circumstances does using a simple interest approximation formula result in the greatest inaccuracy compared with using a compound interest formula?

**6.** An investment offers a nominal rate of 7 percent. Would the annual effective rate be higher if interest is compounded daily or monthly? Explain, using illustrative calculations to support your answer.

**7.** What are the factors the financial analyst must assess in arriving at an appropriate discount rate for risky short-term decisions having multiyear effects?

**8.** Why is it difficult to determine the best discount rate to use in short-term decision making? Is it simpler than determining the discount rate for evaluating long-lived capital projects? Why or why not?

**9.** What effect, if any, does capital market efficiency have on a company's cost of capital? Does market efficiency necessarily characterize a company's short-term borrowing market?

**10.** Explain each term of the risk-adjusted discount rate equation (Equation 3.10) and how one could arrive at the appropriate numerical value for that term.

**11.** Explain how the risk class of a potential venture can be used to determine a discount rate. To what risk class would you assign each of the following decision situations?

**a.** Changing the credit terms you offer to your customers

**b.** Adopting a "just-in-time" inventory management system

**c.** "Stretching your payables" 25 days beyond their due date

**d.** Initiating a hedging strategy for all receivables denominated in a foreign currency

**12.** What are risk-adjusted discount rates? How might one go about determining the specific amount of risk adjustment for a particular decision?

**13.** Summarize the findings of recent studies of corporate capital allocation practices.

## PROBLEMS

*Note: To ensure comparability and consistency when discounting or compounding, use 31 days for a month, 182.5 days for six months, 273.75 days for nine months, and 365 days for a year.*

**1.** Kiernan Enterprises, a small manufacturer located in the eastern part of the United States, uses EVA™ as part of its performance measurement and evaluation system. Below are data from its last two annual reports. The latter year, 2005, is Kiernan's most successful ever, a year in which the company improved its management of cash, inventory, and accounts receivable. The company was able to pay off its short-term debt entirely in 2005 due to the working capital management improvement. Its tax rate is 40 percent.

**a.** Calculate the EVA™ for 2004 and 2005. Comment on the difference in the EVA™ amounts.

**b.** Suggest how improved working capital may increase EVA™ by increasing operating profit *and* reducing capital employed.

Kiernan Enterprises
Selected Financial Data

| | 2004 | 2005 |
|---|---|---|
| *Revenue and Expense Data:* | | |
| Revenues | $3,000,000 | $4,500,000 |
| Cost of goods sold | 2,000,000 | 2,800,000 |
| Gross profit | $1,000,000 | $1,700,000 |
| Operating expenses | 700,000 | 850,000 |
| Operating profit (EBIT) | $ 300,000 | $ 850,000 |
| *Balance Sheet Data:* | | |
| Cost of Capital | 8% | 8% |
| Short-term and long-term capital employed | $1,500,000 | $1,350,000 |

2. Christy anticipates receiving a check for $10,000 in six months. What is the present value of this amount if the interest rate Christy could earn on short-term investments is 12 percent per year?
   a. Use the exact formula, with daily compounding of interest.
   b. Use the simple interest approximation formula.
   c. Comment on the difference between your results in parts **a** and **b**.
3. Julie needs to pay a $5,000 tuition bill nine months from now. She has some money saved up that she could invest, but she is also considering a trip to Europe. She remembers reading something about how money grows over time, and she wonders if maybe she should just go ahead and invest some money today to pay the tuition bill.
   a. How much would Julie invest today to have $5,000 nine months from now if she can invest at a 10 percent annual rate? Use the simple interest approximation formula.
   b. Assuming Julie goes to Europe and waits six months to do her investing, how much would she need to invest then, again assuming a 10 percent annual rate and using the simple interest formula?
   c. Redo **a** and **b** using the daily compound interest formula, and compare your results to the simple interest results.
4. Anthony Rice was recently hired as a financial analyst in global cash management for BaurCorp, a Canadian-based multinational corporation. He has been assigned a collection float comparison analysis. He understands check float to be the total time elapsing between when the payor (check writer) mails the check and when BaurCorp receives available (spendable) funds at its bank. BaurCorp is trying to figure out the loss in value if it has a British £-denominated check sent to it, as opposed to a draft denominated in Canadian dollars. (A draft is a check-like payment instrument that must be approved by the payor or one of its agents before it is honored.) The first step Anthony wishes to take in the analysis is to determine the difference in float between the alternative payment methods. He finds that BaurCorp receives average daily remittances of 100,000 £ from its British customers. At current exchange rates, one £ will convert into 2.30 Canadian dollars. BaurCorp's weighted-average cost of capital, which it uses as a required rate of return on its investment decisions, is 12 percent. The number of mail days will be eight calendar days in either case. On average, it would take 1.5 calendar days to process a draft before getting it deposited but 2.5 calendar days to process a lira-denominated check. After deposit, BaurCorp does not get to spend the deposited amount until two days later for the draft or until ten days later for the lira-denominated check (the check must be routed back to England and presented to the bank on which it was drawn). To simplify the analysis, assume that the latter amounts are also calendar days. Anthony is advised by the analyst who formerly did the analysis to use the following formula:

$$\text{Annual Interest Gain/(Loss) of Collections} = \text{Difference in Days of Float} \times \text{Average Daily Remittance Amount} \times \text{Weighted Average Cost of Capital}$$

**a.** What is the annual interest gain or loss if BaurCorp allows payment by pound-denominated checks instead of Canadian dollar drafts?

**b.** Is the number calculated in part **a** really a value effect? Explain.

**5.** The BMX Bike Co. figures it would experience an increase in NPV of $0.75 per day if it adopts new credit terms.

**a.** If its annual opportunity cost of capital is 10 percent, what would be the total increase in shareholder value?

**b.** Redo part **a** with an opportunity cost of 12 percent. Comment on the reason you get different results from that computed in **a.**

**6.** J. Walker Manufacturing Co. is financially distressed and must pay "cash before delivery" for its raw materials. It pays $40 per assembly at the time of order. The parts are received 30 days after the order. Five days after they are received they are taken out of inventory and used in the manufacturing process. Walker incurs additional processing costs of $6.50 per assembly at the point in time when it manufactures its finished products. On average, it sells each finished assembly 95 days after manufacturing takes place.

**a.** Draw a cash flow timeline of the events above, being careful to denote which flows are negative and which are positive.

**b.** Figure out how much Walker must sell each assembly for to break even on a present value basis. Use a discount rate of 15 percent. You may use trial and error, or use the Goal Seek command in the Tools menu in Microsoft Excel™.

**c.** Now assume that Walker decides to sell the finished goods for $48.50. How high could the discount rate be for Walker to still break even on a present value basis? You may use trial and error, or use the Goal Seek command in the Tools menu in Microsoft Excel™.

**7.** Medsco financial analyst Joshua Brown estimates that the relevant up-front investment necessary to convert to and complete installation of a "just-in-time" inventory system is $40,000. Joshua figures that a risk-adjusted discount rate should be used. He looks in a financial newspaper and finds that the risk-free rate is 4 percent. The company's typical project carries a 3 percent risk premium above the risk-free rate. Joshua believes that this is a moderate-risk project, which generally implies a 1 percent reduction from the company's weighted average cost of capital to get a reasonable project discount rate. Joshua does not believe that there will be any revenue effects of the change-over in systems. Assume that the cost savings are a level perpetual stream.

**a.** How much must the annual cost savings be to make the investment a winner? Ignore any nonfinancial considerations.

**b.** Do you think Joshua's assumption that there will be no revenue effects is valid?

**c.** What nonfinancial considerations should Joshua take into account in evaluating this project?

**d.** Redo the analysis from **a**, assuming now that the cost savings occur only for each of the next five years. Contrast your results to that in **a**, and comment on the difference.

**8.** Brandon is head of the accounts payable department at an Idaho-based manufacturer, Schooley & Company. He just read in a trade association publication that one of his competitors recently renegotiated longer credit terms with a vendor from which his company also buys raw materials. Brandon wonders what increase in value his company would experience if he is able to successfully renegotiate his payable terms. Use the information below to help Brandon quantify the financial impact.

| | |
|---|---|
| Present payment terms | net 30 |
| Renegotiated payment terms | net 45 |
| Purchases (once each six months) | $150,000 |
| Annual opportunity cost of funds (nominal rate) | 12% |

**a.** What is the present value savings of one purchase made under the renegotiated terms?

**b.** Assuming the new terms become permanent, what is the value effect (NPV) of the new terms?

c. *Optional.* Brandon recalls that raw material costs have been going up at a 5 percent annual rate on the items purchased. Redo the analysis with this new assumption. (*Hint:* Utilize a formula used for valuing a constantly growing dividend stream, modified for the six-month cash flow stream.)

9. Mississippi Delta Inc. has been selling switching equipment to computer companies on net 30 terms, in which payment is expected by 30 days from the invoice date. Concerned about deteriorating collection patterns, the credit manager has divided customers into two groups for examination purposes: prompt payors and laggards. Prompt payors (80 percent of Mississippi Delta's customers) pay, on average, in 35 days, versus a 72-day average for the laggards. The manager wonders if the credit terms should be modified to include a 2 percent cash discount on invoices paid within 10 days. The average invoice is the same for both groups, roughly $4,000. The manager expects 50 percent of the prompt payors to pay in exactly 10 days and the average on the other half to slip to 40 days. He thinks that 20 percent of the laggards will pay in 10 days and the average on the others will slip to 70 days. Given these forecasts, he is not sure that the lost revenue from discount takers (who would then pay only 98 percent of the invoiced dollar amount) justifies the improved collection. The company's annual cost of capital is 11 percent.
   a. Using NPV calculations, show the present value of the present collection experience.
   b. Calculate the NPV of the proposed 2/10, net 30 terms.
   c. Based on your NPV analysis, should Mississippi Delta Inc. adopt the cash discount?
   d. What other factors should be taken into account before Mississippi Delta Inc. makes a switch, assuming such is justifiable on an NPV basis?
   e. Sensitivity analysis involves varying the key assumptions, one at a time, and observing the effect on the key decision criterion—such as profits or NPV. In the NPV analysis above, how could one carry out sensitivity analysis? (If you have a financial spreadsheet available, conduct a sensitivity analysis that varies the number of prompt payors who will pay in exactly 10 days and report your findings.)

## REFERENCES

Gerald A. Achstatter, "EVA: Performance Gauge for the 1990s?" *Investor's Business Daily* (June 21, 1995), p. A4.

Anil Arya, John C. Fellingham, et al., "Capital Budgeting: Some Exceptions to the Net Present Value Rule," *Issues in Accounting Education* (August 1998), pp. 499–508.

Stanley Block, "Capital Budgeting Techniques Used by Small Business Firms in the 1990s," *Engineering Economist* (Summer 1992), pp. 289–302.

Patricia Chadwell-Hatfield, Bernard Goitein, Philip Horvath, and Allen Webster, "Financial Criteria, Capital Budgeting Techniques, and Risk Analysis of Manufacturing Firms," *Journal of Applied Business Research* (Winter 1996–1997), pp. 95–104.

Aswath Damodaran, "Value Creation and Enhancement: Back to the Future," *Contemporary Finance Digest* (Winter 1998), pp. 5–51.

Ray Dillon and James E. Owers, "EVA as a Financial Metric: Attributes, Utilization, and Relation to NPV," *Financial Practice and Education* (Spring/Summer 1997), pp. 32–40.

Avinash K. Dixit and Robert S. Pindyck, "The Options Approach to Capital Investment," *Harvard Business Review*, 73 (3 May/June 1995), pp. 105–116.

Kenneth Eades, Robert Bruner, Robert Higgins, and Robert Harris, "Best Practices in Estimating the Cost of Capital: Survey and Synthesis," *Financial Practice and Education* (Spring/Summer 1998), pp. 13–27.

Edward J. Farragher, Robert T. Kleiman, and Anandi P. Sahu, "Current Capital Investment Practices," *The Engineering Economist*, 44 (1999), pp. 137–150.

Erika Gilbert and Alan Reichert, "The Practice of Financial Management Among Large United States Corporations," *Financial Practice & Education* (Spring/Summer 1995), pp. 16–23.

John Graham and Campbell Harvey, "The Theory and Practice of Corporate Finance: Evidence from the Field," *Journal of Financial Economics*, 60 (2001), pp. 187–243.

Roy E. Johnson, "Scrap Capital Project Evaluations," *CFO* (May 1998), p. 14.

Yong H. Kim and Joseph C. Atkins, "Evaluating Investments in Accounts Receivable: A Maximizing Framework," *Journal of Finance* (May 1978), pp. 402–412.

Yong H. Kim and Kee H. Chung, "An Integrated Evaluation of Investment in Inventory and Credit: A Cash Flow Approach," *Journal of Business Finance and Accounting* (Summer 1990), pp. 381–390.

Wilbur C. Lewellen, John J. McConnell, and Jonathan A. Scott, "Capital Market Influences on Trade Credit," *Journal of Financial Research* (Fall 1980), pp. 105–113.

Charles M. Linke and J. Kenton Zumwalt, "Estimation Biases in Discounted Cash Flow Analyses of Equity Capital Cost in Rate Regulation," *Financial Management* (Autumn 1984), pp. 15–21.

Timothy A. Luehrman, "A General Manager's Guide to Valuation," *Harvard Business Review* (May/June 1997), pp. 132–142.

Ann Monroe, "Financials Are King in Evaluating an IT Project," *Finance IT* (January/February 2000), p. 21.

Lee Pinkowitz and Rohan Williamson, "What Is a Dollar Worth? The Market Value of Cash Holdings," *Working Paper*, Georgetown University (2002).

Kenneth D. Riener, "The Analysis of Credit Policy Changes with Growing and Seasonal Sales," In: Yong Kim (ed): *Advances in Working Capital Management*, Vol. 4. Oxford, U.K.: Elsevier Science Ltd. (2001), pp. 123–135.

Patricia A. Ryan and Glenn P. Ryan, "Capital Budgeting Practices in the Fortune 1000: How Have Things Changed?" *Journal of Business and Management* 8 (Winter 2002), pp. 355–364.

Kanwal S. Sachdeva and Lawrence J. Gitman, "Accounts Receivable Decisions in a Capital Budgeting Framework," *Financial Management* (Winter 1981), pp. 45–49.

William L. Sartoris and Ned C. Hill, "A Generalized Cash Flow Approach to Short-Term Financial Decisions," *Journal of Finance* (May 1983), pp. 349–360.

William L. Sartoris and Ned C. Hill, "Evaluating Credit Policy Alternatives: A Present Value Framework," *Journal of Financial Research* (Spring 1981), pp. 81–89.

Neil Seitz and Mitch Ellison, *Capital Budgeting and Long-Term Financing Decisions*, Fifth Edition, (2005), Cincinnati: South-Western.

H. Joseph Wen and David D. Yen, "Methods for Measuring Information Technology Investment Payoff," *Human Systems Management*, 17 (1998), pp. 145–153.

John Zietlow, "8 Principles to Practical Finance," *AFP Exchange* (September/October 2003), pp. 17–20.

# APPENDIX 3A

## Advanced Present Value Analysis

We cover three advanced topics in this appendix: (1) the interaction between accounts receivables and inventories, (2) valuation theory and short-term financial decisions, and (3) risk adjustment in the valuation model. These aspects combined make the decision-making process more realistic.

### RECEIVABLES AND INVENTORY INTERACTIONS

Decisions that have an impact on a company's accounts receivable often affect its inventory position, and vice versa. The analyst is cautioned to consider the specific effect of each decision on all working capital accounts so as not to maximize the value effect of one area while overlooking value-reducing effects of that same decision on other areas. For example, more lenient credit terms may directly increase sales and profits yet lead to larger inventory positions, which will offset some of the profit increase. Inventory used currently in production gets captured in the cash flow timeline NPV analysis (where the associated cash outflow is shown), but there may be permanent "cushion" amounts of inventory held as safety stock as well (see Chapter 4). Proper decision making requires that all effects of a decision be considered, including semivariable cost disbursements and side effects.[1] The wide availability of financial spreadsheets facilitates the more comprehensive analysis that we advocate.

### VALUATION THEORY AND SHORT-TERM FINANCIAL DECISIONS

Consider a company whose cash receipts and cash disbursements are perfectly synchronized and totally predictable (no forecast error)—one in which cash receipts provide just enough funds, at just the time needed, to pay employees, vendors, taxes, dividends, interest, principal repayments, lease payments, and all other bills. The company neither sells nor buys using trade credit, so it has no receivables or payables. It does not prepay, accrue, or defer any expense or revenue. It only purchases finished goods inventories and direct ships them to customers so as not to have any inventories. You find the following balance sheet for our fictitious company surprising:

| CURRENT ASSETS | | CURRENT LIABILITIES | |
|---|---|---|---|
| Cash | $ 0 | Accounts payable | $ 0 |
| Short-term invest. | 0 | Accrued expenses | 0 |
| Inventories | 0 | Notes payable | 0 |
| Accounts rec. | 0 | Current portion of long-term debt | 50 |
| Prepaid expenses | 0 | | |
| *Current Assets* | $ 0 | *Current Liabilities* | $ 50 |
| Property, plant, & equipment | 1,000 | Long-term debt | 450 |
| | | Equity | 500 |
| *Total Assets* | $1,000 | *Total Liab. & Equity* | $1,000 |

You are probably thinking this is pretty far from reality, and you are right. Our exercise would be trivial except for one very sobering fact: this is exactly the type of world envisioned by the prevailing finance theories of valuation. These long-run theories posit that in a world of certainty, information symmetry, and perfect markets, required return (and value) can be linked to market risk (CAPM) or several risk factors (arbitrage pricing theory). There is no recognition of the uncertain, unsynchronized, uneven cash inflows and outflows that cause companies to hold cash and short-term investments as well as to contract for short-term credit lines. Market uncertainty and other imperfections causing companies to hold inventories or to offer and take advantage of trade credit are absent from these traditional valuation frameworks. The fact is that operating decisions, which implement capital projects through astute management of current assets and current liabilities, create value.

[1] Even the pricing policy should be brought into short-term financial decisions, as noted in the Kim and Chung article listed in the Chapter 3 references. Their model is necessarily complex and beyond the scope of our presentation.

Gentry,[2] as developed further in Gentry and Lee,[3] has expanded the NPV approach we used in Chapter 3 to include the large number of real variables that are continually changing. Gentry divides effects into a 4 × 4 matrix that classifies causal variables (henceforth termed drivers) as operational or other and as either influencing cash inflows or cash outflows. Some of the drivers making up the value creation process are:

| | OPERATIONAL | OTHER |
|---|---|---|
| Cash Inflow Drivers | Sales patterns<br>Collection patterns<br>ST investment returns<br>Credit terms | Short- or long-term borrowing<br>Sale of stock<br>Sale of fixed assets |
| Cash Outflow Drivers | Purchasing patterns<br>Payment patterns<br>Compensating balances<br>Delivery and storage costs | Capital expenditures<br>Share repurchase |

Gentry and Lee then formulate the general NPV model, which we have modified slightly to allow for differential growth rates for cash inflows and cash outflows:

$$NPV = \frac{CI - CO}{1 + r} + \frac{CI(1 + g_I) - CO(1 + g_O)}{(1 + r)^2} + \cdots + \frac{CI(1 + g_I)^n - CO(1 + g_O)^n}{(1 + r)^n}$$

Where:
$NPV$ = net present value
$CI$ = cash inflows
$CO$ = cash outflows
$r$ = risk-adjusted cost of capital (discount rate)
$g_I$ = growth rate of cash inflows
$g_O$ = growth rate of cash outflows

This model demonstrates the reality that value can be created (positive NPV) or destroyed (negative NPV) by changes in short-term financial policies, product demand, or production costs. *Any policy or action that speeds up (affects the timing of) cash inflows or increases the amount (level) of those inflows will create value. Speeding up cash outflows or increasing the amount of outflows (e.g., absorbing a cost increase from a supplier) erodes value, all other things held equal.* Gentry and Lee point out that the competitive position of a company influences its cash conversion cycle by determining its credit terms on the selling side (affecting receivables) as well as on the buying side (affecting payables).

This NPV model is attractive in that it incorporates the value-enhancing activities of cash managers, credit managers, purchasing agents, and others working on short-term financial decisions. However, Gentry and Lee note that NPV models do not explicitly include a financial market risk measure.[4] Thus, it is conceivable that the risk-adjusted discount rate used in the NPV model is based on project (standalone) risk, not market risk (which the CAPM would identify as systematic or nondiversifiable risk measured by beta), as might be the case if one was doing a divisional cost of capital for long-term capital projects. The disparate treatment of short-run and long-run projects may be bothersome. The linkage between short-run financial decision making and long-run financial decision making is unclear at best and nonexistent at worst. We return to this concern in the concluding section ("CAPM-Based Discount Rates") after dealing with risk in general terms.

## RISK CONSIDERATIONS

Short-term financial decisions also affect the business and financial risk of the organization. Business risk refers to the variability in operating revenues and costs and is linked to use of assets with fixed operating costs. To the extent a decision requires a permanent increase in investment in cash, receivables, or inventories, it results in higher fixed operating costs, which magnify the effect of any change in revenue on operating profit. Bank fees are a fixed cost of holding cash. Inventory-related fixed costs include shrinkage due to theft or perishability and obsolescence due to technological advance or new product design. Receivables-related fixed costs include the computer hardware and the staffing cost for credit personnel that must be added to service new accounts. Financial risk is also affected by short-term decisions.

[2] James A. Gentry, "Short-Run Financial Management," Section 3C in Dennis E. Logue, *Handbook of Modern Finance*, 1996 ed. (Boston: Warren, Gorham, & LaMont, 1996), pp. C3-1–C3-43.

[3] J. A. Gentry and H. W. Lee, "An Integrated Cash Flow Model of the Firm." Faculty Working Paper 1314, College of Commerce and Business Administration, University of Illinois, Champaign, IL, December 1986.

[4] Gentry (1990) predicts that yet-to-be-developed simulation, simultaneous equations, and control theory models will lay the groundwork for new theoretical linkages between short-term financial and long-term, value-based decision making.

Financial risk is defined as the variability in "bottom-line earnings"—which could be net income or earnings per share. It is largely based on the amount of debt financing or leasing an organization takes on. Any investment in a current asset account must be financed, except in the rare instance in which another current asset account is reduced by an equal amount. The financing decision of interest here is what portion of the current asset increase is financed by short-term financing as opposed to long-term debt or lease financing or equity financing. Any change in debt financing, whether involving short-term or long-term debt, changes the financial risk posture of the organization. Within the debt category, short-term debt is considered more risky than long-term debt. There are two reasons for this:

- Long-term debt is usually "fixed rate," (i.e., the interest rate does not change from year to year), whereas every time short-term debt matures, it is replaced at a different, possibly higher, interest rate.
- Continued availability of short-term financing is uncertain when the business's financial position or general economic conditions change. Banks or other short-term funds providers might be unwilling to continue to provide funds to the business (as is increasingly true with small business commercial lending in several areas of the country in the early 2000s).

The consequences of a large increase in the short-term interest rate paid or of being closed out of the short-term credit market are quite severe. Companies are often pushed into bankruptcy when they are denied access to their short-term borrowing facilities.

The risk effects that we are addressing here are important because they bear on the appropriate discount rate to be used for valuing financial decisions.

### Discount Rate and Market Efficiency

The concept of opportunity cost is related to the investor's required rate of return for the company. Based on their perceptions of the average risk of the capital projects invested in by the firm, stock and bond investors collectively determine the return from the company's stocks and bonds that would be necessary for them to provide capital to the firm. Thus, the opportunity cost of investing in Ford stock is the return that would have been earned by investing in another stock of similar risk. When financial markets are efficient, meaning prices change freely and instantly in response to supply and demand and are not significantly affected by poor information or tax code barriers, a company's cost of capital should reflect the required rate of return, which should, in turn, reflect the riskiness of its typical capital projects. Efficiently priced securities give rise to an accurate cost of capital, which then becomes a hurdle rate against which one can compare the rates of return of long-lived capital projects—and a discount rate for determining the present value of future cash flows.

The CAPM can be used to determine (1) the appropriate cost of equity or (2) a decision-specific cost of capital to use in discounting cash flows. Although the exact relationship between business or financial risk and the discount rate is unknown, an increase in either one should increase the market risk, and hence the discount rate.

## CAPM-BASED DISCOUNT RATES

The CAPM is a theoretical formulation of how common stock returns are determined. If a company is maximizing value, it is giving the highest possible returns to its common shareholders. If the stock market is "efficient," the CAPM says, the expected returns of any company's stock would be based on just one factor—systematic, or market-related, risk. As the market moves, so, too, do the individual stocks making up the market, but to varying degrees. The degree of a stock's sensitivity to market movements is called its systematic risk. Systematic risk is measured by beta.[5] The key point to observe is that CAPM can give us a required rate of return for equity, which can then be combined with the cost of debt and the cost of preferred stock (if any) to derive the weighted-average cost of capital for the organization. The CAPM does this by modeling the equity rate of return as a function of systematic risk, or beta.

$$k_j = k_{rf} + \beta_j(k_m - k_{rf}) \tag{3.1A}$$

Where: $k_j$ = required return for stock j
$k_{rf}$ = risk-free rate of return
$\beta_j$ = stock's systematic risk
$k_m$ = required return on the market portfolio

[5] Two excellent sources of basic information for anyone unfamiliar with beta or the CAPM are Scott Besley and Eugene F. Brigham, *Essentials of Managerial Finance, 12th ed.* (Cincinnati: South-Western, 2000), and Lawrence J. Gitman, *Principles of Managerial Finance, 10th ed.* (Reading, MA: Addison Wesley Longman, 2002). Advanced material may be found in Haim Levy and Marshall Sarnat, *Capital Investment and Financial Decisions, 4th ed.* (Englewood Cliffs, NJ: Prentice-Hall, 1990), pp. 286–312; or in John J. Clark, Thomas J. Hindelang, and Robert E. Pritchard, *Capital Budgeting: Planning and Control of Capital Expenditures, 3rd ed.* (Englewood Cliffs, NJ: Prentice-Hall, 1989), pp. 215–224 and 269–319.

Expressed in words, the CAPM asserts that the required rate of return for security $j$ is the expected **risk-free rate** plus a risk premium that is the product of beta and the overall "market risk premium." Analysts typically use historical data or surveys to proxy for unobservable expectations for both the risk-free rate ($k_{rf}$) and the required return on the market ($k_m$), but Jagannathan and Meier note that the market risk premium ($k_m - k_{rf}$) has been about 2–4 percent during the last two decades—significantly below the 1951–2000 average of 7.43%.[6] Illustrating this approach, if the most recent 3-month moving average of Treasury bill or bond rates is 4 percent, the stock market return has averaged 10.5 percent per year over the past 60 years, and a company's beta ($\beta_j$) is 1.5, then the required return would be:

$$k_j = k_{rf} + \beta_j(k_m - k_{rf})$$
$$k_j = 4\% + 1.5(10.5\% - 4\%)$$
$$k_j = 4\% + 9.75\%$$
$$k_j = 13.75\%$$

Beta estimates are available from some online services, major stock brokerage houses, the Standard & Poor's *Stock Record*, or the Value Line *Investment Survey*. The difficult task is risk-adjusting beta to arrive at a new risk-adjusted required return on common equity. One approach is to set up risk classes, in which risky projects are simply assigned a higher required rate of return (and discount rate) or the CAPM beta is arbitrarily adjusted upward by several percentage points. Lower-risk projects would be assigned a rate lower than the company's cost of capital.

Instead of making such an adjustment, some analysts argue for a "project-specific" application of the CAPM. Here, one determines an appropriate "asset" beta, in lieu of the standard beta calculated on the company's stock. The asset beta, ideally, would be the sensitivity of the project under review to stock market returns. How to determine such a beta is somewhat difficult for large capital projects and even more troublesome for short-term financial decisions.[7] Until finance theory more effectively addresses the relationship of liquidity to shareholder value, the CAPM will not enjoy widespread use for risk adjustment purposes in short-term decision-making.[8] Shin and Stulz[9] note that an increase in a firm's cash flow volatility has a detrimental effect on shareholder wealth for two reasons: (1) it decreases the present value of the firm's tax shields from debt and (2) it increases the present value of costs of financial distress. They find that a one standard deviation increase in a firm's equity volatility results in a reduction of shareholder wealth of approximately 16.3 percent. So total risk, not merely systematic risk, matters to stockholders—and therefore to managers making decisions in stockholders' best interests. Stulz[10] recommends the estimated NPV of a project that increases a firm's total risk be reduced by the cost of the project's impact on the firm's total risk. Shin and Stulz suggest considering newly developed techniques such as "cash flow at risk" to help in this adjustment. Stulz's comment about the uncritical use of such techniques as CAPM for equity risk estimation is instructive:[11]

> It is a peculiarity of finance that we spend so much time on teaching about a world without frictions when everything that makes finance interesting has to do with what happens in the presence of frictions. It is time to reverse the order of things and focus on the real world first.

To summarize this section, finance theorists generally recommend using a company's weighted-average cost of capital to discount capital investment cash flows. We concur that such an approach is advisable for evaluating most working capital policies having multiyear cash flows, in that these projects have a demonstrable value. We do not want to minimize the difficulty of arriving at an appropriate discount rate for such decisions, however. A risk-class approach, as was illustrated in Exhibit 3–9, might be optimal. The analyst should also take into account the effect of large-impact decisions on a firm's total risk.

---

[6] Ravi Jagannathan and Iwan Meier, "Do We Need CAPM for Capital Budgeting?" *Financial Management* (Winter 2002), pp. 5–27.

[7] With the increasing use of "project financing" of long-term capital projects, in which the company lines up financing for a specific project, this approach is quite attractive. The authors know of no instance in which this has been done to finance a change in inventories, receivables, or cash management systems, however.

[8] See the article by James Morris [J. R. Morris, "The Role of Cash Balances in Firm Valuation," *Journal of Financial and Quantitative Analysis* (December 1983), pp. 533–545] for an attempt at integrating short-term liquidity into the CAPM valuation theory. Morris noted that cash outflows resulting in cash position shortfalls force the firm to borrow, increasing the systematic risk of an end-of-period dividend payout.

[9] Hyan-Han Shin and René Stulz, "Shareholder Wealth and Firm Risk," Working Paper, The Ohio State University, December 2000.

[10] René M. Stulz, "What's Wrong with Modern Capital Budgeting?" Address delivered at the Eastern Finance Association meeting, April 1999.

[11] Ibid., p. 10.

# INTEGRATIVE CASE—PART 1

## *Bernard's New York Deli*

**Steven M. Dawson**
University of Hawaii

These deli-bucks are for cash flow what chicken soup is for a cold, thought Bernard Horowitz as he opened the package the printer had dropped off. Three months earlier he had moved his restaurant, Bernard's New York Deli, to a new location in the upscale Ward Centre shopping area. Faced with needing $30,000 to remodel and buy new equipment, a shortage of cash after the move, and the refusal of his bank to lend more, the deli-bucks were, he sensed, a brilliant inspiration. Customers could buy them for $8 each and after 90 days redeem them to pay for $10 worth of purchases. "Where else could people get 20 percent on their money in 90 days?" Bernard asked a reporter who had heard about them. If it all worked as planned, he would have the $30,000 cash, the remodeling would be financed, and he'd have a lot of customers coming back.

### Background

To build rapport and loyalty with customers, Bernard was advised by a friend in public relations to "tell them your story." He did so by preparing a brochure and placing it at the Deliís entrance. Customers who read it learned that Bernard Horowitz, namesake but not kin of the legendary pianist, had grown up in the Crown Heights neighborhood of Brooklyn. When he was a kid, he had often followed his nose into the kitchen where his mother chopped, mixed, kneaded, and roasted the family meals. Under her guidance Bernard had learned a thing or two which he'd later put to good use. Bernard's first job, at the age of 13, was as a part-time clerk behind the deli counter of the local food market. "An education like that you don't get in school," he observed later.

In 1974, Bernard went to Hawaii on vacation. Like so many others, before and since, he fell in love with the place. He returned home only to quit his job, pack his things, and move to Hawaii for good. It wasn't long before he was hired to manage Hawaii's first Burger King. Over the next 12 years, he had opened and managed several more and then became the Hawaii district manager. He had learned a lot about food, about managing people and restaurants, and about working for someone else.

In those days whenever he took a trip to the mainland, he had returned with a suitcase of deli food. "There was no other way to get stuff like that in Hawaii in those days," he recalled. Recognizing the need to "nosh," Hebrew for snack, he quit his job at Burger King, took out a second mortgage, and set to work. He used the New York City *Yellow Pages* to locate suppliers of everything from meats (Hebrew National) and gelfilte fish (Manischewitz) to soda (Dr. Brown's). In August 1986, "Bernard's New York Deli" opened in a tiny storefront near the University. There was room, barely, for table seating for 36 customers. He did take-out business, sold foods not available elsewhere, and acquired a following that craved New York deli specialties. Three years later he moved to suburban Kahala Mall. Room there was even smaller, just seating for 29, but the new location meant he could cater not only to the normal breakfast, lunch, and dinner clientele but also to the late-night movie crowd. "What more could a New Yorker want," Bernard recalled, "than the opportunity to work longer hours?"

### A New York Deli in Hawaii?

Hawaii, led by a diverse tourism industry, was a gourmet's delight. Residents and visitors pampered their palates with dishes whose origins evoked the far reaches of the Pacific Rim: kim chee from Korea and sateh from Thailand to local delicacies like poke and poi. In recent years, a distinctive new Euro-Asian cuisine developed by Sam Choy, Alan Wong, and Roy Yamaguchi had put Hawaii prominently on the culinary map.

---

This case was prepared by Steven M. Dawson as a basis for classroom discussion rather than to illustrate either effective or ineffective handling of an administrative situation. Source: Steven M. Dawson, Bernard's New York Deli, Case Research Journal.  **http://casenet.thomsonlearning.com/casenet_global_fr.html.**

For information regarding this and other CaseNet® cases, please visit CaseNet® on the World Wide Web at **http://casenet.thomsonlearning.com**.

You may wish to consult Chapter 12 if you are not familiar with the cash budgeting process.

What had been missing in Hawaii for the two centuries since the arrival of Captain James Cook in 1778, and more than a millennium since its first settlement by Polynesian explorers, was a real, Jewish-style deli. It took a malihini, Hawaiian for "newcomer," from Brooklyn to see the opening. When Bernard opened his New York Deli, he brought more than just a "bite of the Big Apple." Most foods in a Jewish-style deli came to New York with immigrants a century ago from the far side of the next ocean, the Atlantic. By bringing a taste of New York, Bernard's actually brought Romania (pastrami), Italy (salami), Germany (sauerkraut and sausage), Ukraine (borscht), and the Baltic (pickled herring and lox).

## On the Move Again

You can't keep a New Yorker away from the Big City for too long, and in January 1997, Bernard closed his suburban deli and moved to Ward Centre, an upscale shopping area located between Waikiki and the downtown business district. The new location had nearly four times the seating—55 seats inside and 66 outside on the lanai. Amused by having a lanai, an outdoor deck, for eating, Bernard wryly observed that not everything had to be like Brooklyn. Colorful pictures, Jewish sayings, street signs from New York, copies of the *New York Times* for sale, and an authentic deli food counter provided the ambience of a New York place-to-be for the action. Parking was ample, and business picked up quickly. Thanks to loyal customers and a feature story in the Sunday newspaper's restaurant section, opening day on January 3 was a big success, and revenues were all Bernard had hoped for. Sales for all of January were $110,000, followed by $100,000 and $105,000 in February and March. Bernard expected that with the existing table setup, sales would average about $95,000 a month.

Good as it was, it could be better. To take full advantage of the new location, the deli needed a little more equipment and a bit of remodeling to increase seating by another 50 customers. "This remodeling will really give us a boost," said Bernard, and he expected a 30 percent increase in sales. Based on the first three months at the new location, and his experience earlier, he expected monthly sales to be as follows:

| | FORECAST | | FORECAST |
|---|---|---|---|
| April | $ 90,000 | November | $100,000 |
| May | 95,000 | December | 140,000 |
| June | 115,000 | January | 140,000 |
| July | 125,000 | February | 125,000 |
| August | 135,000 | March | 130,000 |
| September | 120,000 | April | 115,000 |
| October | 110,000 | May | 120,000 |

In June, sales would be 15 percent higher than without the remodeling, and starting in July the increase would be 30 percent.

The bigger-size restaurant at Ward Centre meant the action behind the counter could be as frenetic as in a New York eatery. It also meant Bernard had a bigger task of managing the finances. Long gone were the days when he had just three other employees beside himself. At Ward Centre, Bernard started with a staff of 30 servers, preparers, and cleanup people, and it would grow to 42 with the expansion.

The two big expenses in the restaurant were food and labor. Bernard priced items so that the food expenses were about 30 percent of revenues. He trained his wait staff to be careful about needlessly wasting food. One time he pointed to four unused butter slices left on a table. "Each costs us five cents and if this happens ten times a day, seven days a week, by the end of a year we've wasted over $700." Provide good service, we need repeat customers, but watch the waste was the message.

Employee labor costs were also about 30 percent of revenues and were of two kinds: those he paid directly as wages to employees, and those he paid elsewhere. Hawaii was a tough place to do business when you had high labor costs, thanks to a state government and business environment that a *Forbes* magazine article had called the "New Socialist Republic of Hawaii." With the last paychecks, Bernard had given all his workers two reports: first, the dollars he had paid them as wages and, second, the dollars he had to pay others for them. For a $1,000 monthly wage payment to an employee, he calculated he paid an additional $277.50 as follows:

| | |
|---|---|
| $ 76.50 | Employer social security withholding |
| 6.50 | State temporary disability insurance |
| 61.00 | State worker's compensation |
| 115.00 | Employer share of mandatory state medical insurance |
| 14.50 | State unemployment insurance |
| 4.00 | Federal unemployment tax |

With three months at the new location and ten years of operating experience, Bernard had a comfortable feel for the relationship of revenues and expenses and did not expect a big change to occur after the remodeling was complete. "You need both more food and more employees when you have a bigger operation." Looking at the big picture and for the range of volume of business he expected to do, food and personnel costs would each be about 30 percent of revenues. Monthly rent at the Centre was $1,500 plus 6 percent of revenues. Other premise expenses, including security, insurance, and utilities, would run about $4,000 plus 6 percent of revenue. Kitchen, dining, and office expenses were 5.5 percent. Selling expenses, including advertising, the 4 percent state excise tax, 1.2 percent credit card charges, and printing, averaged 10.5 percent of revenues. Depreciation averaged $1,500 now and would rise to $2,000 a month in July when the expansion was done. It roughly equaled outlays for new or replacement equipment. Monthly payments on the bank loan were $3,210. All except the rent and food expenses were paid during the month incurred. Food generally had net 30-day terms with no discounts for early payment. Bernard didn't pay himself a regular salary. The Deli was organized as a Subchapter S corporation, and when surplus cash was available at the end of the month above the $5,000 he thought was a comfortable minimum, he took it out. "If my good wife didn't have a job, there'd be some really tough times."

The remodeling and expansion would cost about $30,000, and this was a problem. The move and startup had absorbed all the available funds. Cash was tight, just $3,000 at the start of April, and the outlook for getting more funds was discouraging. April and May usually were slow months for restaurants in Hawaii. Bernard believed it was a combination of the seasonal tourism slowdown and the preoccupation of customers with making tax payments. This meant internal funds would not supply the needed expansion capital and, to make it worse, near-term revenue projections wouldn't look good to the bank. Bernard already had a $160,000 bank loan at an interest rate of 10.75 percent. When he discussed increasing the loan, his loan officer replied, "Not at this time. You've maxed out until we see how the new location goes." Bernard wasn't surprised. "The banks in Hawaii, just like the state authorities, are not pro small business."

## Deli-Bucks

Bernard's solution to the shortage of funds came from the gift certificates he'd sold at his very first location to help him get started. Why not use them again, but modified so they could fund the remodeling? Ordinary gift certificates could be redeemed right away and, therefore, would not fill the bill because the money was needed first for remodeling. The solution: deli-bucks. He'd sell deli-bucks with a 90-day delay before they could be redeemed and a one-year life from date of purchase. Ninety days didn't seem unreasonably long and that would give him time to get the remodeling done. Any longer and it might seem too long to customers. The one-year limit would keep the redemption from dragging out forever.

Customers obviously wouldn't see much sense in paying now instead of paying later. They needed an incentive and a discount would do it. Playing with the numbers, Bernard decided on selling $10 deli-bucks for $8. Ten dollars was a reasonable size for an order, putting out $8 was not a big outlay, and a 20 percent discount seemed enough to offer something of value to customers. With the 30 percent food cost, he felt he had a lot of room to maneuver in giving a discount for early purchase. Whether the deli-bucks were more costly than other sources of funds, such as the bank loan if it had been available, was a question Bernard didn't take time to consider. After all, customers would redeem the certificates for food, not cash. A bank loan in contrast would require a cash repayment. How soon after 90 days the certificates would be redeemed was tough to forecast. Based on his earlier experience with gift certificates, Bernard figured it would take him about three months to sell all the delibucks, with 50 percent being sold in April, the first month; 30 percent the second; and 20 percent the third. At this rate, cash collections would approximately match remodeling payments. In accounting terms the deli-buck receipts would be placed in a "precollected revenue" account, with the impact on rent, the state excise tax, and other expenses, except for credit card charges, occurring at redemption. Redemptions would begin in month four and would be at the rate of 50 percent the first eligible month, 10 percent the next, and then 5 percent per month for the remaining seven months of the year. The remaining 5 percent would probably be lost, forgotten, or even kept as souvenirs. For deli-bucks sold in April, 50 percent would thus be redeemed in July, 10 percent in August, and so on. Bernard guessed that 75 percent of the deli-bucks would be redeemed by regular customers and 20 percent by customers who would not otherwise have come to the restaurant. Furthermore, 45 percent of the deli-bucks would be redeemed by regular customers who increased their purchases by an average of $2. The deli-buck redemption expectations are already included in Bernard's forecast of revenues. Not having to pay for the first $10 would make it tempting to take an extra bagel home, to get a more expensive sandwich, or to splurge on dessert. He'd seen this happen earlier with the gift certificates.

Designing the deli-bucks was easy and a good opportunity to mix marketing with finance. Made to look like oversized currency, the certificates on one side had Bernard's picture, a fancy border with $10 signs in the corners, and the notation that the purchase cost was $8 and the value was $10 in food purchases with no redemption for cash. The other side had the logo for

Bernard's New York Deli, a bright red apple with a bite taken out, more $10 signs, and the message "Pay now . . . eat later. These deli-bucks will be used to further our expansion and purchase additional equipment and more seating to make your experience more enjoyable. You will in turn receive a 20% discount on your future purchases." Each certificate had its own serial number so it could be tracked and to discourage counterfeiting.

After hearing about the deli-bucks, Joann Kapololu, manager of the Waikiki Beachcomber restaurant, praised Bernard's idea. "He obviously has a passion for what he does, and came up with something very creative. This brings dollars into his business, allows him to finance his dream, and the people who enjoy his food will be all over it."

The certificate package from the printer held enough of the deli-bucks to raise $30,000, and Bernard prepared an attractive poster to be placed near the restaurant entrance telling customers about them. The wait staff was briefed to respond favorably when customers asked about the certificates. All was ready.

PART

2

# Management of Working Capital

The focus of Part 2 is on the management of the four major working capital accounts including inventory, receivables, payables and accruals. Proper management of these working capital accounts provides a profitable firm with a continual flow of cash and the necessary liquidity to achieve management's operating plan. Part 2 begins with Chapter 4, Inventory Management; the management of credit and receivables is discussed in Chapters 5 and 6. Finally, Chapter 7 studies the management of payables and accruals. As discussed in Part 1, the management of working capital involves the management of the transformation process of resources from the cash invested in inventory once payables and operating accruals are paid, through the operations or production process, followed by the selling process, and finally, the credit collections process. The management of this transformation process has a profound impact on the liquidity position of the firm.

CHAPTER 4

# Inventory Management

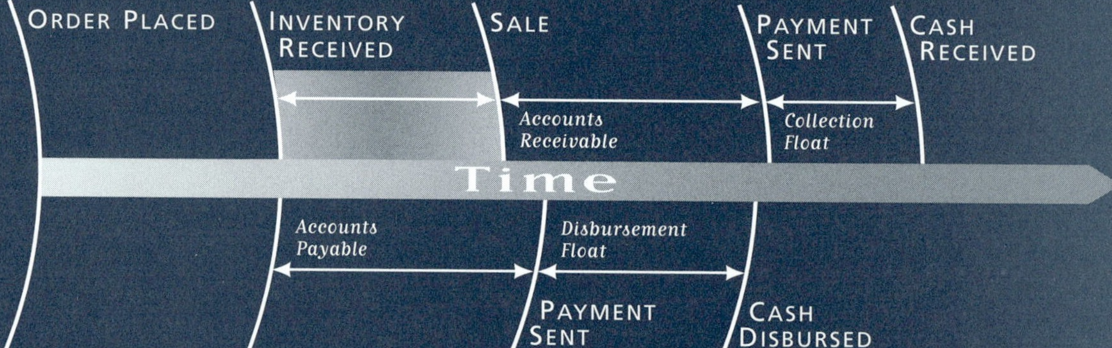

## OBJECTIVES

*After studying this chapter, you should be able to:*

- better understand the role that holding and ordering costs play in the determination of the appropriate inventory order quantity.
- adjust the traditional EOQ model for quantity discounts.
- appreciate how just-in-time concepts can be incorporated into the inventory order decision process.
- assess the impact that different order quantities have on the timing and amount of cash flows related to the inventory purchase decision.
- learn how to assess the actual behavior of inventory flows through the use of balance fraction measures rather than inventory turnover ratios.

The management of inventory plays an important role in the management of the firm's cash flow timeline. Keeping smaller inventory balances means less idle investment, but it requires many more orders of inventory, which results in more disbursements of cash but each of a relatively small amount. However, keeping minimal inventory balances increases the likelihood of inventory shortages. As an alternative, keeping larger inventory balances means more idle investment in inventory. Fewer orders, each of a large quantity, are placed, resulting in larger cash balances being disbursed but over longer intervals of time. This inventory strategy will result in a lower probability of inventory shortages.

### FINANCIAL DILEMMA

Can Placing Fewer Orders Save Money?

The treasurer of Lube-Rite, Inc., a nationwide chain of lube centers, was just informed by the purchasing manager that one of the firm's suppliers of petroleum products has just initiated a quantity discount program. Although the purchasing manager was excited about the prospects, the treasurer realized that the order quantity required to receive the discount would greatly increase the firm's investment in inventory. Larger orders would reduce ordering costs, but the larger quantities would increase the holding costs and opportunity costs of the inventory investment. She wondered if the cost trade-off was worth the quantity discount received.

Inventory is a difficult item to manage because it crosses so many lines of responsibility. The purchasing manager is responsible for supplies of raw material and would like to avoid shortages and to purchase in bulk to take advantage of quantity discounts. The production manager is responsible for uninterrupted production and wishes to keep enough raw materials and work-in-process inventory on hand to avoid disrupting the production process. The marketing manager is responsible for selling the product and therefore wishes to minimize the chances of running out of inventory. The financial manager is concerned about achieving an appropriate rate of return on invested capital. Funds invested in inventory are idle and do not earn a return. In fact, because of the interrelatedness of these diverse areas, **supply chain management** has developed as a field in and of itself. Sometimes referred to as distribution or logistics, supply chain management, the process by which companies move materials and parts from suppliers through the production process and on to consumers, is now placed near the top of corporate strategic agendas. It is not uncommon to find companies cutting delivery time and reducing distribution costs, while at the same time increasing sales as they focus on the overall supply chain as a system rather than trying to manage separately the individual pieces of the logistics puzzle. A striking example of the impact of this kind of focus is the transformation that Dell Computer Corporation underwent during the 1990s. As a result of focusing on its supply chain, Dell was able to hold its inventory level almost constant while increasing sales from $18

## FOCUS ON PRACTICE

### *A Close Shave*

Perhaps no stronger link can be made between working capital management and the value of a firm than that expressed recently by the treasury team at Gillette Company. The team told Wall Street analysts that it would lift its depressed stock price through a restructuring and reorganization plan that includes a reduction of working capital by $1 billion over an 18-month time period. Reduction in inventory is a major component of this restructuring plan because it will cut down on storage and financing costs as well as reduce the length of the production cycle. Analysts had been concerned about the rise in inventories and receivables at Gillette.

*Source:* "Gillette Shaves Inventory Costs," *Treasury and Risk Management* (April 2000), Vol. 10, Issue 3, p. 14.

billion in 1999 to over $35 billion in 2003. During this time frame the number of days inventory was held fell from 7 days to only 3.87 days.

This chapter does not attempt to teach you new inventory management techniques. Rather, the purpose of this chapter is to discuss the impact of inventory management on the cash cycle of the corporation. Presented are some basic techniques that can be used by the financial manager to effectively manage this important component of the cash cycle. Poor inventory management results in a less liquid corporation—one that must continually borrow in order to have enough operating cash on hand. Properly managed, the turnover of inventory releases cash in a timely manner, and this cash flow is then used to make payments on payables and other financial obligations as they come due, which ultimately enhances the value of the firm.

## THE CONCEPT OF INVENTORY

A major problem with managing inventory is that the demand for a corporation's product is to a degree uncertain. The supply of the raw materials used in its production process is also somewhat uncertain. In addition, the corporation's own production schedules contain some degree of uncertainty due to possible equipment breakdowns and labor difficulties.

Because of these possibilities, inventory acts as a shock absorber between product demand and product supply. If product demand is greater than expected, inventory can be depleted without losing sales until production can be stepped up enough to match the unexpected demand.

Three basic types of inventory must be managed: **raw materials inventory**, **work-in-process inventory**, and **finished goods inventory**. Raw materials inventory represents the initial input into the production process. For example, scrap metal or iron ore is used to make the metal necessary in the production of automobile frames and bodies, and chemicals represent the raw material necessary for the production of fertilizer. If a corporation such as Monsanto were to run out of the basic chemicals used in the production of fertilizer, that entire production process would have to be shut down.

Work-in-process inventory represents items that are beyond the raw materials stage but not yet at the completed product stage. For example, General Motors would consider an engine to be a part of its work-in-process inventory as it waits to be installed onto the frame of an automobile. The need for work-in-process inventory is obvious when the complexities of the typical production line are considered. For instance, assume that the production process of an automobile firm consists of two production lines—one to build the frame and body and the other to build the engine. The production line building the engine feeds into the production line building the car body. If work-in-process inventory (which consists of car engines) was not created, the two production lines would have to be perfectly synchronized at all times. Otherwise, the car body production line would be disrupted whenever the engine production line experienced any problems. With a stock of engines to draw upon, the car body production line can continue to operate drawing down the work-in-process inventory of engines until the problems with the engine production line can be resolved.

To carry this example one step further, a finished goods inventory consists of completed automobiles. An inventory of finished goods must be maintained because of the uncertainty with consumer demand for the product and because of management's desire not to run out of inventory for sale.

We should also mention a fourth type of inventory at this point: cash. The stock of cash held by a firm is a special type of inventory that uncouples the payment of bills from the collection of accounts receivable. This chapter focuses on the management of physical inventory, while Chapter 15 discusses the management of the stock, or inventory, of cash.

Three basic motives exist for holding inventory. First, firms hold inventory in relation to the level of operating activity they expect in the near future. This is referred to as the **transaction motive**. For example, a grocery store receives periodic shipments of fresh produce in anticipation of customer demand over the next several days. Customers are not eager to take "rain checks" for such items as produce and meat; they will simply go to another store. A second motive is a **precautionary motive**. Our grocery store manager may order an additional quantity of goods as a cushion for an unexpected increase in demand. Of course, a precautionary balance of canned goods would be more easily managed than a precautionary balance of fresh fruit. The third motive for holding inventory is the **speculative motive**. Suppose the citrus orchards in Florida were devastated by a hard freeze. The grocery store manager might anticipate a future shortage of oranges and purchase a large quantity of frozen orange juice, hoping to have a competitive advantage in the future if a shortage of oranges does occur.

## BASICS OF MANAGING THE AVERAGE INVENTORY BALANCE[1]

Stocking inventory requires a financial investment. From the viewpoint of a financial manager, the investment in inventory should be related to the demand for inventory, the cost of holding inventory, and the cost of ordering the inventory units. For example, the greater the consumer demand for the corporation's product, the greater is the corporation's demand for raw materials, work-in-process, and finished goods inventory. If the cost of holding inventory increases, the financial manager will tend to stock less inventory. If the cost of ordering inventory items increases, the financial manager will tend to order more items per order and to place fewer orders. Given a demand for the inventory items, there is a trade-off between the cost of stocking inventory and the cost of holding inventory.

[1] This section reviews the basic EOQ inventory management model. Those students familiar with this model may wish to skip or skim this section. Those less familiar with the EOQ model will find this section provides a step-by-step development of the EOQ model.

## The Cost of Managing Inventory

Demand for inventory, **holding costs**, and **ordering costs** can be combined into an equation to compute the total cost of managing inventory. As Equations 4.1 and 4.2 show, the total cost of managing inventory has two components: the cost of ordering inventory and the cost of holding inventory.

$$\text{Total cost} = \text{Total cost of ordering inventory} + \text{Total cost of holding inventory} \tag{4.1}$$

$$\text{Total cost} = \left(\text{Order cost per order} \times \text{Number of orders}\right) + \left(\text{Holding cost per inventory item} \times \text{Average inventory balance}\right) \tag{4.2}$$

The first part of Equation 4.2 calculates the total cost of ordering inventory by multiplying the ordering cost per order by the number of orders placed. The number of orders placed is equal to the total number of inventory items demanded over the course of the planning period, such as a year, divided by the number of inventory units ordered with each order.

The second part of Equation 4.2 calculates the holding cost of the average inventory balance. This component of the total cost equation can be developed further if it is assumed that the corporation receives its ordered inventory items on the day its current inventory stock is exhausted and that the inventory items are used up at a constant rate. These two simplifications make the average inventory balance equal to the amount of inventory ordered and received plus the amount of ending inventory, which is zero, divided by two.

To reduce the verbiage in the total cost equation, we employ the following symbols and rewrite the total cost equation as shown in Equation 4.3.

| | |
|---|---|
| Total inventory units demanded | $T$ |
| Order quantity | $Q$ |
| Fixed order cost per order | $F$ |
| Holding cost per inventory unit[2] | $H$ |

$$\text{Total cost} = (F \times T/Q) + (H \times Q/2) \tag{4.3}$$

Careful inspection of Equation 4.3 shows the trade-off between ordering costs and holding costs that presents an interesting challenge for the financial manager. Notice how a larger quantity ordered, $Q$, reduces the ordering costs ($Q$ is in the denominator) by reducing the number of orders placed, while a larger quantity ordered results in a larger holding cost ($Q$ is in the numerator) by increasing the size of the average inventory balance.

These relationships are illustrated by a graph in Exhibit 4–1. The number of inventory units ordered per order is on the horizontal axis and dollar cost is on the vertical axis. As more units are ordered, the total ordering costs fall because fewer orders are placed, while holding costs increase because the average inventory balance gets larger. As the exhibit shows, the total cost curve, which is the sum of ordering costs and holding costs, first falls as units ordered increase and then it begins to increase. The optimal number of units to order is that order quantity that minimizes total costs.

## The Optimal Quantity to Order

The goal of the financial manager is to choose that order quantity level that will result in an optimal trade-off between ordering costs and holding costs such that the total cost of

---

[2] Holding cost per unit may include not only costs such as storage and insurance but also opportunity costs, such as lost interest earnings on funds invested in inventory.

Exhibit 4–1

*The Trade-Off between Ordering Costs and Holding Costs*

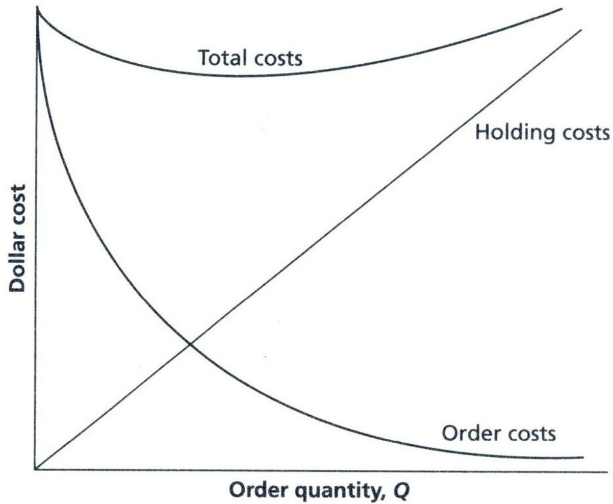


managing inventory is minimized. The order quantity that minimizes the total cost of managing inventory is generally referred to as the **economic order quantity (EOQ)**.

This EOQ level can be derived by differentiating the total cost Equation 4.3 with respect to $Q$ and setting the first derivative equal to zero in order to locate the minimum point on the total cost curve. The optimum inventory order quantity equation derived by doing this is shown in Equation 4.4.

$$\text{EOQ} = \sqrt{\frac{2 \times T \times F}{H}} \tag{4.4}$$

The economic order quantity is that quantity of inventory items that should be ordered each time an order is placed; it is the order quantity that minimizes the total cost of managing the corporation's inventory. The basic EOQ model, as represented by Equation 4.4, is based on some rather restrictive assumptions. First, this basic model requires a near perfect forecast of inventory units demanded, $T$, and a constant rate of inventory usage. In addition, there must be a constant or fixed order cost, $F$, and a constant cost of holding each item of inventory. These assumptions are too restrictive for the model to be used in general. In a later section we will develop a way for the model to work in a more realistic setting. But before we develop extensions of the basic model, we will demonstrate how the basic model works.

## An Example Using EOQ

Cory Manufacturing forecasts that its production process will require 500,000 tons of scrap metal over its planning period. Demand for Cory's products is not affected by seasonal variations and remains quite stable. Ordering costs amount to an average of $20 per order which includes clerical and computer time, phones, and mail. Holding cost per ton of scrap metal is estimated at $1.25. The costs are minimal given that the metal can be stored outside and management has never seen the need for insurance.

Given this information, we can calculate the EOQ for Cory Manufacturing.

$$\text{EOQ} = \sqrt{\frac{2 \times 500{,}000 \times \$20}{\$1.25}}$$

$$\text{EOQ} = 4{,}000 \text{ tons}$$

The optimal order size, that which minimizes total inventory costs, is 4,000 tons per order. Therefore, the financial manager should recommend that 4,000 tons of scrap be ordered with each order. The number of orders placed can be determined by dividing the total inventory units required, 500,000, by the number of tons ordered with each order, 4,000.

$$\text{Number of orders} = \frac{\text{Total inventory requirements}}{\text{Order size}} = \frac{500{,}000}{4{,}000} \quad (4.5)$$

$$\text{Number of orders} = 125$$

The number of orders that Cory must place over the production period is 125 orders. The average inventory balance can also be calculated. As discussed earlier, it is equal to the order quantity divided by 2, as shown below.

$$\text{Average inventory balance} = \frac{\text{EOQ}}{2} \quad (4.6)$$

$$\text{Average inventory balance} = 2{,}000 \text{ tons}$$

The inventory management problem is shown graphically in Exhibit 4–2. Ordered inventory arrives on the day the inventory balance reaches zero. Therefore, on that day, the inventory balance is equal to the amount ordered, which is the economic order quantity. On the next day, the inventory balance begins to drop at a constant rate due to the assumption of the constant rate of usage. This **usage rate** can be calculated by dividing the total inventory units required, *T*, by the number of days in the planning or production period. For this example, let's assume a production run that encompasses 375 working days. Equation 4.7 shows how to calculate the daily usage rate.

$$\text{Usage rate} = \frac{\text{Units of inventory required}}{\text{Number of days in the planning period}} \quad (4.7)$$

$$\text{Usage rate} = \frac{500{,}000}{375}$$

$$\text{Usage rate} = 1{,}333 \text{ tons per day}$$

**Exhibit 4–2**

*Inventory Balance and the Reorder Point*

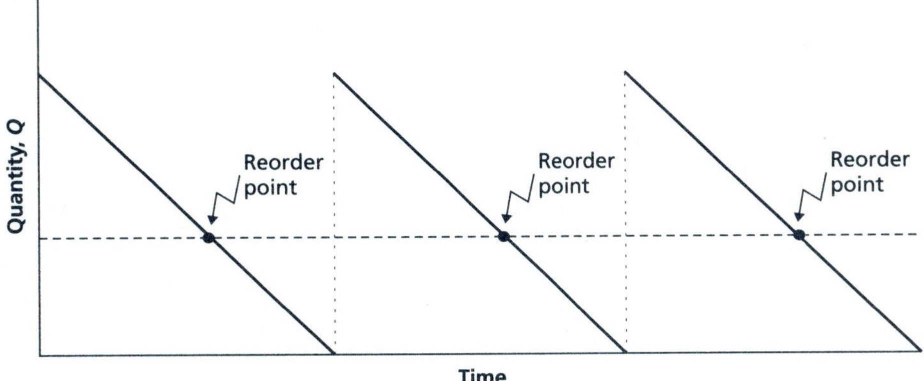

The daily usage rate is used to calculate the point at which Cory's management should place an order. The inventory level at which an order should be placed is called the **reorder point**. To calculate this inventory level, two items must be known. The first item is the daily usage rate that was calculated above. The second item is the number of days it takes to receive the shipment of inventory once the order is placed. In the past, Cory has experienced an average of two days' delivery time. The calculation for the reorder point based on the usage rate and delivery time is shown in Equation 4.8.

$$\text{Reorder point} = \text{Daily Usage Rate} \times \text{Delivery Time} \tag{4.8}$$

$$\text{Reorder point} = 1{,}333 \times 2$$

$$\text{Reorder point} = 2{,}666 \text{ tons}$$

When the inventory balance reaches 2,666 tons, management should place an order for 4,000 tons of scrap metal, which is the economic order quantity. In two days, the inventory will be depleted (two days at a daily usage rate of 1,333 tons per day) and Cory will receive its shipment of scrap metal before it begins operation on the next day.

What would happen to Cory's production process if the shipment was delayed or if the daily usage rate of inventory increased due to an unexpected demand for its products? The next section will develop some extensions of the basic EOQ model.

## Extensions of the Basic EOQ Model

At this point, there are two extensions of the basic EOQ model that need examined: the concept of safety stock and the impact of quantity discounts.

*SAFETY STOCK CONSIDERATIONS* Suppose that sales are not stable or that the production cycle or delivery time is uncertain. Under such conditions, extra inventory is warranted to guard against an inventory shortage. This extra inventory balance acts as insurance against running out of inventory and is often referred to as a **safety stock.**

Exhibit 4–3 demonstrates the importance of safety stock.

**Exhibit 4–3**

*Showing How Safety Stock Can Be Incorporated into the EOQ Model*

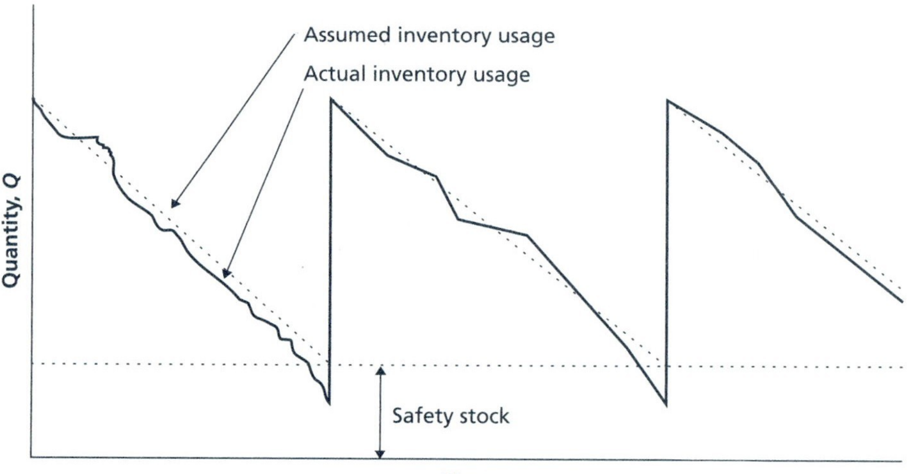

## FOCUS ON PRACTICE

### *Buffer Stocks*

After the initial shock of the tragic events of 9/11 were digested, corporate managers had to turn back to try to keep their supply chains from collapsing. Given the shock to our economic system and the increased border security, serious issues concerning parts delivery and availability had to be addressed. U.S. automakers depend on routine deliveries by truck from Canada and Mexico, yet the trucks were being stuck at border crossings. As a result, assembly line disruptions occurred at U.S. auto manufacturing sites. One consultant for the auto industry said, "We really have regressed to the stage where we're asking plants to carry more buffer inventory."

*Source:* "Chrysler Averts a Parts Crisis," *The Wall Street Journal* (September 24, 2001), p. B1.

The dashed line represents a constant rate of inventory usage, and the solid line represents actual usage. Note how a portion of the safety stock was used prior to receiving shipment of the inventory ordered.

A formal model for determining the optimal safety stock will not be developed here, but there are two basic factors that affect the amount of safety stock needed. First, as mentioned above, variability of demand, the production process, and delivery time will tend to increase the optimal size of the safety stock. The greater the uncertainty, the greater the need for the type of insurance provided by safety stocks. Second, high inventory carrying costs will tend to reduce the size of the safety stock, holding stock-out costs constant. However, stock-out costs are a function of the total inventory level held. Thus, the financial manager must assess the variability of the demand and usage of inventory and analyze the trade-off between the costs of running out of inventory and the costs of holding a safety stock of inventory.

The presence of safety stock does not affect the calculation of EOQ, which is calculated ignoring the safety stock level. But it does affect the calculation of the average inventory balance and the reorder point. The average inventory balance becomes

$$\text{EOQ}/2 + \text{Safety stock}$$

and the reorder point becomes

$$\text{Daily usage rate} \times \text{Delivery time} + \text{Safety stock}$$

We add the desired safety stock to the previously determined average inventory balance to determine average inventory. Then, we add the desired safety stock to the original reorder point to determine the new reorder point.

The EOQ model is a useful financial management tool because it indicates the proper level of inventory to order based on the trade-off of the ordering costs and holding costs of inventory. Proper inventory control is necessary when the actual usage rate differs from that forecasted, so the order quantity can be adjusted to avoid inventory excesses or shortages.

*Adjusting for Quantity Discounts* Often a supplier will offer a discount for volume purchasers referred to as a **quantity discount**. The purchaser must decide whether the discount for purchasing a larger quantity justifies incurring the additional holding costs for storing the surplus inventory.

To account for the quantity discount opportunity, a third variable must be added to the total cost equation first developed as Equation 4.3. The additional variable is the dollar cost of inventory as shown below in Equation 4.9. C′ is the dollar cost of inventory for a given quantity and T is the total volume of inventory required over the planning period. Note that C′ is not a constant, rather it is a function of Q, the volume of inventory purchased with each order.

$$\text{Total cost} = (F \times T/Q) + (H \times Q/2) + (C' \times T) \tag{4.9}$$

To demonstrate the application of Equation 4.9, we will continue with the example we have been working with and will assume that our supplier offers the following quantity discounts.

| Quantity (Q) | Cost per Unit (C′) |
|---|---|
| 0–999 units | $0.50 |
| 1,000–2,999 units | 0.48 |
| 3,000–4,999 units | 0.45 |
| 5,000+ units | 0.40 |

Exhibit 4–4 presents a table showing the total inventory cost and the component costs for a range of order quantities from 500 units to 6,000 units. Notice that our original solution for the EOQ of 4,000 units is far from the optimal when quantity discounts are offered. Total cost is $246,250, with holding costs of $1,250 and ordering costs of $5,000. The optimal order quantity considering quantity discounts is 5,000 units with a total cost of $205,125. Holding costs are $3,125 and ordering costs of $2,000.

## INVENTORY MANAGEMENT AND THE CASH FLOW TIMELINE

From the financial manager's point of view, inventory represents an idle investment of corporate resources. If the inventory is purchased with cash, then there is an opportunity

### Exhibit 4–4

*Total and Component Inventory Costs Considering Quantity Discounts**

| Q | Total Costs | Order Costs | Holding Costs | Purchase Cost |
|---|---|---|---|---|
| 500 | $270,313 | $20,000 | $ 313 | $250,000 |
| 1,000 | 250,625 | 10,000 | 625 | 240,000 |
| 1,500 | 247,604 | 6,667 | 938 | 240,000 |
| 2,000 | 246,250 | 5,000 | 1,250 | 240,000 |
| 2,500 | 245,563 | 4,000 | 1,563 | 240,000 |
| 3,000 | 230,208 | 3,333 | 1,875 | 225,000 |
| 3,500 | 230,045 | 2,857 | 2,188 | 225,000 |
| 4,000 | 230,000 | 2,500 | 2,500 | 225,000 |
| 4,500 | 230,035 | 2,222 | 2,813 | 225,000 |
| 5,000 | 205,125 | 2,000 | 3,125 | 200,000 |
| 5,500 | 205,256 | 1,818 | 3,438 | 200,000 |
| 6,000 | 205,417 | 1,667 | 3,750 | 200,000 |

*Numbers are rounded to the nearest dollar.

Exhibit 4–5

*A Cash Timeline for Inventory*

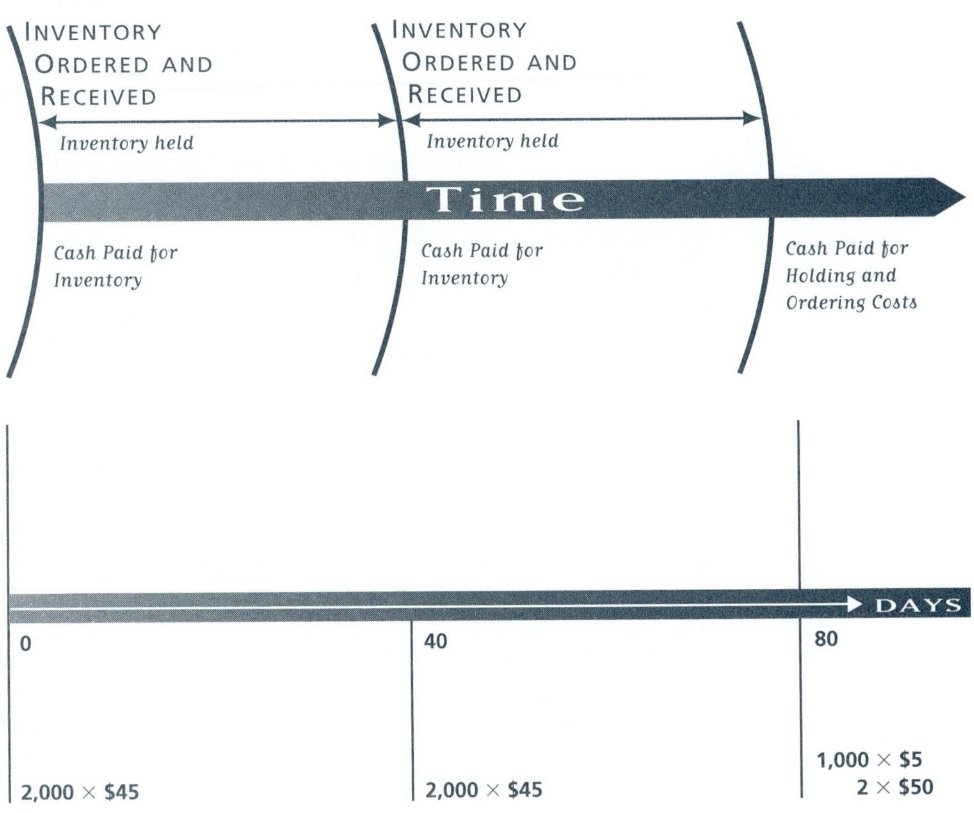


cost of the funds expended. If inventory is purchased on credit, then the firm incurs additional debt, interest expense, and its unused borrowing capacity is diminished.

Suppose a firm requires a total of 4,000 units of inventory for a production run. Further assume that two orders for inventory are placed for 2,000 units each. Inventory would be paid with cash, and ordering and holding costs would be paid at the end of the production run. A cash flow timeline, shown in Exhibit 4–5, depicts these transactions.

The financial manager of the firm wants to make certain that this inventory order quantity minimizes the present value cost of managing the inventory process while still meeting the needs of the production process. To calculate the present value of this inventory management policy, assume the following data:

| | |
|---|---|
| Cost of capital, $k$: | 10% |
| Inventory cost, $C$: | \$45 per unit |
| Order costs, $F$: | \$50 per order |
| Holding costs, $H$: | \$5 per average inventory unit |

Further, assume that the inventory is consumed at a steady rate and the production run period is 80 days. Thus, the average daily usage rate of the inventory is 50 units per day (4,000/80). Since two orders will be placed, each for 2,000 units, and assuming that the orders are placed so that each inventory shipment arrives at the same time that the current inventory balance is used up, there are 40 days separating inventory arrivals. Therefore, the average inventory balance is 1,000 units.

Calculating the present value cost of the current inventory policy is fairly straightforward. We will use simple interest to account for the time value of money.

$$\text{PV Day 0 Cost} = 2{,}000 \times \$45 \times \frac{1}{1 + (0 \times 0.10/365)}$$
$$= \$90{,}000$$

$$\text{PV Day 40 Cost} = 2{,}000 \times \$45 \times \frac{1}{1 + (40 \times 0.10/365)}$$
$$= \$89{,}024.39$$

$$\text{PV Day 80 Cost} = \left(1{,}000 \times \$5 \times \frac{1}{1 + (80 \times 0.10/365)}\right)$$
$$+ \left(2 \times \$50 \times \frac{1}{1 + (80 \times 0.10/365)}\right)$$
$$= \$4{,}990.62$$

$$\text{Total PV Cost} = \text{PV Day 0 Cost} + \text{PV Day 40 Cost} + \text{PV Day 80 Cost}$$
$$= \$90{,}000 + \$89{,}024.39 + \$4{,}990.62$$
$$\text{Total PV Cost} = \$184{,}015.01$$

What if smaller, but more frequent, orders were placed, resulting in more payments but each of a smaller size? The financial manager would pay less money up front for inventory and thus would incur a smaller opportunity cost for those funds. In addition, the inventory carrying costs would decline because less inventory is being held. However, order costs would increase due to the increased number of orders placed. With the changing size and timing of the various cash flows, the only way to assess if a change in inventory policy will enhance shareholder wealth is to calculate the present value of the cash flows. The policy with the minimum present value cost should be the one that results in the greatest enhancement to shareholder wealth.

We can develop a general formulation to assess the cost of inventory management using a present value timeline approach as shown in Equation 4.10.

$$\text{Total Cost} = [(F \times T/Q) + (H \times Q/2)] \div [1 + (i \times D)] + \sum_{t=0}^{(T/Q)-1} (Q \times C)/\{1 + [i \times (t \times Q \times D/T)]\} \quad (4.10)$$

Where:

$T$ = Number of inventory units required

$D$ = Number of days in the production period

$Q$ = Inventory order quantity

$C$ = Cost of each inventory unit

$F$ = Fixed order cost per order

$H$ = Holding cost per unit of inventory

$i$ = Daily opportunity cost

To understand Equation 4.10, note that the first term in the equation is the present value of the ordering costs, $F \times T/Q$, and the holding costs, $H \times Q/2$, assumed to be paid at the end of the production period. The simple interest present value factor is $1/[1 + (i \times D)]$. The second term is a summation of the present value of the cash flows to pay for each inventory lot purchase. The cost of each inventory lot purchase is $Q \times C$. The present value factor accounts for the timing of each purchase. The first purchase is at the beginning of the production period and $t = 0$. Thus, the simple interest factor is $1/(1 + 0)$, or 1. The second purchase, $t = 1$, is on day $[t \times (Q \times D/T)]$. To understand this, first note that the daily usage rate of inventory is T/D. When Q is ordered, it takes Q/daily usage rate, or $Q \div T/D$ days to use it up. This can be rewritten as $[Q \times D/T]$. Inventory purchases are made on day $[t \times (Q \times D/T)]$ for $t = 0,1,2,3,...(T/Q) - 1$.

## FINANCIAL DILEMMA REVISITED

An example will illustrate this equation. Returning to LUBE-RITE's dilemma at the beginning of the chapter, we can now help the treasurer assess the value of the quantity discount offered through the use of the cash flow timeline formulation of the inventory decision. Assume the following values for the inventory decision variables prior to the discount offer.

$$T = 1{,}000$$
$$D = 100$$
$$Q = 200$$
$$C = \$10$$
$$F = \$5$$
$$H = \$2.50$$
$$i = 0.15/365 = 0.00041$$

Using these numbers yields the following values:

Total inventory holding costs = \$250, $H \times Q/2$
Total ordering costs = \$25, $F \times T/Q$
Cost of each purchase lot = \$2,000, $C \times Q$

| $t$ | Inventory purchase day $t \times Q \times D/T$ | Present value factor $1/[1 + i\,(t \times Q \times D/T)]$ | Cash flow | Present value holding and ordering costs | Present value of purchase cost |
|---|---|---|---|---|---|
| 0 | 0 | 1.0000 | \$2,000 | | \$2,000 |
| 1 | 20 | 0.9918 | 2,000 | | 1,984 |
| 2 | 40 | 0.9838 | 2,000 | | 1,968 |
| 3 | 60 | 0.9759 | 2,000 | | 1,952 |
| 4 | 80 | 0.9682 | 2,000 | | 1,936 |
| | 100 | 0.9606 | 275 | \$264 | |
| Total | | | | \$264 | \$9,840 |

Total Present Value Cost = \$264 + \$9,840
= \$10,104

Now assume that the supplier is willing to discount the price per unit to \$9.50 for purchase quantities of 500 units.

Total inventory holding costs = \$625, $H \times Q/2$
Total ordering costs = \$10, $F \times T/Q$
Cost of each purchase lot = \$4,750, $C \times Q$

| $t$ | Inventory purchase day $t \times Q \times D/T$ | Present value factor $1/[1 + i(t \times Q \times D/T)]$ | Cash flow | Present value holding and order costs | Present value of purchase costs |
|---|---|---|---|---|---|
| 0 | 0 | 1.0000 | $4,750 | | $4,750 |
| 1 | 50 | 0.9799 | 4,750 | | 4,655 |
| | 100 | 0.9606 | 635 | $610 | |
| Total | | | | $610 | $9,405 |

$$\text{Total present value cost} = \$610 + \$9{,}405$$
$$= \$10{,}015$$

The present value cost of the inventory can be reduced from $10,104 to $10,015 by taking advantage of the quantity discount. In this case, the reduced cost of the inventory more than offsets the additional holding costs and the larger initial payment for the inventory lot ordered.

This approach can be used to solve for the least cost order quantity, $Q$, in a similar fashion to the approach used by the quantity discount model. A simple solution is not possible since the present value factors for inventory costs, $Q \times C$, are functions of the quantity ordered, $Q$, which determines the timing of the purchases.

The traditional EOQ model is insensitive to the impact on present value cost of the changes in the timing of cash flows resulting from different order quantities and different payment terms. In other words, if one supplier offered a combination of quantity discounts and payment terms different from another supplier, the basic EOQ model would not be able to adequately assess the differences between the present value costs of the two options. Only the present value timeline approach can accurately gauge the true cost differences between alternative inventory ordering strategies.

## MONITORING THE INVENTORY BALANCE

Once an inventory policy has been established, the financial manager must constantly monitor the inventory balance to ensure that the firm is maintaining a proper investment in inventory. The financial manager should be concerned if the resulting investment in inventory is either greater than or less than that expected to result from the accepted policy. This section will present a variety of approaches that can be helpful in monitoring the firm's investment in inventory.

### Inventory Control Systems

One of the most difficult areas of inventory management is inventory control. Consider a large department store chain and the thousands of inventory items that must be managed. It is now common for point-of-sale terminals linked to central computers to be used as a means of controlling inventory. For example, today it is common for department stores such as J.C.Penney to use electronic cash registers that are linked to a corporate central computer as a means of controlling its inventory. At the checkout counter, salesclerks scan relevant product data such as product code, number of items purchased, and the price, and the computer system keeps track of the inventory balance. Such a system lets management know exactly what is or is not selling and where. Inventory pileups or shortages can then be quickly averted.

### Inventory Turnover Approach

The traditional approach to measuring a firm's investment in inventory is based on the firm's **inventory turnover ratio**. The inventory turnover ratio is found by dividing cost of

## FOCUS ON PRACTICE

### *J.C.Penny Cashes In On Supply Chain Management*

On a Saturday afternoon in August, Carolyn Thurmond walked into a J.C.Penney store in Atlanta's Northlake mall and bought a white Stafford wrinkle-free dress shirt for her husband, size 17 neck, 34/35 sleeve. On Monday morning, a computer technician in Hong Kong downloaded a record of the sale. By Wednesday afternoon, a factory worker in Taiwan had packed an identical replacement shirt into a bundle to be shipped back to the Atlanta store. This speedy process, part of a streamlined supply chain and production system for dress shirts that was years in the making, has put J.C.Penney at the forefront of the continuing revolution in U.S. retailing. In an industry where the goal is speedy turnaround of merchandise, J.C.Penney stores now hold almost no extra inventory of house-brand dress shirts. Less than a decade ago, J.C.Penney would have had thousands of them warehoused across the United States, tying up capital and slowly going out of style. The new process is one from which J.C.Penney is conspicuously absent. The entire program is designed and operated by TAL Apparel Ltd., a closely held Hong Kong shirt maker. TAL collects point-of-sale data from J.C.Penney's shirts directly from its stores in North America, and then runs the number through a computer model it designed. The Hong Kong company then decides how many shirts to make and in what styles, colors, and sizes. The manufacturer sends the shirts directly to each J.C.Penney store, bypassing the retailers' warehouses—and corporate decision makers.

*Source:* "Invisible Supplier Has Penney's Shirts All Buttoned Up," *The Wall Street Journal* (September 11, 2003), p. A1.

goods sold (COGS) (although sometimes sales is used) over a given time period, such as a year, by the inventory balance held during that same time period. For example, suppose the annual cost of goods sold for Ureadem, Inc., a book publisher, was $100,000 and the year-end inventory balance was $18,000. The inventory turnover ratio is 5.55 ($100,000/$18,000).

A related inventory activity measure is **days inventory held**. This can be found by first calculating average daily cost of goods sold. Since we used annual cost of goods sold above, average daily cost of goods sold is found by dividing annual cost of goods sold by 365. Average daily cost of goods sold is $273.97 ($100,000/365). The number of days of inventory held is then found by dividing the inventory balance, $18,000, by average daily cost of goods sold, $273.97. The days inventory held is equal to 65.70 days ($18,000/$273.97). The greater this number, the greater the investment in inventory and the slower the inventory turnover.

Rather than monitoring the inventory balance using annual data, management must monitor the resources tied up in inventory over a shorter time frame such as monthly, weekly, or daily. If inventory movement is slowing, the trend must be detected early enough to take corrective action. Suppose the financial manager collected the following data for the past six months. The first two line items, cost of goods sold and ending inventory, are taken directly from the firm's monthly financial statements. The next two line items are based on calculations using the first two line items. Average daily COGS is calculated using the total dollar amount of cost of goods sold over an arbitrarily chosen time period, such as the quarter just completed divided by the number of days in that quarter. In the following table, the chosen time period is the most recent quarter and the number of days in a month is assumed to be 30. Thus, average daily COGS for the quarter ending March is $3.35 [(85 + 110 + 107)/90]. Finally, average days COGS in inventory is calculated by dividing the ending inventory balance by the average daily COGS. The result is the average number of days of COGS held in the ending inventory balance.

| | Jan. | Feb. | Mar. | Apr. | May | June |
|---|---|---|---|---|---|---|
| Cost of goods sold | 85 | 110 | 107 | 93 | 73 | 68 |
| Ending inventory | | | 68 | 55 | 42 | 44 |
| Average daily COGS (quarterly) | | | 3.35 | 3.44 | 3.03 | 2.60 |
| Average days COGS in inventory | | | 20.3 | 15.9 | 13.8 | 16.9 |

From March through May, there is a decreasing number of days inventory is held, which is a good sign. However, average days of COGS invested in inventory does jump up to 16.9 days in June, the second highest level for the four-month period.

## A Balance Fraction Approach

The following table shows the monthly dollar amount of purchases from January through June. In addition, the table shows the dollar amount of inventory left in each successive month after purchase. For example, in February, $120 of inventory was purchased. At the end of February, $60 of inventory remained in stock. Of the $120 of inventory purchased in February, $18 remained in stock at the end of March. The balance of the inventory purchased in February was sold in April. Summing up each column results in the dollar amount of total ending inventory for each month. The table clearly shows that ending inventory for each month consists of inventory items purchased over different time periods. For example, ending inventory for March consists of $50 of items purchased in March and $18 of items purchased in February.

| Month of Purchase | Purchase Amount | Jan. | Feb. | Mar. | Apr. | May | June |
|---|---|---|---|---|---|---|---|
| January | $100 | $50 | $15 | | | | |
| February | 120 | | 60 | $18 | | | |
| March | 100 | | | 50 | $15 | | |
| April | 80 | | | | 40 | $12 | |
| May | 60 | | | | | 30 | $ 9 |
| June | 70 | | | | | | 35 |
| Total inventory | | NA | $75 | $68 | $55 | $42 | $44 |

To make this table useful for analysis purposes, we need to convert the dollar inventory balances to **balance fractions**, dollar inventory balance as a percent of inventory purchases. Let's use an example to help demonstrate this concept. Look at the dollar figures for January in the table. Inventory in the amount of $100 was purchased in January. At the end of January, $50 of the January purchase remained as a balance. At the end of February, $15 of the January purchase remained as a balance. Thus, 50 percent of January purchases remained as balance ($50/$100) at the end of January, and 15 percent, ($15/$100), remained as a balance at the end of February. The next table shows the balance fraction calculations for the rest of the months. Notice that the balance fractions are constant. There is a steady use of inventory resulting in 50 percent of a month's purchase remaining at the end of the purchase month and 15 percent remaining at the end of the month following the purchase month.

| Month of Purchase | Purchase Amount | Jan. | Feb. | Mar. | Apr. | May | June |
|---|---|---|---|---|---|---|---|
| January | $100 | 50% | 15% | | | | |
| February | 120 | | 50% | 15% | | | |
| March | 100 | | | 50% | 15% | | |
| April | 80 | | | | 50% | 15% | |
| May | 60 | | | | | 50% | 15% |
| June | 70 | | | | | | 50% |

We can conclude from this analysis that inventory use has been stable, with no accumulation or depletion of inventory. This finding is in conflict with the conclusion drawn by the analysis based on the number of days inventory was held. This measure uses total inventory in the numerator. If sales or COGS are falling, then inventory will generally be lower, as management adjusts its inventory purchasing to the new lower sales volume. In the denominator, if sales, or correspondingly COGS, are falling, the average daily cost of goods sold will be artificially high because the averaging period will include COGS from an earlier period. This is especially true the longer the averaging period. Thus, the number of days COGS held in inventory will generally fall as sales and purchases fall, not because of increased inventory usage but because of the sales and purchasing trend and the period chosen over which to calculate average daily COGS. The balance fraction method of monitoring inventory is not affected by sales and purchasing trends and is therefore a more accurate measure of inventory usage.

## REDUCING THE SIZE OF THE INVENTORY INVESTMENT

In the past, inventory has been viewed as an asset. And, like any other asset, the more of it that shows up on the balance sheet, the better. More recently, however, inventory has begun to be viewed as an expense and, therefore, as an item to reduce or even eliminate. Earlier, we talked about the shock-absorbing role that inventory plays in the production and sales areas. If this shock-absorbing role could be reduced, then the level of inventory could be reduced. This is the essence of the **just-in-time inventory management system** developed in Japan. The focus of the just-in-time method is on redesigning the production system, not reducing inventory, to streamline the ordering process and to eliminate waste and production errors, thereby improving quality of the production process. Reduced investment in inventory typically comes as a result of this reengineering process.

A just-in-time system demands a commitment to problem solving. With no inventory, inefficiencies and production flow design problems quickly surface. In the past, adding a greater stock of raw materials or work-in-process inventory solved these problems. The just-in-time approach attacks the problem at its source, even to the extent of redesigning the production flow process.

Quality and loyalty are demanded throughout all stages of production if the just-in-time system is to work. Suppliers must be reliable and provide a high-quality product or service. Employees must be efficient and dedicated to quality, and they must be willing to be cross-trained in order to perform a variety of functions and tasks.

Not all industries or firms are adaptable to this type of production process. Prime candidates are those firms that are large, with a major market share, and that have a relatively stable product demand or demand such that a master production plan can be developed and adhered to.

The just-in-time inventory system is one approach to managing the production flow. The more traditional approach has been to stock inventory. Which approach is best for management must subjectively assess a given firm within a given culture. The just-in-time system has its own set of costs in terms of worker education and a significant investment in capital equipment, including a very sophisticated information system. For a given firm, incurring these costs may exceed the costs incurred under an alternative inventory system. Perhaps the most important aspect of the development of alternative production/inventory systems, such as just-in-time, is that it has caused us to change our inventory management philosophy from that of managing an asset to that of managing an expense or liability.

The inventory strategy followed by Toys "R" Us, the retail toy outlet based in Paramus, New Jersey, is in contrast to the just-in-time inventory system. Toys "R" Us uses inventory as a competitive advantage by offering the widest toy selection available on a year-round basis. In addition, they are able to offer prices at about 75 percent of depart-

## FOCUS ON PRACTICE

### *Just-in-Time Inventory Management*

Just-in-time inventory management (JIT) has literally become a household word. The concept has transformed inventory management from managing an asset to managing a process. Companies view inventory as an expense that can and should be reduced. JIT involves the development of sophisticated information systems that provide a forecast of inventory needs for the manufacturer and electronic communications between the manufacturer and its suppliers. Quality control is an essential element of JIT because one of the ingredients of a successful JIT system is reliability.

Major U.S. companies from General Electric to Harley-Davidson have endorsed the JIT concept. In the case of Harley-Davidson, its business has essentially been reborn. Key benefits include:

- significant reduction in plant size, which saves overhead as well as construction costs.
- increased productivity through the use of electronic data interchange systems between manufacturer and supplier.
- cost savings through less investment in inventory and lower financing costs. GE was able to trim inventory by 70 percent, while Harley-Davidson trimmed several million dollars from its work-in-process inventory investment.

While it may seem that JIT inventory management invalidates the EOQ concept, the two systems are actually quite compatible. JIT maintains the same focus on ordering and holding costs but redefines the production process, substantially altering the relative magnitudes of the cost components used in calculating EOQ. As a result, inventory shipments may be received daily or hourly rather than weekly or even more sporadically. For example, the retailing company The Gap employed many of the concepts of JIT. The company boosted quality, strengthened ties with manufacturers, and redesigned its distribution system, enabling it to supply its stores in New York City daily. This procedure ensures that the stores never run out of the hottest items.

ment store prices because of their volume purchases. This winning combination of wide assortment and discount prices has fueled the company's growth. Thus, while minimizing inventory stocks may be appropriate in some cases, stocking inventory may be appropriate in other situations. Inventory management decisions must correspond with competitive opportunities and the firm's strategic plan.

Technology allows management to design systems to more efficiently manage its operations, which ultimately impacts the inventory area. Order costs are reduced, with less costly and faster information systems. According to Stone, "firms that place orders, receive acknowledgments, make confirmations, and process shipping and delivering information through electronic data interchange transactions eliminate time delays, lower costs, and reduce errors."[3]

While many companies have successfully redesigned and integrated their operations on a domestic basis, the challenge remains to integrate on a global basis. For companies to compete effectively internationally, global integration of operations becomes a necessity. This means that a company manages its operations worldwide as a single entity to maximize competitive advantage in all of its markets on a global basis. One leader in global integration is Xerox. It standardized product development procedures for all markets,

[3] "Just-In-Time: The Risk/Reward Trade-Off May Not Be What It Seems" (full citation in the end-of-chapter references).

## FOCUS ON PRACTICE

### Supply Chain Management

Wal-Mart, the world's largest retailer, has a goal of selling its merchandise so quickly that products are out of the store before it has to pay its suppliers. In fact, this strategy of quick inventory turnover is one reason Wal-Mart's profitability has grown faster than sales. In order to accomplish this, the company is building faster distribution centers and providing suppliers with more sales data on products so they can better match their production to Wal-Mart's peak selling seasons. The company also aggressively cut back on slow-moving inventory items. As a result, over 60 percent of Wal-Mart's inventory is sold before payments are made to suppliers. The goal is 100 percent!

A good example of Wal-Mart's distribution system is how it handles Crest toothpaste. At Wal-Mart's new distribution centers, products from Procter & Gamble's trucks are unloaded directly onto trucks headed for Wal-Mart stores (the product is never put on warehouse shelves). Once a truck is full, it heads for the stores, where product is set on the store shelves in less than four hours and sold within 24 hours. Payment to P&G is generally made in 10 days.

*Source:* Emily Nelson, "Wal-Mart May Cut Costs, Boost Earnings by Changing Merchandise Handling," *Dow Jones Business News* (November 10, 1999).

rather than developing products for one market and then reengineering those products for other markets worldwide, resulting in a dramatic saving in product development time. But the company did not stop there. Next, Xerox standardized plant facility requirements worldwide to facilitate the comparison of product cost and inventory data at its plants worldwide. Finally, distribution centers were strategically located worldwide rather than by specific markets in isolation.[4]

As stated earlier, inventory management has really evolved as a byproduct, with the main focus of attention being the redesign of the entire supply chain with increasing focus on quality and efficiency. One example of a company taking an aggressive approach to managing its supply chain is Wal-Mart, as discussed in the Focus on Practice box. The company has been able to enhance its profitability through inventory reduction by effectively redesigning its supply chain management system in alliance with its suppliers. Inventory, then, results when it becomes the cheaper alternative to the costs associated with improving the efficiency of the supply chain process.

Sophisticated systems such as those used by Wal-Mart require a comprehensive information system. It is now common for information systems technology to play a critical role in the management of a firm's entire supply chain and, therefore, the management of inventory. For example, an inventory planning system known as **material requirements planning (MRP)** focuses on the amount and timing of finished goods demanded and translates that into the derived demand for raw materials and subassemblies at various stages of production. MRP provides computer-based support for planning and control of operations from receipt of materials to shipment of orders. Users report significant improvement in their competitive and financial positions, customer service levels, and production scheduling. About half of the users were able to cut inventory levels, manufacturing costs, production lead times, and component shortages. With such a system, if a major customer

---

[4] Robert E. Markland, Shawnee K. Vickery, and Robert A. Davis, *Operations Management: Concepts in Manufacturing and Services* (full citation in the end-of-chapter references), p. 99.

defers an order by a month or so, the MRP system immediately readjusts materials purchases and related production schedules.

The evolution of resource requirements planning systems saw material requirements systems (now referred to as MRP I) merge into **manufacturing resource planning systems** (referred to as **MRP II**), a much broader and all-encompassing concept. Manufacturing resource planning systems are made up of a variety of functions linked together: business planning, sales and operations planning, production planning, master production scheduling, material requirements planning, capacity requirements planning, and the execution support systems for capacity and material. Output from these systems is then integrated with financial reports such as the business plan, purchase commitment report, shipping budget, inventory projections in dollars, etc. And the evolution and sophistication of such systems continues today with MRP II systems evolving into systems referred to as **enterprise resources planning**, or **ERP**. ERP systems are accounting-oriented information systems used for identifying and planning the enterprise-wide resources needed to take, make, ship, and account for customer orders. ERP systems consist of software modules that help manage the many different activities in different functional business areas. Vendors such as SAP, Baan, and PeopleSoft are leaders in providing such software systems.[5]

## SUMMARY

In this chapter we have seen that proper inventory management decisions, from the perspective of the financial manager, should be based on the cost of holding the inventory, the cost of ordering inventory, the opportunity cost of funds invested in inventory, and cost considerations based on quantity discounts. The final inventory decision should then take into consideration whether or not this minimum cost order quantity is workable within the inventory management system so that stock-outs are avoided.

Inventory is a major component in the supply chain of the firm and must also be viewed as a critical component in the cash flow cycle of a corporation. If improperly managed, inventory can be a major contributor to cash flow problems experienced by the organization. The level of inventory needed by an organization is a direct result of the design of its operation or production process. Monitoring the resulting inventory levels, then, is important so that management can continually gauge the status of operations. We learned that some of the traditional inventory monitoring tools such as inventory turnover and days' inventory held are biased by sales and production trends. A suggested improvement was to use a balance fraction approach.

There is anecdotal evidence that the growing success of supply chain management systems in the United States is impacting inventory management. Ratios such as inventory-to-sales, especially in the work-in-process and materials and supplies categories, have been falling steadily over the last decade.

## USEFUL WEB SITES

A great Web site for articles and news on working capital management:
**http://www.gtnews.com**

American Productivity and Quality Center: **http://www.apqc.org**

Industry Week Magazine: **http://www.industryweek.com**

---

[5] Norman Gaither and Greg Frazier, *Production and Operations Management, 8th Edition*, South-Western College Publishing, Cincinnati, Ohio, 1999, pp. 417–418.

## QUESTIONS

1. What is inventory management's primary concern?
2. Why is inventory such a difficult item to manage?
3. Why is inventory needed? What role does it play?
4. What are the three different types of inventory and what role does each play?
5. What are the financial manager's concerns related to inventory management?
6. Explain what the EOQ solution represents.
7. How is risk handled by the EOQ model?
8. What three factors affect the amount of safety stock needed? How does each factor differ from the other?
9. Compare the EOQ solution to the present value timeline solution.
10. Discuss how the dollar amount of inventory can be reduced.
11. How can days COGS held in inventory be a misleading monitoring tool?
12. How is a balance fraction approach to inventory monitoring an improvement over the measure days COGS held in inventory?

## PROBLEMS

1. Ardmore Farm and Seed has an inventory dilemma. It has been selling a brand of very popular insect spray for the past year. It has never really analyzed the costs incurred from ordering and holding the inventory and currently faces a large stock of the insecticide in the warehouse. Ardmore estimates that it costs $25 to place an order and $0.25 per gallon to hold the spray. The annual requirements total 80,000 gallons for a 365-day year.
   **a.** Assuming that 10,000 gallons are ordered each time an order is placed, estimate the annual inventory costs.
   **b.** Calculate the EOQ.
   **c.** Given the EOQ calculated in **b**, how many orders should be placed and what is the average inventory balance?
   **d.** If it takes seven days to receive an order from suppliers, at what inventory level should Ardmore place another order?
2. Lott Manufacturing Inc. has been ordering parts for its production process in lots of 10,000 units. Each order costs the firm $50 to place, and holding costs per unit average $3. Lott uses 200,000 units every 250 days.
   **a.** Calculate the EOQ.
   **b.** What is the difference in inventory costs between the EOQ and the current order quantity of 10,000 units?
   **c.** Given the EOQ calculated in **a**, how many orders should be placed and what is the average inventory balance?
   **d.** If it takes two days to receive an order from suppliers, at what inventory level should Lott place another order?
3. Ardmore Farm and Seed (Problem 1) was recently approached by its supplier with a new quantity discount program. The supplier offered the following quantity discounts.

| Quantity | Cost per Unit |
|---|---|
| 0–4,999 | $40 |
| 5,000–9,999 | 39 |
| 10,000–19,999 | 37 |
| 20,000+ | 35 |

Ardmore believes that these quantity discounts would give it a real competitive edge but realizes that other costs would be affected, such as ordering costs and holding costs.

**a.** What quantity should Ardmore order based on the quantity discounts offered?

**4.** Lott Manufacturing (Problem 2) was recently approached by its supplier with a new quantity discount program. The supplier offered the following quantity discounts.

| Quantity | Cost per Unit |
|---|---|
| 0–1,999 | $5.00 |
| 2,000–3,999 | 4.99 |
| 4,000–5,999 | 4.98 |
| 6,000–7,999 | 4.97 |
| 8,000–9,999 | 4.96 |
| 10,000+ | 4.95 |

**a.** What order quantity is optimal for Lott to place considering the quantity discounts?

**5.** Ardmore Farm and Seed's (Problems 1 and 3) new treasurer has suggested that the inventory decision should include consideration of the firm's opportunity cost of capital. The firm's cost of capital is currently estimated at 15 percent. Using the information in Problems 1 and 3, estimate the optimal order quantity.

**6.** Lott Manufacturing's treasurer suggests that the true optimal order quantity should consider the firm's cost of capital, which is currently estimated at 20 percent. Using the information in Problems 2 and 4, estimate the optimal order quantity.

**7.** Beverly Cosmetics is a cosmetic retailer. The company orders namebrand cosmetics wholesale and sells them at retail, generally through leased spaced in large malls. Beverly's management is trying to determine the optimal order quantity of one particular brand of perfume. The perfume wholesales for $10.00 per ounce and sells for $20.99 per ounce. Order costs are estimated at $75.00 per order, and holding costs are relatively small, at only $0.15 per ounce. Beverly's supplier offers quantity discounts of $0.05 for order increments of 500 ounces. For example, the cost per ounce is $10.00 for order quantities of 1 to 499 ounces, $9.95 per ounce for order quantities of 500 to 999 ounces, etc. Beverly's sells about 50,000 ounces of the perfume each year (365 days). Beverly's cost of capital is 25 percent.

**a.** What is the EOQ solution?

**b.** What is the optimal order quantity ignoring the cost of capital?

**c.** What is the optimal order considering the cost of capital?

**d.** Compare the three answers and discuss whether or not they make sense to you.

**8.** The following table presents data for cost of goods sold and ending inventory for the first six months of 2005 for EBCO, Inc.

| | Jan. | Feb. | Mar. | Apr. | May | June |
|---|---|---|---|---|---|---|
| Cost of goods sold | 100 | 150 | 225 | 200 | 125 | 90 |
| Ending inventory | 40 | 50 | 62 | 62 | 42 | 28 |

Assume that each month has 30 days.

**a.** Calculate the number of days of cost of goods sold held in inventory for March, April, May, and June assuming quarterly cost of goods sold is used to calculate average daily cost of goods sold.

**b.** Discuss your findings in **a.** What is happening with the firm's investment in inventory?

**c.** The following purchasing schedule shows the dollar amount of those purchases remaining as an inventory balance for successive months. Calculate a balance fraction matrix, and discuss what it shows about the firm's management of its inventory balance.

| | | Ending Inventory Balances | | | | |
|---|---|---|---|---|---|---|
| | Purchases | Feb. | Mar. | Apr. | May | June |
| February | 160 | 31 | 15 | | | |
| March | 237 | | 47 | 23 | | |

*continued*

| | Purchases | Ending Inventory Balances Feb. | Mar. | Apr. | May | June |
|---|---|---|---|---|---|---|
| April | 200 | | | 39 | 19 | |
| May | 105 | | | | 23 | 11 |
| June | 76 | | | | | 17 |
| End-of-month inventory | | NA | 62 | 62 | 42 | 28 |

**d.** Explain the disparity between the conclusions reached in **b** and **d.** Which monitoring tool is more accurate?

**9.** The table below presents data for cost of goods sold and ending inventory for the first six months of 2005 for Wynn Manufacturing, Inc.

| | Jan. | Feb. | Mar. | Apr. | May | June |
|---|---|---|---|---|---|---|
| Cost of goods sold | 1,000 | 1,500 | 2,100 | 2,700 | 3,500 | 4,800 |
| Ending inventory | 300 | 450 | 630 | 810 | 1,050 | 1,440 |

Assume that each month has 30 days.

**a.** Calculate the number of days of cost of goods sold held in inventory for March, April, May, and June assuming quarterly cost of goods sold is used to calculate average daily cost of goods sold.

**b.** Discuss your findings in **a.** What is happening with the firm's investment in inventory?

**c.** The following purchasing schedule shows the dollar amount of those purchases remaining as an inventory balance for successive months. Calculate a balance fraction matrix, and discuss what it shows about the firm's management of its inventory balance.

| | Purchases | Ending Inventory Balances Feb. | Mar. | Apr. | May | June |
|---|---|---|---|---|---|---|
| February | 1,650 | 330 | 174 | | | |
| March | 2,280 | | 456 | 234 | | |
| April | 2,880 | | | 576 | 302 | |
| May | 3,740 | | | | 748 | 402 |
| June | 5,190 | | | | | 1,038 |
| End-of-month inventory | | NA | 630 | 810 | 1,050 | 1,440 |

**d.** Explain the disparity between the conclusions reached in **b** and **d.** Which monitoring tool is more accurate and why?

**10.** Float-Rite, Inc., makes float tubes for fly-fishermen. The data below displays three months of sales, cost of goods sold, and ending inventory data. Calculate the days COGS held in inventory for August for three different averaging periods of 30 days, 60 days, and 90 days.

| | June | July | August |
|---|---|---|---|
| Sales | $50,000 | $35,000 | $20,000 |
| Cost of goods sold | 25,000 | 17,500 | 10,000 |
| Ending inventory | 7,000 | 5,000 | 3,000 |

## REFERENCES

Yong Kim, George C. Philippatos, and Kee H. Chung, "Evaluating Investment in Inventory Policy: A Net Present Value Framework," *The Engineering Economist* (Winter 1986), pp. 119–136.

Robert E. Markland, Shawnee K. Vickery, and Robert A. Davis, *Operations Management: Concepts in Manufacturing and Services* (West Publishing: Minneapolis/Saint Paul), 1995.

K. Vinodrai Pandya and J. Boyd, "Appraisal of JIT Using Financial Measures," *International Journal of Operations and Production Management*, Vol. 15, No. 9 (1995), pp. 200–209.

A. Snyder, "Principles of Inventory Management," *Financial Executive*, Vol. 32, No. 4 (April 1964), pp. 13–21.

Bernell K. Stone, "Just-In-Time: The Risk/Reward Trade-Off May Not Be What It Seems," *Journal of Working Capital Management* (Fall 1995), pp. 32–36.

R. C. Walleigh, " What's Your Excuse for Not Using JIT?" *Harvard Business Review* (March–April 1986), pp. 38–54.

FOCUSED CASE

# Fletcher Company

### Background

Fletcher Company was originally founded by Eugene Fletcher some 50 years ago. The company recently celebrated its "Golden Anniversary" with the first-ever family reunion organized to coincide with the annual company picnic. Ira Fletcher, the son of the founder, serves as President and CEO for the firm. The company has been managed by various members of the extended family but over the last decade the company experienced such tremendous growth that a treasury function was recently created out of the controller's office and a Chief Financial Officer was hired from the outside, the first professional manager not part of the family.

The company has a very strong customer orientation and is very operations oriented. Jake Fletcher, one of Ira's two sons, heads up operations and is very proud of the fact that the company has never had to shut down its production lines because of inventory shortages or failure to meet customer demand. Jake's aunt is controller and has served in that position for 20 years. The company has a very good cost accounting system and the company continually receives praise from the outside auditors on the company's internal control systems that she has installed over the years.

Ira recently discovered that Fletcher's working capital requirements to sales ratio was seemingly out of line with the rest of the firms in the industry. A recent article in a trade publication indicated that Fletcher's WCR/S ratio averaged .10 over the last three years while the rest of the industry averaged .05[1] and for 2001 it was at an all time high of .115. Although Ira did not fully understand the significance of this measure, he was concerned that his company's ratio was so far out of line from the industry performance.

## OPERATIONS

Jake Fletcher, VP for Operations has instituted a very strong and reliable supplier network. Each crate of components has an invoice price of $8,000. Currently, Jake orders 750 crates at a time. The company's operations run at a relatively steady rate throughout the year and the company operates 7 days a week, 52 weeks each year.

## CREDIT MANAGEMENT

Sue Fletcher, the youngest of the three Fletcher children, has served as corporate credit manager ever since she took over the position from her mother five years ago. Sue enjoys the credit area and particularly enjoys working with the company's customers. Although working with slow payers is a challenge, she receives a lot of satisfaction from the required negotiations and seeing the flow of payments come in from what originally seemed like impossible situations. She is a member of the National Association of Credit Management (NACM) and is actively involved in her local industry trade credit group. The company's days sales outstanding average 50 days and is only marginally higher than the industry average. Fletcher offers terms of net 45 days; although one or two of the larger firms in the industry offer terms of 1/10, net 30, most of the firms the size of Fletcher offer no discount and the net terms average about 45 days.

## PAYABLES

The payables area is under the controller function and is run in a very efficient manner. The typical credit terms received by Fletcher were 1/10, net 45. The company does not currently take the cash discount, fearing that paying cash 10 days after purchase would excessively strain the company's liquidity position given the relatively long operating cycle. The company has a policy of paying its bills when due and has followed the policy for the last several years, at least since the last major recession.

## TREASURY

The newly hired CFO, John Cummings, previously served as treasurer at one of Fletcher's suppliers. John

[1] *Working capital requirements* is defined as the difference between the sum of accounts receivable, inventory, and other current assets and the sum of accounts payable and operating accruals. For more information on this ratio see Chapter 2. The resulting amount is a dollar amount. To standardize this measure, it is divided by annual sales to make comparisons between different companies.

is a member of the local chapter of the Association for Financial Professionals (AFP) and received his Certified Cash Management (CCM) designation about five years ago. The treasury department he came from was well developed and had been instrumental in moving the company to incorporate economic value added (EVA) as a management philosophy and the company was very cash-flow focused. John's immediate project was to conduct a review of Fletcher's working capital policies and to determine their respective impacts on the Company's cash cycle. The Company seemingly stocked significant inventory as a result of ordering only five times per year. Because inventory figured so prominently in the calculation of the WCR/S ratio and the collections area seems to be managed consistent with industry practice, John decided to focus initial attention on the operations area and in particular to the area of inventory management. John determined that the after-tax cost of capital for Fletcher is 15 percent based on after-tax cost of debt and an equity cost based on the capital asset pricing model. The company's long-term borrowing rate has averaged about 10 percent and its short-term borrowing rate has been prime + 1 percent. Prime is currently 7.5 percent.

## Data Collection

The CFO put together a small project team to study the operations area. He requested that the team calculate the annual cost of the company's current inventory policy. The team discovered that the company was placing five orders per year purchasing inventory in lots of 750 crates, which generated a rather significant average inventory balance. However, the operations manager reiterated that the company has never run out of materials and he reminded the team of the quantity discount that was received.

The inventory was stored in a rented warehouse owned by a local real estate developer. The annual warehouse rental was $120,000 and the annual insurance bill to cover the inventory was $5,000 for theft and fire coverage. In addition, it was estimated that annual costs involved in the current order processing system, including personnel time and communication costs, totaled $1,600. These costs were included in operating costs on the income statement.

John was wondering how the current system would compare with instituting a type of just-in-time inventory management. The project team, in exploring this approach found that the supplier was very willing to consider the change in strategy. To implement such a strategy, the supplier would require an accurate forecast of the units required well in advance, perhaps as much as 6 months in advance, to plan production. In addition, significant transportation planning would be needed to make the strategy successful to ensure against stockouts.

The plan would be to order 110 crates about every week and a half. While this was not a true just-in-time system, John felt that it was a reasonable compromise given the transportation issues that the project team uncovered in their analysis. The team computed that the order costs would increase about $50 per order from the current level as a result of implementing a forecasting system into the order processing system.

The company's financial statements are present below.

| 2001 PROFIT AND LOSS STATEMENT | |
|---|---|
| Revenues | $50,000,000 |
| Cost of goods sold | $30,000,000 |
| Gross profit | $20,000,000 |
| Operating expenses | $18,000,000 |
| Depreciation | $650,000 |
| Operating profit | $1,350,000 |
| Interest | $550,000 |
| Taxes | $200,000 |
| Net income | $600,000 |
| Dividends | $200,000 |

BALANCE SHEET
DECEMBER 31, 2001

| Assets | | Liabilities and Net Worth | |
|---|---|---|---|
| Cash | $500,000 | Accounts payable | $4,100,000 |
| Receivables | $6,850,000 | Notes payable | $1,400,000 |
| Inventory | $3,000,000 | Mortgage | $5,000,000 |
| Net fixed plant | $7,150,000 | Equity: | |
| | | Common stock | $2,000,000 |
| | | Retained earnings | $5,000,000 |
| Total | $17,500,000 | | $17,500,000 |

## REQUIRED

1. Compute the order cost per order and the operational holding cost per unit of inventory given the current ordering system.
2. Compute the annual cost of the current inventory management system including the cost of capital.

3. Compute the annual cost of the proposed system including the cost of capital.
4. What impact would the new system have on the company's WCR/S ratio? John also wondered what the new balance sheet might approximately look like if the new inventory management system was put in place?
5. How should the issues raised by Jake Fletcher be addressed? What are the risks that would be assumed if the "just-in-time" inventory system is adopted?
6. Which system do you recommend Fletcher adopt and why?

CHAPTER 5

# Accounts Receivable Management

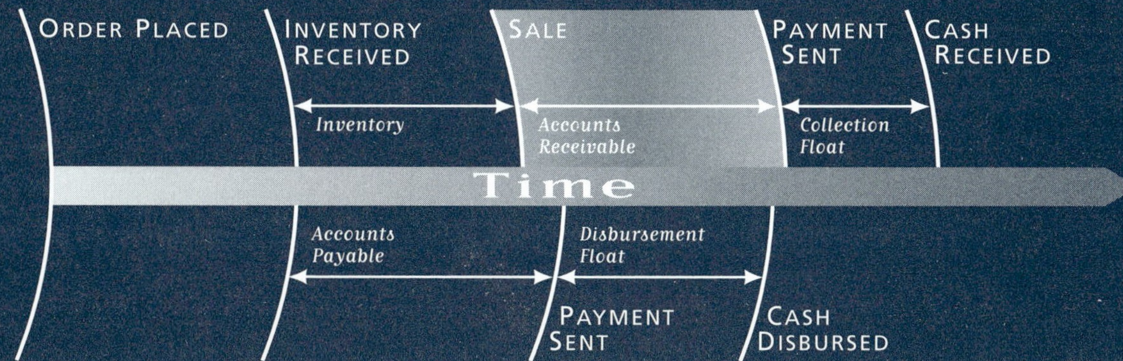

## OBJECTIVES

### *After studying this chapter, you should be able to:*

- define credit policy and indicate its components.
- describe the typical credit-granting sequence a company would follow.
- apply net present value analysis to credit extension decisions.
- define credit scoring and explain its limitations.
- list the elements in a credit rating report.
- describe how receivables management can benefit from electronic data interchange.

Michael Shane first learned about the business world by selling jeans and women's wigs. In a stroke of genius, he foresaw the emergence of a new market selling clones of brand-name personal computers—and Leading Edge was born. At one point, Leading Edge had captured 6 percent of the market for PC clones. Shane suddenly sold out early, however, when the combination of tough competition, quality problems, and his poorly executed credit management strategy undercut the company's profitability. According to published reports, Shane's approach to doing business included forcing retailers to pay him as many as four weeks *before* receiving the computers, leading one analyst to suggest the company was universally hated by its dealers.

Shane's reversed credit policy (his company had a negative days' sales outstanding) was made possible because of the customer demand spawned by the "Best Buy" rating accorded to Leading Edge machines by Consumer Reports. This unusual approach to accounts receivable management provided readily usable funds to fuel Leading Edge's rapid production and inventory expansion. In this chapter, we survey credit management, the essentials of credit policy, sources of credit analysis information, and the credit-granting decision. We show how net present value (NPV) analysis can be applied to a single credit extension decision and how to refine that analysis to incorporate risk. Chapter 6 addresses the application of NPV analysis to overall credit policy, monitoring accounts receivable, and collection procedures. The major credit management issue that you learn about in this chapter is the credit-granting decision, as illustrated in the financial dilemma.

## FINANCIAL DILEMMA

How Can I Make Sense of the Changing World of Receivables Management?

Brandon, assistant credit manager at a Fortune 1000 company, just returned from the National Association of Credit Management annual meeting and is going through his notes. He opens up to some predictions made by credit executives about business credit practices in the future:[1]

- "Credit will consist of fewer, but more highly educated and skilled individuals."
- "Data will be received and deployed electronically via the Internet."
- "Credit will be part of a seamless automated process from order generation through cash application."
- "Credit will have more analytical responsibilities including, but not limited to, portfolio analysis and capital forecasting."
- "The majority of credit risk will not be outsourced to banks, credit insurers, and credit card companies."
- "Credit will not become a sales/marketing function."

As Brandon puts the report aside, some questions crop up in his mind: How valid are these trends? How can credit add value for shareholders? Why is it done in the finance area? and How can I best prepare myself to be successful in the new environment?

[1] Rod Wheeland, "The Future of Business Credit," *Business Credit* (July 1997), pp. 53–54.

## TRADE CREDIT AND SHAREHOLDER VALUE

**Trade credit** arises when goods are sold under delayed payment terms. When credit terms are offered, the seller is exchanging the title to the goods for the buyer's promise to pay at an agreed-upon later date. Selling goods on delayed terms has been traced back to the Roman Empire, when credit billing was relied on to reduce the obstacles faced in transferring money through unorganized trading areas.[2] The practice of selling goods to other companies without demanding cash payment is taken for granted today. Many companies have large investments in receivables. Great Dane Trailers Inc., the largest U.S. manufacturer of highway truck trailers, has $73,000,000 invested in receivables (26 percent of total assets and 47 percent of current assets), as compared to $435,000 in cash and securities. Dun & Bradstreet (D&B) and Risk Management Associates (RMA, formerly Robert Morris Associates) data covering 302 industries indicates that average receivables as a percentage of total assets hover around 25 percent. Receivables are normally the largest asset of businesses that sell on credit, on average constituting 21 to 34 percent of companies' assets across various industries. Receivables constitute a significant working capital investment for service companies as well as manufacturing companies. Yet, surprisingly, a recent survey finds almost half of companies lack a formal and written receivables and

[2] For an excellent survey of the development of credit, see Chapter 1 of Christie and Bracuti, *Credit Executives Handbook* (cited in the end-of-chapter references).

credit extension policy and of the ones that do have a policy, 43 percent do not adhere to that policy. Many companies (57 percent) fail to set performance objectives for receivables management, and one-third of those having objectives don't monitor performance against those objectives.[3] Lack of adequate human resources is the most commonly given reasons for these shortfalls.

The financial manager can add value for the company's shareholders by properly influencing three areas: the company's aggregate investment in receivables, its credit terms, and its credit standards. Exhibit 5–1 shows us that these decision areas are not the exclusive domain of the financial manager but are influenced by the company's marketing strategy and the corresponding sales and market share objectives. Very recent evidence informs us that credit professionals are working almost as much with marketing and sales departments as with other finance personnel.

## FINANCIAL DILEMMA REVISITED

As we consider Brandon's question about how credit management adds value for the company, and the role of finance, let's refer to Exhibit 5–1. The diagram indicates the

**Exhibit 5–1**

*The Influence of Receivables Management on Shareholder Value*

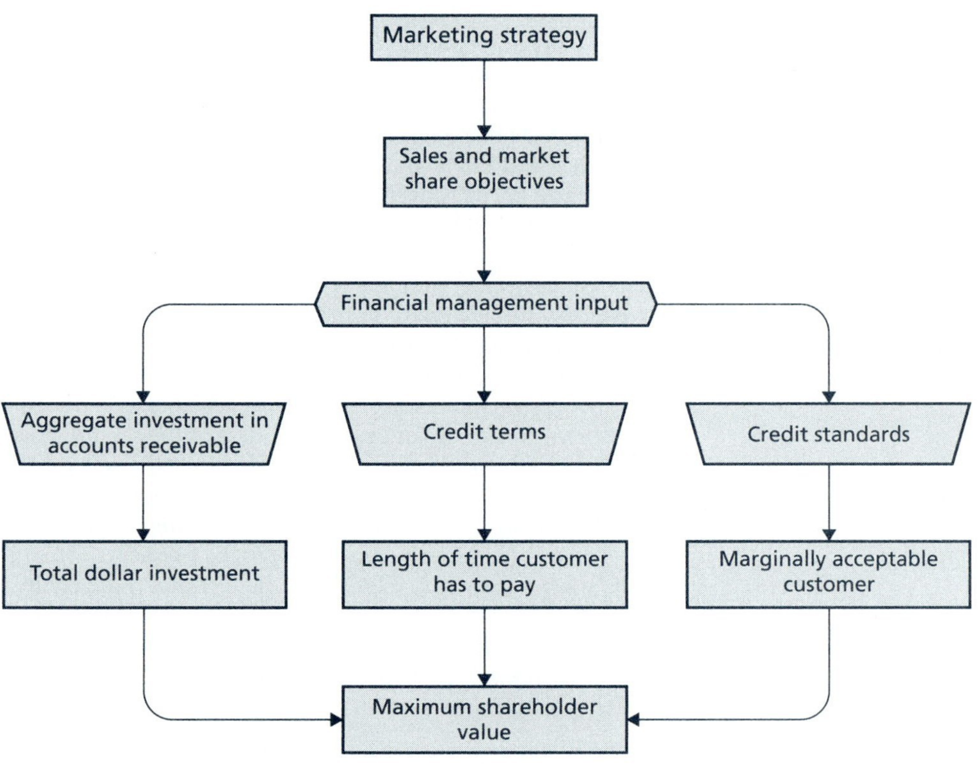


[3] Industry and survey data is from a 2003 PricewaterhouseCoopers survey. See AFP, "Accounts Receivable: The Forgotten Asset," *AFP Exchange* (September/October 2003), p. 11.

major issues addressed by the financial manager, each with a potential impact on share value. Overinvesting in receivables can be costly because the investment is typically financed by short-term borrowing and it may signal acceptance of late-paying customers. Furthermore, if not monitored, a company's investment in receivables can grow rapidly out of control, triggering a liquidity crisis. If the credit terms (cash discount and period allowed for payment) are not competitive when compared with other sellers in the same industry or are misaligned with the product line profitability (a long credit period on product having a slim profit margin), they can diminish shareholder value. Setting an incorrect credit standard for customers diminishes shareholder value because of lost sales (when too stringent) or uncollectible sales (when too lenient). Summarizing, the credit and collections function wants to control bad debts and outstanding receivables, maintain financial flexibility, optimize the mix of company assets, convert receivables to cash on a timely basis, analyze customer risk, and respond to customer needs.[4] Credit managers must accomplish this while holding down the cost of administering the function and ensuring the speed and accuracy of credit-related information. In a later section we will cover some of the credit management trends of which Brandon and other credit professionals should be aware.

## Trade Credit versus Bank Credit

The term *trade credit* generally applies to credit extended by manufacturers and wholesalers to their customers. As of the end of 2002, Federal Reserve Board statistics indicate that, for every dollar of short-term bank credit extended to businesses, \$2.02 of trade credit is extended by suppliers, up from a ratio of \$1.66 to \$1 in early 2001.

Practitioners defend trade credit on two grounds: cost/efficiency and revenue. Although a business's customers could get the same funding from banks, those bank loans often come at a greater cost, with less efficiency, and more slowly. Some mistakenly view trade credit as a "free lunch," because there is no explicit interest charge specified, but its cost is one of the costs of doing business and is built into the product's price.

Marketing and credit managers often advocate trade credit extension on two sales-related grounds: (1) its convenience may trigger larger purchases, increasing the company's overall sales, and (2) it builds goodwill and gives the seller greater stability because of more consistent repeat sales. Some merchants further argue that credit customers are more stable than cash customers and might become reliable repeat purchasers once they have been approved for a specific credit limit by the seller.

Credit sellers have three advantages over banks in extending financing to buyers.[5] The *information advantage* refers to the fact that the seller observes buyers, has industry contacts, and sees payment behavior (including whether cash discounts are taken)—and much of this information comes at low cost as part of the selling process. The *control advantage* occurs when the buyer is dependent upon either the seller or the seller's network for its future supplies, giving it a strong rationale to continue to pay on its trade credit. The *salvage value advantage* is the ability of the seller to repossess and resell goods in a less costly manner than a bank, when buyers do not make payments. Other reasons trade credit might substitute for bank credit are linked to the fact that trade credit offered by businesses differs in some significant ways from the credit typically offered by banking institutions. Exhibit 5–2 illustrates some of the key differences. Note particularly the "security" and "resource transferred" contrasts.

---

[4] This summary is based on Rose Marie Bukics, "Credit Policy: Successful Policy for the Global Marketplace," *Credit and Financial Management Review*, 1 (1995), pp. 58–59.

[5] See Petersen and Rajan (1997), cited in the end-of-chapter references.

**Exhibit 5-2**

*Differences between Trade Credit and Bank Credit*

| ATTRIBUTE | TRADE CREDIT | BANK CREDIT |
|---|---|---|
| Length of terms | Relatively short—usually 30, 60, or 90 days. | Longer and extended and repaid on a seasonal basis. |
| Security | Usually unsecured, somewhat more lenient in extending credit. | Higher standards for unsecured loans; otherwise secured. |
| Amounts involved | Smaller, especially if customer buys from several sources. | Larger, especially for large companies or those dealing with a small number of banks. |
| Resource transferred | Goods or services. | Money. |
| Extent of analysis | Extensive when size of transaction is large, involving large credit exposure. | Bank's needs for liquidity to meet deposit withdrawals necessities in-depth analysis regarding safety and collectibility. |

## Evaluating the Motives for Trade Credit

Formal studies of the rationale for the extension of trade credit go beyond the basic reasons cited above. Four major motives have been identified;[6] we illustrate each motive with Ford's credit extension to car buyers.

- *Financial motive.* Sellers charge a higher price when selling on credit, generating a greater present value profit based on the implicit interest rate charged; also, sellers raise capital at lower rates than their customers and have cost advantages vis-á-vis banks due to (1) the similarity of customers, (2) the information gathered in the selling process (size and frequency of orders, whether the cash discount is taken, timeliness of payments), (3) a lower probability of default (because the purchased goods are part of a product that is an integral part of the buyer's business and the buyer needs to continue paying to maintain supply), and (4) a greater value of collateral to sellers than to banks in that they can rework and resell the product without much difficulty or expense. Ford has a much better understanding than do banks of car buyer default probabilities and repossession resale value and has an established dealer network for resale of repossessions.
- *Operating motive.* Here, suppliers respond to variable and uncertain demand in how they extend trade credit, instead of using more costly responses such as installing extra capacity, building or depleting inventories, or forcing customers to wait in line. Ford uses attractive lease terms and cut-rate financing (interest rates lower than the customer's bank rate) to stimulate sales if production exceeds sales and inventories are beginning to accumulate.[7]
- *Contracting cost motive.* Sales contracting costs between buyers and sellers are reduced for buyers because they can inspect the quantity and quality of goods before payment and reduce the payment if some goods are missing or defective. Sellers

[6] For more on this, see the excellent reviews in Emery (1988), Long, Malitz, and Ravid (1993), Mian and Smith (1994), and Pike and Cheung (2002), cited in the end-of-chapter references.

[7] Some economists contend that the spread of retail incentives and the aggressive way in which automakers use them allow the auto industry to minimize the effects of interest rate increases—at least for a while, and while the increases are fairly small. See Bradshaw (1999), cited in the end-of-chapter references.

have less employee or third-party theft because goods are less liquid than cash and collection is not made at the time of delivery, while the separation of the collection and delivery functions allows sellers to achieve efficiency gains due to the specialization of labor. Furthermore, sellers gain valuable buyer creditworthiness information by observing whether credit buyers take cash discounts, when offered. Ford recognizes that some buyers exercise their option to quit making payments when warranty-period repairs are unsatisfactory. Buying on credit provides "lemon insurance," and if no bank is involved, the resolution of customer dissatisfaction is simpler.

- *Pricing motive.* Sellers in certain industries are unable to alter their prices, perhaps because they are part of an oligopoly (and face a kinked demand curve or are part of a collusive agreement) or due to governmental regulation; unpublished variations in credit policy allow these sellers to charge varying amounts to their customers. Furthermore, normally credit-constrained buyers might be offered the same credit terms as more creditworthy buyers—in a sense, lowering the effective price for them. When Ford does lower its prices through rebates, it will often give a choice of the price reduction or cut-rate financing. Customers can choose their preferred offer, based on their local financing options and present cash position.

Financial market or product market imperfections stand behind all these motives, which represent company responses to the imperfections. In each case, trade credit is considered more economical and efficient than using other responses open to the companies. These motives are difficult to test in the real world, and it is very hard to say which of these motives dominates as the rationale behind most trade credit. Studies by Long, Malitz, and Ravid (1993) and Deloof and Jegers (1996) provide strong support for the contracting cost motive. Trade credit gives customers time to inspect and determine the quality of merchandise. Moderate support is also provided for the operating motive. A comprehensive study by Ng, Smith, and Smith (1999) finds no support for the operating motive, limited support for the pricing motive, and strong support for the contracting cost motive. They note that payment terms are market responses to the information problems plaguing business-to-business transactions.

## Trends Affecting Trade Credit

Company-level trade credit outstanding may be trending downward in the United States due to three interrelated trends: adoption by some companies of a zero net working capital objective, integration of receivables management with inventory management and enterprise resource planning (ERP) systems, and greater use of electronic commerce.

*ZERO NET WORKING CAPITAL OBJECTIVE* Because many companies are explicitly adopting a "zero net working capital" goal or implicitly striving to reduce the order-to-cash cycle, the relative amount and duration of receivables may be expected to decline. Companies are more sensitive to the asset tie-up in receivables due to the use of economic value added (EVA™) metrics, as we noted in Chapter 3. Reduced investment in receivables adds value by allowing investment in more profitable long-term assets and/or reductions in financing costs.

*IMPROVED INTERNAL AND EXTERNAL CREDIT-RELATED INFORMATION* *Internally*, companies have integrated receivables management with inventory management and Enterprise Resource Planning (ERP) systems. ERP systems, sometimes called enterprise systems, help corporate analysts see "the big picture." Illustrating, the SAP R/3 system has a financials module available that includes the accounts receivable and accounts payable functions and a credit control feature that incorporates credit limits and an aging sched-

**Exhibit 5–3**

*The Role of Credit Today*

| Core Functions (Common to All Companies) | Expanded Functions (Some Companies) | Emerging Opportunities (Few Companies) |
|---|---|---|
| Developing Credit Policy | Customer Visits | Inventory Control |
| Collections | Purchasing/Vendor Analysis | Product Development |
| Credit Analysis | Banking Relationship | Accounts Payable |
| Setting Credit Terms | Analysis (Beyond Credit) | Working Capital Management |
| Management Reporting | Billing/Invoicing | MIS Data Warehouse |
| Accounts Receivable | Developing Credit-Scoring Model | Cash Forecasting |
| Legal Bankruptcy | Global Risk Management | Profit/Loss Responsibilities |
| Cash Application | | |

ule (covered in Chapter 6). It also has a sales and distribution module that includes order transactions, providing information necessary for determining receivables balances. It appears that the role of the credit function is expanding, according to Wheeland (see Exhibit 5–3). Notice that billing and invoicing improvements, which cut down on disputes and delays that often stand behind late payments, as well as inventory control and working capital management, are being addressed by credit managers in some companies. *Externally*, expanded and readily accessible information has made it easier to assess creditworthiness and exposure to credit problems.

*ELECTRONIC COMMERCE* Value increases come as the order-to-cash cycle shrinks due to electronic, automated procedures:

- Electronic ordering
- Electronic credit application and evaluation
- Electronic credit approval notification
- Electronic order filling instructions
- Electronic shipment documents, including advance shipping notices
- Electronic processing of shipments received information
- Electronic invoicing
- Electronic payment initiation and execution

And, to start the next cycle more quickly:

- Electronic cash application

The result is that financial markets are becoming more efficient, and some of the outstanding trade credit that is specifically linked to financial market inefficiency will be permanently eliminated. As noted in the following Focus on Practice box, credit markets are becoming more efficient and effective as bank and nonbank service providers facilitate all phases of the cash-to-cash cycle.

## MANAGING THE CREDIT FUNCTION

**Credit administration** involves the establishment of credit policy, along with planning, organizing, directing, and controlling all aspects of the credit function. **Credit policy**

# FOCUS ON PRACTICE

## *Information Technology Transforms Credit Decision Making*

Manual processing of credit decisions is becoming a thing of the past for many companies. A software company called eCredit.com is offering businesses the ability to process credit applications in seconds, rather than days, by completely automating credit. Not only will the software indicate whether and how much credit to extend, it will also help increase revenue by assisting the sales and marketing departments. Here's how: Ryder System Inc. gets 70,000 to 75,000 credit requests a year and about $2.5 billion in revenue from commercial truck leasing. Before using eCredit software, a salesperson would quote a price and book a tentative order, but after doing a credit analysis, Ryder might decide to withdraw the offer or ask for "credit enhancement" (some type of backup for the buyer's payment potential). Now, Ryder uses software that allows information to be pulled from Dun & Bradstreet credit data files, which is then fed into a risk-rating model that scores the buyer on a scale between 1 and 5, and the rating determines a "risk-based price." High-risk customers are charged higher prices to compensate for the increased probability their accounts could deteriorate to a "bad debt"—and this evaluation occurs within minutes. This evaluation process occurs so quickly that it allows deals to be finalized at the point of sale. Ryder estimates its "enhanced revenues" from using this software to be $6 million a year. Graybar Electric Company uses the software to cut credit application turnaround from 2–3 days to 2–3 minutes. Other users have found that fewer customers cancel their orders, now that credit approval and credit line assignment occur so quickly. Companies find that their credit processes and customer data are now more standardized and consistent across various departments and divisions. Credit automation software permits the credit function to become a revenue-generating activity, by being placed at the front of the sales cycle (see diagram below). Sales reps don't have to waste time trying to make sales that will later be rejected by the credit department. This occurs when sales leads are prequalified. The next step in the development of credit automation may be the pairing of the financing function with the credit extension. In this way, the seller would not have to carry receivables, as a third-party financing source would be located and established by the software. eCredit's founder, Dr. Venkat Srinivasan, believes that companies will increasingly outsource receivables to the point where receivables investment by nonfinancial companies will be very small.

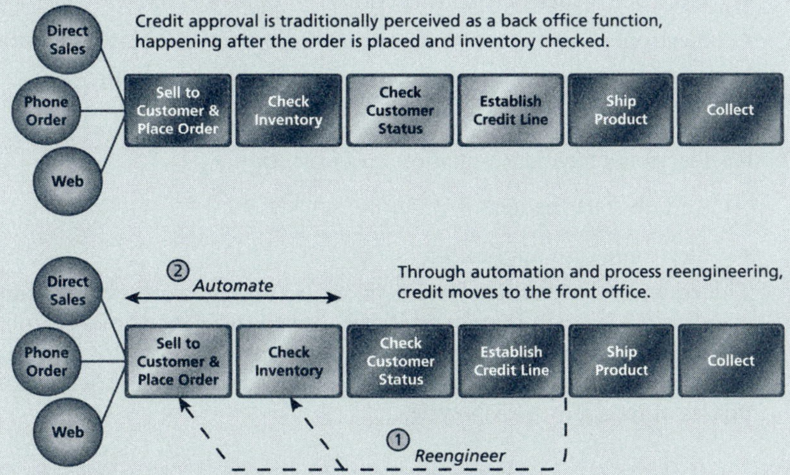


*Sources:* Kelly Cundiff, "Moving Credit into the Front Office: How Credit Risk Scoring Drives Revenues," *Business Credit* (March 2003), pp. 53–54; Kit Ludwig, "E-Biz Applications Boost Credit and Sales," *Collections & Credit Risk* (January 2003), pp. 40–41; and Samuel Greengard, "Standardizing Thorny Credit Decisions," *Business Finance* (September 2003). Accessed online 12/22/2003 at www.businessfinancemag.com.

includes credit standards, setting credit limits, the company's approach to credit investigation, credit terms, and the collection activity. In the remainder of this chapter and in Chapter 6, we will investigate each of these dimensions of credit policy. We begin by defining the credit decision process. The **credit decision process** begins with the marketing contact with potential customers and ends with the approval or disapproval of credit and setting of the credit limit for approved customers. In between these points are credit investigation, contacts with the customer for information, finalizing written documents such as security agreements, establishment of the customer's credit file, and financial analysis. We return to the financial analysis aspects of credit extension in a later section of this chapter.

## Overview of Credit Granting

We can gain a greater appreciation for the credit-granting process if we know the sequence of events initiated when a business makes a credit sale. The activity flowchart in Exhibit 5–4 shows a typical credit sequence. On receipt of orders from a new customer or from an existing customer with insufficient preapproved credit, the seller must determine whether to launch a credit investigation of the buyer. If it investigates, the seller might consult various information sources and tailor the depth of the investigation to the size of the account.[8] Assuming credit is approved, the credit department must also set a credit limit for a new customer, which is the maximum amount of outstanding purchases that the customer may have at any point in time. Items ordered are then shipped. For domestic customers, credit is granted "on open book," which involves sending an invoice and establishing an account receivable for this new customer. (A trade acceptance, which is a more formal credit agreement, is usually set up for foreign customers.[9]) When the buyer receives the goods or services, he or she inspects and checks the order and sets up an account payable to represent the amount owed. The buyer determines whether to pay within the cash discount period if that is part of the seller's credit terms.

If the cash discount is not taken, payment will probably be made near the end of the allotted credit period, typically 30 or 60 days. When the buyer does remit payment, usually with a check, the seller wants to deposit that amount and credit the account receivable quickly: Quick deposits mean quicker availability of funds at the bank. Crediting the account, a process known as **cash application**, frees up that amount of the credit limit for additional orders from this customer—some of which might be backlogged awaiting credit approval. Of course, if the customer does not pay within the credit terms, the seller will send warning letters and follow other predetermined collection procedures, possibly involving an outside collection agency. As long as payments are received in a timely matter, the credit-granting process is a continuous flow of alternating orders and payments.

## Analysis of a Single Credit Extension

Before detailing credit limits and credit terms, we show how one can make proper **credit-granting decisions**. We assume that a complete credit analysis has already been conducted

---

[8] When information cost is large relative to prospective account size and profitability, the manager can use a decision tree approach to credit investigation and granting, as demonstrated originally by Mehta and in more detail by Vander Weide and Maier (see citation in the end-of-chapter references). Stowe (see the end-of-chapter references) presents an integer programming model to make the joint decision of how much information to gather and whether credit should be approved. This work has been expanded on in Scherr (1992; also 1996) in an appealing and logical fashion (see the end-of-chapter references). An elegant spreadsheet solution to this problem is in Ogden and Sundaram (see the end-of-chapter references).

[9] Acceptances and other international credit management differences are covered in more detail in Chapter 6.

Exhibit 5–4

*The Credit-Granting Sequence*

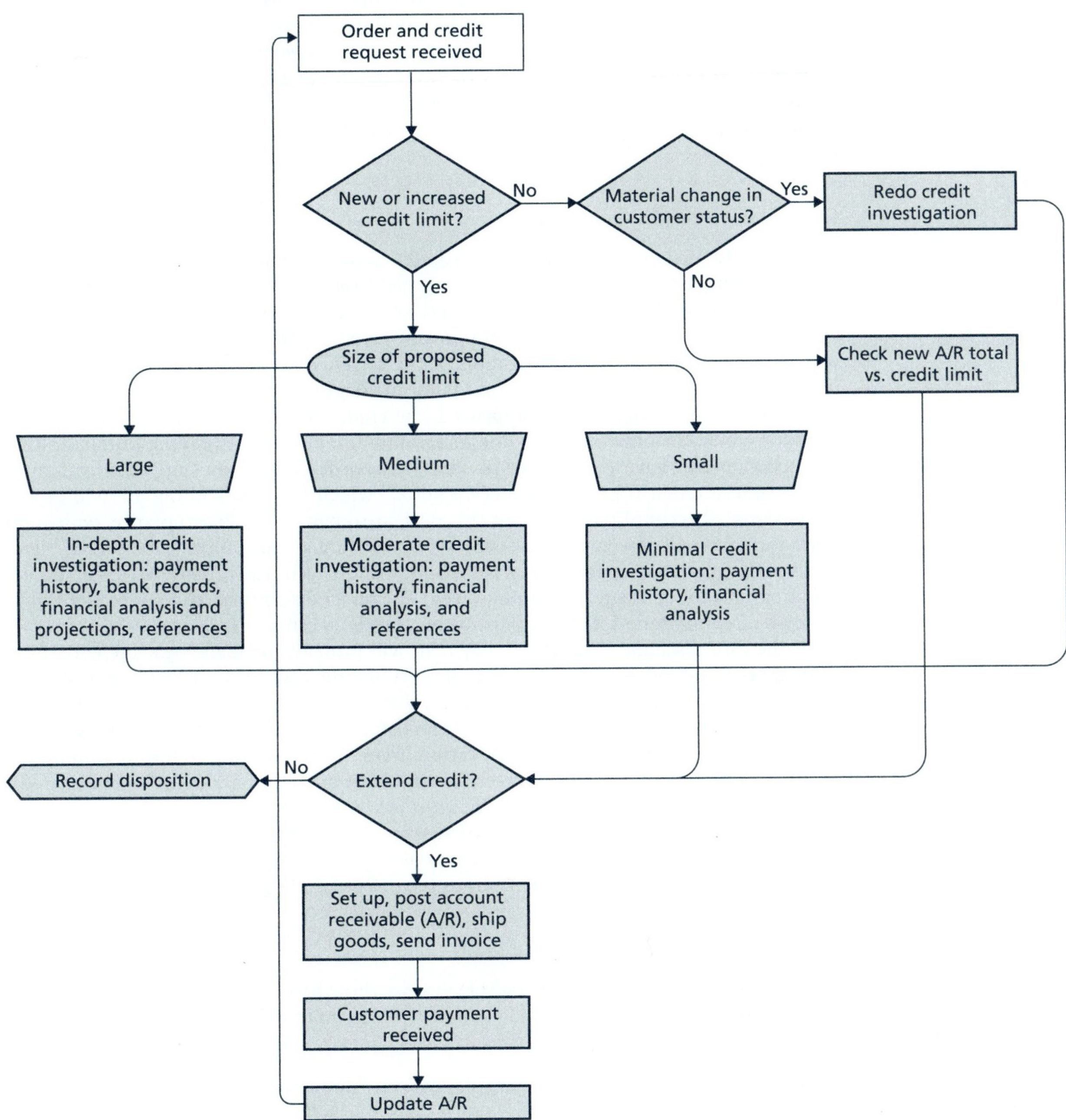


on each credit applicant. Our analysis will be simplified, in that it shows the value effect of a one-time credit extension to a single customer. We use the valuation tools from Chapter 3 to model the credit-granting decision for an *individual customer* and defer our discussion of overall credit policy to Chapter 6.

The definition of a **credit extension** is to allow deferred payment to a customer. The acceptability of a single credit extension is evaluated by calculating the NPV of the potential credit sale. If the credit manager knew that the payment would be made, and exactly when, the NPV model (on a before-tax basis) would be simple. Survey evidence indicates that U.S. firms will vary credit terms to get large new accounts. Too, many U.K. firms will vary terms to attract a new customer and occasionally to help a customer that is experiencing cash flow problems.[10] For a one-time credit extension and assuming that the credit administration and collection expenses occur at the end of the credit period, the model shown as Equation 5.1 would apply.

$$NPV = \frac{S - EXP(S)}{1 + iCP} - VCR(S) \tag{5.1}$$

Where: $NPV$ = net present value of the credit sale
$VCR$ = variable cost ratio, per \$1 of sales
$S$ = dollar amount of the credit sale
$EXP$ = expenses for credit administration and collection, per \$1 of sales
$i$ = daily interest rate
$CP$ = collection period for the sale

In words, we start with the present value of the sales revenue, then subtract the present value of the direct credit-related costs, and then subtract the variable costs (labor and raw material). What is left is the NPV of the credit sale. The discount rate $i$ is the required return on capital, expressed on a per-day basis ($k/365$). The annual rate of interest, here a nominal interest rate $k$, should be the opportunity cost of funds tied up in receivables. Often, the annual rate companies use is the company's weighted-average cost of capital.

The decision rules would then be as follows:

If $NPV > 0$ Extend credit
If $NPV = 0$ Probably extend credit (marginally acceptable)
If $NPV < 0$ Do not extend credit

Illustrating, credit analyst Mike Grossman is considering a \$1,000 order from a new customer, which would be eligible for his company's standard 30-day credit terms. The company's weighted-average cost of capital is 13 percent. He assembles the following information:

$$VCR = 0.70$$
$$S = \$1,000$$
$$EXP = 0.04$$
$$i = 0.13/365 = 0.0003562$$

Substituting these values into Equation 5.1, we compute the NPV of the proposed credit sale to be

$$\begin{aligned} NPV &= \frac{\$1,000 - 0.04(\$1,000)}{1 + (0.0003562 \times 30)} - 0.70(\$1,000) \\ &= \$949.85 - \$700 \\ &= \underline{\underline{\$249.85}} \end{aligned}$$

[10] Paul Wetherhill, "B2B Credit: A Strategic Tool for the New Economy," *Credit Management (U.K.)* (November 2000), pp. 38–40.

Because the NPV is positive, the credit sale would add to shareholder value and should be made. Once the sale is made, the focus shifts to processing customer payments and monitoring payment status of outstanding receivables.

## Importance of Cash Application

Accuracy and speed are both important in crediting customers' accounts. Ideally, the credit and accounts receivable system will be automated to better accomplish both of these objectives. The system should enable the credit manager to:

- determine whether invoices are being paid according to terms of sale.
- know the status of unshipped, previously approved orders.
- determine the payment status and total exposure of any customer.
- enter updated data into a centralized database from remote locations.
- route the order approval instructions quickly if a customer's economic or payment status changes.

One of the greatest advantages of an automated system is cash application: the ability of that system to credit outstanding customer invoices quickly and accurately. The open account system requires that each check or electronic payment received be carefully applied against the specific invoices being paid. Application of payments includes getting the necessary information, identifying the payor, applying the payment to invoice(s), updating the permanent file, and generating reports. Electronic commerce is advancing to the point where more companies and their banks can send and receive electronic payments with remittance information attached. The latter information enables automatic updating of customer accounts without manual rekeying and visual inspection.

*GATHERING INFORMATION* The source of information for applying payments might be punch cards returned with payments, a computer-generated printout of open items, or a listing of open items on a PC, terminal, or microfilm/microfiche reader.

*PAYOR IDENTIFICATION* A check's bottom line, called the magnetic ink character recognition (MICR) line, is one way of identifying the payor. The MICR line contains the check number, the bank's Federal Reserve transit routing number, the bank account number, and the amount of the check. Another way of identifying the payor is through an enclosed document called a **remittance advice**, which might be a prepunched card or tear-off section from the invoice, containing customer account number, date, and dollar amount. Sometimes the customer simply includes a memo indicating what is being paid. Later in the chapter we cover EDI transmission of advices.

*CASH APPLICATION* Companies using MICR line data have a cross-reference from the MICR numbers to the customer's account number. Companies using prepunched cards or tear-off invoice segments feed these into the appropriate optical scanning devices to read payment amounts into a computer. A preset routine, called an algorithm, checks amounts paid against outstanding amounts owed to apply the payment and credit the account accurately. If no match is made, the computerized report will signal the need for manual processing by a receivables clerk.

We have completed our overview of management of the credit function. We turn our attention to the question of whether credit should be offered by a company and a deeper analysis of the major aspects of a credit policy.

## MANAGING THE CREDIT POLICY

We have seen that there are valid reasons for companies to offer credit in certain situations. We now consider whether it is in the best interests of a specific company to offer credit terms, and if so, what aspects of a credit policy should be set. Our discussion includes credit standards, credit terms, the credit limit, and the use of expert systems to assist in these areas.

### Should We Extend Credit?

To a large extent, a company will follow the lead of other firms in its industry when deciding whether to sell on credit. What is less clear is the form and extent of the credit offer. Rather than detailing a checklist of factors to consider, we illustrate the complexity of the decision, as well as several of the interrelated factors involved, by viewing three separate decision situations (see "Focus on Practice" box).

These situations illustrate the practical and theoretical factors in the credit-offering decision. Market imperfections, mentioned earlier in the chapter, provide the main theoretical impetus for offering credit terms to potential customers.

### Credit Policy Components

There are four major components of credit policy: credit standards, credit terms, the credit limit, and collection procedures. In this section, we briefly define these components; each is developed in greater detail in the following sections.

*DEVELOPMENT OF CREDIT STANDARDS* The profile of the minimally acceptable creditworthy customer defines the selling business's **credit standards**. Based on financial analysis and nonfinancial data, the credit analyst determines whether each credit applicant exceeds the credit standard and thus qualifies for credit. Credit extension for marginally acceptable customers may be for a much smaller dollar amount, for a short probationary period, or might need to be backed up by collateral or a bank's standby letter of credit, which guarantees the bank will pay invoices up to a predetermined dollar amount if the customer does not pay. The latter substitutes the creditworthiness of the bank for that of the customer buying on credit in the event of a payment default.

*CREDIT TERMS* The credit period, stipulating how long from the invoice the customer has to pay, and the cash discount (if any) together comprise the seller's credit terms. A company's credit terms are usually very similar to that of other companies in its industry.

*CREDIT LIMIT* If credit is extended, the dollar amount that cumulative credit purchases can reach for a given customer constitutes that customer's **credit limit**. The customer periodically pays for credit purchases, freeing up that amount of the credit limit for further orders. Almost 60 percent of firms in the Credit Research Foundation's 1999 survey indicated that, if initial orders are small relative to the seller's business conditions, blanket approval may be given for orders below a specified dollar amount (for 25 percent of the sellers, that amount was $1,500)—the remaining firms will not ship to a new customer without a credit investigation. Twenty-seven percent of respondents use agency ratings to map into a credit limit. The two primary determinants of the amount of a customer's credit limit are requirements for the supplier's products and the ability of the customer to pay its debts. The latter factor is based primarily on the customer's recent payment record with the seller and others and a review and analysis of the customer's most recent financial statements. About 30 percent of companies inform their customers of the amount

## FOCUS ON PRACTICE

**Should a Retailer Offer an In-House Credit Card?** A retailer might choose to offer its own in-house credit card, allow only the use of bank cards (MasterCard, VISA, etc.), or allow the use of either. Retailers' negative experience with their own credit cards in recent years has pushed them away from reliance on in-house ("private label") credit cards.[11] The key tradeoff for department stores has been the additional sales stimulus of credit versus the "back office" cost of running the in-house credit department. A major uncertainty has been whether customers will buy more or less merchandise if allowed to use a bank card as opposed to the retailer's credit card. Specifically, is J.C.Penney's or Dillard's customer traffic increased and customer loyalty enhanced when many of the target customers possess their credit cards? Answers to such questions are difficult to pinpoint without experimenting.

**Should Receivables Be Sold to a Factor?** Credit department costs can be eliminated and cash advances received by selling receivables to a company specializing in such purchases. Called **factors**, these companies buy receivables from the firm at a discount from face value, possibly giving the selling firm a cash advance on the anticipated collections. Usually the receivables are bought on a **nonrecourse** basis, meaning that the factor now bears the risk of nonpayment. Mian and Smith find that economies of scale in credit-granting and credit-collection functions explain why small firms (especially those with sales below $5 million) commonly outsource credit to factors. Canterbury Belts, Inc., which sells to 6,000 small specialty stores, estimates that it would have to hire between 12 and 15 people to do the credit processing presently done by its factor. Asselbergh finds, using a sample of Belgium firms, that less liquid companies, those with longer collection periods, those with high capital spending needs, and those with unbalanced product portfolios (thus with higher business risk) tend to use factors.[12] Smith and Schnucker note that firm-specific investment by a seller in a trade relationship *lessens* the use of factoring, as the seller protects that investment by offering flexible payment terms to a financially troubled buyer. They also find that the use of factoring *increases* when information and monitoring costs increase, as in two different cases: when a product line is customized (the factor can assess its value better than the buyer), and with geographically dispersed buyers and few repeat sales (due to the high information and monitoring cost for individual sellers in such cases).[13]

**How Should the Credit Activity Be Organized?** Manufacturers selling durable goods such as automobiles and farm machinery often decide to set up their credit activity as a captive finance subsidiary. This arrangement separates the financing arm of the company from the selling arm. Advocates claim this enhances efficiency and increases the overall debt capacity of the company. The General Motors Acceptance Corporation would rank as one of the largest banks in the United States in total assets were it a bank. Although company founder Henry Ford disdained financing cars, Ford Motor Credit Corporation extends so much credit that it now has the highest loan loss ratio of any finance subsidiary. Ford credit executives cite the increase in sales as the major advantage of the subsidiary arrangement, countered by the possibility of large loan losses in a recessionary environment as the chief shortfall. Nationally, surveyed credit executives believe that the debt capacity of the total company (parent plus subsidiary) is higher when the credit area is separate, and they generally argue that sales are higher as well.[14] Mian and Smith find evidence that large firms, especially those with rapidly growing receivables, are more likely to establish captive finance subsidiaries. They attribute this to economies of scale in assessing credit risk. They also document an increase in financial flexibility for companies establishing these subsidiaries.[15]

---

[11] "Retailers Tiring of Involvement with Credit Cards," *Investor's Business Daily* (April 16, 1990), p. 33.

[12] See Asselbergh, cited in the end-of-chapter references.

[13] See Smith and Schnucker, cited in the end-of-chapter references.

[14] For executives whose companies had established captive finance subsidiaries, there was uniform agreement regarding the increased debt capacity. For a matched group of companies that had not organized the credit function separately, however, the main reason cited for not doing so was "no real benefits derived" from setting up a subsidiary. See the Roberts and Viscione article, cited in the end-of-chapter references, for more on their survey conclusions.

[15] Mian and Smith (1992), cited in the end-of-chapter references.

of the credit limit. Four of five credit executives use credit limits for most of their customers.[16]

*Collection Procedures* Detailed statements regarding when and how the company will carry out collection of past-due accounts make up the company's **collection procedures**. These policies specify how long the company will wait past the due date to initiate collection efforts, the method(s) of contact with delinquent customers, and whether and at what point accounts will be referred to an outside collection agency.

Having established a basic understanding of credit policies, we are ready to launch into a deeper and more comprehensive discussion of the first three topics in the context of the manager's credit-granting decision. Collections are analyzed as part of Chapter 6.

## The Credit-Granting Decision

Deciding whether and how much credit to give customers involves four distinct steps: developing credit standards, gathering necessary information about customers, applying credit standards, and setting credit limits. Decisions should be consistent with the credit policy.

*Developing Credit Standards* The minimum standards a customer must meet to be extended credit are usually based on the **five C's of credit**: character, capital, capacity, conditions, and collateral. *Character*, thought to be the most important criterion, refers to moral uprightness, integrity, trustworthiness, and quality of management. Willingness to pay is tested when times are bad and there is pressure to compromise one's integrity. Past payment records and insights from a customer's existing suppliers are often all the information the credit analyst has on which to base an assessment. *Capital* refers to net worth, or the difference between total assets and total liabilities. It measures the cushion with which the business exists, or how much it has in assets over and above what is necessary to pay creditors. The seller should not place too much confidence in this figure, however, because in a liquidation the assets would generally be sold for less than the amount shown on the books. *Capacity* is the ability to repay debts when due, as measured by the company's ability to generate cash flows. This often includes a subjective analysis of the borrower's management and future outlook, both in normal and pessimistic economic conditions. Critical evaluation of the borrower's projected cash budget and most recent statement of cash flows is instrumental here. The general economy and industry environment, as well as the reason for the loan request, comprise the *conditions*. Some of the specific issues the credit analyst should raise involve economic analysis, as seen in Exhibit 5–5. The last consideration, and least important for the trade credit situation, is collateral. Assets pledged as security to back up a credit sale or loan are called *collateral*. The creditor holds claim to these assets in the event the borrower does not pay and the creditor must sell them to make up for amounts owed but not collected. Although it would be rare to hold collateral on trade credit, receivables held on the books are often held as collateral for bank loans.

Although the five C's provide a framework for developing credit standards and for credit investigation, this framework does not give any guidance as to the exact credit standards that would maximize shareholder value. Furthermore, the framework does not specify how much information should be gathered, nor does it indicate when to reject applicants. Setting credit standards is one of the most difficult decisions a credit manager

[16] Besley and Osteryoung (1985); these findings were confirmed in Beranek and Scherr (1991) and Ricci (1999), who further finds that 39% of firms set credit limits for all of their customers (see citations in the end-of-chapter references). The other statistics are from Credit Research Foundation, "Current Trends in the Practice of Credit Review Policies and Limits for Good Accounts" (August 1999).

### Exhibit 5–5

*Useful Questions for Assessing Credit Conditions*

1. At which stage of the business cycle—expansion, peak, recession, trough—are we? How does the customer relate to it?
2. Does the customer's business track the business cycle, or does it fluctuate so much as to move independently? Does it change direction before (lead) or after (lag) the business cycle?
3. What is the anticipated lifespan of the customer's industry cycle, and at what stage is it now? Is there serious overcapacity? Is industry activity tapering off?
4. Is the customer in a new product business that is subject to booms or busts?
5. What is the customer's main business, and how does it relate to the industry cycle?
6. Is the industry function performed by the customer one that will endure, or is the customer's role losing ground?
7. Are industry consolidations taking place?
8. What are the distinct risk characteristics of each of the customer's business segments? What must the customer do well to succeed?
9. At what stage of the business cycle is the customer most strongly affected? How is the customer's performance affected by those cyclical pressures?
10. What is the customer's historic ability to weather recession?

*Source:* Adapted from P. Henry Mueller, "What Every Lender Should Know About Economics," *Journal of Commercial Bank Lending* (December 1978); reprinted in William W. Sihler, ed., *Classics in Commercial Bank Lending* (Philadelphia: Robert Morris Associates, 1981), pp. 47–56.

must make; trial and error or setting smaller credit limits for riskier applicants are two ways to resolve the inherent difficulty. Existing NPV modeling attempts are for a single order only, but estimates of default risk and payment timing may be expected to improve over time—meaning that future orders become relevant to the initial credit decision (Scherr, 1996).

After setting credit standards, the credit executive must determine a risk classification system and then link individual customer evaluations to the credit standards. This system has three components: a listing of risk classes, description of the types of customers that fit each class, and the credit policy for each class.

A customer that is large and has an impeccable credit record would be assigned to the top rating class; a customer in a volatile industry but with good payment practices would be assigned to the second class; and a high-risk, financially weak customer would be assigned to the lowest class. Top-class customers are low risk and would be allowed to order even large dollar amounts without credit approval, as long as the outstanding balance did not exceed the credit limit. (The 1999 Credit Research Foundation survey evidence indicates that only 17 percent of sellers have a policy in place to restrict maximum credit exposure for good customers, regardless of perceived risk—and only one-half of those restricting customers have a definable dollar amount for their restriction, which is typically $5 million.) Bottom-class customers, being high risk, would be forced to provide a payment guarantee (possibly through a bank letter of credit) or would not receive any credit and would be required to provide cash on delivery or even cash before delivery. For all classes except the lowest, credit approval might be automatic for small orders.

*Gathering Necessary Information* Available information should be gathered to help evaluate credit applicants up to the point where the cost of additional information exceeds the decision-making benefit offered by having that information. Information sources include credit reporting agencies, credit interchange bureaus, bank letters, references from other suppliers, financial statements and other applicant-supplied data, and field data provided by sales representatives.

**Credit reporting agencies**, most notably D&B, are the major source of credit information. D&B provides computer (including e-mail), fax, mail, or telephone access to many of its products, including its "Business Information Reports." D&B maintains files on more than 20 million North American firms and an additional 36 million outside North America; it also offers an investigation service that can provide credit managers with information on almost any company. It now has files on companies in 200 countries. An example of an electronic Business Information Report (eBIR) is shown in Exhibit 5–6. This product sells for approximately $20. Note the "Payments Reported" section, which shows speed of payment (whether the customer has taken a discount, has been prompt or slow), the dollar amount of high credit extended, dollar amounts either presently owed or past due, selling terms, and the date of the last sale. The PAYDEX score of 36 is a payment index showing that only 36 percent (about 1/3) of its payments are made within credit terms. A score of 80 is considered very good, and scores above 85 are rare. Further explanation of the PAYDEX score is given in Exhibit 5–7. Also notice the "Banking" section, which can provide average balances, present balances, or both (stated in terms such as "middle five figures," which might be $60,000), size of bank credit line or loans outstanding, whether borrowing is secured or unsecured, and how these amounts will be repaid. By evaluating all the information in the Business Information Report, the credit manager can assess whether the customer is already overextended on bank credit, the degree of lateness in its payments to other sellers, and other significant legal or operating risks that might affect the ability of the customer to repay credit purchases.

When available in some reports, D&B also provides a useful credit rating. The first part of the rating, the estimated financial strength, consists of a number and letter or two letters and is based on rateable net worth. The rating's second part—a number from 1 to 4—represents D&B's composite credit appraisal of the business. The latter score is helpful to the credit manager for account risk classification purposes. A rating of CB2, for example, suggests the company's estimated financial strength is between $125,000 and $199,999, with a "good" overall credit appraisal (see the last section of Exhibit 5–7 for a legend explaining these categories). If a rating is 3A3, the latter 3 indicates a "fair" payment performance. About 27 percent of businesses surveyed by the Credit Research Foundation in 1999 use a matrix of credit reporting agency ratings to assign a credit line to business customers. Kallberg and Udell (2003) find that D&B data adds value beyond what the credit analyst could discern by using financial statements alone, although they used a very limited set of five solvency ratios and a variable to capture dividend paying behavior. The reason given for the small number of financial ratios is that firms are very reluctant to divulge income statement data to D&B. The PAYDEX score was the most critical discriminator between failed and nonfailed firms in their analysis. Wilson, Summers, and Hope (2000), using U.K. credit report payment behavior data, also find that this data adds new and valuable information to corporate failure prediction models and can be used to accurately predict future payment behavior for trade creditors.

D&B also provides more than 100 products and services with different levels of analysis and content. For example, every 60 days, it publishes the *Dun & Bradstreet Reference Book of American Business*, which includes summary information on more than three million businesses in the United States, Puerto Rico, and the Virgin Islands. It tells you a company's line of business, its location, and telephone number, as well as unresolved public filings, including suits, liens, judgments, or bankruptcy proceedings. When available, it provides a company's estimated financial strength and composite credit appraisal. D&B also publishes *Industry Norms and Key Business Ratios*, which is a database of nearly one million public and private companies in over 800 lines of business with calculated financial norms and ratios.

Exhibit 5-6

*Dun & Bradstreet Reports*

## Business Information Report



ATTN: **John Q. Public** Report Printed:

**Business Summary**

**Gorman Manufacturing Company, Inc**
**492 KOLLER STREET**
**SAN FRANCISCO, CA 94110**

D&B's Credit Limit Recommendation NEW!
**How much credit should you extend to this business?**
Learn More Try now for **FREE**

Do not confuse with other Gorman companies, this is a fictitious company used by D&B for demonstration purposes.
This is a headquarters location. Branch(es) or division(s) exist.

| | |
|---|---|
| **Telephone:** | 650 555-0000 |
| **Manager:** | LESLIE SMITH |
| **Year started:** | 1965 |
| **Employs:** | 110 (100 here) |
| **Financial statement date:** | DEC 31 2000 |
| **Sales F:** | $19,683,736 |
| **Net worth F:** | $3,160,644 |
| **History:** | CLEAR |
| **Financing:** | SECURED |

| | |
|---|---|
| **D-U-N-S® Number:** | 80-473-5132 |
| **SIC:** | 2752 |
| **Line of business:** | COMMERCIAL PRINTING |
| **D&B Rating:** | -- |
| **D&B PAYDEX®:** | |

**12-Month D&B PAYDEX: 36**
When weighted by dollar amount, payments to suppliers average 72 days beyond terms.

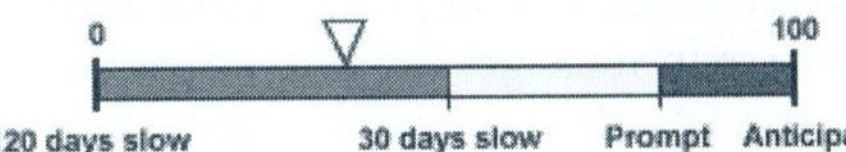


Based on trade collected over last 12 months.

**Special Events**

05/17/2002
On Mar 26, 2001 the subject experienced a fire due to an earthquake. According to Leslie Smith, president, damages amounted to $35,000 which were fully covered by their insurance company. The business was closed for two days while employees settled personal matters.

**Summary Analysis**

**D&B Rating:--**

The blank rating symbol should not be interpreted as indicating that credit should be denied. It simply means that the information available to D&B does not permit us to classify the company within our rating key and that further enquiry should be made before reaching a decision. Some reasons for using a "-" symbol include: deficit net worth, bankruptcy proceedings, lack of insufficient payment information, or incomplete history information. For more information, see the D&B Rating Key.

Below is an overview of the company's rating history since 04/04/01:

| D&B Rating | Date Applied |
|---|---|
| -- | 04/04/01 |

The Summary Analysis section reflects information in D&B's file as of May 20, 2002.

## Customer Service

If you have questions about this report, please call our Customer Resource Center at 1.800.234.3867 from anywhere within the U.S. If you are outside the U.S. contact your local D&B office.

*** Additional Decision Support Available ***

Additional D&B products, monitoring services and specialized investigations are available to help you evaluate this company or its industry. Call Dun & Bradstreet's Customer Resource Center at 1.800.234.3867 from anywhere within the U.S. or visit our website at www.dnb.com.

## History

The following information was reported **05/17/2002**:

**Officer(s):** LESLIE SMITH, PRESIDENT
KEVIN J HUNT, SEC-TREAS

**DIRECTOR(S):** THE OFFICER(S) and Corporate details under investigation.

Corporate details under investigation.

Business started 1965 by Leslie Smith and Kevin J Hunt.

LESLIE SMITH born 1926. Graduated from the University of California, Los Angeles, CA, in June 1947 with a BS degree in Business Management. 1947-65 general manager for Raymor Printing Co, San Francisco, CA. 1965 formed subject with Kevin J Hunt.

KEVIN J HUNT born 1925. Graduated from Northwestern University, Evanston, IL in June 1946. 1946-1965 was general manager for Raymor Printing Co, San Francisco, CA. 1965 formed subject with Leslie Smith.

---

**AFFILIATE:**
The following is related through common principals, management and/or ownership. Gorman Affiliate Ltd, San Francisco, CA, started 1965. Operates as commercial printer. Intercompany relations: None reported by management.

## Corporate Family

**The following list is updated monthly.**

Click below to buy a Business Information Report on that family member.
For more details on the Corporate Family, use D&B's Global Family Linkage product.

**Global Ultimate:**

| Gorman Co. Inc. | London, UK | DUNS # 81-478-5122 |
|---|---|---|

**Domestic Ultimate:**

| Gorman International Inc. | San Diego, CA | DUNS # 81-478-5122 |
|---|---|---|

**Parent:**

| Gorman Brothers Inc. | San Diego, CA | DUNS # 81-478-5122 |
|---|---|---|

**Headquarters:**

| Gorman Co. Inc. | San Francisco, CA | DUNS # 81-478-5122 |
|---|---|---|

*continued*

**Subsidiaries:**

| | | |
|---|---|---|
| Gorman Co. Inc. | San Francisco, CA | DUNS # 81-478-5122 |
| Gorman Co. Inc. | San Francisco, CA | DUNS # 81-478-5122 |
| Gorman Co. Inc. | San Francisco, CA | DUNS # 81-478-5122 |
| Gorman Co. Inc. | San Francisco, CA | DUNS # 81-478-5122 |
| Gorman Co. Inc. | San Francisco, CA | DUNS # 81-478-5122 |
| Gorman Co. Inc. | San Francisco, CA | DUNS # 81-478-5122 |

More than 25 subsidiaries are available for this business.
For the complete list, use D&B's Global Family Linkage product.

---

**Branches:**

| | | |
|---|---|---|
| Gorman Co. Inc. | San Francisco, CA | DUNS # 81-478-5122 |
| Gorman Co. Inc. | San Francisco, CA | DUNS # 81-478-5122 |
| Gorman Co. Inc. | San Francisco, CA | DUNS # 81-478-5122 |
| Gorman Co. Inc. | San Francisco, CA | DUNS # 81-478-5122 |
| Gorman Co. Inc. | San Francisco, CA | DUNS # 81-478-5122 |
| Gorman Co. Inc. | San Francisco, CA | DUNS # 81-478-5122 |

More than 25 branches are available fo this business.
For the complete list, use D&B's Global Family Linkage product.

## Business Registration

CORPORATE AND BUSINESS REGISTRATIONS PROVIDED BY MANAGEMENT OR OTHER SOURCE

The Corporate Details provided below may have been submitted by the management of the subject business and may not have been verified with the government agency which records such data.

**Registered Name:** Gorman Manufacturing Company, Inc.

**Business type:** CORPORATION
**Corporation type:** PROFIT
**Date incorporated:** MAY 21 1965
**State of incorporation:** CALIFORNIA
**Filing date:** MAY 21 1965
**Registration ID:** testcase102

**Common stock**
Authorized shares: 200
Par value:

**Where filed:** SECRETARY OF STATE/CORPORATIONS DIVISION, SACRAMENTO, CA

## Operations

05/17/2002

**Description:** Commercial printing specializing in advertising posters, catalogs, circulars and coupons.

ADDITIONAL TELEPHONE NUMBER(S): Facsimile (Fax) 512 794-7670.

Has 200 account(s). Net 30 days. Sells to commercial concerns.

Nonseasonal.

**Employees:** 110 which includes partners. 100 employed here.

**Facilities:** Rents premises in a one story cinder block building.

**Location:** Central business section on well traveled street.

**Branches:** Subject maintains a branch at 1073 Boyden Road, Los Angeles, CA.

## SIC & NAICS

**SIC:**
Based on information in our file, D&B has assigned this company an extended 8-digit SIC. D&B's use of 8-digit SICs enables us to be more specific to a company's operations than if we use the standard 4-digit code.

The 4-digit SIC numbers link to the description on the Occupational Safety & Health Administration (OSHA) Web site. Links open in a new browser window.

27520000 Commercial printing, lithographic

**NAICS:**
323110 Commercial Lithographic Printing

## D&B PAYDEX

The D&B PAYDEX is a unique, dollar weighted indicator of payment performance based on up to 266 payment experiences as reported to D&B by trade references.

**3-Month D&B PAYDEX: 23**
When weighted by dollar amount, payments to suppliers average 111 days beyond terms.

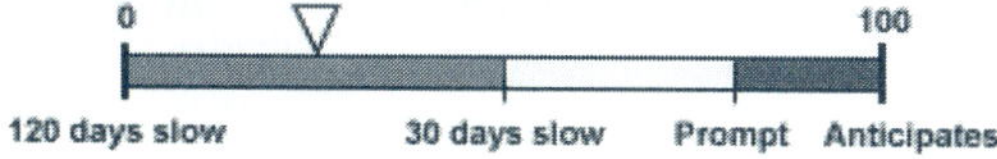


Based on trade collected over last 3 months.

**12-Month D&B PAYDEX: 36**
When weighted by dollar amount, payments to suppliers average 72 days beyond terms.

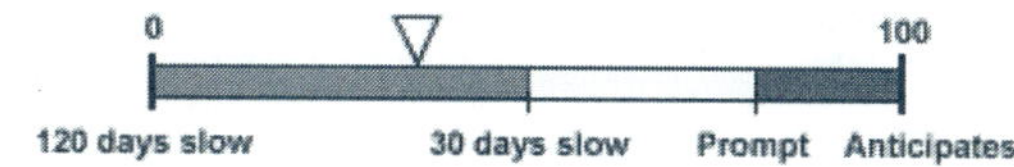


Based on trade collected over last 12 months.

When dollar amounts are not considered, then approximately 13% of the company's payments are within terms.

## Payment Summary

The Payment Summary section reflects payment information in D&B's file as of the date of this report.

Below is an overview of the company's dollar-weighted payments, segmented by its suppliers' primary industries:

| | Total Rcv'd (#) | Total Dollar Amts ($) | Largest High Credit ($) | Within Terms (%) | Days Slow <31 (%) | 31-60 | 61-90 | 90> |
|---|---|---|---|---|---|---|---|---|
| **Top industries:** | | | | | | | | |
| Misc business service | 7 | 319,250 | 250,000 | 94 | - | 1 | 5 | - |
| Misc equipment rental | 4 | 345,000 | 200,000 | 42 | - | - | 58 | - |
| Misc business credit | 3 | 302,500 | 200,000 | 1 | - | 99 | - | - |
| Mfg telephone equip | 2 | 2,050,000 | 2,000,000 | - | 2 | - | 98 | - |
| Nonclassified | 2 | 1,020,000 | 1,000,000 | 98 | - | 2 | - | - |
| Custom programming | 2 | 270,000 | 250,000 | 7 | - | 93 | - | - |
| Computer system desgn | 1 | 1,000,000 | 1,000,000 | - | - | - | 100 | - |
| Mfg malt beverages | 1 | 500,000 | 500,000 | 100 | - | - | - | - |
| Mfg alum extrud prdts | 1 | 400,000 | 400,000 | - | - | - | - | 100 |
| Natural gas distrib | 1 | 250,000 | 250,000 | - | 100 | - | - | - |
| OTHER INDUSTRIES | 87 | 1,380,750 | 100,000 | 35 | 16 | 14 | 32 | 3 |

*continued*

| **Other payment categories:** | | | |
|---|---|---|---|
| Cash experiences | 0 | 0 | 0 |
| Payment record unknown | 15 | 240,500 | 100,000 |
| Unfavorable comments | 21 | 701,250 | 250,000 |
| **Placed for collections:** | | | |
| With D&B | 0 | 0 | |
| Other | 119 | N/A | |
| Total in D&B's file | 266 | 8,779,250 | 2,000,000 |

The highest **Now Owes** on file is $2,000,000
The highest **Past Due** on file is $1,000,000

Dun & Bradstreet has 266 payment experiences in its file for this company. For your convenience, we have displayed 80 representative experiences in the PAYMENTS section.

## Payment Details

### Detailed payment history

| Date Reported (mm/yy) | Paying Record | High Credit ($) | Now Owes ($) | Past Due ($) | Selling Terms | Last Sale Within (months) |
|---|---|---|---|---|---|---|
| 03/02 | Disc | 10,000 | 500 | 0 | | 2-3 mos |
| | Ppt | 30,000 | 0 | 0 | N90 | 2-3 mos |
| | Ppt | 7,500 | 1,000 | 0 | N10 | 1 mo |
| | Slow | 50,000 | 50,000 | 50,000 | N30 | 6-12 mos |
| | Slow 30 | 15,000 | 0 | 0 | N30 | 1 mo |
| | Slow 60 | 200,000 | 50,000 | 50,000 | | 1 mo |
| | Slow 60 | 20,000 | 5,000 | 5,000 | N30 | 2-3 mos |
| | Slow 60 | 2,500 | 0 | 0 | | 1 mo |
| | Slow 90 | 200,000 | 100,000 | 5,000 | | 1 mo |
| | Slow 60-90 | 2,500 | 1,000 | 1,000 | | 2-3 mos |
| | Slow 90 | 2,500 | 2,500 | 2,500 | N30 | 2-3 mos |
| | Slow 90 | 500 | 500 | 500 | N30 | 1 mo |
| | Slow 60-120 | 2,500 | 750 | 750 | | 1 mo |
| | Slow 30-120 | 2,500 | 2,500 | 2,500 | | 1 mo |
| | Slow 160 | 1,000 | 500 | 500 | N30 | 6-12 mos |
| | (016) | 250,000 | 250,000 | 250,000 | | 1 mo |
| | Placed for collection. | | | | | |
| | (017) | 100,000 | 100,000 | 100,000 | | 6-12 mos |
| | Placed for collection. | | | | | |
| | (018) | 40,000 | 20,000 | 20,000 | | 6-12 mos |
| | Placed for collection. | | | | | |
| | (019) | 20,000 | 20,000 | 20,000 | | 1 mo |
| | Placed for collection. | | | | | |
| | (020) | 7,500 | 2,500 | 2,500 | | 1 mo |
| | Placed for collection. | | | | | |
| | (021) | 5,000 | 500 | 500 | | 4-5 mos |
| | Account in dispute. | | | | | |

| | | | | | | |
|---|---|---|---|---|---|---|
| | (022)<br>Placed for collection. | 5,000 | 5,000 | 5,000 | | 1 mo |
| | (023)<br>Placed for collection. | 5,000 | 5,000 | 5,000 | | 1 mo |
| | (024)<br>Placed for collection. | 2,500 | 2,500 | 2,500 | | 6-12 mos |
| | (025)<br>Placed for collection. | 1,000 | 1,000 | 1,000 | | 1 mo |
| | (026)<br>Placed for collection. | 1,000 | 1,000 | 1,000 | | 1 mo |
| | (027)<br>Placed for collection. | 1,000 | 1,000 | 1,000 | | 1 mo |
| | (028)<br>Placed for collection. | 1,000 | 1,000 | 1,000 | | 1 mo |
| | (029)<br>Placed for collection. | 500 | 500 | 500 | | 1 mo |
| | (030)<br>Placed for collection. | 500 | 500 | 500 | | 1 mo |
| | (031)<br>Placed for collection. | 500 | 500 | 500 | | 1 mo |
| | (032)<br>Placed for collection. | 500 | 500 | 500 | | 1 mo |
| | (033)<br>Placed for collection. | 250 | 250 | 250 | | 2-3 mos |
| | (034)<br>Placed for collection. | 100 | 100 | 100 | | 2-3 mos |
| | (035)<br>Placed for collection. | 100 | 100 | 100 | | 2-3 mos |
| | (036)<br>Placed for collection. | 0 | | | Sales COD | 2-3 mos |
| 02/02 | (037)<br>Credit refused. | 20,000 | 20,000 | 20,000 | | 6-12 mos |
| 01/02 | Slow 90 | 500 | 500 | 500 | N30 | 2-3 mos |
| | (039)<br>Placed for collection. | 20,000 | 20,000 | 20,000 | | 6-12 mos |
| | (040)<br>Placed for collection. | 2,500 | 1,000 | 0 | | 2-3 mos |
| 12/01 | Ppt | 100,000 | 65,000 | 0 | Lease Agreemnt | 4-5 mos |
| | Ppt | 75,000 | 40,000 | 0 | N30 | |
| | Ppt | 5,000 | 5,000 | 0 | | 1 mo |
| | Slow 90 | 500 | 500 | 500 | N30 | 6-12 mos |
| | Slow 15 | 500 | 500 | 500 | N30 | 2-3 mos |
| | Slow 15-90 | 80,000 | 80,000 | 80,000 | N30 | |
| | Slow 70-90 | 7,500 | 5,000 | 5,000 | N30 | 2-3 mos |
| | Slow 60-120 | 35,000 | 10,000 | 10,000 | N30 | |
| | (049)<br>Placed for collection. | 10,000 | 10,000 | 10,000 | | |

*continued*

| | | | | | | |
|---|---|---|---|---|---|---|
| | (050) | 10,000 | 10,000 | 10,000 | | 6-12 mos |
| | Placed for collection. | | | | | |
| | (051) | 5,000 | 5,000 | 5,000 | Special Agreemnt | 6-12 mos |
| | Placed for collection. | | | | | |
| | (052) | 5,000 | 5,000 | 5,000 | | 2-3 mos |
| | Placed for collection. | | | | | |
| | (053) | 2,500 | 1,000 | 1,000 | | 6-12 mos |
| | Account in dispute. | | | | | |
| | (054) | 2,500 | 2,500 | 2,500 | | 6-12 mos |
| | Placed for collection. | | | | | |
| | (055) | 2,500 | 250 | 250 | | 6-12 mos |
| | Insufficient funds. | | | | | |
| | (056) | 2,500 | 2,500 | 2,500 | | 6-12 mos |
| | Bad debt. | | | | | |
| | (057) | 1,000 | 1,000 | 1,000 | | 2-3 mos |
| | Placed for collection. | | | | | |
| | (058) | 1,000 | 1,000 | 1,000 | | 6-12 mos |
| | Placed for collection. | | | | | |
| | (059) | 1,000 | 1,000 | 1,000 | | 6-12 mos |
| | Bad debt. | | | | | |
| | (060) | 1,000 | 1,000 | 1,000 | | 6-12 mos |
| | Placed for collection. | | | | | |
| | (061) | 1,000 | 1,000 | 1,000 | | 6-12 mos |
| | Placed for collection. | | | | | |
| | (062) | 500 | 500 | 500 | | 6-12 mos |
| | Placed for collection. | | | | | |
| | (063) | 500 | 500 | 500 | | 6-12 mos |
| | Placed for collection. | | | | | |
| 11/01 | (064) | 20,000 | 20,000 | 20,000 | | 2-3 mos |
| | Placed for collection. | | | | | |
| | (065) | 20,000 | 20,000 | 20,000 | | 1 mo |
| | Placed for collection. | | | | | |
| 10/01 | Ppt | 30,000 | 0 | 0 | N30 | 1 mo |
| | Ppt | 20,000 | 20,000 | 15,000 | N10 | 1 mo |
| | Ppt | 2,500 | 0 | 0 | | 1 mo |
| | Ppt | 500 | 0 | 0 | | 2-3 mos |
| | Ppt | 0 | 0 | 0 | N10 | |
| | Slow 120 | 100,000 | 75,000 | 7,500 | | 1 mo |
| | Slow 15 | 5,000 | 5,000 | 5,000 | N15 | |
| | Slow 90 | 10,000 | 10,000 | 10,000 | N30 | 1 mo |
| | Slow 90 | 5,000 | 5,000 | 5,000 | N30 | 2-3 mos |
| | (075) | 75,000 | 50,000 | 5,000 | | 6-12 mos |
| | Bad debt. | | | | | |
| | (076) | 20,000 | 20,000 | 20,000 | | 1 mo |
| | Bad debt. | | | | | |
| | (077) | 15,000 | 1,000 | 1,000 | | |
| | Placed for collection. | | | | | |
| 09/01 | Antic | 10,000 | 5,000 | 0 | 1 15 N30 | 1 mo |

| | | | | | | |
|---|---|---|---|---|---|---|
| 06/01 | (079) Placed for collection. | 500,000 | 500,000 | 500,000 | | 4-5 mos |
| 05/01 | (080) Satisfactory. | 50 | 0 | 0 | | 1 mo |

Accounts are sometimes placed for collection even though the existence or amount of the debt is disputed.

Payment experiences reflect how bills are met in relation to the terms granted. In some instances payment beyond terms can be the result of disputes over merchandise, skipped invoices etc.

Each experience shown is from a separate supplier. Updated trade experiences replace those previously reported.

## Finance

**05/17/2002**

**Three-year statement comparative:**

| | Fiscal Dec 31 1998 | Fiscal Dec 31 1999 | Fiscal Dec 31 2000 |
|---|---|---|---|
| Current Assets | 5,735,650 | 6,022,432 | 6,383,778 |
| Current Liabs | 4,521,811 | 4,747,902 | 5,032,776 |
| Current Ratio | 1.26 | 1.27 | 1.27 |
| Working Capital | 1,213,839 | 1,274,530 | 1,351,002 |
| Other Assets | 2,623,143 | 2,754,300 | 2,920,416 |
| Net Worth | 2,838,982 | 2,980,930 | 3,160,644 |
| Sales | 17,685,297 | 18,569,562 | 19,683,736 |
| Long Term Liab | 998,000 | 1,047,900 | 1,110,774 |
| Net Profit (Loss) | 584,077 | 613,280 | 650,077 |

**Fiscal statement dated DEC 31 2000:**

| Assets | | Liabilities | |
|---|---|---|---|
| Cash | 829,185 | Accts Pay | 2,845,063 |
| Accts Rec | 2,020,011 | Bank Loans | 1,012,830 |
| Inventory | 1,670,307 | Notes Pay | 445,200 |
| Other Curr Assets | 1,864,275 | Other Curr Liabs | 729,683 |
| **Curr Assets** | **6,383,778** | **Curr Liabs** | **5,032,776** |
| Fixt & Equip | 2,212,435 | L.T. Liab-Other | 1,110,774 |
| Other Assets | 707,981 | COMMON STOCK | 50,000 |
| | | RETAINED EARNINGS | 3,110,644 |
| **Total Assets** | **9,304,194** | **Total** | **9,304,194** |

From JAN 01 2000 to DEC 31 2000 annual sales $19,683,736; cost of goods sold $15,837,499. Gross profit $3,846,237; operating expenses $3,196,160. Operating income $650,077. Net income $650,077.

Submitted MAY 18 2001 by Leslie Smith, president. Accountant: Johnson, Jordan & Jones CPAs.

**ACCOUNTANT'S OPINION**
A review of the accountant's opinion indicates the financial statements meet generally accepted accounting principles and that the audit contains no qualifications.

*continued*

**BALANCE SHEET EXPLANATIONS**

**OTHER CURRENT ASSETS**
Consist of prepaid expenses and a loan receivable.

**OTHER ASSETS**
Consists of deposits.

**BANK LOANS**
Due to the bank at prime interest rate, are secured by accounts receivable and inventory and will mature in 3 years.

**NOTES PAYABLE**
Due on printing equipment.

**OTHER CURRENT LIABILITIES**
Consist of accrued expenses and taxes.

**LONG TERM DEBT**
Consists of the long term portion of the equipment note.

On May 16, 2002, Diane Tester, CEO, confirmed company name, address, principals, annual sales and operational information using Dun & Bradstreet's Internet-based update method (eUpdate) at www.dnb.com.

## Key Business Ratios

**Statement date:** DEC 31 2000
**Based on this number of establishments:** 24

| **Firm** | | **Industry Median** | |
|---|---|---|---|
| Return of Sales: | 3.3 | Return of Sales: | 3.5 |
| Current Ratio: | 1.3 | Current Ratio: | 1.5 |
| Assets / Sales: | 47.3 | Assets / Sales: | 51.1 |
| Total Liability / Net Worth: | 194.4 | Total Liability / Net Worth: | 155.9 |

## Banking

(05-01) Balances average in a low 7 figure amount. At Dec 31 2000, a low 7 figure was outstanding under short-term lines of credit which are secured by accounts receivable and inventory.

## Public Filings

---

The following Public Filing data is for information purposes only and is not the official record. Certified copies can only be obtained from the official source.

## Judgments

| | |
|---|---|
| **Judgment award:** | **$100** |
| **Status:** | **Unsatisfied** |
| **DOCKET NO.:** | 94CV321 |
| **Judgment type:** | Default judgment |
| **Against:** | GORMAN MANUFACTURING COMPANY, INC |
| **In favor of:** | JOHN SMITH |
| **Where filed:** | CONTRA COSTA COUNTY SUPERIOR COURT/MARTINEZ, MARTINEZ, CA |
| **Date status attained:** | 08/13/1996 |
| **Date entered:** | 08/13/1996 |
| **Latest Info Collected:** | 03/14/2001 |

## Suits

| | |
|---|---|
| **Suit amount:** | **$1,000** |
| **Status:** | **Pending** |
| **DOCKET NO.:** | 96CV123 |
| **Plaintiff:** | JOHN SMITH |
| **Defendant:** | GORMAN MANUFACTURING COMPANY, INC |
| **Cause:** | Civil Rights |
| **Where filed:** | CONTRA COSTA COUNTY SUPERIOR COURT/MARTINEZ, MARTINEZ, CA |
| **Date status attained:** | 08/13/1996 |
| **Date filed:** | 08/13/1996 |
| **Latest Info Collected:** | 02/28/2001 |

| | |
|---|---|
| **Suit amount:** | **$20,000** |
| **Status:** | **Pending** |
| **DOCKET NO.:** | SC19951218 |
| **Plaintiff:** | DUN & BRADSTREET, BETHLEHEM, PA |
| **Defendant:** | GORMAN MANUFACTURING COMPANY, INC |
| **Cause:** | Breach of contract |
| **Where filed:** | KERN COUNTY MUNICIPAL COURT / WEST DISTRICT, BAKERSFIELD, CA |
| **Date status attained:** | 12/18/1995 |
| **Date filed:** | 12/18/1995 |
| **Latest Info Collected:** | 03/12/2001 |

If it is indicated that there are defendants other than the report subject, the lawsuit may be an action to clear title to property and does not necessarily imply a claim for money against the subject.

## Liens

A lienholder can file the same lien in more than one filing location. The appearance of multiple liens filed by the same lienholder against a debtor may be indicative of such an occurrence.

| | |
|---|---|
| **Status:** | **Open** |
| **CASE NO.:** | IN5678 |
| **Type:** | State Tax |
| **Filed by:** | State of Ca-Test match Code |
| **Against:** | Gorman Manufacturing Company Inc |
| **Where filed:** | LOS ANGELES COUNTY RECORDER'S OFFICE, NORWALK, CA |
| **Date status attained:** | 12/14/2001 |
| **Date filed:** | 12/14/2001 |
| **Latest Info Received:** | 12/14/2001 |

| | |
|---|---|
| **Amount:** | **$100** |
| **Status:** | **Open** |
| **CASE NO.:** | inn1234 |
| **Type:** | State Tax |
| **Filed by:** | State of CA- test Mtch Code (unmatched thru SO) |
| **Against:** | Gorman Manufacturing Company, Inc |
| **Where filed:** | LOS ANGELES COUNTY RECORDER'S OFFICE, NORWALK, CA |
| **Date status attained:** | 12/14/2001 |
| **Date filed:** | 12/14/2001 |
| **Latest Info Received:** | 12/14/2001 |

*continued*

| | |
|---|---|
| **Amount:** | **$100** |
| **Status:** | **Open** |
| **CASE NO.:** | IN1234 |
| **Type:** | State Tax |
| **Filed by:** | State of Ca-Test Match Code |
| **Against:** | Gorman Manufacturing Company, Inc |
| **Where filed:** | LOS ANGELES COUNTY RECORDER'S OFFICE, NORWALK, CA |
| **Date status attained:** | 12/14/2001 |
| **Date filed:** | 12/14/2001 |
| **Latest Info Received:** | 12/14/2001 |

---

| | |
|---|---|
| **Status:** | **Open** |
| **CASE NO.:** | inn5678 |
| **Type:** | State Tax |
| **Filed by:** | STATE OF CA- TET MTCH CODE (THRU SO) |
| **Against:** | GORMAN MANUFACTURING COMPANY, INC |
| **Where filed:** | LOS ANGELES COUNTY RECORDER'S OFFICE, NORWALK, CA |
| **Date status attained:** | 12/14/2001 |
| **Date filed:** | 12/14/2001 |
| **Latest Info Received:** | 12/14/2001 |

---

| | |
|---|---|
| **Amount:** | **$10** |
| **Status:** | **Released** |
| **DOCKET NO.:** | test1 |
| **Type:** | County Tax |
| **Filed by:** | Test Record |
| **Against:** | Groman Manufacturing Co Inc |
| **Where filed:** | ORLEANS PARISH DISTRICT COURT, NEW ORLEANS, LA |
| **Date status attained:** | 08/22/2001 |
| **Date filed:** | 06/07/2001 |
| **Latest Info Collected:** | 10/29/2001 |

---

| | |
|---|---|
| **Amount:** | **$10** |
| **Status:** | **Released** |
| **DOCKET NO.:** | s0123 |
| **Type:** | State Tax |
| **Filed by:** | test 3 |
| **Against:** | gorman manufacturing co inc |
| **Where filed:** | ORLEANS PARISH DISTRICT COURT, NEW ORLEANS, LA |
| **Date status attained:** | 08/22/2001 |
| **Date filed:** | 06/07/2001 |
| **Latest Info Collected:** | 10/29/2001 |

---

| | |
|---|---|
| **Amount:** | **$10** |
| **Status:** | **Released** |
| **DOCKET NO.:** | 01-1111 |
| **Type:** | State Tax |
| **Filed by:** | test 2 |
| **Against:** | Gorman Manufacturing co inc |
| **Where filed:** | ORLEANS PARISH DISTRICT COURT, NEW ORLEANS, LA |
| **Date status attained:** | 08/22/2001 |
| **Date filed:** | 06/01/2001 |
| **Latest Info Collected:** | 10/29/2001 |

---

| | |
|---|---|
| **Amount:** | **$10** |
| **Status:** | **Released** |
| **BOOK/PAGE:** | 55/32 |
| **Type:** | County Tax |
| **Filed by:** | test 4 |
| **Against:** | gorman manufacturing co inc |
| **Where filed:** | ORLEANS PARISH DISTRICT COURT, NEW ORLEANS, LA |

| | |
|---|---|
| **Date status attained:** | 08/02/2001 |
| **Date filed:** | 06/01/2001 |
| **Latest Info Collected:** | 10/29/2001 |

---

| | |
|---|---|
| **Status:** | **Open** |
| **FILING NO.:** | 1145279 |
| **Type:** | State Tax |
| **Filed by:** | arizona dept of revenue |
| **Against:** | gorman manufacturing test |
| **Where filed:** | ORLEANS PARISH DISTRICT COURT, NEW ORLEANS, LA |
| **Date status attained:** | 10/30/2000 |
| **Date filed:** | 10/30/2000 |
| **Latest Info Received:** | 06/22/2001 |

---

| | |
|---|---|
| **Status:** | **Open** |
| **FILING NO.:** | 1143348 |
| **Type:** | State Tax |
| **Filed by:** | az dept of economic security |
| **Against:** | gorman manufacturing |
| **Where filed:** | ORLEANS PARISH DISTRICT COURT, NEW ORLEANS, LA |
| **Date status attained:** | 10/24/2000 |
| **Date filed:** | 10/24/2000 |
| **Latest Info Received:** | 06/22/2001 |

**UCC Filings**

| | |
|---|---|
| **Collateral:** | All Inventory including proceeds and products - All Account(s) including proceeds and products - All Chattel paper including proceeds and products - All General intangibles(s) including proceeds and products - and OTHERS |
| **Type:** | Original |
| **Sec. party:** | PEOPLE'S SAVINGS BANK OF BROCKTON, NEW BEDFORD, MA |
| **Debtor:** | TARSAGIAN VICTORIA S. |
| **Filing number:** | 000730 |
| **Filed with:** | SECRETARY OF STATE/UCC DIVISION, PROVIDENCE, RI |
| **Date filed:** | 07/31/2001 |
| **Latest Info Received:** | 09/13/2001 |

---

| | |
|---|---|
| **Collateral:** | All Inventory including proceeds and products - All Accounts receivable including proceeds and products - All Fixtures including proceeds and products |
| **Type:** | Original |
| **Sec. party:** | ABC COMPANY |
| **Debtor:** | GORMAN MANUFACTURING COMPANY, INC |
| **Filing number:** | 123456 |
| **Filed with:** | SECRETARY OF STATE/UCC DIVISION, SACRAMENTO, CA |
| **Date filed:** | 10/05/1998 |
| **Latest Info Received:** | 04/11/2001 |

---

| | |
|---|---|
| **Collateral:** | Equipment - Fixtures |
| **Type:** | Original |
| **Sec. party:** | WELLS FARGO FINANCIAL, EAST PROVIDENCE, RI |
| **Debtor:** | REED ROBERT |
| **Filing number:** | 000758 |
| **Filed with:** | SECRETARY OF STATE/UCC DIVISION, PROVIDENCE, RI |
| **Date filed:** | 08/01/2001 |
| **Latest Info Received:** | 09/13/2001 |

---

| | |
|---|---|
| **Collateral:** | Specified Equipment and products |
| **Type:** | Original |
| **Sec. party:** | XYZ COMPANY |

*continued*

| | |
|---|---|
| **Debtor:** | GORMAN MANUFACTURING COMPANY, INC |
| **Filing number:** | 222222 |
| **Filed with:** | SECRETARY OF STATE/UCC DIVISION, SACRAMENTO, CA |
| **Date filed:** | 10/06/1998 |
| **Latest Info Received:** | 04/11/2001 |

The public record items contained in this report may have been paid, terminated, vacated or released prior to the date this report was printed.

**Government Activity**

**Activity summary**

| | |
|---|---|
| Borrower (Dir/Guar): | NO |
| Administrative debt: | NO |
| Contractor: | YES |
| Grantee: | NO |
| Party excluded from federal program(s): | NO |

**Possible candidate for socio-economic program consideration**

| | |
|---|---|
| Labor surplus area: | N/A |
| Small Business: | YES (2001) |
| Woman-owned: | N/A |
| 8(A) firm: | N/A |
| Minority-owned: | YES (2002) |

The details provided in the Government Activity section are as reported to Dun & Bradstreet by the federal government and other sources.

*Source:* Copyright 2003 by Dun & Bradstreet, a company of The Dun & Bradstreet Corporation, **http://www.dnb.com/us**.

Another major source of information is the network of **credit interchange bureaus**. These bureaus are departments of local credit associations that provide information in the form of "Business Credit Reports" and "Credit Interchange Reports." These credit associations are part of the National Association of Credit Management (NACM), and their reports are available only to NACM members. Major inputs to NACM reports include ledger experience information from NACM members' receivables files, bank information, and some public record information. Optionally, anyone accessing the NACM database can also request data from the Standard & Poor's (S&P) financial statement data on 6,000 publicly held companies and key business facts on more than 30,000 publicly and privately held companies.

*Trade associations* also compile factual trade information from the companies in the association. A trade association is made up of companies in a single industry or in several closely related industries. For an annual fee, subscribers receive a report that summarizes financial data for companies in the association. The Financial Executives Division of the National Retail Merchants Association, for example, publishes annually the financial and operating results of department and specialty stores. Some of the data is split out for department stores versus specialty stores or for stores within a certain size bracket.

Finally, banks are a vital source of credit information. The credit executive can ask a bank officer at his or her bank to check with the customers' major banks to verify customer-supplied information and get loan payment and average deposit balance histories.[17] The customer may or may not be notified at the time it applies for credit that its bank will be consulted, but it is standard procedure to get the customer's permission first.

[17] Banks are restricted in their provision of such information, however. Some banks will not provide this information via fax or phone because of security risks.

Some banks include a permission clause allowing disclosure of such information when a business opens an account, stating that the bank may disclose information about the account's existence and condition to a third party such as a credit bureau or merchant.

Ricci (1999) found that 79 percent of surveyed companies get information from D&B, and most companies get information from the potential buyer as well as part of their credit investigation.

Credit information is not always accurate or timely. The managerial questions asked in the "Focus on Practice" box on page 159 underscore some of the concerns credit executives share.[18]

## Exhibit 5–7

*Dun & Bradstreet Paydex and Rating Score Interpretations*

### D&B Rating Interpretation Table

The US 5A to HH ratings reflect company size based on net worth or equity as computed by D&B. These ratings are assigned to businesses that have supplied D&B with current financial information.

The 1R and 2R ratings categories reflect company size based on the total number of employees for the business. They are assigned to business files that do not contain a current financial statement. For 5A to HH Ratings, the Composite Credit Appraisal is a number between 1 and 4 that makes up the second half of the company's Rating and reflects an overall assessment of creditworthiness. Our creditworthiness assessment is based on both payments and financial stability. In 1R and 2R Ratings, the 2, 3, or 4 creditworthiness indicator is based on analysis by D&B of public filings, trade payments, business age and other important factors. 2 is the highest Composite Credit Appraisal a company not supplying D&B with current financial information can receive.

| Financial Strength | | Composite Credit Appraisal | | | |
|---|---|---|---|---|---|
| Rating | US$ | High | Good | Fair | Limited |
| 5A | 50,000,000 and over | 1 | 2 | 3 | 4 |
| 4A | 10,000,000 to 49,999,999 | 1 | 2 | 3 | 4 |
| 3A | 1,000,000 to 9,999,999 | 1 | 2 | 3 | 4 |
| 2A | 750,000 to 999,999 | 1 | 2 | 3 | 4 |
| 1A | 500,000 to 749,999 | 1 | 2 | 3 | 4 |
| BA | 300,000 to 499,999 | 1 | 2 | 3 | 4 |
| BB | 200,000 to 299,999 | 1 | 2 | 3 | 4 |
| CB | 125,000 to 199,999 | 1 | 2 | 3 | 4 |
| CC | 75,000 to 124,999 | 1 | 2 | 3 | 4 |
| DC | 50,000 to 74,999 | 1 | 2 | 3 | 4 |
| DD | 35,000 to 49,999 | 1 | 2 | 3 | 4 |
| EE | 20,000 to 34,999 | 1 | 2 | 3 | 4 |
| FF | 10,000 to 19,999 | 1 | 2 | 3 | 4 |
| GG | 5,000 to 9,999 | 1 | 2 | 3 | 4 |
| HH | Up to 4,999 | 1 | 2 | 3 | 4 |

*continued*

[18] Information regarding consumer credit scores is from Avery et al., "An Overview of Consumer Data and Credit Reporting," *Federal Reserve Bulletin* (February 2003), pp. 47–73. Available online at **http://www.federalreserve.gov/pubs/bulletin/2003/0203lead.pdf.** For more information, see Robert M. Hunt, "What's in the File? The Economics and Law of Consumer Credit Bureaus," *Business Review, Federal Reserve Bank of Philadelphia* (second quarter, 2002), pp. 17–24. Information on corporate credit reports is from "Dun's Credit Reports, Vital Tool of Business, Can Be Off the Mark," *The Wall Street Journal,* (October 5, 1989), p. A1. Information on small business credit reports, available online from Experian, is contained in Lawrence J. Magid, "Online Credit-Rating Reports are Not Always Credible," *Los Angeles Times* (August 19, 1998), p. 6.

| Rating Classification | | Composite Credit Appraisal | | | |
|---|---|---|---|---|---|
| **Rating** | **Number of Employees** | **High** | **Good** | **Fair** | **Limited** |
| 1R | 10 employees and over | | 2 | 3 | 4 |
| 2R | 1 to 9 | | 2 | 3 | 4 |

| Alternative Ratings Used | |
|---|---|
| INV | Indicates that D&B is currently conducting an investigation to gather information for a new report. |
| DS | Indicates that the information available does not permit D&B to classify the company within our rating key. |
| -- (blank) | The blank symbol should not be interpreted as indicating that credit should be denied. It simply means that the information available to D&B does not permit us to classify the company within our rating key and that further enquiry should be made before reaching a decision. Some reasons for using a "-" symbol include: deficit net worth, bankruptcy proceedings, lack of insufficient payment information, or incomplete history information. |
| ER | Certain lines of business, primarily banks, insurance companies and government entities do not lend themselves to classification under the D&B Rating system. Instead, we assign these types of businesses an Employee range symbol based on the number of people employed. No other significance should be attached to this symbol. ERN should not be interpreted negatively. It simply means we do not have information indicating how many people are employed at this firm. |
| NQ | Not Quoted. This is generally assigned when a business has been confirmed as no longer active at the location, or when D & B is unable to confirm active operations. It may also appear on some branch reports, when the branch is located in the same city as the headquarters. |
| **US Employee Range Designation** | |
| ER1 | 1000 or more employees |
| ER2 | 500 to 999 employees |
| ER3 | 100 to 499 employees |
| ER4 | 50 to 99 employees |
| ER5 | 20 to 49 employees |
| ER6 | 10 to 19 employees |
| ER7 | 5 to 9 employees |
| ER8 | 1 to 4 employees |
| ERN | Not Available |

## D&B Score Interpretation Table

| D&B Score Interpretation Table | |
|---|---|
| **D&B PAYDEX Score** | **Payment Habit** |
| 100 | Anticipate |
| 90 | Discount |
| 80 | Prompt |
| 70 | 15 days beyond terms |
| 60 | 22 days beyond terms |
| 50 | 30 days beyond terms |
| 40 | 60 days beyond terms |
| 30 | 90 days beyond terms |
| 20 | 120 days beyond terms |
| UN | Unavailable |

## FOCUS ON PRACTICE

**Can I Rely on Consumer Credit Information?** An individual consumer's credit scores from the three major consumer credit reporting agencies in the United States—Experian, TransUnion, and Equifax—can vary widely. (According to Experian, a credit report contains "information about a consumer's identity, credit relationships, some court actions, consumer's statements, and previous inquiries into that file" (**http://scorecard.experian.com/**). In the spring of 2003, the Federal Reserve Board of Governors released a study of credit reports. It based its findings on a review of 248,000 credit reports and stated that about 70 percent of consumers had at least one account report with incomplete information. A key gauge used in credit evaluation, "utilization," was impossible to calculate properly for about 30 percent of the open revolving accounts in the sample due to the fact that the credit limit was not reported by the creditor. About 70 percent of the consumers' reports were missing a credit limit for at least one of their revolving accounts.

One auto loan financing company notes that one of these three agencies has consistently much lower scores than the other two. The financing company averages the three agencies' scores to come up with an aggregate score with which to make its credit extension and interest rate decisions.

**Can I Rely on Corporate Credit Reports?** Controlling 90 percent of the commercial credit market, D&B data is vital as an input into many lending or credit-extension decisions. Perhaps due to the large number of reports that must be put together quickly, a significant minority of D&B corporate credit reports were found to be inaccurate or outdated according to a published report in 1990. Some credit reporters working at D&B stated at the time that they were responsible for as many as 20 reports per day. Courts have generally held that D&B is not liable for errors in reports. Much of the information is based on interviews with a company's top officials, which are not checked for accuracy. Some information comes from bankruptcy court proceedings; the rest is estimated, especially when the company refuses to provide information. D&B, working to improve its performance, has instituted a computer system to monitor reporters' performance and, since 1986, has sent copies of its reports to the companies to cut down on errors.

*Applying Credit Standards: Credit Analysis* Once the appropriate information has been gathered, a decision must be made about whether to extend credit to the applicant, and if so, how much to extend. Earlier in the chapter, we gave a general diagram for the credit-granting sequence. Exhibit 5–8 illustrates how one major corporation actually makes its credit decisions. It determines the applicant's risk classification based on financial analysis and trade experience. Although a customer's initial credit limit would be based on this information, the customer's credit limit is periodically reset based on its purchasing patterns. When each new order is received, the risk classification and credit limit help to determine approval. If approved, the order is automatically filled. If the risk classification and credit limit data indicate nonapproval, there is a manual override possibility to allow an exception to be made and the order to be filled anyway.

Credit executives consider both nonfinancial and financial factors in determining whether to extend credit and how much credit to extend. Nonfinancial analysis is primarily concerned with the *willingness* to pay and assesses the *character* of the applicant. Subjective analysis of the lending situation is also involved.

The other four C's, *capital, capacity, collateral,* and *conditions*, are assessed primarily in financial ratio analysis, and address the *ability* to pay. The seller may buy a third-party analysis, such as the D&B report in Exhibit 5–6, do its own analysis, or combine both sources. The objectives of a complete financial analysis are threefold:[19] (1) to assess the

[19] For a good introduction to financial analysis, see Chapters 1–3 of Erich A. Helfert, *Techniques of Financial Analysis, 11th ed.* (Homewood, Ill.: McGraw-Hill Irwin, 2003).

Exhibit 5-8

*Example of Corporate Credit Analysis*

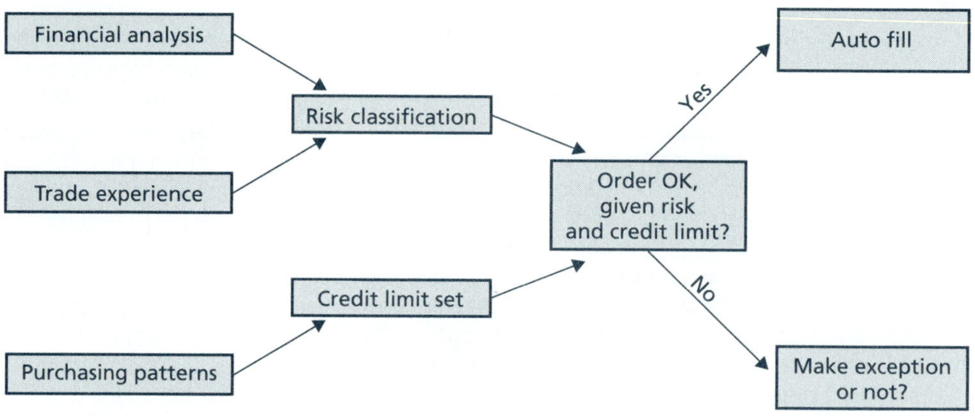


company's financial information, (2) to interpret comparative data regarding the company's competitors and economic conditions, and (3) to conduct financial market analysis to better understand the company's stock price patterns and valuation. The credit analyst is most interested in steps 1 and 2, although sometimes the best early warning of impending bankruptcy or credit rating downgrade is a drop in the company's stock or bond prices. A complete discussion of financial ratio analysis is beyond the scope of this book, but Exhibit 5–9 includes many of the liquidity measures you learned about in Chapter 2 and provides a summary of the major components that would be analyzed. Recent studies have identified some shortcomings in several of these ratios.[20]

The analyst would study both the trends in the company's ratios and how the ratio values compare with those of key competitors or the industry average. The weaknesses of financial ratio analysis are:

- the noncomparability of data for companies using different accounting techniques.
- the difficulty of deciding what the optimum value of a particular ratio should be.
- the ambiguity of whether calculated ratios signal credit approval or nonapproval (for example, KB Toys had trouble paying its vendors in December 2003, but this was due to sales coming in below forecast because of an unusually early price war initiated by Wal-Mart in late September—something that would not be captured in ratios).

Of these weaknesses, the latter is the most troublesome. A financial ratio analysis may reveal an applicant who looks good in certain areas but weak in others. Because financial ratio analysis looks at only one variable at a time (is *univariate*), it does not give a clear signal on whether to approve or reject such a customer. The best advice we can give for the beginning analyst is to watch the trend and then ask probing questions. A *multivariate* model, which simultaneously accounts for several predictor variables, improves the credit analysis.

[20] See Joseph J. Kiernan, "A Model for Working Capital Requirements and Corporate Liquidity Management," *The Credit and Financial Management Review* (Third Quarter 1999), pp. 11–20; Gary W. Emery, "Cash Flow Measures of Credit Risk," *The Credit and Financial Management Review* (First Quarter 1999), pp. 51–62; and Matthew A. Walker, "On the Use of the Cash Conversion Cycle in Working Capital Analysis and Credit Analysis," *The Credit and Financial Management Review* (Fourth Quarter 1998), pp. 30–39.

## Exhibit 5–9

*Key Financial Ratios for Credit Analysis*

| CATEGORY | FINANCIAL RATIO | FORMULA | INTERPRETATION | WARNING SIGNS |
|---|---|---|---|---|
| *LIQUIDITY* | 1. Current Ratio | $\frac{\text{Current Assets}}{\text{Current Liabilities}}$ | Higher is better, indicating increased ability to cover payables. | Watch out for values that are artificially inflated due to slow-moving, perishable, or obsolete inventory. |
| | 2. Net Working Capital | Current Assets − Current Liabilities | Higher is better, indicating increased ability to cover payables. | Must evaluate in light of size of company; also watch out for values that are artificially inflated due to slow-moving, perishable, or obsolete inventory. |
| | 3. Quick Ratio | $\frac{\text{Current Assets} - \text{Inventory}}{\text{Current Liabilities}}$ | Measures the company's ability to pay current obligations with its most liquid assets. More conservative measure than #1 or #2; again higher is better, indicating increased ability to cover payables. | Flow concepts and receivable/payable synchronization must also be evaluated. The quick ratio still does not capture the unsynchronized nature of receipts and disbursements (e.g., situation where only CA are receivables, only CL are payables: if Q.R.= 1, you collect receivables in 60 days but pay payables in 30 days and thus will be unable to meet payables). |
| | 4. Cash Flow to Total Debt | $\frac{\text{Net Income} + \text{Depreciation Expense}}{\text{Short-Term Debt} + \text{Long-Term Debt}}$ *or* $\frac{\text{Net Income} + \text{Depreciation Expense}}{(\text{Current Liabilities} - \text{A/P} - \text{Accrued Expenses}) + \text{Long-Term Debt}}$ | Higher is better, indicating ability to cover debt service (interest and principal repayments). | Low ratio often foreshadows bankruptcy. Company may be able to use large cash and securities position to offset temporary declines in cash flow. |
| | 5. Cash Flow from Operations (CFFO) | Net Income + Noncash Charges + Change in Operating Current Liabilities − Change in Current Assets (or just pull # from Statement of Cash Flows) | Larger amount is better. Gives flow concept of ability of company to generate cash from operations. Much better measure of additions to liquidity than earnings when company is capital-intensive or growing rapidly. | Negative CFFO signals increasing inability to pay payables. Unhealthy firm must fund negative CFFO by selling off assets or issuing new liabilities; so, compare investing and financing cash flows from SCF to give depth to analysis. |

(continued)

**Exhibit 5–9 (continued)**

*Key Financial Ratios for Credit Analysis*

| CATEGORY | FINANCIAL RATIO | FORMULA | INTERPRETATION | WARNING SIGNS |
|---|---|---|---|---|
| *LIQUIDITY CONT.* | 6. Cash Cycle *(CC; also called Cash Conversion Period)* | *CC* = (Days Inventory Held + Days Sales Outstanding − Days Payables Outstanding) *or, equivalently,* *CC* = Inventory Conversion Period + Receivables Conversion Period − Payables Deferral Period | Shorter is better. Longer CC signals more of company's cash being tied up in operations. For any given balance sheet liquidity position, a longer CC indicates more of that liquidity is encumbered by operational working capital needs. Further, the CC indicates the dependence on outside financing. | Any unexpected lengthening of CC is bothersome. Determine the source of deterioration (inventory conversion taking longer, collection experience deteriorating) to evaluate seriousness. Creditor may begin to stretch payables to compensate for longer operating cycle (OC = DIH + DSO). Controlling for size, bankrupt firms are more likely to successfully emerge from bankruptcy with higher receivables-to-total debt and lower payables-to-total debt ratios (Tucker and Moore, 2000). |
| | 7. Cash Turnover | *CT* = 365/CC | Higher is better. Measures how many "turns" company gets on cash tied up in operations. Views cash as inventory. More cash tied up in operations means more nonearning assets. | |
| | 8. Net Liquid Balance | NLB = (Cash + Short-Term Investments) − (Notes Payable + Current Portion of Long-Term Debt) | Larger amount is better. Shows ability of nonspontaneous current assets to cover nonspontaneous (arranged) debts. Is unaffected by collectibility of receivables or salability of inventories. In effect, assumes operating cycle (Accounts Receivable and inventories) is exactly matched by Accounts Payable, and prepaid expenses are exactly matched by accruals. Hypothetically, if CC = 0, how much residual liquidity does the organization have? Offers credit analyst incisive supplement to CC. Gives insight into financial flexibility. | Watch for near-term principal repayments beyond one-year cutoff that separates Current Liabilities from Long Term Debts. This applies to revolving credit agreements, term loans, and bonds. Companies also may use leases in lieu of debt. |
| | 9. Defensive Interval *or* "Time to Ruin" | $\frac{\text{Cash + Short-Term Investments}}{\text{Daily Operating Expenses}}$ *where* Daily Operating Expenses = (COGS + Selling, General, & Administrative Expenses − Depreciation Expense)/365 | Higher is better, showing how long company can pay bills if it has a strike or other disruption of revenue stream, assuming it has lengthy DSI and DSO and has no short-term borrowing capacity. When company has significant untapped short-term borrowing capacity, this measure is overly conservative. Also, the greater the proportion of short-term debt as a percent of total financing, the less protection the cash value represents (interest and principal flows are not included in the measure's formula). | Watch for deterioration in this number as a relative liquidity indicator. When labeled as "time to ruin," it provides an indicator of efficacy of hedging strategies used by the company. If the company's hedges do not significantly increase the "time to ruin," its hedging strategy is flawed. The latter consideration applies to creditors having significant commodity price exposure, foreign exchange transaction exposure, or interest rate exposure. |

| CATEGORY | FINANCIAL RATIO | FORMULA | INTERPRETATION | WARNING SIGNS |
|---|---|---|---|---|
| *DEBT MANAGEMENT & COVERAGE* | 1. Times Interest Earned | EBIT / Interest Expense *or* Operating Profit / Interest Expense | Higher is better. How many times over could we pay the interest expense from the pool of funds available to pay it? If we take 1 − (1/TIE), we get the % reduction in operating profits that company could experience while yet allowing it to cover its interest payments. For example, if TIE is 4, company's operating profit could drop 75% [= 1 −(1/4)] before its ability to pay interest is impaired. Smaller values indicate reduced financial flexibility, increasing risk to other creditors (including trade creditors). | Provides an inaccurate indicator of ability to service debt. It overstates that ability to a degree, in that accrual basis for EBIT recognizes revenue before cash is received and recognizes expenses after cash expenditures for labor and materials are made. Furthermore, lease payments, principal repayments, and preferred dividends are also financing-related cash outflows that must be covered, and these are not included in the formula. On the other hand, capital-intensive companies would see this ratio as understating cash generated and might add back depreciation and amortization to get a better picture of cash generated (yielding EBITDA). May wish to supplement with Cash from Operating Activities (from Statement of Cash Flows) divided by Interest Expense or use a "fixed charges coverage ratio" to include sinking fund payments, lease payments, and preferred stock dividends in the denominator. Also, consider plans for new debt issues. |
| | 2. Long-Term Debt to Capital | Long-Term Debt / Long-Term Debt + Equity *where* Long-Term Debt includes long-term notes and bonds, term loans, and capital lease obligations | Lower is better. We are measuring the percent of long-term financing that is borrowed. More debt reduces financial flexibility and increases risk to other creditors including trade creditors. | This ratio does not account for ability of large operating cash flows to service debt. It is really measuring the relative use of debt and financial flexibility remaining (untapped borrowing capacity) more than the drain on cash flow related to debt service. Short-term debt, operating leases, new/planned borrowing, and preferred stock dividends should be evaluated for more complete analysis. |
| | 3. Total Liabilities to Total Assets | Total Liabilities / Total Assets | Lower is better, for the same reasons indicated for #2. High values show proportionately greater use of borrowed money (less equity), which must be paid back with interest. This ratio is related to the "equity multiplier" that many companies use as a "ROE profit driver" in DuPont modeling: TL/TA =(EM − 1/EM) | Other than the fact that this ratio includes short-term debt, same concerns as for #2. Further comment is necessary because of the linkage to ROE: if the company's "operating return-on-assets" (EBIT/Assets) exceeds the interest rate on debt, it can effectively "lever up" ROE by using more debt. The increased profits and cash flows are offset, from the trade creditors' vantage, by increased financial risk. |

*(continued)*

**Exhibit 5–9 (continued)**

*Key Financial Ratios for Credit Analysis*

| CATEGORY | FINANCIAL RATIO | FORMULA | INTERPRETATION | WARNING SIGNS |
|---|---|---|---|---|
| *PERFORMANCE* | 1. Return on Equity (ROE) | $\frac{\text{Earnings Available to Shareholders}}{\text{Common Equity}}$<br>*where*<br>Earnings Available = (Net Income − Preferred Stock Dividends − Sinking Fund Payments − Amortization) | Higher is better, assuming it does not come with too much risk. This is a profit and performance scorecard for stockholders. It shows the ability to generate profits, from the stockholders' perspective. | Market value added, economic value added, and realized shareholder returns are better performance metrics. Net income is not the same as cash flow. Risk may be high. Prospects for continued profits and cash flows more important from trade creditors' perspective. |
| | 2. Profit Margin on Sales (or Net Profit Margin) | $\frac{\text{Net Income}}{\text{Revenues}}$ | Higher is better. Measures ability to generate profits from each $1 of sales. | Same concerns as in #1. |
| | 3. Return on Total Assets (ROA) | $\frac{\text{Net Income}}{\text{Total Assets}}$ | Higher is better. Measures ability to generate profits from each $1 of assets. Decompose into:<br>NI/TA = NI/Sales × Sales/TA<br>This shows us the two drivers for ROA:<br>1. Profit Margin on Sales (#2 above)<br>2. Total Asset Turnover, which shows us asset use efficiency. Turnover is diminished by overinvestment in fixed assets as well as working capital such as receivables and inventory. | Same concerns as in #1 and #2. |

*Source:* Fair Isaac Corporation, **http://www.fairisaac.com/fairisaac**.

**Credit scoring models** weight variables depending on their helpfulness in discriminating between good and bad applicants, based on past payment histories. A "bad" applicant is one who would likely pay bills in a severely delinquent manner, usually defined as more than 90 days past due. Scoring models are developed with the assistance of computerized statistical techniques such as multiple discriminant analysis. Years of past financial data and ordering and payment data for many customers are used to determine which financial or nonfinancial variables best predict whether a customer will pay bills in a timely fashion. A very simple model might look like the following:[21]

$$Y = 0.000025(INCOME) + 0.50(PAYHIST) + 0.25(EMPLOYMT) \tag{5.2}$$

Where:

$Y$ = the applicant's weighted score

$INCOME$ = the applicant's income for past year

$PAYHIST$ = the number assigned to represent the applicant's past payment habits, with 0 being poor, 0.5 okay, and 1 good

$EMPLOYMT$ = the employment status, with 0 meaning unemployed, 0.5 meaning employed part-time, and 1 meaning employed full-time

If Marcia earned $25,000 last year, has a good payment history, and is employed full-time, her score would be

$$\begin{aligned} Y &= (0.000025 \times \$25{,}000) + (0.50 \times 1) + (0.25 \times 1) \\ &= 0.6250 + 0.50 + 0.25 \\ &= 1.375 \end{aligned}$$

This calculated score would then be compared with a cutoff score to determine whether Marcia should be extended credit. Assuming that past experience has shown that most applicants with a score of at least 1.25 are good credit risks, Marcia would then be extended credit. If her score were close to 1.25, judgment would be applied to determine whether she should be approved, and a score below that signals nonapproval.

*A Sample Credit Scoring Model* A company selling to many small businesses might use the sample credit scoring model shown in Exhibit 5–10. Note the factors that might go into a typical credit score. In this model, the higher the final score, the better one's chances of approval. Perhaps a minimum score of 100 would be necessary for an initial credit extension, and that might be limited to a small dollar amount such as $5,000. Recognize that the actual criteria and how important each criterion is would vary from model to model and lender to lender.

At present, credit scoring is used primarily in consumer (as opposed to industrial) credit evaluation, in which there are a large number of applicants under review at any point in time. Scoring models are being used in bank loans to small businesses, and we saw in the Focus on Practice box on page 134 they are now being used to automate B2B credit approvals and risk analyses. Any time the seller has many potential customers and the dollar amounts involved with most customers is small, using scoring is a necessity. Furthermore, it enables the seller to quantify the risk being taken. The credit score is based on variables such as financial condition, payment history, public filings, financial standing relative to competitors in the industry, years in business, number of employees, revenues, and industry risk. In credit evaluations, credit scoring models are best used as an

[21] The Equal Credit Opportunity Act, as implemented by the Federal Reserve Board's Regulation B, prohibits the use of information on race, gender, or marital status in scoring models, and age can only be used positively (for applicants 62 years and older).

**Exhibit 5–10**

*Sample Credit Scoring Model*

| Characteristics | Attributes with Hypothetical Weights | | | |
|---|---|---|---|---|
| **Credit History Principal(s)** Data: Consumer Credit Report | Major Derog (bankruptcy, collections) −40 pts. | Minor Derog (minor delinquencies) −10 pts. | Satisfactory 15 pts. | No Record 0 pts. |
| **Unused Credit** Data: Consumer Credit Report | ≥ 75% of Available 40 pts. | 74%–33% of Available 30 pts. | < 33% of Available 20 pts. | No Record 0 pts. |
| **Credit History of Business** Data: Business Credit Report | Major Derog −40 pts. | Minor Derog −10 pts. | Satisfactory 15 pts. | No Record 0 pts. |
| **Industry Type** Data: Federal SIC Code | Group A (manufacturing, with hard assets) 50 pts. | Group B 40 pts. | Group C 35 pts. | Group D (high risk, e.g., restaurant) 20 pts. |
| **Available Liquid Assets of Business** (e.g., bank balances) Data: Loan Application | <$6K 15 pts. | $6–$19K 20 pts. | $20–$49K 40 pts. | $50K & up 45 pts. |
| **Net Worth of Principal(s)** Data: Loan Application | <$50K 10 pts. | $50–$100K 20 pts. | $100–$250K 30 pts. | $250K & up 40 pts. |

*Source:* Fair Isaac Corporation, **http://www.fairisaac.com/fairisaac.**

initial screening device to separate out clearly good or clearly bad applicants, leaving the remaining 15–20 percent of applicants for a trained credit analyst to decide. Another possibility is to use the model as a "second opinion," in which case the credit analyst uses the model as a check on his or her decisions. Recommendations that the model and the credit analyst disagree on could be studied further.

Scoring models have tended to focus almost exclusively on capacity and capital. By doing so, they overlook collateral, conditions, and character. Additionally, by focusing on risk, they also overlook expected return.[22] Finally, they do not allow exceptional strengths in one or two areas to offset a glaring deficiency on a variable that is weighted heavily in the scoring equation, even though you might logically expect that applicant to be a good credit risk.

In their 1988 Fortune 500 survey, Smith and Belt found that evaluation of the C's of credit and credit scoring models were the most popular techniques used in the credit-

[22] In response to these weaknesses, a conjoint analysis model has been developed to integrate all of these variables. Conjoint analysis is a multivariate statistical technique that allows the measurement of the joint (simultaneous) effect of two or more independent variables on the ranking of a dependent variable. In this case, the dependent variable is overall loan attractiveness. Although it holds promise, it is too early to tell if this application will be substantially better than present scoring models. For more on the application of conjoint analysis, see the article by Zinkham in the end-of-chapter references.

granting decision.[23] Some firms follow a sequential investigation process, whereby more information is gathered only if the possible benefits of getting that information exceed the cost. Such an approach is strongly advocated because it allows marginal costs and benefits of information gathering to be equated, which, in theory, determines the right amount of information gathering. It will be interesting to see how the amount and type of information collected changes, as a 2002 Credit Research Foundation survey finds that, subsequent to the Enron and WorldCom events, 72 percent of credit professionals are "somewhat more concerned" and an additional 15 percent are "very concerned" about the information they receive regarding their customers' financial condition. Ricci (1999) found that the majority (55 percent) of the surveyed Business Week Global 1000 companies use more than one method, mostly ratio analysis and credit scoring, to decide how to grant credit. Almost 80 percent of the respondents use ratio analysis (at a minimum) in granting credit. Ricci also found that most companies base the scope of the credit investigation on the size of the potential sale, rather than following a uniform or sequential investigation process. A Credit Research Foundation survey in 2003 found that about one-third of business-to-business sellers are using credit scoring at present, although many more are considering its use. Companies with over $1 billion in sales and 7,500 or more active accounts were likely to use scoring. Respondents see scoring as a way to do their job more efficiently, with fewer human resources. A credit decision may be made in minutes, and up to 85 percent of all new account applicants can be assigned a line of credit effectively and accurately—with 75 percent receiving credit and 10 percent being denied credit. This leaves further analysis on only 15 percent of applicants. More Web-based sales will certainly expand the adoption of automated credit scoring. The Foundation foresees eight benefits of credit scoring for the credit department: (1) speed, (2) accuracy, (3) consistency, (4) reduction in bad debts, (5) prioritization of collection activities, (6) reduction of time for risk assessment, (7) identification of potentially fraudulent accounts, and (8) evaluation of overall quality and bad debt exposure for the receivables portfolio.

*EXPERT SYSTEMS* Businesses are increasing their use of rule-based computerized applications of artificial intelligence to credit decision making. The applications are very similar to the credit scoring models we discussed earlier. The credit-granting decision is one area in which pioneering work has been done.[24] The decision-making process of a veteran credit professional is mimicked by a computer in what is termed an **expert system**. The computerized database supporting this system might include complete customer information as well as a model to determine the appropriate credit limit (if any) for each potential customer. An expert system has three main components: a knowledge base that includes all the facts and rules, an "inference engine" that combines the facts and rules to draw a conclusion, and an interface that enables users to determine the reasoning behind the decision and add or update information online. The latter feature enables these systems to be used to train credit analysts. Advantages of the application of expert systems include increased productivity and lower costs of credit evaluation, higher quality of decisions by providing factual support without taking the decision out of the hands of the credit analyst, more consistent application of credit standards, reduced training costs when credit managers retire or leave the company, and use as a training tool to teach newly hired credit analysts how credit evaluation is done by the company. Also, strength in one or more variables may compensate for relatively poor standing on one variable. Here is an example of a credit extension decision rule from an expert system used in a consumer credit card decision model:[25]

---

[23] Smith and Belt (cited in the end-of-chapter references).

[24] See the articles by Srinivasan and Kim (cited in the end-of-chapter references).

[25] Ehsan Nikbakht and Mohammed H. A. Tafti, "Application of Expert Systems in Evaluation of Credit Card Borrowers," *Journal of Managerial Finance 15* (1989), pp. 19–27.

If gross income is equal to or greater than $20,000 and the applicant has not been delinquent and gross income per household member is equal to or greater than $12,000 and debt/income ratio is equal to or greater than 30 percent but less than 50 percent and personal property is equal to or greater than $50,000, then accept application (grant credit).

The expert system offers helpful guidance to the credit analyst, presumably leading to better decisions. Notice how the expert system allows a series of conditional rules to be combined to make the credit extension and credit limit decisions. The credit scoring models prescribed earlier in the chapter are limited to one-step decision making based on weighted averages of financial and nonfinancial data. Computer-aided decisions, particularly based on expert systems, offer the credit analyst significant information-processing capabilities. Human judgment is enhanced, not replaced.

Let's say that we see this applicant as more risky than the typical applicant, based on our assessment of a credit applicant, done with a subjective appraisal of the five C's, financial ratio analysis, or a credit scoring model. How can we conduct risk analysis of the credit extension decision? We return to our credit extension example once again to demonstrate risk analysis.

*Risk Analysis* Our earlier simple analysis of the NPV of a credit extension has implicitly made several key assumptions. First, we assumed that the customer would pay on the 30th day. In reality, the customer may pay early, on time, or late. Second, we have assumed a 100 percent certainty that the payment would be made on that date. The assumed certainty of that payment is unrealistic. Risk can be incorporated into the analysis by utilizing a probability distribution of payment dates. Third, we have assumed that the credit administration and collection expenses do not change regardless of when the customer pays.

Returning to our earlier credit extension decision, we can now make more realistic assumptions to illustrate the incorporation of uncertainty into the NPV analysis.[26] The question we address is, will the probabilities of late payment and need to refer delinquent accounts to a collection agency negate the positive NPV of the credit extension? We will assume that the following collection experience mirrors customers such as the present applicant:

| PAYMENT TIMING | PROBABILITY |
|---|---|
| 30 days or less | 0.40 |
| During second month | 0.40 |
| 3–4 months | 0.15 |
| After four months | 0.05 |
| | 1.00 |

If we assume that payments are received evenly over these time periods, we can closely approximate actual cash inflows by substituting the midpoint of each time frame into the NPV analysis. We also need to know what the credit administration and collection expenses (EXP) would be. Research of past company collection records reveals that variable costs incurred are approximately $40 per month, starting in the second month and extending not beyond the fourth month. After the fourth month, the company gives up hope of ever collecting on its own and refers the account to a collection agency. The collection agency is able to collect $800 on average (based on the fact that it collects nothing on some of the accounts and partial amounts from others), but legal and agency fees consume 25 percent of the amount initially collected. Consequently, on average, the company comes

[26] Risk analysis of this type was first developed in Friedland (see the end-of-chapter references).

out with an added cost of $200 on each referred $1,000 sale. The credit manager insists the company refer accounts for collection, however, to signal other accounts that the company is serious about its collections.

The data are shown in Exhibit 5–11. The net collection cash flow (Column 5) is computed as ($1,000 − *EXP*) except for the referred accounts in the "more than four months" row. For the referred accounts, the company collects $800 but pays the collection agency $200 in addition to the $120 of monthly collection costs it has already incurred (during the second, third, and fourth months). In Column 6, the discounted value of the net collection cash flow is computed, and the variable production cost (which is not discounted because it takes place at time 0) is subtracted. Finally, in Column 7, the expected present value of the credit sale is calculated. The payment probabilities from Column 3 are multiplied by the present values from Column 6 and then added. The expected present value of the credit extension, shown at the bottom of Column 7, is $232.30. Although not as large as the NPV ($249.85) in the certainty analysis done earlier in this chapter, it is still positive, so the credit analyst would recommend that the sale be made. The credit analyst may want to modify the probabilities for new accounts with lower D&B ratings, worse financial ratios, or lower credit scoring values. Studying the payment histories of customers similar to the credit applicant proves helpful in this analysis.

**Exhibit 5–11**

*Credit Extension with Uncertain Collection Experience*

*Background Information:*

| | |
|---|---|
| Terms: | net 30 days |
| Projected Invoice Amount: | $1,000 |
| Variable Production Costs: | $700 |
| Monthly Collection Agency Fee: | $40 |
| Interest Rate (13% annual): | 0.0003562 |

| (1)<br>Collection Period (*CP*, in months) | (2)<br>Collection Period Midpoint (Months) | (3)<br>Payment Probability | (4)<br>Collection Costs (*EXP*) | (5)<br>Collection Cash Flow [$1,000 − (Col. 4)] | (6)<br>Present Value of Credit Sale [P.V. of (Col. 5) − (*VCR*)(*S*)] | (7)<br>Expected Present Value (Col. 3) × (Col. 6) |
|---|---|---|---|---|---|---|
| One month or less | 0.5 | 0.40 | $ 0 | $1,000 | $ 294.69 | $117.88 |
| During second month | 1.5 | 0.40 | $ 40 | $ 960 | $ 244.85 | $ 97.94 |
| 3–4 months | 3 | 0.15 | $ 80 | $ 920 | $ 191.42 | $ 28.71 |
| More than four months | — | 0.05 | $200 + $120* | $ 480** | $(244.65)*** | $ (12.23) |
| | | | Expected NPV of Credit Extension | | | $232.30 |

*This is oversimplified; the $120 actually gets paid out earlier than after five months.

**Assuming it takes one month from the time of referral for the agency to collect.

***The NPV is based on the five-month delay and is calculated as the present value of $480 (= $800 − $320), less the $700 production cost:

$$\$244.65 = \left(\frac{\$480}{1 + (0.0003562)(152)}\right) - \$700$$

*Establishing Credit Limits* Once the decision has been made to grant credit, the manager must determine the maximum credit balance allowable for the customer. Survey evidence provided by Besley and Osteryoung suggests the following are the major reasons companies impose credit limits and identifies "control risk exposure" as the primary reason:[27]

| PRIMARY REASON FOR CREDIT LIMIT | NUMBER | PERCENTAGE |
|---|---|---|
| Control risk exposure | 120 | 53.1 |
| Customer financial position | 63 | 27.9 |
| Experience with customer | 13 | 5.8 |
| Other reasons | 11 | 4.9 |

How high should the credit limit be? Traditional approaches to setting the credit limit include setting it equal to customer need, at 10 percent of customer net worth, at a percentage of high credit reported by other suppliers or banks (as shown earlier on the D&B Business Information Report), or by judgment (gut feeling). Evidence suggests that judgment is used predominantly (53 percent of surveyed firms), with ratio analysis (21 percent), and agency ratings (7.5 percent) the next most frequent—but the latter percentage has increased recently, as noted earlier. Beranek and Scherr surveyed practitioners and found that, for some or all buyers, about 30 percent of sellers believe that the probability of payment decreases with the amount of credit granted. This suggests that credit granting and credit limit setting are simultaneously determined in many cases. Improvement in decision quality and objectivity might be possible through the use of a formula approach; with the advent of computerized expert systems in credit management (covered earlier), the trend is clearly in this direction.[28]

*Credit Terms* Specification of when invoiced amounts are due and whether a cash discount can be taken for earlier payment are known as **credit terms**. The **credit period** is the length of time allowable for payment of the invoice amount. Determining whether a customer has adhered to the stated period is based on the seller's calculation of the actual payment period. Customer payment period usually starts with the invoice date, but in some industries, the clock starts when the customer receives the goods. Sellers usually consider payment to have been made as of the date on which mailed payments are received at the assigned remittance address.[29] The length of the credit period varies by industry and according to product and marketing situation within an industry. Differences are linked to product characteristics as well as market structure and market condition; Exhibit 5–12 highlights some of the factors associated with observed credit terms. Kluger (2001) models optimal credit terms in a competitive pricing model and finds that more rapid-selling goods have shorter terms. Credit terms are often set based on competitive conditions and are rarely challenged, being taken as "givens" to most sellers. Note, how-

---

[27] Besley and Osteryoung also found that a few firms limited the total amount of credit extended to all customers because of a desire to avoid large debt exposure and because of other, more profitable, capital investment alternatives. The balancing of risk and return most often involves controlling individual account exposure.

[28] See Beranek and Scherr (1991; cited in the end-of-chapter references). Use of formulas to set credit lines was stimulated by the publication of "Credit Limits Established by Formula and Computer" by the Credit Research Foundation in 1970. See Wey (1983; cited in the end-of-chapter references) for arguments in favor of a formula-based model. Wey's model included nonfinancial, qualitative variables, applied to both wholesalers and manufacturers, and resulted in absolutely consistent risk classification and credit line recommendations.

[29] Almost 80 percent follow this procedure, according to survey findings in Ricci (1999; cited in end-of-chapter references).

**Exhibit 5–12**

*Factors Affecting Credit Terms*

| FACTOR | INFLUENCE(S) |
|---|---|
| **Market Share and Industry Structure** | |
| Competition | 1. Meet terms of competition. Less need to do so when the seller has a large market share or prices its output measurably lower than the competition.<br>2. Offer longer terms in buyer's market. |
| **Product and Market Characteristics** | |
| Operating cycle | Terms should match length of time for customer to process material, sell it, and collect funds from sale, but in practice, some of that cycle is usually funded by the customer. |
| Type of good | 1. Raw material sold to manufacturers on shorter terms than intermediate or finished goods.<br>2. Terms generally would not exceed sum of manufacturing time plus storage time. |
| Perishability | 1. Short shelf life is associated with rapid turnover and short selling terms.<br>2. Canned goods and processed food products, with longer turnover period, have longer terms (can be stocked in larger quantities by the retailer). |
| Seasonality of demand | 1. When demand is seasonal, longer terms are given during the off-season, as compared with the active sales period.<br>2. Supplier trades off financing costs related to these terms with the more even production this policy allows and the lower storage costs during the off-season. |
| Consumer acceptance | 1. More rapidly selling products accorded shorter terms because of rapid turnover.<br>2. Trademarked goods have higher acceptance and sell more rapidly than unknown brands. |
| Cost and pricing | More expensive items, such as diamonds and jewelry (which have longer operating cycle), given four- to six-month terms; relatively inexpensive items, such as pharmaceuticals, have shorter terms. |
| Customer type | Same product has different terms depending on whether customer is a retailer, wholesale jobber, or institutional buyer (latter gets shorter terms than retailer since purchasing for its own use rather than to resell). |
| Profitability | Higher profit margins allow for longer terms. However, competition may force the seller to offer longer terms even though output prices are depressed, yielding negligible profits or even losses. |

*Sources:* Credit Research Foundation, "Logistics of Payment Terms," (November 2002); and Christie and Bracuti, pp. 386–388, cited in the end-of-chapter references.

ever, that sellers with large market shares and/or a "low price" market position have greater latitude to unilaterally change terms. Large customers may use market power and low gross margins to unilaterally challenge and change the seller's terms to fit their preferences—lengthening the seller's credit period to the buyer's liking. Wal-Mart, Kmart, and Sears have each pursued such a strategy in recent years. In general, though, once terms of sale are established, they are quite slow to change.

Credit terms also include the **cash discount**, the percentage amount that can be subtracted from the invoice if the customer pays within the discount period. Terms of 1/10, net 30 allow a 1 percent cash discount for those paying within ten days; otherwise, the face amount of the invoice is due in 30 days. Credit executives believe that payments on average are more prompt under 1/10, net 30 terms than under net 10 terms, which makes sense given the financial incentive to take the cash discount. A 2001 Credit Research Foundation survey indicates that the discount offered may vary according to the supplier, the buyer's creditworthiness and payment history, order size, and season. Most companies do not allow customers to take unearned discounts, granting only a few days' grace beyond the stated discount period—the median is 5 days offered. That has not stopped many payors from trying, however! In that event, most companies (89 percent) also charge back the discount amount, whereas a minority return the customer's payment, indicating that it is an underpayment. The median amount of unearned discounts recovered is 50 percent, and only 38 percent of firms very aggressively or aggressively pursue unearned discounts. One-half of companies now put customers on credit hold when they violate payment terms, and 89 percent feel that customers are "pushing" suppliers harder today than ever before.[30] Even so, only 43 percent of sellers indicate that more than 75 percent of customers offered cash discounts take them.

Do not confuse cash discounts with trade discounts. Companies will sometimes offer a trade discount, which is a price break given to customers for (1) large quantity purchases or (2) simply because other suppliers offer these concessions. An example of the latter is the industry standard 8 percent trade discount that ladies' apparel makers offer to retailers, which amounts to a permanent price reduction—and illustrates how credit terms can substitute for price changes. Liz Claiborne, Inc., provides a classic example of what may happen when a company without sufficient market power attempts to unilaterally change the discount. Liz Claiborne increased the trade discount to 10 percent in 1990 in an attempt to gain competitive advantage but realized it was not generating sufficient additional sales to cover the 2 percent reduction in its gross margin and returned to the industry's 8 percent discount in late 1995. Trade discounts may be offered instead of or in addition to cash discounts.

In addition to giving an incentive to pay early, credit professionals must decide whether to use the "stick approach" for late payors. Companies are more commonly charging penalties for payments made beyond the credit period. A 2001 Credit Research Foundation online survey indicates 35 percent of firms assess a charge to late paying customers and, of those, 44 percent label it a service charge, 25 percent label it a late payment charge, and 20 percent label it an interest charge. A majority of firms assessing this charge do not assess it to all late paying customers, however. When they do, 23 percent begin to assess charges when the account is 1–5 days past due, 9 percent when it is 6–10 days past due, 15 percent when 11–30 days past due, and the remainder when it is 30+ days past due. About 6 in 10 firms assessing these late fees collect less than half of the fees assessed. Another international survey finds that U.S. and U.K. firms are being paid 14 days late, on average, and Australian firms are paid 11 days late, on average. In all three countries, major and larger firms have lower past-due numbers, as do sellers with relatively long average payment periods for their purchases. Opposite to the latter effect, there is also a domino effect, whereby sellers getting stretched by their customers are also likely to stretch their payables.[31]

U.S. and U.K. surveys of credit executives indicate that most do not believe sales would increase much as a result of lengthening the credit period, and they seem to be more concerned about the effect of a change on the company's profits (perhaps because of changes in bad debt losses) than on sales.

---

[30] Credit Research Foundation, "Logistics of Payment Terms" (November 2002), pp. 8–9.

[31] Pike and Cheung (cited in the end-of-chapter references).

Common credit terms of 2/10, net 30 allow the customer to pay $98 per $100 invoiced amount if the invoice is paid in ten days. The main seller benefits include less short-term borrowing or more short-term investing due to the earlier receipt of cash and a possible increase in sales volume because the cash discount is equivalent to a price reduction. Should a seller offer a cash discount, and if so, how large? The Credit Research Foundation 2001 survey finds that almost 60 percent of companies offer a cash discount, but this may not apply to all customers: 38 percent offer it to less than one-quarter of their customers, and only 51 percent offer it to more than three-fourths of their customers. Analysis of the optimal cash discount has led to the following conclusions:[32]

1. The optimal cash discount depends on a product's variable cost—the lower a product's variable cost, the higher the feasible discount. There is some evidence that companies with lower gross margins are the most likely to reduce or eliminate their cash discount.
2. Logically, the cash discount offered should be based on the offering company's cost of funds; when the opportunity cost of funds changes, so should the cash discount. However, the 2001 CRF survey finds that only 19 percent of companies change the percentage discount in such cases.
3. Both the timing effect of the payments for discount takers and the effect for those not taking the discount must be considered when setting or changing the discount. In the 2001 CRF survey, only 19 percent of sellers had measured the impact of the cash discount on DSO; of these, 53 percent of respondents thought the cash discount reduced DSO by 1–5 days, 24 percent gauged the reduction to be 6–10 days, 13 percent thought 11–15 days, and 11 percent thought 16–20 days. Of firms not measuring discount effects on DSO, two-thirds believe it has improved DSO, 15 percent don't believe it has improved DSO, and 17 percent stated they really don't know.
4. The size of the cash discount should be based on the product's price elasticity of demand or, in this context, how responsive sales are to changes in the cash discount. Rashid and Mitra (1999) demonstrate that price-elastic demand leads to a higher optimal cash discount rate. Only 36 percent of sellers indicated they reevaluate their discount percent as market conditions change, according to the 2001 CRF survey.
5. The higher the rate of bad debt losses being experienced, the higher the optimal cash discount percentage.
6. Computer simulations indicate that the optimal cash discount is between 2 and 3 percent.

Because the cost of *not* taking a cash discount is so high (see Chapter 7), it is surprising that customers do not automatically take the discount. Smith and Sell found that 51 percent of companies surveyed regarding their payment policies always take the cash discount, 40 percent sometimes take the discount, and the remaining 9 percent take the discounts even though they pay after the discount period. We noted above the CRF survey finding that only 43 percent of sellers indicate that more than 75 percent of customers offered cash discounts take them. Credit executives would benefit from a more careful evaluation of their cash discounts. When evaluating the alleged sales-increasing effects of the cash discount, Frantz and Viscione[33] estimated that four of five firms would be more prof-

---

[32] For more on cash discounts, see the Hill and Riener citation in the end-of-chapter references. On elasticity of demand, see Muhammed Rashid and Devashis Mitra (1999), cited in the end-of-chapter references. The optimal discount range of 2%–3% is documented in Stephen Borde and Daniel McCarty (1998), cited in the end-of-chapter references.

[33] "What Should You Do about Cash Discounts?" (cited in the end-of-chapter references).

itable if they eliminated their cash discounts, and Bockhorn and Harris[34] estimated that over half of the farm supply firms they surveyed had unprofitable cash discounts. Other studies also have found some practices that are inconsistent with profit or shareholder wealth maximization, noting that companies generally respond as follows:

- They change the cash discount if competitors do but do not change the cash discount when inflation, interest rates, or economic conditions change (contrary to 1, 2, and 5 above).
- When having higher contribution margins, they are *not* more prone to respond to competitive changes in discounts, but such should be the case.
- Companies do not think a 2 percent cash discount is equivalent to a 2 percent price cut, with the latter thought to have a greater impact on sales.
- When having relatively high levels of receivables on their books, companies are *not* more likely to assess a penalty fee for late payment, but such should be the case.
- When having relatively high levels of receivables, they should reevaluate credit policies more often, but in actuality, there is no apparent relationship between the level of receivables and the frequency or recency of reevaluation.

A recent study addressing cash discounts finds a theoretical basis for observed practices. An empirical study by Ng, Smith, and Smith (1999) finds that cash discounts (1) elicit information about buyer credit quality, in that not taking the discount signals higher risk of customer nonpayment, (2) are for shorter periods when the buyer should be able to sell the merchandise quickly, (3) are for longer periods for international customers (who would need longer to inspect the goods and to arrange payment), and (4) are a higher percentage when product value is fast-changing (due to uncertain demand and the doubtful collateral value).

We have surveyed credit management and its relationship to value maximization. We turn now to a final topic of great importance to the successful execution of credit strategy: the interface with collections and electronic data interchange (EDI).

## RECEIVABLES, COLLECTIONS, AND EDI

The usual distinction between receivables management and the cash collection function is blurring. Credit managers must take part in the structuring of sales terms to take advantage of the advances in EDI. When negotiating price, other factors such as credit terms, purchase volume, gross profit margins, and risk are intertwined. Furthermore, if credit approval is delayed, buyers using EDI purchase orders and just-in-time manufacturing can encounter serious problems. Companies are now able to ship products within two hours of receiving an order, and the seller must be able to handle electronically transmitted orders. Preferably, it can also issue electronic invoices, and be paid electronically, using a bank that is "EDI-capable"(can capture and report remittance detail as well as send and receive electronic payments) so that remittance information that can be automatically read by the seller's accounts receivable system may be bundled with the electronic Automated Clearing House (ACH) or wire payment. The most recent development in EDI is linked to the use of Extensible Markup Language, or XML. This use of Internet forms where numbers are identified by software as being a specific item—such as units ordered—is facilitating the automation of receivables and payables data processing.

One of the trends in receivables management is the use of data transmission to automate the cash application process. The lockbox bank or other lockbox provider captures the MICR line information on each customer's check. Other remittance information that

[34] "Are Cash Discounts in the Farm Supply Industry Profitable?" (cited in the end-of-chapter references).

the seller needs for posting payments to its receivables system is entered manually by the lockbox provider, and then an electronic data file is sent to the seller's computer by the provider. These "electronic remittance services" not only reconcile the company's cash deposits to its posted payments but also speed up the payment posting process and greatly reduce clerical work. Payment files can be uploaded directly into the company's A/R cash application system, updating receivables with no rekeying. The posting of payments occurs in the evening; in the morning, the seller's receivables staff deals with the exception items first by manually applying the items. Because the MICR information received from the bank uniquely identifies the payor, much of the receivables updating can take place automatically. The "hit rate," reflecting the items that automatically apply, may be as high as 95 percent when the seller (1) modifies its billing system, (2) enhances receivables software, and (3) designs highly tailored data capture procedures with its bank or third-party lockbox provider. Ricci (1999) finds that a majority (55 percent) of surveyed Business Week Global 1000 companies did not yet have any of their receivables processes automated.

When its customers are not EDI/EFT capable, the seller may set up an ACH debit program. With the paying company's consent, the collecting company instructs its bank to collect funds from the paying company's bank, much like a check remittance. The seller (and to some extent, the buyer) avails itself of lower costs, improves cash flows, and guarantees payment. The buyer realizes advantages by way of costs savings in accounts payable processing and the reduction in lost checks.

Since more corporate customers are now using "corporate cards" (covered in Chapter 11), sellers are evaluating whether to now accept credit card payments. Interestingly, some buyers are now requesting card payment in order to rack up frequent-flyer miles. Some buyers wish to use cards for payment, even when taking cash discounts—adding another 1.5–3 percent in expense to the transaction.

The Internet is increasingly being used for all aspects of receivables management, including accessing applicant company data and D&B information. Gartner, Inc., estimates that the typical large U.S. company could save $2.7 million per year on its billing costs if all business bills were delivered via the Web. If just half of all disputes were handled online, this would save an additional estimated $1.6 million. Gartner estimates that an average B2B biller could save $10.1 million, in total, for automating the delivery of all bills, disputes, payments, and phone calls (via Web-based self service) to the Internet (Hansen, 2003).

## SUMMARY

Investments in accounts receivable, particularly for manufacturing companies, represent a significant part of short-term financial management. This chapter offered the background concepts necessary for a proper understanding of a company's accounts receivable management. The key aspects of credit policy, credit standards, the credit-granting sequence, credit limits, and credit terms were all detailed. We noted the key sources of information, particularly for corporate credit evaluation. The major tools now being used by businesses to analyze the risk of customer nonpayment—credit scoring, financial ratio analysis, and expert systems—also were profiled. Used in concert, these tools give the analyst clues regarding whether it is necessary to conduct risk analysis of credit extension and credit limit decisions and, if so, how much of a risk adjustment to make.

To recap, much of what we see practiced by credit managers is linked to what competitors are doing, and at times, this conflicts with profitability or shareholder value maximization. Information can clearly offer a competitive advantage to the credit-granting firm. Greater use of automated credit scoring and expert system methods enable the credit manager to improve information processing efficiency and accuracy. Proper incorporation of the time value of money and proper use of net present value techniques can ensure that cost, revenue, and payment likelihood estimates are used correctly to enhance shareholder value in credit-granting decisions.

In the next chapter, we look at an NPV decision-making model that might be used to improve decisions regarding the seller's overall credit policy. That chapter also discusses receivables monitoring and collection and benchmarks for credit performance evaluation.

## USEFUL WEB SITES

| | |
|---|---|
| Center for Research in Electronic Commerce | **http://cism.bus.utexas.edu** |
| Credit Research Foundation* | **http://www.crfonline.org** |
| Dun & Bradstreet | **http://www.dnb.com** |
| Dun & Bradstreet Business Information Report demo | **http://www.dnb.com/demos/ebir/index.asp** |
| ecredit.com | **http://www.ecredit.com** |
| eCFO | **http://www.ecfonet.com** |
| National Association of Credit Management (NACM) | **http://www.nacm.org** |
| NACM Business Credit Magazine online | **http://www.nacm.org/bcmag/bcm_index.html** |
| NACM Certifications | **http://www.nacm.org/education/certification/certification.html** |
| NACM Credit Management Links | **http://www.nacm.org/resource/usefulsites.shtml** |

*The Credit Research Foundation represents a body of knowledge emphasizing the impact and contribution of the credit function on individual businesses and the national economy. Its forums, reports, surveys, and other material provide valuable information on new technique and trends in credit, accounts receivable, and customer administration and practices. Furthermore, they are a resource for the information technology applications to support the credit, accounts receivable, and customer management functions. Membership in The Credit Research Foundation is open to all those invididuals and businesses who have a vested interest in the credit, accounts receivable, and customer financial relationship.

## QUESTIONS

1. What major arguments do credit and marketing professionals make for the extension of trade credit?
2. Is trade credit "free"? Explain.
3. List and explain the four major motives financial theorists have attributed to the extension of trade credit.
4. Regarding cash application:
   a. What is it?
   b. Why should a supplier ensure that cash application is rapid as well as accurate?
   c. Does rapid cash application on a given credit sale shorten the days' sales outstanding for that sale?
5. How do credit managers set credit limits for customers?
6. Why do you think character is considered to be the most important of the "five C's"? How might it be assessed?
7. Summarize the major items offered on a D&B Business Information Report, indicating which one(s) you think is (are) most important for evaluating a new credit applicant.
8. Bank executives consider liquidity and debt ratios to be most important when evaluating a loan applicant. What ratios are they referring to, and why would these be so important in bank credit and trade credit decisions?

**9.** What are credit scoring models? Why do companies that sell to a large number of customers use them?

**10.** A finance company that lends to "high risk" automobile buyers finds the following variables important in classifying default probabilities: time at present residence, prior bankruptcy filing (yes or no), time in present job, monthly income, phone in name (yes or no), prior repossession of item purchased on credit (yes or no), and type of residence (e.g., apartment, rent house, purchasing house). Listing each variable, suggest whether each variable increases (+) or decreases (−) anticipated default risk and how you would evaluate the type of residence in assigning creditworthiness to applicants.

**11.** Summarize the survey findings regarding credit terms and cash discounts.

**12.** Why are credit departments in banks and major corporations implementing expert systems? Indicate what advantages and disadvantages companies that implement such systems might anticipate.

## PROBLEMS

**1.** Nast Stores has derived the following consumer credit scoring model after years of data collecting and model testing:

$$Y = (0.20 \times \text{EMPLOYMT}) + (0.4 \times \text{HOMEOWNER}) + (0.3 \times \text{CARDS})$$

Where: EMPLOYMT = 1 if employed full-time, 0.5 if employed part-time, and 0 if unemployed

HOMEOWNER = 1 if homeowner, 0 otherwise

CARDS = 1 if presently has 1–5 credit cards, 0 otherwise

Nast determines that a score of at least 0.70 indicates a very good credit risk, and it extends credit to these individuals.

**a.** If Janice is employed part-time, is a homeowner, and has six credit cards at present, does the model indicate she should receive credit?

**b.** Janice just got a full-time job and closed two of her credit card accounts. Should she receive credit? Has her creditworthiness increased or decreased, according to the model?

**c.** Your boss mentions that he just returned from a trade association conference at which one of the speakers recommended that length of time at present residence (regardless of homeownership status) be included in credit scoring models. If the weight turns out to be 0.25, how do you think the variable would be coded (i.e., 0 stands for what, 1 stands for what, etc.)?

**d.** Suggest other variables that Nast might have left out of the model, and tell how you would code them (i.e., 0, 1, 2 are assigned to what conditions or variables?).

**2.** Refer to Exhibit 5–10 to answer this question. A business credit applicant has the following profile:

| | |
|---|---|
| Credit History | Minor delinquencies |
| Unused Credit | 30% available |
| Credit History of Business | Satisfactory |
| Industry Type | C |
| Available Liquid Assets of Business | $11,500 |
| Net Worth of Principal | $55,000 |

If the cutoff score for extending credit is a score of at least 100 points, should this applicant receive credit?

**3.** Tricia Velasquez wishes to apply NPV analysis to a newly received order. The company's credit terms are net 45 days. Its opportunity cost of funds is 12 percent. The order dollar amount is $30,000. She finds out from the cost accounting department that variable costs are approximately 65 percent of sales and that incremental credit administration and collection expenses approach 1 percent of sales.

**a.** Assuming that the customer will pay according to the credit terms, with perfect certainty, should Tricia approve the order?

**b.** Assume that further research indicates that payment probabilities and timing for accounts similar to the credit applicant are as follows:

| Payment Timing | Probability |
|---|---|
| Within 45 days | 0.50 |
| 45–60 days | 0.30 |
| 61–90 days | 0.15 |
| Over 90 days | 0.05 |

Assume that payments are received evenly within the above time brackets. The company's experience is that payment received after 90 days occurs only after referral to a collection agency. The agency charges 30 percent of the dollar amount of the invoice. It collects, on average, 65 percent of the invoice amount, about one month after referral. Before the agency referral at day 90, and after the 45 days, the company incurs an additional $125 collection cost every 15 days. Based on the expected NPV of the revised situation, should Tricia recommend credit extension?

**4.** Below is a modified cash flow timeline that includes "invoicing float," the credit period, and "collection float" on mailed payments.

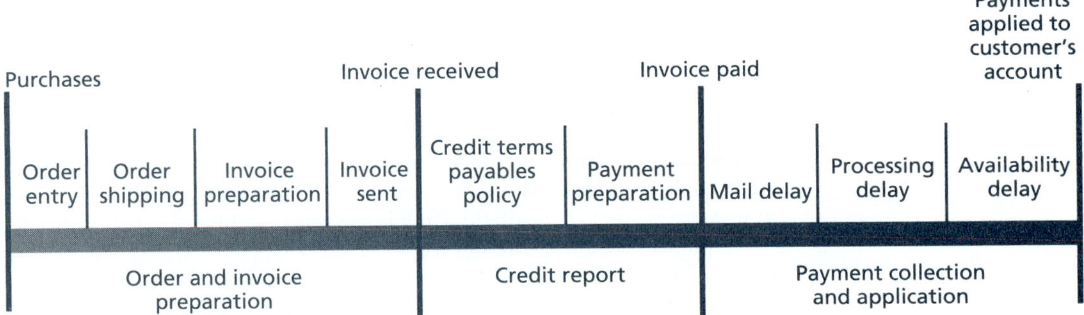


*Source:* © 1997 by The Treasury Management Association. All Rights Reserved. Used with Permission.

Use the following numbers to answer **a** through **d.** Assume that the goods sold are already in inventory before the order placement.

| | |
|---|---|
| *Order & Invoice Preparation:* | |
| Order Entry and Shipping | 5 days |
| Invoice Preparation & Sending ("Invoicing Float") | 3 days |
| *Credit Period:* | |
| Credit Terms | 30 days |
| Added Delay (related to customer's payables policy) | 2 days |
| Payment Preparation | 1 day |
| *Payment Collection & Application:* | |
| Mail, Processing, Availability Delays ("Collection Float") | 6 days |
| Cash Application | 0 days |
| Total Delay from Purchase Communication to Cash Application: | _____ days |

**a.** Calculate the total delay from purchase communication to cash application.
**b.** From the seller's perspective, what part of the total delay represents cash tied up?
**c.** Why should the seller be concerned about the order and invoice preparation delays?
**d.** What fraction of the total delay in your answer to **a** is made up of the credit terms? Based on your answer, comment on the importance of managing all parts of the cash flow time-line.

**5.** Presented below are a balance sheet, income statement, and statement of cash flows for Jordan-Wagner Enterprises. Use this information to calculate the ratios provided in Exhibit 5–9. Using both balance sheets, calculate ratio values for both years for each ratio that has both a balance sheet numerator and denominator. Comment on the trend of each of the balance sheet ratios. Calculate any other ratios in Exhibit 5–9 for which you have adequate data; where necessary, assume the statement of cash flows data will be the same in the coming year as it was in the sample year. Comment on the creditworthiness of Jordan-Wagner Enterprises.

Jordan-Wagner Enterprises Year-End Income Statement

| | |
|---|---|
| Revenues | $16,000,000 |
| Less: Cost of Goods Sold | 9,200,000 |
| Gross Profit | $ 6,800,000 |
| Less: Operating Expenses | 4,000,000 |
| Less: Depreciation | 200,000 |
| Operating Profit | $ 2,600,000 |
| Less: Interest Expense | 300,000 |
| Net Profit before Taxes | $ 2,300,000 |
| Less: Provision for Income Taxes | 450,000 |
| Net Income | $ 1,850,000 |
| Earnings Available for Common Shareholders | $ 1,850,000 |
| Less: Common Stock Dividends Paid | 250,000 |
| Addition to Retained Earnings | $ 1,600,000 |
| Earnings per Share (200,000 shares outstanding) | $ 8.00 |

Jordan-Wagner Enterprises Balance Sheets (Current and Prior Year)

| ASSETS | Current Year | Prior Year | Change |
|---|---|---|---|
| Cash | $ 2,500,000 | $ 1,000,000 | $1,500,000 |
| Short-Term Investments | 1,300,000 | 1,500,000 | (200,000) |
| Accounts Receivable | 1,700,000 | 1,300,000 | 400,000 |
| Inventory | 2,600,000 | 2,100,000 | 500,000 |
| Prepaid Expenses | 900,000 | 900,000 | 0 |
| Total Current Assets | $ 9,000,000 | $ 6,800,000 | $2,200,000 |
| Property, Plant, & Equipment | 7,500,000 | 6,800,000 | 700,000 |
| **Total Assets** | **$16,500,000** | **$13,600,000** | **$2,900,000** |

| LIABILITIES AND OWNERS' EQUITY | Current Year | Prior Year | Change |
|---|---|---|---|
| Accounts Payable | $ 1,600,000 | $ 1,200,000 | $ 400,000 |
| Short-Term Notes Payable | 1,800,000 | 1,300,000 | 500,000 |
| Total Current Liabilities | $ 3,400,000 | $ 2,500,000 | $ 900,000 |
| Long-Term Debt | 3,900,000 | 3,500,000 | 400,000 |
| Total Liabilities | $ 7,300,000 | $ 6,000,000 | $1,300,000 |
| Common Stock at Par Value | $ 200,000 | $ 200,000 | $ 0 |
| Paid-In Capital | 3,600,000 | 3,600,000 | 0 |
| Retained Earnings | 5,400,000 | 3,800,000 | $1,600,000 |
| **Total Liabilities & Equity** | **$16,500,000** | **$13,600,000** | **$2,900,000** |

Jordan-Wagner Enterprises Statement of Cash Flows

| | | | |
|---|---|---|---|
| **Cash Flows from Operating Activities** | | | |
| Net Income | | $1,850,000 | |
| Adjustments to Reconcile Net Income to Net Cash | | | |
| Depreciation | $ 200,000 | | |
| Increase in Accounts Receivable | (400,000) | | |
| Increase in Inventories | (500,000) | | |
| Increase in Accounts Payables | 400,000 | (300,000) | |
| *Net Cash Provided (Used) by Operating Activities* | | | $1,550,000 |
| **Cash Flows from Investing Activities** | | | |
| Capital Expenditures | | $ (900,000) | |
| Decrease in Short-Term Investments | | 200,000 | |
| *Net Cash Provided (Used) in Investing Activities* | | | (700,000) |
| **Cash Flows from Financing Activities** | | | |
| Net Borrowing (Bank Line of Credit Agreement) | | $ 500,000 | |
| Proceeds from Issuance of Long-Term Debt | | 400,000 | |
| Dividends Paid | | (250,000) | |
| *Net Cash Provided (Used) by Financing Activities* | | | $ 650,000 |
| **Net Increase (Decrease) in Cash** | | | |
| Cash—Beginning of Year | | | $1,000,000 |
| Cash—End of Year | | | 2,500,000 |
| *Net Cash Increase (Decrease)* | | | $1,500,000 |

## REFERENCES


Margereta Asselbergh, "Factoring Accounts Receivable Management: An Integrated Approach" (1999). Presented at the annual meeting of the Financial Management Association, Orlando, Fla.

Moshe Ben-Horim and Haim Levy, "Management of Accounts Receivable Under Inflation," *Financial Management* (Spring 1983), pp. 42–48.

William Beranek and Frederick C. Scherr, "On the Significance of Trade Credit Limits," *Financial Practice and Education* (Fall/Winter 1991), pp. 39–44.

Scott Besley and Jerome S. Osteryoung, "Accounts Receivable Management: The Development of a General Credit-Granting Algorithm for Determining Credit Limits Under Funds Constraints" (1984). Presented at the annual meeting of the Financial Management Association, Atlanta, GA.

Scott Besley and Jerome S. Osteryoung, "Survey of Current Practices in Establishing Trade-Credit Limits," *The Financial Review* (February 1985), pp. 70–82.

M. Bockhorn and K. Harris, "Are Cash Discounts in the Farm Supply Industry Profitable?" *Agribusiness* (March 1989), pp. 87–94.

Stephen F. Borde and Daniel E. McCarty, "Determining the Cash Discount in the Firm's Credit Policy: An Evaluation," *Journal of Financial and Strategic Decisions* (Fall 1998), pp. 41–49.

Keith Bradshaw, "Why Higher Interest Rates Haven't Fazed Automakers," *New York Times* (October 10, 1999) section 3, p. 5.

George N. Christie and Albert E. Bracuti, "Credit Executives Handbook" (1986), Lake Success, NY: Credit Research Foundation.

J. Chua. "A Trade Credit Decision Model with Order Size Dependent Credit Risks," Calgary: University of Calgary Working Paper.

Thomas E. Copeland and Nabil Khoury, "A Theory of Credit Extensions with Default Risk and Systematic Risk," *The Engineering Economist* 1 (26) (1981), pp. 35–51.

Marc Deloof and Marc Jegers, "Trade Credit, Product Quality, and Intragroup Trade: Some European Evidence," *Financial Management* (Autumn 1996), pp. 33–43.

Gregory E. Elliehausen and John D. Wolken, "The Demand for Trade Credit: An Investigation of Motives for Trade Credit Use by Small Businesses" (1993), Washington, DC: *Staff Studies 65*, Board of Governors of the Federal Reserve System.

Gary W. Emery, "A Pure Financial Explanation for Trade Credit," *Journal of Financial and Quantitative Analysis* (September 1984), pp. 271–287.

Gary W. Emery, "Positive Theories of Trade Credit," in Yong Kim (ed): *Advances in Working Capital Management*, Vol. 1 (1988), Greenwich, CT: JAI Press, pp. 115–130.

Gary W. Emery and Nandkumar Nayar, "Product Quality and Payment Policy," *Review of Quantitative Finance and Accounting*, 10 (1998), pp. 269–284.

Murray Frank and Vojislav Maksimovic, "Trade Credit, Collateral, and Adverse Selection," *University of British Columbia Working Paper* (1998).

F. Frantz and J. A. Viscione, "What Should You Do about Cash Discounts," *Credit & Financial Management* (May 1976), pp. 30–36.

Seymour Friedland, "Economics of Corporate Finance" (1966), Englewood Cliffs, NJ: Prentice-Hall.

Fay Hansen, "Global E-Commerce Growth," *Business Credit Magazine* (October 2003), pp. 58–60.

Ned C. Hill and Kenneth D. Riener, "Determining the Cash Discount in the Firm's Credit Policy," *Financial Management* (Spring 1979), pp. 68–73.

Ned C. Hill, William L. Sartoris, and Daniel Ferguson, "Corporate Credit and Payables Policies," *Journal of Cash Management* (July/August 1984), pp. 56–63.

Jarl G. Kallberg and Gregory F. Udell, "The Value of Private Sector Business Credit Information Sharing: The U.S. Case," *Journal of Banking and Finance* (March 2003), pp. 449–469.

Yong H. Kim and Joseph C. Atkins, "Evaluating Investments in Accounts Receivable: A Wealth Maximizing Framework," *Journal of Finance* (May 1978), pp. 403–412.

Brian D. Kluger, "Constrained Optimal Trade Credit Terms in a Competitive Pricing Model," in Yong Kim (ed): *Advances in Working Capital Management*, Vol. 4 (2001), Greenwich, CT: JAI Press, pp. 109–121.

Joshua Levant and Ashwinpaul Sondhi, "Finance Subsidiaries: Their Formation and Consolidation," *Journal of Business Finance and Accounting* (Spring 1986), pp. 137–148.

Wilbur G. Lewellen, John J. McDonnell, and Jonathan A. Scott, "Capital Market Influences on Trade Credit Policies," *Journal of Financial Research* (Fall 1980), pp. 105–113.

Michael S. Long, Ileen B. Malitz, and S. Abraham Ravid, "Trade Credit, Credit Guarantees, and Product Marketability," *Financial Management* (Winter 1993), pp. 117–127.

Ileen Malitz, "A Reexamination of the Wealth Expropriation Hypothesis: The Case of Captive Finance Subsidiaries," *Journal of Finance* (September 1989), pp. 1039–1047.

Giuseppe Marotta, "When Do Trade Credit Discounts Matter? Evidence from Italian Firm-Level Data" (2003), *Universita di Modena e Reggio Emilia Working Paper.*

Dileep Mehta, "The Formulation of Credit Policy Models," *Management Science* (October 1968), pp. B30–B50.

Shehzad L. Mian and Clifford W. Smith, Jr., "Accounts Receivable Management Policy: Theory and Evidence," *Journal of Finance* (March 1992), pp. 169–200.

Shehzad L. Mian and Clifford W. Smith, Jr., "Extending Trade Credit and Financing Receivables," *Journal of Applied Corporate Finance* (Spring 1994), pp. 75–84.

Chee K. Ng, Janet Kiholm Smith, and Richard L. Smith, "Evidence on the Determinants of Credit Terms Used in Interfirm Trade," *Journal of Finance* (June 1999), pp. 1109–1129.

Ehsan Nikbakht and Mohammed H. A. Tafti, "Application of Expert Systems in Evaluation of Credit Card Borrowers," *Journal of Managerial Finance* 15 (1989), pp. 19–27.

William A. Ogden, Jr. and Srinivasan Sundaram, "A Spreadsheet Solution for the Optimal Credit Investigation/Granting Sequential Decision," *The Credit and Financial Management Review* 1(1) (1995), pp. 14–17.

Mitchell A. Petersen and Raghuram G. Rajan, "Trade Credit: Theories and Evidence," *Review of Financial Studies* 10 (1997), pp. 661–691.

Richard Pike, "Managing Trade Credit to Sustain Competitive Advantage," *Management Accounting (U.K.)* (June 1998), pp. 28–31.

Richard Pike and Nam Cheung, "Trade Credit, Late Payment and Asymmetric Information," *Bradford University School of Management Working Paper No. 02/09* (May 2002).

Muhammed Rashid and Devashis Mitra, "Price Elasticity of Demand and an Optimal Cash Discount Rate in Credit Policy," *The Financial Review* (August 1999), pp. 113–120.

Alan K. Reichert, Chien-Ching Cho, and George M. Wagner, "An Examination of the Conceptual Issues Involved in Developing Credit Scoring Models in the Consumer Lending Field," *Federal Reserve Bank of Chicago Staff Memoranda* (1981), pp. 81–83.

Cecilia Wagner Ricci, "Receivables Practices in American Corporations," *Business Credit* (April 1999), pp. 32–35.

Gordon S. Roberts and Jerry A. Viscione, "Captive Finance Subsidiaries: The Manager's View," *Financial Management* (Spring 1981), pp. 36–42.

Frederick C. Scherr, "Credit-Granting Decisions Under Risk," *Engineering Economist* (Spring 1992), pp. 245–262.

Frederick C. Scherr, "Optimal Trade Credit Limits," *Financial Management* (Spring 1996), pp. 71–85.

R. Schwartz, "An Economic Model of Trade Credit," *Journal of Financial and Quantitative Analysis* (September 1974), pp. 643–657.

Arjit Sen, "Seller Financing of Consumer Durables," *Journal of Economics and Management Strategy* (Fall 1998), pp. 435–460.

Janet Kiholm Smith, "Trade Credit and Informational Asymmetry," *Journal of Finance* (September 1987), pp. 863–872.

Janet Kiholm Smith and Christjahn Schnucker, "An Empirical Examination of Organizational Structure: The Economics of the Factoring Decision," *Journal of Corporate Finance* (March 1994), pp. 119–138.

Keith V. Smith and Brian Belt, "Working Capital Management in Practice: An Update," West Lafayette, Ind.: Purdue University, Krannert School of Management Working Paper 951 (March 1989).

Keith V. Smith and Shirley Blake Sell, "Working Capital Management in Practice," in Keith V. Smith (ed): *Readings on the Management of Working Capital, 2d ed.* (1980) St. Paul, Minn.: West Publishing, pp. 51–84.

Venkat Srinivasan and Yong H. Kim, "Credit Granting: A Comparative Analysis of Classification Procedures," *Journal of Finance* (July 1987), pp. 665–681.

Venkat Srinivasan, "Designing Expert Financial Systems: A Case Study of Corporate Credit Management," *Financial Management* (Autumn 1988), pp. 33–43.

John Stowe, "An Integer Programming Solution for the Optimal Credit Investigation/Credit Granting Sequence," *Financial Management* (Summer 1985), pp. 66–76.

James W. Tucker and William T. Moore, "Accounts Receivable, Trade Debt and Reorganization," *Journal of Financial and Strategic Decisions* (Summer 2000), pp. 39–43.

James Vander Weide and Steven F. Maier, "Managing Corporate Liquidity: An Introduction to Working Capital Management" (1985), New York: John Wiley & Sons, pp. 259–266.

Frank W. Wey, "Establishing Credit Lines by Formula," *Credit & Financial Management* (May 1983), pp. 24, 26.

Nicholas Wilson, Barbara Summers, and Robert Hope, "Using Payment Behaviour Data for Credit Risk Modeling," *International Journal of the Economics of Business* 3 (2000), pp. 333–346.

John Winginton, "A Note on the Comparison of Logit and Discriminant Models of Consumer Credit Behavior," *Journal of Financial and Quantitative Analysis* (September 1980), pp. 757–771.

Diana Yatsko and Frederick Scherr, "Replacing Defaulted Customers: The Hidden Cost of Default," *The Credit and Financial Management Review*, 9 (3) (2003), pp. 5–8.

F. Christian Zinkhan, "A New Approach for Jointly Evaluating the 'Six Cs' of Loan Analysis," *Akron Business and Economic Review* (Spring 1990), pp. 8–17.

FOCUSED CASE

# Y. Guess Jeans

*You may wish to consult the end-of-book Glossary and parts of Chapter 16 if you are unfamiliar with bank lending terms that are included in this case.*

You are the credit analyst for Y. Guess jeans. One of your major retail accounts, County Seat, has just asked for a credit limit increase of 20 percent. You presently are one of County Seat's largest suppliers of jeans and casual tops. At present, County Seat buys $2.5 million merchandise per month from you. Below are the financials that County Seat provides. Before you reach for the D&B report or check their payment history, you want to arrive at an independent appraisal based strictly on their financial ratios, financial statements, and supplemental information.

Should the credit limit increase be approved? Provide guidance to the credit manager, indicating which indicators or financial ratios you see as most important in supporting your recommendation.

| | |
|---|---|
| SUBMISSION TYPE: | 10-Q www.sec.edgar.com |
| PERIOD OF REPORT: | 1996/08/03 |
| FILED AS OF DATE: | 1996/09/17 |
| COMPANY DATA: | |
| COMPANY NAME: | COUNTY SEAT, INC |
| STANDARD INDUSTRIAL CLASSIFICATION: | RETAIL-DEPARTMENT STORES [5311] |
| FISCAL YEAR END: | 01/29 |
| FORM TYPE: | 10-Q |

**As of September 17, 1996, 3,327,042 shares of Common Stock were outstanding.**

**Consolidated Financial Statements**
**COUNTY SEAT, INC. AND SUBSIDIARY**
**CONSOLIDATED BALANCE SHEETS**
**(Amounts in Thousands, Except Share Amounts)**
**(Unaudited)**

| | August 3, 1996 | July 29, 1995 | February 3, 1996 |
|---|---|---|---|
| ASSETS | | | |
| Current Assets: | | | |
| Cash and cash equivalents | $ 10,603 | $ 8,125 | $ 8,166 |
| Receivables | 1,486 | 2,778 | 2,658 |
| Merchandise inventories | 132,580 | 143,474 | 110,744 |
| Prepaid expenses | 10,985 | 11,371 | 11,339 |
| Deferred tax benefit | 2,930 | 12,006 | 989 |
| Total current assets | $ 158,584 | $177,754 | $ 133,896 |
| Property and equipment, at cost | $ 119,425 | $117,466 | $ 120,277 |
| Less—Accumulated depreciation and amortization | (65,943) | (52,128) | (61,674) |
| Property and equipment, net | $ 53,482 | $ 65,338 | $ 58,603 |
| Other Assets, net: | | | |
| Debt issuance costs | $ 3,816 | $ 3,408 | $ 3,073 |
| Deferred income taxes | 2,111 | 6,455 | 2,486 |
| Excess of purchase price over net assets acquired | | 75,215 | |
| Other | 814 | 1,408 | 1,303 |
| Total other assets, net | $ 6,741 | $ 86,486 | $ 6,862 |
| Total assets | $ 218,807 | $329,578 | $ 199,361 |

*continued*

**Consolidated Financial Statements (continued)**
**COUNTY SEAT, INC. AND SUBSIDIARY**
**CONSOLIDATED BALANCE SHEETS**
**(Amounts in Thousands, Except Share Amounts)**
**(Unaudited)**

| | August 3, 1996 | July 29, 1995 | February 3, 1996 |
|---|---|---|---|
| LIABILITIES AND SHAREHOLDERS' EQUITY (DEFICIT) | | | |
| Current Liabilities: | | | |
| Borrowings under credit agreement | $ 81,800 | $ 43,700 | $ 27,000 |
| Current maturities of long-term debt | 26 | 29 | 25 |
| Accounts payable | 47,397 | 65,472 | 36,754 |
| Accrued expenses | 22,477 | 19,489 | 20,526 |
| Accrued income taxes | 1,348 | 1,962 | 1,111 |
| Total current liabilities | $ 153,048 | $130,652 | $ 85,416 |
| Long-term debt | $ 122,640 | $152,099 | $ 147,365 |
| Other long-term liabilities | 11,966 | 11,752 | 12,044 |
| Commitments and contingencies | | | |
| Minority interest—redeemable preferred stock of Stores | 48,521 | 40,389 | 44,319 |
| Redeemable preferred stock of CSI | 64,210 | 53,637 | 58,628 |
| Shareholders' Equity (Deficit): | | | |
| Preferred stock: par value $0.01 per share; 5,000,000 shares authorized; no shares issued and outstanding | | | |
| Common stock: par value $0.01 per share; 50,000,000 shares authorized; 3,327,042, 3,327,042 and 3,327,042 shares issued and outstanding, respectively | $ 33 | $ 33 | $ 33 |
| Paid-in capital | 22,193 | 22,193 | 22,193 |
| Warrants | 2,600 | 2,600 | 2,600 |
| Common stock notes receivable | (5,139) | (4,973) | (4,982) |
| Accumulated deficit | (201,265) | (78,804) | (168,255) |
| Total shareholders' equity (deficit) | $(181,578) | $ (58,951) | $(148,411) |
| Total liabilities and equity | $ 218,807 | $329,578 | $ 199,361 |

**COUNTY SEAT, INC. AND SUBSIDIARY**
**CONSOLIDATED STATEMENTS OF OPERATION**
**(Amounts in Thousands, Except Share Amounts)**
**(Unaudited)**

| | 13 Weeks Ended | | 26 Weeks Ended | |
|---|---|---|---|---|
| | August 3, 1996 | July 29, 1995 | August 3, 1996 | July 29, 1995 |
| Net sales | $ 121,727 | $ 130,110 | $ 243,331 | $ 254,299 |
| Cost of sales, including buying and occupancy | 90,283 | 95,123 | 185,812 | 190,061 |
| Gross profit | $ 31,444 | $ 34,987 | $ 57,519 | $ 64,238 |
| Selling, general and administrative expenses | 33,668 | 32,189 | 64,990 | 62,094 |
| Depreciation and amortization | 2,956 | 3,531 | 5,915 | 6,787 |
| Loss from operations | $ (5,180) | $ (733) | $ (13,386) | $ (4,643) |

**COUNTY SEAT, INC. AND SUBSIDIARY (continued)**
**CONSOLIDATED STATEMENTS OF OPERATION**
**(Amounts in Thousands, Except Share Amounts)**
**(Unaudited)**

| | 13 Weeks Ended | | 26 Weeks Ended | |
|---|---|---|---|---|
| | August 3, 1996 | July 29, 1995 | August 3, 1996 | July 29, 1995 |
| Interest expense, net | 5,742 | 5,865 | 11,098 | 11,638 |
| Minority interest—dividends and accretion of redeemable preferred stock of Stores | 2,143 | 3,022 | 4,202 | 4,715 |
| Loss before income taxes and extraordinary items | $ (13,065) | $ (9,620) | $ (28,686) | $ (20,996) |
| Income taxes | 4,095 | (2,661) | (1,258) | (6,941) |
| Loss before extraordinary items | $ (17,160) | $ (6,959) | $ (27,428) | $ (14,055) |
| Extraordinary items, net of income tax benefit | | 9,997 | | 9,997 |
| Net Loss | $ (17,160) | $ (16,956) | $ (27,428) | $ (24,052) |
| Redeemable preferred stock dividends and accretion | $ (2,950) | $ (2,869) | $ (5,582) | $ (5,045) |
| Net loss applicable to common shares | $ (20,110) | $ (19,825) | $ (33,010) | $ (29,097) |
| Per common share: | | | | |
| Loss before extraordinary items | $ (6.04) | $ (2.95) | $ (9.92) | $ (5.74) |
| Extraordinary items | | (3.01) | | (3.01) |
| Net loss per common share | $ (6.04) | $ (5.96) | $ (9.92) | $ (8.75) |
| Weighted average shares outstanding | 3,327,042 | 3,326,874 | 3,327,042 | 3,326,705 |

**COUNTY SEAT, INC. AND SUBSIDIARY**
**CONSOLIDATED STATEMENTS OF CASH FLOWS**
**(Amounts in Thousands)**
**(Unaudited)**

| | 26 Weeks Ended | |
|---|---|---|
| | August 3, 1996 | July 29, 1995 |
| Cash Flows from Operating Activities: | | |
| Net loss | $(27,428) | $ (24,052) |
| Adjustments to reconcile net loss to net cash used for operating activities: | | |
| Extraordinary items | | 9,997 |
| Depreciation and amortization | 5,915 | 6,787 |
| Amortization of debt issuance costs and discount | 780 | 1,201 |
| Minority interest—dividends and accretion of redeemable preferred stock of Stores | 4,202 | 4,715 |
| Rent expense in excess of cash outlays, net | 53 | 189 |
| Deferred tax benefit | (1,258) | (5,590) |
| Changes in operating assets and liabilities: | | |
| Receivables | 625 | 2,371 |
| Merchandise inventories | (21,836) | (47,203) |
| Prepaid expenses | 313 | (1,236) |
| Accounts payable | 11,211 | 25,358 |
| Accrued expenses | 2,746 | (4,047) |
| Accrued income taxes | (70) | (1,865) |
| Other noncurrent assets and liabilities | 15 | (971) |
| Net cash used for operating activities | $(24,732) | $ (34,346) |

*continued*

| | 26 Weeks Ended | |
|---|---|---|
| | August 3, 1996 | July 29, 1995 |
| **Cash Flows from Financing Activities:** | | |
| Borrowings under the Credit Agreement, net | $29,800 | $ 73,700 |
| Issuance of long-term debt | | 104,943 |
| Debt and equity issuance costs and prepayment premiums | (1,257) | (6,781) |
| Principal payments on long-term debt and capital leases | (12) | (20) |
| Repayment of long-term debt | | (150,795) |
| Issuance of common stock | | 104 |
| Repayment of common stock notes receivable | | 160 |
| Net cash provided by financing activities | $28,531 | $ 21,311 |
| **Cash Flows from Investing Activities:** | | |
| Capital expenditures | $ (1,365) | $ (9,313) |
| Proceeds from disposal of property and equipment | 3 | 14 |
| Net cash used for investing activities | $ (1,362) | $ (9,299) |
| **Net Increase (Decrease) in Cash and Cash Equivalents** | $ 2,437 | $ (22,334) |
| **Cash and Cash Equivalents:** | | |
| Beginning of period | 8,166 | 30,459 |
| End of period | $10,603 | $ 8,125 |
| **Cash Paid During the Period For:** | | |
| Interest | $ 9,982 | $ 13,570 |
| Income taxes | $ 70 | $ 514 |

## ORGANIZATION AND NATURE OF BUSINESS

The accompanying interim consolidated financial statements represent those of County Seat, Inc. ("CSI") and its wholly owned subsidiary, County Seat Stores, Inc. ("Stores") (together, "the Company" or "County Seat"). The activities of CSI consist principally of its investment in Stores.

The Company is the nation's largest specialty retailer selling both brandname and private-label jeans and jeanswear. The Company operated 740 stores in 48 states as of August 3, 1996. The Company's 681 County Seat stores, located almost exclusively in regional shopping malls, offer one-stop shopping for daily casual wear featuring a contemporary jeanswear look. The Company's wide selection of designer brands, including Girbaud, Guess?, Calvin Klein, Tommy Hilfiger and popular national brands such as Levi's as well as its proprietary brands, County Seat®, Nuovo® and Ten Star® makes County Seat a destination store for jeans. The Company operates 34 County Seat Outlet stores, offering discount pricing on special purchase and clearance merchandise, and 21 Levi's Outlet stores under license from Levi Strauss & Co., offering a full range of Levi's and Docker's off-price merchandise for both adults and children. The Company also operates four The Old Farmer's Almanac General Stores, a new retail concept selling products associated with American country living, under license from Yankee Publishing, Inc., the publisher of The Old Farmer's Almanac.

### Credit Agreement

The Credit Agreement is funded through a syndicate of commercial lenders providing a senior-secured reducing revolving credit facility to fund seasonal working capital requirements and the May 1995 redemption in full of all of the Company's then outstanding senior notes.

The Credit Agreement and the indenture for Stores' 12 percent Senior Subordinated Notes (the "Indenture") contain certain covenants, which, among other things, limit the amount of debt of the Company, restrict the payment of interest on CSI's 9 percent Exchange Debentures, restrict the payment of cash dividends on Stores' Series A senior exchangeable preferred stock and the CSI Series A junior exchangeable preferred stock, limit expenditures for property, equipment and rent under operating leases, and require the Company to maintain certain financial ratios. The most restrictive financial covenants at August 3, 1996, for the Company included, as defined, a minimum current ratio (1.10 to 1.0); minimum interest coverage ratio (0.90 to 1.0); minimum adjusted net worth, as defined ($30,000,000 including redeemable preferred stock); minimum EBITDA, as defined ($24,800,000), and minimum fixed charge coverage ratio (1.15 to 1.0). The Credit Agreement limits the level of capital expenditures to $4,000,000, $3,600,000, $5,000,000, and $5,000,000 in fiscal 1996, 1997, 1998, and 1999, respectively. The permitted capital expenditures will be increased if the Company generates defined excess cash flow levels.

Effective February 3, 1996, the Company amended the Credit Agreement to provide an increased borrowing commitment, to secure borrowings with all assets of the Company, to make certain financial covenants less restrictive, and to further limit capital expenditures. The Company incurred fees and expenses of approximately $1,300,000 in the first quarter of fiscal 1996 related to the amendment to the Credit Agreement, which will be amortized over its remaining term.

The Company has obtained an amendment effective August 3, 1996, and a discretionary waiver effective August 31, 1996, with respect to trailing 12-month EBITDA requirements under the Credit Agreement. The waiver will expire September 24, 1996, unless extended, and is revocable at the election of the requisite banks under the Credit Agreement. In the absence of a current amendment, it will likely be necessary for the Company to obtain amendments or waivers of covenants with respect to the remaining quarters of fiscal 1996 and thereafter. The Company is in the process of meeting with the members of its bank group to discuss additional changes to the Credit Agreement to modify its financial covenants and other terms. A semiannual interest payment on the Company's 12 percent Senior Subordinated Notes is due October 1, 1996. In the absence of an amendment or extension of the waiver, the requisite banks will be permitted to prevent such payment. Failure to make such payment, whether or not prevented by the banks, will constitute a default under the Indenture after the 30-day grace period provided in the Indenture has expired. The Company has initiated discussions with certain holders of the 12 percent Senior Subordinated Notes with respect to a possible financial restructuring and is evaluating such other financial alternatives as may be necessary. In addition, if an appropriate amendment or waiver is not obtained, Stores will not be permitted to advance funds to permit CSI to make the interest payment due November 30, 1996, on CSI's 9 percent Exchange Debentures. No assurance can be given that satisfactory amendments, modifications, or waivers to the terms of the Credit Agreement or the 12 percent Senior Subordinated Notes can be negotiated.

The commitment under the Credit Agreement provides for borrowings up to $135,000,000 including a $50,000,000 letter of credit facility. Availability under the Credit Agreement is limited to the lesser of certain percentages of eligible inventory or $135,000,000 through December 31, 1996. The commitment under the Credit Agreement will reduce to $125,000,000 on December 31, 1996. In addition, the commitment will be reduced if the Company generates defined excess cash flow levels. The Credit Agreement matures on December 31, 1999. Availability is reduced by any amounts drawn under the facility as well as outstanding letters of credit. The Credit Agreement also requires that for a period of 30 consecutive days after each December 15 and before each February 15 of the following year, the Company must not have any aggregate borrowings (including Bankers Acceptances) outstanding under the Credit Agreement, less cash on deposit, in excess of $50,000,000. The permitted aggregated borrowings during this 30-day period will be reduced if the Company generates defined excess cash flow levels. Borrowings under the facility are secured by the assets of Stores and guaranteed by CSI. CSI's guarantee is secured by a pledge of its primary asset, the outstanding common stock of Stores.

In connection with the amendment effective August 3, 1996, the interest rate on borrowings under the Credit Agreement has been increased by 0.5 percent. At the option of the Company, interest is payable on borrowings under the Credit Agreement at a prime rate plus 2.0 percent or a Eurodollar rate plus 3.0 percent. The Credit Agreement provides for a commitment fee during the period prior to maturity of 0.5 percent of the unutilized commitment under the Credit Agreement. Due to the revocable nature of the current waiver, all loans under the Credit Agreement were classified as a current liability as of August 3, 1996. Borrowings of $30,000,000 and $25,000,000 under the Credit Agreement were classified as long-term debt as of July 29, 1995, and February 3, 1996, respectively.

Loans, borrowing base, and letter of credit commitments under the Credit Agreement were as follows (dollars in thousands):

| | 26 Weeks Ended August 3, 1996 |
|---|---|
| *At Period-End* | |
| Loans outstanding | $ 81,800 |
| Borrowing base | 132,721 |
| Available borrowing base | 10,078 |
| Letter of credit commitments outstanding | 22,201 |
| *During the Period* | |
| Days loans were outstanding | 182 |
| Maximum loan borrowing | $ 91,000 |
| Average loan borrowing | 66,490 |
| Weighted average interest rate | 8.22% |

## MANAGEMENT'S DISCUSSION AND ANALYSIS OF FINANCIAL CONDITION AND RESULTS OF OPERATIONS

### Results of Operations

The following table sets forth the Company's operating results as a percentage of net sales for the periods indicated:

| | 13 Weeks Ended | | 26 Weeks Ended | |
|---|---|---|---|---|
| | August 3, 1996 | July 29, 1995 | August 3, 1996 | July 29, 1995 |
| Statement of Operations Data: | | | | |
| Net sales | 100.0% | 100.0% | 100.0% | 100.0% |
| Cost of sales, including buying and occupancy | 74.2 | 73.1 | 76.4 | 74.7 |
| Gross profit | 25.8 | 26.9 | 23.6 | 25.3 |
| Selling, general, and administrative expenses | 27.7 | 24.7 | 26.7 | 24.4 |
| Depreciation and amortization | 2.4 | 2.8 | 2.4 | 2.7 |
| Loss from operations | (4.3) | (0.6) | (5.5) | (1.8) |
| Interest expense, net | 4.7 | 4.5 | 4.6 | 4.6 |
| Minority interest—dividends and accretion of redeemable preferred stock of Stores | 1.7 | 2.3 | 1.7 | 1.9 |
| Loss before income taxes and extraordinary items | (10.7) | (7.4) | (11.8) | (8.3) |
| Income taxes | 3.4 | (2.1) | (0.5) | (2.7) |
| Loss before extraordinary items | (14.1) | (5.3) | (11.3) | (5.6) |
| Extraordinary items | | 7.7 | | 3.9 |
| Net loss | (14.1)% | (13.0)% | (11.3)% | (9.5)% |
| Number of Stores: | | | | |
| Openings | 1 | 10 | 5 | 24 |
| Closings | (5) | (4) | (10) | (5) |
| Net increase (decrease) | (4) | 6 | (5) | 19 |
| End of period | 740 | 720 | 740 | 720 |

Net sales for the second quarter of fiscal 1996 were $121.7 million, $8.4 million or 6.5 percent below net sales of $130.1 million reported in the second quarter of fiscal 1995. A $13.1 million decrease in sales from comparable stores and a $1.8 million reduction in sales due to store closings were partially offset by a $6.5 million increase in net sales from new store locations. Comparable store sales in the second quarter of fiscal 1996 decreased 10.2 percent from the second quarter of fiscal 1995. Men's apparel and accessories contributed a decrease of 7.7 percent, and women's apparel and accessories contributed a decrease of 2.5 percent to the comparable store sales results. The Company defines comparable stores to be stores that have reached their thirteenth full month of operations, excluding closed stores. Stores open less than 13 full months are defined as new stores.

Net sales for the first six months of fiscal 1996 were $243.3 million, $11.0 million or 4.3 percent below net sales of $254.3 million in the first six months of fiscal 1995. A $22.4 million decrease from comparable store sales and a $3.4 million reduction in sales due to store closings were partially offset by a $14.8 million increase in net sales from new store locations. Comparable store sales decreased 9.0 percent in the first six months of fiscal 1996 in comparison to the first six months of fiscal 1995. Men's apparel and accessories and women's apparel and accessories contributed decreases of 7.9 percent and 1.1 percent, respectively, to the comparable store sales results.

Selling, general, and administrative expenses ("SG&A") increased 4.6 percent, in the second quarter of fiscal 1996 compared to the second quarter of fiscal 1995. For the first six months of fiscal 1996, SG&A was $2.9 million or 4.7 percent above the first six months of fiscal 1995. The increase was primarily due to store operating expenses associated with new stores opened in fiscal 1996 and 1995. In the second quarter of fiscal 1996, the Company recorded expenses of $1.1 million to recognize deferred costs related to an executive severance agreement with Barry Parker, former Chief Executive Officer of the Company. In the first six months of fiscal 1995, SG&A included a $1.0 million consulting fee related to the evaluation of the Company's financial structure. SG&A as a percentage of net sales increased to 27.7 percent in the second quarter of fiscal 1996, compared to 24.7 percent in the second quarter of fiscal 1995. For the first six months of fiscal 1996, SG&A as a percentage of net sales was 26.7 percent, compared to 24.4 percent in the first six months of fiscal 1995. The increase in SG&A as a percentage of net sales was primarily due to comparable stores reporting lower sales combined with approximately constant operating expenses.

Net interest expense decreased $0.2 million to $5.7 million in the second quarter of fiscal 1996, from $5.9 million the second quarter of fiscal 1995. Interest expense decreased $0.5 million to $11.1 million in the first six months of fiscal 1996, from $11.6 million in the first six months of fiscal 1995. The decrease for the first six months of fiscal 1996 was primarily due to lower interest expense and issuance cost amortization of $1.9 million on the Senior Notes, reflecting the May 1995 redemption of the Senior Notes, partially offset by a $1.5 million increase in interest expense on borrowings under the Credit Agreement. Additional interest expense related to higher total debt outstanding was substantially offset by a lower net effective interest rate. Other net interest expense decreased by $0.1 million, primarily due to lower discount and issuance cost amortization. The extraordinary charges in the second quarter of fiscal 1995 related to the redemption of the Senior Notes and the exchange of the then-outstanding 12 percent Senior Subordinated Notes for new 12 percent Senior Subordinated Notes.

## Liquidity and Capital Resources: Financing and Operating Activities

Cash provided by operating activities is the primary source of liquidity and capital for the Company. After the impact of cash interest payments, cash used for operations for the 26 weeks ended August 3, 1996, and July 29, 1995, was $24.7 million and $34.3 million, respectively. The Company made cash interest payments of $10.0 million and $13.6 million in the 26 weeks ended August 3, 1996, and July 29, 1995, respectively. Because of the seasonal nature of the Company's business, positive net cash flow from operations is typically not generated through the first three quarters of the fiscal year. The decrease in cash used for operations in the 26 weeks ended August 3, 1996, compared to the 26 weeks ended July 29, 1995, was primarily due to lower net spending on merchandise inventories, partially offset by reduced cash generated from operations. Additional liquidity to fund working capital activities is provided through borrowings under the Credit Agreement and open account trade terms from vendors. While the Company has historically negotiated open trade terms with the majority of its domestic vendors, recent financial circumstances have caused the Company to rely more extensively on letters of credit for its domestic purchase terms. Trade terms are negotiated with each vendor and may be modified from time to time. County Seat is not dependent upon factors to support the Company's purchases from its suppliers. County Seat generates cash on a daily basis by selling merchandise for cash or payments with national credit cards. County Seat does not offer its own credit card.

At August 3, 1996, the Company had cash borrowings outstanding of $81.8 million, $10.1 million available for borrowing under the Credit Agreement, banker's acceptances outstanding of $18.6 million, and outstanding commitments under the letter of credit facility of $22.2 million. Fluctuations in market interest rates affect the cost of the Company's borrowings under the Credit Agreement. The impact of fluctuations in market interest rates in the 26 weeks ended August 3, 1996, were not significant to the operating results of the Company. At August 3, 1996, borrowings under the Credit Agreement accrued interest at a rate of 8.6 percent.

CSI is a holding company, the primary asset of which is the common stock of Stores. Substantially all of CSI's operations are conducted through Stores, and CSI is dependent on the cash flow of Stores to meet its payment obligations with respect to obligations under CSI's 9 percent Exchange Debentures. In the 26 weeks ended August 3, 1996, Stores paid dividends of $1.1 million to CSI to fund semiannual interest payments on CSI's 9 percent Exchange Debentures. Remedies available to the holders of CSI's 9 percent Exchange Debentures for failure to make required interest payments include the right to accelerate such indebtedness. In the event of a failure to repay such defaulted indebtedness, the holders of the 9 percent Exchange Debentures could foreclose upon the assets of CSI including the common stock of Stores, which would constitute an event of default under the Credit Agreement and the Indenture. No assurance can be given that the Company will have access to resources sufficient to repay defaulted indebtedness if so required.

CHAPTER

6

# Credit Policy and Collections

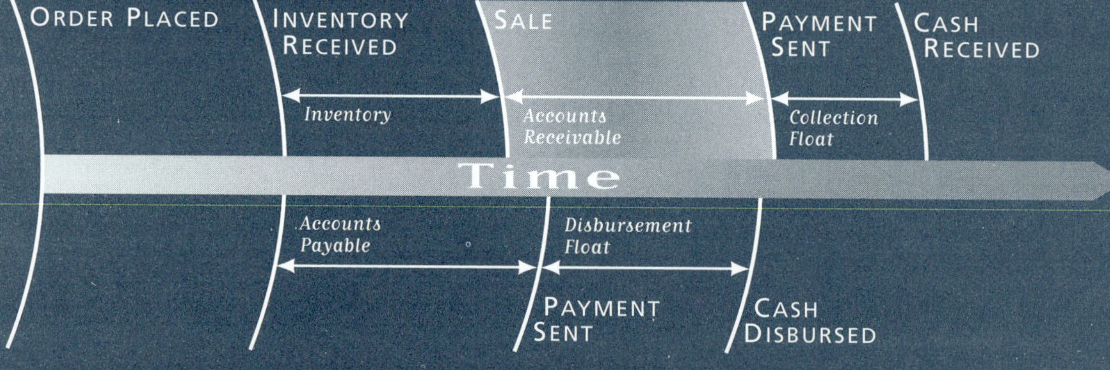

## OBJECTIVES

### *After studying this chapter, you should be able to:*

- specify the advantages of using the net present value approach in evaluating credit policy alternatives.
- calculate the net present value of proposed and existing credit policies, and select the best policy.
- identify the three major traditional measures of collection patterns, calculate them, and indicate the conditions under which they give biased signals.
- calculate and interpret uncollected balance percentages, and indicate why their use is the preferred method for monitoring collection patterns.
- describe present corporate credit policy practices.
- list and explain the major differences encountered through international extension of credit.

The 1980s was a decade of financial restructuring in which companies took on massive amounts of debt financing. Bankruptcies increased sharply in the early 1990s, and credit standards had to be revised to face the new realities. Suppliers found themselves facing new challenges regarding credit extension and receivables monitoring, as illustrated by the apparel industry in the accompanying Financial Dilemma.[1] In the new millennium, despite a very long economic boom, late payments and nonpayment are serious problems for corporations, while credit policy is as important as ever. In 2002, 186 public companies (the largest total ever), with an incredible $368 billion in assets, filed for bankruptcy in the United States. Imax Corporation, the big-screen movie-system concern, saw its revenues fall off and its debt downgraded to a "low junk" status in 2000, specifically due to difficulty in collecting upfront lease payments from large theater companies that are either already in or near bankruptcy status. Considering that U.S. companies' financial statements show an estimated $6 trillion in accounts receivable, including an estimated $2.72 trillion in trade receivables extended by nonfinancial firms, the importance of credit policy and collections becomes abundantly clear. This is not just an American problem—about 25 percent of Britain's annual business failures are linked to delays in payment, with small businesses being the most adversely affected. A law was recently enacted allowing firms to begin charging interest on late trade payments, a practice previously not permitted in the United Kingdom. In this chapter, we continue the study of receivables management begun in Chapter 5, addressing how to make credit policy decisions that enhance shareholder value, monitor investments in accounts receivable, and manage the collections process. Monitoring receivables and managing collections falls near the end of the cash flow timeline.

[1] See 1990. "Stores 'Went from Bad to Worse' as Economy Deteriorated in 1990," *Investors Business Daily* (December 27), p. 21. Aggregate past-due statistics for the entire economy are provided later in the chapter.

## FINANCIAL DILEMMA

How Should Customers' Financial Positions Be Monitored?

The financial strength of U.S. retailers has diminished so greatly that apparel manufacturers are faced with a new challenge. Relevant questions include how often to update information on this group of customers and how best to organize the monitoring function. "Historically, suppliers would review credit monthly, but now it's being checked daily," noted one apparel industry consultant. Many apparel companies have responded to the need for immediate knowledge of changes in their customers' financial status by establishing credit departments for the first time. The added fixed costs of making these adjustments are believed to be more than compensated for by quicker response times. Debt-laden customers are risky to do business with, and these suppliers have responded with decision making based on frequently updated and more accurate credit-related information.

---

In the previous chapter, we developed strategies for assessing individual credit applicants. Our focus was on making individual credit extension "go-no go" decisions that add to shareholder value. We now extend the analysis to the level of credit policy decisions affecting all customers, including using the net present value (NPV) model to evaluate credit policy changes. Next we turn to monitoring the receivables portfolio and provide means for assessing the efficiency of collections and the credit department. The chapter concludes with some complications that can arise in conducting credit operations in foreign countries. Several advanced receivables monitoring techniques are presented in the chapter appendix.

## EVALUATING CHANGES IN CREDIT POLICY: THE CASH FLOW TIMELINE

Credit management offers great potential for reducing the amount of cash tied up by a company's operations. The cash flow timeline is a convenient mechanism for viewing all of the cash flow effects of a change in credit policy, facilitating a capital budgeting valuation of those flows. The timeline includes days sales outstanding (DSO), which, as noted in Chapter 2, is one of the key components of a company's cash conversion period. Credit policies reducing DSO generally add value, but our framework illustrates that some policy changes add value even though they result in a higher DSO. See *Monitoring Receivables* later in this chapter for an explanation on calculating the DSO. We begin with survey evidence regarding which variables credit executives believe are important in making policy decisions and then suggest two ways they can evaluate the effects of different policies. Finally, we conclude with several numerical examples.

### Credit Policy Decision Variables

Financial managers may initiate a reevaluation of credit policy after conducting an internal receivables portfolio analysis (illustrated later in the chapter) or in response to a competitor's change in credit terms. When a company is thinking about lengthening its credit period or increasing its cash discount, what variables should it take into consideration? The Smith and Belt survey found that marketing and bad debt loss considerations were predominant, with production capacity, inventory requirement, and degree of operating leverage (risk linked to asset-related fixed operating costs) being secondary considerations. Managers ranked the criteria variables they deemed important when evaluating credit terms changes (in descending order of importance) as follows: (1) effect on dollar profits, (2) sales effect, (3) receivables effect, and (4) return on investment effect. Because profits correlate closely with cash flows in short-term decisions, decisions that maximize profits tend to increase shareholder value. Risk considerations, although very important to investors, were not explicitly mentioned by the surveyed managers.[2] Recent evidence tells us that many credit managers are now as much aligned with the marketing function as with the finance function, as customer-focused companies use credit terms to compete in markets, add sales, build loyalty, and gather customer intelligence.

Practicing credit executives believe they can estimate the effects of policy changes on profit, sales, and receivables levels. More than 84 percent of the credit executives surveyed by Besley and Osteryoung[3] stated that they could adequately estimate default probability, delinquency probability, credit limits, opportunity cost of funds invested in receivables, and the company's overall cost of capital. The good news here is that either of the latter two variables might be used as a discount rate for discounting (valuing) cash flows, and the discount rate used can presumably be adjusted for risk. Thus, managers are able to incorporate credit policy when making decisions about credit terms.

## Incremental Profits versus NPV

Scholars continue to debate whether the best overall criterion for evaluating credit policy changes is incremental profits, evaluated by using the financial statement approach, or NPV. The financial statement approach, sometimes termed a "heuristic approach," involves projecting condensed income statements for each alternative and then selecting the alternative with the highest profits. As we saw in Chapter 3, this model typically involves three steps: (1) determining the incremental receivables investment, (2) calculating the change in per-unit and total profits, and (3) computing the change in bad debt expense. Although the financial statement approach often gives the same accept-or-reject signals as the NPV approach, it is not quite as accurate and does not indicate the anticipated value effect of a credit policy decision.[4] Furthermore, the NPV approach has been formulated so that, with the proper data, the analyst can determine the optimal credit period and the optimal cash discount. After developing the model, we apply it to changes in a company's credit standards, credit period, and cash discount.

*NPV Approach* We noted in our valuation presentation in Chapter 3 that the NPV approach is preferable for investment decisions because it is consistent with value maximization. Net present value is the difference between the present value of the cash inflows and the present value of the cash outflows. When choosing between several mutually exclusive credit policy alternatives, the decision rule is to select the credit policy that maximizes NPV. If no credit policy alternative gives a positive NPV, we do not offer credit to

---

[2] Smith and Belt, cited in the end-of-chapter references.

[3] Besley and Osteryoung survey, cited in the end-of-chapter references. Company size and industry apparently had very little effect on the accuracy of the estimation.

[4] The financial statement approach does not properly recognize the timing of account losses. Furthermore, it uses an average cost of capital as a discount rate, which some believe is too high when computing the opportunity cost of the incremental investment in receivables.

our customers, implying that we will sell to them on a cash basis only.[5] The NPV model can be used to make value-maximizing decisions, and we illustrate its use in connection with the cash flow timeline to evaluate several policy decisions facing the credit manager.

The model we use for evaluating credit policy decisions shows the change in NPV from adopting a new or proposed policy and is adapted from the NPV model used in capital budgeting. The model is developed in several equations, beginning with the NPV of a newly proposed credit policy. We find the NPV of one day's sales under a newly proposed policy as:

NPV average daily sales = PV of sales to discount-takers + PV of sales to non-discount-takers − Variable operating costs − Variable credit & collection costs

You will find it much easier to work with this NPV formula if you break it into a separate step for each term of the equation. Step 1 involves computing the PV of the cash discount sales (if any); Step 2 computes the PV of the nondiscount sales (customers paying full invoice amount at or after the standard credit period); Step 3 calculates the variable operating, or noncredit, costs; and Step 4 determines the PV of the credit administration and collection costs.

In symbols, the NPV of one day's sales, under the new policy (Equation 6.1), is denoted by $Z_N$:

$$Z_N = \frac{[(1+g)S_E](1-d_N)p_N(1-b_N)}{(1+iDP_N)} + \frac{[(1+g)S_E](1-p_N)(1-b_N)}{(1+iCP_N)} - VCR[(1+g)S_E] - \frac{EXP_N[(1+g)S_E]}{(1+iCP_N)} \quad (6.1)$$

In which: $Z_N$ = NPV of new credit policy, one day's sales

$g$ = percent growth of credit sales caused by new policy

$S_E$ = existing credit sales under present policy, per day

$d_N$ = cash discount offered in new policy

$p_N$ = percent of credit customers expected to take new cash discount

$b_N$ = bad debt loss percent under new policy

$i$ = daily interest rate

$DP_N$ = cash discount period under the new policy

$CP_N$ = average collection period of paying customers under new policy

$VCR$ = variable cost rate, per dollar of sales

$EXP_N$ = variable collection/credit administration cost ratio under new policy

Notice that each term of the equation includes $(1 + g)S_E$, which is a shortcut for getting the new sales level. Three symbols merit closer attention in Equation 6.1. First, $i$ is the daily interest rate (the annual rate, $k$ divided by 365, or $k/365$) at which the seller finances receivables or at which the seller invests monies freed up from a smaller receivables investment. The formula assumes interest is added to the account once a year, even though it is based on daily principal amounts (simple interest based on annual compounding). Second, there is no reason to assume that the ratio of noncredit variable costs to sales

[5] This presupposes that nonfinancial or nonquantifiable considerations do not override the recommendation based on the financial analysis. Also, there is another context in which a negative NPV project would be accepted: when considering several alternative means of performing a necessary function and the only cash flows involved are outflows. These outflows represent costs, and the alternative with the highest NPV would still be selected, which in this situation would be the negative NPV value closest to zero. Selecting from several electronic data interchange (EDI) or receivables-monitoring software packages is an example of this type of decision context.

($VCR$) would change under a new credit policy, so we do not attach an $N$ subscript to $VCR$. Third, the value used for $DP_N$ should be how long, on average, the cash discount-takers actually take to pay. When evaluating a cash discount in a case in which the company has not previously offered a discount, the analyst may simply use the cash discount period instead of a historical pattern.

Unless a company is offering credit for the first time, the attractiveness of a new credit policy must be determined in reference to the existing credit policy. Again, we solve for the daily NPV of the policy as follows:

NPV average daily sales = PV of sales to discount-takers + PV of sales to non-discount-takers − Variable operating costs − Variable credit & collection costs

We can change the subscripts in Equation 6.1 for each of the variables from $N$ to $E$ to denote the existing policy situation, and the NPV of one day's sales under the existing policy $Z_E$ is found in Equation 6.2.

$$Z_E = \frac{S_E(1 - d_E)p_E(1 - b_E)}{(1 + iDP_E)} + \frac{S_E(1 - p_E)(1 - b_E)}{(1 + iCP_E)} - VCR(S_E) - \frac{EXP_E}{(1 + iCP_E)} \tag{6.2}$$

$Z_E$ is the daily $NPV$ of the existing credit policy. Although the VCR should take the same numerical value as in Equation 6.1, and $S_E$ is obviously the same, all other variables will likely take on different values than those used in Equation 6.1. In many cases, the discount rate $i$ is kept the same, but if the proposed and present credit policies directly affect the likelihood of the estimated sales levels being achieved, the analyst might apply a different discount rate in Equations 6.1 and 6.2. As in Equation 6.1, if there is no discount policy under the existing credit policy, $d_E$ and $p_E$ are both zero; this makes the whole first term zero (PV of sales to discount-takers) so it need not be considered. To get the change in daily $NPV$ when going from the existing to the new credit policy, simply take the difference between the daily net present values of the new and existing policies. In words, that is:

Daily NPV of policy change = NPV per day of new policy − NPV per day of existing policy

In symbols, we take the difference in the NPVs of Equations 6.1 and 6.2, as shown in Equation 6.3.

$$NPV\ per\ day = \Delta Z = Z_N - Z_E \tag{6.3}$$

Equation 6.3 gives us the change in daily NPV for a 1-day period, based on average daily sales. Because $\Delta Z$ reveals the change when going to the new credit policy, we recommend acceptance of the new policy when $\Delta Z$ is positive, indifference between the new and existing policies when $\Delta Z$ is zero, and rejection of the new policy when $\Delta Z$ is negative.

Decision Rule: If $\Delta Z > 0$, accept policy change.
If $\Delta Z = 0$, indifferent about policy change.
If $\Delta Z < 0$, reject policy change.

Finally, we need a formula to convert a 1-day NPV effect, which is based on average daily sales, to the total effect on shareholder wealth resulting from the multiyear effect of the new policy. If the change has a permanent effect, Equation 6.4 results, which gives us a close approximation of the total NPV created by switching from the existing policy to the new policy.[6]

[6] The NPV calculated from Equation 6.4 is not exact because of the simple interest formula used in the denominator of Equations 6.1 and 6.2. Except when there is a substantial dollar amount of daily sales or a very large change in daily NPVs, the approximation will be very close to the actual ΔNPV. We will compute the difference between the approximation and the actual ΔNPV when we evaluate the case of loosened credit standards, the first illustration of Equations 6.1 through 6.4.

$$\Delta NPV = \frac{\Delta Z}{i} \tag{6.4}$$

In words, Equation 6.4 tells us that the total NPV of a policy switch is the present value of all future daily NPVs.

Several comments should be made about the NPV model. First, the 1-day incremental to value, $\Delta Z$, signals whether the alternative policy will be preferable. If it is positive, $\Delta NPV$ will be positive as well.[7] Second, because $\Delta Z$ constitutes a perpetuity of daily NPVs, to arrive at its aggregated present value we divide it by a discount rate expressed in terms of the same period.[8] Dividing the 1-day value increment by the daily interest rate gives us the change in value for the company NPV. Third, if given an annual interest rate, $k$, we can determine the daily rate assuming simple interest (annual compounding) by dividing $k$ by 365.[9] Although we are not compounding the calculated $i$ on a daily basis in Equations 6.1 and 6.2, we can easily do so to get an exact value for $Z$. By using an exact daily equivalent to the annual rate $k$, we gain a closer approximation to NPV in Equation 6.4, in which the value of $i$ really matters. Fourth, there are several simplifying assumptions in this model.

*Assumption 1* All sales are credit sales. Notice that Equations 6.1 and 6.2 both address daily credit sales. For the value effect shown in Equation 6.4 to apply, the credit policy change cannot affect cash sales—meaning no existing customer can switch between paying at the point of purchase and waiting until the end of the credit period. Companies with only industrial sales may have negligible cash sales, but retailers clearly must consider switching effects when changing credit availability. Obviously, situations in which a company is considering offering credit terms for the first time, or for the first time to a group of formerly cash-paying customers, constitute a violation of the assumption; however, this violation can be handled very simply. Instead of using $(1 + g)S_E$ in each term of Equation 6.1, substitute $g(S_E)$, which represents the additional sales expected. Because Equation 6.2 is irrelevant in this situation, this revised Equation 6.1 gives the $\Delta Z$ needed to make the acceptance decision. Recapping, for companies offering credit for the first time, or when they only have information regarding the incremental sales that might arise from a policy change, they can replace $(1 + g)S_E$ with $g(S_E)$ in each term of Equation 6.1, and the revised Equation 6.1 gives us the change in value rising from one day's sales (and Equations 6.2 and 6.3 will be unnecessary). For customers that are normally sold to on "cash only" terms, ongoing sales are $S_E$ and the incremental sales brought about by now selling on credit are $gS_E$—with the latter sales being the ones for which we are determining the value effect.[10]

*Assumption 2* The bad debt loss rate used for the proposed credit terms is the forecasted average of loss rates for new and existing customers, and there is no difference in

---

[7] Recall from Chapter 3 that this property holds as long as there is no change in the growth rate of revenues or costs, or any fixed costs subsequent to the initial outlay necessary to implement the project.

[8] For a review of basic time value formulas, see the appendix at the end of the book.

[9] The interest rate if the company is getting paid daily interest on invested funds is lower than if the company is paying daily interest on borrowed funds. Also, Equation 6.4 gives the correct change in NPV if Equations 6.1 and 6.2 are based on $(1 + i)^{\text{no. of days}}$ instead of $(1 + i \times \text{number of days})$. Using $n = 30$ and $k = 10\%$ $(0.10/365 = 0.00027397)$, divide by $(1 \times 0.00027397 \times 30) = 1.00821910$ using simple interest versus $(1 + .00027397)^{30} = 1.00825183$ using compound interest. On a $1,000 future value, the difference in present values is only 3¢. Equation 6.4 then reflects the true value effect of the policy change's perpetuity of cash flows. Those uncomfortable with assuming that the cash flows really last "forever" should recognize that a very high percentage of the present value of the perpetual steam occurs in the first several years.

[10] Implicitly, we also assume the seller can replace the customers switching from cash to credit with new cash only customers without a significant change in any cost element. If that is unrealistic, another term must be added to account for the now-lower profitability from new cash only customers that replace switching customers in $S_E$, unless the only added costs are fixed costs, in which Equation 6.5 is used.

the loss rate for buyers taking the cash discount versus those paying at the end of the credit period. When forecasts of new customer sales are very uncertain, merging new and existing customer bad debt loss rates may cause a decision maker to choose a policy that would not be chosen were the risk made explicit. Regarding the second consideration, the loss rate for customers normally taking cash discounts may be lower in reality. This reflects discount-takers' superior financial position. Furthermore, if the seller can induce some slow payers who are financially strapped to pay early, the probability of not ever getting paid diminishes. Correspondingly, Equation 6.1 could be altered to use different values for $b_N$ in the first two terms.

*ASSUMPTION 3* Other than the change in receivables investment, the new policy does not necessitate additional investment outlays for inventories or fixed assets, nor does it change the *VCR*. However, for a manufacturing firm, inventories increase spontaneously with sales. If sales are expected to increase because of the new policy, the company must operate below capacity to avert increased fixed assets. To see how to incorporate the financial effects of these outlays, we must distinguish between one-time permanent investments and ongoing fixed cost increases. Permanent investments in fixed assets or working capital items, such as inventory, that are caused by a proposed credit policy are subtracted from the calculated $\Delta NPV$, in that they represent time 0 outflows. Ongoing periodic fixed costs related to these investments, such as warehousing fees or security and insurance expenses, must be discounted to their present value. To handle the increased fixed costs, we must calculate the difference between $PVFC_N$, the fixed costs under the new terms (on a present value basis), and $PVFC_E$, the fixed costs under existing terms. We see the net effect in Equation 6.5.

$$\Delta PVFC = (PVFC_N - PVFC_E) \tag{6.5}$$

We can then calculate a revised $\Delta Z$, which we will call $\Delta Z'$ in Equation 6.6.

$$\Delta Z' = \Delta Z - \Delta PVFC \tag{6.6}$$

The value effect for the company, $\Delta NPV'$ (Equation 6.7), would then be:

$$\Delta NPV' = \frac{\Delta Z'}{i} \tag{6.7}$$

Regarding the *VCR*, it is probably safe to assume that no change will occur unless the company is now receiving larger (smaller) quantity discounts as sales volume increases (decreases) as a result of the new credit policy.

*ASSUMPTION 4* The analyst is able to forecast each of the variables' future values with certainty. As was implied in Assumption 2, forecasts of sales for new customers or under a new credit policy should not have the same credibility as those for existing customers under the existing credit policy. This uncertainty, or the risk inherent in changing the credit policy, is never brought into the analysis. To do so requires assignment of probabilities, and the recommended alternative must recognize the decision maker's view of risk.

We may need to relax one or more of the first three assumptions as we consider several common credit policy decisions; uncertainty considerations are discussed briefly in a later section. We turn our attention to representative management decisions regarding credit standards, credit period, and a cash discount.

## Decision 1: Loosening Credit Standards

Regents Manufacturing is considering loosening its credit standards, thereby extending credit to marginal customers it currently sells to on a cash only basis. It presently has excess capacity and therefore does not anticipate any change in fixed costs resulting from the higher sales triggered by the more lenient standards. Sharif Baskerville, a business school graduate recently hired by Regents, has determined that sales will increase by $10 million (sales are presently $100 million and would increase by 10 percent). The VCR as a percent of sales is 0.65. For the new customers, the bad debt loss rate will be 4 percent, and the average collection period (or DSO) of paying customers will be 45 days (5 days longer than the DSO of present paying customers).[11] The company does not actively pursue the collection of late accounts, so the variable collection and credit administration expense will be negligible. The company's annual cost of capital is presently 15 percent. Regents does not offer a cash discount.

SOLUTION Sharif begins by determining the daily interest rate, $i$, equivalent to the 15-percent annual rate. The daily rate, assuming annual compounding, will be:

$$i = 0.15/365 = \underline{\underline{0.0004110}}$$

We can illustrate this situation on a cash flow timeline (see Exhibit 6–1), showing the present value of the additional sales on a daily basis.

Because Regents does not presently offer credit to these customers, $Z_E$ is zero and $\Delta Z$ simplifies to $Z_N$. As noted in Assumption 1, Equation 6.1 gives the change in value for one day's sales, assuming Regents adopts the new credit standard. Sharif determines that the cost outflow for one day's sales is:

$$\begin{aligned}\text{Variable cost outflow} &= -VCR(gS_E) = -0.65\ (0.10 \times \$100\text{ million}/365)\\ &= \underline{\underline{-\$17{,}808.22}}\end{aligned}$$

Regents does not offer a cash discount, so the first term of Equation 6.1 is equal to zero and thus drops out. Sharif figures the cash inflow from an average day's sales, 45 days from now, using the numerator of the second term in Equation 6.1.

Exhibit 6–1

*Regents Credit Easing Cash Flow Timeline*

[11] DSO should be based on an averaging technique or calculated based on a weighting technique, as we demonstrate later in the chapter.

$$\text{Day 45 inflow} = [g(S_E)(1 - p_N)(1 - b_N)] = [(0.10 \times \$100 \text{ million}/365)(1 - 0)(1 - 0.04)] = \underline{\underline{\$26{,}301.37}}$$

The credit administration and collection expenses are negligible and do not need to be arrayed on the timeline. We arrive at the timeline shown in Exhibit 6–1.

Sharif substitutes the numbers into the NPV model (using Equation 6.1) to determine the change in value Regents' shareholders can anticipate from loosening credit standards.

$$Z_N = \left\{\frac{[(0.10)\$100{,}000{,}000/365](1 - 0)(1 - 0.04)}{[1 + 0.0004110(45)]}\right\} - \left\{0.65\left[\frac{(0.10)\$100{,}000{,}000}{365}\right]\right\}$$
$$= \$25{,}823.76 - \$17{,}808.22$$
$$= \underline{\underline{\$8{,}015.54}}$$

Because the 1-day change in NPV of the proposed relaxed credit standards is positive, Sharif recommends its adoption to the credit manager. The addition to shareholder value, given by the aggregate change in NPV ($\Delta NPV$), is found using Equation 6.4.[12]

$$\Delta NPV = \frac{\$8{,}015.54}{0.0004110} = \underline{\underline{\$19{,}502{,}530.41}}$$

## Decision 2: Lengthening the Credit Period

Flying High Hang Gliders, Inc., is contemplating lengthening its credit period from the existing net 30 terms to net 60 terms. Reggie Miller, the credit analyst assigned to review the proposed credit change, has determined that the VCR ratio will be the same for existing and additional sales.[13] He estimates the additional sales to be $5 million. Reggie collects the following information from Flying High personnel:

| | |
|---|---|
| Variable costs as a percent of sales | 70% |
| Existing sales | $30 million |
| Bad debt loss rate now | 5% |
| Bad debt loss rate under 60-day terms | 6% |
| Days sales outstanding now | 45 days |
| Days sales outstanding under 60-day terms | 68 days |
| Credit & collection expenses now | 2% of sales |
| Credit & collection expenses under 60-day terms | 2.5% of sales |
| Opportunity cost of funds | 14% |

[12] If the company receives interest on freed-up funds and pays daily interest on funds borrowed to support the receivables investment, the cash flow discounting should be modified slightly. Solve for the equivalent 45-day interest rate assuming daily compounding by taking $[(1 + 0.15)^{45/365}] = 1.0173802$. Or, we could solve for the daily rate and then raise that rate to the 45th power: $[(1 + 0.15)^{1/365} - 1] = 0.000382983$; $[(1 + 0.000382983)^{45}] = 1.0173802$. Substituting into Equation 6.1, $25,852.06 is found as the value for the first term, and $8,043.84 as $\Delta Z$. Using Equation 6.4 and the rounded daily rate of 0.0003830, the aggregate value effect $\Delta NPV$ is:

$$\$8{,}043.84/0.0003830 = \$21{,}002{,}193.21$$

Thus, simple interest formulas understate the true daily and aggregate value effects if used when daily compounding applies.

[13] This is not to say that variable costs related to credit and collection will not change, however. The variable costs incurred when changing the credit policy are categorized as credit administration and collection expenses, which we have denoted $EXP_N$ for credit sales under the new policy (in Equation 6.1) and $EXP_E$ for credit sales under the existing policy (in Equation 6.2).

SOLUTION First, Reggie finds $i$, the daily equivalent to $k$:

$$i = 0.14/365 = \underline{\underline{0.0003836}}$$

Next, he structures the information provided into the NPV model:

$$\begin{aligned} VCR &= 0.70 \\ S_E &= \$30 \text{ million}/365 \\ S_N &= \$35 \text{ million}/365 \\ b_N &= 0.06 \\ b_E &= 0.05 \\ CP_N &= 68 \text{ days} \\ CP_E &= 45 \text{ days} \\ k &= 14\% \\ EXP_N &= 0.025 \\ EXP_E &= 0.02 \end{aligned}$$

Third, he notes that the new sales level, shown as $(1 + g)S_E$ in the equations, is \$35 million (\$30 million + \$5 million; $g$ in this case is \$5/\$30, or 0.16667). $CP_N$ will increase to 68 days, meaning on average paying customers will pay 8 days late. This compares to 15 days late under the present 30-day period. Because there is no cash discount in the present or proposed terms, we can drop the first term in Equations 6.1 and 6.2. Substituting the above values into Equation 6.1, Reggie finds $Z_N$:

$$\begin{aligned} Z_N &= \frac{(\$35{,}000{,}000/365)(1 - 0)(1 - 0.06)}{1 + 0.0003836(68)} - 0.7\frac{\$35{,}000{,}000}{365} - \frac{0.025(\$35{,}000{,}000/365)}{1 + 0.0003836(68)} \\ &= \$87{,}845.55 - \$67{,}123.29 - \$2{,}336.32 \\ &= \underline{\underline{\$18{,}385.94}} \end{aligned}$$

Reggie calculates $Z_E$ in the same fashion, making the four necessary changes in the numerical inputs:

$$\begin{aligned} Z_E &= \left[\frac{(\$30{,}000{,}000/365)(1 - 0)(1 - 0.05)}{1 + 0.0003836(45)}\right] - 0.7\left(\frac{\$30{,}000{,}000}{365}\right) \\ &\quad - \left[\frac{0.05(\$30{,}000{,}000/365)}{1 + 0.0003836(45)}\right] \\ &= \$76{,}757.21 - \$57{,}534.25 - \$1{,}615.94 \\ &= \underline{\underline{\$17{,}607.02}} \end{aligned}$$

The 1-day change in value, $\Delta Z$, is then the difference between $Z_N$ and $Z_E$, using Equation 6.3.

$$\Delta Z = \$18{,}385.94 - \$17{,}607.02 = \underline{\underline{\$778.92}}$$

Because the 1-day value effect of \$778.92 is positive, the financial analysis supports lengthening the credit period. Substituting $\Delta Z$ in Equation 6.4 determines the aggregate value added by the lengthened terms ($\Delta NPV$), assuming the daily improvement persists indefinitely into the future:

$$\begin{aligned} \Delta NPV &= \frac{\$778.92}{0.0003836} \\ &= \underline{\underline{\$2{,}030{,}552.66}} \end{aligned}$$

Noting that the incremental *NPV* is large and positive, Reggie recommends adoption of the proposed change to net 60 terms because of the anticipated addition to shareholder value.

## Decision 3: Offering a Cash Discount

Siegel Apparel Mills is wondering whether to offer its customers, ladies wear retailers, a 2-percent cash discount if they pay within 10 days. At present, it has net 30 terms. Top management has also asked what the optimal cash discount would be, should a cash discount be advisable. Rosa Kim is evaluating the proposed new terms of 2/10, net 30 versus the present net 30. Under the proposed terms, she anticipates a 3-percent increase in sales volume and a 0.5 percent reduction in the bad debt loss rate, from 3 percent to 2.5 percent. She estimates that the percent of sales made to cash discount-takers will be 40 percent, with the remaining 60 percent continuing to pay in 35 days (the present average collection period). She notes that Siegel does not charge interest for late payments. Thus, the collection period for non-discount-takers equals the existing collection period. Rosa decides that customers taking the discount will pay, on average, on the 10th day after the invoice date. Siegel's marketing activity has forecast sales for the upcoming year to be $20 million, assuming no change in the credit policy. The cost accounting department estimates the *VCR* to be 0.60 and the credit/collection cost to be 4 percent of sales. Rosa believes each of these variable cost elements will retain the same relationship to sales under the new terms. Siegel presently has a 12-percent cost of capital.

SOLUTION Rosa first determines the daily discount rate, $i$: 0.12/365 = 0.0003288. Reminding herself that in her situation $CP_N = CP_E$, Rosa calculates $Z_N$, $Z_E$, and the incremental *NPV* of one day's sales, $\Delta Z$. This is structured as the present value of the cash receipts from the discount-takers plus the present value of the cash receipts of the non-discount-takers, less the variable costs and less the credit and collection costs.

$$\begin{aligned} Z_N &= \left[\frac{(1+0.03)(\$20{,}000{,}000/365)(1-0.02)(0.40)(1-0.025)}{1+0.0003288(10)}\right] \\ &+ \left[\frac{(1+0.03)(\$20{,}000{,}000/365)(1-0.40)(1-0.025)}{1+0.0003288(35)}\right] \\ &- 0.60\left[\frac{(1+0.03)\$20{,}000{,}000}{365}\right] - \left[\frac{0.04(1+0.03)(\$20{,}000{,}000/365)}{1+0.0003288(35)}\right] \\ &= \$21{,}500.05 + \$32{,}640.81 - \$33{,}863.02 - \$2{,}231.85 \\ &= \underline{\underline{\$18{,}045.99}} \end{aligned}$$

Rosa then computes $Z_E$, the *NPV* of the present terms, using Equation 6.2. The first term of Equation 6.2 is not relevant because there is no cash discount at present.

$$\begin{aligned} Z_E &= \left[\frac{(\$20{,}000{,}000/365)(1-0)(1-0.03)}{1+0.0003288(35)}\right] \\ &- 0.60\left[\frac{\$20{,}000{,}000}{365}\right] - \left[\frac{0.04(\$20{,}000{,}000/365)}{1+0.0003288(35)}\right] \\ &= \$52{,}546.00 - \$32{,}876.71 - \$2{,}166.84 \\ &= \underline{\underline{\$17{,}502.45}} \end{aligned}$$

The 1-day incremental *NPV*, based on Equation 6.3, is then $543.54.

$$\Delta Z = \$18{,}045.99 - \$17{,}502.45 = \underline{\underline{\$543.54}}$$

The aggregate *NPV* for the perpetuity of 1-day value effects, assuming that the credit terms change has incremental effects that last indefinitely, is given by substituting into Equation 6.4.

$$\Delta NPV = \frac{\$543.54}{0.0003288} = \underline{\underline{\$1,653,102.19}}$$

Because of the positive *NPV*, Rosa recommends the 2-percent cash discount. Management's second question is now pertinent: What cash discount percentage (if any) would be optimal, in the sense of having the maximum, positive *NPV*? If sales do not change and the proportion of customers taking the cash discount bears a constant relationship to sales (e.g., 10 or 20 times the decimal equivalent of the discount), then the optimal discount $D^*$ for a present or proposed 10-day discount period ($DP_N = 10$) is:[14]

$$D^* = \frac{[1 - (1 + i)^{(DP_N - CP_N)}]}{2} \tag{6.8}$$

Rosa recalls that the daily discount rate is 0.0003288. She plugs this value, along with the cash discount period and the normal credit period, into Equation 6.8:

$$\begin{aligned} D^* &= \frac{[1 - (1 + 0.0003288)^{(10-35)}]}{2} \\ &= \frac{[1 - (0.9918150)]}{2} \\ &= \underline{\underline{0.0040925}} \end{aligned}$$

Because the calculated $D^*$ of roughly 0.4 percent rounds to zero, it appears to Rosa that Siegel would be better off *not* offering a cash discount, assuming sales do not change.[15] We note here that this optimization model (Equation 6.8) normally estimates lower optimal cash discounts than what have been observed in practice, and a recent computer simulation study found that the optimal cash discount for most companies when using a more general model is actually in the 2–3 percent range.[16]

Up to this point, we have worked only with projected data assumed to be known with certainty. This is tantamount to saying that there is no forecast error and that outside influences, such as competitive reaction, can be perfectly anticipated. Analysts choosing to introduce the variability of the inputs used in the *NPV* model might elect to risk-adjust the discount rate ($i$) used, but there is no obviously correct rate to use. Alternatively, they might evaluate credit policy decisions using the certainty equivalent version of the capital

---

[14] Hill and Riener (see the end-of-chapter references). This is a one-period model and does not ensure that the policy is optimal over a multiperiod horizon. See the Lee and Stowe citation in the end-of-chapter references. Lee and Stowe developed a model that explains paradoxical observed discount practices, such as different discounts in the same product market. Behavior such as this may be rational, with asymmetric information about product quality communicated via the cash discount offered. See the discussion on trade credit theories in Chapter 5 for more on product quality and trade credit.

[15] Relative to the solution demonstrated, inflation increases the optimal cash discount slightly. Buyers are more prone to wait until the end of the credit period when inflation is significant, because they are repaying less in real (inflation-adjusted) terms. To keep the cash discount equivalent in real terms, terms of 2/10, net 30 established in a noninflationary era should be adjusted to 2.27% if inflation is 5%, 2.52% if inflation is 10%, and 2.99% if inflation is 20%. For 3/10, net 60 terms, the differences are even more dramatic: 3.66% with 5% inflation, 4.28% with 10% inflation, and 5.43% with 20% inflation. These results are shown in Ben-Horim and Levy (see the end-of-chapter references).

[16] Borde and McCarty (cited in the end-of-chapter references). They used the most general form of the maximum cash discount model developed by Hill and Riener (cited in the end-of-chapter references), which allows for estimates of sales fractions, collection periods, and bad debt experience for both discount- and non-discount-takers. The optimal cash discount is higher when demand is price-elastic (Rashid and Mitra, cited in the end-of-chapter references).

## FOCUS ON PRACTICE

### *Speeding Collections Deemed Most Important Short-Term Financial Management Action*

Companies in the Fortune 1000 were asked by Smith and Belt to rank various short-term financial management practices according to importance. Based on a ranking of 1 being most important to 5 being least important, the results indicated that speeding collection of accounts receivable is the single most important action. Speeding collections was considered slightly more important than minimizing inventory investment, and moderately more important than minimizing bank balances or slowing disbursements for accounts payable. Only three respondents indicated "other" actions to be important. The tabulated results, including number of respondents selecting each action and their average ranking, are as follows:

| Action | Number of Responses | Average Ranking |
|---|---|---|
| Speed collection of receivables | 96 | 1.73 |
| Minimize investment in inventory | 98 | 1.85 |
| Minimize bank balances | 83 | 2.75 |
| Slow payment of payables | 74 | 3.26 |
| Other | 3 | 3.00 |

*Source:* Kevin V. Smith and Brian Belt, "Working Capital Management in Practice: An Update," Krannert School of Management (Purdue University), *Working Paper 951*, March 1989.

asset pricing model or the options pricing model.[17] At a minimum, analysts should conduct sensitivity analyses of the sales estimate, bad debt loss rate, and any other input variable that is uncertain.

Once the credit policy is in place, the credit management process focuses on monitoring and collections of credit sales. The next section develops the monitoring measures a manager can use and provides several measures for assessing credit department effectiveness and efficiency.

## MONITORING COLLECTIONS

The most carefully devised credit policy cannot keep a company's credit activity from becoming a problem area if the company does not diligently collect the receivables. Late payments require an increase in working capital for the seller and erode shareholder value because of the need to obtain financing from one of four sources [Chittenden and Bragg (1997), p. 28]: increased debt, which leads to higher interest payments, reduced profits, and reduced borrowing capacity; increased equity, which dilutes and devalues existing investors' stakes if stockholder returns are unchanged; reduced capital investment in the future, limiting the seller's long-term business performance; or an increase in the length

[17] Both of these are implemented for a credit policy decision in Richard L. Meyer and Scott Besley, "A Normative View of the Credit Policy Decision." Paper presentation at the Fifth Annual Symposium on Cash, Treasury, and Working Capital Management, Boston, MA, October 1989.

(and therefore the amount) of trade credit taken from suppliers. Cisco Systems, the world's largest networking equipment company, found this out in 2001 as some of its prime customers declared bankruptcy—reducing Cisco's sales and making a number of its "vendor financing" loans uncollectible. As noted in the Focus on Practice, financial executives believe that accelerating collections is the single most important short-term financial management action a company can take. Delayed payments deny the seller the use of the money, result in increased collection costs, and increase the risk that payment will never occur. In this section, we see how a company can monitor the receivables balance and the steps it can take to improve on collection of amounts due or past due.

## Monitoring Receivables

Three traditional approaches to monitoring the receivables balance include DSO (also known as the average collection period), accounts receivable turnover, and the aging schedule. More recently, analysts have advocated the payments pattern approach, which shows uncollected balances based on the month in which the credit sales originated. We will discuss and illustrate each of these tools briefly.

The **days sales outstanding (DSO)** measure is computed by taking the latest period's accounts receivable balance and dividing it by daily credit sales, as shown in Equation 6.9. Daily credit sales, in turn, are computed by taking the period's sales and dividing by the number of days in the period—365, when computing DSO over a yearly period. The equation typically used for DSO is as follows:

$$DSO = \frac{\textit{Accounts receivable}}{(\textit{Annual credit sales}/365)} \tag{6.9}$$

The analyst then compares the DSO for the latest period to earlier periods, to the credit terms offered to customers, and possibly to a management target or an industry average. The Credit Research Foundation (CRF)[18] published a benchmark (for comparison purposes) calculation formula as shown in Equation 6.10. It bases the $DSO_{CRF}$ calculation on the most recent three months:

$$DSO_{CRF} = \frac{(\textit{Average trade receivables balance for last 3 months-ends} \times 90)}{\textit{Credit sales for last 3 months}} \tag{6.10}$$

The $DSO_{CRF}$ uses the last three months of data to "smooth" the data, or balance out an unusual receivables balance that might have occurred in one of the months.

However calculated, the computed $DSO$ value is interpreted as the number of days of credit sales remaining uncollected, or how many days, on average, it takes for the company to collect credit sales. The latter interpretation suggests why this number is sometimes called the **average collection period**. If retailer C. J. Nickel's credit sales for January, February, and March were \$100,000, \$125,000, and \$150,000, respectively, and the receivables balance at the end of March was \$140,000, the calculation for DSO using Equation 6.9 would be as follows:

$$\begin{aligned} DSO &= \frac{\$140{,}000}{(\$375{,}000/90)} \\ &= 33.6 \text{ days} \end{aligned}$$

[18] The Credit Research Foundation represents a body of knowledge emphasizing the impact and contribution of the credit function on individual businesses and the national economy. Its forums, reports, surveys, and other material provide valuable information on new techniques and trends in credit, accounts receivable, and customer administration and practices. Furthermore, they are a resource for information technology applications to support the credit, accounts receivable, and customer management functions.

Notice that we have simplified our calculation by assuming each month in the period has 30 days, giving us 90 days for the 3-month period, which is used in converting the period's sales to a daily rate.

In a planning framework, DSO can be used to determine the average receivables needed to support a forecasted sales level, as seen in Equation 6.11.

$$\textit{Average receivables} = (\textit{Credit sales/365}) \times \textit{DSO} \tag{6.11}$$

To illustrate, if credit sales are $100 million, and DSO is 33.6 days, average receivables are $9,205,479.36; this is found by taking $100 million divided by 365 and multiplying by the DSO:

$$\$9{,}205{,}479.36 = \$273{,}972.60 \times 33.6 \text{ days}$$

**Accounts receivable turnover** is simply DSO divided into the number of days in the calculation period, usually 365. If DSO calculated for the past year is 33.6 days, accounts receivable turnover is 365/33.6 = 10.86 times. Receivables turnover is interpreted as how many times a company's investment in accounts receivable "turned over" into sales during the period (on an annualized basis). A slightly different interpretation of the turnover is how many dollars of sales a dollar invested in receivables supports. In our illustration, each dollar invested in receivables supports almost $11 of sales. Similarly to DSO, as seen in Equation 6.12, this relationship can be used in a planning framework to determine the average receivables that are required to support a given level of sales.

$$\text{Average receivables} = \text{Credit sales/Accounts receivable turnover} \tag{6.12}$$

Because it does not give any information not already available with DSO and does not tell us the average number of days customers are taking to pay, the analyst who already knows DSO need not calculate receivables turnover unless comparing to an external receivables turnover benchmark.

The **aging schedule** shows a percent breakdown of present receivables, with the categories shown typically as follows: current, 0–30 days past due, 31–60 days past due, 61–90 days past due, and over 90 days past due. In Exhibit 6–2, we show a spreadsheet that a company might use to compute the percentage breakdown, followed by the aging schedule itself. The percentages shown at the bottom of the aging schedule are as a percentage of the receivables balance as of the date of the report. June's 46 percent (rounded) is based on the $245,000 of credit sales made in June divided by the June 30 accounts receivable balance of $538,000 (shown at far right of Panel B). Some companies develop multiple aging schedules, one of which shows account aging by risk class and another that shows aging by account size. Regardless of format, aging schedules are considered key pieces of information regarding collection efficiency by factors (companies that buy receivables from and then collect them for the original seller) and banks.

The uncollected receivable percentages (right column in the accounts receivable schedule) are based on the period-ending receivables balance, not the sales in the month the receivables originated. We see that $45,000 of January's credit sales remain uncollected as of June 30, constituting 8.36 percent of the June 30 receivables balance of $538,000. Also notice that all uncollected sales from February or previous months are lumped together in the aging schedule because they are 90 days or more overdue.

The three measures we have mentioned serve a twofold purpose. First, they can be compared to various standards that are based on the same period. Standards might include a key competitor's values, management targets, or the industry average. Second, each of the measures might be compared to the trend for that measure. Here the values for several previous periods are used to determine the historical trend to better assess the meaning of the current value.

Surveyed managers indicate a strong preference for using the aging schedule to monitor receivables, with the DSO nearly as popular, and accounts receivable turnover

## Exhibit 6–2

*Development of an Aging Schedule*

Micro Toys, Inc., manufactures and sells miniature toy cars and trucks. It sells these on net 30 terms to toy retailers. Below (Panel A) are the last six months' sales and the accounts receivable balances at the end of June, the present (report) month.

### Panel A: Spreadsheet Containing Sales and Accounts Receivable Data

Accounts Receivable Schedule
Micro Toys, Inc.
June 30, 20XX

| Month | Credit Sales (000s) | Uncollected Amount (000s) | Uncollected as Percent of June 30 Accounts Receivable* Amount |
|---|---|---|---|
| January | $275 | $ 45 | 8.36% |
| February | 350 | 50 | 9.29 |
| March | 400 | 55 | 10.22 |
| April | 400 | 65 | 12.08 |
| May | 450 | 78 | 14.50 |
| June | 500 | 245 | 45.54 |
| June 30 A/R* balance: | | $538 | 100.00% |

*A/R = Accounts receivable

From this raw material, an aging schedule can be developed (Panel B). Notice how the bottom row of Panel B corresponds to the lower part of the rightmost column from Panel A.

### Panel B: Aging Schedule

Aging Schedule*
Micro Toys, Inc.
June 30, 20XX

| Age | Current | 0–30 Days Overdue | 31–60 Days Overdue | 61–90 Days Overdue | Over 90 Days Overdue | |
|---|---|---|---|---|---|---|
| Month of sale | June | May | April | March | February and Prior | Total |
| Accounts receivable (000s) | $245 | $78 | $65 | $55 | $95 | $538 |
| Percentage of June 30 A/R balance | 46% | 15% | 12% | 10% | 17% | 100% |

*For ease of calculation, all months are assumed to have 30 days.

ranking far behind. Many credit departments use multiple measures: recent evidence points to fewer than one in four companies using only aging schedules, with 70 percent of companies using multiple monitoring methods.[19] Unfortunately, all three measures we have looked at share serious flaws. Days sales outstanding and receivables turnover are sensitive to recent sales patterns and are reliable measures of a changing collection experience only if the credit sales patterns for current and preceding periods are identical. To depict the bias of DSO when sales are not constant, in Exhibit 6–3 we have constructed an example in which sales first increase and then decrease, but the collection pattern is held constant: 60 percent of credit sales is collected in the month of sale, and the remaining 40 percent is collected the following month. Yet DSO first increases, then decreases, indicating a seemingly worsening, then improving, collection experience. Exhibit 6–3 graphically illustrates the biased signal given by DSO when sales are not constant. Rising sales produce a larger DSO, and declining sales produce a smaller DSO, even though no change has taken place in how rapidly credit sales are collected. The credit manager was signaled to take corrective action when there was no need to do so.

A further dilemma facing the analyst is the appropriate period from which to make the DSO or receivables turnover calculations. It turns out that the measures give quite different readings depending on whether they are figured from monthly, quarterly, or annual data.[20] The aging schedule is likewise plagued with sensitivity to the sales pattern, even when collection rates are stable. The higher the proportion of more recent sales, the heavier the weighting for collections of recent accounts, and the more favorable the aging schedule appears. The higher percentages reported in the current or slightly past-due categories result from increasing sales, not from a better collection experience.

**Exhibit 6–3**

*Bias in Days Sales Outstanding Induced by Sales Pattern*

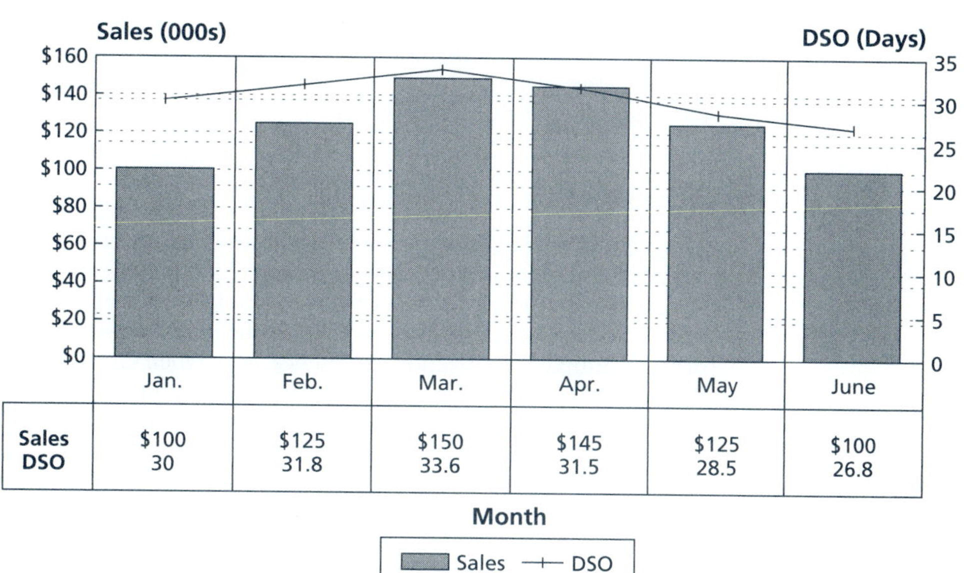


| | Jan. | Feb. | Mar. | Apr. | May | June |
|---|---|---|---|---|---|---|
| **Sales** | $100 | $125 | $150 | $145 | $125 | $100 |
| **DSO** | 30 | 31.8 | 33.6 | 31.5 | 28.5 | 26.8 |

[19] Ricci (1999), cited in the end-of-chapter references.

[20] A weighted DSO that overcomes both biases has been recommended by Carpenter and Miller (cited in the end-of-chapter references). Implementing this approach is based on determination of a standard receivables composition and a weighted DSO for every past month.

Exhibit 6–4

*A Typical Accounts Receivable Portfolio Monitoring System*

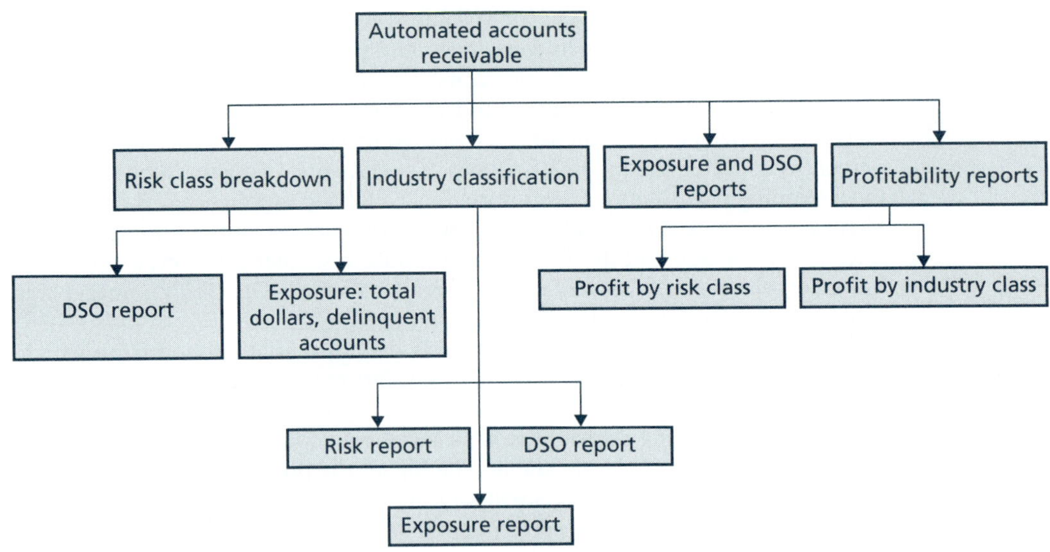


One company's receivables portfolio monitoring system, illustrated in Exhibit 6–4, shows the dollar amounts invested in receivables ("exposure"), DSO, and profitability by risk class and by industry. It exemplifies how the DSO and aging schedule measures might be integrated into an overall receivables analysis. It also enables a company to evaluate and revise its credit policies.[21] The goal is to achieve better-than-industry-standard credit losses as well as superior revenue generation, leading to higher earnings and cash flows, return on equity, and stock valuation. Later in the chapter, we will show how companies use key account management systems and improvement initiatives to improve management of credit and the resulting receivables.

## Uncollected Balance Percentages

The pitfalls of DSO, accounts receivable turnover, and the aging schedule have led to the development of an improved measure, in which the uncollected balances for each month are divided by the credit sales in the month when the receivables originated. Sometimes called the "payments pattern approach," the **uncollected balance percentages** accurately depict a company's collection experience, even when sales are changing. Exhibit 6–5 shows the earlier Micro Toys, Inc., receivables example, but now the far right column (Column 4) shows uncollected monthly receivables computed as a percent of the credit sales in the

---

[21] Space does not permit more complete treatment of credit portfolio management. A good basic introduction is given in Knerr (cited in the end-of-chapter references). Exciting developments on the linkage of portfolio management to shareholder value are profiled in "The Customer Value Imperative: Creating Shareholder Value through Consumer Credit Portfolio Management: An Industry Best Practices Report," a study conducted in 1999 by strategy consulting firm Oliver, Wyman & Company for the financial services association *The Risk Management Association (RMA)*. Some companies use modern portfolio theory to find risk-diversifying opportunities in their consumer credit portfolios and commercial credit exposures. At the time of this writing, an executive summary of the report was available online at **http://www.rmahq.org/Publications/custval_execsum.html**.

## Exhibit 6–5

*Uncollected Balances Schedule*

Micro Toys, Inc., manufactures and sells toy cars and trucks on net 30 terms to toy retailers. Below are the last six months' sales and the accounts receivable balances at the end of June, the present (report) month.

Uncollected Balance Percentages
Micro Toys, Inc.
June 30, 20XX

| (1) Month | (2) Credit Sales (000s) | (3) Amount Uncollected (000s) | (4) Uncollected Balance Percentage |
|---|---|---|---|
| January | $275 | $ 45 | 16.36% |
| February | 350 | 50 | 14.29 |
| March | 400 | 55 | 13.75 |
| April | 400 | 65 | 16.25 |
| May | 450 | 78 | 17.33 |
| June | 500 | 245 | 49.00 |
| June 30 accounts receivable balance | | $538 | *Payment index: 126.98* |

month they originated. The uncollected balance percent is calculated by dividing the portion of the present receivables balance attributable to an earlier month's sales (Column 3) by that month's sales (Column 2). Given that January's credit sales were $275,000, 16.36 percent ($45,000/$275,000) of Micro's January credit sales remain uncollected as of June 30.

To conduct a trend analysis, the most recent uncollected balances percentages can be compared with the comparable month-earlier percentages. Once the July 31 report becomes available, we can see if the collection rate for credit sales made five months earlier (February, in that case) has changed. If the percent uncollected is higher than the 16.36 percent seen in the June report, then this signals a worsening collection experience.

Notice that an overall payment index can also be determined to check on the aggregate collection experience, shown at the bottom of Column 4. In our illustration, the index stands at 126.98. If this number increases, we usually conclude that a greater percentage of previous months' sales remains uncollected. However, analysts must be careful in interpreting this index when offsetting changes sum to the same total while masking a greatly altered collection pattern. As the most recent month is added to the analysis and the earliest month is dropped, offsetting changes in the uncollected balance percentages for the earliest month and most recent month produce the same index value, but obviously, these should not be viewed identically by the credit manager.

Many companies use more than one collection efficiency measure, and analysts should be familiar with several approaches and their relative value. Using our earlier examples (Exhibits 6–2 and 6–5), with the same company's collection experience six months later, let's see how using all three measures either clarifies or muddies the analysis of collection efficiency (see Exhibit 6–6).

The aging schedule misidentifies the problem by making it appear that receivables 91+ overdue are the primary issue, when the problem is with those over 30 and over 60 days due. However, it does accurately show that there is a problem in the 0–30 and 31–60 days overdue categories. DSO misidentifies slightly worse collection experience with a

## Exhibit 6–6

*Using the Aging Schedule, DSO, and Uncollected Balance Percentages to Evaluate Collection Efficiency*

*This is the situation Micro Toys, Inc., faces three months after the original schedule.*

Development of the Aging Schedule (*Steps 1 and 2*)

1. Accounts Receivable Schedule with Aging Percentages:

Panel A

Accounts Receivable Schedule
Micro Toys, Inc.
September 30, 20XX

| Month | Credit Sales ($000s) | Uncollected Amount ($000s) | Aging Percents: Uncollected as Percentage of June 30 A/R Amount |
|---|---|---|---|
| April | $400 | $ 65 | 15.47% |
| May | 450 | 64 | 15.19 |
| June | 500 | 69 | 16.25 |
| July | 450 | 90 | 21.27 |
| August | 400 | 80 | 18.91 |
| September | 350 | 55 | 12.91 |
| ***September 30 A/R Balance:*** | | **$423** | **100%** |

2. Paste Aging Percents into Aging Schedule:*

Panel B

| Age | Current | 0–30 Days Overdue | 31–60 Days Overdue | 61–90 Days Overdue | More Than 90 Days Overdue | Total |
|---|---|---|---|---|---|---|
| *Month of sale:* | September | August | July | June | May and Prior | — |
| Accounts receivable (000s) | $55 | $80 | $90 | $69 | $129 | $423 |
| Percentage of September 30 Accounts receivable balance | 12.91% | 18.91% | 21.27% | 16.25% | 30.66% | 100% |

*For ease of calculation, assume each month has 30 days.

*Step 3:*

3. Calculate Uncollected Balance Percentages by Dividing a Month's Uncollected Amount in Panel A by Credit Sales for that Month.

Panel C

| Month | Uncollected Balance Percentage |
|---|---|
| April | 16.36% |
| May | 14.29% |
| June | 13.75% |
| July | 20.00% |
| August | 20.00% |
| September | 15.60% |

Panel D

***DSO-6 months: (180 days)* A/R/[(Sum of 6 months' credit sales)/180]**

1. **DSO as of June 30 (based on Exhibit 6–2):** *40.77 days*
2. **DSO as of September 30 (based on above data):** *29.87 days*

signal of much better collection experience. Uncollected balance fractions show that the true picture is deterioration in the current month, which has spilled over into 1-month and 2-month late payments. The collection situation must be addressed immediately, but not in the "over 91 days overdue" category suggested by the aging schedule. In this situation, then, the uncollected balance fractions—and for near-term collections, the aging schedule—give insight to the collections analyst.

## FINANCIAL DILEMMA REVISTED

Where does that leave the credit manager selling to an industry with a deteriorating financial condition, such as the apparel retailers in the opening Financial Dilemma? Overall exposure to bad debt losses can be monitored with the uncollected balance percentages. A key account approach to individual customer monitoring, in which the payment patterns of the customers accounting for much of the company's sales are scrutinized, is a necessity. Using online credit agency data enables the credit manager to watch how the customers are paying other companies with which they do business. Even careful oversight cannot prevent all losses, however, as a consumer goods company realized when absorbing a $5 million loss subsequent to Macy's bankruptcy. Credit managers are in the difficult position of not wanting to jeopardize continued business with their best customers, yet wanting to avoid a large loss exposure. Effective collection practices help keep losses to a manageable level.

To summarize our discussion of receivables monitoring, we acknowledge the popularity of the DSO and aging schedule measures while pointing out their unreliability when sales are changing. An improved measure, uncollected balance percentages, is recommended as a better approach to monitoring the collection experience. These percentages can be compared over time to reliably alert the credit manager to improving or deteriorating collections. Recent developments, which are more sophisticated than the above techniques, are profiled in the chapter appendix.

## COLLECTION PROCEDURES

The collection procedures a company uses are triggered when the monitoring system shows an invoice is past due, or delinquent. The guiding principle behind collections is to collect the amount owed as close to the credit terms as possible, trying to preserve customer goodwill when doing so. Customers that are delinquent in payments may be experiencing temporary problems, in which case the seller often renegotiates the terms, stressing that the revised terms must be met. Partial payments are solicited where the full invoice cannot be paid. At some point, particularly when the outstanding invoices are very large, the seller will push for payment even at the risk of alienating the customer. The rationale is that a customer not intending to pay its legal obligations is not worth retaining.

### Collection Effort

Normally, initial contact is made with the customer within 10 days of delinquency. In the initial mailing, the seller often includes a statement of account, which is a listing of amounts sold to this customer recently, usually including the buyer's purchase order number(s). A copy of the unpaid invoice(s) may also be sent. A reminder letter may be followed up by phone or even personal contact, with referral to a collection agency and/or legal action as a last resort. Duplicates of either or both of these documents may be sent with follow-up mailings. The seller's sales force is kept informed about the situation and may be asked about any unusual circumstances or conditions affecting the late-paying customer.

The normal collection cycle lasts two or three months. Companies typically leave 10 to 15 days between their successive collection efforts. In the intermediate stages, the need for cooperation and fairness and the importance of prompt payment on the part of the buyer for maintaining or improving its credit record are emphasized. Attempts are made to formulate specific payment arrangements. In the final stages, a semifinal letter will be sent, warning of the possibility of involving external parties (collection agencies or lawyers) in the collection. The final letter might state that unless payment is received the account will be placed for collection in 10 days. Sometimes, having this letter signed by a senior officer in the company or the company's general attorney helps set the tone. If payment is still not received, documents pertaining to the account are sent to a collection agency or to the company's law firm. The customer is generally notified of this action and given a final opportunity to pay. The systematic follow-up throughout all collection stages communicates the seriousness of the customer's obligation as well as the importance of those obligations from the seller's viewpoint.

*USING A COLLECTION AGENCY* Hiring a collection agency frees up time and resources for the seller and should increase the chance of actually receiving payment. For example, for an agency charge of $10 per account to get the current address and phone number for a delinquent account, plus 15 to 50 percent of the amount collected (the percentage varying based on the amount and age of the claim and the location of the debtor), the agency will locate the debtor and attempt to collect the money the seller is owed. An agency may use a compensation structure of 100 percent commissions to motivate its collectors and will forward accounts on which it is unable to collect to its network of attorneys, either having the client pre-pay the legal fees or it may pay the fees itself and build those charges into the contingency fees. The contingency nature of the agency's charges (excluding the attorney fees, which may be partially or fully contingent) implies "no collection, no fee." The national average recovery rate for collection agencies in the United States is 11 percent, but some firms boast rates of 25 percent and even higher.

Collections pose special problems for smaller businesses, especially service firms. The Focus on Practice provides some techniques that are helpful in such cases.

*EVIDENCE ON COLLECTION PRACTICES* We noted in our credit policy presentation in Chapter 5 that many companies levy service charges for late payment. We now survey evidence that addresses several other collections-related questions. First, consider two related questions: Are companies more aggressive in their collection effort when their level of accounts receivable grows relatively large,[22] and do companies behave as if they understand the goodwill tradeoff when selecting their collection methods?[23] The answer to both of these questions is *yes.* One exception discovered when investigating the second question was that companies use techniques such as garnishment (creditors have amounts owed taken out of the delinquent payer's wages), which are very effective in collecting amounts owed, even though consumers dislike these techniques. State and national laws also have a clear impact on what remedies are used in collecting delinquent amounts.

Second, when asked about the most effective means of collecting receivables, most companies replied that they use more than one method, most commonly letters and phone calls. These techniques are effective only to the degree that invoices and billing statements are accurate and timely. Using data from larger U.S., U.K., and Australian companies, Pike and Cheung[24] note that between 83 and 90 percent of firms send an invoice within three days of shipment, and between 41 and 53 percent send statements within three days after

---

[22] Importance is measured both by accounts receivable as a percent of total assets and by the DSO, and reported in Sartoris and Hill (1988), cited in the end-of-chapter references.

[23] This hypothesis was studied by Richard L. Peterson, cited in the end-of-chapter references.

[24] Pike and Cheung (2002), cited in the end-of-chapter references.

## FOCUS ON PRACTICE

### Ten Ways to Get Paid

1. *Get it in writing.* Before starting the job, establish a fee agreement that explains finance charges, interest charges, hourly rates, and refundable or nonrefundable retainers.
2. *Bill immediately.* Right after work is completed, not at the end of the month. Send bills to a physical address, not a P.O. box, and mark envelopes "Do Not Forward—Address Correction Requested."
3. *Charge interest.* To avoid having your bill put at the bottom of your customer's pile of unpaid bills, and especially if yours is a service company and you obviously cannot "repossess" already-delivered service.
4. *Offer a cash discount.*
5. *Work on retainer.* Get cash up front before doing service work, especially if this your first work for the customer.
6. *Get references.*
7. *Establish a write-off policy.* For debt that is too difficult to collect, recognize that you may accept some level of bad debt.
8. *Follow up frequently.* More often than once a month.
9. *Legalize your faxes.* Insert a clause such as "Fax is as original" to ensure it can serve as a legal document.
10. *Follow your billing procedure.* Be pleasant but firm. Call and restate the terms at the first signs of delinquency, insisting on a firm payment plan and definite arrangements. In some cases, accept a settlement less than payment in full to ensure getting some payment.

*Source:* From Robyn Nissim, "Ten Ways to Get Paid," *Entrepreneurial Edge* (Summer 1996), pp. 22–23.

a period's end. Almost 90 percent of U.S. companies involve sales staff in collections, versus about 70 percent of U.K. and Australian companies.

Third, what factors determine the past-due statistics across firms? Pike and Cheung found that more rapid collections for credit sellers (smaller past-due numbers) were identified with larger sellers, sellers receiving credit periods from their suppliers that were longer than those they extend (a surprise), a narrower customer base, getting bank references for new smaller customers, less use of debt collection agents (once overdues get high, companies tend to use these target-related incentives), less use of incentives for internal collectors (again, once overdues get high, companies tend to use these target-related incentives), and offering cash discounts (almost four days' reduction in past-due numbers). Turning the focus to payor motivations, the character issue again looms large in explaining why some firms pay on time (median past-due of one day) while others routinely pay late (median past-due of 15 days). Study Exhibit 6–7 to see what percentages of prompt payors and late payors rated each factor as "important" or "very important" (these were grouped together to develop the bar chart). While this is a U.K. survey, stretching payables is likely the most unethical practice in corporate America as well, and motivations for paying are probably quite similar to those reported here.

Finally, in what way and how often is credit insurance used? The benefit of having credit insurance is that it indemnifies the seller against losses from nonpayment of receivables. This may allow the company to make incremental sales and possibly increase bank credit line borrowing. Credit insurers may be located in various geographic areas, close to potential buyers, and may research and evaluate buyer information before

Exhibit 6–7

*Importance of Reasons for Prompt Payment*

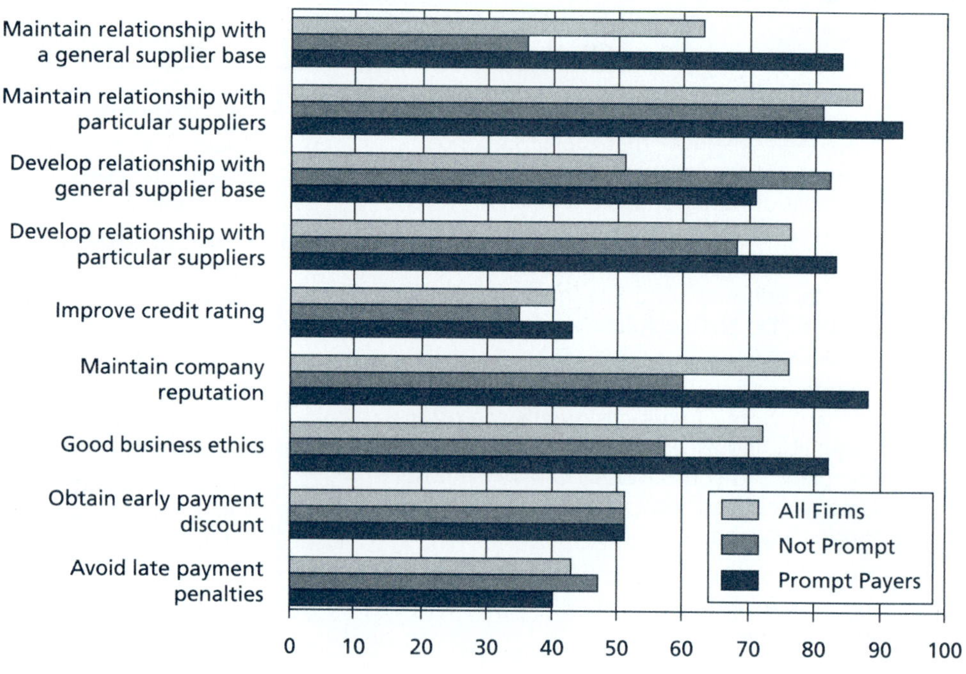


*Source:* Nick Wilson, Barbara Summers, and Paul Wetherhill, "Better Payment Practice: The Benefits of Prompt Payment," **http://www.cmrc.co.uk/documents/promptpayment.pdf** (accessed online 1/2/2004).

making credit extension and credit limit decisions. The insurer will also monitor risks on an ongoing basis. Larger buyers are analyzed individually, with a credit limit assigned for insurance coverage, and smaller buyers are handled under a blanket policy—when one of these buyers does not pay, the insurer will pay (typically within 60 days) the policyholder a claim up to a predetermined amount set in the policy. Almost 40 percent of large U.K. firms purchase credit insurance, versus 14 percent of large U.S. and 19 percent of large Australian firms.[25]

## Legislation and Regulation

Many state and federal laws and regulations govern the extension of credit, the use and communication of credit information, and the procedures used in collection. The National Association of Credit Management annually publishes an extensive volume on this subject entitled *Credit Manual of Commercial Laws.* It includes general information on the legal aspects of security and collections, and state-by-state differences on topics such as contracts, secured transactions, truth-in-lending legislation, bankruptcy proceedings, collection agency requirements, and bad check laws. The manual's chapters on antitrust and trade regulation laws and legal phases of collections provide essential information for the credit administrator.

[25] Pike and Cheung (2002), cited in the end-of-chapter references.

## EVALUATING THE CREDIT DEPARTMENT

The credit manager is also concerned about the efficiency with which the credit department's operations are carried out. Briefly, a review of the departmental operations should include a study of staffing, employee performance, and expense ratios. Exhibit 6–8 illustrates the measures that might be tabulated. Ratio values for a company can be compared to its past years' experience as well as to the values for comparably sized sellers in its industry. From 1960 through 1997 in the United States, percent current has been 81 percent, average (median) days delinquent has been 8.1 days, and the percent over 91 days past due has been 1.8 percent.[26] Trade associations are generally the best source of data on industry experience. Recent evidence points to the use of between two and four measures in management reporting of receivables positions, including DSO, aging schedules, uncollected balance percentages, and exception reports.[27] DSO and aging schedules were most prevalent.

The efficiency of collections is important, but so too is the efficiency of the credit department's processes. The U.K. Credit Management Research Centre estimates that the typical credit department spends over 80 percent of its time on routine activities, and almost 50 percent of the time is spent on collecting sales revenue and chasing down late payments. Exhibit 6–9 provides some benchmark measures of credit department efficiency. In the middle of the column, you see overlap with the collection benchmarks in Exhibit 6–8. In 2002, CRF added another benchmark measure: the index of collection productivity. Briefly, it compares ending receivables ("output") to both employees in the collections area and to cost of capital investment in technology (inputs).

Companies are increasingly using EDI to outsource their invoicing and/or receivables reconciliation to take advantage of expensive new technology, reduce staff time, improve customer service, and speed up exception handling. One approach to outsourcing involves providing your bank with a file of open (unpaid or partially paid) items. The bank keys the data necessary to post paid items to the company's system. The bank has access to company files to verify that the invoice numbers are correctly entered. It may also create and distribute paper or electronic invoices from company-provided billing files. As payments are received, the bank updates the company's customer records and sends them an updated electronic file. Ideally, the "hit ratio" of automatically updated receivables records exceeds 90 percent. A second outsourcing approach, customized and typically more limited in scope, entails services developed to fit the company's credit and receivables situation. The bank may go online with the company's receivables system to update the files (instead of merely transmitting a file and having the company do the update).

Improving efficiency and effectiveness in credit management is accomplished by reducing the investment in receivables, covered in the next section, and by integrating credit management with marketing and customer concerns, covered in the subsequent section.

### Reducing the Investment in Receivables

The zero net working capital objective introduced in Chapter 1 and the cash conversion period objective presented in Chapter 2 both strongly influence accounts receivable policy setting. Key to both objectives is the goal of reducing investment in receivables. Companies attempt to pare receivables to an optimal level by:

1. Reducing invoicing float (the time elapsing between order shipment and invoicing) and ensuring that invoices are accurate and state when the invoice payment terms

---

[26] Ochs and Parkinson, cited in the end-of-chapter references.

[27] Ricci, cited in the end-of-chapter references.

## Exhibit 6–8

*Credit Management and Credit Department Benchmarks*

### Credit Management Benchmarks

| Turnover | | Memo: Third Qtr., 2003 |
|---|---|---|
| Days sales outstanding (*DSO*) | | *43.5 days* |
| Best possible DSO (*BP*) | | *32.2 days* |
| Average days delinquent (*ADD*) | Benchmark value: 8.1 days | *8.8 days* |
| Percent current (*PC*) | Benchmark value: 81% | *79.26%* |
| Percent over 91 days past due (*Over 91*) | Benchmark value: 1.8% | *1.50%* |
| Collection Effectiveness Index | | *78.75* |

**Loss Control**

Percent of gross bad debt to sales (*GBD*)

Percent of net bad debt (net of recoveries) to sales (*NBD*)

**Cost**

Credit cost per sales dollar (*$ Sales*)

**Glossary:**

Credit sales refers to actual billings and therefore includes freight, taxes, and containers.

Total trade receivables refers to all domestic accounts and notes and includes past-due billings and accounts placed for collection.

Current trade receivables refers to the portion of domestic open accounts and notes not yet due.

Average trade receivables beyond 91 days refers to monthly average of trade receivables 91 days or more past due, aged on actual due date.

Collection effectiveness index is based on beginning quarterly A/R and end of quarter, A/R, and is calculated as follows:

$$\text{CEI} = \frac{\text{Beginning total receivables} + (\text{Quarterly credit sales}/3) - \text{Ending total receivables}}{\text{Beginning total receivables} + (\text{Quarterly credit sales}/3) - \text{Ending current receivables}} \times 100$$

$$\text{Days sales outstanding} = \frac{\text{Last three months ending total receivables balance}}{\text{Credit sales for quarter}} \times 30$$

$$\text{Best possible DSO} = \frac{\text{Last three months ending current receivables balance}}{\text{Credit sales for quarter}} \times 30$$

$$\text{Percent over 91 days past due} = \frac{\text{Average receivables over 91 days}}{\text{Average total receivables}}$$

*Sources:* Ronald K. Chung, "Structural Reengineering of the Credit Process: Strategic Influence and Financial Control," *Credit and Financial Management Review* (1) (1995), p. 5. Reprinted with permission. Benchmark data are based on overall data from domestic trade receivables in the United States from 1960 to 1997, as tracked by the Credit Research Foundation (CRF), and are mostly from manufacturers. Data were published in Joyce R. Ochs and Kenneth L. Parkinson, "Collections: What the Data Shows—A Conversation with CRF's Terry Callahan," *Business Credit* (June 1998), pp. 20–21. Recent data are from CRF.

begin (an October 2002 CRF survey found that 69 percent of U.S. firms state this, with about 50 percent indicating this on the invoice and/or credit application and 96 percent indicating this on the invoice);

2. Fine-tuning credit administration and credit policy, including credit standards, by reviewing the profit and bad debt tradeoff periodically and considering the use of key account management systems (covered next);

**Exhibit 6–9**

*Credit Department Efficiency Measures*

**I. FINANCIAL PERFORMANCE METRICS**
DSO
Best Possible DSO
Average Days Delinquent
Collection Effectiveness Index
Percent Current
Percent AR Greater Than 60 Days
Percent AR Greater Than 180 Days
Gross Bad Debt as % of Sales
Bad Debt Recovery as % of Sales
Net Bad Debt as % of Sales
Deductions as % of AR $
Deductions as % of AR Items

**II. CUSTOMER METRICS**
Top 10 Customers as % of Sales
Top 20 Customers as % of Sales
Invoice Size
Number of Invoices per Customer
Number of Active Customers
Primary Customer Type

**III. DEDUCTION METRICS**
Number of Deductions Processed per Deduction Processing Employee
Deduction Processing Costs as % of Sales
Deduction Turnover
Deductions Salary per Deductions Employee
Deductions as % of Sales
Deduction Balances Included in AR Portfolio

**IV. EFFICIENCY METRICS**
Various costs per transaction, employee, salary for Credit/Risk, Cash Application, Collections, etc.

**V. OUTSOURCING METRICS**
Percent of Workload that is Outsourced for Credit Risk, Cash Application, Collections, Deduction Processing, etc.

**VI. COST ANALYSIS METRICS**
Collection Expenses
Outside Services
Outsourcing
Travel
Occupancy or Rent
IT Systems
Depreciation/Amortization
Total Cost as % of Sales, % of FTE Salary Benefits, per Customer and per Employee

**VII. BUSINESS PRACTICES METRICS**
% of Companies Charging Late Payment Fee
% of Companies that Accept Credit Cards
% of Companies Allowing Anticipation Payment Discount
% of Late Payment Charges Ultimately Collected
Annual $ of Credit Card Sales as % of Sales
Electronic Invoicing
Electronic Payments
Auto Write-off
Use of Auto-cash Systems including Auto-cash Hit Rates
$ Amount Shipped Automatically to New Customers with No Credit Investigation
% of Customers in Highest (Top Third) Risk Category

**VIII. ORGANIZATIONAL STRUCTURE / RESPONSIBILITIES**
Reporting Relationships
Where Various Functions are Primarily Performed within the Organization
Department Responsibilities

**IX. SYSTEMS INFORMATION**
AR or ERP Systems Used
Use of Bolt-on Deduction Management, Collection Management Systems and Credit Scoring Systems

Source: Credit Research Foundation, Benchmarking the Credit and Accounts Receivable Functions, **http://www.crfonline.org/surveys/benchmarking/be**.

3. Outsourcing and automating, which might address credit evaluation via credit scoring (Ricci's survey found that few companies have automated this step, which motivates outsourcing of this activity), or factoring, which varies significantly by seller's industry and size (and can be done by banks, trade factoring firms, or nonbank intermediaries);
4. Reducing discrepancies and deductions, which represent disagreement between order and actual shipment made, possibly resulting from inaccurate or delayed order fulfillment (some practitioners have found that invoices that are "at issue" constitute the primary reason for late payments);
5. Improving monitoring and collections, by using benchmark data as standards of comparison, using multiple methods, and employing rapid and effective late-payor follow-up.

These methods generally reduce the time uncollected payments are outstanding and increase the quality (collectibility) of those amounts that are outstanding. Many U.S. companies have made strides in reducing DSO, but not to the extent of the reductions in days inventory held (DIH): from 1980 through 2001, the DIH period was reduced from 73 days to 48 days (25-day reduction) while DSO moved down only from 68 days to 57 days (11-day reduction).[28]

### Organizational Integration of Credit Management: Key Account Management Systems

Continuously improving credit management to meet or exceed benchmark standards demands a holistic approach to credit, in which marketing and finance considerations are combined. The opening discussion in Chapter 5 demonstrated that credit is an integral part of the marketing function as well as the finance function. The opening flowchart in that chapter (Exhibit 5–1) illustrated this connection by beginning with marketing strategy. Businesses have begun to see the need to improve all business processes—including credit standard setting, credit evaluation, credit extension, and collections—which support their key customer accounts. These are large and/or growing customers that are important to the continued success of the seller.

As a seller's level of involvement with its customers increases from simple to complex and the nature of its customer relationships evolves from "just transacting business" to being collaborative, customer loyalty may be built by:

- Developing a better understanding of the needs and wants of the key accounts,
- Prioritizing accounts according to their potential value and the seller's available resources, and
- Making credit terms and policies an integral part of a well-designed sales and marketing offering.

Credit management benefits from and adds to a well-designed key account management system in much the same way that materials requirement planning (MRP) influences inventory management. Objectives pursued with key accounts include market share, profit, sales growth, and DSO. To illustrate, Kodak's Office Imaging business unit seeks to drive shareholder satisfaction by committing to performance objectives in revenue, margin, and account objectives. Changes in the way receivables management is conducted will be triggered by advances in key account management sophistication and penetration.

## INTERNATIONAL CREDIT MANAGEMENT

The final section in this chapter is a brief survey of the international complications of credit management. The three major considerations are currency variations, the often arbitrary timing of customer payments, and the legal and economic environment. Currency variations are changes in the exchange rate at which the company can convert the cash from the receivable collection into the parent company's home currency. Mainly, the devaluation (reduced value of the foreign currency) that the domestic manager is concerned with arises from higher inflation rates and/or more rapid money supply growth in the foreign country. Customer payment timing is problematic because of different religious and cultural norms regarding the acceptability of late payment, the added complexity of international payment instructions, and the longer collection cycle inherent in most international

[28] Mellyn and De Groeve (2002), cited in the end-of-chapter references.

transactions. Recent evidence from the U.K. Credit Management Research Centre bears this out, noting that prompt credit *payors* have a significantly lower percentage of export customers. Finally, the legal and economic environment creates problems caused by foreign exchange controls, country risk, widely varying credit laws, and poor customer credit history data. These three problem areas compound the level of difficulty in both credit policy decision making and monitoring and collections efforts.

## Modifying Credit Policy Analysis

The added complexity of international credit management is evident whenever credit managers seek to alter the company's credit policy. For example, easing the credit policy—whether through a longer credit period or a lower credit standard—is riskier for foreign sales because of the increased uncertainty about the dollar value of cash flows arising from foreign currency devaluation. Although an easing of credit standards or longer credit period should generate more sales, it also results in increased default risk and the possibility of the receivables deteriorating in dollar value as a result of foreign inflation and currency devaluation.[29] Part of this reduced value can be offset by an increase in the company's selling price because of the economy-wide inflation and the newly liberalized terms. Furthermore, regardless of the credit policy, the exporter may require a stronger assurance that payment will be received. Although the majority of sales made by U.S. companies to established foreign companies are on open account, a significant portion of sales to new or less-established accounts use documentary collections or letters of credit, or those sales may have their receipts guaranteed by seller-purchased credit insurance offered by a third party.

Applying the credit policy is also more difficult. A company's in-house credit analyst may not be able to get a client D&B rating for many overseas clients, and bank credit information might also be less easily obtained. Although international credit decisions are more difficult, D&B can provide commercial credit information about many businesses worldwide. D&B's products and services draw on a foreign database of more than 36 million foreign companies, and it gathers business information in 200 countries around the world. Some countries have cross-border data limitations that prohibit a U.S.-based multinational company from transmitting creditworthiness and/or payment history data back to the United States.

## Modifying Monitoring and Collections

In addition to the typical collection probability and timing estimates, credit managers must monitor currency exposure of foreign receivables. This refers to the vulnerability of the company to a decline in the value of the receivables at the time they are collected or when they are translated back into the parent company's home currency. Perhaps in conjunction with other treasury department personnel, they should develop a strategy for monitoring and possibly hedging (protecting the company against) the risk. The absolute size of the exposure of the receivables denominated in various currencies is a starting point. However, the potential for reducing that exposure should also be highlighted. One approach is to weight the dollar equivalent of each currency's exposure by dividing it by the DSO or by the uncollected balance percentage index. The currencies with the highest quotients are then targeted for improved collection efforts.[30] Credit managers especially push

[29] Shapiro (see the end-of-chapter references) has developed a model to determine the expected marginal cost (in dollars) of extending one dollar's worth of credit by one period.

[30] For more on this issue, see the approach to managing foreign subsidiaries' receivables in Turner (cited in the end-of-chapter references).

for timely or even early payment (which is called "leading") when foreign currencies are expected to decline in value relative to the home currency. Note, however, that the manager's forecasting ability may not be better than the market's, and hedging the transaction exposure may be a better way of addressing the depreciation risk (see Chapter 17). Repayment practices abroad often seem arbitrary to U.S.-based managers, who observe payment patterns in the United States that are fairly stable except during recessions. Traditions regarding payment of amounts owed may be much different abroad. This helps explain why credit insurance is much more predominant in Europe than in the United States.

Finally, legal and economic environments vary in foreign countries, constraining multinational managers in the control phase of credit management. Because receivables constitute part of the multinational's asset investment in a foreign country, credit managers should analyze the country's political risk. Risk factors range from the possibility of fund flows being blocked, to the entire operation being nationalized, with the company's remitted profits and asset investment being reduced or totally eliminated. Also, the legal remedies for late payment or nonpayment differ by country.

We conclude with two important observations about improving international credit management. First, a company should manage the entire cash flow timeline. Order-to-invoice delays in foreign subsidiaries have been a major problem area for U.S.-based multinationals, according to a survey of treasurers conducted by the Financial Executives Research Foundation.[31] Widely dispersed sales offices may mail billing information to a company's headquarters, greatly slowing the invoicing process. Computer hookups are a simple solution for such a problem. One food producer's German subsidiary had a 6- to 10-day lag from order-to-invoice, which was cut to one or two days after computer terminals were installed at the warehouses. This saved the company an estimated $40,000 per year in interest, when converted to U.S. dollars.

Second, and closely related to the first point, the entire credit evaluation, granting, monitoring, and collections process should be automated. A U.S. paper manufacturer reduced its DSO from 100 to 72 days, and its bad debt loss rate from 1.2 percent to 0.4 percent of net sales by setting up a computer database of customer credit histories and by automatically generating invoices when orders are entered. An added advantage to an automated system is that the treasurer of a multinational company can net accounts payable and accounts receivable for each currency, arriving at a net exposure by currency.

## SUMMARY

Our second credit management chapter developed the framework for applying the net present-value model to credit policy decisions. This capital budgeting approach is recommended for valuing the impact of credit policy decisions because it properly incorporates cash flow timing and risk. The model is applied to changes in credit standards, the credit period, and the cash discount.

Once the credit policy is in place, the attention shifts to collecting receivables. This effort begins with proper monitoring of the receivables portfolio. Monitoring collection patterns is the credit manager's ongoing responsibility. The manager has several tools to aid in this oversight, including the aging schedule, DSO or the average collection period, accounts receivable turnover, and the uncollected balance percentages. Of these, the uncollected balance percentages are the only reliable and unbiased measure of customer payment patterns; the other measures are biased by changing sales patterns and are sensitive to the averaging period chosen for the calculations. Recent advances in monitoring are presented in the chapter appendix.

---

[31] Business International, *"Automating Global Financial Management,"* New York: John Wiley & Sons (1988).

When the monitoring approach used (such as *DSO*) signals slowed collections, the credit manager initiates a series of contacts with the customer(s) involved. A form letter is often the first contact vehicle, followed by other letters, telephone calls, and initiation of outside collection efforts such as referral to collection agencies or litigation.

The chapter concluded with pointers on how to evaluate the efficiency of the credit department and some warnings regarding receivables management in the international arena. International considerations meriting special focus are foreign currency exposure; payment system particularities; and legal, cultural, and environmental differences.

## USEFUL WEB SITES

*Also see Web sites referenced at the end of Chapter 5.*

| | |
|---|---|
| Business Credit Magazine | **http://www.nacm.org/bcmag/bcarchives/bcarchives.html** |
| Benchmarking | **http://www.crfonline.org/surveys/benchmarking/benchmarking.asp** |
| Performance measures | **http://www.crfonline.org/orc/ca/ca-7.html** |
| U.S. bankruptcy statistics | **http://www.credit-to-cash-advisor.com/document_50.html** |
| DSO statistics—U.S. | **http://www.crfonline.org/surveys/dso/dsoresults.html** |
| State collections laws | **http://www.commercialbar.com/sumcoltn.htm** |
| International collections | **http://www.credit-to-cash-advisor.com/news_91.html** |
| Credit industry news | **http://www.creditworthy.com/** |
| Jobs in credit function | **http://www.creditjobstoday.com/** |

## QUESTIONS

1. What are the key variables for evaluating credit policy changes, according to credit managers? Are managers able to estimate the values for these variables adequately? Compare and contrast the incremental profit and NPV approaches to evaluating credit policy decisions.
2. List the assumptions of the NPV model. Are these assumptions valid when a company is considering extending its credit period from 30 to 90 days, if all of its competitors retain a 30-day credit period?
3. What are the two major shortcomings of DSO and accounts receivable turnover? Which of these also plagues the aging schedule?
4. What is the relationship between DSO and total accounts receivable on a given company's balance sheet?
5. Why might it be argued that uncollected balance percentages are superior to other measures used to monitor customer payment patterns?
6. What collection monitoring measures do managers express a preference for in actual practice?
7. With the aging schedule, receivables amounts from past months are related to the present total accounts receivable balance. To what are the receivables amounts related when computing uncollected balance percentages? Why is this distinction important when evaluating collection efficiency?
8. Interpret the payment index shown at the bottom right of the uncollected balances schedule (see Column 4 in Exhibit 6–5).

9. Why shouldn't a credit manager be overly aggressive when first contacting a customer who has just missed a payment due date?
10. What are the steps followed in the collection effort, along with their approximate timing?
11. What collection practices are actually used by businesses, according to evidence cited in the chapter?
12. What are the main differences faced by U.S. credit managers when selling on credit abroad?

## PROBLEMS

*Note: Round calculations to the seventh decimal place when calculating daily interest rates. Use the simple interest rate unless otherwise specified.*

1. Norton Wrench, a machine tool company, recently found out that one of its main competitors has tightened its credit standards. Norton's chief operating officer has asked you to make a recommendation to the executive policy committee on whether the company should tighten its standards. The marketing department estimates that annual sales will drop $20,000 from the present level of $275,000. The variable cost ratio is 0.7 and will not change, according to one of the cost accountants. Variable expenses related to collections and credit administration are projected at 1.25 percent of sales under the existing standards but 1.45 percent of sales under the proposed standards. The bad debt expense rate on both existing and incremental (lost) sales is estimated to be 7 percent. The DSO of 56 days is not expected to change and can be applied to any sales gained or lost due to a change in credit standards. The company's annual cost of capital is 15 percent.
   - **a.** Draw a cash flow timeline for one day's sales under the proposed standards.
   - **b.** What is the value effect ($\Delta Z$) of this decision on one day's sales?
   - **c.** What is the overall value effect ($\Delta NPV$)?
   - **d.** Are there any nonfinancial considerations about which you believe the executive policy committee should be warned?
2. Evans Knitwear's president is convinced that the company must lengthen the credit period it offers to its customers, upscale mens wear retail stores. She suggests to the credit executive that the stores have become less liquid and more indebted and need longer to pay their bills. As the analyst assigned to "run the numbers," you have determined that such a move will increase sales from $100 million to $105 million per year. The VCR is 0.65 and will not change, and the credit and collection expenses will increase from 2 percent to 2.5 percent under the proposal. DSO under the present 30-day terms is 42 days; under the proposed 45-day terms, it will be 52 days, according to your best estimate. The bad debt loss rate is 2.5 percent, and it will not change for the additional sales. The company's annual cost of capital is 12 percent.
   - **a.** Calculate the decision's 1-day change in value.
   - **b.** Calculate the decision's NPV.
   - **c.** Do you recommend lengthening the credit period?
   - **d.** If the bad debt loss rate under the new credit terms is higher (3.5 percent versus 2.5 percent), does this change your recommendation?
3. J. James Book Publishers is trying to decide whether to offer a 3-percent cash discount for payments made within 10 days, making its new terms 3/10, net 30. On average, its paying customers currently pay in 40 days under its present terms of net 30. A sales analyst estimates that sales will stay the same. The existing bad debt loss rate is 3 percent; the rate under the new policy will be the same. It is estimated that 40 percent of J. James' paying customers will take the discount and pay on the tenth day, on average. The remaining paying customers will continue to pay in 40 days, on average. The company's annual cost of capital is 10 percent. Annual sales will remain unchanged at $250 million, and the variable cost ratio will continue to be 60 percent. The variable expenses for credit administra-

tion and collections will drop from 5 percent to 4 percent if the cash discount is implemented.

**a.** What is the 1-day change in value related to the proposed terms?
**b.** What is the change in daily net present value related to the proposed terms?
**c.** Do you recommend that J. James initiate the cash discount?
**d.** What is the optimal cash discount percent for J. James?

**4.** For each of the following financial situations, calculate the optimal cash discount percentage.
**a.** Cash discount period = 5 days, credit period = 75 days, and annual cost of capital = 15 percent.
**b.** Cash discount period = 10 days, credit period = 30 days, and annual cost of capital = 12 percent.
**c.** Cash discount period = 10 days, credit period = 45 days, and annual cost of capital = 18 percent.
**d.** Cash discount period = 10 days, credit period = 30 days, and annual cost of capital = 22 percent.

**5.** Rework the Flying High Hang Gliders, Inc., text example, assuming daily compounding instead of the simple interest stated in the text. (*Hint:* See footnotes 6 and 9 in the text.)
**a.** How does the 1-day value effect change?
**b.** How does NPV change?
**c.** Comment on the reason for the differences in your answers as compared to the simple interest solutions shown in the text.

**6.** Rework the Siegel Apparel Mills text example, assuming daily compounding instead of the simple interest stated in the text. (*Hint:* See footnotes 6 and 9 in the text.)
**a.** How does the 1-day value effect change?
**b.** How does the decision's NPV change?
**c.** Comment on the reason for the differences in your answers as compared to the simple interest solutions shown in the text.

**7.** You have been presented with the following accounts receivable information from Besley, Inc. Construct an aging schedule and calculate DSO and accounts receivable turnover for the 6-month period, using 180 days to calculate average daily credit sales.

Besley, Inc., manufactures and sells wallboard for use in construction of modular homes. It sells on net 30 terms to contractors. Following are the last six months' sales and the accounts receivable balances at the end of June, the present (report) month.

Accounts Receivable Schedule
Besley, Inc.
June 30, 2005

| Month* | Credit Sales | Uncollected Amount |
|---|---|---|
| January | $ 75,000 | $ 5,000 |
| February | 50,000 | 5,000 |
| March | 100,000 | 6,000 |
| April | 40,000 | 6,000 |
| May | 45,000 | 8,000 |
| June | 50,000 | 12,000 |
| | **June 30 A/R balance:** | **$42,000** |

*Assume all months have 30 days.

**8.** Calculate the uncollected balance percentages for the company in Problem 7. Discuss the insights you gain from this schedule relative to what you found in your analysis in Problem 7.

**9.** The following table gives the receivables data for Besley, Inc., (see Problem 7) for the same six months, exactly one year later.

Accounts Receivable Schedule
Besley, Inc.
June 30, 2006

| Month* | Credit Sales | Uncollected Amount |
|---|---|---|
| January | $100,000 | $10,000 |
| February | 90,000 | 10,000 |
| March | 80,000 | 12,000 |
| April | 200,000 | 12,000 |
| May | 100,000 | 16,000 |
| June | 150,000 | 24,000 |
| | **June 30 A/R Balance:** | **$84,000** |

*Assume all months have 30 days.

For **a–d**, what conclusions can you draw based on your computations?

**a.** DSO

**b.** Accounts receivable turnover

**c.** The aging schedule

**d.** Uncollected balance percentages

**e.** Explain why your conclusions in **d** might give a slightly different picture than those reached in **a–c**.

1. You have been informed that Besley's credit terms in both years were net 30. Are most of Besley's customers paying on time? Paying late?
2. What steps might Besley's credit personnel take to improve the success of their collection efforts?
3. Compute the accounts receivable turnover Besley should have experienced had all of its customers paid on the due date. How much of a reduction in outstanding total receivables would this have implied?

## REFERENCES

Moshe Ben-Horim and Haim Levy, "Management of Accounts Receivable under Inflation," *Financial Management* (Spring 1983), pp. 42–48.

Scott Besley and Jerome S. Osteryoung, "Survey of Current Practices in Establishing Trade-Credit Limits," *The Financial Review* (February 1985), pp. 70–82.

Stephen F. Borde and Daniel E. McCarty, "Determining the Cash Discount in the Firm's Credit Policy: An Evaluation," *Journal of Financial and Strategic Decisions* (Fall 1998), pp. 41–49.

Michael D. Carpenter and Jack E. Miller, "A Reliable Framework for Monitoring Accounts Receivable," *Financial Management* (Winter 1979), pp. 37–40.

Francis Chittenden and Richard Bragg, "Trade Credit, Cash-Flow and SMEs in the U.K., Germany, and France," *International Small Business Journal* 16(1) (1997), pp. 22–35.

Ginger Conlon, Lisa Napolitano, and Mike Pusateri, editors, "Unlocking Profits: The Strategic Advantage of Key Account Management," Chicago: National Account Management Association (1997).

Credit Research Foundation, "Credit Professional's Handbook: The Technical Reference Manual for Credit and Customer Financial Managers," Columbia, MD: Author (1999).

James Fairrie, "2010: The Role of Credit Insurance in Credit Management and Debtor Finance," *Business Credit* (July/August 2000), pp. 48–49.

Ned C. Hill and Kenneth D. Riener, "Determining the Cash Discount in the Firm's Credit Policy," *Financial Management* (Spring 1979), pp. 68–73.

Jeff Keller, "Best Practices in Accounts Receivable," *TMA Journal* (January/February 1995), pp. 34–37.

Joe Ketzner, "Credit Insurance: An Asset in Today's Marketplace," *Business Credit* (April 2003), pp. 22–23.

Sang-Hoon Kim and William Feist, "Examination of the Equivalent Relationship between the Two Credit Policy Approaches: The Opportunity Cost and NPV Approaches," *Financial Review* (November 1995), pp. 711–737.

Yong H. Kim and Joseph Atkins, "Evaluating Investments in Accounts Receivable: A Wealth Maximizing Framework," *Journal of Finance* (May 1978), pp. 403–412.

Ruby Knerr, "Gaining an Understanding of Your Customers Using Portfolio Analysis," *Business Credit* (July–August 1998), pp. 43–47.

Yul W. Lee and John D. Stowe, "Product Risk, Asymmetric Information, and Trade Credit," *Journal of Financial and Quantitative Analysis* (June 1993), pp. 285–299.

William Lim and Muhammad Rashid, "An Operational Theory Integrating Cash Discount and Product Pricing Policies," *Journal of American Academy of Business* (March 2002), pp. 282–288.

Kevin Mellyn and Bernard De Groeve, "The Argument for Financial-Chain Management." Available online at **http://www.cfo.com**. (December 1, 2000). [Accessed online January 5, 2004.]

Joyce R. Ochs and Kenneth L. Parkinson, "Collections: What the Data Shows," *Business Credit* (June 1998), pp. 20–21.

Rob Olsen, "Measures of Performance: Credit Collections and Accounts Receivable." Columbia, MD: National Association of Credit Managers (1994).

Richard L. Peterson, "Collectors' Use of Collection Remedies," *Journal of Financial Research* (Spring 1986), pp. 71–86.

Richard Pike and Nam Cheung, "Trade Credit, Late Payment, and Asymmetric Information," *Bradford University School of Management Working Paper No. 02/09* (May 2002).

Muhammad Rashid and Devashis Mitra, "Price Elasticity of Demand and an Optimal Cash Discount Rate in Credit Policy," *The Financial Review* (August 1999), pp. 113–126.

Cecilia Wagner Ricci, "A Survey and Analysis of Accounts Receivable Practices in American Corporations," *Financial Practice & Education* (Fall/Winter 1999), pp. 111–120.

Kenneth D. Riener, "The Analysis of Credit Policy Changes with Growing and Seasonal Sales," in Yong Kim (ed): *Advances in Working Capital Management, Vol. 4.* Greenwich, Conn.: JAI Press (2001), pp. 123–135.

R. Schwartz, "An Economic Model of Trade Credit," *Journal of Financial and Quantitative Analysis* (September 1974), pp. 643–657.

Alan Shapiro, "Optimal Inventory and Credit-Granting Strategies under Inflation and Devaluation," *Journal of Financial and Quantitative Analysis* (January 1973), pp. 37–46.

Michael D. Sherman and Brian Fisher, "An Evaluation of the Statistic Accuracy of Monitoring Outstanding Accounts Receivable," *Proceedings of the 8th International Symposium on Cash, Treasury & Working Capital Management*, San Francisco, October 2, 1992.

Keith V. Smith and Brian Belt, "Working Capital Management in Practice: An Update," *Krannert School of Management (Purdue University), Working Paper 951*, (March 1989).

Charles R. Turner, "Key to Managing Foreign Subsidiaries' Locally-Generated Trade Receivables," *Credit and Financial Management* (January 1981), pp. 26–28.

Paul Weatherhill, "B2B Credit: A Strategic Tool for the New Economy," *Credit Management* (November 2000), pp. 38–40.

FOCUSED CASE

# Kimball International, Inc.

Kimball International, Inc., (NASDAQ symbol: KBALB) is a diversified furniture and electronics manufacturer that sells wood and metal office furniture, lodging furniture, and electronic assemblies (including computer keyboards and mouse pointing devices).* The Lodging Group (part of the "Furniture and Cabinets" segment) is experiencing dramatic growth in sales and income, increasing market share at the same time that the hospitality industry is continuing its refurbishing cycle. The assistant treasurer is considering increasing the company's investment in this high-growth area. He believes if the company changes its credit standards and credit period, it will add profitable sales. Along with the rest of the top management staff and the board of directors, he is concerned about the slowly growing or declining sales and/or market share in some of Kimball's segments [such as the original equipment manufacturers (OEM) Furniture and Cabinets unit]. Sales continued to grow at a moderate pace in the larger two of the company's three business segments—(Furniture and Cabinets, and Electronic Contract Assemblies), but sales in the company's smallest business segment—(Processed Wood Products and Other) declined from the prior year's first quarter. According to the company's 10-K annual report of its financial statements and operating results (as filed with the Securities and Exchange Commission, p. 9):

> "Sales of Original Equipment Manufacturer (OEM) product lines, primarily television cabinets and stands, audio cabinets, and residential furniture, decreased in the 3-month period when compared with one year earlier. Lower sales volume of cabinets were caused by a major cabinet customer experiencing lower market demand for their products. Although certain other cabinet customers increased their volumes, this product line experienced an overall decline in sales volume. Production flexibility is inherent in the OEM supplier market and may cause short-term fluctuations in any given quarter. Volumes of contract residential furniture increased from the prior year. Some OEM production capacity was used for production of hospitality furniture during the quarter. OEM operating income declined from the prior year's level as a result of the decrease in sales volume and, to a lesser extent, an unfavorable sales mix toward lower margin products."

The assistant treasurer believes that the company's future is linked to significant growth in a few areas such as the Lodging Group. He has asked for your advice as the senior credit analyst in the credit department.

At present, the company holds roughly 25 percent of its $557 million asset base in the form of cash and marketable securities. Its present average credit period for paying customers of the Lodging Group is 54 days. The company extends 45-day terms to its customers. The bad debt losses on the Group's sales are a respectable 1.7 percent. Sales in the Lodging Group are $85 million, almost one-tenth of the company's $983 million sales. The variable costs for lodging furniture, excluding credit administration and collection costs, average 45 percent. The company's weighted average cost of capital is 10 percent. It presently has surplus funds invested at an average rate of 6.5 percent. Sales estimates under two independent proposals for changes in the credit policy are as follows:

Proposal A: Lengthen credit period to 60 days.

Proposal B: Ease up on credit standards.

Proposal C: Implement both Proposals A and B.

Other relevant aspects of the company's financial position were also provided to the credit analyst from the management discussion in the 10-K report (pp. 10–11).

> Consolidated selling, general and administrative expense, as a percent of sales, increased 1.2 percentage points for the 3-month period (compared to the year earlier), primarily as a result of moderate additions to the Company's existing infrastructure supporting the higher sales volume, additions as the result of acquiring ELMO Semiconductor in the latter half of the prior fiscal year, and certain other costs that are variable with earnings.
>
> Operating income for the first quarter of 1997 was $19,183,000, increasing 2.8 percentage

*The company and its attributes are real, but the credit policy aspects are fictitious. Check with your instructor to see if he or she wishes to have you supplement the case data gathered from other print or electronic sources.

| Policy | Lodging Group Sales | Bad Debt Expense Rate (% of revenue) | Credit Administration & Collection Expense (% of revenue) | Paying Customers' Collection Period |
|---|---|---|---|---|
| Present | $85 million | 1.7% | 2% | 54 days |
| Proposal A | $95 million | 2.0% | 2.1% | 66 days |
| Proposal B | $100 million | 2.3% | 3% | 63 days |
| Proposal C | $105 million | 2.15% | 2.5% | 68 days |

points, as a percent of sales, when compared to the first quarter of 1996, primarily as a result of sales volume increases, the diminished effects of material price increases that were experienced in the prior year's first quarter, and manufacturing efficiency improvements, including benefits from quality and cost containment initiatives.

Investment income for the first quarter remained flat when compared to the same period in the previous year, as higher investment balances were offset by a lower effective yield. Other—net includes $3.8 million related to a loss on the sale of a foreign subsidiary in the current year, which is offset by a $3.8 million income tax benefit recorded in Taxes on Income. The remaining decrease in Other income or expense—net is primarily due to larger gains realized on the sale of assets in the prior year.

Taxes on Income includes a $3.8 million tax benefit relating to the sale of a foreign subsidiary in the current year's first quarter. This tax benefit was the result of a higher U.S. tax basis in this subsidiary as a result of previously undeductible losses on the investment in this U.K. subsidiary. Excluding this tax benefit, the effective income tax rate decreased 1.3 percentage points in the 3-month period when compared with the prior year partly as a result of reduced European operating losses that provide no immediate tax benefit.

The company achieved net income of $13,521,000, or $0.65 per share, for the first quarter of the 1997 fiscal year, a 61% increase over the prior year's first quarter net income of $8,418,000, or $0.40 per share.

LIQUIDITY AND CAPITAL RESOURCES

Cash, Cash Equivalents and Short-Term Investments totaled $140 million at September 30, 1996, as compared with $117 million one year earlier. Liquidity remained strong with working capital and the current ratio at $230 million and 2.7 to 1, respectively, at September 30, 1996, as compared with $204 million and 2.7 to 1, respectively, one year earlier.

Operating activities continued to generate positive cash flow, which amounted to $38 million for the three months ended September 30, 1996. Portions of the company's cash flow from operations were reinvested in the business to fund $9 million of capital investments for the future, primarily production equipment upgrades and improvements in the company's business information systems. Five million dollars was used for financing activities, primarily to pay dividends. Net cash flow, excluding purchases and maturities of short-term investments, amounted to a positive $26 million for the 3-month period ended September 30, 1996.

The company anticipates maintaining a strong liquidity position throughout the 1997 fiscal year with cash needs being met by cash flows provided by operations, available cash balances, and short-term investments on hand.

1. Which proposal, if any, should Kimball adopt? Defend your position based on the value effect and the present financial position of the company. Indicate why you chose the discount rate used in the analysis.
2. How does the financial position of the company strengthen or weaken the recommendation you made in **1**?
3. The assistant treasurer indicates to you that one of the Electronic Products senior managers thinks capital should be allocated to his unit instead of to the Lodging Group. How should the assistant treasurer respond to this concern? (You may use any business concept or approach to answer this, not limiting the answer to the credit policy proposals.)
4. What competitor reactions are likely if Kimball unilaterally makes one or both credit policy changes? How might this be incorporated into the present analysis?

# APPENDIX 6A

## Sophisticated Receivables Monitoring Techniques

Several different approaches have been developed or refined recently to better monitor (and forecast) collections. These are the decomposition method, the variance analysis model, the Markov chain approach, the lagged regression model, and the recursive regression model. The **decomposition method**, developed by Gentry and De La Garza[1], involves segregating the period-to-period changes in receivables into three effects: the collection effect, the sales effect, and the interaction effect. The interaction effect refers to the joint influence of sales and collections. The philosophy behind this method is very similar to that used in management accounting, in which budget variances are divided into price, volume, and mix categories. A notable difference is with what we are comparing recent receivables experience; in this case, it is the last period's experience instead of budgeted amounts. The credit manager wishes to know the change in the controllable variable(s), which, in this case, is the collection effect and part of the interaction effect. Deterioration in the collection pattern signals corrective action. Although it takes time to construct the analysis schedule, this approach does help the analyst in determining when and how substantially the collection pattern has changed.

The **variance analysis model** builds on the decomposition model and compares actual receivables performance to the budgeted amounts.[2] If the budget captures the unique conditions and sales levels a company is experiencing, or is so adjusted after the period is over ("flexible budgeting"), then the true reason(s) for changes in receivables levels can be discerned. The budgeted amount is calculated as expected sales multiplied by expected DSO.

Actual sales can be used instead of expected sales, once the period is over, to get a revised (or flexible) budgeted amount. The model separates the collection experience variance (actual DSO minus budgeted DSO) from the sales effect variance (actual daily sales minus budgeted daily sales). If the collection experience variance is positive, or unfavorable, the analyst is prompted to determine the possible reasons and suggest some corrective actions the company might take. Additionally, the model separates the sales effect variance into its two components: the sales mix effect and the sales quantity effect. The sales mix effect is relevant because the company might sell different products with different credit terms, and the analyst should not fault the collection effort for the resultant increase in receivables.

**Markov chain analysis** is an elaborate means of identifying changes in the collection experience. It is related to the uncollected balance percentages presented earlier in the chapter, which are actually a simple application of Markov chains. This technique is applied by (1) identifying each possible payment stage where an account might be, such as already paid, current, one month past due, two months past due, three months past due, or written off as bad debt; (2) specifying the "transition probabilities" for the average account, which is the probability it will move from one of the stages to any of the other stages; (3) using the results from Stage 2 to estimate what the DSO, collection amount, and receivables amount should be; and (4) noting whether the actual experience mirrors what was expected from Stage 3. Historical data or a forecasting technique such as exponential smoothing might be used to develop the Stage 2 transition probabilities.[3]

A quick and relatively inexpensive way of determining a company's collection experience involves **lagged regression analysis**.[4] The amounts collected this

[1] J. A. Gentry and J. M. De La Garza, "Monitoring Accounts Receivable Revisited," *Financial Management* (Winter 1985), pp. 28–38.

[2] A variance is defined as the actual dollar amount minus the budgeted dollar amount. This technique was developed in George W. Gallinger and A. James Ifflander, "Monitoring Accounts Receivable Using Variance Analysis," *Financial Management* (Winter 1986), pp. 69–76.

[3] See Jarl G. Kallberg and Anthony Saunders, "Markov Chain Approaches to the Payment Behavior of Retail Credit Customers," *Financial Management* (Summer 1983), pp. 5–14. See also Jarl G. Kallberg and Kenneth Parkinson, *Current Asset Management: Cash, Credit, and Inventory*. New York: John Wiley & Sons, pp. 180–184, 190–192.

[4] This was suggested by B. K. Stone (1976; cited in end-of-chapter references); it was implemented by J. K. Shim, "Estimating Cash Collection Rates from Credit Sales: A Lagged Regression Approach," *Financial Management* (Winter 1981), pp. 28–31.

period are model-determined percentages multiplied by sales made in this and previous months. The percentages are the regression coefficients $b$:

$$C_t = b_1S_{t-1} + b_2S_{t-2} + b_3S_{t-3} + b_iSt_{t-i} + e_t \qquad (6.1A)$$

In which: $C_t$ = the amount collected during the present month, month $t$

$S_t$ = the company's credit sales made in month $t$

$b_t$ = the month $t$ collection percentage of a given month's sales

$i$ = the number of periods lagged

$e_t$ = an error term to capture bad debt losses and unpredictable variations in collections

The $i$ subscripts for the collection percentages are a bit tricky. The percent of last month's sales being collected this month is represented by $i = 1$; when $i = 2$, we are referencing the sales from two months ago, and so on. In practice, the constant term one typically includes in a regression equation is omitted, which is equivalent to forcing the regression line through the origin. The error term picks up unpredictable influences, and to the degree that $b$ terms sum to less than 100 percent, it would also incorporate the bad debt loss rate. Ignoring unpredictable influences and omitted variables, we have an expression for computing the bad debt loss rate $b$ as shown in Equation 6.2A:

$$b_E = 1 - (b_1 + b_2 + b_3 + \cdots + b_i) \qquad (6.2A)$$

Equation 6.3A is equivalent:

$$b_E = 1 - \sum_{1}^{i} b_i \qquad (6.3A)$$

To implement the lagged regression approach, the analyst gathers the dollar amounts of monthly credit sales and collections for at least three years and inputs these to a statistical package or a financial spreadsheet. (For example, in Excel select Tools, then select Data Analysis, and finally select Regression; make sure you have installed the data analysis add-in within Excel by selecting Tools/Add Ins/Analysis ToolPak before initiating the regression routine.) The computer calculates the $b_i$'s, which are the percentages of each past month's sales that were collected during a particular month. These percentages can be monitored through time to see if they are changing. They can also be used to forecast cash collections in upcoming months. Using only 21 months of actual sales and collection data for one company, Shim and Siegel[5] fit the following equation:

$$C_t = 60.6\%(S_{t-1}) + 24.3\%(S_{t-2}) + 8.8\%(S_{t-3})$$

The $r^2$ for the model is 0.754, which indicates the goodness of fit was quite good. The $t$ statistics for the first two $b$'s were both 0.05 or less, and the third coefficient, $b_3$, was not significant at the 5 percent significance level. The latter was still judged acceptable, because such a small sample size was used to fit the regression equation. In practice, the analyst should use a larger sample. Finally, using either Equation 6.2A or 6.3A, we find that the bad debt loss percentage $b_E$ was $[1 - (0.606 + 0.243 + 0.088)] = 0.063$, or 6.3%.[6] Another application of this model to a large department store chain found the goodness of fit ($r^2$) to increase significantly when including four months of sales data in the model, as compared with only one month ($r^2$ increased to 0.5875 from 0.3805).[7]

A critique of the ordinary least squares (OLS) regression model does not aid the analyst in recognizing when there are significant changes in collection patterns, as opposed to minor and/or seasonal changes. Although a complete discussion is beyond the scope of this text, we mention that the **recursive least squares (RLS) regression model** remedies this shortcoming. Essentially, this model allows the estimated collection fractions (the regression coefficients) to change over time.[8] Although the OLS model can be reestimated many times, such an approach is limited because pattern changes occurring during the model's estimation period contaminate the estimated fractions, and even after receiving the model results and realizing that the pattern has changed, the analyst cannot know when the change occurred. Even if the analyst could identify the timing of the pattern change, it would be necessary to wait a long time before having enough new data to refit a revised model. The RLS lagged regression model has a built-in method of updating an initial set of coefficient estimates, which, in this case, are the collection fractions. Errors observed in actual observations feed back into the model to enable an automatic adjustment of coefficients. Visual inspection of the coef-

[5] See Jae K. Shim and Joel G. Siegel, "Handbook of Financial Analysis, Forecasting, and Modeling," Englewood Cliffs, NJ: Prentice-Hall (1988), pp. 331–332.

[6] The Durbin-Watson statistic when testing for autocorrelation was 2.52, indicating a lack of autocorrelation. The standard error of the estimate for the equation was 11.63.

[7] Kallberg and Parkinson, cited earlier, p. 189.

[8] The only known application of this technique to receivables monitoring is in Michael J. Gombola and Douglas R. Kahl, *"Identifying Changes in Receivables Collection Patterns."* Paper presentation at the Financial Management Association 1989 Annual Meeting, Boston, MA. Their model allows the collection fractions to vary over time, as opposed to the fixed coefficients OLS model presented earlier. The model is appealing because it is precisely the fact that collections fractions might change over time that interests the credit manager.

ficients on a computer printout enables the analyst to see when the collection experience changed.

The careful reader has perhaps noticed a common omission shared by all of the above techniques. Although each method helps to uncover changes in the collection experience, none tells us why the change occurred. Knowing whether to take corrective action certainly depends on the permanence of and reason(s) for the change. It is generally recommended that collection fractions be regressed on factors that might logically cause them to change. Factors suggested include the level of consumer confidence, buying power indices, the unemployment rate, current stage of the business cycle, health of the customers' industries, and many others. Results of this further regression modeling might help answer questions about permanence and aid in forecasting future collection patterns.

CHAPTER

7

# Managing Payables and Accruals

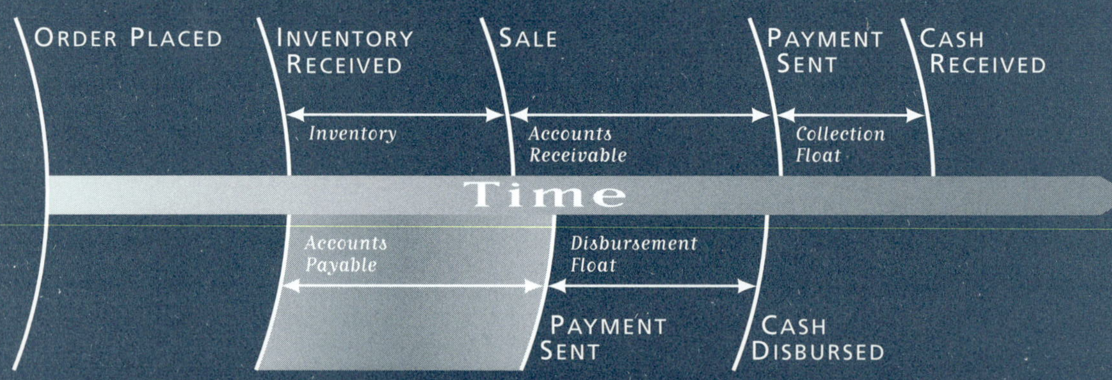

## OBJECTIVES

*After studying this chapter, you should be able to:*

- apply time value of money principles to the payment of accounts payable.
- decide when to take a cash discount for early payment and when to pay at the end of the credit period.
- better understand the ethical issues involved in the payment decision.
- have a better appreciation for the role that information systems play in the management of accounts payable.
- better assess the status of a firm's accounts payable balance through the use of balance fractions rather than using more traditional but less accurate measures such as payables turnover ratios.

In early January, Macy's 20,000 suppliers got the bad news. They were informed that they would have to wait several more weeks to receive payment on the shipments they sent to R. H. Macy & Co. prior to the Christmas holiday season. As January wore on, Macy's financial position deteriorated even more and by the end of the month Macy's declared bankruptcy under Chapter 11. Macy's, struggling under a heavy debt burden as a result of a leveraged buyout and a holiday shopping season with less than expected sales, simply did not have the cash to pay its suppliers.

This chapter focuses on the third leg of the working capital cycle, the management of accounts payable and accrued operating expenses. As we have seen, a firm's working capital cycle begins with the purchase of inventory. This purchase generally initiates an accounts payable balance, and the firm begins accruing expenses such as wages, salaries, and taxes. Inventory is then sold, creating an accounts receivable balance. At a future point in time, generally before the receivables are collected in cash, the payables and accruals are paid. These outflows are then "reimbursed" by the collection of the outstanding receivables. This cycle is continually replayed. However, in Macy's case, the cycle came to a halt, as more cash was needed to pay creditors and suppliers than Macy's had collected from its sales.

Thus far in this text, we have discussed the management of inventory and receivables. We now turn our attention to the proper management of the payables and accruals generated by the operations of the firm. In this chapter, we will discuss how payables and accruals represent sources of financing for the firm's investment in its working capital. We will also discuss how to make proper financial decisions regarding the timing of payment for payables and accruals and some of the institutional aspects of structuring the information systems required for making such payments. The chapter concludes by discussing the importance of monitoring the payables balance so that payments are made in a time frame appropriate to the firm's policies regarding its payables.

### FINANCIAL DILEMMA

Why Pay Early?

The financial manager of BBC, Inc., just received an invoice from a new supplier with the terms 2/5, net 45. He understood that these terms allowed him to take a 2-percent discount from the face amount of the invoice if paid by the 5th day after the invoice date. Otherwise, payment for the full invoice price is due on the 45th day from the invoice date. The financial manager was stumped because, while the discount seemed enticing, it did force him to make the payment 40 days ahead of the actual due date.

## SPONTANEOUS SOURCES OF FINANCING

A spontaneous source of financing is one that occurs automatically as a result of operations. Two common **spontaneous financing** sources are payables and accruals.

An example will help to better understand how these spontaneous sources work. Suppose Ajax Chemical Company purchases a truckload of packaging materials from one of its suppliers. These materials are used to package its shipments of chemical products. When the delivery arrives at Ajax, an invoice is enclosed stating the terms of credit, but Ajax has the materials and can begin using them immediately without making payment of funds.

In this sense, the supplier is extending credit to Ajax as a result of the Ajax order. Ajax can begin using the packaging materials to ship its products and only after the payables credit period is up does Ajax have to pay for its purchases. This allows Ajax to better match its receipt of cash from sales of its products with cash disbursements for its purchases.

## ACCOUNTS PAYABLE

**Accounts payable**, also referred to as trade credit, is considered a spontaneous financing source because it is generated by the normal day-to-day operations of the firm. If there is demand for the firm's product, the firm will produce in order to satisfy that demand and in so doing must order materials and supplies for its production or service processes. If the materials and supplies are purchased on credit, a source of financing is created. Through the sale of the product, the corporation gains a resource that will eventually generate a cash inflow enabling the spontaneously generated liability, the account payable, to be paid off.

### Types of Purchase Terms

A multitude of purchase terms is available. Chapter 5 presented a detailed discussion of credit terms, which are the same as purchase terms, except from the perspective of the seller. This section will not reiterate the various credit terms available, except to highlight some of the more typical forms.

The exact terms depend on the product being purchased and the industry involved. For example, a gas station purchasing gasoline generally gets no longer than 10 days to pay for the purchase because the product is sold so quickly. Likewise, perishable products generally carry short credit periods. On the other hand, the purchase of heavy industrial equipment may carry much longer credit periods. These products are more durable and can be reclaimed if payment is not made.

One common credit arrangement is an **open account**. Under this type of an arrangement, once a customer has been approved for credit, the customer can make repeated purchases without applying for credit each time. When the goods are purchased, they are sent with payment due at a specified time after receipt of invoice. An example is net 30 days. In this case, the full amount of the invoice is due 30 days after the invoice date.

Another common set of credit terms involves offering a **cash discount** for early payment. An example is 2/10, net 30, which means that if payment is made 10 days after the invoice date, a 2-percent discount from purchase price can be taken. Otherwise, the full invoice price is due 30 days from the invoice date.

Not all credit terms are based on the invoice date. For example, some industries quote credit terms on a **prox** basis. Such terms allow payment on a specific date in the following month. For example, terms of 2/10, prox net 30 mean payment is due on the 30th day of the following month or a cash discount of 2 percent can be taken if payment is received on the 10th day of the following month.

Other forms of credit purchases are seasonal dating and consignment. **Seasonal dating** is common in the toy industry and other seasonal businesses. Seasonal dating allows retail outlets to purchase inventory before the peak buying season and defer payment until after the peak season. For example, toy manufacturers allow retail outlets to purchase toys months before Christmas but pay for the inventory during January and February. The advantage to the manufacturer is to permit the production of the items over a longer period of time without excessive inventory buildup. An example of seasonal dating terms is 2/10, net 30, dating 90. In this case, the clock starts running 90 days after the invoice date. The purchaser can then take the cash discount if paid in 10 days with full payment due in 30 days after the 90-day period is up.

**Consignment** is an arrangement whereby a retailer obtains an inventory item without obligation. That is, if the item is sold, payment is due. If the item is not sold, the retailer can simply return the item without penalty. An example of this type of an arrangement is common in the college textbook industry. Book publishers send their books to college bookstores only to have them returned if they are not sold.

Finally, a growing number of companies are allowing discounts if their customers permit the electronic debiting of their accounts. This type of payment system will be discussed more fully in Chapters 11 and 19.

## The Cash Flow Timeline and Accounts Payable

A financial manager purchasing materials or services on credit gains an advantage by being able to utilize the goods or services in order to earn a profit without first having to pay for them. The time period between receipt of the goods or services and the date on which cash payment is made constitutes what is termed **positive float**. The longer the payment delay, the better off the firm as long as payment is not delayed past the credit period. If payment is not made within the prescribed credit period, suppliers will often impose a penalty of 1 to 1½ percent per month until payment is made. In addition, when a delinquent purchaser places another order, the order will not be sent until overdue balances are paid. In general, financial managers should delay payment as long as possible while remaining within the stated credit period.

How long should the financial manager delay payment? This question can be answered in the context of the cash flow timeline such as the one presented in Exhibit 7–1 showing the important payment decision dates.

**Exhibit 7–1**

*Cash Flow Timeline for Disbursements*

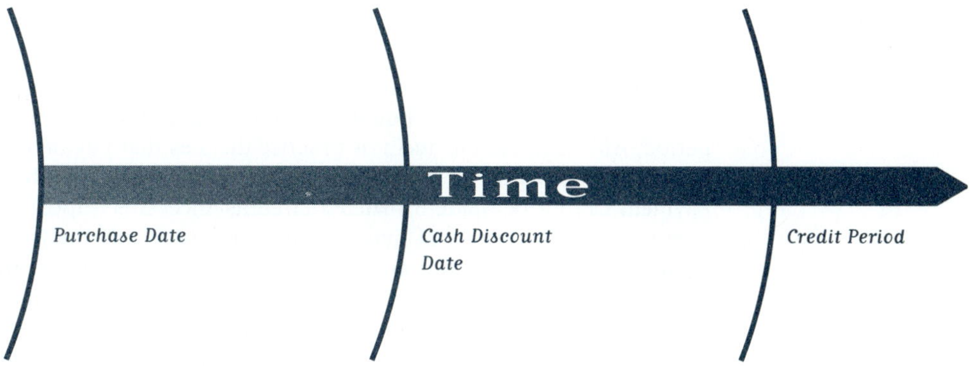

Time

Purchase Date

Cash Discount Date

Credit Period

The financial manager has several payment options. First, payment could be made on the date of purchase. Second, payment could be made on or before the cash discount period. Third, payment could be made on or before the end of the credit period but after the cash discount period. Fourth, payment could be made after the credit period has expired.

How should the financial manager formulate the payment decision? First, consider some basic financial management principles related to the payment of accounts payable. We will develop a payment decision model to support these principles.

- A payable should never be paid until the last day of the discount period or at the end of the credit period and should never be paid early.
- A discount should be taken only when the effective interest rate implied by the discount rate and payable terms exceeds the opportunity cost of short-term funds over the same time period.
- A payable should not be stretched past the credit period.

The payment decision model is relatively straightforward and involves the following variables:

$IP$ = Dollar invoice price

$DD$ = Number of days that payment is delayed from date of purchase

$DP$ = Discount period

$CP$ = Credit period

$d$ = Discount rate

$k$ = Annual opportunity rate

$k_b$ = Annual borrowing rate

$fee$ = Annual fee and intangible cost of late payment

These variables can now be arranged in order to arrive at the present value of delayed payment beyond the purchase date. The three net present value (NPV) models differ only by the assumed date of payment and the amount paid (either the invoice price or the invoice price less the cash discount). The first model, Equation 7.1, calculates the NPV, assuming that payment is made before the end of the discount period.

$$NPV = IP \times (1 - d)/\{1 + [DD \times (k/365)]\} \text{ (if } DD \leq DP) \tag{7.1}$$

Here, the NPV is equal to the present value of the discounted invoice price, assuming that payment is made by the end of the discount period.

The second NPV model, Equation 7.2, assumes that payment is made after the discount period but no later than the end of the credit period.

$$NPV = IP/\{1 + [DD \times (k/365)]\} \text{ (if } DP < DD \leq CP) \tag{7.2}$$

Here, the NPV is equal to the present value of the full invoice price, assuming that payment is made after the discount period but no later than the end of the credit period.

The third NPV model, Equation 7.3, calculates the impact of paying after the credit period. Although ethical business practice dictates that payment should be made no later than at the end of the credit period, a financial manager may be in such a cash bind that payment cannot be made. In such a circumstance, it is important for the financial manager to estimate the cost of making payment late. While the following equation includes a late payment fee, which is an explicit cost of late payment, another cost is the lost goodwill of the supplier that will occur if stretching payments becomes typical behavior. Good business practice dictates that if payments are to be stretched, the financial manager should contact the credit manager at the supplying firm to work out a payment schedule.

$$NPV = IP \times [1 + (DD - CP) \times (fee/365)]/\{1 + [DD \times (k/365)]\} \text{ (if } DD > CP) \quad (7.3)$$

Here, the NPV calculation determines the present value of the invoice price plus the late payment fee.

Before entering numbers into the NPV model, let's discuss its logic. First, suppose that DD = 0, indicating that payment is made on the purchase date. In this case, the value of the cost of paying the payable is simply the discounted invoice price. Next, suppose that payment is made on the discount date. Then NPV is reduced because the same payment is made, but now it is made at a later date and the present value of a later payment is less than an equivalent payment made earlier. Next, suppose that payment is made at the end of the credit period. In this case, NPV is equal to the present value of the invoice price ignoring any discount. Whether this NPV is less than the NPV taking the discount depends on the relative sizes of the cash discount rate and the firm's opportunity rate. We will explore this relationship later. Finally, suppose that payment is made after the credit period. In this case, NPV is equal to the present value of the invoice price and late payment penalty.

Theoretically, the cost of the lost goodwill should also be added to the numerator of the NPV expression. However, this can be difficult to assess. We will reiterate that the financial manager should only stretch the payment of an invoice when the company's financial situation prevents payment from occurring within the credit period.

Using the NPV model, the financial manager should continue to delay payment for an additional day up to the end of the credit period as long as the NPV continues to fall. The objective is to pay on the day that minimizes the present value cost of the invoice.

## FINANCIAL DILEMMA REVISITED

Remember the dilemma faced by the financial manager of BBC, Inc.? He was faced with trying to decide whether it was worth taking a cash discount or keeping the funds invested and possibly even stretching the payable. Using the NPV model, the financial manager can arrive at the proper decision. Let's see what that decision should be.

The terms offered were 2/5, net 45. We may assume that the firm's investment rate is 10 percent, the cost of borrowing is 12 percent, the annualized late payment fee is 18 percent, and the invoice in question is for $10,000. Exhibit 7–2 shows the calculated value for NPV over various time periods. From the NPV results, the obvious answer to BBC's dilemma is to take the discount and pay on the 5th day. This action minimizes the present value cost of making the payment. Payment on any other day incurs a higher present value cost for BBC.

The NPV model can be simplified when payment is either going to be made on the discount date or the credit period date. If these are the only two choices, then the following simplified payables decision model can be developed. The cash discount should be taken and payment made at the end of the cash discount period if the relationship shown in Equation 7.4 is true.

$$IP \times (1 - d) < IP/[1 + (CP - DP) \times (k/365)] \quad (7.4)$$

Payment should be made at the end of the discount period if the discounted invoice price, [IP × (1 − d)], is less than the present value of the full invoice price. Present value is calculated at the end of the cash discount period. This relationship can be simplified by solving for $k$ as shown in Equation 7.5.

$$k < [d/(1 - d)] \times [365/(CP - DP)] \quad (7.5)$$

Thus, if the firm's opportunity rate, $k$, is less than the annualized cash discount rate, it is better to take the cash discount and pay by the discount date. Delaying payment allows

**Exhibit 7–2**

*Calculated Value of NPV Assuming a Ten Percent Investment Rate*

| Days Delayed from Invoice Date | NPV |
|---|---|
| 0 | $9,800.00 |
| 1 | 9,797.32 |
| 2 | 9,794.63 |
| 3 | 9,791.95 |
| 4 | 9,789.27 |
| 5 | 9,786.59 |
| 10 | 9,972.68 |
| 15 | 9,959.07 |
| 20 | 9,945.50 |
| 25 | 9,931.97 |
| 30 | 9,918.48 |
| 35 | 9,905.02 |
| 40 | 9,891.60 |
| 45 | 9,878.21 |
| 46 | 9,880.41 |
| 47 | 9,882.61 |
| 48 | 9,884.80 |

the paying firm to keep its funds invested at the annualized rate of $k$. If this rate is less than the annualized cash discount rate offered by the supplier, then taking the cash discount can enhance value. Otherwise, the funds should be invested and payment only made at the end of the credit period date. The difference between the invoice price and the discounted invoice price is in essence a finance charge for delaying payment from the discount date to the credit period date. If this charge is greater than what the firm can earn on its money by delaying payment, then it should take the discount.

What happens if the firm does not have the cash to pay the payables on the discount date and therefore there is no opportunity to invest the funds? In this case, the firm needs to consider whether or not it is profitable to borrow the funds from a bank in order to take the cash discount assuming that funds to repay the bank will be available by the end of the credit period. In this case, as long as the annualized borrowing rate, $k_b$, is less than the annualized cash discount rate computed above, then it would be profitable to borrow the funds to pay the discounted invoice price on the discount date. This relationship is shown in Equation 7.6.

$$k_b < [d/(1 - d)] \times [365/(CP - DP)] \tag{7.6}$$

Suppose that BBC's investment rate is 20 percent. Exhibit 7–3 displays the calculated values for NPV over the same period of time as that shown in Exhibit 7–2.

In this case, the decision would be to forgo the cash discount since the investment rate, $k$, of 20 percent exceeds the annualized cash discount rate, $[d/(1 - d)] \times [365/(CP - DP)]$, of 18.62 percent. And, in addition, since the investment rate exceeds the explicit penalty fee, the NPV expression decreases with each additional day of nonpayment. This, of course, ignores any assessment of the implicit loss of goodwill with the supplier. The bottom line is that even if NPV declines past the credit period, the firm basically has agreed to a contract to pay no later than at the end of the credit period, and payment should be made regardless of the financial consequences.

## Exhibit 7–3

*Calculated Value of NPV Assuming a Twenty Percent Investment Rate*

| Days Delayed from Invoice Date | NPV |
|---|---|
| 0 | $9,800.00 |
| 1 | 9,794.63 |
| 2 | 9,789.27 |
| 3 | 9,783.92 |
| 4 | 9,778.57 |
| 5 | 9,773.22 |
| 10 | 9,945.50 |
| 15 | 9,918.48 |
| 20 | 9,891.60 |
| 25 | 9,864.86 |
| 30 | 9,838.27 |
| 35 | 9,811.83 |
| 40 | 9,785.52 |
| 45 | 9,759.36 |
| 46 | 9,758.95 |
| 47 | 9,758.55 |
| 48 | 9,758.14 |

These numerical examples demonstrate the three principles of managing the payment of accounts payable presented earlier. Through the use of the NPV model, we verified that payment should not be made until at least the end of the discount period. Then, the discount should only be taken if the annualized discount rate implied by the credit terms exceeds either the investment rate or the borrowing rate. Finally, while the NPV model can easily calculate the impact of late payment, payment should only be stretched past the credit period if the firm is financially unable to make payment.

The variable *fee* has both tangible and intangible components. Many firms will specify a late fee. This is a tangible cost of paying past the credit period. However, intangible costs include the ill will generated by consistently stretching payments past the credit period. This cost is difficult to measure but should be factored into the analysis so that the true cost of stretching can be assessed.

### Ethics and the Payment Decision

Earlier, it was suggested that a firm not stretch the payment beyond the end of the credit period. At times, it may appear that the NPV of stretching is a financially positive decision, especially when the late payment fee is less than the firm's opportunity investment rate. However, when the credit terms were accepted, a contract to pay by a specific date was also accepted, and good business practice dictates that contracts be honored.

Exhibit 7–4 presents three tiers of ethical standards by which to judge one's actions. The lowest tier basically asks if the action is legal or is consistent with the intent of the law. The middle tier asks if you could explain to your parents what you do for a living, the business decisions you make, your business philosophy, and your rationale for your actions and decisions. The top tier of ethical standards says to commit to enhance the well-being of the people you do business with, even if there is some cost to you.

Each tier, moving from the bottom to top, requires additional commitment on the part of the decision maker to make those decisions that enhance the business relationship.

Exhibit 7–4

*Tiers of Ethical Standards*

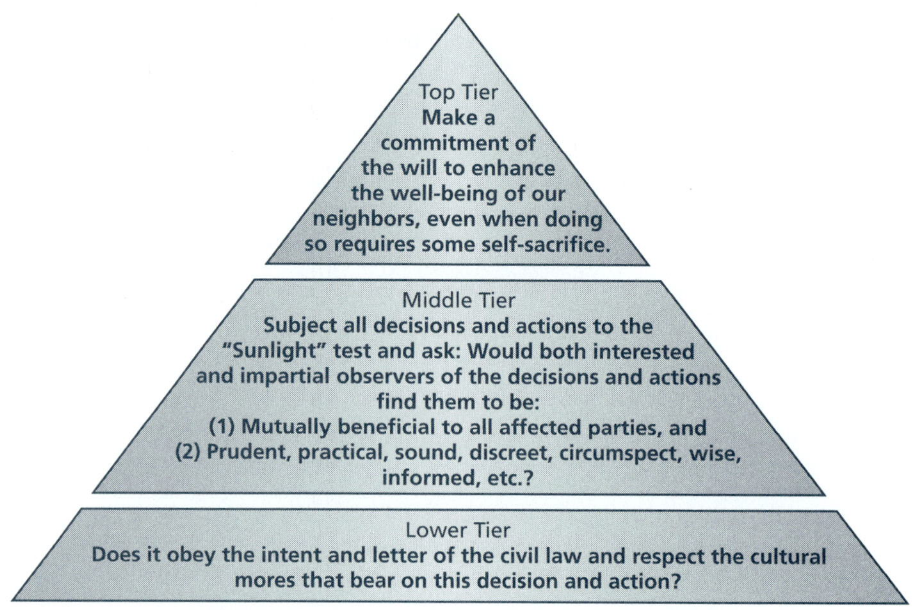

Top Tier
Make a commitment of the will to enhance the well-being of our neighbors, even when doing so requires some self-sacrifice.
Middle Tier
Subject all decisions and actions to the "Sunlight" test and ask: Would both interested and impartial observers of the decisions and actions find them to be:
(1) Mutually beneficial to all affected parties, and
(2) Prudent, practical, sound, discreet, circumspect, wise, informed, etc.?
Lower Tier
Does it obey the intent and letter of the civil law and respect the cultural mores that bear on this decision and action?


*Source:* Richard Chewning, unpublished notes. Interested readers may also read Mary L. Woodell, "Fraud? Imagine You're in the Spotlight," *New York Times* (November 24, 1991), F11. In this article, Woodell offers three tests to help you decide what is right. *The smell test:* Can you convince yourself it is right? *The what-would-your-parents-say test:* Could you explain your actions to your parents and retain their respect? *The deposition test:* Could you defend your actions in a televised trial shown nationwide?

At a minimum, do what is legal according to the civil code, but always strive to make those decisions that build up relationships rather than tear them apart.

In fact, stretching payables may ultimately do more harm than good by potentially driving suppliers into a liquidity crisis. Actually, many financial managers realize that the economic health of a company's suppliers is in the best interest of their companies. Increasing DPO by too many days potentially impedes the ability of the suppliers to cooperate with purchasers to help manage inventory levels. Recognizing this interdependence seems to be reflected by a general decline in DPO in the 2002 Working Capital Survey.[1] In this survey, average DPO across all industries dropped by 5 days to 32 days.

## Information Systems and Accounts Payable Management

As of 2002, an estimated 95 percent of all business-to-business transactions are still settled with paper invoices and checks. Considering that there are approximately 40 billion business transactions annually at an average cost of $50 per transaction, it's no wonder that treasury departments are moving toward trying to automate the financial settlement process. Having an effective accounts payable system requires an integrated information system not only internally, but also with all trading partners. For example, when an invoice is received, it must first be validated. That is, does the invoice represent an order

[1] "We Can Work It Out: The 2002 Working Capital Survey," *CFO* (August 2002), pp. 46–52.

## FOCUS ON PRACTICE

### *Is It Paid, or Is It Not Paid?*

One interesting problem in the payment processing is the criteria for deciding when payment is made. In one survey, Hill, Sartoris, and Ferguson discovered that there is an apparent divergence of opinion between payors and payees regarding the date payment is made.* Credit managers, the payees, generally define date of payment as the day payment is received at the lockbox or collection location. Payables managers, the payors, on the other hand, generally view payment as being made on the postmark date or day sent. Very few firms define payment date as the day they receive goods or collected funds, ie., cash in the bank. In most cases, a grace period is allowed which reduces the conflict over the divergence of opinion related to the date payment is made. This conflict may go away in the near future as more payments are made electronically. Recently, the Financial Services Technology Consortium (FSTC) ushered in a new era of electronic payments with its e-check. E-checks can be issued on the day payment is due to the supplier and e-mailed to allow posting in as little as a few hours. The good thing is that this allows the payor to have control of the funds until the last minute possible yet still meet the supplier's terms.**

Finally, the survey asked if a supplier would charge a late payment fee if a customer paid 25 days late. Approximately 66 percent of the respondents indicated that they would generally not do so. Almost 25 percent of the respondents indicated that it would be likely that a late payment fee would be assessed.

* Ned C. Hill, William L. Sartoris, and Daniel M. Ferguson, "Corporate Credit and Payables Policies: Two Surveys," *Journal of Cash Management* (July/August 1984), pp. 56–62.

** Linda Coven, "The E-Check Cometh . . . as a Replacement for Paper Checks," *Business Credit*, Vol. 101, Number 9 (October 1999), pp. 34–38.

that was actually placed? Is the price or quantity correct? Also, did the firm receive the goods, did the complete shipment arrive, and was it undamaged? Thus, the invoice must be compared to the original purchase order. In addition, shipping documents and the receiving office documents must be checked to verify the receipt and condition of the shipment. Once verified, the invoice is then scheduled for payment. That is, a decision must be made as to the appropriate date to write and send the payment. Will the payment be made in time to take the discount, will the payment be scheduled to meet the credit period, or will payment be stretched, and for how long? We have already discussed the decision-making process for this decision, but the point here is that the payment policy must be linked to the system involved in the actual scheduling of invoice payments.

This information system must be efficient in order to take advantage of cash discounts especially for discount periods less than 10 days. An inefficient information system will simply cause the payor to miss many potentially lucrative cash discount opportunities; indeed, many payables systems just cannot receive a paper invoice through the mail, approve it, resolve exceptions, process the check, and mail payment to the supplier within a 10-day discount period. Today, many firms are moving toward electronic invoice presentment and payment (EIPP) systems to help manage their payables systems. As of 2002, approximately 16 percent of the Fortune 1000 are using some form of EIPP, and it is estimated that this usage rate will move to 20 to 25 percent by 2004.[2]

[2] Jerry Ulrich, "Payables Automation and Electronic Settlement: The Time Is Now," *AFP Exchange* (July/August 2002), p. 45.

FOCUS ON PRACTICE

## The Economic Benefits of Payables Automation

As an early adopter, Sprint Corporation has begun to reap the benefits of payables automation and electronic settlement. Sprint estimates that its costs to process an invoice and issue payment dropped by more than 80 percent by moving from paper invoices and paper checks to an electronic solution.

Due to automated invoice and payment processing, Sprint expects to reallocate between 10 to 15 percent of employees focused on managing supplier invoices to more value-added business activities. In addition, Sprint's suppliers have responded enthusiastically to the business process improvements from an electronic settlement solution.

Finally, as the solution becomes mainstream, the opportunity for Sprint to capture substantial amounts from early payment discounts will drive the return on the modest cost of the solution to very high levels.

*Source:* Jerry Ulrich, "Payables Automation and Electronic Settlement: The Time is Now," *AFP Exchange* (July/August 2002), p. 46.

Another facet of a good information system is that once the payment of an invoice is scheduled, that information can be fed into the company's cash forecast system and the forecast of future cash disbursements updated automatically. This forecast linkage will be discussed more fully in Chapter 13.

### Monitoring the Accounts Payable Balance

Once a firm's payment policy has been determined, the execution of that policy should be monitored on a routine basis. This section will present two ways to monitor the payment pattern and discuss the advantages and disadvantages of each. This material follows directly from the monitoring approaches discussed for inventory and receivables.

*PAYABLES TURNOVER APPROACH* The traditional approach to monitoring a firm's accounts payable balance is based on the firm's **payables turnover ratio**. The payables turnover ratio is found by dividing Purchases over a given time period (sometimes Cost of goods sold is used), such as a year, by the payables balance held during that same time period.[3] For example, suppose that PAYRITE, Inc., showed purchases for a year to be $100,000 and the year-end balance in accounts payable was $18,000. The payables turnover ratio is 5.55 = $100,000/$18,000.

A related payables activity measure is the **number of days of purchases outstanding**, or **DPO**. This can be found by first calculating average daily purchases. Since we used annual purchases above, average daily purchases is found by dividing annual purchases by 365. Average daily purchases is $273.97 = $100,000/365. The number of days of purchases outstanding is then found by dividing the payables balance, $18,000, by average daily purchases, $273.97. The DPO is equal to 65.70 days ($18,000/$273.97).[4] The greater this number, the slower the payables turnover and the longer the firm is taking to pay its suppliers.

[3] It is not uncommon to find average payables used in place of ending accounts payable balance. If the payables balance is growing or declining over the analysis period, average payables gives a better measure of the accounts payable balance than does the ending payables balance.

[4] A shortcut to finding this is to divide the number of days in a year, 365, by the payables turnover ratio. The equation 365/5.55555 results in the number of days of purchases outstanding, which is equal to 65.70 days.

Rather than monitoring the payables balance using annual data, the financial manager should monitor the resources provided by the payables area over a shorter time frame such as monthly or even weekly. It is important for the financial manager to control payables so that appropriate cash discounts are not lost and that full-term payables are paid by the desired time.

Suppose the financial manager collected the following data for the past six months. The dollar amount of monthly purchases would be collected from the firm's purchasing records, and the ending payables balance is based on the firm's monthly balance sheet data. Average daily purchases is calculated by summing the dollar amount of purchases over a predetermined time period such as the most recent month or quarter. In this case, the most recent quarter is used. This sum is then divided by the number of days in the summation period, 90 days for a quarter based on a 360-day year. The result is the average daily purchases. The next line, days purchases outstanding, is calculated by dividing ending payables by the average daily purchases.

| | January | February | March | April | May | June |
|---|---|---|---|---|---|---|
| Purchases | $100 | $120 | $100 | $80 | $60 | $70 |
| Ending payables | | | $ 68 | $55 | $42 | $44 |
| Average daily purchases (quarterly) | | | 3.56 | 3.33 | 2.67 | 2.33 |
| Days purchases outstanding | | | 19.1 | 16.5 | 15.7 | 18.9 |

From March through May, the decreasing days purchases outstanding indicates that payments for outstanding payables are being paid more quickly. However, DPO does jump up to 18.9 days in June, the second highest level for the four-month period.

*A BALANCE FRACTION APPROACH* The following table shows the monthly dollar amount of purchases from January through June. In addition, the table shows the dollar amount of payables left in each succeeding month after purchase. For example, in January, $100 of inventory was purchased. At the end of January, $50 of payables remained unpaid. Of the $100 of purchases in January, $15 remained unpaid at the end of February. The balance of the January purchases was paid in March.

Summing up each column results in the dollar amount of total ending accounts payable for each month. The table clearly shows that ending payables for each month consists of purchases over different time periods. For example, ending payables for March consists of $50 of items purchased in March and $18 of items purchased in February.

| Month of Purchase | Purchase | January | February | March | April | May | June |
|---|---|---|---|---|---|---|---|
| January | $100 | $50 | $15 | | | | |
| February | 120 | | 60 | $18 | | | |
| March | 100 | | | 50 | $15 | | |
| April | 80 | | | | 40 | $12 | |
| May | 60 | | | | | 30 | $ 9 |
| June | 70 | | | | | | 35 |
| Total payables | | NA | $75 | $68 | $55 | $42 | $44 |

To make this table useful for analysis purposes, we need to convert the dollar payables balances to **balance fractions**, dollar payables balance as a percent of purchases. Let's look at an example to help demonstrate this concept. Look at the dollar figures for January in the preceding table. Inventory of $100 was purchased in January. At the end of January, $50 of the January purchase remained unpaid. At the end of February, $15 of the January purchases remained as a payables balance. Thus, 50 percent ($50/$100) of January purchases remained as unpaid at the end of January, and 15 percent ($15/$100) remained unpaid at the end of February. The next table shows the balance fraction calculations for the rest of the months. Notice that the balance fractions are constant. There is a steady pay down of outstanding payables resulting in 50 percent of a month's purchase remaining at the end of the purchase month and 15 percent remaining at the end of the month following the purchase month.

| Month of Purchase | Purchase | January | February | March | April | May | June |
|---|---|---|---|---|---|---|---|
| January | $100 | 50% | 15% | | | | |
| February | 120 | | 50 | 15% | | | |
| March | 100 | | | 50 | 15% | | |
| April | 80 | | | | 50 | 15% | |
| May | 60 | | | | | 50 | 15% |
| June | 70 | | | | | | 50 |

We can conclude from this analysis that payment practice has been stable with no variation in payment pattern of the firm's accounts payable. This finding is in conflict with the conclusion drawn by analysis based on days payables outstanding. DPO uses total payables in the numerator. If purchases are falling, then payables will generally be lower. In the denominator, if purchases are falling, then the average daily purchases will be artificially high because the averaging period will include relatively higher purchases from an earlier period. Thus, turnover will generally fall as purchases fall, not necessarily because of a slower payment pattern, but because of the purchasing trend and the period chosen over which to calculate average daily purchases.

## ACCRUALS

An **accrual** is an expense that has been incurred but has not yet been paid. Basically, two forms of accruals provide a source of short-term financing for the firm: (1) accrued wages and salaries and (2) accrued taxes. Accruals represent a source of financing because, for example, accrued wages represent a service performed by the firm's employees without an immediate payment for the services rendered. Likewise, the government provides financing to business firms because it requires payment for taxes quarterly. The fact that a firm is able to use these tax dollars for a full three months constitutes a source of financing.

A firm can increase its financing through accruals by paying its employees biweekly instead of weekly, or monthly instead of biweekly. However, the financial manager must take into consideration the reaction of employees if he or she decides to change the frequency of wage or salary payments.

Accruals represent a spontaneous source of financing in that as the business expands, the level of operations expands, as does the level of accrued wages and taxes. This source likewise decreases as the level of business activity declines.

## SUMMARY

This chapter approached the determination of an accounts payable model from a present value perspective. We discovered that on the basis of time value of money considerations, a cash discount should be taken whenever the firm's investment rate is less than the annualized cash discount rate. In addition, the firm should borrow to take a cash discount when the borrowing rate is less than the annualized cash discount rate. If neither of these situations exists, then the firm should not pay until the end of the credit period. We also concluded that stretching payment past the credit period date should not be a normal business practice and should only happen when financial resources are not available to make a timely payment.

Technology is beginning to impact the payables area through the development of EIPP systems. Evidence indicates that days payables outstanding is declining across industries, which can partly be explained by increasing efficiencies brought about by technology through more effective information systems and recognition by financial managers of the importance of supplier relationships in the overall supply chain organization.

The chapter concluded by presenting three payables monitoring tools. The balance fraction method is preferred over the payables turnover method and days payables outstanding since they are both influenced by seasonal purchasing trends.

## USEFUL WEB SITES

Online marketplace example: **http://www.tradecard.com**

Payables articles: **http://www.treasury.pncbank.com**

## QUESTIONS

1. What role do payables and accruals play in the working capital or cash cycle?
2. Explain how payables and accruals represent spontaneous sources of financing.
3. Why should firms offer cash discounts?
4. How long should accounts payable be held before payment is made?
5. What is the conceptual relationship between the firm's investment rate, the late payment penalty fee, and the discount rate in determining the appropriate date to make payment?
6. What are the tangible costs related to late payment, and what are some of the intangible costs?
7. What role do information systems play in the payment process?
8. How does the balance fraction approach to monitoring payments improve accuracy of the monitoring information compared to the payables turnover approach?
9. How do accruals represent a source of financing?
10. How manageable are accruals? How does the management of accruals differ from that of payables?

## PROBLEMS

1. For the following set of terms, state whether you should take the cash discount or pay at the end of the credit term period assuming your investment rate is 10 percent.
   - **a.** 1.5/20, net 80
   - **b.** 1/5, net 60
   - **c.** 2/10, net 45
   - **d.** 2/10, net 30
2. You are currently re-evaluating your payables policy. Your current supplier offers terms of 1.5/10, net 40 with a late payment fee of 1.5 percent per month. A supplier wanting your business is willing to offer terms of 2.5/5, net 60 with no stated late payment fee. Your annual borrowing rate is 18 percent. Assume a 365-day year.
   - **a.** How long should you delay payment given the terms of your current supplier? Prove your answer by relating the annualized cost of the discount to your investment or borrowing rate.

**b.** How long should you delay payment given the terms of the competing supplier? Prove your answer by relating the annualized cost of the discount to your investment or borrowing rate.

**c.** Based on an average invoice of $100,000, which supplier should you purchase from, i.e., which set of terms results in the minimum net present-value cost?

**3.** You are currently re-evaluating your payables policy. Your current supplier offers terms of 3/10, net 30 with a late payment fee of 1.5 percent per month. A supplier wanting your business is willing to offer terms of 1/5, net 60 with a late payment fee of 1.5 percent per month. Your annual borrowing rate is 16 percent. Assume a 365-day year. Base your analysis on an assumed $100,000 purchase.

**a.** How long should you delay payment given the terms of your current supplier? Prove your answer by relating the annualized cost of the discount to your investment or borrowing rate.

**b.** How long should you delay payment given the terms of the competing supplier? Prove your answer by relating the annualized cost of the discount to your investment or borrowing rate.

**c.** Based on an average invoice of $100,000, which supplier should you purchase from, i.e., which set of terms results in the minimum net present-value cost?

**4.** Collen Avenue Bakery purchases flour from a mill on a regular basis. The monthly purchase scheduling and ending payables follow.

| | Dec. | Jan. | Feb. | Mar. | Apr. | May | June |
|---|---|---|---|---|---|---|---|
| Purchases | $25 | $45 | $80 | $120 | $100 | $90 | $50 |
| Ending payables | | 50 | 60 | 80 | 85 | 70 | 50 |

**a.** Calculate the days purchases outstanding for March, April, May, and June using quarterly purchases to calculate the average daily purchases.

**b.** What is your conclusion regarding the firm's payment behavior?

**c.** The following table shows the amount of payables remaining in successive months for purchases made during the January through June period of operations. Convert the table to a balance fraction matrix and discuss the firm's payment pattern as represented by the balance fraction table.

| | | Accounts Payable Balances | | | | | |
|---|---|---|---|---|---|---|---|
| | Purchases | Jan. | Feb. | Mar. | Apr. | May | June |
| Jan. | $ 45 | $20 | $22 | | | | |
| Feb. | 80 | | 38 | $20 | | | |
| Mar. | 120 | | | 60 | $30 | | |
| Apr. | 100 | | | | 55 | $17 | |
| May | 90 | | | | | 53 | $15 |
| June | 50 | | | | | | 35 |
| | | NA | $60 | $80 | $85 | $70 | $50 |

**d.** What is your conclusion about the firm's payment pattern?

**5.** Wycliff Contractors, Inc., has the following monthly purchasing schedule and ending accounts payable.

| | Dec. | Jan. | Feb. | Mar. | Apr. | May | June |
|---|---|---|---|---|---|---|---|
| Purchases | $400 | $375 | $350 | $325 | $400 | $500 | $650 |
| Ending payables | | 342 | 320 | 297 | 345 | 430 | 555 |

**a.** Calculate the days payables outstanding for March, April, May, and June using quarterly purchases to calculate the average daily purchases.

**b.** What is your conclusion regarding the firm's payment behavior?

**c.** The following table shows the amount of payables remaining in successive months for purchases made during the January through June period of operations. Convert the table to a balance fraction matrix and discuss the firm's payment pattern as represented by the balance fraction table.

| | | Accounts Payable Balances | | | | | |
|---|---|---|---|---|---|---|---|
| | Purchases | Jan. | Feb. | Mar. | Apr. | May | June |
| Jan. | $375 | $262 | $ 75 | | | | |
| Feb. | 350 | | 245 | $ 70 | | | |
| Mar. | 325 | | | 227 | $ 65 | | |
| Apr. | 400 | | | | 280 | $ 80 | |
| May | 500 | | | | | 350 | $100 |
| June | 650 | | | | | | 455 |
| | | NA | $320 | $297 | $345 | $430 | $555 |

**d.** What is your conclusion about the firm's payment pattern?

## REFERENCES

James A. Gentry and Jesus M. De La Garza, "Monitoring Accounts Payable," *The Financial Review*, Vol. 25, No. 4 (November 1990), pp. 559–576.

John F. Guilding, "Redesigning Accounts Payable," *Management Accounting* (September 1983), pp. 42–46.

Ned Hill, William Sartoris, and Daniel Ferguson, "Corporate Credit and Payables Policies: Two Surveys," *Journal of Cash Management* (July/August 1984), pp. 56–62.

# INTEGRATIVE CASE—PART 2

## *Smyth Appliance, Inc.*

Smyth Appliance, Inc., is a wholesale appliance store selling to contractors. The company has been in operation for more than 30 years and was started by Ted Smyth's grandfather. Ted is the company's chief financial officer (CFO). Ted has been with the company for 5 years, having come from a local bank as one of its lending officers. Five years ago, his father, then chief executive officer (CEO), died unexpectedly, and his brother Ralph took over as CEO, having been with the company since graduating from college. Ralph felt very comfortable with the operating and marketing/sales side of the business, but was very uncomfortable with the financial side of the business. Soon after he took over, he talked Ted into leaving the bank and joining the family business as its CFO.

The company historically has been very profitable, but has been experiencing increasing cash flow problems lately, partly as a result of the recession in the building industry. It seems as though more and more of Smyth's customers are delaying payment of their invoices.

This morning, Ralph has a sales forecast for the coming year on his desk as a result of an intense executive meeting last week. The report includes an analysis of one of Smyth's product lines, kitchen units for manufactured housing. A kitchen unit consists of an oven, dishwasher, and refrigerator set. According to the report, Smyth can expect to sell 1,800 kitchen units during the coming year, which is identical to the level of sales for the current year just ending. Sales are evenly distributed throughout the year.

### Inventory Purchase and Payables

One of Smyth's suppliers is offering an aggressive price/quantity program on the kitchen unit. If Smyth orders 450 kitchen units at a time, the wholesale price that Smyth pays will drop 2 percent from the normal wholesale price of $700 per unit. Smyth currently places an order of 60 units 30 times a year. Smyth prices the kitchen unit at $1,050 to its customers. The best estimate is that placing an order costs about $150, including clerical time, follow-up, inquiries, paper, and computer and telephone expense. Storage or holding costs are estimated to run about $20 per unit, which includes insurance as well as charges for space allocation in the warehouse where space is leased to handle inventory.

In addition to the quantity discount program, the supplier also offers a different set of credit terms to those customers accepting the new quantity discount program. The new terms are justified given the cost savings to the supplier. The new credit terms will become net 60 days rather than the existing net 30 days. The supplier currently does not charge a late payment fee, but will do so under the new policy. A 28 percent annual fee will be charged (accruing interest on a simple interest basis daily) for payments received later than 60 days from invoice date. The supplier indicates that the late payment fee will be stringently applied. Under the old terms, Smyth had been paying 90 days past the invoice date with no late fee and continued good service. However, given the industry conditions, management at Smyth is aware that that they may not be able to expect the same kind of service given their past payment pattern. Net 30 days terms will remain for those customers not taking the cash discount, but they will begin to incur the same late payment fee.

### Credit Terms and Accounts Receivables

Janet Sowell heads up the credit department for Smyth and has been in that position for almost 8 years. Smyth's credit policy is to sell to approved customers on the basis of net 60 days. Smyth's days sales outstanding (DSO) generally runs 90 days and Sowell has been reluctant to be too aggressive about collections, fearing loss of customers, especially in the current economic climate.

Sowell recently learned that several appliance wholesalers have started offering a 2 percent cash discount for payment within 10 days of the invoice date and net terms of 50 days. Her main concern is that if Smyth does not respond with a similar set of competitive terms, the company may begin to lose sales. In fact, she already has had several inquiries regarding a change in credit terms.

As she returns to her office from a meeting, she sees a phone message from Joe Moore, one of her better customers, on her desk asking her to return his call. Janet feels sure that he is inquiring about the possibility of a cash discount. She guesses that, based on the interest her current customers have shown in such a program thus far, about 30 percent will take the cash discount if offered. Those not taking the cash discount will still pay on average in 90 days. Sowell realizes that offering a cash discount of 2 percent reduces cash receipts, but she wonders how that will be offset by receiving the cash earlier, particularly because she sees the change in credit terms as only maintaining the current sales level. Janet is also aware of the discussion going on between the purchasing and inventory managers regarding the quantity discount program and wonders how that might affect her dilemma with the credit terms.

## The Chief Financial Officer

In their weekly executives' meeting, Ted received all the information discussed above and is trying to sort it out. He wants to try to approach the problem by looking at the present-value impact of the decisions in the different areas. To calculate a present value, he will use a required rate of return of 20 percent and wants to evaluate the impact on cash flows for the kitchen unit product line over the coming year (a 360-day year). He figures that the best decision will be the one that increases the net present value (NPV) of the kitchen unit line's direct cash receipts net of direct disbursements.

### Required

a. To start, calculate the EOQ using the basic EOQ equation in Chapter 4.

b. Now decide the optimum order quantity, assuming the firm's current situation (not considering the quantity discount program or change in receivables terms). Choose from order quantities of 10, 20, 30, 60, 100, or 120 units. Explain why this optimal order quantity may be different from the EOQ answer found in part (a).

c. Ted realizes that it is imperative to match credit terms with Smyth's competitors, so all cases analyzed will consider the new credit terms. He decides to consider the four cases indicated below:

**CASE 1:** New A/R terms
Maintain old A/P, paying in 90 days with late fee
Order the current quantity

**CASE 2:** New A/R terms
Maintain old A/P terms but pay in 30 days
Order the current quantity

**CASE 3:** New A/R terms
New A/P terms, paying in 60 days
Order the new higher quantity to receive discount

**CASE 4:** New A/R terms
New A/P terms, paying in 90 days rather than 60 days
Order the new higher quantity to receive discount

To properly evaluate each case, Ted calculates the NPV based on a 360-day year.

d. As Ted is winding up his analysis of the four cases, he discovers that a competing supplier has offered a novel purchase plan. The supplier would like to set up a just-in-time-type inventory program with Smyth. Because Smyth's orders occur at a relatively constant rate throughout the year, the supplier suggests that if Smyth can provide a year-ahead estimate of inventory needs, the supplier can ship units on a daily basis, eliminating Smyth's need to accumulate inventory. In essence, the order quantity will be 5 units. The supplier estimates that ordering costs will be only \$180 a year or about \$.50 per order, and that inventory holding cost will be totally eliminated. The supplier also offers net 90 day credit terms with a 28 percent late fee (accruing daily).

Ted's main concern about this proposal is the risk of contracting for a year's volume of inventory, but he decides that this risk can be accounted for by adjusting the required rate of return up to about 25 percent. How does this alternative compare with the best of the four cases analyzed in part (c)? In addition to the NPV calculation, what additional factors should Ted consider before making his decision?

PART

# Corporate Cash Management

Part III focuses on the heart of corporate short-term financial management—the efficient collection, movement, and disbursement of cash. Effective management of payables, inventories, and receivables frees up cash, but the ultimate benefit is predicated on the effectiveness of the company's cash management systems. In Part III, the costs and benefits of corporate cash management systems are presented to facilitate value-maximizing decision making. The context of cash management decisions is presented in Chapter 8. Chapter 8 introduces the U.S. payment system and presents several differences found in foreign payment systems. It also details the company's relationship with its banks and how best to manage that relationship. Chapter 9 develops several methods by which companies can efficiently collect cash. In Chapter 10, we indicate how to move the collected cash into one or more accounts to make investments, pay down borrowings, or cover disbursements. Finally, in Chapter 11, we build on the general payment system and bank information to show how to establish value-enhancing disbursement systems.

CHAPTER

8

# The Payment System and Financial Institution Relationships

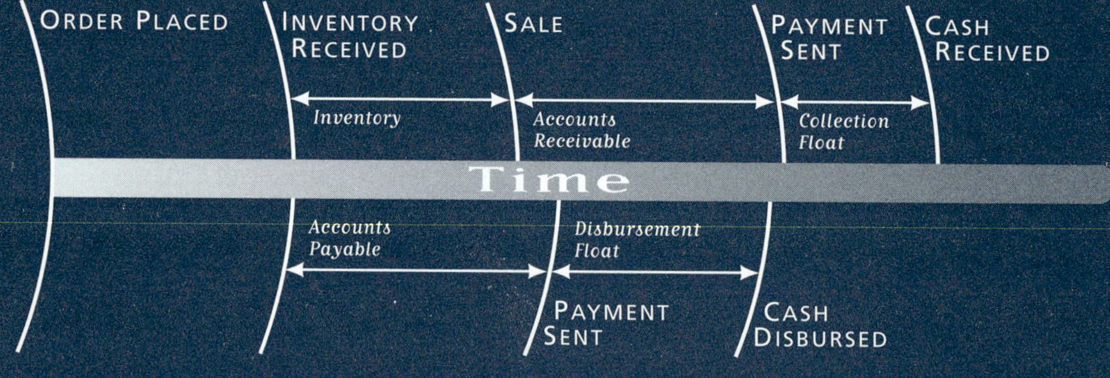

# OBJECTIVES

## *After studying this chapter, you should be able to:*

- explain the concept of float, and calculate its value, indicating why it arises in the U.S. payment system.
- specify and explain the roles of the two major components of the payment system.
- describe the major paper-based and electronic-based payment systems.
- describe how an automated clearinghouse transaction works and how it fits in with electronic data interchange.
- use an availability schedule to calculate availability on deposited checks.
- explain the uses of an account analysis statement and balance requirements to compensate financial institutions for service fees.

Understanding the payment system is very important for the financial manager. Ninety percent of U.S. corporate payments continue to be made by writing checks, but cash managers are increasing their use of electronic payment methods. Collecting and disbursing cash involves several decisions regarding the best payment system methods to use. These decisions can add value to the corporation, as the following Financial Dilemma illustrates.

### FINANCIAL DILEMMA

#### Should We Get on the Electronic Payments Bandwagon?

Organizations have several alternatives for moving funds and paying bills. Checks could be written, or funds could be moved around electronically via electronic funds transfer systems. A related issue is how to handle available funds before paying bills. For Ann Richards, former treasurer of the state of Texas, this was the $1 billion question. By shifting from a paper-based system to a highly automated electronic funds transfer system, she was able to earn the state $1 billion in additional interest within five years. The 49 "Rapid Deposit" programs she initiated move an estimated $10 billion annually. Indicating how things were done before, Richards tells how the previous state treasurer carried a bond issue proceeds check for several hundred million dollars from New York to Austin in the pocket of his sports coat. "The former treasurer did not get mugged, but the people of Texas did," Richards declared, adding that the episode cost the state $20,000 in lost interest.

Cash managers wishing to emulate Richards' accomplishments are faced with several questions: Would the costs outweigh the benefits for our organization? Would parties we deal with be receptive to our new procedures? Does our present banking network allow for expedited and innovative payment methods?

Cash managers repeatedly have demonstrated that understanding the impact of payment mechanisms on the cash flow timeline can enhance profitability and shareholder value. We develop the unifying concept of float in this chapter and also provide a background for later chapters on cash collection, concentration, and disbursement systems. We accomplish this by covering the banking system, paper- and electronic-based payment systems, and the international payment system. U.S. banking regulations that explain the popularity of several corporate cash management techniques are listed. We also describe payment system trends and argue that despite rapid advances in electronic commerce, a cashless, checkless society is not in the foreseeable future. Finally, we show how to manage the corporate banking relationship. This is a lengthy chapter, but this material must be understood because it explains the motivation for so many cash and working capital management techniques.

## VALUE OF FLOAT

The single most important aspect of the U.S. payment system when considering cash management is the existence of **float** on mailed checks. From the payor's perspective, float refers to the delay in value transfer from the time a check is written until it finally is charged to the payor's account. The cash manager can apply the valuation approach to calculating the value of float. Once again, we can use the cash flow timeline to illustrate a realistic situation and how to anchor the dates for our calculation appropriately.

We set up a cash flow timeline in the example that follows, illustrating changes in float and their value effect. We use a simple interest present value calculation for a company considering using newly available bar coding of ZIP codes, which leads to less mail time due to reduced Postal Service handling.

*EXAMPLE* Crown Corporation collects $1,000,000 daily. It is presently considering investing in a machine that will both bar code ZIP + 4 on outgoing envelopes and presort by destination. The Postal Service has already shown the cost savings for the machine in terms of reduced postage (about three cents per first-class item). Management wonders if there is a significant additional savings from the one-third day savings in mail float the Postal Service guarantees for companies doing the bar coding. Collection float at present is three days mail float, two days processing float, and two days availability float. Assume Crown's cost of capital is 10 percent per year.

The cash flow timeline at present is graphed as follows:

How much value can be gained by Crown due to the reduced mail float?

*SOLUTION* The revised cash flow timeline appears as follows:

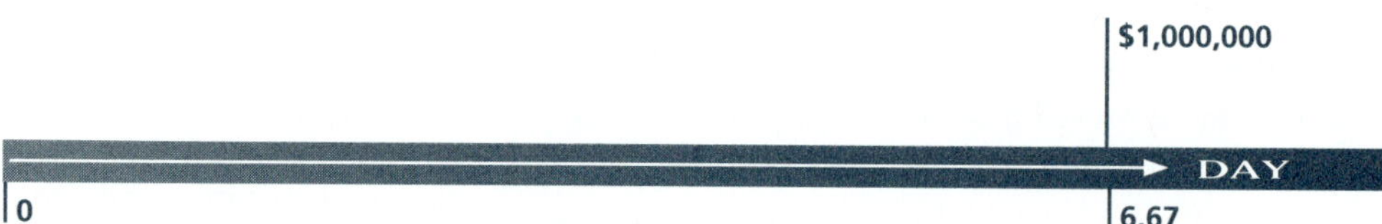


Two approaches can be used to see the value effect of the reduced float: the first gives the present value of one day's collections, and the second uses that result to calculate the total effect.

### Calculate the PV of One Day's Collections under Both Mail Float Situations

The simple interest discounting formula presented in Chapter 3 (Equation 3.2) is reproduced here as Equation 8.1.

$$PV = \frac{CF}{1 + (i)(n)} \tag{8.1}$$

Substituting for the present situation of a 7-day wait until cash is received gives us the present value of the collection float.

$$PV = \frac{\$1,000,000}{1 + (0.10/365)(7)}$$
$$= \$998,085.86$$

The present collection float of seven days has a present dollar value to the corporation of \$998,085.86. To see if the present value would increase on adoption of the new terms, we make the same calculation for the proposal. Based on the anticipated collection float of 6.67 days, we have

$$PV = \frac{\$1,000,000}{1 + (0.10/365)(6.67)}$$
$$= \$998,175.94$$

With the proposal, the collection float reduction to 6⅔ days results in a present value of daily collections of \$998,175.94. Thus, Crown would gain about \$90 *per day's* collections on a present value basis. This first calculation simply indicates the value effect of one day's transactions. To find the total value effect, assuming the savings will last into the indefinite future, we need to calculate the present value of a perpetuity of such flows.

## Calculate the NPV of a Perpetual Stream of Daily Collections

The procedure for determining the present value in total of a daily perpetuity is presented in the appendix at the end of the text and is reproduced here as Equation 8.2. In words, we take one day's cash flow and divide it by the daily equivalent of the nominal interest rate.

$$PV = \frac{CF}{i} \tag{8.2}$$

Because we have the difference in daily cash flow (\$90.077272) from the reduced mail float, we can get the present value of the reduced float bar coding and presorting proposal as follows:

$$PV = \frac{\$90.077272}{0.10/365}$$
$$= \$328,782.04$$

The system is worth \$328,782 to the company, on a present value basis. Notice that there is an implicit assumption that the difference in float is permanent. If we had reason to expect that three years from now float would drop to 6.67 days regardless of company preprocessing, we would discount the daily cash flow as a 3-year daily annuity.[1]

To determine if the proposal should be adopted, we would compare the present value of the benefits, roughly \$329,000, plus the reduced mailing costs, to the installed cost of the bar coding and presorting system. If the combined cost is less than \$329,000, the proposal would have a positive net present value (NPV) and should be implemented. We present a more advanced present value analysis in our discussion of disbursement systems in Chapter 11, in which we compute the value effect of paying suppliers electronically instead of by check.

[1] An approximation formula for the annual benefit of the days saved is Annual benefit = (Days saved) × (Daily cash flow) × ($k$), where $k$ is the annual interest rate. The intuition here is that the product of the first two terms gives an amount that may be continuously invested over time. In our example, the annual interest benefit would be \$33,333: \$33,333 = (0.33333 × \$1,000,000 × 0.10). This simplified formula ignores the compounded effect of daily savings throughout the period over which the total value effect is computed. If the effects of a proposal will last only one year, this approximation will be fairly accurate.

# U.S. PAYMENT SYSTEM

The two components of the U.S. payment system are the banking system (which includes the Federal Reserve System) and the set of payment mechanisms.[2] This system is unique in that most other countries have only a handful of banks and use the postal system to assist in collecting and depositing payments. The U.S. payment system is the backbone of our banking and financial markets, which in turn facilitate the growth and stability of our economy. In this section, we survey the major types of depository financial institutions, explain the payment responsibilities of the Federal Reserve System, and identify the means by which most payments are processed through the payment system.

## Financial Institutions

The financial institutions that participate in the economy's payment process are commercial banks, savings and loan associations, mutual savings banks, and credit unions. All four of these depository institutions, which we simply refer to as banks, are involved in handling checks as well as electronic payments. Commercial banks continue to dominate the banking industry. Roughly 7,800 commercial banks continue to operate in the United States, compared with 1,425 savings and loan associations, 489 stock or mutual savings banks, and 10,000 credit unions. Because so many of a company's cash management activities are linked to banks and banking regulation, the regulatory environment is a key component of the payment system. We subdivide our remaining discussion of financial institutions into product differences, geographic restrictions, and safety considerations.

*PRODUCT DIFFERENCES* Each type of financial institution has a slightly different thrust. Commercial banks are more oriented toward corporate services, savings and loan associations toward real estate development and mortgage finance, mutual savings banks toward mortgage finance, and credit unions toward consumer loan and deposit services. These institutions are becoming more like one another. The ability of savings and loan, mutual savings banks, and credit unions to operate more like commercial banks has come as a result of the passage of the **Depository Institution Deregulation and Monetary Control Act of 1980**. The major product-related provisions of that act are summarized in Exhibit 8–1.

*It is essential to note that business firms (except sole proprietorships) are prohibited by law from receiving interest on bank checking accounts;* this Federal Reserve **Regulation Q** provision limits them to using demand deposit accounts for transactions and disqualifies them from holding negotiated order of withdrawal (NOW), SuperNOW, or **money market deposit accounts (MMDAs)**. One of the most important principles of cash management, that of minimizing idle cash balances, is premised on the opportunity cost of forgone interest linked to this legislation. Businesses with deposit account balances large enough to justify the fixed monthly cost use daily transfers into "**sweep accounts**" to get paid overnight interest on deposit balances. Small businesses able to keep very small deposit balances, particularly those not requiring bank loans, may keep most of their transaction balances in money market mutual funds. Because these funds are not covered by deposit insurance, some cash managers use money funds investing exclusively in government securities.

---

[2] Lewis and Davis (1987) distinguish between cash and noncash payment systems, formally defining a noncash system as a mechanism by which there is (1) a transfer of ownership of claims (a check representing a claim to cash), (2) conversion of those claims to a preferred form, and (3) settlement of debts incurred by asset exchanges between the claims issuers. Our discussion centers on checking and electronic noncash payment systems because they account for most nonretail corporate payment and collection transaction.

**Exhibit 8–1**

*Product Deregulation in the Depository Institutions Deregulation and Monetary Control Act*

| Type of Financial Institution | New Conditions |
|---|---|
| **Commercial banks** | Can now offer consumers, sole proprietorships, and not-for-profit organizations:<br>1. Negotiated order of withdrawal (NOW) accounts, which are interest-bearing checking accounts.<br>2. Money market deposit accounts (MMDAs), accounts with a higher interest rate and a limit on the number of checks that can be written against them each month. These were meant to offer banks a competitive tool to stem the deposit outflows to money market mutual funds.<br>3. **SuperNOW accounts**, with higher minimum balances than NOW accounts. The minimum balance differences were left to each bank's discretion beginning in the mid-1980s.<br>**Note:** The MMDA and SuperNOW accounts were actually implemented subsequent to the Garn-St. Germain Depository Institutions Act of 1982. |
| **Savings and loan associations** | In addition to being able to offer NOW, SuperNOW, and MMDAs:<br>1. Can lend up to 20 percent of total assets in consumer and commercial loans.<br>2. Can issue credit cards.<br>3. Can offer **trust services** (investment of funds left by an estate, for example). |
| **Mutual savings banks** | In addition to the NOW, SuperNOW, and MMDAs:<br>1. Can offer business accounts.<br>2. Can lend up to 5 percent of total assets in commercial loans.<br>3. Can offer trust services.<br>4. Can issue credit cards. |
| **Credit unions** | In addition to the NOW (in this instance called "share draft" accounts), SuperNOW, and MMDAs:<br>1. Can issue certificates of deposit (CDs).<br>2. Can offer student loans.<br>3. Can offer safety deposit boxes.<br>4. Can offer automated teller machines (ATMs).<br>5. Can issue credit cards.<br>6. Can pay interest on business checking accounts (primarily to members running a business), which any other type of depository institution cannot do. |

Further alterations enacted as part of the **Garn-St. Germain Depository Institutions Act of 1982** allowed depository institutions to pay interest on MMDAs to compete with money market mutual funds and allowed savings and loan associations to lend to businesses. Although banks continue to set higher minimum balance requirements for SuperNOW accounts than for NOW accounts, in 1986 regulators removed interest rate distinctions between the accounts by eliminating the maximum NOW rate of $5\frac{1}{4}$ percent. In 1989, the **Financial Institutions Reform, Recovery, and Enforcement Act**, which was mainly addressed to failing savings and loan institutions, further blurred the lines between depository institutions by allowing bank holding companies (the parent firm over several banks) to buy healthy savings and loan associations (S&Ls).

Nonbank institutions are also becoming players in the payment system. Brokerage firms, in particular, have either acquired banks or established **nonbank banks**, which accept deposits or make loans (but not both). These banks are used to consolidate and invest idle cash balances for the brokerage firm's customers. The **Competitive Equality Banking Act of 1987**, while allowing existing nonbank banks to continue to operate, prohibits the establishment of new nonbank banks. Small businesses, in particular, have benefited from the competitive Merrill Lynch "Working Capital Management Account" and lending and investing services offered by American Express.

The most recent legislation affecting the banking landscape is the **Financial Services Modernization Act of 1999** (also known as Gramm-Leach-Bliley). This law repeals the 1933 Glass-Steagall Act's prohibitions on bank-investment company affiliations:

- Banks can now affiliate with investments and insurance firms.
- A new organizational form, called a financial holding company, allows banking organizations to carry out new powers through nonbanking subsidiaries that are permitted to sell insurance and underwrite securities.
- Banks having a federal charter can conduct some of the insurance and securities activities through "financial subsidiaries."[3]

Furthermore, the nonbank banks mentioned earlier, mostly set up as part of a "unitary thrift holding company" structure, were limited. Regulators were forbidden from approving any new applications received after May 4, 1999. The intended effect was to prevent Wal-Mart from taking on this charter, and thereby initiating large-scale consumer lending.

*GEOGRAPHIC RESTRICTIONS* Past regulatory limits on interstate branching are the major reason corporate cash management systems have included multiple banks. Interstate branching refers to the ability of a bank headquartered in one state to open branches in other states. If one bank could set up branches wherever it wished, there might not be a need for the cash manager to establish relationships with multiple banks for check clearing and cash concentration. Originally, limits on interstate branching were linked to fears of a concentration of financial power and a reduction of lending to businesses in small towns.

The **McFadden Act**, passed in 1927 and amended in 1933, limited bank branching by national banks to the same areas where state-chartered banks in that state were permitted to branch. This effectively prohibited interstate branching.

Banks got around this limitation to some degree by setting up holding companies, which are controlling organizations owning 100 percent of the stock in separately chartered banks. The **Bank Holding Company Act of 1956** addressed this issue by prohibiting any further interstate acquisition by holding companies unless specifically allowed by state law in the state of the proposed acquisition. Because no state allowed these acquisitions at that time, only the very limited networks set up before 1956 existed, until Maine passed an enabling law in 1978. As part of "regional compacts," most other states have since enabled bank holding companies from selected other states to acquire their banks, as long as those states offer reciprocal privileges. The Garn-St. Germain Depository Institutions Act of 1982 allows interstate acquisitions of failed or failing banks or thrifts, primarily to reduce the costs of government bailouts of troubled institutions.

The mid-1990s experienced a final crumbling of the walls prohibiting interstate acquisitions and interstate branching. The key piece of legislation was the 1994 passage of the **Interstate Banking and Branching Efficiency Act (IBBEA)**. Key provisions included:

---

[3] There is a real concern that the failure of a nonbanking firm controlled by a bank may now jeopardize the entire banking organization. For more on this and other issues related to the Financial Services Modernization Act of 1999, see the special issue of the Federal Reserve Board of Minneapolis special issue of *The Region* (March 2000). It is available online at **http://minneapolisfed.org/pubs/region/00-03/**.

## FOCUS ON PRACTICE

### What Effect Is Interstate Banking and Bank Consolidation Having in the United States?

The Treasury Management Association (now called the Association for Financial Professionals) conducted a survey of 4,000 members in early 1999 and got the following responses from 587 corporations:

- Bank consolidation, mostly due to mergers and acquisitions, resulted in increased delays in bank decision making, more errors in monthly bank statements and/or account analysis statements, and some operational disruption in corporate treasury departments. Almost half of the respondents saw banks as now being less loyal to their business customers and believed that their business relationship was of diminished importance to their banks.
- Interstate banking was advantageous to 314 of the respondents, with half of these companies consolidating services within existing banks (primarily local depository services, cash concentration services, and balance reporting services) or moving services to other banks (67 respondents had discontinued relations with one or more banks due to those banks' inability to offer interstate banking capability). Of the 87 companies divulging their annual cost savings, three-fourths were saving $36,000 or less, but 23 respondents were saving an average of $247,200 annually. Primary benefits cited for interstate banking were mainly "fewer banks and services to monitor" and "improved collection and concentration," with some organizations seeing "reduced local account balances" as well.
- The most likely trends for the future, with the percentage of corporate respondents agreeing with the statement, are:
  - likely or very likely that bank services will become more commoditized (90 percent).
  - likely or very likely that monopolistic pricing will occur (80 percent), possibly due to specialization in certain service areas.
  - likely or very likely that there will be fewer sources of credit (80 percent).
  - likely or very likely that there will be faster convergence of technology standards (79 percent).

These findings are linked to the passage in 1994 of the Interstate Banking and Branching Efficiency Act, covered earlier.

*Source:* Aaron L. Phillips, "Bank Consolidation and Interstate Banking: Effect on Treasury Management," *TMA Journal* (March/April 1999), pp. 40–43.

- Bank holding companies were permitted to acquire a bank located in any state beginning September 1995 (interstate banking).
- Banks in one state could merge with banks in another state beginning June 1997, unless either of the two states had prohibited interstate mergers between the law's enactment and the end of May 1997.
- Banks could establish new branches in states where they had not previously had a branch if the host state expressly passed a law permitting such branches (interstate branching).

With interstate branching allowed, corporations will use far fewer banks, eventually making it possible to use one large bank with nationwide branches to both accept deposits and clear checks. Short-term financial management will become less costly and more efficient as deposits are granted immediate or next-day availability in almost all cases, much like the Canadian system. Transfers, including account funding and concentration account transfers, will be greatly reduced because balances will be automatically pooled in a bank's bookkeeping system. We are already seeing these effects, as noted in the Focus on Practice.

*SAFETY CONSIDERATIONS* Bank safety is also important because banks play such a vital check-clearing role in the payments system. The past decade has been very positive for banks. In 1991, the Federal Deposit Insurance Corporation (FDIC) had 1,426 banks and savings associations on its problem list, but by year-end 2003 this number had declined to only 116 institutions, holding $30 billion in assets. In 1990, there were 382 institutions that had failed, but only two institutions closed their doors in 2003. These troubled banks pose special problems for their depositors. The FDIC only guarantees the first $100,000 of a depositor's money in the event of bank failure. The too-big-to-fail doctrine practiced before 1991 ensured that depositors with money in very large banks would be covered even above the $100,000 limits. However, in the **Federal Deposit Insurance Corporation Improvement Act of 1991**, coverage of uninsured deposits is less certain. The FDIC must give acquirers of failed banks a choice of whether to bid for all the deposits or just the insured deposits. Acquirers have been prone to bid for the insured deposits, meaning uninsured depositors receive only part of their deposited funds back as the FDIC liquidates the assets. For example, in the closure of the First National Bank of the Panhandle (Panhandle, Texas), there was a total exposure of about $752,000 in 102 accounts exceeding the $100,000 insured limit. Under federal law, these depositors and creditors holding deposit claims receive priority in payment from the subsequent sale of assets of the failed bank (over creditors holding nondeposit claims).

The FDIC continues to take over large banks when there is agreement among federal regulatory agencies that defaulting on uninsured deposits would pose a substantial risk to the payments system. International capital standards for banks, phased in during 1992 in the United States, further regulate bank soundness. Developed in 1988 by a committee of bank regulators from seven countries, the Basel Accord standards require banks to have $3 of Tier 1 capital (common and perpetual preferred stock and minority interests, minus goodwill) for every $100 of total assets. Tier 1 plus Tier 2 capital (other preferred stock, mandatory convertible debt, and long-term subordinated debt) must be at least $8 for every $100 of risk-weighted assets. Risk weightings are 100 percent for business loans, 50 percent for home mortgages, and 0 percent for Treasury securities. Not surprisingly, banks have become more conservative in their business lending. One short-term finance implication is that cash management services may not be priced as attractively because banks need to make more fee income to compensate for diminished corporate loan profitability. Proposed Basel II Accord standards, to be phased in by year-end 2006, further define "risk-weighted assets." For example, past-due loans are risk-weighted at 150 percent, and banks must rely more heavily on external credit assessments done by third parties such as export credit agencies and private rating agencies. More important for our focus, banks must now consider operational risk: "the risk of loss arising from inadequate or failed internal processes, people and systems, or external events."[4] Banks must calculate required capital for each business line, summing these amounts to arrive at total operational risk capital. Basel II standards will likely mean lower capital allocations for risk assets, but offsetting higher capital allocations for operational risk. This may result in higher cash management prices, less product innovation, some banks pruning some product lines, and a possible competitive advantage for nonbank providers which are not subject to Basel standards.

---

[4] Bank for International Settlements, "Overview of the New Basel Capital Accord" (April 2003), p. 8. For more on this, see Ron Chakravarti, "Basel II: Trouble for Treasurers?" (October 29, 2003). Available online at **http://www.gtnews.com**.

## Federal Reserve System

The **Federal Reserve System**, or the **Fed**, is the nation's central bank. As the "banker's bank," it:

- Acts as lender of last resort, lending money to banks through the "discount window."
- Is one of several bodies that supervises and regulates banks.
- Facilitates the payments mechanism.

The nationwide Panic of 1907, which saw a breakdown in the nation's payment system and a full-scale run on banks, led to the passage of the **Federal Reserve Act** in 1913. We will further our understanding of the Fed by discussing its organization, its functions, and its present and future involvement in the payment system.

*ORGANIZATION* The Federal Reserve System is made up of the Board of Governors, the Federal Open Market Committee, the Federal Advisory Council, Federal Reserve District Banks, and member banks (Exhibit 8–2).

The Fed is run by the 7-member **Board of Governors**, which is appointed by the President and confirmed by the U.S. Senate. Terms of office for this federal government agency are 14 years, with one of the seven terms expiring every two years. The chairperson (Alan Greenspan, at the time of this writing) and vice-chairperson hold 4-year, renewable terms.

Exhibit 8–2

*Organization of the Federal Reserve System*

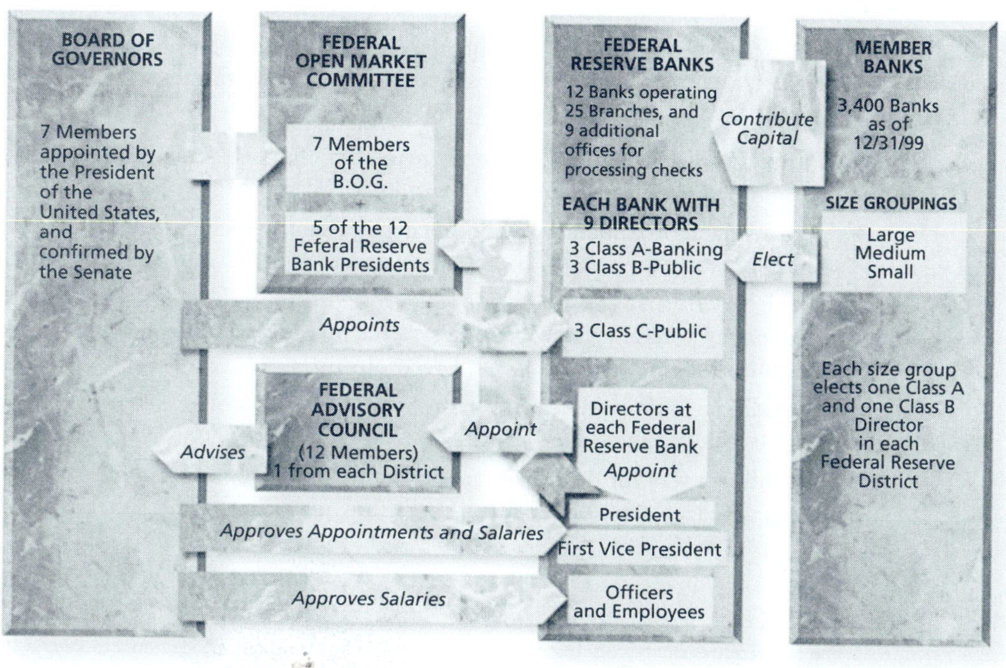


*Source:* **http://www.rich.frb.org/pubs/frbaction/**
Board of Governors of the Federal Reserve System. Reprinted from *The Federal Reserve Today*, 15th ed., 2003.

The seven members of the Board of Governors are also members of the **Federal Open Market Committee (FOMC)**, which makes most of the monetary policy for the United States in its eight meetings per year. The FOMC does so by buying and selling Treasury securities (open market operations), which affects the reserve positions of banks, and, ultimately, the money supply. The **Federal Advisory Council** is made up of prominent commercial bankers and meets at least four times per year with the Board of Governors.

The Fed, unlike the single central bank in most countries, is comprised of 12 district **Federal Reserve Banks (FRBs)**, with 25 regional branches spread across the country. There also are six **regional check processing centers (RCPCs)** set up to help clear checks. Together, most of the 12 district banks, most of the 25 regional branches, and six RCPCs give the Fed a network of 32 offices to clear checks as of the end of 2004. Exhibit 8–3 shows a map of the districts and branches. The Federal Reserve Banks are private organizations, with a corporate structure very similar to that of a commercial bank. Each Reserve Bank issues stock and has a board of directors that elects the bank's officers and oversees the bank's operations. The buyers of that stock, and thus the true owners of the Fed, are the member commercial banks.

The Reserve Banks differ from commercial banks in that their primary responsibility is to promote society's interest, not the interest of member bank stockholders who contribute the capital (refer to Exhibit 8–2). Furthermore, the Board of Governors supervises the district banks, limiting to some extent the powers and privileges of their stockholders.

The final component of the system is the group of **Federal Reserve member banks**. Being a member of the Federal Reserve System has been a requirement of all national banks, and many state-chartered banks have joined voluntarily. Subsequent to the 1980 Monetary Control Act, membership has been much less important because all depository institutions may receive Fed payment services, must adhere to Reserve requirements, and may now borrow from the Fed.[5]

*Involvement in the Payment System* The Federal Reserve's official role in the payment system is "to promote the integrity and efficiency of the payments mechanism and to ensure the provision of payment services to all depository institutions on an equitable basis, and to do so in an atmosphere of competitive fairness."[6] The Fed's participation in the payment system includes:

- Putting into circulation new money printed by the U.S. Treasury Department and withdrawing damaged coins and worn bills.
- Processing approximately 16 billion checks a year, which consists of moving, sorting, and tabulating the checks, and debiting and crediting the proper depository institution's account.
- Supporting several private clearing systems by offering settlement services through its nationwide network of account relationships.
- Providing a nationwide electronic network for small-dollar electronic payments [automated clearinghouse (ACH)].
- Providing a way for depository institutions to quickly transfer large-dollar amounts using wire transfers via "Fedwire," a nationwide wire transfer system.

[5] The Fed requires depository institutions with check-like (transaction) accounts to keep a stipulated percentage of the dollar amount of these accounts on reserve as deposits with a Federal Reserve Bank (Fed Regulation D). The Fed's control over the amount of reserves deposited helps it to control the amount of money in circulation.

[6] "The Federal Reserve in the Payments System," *Federal Reserve Bulletin* (May 1990), p. 293.

**Exhibit 8–3**

*Boundaries of Federal Reserve Districts and Their Branch Territories*

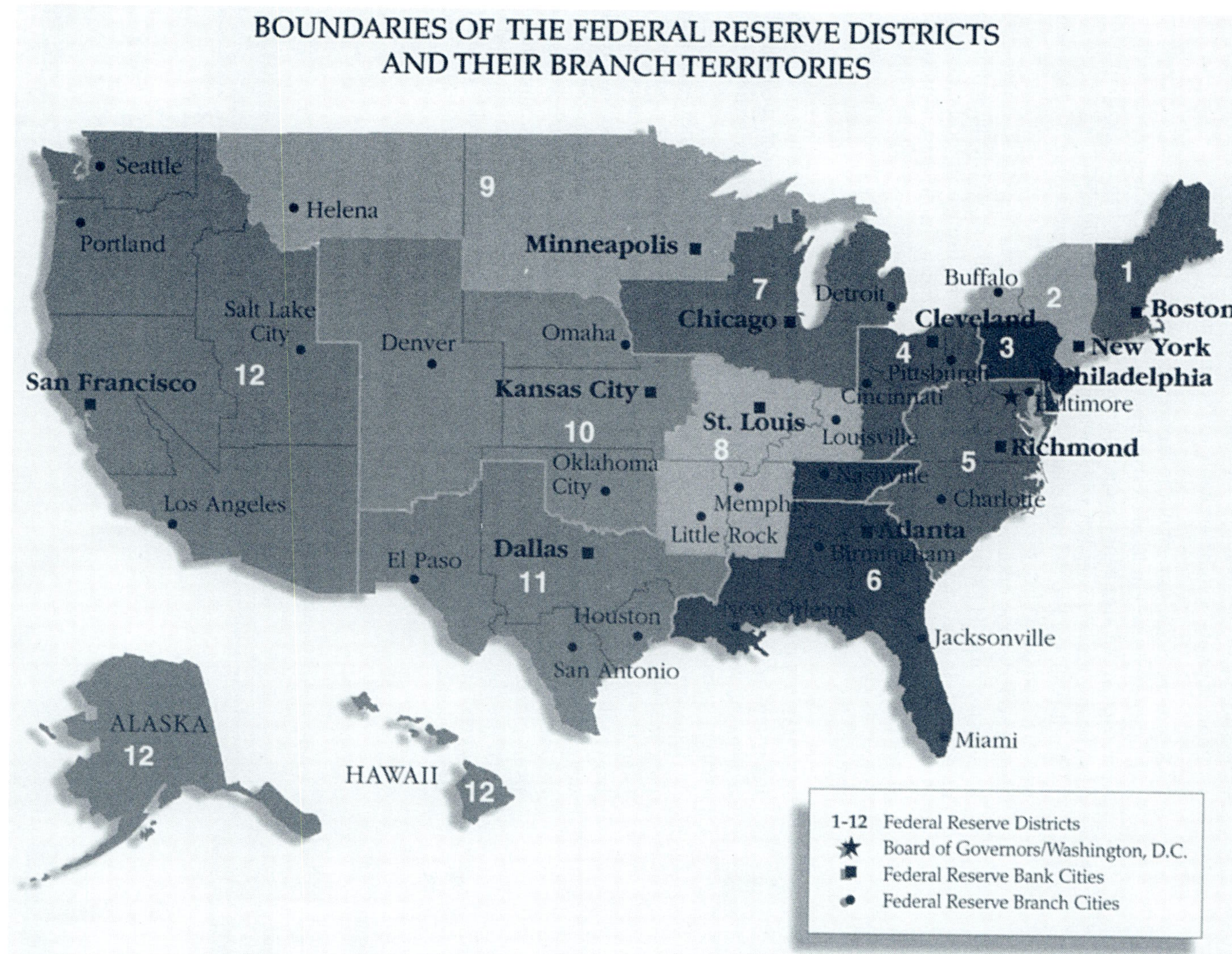


*Source:* Reprinted from *The Federal Reserve Today*, 13th ed., 1999.

- Regulating the availability schedules of banks, which indicate when checks or electronic deposits become available to the customer.

Before the establishment of the Federal Reserve System, banks settled checks drawn on each other exclusively at local clearinghouses. A **clearinghouse** is a central location where representatives of area banks meet, and each bank settles its balances with one institution (the clearinghouse) instead of with each other bank individually.

Until 1980, the Fed did not charge banks for its check processing. The Monetary Control Act mandated that the Fed begin charging for its services, partly to spur private-sector check clearing initiatives. Increasingly, banks are sending checks drawn on banks in another region to (1) a large bank ("correspondent bank" at which the sending bank has an account) in that region, which processes the checks through its local clearinghouse, or (2) directly to the bank on which the checks are drawn. In the past, almost all interregional checks would have been sent to the district Federal Reserve Bank. This circumvention of its check clearing system and the increased volume of electronic payments have reduced the Fed's role in U.S. check processing.

*Mechanics of Check Clearing* We can gain an understanding of the check clearing system by observing the life of a check. A check processed through the Federal Reserve System will serve as our example. Consult Exhibit 8–4 as we follow a check through the clearing system.

Barbara is on vacation in Atlanta, escaping the cold winter of Minneapolis. While shopping at Saks Fifth Avenue, she buys a coat. She writes a check for the purchase amount (step 1). Saks receives the check in its processing area (step 2). That evening, Saks deposits her check at its bank, Wachovia Bank, along with many other checks Saks received that day (step 3). Referred to as the **collecting bank**, Wachovia first encodes the dollar amount in magnetic ink on the bottom right-hand side of the check, then batches this check with many others it has received that were written on banks outside the Atlanta area. It transports the checks to the Atlanta Federal Reserve Bank (step 4). The Atlanta Fed sorts this check and other unsorted checks it has received, according to the check's destination (the **drawee bank**, which in our example is the Wells Fargo Bank in Minneapolis). The Atlanta

Exhibit 8–4

*Steps in Check Clearing*

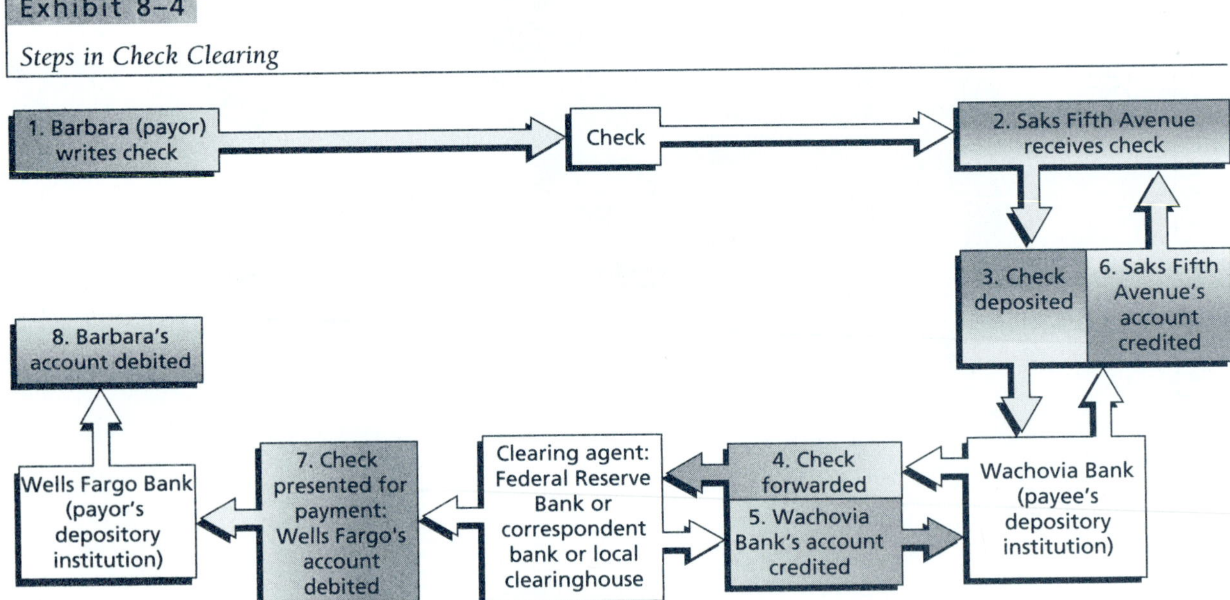

Fed settles accounts, crediting Wachovia Bank's reserve account according to a prearranged "availability schedule" (step 5). After settlement, checks drawn on banks in the Ninth District (Minnesota, North and South Dakota, part of Wisconsin) are grouped and sent to the Minneapolis Fed (step 6). The Minneapolis Fed, in turn, returns Barbara's check to Wells Fargo and debits Wells Fargo's reserve account (step 7, called **presentment**). Wells Fargo then debits Barbara's checking account (step 8).

The **clearing agent**, often a Federal Reserve Bank, branch, or RCPC, uses the information printed at the bottom of the check to process the check. Known as the **magnetic ink character recognition (MICR) line**, this information can be read by scanning machines and indicates several items (see example in Exhibit 8–5).

1. The Federal Reserve Bank code (10) indicates which Federal Reserve district the check will be routed back to, if the Fed's check clearing system is used. Here, it signifies the Tenth District, for which the Kansas City Federal Reserve is the district bank.
2. The Federal Reserve office code indicates the Fed branch assigned to handling the drawee bank and, if followed by a second digit, what the availability classification is for that bank (0 or 9 denote that same-day availability might be extended by the Fed to the bank of first deposit). (Notice that items 1 and 2 are combined in the denominator of the fraction included at the top right of the check underneath the date. This area is used for manual processing in the event the depositing bank does not have or cannot use automated check processing equipment.)
3. American Banker's Association (ABA) bank identification number for the bank on which the check was written, or drawn (known as the *drawee bank*). This number

**Exhibit 8–5**

*Sample Check*

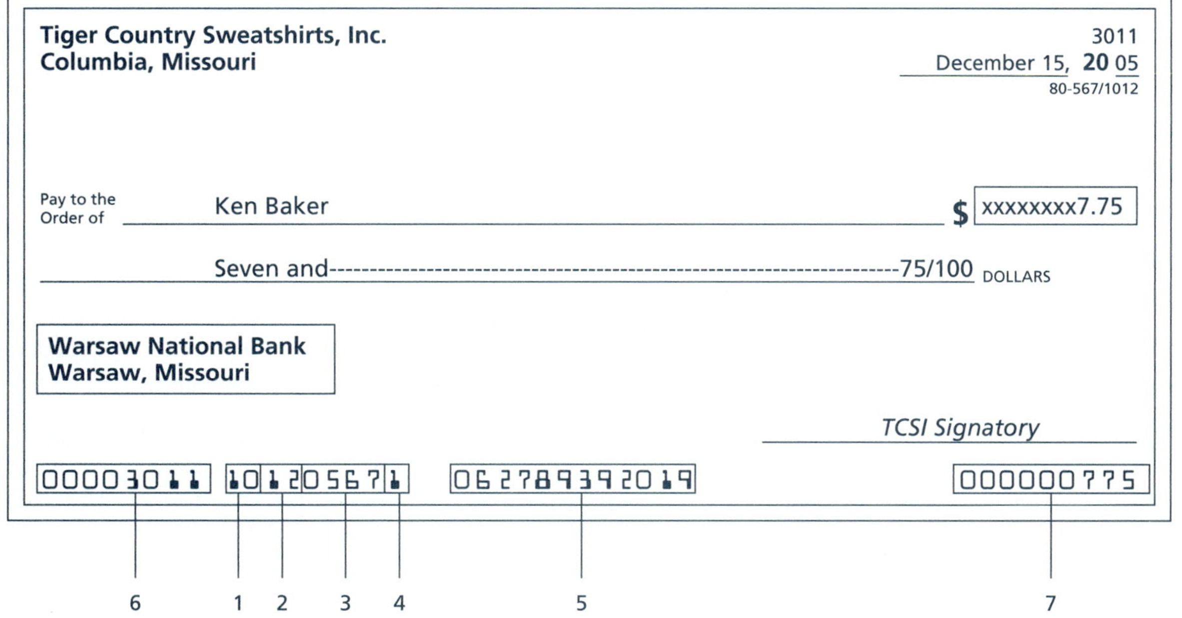
Tiger Country Sweatshirts, Inc.
Columbia, Missouri

3011
December 15, 20 05
80-567/1012

Pay to the Order of Ken Baker $ xxxxxxxx7.75

Seven and------------------------------------------------------------75/100 DOLLARS

Warsaw National Bank
Warsaw, Missouri

TCSI Signatory

also appears in the numerator of the fraction at the top right of the check underneath the date; the 80 preceding it is a unique identifier for the state of Missouri.

4. A verification digit that is used in conjunction with the other numbers to detect processing errors.
5. Account number of the payor, assigned by the drawee bank at the time the account is opened.
6. The sequence number (also called an auxiliary on-us field) may appear at the far left or next to the account number and is usually the check number. It enables the drawee bank to sort cleared checks before returning the checks (or a sorted statement listing of them) to the payor.
7. The check's encoded amount, which indicates in dollars and cents the amount written or typed on the check by the payor. It is encoded by the bank at which the check is first deposited.

Items 1–4, taken together, make up the Federal Reserve District/American Banker's Association (FRD/ABA) bank ID number, which is often called the **transit routing number**. We find out more about the use of this important number in our later section on paper-based payments. We conclude our discussion of the mechanics of check processing by identifying an important banking trend that has an effect on corporate depositors and their deposit items.

As many as 70 percent of all interbank checks do not clear through the Federal Reserve System. We noticed in our earlier example (Exhibit 8–4) that the clearing agent may be a correspondent bank or a local clearinghouse. The bank of first deposit will select the clearing mechanism based on: (1) the location of the drawee bank (which defines the options it has available for processing checks drawn on that bank), (2) the availability schedule associated with each of these options (which indicates when it will be given credit for the deposited amount), (3) the time of deposit, (4) the dollar amount of the check, and sometimes (5) the desires of the depositor. We now consider the various ways that a check might be cleared.

## Clearing Mechanisms

A check might follow numerous routes as it clears from the receiving bank where it is first deposited back to the drawee bank on which it was written. Exhibit 8–6 shows us the options the receiving bank faces. After checks are coded, sorted, and verified ("proofed"), the bank must decide how best to route the check to get it cleared back to the drawee bank.

*HOUSE/ON-US CHECKS* For a check written **on-us**, meaning the payee deposits the check in the bank on which it is drawn, the bank simply credits the depositor's account and debits the payor's account. It later returns the checks, or possibly a simple record of all checks written during a period, to the payor. If the payee cashes the check, obviously the bank would not credit the payee's account. Approximately 30 percent of all checks are on-us, and this percent will grow as banks merge and branch nationwide.

*LOCAL ITEMS* For a check written on other banks in the receiving bank's geographic area, the receiving bank might handle check clearing in one of three ways. First, it might send it by courier, with a group of other checks drawn on the same bank, to be swapped for checks drawn on itself that the other bank has received. This arrangement makes sense when many checks ordinarily flow between two banks in the same geographic area. It may seem unusual that banks would have accounts at other (competing) banks, but these cor-

*Bank Check Processing Flow Chart*

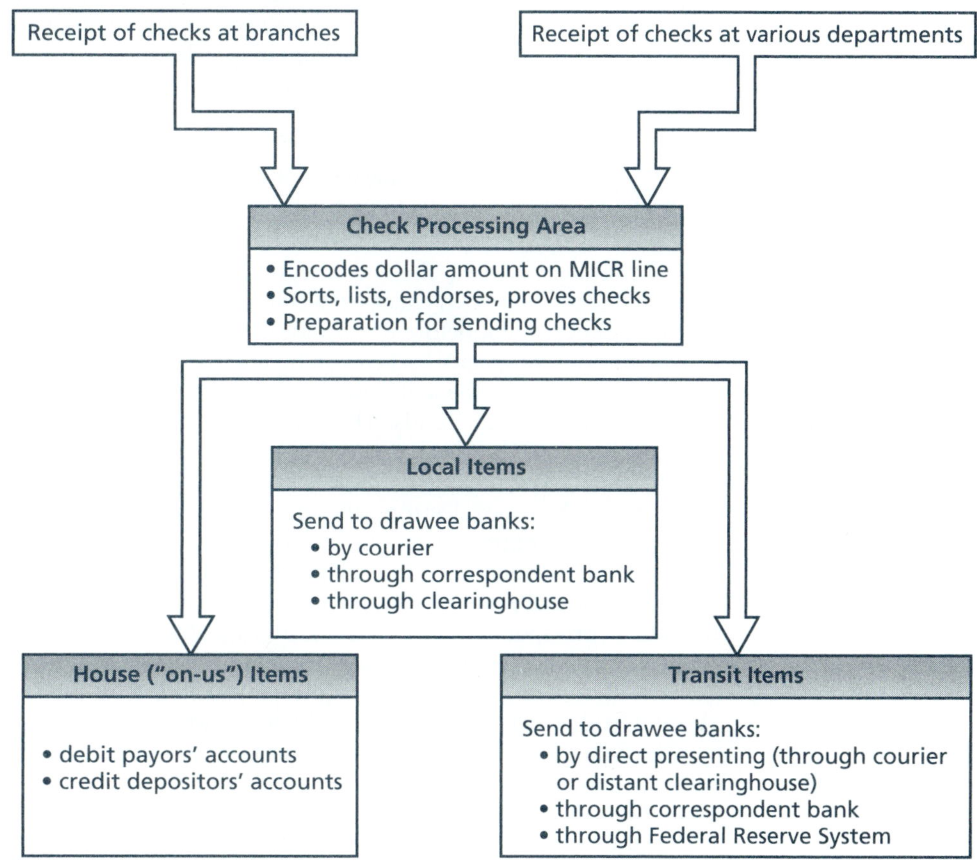


*Source:* Copyright © 1994 by the American Banker's Association. Reprinted with permission. 

respondent accounts can be debited or credited in one transaction to efficiently clear many checks drawn on each. Second, the checks may be processed through a correspondent bank, which in turn may be engaged in large-volume check swapping with the major banks in a locality. Third, a local clearinghouse may be used. Each day, representatives from each bank that is a part of the clearinghouse meet to present checks to each other. The net value is debited or credited either to each bank's correspondent account or Federal Reserve account at the end of each business day.

*TRANSIT ITEMS* Checks drawn on banks that do not participate in a bank's local clearinghouse or exchange are called **transit items**. These are sometimes called "out-of-town" checks. Formerly, many of these were cleared by **direct presenting** hand-carried checks via courier, but the sorting and courier expense had greatly reduced the practice except on large checks. Larger banks have started direct presenting more checks, with such arrangements often made with other large banks in reciprocal arrangements. The courier may present the checks to the drawee bank directly, or indirectly through the drawee bank's clearinghouse. The **clearing bank** would need to have a large volume of checks drawn on banks in the area to make membership in a remote clearinghouse pay off. Direct presenting might still be used when the dollar size is large enough to warrant gaining a day or two of speedier availability, the depositor is willing to pay for the extra expense (particularly air travel for the courier), and the local Fed cutoff for receipt of checks will be missed (and direct presenting will therefore get the check to the drawee bank much sooner). For example, on a $2 million check, a savings of one day of float, assuming the company's cost of capital is 10 percent, is approximated using Equation 8.3.

$$\textit{Interest earned} = \textit{Amount per day} \times \textit{Number of days} \times \textit{Daily interest rate} \qquad (8.3)$$

$$\textit{Interest earned} = \$2{,}000{,}000 \times 1 \text{ day} \times 0.10/365$$
$$= \$547.95$$

Effective January 1, 1994, the Fed amended Regulation CC to promote **same-day settlement** of directly presented checks. If a collecting bank presents checks to the place of business of a drawee bank before 8 A.M. local time, the paying bank must return the checks or pay the collecting bank by Fedwire by the close of business that day. The drawee bank can no longer charge the collecting bank a fee or force it to wait until the next business day to receive available funds. This has stimulated a resurgence in direct presenting, as mentioned earlier. Fed check processing volumes have fallen 12 percent as a result of same-day settlement. With the new Check 21 law going into effect in late 2004, many banks will move the check images electronically and either present those images directly to the drawee bank or have them printed out in a location near to the drawee bank and then presented physically for payment. We will say more about this law later.

The second alternative for clearing checks written on out-of-town banks is to send them to a correspondent bank located near the drawee bank. The main advantage of this arrangement is a later deposit deadline, or **cutoff time**, than would be offered by the nearest Fed office. This translates into quicker availability of the deposited funds, which the clearing bank generally passes on to the depositor.

The final possibility for handling transit items is to send them through the Federal Reserve System, which continues to process about 30 percent of all interbank U.S. checks. Here there are two possibilities: send them through the local Fed (the usual process), or bypass the local Fed and send them directly[7] to the Federal Reserve check clearing office nearest the drawee bank. The last alternative would be pursued when it would mean speedier availability and when the size of the check(s) justifies the added expense. One curiosity here is that the local Fed will allow the bank to **piggyback** the check(s) and accompanying listing (called a **cash letter**) with whatever checks that office is sending to the distant Fed office. This way the clearing bank can miss the local Fed's cutoff time but still meet the distant Fed's cutoff. The credit is still made to the bank's account at the local Fed, however.

The fact that the Fed grants the depositing bank credit according to a preset availability schedule but is not always able to present the check (debit the drawee bank) within that same period gives rise to float. For a private bank, float refers to items taken on deposit but not yet collected. Float has made it profitable for depositors or banks to try to "beat the system," striving for quick availability on deposits and slowed presentment on checks written. The availability schedule is an important document for the corporate cash manager for this reason, and we return to a fuller discussion later in this chapter. After gaining a deeper perspective on float and the Fed's attack on it, the remainder of this chapter discusses paper-based payments, electronic-based payments, the international payments system, and managing corporate banking relationships.

---

[7] Any routing that does not go through the Federal Reserve System facility nearest to the clearing bank might be labeled a "direct send."

## CONCEPT OF FLOAT

The treasurer must first distinguish between collection float and disbursement float. **Collection float** refers to the elapsed time between when a customer writes a check and when the company is granted available or collected funds after depositing the check. **Disbursement float** is slightly different: It is the delay between the time when the company writes the check and the time when its bank charges the checking account for the amount of the check. On the same check, disbursement float may be slightly more because the Fed may grant the depositor's bank availability before it debits the drawee bank. At times, collection float is longer because the "hold" placed on the check by the depositor's bank (delay in availability) may exceed the time it actually takes to present the check to the drawee bank (which usually debits the drawee's checking account the same day). This is justified by the depositor's bank based on its concern about whether a given check might be returned (the check "bounces"), but Regulation CC places strict limits on hold periods otherwise. We can gain a better appreciation for the management of collection or disbursement float if we break them down into their component parts.

### Components of Float

There are three basic components to collection or disbursement float: mail float, processing float, and clearing float.

*MAIL FLOAT* The time that elapses from the point when the check is written until it is received by the payee is termed **mail float**. It may range from a day for local checks mailed out immediately to 10 days for a check sent to New York from Rome, Italy. Companies not having the time or clerical staff to monitor mail times can get the information in two other ways. First, the U.S. Postal Service has published guidelines for delivery times on first-class mail and has contracted with PriceWaterhouseCoopers to provide an outside measurement system to indicate success in meeting those targets. Additionally, consulting firm Phoenix-Hecht provides clients with mail times for many different "mailed from–mailed to" combinations.

The U.S. Postal Service has reduced the time it takes to deliver nonlocal mail by four hours since 1996, according to Phoenix-Hecht. It has improved service consistency as well and is able to deliver according to its published schedule 85 to 95 percent of the time. Companies that invest in specialized machinery that make bar codes representing ZIP codes (in ZIP + 4 format) and presort outgoing mail can reduce Postal Service processing time by one-third of a day.

*PROCESSING FLOAT* The amount of time that transpires from the time the check is received at a post office box or company mailroom and when the check is deposited at the bank is termed **processing float**. Smaller companies, governments, and nonprofits have characteristically been the slowest in posting credits to the receivables file and transmitting the checks to the bank. Companies with a lockbox arrangement with a bank can eliminate much of this float. This is because bank personnel empty the post office box several times a day and begin processing the checks and crediting the company's bank account the same day, perhaps even after normal business hours.

*CLEARING FLOAT* Sometimes called "availability float," **clearing float** is the delay in availability incurred after deposit. The length of this component of float is linked to the bank's availability schedule in connection with the location of the payor's bank. When considered as part of disbursement float, it has a somewhat different meaning: The time lag is from the point when the payee deposits the check until the Fed or local clearinghouse presents the check to the drawee (disbursing company's) bank, and the bank in turn debits the payor's checking account.

Part of the clearing float is then properly labeled **Fed float**, because the Fed may grant availability to the clearing bank before it presents the check to (and debits the account of) the payor's bank. Fed float has been greatly reduced since 1980, because the 1980 Monetary Control Act mandated that the Fed eliminate or charge for Fed float. The Fed processes checks more quickly and has become more consistent in its clearing times. The Fed has several methods it uses to reduce float.

- **Check truncation.** This involves expediting clearing by scanning the data on the check's MICR line and then processing only that data back to the payor's bank. This is called *electronic presentment* and is primarily done with large checks. Illustrating, the 12th Federal District (San Francisco region) presented about 15 to 17 percent of its volume electronically in 2000. The practice of check truncation is about to explode in the United States due to the late 2003 passage of the Check 21 law (**Check Clearing for the 21st Century Act**). It encourages banks to transmit check images electronically to print centers located near the paying banks, where substitute checks are created from the images of the original checks and the MICR information. These substitute checks (a.k.a. Image Replacement Documents, or IRDs) function as the legal equivalent of the original checks and are then presented to the banks for payment. By going to image-based check exchange and eliminating the need to physically transport checks, Check 21 speeds presentment while reducing risk.
- **High-dollar group sort.** This is a special expediting of large-dollar amounts through the clearing system, with the Fed granting the depositing bank immediate (same-day) credit if it deposits the check early in the morning. The Fed targets any noncity drawee bank getting at least $10 million of daily presentments from outside its Fed district.[8]
- **Interdistrict transportation system.** This simply means the Fed redesigned its air transit routing modes and techniques to shorten delays and minimize systemwide float.
- **Later presentments and deposit deadlines.** The Fed initiated a second, mostly electronic, presentment of checks later in the morning to supplement its standard early morning presentment, and it also allowed banks to deposit checks as late as 2:30 A.M. (instead of at midnight) for some items that will be processed through RCPCs. It charges an extra fee to banks using the later deposit deadline.

The upshot of the Fed's initiatives is that float, a major reason to use checks when paying and to avoid collecting through checks, has become much less of a factor in the U.S. payment system. Fed float has declined in the 1990s and early 2000s to a few hundred million dollars (although it temporarily spiked to $47 billion when planes were grounded after the September 11 tragedy) due to fewer paper checks being sent to the Federal Reserve; this reduces holdover float. More use of electronic payments, particularly direct deposited payrolls, has speeded payments and reduced float. Some paying banks are opting to accept electronic presentment of checks drawn on them, which leads to faster debiting of those banks' reserve accounts, and again reduces Fed float. Now the Federal Reserve claims the ability to collect over 90 percent of the value of all checks deposited with it within one day after they are deposited in the collecting bank. The use of check image presentment, which is rapidly expanding due to the late 2004 phase-in of the Check 21 legislation, should

[8] An example listing for the Fed's San Francisco listing may be found at: **http://www.frbsf.org/fiservices/feeschedules/hdpresnt.pdf**.

reduce remaining check float significantly, giving disbursing companies even less incentive to use checks for their float value.

## PAPER-BASED PAYMENTS

The two major paper-based payment mechanisms are checks and drafts. These clear through the same channels and, to a large degree, substitute for each other. Except for small purchases, checks remain the most popular means of payment. An estimated 40 billion checks were written in 2002, with a total dollar amount of close to $47 trillion. Individuals write 51 percent of the checks, businesses 44 percent, and government 5 percent. Exhibit 8–7 shows the growth in the dollar value of interbank checks processed as well as the use of electronic payment mechanisms. The number of checks is now estimated to be declining at about 2 percent per year, while electronic payments using ACH and large-value funds transfers done through Fedwire and CHIPS are growing at accelerated rates. (These latter electronic payment systems are discussed later in this chapter.) In 1979, the ratio of checks to ACH payments in dollar terms was $10 to $1, but in 2000 that ratio had plummeted to $2 to $1.

Although we will not go into detail on coin and currency payments, we note that these cash payments remain important for consumer purchases.[9] A recent study of consumer retail spending found that cash and checks account for 41 percent of in-store transactions by consumers, with debit cards accounting for almost one out of three in-store purchases. Exhibit 8–8 shows the entire breakdown, which indicates that cash and checks are being used less and credit cards at about the same rate as before. Prepaid cards and check truncation (where the consumer's check is turned into an electronic debit to his or her account) account for the 2 percent "other" category.

The same study found that consumers still predominantly pay their bills by check, but electronic methods are gaining in popularity. In 2001, consumers made 72 percent of recurring bill payments with checks; today, this percentage has dropped to 60 percent. In-

**Exhibit 8–7**

*Growth of Payment Types in the United States*

| | (in trillions of dollars) | | | |
|---|---|---|---|---|
| Type of Payment | 1990 | 1994 | 1998 | 2002 |
| Check | $ 43.5 | $ 50.6 | $ 56.1 | $ 47.0 |
| ACH | 4.7 | 9.1 | 18.1 | 24.4 |
| CHIPS and wires* | 421.1 | 506.6 | 679.1 | 721.4 |
| Total | $469.3 | $566.3 | $753.3 | $792.8 |

*Wires are for funds transfers only (exclude Securities transfers).
*Source:* 1990–1994 data are adapted from Table 2, p. 13, of Bruce J. Summers and R. Alton Gilbert, "Clearing and Settlement of U.S. Dollar Payments: Back to the Future?" *Federal Reserve Bank of St. Louis Review* 78 (September/October 1996), pp. 3–27. Summers and Gilbert gathered these data from Annual Reports of the Board of Governors of the Federal Reserve System and the Bank for International Settlements. Check data for 1998–2002 are estimated by Green Sheet, Inc. 1998–2002 ACH data are from NACHA, and 1998–2002 CHIPS and wire data are from the Bank for International Settlements.

[9] **Coins** are important for their use in vending machine purchases and are produced by the U.S. Mint as needed. **Currency** refers to paper bills issued by the Federal Reserve and is considered a liability of the issuing Federal Reserve District Bank.

Exhibit 8–8

*Consumer Retail Spending by Method*

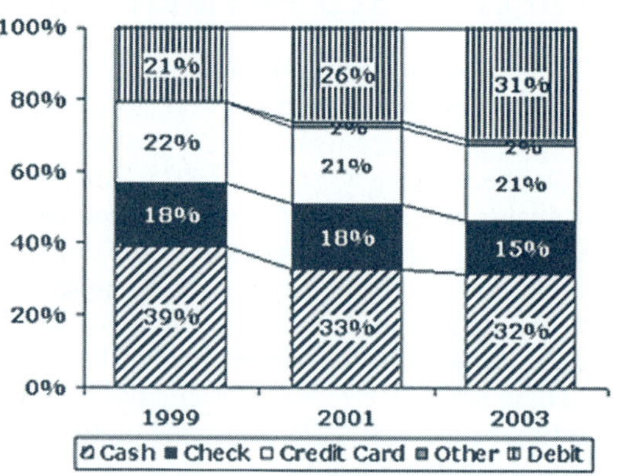


*Source:* 2003/2004 Study of Consumer Payment Preferences by the American Bankers Association and Dove Consulting, **http://www.consultdove.com/PR-2003-12-10CPPS.htm**.

creasing consumer adoption of automatic payment and online bill payment explains this trend. Currently, 60 percent of consumers use automatic payment, with only 30 percent of consumers having never tried automatic payment. Online bill payment adoption is lower than automatic payment—about four in 10 consumers currently use online bill payment—but it is growing rapidly.

The preference for paying bills by check is more pronounced for business-to-business (B2B) transactions (consultant Celent Communications estimates that 82 percent of transactions used checks, at an average amount of $2,738, accounting for 65 percent of the dollar value of the payments), although some large companies now require their suppliers to be paid electronically. Projections for the United States in 2010 are for about equal unit volumes of B2B checks and electronic payments, even though electronic payments already account for 95 percent of the value of total noncash payments in Germany, the Netherlands, and Switzerland.

## Checks

Some people think that the amount of money showing in their checking account balance is held in the bank's vault, but this is not the case. Your checking account balance is actually a computer entry, an electronic record representing how much the bank is committed to pay on the checks you write. Traditional, non-interest-bearing checking accounts are thus termed **demand deposit accounts**. Since early 1981, banks have offered checking with interest, or a **negotiated order of withdrawal (NOW) account**, to individuals, sole proprietorships, and nonprofit organizations.[10] Either type of account obligates the bank on which the item is drawn to honor requests for withdrawals on demand. This simply means that the bank will pay the check when presented with it, unless the account balance is insufficient.

[10] The formal name for such accounts is "negotiated order of withdrawal," or NOW accounts. They are authorized by the Monetary Control Act of 1980.

Only one of every 200 checks is not honored. Banks therefore assume that the drawee bank will honor deposited checks. They call the deposited checks **cash items** and give depositors immediate provisional credit for them. "Immediate" means the bank credits the depositor's account balance on the day the check is received, and "provisional" implies the bank can reverse the credit if the payor has insufficient funds or if for any other reason the check is not honored at the time the check is presented to his or her bank.

Does this mean the depositor gains available or spendable funds equal to the amount of the deposit? Not always. We need to distinguish between ledger balances and collected balances. The **ledger balance** reflects all credits and debits posted to an account as of a certain time, but this balance may not be entirely spendable. If a person deposits checks before his or her bank's daily cutoff time, he or she may not be able to withdraw some or all the amount of the total deposit. The **collected balance** (sometimes called the available balance) may be somewhat less than the ledger balance because of availability delays applied to the checks by the bank.[11] These "holds" placed on checks are spelled out in the bank's availability schedule, and when greater than one or two business days, apply primarily to consumer checking accounts. One bank's policy is:

> A deposit made before closing time on a business day (except holidays) is credited to your account that day. We will make funds from your deposits available to you on the first business day after we receive your deposit. Depending on the type of check you deposit, funds may not be available until the fifth business day after the date of your deposit. However, the first $100 of your deposit will be available the first business day.

The Federal Reserve has dealt with a major concern of check depositors by shortening the maximum allowable hold period banks can place on checks. Effective September 1990, the Fed's **Regulation CC** stipulates that from the day of deposit local checks must be given availability within two business days and nonlocal checks within five days.[12] Regulation CC implemented the mandate of the **Expedited Funds Availability Act of 1987**, which required that shorter availability schedules be put in place. Banks still have the right to delay availability for a longer period when they believe the deposit will not be paid (the check will not be honored after being presented to the drawee bank), you deposit more than a certain dollar amount on one day, you redeposit a check that was returned unpaid, you have repeatedly overdrawn your account, or there is a computer or communications system malfunction. When checks do bounce, they are called **return items**. Whereas from the time of deposit checks only take one to five days to be presented to the drawee bank, physically returned checks may take five to 10 days to work back to the clearing (depositing) bank. This is because any endorsements are verified as the check works back to each bank that handled it.[13] Banks increasingly use an electronic debit transaction (called a "represented check entry," or RCK) to redeposit a check that had been

---

[11] Some banks will honor checks up to the ledger balance, even though technically they only have to pay checks summing to the available balance. Banks do this to preserve customer goodwill and may not have made the policy known to customers in the past. Under Regulation CC, banks are required to publish their availability schedules and abide by them, but they may offer different availability to various classes of customers.

[12] Local checks are those deposited in a bank located in the drawee bank's Federal Reserve check processing zone.

[13] Potentially, Regulation CC could have an important effect on the way checks are cleared. To speed up check clearing, a group of 11 large banks have formed the Electronic Check Clearing House Organization (ECCHO). This enables the banks to process information from each other's checks using the electronic information from the MICR line, instead of waiting for the physical check to be presented. This notifies banks about a day earlier of incoming presentments, allowing banks to identify returned items more quickly. Return identification, in turn, aids banks trying to prevent check fraud: bogus checks may be deposited and the funds withdrawn before the depositor's bank realizes the checks will not be honored.

returned due to insufficient or uncollected funds. Using RCK electronic debits greatly reduces "insufficient funds" bank fees, and return notices are received in at most a few days as compared to up to 10 days for paper checks. These insufficient funds items can be resubmitted much more quickly, increasing the likelihood of being able to collect the returned check. Coupled with the more rapid initial presentment that will take place due to Check 21 image presentments, the handling cycle of return items will be greatly reduced.

## Drafts

A **draft** is a written order to make payment to a third party, in which the entity ordered to pay the draft is usually a bank. Any party holding a credit balance for the person writing the draft may have a draft drawn on it. For example, a store may draft on another store, or a bank may draw a draft on another bank. A draft is similar to a check: It is an order to pay and involves three parties. This distinguishes it from a note, which is a promise to pay involving only two parties. When drawn on a bank, the draft differs from a check because the payor's bank will pass it on to the payor for approval before the payor has to make funds available to pay the draft amount.

Drafts also differ from checks in three other ways. First, drafts are not necessarily drawn on a bank, whereas checks are. Second, drafts are not always payable on demand. **Sight drafts** are payable on demand, but **time drafts** are payable at some future date. Third, the purposes for which drafts are written are often different. Sight drafts often must have documentation attached to verify that conditions for payment (receipt, or "sight" of goods) have been met. Time drafts are usually dated after verification of a shipment of goods. These are commonly used in export sales due to uncertainty about the creditworthiness of the buyer and to give the buyer the time to inspect the shipment before taking title to the goods.

Three forms of the draft concept merit our attention. A common variety of draft called a **payable through draft (PTD)** gives the payor 24 hours to decide whether to honor or refuse payment after it has been presented to the payor's bank. They are used for claim reimbursement by insurance companies, which use the 24-hour period to verify the signature and endorsements. A **government warrant** is essentially a PTD issued by a government agency. Finally, a **preauthorized draft** is initiated by the payee, who has been authorized to draw against the payor's account. Banks sometimes collect mortgage payments this way.

Drafts can cause special problems for the cash manager using them for payment:

- Drafts must be handled by the company (and usually as well by its bank), adding to the company's clerical workload.
- The extra processing time and the 24-hour delay results in a delay in funds availability to the payee, which may create ill will.
- The bank might impose an extra balance requirement (larger compensating balance) or processing fee for its part in handling the draft; this offsets some or all of the benefit of the delay in debiting the payor's account.

## Future of Paper Payments

Some observers have labeled the check a dinosaur and foresee a checkless society in the near future. Check usage in the United States is projected to drop by one billion per year, yet check usage will remain prominent for the foreseeable future. The increasing use of plastic debit cards, which allow consumers to pay grocery and other bills through an electronic charge to their bank accounts, is definitely slowing the growth in the number of checks written, as is the federal government's decision to no longer pay any of its bills by check (with the exception of some benefit transfers), effective since 1999. **Electronic check presentment (ECP)**, in which paying banks have the option of converting scanned checks into electronic presentments at the Federal Reserve or as direct presentments to the drawee bank, is allowing checks to be debited more quickly. Coupling ECP with the granting of "same as check" legal status to check substitutes (images printed out as "image replacement documents") from Check 21 legislation, U.S. payment system participants are signaling a desire to continue to work around the inefficiencies of a paper-based system.

## ELECTRONIC-BASED PAYMENTS

The delays in check collection and presentment have spurred the development of faster means of moving funds. These electronic funds transfer techniques transfer value in a paperless, or electronic, form. The three major methods are wire transfers, EDTs, and automated debits and credits. Wire transfers are conducted through the Federal Reserve's Fedwire system, whereas EDTs and automated debits and credits are processed through automated clearinghouses.

### Wire Transfers

The best way to quickly move money from one place to another is with a wire transfer. A **wire transfer** is a bookkeeping entry that simultaneously debits the payor's account and credits the payee's account. The only thing that is "wired" is the encoded message requesting the transfer, which is sent via telephone lines. Value is transferred immediately, which is the distinguishing feature of wire transfers. Formerly, domestic wire transfers took place over Bankwire (a private network of banks) and Fedwire (the Federal Reserve's system), but Bankwire is now defunct.[14] **Fedwire** is a linked network of the 12 Federal Reserve district banks that transfers funds for banks (and by extension their customers) by debiting or crediting the banks' reserve accounts.

The number of wire transfers is small relative to other payment systems, but the dollar volume is very large compared to that of checks. The dollar volume continues to grow annually, with over $1.6 trillion being transferred on an average day. The Clearing House Interbank Payment System (CHIPS) also involves wire transfers but is primarily an international payment system and is considered in that section of the chapter.

*Wire Transfer Uses* Companies and banks opt for wire transfers when they want to gain immediate access to large-dollar amounts. The median wire transfer in the United States is $30,000. Small-dollar amounts are not transferred because the Fed charges banks for the service it provides. Banks will pass the cost on to the customer in the form of a fee ($10 charged to the initiating party; $7 to $10 charged to the recipient) or require a higher balance in the company's non-interest-bearing checking account. When banks borrow overnight from customers (via repurchase agreements) or each other (via Fed funds borrowing), the money must be transferred one day and transferred back the next.[15] This necessitates rapid and efficient movement of funds, which at present can only be accomplished by wire transfers. Settlement is immediate and final for such transfers, meaning

[14] Although not used much by businesses, Western Union offers wire transfers to customers. An individual conveys a payment order to a local Western Union office, which enters the message into its personal computer and conveys the order to another office in the vicinity of the payee. The receiving office picks up the message on its PC and issues a check to the order of the payee. The payee can then come by and pick up the check and take it to be cashed or deposited.

[15] To the customers or lending banks, this is viewed as an overnight investment.

there is no availability delay and no worry about the transfer bouncing. Companies find wire transfers economical for moving balances from several banks to a concentration bank, where the total amount can be used to pay down borrowings or invested in a higher-interest, large-denomination investment. Municipalities such as the city of Philadelphia have eased cash flow crises by having the state wire transfer payments that routinely are made in support of city services. Wires are also commonly used in large real estate transactions and occasionally to collect disputed amounts.

*MECHANICS OF WIRE TRANSFERS* The steps involved in a wire transfer are diagrammed in Exhibit 8–9. The customer wanting to make payment (the originator) may contact his or her bank in one of several ways: telephone, specialized telex machine or facsimile machine, telegram, or personal computer (Web site or electronic mail). Some type of account number or authorization code validates the identity of the originator to prevent fraud. Formally, when the originating customer requests that money be paid to a beneficiary, this is called a payment order (step 1). The customer's bank (Bank A) will then deduct the amount of the requested payment from the customer's available balance (step 2). At this point, the customer's bank (originating bank) communicates the payment order to the Fedwire office at the nearest Federal Reserve District Bank (step 3),[16] which then subtracts (debits) the amount of the transfer from the originating bank's balance at the Fed (reserve balance) and adds to (credits) the account of the beneficiary's bank (Bank B; step 4). The Fed also notifies Bank B of the transaction.[17] Bank B will then credit the beneficiary's ledger and available balances and notify the beneficiary by phone, in writing, or through a new balance report (step 5).

*ADVANTAGES AND DISADVANTAGES OF WIRES* Wire transfers have several advantages. They can be completed in a matter of minutes and are the best method for quickly

**Exhibit 8–9**

*Diagram of a Wire Transfer*

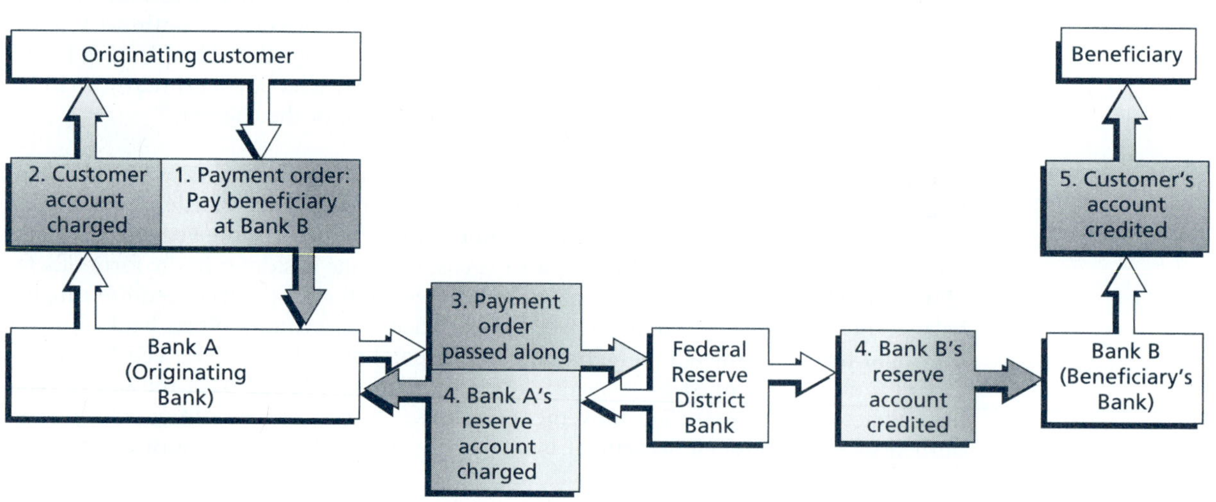


[16] Small banks not connected to the Fedwire computer can instruct larger correspondent banks to initiate wire transfers on behalf of their customers or initiate the transfers by telephoning or sending a message via a personal computer telephone hookup to the nearest Fed.

[17] When Bank B is in a different Federal Reserve District than Bank A, the payment order information is communicated through the FedNet communication system to Bank B's Federal Reserve District Bank.

moving large sums of money. They accomplish immediate final transfer of value without the worry of whether the check will bounce or ACH be reversed. When collecting a large sum of money from a customer of questionable creditworthiness, this finality is an appreciable advantage to the seller. However, because of the number of parties and necessary confirmations and other supportive tasks, they are also the most expensive on a per-transaction basis. The expense mounts when two entities within the same company are originator and beneficiary, respectively (as in the case of wiring money to concentrate into a larger balance), and the company must incur fees on both the sending and receiving ends.[18] As ACH transfers move toward same-day transaction, their lower cost will result in the displacement of many wires.

## Automated Clearinghouses

A fast and relatively inexpensive means of processing large numbers of routine transactions was developed in the early 1970s. Known as **automated clearinghouses (ACHs)**, this system is comprised of a loose network of associations spread across the country. The 20 ACH associations include more than 12,000 member financial institutions and hundreds of corporations. The associations provide information about ACH transactions, along with the benefits and costs. However, these associations do not actually make the electronic transfers; all transactions must be handled by an ACH operator. The Fed is the primary operator of the underlying value transfer system, processing 85 percent of all ACH transactions, the others handled by Electronic Payments Network, a private-sector operator. The most popular uses for entities conducting ACH transactions are the automatic (direct) deposit of paychecks and Social Security checks, explaining why the average ACH transaction amount is $2,850. Over 20,000 financial institutions and 725,000 companies use the ACH system to transfer funds electronically.

**Electronic depository transfer checks (EDTs)** are a common payment mechanism that uses the ACH system. EDTs are not really checks but are paperless, unsigned payments ("electronic debits") that transfer funds using the ACH system. They are often communicated via a personal computer and usually are accompanied by an electronic (paperless) message encoded in a specialized format. EDTs involve the payor's bank producing a computer file of payees, which is sent to one of the ACH operators, for availability to the payee either the next day or the day following. When used for concentrating funds from various depository accounts, the local or regional account is debited electronically and the funds are sent through an automated clearinghouse to the concentration bank account. Next-day availability is desirable for transfers used in deposit concentration, so that monies can be invested more quickly.

Payors know at the time of order initiation exactly when they will have their accounts charged for the dollar amount of each transaction. Two complicating factors affect the timing of order initiation, however. First, not all banks are members of the ACH system. Thus, a company wishing to pay all its employees through direct deposit will likely have to pay a few by means of checks. Second, not all banks have systems that enable them to electronically transmit payment orders (and accompanying information) to the appropriate ACHs.

*Growth of ACH Transactions* Referring back to Exhibit 8–7, it is evident that ACH volume is a fast growing payment system. Growth in dollar volume remained strong

---

[18] When the entity being paid (beneficiary) initiates the wire transfer, as is the case when a company's headquarters initiates concentration of funds from several distant banks, the transaction is called a "**wire drawdown**."

## FOCUS ON PRACTICE

### *New ACH Formats Triggering More Electronic Payments in the United States*

ACH Network E-Check Applications

*Internet-Initiated Entries (WEB):* A consumer accountholder authorizes, via the Internet, a company to debit their checking account. Accountholder authenticates their identity by entering a PIN code or answering a secret question.

*Telephone-Initiated Entries (TEL):* A consumer authorizes, via the telephone, a company to debit their account. Specific rules guide companies and financial institutions as to proper authorization procedures for the consumer.

*Point-of-Purchase Entries (POP):* A consumer's check is converted to an ACH transaction at the point of sale or purchase. The merchant scans the check through an electronic terminal, capturing the MICR information at the bottom of the check. The check is voided and an authorization form prints. The consumer signs the authorization assenting to the transaction. The consumer receives back the voided check and a copy of their signed authorization.

*Accounts Receivable Entries (ARC):* A consumer's check is converted to an ACH transaction by a lockbox or dropbox operator. The consumer is notified in advance that his or her check will be converted.

*Source:* Ian Macoy, "Arm Your Frontline Staff with ACH Training," NACHA—The Electronic Payments Association, **http://www.nacha.org/OtherResources/Arm_article/arm_article.htm**. 

from 1998–2000, when volume was growing at a compound annual growth rate of 7.75 percent per year. The annual number of ACH transfers in the United States grew from 850 million to almost 7.5 billion from 1989 to 2003—reflecting the fact that the number of companies using the ACH system grew from 100,000 to over 750,000. Growth would have been even faster had potential users been offered more inducement to use the system. The company or individual paying through an ACH debit loses the advantage of disbursement float, the delay between the time the check is written and when funds are subtracted from the account. Unless there is some offsetting benefit such as a longer credit period before payment (the ACH debit) is initiated, the customer lacks a strong reason to switch over. State governments have started mandating ACH payment of taxes owed, choosing the stick approach over the carrot approach. The ACH system has innovated to meet user needs, and there are new ways to initiate ACH payments. The Focus on Practice lists these new e-check ACH entry classes that promise to account for even faster growth in the future. The ACH network processed 518 million e-check transactions in 2002, about 6 percent of the ACH transactions processed, and well over double the number of 2001 e-check transactions.

*Purpose of the ACH System* The Fed is strongly encouraging greater use of electronic deposits and payments through the ACH system for two reasons. First, the payments are paperless, saving banks large amounts of money and back-office time. ACH transactions save financial institutions an estimated 30 to 35 percent compared to checks. The second advantage is related—the recipient of the payment gains faster availability and can credit the payor more quickly than would be the case for checks. ACH processing is ideal for payroll deposits, insurance premium collections, and corporation-to-corporation payments. Public and nonprofit organizations, particularly governments, have also found ACH collections attractive. Fund-raising consultants are beginning to advocate automated collection of pledges.[19] The major disadvantage to using ACH transactions is that the payor loses the customary float when writing checks, and payment terms may have to be renegotiated to induce payor participation.

*Mechanics of ACH Transactions* Exhibit 8–10 illustrates the mechanics of an ACH transaction and identifies the players involved. Two clarifying comments will aid in our understanding of the ACH. First, there is no physical clearinghouse, as would be the case with a local clearinghouse used in check swapping. Instead, the entries are debited and credited to the appropriate banks' accounts on the clearinghouse operator's computer. Second, all transactions eventually culminate in financial institution debits and credits at a Federal Reserve District Bank. All but one of the ACH operators is housed in Federal Reserve facilities, which settle ACH transactions by debiting or crediting the appropriate banks' reserve accounts. Even for the private operator, which processes ACH transactions (which are basically just information flows), settlement of the funds transfers still takes place at a Federal Reserve location. The net effect of all transfers involving a particular bank is handled by a debit (if the total is negative) or credit (if positive) to that bank's Federal Reserve account.[20]

Payroll processing illustrates the steps involved in an ACH transfer. Let's say Consolidated Freightliners (the originator) pays its employees monthly. It first prepares a computer file of electronic entries, which include the company's and employees' account numbers and bank transit routing numbers, as well as the dollar amount of the payments. It then sends the file electronically (via Internet or PC and telephone line) or manually (courier hand-carries a computer magnetic tape or disk) to Consolidated's bank [**originating depository financial institution (ODFI)**]. The bank sorts out the on-us credits for employees having checking accounts at that bank and credits their accounts. If it has any, the bank will then combine the other entries with those submitted by other companies and send Consolidated's remaining entries on a computer tape to the local ACH. The ACH operator must first sort the transactions involving the banks in its area and then send nonlocal transactions to other ACHs. The ACH then credits the employees' banks [called **receiving depository financial institutions (RDFIs)**] according to whether Consolidated has selected 1-day (next-day) or 2-day settlement.[21] The ODFI's account is likewise charged for the total amount of the payroll being processed through the ACH. Consolidated must be certain to have adequate funds in its checking account, as the bank will in turn debit Consolidated's account. The ACH will then send a data transmission to each RDFI bank, including all account numbers and dollar amounts of employees having accounts at that bank. The RDFI credits each employee's checking account appropriately. Consolidated's bank will provide it with periodic bank statements and/or daily deposit reports so that its treasurer can monitor the company's cash position.

---

[19] Organizations can get higher pledge amounts, guaranteed fulfillment of pledges, automatic pledge renewal, reduced solicitation costs, and more predictable cash inflows simply by having donors preauthorize automated debits to their checking accounts each month. For more on this, see Beverly Kempf, "Moving Donors to EFT," *Fund Raising Management* 4 (November 1990), pp. 51–52, 62.

[20] Do not confuse ACH operators with the 20 regional ACH associations. ACH associations, like other trade associations, include banking and corporate participants in a geographic area that participate in ACH payments or collections.

[21] More precisely, the ACH operator nets all transactions affecting a bank for a given settlement day and then has the Federal Reserve account of the bank debited or credited for the amount of the net balance. For an ODFI, 1-day settlement implies that an ACH processed Friday results in a debit for the total dollar amount on Monday, assuming it is not a bank holiday.

## Exhibit 8–10

*Mechanics of ACH Transactions*

### PARTICIPANTS

Five entities participate in the ACH system. They are defined as:

1. *Originator.* The originator is the entity that agrees to initiate ACH entries into the payment system according to an arrangement with a receiver. The originator is usually a company directing a transfer of funds to or from a consumer's or another company's account. In the case of a customer initiated entry, however, the originator may be an individual initiating funds transfer activity to or from his or her own account.
2. *Originating depository financial institution.* The originating depository financial institution (ODFI) is the institution that receives the payment instructions from originators and forwards the entries to the ACH operator. A DFI may participate in the ACH as a receiving depository financial institution (RDFI) without being an ODFI; however, if a DFI chooses to originate ACH entries, it must also agree to act as an RDFI.
3. *Automated clearinghouse operator.* An automated clearinghouse (ACH) operator is the central clearing facility, operated by a Federal Reserve Bank or a private organization, that receives entries from ODFIs, distributes the entries to appropriate RDFIs, and performs the settlement functions for the affected financial institutions.
4. *Receiving depository financial institution.* The receiving depository financial institution (RDFI) is the DFI that receives ACH entries from the ACH operator and posts them to the accounts of the depositors or payees (receivers).
5. *Receiver.* A receiver is a natural person or an organization that has authorized an originator to initiate an ACH entry to the receiver's account with the RDFI.

The flow chart depicts the system participants and their relationships.

System participants

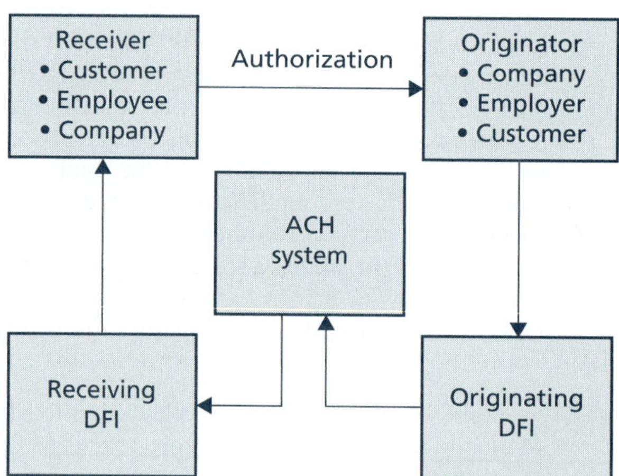


### Payment Applications

The ACH network supports a number of different payment applications. Unlike the wire transfer and check systems, the ACH is both a credit and a debit payment system. ACH credit transactions transfer funds from the originator to the receiver. ACH debit transactions, on the other hand, transfer funds (collect funds) from the receiver to the originator.

*Source:* Adapted with permission from materials provided by NACHA The Electronic Payments Association, **http://www.nacha.org/**.

Banks will charge slightly less for a 2-day settlement cycle than for transactions processed on a 1-day cycle. In fact, different banks will have different cutoff times by which originators must submit the computer file, and each bank may charge a different amount for the same ACH origination service.

*SUMMARY OF ACH ADVANTAGES AND DISADVANTAGES* Proponents claim numerous advantages for using the ACH system. Among them are the following:[22]

1. Reduced costs for banking, reconciliation and cash application, and handling return items.[23] The per-item fees companies pay for ACH debits and credits range from six cents to 15 cents. Banks are able to process ACH debits for about one-half the cost of processing a check and pass the savings on to companies. Banks much prefer to collect loan payments electronically, with estimated savings of up to $4.11 per payment, by eliminating loan coupons and other processing costs.
2. Faster inflows because of the possibility of collecting insurance premiums and other payments through the ACH; check-related mail and processing delays are eliminated.
3. More reliability, resulting in better service to customers and employees, due to the control over payment timing and the fact that fewer exception items must be dealt with.
4. Greater security, because checks can be tampered with and lost in the mail.
5. More accurate forecasting of funds availability, because of certainty as to when the transaction will take place.

Disadvantages for ACH usage offset the above advantages somewhat:

1. Disbursement float and control are reduced for the payor, which may lead to a renegotiation of all payment terms.
2. Up-front systems costs may be very high for the necessary investment in computer hardware and software, especially for a smaller bank or originator; recent movement toward PCs has reduced the hardware costs considerably.
3. Lack of uniform notification practices and payment formats has plagued the ACH industry. Some depository institutions are not timely in their notification of customers, and presently there are several different formats for transmission of payment data.

The relative advantage or disadvantage of using ACH depends on the application and the size of the company. Direct deposit and automated state tax payments are used by companies of all sizes, but other ACH uses vary significantly depending on company size. Notice in Exhibit 8–11 the results of the Phoenix-Hecht 1998 survey. The biggest change in the past several years has been the substantial increase in companies using the ACH for state tax payments. Corporate trade payments are increasingly made electronically, but almost twice as many large companies (sales in excess of $2.5 billion) as smaller companies (sales less than $250 million) use electronic payments. It is also noteworthy that most companies now use ACH debits for concentrating their cash to a central bank account.

ACH use continues to grow, and recent developments such as weekend acceptance of payment files for Monday settlement and all-electronic transmittal and receipt of payment flows should increase usage in the future.

---

[22] This discussion is based on material found in the Association for Financial Professionals' *Essentials of Cash Management, 7th ed.*

[23] The Fed charges a bank $1.60 to $2.00 for handling a returned check but only 50 cents for a returned ACH transaction.

**Exhibit 8–11**

*ACH Service Usage by Company Size*

| Service | Sales | | | | | All Respondents |
|---|---|---|---|---|---|---|
| | <$250M | $250M–$499M | $500M–$999M | $1B–$2.49B | $2.5+B | |
| Direct deposit of payroll | 73.0% | 74.9% | 79.3% | 84.8% | 79.8% | 75.4% |
| Automated state tax payments | 70.3% | 72.7% | 80.8% | 78.6% | 80.3% | 73.4% |
| ACH debits for cash concentration | 58.4% | 65.4% | 69.1% | 79.5% | 78.4% | 64.5% |
| Corporate trade payments | 38.2% | 46.6% | 52.7% | 63.2% | 70.6% | 46.1% |
| Consumer debits | 15.4% | 17.7% | 18.5% | 22.7% | 25.4% | 17.6% |
| Direct deposit of dividends/pension | 10.1% | 11.8% | 16.2% | 20.5% | 21.7% | 12.8% |

*Source:* "Cash Management Monitor™: Report to Corporations" (1998), Phoenix-Hecht, p. 16. **http://www.phoenixhecht.com**

## FINANCIAL DILEMMA REVISITED

Should your company get on the electronic payments bandwagon? Unquestionably. Despite the expenditures to get up and running, the advantages far outweigh the costs. Furthermore, a large customer or supplier will soon force the issue for you because of their preferences for electronic commerce applications, including financial EDI. The federal government has mandated that all of its vendors be paid electronically, and federal withholding taxes and some states' corporate taxes must be paid electronically by many businesses. Financial institutions and the regional or national ACH association will provide much needed help to guide your implementation process. A good illustration of how electronic payments can benefit a company is retailer user of "electronic checks." An estimated 110 million checks written by consumers at retail check-out stations were converted to ACH debits in 2003—up from 25 million point-of-purchase check conversions in 2000. When a consumer writes a check at the check-out, the merchant runs it through an electronic reader that captures the bank account number and routing information, along with the check serial number. The check is marked or stamped "Void" and handed back to the consumer. The consumer signs a receipt authorizing the electronic transaction and keeps a copy for his or her records. The merchant initiates an ACH debit using the check information and transaction amount. The consumer receives a brief listing of the transaction on his or her monthly bank statement. Now, accounts receivable conversions are being done of consumer bill payments received at lockbox locations, giving companies at most 1-day availability to all consumer check payments. Amazon.com plans to allow online purchasers to enter their checking account information and make a Web-based payment from their account, instead of a credit card or debit card payment.

### Point-of-Sale Transactions Using Debit Cards

Increasingly, consumers are using debit cards to make purchases: one in three in-store transactions are now paid for with a debit card in the United States. A **debit card** is very similar to a credit card, but the transaction is processed through an online hookup to local banks (36 percent of transactions and 40 percent of dollar value in 2000) or offline through the ACH system (64 percent of transactions and 60 percent of dollar value) and the amount is immediately (or if ACH within two business days) subtracted from the customer's checking account. By contrast, a credit card transaction is not a payment but is a loan from the credit card issuer. The number of merchants accepting debit cards exploded from only 50,000 in 1990 to hundreds of thousands today, as two in three Americans now have at least one debit card. Over 8.3 billion debit card transactions with a dollar value of $348 billion were made in 2000.

## INTERNATIONAL PAYMENT SYSTEMS

Companies selling or purchasing goods abroad are aware of several important differences in foreign payment systems. A complete discussion of other countries' payment systems is beyond the scope of this text,[24] and we present only the basic aspects of international paper-based and electronic payment systems.

In one sense, doing business abroad is much simpler, because there are far fewer banks in each country. One must pay attention to the customs and conventions of the different countries, however. Cross-border check processing is especially problematic, taking from several days to several weeks for clearing. Several correspondent banks might be involved, which slows the process while adding to the expense. Banks also may charge a service fee for the transfer that varies with the amount involved; within the United States, a fixed charge applies regardless of dollar amount. Drafts also are used much more in international trade, a topic we return to in our later chapter on collections. Finally, many countries restrict data and/or currency outflows, complicating the task of the multinational corporation treasurer.

### Paper-Based Payments

Checks are used in foreign countries but are not quite as popular. The major difference one sees abroad is the prevalence of giro systems, particularly in Europe. The **giro system** is a centralized payment system, usually linked to the postal service, used primarily for retail payments. To use it, a company mails a bill to the customer with a stub attached to it that includes the seller's bank and account number. Called a **giro acceptance**, this computer-processable stub card is signed by the customer, who then takes it to the post office. The post office transmits what now amounts to a payment order to the customer's bank, which then debits the customer's account and arranges for this and other payments from this customer to be credited to the seller's bank. The seller's bank then credits the seller's account and notifies the seller of the payment(s). The main advantage of the giro system is very little delay, or float, in a company's collections. The main disadvantage is that the seller is at the mercy of the buyer for payment initiation timing.

The use of checks is also reduced where postal systems are unreliable or consumers do not have checking accounts. In Latin America, for example, mail systems are too unreliable for sending checks, and fewer than 30 percent of households have checking accounts (compared to 87 percent in the United States). Until recently, check clearing occurred by arrangements between individual banks, because many central banks had no centralized check clearing systems, and in-country transportation was unreliable. Business-to-business payments were usually made by check, but these were either delivered or picked up by couriers, or deposited by the payor into the payee's account using a special deposit ticket. Consumers typically pay in person by cash or less frequently by check, either at a bank or the company's office. In Middle Eastern countries, central banks maintain control over the domestic clearinghouses, and manual check clearing occurs in each country except Saudi Arabia. As a result, most corporate payments occur by check, which will take

[24] Excellent surveys of various countries' payment and banking systems may be found in Back's book (see the end-of-chapter references) and various issues of the *AFP Exchange.*

from one to three business days to clear in the major cities and anywhere from five to 10 business days outside of the central clearing systems.

**Value dating** is another practice commonly used in foreign countries. Because banks abroad are allowed to (and do) pay interest on checking accounts, they must make up for the added interest expense by either charging fees for services rendered or engaging in value dating, which entails delaying the availability of deposited checks and retroactively advancing the debit date for cleared checks (the latter is called back valuing). The number of days a customer loses is sometimes negotiable and may vary by customer type, by bank, and by country. When a company is subject to back valuing by its banks, monitoring the company's bank balance becomes difficult and the company must do additional forecasting. Fortunately, banks in many countries offer automatic overdraft protection, so that the company is simply charged interest on overdrafted amounts as if it has taken out a small loan.

*EFFECT OF THE EURO* The single currency in Europe, the euro, and the single European market for financial services are changing European cash management. First, large amounts can be transferred on a same-day basis with no value dating—enabling concentration and **pooling** of funds into a single currency. Second, the development of between-country transfers that are not value dated is causing banks to begin dropping value dating on domestic payments. Third, the increased competition in banking services has lowered bank fees. Coincidentally, electronic balance reporting and payments initiation services are now being offered with Windows and Internet-based platforms. Cash management processes and receivables and payables management will continue to become more centralized and efficient.

## Electronic Payments

ACH systems are not generally available abroad, because of the prevalence of the giro system. Countries that are notable exceptions include Austria, Germany, the United Kingdom, the Netherlands, Switzerland, Canada, Brazil, and Mexico. U.S. companies can now initiate cross-border ACH payments to Canadian payees using a single computer-generated, **NACHA**-formatted file, and beginning in 2004 were able to do so to Mexico (with 2-day guaranteed settlement) and for credit transfers on a pilot basis to five European countries as well (with a maximum transfer cost estimated to be less than $3). The added complexity in these transactions is the U.S. dollar-to-foreign currency exchange rate calculation. Payments from Canadian companies can be received in a similar manner. Settlement is one or two days for credits and one day for debits, the cost to the originating bank is less than a nickel per transaction, and the receiver of the transaction is not charged anything. Mexico introduced ACH via a bank-owned ACH operator, Cecoban, in the 1990s. ACH systems are being developed in Argentina, Chile, Colombia, and Panama. In Europe, the Eurogiro system has been developed recently. **Eurogiro** is an electronic payment network established to enable financial institutions to exchange transactions. Eurogiro is tailored toward making cross-border transactions for small currency amounts, characterized by the following:

- Four business days is the standard transfer time from debiting the sender's account until the receiver's account is credited.
- Urgent cash payments are possible for rapid transfer within minutes (Western Union).
- Transfers are possible to and from more than 150 million giro accounts plus most bank accounts in Europe and in the United States.

Eurogiro handled 1,800,000 transactions in 2002. The Euro Bankers Association is now upgrading TARGET (Trans-European Automated Real-Time Gross Settlement Express

Transfer system), the European Union's electronic funds transfer network, to enable it to serve as a pan-European ACH system.

Wire transfers are commonly used to transfer large-dollar amounts internationally. We limit our discussion to CHIPS and SWIFT, the two international wire transfer mechanisms.

**CHIPS**, short for Clearing House Interbank Payment System, was established in 1970 to handle interbank transactions needed to settle international transactions. CHIPS is a private association of banks that operates through the New York Clearinghouse Association. Much of the flow of funds related to buying and selling dollar-denominated investments in major foreign financial centers (Eurodollar investments) is processed through CHIPS. Participating banks relay and receive payment messages over leased telephone lines to the CHIPS computer. CHIPS handles about 240,000 transactions daily, totaling $1.2 trillion.

CHIPS now provides intraday payment finality through a real-time system, meaning that each payment is considered final as soon as it is made. CHIPS settles small payments, which can be accommodated by the participating banks' available balances, individually. It uses bookkeeping entries to net other payments bilaterally (e.g., when Bank Y has to pay $250 million to Bank Z, and Bank Z has to pay $250 million to Bank Y), eliminating any actual movement of funds between the participants. Each participant pre-funds a deposit amount each morning, and when it has an end-of-day balance owed, the amount is taken out of the deposit. There is a 30-minute window of time to add to that position if the total amount owed exceeds the morning deposit. Banks with a credit balance receive that amount by Fedwire. CHIPS now has electronic data interchange capability attached to its payment message format. EDI allows participants to send business information (such as the purpose of the payment) along with their funds transfers.

**SWIFT**, the Society for Worldwide Interbank Financial Telecommunications, is really just a communication network. Its services are used by parties in 192 countries, and over 7,125 banks are connected to the network. It facilitates international payment orders because of a partly standardized message format and the ability to include additional payment messages with the payment order. At present, almost 1.3 billion messages are processed annually. Recent improvements, packaged as SWIFT II, include the ability to conduct interactive communications and a doubling of the number of characters the messages can include to 4,000. The messages only cost 38 cents each, regardless of source or destination. Settlement of the orders is made through correspondent banks or CHIPS; in the latter case, it would cost about $12 to the payor. A newer SWIFT message code enables banks to report balances to companies, with most international banks able to convey this information.

We can illustrate the workings of SWIFT by a simple example. Let's say a company in Australia wants to pay IBM for a computer. It would instruct its Australian bank to wire money to IBM. The bank might then cable the message across SWIFT to a correspondent bank in New York, which would debit the Australian bank's correspondent account for the amount of the transfer plus any fees. The U.S. correspondent bank would then pay IBM's bank, possibly working through yet another correspondent bank with which both of the banks have accounts.

## MANAGING THE BANK RELATIONSHIP

Corporate treasurers are responsible for not only understanding the payment system but also for selecting the best bank(s) to conduct business with and then maintaining good relationships with those banks. We will survey the five major types of services that banks can provide, the key documents treasurers use to evaluate banks, and how banks charge for their services. We take an in-depth look at how treasurers select a bank or bank network for cash management and other services. We also introduce the major trends affecting banks' provision of corporate services.

The objective treasurers strive to achieve when managing the bank relationship is to ensure that all the company's banking services are provided reliably at a reasonable cost. Note that we did not say "at a *minimal* cost," because reliability of the corporate/bank relationship and adequate compensation of the company's banks take precedence over cost minimization. Value is created for a corporation by wise selection of banks, followed up by careful monitoring of the banks, with new arrangements being made when necessary. The remainder of the chapter is laid out as follows. The first section provides background information regarding the major services banks offer to corporations, giving a logical starting point for treasurers determining which banks to do business with. The second section incorporates this information into a discussion of the bank selection process and principles regarding the management of the corporate/bank relationship. The chapter concludes with sections on banking system trends in the United States and abroad, including the increasing prominence of nonbank service providers, the ongoing unification of Europe's economic system, and the globalization of financial services provision.

## SERVICES PROVIDED BY BANKS

Banks offer five major types of services that are of interest to the financial manager responsible for short-term financial management decisions.[25] The first three fall under the umbrella of "cash management" services: collections services (including the concentration of funds), payments services, and information services. The other two services are closely linked to the cash management services, as corporations that run short on cash need credit services, and corporations with excess cash use banks' investment services. Exhibit 8–12 summarizes the five banking services. We limit our present discussion to the bank pricing and provision of cash management services; Chapters 9 and 10 cover collection and mobilization services, Chapter 11 covers payment services, Chapters 14 and 15 address investments, Chapter 16 discusses borrowing, and Chapter 19 covers information services.

To better understand this, we present the organization of the **corporate services** division in a typical bank. The treasury professional can understand the role and significance of cash management and related services when seeing the role and location of cash management in the typical bank's organizational structure. Throughout our discussion, when we use the term "bank," we are referring to any financial institution that offers the particular service being discussed.

### Banking Perspective on Corporate Services

Banks sometimes label services provided to corporate customers as "wholesale" services. Banks formerly used services such as cash management as a low-priced "loss leader" to gain a foothold with corporate clients, hoping to later add profitable lending arrangements. Corporations increasingly shifted borrowing to nonbank sources in the 1980s, however, and bank loan profitability declined. During the same time period, cash management services experienced a 19-percent growth, and both factors led to a repricing of cash management and related services. Three hundred banks presently offer cash management services, leading many observers to predict a shakeout and resultant exit by some of the

---

[25] Some "long-term" services we are not concerned with include leasing, investment banking, merger/acquisition counseling, and dividend-related services.

Exhibit 8–12

*Major Banking Services*

banks. The growth rate slowed in the 1990s and 2000s to single digits, and the banks' offerings are so similar that some consider cash management services a commodity-type product. If so, the implication for banks is serious: more shopping around by corporate clients, leading to lower prices and less profitability.[26] The profitability of the overall relationship with the client, which encompasses all services a bank provides for the client, is the bank's proper focus.

*Organization of Cash Management in Banks* Organizationally, the cash management group is usually a separate department in the bank's corporate services division. Within the cash management group, there might be three distinct subgroups: sales, product development/management, and customer service.[27] The sales group generates income by selling cash management products to corporate clients, the product group develops new products and improves on existing ones, and the customer service group strives to quickly and accurately resolve client inquiries and complaints.

*Value of Banks to Corporate Treasurers* Corporate treasurers generally find banks' cash management officers very helpful with advice and information. This advice is most often oriented toward positioning the bank in the most favorable light, however. Conversely, bankers' major complaints regarding treasurers are that they are sometimes defensive, cover up ignorance of complex products, are unfair and tactless when having banks bid against one another, or overlook the fact that banks must make a profit on the total client relationship (and cannot accept thin margins on all services). Banks also expect to be informed as soon as possible of any adverse changes in the client's financial position and consider the treasurer to be the main source of information regarding the company and its banking needs. Many banks assign one individual to the overall client relationship; this involves overseeing all services provided to the client. Accounts (clients) that are large and profitable to the bank naturally have the best bank personnel assigned to them. With this banking environment context in mind, we now consider the five major corporate services provided by banks: collection, payment, information, lending, and investment.

## Depository Services and the Availability Schedule

**Standard check processing** involves verifying the depositor's cash letter—which lists the checks and their amounts—and then encoding the dollar amount on the MICR line and

[26] Quality of service should also become more important, and banks are devoting more attention to quality aspects such as speedy customer complaint handling.

[27] Many banks have a centralized customer service department that would not only handle cash management inquiries but would also handle complaints and questions about all other services used by a client. Very technical questions are referred to product managers. Also, a bank's operations area actually does the wire transfers and other transactions for the client.

sending the checks to a correspondent bank or the nearest Federal Reserve facility[28] to be cleared back to the bank on which the check was written. The depositor's ledger balance is credited, but the portion of the total deposit available as "good funds" ready to be spent varies according to the bank's **availability schedule**. Exhibit 8–13 illustrates part of the availability schedule offered by Fifth Third Bank, a Cincinnati bank. Notice that the schedule applies to checks deposited from Monday through Thursday, and that Friday deposits get Monday or Tuesday availabilities. It lists all checks that will receive 0-day (same-day), or immediate availability, other than on-us checks. It then shows availability by drawee bank Fed district. The absolute latest ledger cutoff time—the time by which a company may deposit pre-encoded checks and get the stated availability is the closing time at—is 8:00 P.M. Saturday or Sunday deposits taken at branches are subject to Monday's cutoff. Checks must be deposited by the stated cutoff time to get the stated availability; otherwise, they would be granted availability as if deposited the next *business* day.

How quickly deposited amounts are made available by the clearing bank is related to the time of deposit, how distant the drawee bank is, whether it is in a Federal Reserve Bank city or an RCPC area, and whether it is in a check swapping agreement or local clearinghouse with either the clearing bank or one of the clearing bank's correspondents. This availability float time lag may not always coincide with the amount of time it takes the check to actually clear, but generally, the two are closely linked. Notice that no check gets longer than a 2-day availability on this Fifth Third availability schedule, which assumes the company has pre-encoded the dollar amount on each check.

Banks will provide **expedited check processing** if the depositor is willing to perform extra tasks or pay the bank the extra charge involved. One task that companies can perform to cut bank processing time and reduce service charges is to pre-encode checks before deposit. This necessitates purchase of an MICR encoder, which is the machine used to imprint the check's dollar amount on the bottom right of the check. After endorsement, pre-encoded checks are bundled together, totaled, and sent to the bank. In addition to reduced per-check fees, the bank also offers a later cutoff time (e.g., 10 P.M.) for availability assignment. Even if the depositor does not perform extra tasks, the bank might offer a courier service to expedite collection of large-dollar checks.

## BANK SELECTION AND RELATIONSHIP MANAGEMENT

### The Bank Selection Process

The **bank selection process** involves assembling a system of banks to efficiently and effectively process all information and cash flows involving the corporation's short-term financial management. Except for very small organizations, corporations deal with more than one bank. Geographically widespread or large firms tend to use the largest number of banks, and particular industries exhibit varying usage of banks, although all groups are consolidating their banking systems toward use of fewer banks. Greenwich data show the typical U.S. company uses seven banks for cash management services, with the larger companies averaging 12 banks and the smaller companies averaging only four. Multiple banks are also utilized abroad: Soenen and Aggarwal (1989) found that half of all U.K. companies they surveyed had 15 or more banking relationships each, and in the Netherlands and Belgium, half of the companies dealt with five or more banks.

In the past, businesses chose banks primarily using a total **relationship approach**, where credit and cash management services were both handled by the chosen bank. In-

[28] Major money center banks clear from 1 to 3 million checks daily in the New York City area alone.

Exhibit 8–13

*Availability Schedule*

**Availability Schedule by ABA Number**
Effective Date: 1/02/04
Processing Center: Cincinnati, Ohio

Frequency: Monday through Thursday

This Availability Schedule supersedes all prior schedules published by this bank.

| ABA | Description | Deadline | Avail | Fraction |
|---|---|---|---|---|
| **Government Items** | | | | |
| 0000-0050,0051 | TREASURIES | 11:00 A.M. | 0 | 100% |
| 0000-0800 | POSTAL M.O. | 11:00 A.M. | 0 | 100% |
| 0000-9000 | SAVINGS BONDS | 11:00 A.M. | 0 | 100% |
| **Federal Reserve District 1** | | | | |
| 0110 | BOSTON CITY | 8:00 P.M. | 1 | 100% |
| 0111 | WINDSOR LOCKS | 8:00 P.M. | 2 | 100% |
| 0112 | BOSTON RCPC | 8:00 P.M. | 1 | 100% |
| 0113 | BOSTON RCPC | 8:00 P.M. | 1 | 100% |
| 0114 | BOSTON RCPC | 8:00 P.M. | 1 | 100% |
| 0115 | BOSTON RCPC | 8:00 P.M. | 1 | 100% |
| 0116 | WINDSOR LOCKS | 8:00 P.M. | 1 | 100% |
| 0117 | WINDSOR LOCKS | 8:00 P.M. | 1 | 100% |
| 0118 | WINDSOR LOCKS | 8:00 P.M. | 1 | 100% |
| 0119 | WINDSOR LOCKS | 8:00 P.M. | 1 | 100% |
| **Federal Reserve District 2** | | | | |
| 0210 | EROC CITY | 8:00 P.M. | 1 | 100% |
| 0211 | WINDSOR LOCKS | 8:00 P.M. | 2 | 100% |
| 0212 | EROC RCPC | 8:00 P.M. | 1 | 100% |
| 0213 | UTICA RCPC | 8:00 P.M. | 1 | 100% |
| 0214 | EROC RCPC | 8:00 P.M. | 1 | 100% |
| 0215 | VIRGIN ISLANDS / PR | 8:00 P.M. | 1 | 100% |
| 0216 | VIRGIN ISLANDS / PR | 8:00 P.M. | 1 | 100% |
| 0217 | EROC RCPC | 8:00 P.M. | 1 | 100% |
| 0219 | EROC RCPC | 8:00 P.M. | 1 | 100% |
| 0220 | UTICA CITY | 8:00 P.M. | 1 | 100% |
| 0223 | UTICA RCPC | 8:00 P.M. | 1 | 100% |
| 0260 | EROC CITY | 8:00 P.M. | 1 | 100% |
| 0270 | EROC CITY | 8:00 P.M. | 1 | 100% |
| 0280 | EROC CITY | 8:00 P.M. | 1 | 100% |
| **Federal Reserve District 3** | | | | |
| 0310 | PHIL CITY | 8:00 P.M. | 1 | 100% |

*continued*

## Exhibit 8–13 (continued)

*Availability Schedule*

| ABA | Description | Deadline | Avail | Fraction |
|---|---|---|---|---|
| 0311 | PHIL RCPC | 8:00 P.M. | 1 | 100% |
| 0312 | PHIL RCPC | 8:00 P.M. | 1 | 100% |
| 0313 | PHIL RCPC | 8:00 P.M. | 1 | 100% |
| 0319 | PHIL RCPC | 8:00 P.M. | 1 | 100% |
| 0360 | PHIL CITY | 8:00 P.M. | 1 | 100% |
| **Federal Reserve District 4** | | | | |
| 0410 | CLEV. CITY | 8:00 P.M. | 1 | 100% |
| 0412 | CLEV. RCPC | 8:00 P.M. | 1 | 100% |
| 0420 | CINN CITY | 8:00 P.M. | 1 | 100% |
| 0421 | CINN RCPC | 8:00 P.M. | 1 | 100% |
| 0422 | CINN RCPC | 8:00 P.M. | 1 | 100% |
| 0423 | CINN RCPC | 8:00 P.M. | 1 | 100% |
| 0430 | PITTSBURGH CITY | 8:00 P.M. | 1 | 100% |
| 0432 | PITTSBURGH RCPC | 8:00 P.M. | 1 | 100% |
| 0433 | PITTSBURGH RCPC | 8:00 P.M. | 1 | 100% |
| 0434 | PITTSBURGH RCPC | 8:00 P.M. | 1 | 100% |
| 0440 | COLUMBUS CITY | 8:00 P.M. | 1 | 100% |
| 0441 | COLUMBUS RCPC | 8:00 P.M. | 1 | 100% |
| 0442 | COLUMBUS RCPC | 8:00 P.M. | 1 | 100% |
| **Federal Reserve District 5** | | | | |
| 0510 | RICHMOND CITY | 8:00 P.M. | 1 | 100% |
| 0514 | RICHMOND RCPC | 8:00 P.M. | 1 | 100% |
| 0515 | CHARLESTON RCPC | 8:00 P.M. | 1 | 100% |
| 0519 | CHARLESTON CITY | 8:00 P.M. | 1 | 100% |
| 0520 | BALTIMORE CITY | 8:00 P.M. | 1 | 100% |
| 0521 | BALTIMORE RCPC | 8:00 P.M. | 1 | 100% |
| 0522 | BALTIMORE RCPC | 8:00 P.M. | 1 | 100% |
| 0530 | CHARLOTTE CITY | 8:00 P.M. | 1 | 100% |
| 0531 | CHARLOTTE RCPC | 8:00 P.M. | 1 | 100% |
| 0532 | COLUMBIA RCPC | 8:00 P.M. | 1 | 100% |
| 0539 | COLUMBIA CITY | 8:00 P.M. | 1 | 100% |
| 0540 | BALTIMORE RCPC | 8:00 P.M. | 1 | 100% |
| 0550 | BALTIMORE RCPC | 8:00 P.M. | 1 | 100% |
| 0560 | BALTIMORE RCPC | 8:00 P.M. | 1 | 100% |
| 0570 | BALTIMORE RCPC | 8:00 P.M. | 1 | 100% |
| **Federal Reserve District 6** | | | | |
| 0610 | ATLANTA CITY | 8:00 P.M. | 1 | 100% |
| 0611 | ATLANTA RCPC | 8:00 P.M. | 1 | 100% |
| 0612 | ATLANTA RCPC | 8:00 P.M. | 1 | 100% |
| 0613 | ATLANTA RCPC | 8:00 P.M. | 1 | 100% |
| 0620 | BIRMINGHAM CITY | 8:00 P.M. | 1 | 100% |
| 0621 | BIRMINGHAM RCPC | 8:00 P.M. | 1 | 100% |
| 0622 | BIRMINGHAM RCPC | 8:00 P.M. | 1 | 100% |
| 0630 | JACKSONVILLE CITY | 8:00 P.M. | 2 | 100% |
| 0631 | JACKSONVILLE RCPC | 8:00 P.M. | 2 | 100% |
| 0632 | JACKSONVILLE RCPC | 8:00 P.M. | 2 | 100% |
| 0640 | NASHVILLE CITY | 8:00 P.M. | 1 | 100% |

## Exhibit 8–13 (continued)

*Availability Schedule*

| ABA | Description | Deadline | Avail | Fraction |
|---|---|---|---|---|
| 0641 | NASHVILLE RCPC | 8:00 P.M. | 1 | 100% |
| 0642 | NASHVILLE RCPC | 8:00 P.M. | 1 | 100% |
| 0650 | NEW ORLEANS CITY | 8:00 P.M. | 1 | 100% |
| 0651 | NEW ORLEANS RCPC | 8:00 P.M. | 1 | 100% |
| 0652 | NEW ORLEANS RCPC | 8:00 P.M. | 1 | 100% |
| 0653 | NEW ORLEANS RCPC | 8:00 P.M. | 1 | 100% |
| 0654 | NEW ORLEANS RCPC | 8:00 P.M. | 1 | 100% |
| 0655 | NEW ORLEANS RCPC | 8:00 P.M. | 1 | 100% |
| 0660 | MIAMI CITY | 8:00 P.M. | 1 | 100% |
| 0670 | MIAMI RCPC | 8:00 P.M. | 1 | 100% |
| **Federal Reserve District 7** | | | | |
| 0710 | CHICAGO CITY | 8:00 P.M. | 1 | 100% |
| 0711 | PEORIA | 8:00 P.M. | 1 | 100% |
| 0712 | CHICAGO RCPC | 8:00 P.M. | 1 | 100% |
| 0719 | CHICAGO RCPC | 8:00 P.M. | 1 | 100% |
| 0720 | DETROIT CITY | 8:00 P.M. | 1 | 100% |
| 0724 | DETROIT RCPC | 8:00 P.M. | 1 | 100% |
| 0730 | DES MOINES CITY | 8:00 P.M. | 1 | 100% |
| 0739 | DES MOINES RCPC | 8:00 P.M. | 1 | 100% |
| 0740 | INDIANAPOLIS CITY | 8:00 P.M. | 1 | 100% |
| 0749 | INDIANAPOLIS RCPC | 8:00 P.M. | 1 | 100% |
| 0750 | MILWAUKEE CITY | 8:00 P.M. | 1 | 100% |
| 0759 | MILWAUKEE RCPC | 8:00 P.M. | 1 | 100% |
| **Federal Reserve District 8** | | | | |
| 0810 | ST LOUIS CITY | 8:00 P.M. | 1 | 100% |
| 0812 | ST LOUIS CNTRY | 8:00 P.M. | 1 | 100% |
| 0813 | LOUISVILLE RCPC | 8:00 P.M. | 1 | 100% |
| 0815 | ST LOUIS CNTRY | 8:00 P.M. | 1 | 100% |
| 0819 | ST LOUIS RCPC | 8:00 P.M. | 1 | 100% |
| 0820 | LITTLE ROCK CITY | 8:00 P.M. | 1 | 100% |
| 0829 | LITTLE ROCK RCPC | 8:00 P.M. | 1 | 100% |
| 0830 | LOUISVILLE CITY | 8:00 P.M. | 1 | 100% |
| 0839 | LOUISVILLE RCPC | 8:00 P.M. | 1 | 100% |
| 0840 | MEMPHIS CITY | 8:00 P.M. | 1 | 100% |
| 0841 | MEMPHIS RCPC | 8:00 P.M. | 1 | 100% |
| 0842 | MEMPHIS RCPC | 8:00 P.M. | 1 | 100% |
| 0843 | MEMPHIS RCPC | 8:00 P.M. | 1 | 100% |
| 0863 | LOUISVILLE RCPC | 8:00 P.M. | 1 | 100% |
| 0865 | ST LOUIS CNTRY | 8:00 P.M. | 1 | 100% |
| **Federal Reserve District 9** | | | | |
| 0910 | MINNEAPOLIS CITY | 8:00 P.M. | 1 | 100% |
| 0911 | MINNEAPOLIS CNTRY | 8:00 P.M. | 2 | 100% |
| 0912 | MINNEAPOLIS CNTRY | 8:00 P.M. | 2 | 100% |
| 0913 | MINNEAPOLIS CNTRY | 8:00 P.M. | 2 | 100% |
| 0914 | MINNEAPOLIS CNTRY | 8:00 P.M. | 2 | 100% |
| 0915 | MINNEAPOLIS CNTRY | 8:00 P.M. | 2 | 100% |
| 0918 | MINNEAPOLIS RCPC | 8:00 P.M. | 1 | 100% |

*continued*

## Exhibit 8–13 (continued)

*Availability Schedule*

| ABA | Description | Deadline | Avail | Fraction |
|---|---|---|---|---|
| 0919 | MINNEAPOLIS RCPC | 8:00 P.M. | 1 | 100% |
| 0920 | HELENA CITY | 8:00 P.M. | 1 | 100% |
| 0921 | HELENA RCPC | 8:00 P.M. | 1 | 100% |
| 0929 | HELENA RCPC | 8:00 P.M. | 1 | 100% |
| 0960 | MINNEAPOLIS CITY | 8:00 P.M. | 1 | 100% |
| **Federal Reserve District 10** | | | | |
| 1010 | KAN. CITY CITY | 8:00 P.M. | 1 | 100% |
| 1011 | KAN. CITY CNTRY | 8:00 P.M. | 2 | 100% |
| 1012 | KAN. CITY CNTRY | 8:00 P.M. | 2 | 100% |
| 1019 | KAN. CITY CNTRY | 8:00 P.M. | 2 | 100% |
| 1020 | DENVER CITY | 8:00 P.M. | 1 | 100% |
| 1021 | DENVER CNTRY | 8:00 P.M. | 2 | 100% |
| 1022 | DENVER CNTRY | 8:00 P.M. | 2 | 100% |
| 1023 | DENVER CNTRY | 8:00 P.M. | 2 | 100% |
| 1030 | OKLA. CITY CITY | 8:00 P.M. | 1 | 100% |
| 1031 | OKLA. CITY CNTRY | 8:00 P.M. | 2 | 100% |
| 1039 | OKLA. CITY RCPC | 8:00 P.M. | 2 | 100% |
| 1040 | OMAHA CITY | 8:00 P.M. | 1 | 100% |
| 1041 | OMAHA CNTRY | 8:00 P.M. | 2 | 100% |
| 1049 | OMAHA RCPC | 8:00 P.M. | 1 | 100% |
| 1070 | DENVER RCPC | 8:00 P.M. | 1 | 100% |
| **Federal Reserve District 11** | | | | |
| 1110 | DALLAS CITY | 8:00 P.M. | 1 | 100% |
| 1111 | DALLAS RCPC | 8:00 P.M. | 1 | 100% |
| 1113 | DALLAS CNTRY | 8:00 P.M. | 2 | 100% |
| 1119 | DALLAS RCPC | 8:00 P.M. | 1 | 100% |
| 1120 | EL PASO CITY | 8:00 P.M. | 1 | 100% |
| 1122 | EL PASO RCPC | 8:00 P.M. | 2 | 100% |
| 1123 | EL PASO RCPC | 8:00 P.M. | 2 | 100% |
| 1130 | HOUSTON CITY | 8:00 P.M. | 1 | 100% |
| 1131 | HOUSTON RCPC | 8:00 P.M. | 2 | 100% |
| 1140 | SAN ANTONIO CITY | 8:00 P.M. | 1 | 100% |
| 1149 | SAN ANTONIO RCPC | 8:00 P.M. | 2 | 100% |
| 1163 | EL PASO RCPC | 8:00 P.M. | 2 | 100% |
| **Federal Reserve District 12** | | | | |
| 1210 | SAN FRAN CITY | 8:00 P.M. | 1 | 100% |
| 1211 | SAN FRAN RCPC | 8:00 P.M. | 1 | 100% |
| 1212 | SAN FRAN RCPC | 8:00 P.M. | 1 | 100% |
| 1213 | SAN FRAN RCPC | 8:00 P.M. | 1 | 100% |
| 1214 | SAN FRAN CNTRY | 8:00 P.M. | 2 | 100% |
| 1220 | L.A. CITY | 8:00 P.M. | 1 | 100% |
| 1221 | L.A. RCPC | 8:00 P.M. | 2 | 100% |
| 1222 | L.A. RCPC | 8:00 P.M. | 2 | 100% |
| 1223 | L.A. | 8:00 P.M. | 2 | 100% |
| 1224 | L.A. RCPC | 8:00 P.M. | 2 | 100% |
| 1230 | PORTLAND CITY | 8:00 P.M. | 1 | 100% |
| 1231 | PORTLAND RCPC | 8:00 P.M. | 2 | 100% |

**Exhibit 8–13** (continued)

*Availability Schedule*

| ABA | Description | Deadline | Avail | Fraction |
|---|---|---|---|---|
| 1232 | PORTLAND RCPC | 8:00 P.M. | 2 | 100% |
| 1233 | PORTLAND RCPC | 8:00 P.M. | 2 | 100% |
| 1240 | S.L.C. CITY | 8:00 P.M. | 1 | 100% |
| 1241 | S.L.C. RCPC | 8:00 P.M. | 2 | 100% |
| 1242 | S.L.C. RCPC | 8:00 P.M. | 2 | 100% |
| 1243 | S.L.C. RCPC | 8:00 P.M. | 2 | 100% |
| 1250 | SEATTLE CITY | 8:00 P.M. | 1 | 100% |
| 1251 | SEATTLE RCPC | 8:00 P.M. | 2 | 100% |
| 1252 | SEATTLE RCPC | 8:00 P.M. | 2 | 100% |

ON FRIDAY ALL POINTS WILL BE AVAILABLE ON MONDAY EXCEPT THE POINTS LISTED AS COUNTRY.
ALL BUSINESS DAY DEADLINES INDICATED ON THIS SCHEDULE ARE BASED UPON ARRIVAL AT PROCESSING CENTER
ALL AVAILABILITY IS STATED IN BUSINESS DAYS AS OF AN 8:00 PM LEDGER CUT-OFF FOR FULLY ENCODED ITEMS.
AVAILABILITY STATED IN THIS SCHEDULE MAY BE ALTERED DUE TO FEDERAL RESERVE BANK HOLIDAYS.
IF DEADLINES ARE DELAYED DUE TO WEATHER, POWER BLACKOUTS OR OTHER ACTS OF GOD,
AVAILABILITY WILL BE PASSED AS IT IT RECEIVED.
ALL FRB/ABA NUMBERS BEGINNING WITH 2XXX OR 3XXX WILL BE ASSIGNED THE SAME AVAILABILITY
AS PREFIXES BEGINNING WITH OXXX OR 1XXX.
ANALYSIS ADJUSTMENTS WILL BE MADE FOR RETURNED AND EXCEPTION ITEMS WHERE FLOAT IS INCURRED.
FIFTH THIRD BANK WILL NOT BE RESPONSIBLE FOR AVAILABILITY LOSSES RESULTING FROM TYPOGRAPHICAL ERRORS
APPEARING IN THIS SCHEDULE.
THIS SCHEDULE IS DESIGNED TO ASSIST YOU IN CLEARING ITEMS,
DEADLINES, ENDPOINTS AND AVAILABILITY ARE SUBJECT TO CHANGE WITHOUT NOTICE.

creasingly, there is a decoupling or "unbundling" of services, popularizing the **transaction approach** whereby the treasurer selects the bank(s) that can best provide a specific service. Banks have developed sophisticated cost accounting and management control systems that enable them to identify profitability by product line and by customer, facilitating exact and competitive pricing of individual cash management services. Procedurally, larger firms often initiate requests for formal bids on cash management service offerings and prices, whereas smaller organizations generally shop around and then negotiate with a small number of select banks.

## Selection Criteria

We will focus on selecting banks for cash management and related services, occasionally noting interfaces with aspects of selecting banks with which to borrow or invest. Because banks are so involved in the payments system, this is a crucial decision for a company. A comprehensive checklist for bank selection is reproduced in Appendix 8A at the end of the chapter. We highlight several of the major criteria companies use when first establishing the bank(s) to utilize for cash management and related services.

- Location
- Bank/Company fit
- Service quality/Breadth (including development of nationwide branch network)
- Bank creditworthiness
- Bank specializations
- Price

More will be said about when and how to negotiate bank selection later in the chapter.

## MANAGING BANK RELATIONSHIPS

Ideally, a corporation should monitor ongoing banking relations in reference to an established bank relationship policy. The **bank relationship policy** establishes the company's objectives, compensation, and review process for the banks it has a relationship with. The policy elements devised by E. F. Hutton subsequent to its legal problems linked to its overly aggressive banking posture are illustrative:[29]

- defining bank relations (tiering)—rank banks in terms of importance to company, ranging from tier one banks used extensively in the past for credit and noncredit services to tier four banks, which are branches and some regional depository banks that typically do not provide credit services.
- establishing compensation ranges—how should banks in each tier be compensated and a reasonable level of compensation.
- establishing a method for adjusting target balances—indicate how bank compensation would be adjusted if a bank exceeds or falls below the target, with a goal of altering the bank's return on assets related to its business with the company.
- defining relationship and communications responsibility—specify who in the corporation is responsible for managing the overall relations with banks (usually the treasurer) and the frequency and form of company-bank communications.
- defining compensation periods—how often the company will review compensation for each tier of banks, which is negotiated and confirmed with each bank, assisting in the overall objective of reaching a target compensation over a certain time frame.
- defining payment methods—for credit services this would normally be in fees and interest charges, while for noncredit services payment might be in fees, compensating balances, or a combination of fees and balances.
- defining compensation agreements and contracts—here the company's position is articulated as a first approach toward negotiating a written agreement or contract with each bank.
- establishing an annual review process—includes an overall rating of the bank, an estimate of the bank's past and projected income and expense on the company's account, potential new business with the banks, target compensation level re-establishment, and whether a bank will remain in the same tier, move to a new tier, or be terminated.

This approach's underpinning logic is to ensure that the bank maintains a satisfactory return on assets on the company's overall account. Prudent companies attempt to negotiate when differences of opinion occur with existing banks, rather than immediately switching banks, to preserve long-term relationships. These relationships create value for the company in the form of predictability, speed, and flexibility of bank response to future company requests.

### Account Analysis Statement

Banks provide corporate customers with an **account analysis statement**, which indicates the services used and the charges assessed the company. The statement provides in-depth balance information, a 12-month balance history, a detailed listing and pricing of services

[29] For more on the Hutton approach, see the Beehler (1987a, 1987b) citations in the end-of-chapter references.

used, and the degree to which the company's actual balances offset fees charged for the services used. The statement is valuable as a cash management tool because it helps company personnel identify whether excess balances are being held and to project balances necessary for avoidance of service charges. The charges are shown on a fee basis and a compensating balance basis by banks following the Association for Financial Professionals (AFP) standard presentation format, established in 1987 to facilitate bank comparisons. The availability schedule to be used may be negotiable in any case, as most banks have two or three different availability schedules (and possibly another one for pre-encoded checks).

Exhibit 8–14 illustrates the most important parts of the account analysis statement used by Bank One, Louisville, KY, which conforms to the AFP format. This particular statement summarizes the activity for December, 2003, for a client, with the net service charge (or credit) computed in the first schedule and individual services used shown in the second schedule. Near the top of the first schedule, starting with (D), is the average monthly ledger balance calculation (see the glossary at the end of Exhibit 8–14 for additional detail on each lettered item). The average float (E), representing checks deposited on which the bank has not yet collected funds, is subtracted from the average ledger balance (D) to arrive at the average collected balance (F).[30] Simplifying the wording slightly, the relationship of collected to ledger balances is shown formally as Equation 8.4.

$$\text{Average collected balance} = \text{Average ledger balance} - \text{Float} \tag{8.4}$$

Bank One distinguishes between collected[31] and investable (available) balances by adjusting the former by the Fed's reserve requirement—10 percent at the time of the schedule. Because the bank must hold reserves in nonearning assets (vault cash or deposits at the Federal Reserve), it does not count this part of the company's balances in the available balance. Near the bottom of the first panel (N), we see the **earnings credit rate (*ecr*)** applied to balances held at the bank, which can be used to offset the service charges.

Recognizing that they are legally prohibited from paying a company interest on demand deposit accounts, banks provide a bookkeeping credit to offset service charges incurred by the company. The *ecr* applied in the statement month was 0.30 percent. The *ecr* shown here is based on the 91-day Treasury bill rate. Banks' earnings credit rates are generally based on a prevailing money market rate (usually somewhat less than the 91-day Treasury bill rate from a recent auction) and a bank's business strategy, but typically are relatively low compared with the rates at which treasurers are able to invest surplus funds.

To see where the Balance Required (J) comes from, we must refer to the "Service Analysis" panel of Exhibit 8–14 as a second schedule. Notice that the services used by the clients during the month, unit prices, and the resultant service charges are shown. In the right-most column, labeled Balance Required, the service charges are converted to the equivalent amount of demand deposit balances. To do so, the *ecr* is first put on a monthly basis by dividing it by 365, then multiplying it by the number of days in the month (in this case,

---

[30] The float, or average uncollected funds, calculation is a function of the bank's availability schedule and its cutoff times. A manager cannot assume that quicker availability implies higher collected balances because a bank may have an earlier cutoff time for assigning ledger credit to checks. Availability of funds on a check deposited at 3 P.M. at Bank A, which has a 1 P.M. cutoff time and assigns 1-day availability, will be the same as at Bank B, which has a 4 P.M. cutoff time and 2-day availability. Deposits made after the cutoff time are not even granted ledger credit until the next business day. Furthermore, some banks base their availability schedules on actual check clearing times for each customer's checks, whereas others use averages based on past periods for the customer or a group of similar customers.

[31] Banks may also subtract from the average collected balance an amount necessary to compensate for loan services provided to the customer, if a lending relationship exists.

Exhibit 8–14

*Account Analysis Statement Example*

Bank One, NA

CAP N N Z 01-07-2004

Account No:

Page 1 of 3

**B** **DEC 1 through DEC 31, 2003**

External

**A** Contact:
Phone:

## Account Analysis Statement

**C** Account No: DEMAND DEPOSIT ACCOUNT

### Balance Analysis

| | | | This Period | Average Year To Date |
|---|---|---|---|---|
| D | Average Ledger Balance | | 7,597,307.76 | 6,954,741 |
| E | Less Average Float | | -6,019,317.30 | -6,208,912 |
| F | Average Collected Balance | | 1,577,990.46 | 745,828 |
| G | Avg Positive Collected Balance | | 1,577,990.46 | 757,320 |
| H | Less Reserve Requirement | Rate: 10.000 | -157,799.04 | -75,732 |
| I | Average Investable Balance | | 1,420,191.42 | 681,588 |
| J | Less Balance Required | | -367,889,112.21 | 307,079,271 |
| K | Excess(Deficit) Invest Bal | | -366,468,920.79 | 306,397,682 |
| L | Reserve Adjustment-Collected | | -40,718,768.97 | -34,044,186 |
| M | Net Collected Balance Position | | -407,187,689.76 | 340,441,869 |
| | **Service Charge Calculation** | | | |
| N | Earnings Credit Allowance | Rate: .300 | 361.85 | 181 |
| O | Total Charge For Services | | -93,736.13 | -81,395 |
| P | Net Charge For Services | | -93,374.28 | -81,213 |
| | **Service Charge Amount** | | **93,374.28** | |

**Exhibit 8–14** (continued)

*Account Analysis Statement Example*

Bank One, NA

CAP N N Z 01-07-2004

Page 2 of 3

**DEC 1 through DEC 31, 2003**

Account No: DEMAND DEPOSIT ACCOUNT

## Service Analysis

| Service | Number Of Units | Unit Price | Charge For Service | Balance Required |
|---|---|---|---|---|
| **Account Services** | | | | |
| FDIC Assessment | 3,877,878 | 3.8500 | 128.56 | 504,563.44 |
| Account Maintenance | 1 | 18.0000 | 18.00 | 70,645.16 |
| DDA Statement Print Additional | 1 | | 0.00 | |
| **Depository Services** | | | | |
| Credits Posted | 832 | 0.4000 | 332.80 | 1,306,150.53 |
| Dep Cks On-Us | 83,909 | 0.0450 | 3,775.91 | 14,819,431.72 |
| Dep Cks Local City | 1 | 0.0600 | 0.06 | 235.48 |
| Dep Cks Local RCPC | 1 | 0.0600 | 0.06 | 235.48 |
| Dep Cks National Frb Other | 19,721 | 0.1000 | 1,972.10 | 7,739,962.36 |
| Dep Cks Encoding | 1 | 0.0400 | 0.04 | 156.98 |
| Dep Cks MICR Reject Repair | 532 | 0.2500 | 133.00 | 521,989.24 |
| Dep Return-Items Returned | 9,133 | 5.0000 | 45,665.00 | 179,222,849.46 |
| Dep Return Redeposit Reclear | 9,982 | 4.0000 | 39,928.00 | 156,706,666.66 |
| Dep Return Detail Reporting | 19,115 | | 0.00 | |
| Proof Corrections | 25 | 5.0000 | 125.00 | 490,591.39 |
| **Disbursement Services** | | | | |
| Debits Posted | 137 | 0.1600 | 21.92 | 86,030.10 |
| **Funds Transfer Services** | | | | |
| FT Voice Outgoing Rep Transfer | 22 | 14.0000 | 308.00 | 1,208,817.20 |
| FT Voice Outgoing Non-Rep Trfr | 22 | 17.0000 | 374.00 | 1,467,849.46 |
| **Information Services** | | | | |
| TOC Prev Day Maintenance | 1 | 55.0000 | 55.00 | 215,860.21 |
| TOC Intraday Maintenance | 1 | 65.0000 | 65.00 | 255,107.52 |
| TOC Prev Day BAI Maintenance | 1 | 55.0000 | 55.00 | 215,860.21 |
| TOC Intraday BAI Maintenance | 1 | 65.0000 | 65.00 | 255,107.52 |
| TOC Special Report Maintenance | 1 | 35.0000 | 35.00 | 137,365.59 |
| BAI2 File Transmsn-Per Acct | 2 | 50.0000 | 100.00 | 392,473.11 |
| BAI2 File Transmsn-Per Item | 673 | 0.0600 | 40.38 | 158,480.64 |
| TOC Prev Day Accounts | 3 | 11.0000 | 33.00 | 129,516.12 |
| TOC Prev Day Items | 454 | 0.1000 | 45.40 | 178,182.79 |
| TOC Intraday Accounts | 3 | 16.5000 | 49.50 | 194,274.19 |
| TOC Intraday Items | 105 | 0.1500 | 15.75 | 61,814.51 |
| TOC Prev Day BAI Accounts | 4 | 11.0000 | 44.00 | 172,688.17 |
| TOC Prev Day BAI Items | 1,624 | 0.1000 | 162.40 | 637,376.34 |

*continued*

**Exhibit 8–14** (continued)

*Account Analysis Statement Example*

Bank One, NA

CAP N N Z 01-07-2004

Page 3 of 3

**DEC 1 through DEC 31, 2003**

Account No: DEMAND DEPOSIT ACCOUNT

## Service Analysis

| Service | Number Of Units | Unit Price | Charge For Service | Balance Required |
|---|---|---|---|---|
| TOC Intraday BAI Accounts | 4 | 16.5000 | 66.00 | 259,032.25 |
| TOC Intraday BAI Items | 815 | 0.1500 | 122.25 | 479,798.38 |
| **Total Charge For Services** | | | **93,736.13** | **367,889,112.21** |

***A*** Bank One Relationship Manager, Account Officer, or Banking Center.

***B*** Beginning/ending date.

***C*** The account(s) to which statement applies.

***D*** The sum of the daily positive and negative ledger balances for the month divided by the number of days in the month. Balances for the last preceding business days are used for weekends and holidays.

***E*** The difference between the average ledger balance and the average collected balance for the month. Bank One assigns float item based on our published availability schedule.

***F*** The sum of the daily positive collected balances for the month divided by the number of days in the month.

***G*** The portion of the positive balances Bank One must keep on deposit at the Federal Reserve. This amount, therefore, is not available to offset service charges.

***H*** The sum of the average positive collected balances less reserve requirements, as defined by Federal Reserve. (Less loan compensating balances, if applicable.)

***I*** The total balances required for services rendered.

***J*** The sum of average investable balance less balances required for services.

***K*** Reserves not used for deposit services are added back to the Excess (Deficit) Investable Balance. For deficit balances, this is the additional reserves required to support deposit services.

***L*** The collected balance position adjusted for credit commitments and other services used. These funds are available to your company to meet other corporate obligations. For deficit balances, this is the additional collected balances required to offset all service charges.

***M*** The dollar credit on the average positive investable balances maintained. If there are negative balances at any time during the month, the applicable bank rate for short-term commercial borrowing will be assessed as a Negative Colleced Balance Fee in the itemized services section of your Account Analysis Statement.

***O*** The total charge for services rendered.

***P*** The amount remaining in dollars after service charges have been deducted from the earnings credit allowance. If negative, this line will show the net charge for services.

*Source:* Reprinted with permission of Bank One (Louisville, KY).

31). Bank One converts each service charge line item to the equivalent balances necessary to cover those charges by applying Equation 8.5.

$$RCMP = \frac{SC}{\left(\frac{ecr}{365}\right)n} \quad (8.5)$$

Where:

$RCMP$ = Required compensating balances

$SC$ = Service charges for the month

$ecr$ = Earnings credit rate (annual)

$n$ = Number of days in month

Equation 8.5 would be modified slightly for banks not distinguishing between the average collected balance and the average investable (available) balance, with the adjustment being made in the denominator to reflect the required reserve ratio (*rr*). Because the required balances must cover required reserves as well as fees, it seems that the balances will be higher. In practice, the bank adjusts the *ecr* upward to make the two approaches equivalent. Equation 8.6 gives us the required compensating balances in light of the reserve ratio.

$$RCMP = \frac{SC}{(1 - rr)\left(\frac{ecr}{365}\right)n} \quad (8.6)$$

Given the company's total service charges owed of \$93,736.13 for December, the Total Charge For Services at the bottom of the second schedule (using Equation 8.5) indicates a required balance of \$367,889,112.21.

$$\$367{,}889{,}112.21 = \frac{\$93{,}736.13}{\left(\frac{0.0030}{365}\right)31}$$

This represents how much in available balances the company would have had to average during July to avoid paying fees for bank services rendered. Returning to the top schedule in Exhibit 8–14, we see \$367,889,112.21 inserted as the Balance Required (M).

The Excess Investable Balance (K) is then computed as the Average Investable Balance minus the Balance Required. At this point, Bank One recognizes that some additional balances may need to be held during the month as compensating balances required to support loans. Item (L) is therefore subtracted from the Excess Investable Balance to arrive at the Net Collected Balance Position (M) of (\$407,187,689.76). The company has held much smaller balances in its checking account than those necessary to compensate for fees and to serve as loan compensating balances.

But what if the company would rather compensate the bank by paying a fee each month? The remainder of the schedule compares the earnings credit applied to the company's balances to the total service charges incurred. Be careful; the Earnings Credit Allowance computation (N) below the Net Collected Balance Position is found by multiplying the Average Investable Balance of \$1,420,191.42 (I) by the monthly *ecr* (0.003/12). The company has "earned" \$361.85 based on its account balances (N), versus the Total Charge For Services (see bottom of Balance Analysis schedule) of \$93,736.13 (O). The difference of \$93,374.28 (P) is an amount due, which is often invoiced or directly debited from the account. When the company has a net service average, or credit, the amount might be carried into future months to offset months when balances are inadequate to cover service charges. If the company would rather compensate the bank by holding larger balances, it may be given several months to make up for a shortfall. Settlement periods over which credits or shortfalls are cumulated might be quarterly, semiannual, or annual (calendar year). Charges would be made on the cumulative shortfall at the period's end.

*Uses of the Account Analysis Statement* In addition to serving as an invoice for bank services rendered, the cash manager can use the account analysis to get an overall view of the company's balance levels and bank activity. Two impediments to interbank comparisons based on account analyses are the lack of uniform presentation formats (which are gradually becoming more standard) and the variety of cutoff times and availability schedules making up banks' float calculations. Despite growing acceptance of the uniform account analysis format developed by the AFP, cash managers complain that many banks have been slow in adopting the voluntary standard. Consequently, cash managers are forced to either manually adjust different banks' statements to compare them or use third-party software that automatically reformats them to a uniform statement.

### How Banks Charge for Services

To maximize value from the company's banking relationships, one must understand how compensating balances work and the relative merits of paying for bank services by balances versus fees. We begin by illustrating the required compensating balance computation for cash management services.

*Calculating Compensating Balances* Compensating balances are minimum or average deposit amounts required by banks as a means of charging for cash management or lending services. Banks formerly required customers to maintain a demand deposit account balance of 10 percent of the credit line or loan principal amount, but competition has forced this figure lower. For large corporations, balances show good will rather than being required. When required on lending arrangements, companies must maintain the balances as well as pay interest on amounts borrowed.

As compensation for each cash management service, the bank will compute the charges for a month's activity, then use a formula to compute the equivalent amount of balances. The formula will look like Equation 8.5 or Equation 8.6. Illustrating, a company being charged \$150 for direct sends during the month would have to have \$150/0.004438356 = \$33,796.30 in compensating balances, assuming a required reserve ratio of 10 percent and an *ecr* of 6 percent (using Equation 8.6).

$$\begin{aligned} \textit{Compensating balances} &= \frac{\$150}{(1 - 0.10)\left(\frac{0.06}{365}\right)30} \\ &= \frac{\$150}{0.004438356} \\ &= \$33{,}796.30 \end{aligned}$$

At the time of this writing, most banks have a small FDIC insurance premium assessed—in the Bank One schedule the FDIC charge that is shown is \$128.56. However, S&Ls and mutual savings banks have larger assessments. Financial institutions that pass along assessments are either including a fee on the service charge schedule or, by further multiplying the denominator of the above formula by (1 − FDIC assessment rate), driving the compensating balance dollar amount even higher.

### Pros and Cons of Balances versus Fees

Banks have generally favored compensating balances over fees as the method of remuneration for services performed, even though a recent survey indicated that just more than half of corporations are paying by fees. Bankers cite the following advantages of compensating balances:

- Compensating balances have the effect of increasing total deposits and assets, which are traditional benchmarks of a bank's success.
- Balances can be re-loaned to another customer, which means that in the case of loan-encumbered balances some of the funds are actually loaned twice: compensating balances required of borrower A are part of the loan made to borrower B.
- Balances form a cushion, so that a loan default is partly recouped by the bank.

Corporate cash managers generally prefer fees, although some balances might be kept in the bank anyway to meet transactions requirements and provide a liquid reserve that can be tapped quickly if needed. Demand deposits (except for sole proprietorships and nonprofit organizations) are non-interest-bearing accounts, which are ideally kept at a minimum, unless the earnings credit rate is greater than the rate that could be earned on alternative investments available to the firm. This accounts for the first of several reasons cash managers favor fee-based compensation:

- Earnings credit rate (*ecr*) is almost always less than the alternative investment rate.
- Lost interest related to the balances is not a tax-deductible expense, but fees charged by the bank are tax deductible.
- Fee-based compensation offers a tangible expense that can be easily monitored and budgeted.
- Fees are directly comparable between banks and are fixed for a year at a time,[32] whereas the *ecr* is a floating rate that is unpredictable.

A final consideration is the possibility of **"double-counting"** of compensating balances. This occurs when a bank counts the same balances as compensation for a loan and as compensation for cash management services, or may occur on intrabank transfers. Double-counting is uncommon at large and medium-sized banks due to their better processing systems, but it may occur at smaller banks. Taking advantage of double-counting without the bank(s) being aware of it is considered unethical by most cash managers—especially in light of the way E.F. Hutton took advantage of its banks by initiating unnecessary lateral transfers to draw on uncollected balances.

## Daylight Overdrafts and the Availability Schedule

**Daylight overdrafts** occur when a bank's Federal Reserve account book balance is negative during the day, possibly because it sends more funds via Fedwire than it receives, before final end-of-day settlements. Many of the overdrafts occur because of international funds transfers of government securities transactions.

Since 1986, a bank whose nonwire transactions add up to a net credit (excluding ACH transactions) receives that credit *retroactive to the opening of business.* This enables the bank to use the credit to offset any wire debits occurring throughout the day. When nonwire transactions add up to a net debit, that total does not have to be covered until the close of business, giving rise to large intraday or "daylight" overdrafts.

The Fed recently changed the handling of such overdrafts, resulting in charges for banks' intraday use of funds. The changes involved charges for bank intraday overdrafts as well as institution of the following posting times:

[32] Most cash management contracts are based on 3-year bids, with a capped inflation adjustment allowable at the end of Years 1 and 2.

1. Treasury and commercial ACH credits at the opening of business
2. ACH debits at 11 A.M. Eastern Time
3. Commercial check transactions and coin and currency deposits beginning at 11 A.M. Eastern Time, and then hourly, with the amounts based on proportions of the deposits drawn on the various endpoints
4. Wire transfers and book-entry (securities) transfers continue to be posted, for overdraft measurement purposes, as they occur

This system should make available to collecting banks approximately half of the value of all check deposits by noon Eastern Time and roughly three-fourths by 1 P.M.

These regulations should reduce banks' daylight overdrafts, an implicit subsidy to paying banks, with several important cash management implications. First, funds are available in smaller amounts throughout each business day, instead of all at once. Second, cash managers have to be careful to avoid intraday overdrafting of checking accounts, which might incur bank charges. A corollary to this is to be careful to delay disbursing funds until check deposits and other nonwire credits are posted and made available. Third, because banks are charged a fee based on the size of their intraday overdraft, they will require account holders to fund check presentments before the Federal Reserve fee is posted to the bank's reserve account. This will have a disproportionate effect on larger banks, which tend to have sizable daylight overdrafts—possibly foreshadowing higher cash management prices from these institutions.

Financial managers are urged to carefully compare existing banks to new bidders to ensure the company is getting maximum value from its banking relationships. The true opportunity cost in terms of interest forgone (due to having to leave extra amounts in checking accounts to compensate banks) is not the Treasury bill rate but either the overnight repurchase rate, commercial paper rate, or money market mutual fund rate offered by banks and brokers. In addition, there are many qualitative factors to examine, including how long the company has done business with its existing bank(s) and the other noncredit and credit services being provided by the bank(s). Exhibit 8–15 summarizes some of the factors to be compared before negotiating a contract.

### Optimizing the Banking Network

Recall the objective for bank relationship management that we started this section of the chapter with: to ensure that all the company's banking services are provided reliably at a reasonable cost. Potentially, if we assume some product differentiation and/or nonuniform pricing on the part of banks, there exists a banking system configuration (or several) that will maximize value for the company. Finding that optimum is elusive, given the role of qualitative criteria such as reliability that enter the objective function. Several theorists have attempted optimization through mathematical models: two of these are presented in Appendix 8B. We simply note here that we should take a systems view of overall bank relationship structure. Lending and cash management services often are tied together, even though some treasurers contend a "do-your-own" lockbox network is less expensive, even when taking loan considerations into account. Further, banks aggressively sell their own and other institutions' securities, and treasurers generally find that the investment services are separable from other bank services. An exception would be the bank sweep product, which is inextricably tied to the checking account balances the corporation holds.

## NONBANK PROVIDERS OF SERVICES

Nonfinancial corporations are increasingly providing what were traditionally banking services. Service offerings are directed at other corporations and consumers and also the

**Exhibit 8–15**

*Checklist for Cash Management Bank Selection*

Prenegotiation Comparison Checklist

1. Is my existing service or relationship so substandard that I am unwilling to invest any more time in trying to improve it?
2. Has my current bank shown little or no interest in this aspect of our relationship?
3. Has my current bank re-categorized our relationship in a way that means our importance has declined?
4. Has my current bank de-emphasized products that are of particular importance to us, in a way that jeopardizes our future satisfaction?
5. Are we looking for an entirely new package of services or trying to establish a new bank account structure?
6. Are these needs the result of an acquisition or major organizational change?
7. If my prices are *meaningfully* above market prices, am I satisfied that this is not the result of customization? Have I already approached my current bank about pricing improvements, to little or no benefit?
8. Have I already exhausted the capabilities or creativity of the bank(s) which have been investing in a true partnership relationship with us?

If you answer yes to any of questions 1–7, *and* yes to question 8, then you probably should bid out your services.

In bidding, the following checklist can help guide you to a complete decision:

1. Confirm that the bank fits your bank relationship philosophy.
2. Confirm that the features you want are already available—and that you know clearly which are still being considered, planned for, or "in development."
3. Make sure you understand all financial components of the deal—all items you'll be charged for, contract terms, permissible price increases, volume discount levels, and penalties for nonperformance (both yours and theirs).
4. Understand what implementation will entail, what resources the bank will commit, what resources you should expect to commit, and what (if anything) you will be charged for.
5. Know exactly who will service your account—from your calling representative to service and problem resolution people.
6. Ask what else the bank hopes to gain from this relationship over time.
7. Understand how your firm fits with the bank's strategic focus.

---

*Source:* Cathryn R. Gregg, Treasury Strategies, Inc., 309 W. Washington St., Suite 1300, Chicago, IL 60606, (312) 443-0840.

providing organization itself—in which the company, in effect, is making versus buying the service. Commercial and industrial conglomerates, such as American Express, Ford, GE, Westinghouse, Sears, and J.C.Penney, are leaders in acquiring financial institutions.

Much of the nonbank activity has taken place in lending. Banks traditionally provided most of the short-term and medium-term loans for businesses, but this has changed. Banks are no longer the dominant players they once were for short-term funding. In 2004 there was $1.3 trillion in commercial paper outstanding (including $108 billion issued by nonfinancial companies), compared to $900 billion in commercial and industrial loans made by banks.[33] Increasingly, banks are moving away from a direct finance role to a risk-sharing role, in which they guarantee the payment of corporations' commercial paper borrowings at maturity. Banks collect fees for providing the guarantee, and the issuer receives a better credit rating with a correspondingly lower interest rate. Almost one-half of all consumer and business loans are now held by nonbank companies. An intriguing if rare example is the $50 million loan PepsiCo made to Marriott, at Marriott's request, reportedly to win a soda-fountain service contract. The nonbank penetration has pushed into nonlending services as well, however.

In the realm of information services, the primary nonbank providers are third-party vendors of balance reporting services. In the collections area, companies are progressively doing part of or all the lockbox work in-house or retaining a nonbank vendor. Consultants providing software to compare banks, mail time analyses, and bank rating services are primary examples of information service providers. Since 1974, payment and investment services have increasingly become the domain of money market mutual funds. From 1987 to the end of 2003, institutional (nonpersonal) assets held in these nonbank accounts grew from $140.4 billion to $1.1 trillion. These accounts serve as interest-bearing payment vehicles, although the minimum check amount is typically $500. An interesting survey of bankers found that 79 percent believed money funds to be an important competitor to their money market deposit accounts, and 83 percent saw them as an important competitor to their CDs (Holmberg and Baker, 1996).

As geographic and product restrictions are lifted in this era of financial services deregulation, financial institutions may regain market share in some of the areas just mentioned or at least hold their own.

## FINANCIAL SYSTEM TRENDS

In this concluding section of the chapter, we profile general financial system trends, then delve into trends in the areas of imaging, information services, Internet banking, and international banking relationships.

We can identify two major trends that have an effect on the bank service areas. One trend is nationwide banking in the United States and the economic unification of Europe, both of which will be catalysts for an ongoing drift toward concentration in the industry and globalized banking. Another trend now unfolding that is related to nationwide banking is consolidation of banking networks. No longer will a company need to have multiple banks operating a collection and concentration network. Imagine a 1-bank collection center, which can also pool and invest or pay down borrowings, instead of sending funds from various field banks to a different lead bank. In addition, this allows for greater pooling from various locations nationwide without the need to actually transfer funds, because the balances can be netted out within one bank's computer records. In the mid-1990s, one analyst projected that there would be 10 banks with nationwide branches as early as the year 2000, but that proved to be far off the mark.

All of Europe stands to gain from the economic unification of Europe and the introduction of the common currency, the euro. We noted in our payment system section some of the effects. The full introduction of the euro in 2002 as the sole European legal tender has reduced cash management inefficiencies and costs. Bank debt is expected to drop from four-fifths of corporate borrowing (in France, Germany, and Italy) down to much lower levels, as a result of the pan-European credit market that develops. Bank mergers will also have major effects. Although the cultural, regulatory, legal, and organizational assimila-

[33] Statistics based on Federal Reserve data.

tion of merged banks takes time, economies of scale will be available in Europe and elsewhere. The Boston Consulting Group estimates the average cost of a wholesale cross-border transaction will drop from $47 to only 40 cents within 10 years; most of this will result from a lower foreign exchange charge. The European Union will further change the corporate banking landscape.

## Imaging

An important trend affecting check routing, collections, and disbursements is **imaging**. Imaging is increasingly being used in two distinct applications: document imaging and check imaging. Document imaging is used for items such as invoices (particularly those processed by lockbox clerks) and loan applications. Check imaging is used for check truncation, as seen earlier in the chapter, as well as to avoid having to send batches of canceled checks back to customers. Instead, a computer image holding numerous miniaturized checks on each page is returned. The image of a questionable check may be inspected online before the paying bank decides to honor the check, as we will discuss further in Chapter 11. Essentially, then, check imaging systems store images of checks in computers. These images can be compressed and printed out when needed. Proponents suggest that storing check images in computers can speed check processing in the following ways:

- Reduce check sorting by allowing for monthly checking account statements to be sent with a page or two of check images attached, instead of enclosing the physical checks.
- Eliminate encoding of documents such as internal debits, credits, and cash tickets.
- Electronically capture the data on adding machine tapes and other documents that accompany large deposits.
- Allow checks to be electronically "called up" on-screen to verify signatures, possibly using automatic signature scanning to compare signatures on the checks with a digitized signature card (which may trigger "dishonoring" of fraudulent checks shortly after their presentment to the drawee bank).
- When there is a problem check, enable the clerk who is in charge of returning checks (to the bank of first deposit) to return an image instead.

## Information Services

Banks offer corporate clients various advisory services. **Advisory services** include all specialized and general financial management consulting that banks might provide to corporations. Several typical advisory services are:

- *Lockbox studies:* The bank uses a computerized model to study the pattern of mailed checks a company receives and advises the company on the best number and locations of lockboxes.
- *Disbursement studies:* Similar to lockbox studies, except the bank advises the client regarding controlled disbursement and zero balance accounts, the best locations of these accounts, and direct deposit.
- *Financial management advice:* Especially for smaller companies and nonprofits, banks may give advice about basics such as cash budgeting, pro forma statements, which cash management services might be cost effective, and the types of bank lending for which the client might be eligible.

- *International cash management studies:* Included here are analyses of foreign countries' payment systems, economies, and the best approach to pooling cash and moving cash into or out of each country.
- *Computerized treasury management information system hardware and software:* In some cases, the bank will serve as a distributor under a license agreement with the developer of the computer system.

## Online Banking

The biggest development in the early 2000s is the explosion of what is variously called online banking, Web-based banking, or Internet banking. Ernst & Young, in its 2000 Cash Management Services survey, discovered that 9 percent of all commercial users of electronic information reporting services received balance and transaction details from their bank via the Internet (Forman and Shafer, 2000); this tripled by the following year (Forman and Shafer, 2002). Many banks also reported either losing clients or being left out of new relationship consideration if they lacked a specific Internet ability. Corporate customers found that being able to access data anywhere they could access the Internet was a major advantage of online banking, with slow response time, scaled-down product offerings, and one-size-fits-all product offerings being the main disadvantages. In its most recent survey of a cross-section of banks' Internet offerings, Ernst & Young found that almost all banks now offer corporate clients balance and information reporting, 91 percent offer between-account transfers at the bank, 75 percent offer ACH transfers and wire transfers, and 41 percent offer image delivery of issued checks (mostly for viewing exception items for a bank's fraud protection service) and lockbox items. Somewhat troubling is the perception on the part of merely 37 percent of corporate users that they could automatically trust that security issues were taken care of by the bank once a bank launched an Internet product. A 2001 survey by the Association for Financial Professionals also indicates that 92 percent of treasury professionals are obtaining information on the Internet, about four in five are using the Internet to communicate with financial service providers, 63 percent are using the Internet to transact business, and 36 percent are selecting service providers with Web information. In Europe, large companies indicate that they are most interested in getting account information, but over half also mentioned using the Web for foreign exchange or disbursement services.

## International Aspects of Banking Relationships

All advising services remain strong, but the brightest aspect for banks is probably the international cash management services they provide. The combination of computerized treasury systems and international account balance inquiry and pooling capabilities is positioning some banks to gain market share by aggressively serving the needs of customers operating multinationally.

U.S. financial executives anticipate worldwide emergence of financial supermarkets, in which very large global "superbanks" compete aggressively against one another. However, anticipating the effect of global trends on U.S. banks is more difficult. To provide U.S. banks equal footing with banks operating in unregulated foreign markets, special organizational structures known as Edge Act branches and International Banking Facilities (IBFs) have been established. Edge Act branches are branches outside the home state of the bank, which must limit their involvement to business abroad or financing foreign trade. The IBFs are not physical bank facilities but are a separate set of books kept by an existing bank. International banking facilities avoid reserve requirements, interest rate ceilings, and deposit insurance, enabling them to survive with much smaller margins. In recent years, the number and scope of Edge Act branches and IBFs have declined, mainly as a result of the foreign loan losses of large U.S. banks. Large U.S. banks continue to operate numerous branches abroad to service multinational customers.

*Global Bank Consolidation* To retain influence with increasingly relationship-driven MNC corporate treasurers, banks are merging and expanding globally. Although three of the 10 largest banks are Japanese, 20 of the top 25 global banks, based on asset size, are U.S. and European banks—each with at least $440 billion in assets.[34] Many of these banks have a presence in 80 to 90 different countries, and Citigroup operates in more than 100 countries and territories. In cash management, the technology-intensiveness has seen strong cash management banks invest more and become stronger. Large banks tend to see cash management as the area that cements corporate relations and offers opportunities to cross-sell other bank services. According to *Global Finance Magazine*, these are the largest banks at the end of 2003, along with their home country and asset size expressed in billions of U.S. dollars:

| | | |
|---|---|---|
| (1) Citigroup | (United States) | $1,097.19 |
| (2) Mizuho Holdings | (Japan) | 1,029.69 |
| (3) UBS | (Switzerland) | 851.69 |
| (4) Sumitomo Mitsui Banking Corporation | (Japan) | 826.60 |
| (5) Deutsche Bank | (Germany) | 795.74 |
| (6) Mitsubishi Tokyo Financial Group | (Japan) | 784.52 |
| (7) J.P. Morgan Chase | (United States) | 758.80 |
| (8) ING Group | (Netherlands) | 751.78 |
| (9) HSBC Holdings | (United Kingdom) | 748.89 |
| (10) BNP Paribas | (France) | 745.41 |

Because of the increasing reach of global banks, U.S.-based multinational corporations have been free to centralize European treasury operations, often selecting London or tax-haven locales such as Dublin Docks (Ireland), Belgium, or Holland to host their finance subsidiaries. The location of a U.S. company's central treasury may be driven by tax treatment, exchange rate risks, or banking and other administrative costs. Illustrating, DuPont has been able to focus its 22-country European services with Bank of America, with Citicorp being its main service provider in all other areas of the world.

## SUMMARY

We have presented the major aspects of the U.S. and international payment systems in this chapter and identified the concept and value of float. The importance of understanding these foundational concepts is illustrated by the improvements made by the treasurer for the city of Seattle.[35] The treasurer set a goal of having all checks and currency invested on the day received and reducing mail float to one day. This meant eliminating office processing float (which had cost $250,000 in lost interest annually) and eliminating availability float—which, combined, totaled five days. Eliminating availability float implied clearing all checks through the bank the same day received. Although it took a year to change banking contracts, retrain staff members, and purchase bar coding and scanning equipment, the city largely was able to achieve its objectives. The city MICR en-

[34] The World's Biggest Banks (2003). *Global Finance Magazine* (January 2004). Accessed online at **http://globalf.vwh.net/content/?article_id=455** on January 11, 2004.

[35] See Lloyd F. Hara, "Seattle's 'No-Float Day,'" *Government Finance Review* (December 1987), pp. 7–10.

codes checks and deposits all on-us items at the various banks' check processing centers. It competitively bid the concentration bank contract and gained collected-funds status in one-half day for checks other than on-us items. All told, the treasurer estimates the changes have reaped a present value benefit of $1.3 million per year for the city. Treasurers of all corporations, governments, and nonprofit organizations would be wise to emulate Seattle's example.

We developed the uniqueness of the U.S. payment system as well as its major components. This system involves many more banks (which are smaller in size) than other countries. This patchwork is primarily related to the banking regulations, which focus on keeping banks from gaining too much economic power. As a result of past restrictions on interstate branching and bank acquisitions, companies must still work with several banks when paying or collecting funds from outside their local area. The $100,000 limit on bank deposit insurance has forced cash managers to limit deposit size and investment denominations when investing in bank-issued securities, although the too-big-to-fail doctrine has protected large bank depositors in the past. The recent change to U.S. banking regulation to allow interstate banking and branching will make cash management less costly and more efficient.

The Federal Reserve System is a key player in the payment system because of its check clearing and regulatory roles. We noted the mechanics of check clearing and the importance of the check's MICR line. Paper-based payments include checks and drafts. Check usage continues despite the regulatory push toward electronic payments. Electronic-based payments using wire transfers, EDTs, and automated debits and credits account for a large percentage of the dollar volume of today's payments. The ACH system is handling more payments and will continue to gain volume at the expense of checks. Popular uses to date include direct depositing of Social Security and employee payrolls.

We developed the banking aspects of the major cash management services used by corporations: depository services and information. Basic elements of these services have been defined and illustrated. Nonbank competition has been most noticeable for borrowing and investing services but promises to heighten in payments, collections (and concentration), and information.

Bank selection and relationship management are extremely important aspects of short-term financial management. We noted that the major factors related to bank selection are location, price, service quality and breadth, bank/company fit, bank creditworthiness, and bank specialties. The banking industry is undergoing major structural changes, partly as a result of continued deregulation of geographic restrictions and partly as a result of technology changes in the areas of imaging, network computing, and the use of the Internet. Furthermore, the increasing economic importance of the Pacific Basin, the Commonwealth of Independent States, Eastern Europe, China, and a newly unified Europe will significantly affect the economies of scale available for banks competing globally.

## USEFUL WEB SITES

| | |
|---|---|
| Association for Financial Professionals | **http://www.afponline.org** |
| Eurogiro | **http://www.eurogiro.com** |
| European Central Bank—TARGET | **http://www.ecb.int/target/target.htm** |
| European Central Bank—TARGET FAQ | **http://www.ecb.int/target/bt/targetfaq.pdf** |
| European Central Bank—TARGET2 | **http://www.ecb.int/pub/pdf/target2en.pdf** |
| Federal Reserve Atlanta Financial Update | **http://www.frbatlanta.org/publica/finan_update/index.html** |

| | |
|---|---|
| Federal Reserve Board | **http://www.federalreserve.gov/** |
| Federal Reserve Board—Interstate Banking | **http://www.federalreserve.gov/generalinfo/isb/** |
| Greenwich and Associates | **http://www.greenwich.com** |
| National Automated Clearing House Association | **http://www.nacha.org** |
| Phoenix-Hecht | **http://www.phoenixhecht.com** |
| Phoenix-Hecht Survey Findings | **http://www.phoenixhecht.com/PDF/CorpMon2000.pdf** |

## QUESTIONS

1. Would small businesses achieve the same benefits from using electronic-based payments as the state of Texas? Explain.
2. Why is there value in reducing float when a company collects payments made by check? Is the value of float reduction as great for the collecting firm when interest rates decline? Explain.
3. What are the two components of the U.S. payment system? What sets it apart from other countries' payment systems?
4. Summarize briefly the major legislation regarding product offerings and geographic scope of depository institutions.
5. Are bank safety considerations more likely to be of concern to the cash manager of a small company or large company? Explain.
6. What roles does the Federal Reserve System play in the payment system? How, specifically, does the Federal Reserve facilitate the payments mechanism?
7. Summarize the mechanics of check clearing. Summarize the various clearing mechanisms used and indicate when direct presenting might be used.
8. What information appears on a check's MICR line? Which, if any, of the items would be helpful to a bank of first deposit as it considers various check clearing options?
9. Define each of the following types of float:
   a. Collection float
   b. Disbursement float
   c. Mail float
   d. Processing float
   e. Clearing float
   f. Fed float
10. List and define briefly the means the Federal Reserve System has used to reduce Fed float. For a given check, what will happen to the difference between the payee's collection float and the payor's disbursement float as Fed float is reduced? Will that difference disappear completely? Explain.
11. Name the two major paper-based payment mechanisms and explain each.
12. Why are coins and currency still used in the modern U.S. economy? Specifically, why are they used instead of checks?
13. Distinguish between a demand deposit account and a NOW account. Which one do businesses use, and why?

14. You just deposited a $1,000 check written on a bank in a neighboring state. Can the deposited funds be considered available funds? In your answer, distinguish between bank ledger balances and collected balances.
15. Summarize the check availability provisions of Regulation CC.
16. Do you think paper payments will disappear in the near future in the United States? Support your opinion.
17. List and define the three major electronic-based payments, giving the usage occasions, advantages, and disadvantages of each.
18. What objective do companies attempt to achieve when managing bank relations?
19. What is an availability schedule? Why should banks' availability schedules be compared by the cash manager, and what should the manager look for in making comparisons?
20. Futurists have long forecast a paperless U.S. economy. Why have they been wrong? Include a discussion of corporate payment practices in your answer.
21. What does the popularity of the transaction approach to bank selection and relationship management imply about the competition among cash management banks? What are the pricing implications of this?
22. From a corporate risk perspective, what does the relationship approach to bank relations offer that the transaction approach does not?
23. Explain what an account analysis statement is and several of the uses it has for cash managers.
24. Define an earnings credit allowance; indicate how it is computed and how it compares with currently available yields on short-term investments. Why is its use so important for the company trying to decide whether to use fee-basis or compensating balances for bank service charge remuneration?
25. What are daylight overdrafts, and why might they be considered a bank credit service?

## PROBLEMS

1. Amax Manufacturing Corp. collects $225,000 per day. The cash manager has just been told of a new collection system using lockboxes that could reduce collection float from seven days to six days by reducing mail and processing float a total of one day. Given the company's opportunity cost of funds of 14 percent and using simple interest formulas,
   **a.** Draw a cash flow timeline for one day's collection under the existing collection system. What is the present value of existing collections? Show your calculations for an average day's collections as well as in total for a perpetuity of daily collections.
   **b.** Draw a cash flow timeline for one day's collection under the proposed lockbox collection system. What is the present value of lockbox-based collections? Again, show the 1-day and the total value effects.
   **c.** Ignoring bank fees to administer the lockbox system, would the cash manager recommend the new system?
   **d.** What will happen to the disbursement float for Amax's customers if the lockbox system is implemented?
2. Rework **a** and **b** of Problem 1 using an opportunity cost of funds of 4 percent. Describe the effect on the difference between the two systems' present values, as compared with your findings in Problem 1.
3. The capital budgeting approach to financial decision making requires comparing the present value of incremental cash inflows with the present value of incremental cash outflows. Given that the present value of the perpetuity of daily collection cash inflows has already been computed in **a** and **b** of each of the above problems, would you recommend adoption of the lockbox collection system if the only cash outflows were bank charges (an initial investment for

Amax) of $175,000? (***Hint:*** *You must first compute the difference in the two perpetuities' cash flows to arrive at the incremental cash inflow.)*

**a.** Assume the opportunity cost of funds was 14 percent (as in Problem 1).

**b.** Assume the opportunity cost of funds was 4 percent (as in Problem 2).

**c.** What is the effect of the lower time value of money in **b** on the present value of the project's net cash flows? (***Hint:*** *What is true of the value of day 2, day 3, and subsequent cash flows, in present dollar terms, when a lower discount rate is used?)*

**4.** Triton Corporation is trying to better manage its bank relationship. It requested and recently received via facsimile an account analysis statement for June. As happens with faxes, several of the line items are illegible, and the treasurer cannot get in touch with the bank liaison. Could you help complete the schedule? Assuming that the statement is done according to the AFP standard format (refer back to Exhibit 8–14), the earnings credit rate is 1.15 percent, the reserve requirement is 10 percent, and Triton does not have any loan-related compensating balances. (Ignore the difference between negative and positive collected balances.)

**a.** Fill in the missing line item labels and dollar amounts (each item shaded below).

**b.** Does Triton owe the bank the amount you have calculated for the net service credit/(debit), or can it carry this amount forward to offset future shortfalls?

| | |
|---|---|
| Average Ledger Balance | $1,130,000 |
| Less: ________ | ________ |
| Average Collected Balance | $ 890,000 |
| Less: ________ | ________ |
| Average Investable Balance | |
| Less: | |
| Balance Required | $1,100,000 |
| Less: | |
| Reserve Adjustment Collected | 0 |
| Net Collected Balance Position | |
| Total Charge for Services | $ 1,040 |
| Net Service Credit/(Debit) | ________ |

**5.** The following schedule has been developed as part of your bank's account analysis statement. Assuming no FDIC assessment, an earnings credit rate (already adjusted for the reserve requirement) of 2 percent, and 31 days in the month,

**a.** Fill in the missing amounts.

**b.** How will the dollar amounts for "total charge for services" (listed at the bottom) be used in the finalized account analysis statement sent out by the bank?

| Type of Service | Number of Units | Unit Price | Service Charge | Required Balance |
|---|---|---|---|---|
| General account services | | | | |
| Account maintenance | 1 | $15.00 | | |
| ZBA master account maintenance | 1 | $20.00 | | |
| Depository services | | | | |
| Deposits | 47 | $ 0.45 | | |
| Deposited checks | 1,000 | $ 0.12 | | |
| Disbursement services | | | | |
| Regular checks paid | 2,250 | $ 0.15 | | |
| Reconciliation services | | | | |
| Full reconciliation surcharge | 1 | $45.00 | | |
| Account reconciliation program checks paid (Note: represents last month) | 2,100 | $ 0.05 | | |
| Total Charge for Services | | | | |

## REFERENCES

Philippa Back, *Corporate Cash Management*, 2nd ed. New York: Nichols (1998).

Paul J. Beehler, "Hutton's Strategy for Managing Bank Relationships," *Journal of Cash Management* (January/February 1987), pp. 16–20.

Andrea Bierce and Kathleen Ekedahl, "The Bank Selection Process," *Journal of Cash Management* (July/August 1989), pp. 13–15.

A. Barry Cappello, "Finding a New Bank," *Small Business Reports* 14(6) (1989), pp. 52–57.

Thomas F. Cargill, "CAMEL Ratings and the CD Market," *Journal of Financial Services Research* 3 (1989), pp. 347–358.

Robert T. Clair and Paula K. Tucker, "Interstate Banking and the Federal Reserve: A Historical Perspective," *Federal Reserve Bank of Dallas Economic Review* (November 1989), pp. 1–20.

Jonathan D. Epstein, "Banks Close In on Goal of Interest-Bearing Accounts," *Treasury & Risk Management* (November 2000), pp. 7–8.

Federal Reserve, "The Federal Reserve in the Payments System," *Federal Reserve Bulletin* (May 1990), pp. 293–298.

Lawrence Forman and David L. Shafer, "From Doubt to Adoption . . . Internet Delivery of Cash Management Services is Changing the Marketplace," *AFP Exchange* (Fall 2000), pp. 104–107.

Lawrence Forman and David L. Shafer, "The Current State of Internet Cash Management Services," *AFP Exchange* (November/December 2002), pp. 15–19.

Lyn Fritter and Robert W. Page, "Evaluating Your Service Provider," *TMA Journal* (July/August 1998), pp. 46–48, 50.

Chris Giodano, "Teaming Up for Implementation Success," *TMA Journal* (September/October 1997), pp. 9–10, 12–13.

John Holland, "Bank Lending Relationships and the Complex Nature of Bank-Corporate Relations," *Journal of Business Finance & Accounting* (April 1994), pp. 367–393.

Stevan R. Holmberg and H. Kent Baker, "Commercial Bank Retail Deposit Strategy: The Role of MMDAs," *Southern Business Review* 22 (Fall 1996), pp. 32–44.

Blair Houchens Miller, "Are You Profitable to Your Bank? Why You Should Care," *TMA Journal* (July/August 1998), pp. 28–30, 32–33.

George R. Juncker, Bruce J. Summers, and Florence M. Young, "A Primer on the Settlement of Payments in the United States," *Federal Reserve Bulletin* 77 (November 1991), pp. 847–858.

Sawaichiro Kamatam, "Managing Risk in Japanese Interbank Payment Systems," *Federal Reserve Bank of San Francisco Economic Review* (Fall 1990), pp. 18–32.

Stephen M. Kearney, "Managing Bank Relations at the U.S. Postal Service," *TMA Journal* (November/December 1998), pp. 64–67.

David Lordan, "Criteria For a Money Mobilization Bank," *The Banking Side of Corporate Cash Management (Stonier Graduate School of Banking Research Study)* Boston, MA: Financial Publishing Company (1973), pp. 51–61.

Steven F. Maier and Larry A. Marks, "Applications and Models: The Three Spires of Excellence," *Journal of Cash Management* (November/December 1988), pp. 84, 86, 88.

Leslie N. Masonson, "Everything You Wanted to Know about Checks," *Management Accounting* (July 1990), pp. 26–29.

Dubos J. Masson, "Essentials of Cash Management," 7th ed., *Association for Financial Professionals*, Bethesda, MD (2001).

David L. Mengle, "The Case for Interstate Branch Banking," *Federal Reserve Bank of Richmond Economic Review* 76 (November/December 1990), pp. 3–17.

Paul S. Nadler, "Choosing a Bank for the 90s," *Journal of Cash Management* (September/October 1990), pp. 50–51.

Aaron L. Phillips, "Migration of Corporate Payments from Check to Electronic Format: A Report on the Current Status of Payments," *Financial Management* (Winter 1998), pp. 92–105.

Aaron L. Phillips, "Bank Consolidation and Interstate Banking: Effect on Treasury Management," *TMA Journal* (March/April 1999), pp. 40–43.

Harley Ranking, Jr., "Selecting a Commercial Bank," In *Treasurer's Handbook*, edited by J. Fred Weston and Maurice B. Goudzwaard. Homewood, IL: Dow-Jones Irwin (1976), pp. 577–593.

Cathy L. Rollins and Anthony J. Carfang, "Negotiate a Better Deal with Your Cash Management Banks," *Corporate Cashflow* (September 1989), p. 58.

Nancy L. Russell, "Payment Systems in the U.S. and Latin America: Contrasts and Similarities," *TMA Journal* (May/June 1999), pp. 48, 50–51.

Warren D. Schlesinger, Fahri Unsal, and M. Raquibuz Zaman, "Attributes of Sound Banking as Perceived by Small Businesses: Results of a Survey," *Journal of Small Business Management* (October 1987), pp. 47–53.

Susan Skerritt, "What Payment Changes Should We Expect from the Euro?" *TMA Journal* (November/December 1998), pp. 24, 26, 28.

Larry D. Wall, "Too-Big-to-Fail After FDICIA," *Federal Reserve Bank of Atlanta Economic Review* (January/February 1993), pp. 1–14.

Note: Each issue of *Financial Update*, a newsletter published by the Federal Reserve Bank of Atlanta, includes articles on the latest regulatory developments and Federal Reserve System payment systems innovations. For information or to subscribe:
**http://www.frbatlanta.org/publica/finan_update/index.html**.

Public Information Department
Federal Reserve Bank of Atlanta
104 Marietta St., N.W.
Atlanta, GA 30303-2713
PH: (404) 521-8788

# APPENDIX 8A

## Checklist for Bank Evaluation

- Bank name
- Address
- Phone number
- Bank contact: Name
- Title/Dept.

I. Financial Strength
- Number of years in business
- Total assets
- Total commercial loans
- Ratio loans/assets
- Other loans:
  - Real estate
  - Consumer
  - International
  - Lease financing
  - Asset based (e.g., factoring)
  - Other
- Loan losses (past five years)
- Earnings history (past five years)
- Return on assets (past five years)
- Comments

II. Operations
- General reputation for service
- Data processing system:
  - Type
  - Date installed
- Rating of operations based on:
  - Automation
  - Number/experience of personnel
  - Error correction system
  - Quality controls
  - Supervision
- Services available:
  - Lockbox
  - Wholesale/retail
- Preauthorized checks
- Special handling for checks
- Concentration account
- Wire transfer
  - Federal Reserve wire
  - International (e.g., SWIFT)
- Balance reporting
  - Via telephone
  - Via terminal
  - Multibank
  - Intraday
- Account reconciliation
  - Full/partial
  - Check storage
- Zero-balance disbursement account
  - Method of funding (e.g., imprest balance, wire transfer, etc.)
- Direct deposit
- Payable through drafts
- Payroll services
- Overdraft privilege
- Remote disbursement
- Controlled disbursement
- Letters of credit
- Foreign exchange
  - Forward contracts
- International branches
- Correspondent banks
  - Domestic
  - International
- Consulting
- Financial planning for executives
- Check cashing service for employees
- Credit investigations
- Investment services
  - Bank's own instruments (e.g., commercial paper, banker's acceptances, etc.)
  - Outside money market vehicles
  - Money market fund
  - Trust service
  - Pension service
- Comments

III. Pricing
- Pricing for key services
- Method of compensation:
  - Compensating balances
  - Fees
  - Combination
- Level of compensating balances for loans
- Earnings allowance rate for compensating balances for services
- Comments

IV. Credit
- Experience with type of financing required
- Line of credit available
- Makeup of bank's other commercial customers
  - Companies in our industry
  - Companies our size
- Comments
- Availability of:
  - Factoring
  - Mortgage financing
  - Long-term loans
  - Export financing
  - Inventory loans
  - Unsecured loans
  - Receivables financing
  - Special financing arrangements
- Interest rate terms (e.g., 1.3 percent over prime)
- Interest due dates
- Conditions of default on loans
- Credit insurance available
- Comments

V. Bank/Company Fit
- Bank location
- Personal relationship with bank contact
- Access to bank executives

---

*Source:* Adapted from CASH MANAGEMENT by John M. Kelly. Copyright © 1985 by Alexander Hamilton Institute. Reprinted with permission of the publisher, Franklin Watts Inc., New York.

# APPENDIX 8B

## Optimizing the Banking Network

Several linear programming models have been developed to best allocate check activity, deposit activity, credit lines (including revolving credit agreements), and planned borrowing levels across a company's banking system.[1] The first attempt, called CASH/ALPHA, has been adapted by a number of companies. It takes as a given the credit-borrowing allocation across banks and specifies the following objective function (Equation 8.1B):

$$\min Z = \sum_{q=1}^{Q} CP_q + k \sum_{q=1}^{Q} (NCB_q - FLT_q) \quad (8.1B)$$

Where: $Z$ = The sum of total cash payments and the cost of total book balances

$q$ = Subscript denoting a particular bank

$Q$ = Total number of different banks being considered

$CP$ = Cash payments for tangible services

$k$ = Opportunity cost of balances (investment rate company could earn)

$NCB$ = Net collected balances

$FLT$ = Net float

The sum of total cash payments made to all banks is calculated in the first term of Equation 8.1B, and the cost of total book balances makes up the second term. The company must attend to five constraints:

(1) NCB ≥ a(LOAN) + b(LINE)
(compensating balance requirement)

(2) CP + *ecr*(NCB) ≥ TSC
(sum of fees and balance credits ≥ total service charges assessed)

(3) CP ≤ α(SC)
(bank's restriction on amount of charges payable by cash)

(4) NCB ≥ MAB
(company's self-imposed minimum balance requirement)

(5) LOAN ≤ LINE
(borrowing cannot exceed total credit line amount)

Where: a = Compensating balance rate on loans

b = Compensating balance rate on credit line

LOAN = Level of the loan ($)

LINE = Level of the line ($)

*ecr* = Earnings credit rate per dollar of net collected balances

α = Fraction of service charges payable by cash

SC = Total tangible service charges for given bank

MAB = Minimum available balance to be maintained (company policy)

Notice in Equation 8.1B that the level of tangible service charges and value of float vary with check and deposit activity levels. This model, and those like it, trade off float improvements with service charges. Modifications and improvements of this model have been developed by Stone; computationally, they can be very cumbersome if the banking system includes numerous banks. Stone has developed two simplified "partial models," which do not guarantee optimization (in terms of cost minimization) but can be implemented in Microsoft Excel™.

Stone subsequently refined the above model to allow for compensation by non-interest-bearing time deposits and for annual settlement periods (surplus balances or shortfalls could be offset much later in the year). The revised model incorporates more bank compensation constraints, cash budgeting variables, and an expanded objective function. The revised objective function involves minimizing the sum of four costs:

[1] See Robert F. Calman, *Linear Programming and Cash Management/CASH ALPHA* (Cambridge, MA: MIT Press, 1986); Gerald A. Pogue, Russell B. Faucet, and Ralph N. Bussard, "Cash Management: A Systems Approach," *Industrial Management Review* (Winter 1970), pp. 55–74; and Bernell K. Stone, "Allocating Credit Lines, Planned Borrowing, and Tangible Services over a Company's Banking System," *Financial Management* (Summer 1975), pp. 65–78. Our presentation is primarily based on the latter source.

Total cost = Short-term debt interest +
Credit commitment fees + Cash fees +
Opportunity cost of balances net of investment income

The model is more realistic, but Stone still calls it a modeling framework instead of an optimization model. Because compensation terms, fees, and borrowing and investment arrangements are subject to company/bank negotiations, the modeling framework serves primarily as a decision aid. It enables simulation of various cash budget scenarios and banking system design configurations, helping the corporate analyst determine where it would be most beneficial to renegotiate terms. Later, as actual cash flows and interest rates vary from the values used in the planning model, the analyst can rerun the model to optimally allocate bank debt. The analyst should be careful to factor in the quality of bank services, in that the model focuses only on costs. Furthermore, the value-maximizing decisions require cash flows in the optimization equation to be discounted to their present values.

CHAPTER

9

# Cash Collection Systems

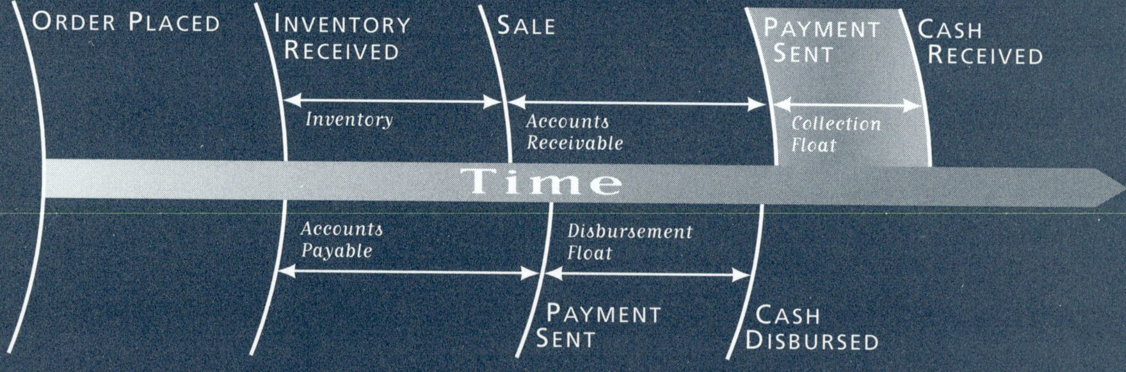

## OBJECTIVES

*After studying this chapter, you should be able to:*

- understand the various options that firms have to collect payments from customers.
- differentiate between the various collection systems, and choose that system best suited to the company's situation.
- collect the basic data necessary for a lockbox study.
- understand how a lockbox model works.

Once a firm has sold a product on credit, the financial manager's attention is turned to receiving cash payment as soon as possible. The credit period offered by the seller is a key source of delay in receiving payment. However, important delays occur even after the customer places the check in the mail. This chapter discusses the types of delays experienced from the time the remittance is mailed until cash is received at the depositing bank. We develop a model approach to designing a system to accelerate the receipt of cash and then design a cash collection system to accelerate the receipt of cash.

### FINANCIAL DILEMMA

How Can a Firm Accelerate Its Cash Collections?

Your firm continually experiences a shortage of cash. You offer the same credit terms as your competitors, yet they don't seem to be experiencing the same liquidity problems. As you survey your industry, you discover that all your competitors use a different method of collecting receivables than you do. Your firm uses a very simple system. Invoices are sent with the orders, and a remittance envelope is included. The corporate headquarters' address is preprinted on the remittance envelope with the credit department's post office box number. Mail is delivered to the credit department once each day at about 11:00 A.M. Several clerical employees open the envelopes and key the invoice data and payment amount into your accounts receivable information system. If the payment agrees with the invoice data, the check is separated from the invoice and placed in a stack to be deposited. If the check amount does not reconcile with the invoice data, the check remains with the invoice and another clerical employee begins the reconciliation process. Once the problem is resolved, the check is separated from the invoice and prepared for deposit. By 3:30 P.M., a deposit ticket is prepared for the growing stack of checks, and a deposit is made at a nearby branch of your firm's bank. Although this system has seemingly worked well for the last twenty years, you wonder why your competitors have adopted what is referred to as a lockbox collection system and whether this could have any impact on your cash flow.

## THE CASH FLOW TIMELINE AND CASH COLLECTION

Exhibit 9–1 displays the cash flow timeline detail related to the cash collection problem. As the exhibit shows, three types of delays can occur between the date the check is placed in the mail and the date the deposited check is cleared and cash is actually available in the bank account. The sum of these three types of delays is referred to as **collection float**. **Float** is the time lag between events.

The first delay is the mail time it takes for a check to arrive at its destination. This is referred to as **mail float**, and the length of the delay is obviously related to the physical distance between the two points. It is also related to holiday periods, weekends, the efficiency of the postal system, and the weather.

Exhibit 9–1

*Cash Flow Timeline Related to Cash Collection Float*

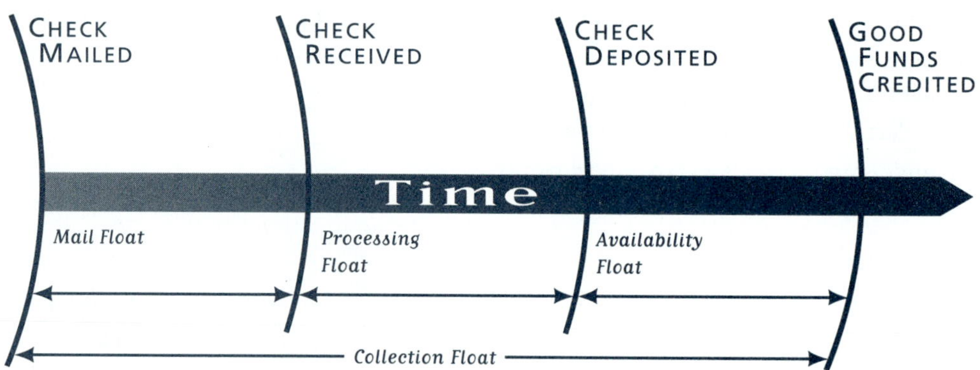


The second delay is **check processing float**. Once the check is received, it must be processed. That is, the envelope must be opened, the check prepared for deposit, and then the check must be physically deposited in the firm's bank.

The final delay is called **availability float**. The deposited check is not immediately converted into cash. Rather, the depositing bank first estimates the time it will take to deliver the check back to the bank on which the check was written. This is determined by scanning the MICR line printed at the bottom of each check. The MICR line contains the transit routing number that identifies the bank on which the check was written. The depositing bank's computers have a database that is used to assign an availability time to each deposited check. The availability time is the estimated time it will take to clear the check once it is deposited. The depositing bank is obligated to give credit to the deposited checks after the elapse of the availability date even if it has been unable to clear the check.

The problem confronting the financial manager is determining how to design a collection system that addresses each of the three components of collection float. Mail float can be anywhere from one to several days. Processing float can generally range from a few hours to one or more days. Availability float can range from immediate availability to as much as five days if weekends and/or holidays are involved. Thus, the financial manager is probably dealing with collection float from one day, at the very best, to as much as a week or more at the extreme. This may seem trivial until you begin to calculate the opportunity cost of these idle funds. For example, assume a firm has $1 million of daily receipts and these remittances take an average of seven days to clear from the date they are mailed. If the annual opportunity cost of money is 8 percent, then the annual cost is $560,000 ($1,000,000 × 7 × 0.08). This relationship indicates that the firm has an average of $7 million of uncollected funds ($1,000,000 × 7 days) at any point of time during the year. Using an 8-percent opportunity cost, the firm is losing $560,000 annually due to the collection process.

## THE COST OF FLOAT

Float refers to the time lag between events. While the time lag is important to the financial manager, the dollar amount of remittances being affected by the time delay is also important. **Dollar-day float** is a measure that incorporates both the time lag and the dollar amount involved. Exhibit 9–2 presents a simple example that shows how to calculate the cost of float. In the example, there are four remittances during a given month totaling

**Exhibit 9–2**

*A Simple Example to Calculate the Cost of Float*

| Remittances | × Collection float | = Dollar-day float |
|---|---|---|
| $ 50,000 | × 2 | = $ 100,000 |
| 1,200,000 | × 5 | = 6,000,000 |
| 500,000 | × 7 | = 3,500,000 |
| 1,000 | × 10 | = 10,000 |
| $1,751,000 | | $9,610,000 |

$$\begin{aligned}\text{Average dollar-day float} &= \text{Dollar-day float/Days in month}\\ &= \$9{,}610{,}000/30\\ &= \$320{,}333.33\end{aligned}$$

$$\begin{aligned}\text{Average collection float} &= \text{Dollar-day float/Remittances}\\ &= \$9{,}610{,}000/\$1{,}751{,}000\\ &= 5.49 \text{ days}\end{aligned}$$

$$\begin{aligned}\text{Annual cost of float} &= \text{Average dollar-day float} \times \text{Rate}\\ &= \$320{,}333.33 \times 0.08\\ &= \$25{,}626.67\end{aligned}$$

$1,751,000. The dollar-day float related to each remittance is calculated by multiplying each remittance by its associated collection float. The total dollar-day float for the month is $9,610,000. The total dollar-day float divided by the number of days in a month results in an average daily dollar-day float of $320,333.33. The remittances and collection float in the example result in an average of $320,333.33 of idle funds daily throughout the month. If the firm's opportunity investment rate is 8 percent per year, the annual cost of the collection float is $25,626.67, assuming the remittances and collection float are replicated throughout the remaining 11 months.

## TYPES OF COLLECTION SYSTEMS

Once a company begins to sell to customers outside of its headquarters city, the problem of collecting payment from geographically dispersed customers becomes an important issue. Should the firm continue to have its customers remit to company headquarters, or should the firm allow its field offices to collect payments? What are the available payment collection alternatives, and what are the advantages and disadvantages associated with these alternatives? This section will discuss the two basic **cash collection systems** available for collecting customer remittances, company processing centers and **lockbox** systems. Since the discussion of company processing centers and lockbox systems focuses on the collection of checks, the section will end with a brief discussion of two alternative collection systems that do not involve checks.

### Collection System Cost Factors

Collection systems incur both a fixed cost and a variable cost. Fixed costs include such items as clerical salaries, account maintenance fees, fees charged to transfer balances from the collection bank to another bank, a deposit notification charge, and a deposit charge. Variable costs include a processing charge per item, a charge for encoding each remittance item, and a deposit charge for each item. A final cost factor is the opportunity cost of float. Equation 9.1 develops a total cost equation for a general cost model of a cash collection system.

$$\text{Total cost} = N \times [(F \times D \times i) + VC] + FC \tag{9.1}$$

Where:

$N$ = The number of remittances processed

$F$ = The average face value of remittances

$D$ = The number of days it takes to clear the check

$i$ = The daily opportunity cost of funds

$VC$ = The variable cost charged for each remittance item

$FC$ = The fixed cost of managing the collection system

## Company Processing Center

A company may decide to do its own processing and depositing of checks. Such a system is referred to as a **company processing center**. If company processing is chosen, then management must decide whether to have a **decentralized processing system** or a **centralized processing system**. Deciding which to use depends primarily on the volume of checks processed and the dollar size of the checks.

*Decentralized Collection Systems* One company processing option available to the corporation is to have its various field offices or stores around the country receive payments from the company's customers. This simple system has two major advantages. First, mail delay is minimal, since the customers and the store or field office are in the same location. Second, availability delay is minimal, since the check is more than likely drawn on a bank in the same location. It is even possible that the customers' accounts are at the same bank used by the store or field office.

The decentralized processing system also has several disadvantages. First, the store or field office staff may get busy and not deposit checks received in a timely manner. This offsets some of the mail float and availability float advantages. Second, the funds deposited will remain in the field office's or store's local bank account until they are transferred to the bank(s) used by corporate headquarters. Only then will the corporate cash manager have use of the funds.

*Centralized Processing System* At the other extreme is the company centralized processing system where corporate headquarters receives all customer remittances. The checks with invoices are mailed to one or two major administrative centers for processing. These centers have high-speed equipment for processing the remittance information and a staff dedicated to this task. The advantage to a centralized processing system is that the processing time is reduced compared to the field office or decentralized alternative. In addition, the corporate cash manager has more control over the system and bank account balances. The account balances, rather than being spread all over the country, are in only one or two locations. The disadvantages are that mail and availability time will generally increase. Because this alternative requires the firm to maintain costly state-of-the-art processing equipment, most consultants consider this alternative only when the monthly remittance volume exceeds 100,000 items per month.

*Cost Analysis* Company processing centers incur both fixed and variable costs. Fixed costs include clerical salaries, equipment rental fees, account maintenance fees, a fee charged to transfer balances from the collection bank to another bank, a deposit notification charge, and a deposit charge. Variable costs include processing charges per item, a charge for encoding each remittance item, and a deposit charge for each item.

Suppose you have estimated the following cost data for a decentralized and a centralized company processing center. Note that the number of days it takes to clear a check, *D*, is less for the centralized system. In this case, the longer processing time taken by the decentralized system does not offset the longer mail time and availability time of the centralized system. The centralized system is able to incur a lower variable processing charge due to using more competitive banks. Finally, the centralized system incurs a higher fixed charge due to equipment costs and salaries for dedicated clerical staff.

| | Common Data | Decentralized | Centralized |
|---|---|---|---|
| $N$ | 1,000 | | |
| $F$ | \$1,500 | | |
| $D$ | | 7 | 6 |
| $i$ | 0.10/365 | | |
| $VC$ | | \$0.25 | \$0.20 |
| $FC$ | | \$100 | \$600 |

$$\begin{aligned}\text{Total cost (decentralized)} &= 1{,}000[\$1{,}500 \times 7 \times (0.10/365) + \$0.25] + \$100 \\ &= 1{,}000(\$2.877 + \$0.25) + \$100 \\ &= \$3{,}127 + \$100 \\ &= \$3{,}227\end{aligned}$$

$$\begin{aligned}\text{Total cost (centralized)} &= 1{,}000[\$1{,}500 \times 6 \times (0.10/365) + \$0.20] + \$600 \\ &= 1{,}000(\$2.466 + \$0.20) + \$600 \\ &= \$2{,}666 + \$600 \\ &= \$3{,}266\end{aligned}$$

Thus, even though the decentralized system, in this example, incurs a longer float period and a higher variable processing cost, the lower fixed costs allow for a lower total cost compared to the centralized system.

## Lockbox Collection System

A **lockbox collection system** is really a blend of the two company processing systems just discussed with the exception that a bank or third party does the processing. A lockbox system is similar to the field office collection system in that the lockbox system consists of dispersed collection sites. It is similar to the centralized collection system in that there are a limited number of collection sites and the deposited funds are transferred from the lockbox collection sites to the corporate headquarters bank on a frequent basis.

The first lockbox system was developed by Radio Corporation of America (RCA) in conjunction with its major bank, First Chicago, in 1947. The primary purpose served by the lockbox system was to allow RCA to reduce its level of bank borrowing.

A lockbox collection system initially consisted of a physical post office box serviced by a bank. The company would send out remittance envelopes with each billing with the post office box preprinted on the envelope. The bank's employees would empty the contents of the post office box several times daily delivering the contents to the bank's lockbox processing area. The remittances would be opened, the checks proofed and deposited, and the invoice material routed to the company.

Today, most banks have a **unique ZIP code** for their lockbox operation and instead of a box, the mail sorted to that ZIP code is bagged and held in a designated area of the post office. Since most of the mail sorting is done at night, the bank staff will make several trips daily to the post office, seven days a week, to retrieve the bags of mail. The

## FOCUS ON PRACTICE

### *The Impact of a Retail Lockbox: The Scotts Company*

The Scotts Company, historically a company providing lawn maintenance products for the "do-it-yourselfer," started up Scotts Lawn Service for the "do-it-for-me" customer. The new service experienced rapid growth and quickly began operations in 60 of the nation's top 100 lawn service markets in the United States. However, the rapid growth created a highly decentralized cash collection system with each branch opening up its own bank account for daily deposits. The system was heavily labor intensive, chewing up a large number of man-hours that included the following activities:

- making daily trips to the post office and bank;
- sorting mail manually;
- opening, extracting, and sorting the remittance contents by payment type;
- removing customer comment cards;
- preparing a deposit slip and endorsing each check;
- obtaining credit card authorizations;
- batching payments for cash application and manually posting receipts to customer accounts; and
- correcting payment errors.

Weekly, corporate treasury would then contact each bank for balances and enter automated clearinghouse transactions into bank software for concentration purposes. As a result, significant idle balances remained in the field banks for days at a time. At the time, Scotts' decentralized cash collection system was processing 50,000 items per month, with a projected 250,000 collection items based on growth estimates. A retail lockbox system was the solution. Local bank accounts were eliminated, saving $90,000 annually. Processing float and mail float were reduced, which allowed the company to reduce its amount of borrowing resulting in an immediate annual interest expense savings of $100,000. Significant personnel costs were also saved that could be redirected to customer service matters.

*Source:* "Scotts' Retail Lockbox Trims Millions in Processing Costs," *AFP Exchange* (July/August 2003), pp. 48–49.

remittances are then processed in batches as received, with the heaviest amount of processing being done by 7:00 A.M. This early morning processing schedule allows the bank to meet same-day settlement deadlines and other check clearing deadlines that accelerate availability of the deposited items.

*Types of Lockbox Collection Systems* There are two basic types of lockbox collection systems. The **retail lockbox system** is structured to handle a large volume of standardized invoice materials, and the remittance checks have a relatively low average dollar face value. The standardized remittance information is a requirement in this system because it allows the bank to reduce its cost of handling the item. Cost reduction is essential, since the average dollar face value per item is low and therefore the value of the float is low. Most consumers receive a standardized monthly invoice resulting from phone calls, gasoline purchases, credit card purchases, etc. Companies with a large consumer base, such as AT&T, Shell, or VISA, send a standardized invoice with a machine readable scan line at the bottom of the remittance ticket.

Contrast a retail lockbox system with a **wholesale lockbox system**. The wholesale lockbox system is designed to process smaller volumes and larger average dollar items with nonstandard remittance information. For example, the average wholesale lockbox receives

400 to 500 payments monthly, valued at $25 to $35 million.[1] Whereas retail lockbox systems are used by companies receiving large volumes of remittances from consumers, wholesale lockboxes are used for business-to-business trade payables.

*Cost Analysis* Lockbox processors charge both a fixed cost and a variable cost. Fixed costs include an account maintenance fee, a fee charged to transfer balances from the collection bank to another bank, a deposit notification charge, and a deposit charge. Variable costs include a lockbox processing charge per item, a charge for encoding each remittance item, and a deposit charge for each item. The other variable cost is not directly bank related. It has to do with the opportunity cost of float.

Suppose you have approached two different lockbox processors, Citibank and Chase, and gathered the following data:

| | Common Data | Citibank | Chase |
|---|---|---|---|
| $N$ | 1,000 | | |
| $F$ | $1,500 | | |
| $D$ | | 6 | 5 |
| $i$ | 0.10/365 | | |
| $VC$ | | $0.45 | $0.50 |
| $FC$ | | $225 | $275 |

$$\begin{aligned}\text{Total cost (Citibank)} &= 1{,}000[\$1{,}500 \times 6 \times (0.10/365) + \$0.45] + \$225 \\ &= 1{,}000(\$2.466 + \$0.45) + \$225 \\ &= \$2{,}916 + \$225 \\ &= \$3{,}141\end{aligned}$$

$$\begin{aligned}\text{Total cost (Chase)} &= 1{,}000[\$1{,}500 \times 5 \times (0.10/365) + \$0.50] + \$275 \\ &= 1{,}000(\$2.055 + \$0.50) + \$275 \\ &= \$2{,}555 + \$275 \\ &= \$2{,}830\end{aligned}$$

Thus, even though Chase charges a higher variable processing cost and a higher fixed cost, the shorter check clearing time provides enough opportunity cost savings to generate a lower total cost. Indeed, the lockbox system offered by Chase is cheaper than the decentralized company processing system alternative analyzed earlier.

Now assume that there are 100,000 checks and a face value of $15 per check (note that the total dollar value is the same).

$$\begin{aligned}\text{Total cost (Citibank)} &= 100{,}000[\$15 \times 6 \times (0.10/365) + \$0.45] + \$225 \\ &= 100{,}000(\$0.0247 + \$0.45) + \$225 \\ &= \$47{,}470 + \$225 \\ &= \$47{,}695\end{aligned}$$

$$\begin{aligned}\text{Total cost (Chase)} &= 100{,}000[\$15 \times 5 \times (0.10/365) + \$0.50] + \$275 \\ &= 100{,}000(\$0.0205 + \$0.50) + \$275 \\ &= \$52{,}050 + \$275 \\ &= \$52{,}325\end{aligned}$$

With the increased number of checks and lower face value, Citibank provides the lower total cost because the float savings are less significant when the dollar value of the check is small. In such a case, the processing costs are the more significant factor in determining total cost.

[1] Richard J. Poje, "The Death and Birth of Wholesale Lockbox," *AFP Exchange* (March/April 2003), p. 61.

FOCUS ON PRACTICE

### Data Transmission Enhances Lockbox Value

A service now being offered by many banks is the electronic transmission of lockbox data. The many benefits from such a service include:

- No computer input preparation by clerical staff
- Same-day accounts receivable updating
- More efficient credit management
- Reduction of potential credit/collection problems
- Greater flexibility when selecting lockbox banks

One of the most important benefits is the reduction in manual data entry in the corporation's accounts receivable area. When a bank provides a hard-copy report with lockbox remittance information, accounts receivable clerks must enter the data into their computer system. Electronic transmission allows a company to feed the data automatically into the system. Such electronic data transmission enables a company to update its accounts receivable system faster, which results in increased control and more efficient credit management.

### Alternative Collection Systems

Company processing systems and lockbox systems are the two major collection systems used today for the collection of check remittances. However, other forms of payment can be used which alleviate the need to process paper checks.

One alternative collection system utilizes **preauthorized payments**. In this situation, the buyer and seller agree to a payment date, such as the 12th of each month, and the seller initiates a request to the buyer's bank for payment of the predetermined amount. Preauthorized payments eliminate mail float, processing float, and availability float and improve the cash flow forecasting ability of both the buyer and seller. A limiting factor is that time is needed to set up the system for each customer, so the transactions handled this way are best suited for regularly recurring payments. For example, insurance companies regularly collect monthly premiums using preauthorized payment systems.

As **electronic corporate trade payments** become more common, wholesale lockboxes, as we know them today, will likely be phased out. Electronic corporate trade payments involve an arrangement between a buyer, a seller, and the banks of the two parties involved so that payment is effected without a paper check being issued. A seller will transmit an electronic invoice to the buyer and payment will occur electronically between the two parties' banks, eliminating the need for wholesale lockboxes. Chapter 19 will discuss this payment alternative in more detail as a part of what is commonly referred to as *electronic data interchange*, or *EDI*. An example of an electronic collection system is an **electronic lockbox**. This collection system is offered by banks for companies to receive payments via wire transfer or ACH rather than by paper checks.

## THE LOCKBOX LOCATION STUDY

How does a corporation decide whether or not to have a lockbox? And, if a lockbox system is desirable, how does a firm decide how many lockboxes to have, where to locate them, and how to allocate the firm's customers among the chosen lockbox sites? The process by which these decisions are made is called a **lockbox study**. Such a study is usually conducted by a commercial bank. Money center banks and many of the large regional commercial banks have a cash management consulting group which markets the banks' cash management services. One way to market such services is through a lockbox study.

A lockbox study involves the collection of data that are fed into a computerized model that determines the optimal number and location of lockbox sites. The data collected consist of a sample of remittance information including the number of checks and the dollar amount, postmark city, postmark date and date received, and the drawee bank's transit routing code for each remittance check. The data sample may include one or more months of remittance information, depending on whether seasonal factors are important.

Let's compare the data gathered to the cost equation shown previously in Equation 9.1 to see how they relate. The number of checks, $N$, and the face value of each check can be used to determine the average face value, $F$. The postmark city, postmark date, and date received are necessary to determine mail float, one component of the total number of days it takes to clear a check, $D$. The other component of $D$ is availability float, and it can be determined given the drawee's bank transit routing number. The consultant's database should include some estimated cost data that may be bank specific or just proxies for variable and fixed costs. Once these data are collected, they are fed into a computerized optimization model to determine the number and location of lockbox sites. As with any type of research study, many choices related to the input data must be made based on judgment. We will now turn our attention to some of the more complicating factors that exist in the data collection effort for the lockbox location study.

## Customer Groups

How should customer groups be determined? One approach is to let each individual customer represent a unique customer group. This may be the best approach for firms with a relatively small number of customers.

But what if the firm has tens of thousands of customers? This results in a very large optimization problem. At this point, it might make sense to organize the firm's customer base into customer regions based on ZIP code. If additional refinement is required, each ZIP code group could be further grouped by size or even by Federal Reserve District.

## Remittance Sample

How large should the remittance sample be? First, the number of items in the sample should reflect the size of the company. Second, consultants usually recommend using a stratified sample technique. The stratified sample technique fully incorporates the largest dollar items. If these items represent about 80 percent of the total dollars being received, then the remainder of the sample may be disregarded. If the small items represent a significant dollar amount, then a sample of the items should be included.

## Mail and Availability Times

Mail times can be estimated using the postmark date of the remittance envelopes and the date the remittance was received. However, this approach has been found to be prone to errors.

One popular source for mail time data is a database provided by Phoenix-Hecht. This company has developed a standardized technique for measuring mail times between central post offices.

Availability times can be obtained from a variety of sources. One source is Federal Reserve Schedules. As we have seen, however, banks may not use the Federal Reserve System for clearing checks. Another source is City Averages, which represent the average of major clearing banks in a particular city. The third and final source of availability data is from published individual bank availability schedules. This source is the most accurate but also the most troublesome to obtain. Most banks, though, are willing to make their availability schedules available for lockbox study purposes.

## FINANCIAL DILEMMA REVISITED

In trying to resolve the Financial Dilemma mentioned at the beginning of this chapter, suppose the cash manager decides to bring in a consulting group to study the firm's cash collection system. The consultant, after reviewing the remittance information, determines the following remittance characteristics.

| Customer Group | Number of Remittances | Average Face Value | Mail and Availability Float | Processing Float |
|---|---|---|---|---|
| 1 | 25 | $ 75,000 | 7 days | 2 days |
| 2 | 10 | 100,000 | 2 | 2 |
| 3 | 5 | 150,000 | 8 | 2 |

Variable processing cost per item: $0.35
Monthly bank account fixed cost: $125

As the sample shows, there are three geographically dispersed customer groups. As the data are analyzed, the consultant finds that customer group 2 is composed of most of the company's original customers and that groups 1 and 3 are customers that have been added more recently as the company has grown and attracted a more geographically dispersed product demand. The consultant determines that remittances take an average of two days to process before they are deposited at the company's bank. The consultant further indicates that this processing delay can be substantially reduced if not completely eliminated by allowing a bank to handle the processing. Currently, all customers mail their remittances to corporate headquarters. The total monthly cost of the current collection system using Equation 9.1 is:

$$\begin{aligned}\text{Total cost} &= [25 \times \$75{,}000 \times 9 \times (0.10/365)] \\ &\quad + [10 \times \$100{,}000 \times 4 \times (0.10/365)] \\ &\quad + [5 \times \$150{,}000 \times 10 \times (0.10/365)] \\ &\quad + [(25 + 10 + 5) \times \$0.35] \\ &\quad + \$125 \\ &= \$7{,}913\end{aligned}$$

The total monthly cost of the float and processing charges amount to $7,913. For a year, this would equal $94,956 ($7,913 × 12).

In the next section, the consultant will estimate the cost of using a lockbox system to collect the company's remittances to see if a lockbox system is cost effective.

## THE LOCKBOX MODEL

Once all the data have been gathered through the lockbox study, the data are entered into a **lockbox optimization model**. Such a model determines the optimal number of lockboxes and their locations. In addition, the model will allocate the customers among the selected lockbox sites.

### Complete Enumeration

A **complete enumeration model** analyzes all possible lockbox sites to determine the optimal combinations that maximize shareholder wealth. For example, if a firm wanted to find the optimal combination of lockbox sites out of a sample of three potential sites, the complete enumeration model would first find the best 1-bank site by comparing the total cost (Equation 9.1) for each of the potential lockbox sites. Then, the model would find the best 2-bank combination. Finally, the model finds the best 3-bank combination. In all, given three possible lockbox locations, seven comparisons are made to determine the site combination with the lowest total cost. In general, the number of different lockbox combinations is $2^n - 1$, where $n$ is the number of different sites. The possible combinations for $n = 3$ are shown below.

- Best 1-Site
  Choose from: Bank A, Bank B, or Bank C
- Best 2-Site Combination
  Choose from: Bank A–Bank B, Bank A–Bank C, or Bank B–Bank C
- Best 3-Site Combination
  Bank A–Bank B–Bank C

The optimal solution is the site combination that provides the lowest total cost. We develop the complete enumeration model through an application of the Financial Dilemma data collected earlier.

As part of the lockbox study, the consulting group presented the following remittance data and collection float data for a sample of three banks. Bank A is the current corporate headquarters' bank. Notice that the variable processing costs and fixed costs are higher for Bank A using a lockbox system compared to the company's current system because of the additional costs incurred related to the lockbox processing activity. Also, days of float include only mail and availability float because a lockbox system essentially eliminates processing float.

| Customer Group | Number of Remittances | Average Face Value | Days of Float | | |
|---|---|---|---|---|---|
| | | | Bank A | Bank B | Bank C |
| 1 | 25 | $ 75,000 | 7 | 3 | 1 |
| 2 | 10 | 100,000 | 2 | 5 | 3 |
| 3 | 5 | 150,000 | 8 | 2 | 4 |
| Variable processing costs | | | $0.45 | $0.35 | $0.75 |
| Fixed costs | | | $275 | $200 | $150 |

The next table shows the total cost matrix for the three customer groups and the three banks. Total cost is calculated using Equation 9.1. The numbers calculated for each combination of customer group and bank represent variable costs computed using the opportunity cost of float and the variable processing costs. The total variable cost for each bank plus the respective bank fixed cost represent the total cost of processing the indicated customer groups for that particular bank. For example, allocating all customers to Bank A generates a monthly total cost of $6,080, compared to the monthly cost of $7,913 computed earlier using your corporate headquarters as the collection site and Bank A for deposit services only. The optimal 1-lockbox system is Bank C, with a monthly cost of only $2,337. This represents a significant saving from the current system.

| Customer Group | Bank A | Bank B | Bank C |
|---|---|---|---|
| 1 | $3,607 | $1,550 | $ 532 |
| 2 | 552 | 1,373 | 829 |
| 3 | 1,646 | 413 | 826 |
| Fixed costs | 275 | 200 | 150 |
| Total cost | $6,080 | $3,536 | $2,337 |

The next step is to compute the total cost for all combinations of two sites. The allocation of customer groups to specific banks is based on the very simple goal of minimizing variable costs. For example, look at Combination 1 below. Customer group 1 is assigned to Bank B because its variable costs of $1,550 are less than the variable costs of $3,607 if it was assigned to Bank A.

| Customer | Combination 1 | | Combination 2 | | Combination 3 | |
|---|---|---|---|---|---|---|
| Group | Bank A | Bank B | Bank A | Bank C | Bank B | Bank C |
| 1 | | $1,550 | | $ 532 | | $ 532 |
| 2 | $552 | | $552 | | | 829 |
| 3 | | 413 | | 826 | 413 | |
| Variable costs | $552 | $1,963 | $552 | $1,358 | $413 | $1,361 |
| Fixed costs | 275 | 200 | 275 | 150 | 200 | 150 |
| Total cost | | $2,990 | | $2,335 | | $2,124 |

The optimal 2-site system is Combination 3, which includes Bank B and Bank C, with a total cost of $2,124. Customer groups 1 and 2 are assigned to Bank C, and customer group 3 is assigned to Bank B. Since the total cost for a 2-site system is less than the total cost for a 1-site system, we conclude that a 2-site system is preferred.

We now analyze a 3-site system. If the minimum cost for a 2-site location exceeded the minimum cost for a 1-site location, then the analysis could end at this point.

| | Combination 1 | | |
|---|---|---|---|
| Customer Group | Bank A | Bank B | Bank C |
| 1 | | | $ 532 |
| 2 | $552 | | |
| 3 | | $413 | |
| Variable costs | $552 | $413 | $ 532 |
| Fixed costs | 275 | 200 | 150 |
| Total cost | | | $2,122 |

A 3-site solution offers the minimum monthly total cost of $2,122, which beats the best 2-site solution by $2, the best 1-site solution by $215, and the current system by $5,791. It's no wonder that the firm has been losing some competitive advantage due to the significantly higher costs related to the centralized company processing cash collection system.

## Other Solution Techniques

The problem with the complete enumeration model is the computational requirements for large problems. It is not uncommon for a lockbox problem to analyze a set of 50 different collection sites and possibly hundreds of different customer locations. Analyzing all possible combinations of bank and customer sites is indeed a large problem. This has led researchers to develop models that find the best combinations of sites without having to analyze all possible combinations. Lockbox models have gone through significant development since the early 1970s. The most popular model used today is the The Collection Model (sometimes referred to as the 5.1 Model or the "Duke" model because of the author's former affiliation with Duke University). The Collection Model is an optimization model that runs on the Windows platform and represents the most advanced collection modeling technology available.[2] The Collection Model used by Phoenix-Hecht is a pro-

[2] *Measuring, Modeling & Monitoring Your Lockbox*, Phoenix-Hecht (1997), p. 19.

prietary model. The appendix to this chapter demonstrates the use of an optimization model by developing a linear programming model that can be used to solve the lockbox location problem using the add-in Solver to Microsoft Excel.

## LOCKBOX BANK SELECTION

Once the lockbox model has chosen the optimal number of and location for lockbox collection sites, the final decision is to decide which banks to contract with for the actual **lockbox services**. While the lockbox database may have included individual bank site mail and availability data and cost data, it is more likely that the database would include mail times between central post office sites and average availability data. Thus, once the optimal sites are chosen, specific banks must then be chosen at the optimal sites.

The U.S. banking system has historically banned nationwide branching, generally endorsing the unit banking structure or statewide branching bounded by state lines. This banking structure has historically caused administrative problems for companies establishing nationwide lockbox systems because a company would potentially have to establish separate bank accounts with a large number of different banks. However, statewide branching is now common, with recent legislation allowing nationwide branching.

To combat these structural inefficiencies, banks have developed several different options from which to choose. Some banks offer a **lockbox consortium**. This system is comprised over several independent banks operating under a contractual agreement to provide lockbox services for each other's customers. A company would choose one bank to act as a lead or concentration bank. Other banks have developed **multiple processing centers**. Processing centers are established around the country to pick up lockbox mail and do the processing while the processed checks are deposited in accounts at correspondent banks in the company's name. Cash is then concentrated in the company's account at the lockbox bank's headquarters.

With the difficulties experienced by the banking system during the 1980s, banking laws had to be amended in order to allow out-of-state banks to absorb failed in-state banks. For example, Bank of America, based in North Carolina, was permitted to purchase the insolvent First Republicbank system in Texas; likewise, the Bank One organization, based in Ohio, was allowed to purchase the insolvent Texas-based MBank system and most recently merged with JP Morgan Chase organization. The insolvency of such a significant number of large regional banks has accelerated the movement to a regional branch banking system, a prelude to nationwide branching, which will create a much more efficient collection system. The advantage of such a system are lower administrative costs, lower internal processing costs, and lower concentration costs. There are disadvantages, however. For one, bundled services may make cost comparisons difficult. Some additional risks may be entailed by having all collection, concentration, and reporting activities done by one bank.

## A LOCKBOX STUDY CASE EXAMPLE

A bank in Dallas, Texas, was asked by the subsidiary of a Dallas-based oil company to evaluate its current cash collection system and to offer suggestions for improvements. The subsidiary did not use a lockbox collection system and currently had all customers remitting to company headquarters in Dallas. Dollar volumes of remittances by state were: Texas (13%), New York (12%), Illinois (10%), California (10%), Pennsylvania (7%), Ohio (6%), and Other (42%). Exhibit 9–3 displays the initial remittance data collected for a 2-month period by the bank's consulting group.

### Exhibit 9–3

*Remittance Data*

| | |
|---|---|
| Number of days in study | 62 (two months) |
| Total dollar value | $53,219,517 |
| Average daily remittance | $858,379 |
| Estimated number of remittances | 1,600 |
| Average remittance size | $33,262 |
| Current system float, days | 4.97 days |
| Current system float, dollars | $4,266,144 |

For the 2-month period, the company received over $53 million in remittances for an average daily remittance of $858,379. The total number of remittances included 1,600 items for an average face value per remittance of $33,262. The current system resulted in 4.97 days of float including mail and availability float. The number of days of float multiplied by the average daily remittance of $858,379 resulted in dollar-day float of $4,266,144. That is, on any given day, the company had over $4 million of idle funds in the remittance/clearing system.

The bank consulting group used the cost data contained in Exhibit 9–4 as an estimate of the total bank charges incurred by different banking systems analyzed. It was estimated that the firm's current cash collection system incurred a banking charge of $100 monthly or a required compensating balance of $18,182, based on an earnings credit rate of 7.50 percent, a bank reserve requirement of 12 percent, and 30 days per month in a 360-day year.

Exhibit 9–5 shows the optimal solutions for 1-box, 2-box, and 3-box systems. An optimization routine is used to determine the best bank combinations for a 1-, 2-, or 3-bank

### Exhibit 9–4

*Lockbox System Monthly Costs*

| Service Item | 1-Box | 2-Box | 3-Box |
|---|---|---|---|
| Account maintenance | $ 15 | $ 30 | $ 45 |
| Lockbox processing (800 × $0.28)[3] | 224 | 224 | 300 |
| Deposit notification | 50 | 100 | 150 |
| Items deposited (800 × $0.04) | 32 | 32 | 32 |
| Encoding (800 × $0.025) | 20 | 20 | 20 |
| Wire transfer—Incoming (22 × $5) | 110 | 220 | 330 |
| Wire transfer—Outgoing (22 × $6) | 132 | 264 | 396 |
| Deposits credited, 2/day (50 × $0.60) | 30 | 60 | 90 |
| Total cost | $ 613 | $ 950 | $ 1,363 |
| Estimated balance requirement | $111,454 | $172,727 | $247,818 |

Note: Estimated balance requirement is calculated using an ECR of 7.50 percent, a 12-percent reserve requirement, 30-day months, and a 360-day year. Thus, for a 1-box system, the firm could choose to pay a fee of $613 or leave balances of $111,454 to compensate the bank for the services rendered.

[3] The lockbox processing fee is different for a 3-bank system assuming that each bank has a $100 minimum per month charge. Dividing the estimated total processing charge of $224 by three banks results in a charge per bank less than the required minimum charge.

Exhibit 9–5

*Comparative System Float and Cost Results*

| Site | Days | Dollar Float | Required Balances | Total Idle Balances | Net Improvement | Investment Earnings, 9% |
|---|---|---|---|---|---|---|
| Current system | 4.97 | $4,266,144 | $ 18,182 | $4,284,326 | | |
| Optimal 1-city systems: | | | | | | |
| Chicago | 3.46 | 2,969,991 | 111,454 | 3,081,445 | $1,202,881 | $108,259 |
| Pittsburgh | 3.52 | 3,021,494 | 111,454 | 3,132,948 | 1,151,378 | 103,624 |
| Optimal 2-city systems: | | | | | | |
| Chicago/Pittsburgh | 3.25 | 2,789,732 | 172,727 | 2,962,459 | 1,321,867 | 118,968 |
| Houston/Pittsburgh | 3.33 | 2,858,402 | 172,727 | 3,031,129 | 1,253,197 | 112,787 |
| Optimal 3-city systems: | | | | | | |
| Chicago/Dallas/Charlotte | 3.11 | 2,669,559 | 247,818 | 2,917,377 | 1,366,949 | 123,025 |
| Chicago/Newark/Charlotte | 3.19 | 2,738,229 | 247,818 | 2,986,047 | 1,298,279 | 116,845 |

system. The cost data, converted to required balances, are then added to the resulting dollar-day float for each system to determine the net improvement so that the optimal number of bank sites can be selected.

Note that the results for the second best solution for each system are also displayed. If the firm wishes to use the second best solution because of a desired bank relationship, the cost of suboptimizing can be easily assessed. As mentioned earlier, the exhibit takes the resulting dollar-day float and adds the required balances to service the bank system cost for a total idle dollar balance resulting from the banking system. Then the benefit of using each lockbox system relative to the current system is estimated based on an assumed opportunity rate of 9 percent. The optimal system is a 3-bank system using banks in Chicago, Dallas, and Charlotte for an annual benefit of $123,025.

## SUMMARY

Once the customer has mailed a remittance, the financial manager can significantly affect the amount of time it takes to get that mailed check converted into usable cash. This chapter has focused on the application of a lockbox system to quickly and efficiently convert the remittance check into cash. A lockbox system reduces mail and availability delay by intercepting the check close to the point at which it is mailed and decreases processing delay by having a bank process the remittance and make deposit within a matter of a couple of hours. The processing bank uses state-of-the-art equipment and a highly trained and dedicated staff.

The lockbox study is an essential ingredient in determining whether a lockbox system is advantageous for a specific situation. The study process collects the necessary data by which to determine the optimal collection system. The firm's staff must work closely with the consulting group in making a wide variety of decisions in the data collection process to determine the size of the remittance sample and the time frame of the sample. Collected data that are not truly representative of the firm's total remittances will cause a less than truly optimal system to be created.

This chapter developed the basics of the lockbox model using a complete enumeration approach. The complete enumeration model, while rather simple, is not very efficient at solving large-scale problems because it analyzes every possible combination. An optimization model is typically used that is based on the same types of cost equations, but is able to find the best solution without evaluating each and every possible site. Appendix 9A provides a linear programming approach to developing a lockbox model.

The chapter ended with a demonstration of many of the principles discussed through the use of a case study. In the case study, a bank consulting group recommended that a company replace its centralized company remittance processing center with a 3-bank lockbox system.

## USEFUL WEB SITES

A good general site for cash management systems is Phoenix-Hecht:
**http://www.phoenixhecht.com**

For information on lockboxes, go to the PNC Bank site and use the search function or index to explore such terms as retail lockbox, wholesale lockbox, etc.:
**http://www.treasury.pncbank.com**

## QUESTIONS

1. Explain the role that each of the following play in the cash collection process:
   **a.** Mail float
   **b.** Processing float
   **c.** Availability float
2. What are the advantages and disadvantages of the following cash collection systems?
   **a.** Decentralized collection
   **b.** Centralized collection
   **c.** Lockbox collection
3. How does a lockbox collection system help a firm's liquidity and cash flow situation?
4. Compare and contrast a retail lockbox system to a wholesale lockbox system.
5. What are the major variables in the total cost function for lockbox processing?
6. What are the major points of inquiry in a lockbox study?
7. How does a lockbox collection system reduce mail delay? How does it reduce processing delay? How does it reduce availability delay?
8. As the U.S. financial system moves to nationwide branch banking, how will this impact the collection systems used by corporations?

## PROBLEMS

1. A company has five remittances for the typical month as listed below. Assume the typical month has 30 days. The days of mail float and availability float for each remittance are also shown. Processing float is negligible.

| Remittance | Mail Float | Availability Float |
|---|---|---|
| $100,000 | 2 | 1 |
| 5,000 | 7 | 2 |
| 300,000 | 1 | 1 |
| 10,000 | 5 | 1 |
| 150,000 | 4 | 2 |

**a.** Calculate the total dollar-day float for the month.
**b.** Calculate the average dollar-day float.
**c.** Calculate the average collection float in days.
**d.** If the annual opportunity rate is 4 percent, calculate the annual cost of float.

**2.** A company has five remittances for the typical month as listed below. Assume the typical month has 30 days. The days of mail, processing, and availability float for each remittance are also shown. Under the firm's current system, remittances of $1 million or more receive expedited processing, while all other remittances receive standard processing.

| Remittance | Mail Float | Processing Float | Availability Float |
|---|---|---|---|
| $ 500,000 | 5 | 1 | 2 |
| 100,000 | 2 | 2 | 1 |
| 50,000 | 5 | 1 | 2 |
| 1,000,000 | 3 | 0.5 | 0 |
| 25,000 | 1 | 2 | 2 |

**a.** Calculate the total dollar-day float for the month.
**b.** Calculate the average dollar-day float.
**c.** Calculate the average collection float in days.
**d.** If the annual opportunity rate is 5 percent, calculate the annual cost of float.

**3.** As cash manager for a sporting goods manufacturer, you are responsible for the firm's cash management activities. One of these activities is the management of the firm's cash collection system. Your firm receives an average of 5,000 remittances per month with an average face value of $10,000.

Your current collection system consists of your customers remitting to your company headquarters. You estimate the average mail delay is three days. The typical remittance remains at headquarters for two days. You are informed that the average deposit receives good funds in two days.

**a.** Based on the given information, compute the monthly total cost for your cash collection system if your firm's opportunity investment rate is 5 percent and your bank charges $0.35 per item and a monthly fixed cost of $150.
**b.** Your bank, interested in selling you a lockbox system, indicates that a lockbox system would reduce mail float by two days, processing float by two days, and availability float by one day. If the system charges a variable cost of $0.80 per item and monthly fixed cost of $500, should you change to the lockbox system? You may assume your opportunity investment rate remains at 5 percent.

**4.** As cash manager for an oil company, you are responsible for the firm's cash management activities. One of these activities is the management of the firm's retail cash collection system. Your firm receives an average of 130,000 remittances per month with an average face value of $285.

Your current collection system consists of your customers remitting to your company headquarters. You estimate the average mail delay is three days. The typical remittance remains at headquarters for one day. You are informed that the average deposit receives good funds in 1.5 days.

**a.** Based on the given information, compute the monthly total cost for your cash collection system if your firm's opportunity investment rate is 4 percent and your bank charges $0.25 per item and a monthly fixed cost of $125.
**b.** Your bank, interested in selling you a lockbox system, indicates that a lockbox system would reduce mail float by two days, processing float by one day, and availability float by 0.5 day. If the system charges a variable cost of $0.75 per item and monthly fixed cost of $425, should you change to the lockbox system? You may assume your opportunity investment rate remains at 4 percent.
**c.** Assume you are negotiating with your bank to lower its lockbox variable cost of $0.75 to make the system more attractive to you. What would be the maximum variable cost you would accept?

5. Your firm sells to wholesalers nationwide. Your bank has just completed a lockbox study of your cash collection system. After a thorough study of your remittance information, they categorized your customers into four groups as shown below. Your opportunity rate is 5 percent.

| Customer Group | Average Monthly Remittances | | Days of Float | | |
|---|---|---|---|---|---|
| | Number | Face Value | Bank A | Bank B | Bank C |
| 1 | 2,000 | $50,000 | 5 | 3 | 1 |
| 2 | 4,000 | 30,000 | 1 | 6 | 4 |
| 3 | 1,000 | 18,000 | 3 | 7 | 5 |
| 4 | 200 | 20,000 | 7 | 1 | 3 |
| Variable processing costs | | | $0.30 | $0.60 | $0.80 |
| Fixed costs | | | $300 | $400 | $150 |

Using the complete enumeration model, determine the optimal number of lockbox sites and the customer allocation among the chosen sites.

6. Your firm sells to wholesalers nationwide. Your bank has just completed a lockbox study of your cash collection system. After a thorough study of your remittance information, they categorized your customers into four groups as shown below. Your opportunity rate is 8 percent.

| Customer Group | Average Monthly Remittances | | Days of Float | | |
|---|---|---|---|---|---|
| | Number | Face Value | Bank A | Bank B | Bank C |
| 1 | 500 | $50,000 | 5 | 2 | 1 |
| 2 | 1,000 | 30,000 | 1 | 5 | 4 |
| 3 | 100 | 18,000 | 3 | 4 | 5 |
| 4 | 50 | 20,000 | 7 | 1 | 3 |
| Variable processing costs | | | $0.25 | $0.70 | $0.50 |
| Fixed costs | | | $500 | $600 | $400 |

Using the complete enumeration model, determine the optimal number of lockbox sites and the customer allocation among the chosen sites.

7. Your firm sells to retail customers nationwide. Your bank has just completed a lockbox study of your cash collection system. After a thorough study of your remittance information, they categorized your customers into three groups as shown below. Notice that the consultants expressed remittance data on an average daily basis assuming 30 days in a month. Your opportunity cost of funds is 8 percent.

| Customer Group | Average Monthly Remittances | | Days of Float | | |
|---|---|---|---|---|---|
| | Number | Face Value | Bank A | Bank B | Bank C |
| 1 | 2,000 | $ 500 | 6 | 2 | 1 |
| 2 | 10,000 | 900 | 5 | 1 | 3 |
| 3 | 4,000 | 1,500 | 1 | 4 | 6 |
| Variable processing costs | | | $0.55 | $0.20 | $0.70 |
| Fixed costs | | | $350 | $550 | $250 |

Using the complete enumeration model, determine the optimal number of lockbox sites and the customer allocation among the chosen sites.

**8.** Your firm sells to retail customers nationwide. Your bank has just completed a lockbox study of your cash collection system. After a thorough study of your remittance information, they categorized your customers into three groups as shown below. Notice that the consultants expressed remittance data on an average daily basis assuming 30 days in a month. Your opportunity cost of funds is 10 percent.

| Customer | Average Monthly Remittances | | Days of Float | | |
|---|---|---|---|---|---|
| Group | Number | Face Value | Bank A | Bank B | Bank C |
| 1 | 50,000 | $ 98 | 5 | 6 | 1 |
| 2 | 100,000 | 55 | 1 | 4 | 3 |
| 3 | 75,000 | 125 | 3 | 5 | 4 |
| Variable processing costs | | | $0.55 | $0.40 | $0.70 |
| Fixed costs | | | $350 | $500 | $250 |

Using the complete enumeration model, determine the optimal number of lockbox sites and the customer allocation among the chosen sites.

## REFERENCES

G. Cornuejols, M. L. Fisher, and G. L. Nemhauser, "Location of Bank Accounts to Optimize Float: An Analytical Study of Exact and Approximate Algorithms," *Management Science* (1977), pp. 780–810.

B. D. Fielitz and D. L. White, "A Two Stage Solution Procedure for the Lockbox Problem," *Management Science* (August 1981), pp. 881–886.

__________, "An Evaluation and Linking of Alternative Solution Procedures for the Lockbox Location Problem," *Journal of Bank Research* (1982), pp. 17–27.

F. K. Levy, "An Application of Heuristic Problem Solving to Accounts Receivable Management," *Management Science*, (February 1966), pp. B236–B244.

S. F. Maier and J. A. Vander Wiede, "A Unified Location Model for Cash Disbursement and Lockbox Collections," *Journal of Bank Research* (1976–1977), pp. 166–172.

__________, "What Lockbox and Disbursement Models Really Do," *Journal of Finance* (May 1983), pp. 361–371.

Larry A. Marks and Denise A. Arnette, "Data Sample Key to Accurate Lockbox Analysis," *CASH-FLOW* (October 1986), pp. 37–38.

R. M. Nauss and R. E. Markland, "Theory and Application of an Optimizing Procedure for Lock Box Location Analysis," *Management Science* (1974), pp. 855–865.

__________, "Solving the Lockbox Location Problem," *Financial Management* (Spring 1979), pp. 21–31.

B. K. Stone, "Design of a Receivable Collection System," *Management Science* (August 1981), pp. 876–880.

# APPENDIX 9A

## Developing a Lockbox Optimization Model

Linear programming (LP) is a mathematical model that optimizes an objective function subject to specified constraints. The objective function and constraints must be linear equations. If a feasible solution exists for the given problem, it can be proven that the LP model will find the optimal answer, the one that maximizes or minimizes the objective function subject to the constraints. One interesting feature about the LP model is that the solution can be found at one of the corner solutions of the constraint region so that not all possible solutions must be examined. Since only a finite number of corner solutions exists in the feasible region, it only takes a computer a relatively small amount of time to find the optimal solution.

Four general classes of business problems are well suited for the LP model. Product mix is a problem situation where the attempt is to combine limited resources to maximize profit. Staff scheduling problems try to meet staffing needs at minimum cost. Optimal routing problems attempt to ship goods from sources to demand points at minimum cost. Lockbox problems fit into this problem classification. Finally, blending mixes of raw materials to meet blending requirements at minimum cost represents the fourth and last general class of business problems that are well suited for the LP model.

The formulation of the objective function for a linear programming application to lockbox application is basically a repeat of the total cost equation developed in the chapter as Equation 9.1. The primary difference here is that the equation is expressed as a total cost function for all customer groups $j$ and for all bank sites $k$.

$$\text{Minimize TC} = \sum_j \sum_k [(N_j \times F_j \times D_{jk} \times i) + (N_j \times V_k)]X_{jk} + \sum FC_k Y_k \qquad (9.1A)$$

Where:

$N_j$ = The number of checks remitted by customer $j$

$F_j$ = The face value of remittances by customer $j$

$D_{jk}$ = Collection float between customer $j$ and bank $k$

$i$ = Daily interest rate

$V_k$ = Variable cost for bank $k$

$X_{jk}$ = 0,1 Variable for customer/bank relationship

$FC_k$ = Dollar fixed cost for bank $k$

$Y_k$ = 0,1 Variable for whether or not a bank is active

The solution or decision variables are $X_{jk}$ and $Y_k$. The $X$'s represent the allocation of customers, $j$, among the banks, $k$; the $Y$'s indicate which banks are included in the optimal solution.

Another characteristic of a linear or integer programming formulation is that the objective function is optimized with respect to a set of constraints. In the case of a lockbox problem, the constraints are generally structured to ensure that all customer remittances are assigned to some lockbox site and that no customer remittances are assigned to a lockbox site that is not "open," that is, one that is not in the solution. For a lockbox solution, Equation 9.1A is minimized subject to the following set of constraints.

Subject to:

$$\sum_k X_{jk} = 1, j \in J \qquad (9.2A)$$

Constraint set 9.2A allows customer $j$ to be allocated to only one bank $k$. There are $J$ constraints, each one summing across $K$ banks.

$$\sum_k Y_k \leq Z \qquad (9.3A)$$

Constraint 9.3A sets the maximum number of bank sites chosen to be less than or equal to some arbitrarily chosen maximum of $Z$. At times, the user may wish to constrain the maximum number of lockbox sites. The model then solves for those sites yielding the minimum cost such that the number of lockbox sites is less than or equal to $Z$.

$$Y_k \in \{0,1\}, k \in K \qquad (9.4A)$$

Constraint set 9.4A specifies that a bank is either in the solution or out of the solution. A bank cannot partially be in the solution. It is either in or it is out. Rather than enter these constraints explicitly in the constraint matrix, the integer constraint is generally handled by special instructions to the optimization model.

$$X_{jk} \in \{0,1\}, j \in J, k \in K \qquad (9.5A)$$

Constraint set 9.5A specifies an integer solution for a customer allocation. There are $J \times K$ constraints such that a given customer's remittances are allocated to only one bank. Rather than enter these constraints explicitly in the constraint matrix, the integer constraint is generally handled by special instructions to the optimization model.

$$\sum_j X_{jk} \leq MY_k, \; k \in K \qquad (9.6A)$$

Constraint set 9.6A specifies that a lockbox bank $k$ must be open for customers to be assigned to it. $M$ is some arbitrary large number such as 100.

The format for the objective function and constraint matrix is shown in Exhibit 9A–1. The $V$ coefficients in the objective function represent the total variable costs related to each $X$. $X$ is a decision variable that has a solution of either zero or one and represents the customer allocation among the possible bank sites. The subscripts are the $jk$ subscripts in which $j$ is the index for the customer group and $k$ is the index for the bank site. $Y$ is a decision variable that also has a solution of zero or one indicating whether or not a bank site is chosen ($Y = 1$) or not chosen ($Y = 0$). The numbers in the body of the constraint matrix represent the coefficients for the variable in the respective column. Exhibit 9A–2 shows the format for the integer programming format using the data for the example problem developed in the chapter.

## PROBLEMS

9A-1. Develop the data matrix for Problem 6 at the end of the chapter. This problem had three bank sites and four customer groups. Solve this problem using an integer programming model.

9A-2. Develop the data matrix for Problem 7 at the end of the chapter. This problem had three bank sites and three customer groups. Solve this problem using an integer programming model.

**Exhibit 9A–1**

*Format of the Integer Progamming Data Matrix*

**Objective Function**

Minimize *TC*

$$V_{11}X_{11} + V_{12}X_{12} + V_{13}X_{13} + V_{21}X_{21} + V_{22}X_{22} + V_{23}X_{23} + V_{31}X_{31} + V_{32}X_{32} + V_{33}X_{33} + F_1Y_1 + F_2Y_2 + F_3Y_3$$

(Note: $V_{jk} = N_j \times F_j \times D_{jk} + N_jVC_k$ represents total variable cost for a given combination *jk*)

Subject to:

| $X_{11}$ | $X_{12}$ | $X_{13}$ | $X_{21}$ | $X_{22}$ | $X_{23}$ | $X_{31}$ | $X_{32}$ | $X_{33}$ | $Y_1$ | $Y_2$ | $Y_3$ | |
|---|---|---|---|---|---|---|---|---|---|---|---|---|
| 9A.2 | | | | | | | | | | | | |
| 1 | 1 | 1 | | | | | | | | | | = 1 |
| | | | 1 | 1 | 1 | | | | | | | = 1 |
| | | | | | | 1 | 1 | 1 | | | | = 1 |
| 9A.3 | | | | | | | | | | | | |
| 0 | 0 | 0 | 0 | 0 | 0 | 0 | 0 | 0 | 1 | 1 | 1 | ≤ Z |
| 9A.6 | | | | | | | | | | | | |
| 1 | | | 1 | | | 1 | | | −M | | | ≤ 0 |
| | 1 | | | 1 | | | 1 | | | −M | | ≤ 0 |
| | | 1 | | | 1 | | | 1 | | | −M | ≤ 0 |

## Exhibit 9A–2

*The Integer Progamming Data Matrix and Solution for the 3-Bank–3-Customer Group Problem*

Let $M = 100$
Let $Z = 3$

**Objective Function**

Minimize $TC$

$$3607X_{11} + 1550X_{12} + 532X_{13} + 552X_{21} + 1373X_{22} + 829X_{23} + 1646X_{31} + 413X_{32} + 826X_{33} + 275Y_1 + 200Y_2 + 150Y_3$$

Subject to:

| $X_{11}$ | $X_{12}$ | $X_{13}$ | $X_{21}$ | $X_{22}$ | $X_{23}$ | $X_{31}$ | $X_{32}$ | $X_{33}$ | $Y_1$ | $Y_2$ | $Y_3$ | |
|---|---|---|---|---|---|---|---|---|---|---|---|---|
| 9A.2 | | | | | | | | | | | | |
| 1 | 1 | 1 | | | | | | | | | | = 1 |
| | | | 1 | 1 | 1 | | | | | | | = 1 |
| | | | | | | 1 | 1 | 1 | | | | = 1 |
| 9A.3 | | | | | | | | | | | | |
| 0 | 0 | 0 | 0 | 0 | 0 | 0 | 0 | 0 | 1 | 1 | 1 | ≤ 3 |
| 9A.6 | | | | | | | | | | | | |
| 1 | | | 1 | | | 1 | | | −100 | | | ≤ 0 |
| | 1 | | | 1 | | | 1 | | | −100 | | ≤ 0 |
| | | 1 | | | 1 | | | 1 | | | −100 | ≤ 0 |

Solution:
$TC$ = $2,122
Customer Allocation: Customer 1 to Bank C, $X_{13} = 1$
Customer 2 to Bank A, $X_{21} = 1$
Customer 3 to Bank B, $X_{32} = 1$

$Y_1 = 1$
$Y_2 = 1$
$Y_3 = 1$

CHAPTER

# 10

# Cash Concentration

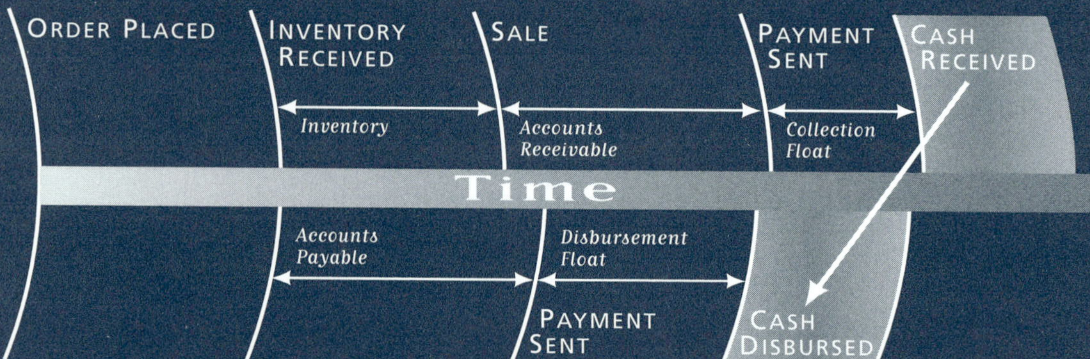

## OBJECTIVES

*After studying this chapter, you should be able to:*

- understand the need for a cash concentration system.
- formulate a cash transfer decision model.
- understand the advantages and disadvantages of the different cash transfer tools.

In the last chapter, we developed an efficient cash collection system that accomplished three things. First, it reduced mail float. Second, it reduced processing delays. Third, it reduced availability float. Given these benefits, the cash collection system, such as the lockbox system, leaves the cash manager with one problem. Multiple deposit accounts are now spread around the country. To combat this problem, the cash manager must design a system to concentrate these deposit balances into the company's major concentration bank or banks so that the collected balances can be used to fund disbursements or be invested.

**Cash concentration** is the process of moving dollar balances from deposit banks to concentration banks. A **concentration bank** receives balance transfers from several deposit or gathering banks. While a corporation's cash management system may have many deposit or collection banks, it generally has only a few concentration banks.

### FINANCIAL DILEMMA

How to Consolidate Collected Balances

The cash management consulting group from your lead bank has just completed a lockbox study of the cash collection system of Tri-Teck Products, Inc. The report suggests that Tri-Teck develop a lockbox collection system using five different lockbox banks. In the past, Tri-Teck has had all customers remit to corporate headquarters. However, the estimated savings in collection float, which translates into increased interest earnings from the additional invested funds generated by the suggested lockbox system, would be significant. The treasurer's office at Tri-Teck is now concerned about the lack of control treasury would have over the dispersed collection system. Tri-Teck's cash manager needs to know how to determine the dollar amount of daily receipts and how to get the funds out of the deposit banks and into the firm's disbursement and investment accounts. Certainly, there are costs and delays in getting the collected balances into usable accounts. Won't these costs and delays offset the benefits generated by the lockbox system?

## THE BASIC STRUCTURE OF A CASH CONCENTRATION SYSTEM

A typical cash concentration system would look very much like the pyramid shown in Exhibit 10–1. At the base of the pyramid are the scores of deposit banks connected with field offices or store outlets. In the middle of the pyramid are the several lockbox collection banks. Finally, at the top of the pyramid are the central or main corporate concentration banks. The funds transferred to these banks are to fund the firm's disbursement accounts with any surplus funds invested. From the base of the pyramid to the top of the pyramid is a continual flow of collected balances and deposit information.

### Cash Transfer Tools

Cash managers transfer funds from accounts at one bank to accounts at another bank using two basic methods. These two methods are:

- electronic depository transfer (EDT) and
- wire transfer.

Each transfer method has its own characteristics regarding cost and performance, and the cash manager

Exhibit 10–1

*A Typical Cash Concentration System*

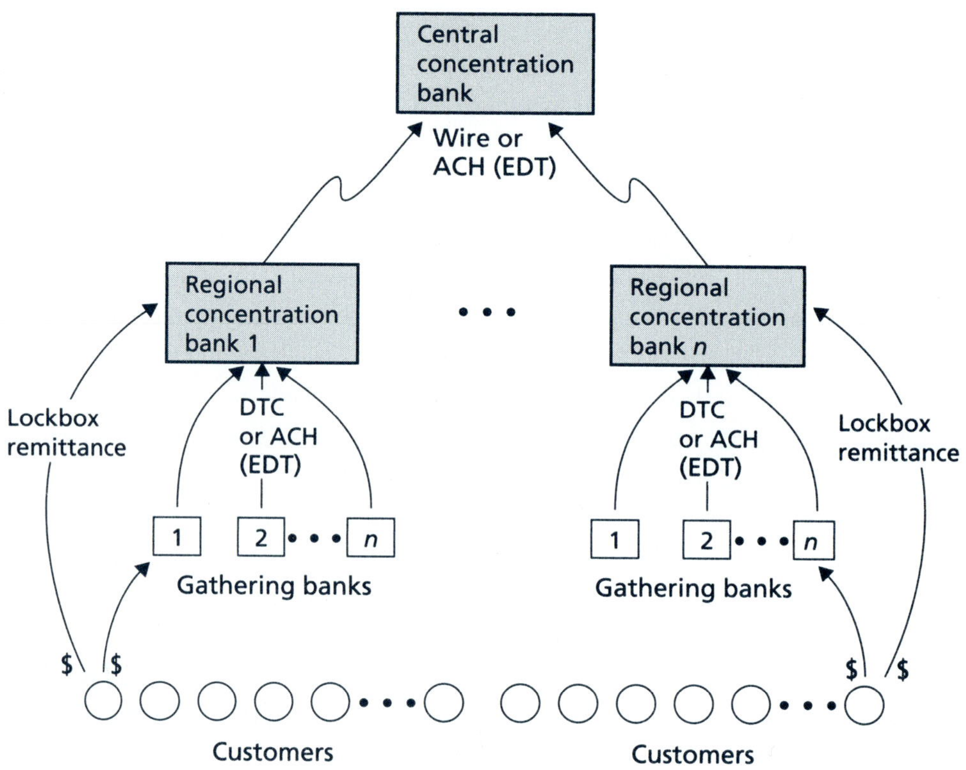


must exercise judgment in selecting the transfer method or combination of methods to properly balance the benefits and costs of each transfer instrument. The transfer instruments will be discussed separately.

Until recently, a third transfer tool called a depository transfer check was used. A **depository transfer check (DTC)** is a nonnegotiable, usually unsigned, check payable only to a single bank account at a particular bank. Firms used these checks to transfer balances from one bank to another. While the DTC was processed via the normal check processing channels, the local checks that were deposited cleared locally. By the time the DTC cleared back, the deposited checks would have cleared and balances were then transferred to the concentration bank. Each DTC cost $1 or more to use and was especially valuable when the dollar amount of funds to be transferred from one bank to another was relatively small, less than $3,000 to $5,000. However, since most banks are now ACH compatible, the DTC has largely disappeared.

*Electronic Depository Transfers (EDT)* An **electronic depository transfer (EDT)**, also known as an **ACH debit**, is handled through the automated clearinghouse network. Automated clearinghouse debit entries are now used in place of DTCs, and this transfer method has largely replaced the use of DTCs. In such a case, the cash manager authorizes the company's concentration bank to originate an ACH debit entry against the company's accounts at various gathering banks for a specified amount. When settlement occurs, one day is the norm, for the company's account at the concentration bank to be credited and for the local gathering bank account to be debited. The advantage of the EDT

**FOCUS ON PRACTICE**

In the early 1990s, treasury operations at International Paper Co. (IP) had become very decentralized as it had expanded its global operations with lots of bank accounts and some $60 million in idle cash balances. Management took aggressive steps to reorganize its treasury and cash management operations after an attempted fraudulent wire transfer was discovered. The first step involved slashing the number of overseas bank accounts from more than 500 to 300 resulting in fewer accounts, lower administration fees, and fewer transactions that yielded a savings of $400,000 per year.

Treasury established its global headquarters in Stamford, Connecticut, and four regional centers in Asia, Europe, Canada, and Latin America. To gain faster control over cash in Europe, IP applied daily zero-balancing concentration for euros and British pounds in accounts controlled by the Belgium coordination center. Fewer accounts systemwide made idle cash more obvious, and the increased investment of cash resources earned the company an additional $1.4 million in interest earnings.

*Source:* "Concentrated Excellence: International Paper Cuts Global Waste," *Treasury & Risk Management* (October 2003) pp. 36–37.

is that collected funds are available at the concentration bank the day after the ACH debit is originated, regardless of the location of the gathering bank.

*WIRE TRANSFERS* A **wire transfer** represents a real-time transfer of account balances. Historically, only bank employees could activate a wire transfer. Today, many treasury work stations allow cash managers to initiate a wire transfer via their own computer terminal. There are two drawbacks related to the use of wire transfers. First, they are relatively expensive. A fee is generally charged by the bank being debited as well as by the bank being credited with the transfer balance. The total charge can be as high as $20 for the complete transaction. Thus, the use of wires is best for larger balances. Second, because wires represent immediate transfer of funds, the deposited balances being transferred must be collected funds, not just ledger balances. Although EDTs clear more slowly, if the cleared EDT matches the availability of the deposited checks, then it is far superior to the wire because it is much cheaper and yields transferred funds as quickly as the wire, given the availability constraint.

### Initiation of the Cash Transfer

The previous section focused primarily on the transfer tools available for the transfer process. This section presents a more detailed look at the two different approaches to the transfer initiation process.

*DECENTRALIZED INITIATION* An example of a **decentralized transfer initiation** process is the field office or store manager who makes a deposit and who initiates the transfer. In this case, the amount of the transfer is generally the amount of the deposit.

*CENTRALIZED INITIATION* **Centralized transfer initiation** is an alternative system in which the timing and amount of the transfer are centralized either at the concentration bank or corporate headquarters. In this case, the field manager simply makes the deposit in the local bank and reports it via a third-party information vendor who transmits the data to the concentration bank and corporate headquarters.

Recently, the information retrieval process has become even more advanced. In some cases, the field offices' cash register terminals are scanned by the corporation's computers on a daily basis to determine the dollar amount of receipts. Thus, a telephone call by the local manager is not even necessary.

### Costs of Running a Concentration System

Three major cost categories are associated with running a cash concentration system. We will examine each of these cost categories separately.

*Opportunity Cost of Idle Balances* It is very difficult to always transfer the balance from the deposit bank to the concentration bank at the exact moment it becomes a collected balance. Deposits may consist of cash, checks of varying availability, and charge card vouchers. Given this variety of availability, it is quite common for idle balances to exist at the deposit bank. When idle balances do occur, they can be used to offset bank service charges.

*Transfer Costs* Actual charges for transferring balances vary, depending on the transfer instrument chosen. Exhibit 10–2 shows the range of charges that are generally associated with the two major transfer instruments. Wire transfers are more expensive, while EDTs are cheaper.

*Administrative Costs* Managing the concentration system is a major cash management responsibility. Receiving and reviewing deposit reports from the gathering banks, third-party information vendors, and concentration banks consume a portion of the cash manager's day. If overdrafts are created or some type of fraud is detected, returned checks are included in the deposit. Another administrative cost is associated with developing and maintaining a cash forecast system if transfer scheduling is based on anticipated deposits.

### Benefits Derived from the Concentration System

Significant benefits associated with a well-designed cash concentration system offset the costs we have just discussed.

*Economies of Scale* It is not efficient or profitable to leave small balances deposited in several deposit accounts spread around the country. It is much more economical to concentrate those balances into one or only a few **concentration accounts** so big blocks of funds can be invested at one time. The cash manager, with sizable funds to invest, can

**Exhibit 10–2**

*Service Charges for the Two Basic Transfer Instruments*

| | Cost per Transfer | Availability |
|---|---|---|
| Wire transfer | \$15–\$20 | Immediate |
| EDT | \$0.25* | One business day |

*Note: This represents the typical charge for just the transfer transaction. Depending on additional information services that the bank may need to perform related to the transfer, the cost may be higher.

find readily available investments in major markets yielding good rates. The field manager in charge of the local deposit account will find only very limited opportunities for short-term investment of balances.

*Enhanced Visibility and Control over Balances* Control is a major advantage afforded the company's cash manager by the cash concentration system. It is impossible for the company's cash manager to effectively control and manage the firm's cash balances if they are spread around the country in several hundred deposit accounts. A concentration system continually concentrates the geographically dispersed balances to a limited number of concentration accounts that are readily controlled by the cash manager.

*Possibility of Dual Balances* A **dual balance** is created when the transfer instrument granted availability at the concentration bank before the transfer instrument clears back against the deposit account. When this happens, the same collected balance exists at both banks. Thus, the cash manager has use of a balance that is twice the size of the transfer. Funds can be invested from the concentration account, and the balance at the original deposit bank remains as a collected balance that can be used to offset bank service charges. The ability for the concentration system to generate dual balances was much more prevalent when DTCs were widely used. Today, the increased efficiency of the payment system has significantly reduced the likelihood of dual balances existing so they are now of little value to the financial manager since they can't be predicted.

### The Future of Cash Concentration Systems

Much of what has been discussed thus far relates to concerns and issues facing the cash manager because of the fragmented banking and payment system that currently exists in the United States. As the banking and payment system evolves toward a nationwide branching system with a relatively small number of national banks, these inefficiencies will begin to disappear. The gathering banks will more likely be branches of the national bank chosen by the corporation. Rather than incurring the transfer and administrative costs involved in moving balances between separately incorporated banks, there will simply be debits and credits between accounts within the same banking organization. Instead of spending time on managing the cash concentration processes between separately incorporated banking institutions, the cash manager will likely focus on managing and improving information flows and forecasting cash flows. Nationwide banking systems, such as Bank of America, essentially incorporate zero-balance accounts at the different levels of the concentration system to daily move balances from the gathering banks to the final concentration accounts.

## CASH CONCENTRATION AND THE CASH FLOW TIMELINE

Exhibit 10–3 displays on a timeline the major time intervals related to cash concentration. Times T3, T5, and T6 are critical because these are the time periods when cash is actually affected by the concentration system. T3 is the time period at which collected balances are credited at the deposit bank. This may either be a lockbox bank or a field office deposit or gathering bank. Collected funds are credited at the concentration bank as a result of the cash transfer at time period T5. Collected funds are debited from the original bank deposit account at time period T6. T6 can come after T5, be contemporaneous with T5, or even come before T5. The normal situation is for T5 to occur contemporaneous with T6. Dual balances are created when T5 occurs before T6.

Exhibit 10–3

*Cash Concentration and the Cash Flow Timeline*

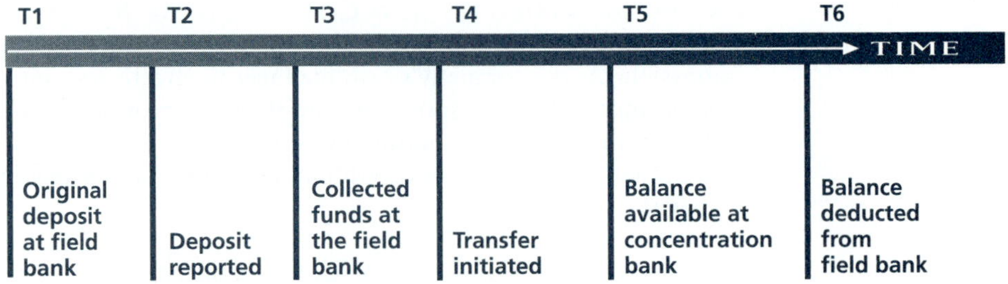


T1 – T3: Availability granted by deposit bank.
T1 – T2: Efficiency and structure of concentration system.
T2 – T4: Efficiency and structure of concentration system.
T4 – T5: Type of transfer mechanism chosen and availability granted by the concentration bank.
T5 – T6: If the balance is deducted from the gathering bank after the balance is available at the concentration bank, then a dual balance is created. Dual balances are generally created by inefficiencies in the payment system.

## CASH TRANSFER SCHEDULING

Several factors complicate the decisions of when to transfer balances and how much to transfer at a time. First, daily deposits generally fluctuate. Second, the deposits may consist of a mixture of currency and checks with immediate, 1-day, or 2-day availability. The deferred availability on a part of the deposit causes the ledger and collected balance to be different, and only collected balances can be transferred. A third complicating factor is the time delay in the transfer instrument and the problem of matching that delay with the availability schedule of the deposits. Fourth, weekends cause a problem in that Friday's ending balances are carried over the weekend and deposits made during the weekend are not credited to the account until Monday. Also, weekends cause delays to occur in clearing the transfer instrument. Finally, two cost trade-offs must be considered: the differences in the cost of each transfer instrument and the differences in the time required to transfer a cash balance. The two types of transfer instruments have very different costs. Wire transfers, which grant immediate availability, are the most expensive; and EDTs, which grant 1-day availability, are the cheapest.

### Calculating the Minimum Balance to Transfer

The higher the cost of the transfer instrument, the larger the balance must be to make the transfer cost effective. Any collected balance that remains in the deposit account incurs an opportunity cost. However, these balances can be used to cover bank service charges through the earnings credit rate (ECR). While the ECR is generally lower than the firm's opportunity investment rate, especially considering the allowance made for the reserve requirement, at least some benefit is derived from collected balances remaining in the deposit accounts.

A simple break-even equation for this aspect of the transfer problem can be developed as shown in Equation 10.1. This equation is derived from the incremental benefit relationship that calculates the incremental benefit of transferring a balance quicker, using one transfer method versus a slower method. Then, Equation 10.1 is developed by setting the incremental benefit relationship equal to the incremental cost of the faster transfer method relative to the alternative slower method.

$$\text{Incremental benefit} = DS \times [k - ECR \times (1 - rr)] \times TBAL$$

Where: $DS$ = The number of days saved with the faster transfer method

$k$ = The firm's investment opportunity rate

$ECR$ = The bank's earnings credit rate

$rr$ = The required reserve rate, generally 12 percent

$TBAL$ = The balance to be transferred

Next, set incremental cost equal to the relationship for incremental benefit.

$$\text{Incremental cost} = \text{Incremental benefit}$$

$$\text{Incremental cost} = DS \times [k - ECR \times (1 - rr)] \times TBAL$$

Finally, solving this equation for TBAL results in the minimum balance required justifying the higher cost transfer instrument:

$$TBAL = \frac{\text{Incremental cost}}{DS \times [k - ECR \times (1 - rr)]} \tag{10.1}$$

Notice that instead of using just the investment opportunity rate, the difference between the investment opportunity rate and the reserve adjusted earnings credit rate is used since collected balances at the deposit bank can earn the earnings credit rate. Of course, this would only be the case once the transferred balances caused the remaining balance to fall below the required balance to compensate the bank for its services. If the balances being transferred are simply excess balances, then the effective ECR is zero and thus irrelevant.

To see how to apply this equation, assume that the financial manager is trying to decide between using a wire transfer and an EDT. The costs of these transfer instruments were shown in Exhibit 10–2. Assume that the firm's opportunity investment rate is 10 percent, the ECR is 8 percent, the EDT takes one day longer to clear, and the reserve requirement is 12 percent. Entering these data into Equation 10.1 results in the minimum balance that must be transferred to justify the incremental cost.

$$TBAL = \frac{\$19.75}{1 \times [0.10 - 0.08 \times (1 - 0.12)]/365}$$

$$TBAL = \$243{,}538.85$$

This balance seems large because the wire transfer only yields a 1-day advantage, and the return is only the increment over the reserve adjusted ECR. If the balance did not earn the ECR, then recalculating Equation 10.1 with ECR = 0 results in a break-even transfer balance of only $72,087.50.

$$TBAL = \frac{\$19.75}{1 \times [0.10 - 0 \times (1 - 0.12)]/365}$$

$$TBAL = \$72{,}087.50$$

## The Transfer Scheduling Decision

The objective of the cash transfer scheduling decision is to minimize cash concentration costs while adequately compensating the deposit banks. The cash concentration costs include the cost of the transfer instrument, generally a fixed charge per transfer, and the costs associated with excess collected balances remaining at the deposit bank. The total cost of the transfer scheduling decision can be expressed as Equation 10.2.

$$\begin{aligned} \text{Total cost} &= FEE + \left(k \times \{ACB - [(SC - FEE)/ECR(1 - rr)]\}\right) \\ &= FEE + [k \times (ACB - RCB)] \end{aligned} \quad (10.2)$$

Where: $FEE$ = The amount of the total service charge, SC, that is paid through fees

SC = The bank service charge related to transfer activity (equal to the charge per transfer times the number of transfers)

$k$ = The firm's investment opportunity rate

$ACB$ = The average collected balance at the gathering bank resulting from the transfer scheduling decision

$RCB$ = The required collected balance to be maintained at the deposit bank to compensate the bank for those services not paid by fees [$RCB = (SC - FEE)/ECR(1 - rr)$]

## FINANCIAL DILEMMA REVISITED

The application of this total cost equation will now be applied to the Tri-Teck problem mentioned in the Management Dilemma at the beginning of the chapter. Exhibit 10–4 presents the daily deposits made at each of the firm's lockbox banks. Tri-Teck's cash manager now must transfer those deposited balances to the firm's lead corporate bank where the major disbursement accounts are located. Two different daily deposit structures will be considered as shown in Exhibit 10–4. The situation presented as Case 1 assumes that deposits occur evenly throughout the week, while Case 2 assumes that daily deposits vary. Note that the total weekly deposits are the same in both cases. Further assume that the cost of an EDT is \$0.25 per transfer and that Tri-Teck's investment opportunity rate is 10 percent.

To understand the basic complexities of the cash transfer scheduling problem, we will apply one of the most basic scheduling rules, transfer daily the dollar amount of the daily deposit, under differing structural assumptions. The **daily transfer rule** is applied to situations involving weekend bank processing and no weekend bank processing; immediate deposit availability and deferred deposit availability; and finally, cash transfers with immediate availability and cash transfers with 1-day availability.

### Exhibit 10–4

*Tri-Teck's Daily Deposits*

| Day of the Week | Case 1 | Case 2 |
|---|---|---|
| Monday | \$ 5,000 | \$ 3,000 |
| Tuesday | 5,000 | 2,500 |
| Wednesday | 5,000 | 5,000 |
| Thursday | 5,000 | 7,000 |
| Friday | 5,000 | 5,500 |
| Saturday | 5,000 | 8,000 |
| Sunday | 5,000 | 4,000 |
| Total | \$35,000 | \$35,000 |
| Daily average | \$ 5,000 | \$ 5,000 |

***Daily Transfer Rule*** This is the simplest and most common transfer rule of the three we will review. The rule is to initiate a daily transfer from the deposit bank to the concentration bank in the amount of the daily deposit. Several factors that complicate the transfer of funds include:

- weekend bank processing schedules,
- availability schedule for deposit items, and
- type of transfer instrument and delay in transfer.

Exhibit 10–5 applies the daily transfer rule to the Case 1 deposit schedule shown earlier in Exhibit 10–4 assuming that banks process items seven days a week, that the total deposit is immediately available, and that the transfer of funds is accomplished on the same day it is initiated. As a result, the deposit availability matches exactly the transfer schedule leaving a zero ledger and a zero available balance. This would necessitate the compensation of the bank for its banking services through the payment of fees since no balances are maintained.

Exhibit 10–6 applies Case 1 deposit data under the same assumptions with the exception that there is no weekend bank processing. The only difference in this situation is that the firm loses interest on the deposits made during the weekend since the bank does not process the deposits. However, on Monday, when the weekend deposits are credited to the account, they are immediately transferred along with Monday's regular deposit.

Exhibit 10–7 applies the Case 1 deposit schedule to the daily transfer rule assuming weekend processing, immediately available funds from deposit but the transfer is delayed one day. The result is that a $5,000 balance is maintained in the ledger and collected funds

**Exhibit 10–5**

*Worksheet for Case 1 Deposit Structure*

| | | Availability | | | | Ending Balances | |
|---|---|---|---|---|---|---|---|
| Day of Week | Daily Deposit | Immediate | 1-Day | 2-Day | Transfers | Ledger | Collected |
| Sunday | | | | | | | |
| Monday | $5,000 | $5,000 | $0 | $0 | $(5,000) | $0 | $0 |
| Tuesday | 5,000 | 5,000 | 0 | 0 | (5,000) | 0 | 0 |
| Wednesday | 5,000 | 5,000 | 0 | 0 | (5,000) | 0 | 0 |
| Thursday | 5,000 | 5,000 | 0 | 0 | (5,000) | 0 | 0 |
| Friday | 5,000 | 5,000 | 0 | 0 | (5,000) | 0 | 0 |
| Saturday | 5,000 | 5,000 | 0 | 0 | (5,000) | 0 | 0 |
| Sunday | 5,000 | 5,000 | 0 | 0 | (5,000) | 0 | 0 |
| Beginning of steady state: | | | | | | | |
| Monday | $5,000 | $5,000 | $0 | $0 | $(5,000) | $0 | $0 |
| Tuesday | 5,000 | 5,000 | 0 | 0 | (5,000) | 0 | 0 |
| Wednesday | 5,000 | 5,000 | 0 | 0 | (5,000) | 0 | 0 |
| Thursday | 5,000 | 5,000 | 0 | 0 | (5,000) | 0 | 0 |
| Friday | 5,000 | 5,000 | 0 | 0 | (5,000) | 0 | 0 |
| Saturday | 5,000 | 5,000 | 0 | 0 | (5,000) | 0 | 0 |
| Sunday | 5,000 | 5,000 | 0 | 0 | (5,000) | 0 | 0 |
| Average, 2nd week | | | | | | $0 | $0 |

## Exhibit 10–6

*Worksheet for Case 1 Deposit Structure: No Weekend Processing*

| | | Availability | | | | Ending Balances | |
|---|---|---|---|---|---|---|---|
| Day of Week | Daily Deposit | Immediate | 1-Day | 2-Day | Transfers | Ledger | Collected |
| Sunday | | | | | | | |
| Monday | $ 5,000 | $ 5,000 | $0 | $0 | $ (5,000) | $0 | $0 |
| Tuesday | 5,000 | 5,000 | 0 | 0 | (5,000) | 0 | 0 |
| Wednesday | 5,000 | 5,000 | 0 | 0 | (5,000) | 0 | 0 |
| Thursday | 5,000 | 5,000 | 0 | 0 | (5,000) | 0 | 0 |
| Friday | 5,000 | 5,000 | 0 | 0 | (5,000) | 0 | 0 |
| Saturday | 0 | 0 | 0 | 0 | 0 | 0 | 0 |
| Sunday | 0 | 0 | 0 | 0 | 0 | 0 | 0 |
| Beginning of steady state: | | | | | | | |
| Monday | $15,000 | $15,000 | $0 | $0 | $(15,000) | $0 | $0 |
| Tuesday | 5,000 | 5,000 | 0 | 0 | (5,000) | 0 | 0 |
| Wednesday | 5,000 | 5,000 | 0 | 0 | (5,000) | 0 | 0 |
| Thursday | 5,000 | 5,000 | 0 | 0 | (5,000) | 0 | 0 |
| Friday | 5,000 | 5,000 | 0 | 0 | (5,000) | 0 | 0 |
| Saturday | 0 | 0 | 0 | 0 | 0 | 0 | 0 |
| Sunday | 0 | 0 | 0 | 0 | 0 | 0 | 0 |
| Average, 2nd week | | | | | | $0 | $0 |

accounts. The firm is losing interest on a perpetual $5,000 balance as a result of the discrepancy between the availability schedule for the deposit items and the availability schedule for the transfer item.

Exhibit 10–8 continues with the assumption of the 1-day delay in the transfer clearing but assumes no weekend bank processing. The major impact is the increase in the collected balance account on Monday from $5,000 to $15,000, resulting in an average weekly collected balance of $6,428 versus $5,000. Daily transfers become costly as deposit availability exceeds transfer clearing time. Lack of weekend processing causes increased opportunity costs as the time discrepancy increases.

Exhibit 10–9 maintains the same transfer schedule and no weekend processing but changes the deposit availability schedule so that only $2,500 (or 50 percent) is immediately available and $2,500 (or 50 percent) has 1-day availability. The impact is to reduce the average collected balance because the availability of the deposit more closely matches the availability of the transfer item. In fact, Exhibit 10–9 demonstrates that if the entire deposit had 1-day availability then the ledger balance would generally be $5,000 and the collected balance would generally be zero.

The total cost for the daily transfer rule for Case 1, based on the assumptions in Exhibit 10–9, is computed on page 356. To compute the total cost, based on Equation 10.2, we further assume that the ECR is 8 percent per year and the reserve requirement is 12 percent. The firm compensates the bank with balances and thus pays no fees. This makes sense based on the average collected balances left in the gathering bank. The required collected balance (RCB) is equal to $\$923.30 = (5 \times \$0.25)/[(0.08/52) \times (1 - 0.12)]$.

## Exhibit 10–7

*Worksheet for Case 1 Deposit Structure: Transfer Clearing Delay*

| Day of Week | Daily Deposit | Availability: Immediate | 1-Day | 2-Day | Transfers | Ending Balances: Ledger | Collected |
|---|---|---|---|---|---|---|---|
| Sunday | | | | | | | |
| Monday | $5,000 | $5,000 | $0 | $0 | $ 0 | **$5,000** | **$5,000** |
| Tuesday | 5,000 | 5,000 | 0 | 0 | (5,000) | **5,000** | **5,000** |
| Wednesday | 5,000 | 5,000 | 0 | 0 | (5,000) | **5,000** | **5,000** |
| Thursday | 5,000 | 5,000 | 0 | 0 | (5,000) | **5,000** | **5,000** |
| Friday | 5,000 | 5,000 | 0 | 0 | (5,000) | **5,000** | **5,000** |
| Saturday | 5,000 | 5,000 | 0 | 0 | (5,000) | **5,000** | **5,000** |
| Sunday | 5,000 | 5,000 | 0 | 0 | (5,000) | **5,000** | **5,000** |
| Beginning of steady state: | | | | | | | |
| Monday | $5,000 | $5,000 | $0 | $0 | $(5,000) | **$5,000** | **$5,000** |
| Tuesday | 5,000 | 5,000 | 0 | 0 | (5,000) | **5,000** | **5,000** |
| Wednesday | 5,000 | 5,000 | 0 | 0 | (5,000) | **5,000** | **5,000** |
| Thursday | 5,000 | 5,000 | 0 | 0 | (5,000) | **5,000** | **5,000** |
| Friday | 5,000 | 5,000 | 0 | 0 | (5,000) | **5,000** | **5,000** |
| Saturday | 5,000 | 5,000 | 0 | 0 | (5,000) | **5,000** | **5,000** |
| Sunday | 5,000 | 5,000 | 0 | 0 | (5,000) | **5,000** | **5,000** |
| Average, 2nd week | | | | | | **$5,000** | **$5,000** |

## Exhibit 10–8

*Worksheet for Case 1 Deposit Structure: No Weekend Processing, Transfer Clearing Delay*

| Day of Week | Daily Deposit | Availability: Immediate | 1-Day | 2-Day | Transfers | Ending Balances: Ledger | Collected |
|---|---|---|---|---|---|---|---|
| Sunday | | | | | | | |
| Monday | $ 5,000 | $ 5,000 | $0 | $0 | $ 0 | $ 5,000 | $ 5,000 |
| Tuesday | 5,000 | 5,000 | 0 | 0 | (5,000) | 5,000 | 5,000 |
| Wednesday | 5,000 | 5,000 | 0 | 0 | (5,000) | 5,000 | 5,000 |
| Thursday | 5,000 | 5,000 | 0 | 0 | (5,000) | 5,000 | 5,000 |
| Friday | 5,000 | 5,000 | 0 | 0 | (5,000) | 5,000 | 5,000 |
| Saturday | 0 | 0 | 0 | 0 | 0 | 5,000 | 5,000 |
| Sunday | 0 | 0 | 0 | 0 | 0 | 5,000 | 5,000 |
| Beginning of steady state: | | | | | | | |
| Monday | $15,000 | $15,000 | $0 | $0 | $ (5,000) | **$15,000** | **$15,000** |
| Tuesday | 5,000 | 5,000 | 0 | 0 | (15,000) | 5,000 | 5,000 |
| Wednesday | 5,000 | 5,000 | 0 | 0 | (5,000) | 5,000 | 5,000 |
| Thursday | 5,000 | 5,000 | 0 | 0 | (5,000) | 5,000 | 5,000 |
| Friday | 5,000 | 5,000 | 0 | 0 | (5,000) | 5,000 | 5,000 |
| Saturday | 0 | 0 | 0 | 0 | 0 | 5,000 | 5,000 |
| Sunday | 0 | 0 | 0 | 0 | 0 | 5,000 | 5,000 |
| Average, 2nd week | | | | | | **$ 6,428** | **$ 6,428** |

**Exhibit 10–9**

*Worksheet for Case 1 Deposit Structure: No Weekend Processing, Deposit Availability Delay, Transfer Clearing Delay*

| Day of Week | Daily Deposit | Availability Immediate | Availability 1-Day | Availability 2-Day | Transfers | Ending Balances Ledger | Ending Balances Collected |
|---|---|---|---|---|---|---|---|
| Sunday | | | | | | | |
| Monday | $ 5,000 | **$2,500** | $ 0 | $0 | $ 0 | $ 5,000 | $2,500 |
| Tuesday | 5,000 | **2,500** | **2,500** | 0 | (5,000) | 5,000 | 2,500 |
| Wednesday | 5,000 | **2,500** | **2,500** | 0 | (5,000) | 5,000 | 2,500 |
| Thursday | 5,000 | **2,500** | **2,500** | 0 | (5,000) | 5,000 | 2,500 |
| Friday | 5,000 | **2,500** | **2,500** | 0 | (5,000) | 5,000 | 2,500 |
| Saturday | 0 | 0 | 0 | 0 | 0 | 5,000 | 2,500 |
| Sunday | 0 | 0 | 0 | 0 | 0 | 5,000 | 2,500 |
| Beginning of steady state: | | | | | | | |
| Monday | $15,000 | **$7,500** | **$2,500** | $0 | $ (5,000) | $15,000 | $7,500 |
| Tuesday | 5,000 | **2,500** | **7,500** | 0 | (15,000) | 5,000 | 2,500 |
| Wednesday | 5,000 | **2,500** | **2,500** | 0 | (5,000) | 5,000 | 2,500 |
| Thursday | 5,000 | **2,500** | **2,500** | 0 | (5,000) | 5,000 | 2,500 |
| Friday | 5,000 | **2,500** | **2,500** | 0 | (5,000) | 5,000 | 2,500 |
| Saturday | 0 | 0 | 0 | 0 | 0 | 5,000 | 2,500 |
| Sunday | 0 | 0 | 0 | 0 | 0 | 5,000 | 2,500 |
| Average, 2nd week | | | | | | $ 6,428 | $3,214 |

The total 1-week cost of the cash transfer system is $4.41, as shown in the following computation.

$$\text{Total cost} = (0.10/52) \times (\$3{,}214 - \$923.30)$$
$$= \$4.41$$

The daily transfer rule applied to Case 2, shown in Exhibit 10–10, is presented for the situation with no weekend processing and deferred availability on the deposits and transfer instrument. Note that a low collected balance of $1,250 occurs on Tuesday and a high collected balance of $7,500 occurs on Monday. When daily deposits vary, the cash manager must be careful to make sure that the amount requested to be transferred does not exceed the dollar amount of collected balances at the time the transfer clears.

MANAGING ABOUT A TARGET Rather than making daily transfers, the **managing about a target rule** makes only one transfer for several days of deposits. This rule is particularly appropriate when a firm has a target collected balance it is trying to maintain in the deposit bank.

Initially, the firm transfers its balance out of the deposit account and thus begins with a zero balance. Then it lets the deposits accumulate until the average daily balance hits the target balance. The accumulated balance is then transferred to the concentration account. This transfer rule has two advantages. First, it allows the firm to make a 1-time transfer out of the deposit account at the time the rule is initiated. Assuming that an initial balance exists, this money represents a permanent 1-time interest earning opportunity for the firm. Second, this rule can reduce the dollar amount of transfer costs because of the reduced number of transfers while maintaining the target balance.

## Exhibit 10–10

*Worksheet for Case 2 Deposit Structure: No Weekend Processing, Deferred Availability on Deposits and Transfers*

| | | Availability | | | | Ending Balances | |
|---|---|---|---|---|---|---|---|
| Day of Week | Daily Deposit | Immediate | 1-Day | 2-Day | Transfers | Ledger | Collected |
| Sunday | | | | | | | |
| Monday | $ 3,000 | $1,500 | $ 0 | $0 | $ 0 | $ 3,000 | $1,500 |
| Tuesday | 2,500 | 1,250 | 1,500 | 0 | (3,000) | 2,500 | **1,250** |
| Wednesday | 5,000 | 2,500 | 1,250 | 0 | (2,500) | 5,000 | 2,500 |
| Thursday | 7,000 | 3,500 | 2,500 | 0 | (5,000) | 7,000 | 3,500 |
| Friday | 5,500 | 2,750 | 3,500 | 0 | (7,000) | 5,500 | 2,750 |
| Saturday | 0 | 0 | 0 | 0 | 0 | 5,500 | 2,750 |
| Sunday | 0 | 0 | 0 | 0 | 0 | 5,500 | 2,750 |
| Beginning of steady state: | | | | | | | |
| Monday | $15,000 | $7,500 | $2,750 | $0 | $ (5,500) | $15,000 | **$7,500** |
| Tuesday | 2,500 | 1,250 | 7,500 | 0 | (15,000) | 2,500 | **1,250** |
| Wednesday | 5,000 | 2,500 | 1,250 | 0 | (2,500) | 5,000 | 2,500 |
| Thursday | 7,000 | 3,500 | 2,500 | 0 | (5,000) | 7,000 | 3,500 |
| Friday | 5,500 | 2,750 | 3,500 | 0 | (7,000) | 5,500 | 2,750 |
| Saturday | 0 | 0 | 0 | 0 | 0 | 5,500 | 2,750 |
| Sunday | 0 | 0 | 0 | 0 | 0 | 5,500 | 2,750 |
| Average, 2nd week | | | | | | $ 6,571 | $3,286 |

ANTICIPATION The **anticipation rule** initiates a transfer before the related deposit is made. This rule is very helpful for those cases where the deposits have a shorter availability than the transfer instrument thus better matching the clearing of the transfer instrument with the availability of the deposit. As we saw with the daily transfer rule using the Case 1 data, the more closely matched the deposit availability is to the availability of the transfer item the lower will be the average collected balance that remains in the deposit account.

While anticipatory transfers can reduce balances, additional costs must be considered. First, additional administrative costs are incurred due to the forecasting system that is required. Second, this type of transfer system is riskier. The dollar amount of the transfer is based on a forecast, which may be different from the actual deposit. As a result, the potential for overdrafts is increased. The likelihood of incurring overdraft costs must be taken into consideration.

WEEKEND TIMING As we have seen, the lack of weekend processing by banks causes a great deal of inefficiency when the cash manager is attempting to minimize the collected balances that remain in the deposit bank. **Weekend balances** should be a critical factor in deciding which transfer rule to use. Under the current U.S. banking system, closing balances on Friday are carried over until Monday. In addition, deposits made during the weekend are not credited to the account until Monday. This means that if Friday's closing balance is expected to be an excess balance, that balance has a 3-day impact. When choosing a transfer rule, the cash manager should consider the impact of Friday balances on the calculated average balance so that excess compensation is avoided.

## E.F. HUTTON: A SYSTEM THAT LOST CONTROL[1]

E.F. Hutton's basic cash concentration system design was the typical cash concentration system shown earlier in Exhibit 10–1. In the early 1980s, Hutton had approximately 400 branch offices located in all parts of the United States. It was common for these offices to receive payments from customers on a regular basis. Therefore, at the bottom of the cash concentration pyramid were the 400 gathering banks. In the middle of the pyramid were a smaller number of regional concentration banks, some of which would be the same bank as one of the gathering banks located in a larger city. At the top of the pyramid were two national concentration banks, one located in Los Angeles and the other in New York.

The cashier at the local office would call the regional cashier with the amount of daily deposits adjusted by an approved formula. Because the clearing of checks in the local deposit bank did not always match with the clearing of the concentration instrument, and because some of the daily deposits contained immediately available items, an adjustment was made in the amount to be transferred to reduce or prevent excess compensation. The formula took this into account so that Hutton would be able to draw down these excess balances. The regional cashier would then deposit a DTC in the regional concentration account. Later the same day, the regional cashier would call the national cash desk and another DTC would be created between one of the two national concentration banks and the regional concentration banks. In this way, balances were continually being transferred from the 400 deposit banks through the regional concentration banks to one of the two national concentration accounts.

Although the basic system just described is very typical and legal, some of Hutton's branch managers began to modify the system. Hutton's branch managers received bonuses based on interest earnings. If a branch could generate additional balances, interest earnings would increase, creating a larger bonus for the branch manager. So, during the early 1980s, some of the branch managers began to modify the formula which determined the size of the cash transfer. In addition, they revised the concentration system design to create multiple transfers in order to more likely generate dual balances. They began to transfer balances among some of the gathering banks on the way to one of the concentration banks.

In 1985, Hutton pleaded guilty in Federal Court to two charges, excessive drawdowns and multiple transfers. When the legal charges were made public, many corporate cash managers became concerned that their cash concentration practices would be seen as illegal. Perhaps one of the biggest concerns focused on the creation of a DTC for an amount different from the related deposit. This is a typical type of activity and is the only way that a cash manager can effectively manage the amount of compensation being paid for bank services. Although the basic practice was deemed appropriate as long as the DTC amount is based on the deposit or the excess balances at the bank, the legal proceedings made it very clear that cash managers should have a written document drawn up with their banks regarding how overdrafts of collected funds will be handled. Many of Hutton's accounts at smaller banks were consistently overdrawn on a collected balance basis, and the banks did not have accounting control systems sophisticated enough to be able to monitor the situation. In fact, Hutton admitted to fraudulently obtaining the use of more than $1 bil-

[1] "What Did Hutton's Managers Know—and When Did They Know It?" *Business Week* (May 20, 1985).
"When E.F. Hutton's Caught, Treasurers Listen," *CASHFLOW* (July/August 1985).
"Post-Hutton Lessons in How to Manage Corporate Cash," *Fortune* (November 11, 1985), p. 134.
"Editorial: Learning from the E.F. Hutton Experience," *Journal of Cash Management* (July/August 1985), pp. 12, 80.
"E.F. Hutton: Reactions and Commentary," *Journal of Cash Management* (July/August 1985), pp. 14–21.
Various issues of the *Leahy Newsletter*.

lion in interest-free funds through its concentration system over the 2-year period that this activity took place.

This case also prompted the Association for Financial Professionals, then known as the National Association of Corporate Cash Managers, to draft a code of conduct for its members. The code is shown in Exhibit 10–11. The second bullet under Integrity of this code relates directly to the Hutton case by stating that the cash manager should, "Avoid intentional abuse of the banking system . . ."[2]

## CASH CONCENTRATION: THE CANADIAN EXPERIENCE[3]

A review of the banking structure and the cash concentration system of Canada may give some insight into where the U.S. banking system might be headed.

**Exhibit 10–11**

*Code of Conduct for the Association for Financial Professionals*

# AFP Standards of Ethical Conduct

The conduct of **Association for Financial Professionals (AFP)** members and/or certified professionals has a direct effect on the reputation of the finance profession. A good reputation is earned on a continuing basis by conducting one's business with competence, appropriate confidentiality, integrity, and by knowledge of and compliance with applicable laws or regulations. **AFP** members and/or certified professionals, therefore, have an obligation to their employers, colleagues, customers, profession and themselves to maintain the highest standards of conduct and to encourage their peers to do the same.

***COMPETENCE***

- Maintain an appropriate level of knowledge and skill in the finance profession
- Perform professional duties in accordance with legal, regulatory, and technical practices in the finance profession

***CONFIDENTIALITY***

- Refrain from disclosing confidential information acquired in the course of professional activities unless legally obligated to do so
- Refrain from using confidential information for unethical or illegal advantage either personally or through third parties

***INTEGRITY***

- Refrain from participating in any activity that would hinder one's ability to carry out professional responsibilities competently, honestly and fairly while avoiding conflicts of interest
- Refrain from intentional abuses of financial systems and markets
- Disclose to relevant parties all information that could reasonably be expected to influence business dealings or decisions
- Refrain from using the Certified Cash Manager (CCM) or any other **AFP** professional designation unless the certification is properly achieved and currently active

***Association for Financial Professionals***

***AFP reserves the right to take appropriate disciplinary action for any breach of these standards.***

*Approved by the Certified Cash Manager (CCM) Committee, March 2000*



---

[2] Code of Ethics for Certified Cash Managers.

[3] Mohsen Anvari, "Alternative Cash Concentration Systems in Canada: An Example of National Banking," *Journal of Cash Management* (June/July 1983), pp. 48–56.

Until 1980, the Canadian banking system consisted of no more than 12 national banks. Revisions in the Bank Act during the early eighties relaxed chartering restrictions so that there are now over 60 banks. Many of the new banks are foreign owned. The original 12 banks, primarily the largest five, dominate the cash concentration effort used by corporations operating in Canada because of their extensive network of branches.

Compared to the current U.S. system, the Canadian payment system is remarkably efficient. Due to their large scale of business, these five major banks have invested in very efficient communications and computer systems that link their branches nationwide. Thus, intrabank check clearing and balance transfers are generally handled on an immediate availability basis. Even interbank clearings are handled in a similarly efficient manner. The Bank of Canada, the country's central bank, assumes no float responsibilities.

Canadian banks and their customers are not encumbered by many of the restrictions common in the U.S. system. For example, there are no interest restrictions on deposits. Therefore, even small deposit balances held at remote branches can earn interest before they are concentrated. Also, overdraft privileges are common, reducing the problem of transfers clearing against insufficient collected balances.

Cash concentration systems include a telephone transfer system, which results in immediate availability of funds. In addition, an automatic transfer system (ATS) is used only for branches within the same bank. A company can specify a wide variety of automated decision rules that are time based, such as once a day, every other day, etc.; or it may be balance based such as setting a trigger level so that once it is reached a prespecified balance is transferred. Finally, Canada has a paperless concentration system that is terminal based. A cash concentration order is entered through the terminal to the company's bank to transfer a specified balance from a deposit account at a branch to a concentration account located at the company's main branch.

One service that reduces the need for cash concentration is the availability of off-set balances. Off-set balances allow companies to specify a group of accounts at different branches to be treated by the bank's accounting system as a single account.

Currently, the U.S. banking system has over 10,000 individually chartered banks. Historically, we have been a country of unit banks, but given the banking crisis in the eighties, we are slowly evolving into a large regional branch banking system. This evolution has been somewhat by default as the Fed has sold insolvent banks to stronger out-of-state banks. As the evolution continues, we may keep our eyes on our neighbor to the north for clues of the cash concentration systems that may evolve as the U.S. banking system moves toward a national branching system.

## SUMMARY

As a financial manager attempts to reduce collection float through the development of a lockbox collection system, a cash concentration system becomes essential in moving the collected deposit balances to banks where the balances can be better managed. An effective cash concentration system provides deposit information to the corporate cash manager that is critical if the cash manager is going to effectively manage the firm's daily liquidity. The improved deposit information allows the cash manager to move the accumulating balances from the original banks of deposit to fewer deposit accounts of greater balances so that the funds can be managed more efficiently.

This chapter discussed the structure of a cash concentration system and emphasized the cost components and benefits. The chapter also developed an objective function for the cash transfer scheduling problem. Three basic transfer scheduling rules were discussed including daily transfer, managing about a target, and anticipation. The problems of weekend timing were also noted.

The chapter concluded by comparing the cash concentration characteristics of the Canadian banking system with those of the U.S. banking system. As the U.S. banking system moves toward a national banking system, the structure of cash concentration systems in the United States will probably take on the major characteristics of their Canadian counterparts.

## USEFUL WEB SITES

PNC Bank: **http://www.treasury.pncbank.com**

Use this site to explore different aspects of cash management services offered by PNC Bank. Click on Search*PNC* and key in *Cash Concentration.* It will return optional pages for you to explore showing a description of the services PNC offers.

## QUESTIONS

1. What are the two principal cash transfer tools, and what are the main differences between them?
2. List the three costs of running a cash concentration system.
3. Identify the benefits derived from a cash concentration system.
4. Briefly discuss the major complicating factors affecting cash transfer scheduling.
5. What advantage does managing about a target have over the simple daily transfer rule?
6. What additional advantages and disadvantages are related to the anticipation rule?

## PROBLEMS

1. The cash manager of Bronco, Inc., is contemplating the choice between using a wire transfer and an EDT. She estimates that her investment opportunity rate is 8 percent. The bank's ECR is currently 5 percent, and the reserve requirement is 12 percent. Her bank account officer informs her that a wire transfer will cost $20 and will provide collected balances one day earlier than the EDT which costs $0.75.
   - **a.** Assume that the balances transferred are above the balances required to compensate the deposit bank for its services. Calculate the minimum transfer balance required to justify the use of a wire transfer.
   - **b.** Assume that the balances transferred are below the balances required to compensate the deposit bank. Calculate the minimum transfer balance required to justify the use of a wire transfer.
   - **c.** Why are the answers in the two preceding parts different?
2. The cash manager of Verematic, Inc., is contemplating the choice between using a wire transfer and a paper-based DTC. He estimates that his investment opportunity rate is 9 percent. The bank's ECR is currently 4 percent, and the reserve requirement is 12 percent. His bank account officer informs him that a wire transfer will cost $15 and will provide collected balances one day earlier than the EDT, which costs $0.30.
   - **a.** Assume that the balances transferred are above the balances required to compensate the deposit bank for its services. Calculate the minimum transfer balance required to justify the use of a wire transfer.
   - **b.** Assume that the balances transferred are below the balances required to compensate the deposit bank. Calculate the minimum transfer balance required to justify the use of a wire transfer.
   - **c.** Why are the answers in the two preceding parts different?

3. You have just been promoted to the cash manager's position at your firm. Your first assignment is to analyze the firm's cash concentration system. You discover that the firm currently compensates the bank with balances and uses an EDT daily (five days per week) to concentrate collected balances. The weekly EDT transactions cost $2.00. The firm's average collected balances equal $35,000 as a result of the transfers. The bank's ECR is 6 percent, and the reserve requirement is 12 percent. Your investment opportunity rate is 12 percent.
   a. Calculate the cost of the current system assuming the bank is compensated 100 percent with balances (no fee is paid).
   b. Now assume that if a wire transfer was utilized, the average daily collected balance could be reduced to zero. However, the weekly transfer costs would increase to $100. Assuming that fees are paid only as needed, estimate the total cost of the revised cash concentration system.
   c. What is your recommendation and why?
4. As the new cash manager for your firm, your first task is to analyze the firm's cash concentration system. You discover that the firm currently compensates the bank with balances and uses a paper DTC daily (five days per week) to concentrate collected balances. The weekly DTC transactions cost $10.00. The firm's average collected balances at the deposit bank equal $15,000 as a result of the transfers. The bank's ECR is 4.5 percent, and the reserve requirement is 12 percent. Your investment opportunity rate is 10 percent, and you may assume 52 weeks in a year.
   a. Calculate the cost of the current system assuming the bank is compensated 100 percent with balances (no fee is paid).
   b. Now assume that if a wire transfer was utilized, the average daily collected balance could be reduced to zero. However, the weekly transfer costs would increase to $100. Assuming that fees are paid only as needed, estimate the total cost of the revised cash concentration system.
   c. What is your recommendation and why?
5. The following data were recently collected by the cash manager at Rayco Department Stores, Inc.

| Day | Dollar Deposit |
|---|---|
| Monday | $ 1,500 |
| Tuesday | 2,000 |
| Wednesday | 1,000 |
| Thursday | 10,000 |
| Friday | 25,000 |
| Saturday | 35,000 |
| Sunday | 10,000 |

   These daily deposits are typical of Rayco's 10 regional stores. Rayco is headquartered in Oklahoma City and concentrates cash from the 10 local deposit banks to its concentration bank in Oklahoma City. You may assume that Rayco's opportunity investment rate is 10 percent, the ECR is 8 percent, and the reserve requirement is 12 percent. Further assume that Rayco uses EDTs to concentrate the cash balances and that the EDT is initiated on the day of deposit and clears the next day. Deposits are made before the daily ledger cut-off time. Also, half of each deposit is cash and half is in checks with 1-day availability. Finally, assume that no bank clearing activity is conducted on the weekends and the beginning ledger and collected balance for the first week are equal to zero.
   a. Assuming that the deposit schedule is typical of each week, create two weeks of deposit and transfer clearing activity similar in format to Exhibits 10–5 through 10–10.
   b. Calculate the average collected balance at the typical deposit bank.
   c. Assuming that each EDT costs $1.00, calculate the dollar amount of collected balances required to compensate the deposit bank.
   d. What is the total cost of the cash concentration system for one bank for one week?
   e. Can you suggest any improvements in Rayco's cash concentration system?

**6.** The following data were recently collected by the cash manager at Wonder Burger, Inc.

| Day | Dollar Deposit |
|---|---|
| Monday | $ 3,000 |
| Tuesday | 2,000 |
| Wednesday | 7,500 |
| Thursday | 5,000 |
| Friday | 12,000 |
| Saturday | 40,000 |
| Sunday | 20,000 |

These daily deposits are typical of Wonder Burger's 150 regional restaurants. Wonder Burger is headquartered in Cleveland, Ohio, and concentrates cash from the 150 different local deposit banks to its concentration bank in Cleveland. You may assume that the opportunity investment rate is 12 percent, the ECR is 7 percent, and the reserve requirement is 10 percent. Further assume that Wonder Burger uses EDTs to concentrate the cash balances and that the EDT is initiated on the day of deposit and clears the next day. Deposits are made before the daily ledger cut-off time. Also, 80 percent of each deposit is cash, and the remaining 20 percent is in checks with 1-day availability. Finally, assume that no bank clearing activity is conducted on the weekends and the beginning ledger and collected balance for the first week are equal to zero.

**a.** Assuming that the deposit schedule is typical of each week, create two weeks of deposit and transfer clearing activity similar in format to Exhibits 10–5 through 10–10.
**b.** Calculate the average collected balance at the typical deposit bank.
**c.** Assuming that each EDT costs $0.20, calculate the dollar amount of collected balances required to compensate the deposit bank.
**d.** What is the total cost of the cash concentration system for one bank for one week?
**e.** Can you suggest any improvements in Wonder Burger's cash concentration system?

**7.** The cash manager at Curry Office Products, Inc., is contemplating changing the company's current cash concentration system from a daily transfer of deposited balances using an EDT system to managing the system based on a target balance. Under the proposed plan, only one transfer would be made weekly using an EDT. The transfer would occur on Thursday. Currently, the company experiences an average daily deposit of $3,700. The earnings credit rate is 6 percent, the bank has a 10-percent reserve requirement, and it charges $0.50 per EDT transaction. Curry's opportunity rate is 12 percent on these balances. The resulting daily collected balances under both plans follow:

Current System Daily Collected Balances

| Mon. | Tues. | Wed. | Thur. | Fri. | Sat. | Sun. |
|---|---|---|---|---|---|---|
| $3,700 | $3,700 | $3,700 | $3,700 | $3,700 | $3,700 | $3,700 |

Proposed System Daily Collected Balances

| Mon. | Tues. | Wed. | Thur. | Fri. | Sat. | Sun. |
|---|---|---|---|---|---|---|
| $14,800 | $18,500 | $22,200 | $25,900 | $3,700 | $7,400 | $11,100 |

Daily receipts and deposits equal $3,700. Under the current system, the company transfers the deposit amount each day (deposit and clearing activities occur seven days a week) using an EDT which clears the next day. Under the proposed system, the accumulated balance of $25,900 is transferred on Thursday of each week using an EDT, which clears the next day.

**a.** Calculate the average daily balance for each system.
**b.** Calculate the required collected balance for each system for one week.
**c.** Calculate the opportunity cost of any excess balances left by each system for one week.
**d.** Calculate the weekly service charge imposed by the bank under both systems.
**e.** Which system should the cash manager choose and why?

## REFERENCES

B. K. Stone and N. C. Hill, "Cash Transfer Scheduling for Efficient Cash Concentration," *Financial Management* (Autumn 1980), pp. 35–43.

Linda A. Zang, "Cash Management at a Mid-Sized Retailer," *Journal of Cash Management* (January/February 1990), pp. 12–15.

FOCUSED CASE

# Gold Star Laundry and Drycleaners, Inc.

Gold Star Laundry and Drycleaners, Inc., is a regional chain of laundry and dry cleaning outlets in the southeast United States. The company is headquartered in Atlanta, Georgia, and has outlets in four states. The company has grown rapidly in the last five years and recently created a treasury office.

Historically, Gold Star had the manager of each local outlet establish a bank relationship with a local bank for deposit of daily cash receipts. The corporate controller would then initiate a deposit transfer once each week to move the funds from the local bank accounts to the corporate headquarters bank in Atlanta. The controller relied on depository transfer checks (DTCs) for this purpose and liked the fact that a paper document existed for an audit trail. DTCs cost $1.50 each and seemed quite economical because only one transfer was made each week.

The chief financial officer (CFO) asked the newly hired treasurer to review the company's existing cash management system and put all recommendations in a report to be submitted by the end of the month. The CFO felt that the company was not as efficient as it might be from a cash management perspective but he did not have any hard data to back up this hunch.

## THE CURRENT SITUATION

The treasurer began to pull together the pertinent information. There were 50 different outlets in four states. The outlets were located in the major cities of these states and each city was serviced by a number of major banks; some of these were referred to as super regional banks because they had branches in all four states. However, the treasurer discovered that, because of the lack of a corporate bank policy, the managers were free to select their own banks and as a result the corporation had relationships with over 15 separately incorporated banking institutions. The following data were computed from the company's records by the analyst staff and represent the typical outlet's weekly cash receipts.

| Day | Cash Receipts |
|---|---|
| Monday | $25,000 |
| Tuesday | 6,000 |
| Wednesday | 8,000 |
| Thursday | 15,000 |
| Friday | 30,000 |
| Saturday | 10,000 |
| Sunday | 0 |

The cash receipts were deposited in the local bank the following day by 9 A.M., and the bank credited the deposit that same day because the receipts consisted of cash and checks drawn on local banks. The outlet manager then sent a DTC on Thursday morning to the corporate headquarters bank in Atlanta in the amount of Thursday's collected balance, which included Wednesday's cash receipts deposited on Thursday morning. The DTC arrived on Friday at the headquarters' bank and is given a 1-business day availability clearing the amount of the DTC out of the depository bank on Monday.

The corporate policy has been to compensate the bank system with balances rather than fees. The treasurer agreed with this policy given the balances maintained at the depository banks, but wondered if this would continue to be a reasonable policy if there was going to be a change in the transfer system in general. In discussions with the headquarters' bank, he learned that the Federal Reserve was currently requiring a 10 percent reserve requirement. The average earnings credit rate among the banks was 4.7 percent, and in most cases, the overnight investment rate offered by the depository banks was about 3.00 percent. The treasurer estimated that the corporation's overnight opportunity rate was about 4.50 percent.

### Scenario One

One option the treasurer easily recognized was to maintain the current transfer system but shift the transfer initiation day from Thursday to Wednesday. If the same DTC system was continued, this 1-day shift would cause the transfer to clear on Friday and would reduce the idle balances carried over the weekend. However, he was not sure how this would impact the average daily collected balance; he did not know if this would be the best solution.

## Scenario Two

The treasurer wondered why the company was not using an automated clearinghouse (ACH) transaction to make transfers, because an electronic depository transfer (EDT) was cheaper and more efficient to use. In most cases, the company's banks charge $0.50 for an EDT with 1-business day availability. Several options exist to transmit the collected balance information. At a minimum, the outlet manager could simply call the treasurer's office with the information. A more expensive option would be to install electronic cash registers/terminals at each outlet; the cash register/terminals can be queried daily by the computer at the headquarters to retrieve the daily cash receipts. The treasurer thought that it might be prudent to defer the more technological alternative as a second step to be investigated more thoroughly in a few months. He settled on having the outlet manager call in the previous day's cash receipts the following morning and then corporate headquarters would contact the headquarters' bank to initiate an ACH in the amount of the previous day's cash receipts. The ACH would be given 1-business day availability and would clear the next day. His plan was for this to happen on a daily basis, and he wondered what impact a daily transfer would have on the collected balances maintained at the bank. He also wondered where this would leave the typical outlet's bank compensation situation and whether there would still be enough balances to compensate the bank.

## Other Alternatives

The treasurer's project team came up with two other alternatives for his consideration. The first alternative was to wire transfer the daily collected balance each day and the second alternative was to purchase a daily cash forecasting software package promoted by a cash management consulting firm. This would allow the daily collected balance to be forecasted and an EDT initiated in advance of the deposit so that the collected balance could be transferred the same day it is collected. The wire transfer would cost $20 for the combined incoming and outgoing wire, and the cost of the forecasting package was estimated at $10,000 plus an annual maintenance contract of $500. Although the treasurer realized that both of these alternatives would have the same impact on the level of collected balances, he wasn't sure how to compare the advantages and disadvantages.

Finally, as the treasurer was putting together his report consisting of his analysis of the various scenarios and alternatives, he wondered what the impact would be on the system he recommends when nationwide branch banking is put into place.

# APPENDIX 10A

## A Linear Programming Cash Transfer Model

The transfer scheduling problem is set up to minimize the total costs associated with the transfer scheduling decision. The two costs are the dollar amount to be paid in fees, *FEE*, and the opportunity cost of leaving average collected balances in excess of required balances, $k \times (ACB - RCB)$, where $k$ is the investment opportunity rate, *ACB* is the average collected balance, and *RCB* is the average required balance. The actual formulation for *RCB* was developed earlier as a part of Equation 10.2. This form of the objective function allows the solution to not only solve the transfer scheduling problem, the dollar amount of the transfer, and the specific days that transfers are initiated, but it also solves the fee versus balance problem by directly solving for the dollar amount of fees to be paid considering the collected balances left on account at the bank. The objective function set to be minimized is thus:

$$TC = FEE + k \times (ACB - RCB) \quad (10.1A)$$

We next must create the constraint equation set. The constraint equations are developed as follows:

$$LB_t = LDEP_t - TF_{t-d} + LB_{t-1} \; t = 1,2,3,4,5 \quad (10.2A)$$

$$LB_t - LB_{t-1} + TF_{t-d} = LDEP_t \; t = 1,2,3,4,5$$

Constraint set 10.2A defines the daily closing ledger balance. The first equation set establishes the ledger balance relationship logic by setting the ledger balance for day $t$ equal to the day $t$'s ledger deposit, *LDEP*, less the transfer clearing, *TF*, plus the previous day's ending ledger balance. The $d$ in the expressions above represents the days of delay from the day the transfer is initiated to the day the transfer actually occurs. The second equation set is the same equation, but it is rewritten to be used in a linear programming problem. This formulation puts all the decision variables on the left-hand side of the constraint equation and all constants or fixed values on the right-hand side of the constraint equation.

$$CB_t = CDEP_t - TF_{t-d} + CB_{t-1} \; t = 1,2,3,4,5 \quad (10.3A)$$

$$CB_t - CB_{t-1} + TF_{t-d} = CDEP_t \; t = 1,2,3,4,5$$

Constraint set 10.3A defines the daily closing collected balance. The first equation set establishes the collected balance relationship logic by setting the collected balance for day $t$ equal to the day $t$'s collected deposit, *CDEP*, less the transfer clearing, *TF*, plus the previous day's ending collected balance. The second equation set is the same equation, but it is rewritten to be used in the linear programming formulation. This formulation puts all the decision variables on the left-hand side of the constraint equation and all constants or fixed values on the right-hand side of the constraint equation.

$$\Sigma\, TF_t = \Sigma\, CDEP_t \quad (10.4A)$$

Constraint set 10.4A constrains the total transfers in a week or some other fixed time period to be equal to the sum of the collected deposits for the same time period.

$$(-M \times TD_t) + TF_t \leq 0 \; t = 1,2,3,4,5 \quad (10.5A)$$

Constraint set 10.5A constrains the transfer day variable, $TD_t$, which is a 0,1 variable, to assume the value of 1 for day $t$ if *TF* is greater than zero on day $t$. $M$ is some arbitrarily chosen number that will be greater than the maximum transfer.

$$\Sigma\, CB_t/7 - \Sigma\, TD_t\,[SC/ECR(1 - rr)] = EXCESS - DEF \quad (10.6A)$$

$$\Sigma\, CB_t/7 - [(\Sigma\, TD_t \times SC) - FEE]/ECR(1 - rr) - EXCESS + DEF = 0$$

Constraint set 10.6A establishes the definition of excess and deficit balance by relating the average daily collected balance to the balance required to compensate the bank for the transfer charges.

$$(\Sigma\, CB_t/7) \times ECR \times (1 - rr) + FEE - (\Sigma\, TD_t \times SC) \geq 0 \quad (10.7A)$$

Constraint set 10.7A constrains the solution result so that the earnings credits earned on the average collected balance plus the fees paid are at least equal to the total bank service charges incurred by the transfer system.

## PROBLEMS

10A-1. Utilizing the model formulation presented in the chapter, solve the cash transfer scheduling problem presented in Exhibit 10–10. Solve for the optimal dollar amount of fees, the optimal balance to leave at the deposit bank, and the transfer schedule and amount to be transferred using Microsoft Solver.

10A-2. Utilizing the model formulation presented in the chapter, solve the cash transfer scheduling Problem 6 at the end of the chapter. Solve for the optimal dollar amount of fees, the optimal balance to leave at the deposit bank, and the transfer schedule and amount to be transferred using Microsoft Solver.

CHAPTER

11

# Cash Disbursement Systems

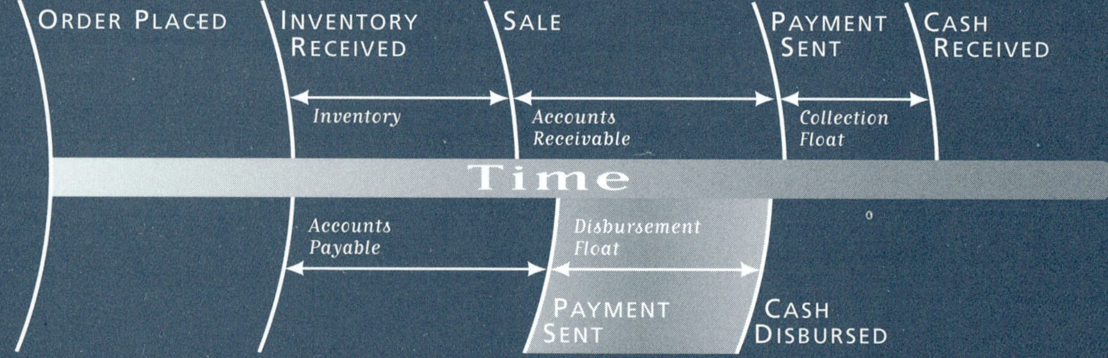

## OBJECTIVES

*After studying this chapter, you should be able to:*

- identify the environmental variables influencing disbursement decisions.
- identify the major disbursement mechanisms, relevant institutional aspects, and major implementation variations.
- specify the major funding alternatives for disbursement accounts.
- conduct valuation of payment mechanism decisions.
- state the contribution of disbursement location model application.

A company's decision regarding the payment methods and systems it will use in various situations is a major financial decision. The payment methods, disbursement banks, and locations chosen make up a company's **disbursement system**. In this chapter, we show how the payment dollar amounts and the location and type of collection system used by the party being paid influence whether a company opts for checks or electronic transfers. The payment methods offered by a company's banking system or by third-party service providers also constrain the paying company's flexibility. The disbursement system chosen affects value by changing the company's cost structure or by altering the payables cycle and thereby the cash conversion cycle. We have already developed major aspects of payables management (Chapter 7) and the payments system and financial institutions (Chapter 8). Using this background, we now analyze the major disbursement systems issues, the context of disbursement decisions, the major disbursing alternatives, funding of the disbursement accounts, site location of the disbursement account(s), and global disbursing.

Good corporate practice dictates that a company have a payments policy. The Financial Dilemma portrays an issue at the center of such a policy. The following Focus on Practice indicates some features that should be included in such a policy.

### FINANCIAL DILEMMA

Is It Time to Go Electronic with Payments and Payment Information?

Many companies are wondering if they should emulate Sears, Roebuck & Company in its implementation of electronic disbursing.[1] After negotiating new payment terms with each of its suppliers, it quickly built up a significant volume of electronic payments: 1,000 transactions, 60,000 invoices, and $500 million in payments per month. When evaluating electronic payments, Sears calculated that it would save $0.40 and the payee as much as $1.10 per payment by going through the automated clearinghouse (ACH). The savings to Sears as payor was based on the difference between the per-check cost and the ACH payment cost (note that the postage cost has gone up significantly since then):

| ACH CORPORATE TRADE PAYMENTS | | CHECKS | |
|---|---|---|---|
| Item | Cost per Transaction | Item | Cost per Transaction |
| Process tape | $0.01 | Check stock | $0.01 |
| Tape delivery | 0.01 | Processing | 0.08 |
| Personnel | 0.03 | Personnel | 0.14 |
| Bank service fees | 0.02 | Postage | 0.22 |
| Tape transmission | 0.05 | Bank charges | 0.14 |
| Return items | 0.01 | | |
| Lost float | 0.06 | | |
| Total | $0.19 | | $0.59 |

Two of the top six goals of Fortune 500 accounts payable managers in 2002 were to (1) install or increase the use of electronic data interchange, evaluated receipt settlement (invoiceless pay in which receipt of goods triggers payment), and electronic invoicing and (2) install or increase the use of electronic payments.[2]

[1] Cited in *The Globecon Group, Ltd.*, "Electronic Data Interchange and Corporate Trade Payments," Morristown, NJ: Financial Executives Research Foundation, 1988.

[2] "Goals in Accounts Payable." Accessed online 1/14/2004 at **http://www.recapinc.com/eap_survey_goals.htm**.

## FOCUS ON PRACTICE

### What Should Be in Your Corporate Payment Policy?

Many companies are thinking about devising a written policy for outgoing payments, triggered in part by Internet and e-marketplace purchases. The Association for Financial Professionals' Payments Advisory Group offers the following suggested elements for inclusion in this policy:

- Which payment methods are authorized?
- What are the circumstances under which each of these payment methods should be used?
- Who is responsible for approving payments?
- What procedures may be used for unusual or urgent situations?
- What is the company's position on the security, efficiency, and cost effectiveness of each payment method?
- Is the treasury department designated by the board of directors and/or senior management as the department responsible for cash, banking relationships, and the control of credit facilities?

*Source:* Adapted from *Report of the AFP Payments Advisory Group.* "Payments Pitfalls II: Learn the Truth and Avoid the Consequences" (October 15, 2001), pp. 4–5.

## DISBURSEMENT POLICY

Four guiding principles should drive corporate disbursement system decisions:

1. *Maximize value through payment timing.* Payments should be timed to add the maximum value to the company. Three observations help us see how to implement this principle. First, this is basically equivalent to asking the decision maker to minimize costs—particularly for the cash-poor company that is typically in a net borrowed (illiquid) position—by paying on terms but not before. Second, the principle implies that a company should take cash discounts when preferable, as demonstrated in Chapter 7. Third, within ethical, legal, and practical constraints, a company may gain information and float advantages offered by strategic location of disbursement banks. You may wish to refer back to Exhibit 10–11 for a review of ethical aspects of cash management. The Federal Reserve System has largely eliminated "Fed float," which is the difference between the availability float experienced by the payee and the presentment float experienced by the payor. This implies that the payor's float gains come solely from a bank's or payee's pocket. Increasingly, abuses of float are considered unethical and poor business practice, because the payee and collecting bank(s) are damaged by it.
2. *Optimize the accuracy and timeliness of information.* Accuracy and timeliness of information are key attributes of disbursement systems. Optimizing a company's configuration of disbursement systems means getting accurate information in a timely manner without incurring excessive costs. Accurate funds balance information received early in the day adds value through access to investments with higher interest rates or better credit quality.
3. *Minimize balances in disbursement accounts.* Although some demand deposit balances may be necessary to support disbursements, as a rule these balances should be

minimized. There are three possible exceptions to this principle. First, nonprofit organizations, governmental agencies, and sole proprietorships are permitted to have interest-bearing checking accounts, and those with low average balances may not lose much interest by leaving funds in the disbursement account. Second, when the company contracts with its bank(s) for a bundled package of services, a global systems approach may negate this principle. The systems approach involves considering the *total* cost and reliability of bank services instead of negotiating the price for each service individually. For banks that have adequate cost accounting systems and will bundle services (sell services as a group), significant cost savings may be possible for the corporate customer. The appropriate focal point is the company's overall banking costs, not the cost of each individual service. Third, compensating balances needed to support a loan may limit how far a company can go in reducing disbursement account balances.

4. *Prevent fraud.* One of the fastest growing crimes in the United States is check fraud. Fraud prevention and detection techniques, as well as greater use of electronic payments, are disbursement system essentials.

Our central focus in applying these principles is the development of a disbursement policy. A company's **disbursement policy**, whether an informal strategy or a formal written document, encompasses the payment policy in the Focus on Practice box; it specifies which payment mechanism to use for a given disbursement type or vendor, when to pay a given invoice,[3] and sets up guidelines for the disbursement system [including which bank(s) might be involved]. The disbursement policy should reflect the application of the four guiding principles. It is important to understand the context within which policy decisions are made as a guide to implementing the principles.

## CASH DISBURSEMENTS AND THE CASH FLOW TIMELINE

Six major factors influence a company's disbursement policy. The economy's payment system is the only factor that is external to the company and therefore uncontrollable. The remaining five factors are internal and mostly controllable: the company's philosophy, its organizational structure, its banking system, its information system and computer capabilities, and the predictability and size of its average daily net cash flow. Before examining these factors, we review the disbursement situation in the context of the cash flow timeline.

### Disbursement Float and the Cash Flow Timeline

Corporations continue to pay most bills with mailed checks. From the time a check is put in the mail by the buyer, there are three major delays that together compose disbursement float: mail float, processing float, and clearance (availability and clearing slippage) float. The length of these components depends on the locations of the mail initiation and destination points, the time it takes the receiver to process it before depositing it at the bank, and the clearance mechanism used. Exhibit 11–1 shows mail, processing, and clearance float. Mail float varies from one to five calendar days, processing float varies from one-half day to three calendar days, and clearance float ranges from zero (e.g., "on-us" checks) to three business days. In the 1970s, companies quite often extended mail float through

---

[3] We do not deal with the payment timing decision here because we discussed managing payables and accruals in Chapter 7, including such decisions as whether to take cash discounts or pay at the end of the normal credit period.

Exhibit 11–1

*Components of Disbursement Float*

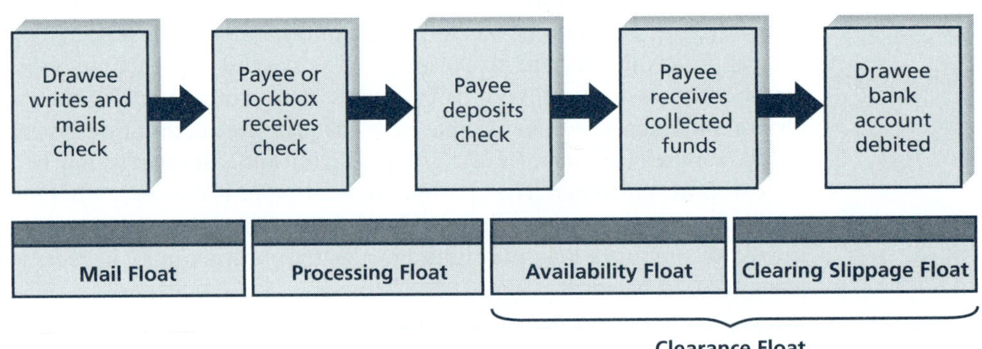


*Source:* Copyright © 1997 by the Association for Financial Professionals. All rights reserved. Used with permission of the Association for Financial Professionals.

remote mailing points[4] or clearance float through remote disbursement banks, but pressure from the Federal Reserve (the Fed) and the Justice Department as well as negative publicity received by Merrill Lynch (which was paying East Coast vendors from West Coast sites, and vice versa) has largely curbed these practices. The Fed has greatly reduced the clearing slippage float, or Fed float, which occurs when it grants availability to the depositing bank before debiting the drawee bank (see Chapter 8). Cash managers now place less emphasis on maximizing float and more emphasis on better control and forecasting of disbursements to minimize idle account balances and prevent fraud.

## Payment System

The payment mechanisms available to a company, their current state of development and relative costs, the available clearing and settlement mechanisms, and the regulatory framework are all important parts of the payment system. Regulatory changes enabling U.S. nationwide banking, European economic integration, and pricing for daylight overdrafts are noted in Chapter 8. At the beginning of 1995, the Federal Reserve implemented **Same-Day Settlement (SDS)**, whereby any bank may present a check for payment to any drawee bank, and the check must be paid by the close of the business day. These checks must be presented by 8:00 A.M. local time at the drawee bank or its designated site (which may be the district's Fed processing center). The checks may be presented using **electronic check presentment** if the depositing and drawee banks participate in this banking industry-developed program. Electronic check presentment involves the bank of first deposit doing a magnetic ink character recognition (MICR) line image capture followed by an electronic transmission of that image to the paying bank (the paper check is forwarded through the usual channels), and if the check is presented after the 8:00 A.M. cutoff, many banks will await physical presentment before paying the check. The Electronic Check Clearing House Organization (ECCHO) and The Small Value Payments Company's Electronic Clearing Services (ECS) are the two private-sector bank groups that participate in elec-

[4] Widespread use at that time of the postmark date as the payment date allowed the remote mailing practice to succeed. Courts have ruled a payment is timely if mailed by the due date on the invoice, in that the payor cannot control the check once it is in the mail.

tronic check presentment. About 24 banks in ECCHO participate in bilateral electronic presentments to each other, along with 27 banks in ECS. The three impediments to greater use of electronic check presentment have been the following: (1) prior to the implementation of the Check 21 legislation (see Chapter 8) in late 2004, many banks and customers would not accept check truncation, so the physical checks had to be transported and presented; (2) the laws in some states previously required the return of canceled checks; and (3) a paper check has historically been necessary to prove a court case.[5] ECP should expand rapidly under the new law: average daily volume is projected to increase from 400,000 to 14 million checks in 10 years.

## Ethics and Organizational Policies

Subsequent to the E.F. Hutton check-kiting fiasco, many companies have formulated or revised disbursement guidelines. A survey of 197 cash managers regarding certain practices that were thought to be either unethical or possibly illegal is shown in Exhibit 11–2. A majority of the managers thought that three practices were unethical and/or possibly illegal: altering checks so they have to be manually processed by bank personnel, drawing on uncollected funds when the paying bank has poor float tracking systems (Uncollected funds 1), and drawing on uncollected funds when not covered by an agreement with a bank (Uncollected funds 2). Less than half the managers thought these practices were unethical or illegal: rotating disbursement points (to add float based on the changed

**Exhibit 11–2**

*Views on Ethics and Legality of Disbursement Practices*

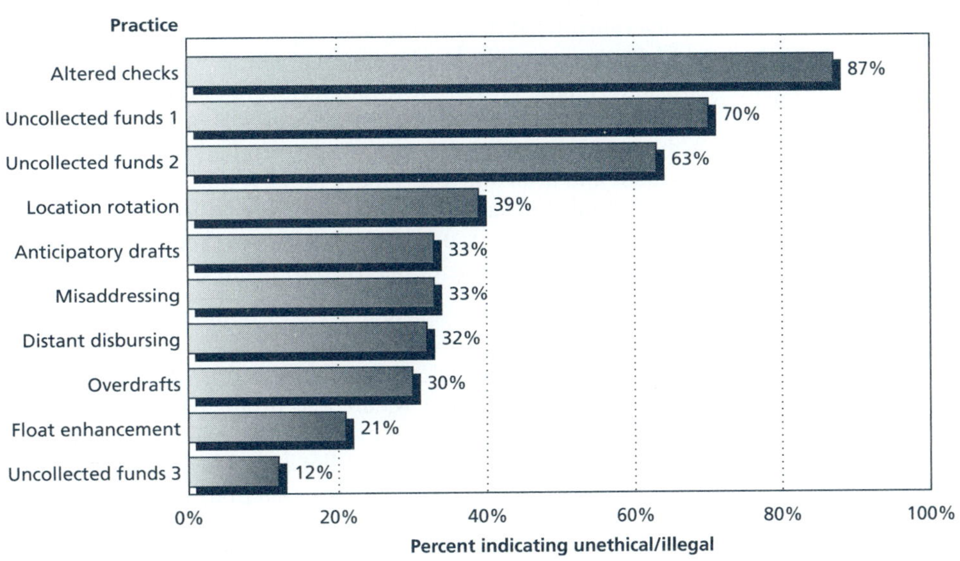


*Source: Cash Management and the Payments System: Ground Rules, Cost, and Risks.* The Globecon Group, 1986, Financial Executives Research Foundation.

[5] "A New Twist to the Old 'Checks-to-Electronics' Question," *AFP Pulse* (October 2000), ec1. The Fed proposed and the 2003 legislation called "Check 21" (implemented in late 2004) implemented a rule that 2-sided images or "substitute checks" be considered legally equivalent to the original checks to get around these issues.

locations of their vendors' lockboxes), writing checks in anticipation of adequate balances by the clearing time, sending checks to a company's office instead of the lockbox designated by the vendor, paying East Coast vendors from West Coast banks and/or mailing points, overdrafts, use of systems designed to extend disbursement float, or using uncollected funds at any time (Uncollected funds 3). It is possible that some of these practices have come to be accepted because of their prevalence in certain industries or during eras of high interest rates. However, it is difficult to rationalize the obvious detriment that many of these practices create for the payees and disbursement banks.

## Decentralization versus Centralization of Disbursements

We saw in earlier chapters how collection and concentration systems might be centralized or localized, and this distinction also characterizes disbursement systems. **Centralized disbursing** allows the corporate headquarters' staff to oversee each disbursement and possibly also initiate each disbursement. Centralized control is a means to ensure disbursement account balance adequacy because the cash manager at headquarters has a better view of the company's cash position than plant or divisional managers. Centralized data allow a more rapid and accurate reading of disbursement timing and amounts, providing a more accurate forecast and better decisions about such things as whether to take a cash discount and how much to "fund" the disbursement account. Generally, disbursement float is higher with central disbursing than when local operating units pay nearby firms from nearby banks. Elimination of duplicate disbursement accounts also reduces costs and deters fraud. If disbursement services are bundled with credit services, the greater size of centralized balances should enable the manager to negotiate lower total (credit and noncredit service) banking costs. Young, small companies and those operating at a single location are centralized and tend to deal with only one bank. Many larger companies are working to centralize disbursing as well.

**Decentralized disbursing** allows payments to be made by divisional offices or individual stores, usually from accounts held at nearby banks. Companies with operations spread throughout multiple locations or even multinationally tend to be decentralized because of the need to pay wages and local bills or to disburse from an overseas subsidiary. Although decentralization may improve relationships with suppliers, who receive both payment and available funds more rapidly, it can severely hamper the efficiency and control of the disbursement accounts. Narrowed investment opportunities may result. The treasurer of ARMCO, a company that switched from centralized to decentralized disbursing, expresses some of his frustrations in the following example.

> "You can never get your controlled disbursements [amount] early enough. If I'm managing anywhere between a $500 million and $1 billion portfolio, I'd like those numbers the night before, but that's not practical. The problem that we have now in our company is that we are decentralizing. I used to have control of the whole position. We worked with one controlled disbursement bank. Now we are setting up three or four divisions, and I'm acting as a short-term lender; an in-house bank, so to speak. Instead of having one system to worry about, I now have three or four. The investment process, which could have started at 9:00 or 9:30 A.M., still starts at 9:00 or 9:15 and continues to around 9:45, or maybe a little later, 10:15 or 10:45, until you've got all four of these pieces, and you finally finish that puzzle up at 11:30. And, as you get later and later into the morning, [investment] rates seldom improve. Quality and supply [of attractive investments] diminish as the day goes on."[6]

Between centralized and decentralized disbursing is a mixed approach, which combines some features of each approach. Here, checks are issued and accounts reconciled at field

---

[6] "Focus on Technology," *Journal of Cash Management* (September/October 1990), p. 20.

operations, but they are written on a central disbursing account. Headquarters does bank selection and disbursement account funding.

## Organizational Structure

Various functional areas within the organization affect a company's disbursement systems. Organizational structure refers to the firm's functional areas and how they are interrelated, chains of command, informational and decision-making flows, and formal and informal groups. The impact on the disbursement activity comes mainly from treasury, purchasing, production, accounts payable, and personnel. These areas can influence disbursement policies and practices because each has responsibility for some aspect of the resource acquisition process. Exhibit 11–3 indicates some of these responsibilities. Because treasurers or cash managers are in a staff position, they do not have direct authority over any of the other departments.

Improvements in disbursement practices, particularly in switching to electronic ordering and payments, are highly dependent on the purchasing department's cooperation. A major study of selected purchasing tasks in different industries found that in a significant number of manufacturing companies, the purchasing area prepared financial forecasts; very often, the purchasing area coordinated its activities with the manufacturing and material planning areas (and, in a few companies, with the marketing area).[7]

**Exhibit 11–3**

*Functional Areas Influencing Disbursements*

| Organizational Unit | Practices/Policies Influenced |
|---|---|
| Treasury Department | ■ Bank relationships<br>■ Bank services<br>■ Disbursement policies<br>■ Funding policies<br>■ Disbursement mechanisms<br>■ Account balance oversight |
| Accounts Payable Department | ■ Disbursement records<br>■ Disbursement policies<br>■ Discount policies<br>■ Invoice information<br>■ Disbursement scheduling/forecasts |
| Production Department | ■ Status of inventory position<br>■ Initiation of orders, quantities<br>■ Initiation of charge-backs |
| Purchasing Department | ■ Negotiation for vendors, prices, terms<br>■ Discount policies<br>■ Assist in determination of orders, quantities<br>■ Vendor relations<br>■ Use of electronic purchase orders, payment |
| Personnel Department | ■ Negotiation of wages, pay periods<br>■ Localized payroll policies<br>■ Direct deposit policies |

[7] Robert E. Shealy, "The Purchasing Job in Different Types of Business," *Journal of Purchasing & Materials Management* 21 (1985), pp. 17–20.

Having other corporate personnel involved with disbursements presents both a problem and an opportunity. The problem arises when the fragmentation in control and oversight causes poor decisions to be made. Assuming equal quality and reliability, the purchasing agent might lean toward selecting the supplier based only on material cost, whereas using a supplier with a slightly higher material cost but who allows electronic ordering and payment might reduce total costs. The opportunity presented is for the treasury area to captain and more heavily influence the overall ordering, invoicing, payment, and crediting process. Put another way, the finance function might gain greater control of the entire cash flow timeline. Given top executive support, the treasury area has the clout to push for implementation of improved systems. Recent changes in many U.S. companies have given treasury departments a bigger voice in the reengineering of business processes.

### Banking System

The ability of a company's banks to provide the appropriate services in the right locations at the right prices is critical to efficient disbursing. The starting point for many disbursement decisions is the flexibility and cost of the company's existing disbursement system, which is highly dependent on its **disbursing banks'** capabilities. The availability of fraud prevention methods such as "positive pay" is also a key consideration. We return to this theme later in the chapter. Many times, the greatest reductions in cost and accompanying increases in value come from modifying the company's use of banking services and/or banks. Just as important in today's payment environment is whether a bank has electronic data interchange capability; in other words, whether it is "EDI-capable." This means that the bank has the capacity to send "dollars and data" together so that the payment and invoice information do not have to be coupled by the payee, and the payee's receivables area can automatically process the cash application. Even companies with extensive experience using financial EDI have only been able to convert about one-third of their total financial transaction volume to EDI, but the browser-based applications promise to change this quickly. However, the Fed is making a low-end financial EDI translation software package available to the many financial institutions that are not EDI-capable. Called Fed*EDI, it is motivated by the Electronics Funds Transfer Act of 1999 initiative to convert all federal payments, except tax refunds, to electronic mode, and a National Automated Clearing House Association rule change. That rule change requires that on the request of the receiver (corporate customer), a receiving depository financial institution must provide all payment-related information within the addenda record *for corporate payments.*[8]

### Treasury Information Systems

The capabilities of the company's management information systems are another limiting factor on a company's disbursement systems. The degree of automation of the accounts payable process varies across companies. Companies are more highly automated in payables than in any other cash management area. Automated systems ensure that bills are paid on time, without manual intervention, achieving substantial cost savings. One foreign subsidiary that had been paying each bill 30 days early estimates that it now saves $250,000 annually resulting from its implementation of an automated system. Ford Motor Company cut its payables processing staff from 200 to 40 after automation. A chemicals company set up a process in which a computer determines disbursement float for each check by matching issue dates with presentment dates. Some vendors yielding disbursement float as long as 10 days were identified and disbursement accounts were funded later, allowing a substantial reduction in account balances.

---

[8] From *The Financial Connection* (July 1998), accessed at **http://www.fms.treas.gov/finconn/fcjul98.html.**

Computerization permits the payables area to speed account reconciliation, initiate and track orders electronically, and initiate electronic payments (PC-initiated ACH payments or wire transfers). The same system can be used by the cash manager to access account balances at concentration and field banks and initiate investment of excess balances or borrowing under prearranged credit agreements. Chapter 19 deals almost entirely with this important topic.

### Cash Flow Characteristics

The final consideration affecting disbursement systems is the nature of a company's cash flows. Cash management systems create value because cash flows are unsynchronized, uneven, and uncertain. Here, our focus is the predictability of those flows and whether the company typically is in a net-invested or net-borrowed cash position. Relatively small or predictable flows generally moderate the need for establishment of sophisticated disbursement accounts with their higher fees. A company with predictable cash flows that is cash-rich prefers a disbursement system in which surplus balances are easily and inexpensively transferred into interest-bearing investments. The company might select banks having the most attractive sweep accounts, in which amounts above compensating balance requirements (or all positive amounts) are automatically transferred to overnight or other short-term investments. Companies that are typically cash-poor, especially those with unpredictable cash flows, prefer banks that link disbursement accounts and services seamlessly to attractive credit facilities. Companies having relatively large cash flows might also bargain for volume-based pricing when negotiating with disbursement banks.

## DISBURSEMENT SYSTEMS

Each of the factors we have mentioned influences the disbursement system that a company establishes. The appropriate disbursement system for a small company with local dealings might be very simple, whereas a large multinational corporation may enhance shareholder value with a complex system. We now investigate simple disbursement systems, complex disbursement systems, and trends in today's environment.

### Simple Disbursement Systems

Simple disbursement systems tend to be manual and paper-based. Standard payment services such as demand deposit accounts, payroll services, and drafts are especially attractive to companies that have small daily cash flows, untrained treasury personnel,[9] minimal computer facilities or skills, and localized business dealings.

These companies may also find it advantageous to use **account reconciliation**, a disbursement-related service in which the company provides the bank with a record of checks drawn. The bank essentially helps balance the company's checkbook, providing the company information regarding which checks have been paid. Cash managers may select from three common types of reconciliation, based on how much information they wish to pay for, beyond what is already being provided in a monthly statement. **Paid-only reconciliation** reports all paid checks by check number, with check number, dollar amount, and date paid. The latter can be compared with the check issue date to determine each indi-

---

[9] A recent study of accountants in small- and medium-sized companies found that next to financial accounting, their largest job responsibility was cash/treasury management—especially in payables and receivables. Bradley M. Roof and Charles R. Baril, "How Does Your Accounting Department Measure Up?" *Management Accounting* (April 1991), pp. 39–42.

vidual check's disbursement float. The total number of checks written and their dollar amount, as well as any stopped payments or miscellaneous debits to the account, are also noted. Companies with automated payables systems can receive this information via PC transmission or on floppy disks and use it to automatically update their payables records. Another form of partial reconciliation, **range reconciliation**, provides subtotals of all checks within a range of check serial numbers. This is especially useful for identifying disbursements from the same account but from several locations. **Full reconciliation** provides detailed "checks outstanding" information, along with the "checks paid" data from company-supplied check issue detail. It generally costs $30 to $40 per month per account more than partial reconciliation.

*PAYMENT MECHANISMS* The major paper-based payment mechanisms are checks and **drafts.**[10] Exhibit 11–4 summarizes the major attributes of each mechanism. Both are considered simple because they are easy to use, do not require a special computer or an advanced information system for payor or payee, do not require special skills to handle, and can be implemented by any financial institution.

Checks have several advantages, including their ability to be cashed or transferred ("negotiability"), their disbursement float, the stop payment feature, and the ability to include extensive remittance detail with mailed checks. Except for recurring, same-dollar payments, they remain the payment method of choice when paying individuals. Negative features include labor and paperwork costs to the issuer and delayed availability to the payee.

**Exhibit 11–4**

*Checks and Drafts*

| Instrument | Clearing Process | Uses |
|---|---|---|
| Checks (Regular demand deposit account) | Deposited by payee, cleared back to drawee bank when they are paid unless a stop payment has been issued or a forgery detected. | Any payment situation except when immediate transfer of value is required. |
| Drafts | Deposited by payee, cleared back to agent ("payable through") bank, which presents check to payor; if payor approves payment, bank pays check. Agent bank is charged for draft amount at the time of presentment and may charge for float from that point until the payor authorizes payment. Alternatively, payor allows all drafts to be paid by agent bank (from demand deposit account), with refused drafts later credited back. | When authorization control is desired over field payments (as in property and casualty insurance, when signature of agent and dollar amount need to be verified) or off-premise purchases by an employee who cannot get the needed second signature on a check. Formerly used by auto manufacturers to get payment from dealers. Deters fraud and misuse of funds. |

[10] The reader may wish to review the discussion in Chapter 8 on paper-based payment systems.

Despite the need to manually handle drafts, bank charges for drafts are as much as 75 percent lower than those for paying checks, primarily because banks do not need to verify signatures or do account reconciliations. Furthermore, because companies that use drafts usually issue many of them, the bank can process and present them as a batch total instead of individually. The issuing company bears full responsibility for record keeping and reconciling drafts issued, which it accepts because of the greater control and lower bank fees. On the downside, many banks will not cash drafts, making payment to individuals problematic. Drafts primarily are used for business-to-business payments because of consumer complaints about difficulty and delays in getting them cashed. Insurance companies use them for large-dollar field claims disbursements because of the extra control and fraud prevention.

*Disbursements Funding* A simple disbursement system also uses basic methods to fund disbursements. Disbursement account funding is provided by existing demand deposit account balances, deposits of daily cash receipts, or maturing investments. Companies may have an automated sweep account, in which balances in excess of the sum of compensation requirements and an average daily disbursement amount are taken out of the account overnight and invested in one of the bank's money market accounts.[11] Depending on the average balance in the disbursement account, the rate of interest earned might be ¼ to ½ percent less than a benchmark rate (usually the Treasury bill or federal funds rate). In low interest rate years, such as in 2004, some banks were inducing corporate customers to leave balances in their accounts by offering an earnings credit rate that was almost as high as the sweep account rate. However, the excess balances left on account are reduced by the Fed's required reserve ratio (presently 10 percent). This leaves only 90 percent of the excess balances to obtain credit.

Cash-poor organizations and organizations that have disbursement accounts at banks that provide their credit lines follow one of two complementary funding approaches. One approach is to leave excess balances in the disbursement account, a buffer that is replenished from daily cash receipts. If this is insufficient, the company draws on its credit line to meet disbursement needs.

*Company Characteristics* Companies using simple disbursement systems generally share several characteristics. First, they are often localized smaller businesses that sell one or a few products. Second, a significant proportion of their funds transfers are local (e.g., paying employees) or between company units. Third, they often operate with a limited treasury department—with limits on skilled personnel, computers, and information systems. Fourth, their trading partners either have not invested in electronic order and remittance capabilities or have not applied pressure for electronic payments. Taken together, these four properties portray companies whose disbursement systems are characterized by paper-based payments and simple funding approaches.

## Complex Disbursement Systems

Complex disbursement systems are characterized by a greater use of electronic payments, specialized disbursement accounts, flexible account funding, and greater control and information capabilities. The additional capabilities come at the expense of higher com-

---

[11] This is not actually an overnight investment, but a 24-hour investment made the next business day based on a day's closing balance. What if a wire drawdown is presented against the account or ACH debits are presented against the account the next morning? Many banks do not charge for an intraday overdraft because they recognize that the necessary funds are coming into the account at the close of the day. In essence, they look at the intraday account balance as collected balances + incoming sweep funds.

pensating balances or fees, but the increases in control, information, and net interest income outweigh the costs. Complex systems often are linked to the company's collection and concentration systems to maximize efficiency of funds movement. Finally, these systems often are the product of elaborate disbursement studies that guide bank selection and may recommend establishment of a disbursement network of strategically sited disbursement accounts.

*PAPER-BASED PAYMENT MECHANISMS* Regular checking accounts play a smaller role in complex systems as a result of inadequacies related to control, cost, and funding uncertainty. These problems are especially acute for larger companies. A company with centralized disbursements but dispersed locations that issues paychecks and supplier payments faces a *control dilemma.* Specialized checks called **multiple-drawee checks** have more than one bank listed on the face of the check; one of the banks is located near the disbursing location (for which the check is an on-us item). These are used by companies located in states that require paychecks to be drawn on an in-state bank, when the companies use a centralized disbursement system with the primary disbursement bank located in a different state. The *cost dilemma* springs from the large number of small-dollar checks that a company issues. This can be handled by attaching a draft to the purchase order, called a **purchase order with payment voucher attached**. Good only up to a specified dollar amount, the draft (voucher) is filled out for the amount of sale and then detached and deposited by the supplier after the goods are shipped. These drafts save payables processing time and expense for the customer and eliminate supplier invoicing and receivables processing. *Funding uncertainty* arises because banks do not generally provide same-day presentment information on regular checking accounts; this has been addressed through specialized checking accounts called controlled disbursement accounts and zero balance accounts.

A **controlled disbursement account** is a checking account for which the bank provides early morning presentment information via a telephone call, fax, Web site or computer message to the cash manager. The bank is able to ensure the total amount is accurate because it receives only one presentment daily[12] and does not permit same-day availability for electronic or physical presentments (direct sends or over-the-counter presentments) after that time. The major advantage to the disbursing company is the ability to maintain zero or minimal balances in the disbursement account. This means that no disbursement forecast needs to be made, and otherwise idle balances can be invested on an overnight basis for a greater yield than would have been earned in a sweep account. The company also picks up a small clearing float increase because the controlled disbursement account is generally located near a regional check processing center or at a country bank. For example, Cleveland's National City Bank runs its accounts through its Ashland, Ohio, affiliate. Companies are careful to avoid the appearance of maximizing clearance float, however, because the practice is considered unethical and is in violation of Justice Department guidelines issued as part of its prosecution of E.F. Hutton.[13]

Controlled disbursement accounts are very popular with mid-sized and larger companies. A 2000 Phoenix-Hecht survey found that almost 90 percent of large corporations

---

[12] Increasingly, as part of the Fed's High Dollar Group Sort program, the bank also receives a late-morning presentment of large checks. The Fed provides the bank with advance warning of this noon presentment by electronic notification of dollar totals so that the bank can pinpoint the day's total presentments and then communicate the figure to the payor while there are still good investment opportunities.

[13] A predecessor of the controlled disbursement account, the remote disbursement account is now used by relatively few companies. It purposefully picks banks in remote areas (hypothetically, "Sneaky Falls," Wyoming), which maximizes clearance float and minimizes prospects of over-the-counter check cashing.

## Exhibit 11–5

*Use of Disbursement Services as Compared with Collection and Information Services*

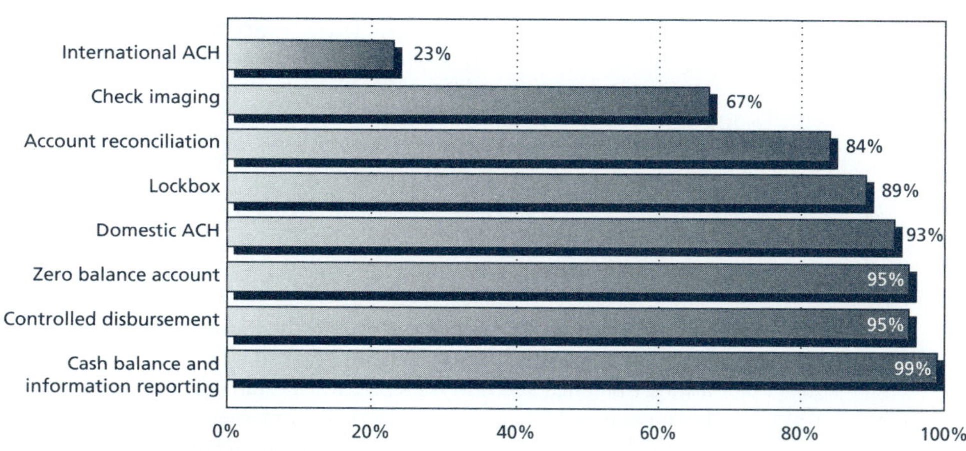


*Source:* Based on Greenwich Associates 2000 study of the cash management practices of large U.S. corporations. Greenwich Associates, Greenwich, CT 06831.

and almost 70 percent of mid-sized corporations used these accounts.[14] Greenwich Associates data (shown in Exhibit 11–5) show 95 percent usage of controlled disbursement accounts by mid-sized and large companies, up from 81 percent in 1990, and 73 percent in 1986. Utilization rates are much lower for smaller companies. The economies of scale inherent in use of software for which a bank pays an annual license fee (representing a fixed cost) increasingly make the controlled disbursement account a competitively priced service. This, in turn, makes it cost beneficial for smaller companies to adopt the controlled disbursement account.

If the controlled disbursement account typically maintains a zero balance (which is actually negative by the amount of the day's presentments until the account is funded), it qualifies as one type of **zero balance account** (ZBA). A ZBA maintains a zero dollar balance because another company account, usually the master or concentration account, automatically funds the total presented against it each day.[15] By special arrangement with the bank, the company may have several ZBAs, each of which is funded from another account at the same bank or a correspondent bank at the time checks are presented (a setup with three ZBAs is depicted in Exhibit 11–6). At all other times, the balance is zero, meaning that no idle funds are left in the non-interest-bearing account. If the ZBA also receives deposits, any positive balances will be transferred to the master or concentration account. In total, the company can have lower deposit balances because the cash flow variability can be managed in the master account instead of holding positive balances in each indi-

[14] Cited in "Cash Management Trends for a New Century: Quality and Consolidation. A Report from the 2000 Cash Management Monitor Survey," by Phoenix-Hecht, 2000. Published online at **http://www.phoenixhecht.com**. Used by permission of Phoenix-Hecht, Inc. This survey targets companies of $40 million or better in sales.

[15] Not all ZBAs are controlled disbursement accounts. Banks do not notify the ZBA holder of daily presentments but automatically debit the master or concentration account to cover the sum of ZBA presentments. With a controlled disbursement account, the advance notification gives the cash manager time to arrange a transfer, sale of securities, or credit line drawdown.

**Exhibit 11-6**

*Typical Zero Balance Account Configuration*

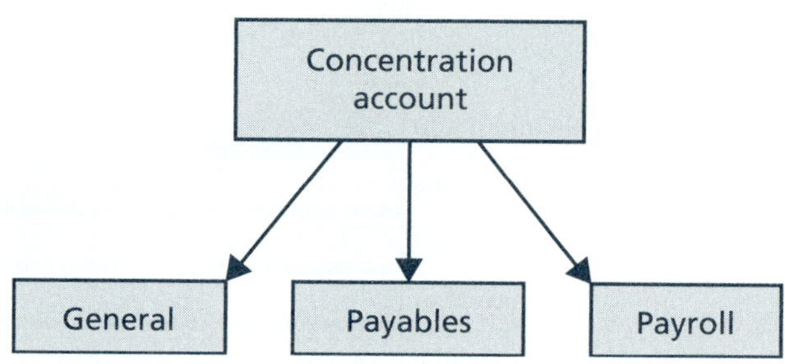


vidual account. Because of the risk to the bank that the corporate account holder will not have adequate funds for the automatic transfer into a ZBA, a pseudo-ZBA (perhaps called a target balance account) is sometimes established instead. This type of account has daily balances equal to an average day's disbursements. Some banks require ZBA account holders to also hold money market investment accounts and/or credit lines at the bank. Cash managers should realize that their company will have to pass a credit review to be approved for a controlled disbursement account or ZBA because the bank is exposed to the risk that a company will be unable to fund the account. The bank's exposure lasts from the time of presentment until the time of funding.

Should a company set up ZBAs or controlled disbursement accounts? The answer depends on many of the factors that we have highlighted throughout this chapter:

- Companies with centralized disbursing can set up controlled disbursement accounts or ZBAs at each subsidiary or division and then fund these from a central master account.
- Either type of account is advisable when a company's cash flows are unpredictable; the account should be tied to an investment account or credit line when cash receipts are volatile.
- Neither account makes sense if the company needs only one disbursement account and receives an earnings credit rate roughly equivalent to the rate at which the company could invest excess balances.
- ZBAs that upstream funds to a concentration account might be preferable for the company whose divisional personnel do not have the time or expertise to determine where to invest freed-up funds.
- A controlled disbursement account generally is used instead of a ZBA when the company has no master account at the disbursement bank, its affiliates, or correspondent banks—implying automatic transfers are not as easily accomplished.
- Companies with tight cash positions might prefer the extra control afforded by the controlled disbursement account, which provides extra flexibility by giving early-morning notification of the day's disbursements.

The number of accounts set up might depend on the number of decentralized disbursement locations and the company's desire to gain additional clearance float. Controlled disbursement accounts typically provide about half a day's additional float; Chase obtains this by disbursing from Syracuse instead of from the customer's concentration account location (New York City).

*ACCOUNT FUNDING* Funding of disbursement accounts in a complex disbursement system is often based on a choice between several vehicles. ZBAs commonly are funded by intrabank transfers from master accounts or concentration accounts, overnight bank loans paid off by next-day funds transfers,[16] and money market funds. Controlled disbursement accounts might be funded in the same ways, as well as by maturing overnight investments (usually repurchase agreements), wire transfers, or ACH debits to a funding account. Until same-day settlement is available through the ACH system, many companies will continue to leave monies equivalent to one day's average disbursements in the disbursement account. ACH funding is preferred over wire transfers because it presently costs $1 or less per transaction, whereas wire transfers involve a total charge of $15 to $17. Most companies use wire transfers or ACH debits for funding controlled disbursement accounts.

*ELECTRONIC DISBURSING MECHANISMS* Companies with sophisticated disbursing systems not only use electronic funds transfers to fund disbursement accounts but also increasingly pay employees and suppliers electronically via ACH transfers. We discuss the electronic payment alternatives from the decision maker's perspective and then devote the following sections to the combination of EDI with electronic fund transfers and international disbursing.

**Direct deposit** of payroll is easily the most popular electronic payment application. Greenwich survey data indicate that two of five companies having sales of $5 to $9 million and four of five companies having sales of at least $250 million use payroll direct deposit.[17] One-half of all ACH transactions in the United States are electronic payroll deposits. The federal government has given a strong impetus to direct deposit by implementing it for a significant proportion of Social Security payments. The company's payroll department provides employees' banks (for employees who have opted for direct deposit) with a computerized listing of employees, their Social Security numbers, bank account numbers, and payment amounts. This is done at least two days before payday. When communicating direct deposit information electronically, the company simply transmits the data to the region's ACH for all employees' banks that are members of the ACH.[18] Advantages include reductions in the number of lost and stolen checks; in payroll processing, check printing, and storage costs; and in disbursement bank charges. Personal computer software can automatically format employee payment data in ACH format. Now, direct deposit applications are being extended with increasing frequency to travel and entertainment reimbursement, dividends, pension payments, and interest. The federal government and Missouri, Pennsylvania, and New Jersey are beginning to use electronic benefit transfer as a way to reduce administrative costs and the risk of fraud.

Paying vendors through ACH debits and credits is increasingly attractive to companies. Although some suppliers are very inefficient in processing customers' check payments, mainly because of slow invoicing or slow check processing before deposit, the disbursement float advantage of paying most suppliers by check has been greatly reduced in recent years. The small remaining float must be weighed against the primary electronic payment advantages: reductions in bank charges, internal processing costs, and decreased potential for fraud or error. Paying suppliers electronically is most often accomplished through an ACH transaction. A major impetus to electronic payment is the insistence by

---

[16] When preauthorized loan arrangements are used, the coverage of presentments achieves the same goal as an overdraft disbursement account, which is common in Europe but cannot be offered in the United States.

[17] Cited in "The Best Bank Monitor," Greenwich Associates (2000).

[18] Nonelectronic direct deposit also is possible and is best accomplished by opening zero balance disbursement accounts at all the employees' banks, so that each bank can transfer funds by making on-us bookkeeping transactions.

## FOCUS ON PRACTICE

### *Pizza Franchises Send the Dough Electronically*

Franchises of a national pizza chain formerly placed their orders for supplies and ingredients with the parent company headquarters and later paid with mailed checks. Now, they order and issue payment instructions electronically. They dial up the company's computer system and key in specific payment and invoice information, such as the store ID number and payment amount using a touch-tone telephone. The parent company creates debit instructions and transmits them to its bank, which in turn initiates an ACH debit to collect the funds from the franchise's bank. The franchises much prefer the new system.

*Source:* Presented in Walter C. Repak, "'What Check?'—Innovative Electronic Payments," *TMA Journal* (November/December 1995), pp. 50–53.

the Internal Revenue Service that any corporation having $47 million or more of payroll taxes (withheld employee income taxes, Social Security, and railroad retirement contributions) per year *must* pay those taxes electronically through the Electronic Federal Tax Payment System (EFTPS). Forty states now have voluntary or mandatory electronic remittance of certain business and withholding taxes.

An **ACH debit** is a payment order originated by the payee, based on the prior authorization by the payor, which is routed through the payee's bank [originating depository financial institution (ODFI)]. If the payee's bank [receiving depository financial institution (RDFI)] is a member of the same ACH as the originating institution, the bookkeeping entries to make the transfer are made by that ACH's computer. Otherwise, the ACH (now called the **originating ACH**) must transmit the payment order to the receiving institution's ACH (termed the **receiving ACH**). Presently, the major uses of debits are the collection of preauthorized dealer and distributor payments and internal cash concentration transfers (see the Focus on Practice). An **ACH credit** is originated by the payor, so the routing bank (originating institution) in this case is the payor's disbursement bank. Direct deposit of payroll or dividends and payment of trade accounts payable are the most common uses of credits.

Companies initiate ACH payments by putting transaction details into standardized computer formats prescribed by the National Automated Clearing House Association and then transmitting the transactions to the originating institution. The five formats that companies can use, and their advantages and disadvantages, are listed in Exhibit 11–7. One of these formats, corporate trade exchange (CTX), is commonly used along with EDI. The most recent addition is the CBR, or corporate cross-border payment. CBR is used for the transmission of corporate cross-border ACH credit and debit entries. Canadian entries are the most common CBRs, but Mexico debits and credits on a regular basis, and credits from the United States to five European nations on a pilot basis became available in 2004. Despite the cost advantages experienced by companies such as Sears, as documented in the opening Financial Dilemma, companies continue to resist abandonment of simple check-based disbursement systems. A 1998 Treasury Management Association (TMA) survey[19] found that the despite the federal and state mandates to have tax payments made electronically (implying at least some corporate familiarity with electronic payments),

[19] Aaron L. Phillips (1998), cited in the end-of-chapter references.

**Exhibit 11-7**

*Corporate ACH Payment Formats*

| Format | Uses | Advantages/Disadvantages |
|---|---|---|
| Prearranged payments and deposits (PPD) | Direct deposit of payroll, automatic utility, or loan bill paying services. | Normally settle in two business days; generally used only for crediting or debiting consumers' accounts. |
| Cash concentration or disbursements (CCD) | Movement of funds to concentration accounts or electronic payment of suppliers. | Electronic depository transfer checks (EDTCs or EDTs) created for next-day settlement. Simple data format and almost universal ability of banks to initiate or receive account for increasing utilization. |
| CCD plus addenda (CCD +) | The federal government uses this format in its Vendor Express payments. This format adds an addendum (up to 80 characters of computer-readable data) to the CDD format, enabling computerized relay of the remittance data into the cash application component of the company's receivables software. | Next-day settlement. Banks may not be able to capture and relay the addenda information, however. |
| Corporate trade exchange (CTX) | Used for intercorporate payments. As many as 4,990 addenda records (an invoice might be one record). A standardized (ANSI X12) format that already is used by numerous companies in dealings with suppliers and customers via EDI. | Next-day settlement and standardized formats. The number of banks that can originate and receive has been an impediment to use, but that number is increasing rapidly. Companies can read and translate ANSI X12 for automatic processing and updating of payments. Encryption and authentication is feasible. |
| Corporate cross-border payment (CBR) | Used for the transmission of corporate cross-border ACH credit and debit entries. | The CBR format is able to include detailed information unique to cross-border payments (e.g., foreign exchange conversion, origination and destination currency, country codes, etc.). |

many companies continue to resist electronic payments because of the lack of vendor (trading partner) capability to receive electronic payment with the associated remittance information, lack of systems integration, and costs of additional technology. Other surveys have indicated that renegotiating credit terms to share the float savings may be an issue. Regarding the latter, one Midwestern hospital supply company added up to 15 days to its credit terms to induce hospitals to pay electronically. An impediment that was not mentioned, but which may surpass all others in importance, is the loss of flexibility when switching to electronic payments. This is especially true for payee-initiated ACH debits. It is much easier to stretch payables ("the check's in the mail") than to delay electronic disbursements. Then, when the check is actually mailed, the disbursement float further delays value loss. The 1998 TMA survey indicates that average mail float was 3.2 days, equal to the average of bank-clearing times for check disbursements.

*Electronic Data Interchange* Prospects for electronic payments are improving because more companies are using EDI. **Electronic data interchange** (EDI) is the electronic transmission of purchase-related data, such as orders, shipping notices, invoices, credits and other adjustments, and payment notices. The data are in standardized computer-readable format.[20] Companies began using EDI for electronic purchase orders and have begun transmitting invoices and shipping receipts electronically. An increasing number of companies were adopting **financial EDI**, which adds electronic disbursing via an ACH transfer to the process, but some of this usage is being replaced by Internet transaction initiation. (A 2002 Phoenix-Hecht survey found that 36 percent of upper-middle market companies and 24 percent of large corporates initiate ACH transactions via the Internet.) One estimate of the total cost to payor and payee of handling the exchange of paper documents and making a single payment by check is $8.33 per payment, as compared to $3 for handling the same transaction using financial EDI. Phoenix-Hecht 2000 survey data document 64 percent large company (sales of at least $500 million) and 50 percent upper-middle company (sales of $100 to $499 million) usage of corporate trade payments. Note in Exhibit 11–8 the increased usage rates of direct deposit of payroll and corporate trade payments as company size increases. It is also noteworthy that from 1996 to 2000 usage rates of electronic disbursing products increased dramatically for companies regardless of size.

In a situation involving product delivery and repeat orders, companies are increasingly paying under **evaluated receipt settlement (ERS)**. In this electronic payment process, the buyer triggers payment on receipt of goods, not invoice arrival. Invoices are eliminated, and price and payment terms are determined in advance. Bar codes on merchandise are scanned when received at the loading dock. That information is transmitted to payables to trigger payment. Evaluated receipt settlement is usually tied to EDI but can be used as a separate process. It is used primarily in the auto industry, but use is expanding to other

**Exhibit 11–8**

*Trends in ACH Payments*

ACH Usage

| | Middle Market | | Upper-Middle Market | | | Large Corporate | | |
|---|---|---|---|---|---|---|---|---|
| | 1999 | 2001 | 1996 | 1998 | 2000 | 1996 | 1998 | 2000 |
| Direct deposit of payroll | 73.2 | 83.7 | 68.0 | 73.8 | 91.1 | 77.5 | 80.2 | 96.5 |
| ACH concentration debits | 51.9 | 53.9 | 58.8 | 61.2 | 62.6 | 74.2 | 74.5 | 74.1 |
| Corporate trade payments | 36.4 | 41.9 | 34.4 | 41.5 | 49.9 | 53.6 | 59.9 | 64.2 |

Middle market—Annual sales $40–$100 million
Upper-middle market—Annual sales $100–$500 million
Large corporate—Annual sales over $500 million

*Source:* Middle Market Monitor Report to Respondents 2001; Cash Management Trends for a New Century—Quality and Consolidation. Phoenix-Hecht Cash Management Monitor™ **http://www.phoenixhecht.com/**. Reprinted with permission of Phoenix-Hecht, Inc.

[20] Electronic mail and facsimile (fax) transmissions are not considered EDIs because they are not in structured form nor are they computer-readable. They are, however, considered part of electronic commerce.

similar industries. As payables management is increasingly automated, EDI and financial EDI or the Internet replacement for it will be more commonly used. We will return to these topics in Chapter 19.

## Disbursement System Trends

We briefly profile four related trends in domestic disbursement systems: comprehensive payables, purchasing cards, payables security and fraud prevention, and use of the Internet for ordering and payment. The first two are forms of **outsourcing**, or contracting with outside companies to do certain business functions, and are mainly cost motivated. Security and fraud prevention are largely responses to the advances in technology that make it easier to issue bogus checks and the shorter availability times mandated under Regulation CC. The fourth trend represents a small but explosively growing mode of EDI and financial EDI.

**Comprehensive payables**, also called integrated payables, involve the outsourcing of part or all of the accounts payable and/or disbursements functions. Some companies outsource payments; others outsource almost the entire payables function. For example, CoreStates, a large eastern bank, offers a "CorePay" service in which it receives from the company a daily payables file in an agreed-on format and then creates paper checks, ACH, or wire transactions for the company. Remittance information can be delivered with the payment or transmitted directly to the payee via a third-party company. Advanced notification may be optionally provided to the payees. From the company's perspective, this service may reduce the internal and external payables costs while streamlining or enhancing the company's payables system. For example, Thrift Drug estimates that it saves $7,000 per month by having a bank handle its pharmacy payments instead of having its own employees process the payments internally. A company may outsource more of the payables function by providing to its banks more extensive payables information, starting as early in the payment process as the original purchase order initiation. Some companies transmit trade payables, employee reimbursement, and employee benefit payment information. The data are provided to the bank, which develops a database of the company's payees, preferred payment methods, transit routing numbers of payees' banks, and other remittance information. The database is periodically updated with new payees or changes to existing payee profiles. First Union, now part of Wachovia, notes four advantages for the paying company:

1. Increased accuracy—elimination of paper documents and manual data entry
2. Improved cash flow management—the use of EDI and financial EDI, and the certain payment timing that results
3. Reduced administrative costs—computer exchange of data instead of human involvement
4. Proactive control—payables transmitted in EDI format include control totals, or if not in EDI format, the company faxes, mails, or e-mails control totals to the bank, ensuring file accuracy and an improved audit trail

Greenwich survey data indicate that 15 percent of companies having $500 million or more in sales are using payables outsourcing. With the recent emphasis on fraud prevention, and given that 90 percent of check fraud is committed against corporations (St. Goar, 1996), moving the liability to a third party is attractive. Even without any reduction in fraud, the net present value of a switch to integrated payables can be impressive, as the Focus on Practice indicates.

**Purchase cards**, also called procurement cards, are another form of outsourcing. Because it costs from $25 to $45 to process a purchase order all the way through payment,

# FOCUS ON PRACTICE

## The NPV of Comprehensive Payables

One of the first considerations for companies considering outsourcing much or all of their payables function is the strategic objectives, possibly including:

- Greater predictability of cash flow
- Use of technology to create efficiencies and allow staff to focus on more important tasks
- Minimization of cost and risk
- Contingency processing and disaster recovery capabilities

These factors seem to favor outsourcing payables, but a complete analysis requires a comparison of the costs and benefits of the company's existing internal payment process with those of the prospective bank partner's comprehensive payables service—all relative to the strategic business objectives. Some items of concern are obvious such as paper stock, postage, and printers, but others are less apparent such as the staff required to initiate and deliver payments and the cost of fraud and potential risk. Another key consideration is the possibility of improved trading partner relationships that could result from better meeting their changing needs and demands. All relevant components, both quantitative and qualitative, must be evaluated in terms of the potential benefits related to cost/profit, cash flow, customer service, or risk exposure. Conversion costs and/or sunk costs of investment in printers, real estate, or personnel may seem to outweigh the possible benefits and often present a barrier to change. However, when viewed for the longer term and in a broader context using net present value, an entirely different picture may emerge, as we see in the following table, which uses hypothetical but realistic company data. The positive NPV signals a value-enhancing investment opportunity.

**Net Present Value Using Sample Data**

| | |
|---|---|
| Check volume per month | 75,000 |
| Total per-check cost (Internal production) | $1.10 |
| Total per-check cost (Outsourced/Integrated payables) | $1.03 |
| Total per-ACH cost (Outsourced/Integrated payables) | $0.50 |
| Assume 15 percent of payments transition from check to ACH: | |
| New check volume per month | 63,750 |
| ACH volume per month | 11,250 |
| Net monthly variance using IP solution | $11,212 |
| Annual variance | $134,544 |
| Cost of process reengineering & conversion | $350,000 |

Assume 12-percent minimum acceptable rate of return and a 5-year annuity period:
Annuity discount factor is 3.605
NPV = $134,544(3.605) − $350,000 = $135,031

*Source:* Adapted from Jennifer B. Dunn, "Integrated Payables Solutions: Understanding the Net Present Value," from *The Accounts Payable Network* at **http://www.theaccountspayablenetwork.com/html.** © 2003, *The Accounts Payable Network* (**http://www.tapn.com**).

companies are eliminating the requirement for requisitions and purchase orders and allowing employees to use a credit card to make purchases of small-dollar maintenance, repair, and operating supplies. Although they may not get much purchase detail on the monthly statement, companies appreciate having to only make one payment instead of hundreds or thousands per month for these items. A list of approved vendors may be kept on an internal database, often an intranet, or the company may allow the employee to buy from any vendor accepting VISA, MasterCard, or American Express credit cards. Phoenix-Hecht survey data in 2000 found that although less than 35 percent of corporations used purchase cards, 49 percent of companies with revenues of $500 million or more (up from 25 percent in 1996) were using them. The main obstacles to further growth, the survey showed, were low management priority, loss of control, time commitment to implement, lack of systems resources, cost, and state sales and use tax issues. A 2003 survey by Treasury & Risk Management found that one-half of companies use p-cards, mostly for office supplies or travel and entertainment purchases, with 30 percent of companies having a $1,500 maximum transaction size and an additional 40 percent having a maximum transaction size of between $2,000 and $5,000. About 6 in 10 respondents expected more users to use p-cards in their particular company in the future. The chief benefit seen by users is reduced administrative burden or paperwork.

One of the biggest trends in the past decade was the increased attention paid to payables security and fraud prevention. Check fraud has grown exponentially in recent years, with FBI estimates for the United States at about $12 billion. A 2003 KPMG survey of 459 U.S. public companies and government agencies determined that 40 percent of respondents have detected check fraud in their organizations, up from 26 percent just five years earlier.[21] Banks absorb about $1 billion of the loss, but corporations suffer $11 billion in loss. In contested cases, corporations usually end up with the loss liability. Consultant Larry Marks of Marks & Associates estimates that not including any losses for fraudulent checks, the cost to a company for just one occurrence of check fraud may be from $4,000 to $5,000![22] This includes reconciliation time, correction (stop payment, possibly reissue), managerial time, and incidental costs. If the firm decides to contest the bank's dishonoring of the check and this entails (internal or external) legal counsel, the cost reaches about $12,000 to $15,000 per occurrence. Marks concludes that the most common occurrence of check fraud is with payroll checks. Some of the steps being taken to prevent fraud include positive pay, reverse positive pay, internal controls (including bonding employees), and greater use of financial EDI. In the case of **positive pay**, a company sends its daily check issue file to its disbursing bank. Before it honors incoming checks, the bank refers to the issue file to see if the payee and check amounts match. If they do not (e.g., because a check issued later in the day was presented as an on-us check), the bank contacts the issuer to see whether the item should be honored. In the case of **reverse positive pay**, the disbursement bank sends the check presentment file to the company to see if all the items should be honored (a system that operates much like payable through-drafts). Banks now offer Web-based or CD-based images so that corporate personnel may look at the image of the front and back of the check before deciding whether to honor the item, and optical character recognition ability at some leading banks now includes an attempted computerized match-up to payee information as part of the initial check issue file data feed. Internal controls include special check stock (e.g., checks that have the word *VOID* showing diagonally across them when photocopied), restrictions on check stock access (or use of laser-printed checks), and restrictions on the checks issued file. Companies are more attuned to internal controls because of the documentation requirements imposed by the Sarbanes-Oxley Act in 2002, as implemented in 2004. A 2003 Treasury Strategies survey found that 80 percent of survey respondents were reviewing controls on treasury-related activities as well as documenting controls and Treasury procedures.[23] Most banks do not sign up a new controlled disbursement account customer without a positive pay or reverse positive pay agreement. Finally, some companies are moving toward ACH payments as a way of reducing the number of checks issued, but this has spawned new concerns about unauthorized ACH debits when debits are used rather than credits for trade payments. A

---

[21] "Seek and Ye Shall Find Fraud," *Treasury & Risk Management* (December/January 2004), p. 14.

[22] Quoted in Zietlow (2003), cited in the end-of-chapter references.

[23] Treasury Strategies, Inc., "The 2003 Corporate Treasury Survey" (2003), p. 9.

Chicago Clearing House study determined that almost 40 percent of large corporations have had unauthorized ACH debits to their accounts, and even some checks returned as part of positive pay services have been converted to ACH debits and successfully charged to the account (although daily reconciliations will catch these and allow for ACH returns, and companies can use debit blocks to thwart these attempts).[24] Bonding (buying a fidelity bond is an insurance policy against embezzlement), positive pay, and direct deposit services help deal with the symptoms of integrity and fraud issues. However, ethics experts suggest that hiring employees committed to integrity is the key step in prevention.

The Internet is probably the single biggest development within the electronic commerce field; most businesses are in the beginning stages of using it for business applications. The Internet may be thought of as a network connecting many computer networks, based on a common communications protocol. An organization known as CommerceNet is bringing a wide range of business services, including financial EDI, to the Internet. This is appealing because most companies already have access to the Internet or can gain access inexpensively, saving the cost of investing in specialized software and of paying a third-party company substantial monthly connect fees. Furthermore, the problems of differing corporate systems and their incompatibilities are eliminated when using the Internet. For example, Lawrence Livermore National Laboratory inserts standard EDI transactions inside secure e-mail envelopes and mails them over the Internet. Digital signatures and encryption are used as security measures (these are discussed further in Chapter 19). Many mid-sized companies use the Internet instead of EDI to get around the message formatting and costs of EDI; Greenwich survey data indicate that 35 percent of mid-sized companies now initiate payments over the Internet, and Phoenix-Hecht survey data bear this out. Furthermore, the Financial Services Technology Consortium has developed an enhanced, all-electronic check for use over the Internet. Businesses and consumers can create "digitally signed checks" (with the help of a secure memory card) and deliver them to authorized recipients by "sending" them (much like an e-mail message) over the Internet. Eventually, it is hoped that recipients will be able to authenticate the payments and deposit them immediately and directly into their bank accounts, without any kind of physical movement.

A separate trend that may use Internet delivery and facilitate positive pay is **check imaging**. Phoenix-Hecht survey data indicate that the most important uses of imaging technology are for long-term storage of paid items and online approval of positive pay items. Imaging for same-day retrieval of recently paid items is also moderately important. All three services are rated slightly more important for larger companies than mid-sized ones. (Imaging is also used on the collection side, with imaging of return documents and checks slightly more important than imaging for long-term storage of paid items.)

Integrated evaluation of the entire purchasing and payables process, not just the payment mechanism used, offers tremendous profit and value enhancement. Most companies that have reengineered their payment methods have also reengineered their receivables and payables, including using EDI to eliminate paper and manual processing and using purchase cards to eliminate purchase orders on small-dollar maintenance, repair, and operating supplies. After a brief discussion of international disbursing, we can see how to calculate the value effects of disbursement decisions.

## GLOBAL DISBURSEMENT STRATEGIES

Our focus in presenting international disbursing is to highlight major elements affecting the international disbursement system: the payment system differences, the additional risks

[24] Richard Gamble (2004), cited in the end-of-chapter references.

involved, and advanced techniques for handling intracompany funds flows. When appropriate, we distinguish between foreign disbursements that are between countries and those that are within a given country. More detailed information on international cash management is provided in Chapter 18.

## Payment System Differences

One very important difference in disbursement systems abroad is the existence of interest-bearing demand deposit accounts, often with an automatic overdraft provision. This makes the minimization of disbursement account balances and careful control of those balances much less important. Not surprisingly, controlled disbursement accounts are rarely available outside the United States. One caution is appropriate: The interest rate on deposit balances may be relatively low, especially relative to the interest rate charged when the account is overdrafted.

A second difference is that disbursement float on checks depends greatly on what currency the check is denominated in and from where it is mailed. Checks must clear back to the country of the currency in which the check is denominated because there is no centralized settlement bank. If Ford Motor Company's German subsidiary sends a dollar-denominated check to a French supplier, the check must clear back to the U.S. bank on which it is written, even if that bank has a European branch. The clearing time could exceed a week in such a case. Furthermore, when a European customer sends a euro-denominated check to a multinational company in the United States, the mail time from a European city to New York City might also exceed a week. But within a given country, check clearing is usually quite rapid because of the smaller geographic area most countries occupy and the smaller number of banks within most foreign countries.

Third, there are two payment mechanisms that are much more prominent in foreign transactions. We have mentioned the giro system that is popular in Europe, which uses postal system clearing of many payments. This and other direct debit systems are very common abroad. We also noted in Chapter 8 the use of drafts in international purchases. Both mechanisms greatly reduce both the importance of and discretion over disbursement float. Value dating, a European practice in which debits of checking accounts may be back-valued to the date on which checks were issued, may further reduce disbursement float. These payment system differences are reflected in the Focus on Practice.

## International Disbursing Risks

Two risks that must be carefully evaluated in administering international disbursements are country risk and foreign exchange risk. **Country risk** refers to the possibility of loss of assets resulting from political, economic, or regulatory instability in the nation in which business is being conducted. Studies of country risk are usually conducted by banks or specialized consultants. **Foreign exchange risk** is the possibility that exchange rates will move adversely, causing foreign business transactions to have a reduced value when converted into the company's home currency. Various strategies are used to manage this risk. A simple strategy is to expedite outgoing disbursements when it is feared that a local currency will weaken (drop in value) against the dollar. The Brazilian subsidiary anticipating paying a dividend to its U.S.-based parent will accelerate the disbursement if a depreciation of the cruzeiro is anticipated. It is hoped that this payment will be made before the depreciation occurs; if not, less dollars will be received on exchange.

## Managing International Intracorporate Payments

Companies can adopt two advanced mechanisms to manage intracorporate payments: netting systems and reinvoicing centers. **Bilateral** and **multilateral netting systems** are cen-

## FOCUS ON PRACTICE

### *Pointers for Making International Payments*

Disbursements outside one's home country can be tricky. Here are six pointers for making international payments:

1. When you begin making payments internationally, look for a provider with global knowledge and international capabilities. It is often more efficient to initiate a new relationship with an international payments bank that has operations in the countries in which you anticipate doing business. This is so because using foreign currency checks for small value payments and wire transfers through a correspondent banking network for high value payments must pass through several banks, increasing expense and reducing speed. Furthermore, the global bank may be able to facilitate payables outsourcing as payment volumes grow.
2. Understand the payment mechanisms and the preferred payment method in each country where you conduct business. Just because a payment mechanism is available in your country does not mean it will be in every country abroad. In Germany, checks account for less than 8 percent of all payments made, both retail and wholesale, and in the Scandinavian countries less than 1 percent of payments are by check. Banks can help in this assessment, or you can go to Web sites such as that offered by the Bank of International Settlements to get this information.
3. Seek alternative ways of providing detailed remittance information. Using in-country local banks for local currency and cross-border payments within a region provides access to less expensive, local clearing systems, but at the price of an inability to move remittance data with the payment through banks and the local clearing systems. The remittance advices may be mailed separately, they may be conveyed via the Internet, or a provider may automatically produce and mail this detail for you.
4. Centralize your accounts payable and consider outsourcing options for all of your payments within a region. Establish a regional headquarters to centralize and control payables, if possible. Some companies outsource payments through a shared service central managed by a regional network bank that operates in the same countries as the company. The bank essentially acts as the company's regional central for funds disbursement.
5. Automate your payables function. Functions may be duplicated at various local sites. One company doing a treasury review found out that its decentralized disbursement process involved more than 800 locations issuing disbursement checks and was able to both reduce risk and cut $400,000 in administrative costs annually (McDonough, 1997). When centralizing payments at a regional headquarters, efficiency is gained but the complexity of making payments in many different payment systems within central bank reporting requirements can be overwhelming. The solution is to automate payments, possibly by having a bank accept a single electronic file of both electronic and check disbursements in one format, which is then reformatted into the various formats required by other countries' clearing systems. The company can also use industry standard formats or common EDI message standards for payment instructions.
6. Work toward creating a "global payments factory." A "super center" may be able to handle a company's payments regardless of their destination worldwide in the not-too-distant future. Several regional centers can be tied together as part of the company's enterprise resource planning (ERP) system. A bank with global payments capability and linkages to all major local clearing systems can pave the way for making the necessary country-by-country modifications of payment instructions.

*Source:* Michael Burn, "Making International Payments—Navigating the Course," *AFP Exchange* (Winter 2000), pp. 62–64.

tralized bookkeeping entries made to eliminate (net out) offsetting amounts owed by divisions or subsidiaries within a company. Only the net amount owed between the entities is actually transferred, and that transfer may only be a bookkeeping transaction, as opposed to an actual funds transfer. These systems greatly reduce the average size and actual number of transfers and simplify the monitoring and control of multinational operations. A bilateral system nets out any two divisions' charges, whereas a multilateral system nets out charges among several entities, with only the net amount owed to (or from) a subsidiary from all other company entities actually being transferred to (or from) that subsidiary. Cash managers should be aware that South American countries may prohibit netting systems as part of their system of foreign exchange controls, and some European countries require that the company establish a formal agreement when setting up a netting system. Netting systems usually are administered in-house but may be operated by one of the company's banks.

Reinvoicing centers include a netting system but also use a centralized foreign exchange monitoring and control capability. A **reinvoicing center** buys raw materials and final products from producing units of the company, then rebills (reinvoices) those items to foreign selling subsidiaries and noncompany customers. The major advantage of reinvoicing is centralized foreign exchange exposure, removing exposure from all subsidiaries. Lesser advantages include better control and monitoring of company cash flows, particularly intracompany payables and receivables, added flexibility of subsidiary-to-subsidiary or subsidiary-to-parent payments, and possible tax advantages if transfer prices are set at a higher level to compensate the reinvoicing center's services.[25] Strategic timing of payables and receivables, illustrated earlier, is greatly facilitated by such an arrangement.

## OPTIMIZING THE DISBURSEMENT SYSTEM

We opened the chapter by defining a company's disbursement system as its payment methods and disbursement banks and disbursing locations and suggesting that the disbursement policy should maximize value through payment timing, optimize the accuracy and timeliness of information, and minimize balances in disbursement accounts. Ideally, the optimal disbursement system is assembled by formulating disbursement strategies and goals while considering the company's collection and concentration systems, selecting the appropriate disbursement mechanisms and account structures, selecting the best disbursement banking network that offers those mechanisms and accounts, establishing a disbursement security and control process, and specifying how and when elements of the company's disbursement system will be re-evaluated. Profitability assessment and valuation of alternatives enable the manager to carry out the second and third steps by showing the financial impact of various alternatives. We demonstrate the financial analysis applicable to disbursement mechanisms and bank selection by detailing three of the four major decisions. Although it would be ideal to si-

[25] Originally, reinvoicing centers were principally motivated by the lower tax rates in particular countries. The U.S. tax code (subpart F) now provides that profits generated by reinvoicing are taxable at the U.S. tax rate whether they are remitted or retained. The U.S. tax code does allow a credit to U.S. corporate income taxes for taxes paid abroad, however, and a U.S.-based multinational company anticipating foreign tax credits in excess of its U.S. tax liability may benefit from reinvoicing. By charging higher transfer prices to subsidiaries located in countries with high tax rates, the subsidiaries' tax payments (and the associated credit) will be reduced. Although the multinational must pay tax at the U.S. rate on the now-higher reinvoicing center's profits, the company saves on balance because the U.S. rate is less than would have been paid in the high-tax countries.

multaneously evaluate all four, it is too complex to do so in practice, and the decisions are treated separately. The four major decisions are:

1. Selection of the optimal disbursing mechanism for a given transaction or transaction type.
2. Establishment of the disbursement network by specifying the number and location(s) of disbursement accounts.
3. Selection of the disbursement bank(s).
4. Selection of the funding mechanism(s) for disbursement accounts.

### Selecting Optimal Disbursement Mechanisms

Recall the chapter's opening Financial Dilemma, in which Sears was used to illustrate the paper check versus ACH disbursing decision. We return to that situation now.

## FINANCIAL DILEMMA REVISITED

In evaluating the choice between paper check disbursement and ACH disbursement, we assume that the payment terms involve roughly equivalent timing of the transfer of value. Although not mentioned in the example, Sears would incur up-front investment costs to enable conversion to ACH disbursing; this initial incremental investment might be $40,000. Based on a perpetuity of 1,000 payments per month, per-payment savings of 40 cents, and an assumed annual cost of capital of 10 percent (which we convert to a monthly rate based on simple interest), the net present value of switching to ACH disbursing would be $8,000.19, as shown below:

$$
\begin{aligned}
NPV &= PV \text{ of net cash flow} - \text{Initial investment} \\
&= \frac{1{,}000 \times \$0.40}{(0.10/12)} - \$40{,}000 \\
&= \frac{\$400}{0.0083333} - \$40{,}000 \\
&= \$48{,}000.19 - \$40{,}000 \\
&= \$8{,}000.19
\end{aligned}
$$

The present value of the cash flows, excluding the initial investment ($48,000.19 in this case), represents the most Sears is willing to pay to implement the new disbursement system. The ACH savings are warranted on economic grounds. We add that a 2000 study found that e-payments cost 40 to 55 percent less than checks.[26]

Our first illustration addressed *company-wide* disbursement practices. A second use of valuation techniques is to determine if electronic payment terms *offered by an individual supplier* are at least as attractive as the present check payment.[27] Here, the objective is to minimize the present value of the outflow. The electronic alternative is preferable if the

---

[26] Humphrey, et al. (2002), cited in the end-of-chapter references. Resistance to electronic payments and how to overcome it is discussed in Wisecup and Zietlow (2003), cited in the end-of-chapter references.

[27] A full discussion of variants of the terms negotiated between supplier and customer is beyond the scope of this text. See the Hill and Ferguson citation in the end-of-chapter references for a more complete discussion.

present value of the outflow, including variable transaction costs, is less than it would be with a check. This hinges on the value transfer date specified in the electronic payment terms. We assume a longer period is given for payment initiation for electronic payments ($n_e$) than for checks ($n_c$) to offset the clearing delay (mail plus clearance float) advantage of checks. Relevant variables are defined as follows:

$A$ = Average payment amount ($)

$n_c$ = Credit period for check payment

$n_e$ = Credit period for electronic payment

$i$ = Daily cost of capital

$c_c$ = Clearing period for check payment

$c_e$ = Clearing period for electronic payment

$VC_c$ = Variable cost per check

$VC_e$ = Variable cost per electronic payment

The present value of the outflow for a check payment, $PV_c$, is given in Equation 11.1; a simple interest formula provides sufficient accuracy here because we are valuing only one payment:

$$PV_c = \frac{A}{[1 + i(n_c + c_c)]} + VC_c \tag{11.1}$$

The present value of the outflow for an electronic payment, $PV_e$, is shown in Equation 11.2:

$$PV_e = \frac{A}{[1 + i(n_e + c_e)]} + VC_e \tag{11.2}$$

Which payment method would be preferable to the payor if the credit period for checks is 30 days and for electronic payments is 31 days, the payor's daily cost of capital is 0.02740 percent (equivalent to 10 percent annually), the clearing period for checks is three days and for electronic payments is one day, the variable cost per check is $2.10 and per electronic payment is $1.00? The accounts payable area informs us that the average payment is $4,500. Substituting the numbers into Equation 11.1, the present value of the outflow when paying by check is:

$$\begin{aligned} PV_c &= \frac{\$4{,}500}{[1 + 0.0002740(30 + 3)]} + \$2.10 \\ &= \frac{\$4{,}500}{1.0090420} + \$2.10 \\ &= \$4{,}459.68 + \$2.10 \\ &= \$4{,}461.78 \end{aligned}$$

The present value outflow if payment is made electronically is found using Equation 11.2:

$$\begin{aligned} PV_e &= \frac{\$4{,}500}{[1 + 0.0002740(31 + 1)]} + \$1.00 \\ &= \frac{\$4{,}500}{1.008768} + \$1.00 \\ &= \$4{,}460.89 + \$1.00 \\ &= \$4{,}461.89 \end{aligned}$$

Because it involves lower present value costs, the check payment is slightly preferable, since $VC_e < VC_c$. This simple model can be extended to include discounts offered by the supplier to induce electronic payment, which in effect is a price change. The relative costs of capital of the customer and supplier are very important in that case; the customer may have a much lower cost of capital than the supplier and be willing to take a lower price but pay immediately. The supplier and customer can negotiate the share of the gains accruing from electronic disbursement in that situation.

## Selecting Disbursement Banks and Locations

Disbursement models used by banks and third-party consultants to assist companies in their selection of disbursement banks and account locations are very similar to lockbox models. Instead of minimizing collection float, the model might maximize disbursement float, or at least specify the float characteristics of various account sites. The disbursement model differs from a lockbox model because it takes into account the location of mailing points as well as of drawee banks. It is usually not advantageous to have disbursement accounts in a very large number of locations because of the cost of the accounts. Disbursement models use as inputs a sample of the company's checks and a proprietary database of clearing times. From this, using built-in computer algorithms, the model determines the optimal set of disbursement banks and assigns suppliers to these banks. To avoid the practice of remote disbursing and yet retain some clearance float, the model can assign all suppliers within a particular geographic area to the closest disbursement site.

We illustrate the process using the Phoenix-Hecht Disbursement Web Optimization Model, which runs on the Internet. The model works basically the same as the lockbox location model presented in Chapter 9, except that float is now maximized instead of minimized. Relatively few companies strictly follow the model's recommendations because of the ethical issues involved in remote mailing and remote disbursing. Exhibit 11–9 shows a comparison of the model's optimal disbursing locations, as compared with the company's one existing location. For the 31-day period sampled, the firm is paying $78,934,771 from its disbursement account in Grand Junction, Colorado. On average, the clearing float is 2.10 days for the present disbursement account. The model compares the float on all the checks presently written for various 1-site and 2-site disbursement combinations. Although a 2-site solution (not shown) of Wewoka, Oklahoma, and Lewistown, Montana, would give the most float, the extra cost of having two locations outweighs the float pickup, compared to disbursing only from the best 1-site location of Lewistown, Montana. Lewistown, Montana, compared to Grand Junction, Colorado, brings an additional 0.75 day of float, on average: 2.85 days versus 2.10 days. This brings an additional $191,808 of interest savings, assuming a 10 percent interest rate.

## Selecting Disbursement Funding Mechanism

Our final decision area is the choice of funding mechanisms for controlled disbursement accounts and zero balance accounts. This decision is very similar to the decision on how to transfer funds to a concentration account. The valuation analysis for this decision amounts to a simple profitability estimate. Basically, the lowest cost approach to funding the account is chosen, taking into account transfer costs and float. In almost every case, transfers from other accounts or ACH transfers are preferable to wire transfers because of the high cost of wires and the zero float aspect inherent in a wire's immediate value transfer.

## Other Factors

In addition to the value considerations we have analyzed, several other factors must be taken into account when optimizing the company's disbursement system. The main

**Exhibit 11–9**

*Optimal Disbursing Location(s) versus Present Locations*

Disbursement Analysis Prepared for Demo
Entire Check Sample

**Proposed System Processing Site Analysis**

| | Dollars | | Items | | Marginal Cost If Site Eliminated | |
|---|---|---|---|---|---|---|
| Site Name | Total | Pct | Total | Pct | Days | @ 10.0% |
| Lewistown, MT | $78,934,771 | 100.0% | 20 | 100.0% | 0.00 | $ 0 |
| Total | $78,934,771 | 100.0% | 20 | 100.0% | | |

**Proposed System**

| Site Name | Days Float | Cost |
|---|---|---|
| Lewistown, MT | 2.85 | $726,882 |
| Total | 2.85 | $726,882 |

**Current System Scheduled**

| Site Name | Days Float | Cost |
|---|---|---|
| Grand Junctn, CO | 2.10 | $535,075 |
| Total | 2.10 | $535,075 |

**Proposed System Savings**

| | Days Float | Cost |
|---|---|---|
| Current System | 2.10 | $535,075 |
| Proposed System | 2.85 | 726,882 |
| Savings | 0.75 | $191,808 |

*Source:* Page 10 of Web Optimization Disbursement Analysis, using Phoenix-Hecht Disbursement Model, Survey 2003–02.


considerations are the company's organizational form or structure, the size and frequency of disbursements, and the nature of the company's existing bank relationships. Risks are inherent in any decision; the moment a supplier finds out about your company's new disbursement sites, it may "deoptimize" the sites by changing lockbox or mail-to locations.

## SUMMARY

In this chapter, we have learned about the major disbursement strategies used by companies. The objective of a company's disbursement system is to pay with the right method, at the right time, in an efficient manner. Efficiency was shown to depend on the company's banking options and its particular characteristics. Some of the most important characteristics are the payment system of the country in which the company is operating, the company's policies and philosophy, its organizational structure, and the size and predictability of its cash flows.

Simple disbursement systems are paper-based and use basic funding mechanisms. Companies for which simple systems are appropriate are those with one or a few products, local operations and business dealings, and small predictable cash flows. If poorly managed, simple systems can be very costly; some companies' systems are so slow that by the time a check is ready to be disbursed, the company has lost the opportunity to take a cash discount.

Sophisticated disbursement systems are prone to use electronic payments, controlled disbursement accounts and ZBAs, and electronic funding of the disbursement account. Such systems also are more likely to be tied in with the company's collection and concentration systems and may be developed from a formal disbursements study.

We recommended valuation as the appropriate method for evaluating disbursement alternatives. Payment mechanism, funding mechanism, and account sites are all important aspects of a company's disbursement system, and the options selected have a measurable impact on the cash flow timeline. However, the disbursements manager must also recognize ethical and other qualitative dimensions of such decisions.

Several important differences in international disbursements were noted, including the use of drafts, overdraft checking accounts, and value-dated transactions. Companies use netting systems and reinvoicing centers to improve their grip on international funds flows.

Disbursement systems should be well coordinated with cash collection and cash concentration systems. The master account used in controlled disbursement is often the concentration account to which surplus cash flows from collections are directed. The entire collection-concentration-disbursement network should be carefully designed to ensure maximum efficiency and value contribution. Managing the financial risks of the company's cash position requires accurate and timely balance information and accurate short-term cash forecasts—the subject of Chapter 12.

## USEFUL WEB SITES

| | |
|---|---|
| AFP—Association for Financial Professionals | **http://www.afponline.org** |
| Greenwich Associates | **http://www.greenwich.com** |
| GT News articles | **http://www.gtnews.com** |
| J.P. Morgan | **http://www.jpmorgan.com/cm/cs?pagename=Chase/Href&urlname=jpmorgan/cash/_home_/northamerica** |
| OCC Check Fraud primer | **http://www.occ.treas.gov/chckfrd/chckfrd.pdf** |
| Phoenix-Hecht | **http://www.phoenixhecht.com** |

## QUESTIONS

1. What is a company's disbursement system, and why is it an important part of that company's short-term financial management? What principles should guide disbursement system decisions?
2. Remote disbursing was widely practiced in the 1970s because the Federal Reserve granted availability much more quickly than it was able to collect from banks in its clearing practices, leading to significant Fed float. Now that much of this type of float has been eliminated, at whose expense are companies achieving their float gains when slowing disbursements? How does the first disbursement system guiding principle apply here?

3. Describe the three components of disbursement float, and indicate whether disbursement float on a given check is always the same as the collection float on that check.
4. Apart from questions of legality, do you agree or disagree with the surveyed cash managers' views on the ethics of various disbursement practices? Use the AFP Standards of Ethical Conduct (Chapter 10) and the payables ethics discussion (Chapter 7) to support your position.
5. What are the advantages achieved by a company switching from decentralized to centralized disbursing?
6. Cash managers generally are part of a company's treasury department. With what other organizational units might cash managers interface to determine disbursement policy and to make day-to-day disbursements?
7. Some observers consider the selection of the company's disbursing bank(s) to be the most important disbursement-related decision. Do you agree or disagree? Support your position.
8. How do a company's cash flow characteristics influence its selection of a disbursement system?
9. What are the major differences between simple and complex disbursement systems? Construct a table showing the important differences.
10. Define a controlled disbursement account, and indicate why it appeals to companies. How is it different from a ZBA?
11. Indicate the major electronic disbursing mechanisms.
12. How are controlled disbursement accounts and ZBAs funded?
13. What are the obstacles to greater use of electronic payments? Which of these is the single most important obstacle?
14. Summarize the payment system differences, risks, and intracompany techniques used in global disbursing.
15. What are disbursement models? How do they differ from lockbox models?
16. If a company radically changes its disbursement systems following the prescriptions flowing from the use of disbursement models, what would the likely effect on shareholder value be? What caution(s) might you offer regarding that anticipated effect?

## PROBLEMS

1. Using the data from the chapter's opening Financial Dilemma, rework the NPV analysis for each of the following situations. For each situation in parts **a–d**, assume all data are the same as that given in the textbook analysis except the one item indicated. In part **e**, assume all four changes indicated in parts **a–d** are applicable. Make a recommendation either for or against the ACH disbursement system in each case. If you have access to spreadsheet software, you can save time by developing a worksheet or by using a preprogrammed worksheet.
   **a.** The initial investment is $60,000 instead of $40,000.
   **b.** The company makes 5,000 payments per month instead of 1,000.
   **c.** The annual interest rate is 5 percent instead of 10 percent.
   **d.** The per-payment savings is $1 instead of $0.40.
   **e.** All the changes in parts **a–d** are applicable.
2. Rework Problem 1 by first using the original data, but using compound interest instead of simple interest. Then rework the analysis for each change listed in part **e** from Problem 1, again using monthly compounding instead of a simple interest formula. To what degree does the calculated NPV change? Is there any situation in which your recommendation changes?
3. ACD, Inc., a computer parts company, presently pays its largest supplier by check and is trying to determine whether to switch to electronic payment. Its present credit period is 45 days. Its opportunity cost for funds is a 12-percent annual rate. The disbursement float on its checks averages four days. It estimates the variable cost per check to be $8.35. Its average

payment to the supplier is $20,000. Using ACH debits initiated by its supplier would result in per-payment charges of $3.00 and clearance float of one day. Its supplier has generously agreed to pay any switchover costs necessary to make ACD "financial EDI-ready." The credit period for electronic payments would be 48 days.

**a.** Should ACD switch to electronic payments?

**b.** ACD decides not to go with the switchover. One year later, the supplier approaches ACD again and asks for a reconsideration. What are the present values of check and electronic payments if the annual opportunity rate on funds has dropped to 8 percent? How does this affect the relative attractiveness of electronic payments?

**c.** Is there any reasonable opportunity cost of funds (i.e., less than 30 percent) for which your recommended payment method would change?

## REFERENCES


"Association for Financial Professionals, Study Finds Apparent Paradox in Procurement Trends," *Finance IT* (April 2001), pp. 1, 6.

Michael Burn, "Making International Payments—Navigating the Course," *AFP Exchange* (Winter 2000), pp. 62–64.

Business International, *Automating Global Financial Management.* New York: John Wiley & Sons (1988).

Beth A. Dubyak, "Outsourcing Payables at Thrift Drug," *TMA Journal* (January/February 1996), pp. 40–44.

"EDI Automates the Paystream," *Journal of Cash Management* (September/October 1990), p. 60.

D. M. Ferguson and S. E Maier, "Reducing the Risk in the Corporate Disbursement System," *The Magazine of Bank Administration* (June 1984), pp. 28–42; (July 1984), pp. 66–72.

Richard Gamble, "Breaking Up Over Fraud," *Treasury & Risk Management* (November/December 1998), pp. 47, 49.

Richard Gamble, "Everyone Is Learning to Love ACH—Including the Crooks," *Treasury & Risk Management* (December/January 2004), pp. 37–38, 42.

Christine Handt, "Creating a Global Payments Platform," *TMA Journal* (May/June 1999), pp. 52–54.

Ned C. Hill and Daniel M. Ferguson, "Negotiating Payment Terms in an Electronic Environment," in Y. H. Kim, V. Srinivasan (eds): *Advances in Working Capital Management.* Greenwich, CT: JAI Press (1988), pp. 131–146.

D. B. Humphrey, L. B. Pulley, and J. M. Vesala, "The Check's in the Mail: Why the United States Lags in the Adoption of Cost-Saving Electronic Payments," *Journal of Financial Services Research* 17, pp. 17–39.

Vicki L. Jones (1992), "Corporate Disbursements Yesterday, Today and Tomorrow," *TMA Journal* (May/June 2002), pp. 41–44.

Steven F. Maier and Jack M. Meckler, "The Current State of Controlled Disbursing," *Journal of Cash Management* (November/December 1990), pp. 37–38, 40, 42–43.

Steven F. Maier and James H. Vander Weide, "What Lockbox and Disbursement Models Really Do," *Journal of Finance* 38, (1983), pp. 361–371.

Stephen G. McDonough, "Internal Treasury Management Reviews," *TMA Journal* (July/August), pp. 28–31.

Betsy Olson (1993), "Corporate Disbursing: A Fresh Look at Strategies and Applications," *Journal of Cash Management* (March/April 1997), pp. 8–12.

Aaron L. Phillips, "Migration of Corporate Payments from Check to Electronic Format: A Report on the Current Status of Payments," *Financial Management* (Winter 1998), pp. 92–105.

Walter C. Repak, "What Check?"—Innovative Electronic Payments," *TMA Journal* (November/December 1995), pp. 50–53.

John T. Soma and Michael C. Tierney, "Cash Management after E.F. Hutton," *Bankers Magazine* 170, (1987), pp. 25–28.

Jinny St. Goar, "Positive Pay Combats Check Fraud," *Treasury & Risk Management* (September 1996), pp. 47–48.

Gerald Stephens, "Don't Let Your Check Fraud Nightmare Come True!," *TMA Journal* (May/June 1998), 28, pp. 30–32.

Kathryn J. White and Mary McKenney, "Payment Systems that Work," *TMA Journal* (March/April 1998), pp. 32–35, 36.

Jon Wisecup and John Zietlow, "Winning the Tech Race: Companies Jockey for E-Payments Acceptance," *AFP Exchange* (May/June 2003), pp. 21–26.

John Zietlow, "8 Principles to Practical Finance: What Businesses and Not-for-Profit Managers Should Know," *AFP Exchange* (September/October 2003), pp. 18–23.

FOCUSED CASE

# Structuring a Payment Decision

Joe Walker just got back from a 1-day conference put on by the regional ACH association in which all of the speakers and some of the audience participants bragged about the benefits of direct deposit. One comparative cost analysis pegged the cost of a payroll check to be $1.90, including $1.25 of lost employee time for those making a trip to the bank on company time, versus a direct deposit per item cost of $0.14. His company, which has only 25 employees, has always paid its employees by check. All employees are presently paid biweekly.

One of the pamphlets passed out at the conference talks about the experience the Social Security Administration (SSA) has had in persuading benefit recipients to accept direct deposit. SSA uses ACH credits to make the payments. Advantages the SSA used to "sell" recipients include:

- No paper check to be lost, stolen, or misplaced.
- No waiting for the check to be delivered.
- Assurance that your money gets to the bank, even if you are sick or traveling at the time the payment is made.
- No special trip to the bank or waiting in line at the bank to cash your check.
- Money is available the same day you would have received a check.

Joe is impressed with the fact that about 60 percent of the 43 million people who get Social Security already receive their benefit by direct deposit. Further, SSA estimates total savings to taxpayers of another $9.6 million a month if the 24 million Social Security *and* Supplemental Security Income recipients who now receive checks switched to direct deposit. Reading further, Joe sees that this estimate is based on an estimate that it costs SSA 42 cents to process and mail each check, as compared to 2 cents for direct deposit.

The combined carrot-and-stick approach SSA is using to enroll additional recipients in the direct deposit program interests Joe. A program recently inaugurated by SSA enables those now receiving paper checks to be automatically enrolled in direct deposit by their bank. The bank sends the recipient's account number directly to Social Security, and the individual does not even have to contact the agency. SSA tells new enrollees that they must be paid by direct deposit. Present recipients were required to switch to direct deposit by a certain point of time in the future. If they didn't have a bank account at that time, a special debit-only checking account was made available to them at a designated bank.

Joe finds the idea of mandating direct deposit appealing, but wonders if state law will permit it. He also wonders if his experience will mirror that of the Social Security Administration. Another question crosses his mind: Do all of my employees have bank accounts?

## QUESTIONS

1. In what ways is Joe's situation similar to that of the Social Security Administration? Different?
2. What additional financial data will Joe need before reaching a decision? Nonfinancial data?
3. What is the effect of time value of money in this situation, if any?
4. Does Joe's company have to be "EDI-capable" to convert to direct deposit? What about his bank's capabilities? What alternative(s) will his company have for implementing direct deposit in the event that appropriate capabilities are unavailable?

# INTEGRATIVE CASE—PART 3

## *Harker Telecommunications, Inc.*

Harker Telecommunications, Inc., is a full-line telecommunications corporation. After graduating from college with a degree in electrical engineering, Ted wanted to join a firm with high-tech products where he could spend his efforts in the research lab generating new products based on the semiconductor. Harker Telecommunications, Inc., seemed to be the ideal employment prospect. It had an immediate opening in their research lab and the company was at the forefront of research.

Julie, Ted's wife, also graduated the same year with a degree in business and was able to join Harker as a treasury analyst. As the company grew, both Ted and Julie's careers took off. Ted is now director of research, and Julie has been promoted from assistant treasurer to treasurer. As treasurer, her main responsibilities are dealing with bank relationships and cash mobilization.

Julie is always trying to find a more efficient way to manage the company's cash receipts and disbursements between its two banks and two administrative financial centers. By December of 2005, Harker had grown into a large corporation with customers and suppliers nationwide. A listing of the typical monthly cash receipt and disbursement activity is shown below.

| CHECKS WRITTEN | CHECK VOLUME | FACE VALUE PER CHECK |
|---|---|---|
| Vendors | 8,000 | $ 400 |
| Payroll | 10,000 | 550 |
| Deposits | | |
| Customer Group 1 | 4,000 | 1,200 |
| Customer Group 2 | 7,000 | 1,200 |

Harker is currently using two banks; Bank 1 is used only for a credit line facility related to the company's seasonal financing needs. Julie has learned that Harker has been paying a fee of $10 per month to maintain the account at Bank 1. However, all daily transactions are currently being conducted out of Bank 2. Julie has the following activity charges for both banks in her cash management project file.

| ACTIVITY | BANK 1 | BANK 2 |
|---|---|---|
| Vendor checks | $.30 | $.50 |
| Payroll checks | $.40 | $.60 |
| Deposits | $.30 | $.50 |
| Earnings credit rate | 8.00% | 10.00% |
| Maximum fee payment | 50% | 50% |
| Monthly maintenance fee | $10.00 | $20.00 |

Julie always makes it a practice to analyze the monthly account statements sent to her from the two banks. The basic statement format follows, showing the most recent month's activity provided for Bank 2.

| | |
|---|---|
| Average ledger balance | $2,308,333 |
| Less: float | 869,667 |
| Average collected balance | 1,438,667 |
| Less: 12% reserves | 172,640 |
| Less compensating balances | 0 |
| Average available balance | 1,266,027 |

| SERVICES RENDERED | PRICE | VOLUME | AMOUNT |
|---|---|---|---|
| Account maintenance | $20.00 | 1 | $ 20.00 |
| Vendor checks paid | 0.50 | 3,367 | 1,683.33 |
| Payroll checks paid | 0.60 | 9,000 | 5,400.00 |
| Deposits posted | 0.50 | 10,217 | 5,108.33 |
| Cost of bank services | | | $13,328.33 |

*Average ledger balance:* Records all transactions (checks paid and deposits posted). Note that half of deposit and disbursement float is mail float and half is availability float. Also, average ledger balance is an average for the month, which is calculated by taking the total ledger balance and dividing by two.

*Float:* Float on the bank statement represents receipt or availability float on checks deposited in the bank but not yet cleared.

*Collected balance:* Average ledger balance less float. This is the average dollar amount of good funds in the bank account.

*Average available balance:* This is the balance on which the bank pays an earnings credit. It is the average collected balance for the month, less the 12 percent reserve requirement, less any other required balances for other activities such as loan compensating balances.

Julie is frustrated because the past treasurer seems not to have kept Harker's balances invested, leaving rather sizable funds idle. She also is irritated to learn that the company has been paying to maintain the account at Bank 1 but has not been using it. Because the company has no balances at Bank 1, the charge has been paid with a fee, violating the bank's requirement that no more than 50 percent of bank service charges can be paid by fee. In fact, the service agreements with both banks call for bank service charges funded by fees not to exceed 50 percent. She wonders, because no fees are paid to Bank 2 at all, whether the firm's idle balances cover the service charges, and if so, how much in overcompensation is being paid. As can be noted by the most recent account analysis statement, the average collected balance is $1,438,667.

Julie has been a member of the local chapter of the Association for Financial Professionals for about 5 years and she recently passed the Certified Cash Management exam. As she studied for the exam she realized it might be possible to reallocate her bank activity to solve some of her more pressing cash management problems. After all, the main reason she was able to determine that Harker was using Bank 2 was that the loan officer at Bank 2 always let the previous treasurer win at golf. Julie prefers fly fishing, so she feels that the time is long overdue to complete a careful analysis of Harker's cash management system. She requests that her bank provide her the following float data for all of her receipt and disbursement activity for a typical month. The data show the days of float between her two administrative financial centers, her two banks, and the two different types of check activity. In addition, the data reveal the differences in float between her two customer groups and her two banks.

Float Characteristics

| ijk | d(ijk) | mk | r(mk) |
|---|---|---|---|
| 111 | 4.5 | 11 | 6 |
| 112 | 5 | 12 | 3 |
| 121 | 6 | 21 | 2 |
| 122 | 3 | 22 | 5 |
| 211 | 4.5 | | |
| 212 | 4.5 | | |
| 221 | 4.5 | | |
| 222 | 3 | | |

i = Administrative financial center (1 or 2)
j = Type of activity
  j = 1, vendor checks
  j = 2, payroll checks
k = bank (1 or 2)
m = customer group (1 or 2)
d = disbursement float in days
r = receipt float in days

She readily notices that Bank 1 charges less to clear checks and to deposit checks, but offers a lower earnings credit rate. She wonders how these differences interact with the differences in float days generated by the two banks. At minimum, given the current allocation of activity, Julie decides that she should determine the appropriate balances to leave and invest the difference at her opportunity investment rate, which is 7.5 percent per year. Second, she would like to see if a reallocation of Harker's receipts and disbursements can generate additional investable fund balances while properly compensating the banks. Currently, the responsibility for writing and sending out vendor and payroll checks is divided evenly between the two administrative financial centers.

## REQUIRED

1. Determine whether Harker should pay in fees, up to the maximum allowed, or pay by balances.
2. Given Harker's current activity allocation, determine if there are idle balances in Bank 2 that could be invested. If so, how much?
3. After studying the bank cost data, the receipt and disbursement float characteristics, and the relative earnings credit rates, intuitively construct a cash management allocation plan disbursing the required number of checks and depositing the appropriate numbers of check receipts among the two banks and two administrative financial centers. Your objective is to pay the appropriate fee levels, leave the appropriate collected balances in the banks, and to earn as much interest incomes as possible. You may wish to take the firm's current situation and incrementally change it to take advantage of any float variations or relative cost differentials.
4. Discuss the results of your intuitive plan relative to the firm's current cash management system. For example, how much additional interest income net of activity charges were you able to generate and why?
5. Now optimize the cash management system using a mathematical optimization program such as Microsoft's Solver. Discuss the results of the optimized plan relative to Harker's current allocation plan and also relative to your intuitive plan. How much improvement did the optimized plan generate? What opportunities for improvement did the optimized plan take advantage of that you failed to recognize in your plan?

## TECHNICAL NOTES FOR THE WORKSHEET MODEL LOGIC

*Objective function: Maximize net profit*

$$(k \times I) - \text{fees} - k \times (ACB - RBL - (SC - \text{fees})/ecr(1 - rr))$$

k = monthly opportunity investment rate
I = average daily investment of surplus collected balances
fees = fees paid to the banks
ACB = average collected balance
RBL = required balances for loans
SC = charges for bank services
ecr = monthly earnings credit rate
rr = reserve requirement

*Average ledger balance*

X = number of checks written
FVC = average face value of checks
Y = number of checks remitted by customers
FVD = average face value of deposits
d = average days of disbursement float
r = average days of receipt float
ALB = average ledger balance
AF = average value of float

$$ALB = ((Y \times FVD \times (1 - .5r/30)) - (X \times FVC \times (1 - d/30)))/2$$

$$AF = Y \times FVD \times (1 - (.5r/30)) \times (.5r/30)$$

$$\text{Number of checks paid} = X \times (1 - d/30)$$

$$\text{Number of deposits posted} = Y \times (1 - .5r/30)$$

The days of receipt float are adjusted by 0.5 assuming that half the float is mail float and half is clearing float. Once the cash management system reaches a steady state, the number of checks paid and deposited will not be adjusted by the float because checks written from the previous month will clear in the current month, offsetting the checks written during the current month but not paid by the bank this month because of float. The changes in float that release cash or soak up cash then reflect the one-shot impact that a change in float causes. For example, an increase in disbursement float allows the payor to conserve a lump sum balance and keep it invested until float characteristics change. If the float characteristics don't change next month, no additional balances are created, but the firm can continue to keep the original balances invested.

The following decision variables are needed for an optimization formulation:

1. X(ijk)
2. Y(mk)
3. FEE(k)
4. Investments(k)

For an optimization formulation, the following constraints are needed:

1. Constraints to ensure that all vendor and payroll checks are written and all remittances are received by one of the banks.
2. Constraints to ensure that the average ledger balance is >= 0.
3. Constraints to ensure that the average collected balance is >= 0.
4. Constraints to ensure that each bank is properly compensated by a combination of fees and balances, and that the payment of fees does not exceed the maximum percentage allowed.

PART 4

# Forecasting and Planning

Now that Part III is concluded, the financial manager has a picture of the cash position of the firm based on daily cash collections and daily cash disbursements. The next step is to invest cash surpluses and borrow to cover cash deficiencies. However, before an investment and borrowing strategy can be developed, the financial manager must look to the future to assess the future cash flow scenario. Chapter 12 develops a process for developing cash forecasts. We first develop a framework, and then we discuss a variety of techniques to generate cash forecasts. Chapter 13 introduces a short-term financial planning model that uses forecasts of cash flows to aid the financial manager in developing a short-term investment and financing strategy.

CHAPTER

# 12

# Cash Forecasting

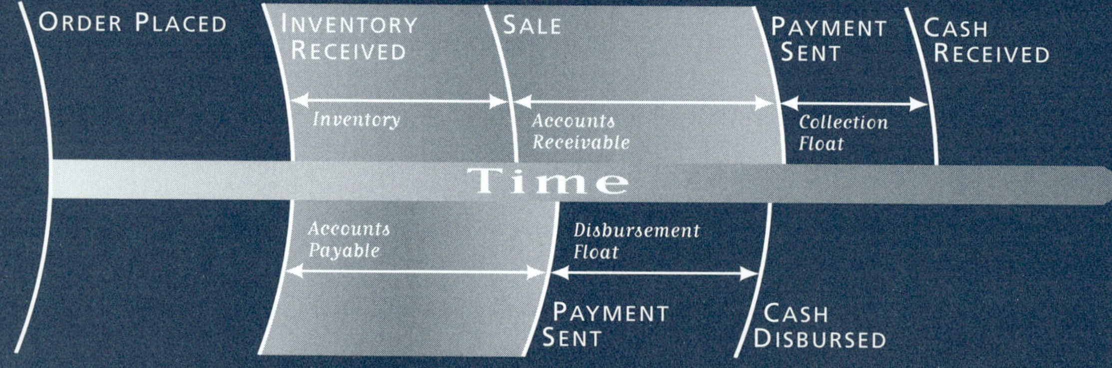

# OBJECTIVES

## *After studying this chapter, you should be able to:*

- explain why companies should emphasize short-term cash forecasts.
- indicate why the monthly cash budget is important to top management, and specify the two objectives for its development.
- indicate how the process of daily cash forecasting differs from that used in monthly forecasting.
- explain the receipts and disbursements, pro forma balance sheet, and distribution methods of cash forecasting.

Online toy retailer eToys missed badly on its sales and cash receipts forecasts in late 2000, estimating double the sales that actually materialized. This led to a revised "out of cash" cash position forecast within three months, a hasty plea for a "substantial cash infusion" that went unmet, and a bankruptcy declaration in early 2001. We noted in Chapter 2 that financial flexibility in the form of unused borrowing capacity can be critical, and eToys found itself lacking that flexibility. One wonders whether eToys might have taken more drastic action to stem losses had its forecasting been more accurate. The treasurer of a consumer goods company once asserted, "Cash forecasts are the most important tool for monitoring and controlling corporate cash. Without them, good cash management is simply impossible."[1] Furthermore, a 1997 survey of over one thousand treasury professionals found that within the whole realm of domestic cash management, knowledge of mathematical statistical forecasting techniques was the most important quantitative skill.[2] A 2003 survey by the Association for Financial Professionals found that the treasury activity the largest percentage of companies have been and will continue to add resources into is cash forecasting (53 percent and 57 percent, respectively).[3] Another 2003 survey by GTNews finds only one in four MNC senior finance professionals report high levels of cash forecasting accuracy.[4] Four factors account for today's renewed corporate emphasis on short-term cash forecasts.

First, cash forecasts drive the short-term investing and borrowing strategies. Selecting the maturity of a short-term investment, when to repay borrowings, or the size of a credit line to request all depend critically on the forecasted cash position. Alternating cash surpluses and shortages occur because cash receipts and disbursements are not synchronized.

Sagner (2000) estimates that a $15 million portfolio will earn an added one-fifth to one-quarter of 1 percent (equal to $37,500 per year) and save an additional $5,500 in transactions costs when moving from overnight (sweep account) investing to 1-month maturities.

Second, as noted in earlier chapters, the forecast is an important input into short-term financial policy decisions, including disbursement policies, credit terms, and bank selection. *Making decisions along the cash flow timeline requires accurate estimation of cash flow size and timing.* Accurately anticipating very near-term cash balances might be less important if the company had a controlled disbursement account (particularly when funding is automated) or sufficient balances (e.g., to compensate for credit or noncredit services) to absorb uncertainties.

Third, cash forecasts function as a control device. Before the beginning of each year, the finance staff develops a cash budget, which is a forecast of cash flows and the

[1] Quoted in Business International, *Automating Global Financial Management*, New York: John Wiley & Sons (1988), p. 172.

[2] Survey reported in Phillips (1997), cited in the end-of-chapter references.

[3] Association for Financial Professionals, "The Evolving Role of Treasury," (November 2003).

[4] GTNews, "Working Capital Survey: Cash Flow Forecasting," (2003). Accessed online 1/19/2004 at **http://www.gtnews.com/workingcapital/wcmsurveycash.cfm**.

cash balance for each month. As the year progresses, deviations of actual cash balances from cash budget projections signal the cash manager to investigate and take corrective action. Sales and marketing managers may use the cash balance variances as an early warning system when declining cash receipts are found to be the cause of the variance. Accurate forecasts can provide added value when they signal a cash shortage and the need for action before problems emerge, or corrective action as actual data become available.

Fourth, effective risk management is impossible without forecasts of the cash flow effects of interest rate changes, commodity price changes, and foreign exchange rate changes.

### FINANCIAL DILEMMA

#### Which Cash Balance Should We Forecast?

The first issue a manager faces when establishing a cash forecasting system is how to define cash. Should cash be based on the company's accrual-based accounting records or on bank balances? Specifically, should cash as shown in the general ledger be forecasted? Or how about cash and cash equivalents as shown by the ledger? Another set of alternatives arises if, instead, the focus is on the cash balance on deposit at the bank. If bank balances are used, should they be bank ledger balances or collected (or available) balances, and how should compensating balances be incorporated into the forecast, if at all?

This chapter provides you with a cash forecasting framework useful for monthly, weekly, and daily cash forecasting. We develop the techniques and approaches used in monthly and daily forecasting. The chapter concludes with a portrayal of state-of-the-art corporate practice. Material on useful statistical techniques and the main forecasting error measures is provided in the chapter appendices. Chapter 13 presents an integrated financial modeling approach that builds on this chapter's material.

## THE CASH FORECASTING PROCESS

Even before beginning the forecasting process, the forecaster must carefully consider the nature and objectives of the task. In most companies, the cash or treasury manager or one of their assistants does this work. Because immediate access to transactions throughout the company that have a cash effect is needed, other corporate personnel in operations, marketing, and purchasing should be consulted in this preliminary stage. Objectives for the cash forecast should be established. An example would be accuracy of ±3 percent for the 3-month forecast. One oil company has daily cash flows of $2 billion and shoots for an error of $5 million or less. Forecasting accuracy is improving in the United States as more and more companies pay electronically, providing more certainty for their cash outflow forecast and their vendors' cash inflow forecasts. However, cash forecasting is still considered to be one of the most inefficient parts of the cash flow process because of a notable lack of integration between operating units and their databases and the amount of labor-intensive administrative work involved in developing accurate forecasts.[5]

[5] Based on a survey administered by Visa U.S.A., found in Brannen (2004), cited in the end-of-chapter references.

Beyond forecast accuracy, other forecasting objectives might address ease of generation, speed of updating, flexibility, and documentation of procedures used. The forecast should be made available to higher-level financial and administrative managers. Minimal requirements relating to what is to be forecast and how often might be prespecified or developed during the forecasting process. The cash forecasting policy adopted by 3M is as follows:

> Accurately forecast cash sources and uses and take whatever actions are deemed appropriate so that adequate cash is on hand at all times and so that daily and long-term liquidity needs are met at the best price.

It is best to view the cash forecasting process as an integrated part of the company's financial management, not simply a separate activity. The forecasting process involves the company in anticipating possible futures and preparing for them. Consequently, the forecasting approaches we now discuss should be developed carefully and communicated to appropriate units within the organization. Carfang[6] lists as his first cash forecasting success factor "endorsement by senior management," which means that senior management gives it priority, allocates necessary resources, stays involved in continuous improvement of the process, and clearly articulates and endorses the cash forecasting process. Affected areas are those that provide input data for the forecast or units that should be alerted to the developing future of cash receipts and disbursements because of their ability to affect the cash flow stream.

Cash managers may use treasury information systems (see Chapter 19) and tap into real-time transaction data, which are now available for many financial variables. The Internet has allowed reporting of cash positions and upcoming payments to become faster, thereby enabling forecasts to be more accurate (Forster, 2000). This allows managers to see their cash positions in (or close to) real time (Webb, 2000), but it does not eliminate the need to forecast cash flows. That conclusion holds even for corporations with extensive supply chain interaction with trading partners. Knowing supplier and customer availabilities and needs reduces uncertainty in regard to disbursements and receipts, respectively, but does not eliminate that uncertainty. A good example is the severe shortage of components in the high-tech electronics industry in 2000, which significantly affected cash flows for suppliers and customers, and was only partially anticipated.[7]

## FORECASTING MONTHLY CASH FLOWS

The most important cash forecast from a top management perspective is the monthly cash forecast. This forecast shows cash receipts and disbursements on a monthly basis for a minimum horizon of one year; when done before the beginning of a new fiscal year, it is called the cash budget. The **cash budget** is a document showing anticipated cash receipts and disbursements for a future period, usually one year. This cash budget is formulated to be consistent with the company's operating budget, which specifies planned sales and operating expenses. Many companies extend the monthly forecast to a 5-year horizon to correspond with the company's long-range financial plan. The level of detail and anticipated accuracy diminishes with longer forecast horizons, however. The Focus on Practice box illustrates cash forecasting, or cash planning, in the U.S. Air Force.

---

[6] A. J. Carfang, "Cash Forecasting," May 20, 1999. Found online at **http://www.treasurystrat.com**.

[7] Some analysts have contended that a movement to "sell-one-make-one" supply replenishment would eliminate inventory needs as well as all demand uncertainty, but this is not the case, as noted by Lapide (2000), cited in the end-of-chapter references.

## FOCUS ON PRACTICE

### Fundamentals of Cash Planning at the U.S. Air Force

Cash budgeting is important in the public and not-for-profit sectors as well as in corporate America. The rationale and some of the components of cash budgeting used by the Air Force Working Capital Fund (AFWCF) include:

- Actual cash inflows and outflows may vary from forecasted results, with AFWCF activities experiencing differing degrees of variability. To minimize the variance between actual and forecasted inflows and outflows, a cash manager must develop a carefully constructed monthly cash plan. The cash plan should begin with projected sales and the pattern of collections as key elements in estimating future cash flows. In addition, the outlay plan should provide a forecast of purchases, disbursements, capital requirements, and net outlays (disbursements minus collections). The cash manager should base his or her forecasts on a combination of historical experience, known events, expected values, and projected financial performance standards.
- A monthly cash plan should identify which activity groups require additional cash, where excess cash will accumulate, and the length of time either of these conditions may exist. The plan must consider timing differences for obligations, sales, billings, collections, and disbursements. Accurately forecasting cash flows affords management the opportunity to develop and subsequently implement alternative strategies for maintaining an appropriate cash position.
- Development of an effective cash plan requires the involvement of all levels of management. Moreover, effective development and execution of that plan requires integrated functional and financial systems that provide timely, accurate, and complete information throughout the organization. Unfortunately, the systems currently in use throughout the AFWCF activity groups and Defense Finance and Accounting Service (DFAS) are neither fully integrated nor use the same standard general ledger. The lack of integrated systems impairs the DFAS's ability to provide the Air Force with timely, accurate financial reports. Thus, manual intervention at the technician level (e.g., through manual billings, reconciliation of error reports, and so on) and closer scrutiny of the financial reports are necessary to manage cash effectively.
- Because timely, accurate, and complete information is not available, AFWCF managers must be proactive in identifying cash problem areas

*continued*

We begin our presentation of the monthly cash forecast by highlighting its importance. This is followed by the underlying objectives and cash forecasting philosophy. We then consider the key decisions a forecaster must make, especially regarding the forecasting horizon, interval, and update frequency. The three major approaches to monthly cash forecasts are then developed in the context of numerical examples. Appendix 12B profiles the main statistical tools that can be used to assist the forecaster.

## Importance to Top Management

The monthly cash forecast serves as a valuable planning tool for top-level managers. First, the typical billing and payment cycle in most industries is monthly. Second, the monthly interval is generally thought to be adequate for anticipating funding requirements. Quarterly forecasts may mask important within-quarter cash receipt and disbursement imbalances, causing the business to underestimate peak funding needs and then arrange too little in external financing. Businesses often assemble the next year's monthly cash budget several months before the start of the year.

rapidly, implementing corrective actions, and effectively managing cash. Cash managers must be alert to internal changes (e.g., lower than expected sales) and external changes (e.g., contingency operations, Department of Defense policy changes) that can affect sales and subsequent collections and disbursements. Proactive cash management can preclude an Anti-Deficiency Act (a law that limits the amount of funds available for obligation and expenditure in an attempt to avoid situations of deficient funding) violation and yield a more efficient and effective AFWCF business.

The cash forecasting requirement is legislated as part of the Department of Defense's Financial Management Regulation, which identifies the requirement to conduct cash outlay planning. Chapter 54 of the regulation identifies the requirement to develop a cash plan to facilitate the cash management process. It states that the plan

> Shall consider collections, disbursements, appropriations, and other cash transactions based on Department of Defense component estimates. This annual plan will be initially developed during the budget process and will be an integral part of the budget document. In addition, a monthly phasing of the cash plan is required to monitor execution. A monthly execution review should increase management's attention on cost reduction, timely billing and collection of revenue, and timely disbursement.

Implementation of forecasting and related cash control functions work their way down to the commander level. Various commanders are responsible for managing their assigned activity groups, divisions, or subdivisions in a manner consistent with their assigned cash outlay targets. Responsibilities include:

1. Developing a cash plan consistent with approved budget levels for revenues or sales, expenditures or costs, investments, and credit policies;
2. Submitting cash plans for approval/disapproval as part of the budget submission or as required;
3. Distributing cash targets to subordinate operating activities;
4. Reviewing, controlling, and adjusting subordinate level cash outlay targets;
5. Preparing necessary budget schedules and analysis related to cash plans;
6. Monitoring collections, disbursements and other transactions to ensure adherence to approved division cash targets.

*Source:* Located online at **http://www.afmc.wpafb.af.mil/HQ-AFMC/FM/FMRS/noframes/chap83a.htm**. Used by permission.

Two comparisons provide valuable information to management once the budget year begins: a comparison of actual cash versus budgeted cash for the most recent month and for the year to date, and an updated cash forecast for the remainder of the year, which includes an explanation of any variance relative to budgeted cash.

The third benefit of the monthly cash forecast is that it alerts management to threats to organizational stability and survival. Particularly for smaller companies and not-for-profit organizations that are growing rapidly and cannot tap external credit, the picture of deteriorating liquidity can give warning while it is still possible to adjust the selling rate or the level of asset investment. However, small companies have organizational attributes that may hinder cash forecasting, as noted in the Focus on Practice box.

## Monthly Cash Forecast Objectives

Two main objectives characterize the monthly cash forecast: accuracy and usefulness. The forecaster wants the forecast to be accurate enough to avert account overdrafts, to determine

## FOCUS ON PRACTICE

### *Organizational Aspects of Small Business Cash Forecasting*

Small businesses often rely on an unsophisticated and informal cash forecasting approach. This happens for several reasons:

- Managers may lack the training and experience to appreciate the importance of cash forecasting.
- The limited number of management and employee team members may not allow for formal systems.
- Senior management experience may substitute for formal forecasting and review processes.
- The business may be easily managed by simple controls, lessening the need for forecasting processes.

In many small companies, the cash forecasting and review process is the weakest part of the cash management system, and analysis might be limited to a quarterly review of performance. There is less automation and more subjectivity than is the case with larger companies.

When small companies develop cash forecasts, they typically start with annual financial forecasts (already developed by the chief financial office, or CFO, with department manager input). A monthly source and use of cash schedule then becomes part of an annual planning package that includes balance sheet and income statement projections. The package is approved by senior management, the board of directors, and all lending institutions. On a weekly basis during the year, departmental cash reports (weekly and year-to-date) may be generated by the controller and distributed to appropriate division heads. Then, perhaps on a semimonthly basis, revised cash projections (with horizons of 30 days, 60 days, 90 days, and 1 year) are developed by the CFO and reviewed with the top management team during staff meetings. To underscore the importance of cash to the organization, each staff meeting might begin with an overview of the company's current cash position. Senior management might proceed to discuss any large variances between forecast and actual, new large cash requirements, and how future cash needs should be prioritized. In smaller companies, managers must collaborate with each other to review and allocate cash.

*Source:* Andrew R. Jassy, Laurence E. Katz, Kevin Kelly, and Baltej Kochar, "Cash Management Practices in Small Companies," *Harvard Business School Teaching Note 9-699-047*, December 4, 1998.

the amount of short-term credit lines, and to aid in the selection of investment maturities when excess cash is projected. Beyond some point, increased accuracy becomes more expensive, and the forecaster must weigh the improved accuracy against the increased cost. On a year-ahead forecast, +/− 5 percent or +/−10 percent are common targets. The usefulness of a forecast involves more than its accuracy. A useful forecast allows timely and appropriate managerial responses to foreseen cash surpluses or shortfalls and specifies the variability of the cash flows and cash position. A forecast allows preemptive managerial responses when it is done with sufficient lead time and at an adequate level of detail. If overly aggregated, it may be impossible to ascertain why cash flow is inadequate or the cash position is deteriorating. With proper detail, the manager can alter the amounts of individual elements making up the forecast and observe the effect on liquidity. The forecast template thus doubles as a decision-making model.

The usefulness of the forecast is further enhanced if the variability of individual elements making up the forecast (or at least the variability of the bottom-line cash position) is specified. From this, management can calculate the probabilities of running short on cash[8] and the need for and potential magnitude of contingency plans. Risk analysis can be implemented by formally recognizing that some items are better characterized as probability distributions, not point estimates (Tezel and McManus, 1999). Contingency plans are actions that can be taken if and when necessitated by deteriorating liquidity. For example, one ladies wear retailer calls its stores and directs them to run 40 percent off storewide sales when the chain's cash position is poor. Variability might be communicated by giving a range of anticipated outcomes, or more formally through sensitivity analysis or simulation.

## Forecasting Philosophy

A company's forecasting philosophy affects the potential accuracy and usefulness of its cash forecasts and the techniques used in making the forecast. The philosophy refers to management's views on the number and type of cash forecasts made, the amount of money the company is willing to spend developing the forecast, whether the company prefers to develop the forecast internally or to use an external forecaster, and the preference for a quantitative (usually computerized) versus a judgmental approach to forecasting.

*NUMBER AND TYPE OF FORECASTS* Companies may have up to three types of cash forecasts: short-term, intermediate-term, and long-term. These forecasts may range from as short as one day ahead to as long as five years ahead. Some companies do no daily forecasting because of lack of time, forecasting expertise, or ignorance of the value of the daily forecast. Likewise, some companies see the 5-year financial plan as meaningless because of its questionable accuracy.

*EXPENDITURE ON FORECASTS* Smaller companies or companies with stable or consistently positive cash flow patterns may not be willing to spend very much for the forecasting function. In any business, top management may not see the value of achieving accuracy in the cash forecast and consequently may underfund or understaff the forecasting function.

*EXTERNAL VERSUS INTERNAL FORECASTS* Companies also differ in their willingness to use an outside third party to develop part or all of the forecast. Macroeconomic

---

[8] If the distribution of the cash balance is normal, a "Z score" can be calculated by subtracting the average cash level from zero (or some other minimum cash balance), taking the absolute value of that difference and dividing the absolute difference by the standard deviation of the cash flows. This Z score is then compared with a critical value from a standard normal distribution table to get the probability of the cash position staying above the minimum cash balance. Assuming an average cash position during the year of $1,000,000, a standard deviation of $425,000 for the annual cash position, and a minimum cash balance of zero, the probability of running below zero during the year is calculated as follows:

$$Z = \frac{(\$0 - \$1{,}000{,}000)}{\$425{,}000}$$

$$= 2.35$$

The probability of staying above a $0 cash position based on this Z value is determined by looking up the probability associated with a Z score of 2.35 in the standard normal table. The probability of falling below $0 in cash is the one-tailed probability of (0.50 − the tabled probability of 0.4906), or 0.0094. The chance of running out of cash is then 0.94 percent, or less than 1 percent. Management will have to determine if this is an acceptably low risk; if not, more than $1,000,000 will have to be maintained in the cash account. The reader is cautioned that existing studies of cash distributions document nonnormality, implying that this calculation only gives a rough approximation of cash shortage probabilities.

forecasts and industry forecasts are commonly provided by consulting agencies such as Data Resources, Inc. (DRI), and Wharton Econometrics (WEFA). Even for cash forecasts, outside help is available in the form of customized computer forecasting models, some of which are integrated with the accounting and inventory management system. When done internally, managerial philosophy may dictate who does the forecast. Increasingly, line personnel are doing strategic long-term forecasting; these same personnel might also develop short-term and intermediate-term forecasts. The rationale is that line managers are "close to the action" and are responsible for implementing the plans, whereas a forecasting staff is neither. Even when the cash manager does the cash forecast, he or she is wise to check with appropriate operating personnel for up-to-date developments that will affect cash receipts or disbursements.

*QUANTITATIVE VERSUS JUDGMENTAL FORECASTING* Some managers favor judgmental forecasting approaches, whereas others favor quantitative approaches. Also called subjective forecasting, the **judgmental approach** relies heavily on intuition to adjust what is known about upcoming cash flows to arrive at the cash forecast. Quite often, preference for the judgmental approach arises from a very short forecast horizon, a distrust of computers, or an inability to understand the statistics that underlie quantitative models. The **quantitative approach** involves the use of a numerical model to forecast and is usually implemented on a computer.[9] Of course, these two approaches may be used in conjunction with one another, in which case the firm is using a **mixed approach**.

## Forecast Parameters

The forecasting philosophies interact with other aspects of the forecasting situation to guide the forecaster in making some of the key decisions regarding the nature and format of the forecast. The four key parameters that we investigate here are the forecast horizon, the forecast interval, the update frequency, and the presentation format. These parameters, in turn, largely determine the forecasting approach used. Before making these key decisions, the forecaster must consider the volatility of the forecast variables and the company's existing planning methods. The inherent uncertainty of the forecast variables indicates whether sensitivity analysis or simulation should be incorporated into the forecast model. Existing planning techniques with which managers already are comfortable are the best candidates for the cash forecast, because managers are reluctant to base decisions on unknown methods. The degree of decentralization in the company also has an effect on the forecast process because of the required aggregation of field or divisional forecasts.

We consider the monthly cash forecast within five steps involved in forecasting: (1) setting the forecast horizon and interval, (2) identifying the variables that need to be forecasted and how they may be measured, (3) formulating a mathematical model, (4) estimating that model, and then (5) validating the model. We expand on the third step, modeling the cash flow sequence, to include the statistical tools from which the forecaster can select. We also highlight practical concerns faced by the forecaster as each step is developed. Because the **forecast interval** is monthly, our first step is reduced to specifying the forecast horizon.

*FORECAST HORIZON* The monthly cash **forecast horizon**, indicating how far ahead the cash balance is being projected, may range from the next month to the next five years.

[9] A survey conducted by Business International in the mid-1980s found that 13 percent of the responding firms had already implemented highly automated forecasting systems, 45 percent said they would have such systems within a few years, and fully 87 percent of the firms anticipated having some aspect of their forecasting computerized in the foreseeable future.

Normally, a forecast is prepared for each month interval within that horizon, but that may change to quarterly forecasts as the horizon moves beyond two years. Short-term forecasts might be made for the next one to three months: Getronics has its 60 worldwide subsidiaries submit 13-week rolling cash forecasts via the corporate Intranet.[10] Most of the events giving rise to cash flows (sales and purchases, leases and rental contracts, dividend declarations and loan arrangements, and salary and wage amounts) are already known for the month-ahead forecast, making this the easiest monthly forecast. Partially offsetting the ease of this forecast is the level of detail required in that horizon, which we reconsider in our discussion of the variable identification step.

The second horizon for the monthly forecast is the intermediate term, encompassing forecasts for 3 to 18 or 24 months into the future. A 1995 survey by Treasury Strategies, Inc., determined that many corporations invest surplus funds in too-short maturities—which one expert attributes to not having cash budgets for the 12–18-month horizon.[11] An example of a cash forecast with a 3-month horizon, without the detail behind the totaled cash receipts and disbursements, appears in Exhibit 12–1. This intermediate-term horizon may have cash flow forecasts tied directly to the organization's budget. The form of intermediate-term forecast used by most firms is the cash budget. One survey of businesses indicated that 95 percent of large (Fortune 500) firms project a cash budget. The cash budget shows the anticipated cash receipts and disbursements for the next 12 months. A recommended accuracy target is ±3 percent, achieved 95 percent of the time.[12]

A possible third horizon is the long-term forecast, from 18 or 24 months to 5 years out. Longer horizons imply less forecast accuracy and greater applicability for statistical forecasting techniques. Far fewer companies provide a monthly breakdown for these more-distant horizons. Instead, they project just the year-end cash balances or the quarterly cash flows. These longer horizon forecasts are used mainly for anticipating financing needs. Correspondingly, companies with substantial intrayear variability in their cash flows find it advantageous to estimate a monthly breakdown because they can identify peak financing needs. The peak needs dictate minimum amounts of short-term or medium-term financing to arrange, because actual needs may exceed anticipations as a result of forecast error.

*VARIABLE IDENTIFICATION* The shorter the horizon, the more detail the cash forecast will show—and therefore the more variables that will be included in the analysis. The company's operating, credit, inventory, capital expenditure, financing, investing, and tax-related decisions give rise to cash flows that must be identified and estimated. Depending

**Exhibit 12–1**

*Simple Cash Forecasting Model*

Simple Cash Forecasting Model

| Item | Jan. | Feb. | Mar. |
|---|---|---|---|
| Cash receipts | $125 | $145 | $150 |
| − Cash disbursements | 85 | 125 | 135 |
| = Cash flow | $ 40 | $ 20 | $ 15 |
| + Beginning cash | 35 | 75 | 95 |
| = Ending cash | $ 75 | $ 95 | $110 |

[10] Van Weezendonk (2003), cited in the end-of-chapter references.
[11] Noted in Gamble (1996), cited in the end-of-chapter references.
[12] Recommended in A. M. Cunningham, "The Accrual Addback Technique for Medium-Term Cash Forecasting," *Journal of Cash Management* (September/October 1988), pp. 46–50.

on the horizon and the forecasting technique used, some or all of the following cash receipt variables might be included: cash sales, cash collections from credit sales, rent, interest, dividends from stock holdings, royalties, asset sales, and proceeds from new borrowings. Cash disbursements might include supplier cash or payables disbursements, wage and salary payments, pension fundings, utility bills, tax payments, capital expenditures, dividend payments, interest payments, principal repayments, and insurance premiums.[13] The forecaster may wish to order the receipt or payment variables based on whether management has any control over the payment amount and timing. This provides a tool for determining when and how to adjust collecting or paying patterns to alter the company's cash position if the plan is untenable or when the actual figures arrive worse than anticipated.

A related decision to be made here is the format of the forecast. One option is to use the statement of cash flows format (as prescribed in Financial Accounting Standards Board Statement 95).[14] One problem posed by the statement of cash flows format is the proper treatment of compensating balances. It is best to treat these balances as cash and to disclose any withdrawal restrictions.

When setting up the format, the forecaster should remember that the forecast will be used later as a monitoring device. Comparisons can be made more easily by setting up a financial spreadsheet model with separate columns for the actual amount, the forecasted amount, and the difference. The amount by which the actual amount is over or under the forecasted or budgeted amount is termed the **variance**. Large dollar or percentage variances stand out and command management attention and remedial action.

*Modeling the Cash Flow Sequence* Once the variables have been defined and the forecaster has determined how each will be measured, he or she is ready to model the cash flow sequence. The present focus is limited to the three major approaches to monthly cash forecasting. Several statistical tools that can assist the implementation of two of these approaches also are developed. The three commonly used cash forecasting approaches are the receipts and disbursements method (sometimes referred to as scheduling), the modified accrual method, and the pro forma balance sheet approach.

The **receipts and disbursements method** involves looking up most of the data variables in company sources and estimating cash effect timing of noncash events. The major noncash events are product sales and material purchases. Usually, receipts are listed separately on a receipts schedule and disbursements on a separate disbursements schedule. The forecaster then combines the receipts and disbursements on a projected schedule (think of it as a projected cash flow timeline) according to anticipated cash flow dates. The layout used may vary from a desk calendar to a fancy computer spreadsheet that is linked to numerous other corporate spreadsheets. Periodic and accurate intracompany communications are critical to the accuracy of the approach. Accuracy suffers when the horizon extends beyond one month, however, and earlier inaccuracies compound into large errors for longer horizons. Yet, many firms project a 12-month rolling forecast of anticipated daily activity using this technique (Gallanis, 2001).

*Format of the Receipts and Disbursements Forecast* A template that might be used for receipts and disbursements is shown in Exhibit 12–2. Note that this format takes into account beginning and ending cash (both calculated by assuming no short-term investments or borrowings), the period's cash flows, and required minimal cash levels.

---

[13] An excellent "user-friendly" guide to practical aspects involved with specifying each of these variables is provided in the Loscalzo citation found in the end-of-chapter references.

[14] Refer to Chapter 2 for a detailed presentation of the statement of cash flows (FASB Statement 95). Under the previous statement of changes in financial position (sometimes called a funds flow statement), many companies reported sources and uses of funds on a working capital basis, which disguised cash fluctuations and was of little help to the individual managing the cash position.

## Exhibit 12–2

*Template for Receipts and Disbursements Method*

World Communications Corp. Cash Receipts and Disbursements

| | JANUARY 2006 | FEBRUARY 2006 | MARCH 2006 |
|---|---|---|---|
| **BEGINNING CASH BALANCE** | $ 1,500,000 | $2,612,050 | $ (4,738) |
| **CASH RECEIPTS:** | | | |
| Cash sales | $ 5,600,000 | $3,500,000 | $3,125,000 |
| Cash collection of prior month's credit sales | 10,200,000 | 8,400,000 | 5,250,000 |
| Cash collection of credit sales made two months ago | 5,750,000 | 3,187,500 | 2,625,000 |
| Interest income received | 9,675 | 2,535 | 0 |
| Cash dividends received | 375 | 245 | 165 |
| Cash from asset sales | 0 | 15 | 0 |
| Cash proceeds from long-term borrowings | 4,500 | 0 | 0 |
| Cash proceeds from equity issuance | 0 | 0 | 0 |
| *TOTAL CASH RECEIPTS:* | $21,564,550 | $15,090,295 | $11,000,165 |
| CASH DISBURSEMENTS: | | | |
| Cash purchases | $ 6,750,000 | $ 2,720,000 | $ 2,500,000 |
| Cash payment for prior month credit purchases | 11,250,000 | 4,533,333 | 4,166,667 |
| Cash payment for credit purchases made two months ago | 0 | 0 | 0 |
| Interest payments | 250 | 250 | 250 |
| Principal repayments | 1,000 | 1,000 | 1,000 |
| Cash dividends paid | 0 | 12,000,000 | 0 |
| Tax payments | 1,250 | 0 | 0 |
| Asset acquisitions | 2,450,000 | 0 | 1,250,000 |
| *TOTAL CASH DISBURSEMENTS:* | $20,452,500 | $19,254,583 | $ 7,917,917 |
| **CASH FLOW (RECEIPTS − DISBURSEMENTS)** | $ 1,112,050 | ($ 4,164,238) | $ 3,082,248 |
| **ENDING CASH (BEG CASH + CASH FLOW)** | $ 2,612,050 | ($ 1,552,238) | $ 1,530,010 |
| LESS: Minimum cash balance | $ 1,000,000 | $ 1,000,000 | $ 1,000,000 |
| **CASH SURPLUS (IF POSITIVE)** | $ 1,612,050 | $ 0 | $ 530,010 |
| **CASH SHORTFALL (IF NEGATIVE)** | $ 0 | $ 2,552,238 | $ 0 |

The ending cash for one month serves as the beginning cash for the following month. The minimum cash balance is a function of management policy that a certain emergency cash stock be held and/or a compensating balance be kept at deposit banks. The bottom line, excess cash or required total financing, is a cumulative total. It represents the account balance of the amount invested or borrowed as of the end of the period. The net cash flow indicates how much additional money is invested or paid back (on outstanding loans), if positive, or the dollar figure of investments liquidated or additional lending, if negative.

An alternative format is to use the statement of cash flows format for the receipts and disbursements, thereby classifying sources and uses of cash according to whether they are operating, investing, or financing cash flows. Because businesses must include the cash flow statement as part of their reporting, monitoring forecast accuracy is simple.

*Interpreting the Receipts and Disbursements Forecast* Take a closer look at Exhibit 12–2 to see how the treasury analyst can use it to make investing and borrowing decisions. The company starts the quarter with $1.5 million in cash and cash equivalents. Everything looks fine after January, with an ending cash position of $2.6 million. Even after subtracting the minimum cash balance of $1 million, there is a large cash surplus. This represents an investable balance, which usually is invested in short-term securities. The large net cash outflow in February, mainly resulting from the dividend payment, causes the company to liquidate the short-term securities but still run short of cash.

Even before considering the required minimum of $1 million, the company is unable to cover the cash outflow. The company will have to borrow more than $2.5 million to maintain the necessary minimum cash. March brings a net cash inflow, large enough to not only pay off the $2.5 million-plus credit line borrowing but also to invest in $0.5 million of short-term securities.

Notice three uses for the monthly cash forecast. First, we are able to anticipate the need for credit and the amount of borrowing that should be prearranged to cover anticipated deficits. In World Communications' case, the company will likely arrange a credit line of at least $3 million because forecasts are never perfect and there might be a smaller receipt total or larger disbursement total in any given month. Or the company may allow the $1 million minimum liquidity to act as a partial buffer against unforeseen cash needs and only borrow $2.5 million. Of course, the analyst looks at least one year ahead, not merely the three months we show here. Second, we are able to project short-term investment amounts and, based on how long cash surpluses will persist, the allowable maturity of those securities. Normally, longer maturities bring higher yields, and the analyst will study the forecast for 6 or 12 months ahead to see how long projected cash surpluses will last. Third, the analyst might use such projections to help establish the company's target cash balance. The company might arrange more long-term borrowing to increase the year-beginning cash position and avoid short-term borrowing altogether. One caution when using monthly cash budgets: This forecast is giving us anticipated *end-of-month* cash balances. These could well mask larger intramonth receipt and disbursement mismatches, and the analyst will look at the historical pattern of cash flows to determine if these have occurred. This provides further motivation to arrange credit lines larger than the largest cumulative month-end cash shortage recorded in the cash forecast.

*Developing the Receipts and Disbursements Forecast* The steps involved in generating the cash forecast using the receipts and disbursements method are straightforward. First, the analyst must develop or look up the company's sales forecast. Preferably, a range of sales forecasts can be developed, linked to likely scenarios for the horizon period. This enables the forecaster to incorporate the uncertainty inherent in the sales forecast through techniques such as simulation. To aid in the sales projection, the analyst may break down the sales revenue forecast into its components, unit sales and selling prices.

Second, the analyst lays out the incoming cash from cash sales, cash collections, asset sales, and other sources. But what if the company offers credit terms and a given month's sales generates cash across several subsequent months? The historical or anticipated payment pattern for the company's customers is used to project the cash receipts from sales. Expanding the receipts and disbursement illustration (Exhibit 12–3) helps.

World Communications first projects sales for its product lines, which we show as a memo item at the top of Exhibit 12–3. Next, it studies historical collection patterns to determine the uncollected balance fractions shown in the second column (these may already

## Exhibit 12–3

*Cash Receipts from Sales Worksheet*

Projecting Cash Collections from Earlier Sales

| | | MONTH SALES | | | | | |
|---|---|---|---|---|---|---|---|
| Item | Proportion | Oct 2005 | Nov 2005 | Dec 2005 | Jan 2006 | Feb 2006 | Mar 2006 |
| *MEMO:* Actual (Forecast) Sales: | | $20,000,000 | $38,333,333 | $21,250,000 | *$17,500,000* | *$10,937,500* | *$ 9,765,625* |
| Cash Sales | 32% | | | | $ 5,600,000 | $ 3,500,000 | $ 3,125,000 |
| Collections of Credit Sales: | | | | | | | |
| Lagged 1 Month | 48% | | | | 10,200,000 | 8,400,000 | 5,250,000 |
| Lagged 2 Months | 15% | | | | 5,750,000 | 3,187,500 | 2,625,000 |
| Lagged 3 Months* | 0% | | | | 0 | 0 | 0 |
| *Total Cash Receipts from Sales* | | | | | ***$21,550,000*** | ***$15,087,500*** | ***$11,000,000*** |

*Bad debt loss rate is 5% (=100%−32%−48%−15%).

be available if the credit department is using them to monitor collection efficiency, as demonstrated in Exhibit 6–6). The key is to determine when cash is received from customers—when does the customer actually make payment? We will include a few months of actual sales in our data, because of the lag in collections. Here, the analyst is making a projection in early January, so we have actual data from October, November, and December, in case there is a 3-month lag in collections. In World Communications' case, October's sales are not used, because 95 percent of sales are collected within two months and the remaining 5 percent are uncollectible. World receives 32 percent in the month of sale, 48 percent in the next month (lag one month), and 15 percent in the second following month (lag two months). These proportions add to 100 percent only if World experienced negligible bad debt losses. Here, as noted, World fails to collect 5 percent of sales (100%−32%−48%−15%). To calculate January's cash receipts from sales, we take 32 percent of January's projected sales of $17.5 million, plus 48 percent of December's sales of $21.25 million, plus 15 percent of November's sales of $38.33 million. The sum is $21.55 million of cash receipts, which constitutes most of January's total cash receipts in Exhibit 12–2.

Third, cash disbursements, including payments to suppliers, employees, governments, and funds providers are arrayed. The difference in the cash receipts and disbursements gives the period's net cash flow. Many forecasters stop here, but, as shown in Exhibit 12–2, it is valuable to go beyond this to add beginning cash, arriving at ending cash. Financing and investments can be handled in two different ways. They can be treated as a residual: If ending cash is negative, arrange this amount of financing; if positive, plan to invest the surplus amount. Or the financing and investing can be built into the forecast to reflect planned financing and investing. Regardless, asset sales and capital investments should be included as separate categories under receipts and disbursements. Strengths of the receipts and disbursements method include simplicity, accuracy for near-term forecasts, and attractiveness as a monitoring and control tool. Weaknesses include the inaccuracy for forecast horizons longer than three months (largely resulting from the cumulation of early errors) and the overreliance on the forecaster's judgment that typifies real-life applications of the technique.

*Modified Accrual Method* A second technique useful for monthly forecasts is the **modified accrual method.** Sometimes called the accrual addback technique or adjusted net income technique, the approach begins with accounting reports or the operating budget and then adjusts these numbers to reflect the timing of cash flows related to these transactions. For small businesses and nonprofit organizations doing their income statements on a cash basis, very few adjustments to the operating budget or projected income statement are necessary. The only problem encountered in that case is if the historical tracker used to develop a forecast is invalidated because of faster or slower processing of invoices, checks received, and so on. In its simplest form, the modified accrual forecast is easily determined, as shown in Equation 12.1.

$$C_t = NI_t + NC_t - CA_t + CL_t \tag{12.1}$$

when for period $t$:

$C_t$ = Cash flow

$NI_t$ = Net income

$NC_t$ = Noncash charges

$CA_t$ = Current asset change

$CL_t$ = Current liability change

EXAMPLE OF THE MODIFIED ACCRUAL TECHNIQUE AMAX Coal has assembled the following condensed pro-forma income statement and parts of its present and pro-forma balance sheets.

| Pro-Forma Income Statement ($ mils.) | |
|---|---|
| Sales | $10,000 |
| − COGS | 6,000 |
| Gross margin | $ 4,000 |
| − Operating exps. | 3,150* |
| Operating profit | $ 850 |
| − Interest exp. | 50 |
| Pretax income | $ 800 |
| − Taxes | 300 |
| Net income | $ 500 |

*Includes depreciation and other noncash charges of $145 million.

| | Present Balance Sheet ($ mils.) | Pro-Forma Balance Sheet ($ mils.) |
|---|---|---|
| ***Current Assets*** | | |
| Cash | $ 10 | *Uncertain; assume to be unchanged.* |
| Accounts receivable | 970 | $ 960 |
| Inventories | 835 | 820 |
| ***Long-Term Assets*** | | |
| Property, plant, and equipment | $12,000 | $11,700 |
| ***Current Liabilities*** | | |
| Accounts payable | $ 745 | $ 730 |
| Notes payable | 500 | 500 |
| Long-term debt | 7,000 | 8,000 |

**Forecast Solution**: Net income and the noncash charges are taken from the projected income statement. Changes in current assets and current liabilities are calculated as (Projected balance sheet amount − Present balance sheet amount). If AMAX Coal projects net income of $500 million, noncash charges of $145 million, decreases in current assets of $25 million (in this case, the change in accounts receivable plus change in inventories), and decreases in current liabilities of $15 million (here, the change in accounts payable), cash flow for the period using our simple equation is:

$$CF_t = \$500 + \$145 - (-\$25) + (-\$15) = \$655 \text{ million}$$

Current asset changes are subtracted because increases in items such as inventories drain cash flow, and current liability changes are added because they represent sources of cash flow. Typical noncash charges are depreciation, amortization of intangibles, and gains or losses on asset sales. Notice that the cash flow formula presented is an operating cash flow forecast. The change, if any, in long-term assets, long-term liabilities, and equity will not affect the forecasted cash flow. If desired, Equation 12.1 easily can be expanded to include anticipated dividends, loan interest or principal payments, acquisitions, and other episodic cash flows. At that point, however, it might be easier to simply change to a projected statement of cash flow format.

The major strength of the modified accrual technique is ease of implementation: The data are already available, in most cases, in the form of a budget or projected income statement. The adjustments to net income to arrive at cash flow are easily made, as shown above. The technique is also relatively accurate for intermediate-term forecasting, when compared with other techniques. However, it suffers from inaccuracy in the short-run horizons and may lack sufficient detail to ensure accuracy.[15]

*PRO-FORMA BALANCE SHEET METHOD* The **pro-forma balance sheet approach** to generating a cash forecast involves determination of the amount of cash and marketable securities by computing the difference between projected assets (excluding cash and marketable securities) and the sum of projected liabilities and stockholders' equity. This approach, very popular for medium-term and long-term forecasting, is illustrated in Exhibit 12–4. Some of the questions such a forecast may answer are:[16]

1. How much money will our foreign subsidiary provide to headquarters over the next two quarters?
2. What is the estimated credit line usage over the next three quarters?
3. What is the projected global cash position at quarter-end?
4. What is the expected level of cash collections of accounts receivable and the corresponding days' sales outstanding at quarter-end?

In projecting the balance sheet, one might predict current liabilities and noncash assets as a percentage of anticipated sales and assume that the long-term liabilities and common stock will remain constant. The change in retained earnings is based on anticipated net income less planned cash dividends. Subtracting the sum of liabilities and stockholders' equity from noncash assets gives us a residual amount labeled "cash and marketable securities," which is our cash forecast. If this amount is negative, additional financing will have to be arranged. Then, the new financing amount would be plugged into the liability section; interest expense, net income, and additions to retained earnings recomputed and a new cash amount calculated. In other cases, the figure may be a large positive amount,

---

[15] In response to this weakness, Alan Cunningham has devised a more elaborate modified accrual technique that he terms the *accrual addback technique* (AAT). Adjusting for uncontrollable elements, the technique has achieved impressive accuracy for intermediate-term horizons. The model is documented and an example provided as part of our text's computer supplement.

[16] Schmidt (2003), cited in the end-of-chapter references.

**Exhibit 12–4**

*Pro-Forma Balance Sheet Method*

Balance Sheet Projection Forecasting Method
Cash and Marketable Securities Residual of Balance Sheet Projection

| | Month | | |
|---|---|---|---|
| ACCOUNT | JAN. | FEB. | MAR. |
| Cash and M.S.* | Plug | Plug | Plug |
| Accounts receivable | $ 35 | $ 36 | $ 36 |
| Inventories | 65 | 66 | 68 |
| Prepaid expenses | 15 | 15 | 16 |
| Current assets | $115 | $117 | $120 |
| Property, plant, & equipment | $210 | $223 | $227 |
| TOTAL ASSETS | $325 | $340 | $347 |
| Accounts payable | $ 30 | $ 31 | $ 31 |
| Notes payable | 25 | 26 | 26 |
| Accrued expenses | 10 | 10 | 10 |
| Current liabilities | $ 65 | $ 67 | $ 67 |
| Long-term liabilities | $ 45 | $ 46 | $ 47 |
| TOTAL LIABILITIES | $110 | $113 | $114 |
| Stockholders' Equity | | | |
| Common stock | $ 5 | $ 5 | $ 5 |
| Paid-in capital | 20 | 20 | 20 |
| Retained earnings | 205 | 220 | 235 |
| EQUITY | $230 | $245 | $260 |
| TOTAL LIABILITIES and EQUITY | $340 | $358 | $374 |

*Calculation of Cash & Marketable Securities Plug Amount
Cash and M.S.
= (Totals Liabilities
+ Stockholders' Equity)
− Total Assets: 340 − 325 = 15 358 − 340 = 18 374 − 347 = 27

whereby some previous borrowings may be paid down, stock repurchased, or greater expansion in fixed assets arranged.[17] The fact that the forecast leads naturally to financial planning demonstrates the value of longer-term cash forecasts. The pro-forma balance sheet approach is well suited for these longer-range cash forecasts.

Basically, the pro-forma balance sheet represents a crude approximation of sources and uses of funds, with funds defined as cash and marketable securities. Liability and equity accounts represent sources of funds; asset amounts represent uses of funds. The major strength of this forecasting approach is its ease of implementation. The major weakness is the difficulty in making accurate monthly forecasts by using balance sheet projections. For annual totals, the technique is acceptable, but for monthly forecasts, the failure to adjust for differences between accrual-based net income (which drives the retained earnings projection) and cash flows arising from that income stream hurts forecast accuracy.

[17] Another way of approaching this exercise, if the primary goal is planning short-term borrowing, is to make Notes payable the plug figure and insert some targeted minimum cash & marketable securities amount.

*MODEL ESTIMATION* Once the variables included in the model have been specified, the forecaster must estimate the model with real data. **Model estimation** includes selecting an appropriate forecasting technique and model calibration. Model calibration refers to fitting the data to the model so that coefficients can be determined. To illustrate, finding the coefficients for a model in the form $Y = a + b(X)$ involves computing the numerical values for $a$ and $b$. It is important to not overlook the fact that forecasts are subject to error, however. To incorporate the uncertainty underlying the cash forecast, the forecaster might supplement the forecast with sensitivity analysis or simulation. **Sensitivity analysis** involves varying the input values for each key assumption, such as the sales level, that bears on the cash forecast. This process reveals which assumptions have the greatest impact on cash flow. The forecaster can then restudy those assumptions to ensure they are accurate or at least have contingency plans ready if, during the middle of the year, they turn out to be overly optimistic or pessimistic. The forecaster also can present a range forecast, indicating the likely span of values that the forecast variable will adopt if sales or interest rates vary from their expected values. Another means of incorporating the underlying forecast uncertainty is through **simulation**. Simulation involves simultaneously varying key input variables, using values corresponding to their historical frequency of occurrence, and noting the effect on the cash position.

*MODEL VALIDATION* We have mentioned at several points the difficulty of detecting breakdowns in the modeled behavior of the forecast variable. The model validation (or validity-checking) stage should have a built-in means of detection, such as the occurrence of a forecast error that is more than one standard deviation from the mean or mean-adjusted-for-trend. Manufacturing and processing firms such as Frito-Lay have successfully used such an approach to detect the need for production machine adjustment in their statistical process control.

## FORECASTING DAILY CASH FLOWS

Forecasters typically use the receipts and disbursements method for daily cash forecasts, especially for short horizons. Statistical tools can be helpful for the recurrent nonmajor elements in the forecast, however. As noted earlier, many smaller and some medium-sized companies do not even forecast on a daily basis and instead rely on funding from investments or credit lines to cover shortfalls. Mid-sized companies not developing daily cash forecasts manage the uncertainty of check clearing with controlled disbursement accounts. As the opportunity cost for suboptimal investing increases as a result of increasing interest rates, more companies find it profitable to do daily forecasts. Before determining the steps in developing the daily cash forecast, we return to our chapter opening Financial Dilemma to consider which cash balance to forecast.

### FINANCIAL DILEMMA REVISITED

An analyst developing the daily cash forecast must first determine how best to measure the company's cash position. For near-term forecasts, it is preferable to measure the company's available cash, which means we wish to forecast the collected bank balance. The level of the bank balance (or balances, in the case of multiple accounts) is what triggers short-term investing or borrowing. Most companies find it too cumbersome to adjust the company's ledger cash balance as shown in its accounting records. In fact, for companies using controlled disbursement accounts, that cash balance typically is negative because checks are charged against cash even though they have not yet cleared because of float. The accrual-based balance must reflect sales revenues that have not yet been collected and expenses for which no disbursement has yet been made, as well as prepaid and deferred expenses. As the forecast horizon increases, the forecast focus shifts to the book balance. The cash balance at future financial statement dates is a book balance forecast.[18]

The second decision relates to what inputs will be used to forecast the collected bank balance. The forecasts of cash receipts and disbursements made by various divisional and field personnel might be aggregated, or the forecaster may use the historical relationship of sales volume to cash receipts and disbursements to statistically forecast the cash position. If the company's bank accounts have been structured properly, the forecaster should be able to forecast cash flow by operating units. A very simple approach, which might be appropriate for a small company with only one account, includes the following variables:

| VARIABLE | HOW MEASURED |
|---|---|
| Cash receipts (*CR*) | Credits to demand deposit account |
| Cash disbursements (*CD*) | Debits to demand deposit account<br>Petty cash disbursements |
| Cash flow ($CF = CR - CD$) | Difference between cash receipts, disbursements |

For example, one U.S. manufacturer has all its subsidiaries forecast each of the following elements: profits before interest, interest, depreciation, inventory, receivables, payables, capital expenditures, dividends, and long-term debt payments. Another company requires each subsidiary to further specify total cash flows by currency.

### Horizon

For most companies doing daily forecasting, the immediate day's cash flows are simply gathered from balance-reporting systems. For the next day and up to two weeks in the future, historical collection and payment patterns can be used in connection with sales and purchases to project cash flows.

### Variable Identification

The shorter the horizon, the more detail that can be shown in the cash forecast. Ideally, the format includes columns for the forecast, the actual amount (as it materializes), the budgeted amount, and variances. Typically, actual-vs.-forecast and actual-vs.-budget variances are calculated. Explanations of likely causes and corrective actions accompany the numbers.

With the requirement to present a statement of cash flows, some companies are finding it fruitful to prepare their cash forecasts with separate subtotals for operating, financing, and investing cash flows. Although the statement of cash flows format might be more appropriate for a monthly forecast, it provides a checklist of line items that should be incorporated into daily forecasts as well.

### Modeling the Cash Flow Sequence

The major differences when it comes to modeling the daily cash flow sequence are a greater reliance on bank-supplied deposit and clearing data, an emphasis on scheduling the upcoming cash flows via the receipts and disbursements technique, and a lesser reliance on

---

[18] For more on this, see Gallanis (2001), cited in the end-of-chapter references.

**FOCUS ON PRACTICE**

## *How Can a Company Measure the Results and Improve the Performance of Its Daily Cash Forecasting System?*

One major industrial company has applied service quality improvement techniques to its treasury department. Comparing actual performance to departmental goals has led to improved intraday forecasts, which have led to smaller and more tightly controlled end-of-day balances. The service improvement effort began with the establishment of "minimally acceptable performance standards" for daily cash forecast deadlines, bank balance forecasts, and presentment notification from disbursement banks. The daily cash forecast minimum standard was set at 10:00 A.M., with 9:45 A.M. as the goal. Major disbursement banks were graded based on the percentage of the total day's presentments making the first presentment deadline (see Chapter 8 for information on the check presentment process). Because daily investing and borrowing decisions are based on the first presentment and large later presentments might lead to an overdraft situation, larger first-presentment percentages are preferable. After the standards were implemented, a "below standard" bank was identified and forced to improve. In line with the forecasting improvements, the company established a minimally acceptable ending daily cash position of $1 million and a goal of $500,000. Performance tracking and adjustments have enabled managers to approach that goal. The company's review and improvement of forecasting and other treasury department processes have saved it an estimated $1 million annually. Companies in the 2000s now strive for even greater savings and forecast accuracy, which is possible because of the richer data and more sophisticated forecasting routines built into global "enterprise resource planning" software used by U.S. multinational corporations.

*Sources:* "Treasury Finds a Tape to Measure Quality, Improve Performance," *Corporate Cashflow* (April 1990), p. 24; Richard H. Gamble, "The Bank Cash/Book Cash Disconnect," *Business Finance* (January 2002).

statistical forecasting techniques. Scheduling upcoming cash receipts and disbursements requires close contact with any corporate personnel having responsibility for or knowledge of impending cash flows. Cash managers who have not yet mastered computer spreadsheets have been known to use their desk calendars to keep track of these flows.

### Structuring the Daily Cash Forecast

Even the structuring of which inflows and outflows to forecast is different in the daily cash forecast.[19] Typically, there are a few large-dollar items and many small-dollar items. For the major flows, such as taxes, dividends, lease and bond payments, and wages, the amount and timing are usually known in advance, and these can be separately projected one to two months into the future. Other major flows may be impossible to anticipate, such as payments from financially distressed firms that are in arrears (and have a large balance

[19] The definitive sources for this topic, on which much of our discussion is based, is B. K. Stone and R. A. Wood, "Daily Cash Forecasting: A Simple Method for Implementing the Distribution Approach," *Financial Management* (Fall 1977), pp. 40–50; and T. W. Miller and B. K. Stone, "Daily Cash Forecasting: Alternative Models and Techniques," *Journal of Financial & Quantitative Analysis* (September 1985), pp. 335–351.

due) and some international remittances. These are often offset through a financial transaction: When unanticipated monies come in, they are used to pay down a credit line or invest overnight; when amounts are debited, these are offset with a transfer from the short-term investments portfolio or a credit line drawdown. In any case, it may be futile to try to pinpoint their timing, as long as contingency plans have been made to handle them. What we *are* interested in is the sum of the many small-dollar flows, and this net cash flow total is amenable to forecasting.

## Distribution Method

One area in which statistics has been instrumental in achieving accuracy is for spreading out (distributing) check clearing or receivable cash effects throughout the days of the week and month. Here, regression analysis has been very useful, in that the day-of-the-week and even day-of-the-month effects can be modeled by assigning each a separate regression coefficient. The regression-based **distribution method** also has been used to model the cash disbursements related to how many business days have elapsed since payroll checks have been issued. In general, distribution simply refers to spreading out the month's cash forecast into daily flows, thereby showing the intramonth cash flow pattern. Analysts not having an understanding of regression may estimate daily proportions by calculating average values from the past. Notice that this method still relies on the monthly cash budget to provide the total dollar amount that is to be distributed.

*USING THE DISTRIBUTION METHOD FOR DISBURSEMENTS* We can illustrate this in the disbursements context by assuming that October's total disbursement is forecast to be \$40 million. Equation 12.2 indicates how we can forecast the disbursements for Friday, October 15, which is the 11th work day of the month:

$$CD_{11} = (d_{11} + w_5) \times MDF \qquad (12.2)$$

In which: $CD_{11}$ = Cash disbursement forecast for the 11th work day of the month

$d_{11}$ = Coefficient for 11th work day (from regression model)

$w_5$ = Coefficient for fifth day of week, Friday (from regression model)

$MDF$ = Month's disbursement forecast (from cash budget)

If regression analysis indicates that historically $d_{11}$ is 0.04 and $w_5$ is 0.015[20] and our best estimate of MDF is \$40 million, we have:

$$\begin{aligned} CD_{11} &= (0.04 + 0.015) \times \$40{,}000{,}000 \\ &= (0.055) \times \$40{,}000{,}000 \\ &= \$2{,}200{,}000 \end{aligned}$$

One can think of the work-day coefficient as the effect of the day-of-the-month effect, holding constant the day of the week, and the day-of-the-week coefficient as that day's effect holding constant the day of the month.

*USING THE DISTRIBUTION METHOD FOR COLLECTIONS* We can also use the distribution method for collections of credit sales. One month's cash and credit sales can be distributed partially across that month (cash sales and cash discount-takers) and the remainder across the following months. Or a typical month-end receivables balance can be

[20] The technique used to estimate the day-of-week or day-of-month effects is regression analysis with dummy variables. See the Appendix 12B discussion of the dummy variable technique and seasonal variations.

distributed across the next 60 or 90 days, with some residual amount left uncollected at the end of that period.

*Example of Distribution Method* We can learn how to develop a 5-day payroll disbursement forecast by looking at an example. This example also illustrates the basics of the distribution method and how proportions can be determined without the help of regression modeling. First, we need to know the total dollar amount of payroll checks being issued. Then, we take the proportions clearing 1, 2, 3, 4, and 5 days after the issue date. To keep things simple, we assume the payroll checks are issued after the ledger cut-off time of the local banks, so that at best the depositor can get 1-day availability. In our example, we analyze check clearings based solely on business days after issuance and overlook the day-of-the-week, day-of-the-month, and whether a holiday intervenes. Here is the background data for a company that issues only monthly payroll checks:

1. Amount of payroll checks issued on Wednesday, June 30: $455,000
2. Historical check clearing data (past five payroll check issuances) and the calculated averages:

Proportion Clearing

| DAYS AFTER ISSUANCE | PAYROLL #1 | PAYROLL #2 | PAYROLL #3 | PAYROLL #4 | PAYROLL #5 | CALCULATED AVERAGE PROPORTION |
|---|---|---|---|---|---|---|
| 1 | 45% | 42% | 47% | 42% | 43% | 44% |
| 2 | 32% | 33% | 31% | 35% | 33% | 33% |
| 3 | 14% | 16% | 10% | 18% | 15% | 15% |
| 4 | 7% | 5% | 10% | 4% | 7% | 6%* |
| 5+ | 2% | 4% | 2% | 1% | 2% | 2% |

*Rounded down to force column total to 100 percent.
+Very small amounts for Days 6 and following are lumped together with Day 5 clearings.

To get the clearing forecast, take the dollar amount of the payroll and multiply it by the calculated proportions:

Next-business-day clearing (Thursday, July 1) $455,000 × 0.44 = $200,200

Second-business-day clearing (Friday, July 2) $455,000 × 0.33 = $150,150

Third-business-day clearing (Tuesday, July 6—banks closed on July 5) $455,000 × 0.15 = $68,250

Fourth-business-day clearing (Wednesday, July 7) $455,000 × 0.06 = $27,300

Fifth-business-day clearing (Thursday, July 8) $455,000 × 0.02 = $9,100

Having the proportions and the total amount of payroll checks issued, the disbursement account clearings are easily obtained. A caution is in order: The simplicity masks some important differences that may alter the historical proportions. In this case, a bank holiday combined with an intervening weekend makes the forecast suspect. Most likely, the Day 1 and Day 2 clearings will be higher than the historical amounts because of quicker deposits triggered by consumer anticipation of the Independence Day weekend and the correspondingly higher spending.

*Final Comments on the Distribution Method* The distribution method works well when the intramonth cash flow pattern is stable so that historical patterns persist into the future. Once the distribution proportions have been determined, it is simple and inexpensive to use them to make the cash forecast. It is generally recommended that receipts be broken into several categories of nonmajor flows and each forecasted separately. Likewise, splitting out categories of nonmajor disbursements and forecasting them separately can help improve disbursement timing accuracy. One layout might be by subsidiary, product group, or product line. Be careful about special events such as bank holidays, since disbursements or deposits do not clear the bank and mail is delayed. Recognize that you may need to gather a large amount of data to estimate the proportions, and then you will have to do it all over again when the pattern changes because of changes in employee or vendor behavior or payment method. Finally, the accuracy of the forecasts obtained is closely linked to the accuracy of the monthly or weekly amount being distributed—an inaccurate total gives inaccurate daily amounts. Thus, monthly and daily cash forecasts are necessarily closely tied together when using the distribution method.

### Model Estimation

We cannot profile model estimation for a receipts and disbursements forecast, because data are gathered through telephone calls and access to the corporate database. For the distribution method of statistical forecasting, regression analysis with dummy variables is used. Additional detail on regression analysis is provided in Appendix 12B.

### Model Validation

Once again, the model validation phase is very similar to the process conducted for monthly forecasting. The primary difference is that the time frame within which the model validation takes place is very compressed. Once inaccuracies are detected, the model must be quickly altered to avoid overdrafts, excess borrowing, or opportunity costs related to very large demand deposit balances. Stone and Wood recommend using a cumulative error measure, in which each receipts or disbursement subtotal and the overall net cash flow forecast errors are cumulated over time. If the monthly forecasts are fairly accurate, the cumulative errors will approach zero. When in error, the cumulative error measure will grow over time. With the daily error cumulative total, if errors grow, a warning flag is raised. This is monitored for each nonmajor component being forecasted. Distribution fractions may be recomputed when it is clear that the pattern (number of elapsed business days, day-of-week, or day-of-month) has changed.

## SUMMARY

We started our presentation of cash forecasting with the philosophy and environment within which cash forecasts are made. Forecasts add value primarily by enabling the company to borrow less or extend investment maturities, resulting in higher investment yields. Even the existence of real-time order, shipment, or payment data does not eliminate the need to forecast. The two major cash forecasting intervals, monthly and daily, were then presented. We demonstrated within those intervals the processes of variable identification, modeling the cash flow sequence, model estimation, and model validation.

We intensively developed the monthly cash forecast by first indicating its importance to senior management. Then, we worked through the process of developing and validating the forecast. Finally, we briefly discussed daily cash forecasting by highlighting how one's approach for this interval differed from the monthly interval. The distribution method for spreading a month's cash receipts or cash disbursements forecast into daily intervals also was demonstrated.

## USEFUL WEB SITES

Association for Financial Professionals: **http://www.afponline.org**

Global Treasury News: **http://www.gtnews.com** (search in Trends or Cash Management sections for articles by McDonough or Sagner)

Treasury Strategies, Inc.: **http://www.treasurystrategies.com**

## QUESTIONS

1. Why do corporations put so much emphasis on cash forecasts? What happens if a company continually relies on inaccurate cash forecasts?
2. How can a company's cash position be measured for forecasting purposes? Why do managers generally prefer using the available bank balance?
3. Why does top management focus more on the monthly cash forecast than the daily forecast?
4. "The cash budget is just a glorified name for a cash forecast." Comment on this statement, indicating whether you agree and why you think the statement was made.
5. What constitutes a useful forecast? What does usefulness include beyond forecast accuracy?
6. Why is a company's forecasting philosophy an important ingredient in determining potential forecast accuracy?
7. Define the receipts and disbursements method of forecasting and briefly explain the process of developing a forecast using this method. Why do most forecasters limit its use to very short-term cash forecasts?
8. Briefly summarize differences between daily cash forecasting and monthly forecasting.

## PROBLEMS

1. Fill in the missing cells in the following simple cash-forecasting template. Explain what the cash flow, beginning cash, and ending cash line items represent. Assume short-term borrowing and investing are not included in any of the cash flow items.

Simple Cash Forecasting Model

| Item | June | July | August |
|---|---|---|---|
| Cash receipts | \$375 | \$345 | \$450 |
| − Cash disbursements | \$295 | \$425 | \$535 |
| = Cash flow | — | — | — |
| + Beginning cash | \$ 35 | — | — |
| = Ending cash | — | — | — |

2. Omega, Inc., has been running short on cash with increasing regularity. The cash manager wants to know why. She determines that the average cash position over the past 12 months has been \$300,000, the standard deviation of that cash position over the same period has been \$275,000, and the distribution of day-ending cash positions is approximately normal. The company's minimum cash balance is \$0. Can you help her? (Note: Consult a standard statistics textbook for any necessary tables using one-tailed probability values.)
3. Below is the sales forecast, in dollars, for the upcoming year for BeachTop Boats, Inc. BeachTop collects 5 percent of each month's sales in cash, 45 percent one month later, and 47 percent the second month after sale. Examination shows that 3 percent of sales are uncollectible. A given month's purchases are 35 percent of the forecasted sales amount for that month and 35 percent of the next month's sales forecast. All purchases are paid on "net 30 terms," so purchases and the associated cash payments on those purchases do not occur within the same

month. The other cash flows for the last quarter of the year (October through December) are $15 interest income to be received in November, a principal repayment of $165 in December, interest payment of $20 in December, tax payments of $40 in December, cash proceeds from asset sales of $35 in October, and payment for asset acquisitions of $75 in November. Beach-Top policy mandates that a minimum of $100 be kept in cash at all times. Ending cash in September is projected to be $165, and the company has no outstanding short-term borrowing or investments at that time.

| Month | Sales Forecast | Month | Sales Forecast |
|---|---|---|---|
| January | $36 | August | $63 |
| February | 38 | September | 57 |
| March | 50 | October | 40 |
| April | 55 | November | 32 |
| May | 59 | December | 45 |
| June | 65 | January | 40 |
| July | 75 | | |

Based on this information, prepare a cash forecast for October through December using the cash receipts and disbursements method. Interpret your projections for the cash surplus (shortage), indicating what actions we should expect the cash manager to take. Then indicate whether a study of the seasonality of sales should have forewarned the cash manager of potential problems in the fourth quarter.

4. Use the data below from a company's sales for January–June to get a forecast for the collection forecast, including cash sales, for June.

| Month | Sales |
|---|---|
| January | $220,000 |
| February | 140,000 |
| March | 150,000 |
| April | 140,000 |
| May | 170,000 |
| June | 150,000 |

Of the sales above, 30 percent are for cash and 70 percent are for credit. Of the credit sales, 55 percent are collected one month later, 30 percent are collected two months later, and 15 percent are collected three months later. What is the collection forecast for June?

5. Here is the background data for a company that issues monthly payroll checks:
   - Amount of payroll checks issued on Monday, April 30: $1,750,000
   - Historical check clearing data (past four payroll check issuances)

| Proportion Clearing | | | | | |
|---|---|---|---|---|---|
| Days After Issuance | Payroll #1 | Payroll #2 | Payroll #3 | Payroll #4 | Average Proportion |
| 1 | 65% | 60% | 58% | 66% | |
| 2 | 32% | 33% | 33% | 32% | |
| 3 | 2% | 6% | 5% | 2% | |
| 4 | 1% | 1% | 3% | 0% | |
| 5+ | 0% | 0% | 1% | 0% | |

Use the distribution method to forecast check clearings for the company.

# REFERENCES

Association for Financial Professionals, "The Evolving Role of Treasury," (November 2003). Bethesda, MD: Association for Financial Professionals.

Paul J. Beehler, *Contemporary Cash Management: Principles, Practices, Perspectives,* 2nd ed. New York: John Wiley & Sons (1983).

Laurie Brannen, "Upfront: The Trouble with Cash Management," *Business Finance* (January 2004), p. 13.

Michael J. Brennan and Thomas M. Carroll, *Quantitative Economics & Econometrics.* Cincinnati, OH: South-Western Publishing (1987).

Brian Coyle, *Cash Flow Forecasting and Liquidity.* Chicago: Glenlake Publishing Co., Ltd. (2000).

Alan M. Cunningham, Dennis James Hogan, and Richard Bort, "Medium-Term Funds Flow Forecasting," in Richard Bort (ed): *Corporate Cash Management Handbook.* Boston: Warren, Gorham, & Lamont (1996).

William Forster, "Treasury Management and the Use of the Internet," (April 6, 2000). Accessed online at **http://www.gtnews.com/articles3/2023.html**.

Michael A. Gallanis, "Seeing Around the Bend," *Treasury Management International* (June 2001), pp. 18–20.

Richard H. Gamble, "Improving the Yield on Short-Term Cash Investments," *Controller Magazine* (September 1996), pp. 37–40.

Richard H. Gamble, "The Cash Forecaster's Almanac," *Controller Magazine* (May 1998), pp. 41–45.

James A. Gentry, "Short-Run Financial Management," in Dennis E. Logue (ed): *Handbook of Modern Finance.* Boston: Warren, Gorham, & Lamont (1996).

Clive W. J. Granger and M. Hashem Pesaran, "Economic and Statistical Measures of Forecast Accuracy," *Journal of Forecasting* 19 (2000), pp. 537–560.

John J. Hampton and Cecilia L. Wagner, *Working Capital Management.* New York: John Wiley & Sons (1989).

W. C. F. Hartley and Yale L. Meltzer, *Cash Management: Planning, Forecasting, and Control.* Englewood Cliffs, NJ: Prentice-Hall (1979).

Monzurul Hoque and James A. Gentry, *Forecasting Daily Cash Receipts and Disbursements.* Paper presented to the Financial Management Association, October 19, 1989.

Jarl G. Kallberg and Kenneth L. Parkinson, *Current Asset Management: Cash, Credit, and Inventory.* New York: John Wiley & Sons (1984).

John M. Kelly, *Cash Management.* New York: Franklin Watts (1986).

Richard P. Kramer, "Corporate Cash: Why Its Meaning Differs Between Treasurers and Controllers," *Financial Executive* 4 (1988), pp. 53–55.

Larry Lapide "New Developments in Business Forecasting," *The Journal of Business Forecasting* (Fall 2000), pp. 15–16.

Eugene M. Lerner, "Simulating a Cash Budget," *California Management Review* 9 (1968), pp. 79–86.

William Loscalzo, *Cash Flow Forecasting.* New York: McGraw-Hill (1982).

Stephen Manthey, "Cash Forecasting: Fictional Facts and Factual Fiction," *TMA Journal* (March/April 1994), pp. 24–26.

Thomas W. Miller and Bernell K. Stone, "Daily Cash Forecasting: Alternative Models and Techniques," *Journal of Financial & Quantitative Analysis* (September 1985), pp. 335–351.

Aaron L. Phillips, "Treasury Management: Job Responsibilities, Curricular Development, and Research Opportunities," *Financial Management* (Autumn 1997), pp. 69–82.

Bennett Quillen, "Effective Cash Flow Forecasting Techniques," *Journal of Cash Management* (September/October 1993), pp. 58–61.

Zinovy Radovilsky and John Ten Eyck, "Forecasting with Excel," *The Journal of Business Forecasting* (Fall 2000), pp. 22–27.

James Sagner, "Cash Forecasting and the Behavior of Interest Rates," (January 7, 2000). Accessed online at **http://www.c-stream.com/www.gtnews.com/articles3/1890.html**.

Jeanne Castro Schmidt, "Developing a Medium-Term Cash Forecast," *AFP Exchange* (July/August 2003), pp. 36–40.

Bernell K. Stone and Robert A. Wood, "Daily Cash Forecasting: A Simple Method for Implementing the Distribution Approach," *Financial Management* (Fall 1977), pp. 40–50.

Bernell K. Stone, Robert A. Wood, and Thomas W. Miller, "Daily Cash Forecasting with Multiplicative Models of Cash Flow Patterns," *Financial Management* (Winter 1987), pp. 45–54.

Ahmet Tezel and Ginette McManus, "Monthly Cash Budget Under Sales and Collections Uncertainty," *Journal of Financial Education* (Fall 1999), pp. 75–82.

Treasury Management Association, "The Practice of Treasury Management," *TMA Journal* (May/June 1997), pp. 8–10, 12, 14.

Sander-Paul van Weezendonk, "Forewarned Is Forearmed: The Importance of Cash Flow Forecasting," *Treasury Management International* (July/August 2003), pp. 14–17.

James H. Vander Weide and Steven F. Maier, *Managing Corporate Liquidity: An Introduction to Working Capital Management.* New York: John Wiley & Sons (1985).

Andy Webb, "All Together Now," (October 11, 2000). Accessed online at **http://www.gtnews.com/articles4/2377.html**.

# APPENDIX 12A

## Measuring Forecast Errors

In this appendix we present five measures of forecast error: the mean absolute error, mean square error, root mean square error, coefficient of determination, and error distribution. A forecaster might use only mean absolute error to gauge cash forecasting accuracy, or some combination of these measures.

Let's reconsider a cash forecasting model's validity. The adequacy of a forecasting model usually is assessed by some measure of forecast error. One use of these measures is to evaluate a model's goodness-of-fit when the model is first calibrated. Observations that were not part of the data used to calibrate the model generally are used in the evaluation.

A second use of the forecast error measures is to quickly detect a breakdown in an established model's adequacy. When large errors occur, the forecaster seeks to determine whether the model is no longer valid—perhaps because a new trend has been established—or whether the errors are a result of unusual and nonrecurring factors.

The five forecast error measures that have been found useful for short-term forecasts are mean absolute error, mean squared error, root mean squared error, coefficient of determination, and error distribution. Arguably the best measure, **mean absolute error (MAE)** is developed first; then, the others are presented for comparison. MAE involves adding the absolute values of the difference between forecasted and actual values and then dividing by the number of forecasts. Equation 12.1A provides a symbolic representation of the MAE calculation.

$$MAE = \frac{\sum_{i=1}^{n} |(a_i - f_i)|}{n} \qquad (12.1A)$$

In which: $MAE$ = Mean absolute error
$n$ = Number of forecasts
$a_i$ = Actual value for period $i$
$f_i$ = Forecast value for period $i$

Exhibit 12A–1 provides a set of forecasted and actual values and illustrates computation of the mean absolute error. Notice that had we simply summed the forecast errors without first taking the absolute values, we would have found the mean error to be $[(-3) + (-1) + 2 + (-1) + 2]/5 = -0.20$. This greatly understates the errors of the model, giving the unwary analyst false confidence. The mean absolute error measure is not distorted by the averaging of offsetting errors, because the absolute value of each forecast error is taken before summing the errors.

Substituting Column 4 values into Equation 12.1A, we arrive at:

$$\frac{[(3 + 1 + 2 + 1 + 2)]}{5} = \frac{9}{5} = 1.8$$

**Exhibit 12A–1**

*Computation of Mean Absolute Error*

| (1) Forecast Value | (2) Actual Value | (3) Difference [(2) − (1)] | (4) Absolute Value of Difference (3) |
|---|---|---|---|
| 15 | 12 | −3 | 3 |
| 17 | 16 | −1 | 1 |
| 19 | 21 | 2 | 2 |
| 21 | 20 | −1 | 1 |
| 23 | 25 | 2 | 2 |
| | | | = 9 |
| | | | $\Sigma/n = 9/5 = 1.8$ |

The analyst can compare forecast accuracy for variables with varying magnitudes by calculating a mean absolute percentage error, which involves dividing each row's Column 4 value by the Column 2 actual value, summing the resulting percent error, and dividing the sum by $n$.[1A]

**Mean square error (MSE)** weights large errors more than small ones and thus favors forecasting models that rarely, if ever, miss by a large amount. The calculation of MSE is shown in Equation 12.2A.

$$MSE = \frac{\sum_{i=1}^{n} (a_i - f_i)^2}{n} \qquad (12.2A)$$

In which: $f_i$ = Forecast value for time period $i$

$a_i$ = Actual value for time period $i$

$n$ = Number of time periods in sample

The MSE shares an advantage of MAE: It handles positive and negative errors in a way that does not bias the model's accuracy. Before averaging, the square of the error is calculated, getting rid of any negative signs. Exhibit 12A–2 illustrates an MSE calculation with the same data used in our earlier MAE computation.

A closely related measure, **root mean square error (RMSE)**, has become increasingly popular in business and economic applications. It simply involves taking the square root of the MSE. RMSE has all the advantages of MSE, plus the added advantage that it is expressed in the same units as the original series being forecasted. Expressing the error measure in percentage or dollars certainly communicates the idea better than expressing it as "percentage squared" or "dollars squared." RMSE is formulated as Equation 12.3A.

$$RMSE = \sqrt{\frac{\sum_{i=1}^{n} (a_i - f_i)^2}{n}} \qquad (12.3A)$$

Using the same numbers as earlier, RMSE is calculated exactly like MSE, with the added final step of taking the square root. Thus, in that example, $RMSE = \sqrt{3.8} = 1.9$.

When regression analysis is used in the forecasting model, an additional error measure often is reported. The **coefficient of determination** ($r$-squared) gives the goodness-of-fit for the fitted regression equation. It indicates the proportion of the total variance of the forecasted variable that is accounted for, or "explained," by the fitted regression equation. Thus, $r^2$ is the regression sum-of-squares (RSS) divided by the total sum-of-squares (TSS); alternatively, it is (1 − [(error sum-of-squares)/(total sum-of-squares)]). When forecast errors have already been calculated, the latter formula can be restated as:

$$r^2 = 1 - \left(\frac{\text{Variance of forecast error}}{\text{Variance of series being forecasted}}\right)$$

$$= 1 - \left[\frac{MSE}{\sigma^2_{a_i}}\right]$$

If forecast errors have not already been calculated, use the equivalent expression for $r^2$ shown in Equation 12.4A, in which $\bar{a}_i$ is the mean of the actual values:

$$r^2 = 1 - \left[\frac{\sum_{i=1}^{n} (a_i - f_i)^2/n}{\sum_{i=1}^{n} (a_i - \bar{a}_i)^2/n}\right] \qquad (12.4A)$$

$$r^2 = 1 - (3.8/19.76)$$

$$= \mathbf{0.81}$$

Using our example data, the mean of the actual values is [(12 + 16 + 21 + 20 + 25)/5] = 18.8. Thus, the variance of the actual values ($a$'s) equals $[(12 - 18.8)^2 + (16 - 18.8)^2 + \cdots (25 - 18.8)^2/5]$, or 19.76.

Substituting the MSE from an earlier calculation, the computed variance gives us:

$$r^2 = 1 - (3.8/19.76)$$

$$= 0.81$$

**Exhibit 12A–2**

*MSE Computation Example*

| (1) Forecasted Value | (2) Actual Value | (3) Difference [(2) − (1)] | (4) Squared Difference [(3)$^2$] |
|---|---|---|---|
| 15 | 12 | −3 | 9 |
| 17 | 16 | −1 | 1 |
| 19 | 21 | 2 | 4 |
| 21 | 20 | −1 | 1 |
| 23 | 25 | 2 | 4 |
| MSE = 19/5 = **3.8** | | | Σ = 19 |

[1A] This would give us a mean absolute percentage error (*MAPE*) of 10.75 percent in our example:

| Period | Percent Error |
|---|---|
| 1 | 3/12 = 0.25 |
| 2 | 1/16 = 0.0625 |
| 3 | 2/21 = 0.0952 |
| 4 | 1/20 = 0.05 |
| 5 | 2/25 = 0.08 |

Sum = 0.5377, or 53.77 percent. Dividing by 5, we get *MAPE* = 53.77/5 = 10.75%.

**Exhibit 12A–3**

*Systematic Forecast Bias in Third Quarter Forecast*

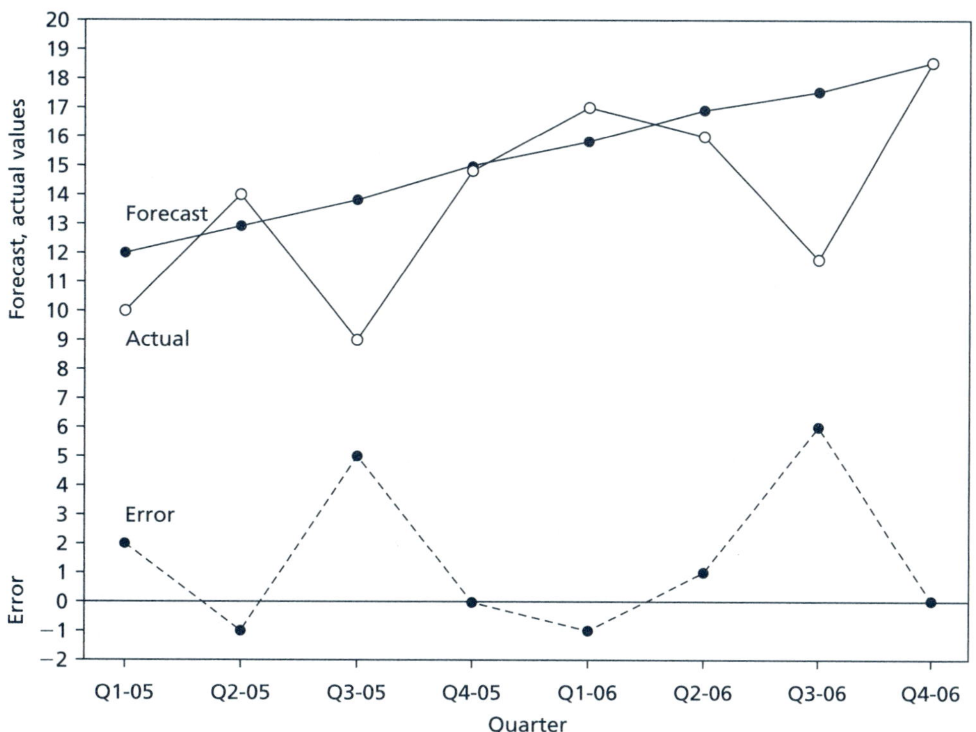


The estimated model, from which the forecasted values were obtained, "explains" 81 percent of the variation in the forecasted variable.[2A]

Our final measure of forecast accuracy is the **error distribution**. The error distribution refers to the shape or pattern of the forecast errors. A graph of forecast errors over time or across values of an important predictor variable sometimes reveals a **forecast bias**. Bias exists when the model systematically underpredicts or overpredicts the forecasted variable. For example, graphical analysis might reveal a systematic overprediction of third-quarter sales, as depicted in Exhibit 12A–3. Although there is no pattern evident for the first, second, or fourth quarters, clearly the third-quarter forecast is missing some important influencing factor(s). Another pattern to watch for is shown in Exhibit 12A–4 in which the model is increasingly underpredicting each value, implying that a new trend is being established. A recalibration of the model is the appropriate course of action in such a case. If forecast accuracy is not adequate when the new model is tested, the analyst must search for new predictor variables to add to the forecast model.

Determining why a forecast is in error is not always easy. It helps to know the error distribution that should be expected for a given forecast variable, in addition to the realized error distribution. Vander Weide and Maier[3A] distinguish between three types of error distributions: normal, causal, and stable. A forecasted variable can be characterized by any one of these or a combination. Normal distributions are characteristic of unpredictable errors, which occur in seemingly random fashion above and below forecasted values. **Causal distributions** characterize situations in which a predictor variable has changed from what was expected, causing the forecasted variable to deviate from what was expected. For example, a key supplier that has always paid

[2A] The reader is cautioned that simply adding an independent variable to the model can increase the coefficient of determination. An adjusted coefficient of determination can be used for cases in which there are multiple independent variables. This is illustrated in the coverage of regression in Appendix 12B.

[3A] See page 128 in the Vander Weide and Maier citation in the end-of-chapter references.

Exhibit 12A–4

*Increasing Bias Over Time: Increasing Forecast Error*

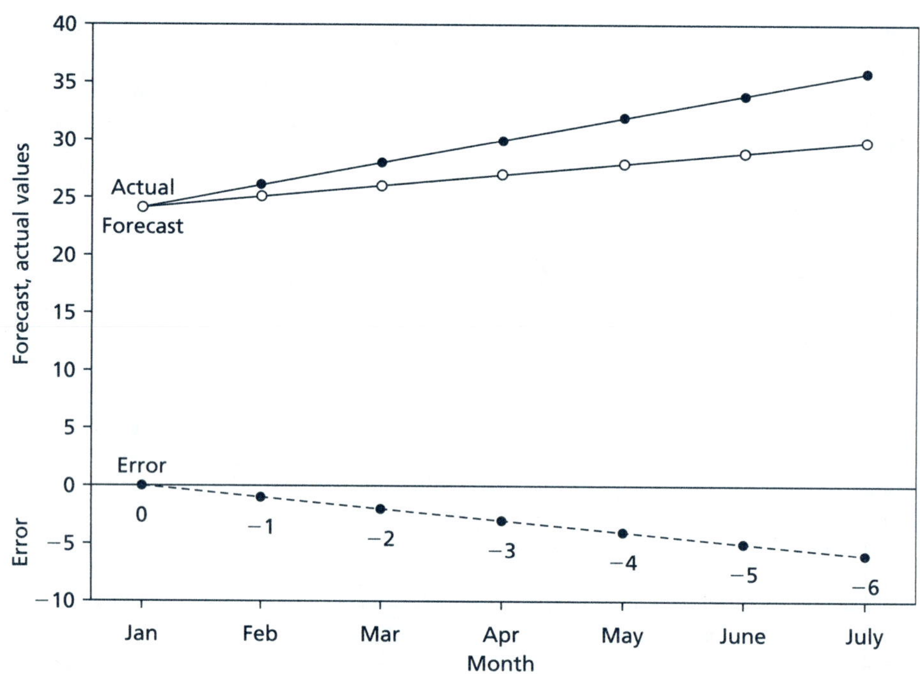


promptly on Day 30 misses its payment for the first time ever, causing the lockbox cash receipts forecast to be off target. Finally, **stable distributions** characterize variables with well-defined consistent trend or seasonal components. Until adjusted, forecasting models will tend to under- or overpredict whenever the trend changes or a new season is entered. Exhibit 12A–4 illustrates such an occurrence when the trend changed. Seasonal swings are sometimes hard to anticipate, especially for retail sales, in which seasonal behavior may be delayed as a result of inclement weather or external shocks. Once recognized, such delays are easily handled by the forecaster, because the period's forecast error can be subtracted from the next period's forecast with some assurance that the historically stable patterns will persist.

Advanced thinking on the subject of forecast accuracy, beyond our scope here, may be found in Granger and Pesaran (2000). They argue that financial forecasters should think more like physical scientists, and link the forecast evaluation to the decision situation. This is borne out by consultant Tony Carfang, who indicates that the precision needed is directly linked to the business decisions that will be based on the forecast (Gamble, 1998).

## PROBLEMS

**12A-1.** Compute the mean absolute error for the following table. Also, determine the mean of actual values ($\overline{a}_i$), and compare the calculated mean absolute error to the mean error. It may help to graph the actual values to aid you in summarizing the reason behind your findings.

| (1) Forecast Value | (2) Actual Value | (3) Difference [(2) − (1)] | (4) Absolute Value of Difference (\|3\|) |
|---|---|---|---|
| 135 | 120 | | |
| 127 | 86 | | |
| 139 | 210 | | |
| 121 | 200 | | |
| 143 | 125 | | |

**12A-2.** Rework Problem A-1 to calculate the following additional error measures:

a. Mean square error

b. Root mean square error

Comment on the meaning of each of these error statistics.

**12A-3.** Locate a data set of at least 30 consecutive observations for a financial or economic variable. Add an independent variable to account for time, with the first observation being assigned a value of 1, the second observation coded as 2, and so on. Conduct regression analysis of the time series using a financial spreadsheet.

a. What is the fitted equation for your financial time series?

b. What is the coefficient of determination of your fitted equation? What does this tell you about the "goodness-of-fit" and possible forecasting accuracy of your equation?

c. Does a high value for the coefficient of determination necessarily imply that the model will provide accurate forecasts of the financial variable? Explain.

# APPENDIX 12B

## Statistical Forecasting Tools

For longer-term forecasts, quantitative modeling can be advantageous. Beehler[1B] cites four advantages to quantitative approaches: The methods can be easily used year after year; variance analysis is facilitated because the forecaster can pinpoint more easily the cause of forecast misses (e.g., the sales forecast was overly optimistic); statistical confidence can be determined based on probability concepts, indicating how much confidence the forecaster can place in the model; and in most cases, the model results provide the basis for decision making. With longer horizons, statistical forecasting is even more valuable because collections and disbursements (and the sales and purchases that give rise to them) are not known but also must be forecasted.

There are two categories of statistical tools: causal and time-series. **Causal techniques** link the forecast values of an effect variable to one or more anticipated causes. Inventory levels should change in response to changes in sales, for example. Two statistical tools that can be used in causal modeling are simple regression and multiple regression. **Time-series techniques** link future movements in the forecast variable to patterns revealed by historical movements in that same variable. The series of historical values over time, therefore, sets the stage for future movements. The moving average, exponential smoothing, time-series regression, statistical decomposition, and Box-Jenkins methods are all time-series tools. Many of these tools can now be implemented without much training or difficulty in Microsoft Excel™ (Radovilsky and Ten Eyck, 2000). We turn now to a brief discussion of these various techniques.

[1B] Cited in the end-of-chapter references.

### REGRESSION

The most important statistical tool used in causal modeling is regression analysis. Regression analysis is often used in **percent of sales** forecasting models, in which an expense or balance sheet amount is expressed as some percentage of sales. **Simple regression** involves just one predictor (independent) variable, whereas **multiple regression** incorporates two or more predictor variables. Regardless, regression analysis finds an equation for the "line of best fit," so that as much variation in the forecasted dependent variable is accounted

**Exhibit 12B–1**

*Causal Model Using Simple Regression*

| Month | Sales (000) | Inventories (000) |
|---|---|---|
| 1 | $295 | $100 |
| 2 | 250 | 86 |
| 3 | 225 | 85 |
| 4 | 265 | 95 |
| 5 | 270 | 100 |
| 6 | 265 | 100 |
| 7 | 275 | 100 |
| 8 | 275 | 100 |
| 9 | 280 | 100 |
| 10 | 310 | 125 |
| 11 | 355 | 170 |
| 12 | 360 | 175 |

for as possible. The simple regression equation is in the following form (Equation 12.1B).

$$Y = a + b(X) + e \qquad (12.1B)$$

In which: $Y$ = Forecasted variable

$a$ = Intercept

$b$ = Slope

$X$ = Independent predictor variable

$e$ = Unpredictable part of movements in $Y$

The unpredictable part of movements in $Y$, symbolized by $e$, might signal that our model omits an important predictor variable. We can illustrate this with sales ($X$) being used to forecast inventories ($Y$). We use the data in Exhibit 12B–1 to calibrate, or fit, the model.

The forecaster commonly views a graph with the values of $Y$ plotted against values of $X$, in the form of an $XY$ graph. Exhibit 12B–2 shows us the plot for the sales and inventory relationship. We see the expected relationship: As sales increase on the $X$ axis, we find increasing inventory levels on the $Y$ axis. Each data point represents a month's observed sales and inventory levels.

Now, conduct a regression analysis to find the equation for the line of best fit. This is easily accomplished using a computer-based statistical package or financial spreadsheet. The output results from a spreadsheet are shown in Exhibit 12B–3, based on a Microsoft Excel™ fit (using the **T**ools/**D**ata Analysis/**R**egression commands). Spreadsheet regression outputs label $a$ the constant and $b$ the $X$ coefficient. The fitted equation is thus:

$$\text{Inventories} = -95.99 + 0.7264\ (\text{Sales}).$$

Once we have the sales forecast for a future period, we plug that amount into the equation and get the forecasted inventory amount. Notice that Excel does not give an error term; simply append this to the end of the equation as a reminder that unpredictable aspects of $Y$ cause the forecasted values to differ from the actual values. Plugging the $X$ values back into the fitted equation, we get forecasted values that can be compared with those actually observed. Because the coefficient of determination is so high ($r^2 = 0.909$, compared with the highest possible value of 1.0), we see the forecasted values being very close to the actual values (consult graph of fitted points versus actual points for months 1 through 12 in Exhibit 12B–4).

**Exhibit 12B–2**

*Relationship between Sales and Inventories*

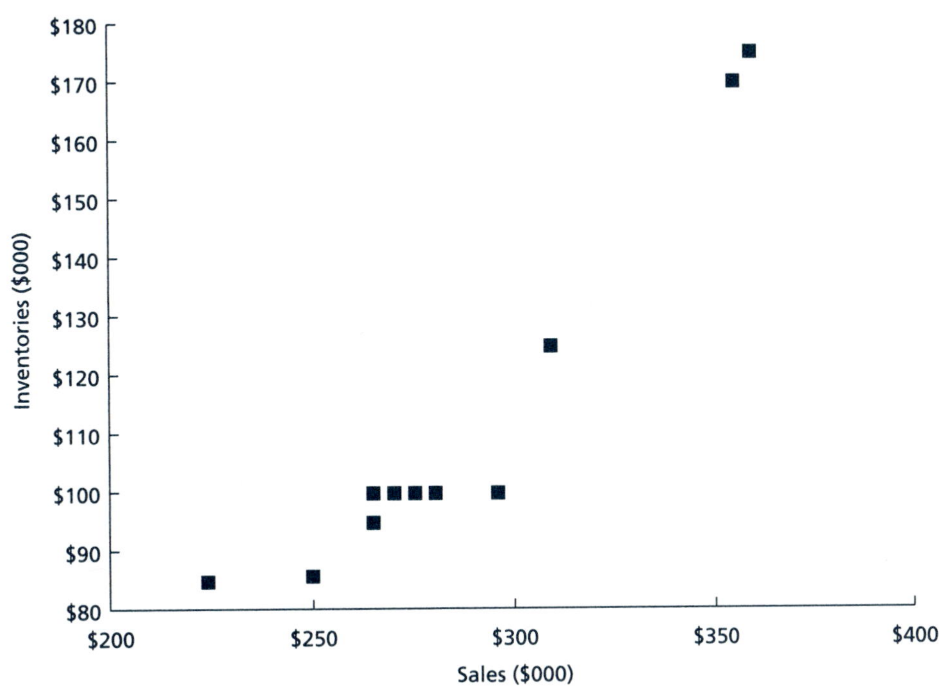

**Exhibit 12B–3**

*Regression Results for Simple Regression of Inventory (Y) on Sales (X)*

SUMMARY OUTPUT

| Regression Statistics | |
|---|---|
| Multiple R | 0.953457533 |
| R Square | 0.909081268 |
| Adjusted R Square | 0.899989395 |
| Standard Error | 9.561158646 |
| Observations | 12 |

ANOVA

| | df | SS | MS | F | Significance F |
|---|---|---|---|---|---|
| Regression | 1 | 9140.50912 | 9140.50912 | 99.98833521 | 1.5904E-06 |
| Residual | 10 | 914.1575466 | 91.41575466 | | |
| Total | 11 | 10054.66667 | | | |

| | Coefficients | Standard Error | t Stat | P-value | Lower 95% | Upper 95% | Lower 95.0% | Upper 95.0% |
|---|---|---|---|---|---|---|---|---|
| Intercept | −95.99278413 | 20.91672334 | −4.589284018 | 0.000996343 | −142.5981561 | −49.38741213 | −142.5981561 | −49.38741213 |
| X Variable 1 | 0.726398076 | 0.072644056 | 9.999416743 | 1.5904E-06 | 0.56453703 | 0.888259122 | 0.56453703 | 0.888259122 |

**Exhibit 12B–4**

*Forecasted Inventory versus Actual Inventory Using Simple Regression*

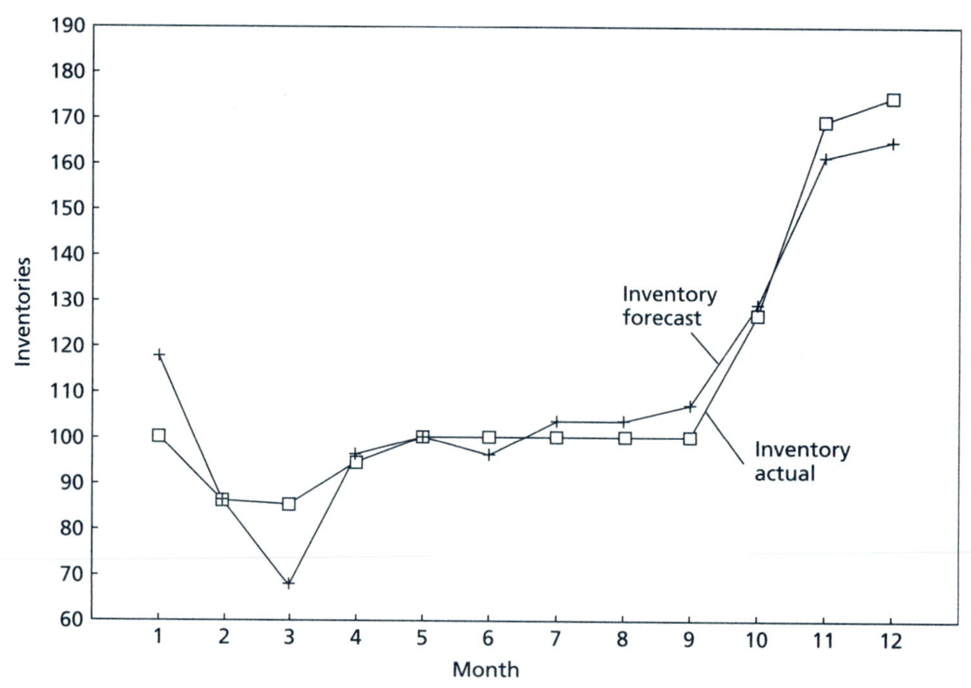

Now that we know the model's $a$ and $b$ coefficients, we can plug next period's sales forecast in and calculate the forecasted value for inventories. If the Month 13 sales forecast is \$375, the inventory forecast is 176.41 [= −95.99 + 0.7264(375)].

In multiple regression, inventories are modeled as a function of sales and some other variable(s). Possible candidates for predictor variables include the existence of quantity discounts (which increase order size and therefore inventory levels) and interest rates (which represent the opportunity cost of having money invested in inventories). We can revise Equation 12.1B to include multiple predictor variables:

$$Y = a + b_1(X_1) + b_2(X_2) + \cdots + b_n(X_n) + e \qquad (12.2B)$$

Several cautions are offered to the forecaster using multiple regression. First, a high $r^2$ value can be attained by simply including more variables—a problem that is especially pertinent in our simplistic example, which includes only 12 data points. A related measure, **adjusted $r^2$**, compensates for this upward bias in goodness-of-fit. Because we have only one predictor variable in our model, our adjusted $r^2$ is almost as high as the original $r^2$ (refer to Exhibit 12B–3).

Second, correlation does not imply causation. Although we are calling ours a causal model, **spurious correlation** might account for our high coefficient of determination. A predictor variable may simply be associated with another predictor variable, which in turn *is* the true cause of the dependent variable.

Third, one must ensure that the data approximately meet the assumptions of regression analysis. Two potential problems in our illustration are **multicollinearity**, which is a correlation between predictor variables, and **serial correlation**, which is the existence of correlated errors through time. **Omitted variables** that could have helped us predict inventories may give rise to the serial correlation. At times, the included predictor variables have a joint effect on the dependent variable, in which case the model should include an interaction term (for example, the product $X_1X_2$). These problems are discussed more fully in forecasting and econometrics textbooks.

## TIME-SERIES METHODS

The noncausal models we address are those that extrapolate past data observations to the future. The historical time path is assumed to persist into the future, although the analyst might override the model-based forecast for known changes. So either the item being forecasted moves upward or downward through time in some consistent pattern, or it is correlated with an unknown or unobserved predictor variable that moves in that consistent pattern over time. Our presentation moves from the simplest method to the most complex: moving average, exponential smoothing, time-series regression, statistical decomposition, and Box-Jenkins (ARIMA) modeling.

A **moving average** evens out temporary ups and downs by taking the mean of the most recent observations. One might calculate a 3-month, 6-month, or 12-month moving average. The average for the period then becomes the forecasted value for the next month. A key advantage of the technique is that the longer the averaging period, the less a recent observation will change the average—and, therefore, the forecast. Exhibit 12B–5 shows a 3-month moving average that illustrates this situation. It is evident that the average lags behind the original series. This may be a disadvantage at times, because there may be a new trend established that the average is slow to incorporate. The result is inaccurate forecasts.

**Exponential smoothing** overcomes this weakness by allowing a greater weighting for more recent data. Specifically, it starts out with a base forecast for the next period and then adjusts that base by the error from last period's forecast. Think of it as a model that learns from its errors. Mathematically, the exponential smoothing model appears as Equation 12.3B.

$$F_{t+1} = F_t + \alpha(A_t - F_t) \qquad (12.3B)$$

In which: $F_{t+1}$ = Forecasted value for next period $(t + 1)$

$F_t$ = Forecasted value for present period, made earlier

$\alpha$ = Smoothing constant $(0 < \alpha < 1)$

$A_t$ = Actual value for present period

The larger the forecast error for the present period, represented by $(A_t - F_t)$, the greater the revision made to the present period's forecast to arrive at the next period's forecast. Also, the larger the smoothing constant $\alpha$, the larger the revision, given the forecast error. Regardless of the value of $\alpha$, actual observations in the distant past are weighted less heavily than recent values. Even so, trend changes or new seasons have a lagged effect on the forecast in the exponential smoothing model.[2B]

---

[2B] Extensions to the basic model to handle trends (Holt's Two Parameter Linear Exponential Smoothing Method) and seasonal variations (Winter's Three Parameter Model) are developed in John E. Hanke and Arthur G. Reitsch, *Business Forecasting* (Boston: Allyn & Bacon, Inc., 1981), pp. 254–264.

Exhibit 12B–5

*Three-Month Moving Average: Sales and Moving Average*

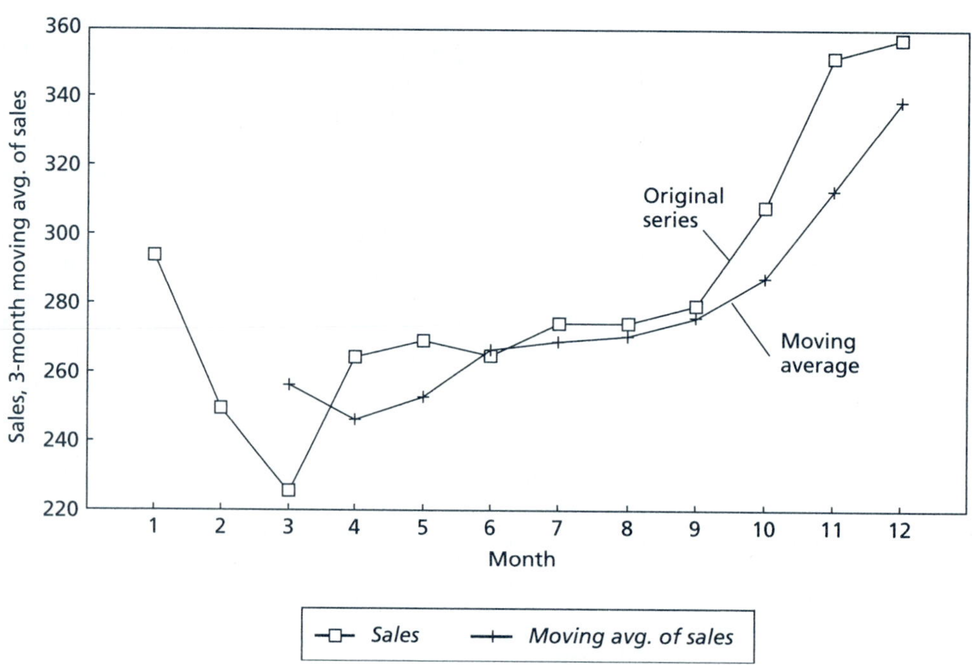


A cash flow series with both trend and seasonal components is tabled in Exhibit 12B–6. Notice the effect on forecast accuracy, as measured by mean absolute error (MAE). The graphs of two exponential smoothing models, one with $\alpha = 0.25$ and the other with $\alpha = 0.75$, are shown in Exhibit 12B–7. The data series is both seasonal and trended. Though neither model is very accurate, the model with the higher $\alpha$ is somewhat more accurate (has a lower mean absolute error) because it adjusts more rapidly to the recent values. The models are particularly inaccurate in the months when the cash flows reach their seasonal highs. Also, note the greater smoothing accomplished by the model with the lower $\alpha$, which is not appropriate for the example data.[3B] Perhaps the failure to use modified exponential smoothing to handle seasonal and trend variations accounts for the low degree of usage for cash forecasting. At a minimum, exponential smoothing can generate naive forecasts, with which users can compare the forecast accuracy of other techniques.

Another extrapolative method is **time-series regression.**[4B] It is a naive modeling approach in the sense that it seems to imply that the mere passage of time causes the forecast variable to change in value. Users of this approach defend it on the grounds that whatever is causally affecting the forecast variable is behaving with a systematic regular effect through time. We reformulate our earlier regression equation to make the time period ($t$) the independent variable:

$$Y_t = a + b(t) + e_t \qquad (12.4B)$$

Here, $Y_t$ is the value that the dependent variable takes on in time period $t$. Coefficients $a$ and $b$ and the error term ($e_t$) for the time period are defined in the same way as earlier, although the interpretation of $b$ is now the change in $Y$ over each time period. The model extrapolates the historical trend based on the set of observations included when fitting the equation.

Using the data from Exhibit 12B–6, in which the month variable is reassigned an integer value from 1 (earliest) to 15 (most recent), we regress actual cash

[3B] For specifics on how to use Microsoft Excel's Solver function to determine the "best" exponential smoothing model, see Radovilsky and Ten Eyck (2000), cited in the end-of-chapter references.

[4B] Although times-series regression can refer to any $X$-$Y$ relationship through time, we are using it in a more limited sense of trend analysis.

## Exhibit 12B–6

*Exponential Smoothing with Two Values for $\alpha$*

Exponential Smoothing: Two Models Fitting a Data Series
(Series exhibits trend, seasonal factors)
Notes: (1) Seed Value for initial forecast is based on moving average.
(2) Forecast errors equal (actual − forecast).

| FORECAST #1 MONTH | FORECAST #1 ACTUAL | FORECAST #2 $\alpha = 0.25$ | FORECAST #2 ERROR | $\alpha = 0.75$ | ERROR |
|---|---|---|---|---|---|
| January | 45 | 40.0 | 5.0 | 40.0 | 5.0 |
| February | 42 | 41.3 | 0.7 | 43.8 | −1.8 |
| March | 40 | 41.4 | −1.4 | 42.4 | −2.4 |
| April | 50 | 41.1 | 8.9 | 40.6 | 9.4 |
| May | 55 | 43.3 | 11.7 | 47.7 | 7.3 |
| June | 60 | 46.2 | 13.8 | 53.2 | 6.8 |
| July | 54 | 49.7 | 4.3 | 58.3 | −4.3 |
| August | 52 | 50.8 | 1.2 | 55.1 | −3.1 |
| September | 64 | 51.1 | 12.9 | 52.8 | 11.2 |
| October | 70 | 54.3 | 15.7 | 61.2 | 8.8 |
| November | 90 | 58.2 | 31.8 | 67.8 | 22.2 |
| December | 100 | 66.2 | 33.8 | 84.4 | 15.6 |
| January | 65 | 74.6 | −9.6 | 96.1 | −31.1 |
| February | 62 | 72.2 | −10.2 | 72.8 | −10.8 |
| March | 60 | 69.7 | −9.7 | 64.7 | −4.7 |
| ***Mean Absolute Error:*** | | | ***11.4*** | | ***9.6*** |

flow on time. The fitted equation is $Y_t = 41.0286 + 2.4464(t)$ and accounts for 51 percent of the variation in cash flow. The forecast for the next period (Period 16) is computed by plugging 16 in for $t$, giving a forecasted cash flow of \$80. For a variable with a stable trend, time-series regression is an accurate technique. However, be careful of two issues when using this technique to forecast. First, few financial variables are characterized by stable trends. This implies that the linear regression model that we are using may have to be adjusted to a more complex (an exponential or polynomial) form, and the forecaster may have to use multiple regression incorporating predictor variables other than time. Second, correlated forecast errors violate an important assumption of regression analysis and must be treated with first differencing or another corrective to ensure efficiency and proper statistical testing of the model's coefficients.[5B] **First differencing** is accomplished by subtracting the previous value for $Y$ from the current value and then using the differences as the dependent variable (instead of the original $Y$ values).

A novel approach to time-series regression estimates the compound annual growth rate of a dependent variable growing continuously at an uneven rate. A growth rate formula that involves **log-linear regression** takes into account all values of the time series. If we have a continuously growing series of cash flows ($C_t$) starting with $C_0$, the relationship between each cash flow and the beginning cash flow is

$$C_t = C_0 \, e^{gt} \qquad (12.5B)$$

in which $e$ is the natural number (approximately 2.71828), $g$ is the growth rate, and $t$ is the number of time periods over which the series has grown. Taking the natural logarithms of each side of Equation 12.5B gives us Equation 12.6B:

$$\begin{aligned} \ln C_t &= \ln C_0 + \ln e^{gt} \qquad (12.6B) \\ &= \ln C_0 + gt \end{aligned}$$

As long as we are careful to later convert predicted $Y$ values from logarithmic units back into dollar cash

[5B] See the Brennan and Carroll citation in the end-of-chapter references for an excellent basic treatment of Durbin-Watson, Cochran Orcutt, and Hildreth Lu correctives and the efficiency and statistical testing ramifications of correlated errors.

## Exhibit 12B–7

*Exponential Smoothing of Trended and Seasonal Series*

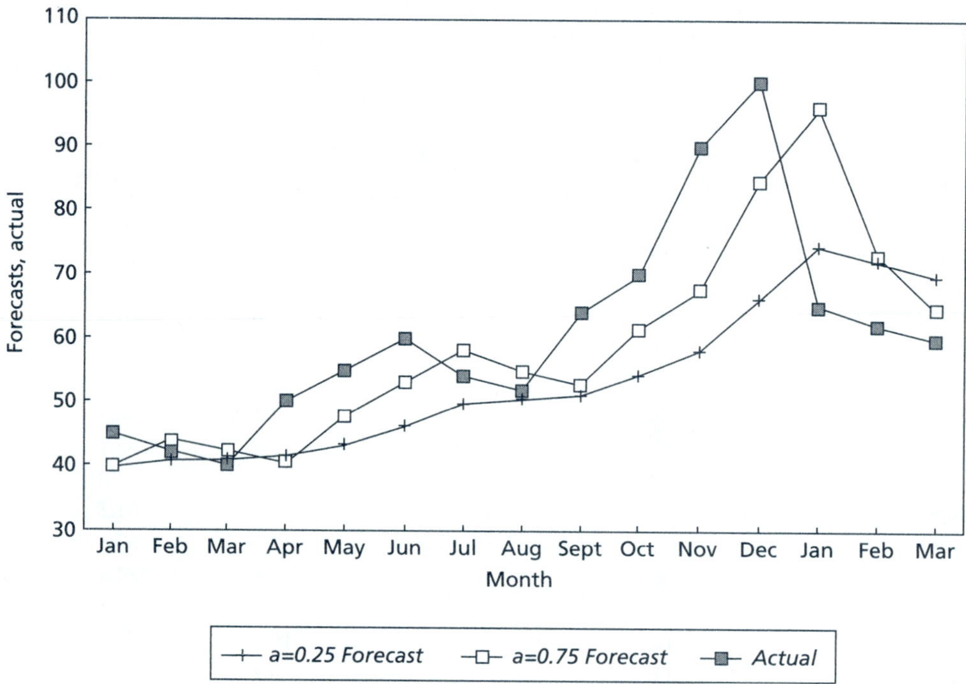


flows, we can set $Y$ equal to the ln $C_t$. This gives us the regression equation shown as Equation 12.7B:

$$Y_t = \ln C_0 + gt \quad (12.7B)$$

Historical cash flow data can be fitted with ordinary least squares regression because the functional form is "linear in the logarithms"—hence the name **log-linear regression.** Plugging a new $t$ value into the fitted equation gives a value for the natural logarithm of the predicted cash flow, which is converted to dollars by raising $e$ to that power. We fit the following data using the log-linear model: \$2.75 ($CF_0$), \$2.48, \$2.85, \$3.15, \$3.55. The coefficients from the regression analysis are 0.926338 for $a$ and 0.074984 for $g$. The *antilog* of the $g$ coefficient is the percentage compound annual growth rate, in decimal form. Plugging in the number 5 to represent a future time period gives us a $Y_t$ value of 1.3012569; taking $e^{1.3012569}$ (using the spreadsheet EXP function) gives us a cash flow forecast of \$3.67 for Period 5.

Seasonal variations, intrayear movements that tend to occur each year, are handled easily by including **dummy variables.** The number of dummy variables included in the regression equation is one less than the number of seasons.[6B] Each dummy variable that is included as an independent variable takes on a value of 1 only when the season it represents is the season for which the forecast is being made; it is 0 at all other times.

The main pitfall plaguing these two time-series regression models is the difficulty of detecting a change in trend. Unfortunately, trend shifts usually are not detected until the incoming actual values reveal very large forecast errors. Even then, the forecaster is at a loss as to how to refit the model, because there is not enough recent data to conduct a valid regression analysis. Model forecasts will have to be subjectively overridden in this event.

A fourth time-series model, **statistical decomposition**, is more complex. Sometimes called Census X-11 decomposition (after the computer software developed

[6B] The reason for this is to be able to retain the intercept ($a$) in the equation and still be able to estimate the $b$ coefficients. In technical terms, including one dummy variable for each season leads to a situation in which the **XxX** matrix does not have an inverse and unique estimators of the regression coefficients cannot be found.

by the Census Bureau), this approach is especially useful for forecasting variables that have trend, seasonal, and cyclical variations. By decomposing the historical observations into trend, seasonal, cyclical, and irregular (unpredictable) components, the separate effect of each is determined. The forecaster can then study each component in arriving at forecasts. The cyclical component, which refers to regular up-and-down phases lasting longer than one year, is ignored when doing short-term and most intermediate-term forecasts.

The decision process begins with trend identification, which is usually done by using time-series regression. The purpose is to "de-trend" the data to isolate seasonal and/or cyclical influences. Next, the seasonal component is identified. This is achieved by first developing a moving average. For a daily forecast, five days' values are averaged; for a monthly forecast, values for 12 months are averaged.

Exhibit 12B–8 gives the computation of a 12-month centered moving average (Column 4) and the seasonal indices (Column 5) for monthly data exhibiting seasonal variation. To get Column 4 numbers, we start with rolling cumulative 12-month numbers in Column 2: the first entry, 772, is the sum of January 2005–December 2005 cash flows, the second entry drops January 2005 and picks up January 2006, and so on. Column 3 takes month-beginning (772 for July 2005) and month-ending (777 for July 2005) numbers and adds them, so that the month's average in Column 4 (64.54 for July 2005) is centered at midmonth. The actual cash

**Exhibit 12B–8**

*Seasonal Indices for Statistical Decomposition*

Statistical Decomposition Using Centered Moving Average

| | (1) | (2) | (3) | (4) | (5) [(1)/(4)] |
|---|---|---|---|---|---|
| Month | Actual Cash Flow | Rolling 12-Month Cumulative | Rolling 24-Month Cumulative | 12-Month Centered Average | % of 12-Month Centered Average |
| Jan. 2005 | 45 | | | | |
| Feb. | 40 | | | | |
| Mar. | 50 | | | | |
| Apr. | 55 | | | | |
| May | 55 | | | | |
| June | 60 | | | | |
| July | 62 | 772 → | 1549 | 64.54 | 96.06% |
| Aug. | 65 | 777 | 1572 | 65.50 | 99.24% |
| Sept. | 65 | 795 | 1600 | 66.67 | 97.50% |
| Oct. | 70 | 805 | 1625 | 67.71 | 103.38% |
| Nov. | 95 | 820 | 1655 | 68.96 | 37.76% |
| Dec. | 110 | 835 | 1685 | 70.21 | 156.68% |
| Jan. 2006 | 50 | 850 | 1714 | 71.42 | 70.01% |
| Feb. | 58 | 864 | 1743 | 72.63 | 79.86% |
| Mar. | 60 | 879 | 1773 | 73.88 | 81.22% |
| Apr. | 70 | 894 | 1808 | 75.33 | 92.92% |
| May. | 70 | 914 | 1838 | 76.58 | 91.40% |
| June | 75 | 924 | 1868 | 77.83 | 96.36% |
| July | 76 | 944 | | | |
| Aug. | 80 | | | | |
| Sept. | 80 | | | | |
| Oct. | 90 | | | | |
| Nov. | 105 | | | | |
| Dec. | 130 | | | | |

flow (Column 1) is then divided by the 12-month centered average (Column 4) and the quotient multiplied by 100 to get the percentage seasonal index in Column 5. Thus, July experiences a very slight seasonal downswing, because the index (96 percent) is slightly less than 100 percent. Notice the pronounced seasonal upswing for this company in November (138 percent) and December (157 percent).

If several years of data are available, the seasonal percentage indices can themselves be averaged to come up with a more reliable estimate. The seasonal indices should sum to 1200 because the 12 values average out to 100 percent each. However, when they are used in arriving at a forecast, they are first converted to decimal form.

Once we have calculated the trend and seasonal indices, we are ready to do our forecast for the next 12 months. Assume the trend is level at a cash flow amount of $75. Our January 2007 cash forecast is made using Equation 12.8B, which includes a subscript for the month for which we are making the forecast.

$$CF_m = T \times S_m \times C \times I \qquad (12.8B)$$

In words, the cash forecast for month *m* is the product of the trend forecast, that month's seasonal index, and the cyclical index (if used). The irregular component is included, but generally no forecast is made for it, implying an irregular component value of 100. Other indices can be added to Equation 12.8B to reflect the effects of other important causal predictor variables, such as interest rates or exchange rates, although this removes the equation from the domain of a purely time-series model. Because we are not concerned about $C$ in the short-term forecast, and by definition we cannot predict $I$, we are left with the following short-term monthly forecast equation:

$$Y = T \times S \qquad (12.9B)$$

Using our trend value of 75 and the January seasonal index of 0.7001, we have our January forecast:

$$52.51 = 75 \times 0.7001$$

For intermediate-term and long-term forecasts, we want to incorporate a cyclical component to reflect, among other things, the phase of the business cycle.[7B]

[7B] The effect of the cyclical component is to increase revenues during the recovery phase of the business cycle and to shave revenues during recessions. Different industries experience cycles of varying length. For the mechanics of cyclical index computation, see Hanke and Reitsch or another business forecasting textbook.

**Box-Jenkins models** are our final class of time-series techniques. Named after two pioneers in the field of time-series modeling, this approach lets the data specify the best model. Multistage development using iterative testing is done to arrive at the final model. Exposition of these models is beyond our scope, but we mention them because forecasts of some items such as interest rates have been best handled by Box-Jenkins models. These models are sometimes called ARIMA models because they combine AutoRegressive,[8B] Integrative, and Moving Average elements into one model. Advanced forecasting sources and econometrics textbooks take up these models in greater detail.

We have completed our statistical technique coverage. These techniques are especially useful for the repetitive, smaller-dollar cash receipts and disbursements. Large and nonrepetitive elements should be handled with the receipts and disbursements method. Many businesses, especially smaller ones, subjectively adjust the statistically generated forecast. Many also rely heavily on field data, collected from field sales representatives and collection banks, to assist in the cash forecast. Field deposit data and information on new orders is especially helpful. These inputs are critical for daily cash forecasts made up to a 2-week horizon. For horizons beyond two weeks, statistical tools begin to pay off with greater accuracy. Because of the widespread use of personal computers, the necessary statistical computations involve a minimal expenditure of time and money.

## SUMMARY

In this appendix we have reviewed some of the statistical tools that a cash forecaster might use in modeling various cash inflow or outflow elements. We subdivided models into causal and time-series categories. In the causal section, we saw how simple or multiple regres-

[8B] Autoregressive modeling specifically accounts for the nature of the correlation between forecast errors through time. The term *autoregressive* refers to the process of determining the correlations by regressing the data series on itself. An advanced use of ARIMA modeling is as a second step to follow up a single equation regression daily cash flow forecasting model. Gentry (1991) and Hoque and Gentry (1989) use the ARIMA structure to extract information from a previous regression fit to improve the forecast model. Background information on how to integrate both regression and ARIMA components into a more general forecasting model is presented in P. Newbold, and T. Bos, *Introductory Business Forecasting*, Cincinnati, OH: South-Western Publishing, 1990, pp. 366–373.

sion analysis can be used to show the impact of a causal variable on the effect (forecasted) variable. Time-series models included in our presentation were moving averages, exponential smoothing, time-series regression, statistical decomposition, and Box-Jenkins. We noted that one might be forecasting sales, receivables, inventories, payables, or net cash flow as part of the short-term financial management process. Any item that can change the organization's future cash position is a candidate for quantitative or judgmental forecasting.

## QUESTIONS

**1.** Contrast causal techniques and time-series techniques. What do the two classes of techniques have in common?

**2.** You have been assigned to develop a cash forecast for Greenlawn, a lawn fertilizing service operating in a medium-sized city. For cash disbursements, you need to develop a sales forecast. Your boss heard somewhere that regression analysis is good for sales forecasting. What causal (predictor) variables will you include in the set of independent variables?

**3.** Joe, one of your old college buddies, just received a pink slip from his first employer. No reason was given for his dismissal, but Joe suspects office politics. He was a sales analyst, responsible for sales forecasts. His last attempt at using regression to predict sales resulted in a reported $r^2$ value of 0.290. He is on the phone with you wondering whether to include his forecasting prowess on his updated resume. A longtime baseball fan, Joe remarks that "a 0.290 batting average sounds major league to me."

a. Should Joe brag about his forecasting accuracy?

b. A month later, Joe is cleaning out his desk, and as he throws out the computer output, he is startled to notice that the $r^2$ on his forecast was 0.79, not 0.29. Reevaluate his forecasting accuracy.

**4.** Describe a data pattern well suited to moving average forecasting.

**5.** What is the effect of using a larger value for $\alpha$ in an exponential smoothing model?

**6.** How is time-series regression different from other regression models?

**7.** Explain briefly how dummy variables are used to model seasonal effects in a regression model.

## PROBLEMS

**12B-1.** The following represent some recent quarterly data available to José Garcia, the credit analyst responsible for reporting the "percent of sales" relationship of accounts receivable to sales. All sales are credit sales. He has a sales forecast for next quarter (Quarter 9) and wishes to know what receivables amount he should forecast.

a. Can you help him out by using regression analysis to determine the relationship? (Hint: Force the constant, or *Y*-intercept, to zero.)

b. Is your regression fit a good one?

c. Graph the receivables data, using the time period as your independent variable. Is there anything that José can do to improve a given quarter's forecast?

| Quarter | Sales | Accounts Receivable |
|---|---|---|
| 1 | $255 | $125 |
| 2 | 265 | 128 |
| 3 | 260 | 127 |
| 4 | 290 | 140 |
| 5 | 275 | 136 |
| 6 | 285 | 140 |
| 7 | 278 | 138 |
| 8 | 310 | 160 |

**12B-2.** Using the template below and a starting forecast of 75, develop the forecasts and evaluate the two exponential smoothing models using mean absolute error. Comment on the effect of the different smoothing constants ($\alpha$'s) used in the two models. For advanced model evaluation, you may wish to compute several of the other error measures presented in Appendix 12A.

| Month | Actual | Forecast #1 $\alpha = 0.20$ | Forecast #1 ERROR | Forecast #2 $\alpha = 0.80$ | Forecast #2 ERROR |
|---|---|---|---|---|---|
| Jan. | 90 | 75.0 | | 75.0 | |
| Feb. | 85 | | | | |
| Mar. | 87 | | | | |
| Apr. | 90 | | | | |
| May | 95 | | | | |
| June | 96 | | | | |
| July | 98 | | | | |
| Aug. | 102 | | | | |
| Sept. | 110 | | | | |

| Month | Actual | Forecast #1 $\alpha = 0.20$ | Forecast #1 ERROR | Forecast #2 $\alpha = 0.80$ | Forecast #2 ERROR |
|---|---|---|---|---|---|
| Oct. | 122 | | | | |
| Nov. | 110 | | | | |
| Dec. | 100 | | | | |
| Jan. | 110 | | | | |
| Feb. | 112 | | | | |
| Mar. | 120 | | | | |
| Mean absolute error | | MAE = | | MAE = | |

**12B-3.** Using the fifteen actual values shown in Problem B-2, calibrate a time-series regression model. Include an intercept ($a$) in your model.

a. Comment on the goodness-of-fit for your model of the 15 months shown, using only the model's $r^2$ (consult the discussion of $r^2$ in the Appendix 12A if necessary).

b. Is it advisable to measure the goodness-of-fit for the model by using only the sample data from which the model coefficients are determined?

c. The next three months (April, May, and June) need to be forecasted. Based on your regression model, what are your forecast values?

d. Compute the mean absolute error for the 15 months in the data sample. Use the regression model coefficients to get the predicted values, and then compare those with the actual values presented in the table.

**12B-4.** A company's sales have exhibited the following pattern (all numbers are in thousands): \$3,050; \$3,250; \$3,125; \$3,500; \$3,975. Apply the log-linear regression model to the data.

a. Comment on the goodness-of-fit for your model (consult the discussion of $r^2$ in the chapter appendix if necessary).

b. What are the forecasts for the next two periods, based on your model?

c. Plot the data. Do you think a simple linear time-series regression model would do as well in fitting the data?

d. Test your hypothesis from part **c** by fitting a linear time-series regression model. Comment on the goodness-of-fit, comparing this model with the log-linear model calibrated in part **a**.

**12B-5.** Beginning with July 2005 and ending with June 2006, fill out Columns 2 through 5 in the format shown below. Indicate the interpretation of the calculated percentages in Column 5 and how they would be used in a forecast based on statistical decomposition.

| Month | (1) Actual Cash Flow | (2) Rolling 12-Month Cumulative | (3) Rolling 24-Month Cumulative | (4) 12-Month Centered Average | (5) [(1)/(4)] Percentage of 12-Month Centered Average |
|---|---|---|---|---|---|
| Jan. 2005 | 125 | | | | |
| Feb. | 140 | | | | |
| Mar. | 150 | | | | |
| Apr. | 155 | | | | |
| May | 175 | | | | |
| June | 160 | | | | |
| July | 168 | | | | |
| Aug. | 175 | | | | |
| Sept. | 165 | | | | |
| Oct. | 170 | | | | |
| Nov. | 190 | | | | |
| Dec. | 220 | | | | |
| Jan. 2006 | 175 | | | | |
| Feb. | 185 | | | | |
| Mar. | 160 | | | | |
| Apr. | 170 | | | | |
| May | 190 | | | | |
| June | 175 | | | | |
| July | 176 | | | | |
| Aug. | 200 | | | | |
| Sept. | 180 | | | | |
| Oct. | 190 | | | | |
| Nov. | 195 | | | | |
| Dec. | 230 | | | | |

CHAPTER

13

# Short-Term Financial Planning

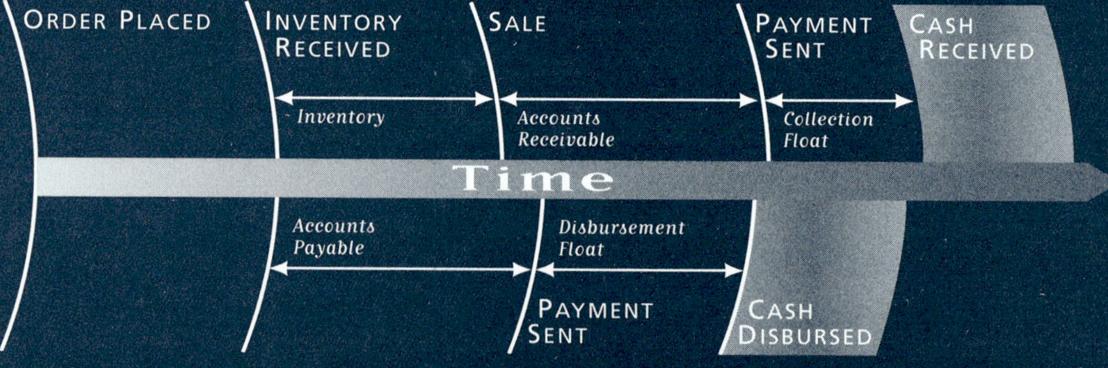

# OBJECTIVES

## *After studying this chapter, you should be able to:*

- implement the six steps involved in the modeling process.
- differentiate between a long-term financial planning model and a short-term financial planning model.
- develop a short-term financial planning model so that different short-term investment and financing strategies can be tested.

In a recent survey of corporate treasury officials, the Association for Financial Professionals (AFP) reported that most senior-level financial executives see the treasury function expanding into new areas including internal consulting, SEC compliance, and strategic financial planning.[1] In the survey, 57 percent of respondents indicated that they are currently dedicating more time and resources to cash forecasting with 53 percent expecting to spend more time and resources on forecasting in the future. This chapter and the previous chapter focus on financial forecasting techniques and modeling.

In this chapter, you will learn how to develop a short-term financial planning model that would help a financial manager better ascertain the overall impact that short-term financial management decisions have on the net operating cash flows of the company. With such a forecast in hand, the financial manager can better plan the firm's short-term investment and financing strategies and optimize the company's financial supply chain.

**Modeling** is the process of establishing a relationship between a set of independent variables in order to produce an estimate of a dependent variable. For example, meteorologists have devised sophisticated computer models to predict weather patterns. Economists estimate econometric models to explain and predict complex relationships dealing with various aspects of the macro economy. As we are all aware, these modeling applications have met with only limited success!

This chapter begins with a general discussion of the modeling process. Then, we develop the logic for a relatively complex short-term financial planning model. This model generates financial statement projections, specifically balance sheets, income statements, and cash budgets for a predetermined planning horizon.

### FINANCIAL DILEMMA

What Does the Future Hold?

Management at Francine's Attic, Inc., a nationwide specialty retail outlet chain in the Southeast just accepted a recommendation to relax its credit terms in order to stimulate sales. However, management was concerned about what the new policy would do to its cash flows and wondered what type of funding contingencies should be arranged over the next six months. The corporate treasurer wanted to try to create a forecast of the firm's cash flow position in order to anticipate the timing and amount of potential financing needs or investing opportunities.

[1] "The Evolving Role of Treasury: Report of Survey Results, November 2003," *Association for Financial Professionals* (**http://www.afponline.org/pub/pdf/AFPTreasury_%20Survey.pdf**).

## TYPES OF MODELS

Models have two basic formats. A model may be **deterministic** or **stochastic**. Data input for a deterministic model is single point estimates, while data input for a stochastic model includes probability distributions for one or more variables. For example, suppose we determine that the accounts receivable balance is forecasted to be 20 percent of sales. Thus, the receivables balance is the dependent variable, and sales is the independent variable. The type of input used for the sales estimate would define whether the model is deterministic or stochastic. If we wanted to find out the level of receivables if sales were expected to be $50,000, then the model would be deterministic. If, instead, we let the sales estimate be drawn from a normal distribution, for example, with a specified mean and standard deviation, then the model would be stochastic. For example, the Lotus or Excel add-in product @RISK allows the modeler to convert a deterministic model into a stochastic model with minimal effort. The models discussed and developed in this chapter are deterministic models but can easily be adapted to include probability distributions for selected variables.

## THE MODELING PROCESS

The first step in designing a model is to determine the question being asked. The modeler must clearly define the objective of the model. For example, a financial manager may wish to create a model to estimate the required level of external financing given a range of sales growth rates. Or, the personnel manager may wish to estimate the number of new entry-level positions that will need to be filled during the coming year. Clearly defining the problem will generally allow the modeler to better determine the appropriate relationships and variables required to model the problem.

Having defined the problem, the next step is to specify the variables to be used in the model. A personnel manager estimating new entry-level positions to fill will need to know how many promotions are expected during the period, growth in business activity, and the number of people leaving the firm for various reasons.

Variable specification is also affected by the time period for the forecast. Does the financial manager wish to estimate the required external funding for the next month, quarter, year, or five years? Defining the time period for the forecast will generally determine the level of detail necessary to model the problem. Determining the funding requirements for the next month requires detailed data about cash collections and cash disbursements. Estimating funding requirements for the coming year or 5-year period would generally require more aggregate data such as estimating the level of total assets.

The third step in the modeling process is determining the relationship between the selected variables. Suppose that a financial manager wishes to estimate cash collections from credit sales for the coming month. Cash collection is the dependent variable. Current and previous months' credit sales would be the independent variables. The relationship between these variables might be expressed as the following:

$$C_t = a_1CS_t + a_2CS_{t-1} + a_3CS_{t-2}$$

This relationship says that cash collection in month $t$, $C_t$, is equal to some fraction, $a_1$, of credit sales during month $t$, $CS_t$, plus some fraction, $a_2$, of credit sales last month, $CS_{t-1}$, plus some fraction, $a_3$, of credit sales two months ago, $CS_{t-2}$.

To estimate cash collection, the financial manager must arrive at an estimate of credit sales for the given month, estimates of the collection percentages, and actual historical data on the previous months' credit sales. In addition to these data, an estimate of the current month's sales is required. This calls for the development of a sales forecast that can be fed into the cash collection forecast model.

Once the variable relationships have been developed, the fourth step is parameter estimation. The cash collection model requires the financial manager to form estimates of the collection percentages, $a_1$ through $a_3$, and the parameters for current and past months' credit sales. This can be done in several ways. One approach is to estimate the collection fractions by calculating a simple average over a historical time period. A more sophisticated approach may involve running a lagged regression model with monthly cash collections as the dependent variable and current and lagged credit sales as the independent variables.[2] Alternatively, the financial manager can treat the collection percentages as policy variables and arbitrarily enter "desired" collection percentages.

Once the model has been developed, the fifth step is validation. The financial manager should "run" the model on a variety of data sets and manually check the results. The sixth and final step is to document the model. The model's logic should be documented so that if errors are subsequently found or if model logic might be changed in the future, it can be more easily edited and modified.

## A SIMPLE PERCENT OF SALES FORECASTING MODEL

We will first apply the modeling principles discussed above by developing a relatively simple financial forecasting model. The example model estimates the needed external funds required for a given sales growth estimate.

The heart of this relatively simple forecasting technique lies in the assumption that current assets and possibly noncurrent or fixed assets as well as current liabilities fluctuate proportionately with sales. For example, if total assets are currently 45 percent of sales and it can be assumed that this relationship will remain roughly the same over the next year or two, then for every additional $1,000 of sales over the current sales level, total assets must increase by $450. This increase in assets must be financed by a source of funds, such as an increase in liabilities or an increase in equity.

One readily available financing source, often referred to as a spontaneous source, is current liabilities. Accounts payable and accrued wages vary with the level of sales. If current liabilities traditionally amount to about 25 percent of sales, then for every $1,000 of sales above the current level, current liabilities (a source of funds) will increase by $1,000 × 0.25, or $250.

We still have an excess of uses of funds (an increase in assets) over sources of funds (an increase in liabilities) in the amount of $200 = $450 − $250. The final source of funds considered is retained earnings. This internal source can be calculated by multiplying the firm's net profit margin, *m*, by the forecasted sales level, *S*, over the planning period multiplied by the fraction 1 minus the dividend payout ratio, *dpo*. This final figure represents the funds from operations that will be retained for internal investment purposes. Note that depreciation is not added back because the asset figure is net of depreciation. At this point, if uses of funds still exceed sources of funds, new external financing will be required over the planning period. This forecasting model for needed external funds (NEF) can be reduced to the relatively simple formula shown below.

$$\begin{aligned} \text{NEF} = {} & (\text{Total assets/Sales}) \times \text{Change in sales} \\ & - (\text{Current liabilities/Sales}) \times \text{Change in sales} \\ & - \text{Sales} \times \text{Net profit margin} \times [1 - (\text{Dividends/Net profit})] \end{aligned}$$

$$\text{NEF} = (\text{TA/S}) \times \Delta\text{S} - (\text{CL/S}) \times \Delta\text{S} - [\text{S} \times \text{m} \times (1 - \text{dpo})]$$

[2] J. K. Shim, "Estimating Cash Collection Rates from Credit Sales: A Lagged Regression Approach," *Financial Management* (Winter 1981), pp. 28–30.

In the previous equation, $\Delta S$ represents the expected change in sales over the planning period.

We will now use an example to show how this forecasting model works. Assume the following data are representative of a company's financial position.

BALANCE SHEET FOR 2004

| | | | |
|---|---|---|---|
| Total assets | $15,580,000 | Current liabilities | $4,261,000 |
| | | Long-term debt | 3,638,000 |
| | | Net worth | 7,681,000 |

INCOME STATEMENT FOR 2004

| | |
|---|---|
| Net sales | $12,250,000 |
| Net profit | 692,000 |
| Dividends | 429,000 |

Thus,

$$\begin{aligned} TA/S &= 1.272 \\ CL/S &= 0.348 \\ m &= 0.056 \\ dpo &= 0.62 \end{aligned}$$

Further assume that management expects sales to increase by \$2.75 million, $\Delta s$, during the coming year, making the expected level of sales, *S*, equal to \$15 million. Plugging these values into the forecasting model yields the following estimate of needed external funds (NEF):

$$\begin{aligned} NEF &= (1.272 \times \$2.75) - (0.348 \times \$2.75) - [\$15 \times 0.056 \times (1 - 0.62)] \\ &= \$3.498 - \$0.957 - \$0.319 \\ &= \$2.222 \end{aligned}$$

If sales increase by \$2.75 million, then total assets will expand by \$3.498 million, current liabilities will expand by \$0.957 million, and retained profits will expand by \$0.319 million. The company's balance sheet would look like the following:

| | | |
|---|---|---|
| Total assets = | $19,078,000 | = $15,580,000 + $3,498,000 |
| Current liabilities = | $5,218,000 | = $4,261,000 + $957,000 |
| Long-term debt = | $3,638,000 | = Assumed held constant |
| Net worth = | $8,000,000 | = $7,681,000 + $319,000 |

Summing up the current liabilities, long-term debt, and net worth, we arrive at a total of \$16,856,000. We can see that total assets are forecasted to be \$19,078,000. Thus, the financing side of the balance sheet is \$2,222,000 short of the funds needed to finance the asset side of the balance sheet as predicted by the NEF equation.

The financial manager now knows that if sales grow as predicted and if the financial and operating policies are such that there should be \$1.272 of assets for each dollar of sales, \$0.348 of current liabilities per dollar of sales, a profit margin of 5.6 percent, and 62 percent of the profits paid as dividends, then the firm must obtain \$2.222 million of outside financing. This new financing may be obtained either through new debt or new equity sources, but that level of funding must be acquired in order to finance the forecasted growth in assets.

## BASICS OF BUILDING A FINANCIAL MODEL

This simple percent of sales forecasting model assigns sales as the **driving variable**. Most financial forecasting models contain a driving variable that is the basis of many of the forecasting relationships. In the simple model presented earlier, the growth in total assets is driven by the change in sales. In addition, current liabilities and retained profits are driven by the change in sales. The change in total assets, the change in current liabilities, and the retained profit are then linked to the driving variable through relationship variables. The relationship variables, or parameters, in the model are the assets to sales ratio, the current liabilities to sales ratio, the profit margin, and the dividend payout ratio. These parameters may also be called policy variables because they are basically relationships that the financial manager has some control over and can change if necessary or desired. The dependent variable is the dollar amount of external funds needed.

There is always the temptation to make a model too detailed. Caution should be used to minimize the number of policy variables and to find the most basic driving variable, the one to which most relationships can be tied.

Building this simple model into an electronic spreadsheet requires careful organization to maximize efficiency and effectiveness of the modeling process. First, the model must be conceptualized as has been discussed earlier and demonstrated through the percent of sales forecasting model. Then, the relationship or policy variables should be entered in a separate area of the worksheet. The layout may be as follows:

| Row | Column A | Column B |
|---|---|---|
| 1 | Assets to Sales | ________ |
| 2 | Current liabilities to Sales | ________ |
| 3 | Net profit margin | ________ |
| 4 | Dividends to Net profit | ________ |
| 5 | Change in sales | ________ |
| 6 | Current sales level | ________ |

The labels for the relationship and driving variables are entered in Column A, and the user can then enter the values for these variables in Column B.

The forecasting model is developed in another part of the worksheet such as Column C on line 50 as shown next. Note that the model is developed using cell references for the relationship or policy variables and the driving variable.

| Row | Column C |
|---|---|
| 50 | (B1 × B5) − (B2 × B5) − [B3 × (1 − B4) × (B5 + B6)] |

Financial models should always be developed using cell references rather than inputting the actual values for the policy variables into the model itself. If the user wishes to see how a change in the value of a policy variable or driving variable affects the result, then the user simply keys in a different number in the cell labeled for that variable, such as in cells B1–B5, and the model, in cell C50, is automatically updated. Otherwise, the user would have to edit the model itself with the danger of inadvertently changing the logic.

You may wonder why the model logic was placed in Column C and on a row below the policy variables. Basically, it is a good idea to do this, as adding or deleting columns in the data entry section could destroy some of the model logic, especially in a model more complex than the one under consideration.

## A SHORT-RUN FINANCIAL PLANNING MODEL

The short-run financial planning model we will now develop is basically a sophisticated percent of sales forecasting model that links a pro-forma income statement, cash flow statement, and balance sheet together for as many months in the future as the user would like to project. The basic driving variable is Sales, as the model ties the financial statement items not controlled by the user to sales. The policy variables over which the user has control are:

Gross profit margin

Level of operating expenses

Receivables collection pattern

Desired ending inventory

Accounts payable payment pattern

Marketable securities maturity structure

Debt maturity structure

Other variables which we will take as given include:

Sales level

Level of fixed assets

Level of depreciation

## MODEL LOGIC

The following material describes the basic logic used to forecast each item on the projected income statement, cash budget, and balance sheet. Spend some time reviewing these relationships. The better you understand the relationship logic, the better you will understand how each account value on the projected financial statements interrelates with other financial statement accounts.

| Pro-Forma Statement Item | Logic |
|---|---|
| | Income Statement |
| **Estimated sales** | $S_t$.<br>Forecasted sales for any pro-forma period will be a given. The purpose of the model is to develop a financial plan based on an assumed level of operations. |
| **Cost of sales** | $S_t \times (1 - gpm_t)$.<br>The user can control the relationship between sales and cost of goods sold by specifying a desired gross profit margin, $gpm_t$. Cost of goods sold is then Estimated sales × (1 − gpm). |
| **Gross profit** | Estimated sales − Cost of sales. |
| **General and administrative expenses** | $G\&A_t$.<br>In our simple model, the user will enter the expected level of operating expenses for each period. |
| **Depreciation** | $DEPR_t$.<br>In our simple model, the user will enter the expected level of depreciation for each period. |
| **Operating profit** | Gross profit − General and administrative expenses (excluding depreciation) − Depreciation. |
| **Interest income** | $MS_{t-1} \times i$. |

**Interest expense** $(STD_{t-1} + LTD_{t-1}) \times i$.
Monthly interest income and expense is equal to the previous period's marketable securities balance times the investment interest rate and the short-term and long-term debt level times the monthly interest rate, respectively.

**Profit before tax** Operating profit − Interest expense.

**Tax liability** $TL_t$ = Profit before tax × (1 − T).

**Profit after tax** Profit before tax − Taxes.

## Cash Flow Statement

**Operating Cash Receipts**

**Sales collections** $(S_t \times cf_t) + (S_{t-1} \times cf_{t-1}) + (S_{t-2} \times cf_{t-2})$.
Cash receipts from sales are estimated by taking current period sales and past period sales ($S_t$) and multiplying the appropriate collection fractions ($cf_t$) by the appropriate period sales.

It is important to remember that the December base period data including the December receivables balance are based on past period collection fractions. If collection fractions for the planning period are to be different, the planning model should use the past collection fractions to apply against the historical period sales in order to properly collect the base period receivables balance during the first month or two of the planning period. If this is not done, then the base period receivables balance will not be properly collected and the balance sheet for the planning period will not generally balance.

**Operating cash receipts** Sum of the above items.

**Operating Cash Disbursements**

**Payment of payables** $(Pur_t \times pf_t) + (Pur_{t-1} \times pf_{t-1}) + (Pur_{t-2} \times pf_{t-2})$.
Cash disbursement resulting from current and prior period purchases is a function of the dollar amount of purchases in the current and past periods ($Pur_t$) and the payment fractions ($pf_t$) assumed by management.

The monthly purchase amount is determined by the level of beginning inventory and the firm's policy related to the desired amount of ending inventory in the current period. This basic accounting relationship is shown below.

Desired ending inventory = Beginning inventory + Purchases − Cost of goods sold.

Solving this accounting relationship for Purchases results in the following equation:

Purchases = Desired ending inventory − Beginning inventory + Cost of goods sold.

The only thing still lacking from making this equation operational is a policy relationship establishing the firm's desired ending inventory. To make this relatively uncomplicated, we will express the desired inventory balance as some relationship to cost of goods sold such as assuming the firm desires to maintain one month's cost of goods sold as ending inventory, or two months' cost of goods sold as ending inventory, etc.

It is important to remember that the December base period data including the December purchase amount are based on past period inventory order policies and the payment of purchases is based on past period payment fractions. If these policies are changed in the planning period, the planning model should use the past payment fractions to apply against the historical period purchases in order to properly disburse the base period purchases during the first month or two of the planning period. If this is not done, then the base period purchases will not be properly disbursed and the balance sheet for the planning period will not generally balance.

| | |
|---|---|
| **General and administrative expenses** | $G\&A_t$.<br>To simplify the model, we will assume that all monthly operating expenses, except depreciation, are paid in the month they are incurred. Thus, the number in the cash budget is taken directly from the number generated in the income statement. |
| **Taxes disbursed** | $TP_t$.<br>Taxes disbursed is equal to the balance sheet account, Taxes payable (TP), if the current month is a tax payment month. We will assume that Month 3, March; Month 6, June; Month 9, September; and Month 12, December are tax payment months. |
| **Operating cash disbursed** | The sum of the above items. |
| **Operating net cash flow** | Operating cash receipts − Operating cash disbursed. |
| **Financial Strategy Section** | |
| **Marketable securities** | Purchase marketable securities, MS, if the ending cash balance exceeds the minimum cash balance. |
| **Notes payable and long-term debt** | Borrow notes payable, NP, or long-term debt, LTD, if the cash balance is less than the minimum cash balance. |
| **Financial Servicing Flows** | |
| **Interest received** | $MS_{t-1} \times i$. |
| **Interest paid** | $(NP_{t-1} \times i) + (LTD_{t-1} \times i)$. |
| **Debt maturing** | $NP_{t-1}$ (based on maturity schedule). |
| **Maturing investments** | $MS_{t-1}$ (based on maturity schedule). |
| **Beginning cash** | $CB_{t-1}$.<br>The beginning cash balance for each month is equal to the previous month's ending cash balance. |
| **Ending cash balance** | $CB_{t-1}$ + Operating net cash flow$_t$ + Interest received$_t$ − Interest paid$_t$ − Debt maturing + Maturing investment + New debt − New investments.<br>The month ending cash balance is equal to last month's ending cash balance plus the current month's operating net cash flow plus investment interest received less interest paid less debt principal due plus maturing investments plus new debt acquired less new investments. |

**Balance Sheet**

| | |
|---|---|
| **Assets** | |
| **Cash** | $CB_t$.<br>The cash account is estimated by the cash budget in the previous section. It is the monthly ending final cash balance. |
| **Marketable securities** | $MS_{t-1}$ + Maturing investments$_t$ − New investments$_t$.<br>The balance for the marketable securities portfolio is taken directly from the financial strategy section of the cash budget. |
| **Accounts receivable** | $S_t \times (1 - cf_t) + S_{t-1} \times (1 - cf_t - cf_{t-1}) + S_{t-2} \times (1 - cf_t - cf_{t-1} - cf_{t-2})$.<br>The accounts receivable balance is determined through the assumed accumulated collection fractions for the appropriate current and prior period sales levels.<br>Another approach to estimating the balance of accounts receivable is the following:<br>$AR_{t-1} + S_t$ − Cash collections from sales$_t$. |

The cash collections from sales is the dollar amount of cash collections from sales estimated in the cash budget.

**Inventory**

$INV_{t-1} + PUR_t - COGS_t$.
The inventory balance is controlled through the inventory policy variable discussed earlier, and the month ending balance is equal to the ending balance for the prior period plus purchases less the cost of goods sold.

**Total current**

Sum of the above.
Note that we implicitly assume that cash, marketable securities, receivables, and inventory are the only current assets on the balance sheet. A more real-world financial planning model would need to include prepaid assets and other current assets.

**Gross fixed assets**

$GFA_t$.
The ending balance for gross fixed assets is equal to the ending balance for the prior month plus any new purchases of gross fixed assets. In order to reduce the complexity of the forecasting model, we will assume that during the planning period no gross fixed assets will be sold off or acquired.

**Accumulated depreciation**

$ADEPR_{t-1} + DEPR_t$.
The ending balance for accumulated depreciation is equal to the ending balance for the prior month plus the depreciation expense for the current month.

**Total assets**

Sum of the above components except accumulated depreciation − accumulated depreciation.

---

**Liabilities and Owners' Equity**

**Accounts payable**

$PUR_t \times (1 - pf_t) + PUR_{t-1} \times (1 - pf_t - pf_{t-1}) + PUR_{t-2} \times (1 - pf_t - pf_{t-1} - pf_{t-2})$.
The accounts payable balance is controlled through the payables payment fractions. An alternate method to calculate the ending balance for current period payables is the following:

$$AP_t = AP_{t-1} + PUR_t - \text{Cash disbursed for purchases}_t.$$

**Notes payable**

$NP_{t-1} + \text{New notes borrowings}_t - \text{Notes retired}_t$.
The ending balance for notes payable is equal to the prior period ending balance plus new borrowings determined by the cash budget and the financing policy variable for long- versus short-term debt and the dollar amount of notes payable retired determined by the maturity of the notes.

**Taxes payable**

$TP_{t-1} + TL_t - \text{Taxes paid}_t$.
The ending balance for the taxes payable account is equal to the ending balance for the prior period plus the new tax liability (TL) determined on the current period income statement less any taxes paid based on the tax payment month. This last number comes directly from the cash budget.

**Total current**

Sum of the above.

**Long-term debt**

$LTD_{t-1} + \text{New } LTD_t$.
The balance of long-term debt outstanding for the current period is equal to the balance for the prior period plus any new long-term debt acquired as a result from cash needs and the firm's assumed financing policy related to short-term versus long-term financing.

**Common stock**

Assumed constant value.

**Retained earnings**

$RE_{t-1} + NI_t$.
Current period retained earnings is equal to the prior period balance plus the net income projected by the income statement. No dividends will be paid.

**Total liabilities and net worth**

Sum of the above components.

## UNDERSTANDING THE MODEL

At this point, you may be a little dazed by all the financial relationships developed to create the short-term financial planning model. However, before we apply the model to the Financial Dilemma presented at the beginning of the chapter, let us think about what the model does. As a company begins producing and selling a product or service, it generates revenues and expenses represented by the income statement. Our financial planning model then transforms the income statement into a cash flow statement by converting revenues into cash receipts based on collections fractions and converting expenses into cash disbursement based on payment fractions. The projected income statement and resulting cash flow statement then impact the balance sheet by changing the level of current assets (cash, receivables, and inventory), current liabilities (accounts payable), accumulated depreciation, and retained earnings. If spontaneous assets grow faster than spontaneous liabilities and equity, then additional financing is required in order to fund the difference. The financial manager is then faced with choosing the type, amount, and maturity of financing that enhances the value of the firm. If spontaneous liabilities and equity grow faster than spontaneous assets, then excess liquidity is generated and the financial manager can either retire debt, pay a dividend, or invest in financial assets. Again, the choice made should be the one that enhances the value of the firm. In our simple optimization model that will be discussed next, firm value will be enhanced by maximizing the net interest income for a given set of constraints.

## FINANCIAL DILEMMA REVISITED

Exhibit 13–1 reviews the base period information, the exogenous/environmental variables, policy variables, and decision variables that will be incorporated into the financial planning model to help solve the dilemma facing Francine's Attic, Inc. This exhibit also displays the assumed data for each of the variables in the financial planning model for the first six months of the new operating year for Francine's, Inc., a specialty retail outlet chain dealing in outdoor recreational equipment in the Southeast. The exhibit presents the base period financial data for the ending month of the prior year, management's expectations for sales, operating expenses, depreciation, and the future monthly term structure of interest rates. In addition, the exhibit presents environmental parameters such as the tax rate and management's policy variables including collection and payment fractions and the desired gross profit margin. Management is relaxing its credit policy and expects that the collection fractions will slow from 10 percent, 60 percent, and 30 percent to 10 percent, 10 percent, and 80 percent for the month of sale, one month after, and two months after sale, respectively. Management is concerned about the financial impact of this decision and wants to know what it will cost the firm in terms of additional financing costs. In addition, management wants to determine the optimal investment and financing plan given the future course of interest rates. Exhibit 13–1 presents the investment instrument and financing instrument options available to the firm along with their respective interest rate forecasts for the next six months.

The financial strategy designed to support the firm's operating plan presented in Exhibits 13–2 through 13–4 is based on an optimization process that will be discussed in the next section. The plan results in a net interest earned for the 6-month planning period of −$99.83 (interest expense exceeds interest income). The financial manager should plan to invest in 30-day and 90-day marketable securities in January at 8 percent and 9.50 percent, respectively, 30-day marketable securities in February at 9 percent, and 30-day marketable securities in April at 9.50 percent. The plan also requires the use of 180-day notes payable financing commencing in January at 10 percent, 90-day notes payable financing commencing in February at 10 percent, and 30-day notes payable in the month of May at

## Exhibit 13–1

*Data Input for the Short-Run Financial Planning Model*

| Base Period Information and Sales Forecast | | | | | | | | | |
|---|---|---|---|---|---|---|---|---|---|
| | Nov. | Dec. | Jan. | Feb. | Mar. | Apr. | May | June | July |
| Sales | $1,400 | $1,500 | $1,700 | $1,800 | $2,000 | $2,600 | $2,400 | $1,900 | $1,400 |
| Operating expenses | | | 250 | 250 | 250 | 250 | 250 | 250 | |
| Depreciation | | | | | | | | 100 | |
| Cash | | 250 | | | | | | | |
| Short-term investments | | 0 | | | | | | | |
| Accounts receivable | | 1,770 | | | | | | | |
| Inventory | | 1,275 | | | | | | | |
| Gross fixed assets | | 4,000 | | | | | | | |
| Accum. depreciation | | 1,200 | | | | | | | |
| Accounts payable | | 1,275 | | | | | | | |
| Notes payable | | 0 | | | | | | | |
| Taxes payable | | 200 | | | | | | | |
| Long-term debt | | 1,000 | | | | | | | |
| Common stock | | 1,000 | | | | | | | |
| Retained earnings | | 2,620 | | | | | | | |

**Exogenous/Environmental Variables**

Tax payment months, March (3), June (6), September (9), December (12)
Tax rate, $T = 40\%$

| | Expected Term Structure of Interest | | | | | |
|---|---|---|---|---|---|---|
| | Jan. | Feb. | Mar. | Apr. | May | June |
| Investment instruments: | | | | | | |
| 30-day marketable securities | 8.00% | 9.00% | 10.00% | 9.50% | 9.00% | 9.00% |
| 90-day marketable securities | 9.50 | 9.00 | 9.50 | 9.00 | 9.50 | 9.50 |
| Financing instruments: | | | | | | |
| 30-day notes payable | 9.00 | 10.00 | 11.50 | 11.00 | 9.50 | 9.50 |
| 90-day notes payable | 9.50 | 10.00 | 11.00 | 11.00 | 10.00 | 10.00 |
| 180-day notes payable | 10.00 | 10.00 | 10.00 | 10.00 | 10.50 | 10.50 |
| Long-term debt | 10.50 | 10.00 | 10.00 | 10.00 | 11.00 | 11.00 |

**Policy Variables**

| | Month of Sale | 1 Month after | 2 Months after |
|---|---|---|---|
| Collection fractions | 10% | 10% | 80% |
| | Month of Purchase | 1 Month after | |
| Payment fractions | 0% | 100% | |

Inventory policy: Ending inventory in month $t$ equal to next month's COGS.

| | |
|---|---|
| Gross profit margin | 25% |
| Minimum cash balance | $250 |

**Decision Variables**

Short-term investment amount and maturity, January–June
Short-term borrowing amount and maturity, January–June
Long-term borrowing amount, January

## Exhibit 13–2

*Projected Income Statement Based on Exhibit 13–1 Data**

| | Jan. | Feb. | Mar. | Apr. | May | June |
|---|---|---|---|---|---|---|
| Sales | $1,700 | $1,800 | $2,000 | $2,600 | $2,400 | $1,900 |
| Cost of goods sold | 1,275 | 1,350 | 1,500 | 1,950 | 1,800 | 1,425 |
| Gross profit | $ 425 | $ 450 | $ 500 | $ 650 | $ 600 | $ 475 |
| General and administrative | 250 | 250 | 250 | 250 | 250 | 250 |
| Depreciation | 0 | 0 | 0 | 0 | 0 | 100 |
| Operating profit | $ 175 | $ 200 | $ 250 | $ 400 | $ 350 | $ 125 |
| Interest income | 0 | 8 | 10 | 6 | 4 | 0 |
| Interest expense | 9 | 18 | 26 | 26 | 26 | 22 |
| Profit before tax | $ 166 | $ 190 | $ 233 | $ 380 | $ 327 | $ 103 |
| Taxes | 67 | 76 | 93 | 152 | 131 | 41 |
| Net income | $ 100 | $ 114 | $ 140 | $ 228 | $ 196 | $ 62 |

* Calculated numbers have been rounded, and thus, some totals may be off by $1.00.

## FOCUS ON PRACTICE

### *Optimizing the Financial Plan*

Forecasting allows companies to make more informed liquidity management decisions. By understanding where cash flow peaks and valleys are, financial managers can more accurately position debt or investment maturities and take advantage of yield curve opportunities. According to Michael A. Gallanis of Treasury Strategies, Inc., a review of recent commercial paper yield data suggests a 30 to 50 basis point spread in overnight versus 30-day rates which equates to an extra $150,000 to $250,000 of annual expense/income on a $50 million portfolio.*

TreasuryPoint.com recently went online with the "Optimizer." The Optimizer is a state-of-the-art analytical system that can be used to optimize a company's daily short-term borrowing and investing decisions given a company's short-term financial position, cash flow forecasts, and risk guidelines. Each day, the Optimizer's analytical engine goes through a systematic analysis of the company's financial position and the current markets. Then, it works within the investment guidelines and borrowing parameters set up by the financial manager to recommend the optimal solution for the company. Based on five case studies of companies with $250 million to $15 billion in sales, the Optimizer generated annualized savings of 10 to 65 basis points versus actual results. In one case study, the Optimizer recommended borrowing from a higher-rate credit line rather than a lower-rate, longer-term borrowing source. It calculated the total cost of borrowing for a few days at the higher rate and compared it to the total cost of borrowing at a lower rate and investing excess borrowings for a longer period of time. The company's Web site can be found at **http://www.treasurypoint.com/**.**

* "Cash Forecasting: Examining the Ups and Downs," *AFP Exchange* (March/April 2003), pp. 15–18.
** "Optimizing Short-Term Cash," *Treasury and Risk Management* (April 2000), p. 20.

Exhibit 13–3

*Projected Cash Budget Based on Exhibits 13–1 and 13–2*

| *Cash Receipts* | Jan. | Feb. | Mar. | Apr. | May | June |
|---|---|---|---|---|---|---|
| Month of sale | $ 170 | $ 180 | $ 200 | $ 260 | $ 240 | $ 190 |
| 1 Month after sale | 900 | 170 | 180 | 200 | 260 | 240 |
| 2 Months after sale | 420 | 450 | 1,360 | 1,440 | 1,600 | 2,080 |
| Total cash receipts | $1,490 | $ 800 | $1,740 | $1,900 | $2,100 | $2,510 |
| Purchases | $1,350 | $1,500 | $1,950 | $1,800 | $1,425 | $1,050 |
| *Cash Disbursements* | | | | | | |
| Month of purchase | $ 0 | $ 0 | $ 0 | $ 0 | $ 0 | $ 0 |
| 1 Month after purchase | 1,275 | 1,350 | 1,500 | 1,950 | 1,800 | 1,425 |
| General and administrative | 250 | 250 | 250 | 250 | 250 | 250 |
| Taxes | 0 | 0 | 436 | 0 | 0 | 324 |
| Total disbursements | $1,525 | $1,600 | $2,186 | $2,200 | $2,050 | $1,999 |
| Operating net cash flow | $ (35) | $ (800) | $ (446) | $ (300) | $ 50 | $ 511 |
| *Investment/Financing Strategy (Decision Variables)** | | | | | | |
| MS (30) | $ 298 | $ 462 | $ 0 | $ 458 | $ 0 | $ 0 |
| MS (90) | 778 | 0 | 0 | 0 | | |
| N/P (30) | 0 | 0 | 0 | 0 | 489 | |
| N/P (90) | 0 | 975 | 0 | 0 | | |
| N/P (180) | 1,120 | | | | | |
| LTD | 0 | | | | | |
| *Financial Flows (Resulting from Decision Variables)* | | | | | | |
| Interest received | $ 0 | $ 8 | $ 10 | $ 6 | $ 4 | $ 0 |
| Interest paid | 9 | 18 | 26 | 26 | 26 | 22 |
| Debt maturing | 0 | 0 | 0 | 0 | 975 | 489 |
| Maturing investments | 0 | 298 | 462 | 778 | 458 | 0 |
| Beginning cash | 250 | 250 | 250 | 250 | 250 | 250 |
| Ending cash balance | 250 | 250 | 250 | 250 | 250 | 250 |

* Note that 90-day marketable securities cannot be purchased in May and June and that 90-day notes payable cannot be obtained in May and June. In addition, January is the only month that 180-day notes payable and long-term debt can be obtained. These restrictions are imposed to keep the financing and investment decisions made during the period related to the excess or surplus cash flows during the period.

9.5 percent. This financing plan allows the firm to meet its desired minimum cash balance of $250 for each month while maximizing the dollar amount of net interest earned.[3]

## OPTIMIZING THE FINANCIAL PLAN

This section will present an optimization formulation of the financial planning model. The optimization focus will be on the financial strategy section choosing the investment amount

[3] The financial manager has already determined that under the current policy an optimal financing and investing strategy would result in a net interest earned for the coming 6-month period of −$64.18.

## Exhibit 13–4*

*Projected Balance Sheet Based on Exhibits 13–1 through 13–3**

| | Jan. | Feb. | Mar. | Apr. | May | June |
|---|---|---|---|---|---|---|
| Cash | $ 250 | $ 250 | $ 250 | $ 250 | $ 250 | $ 250 |
| MS (30) | 298 | 462 | 0 | 458 | 0 | 0 |
| MS (90) | 778 | 778 | 778 | 0 | 0 | 0 |
| Accounts receivable | 1,980 | 2,980 | 3,240 | 3,940 | 4,240 | 3,630 |
| Inventory | 1,350 | 1,500 | 1,950 | 1,800 | 1,425 | 1,050 |
| Gross fixed assets | 4,000 | 4,000 | 4,000 | 4,000 | 4,000 | 4,000 |
| (Accum. depreciation) | 1,200 | 1,200 | 1,200 | 1,200 | 1,200 | 1,300 |
| Total assets | $7,456 | $8,771 | $9,018 | $9,248 | $8,715 | $7,630 |
| Accounts payable | $1,350 | $1,500 | $1,950 | $1,800 | $1,425 | $1,050 |
| Taxes payable | 267 | 343 | 0 | 152 | 283 | 0 |
| N/P (30) | 0 | 0 | 0 | 0 | 489 | 0 |
| N/P (90) | 0 | 975 | 975 | 975 | 0 | 0 |
| N/P (180) | 1,120 | 1,120 | 1,120 | 1,120 | 1,120 | 1,120 |
| Long-term debt | 1,000 | 1,000 | 1,000 | 1,000 | 1,000 | 1,000 |
| Equity | 3,720 | 3,834 | 3,974 | 4,202 | 4,398 | 4,460 |
| Liabilities and net worth | $7,456 | $8,771 | $9,018 | $9,248 | $8,715 | $7,630 |

* Calculated numbers have been rounded, and thus, some totals may be off by $1.00.

and maturity and the financing amount and maturity with the goal of maximizing the net interest income over the 6-month period.

The decision variables include 10 investment decision variables and 11 financing variables for a total of 21 decision variables. The 10 investment decision variables include six 30-day marketable securities variables, for January through June, and four 90-day marketable securities variables, for January through April. The 11 financing variables include five 30-day notes payable variables, for January through May, four 90-day notes payable variables, for January through April, one 180-day notes payable variable for January, and one long-term debt variable for January.

The objective function of the optimization model is to maximize the net interest income over the 6-month planning horizon. This is formulated as the sum of the interest received row less the sum of the interest paid row on the cash flow statement.

### OBJECTIVE: Maximize Net Interest Income for the 6-Month Period

Some of the relevant constraints have already been programmed into the spreadsheet relationships. For example, the decision variable cells are referenced in the financial flow section of the cash flow statement so that new notes payable automatically mature in the appropriate month creating a new cash disbursement draining cash. Likewise, marketable security investments in a given month are referenced to automatically mature in the appropriate month providing additional cash receipts.

The only constraint that is not explicitly considered in the financial planning model is the minimum cash balance constraint. This constraint indicates that the ending cash balance for any given month must equal the minimum cash balance for that month. Any cash over the minimum will be invested, and any cash shortage will be borrowed. The optimization program will then solve for the combination of financing and investment decision variables that maximize the objective function subject to the restrictions considered in the worksheet relationships and the explicit minimum cash balance constraint. The minimum balance constraint is shown below.

Subject to:

$$CB_{t-1} + ONCF_t + \text{Interest Received}_t - \text{Interest Paid}_t - NMS(30)_t + NMS(30)_{t-1} - NMS(90)_t + NMS(90)_{t-3} + NNP(30)_t - NNP(30)_{t-1} + NNP(90)_t - NNP(90)_{t-3} + NNP(180)_{Jan} + NLTD_{Jan} = MIN_t \text{ for } t = 1 - 6$$

Where:

CB = Cash balance

ONCF = Operating net cash flow

NMS = New marketable securities

NNP = New notes payable

NLTD = New long-term debt

MIN = Minimum cash balance

Additional constraints can easily be added to the model. For example, if there are upper limits on the amount of financing outstanding for the various borrowing categories, these can be added as follows:

$$NP(90)_t \leq 700, \text{ for } t = 1 - 4.$$

This equation constrains the dollar amount of 90-day notes payable outstanding to be no more than $700 for any of the first four months of the planning period. The NP variable is the one on the balance sheet. Thus, new 90-day notes payable for any given month would be constrained such that the total balance for this loan category does not exceed the $700 maximum. Exhibit 13–3 indicates that without this constraint, 90-day notes payable will equal $975 beginning in February. Adding this constraint will cause 90-day notes payable to equal $700 in February, and some other source of financing will be increased. The objective function will also be reduced in value since adding additional constraints such as this one will add costs. Other possible constraints might include setting minimum levels for ratios such as the current ratio or the level of net working capital. Using such a model as discussed in this chapter can help the financial manager enhance the value of the firm by choosing those financing and investment alternatives that maximize the net interest earned for a given financial position and operating cash flow forecast.

## SUMMARY

This chapter began by discussing financial modeling in general. Then a simple percent of sales forecasting model was developed and discussed. This type of forecasting model was discussed because its logic is at the heart of many financial planning models. Finally, the chapter developed the logic for a fairly detailed short-run financial planning model. This model forecasts a firm's monthly balance sheet, income statement, and cash flow statement for an assumed 6-month time period. The chapter concluded by discussing the basic logic for each item on the forecast income statement, cash budget, and balance sheet and presenting a financial strategy based on optimizing the financial plan using an optimization program.

## USEFUL WEB SITES

Two sites covering short-term financial modeling are:

Treasury Point **http://www.treasurypoint.com**

Wisdom Corporation **http://www.wisdomcorp.com**

## PROBLEMS

1. Summit, Inc., just completed its best year ever. Sales for 2004 were $5.5 million. Its year-end balance sheet is shown below.

**Balance Sheet for 2004**

| | | | |
|---|---|---|---|
| Current assets | $1,000,000 | Current liabilities | $ 500,000 |
| Net fixed assets | 2,000,000 | Long-term debt | 1,500,000 |
| | | Owners' equity | 1,000,000 |
| Total | $3,000,000 | | $3,000,000 |

**Income Statement for 2004**

| | |
|---|---|
| Sales | $5,500,000 |
| Cost of goods sold | 3,500,000 |
| Gross profit | $2,000,000 |
| Operating expenses | 1,000,000 |
| Interest | 170,000 |
| Taxes | 350,200 |
| Net profit | $ 479,800 |
| Dividends | $ 400,000 |

Summit's financial manager would like to forecast the dollar amount of external financing the firm will need in 2005. The financial manager assumes that sales will increase 30 percent and that since the firm is operating at capacity, total assets will stay in the same proportion to sales in 2005 as in 2004. In addition, all current liabilities are assumed to be spontaneous.

**a.** Forecast the dollar amount of external funds needed in 2005.

**b.** How might the firm reduce its reliance on external funds?

2. Program the financial planning model developed in this chapter using spreadsheet software such as Lotus 1-2-3 or Microsoft Excel. Exhibits 13–2 through 13–4 present the optimized financial plan given management's assumptions and policy variables. Enter your own financing and investment plan in the financial strategy section of the plan based on your analysis of the operating cash flow needs and management's interest rate scenario. In other words, try to intuitively determine the best plan without using an optimization program. Make sure that your plan meets the minimum cash balance requirement. Compare the resulting net interest income from your revised plan with that occurring from the optimized plan. Interpret the financing plan logic of the optimized plan shown in the exhibits in relation to the logic you used to devise your plan.

3. Program the financial planning model using spreadsheet software such as Lotus 1-2-3 or Excel. Put zeros for the financing and investment variables and use an add-in optimization program such as Solver for Microsoft Excel to determine the optimal solution. Check your answers against those presented in Exhibits 13–2 through 13–4. Change your input for collection fractions to the company's original policy of 10 percent, 60 percent, and 30 percent for the month of sale, month after sale, and two months after sale and compare the net interest income to the optimal net interest income for the new terms. Assume that projected sales under the old terms were the following:

| | |
|---|---|
| January | $1,600 |
| February | 1,600 |
| March | 2,000 |
| April | 2,500 |
| May | 2,400 |
| June | 1,800 |

How much does the new credit policy cost the company? Is the change in credit policy advantageous to the firm?

4. Using the financial planning model developed in Problem 2, assume that the bank will allow a maximum 180-day note payable of $500. Implement this new constraint into the model and re-optimize the financial plan. What is the resulting net interest earned from the revised plan? Explain the logic of the result.
5. Beginning with the financial planning model as developed in this chapter, discuss how the model would be adjusted to include a line of credit as a financing choice rather than the various maturities of notes payable. The firm would be able to draw down the line as needed on a monthly basis but could also repay the line as surplus funds occur. Assume the line has a monthly fee that would need to be paid the month after it is incurred, the line requires a minimum monthly compensating cash balance of X percent of the amount borrowed, and that interest is paid the month following the borrowing. The required compensating balance will be effective the month following the borrowing since it is assumed that borrowing occurs at the end of each month.

FOCUSED CASE

# Jones Salvage and Recycling, Inc. (Case A)

Jones Salvage and Recycling, Inc., was started by Mr. John Jones in 1985. Mr. Jones was concerned about the industrial impact on the world's environment and felt that it was time to be proactive in attempting to save the world's decreasing natural resources. His company takes scrap metal and compresses it into 4-ton blocks. His company then ships the blocks to steel mills that melt it down to take out the impurities and recycle it back into bars and pipes for the construction industry. Jones also recycles glass bottles and jars. They crush the glass into fine powder and ship it to a local glass company that recycles the glass powder into new bottles, which saves natural resources as well as energy. Although Mr. Jones is convinced that this type of business is the wave of the future, the business has not prospered and at times he feels he is out in front of the wave rather than riding it.

The financial manager at Jones Salvage and Recycling, Inc., is attempting to estimate the financial needs of the company for the first half of the new year. The company's end-of-year balance sheet is presented below.

| Assets | | Liabilities and Net Worth | |
|---|---|---|---|
| Cash | $ 1,000 | Accounts payable | $ 65,000 |
| Marketable securities (30-day) | 84,000 | Taxes payable | 0 |
| Accounts receivable | 75,000 | 30-day notes payable | 71,000 |
| Inventory | 65,000 | Mortgage loan | 150,000 |
| Gross fixed assets | 251,000 | Common stock | 100,000 |
| Accumulated depreciation | (25,000) | Retained earnings | 65,000 |

All sales are made on credit with terms of net 30 days, which is standard for the industry. However, the following cash collection schedule for the most recent six months is pretty typical.

| Month | Credit Sales | Cash Collections Month of Sale | Cash Collections 1 Month After Sale | Cash Collections 2 Months After Sale |
|---|---|---|---|---|
| July | $60,000 | 0 | $15,000 | $25,000 |
| August | 90,000 | 0 | 30,000 | 15,000 |
| September | 75,000 | 0 | 45,000 | 30,000 |
| October | 100,000 | 0 | 37,500 | 45,000 |
| November | 100,000 | 0 | 50,000 | 37,500 |
| December | 25,000 | 0 | 50,000 | 50,000 |

Jones purchases materials on terms of net 30 days and pays when due. He purchases enough materials in any given month based on a desired inventory policy of ending each month with enough inventory to satisfy next months' sales at cost. His gross profit margin is 35 percent.

General and administrative costs run about $30,000 per month, and taxes are paid quarterly at the end of March, June, September, and December. The tax rate is 40 percent. Depreciation expense runs $1,000 per month. Jones is currently required to leave a minimum of $1,000 in the company's bank account. Jones forecasts sales for the next eight months to be:

| Month | Forecasted Sales |
|---|---|
| January | $ 80,000 |
| February | 180,000 |
| March | 300,000 |
| April | 200,000 |
| May | 160,000 |
| June | 120,000 |
| July | 100,000 |
| August | 90,000 |

## Required

1. Using the financial planning model provided to you by your instructor or the model you created yourself, enter the necessary data from the information presented and forecast Jones' monthly cash flow position for each month of the 6-month period January through June. You should also construct a monthly income statement, cash budget, and balance sheet for the 6-month planning period.
2. Ignoring any interest expense or interest income, what is the total amount of financing that Jones' financial manager must plan for to cover the coming 6 months?

# INTEGRATIVE CASE—PART 4

## *Toy World, Inc.*

Grace Jones, the recently hired treasurer of Toy World, Inc., a manufacturer of specialty toys, was summoned to the office of Dan Culbreth, the president and chief executive officer. When she got to Dan's office, Grace found him shuffling through a set of worksheets. He told her that because of a recent tightening of credit by the Federal Reserve, and hence, an impending contraction of bank loans, the firm's bank has asked each of its major loan customers for an estimate of their borrowing requirements for the remainder of 1995 and the first half of 1996. Also, Dan informed Grace that the bank planned to continue its practice of charging a commitment fee of 1.5 percent per year (0.1250 percent per month) on any unused committed funds.

Dan had a previously scheduled meeting with the firm's bankers the following Monday, so he asked Grace to produce an estimate of the firm's probable loan requirements that he could submit at that time. Dan was going away on a white-water rafting expedition, a trip that had already been delayed several times, and he would not be back until just before his meeting with the bankers. Therefore, he asked Grace to prepare a cash budget while he was away.

Because of Toy World's rapid growth over the last few years, no one had taken the time to prepare a cash budget recently, so Grace was afraid she would have to start from scratch. From information already available, Grace knew that no loans would be needed from the bank before January, so she decided to restrict her budget to the period of January through June 1996.

As a first step, she obtained the following sales forecast from the marketing department:

| | | |
|---|---|---|
| 1995 | November | $800,000 |
| | December | 925,000 |
| 1996 | January | 500,000 |
| | February | 300,000 |
| | March | 280,000 |
| | April | 225,000 |
| | May | 200,000 |
| | June | 250,000 |
| | July | 350,000 |
| | August | 400,000 |



Note that the sales figures are before any discounts; that is, they are not net of discounts. Also, the marketing people cautioned Grace to recognize that actual sales could vary substantially from the forecasted levels because kids are fickle in their choice of toys.

Toy World's credit policy is 2/15, net 30. Hence, a 2 percent discount is allowed if payment is made within 15 days of the sale; otherwise, payment in full is due 30 days after the date of sale. On the basis of a previous study, Grace estimates that, generally, 35 percent of the firm's customers take the discount, 60 percent pay within 30 days, and 5 percent pay late, with the late payments received about 60 days after the invoice date, on average. For monthly budgeting purposes, discount sales are assumed to be collected in the month of the sale, net sales in the month after the sale, and late sales 2 months after the sale. Of course, variances could occur from all of these figures.

Toy World begins production of goods 2 months before the anticipated sale date. Variable production costs are made up entirely of purchased materials and labor, which total 70 percent of forecasted sales—30 percent for materials and 40 percent for labor. Again, these figures could change if operating conditions depart from norms. All materials are purchased just before production begins, or 2 months before the sale of the finished goods. On average, Toy World pays 60 percent of the materials cost in the month when it receives the materials, and the remaining 40 percent the next month, or 1 month before the sale. Half of the labor expenses are paid 2 months before the sale, and the remaining 50 percent is paid 1 month before the sale.

Toy World pays fixed general and administrative expenses of approximately $95,000 a month, and lease obligations amount to $60,000 per month. Both expenditures are expected to continue at the same level throughout the forecast period. The firm estimates miscellaneous expenses to be $40,000 monthly, and fixed assets are currently being depreciated at the rate of $47,500 per month. Toy World has $1,600,000 (book value) of bonds outstanding. They carry a 10 percent semi-annual coupon, and interest is paid on January 15 and July 15. Also, the company is planning to replace an old machine in June with a new one expected to cost $100,000. The old machine has both a zero book and a zero market value. Federal and state income taxes are expected to be $90,000 quarterly, and payments must be made on the 15th of December, March, June, and September. Toy World has a target minimum cash balance of $450,000, and this amount will be on hand on January 1, 1996.

Assume that you were recently hired as Grace Jones's assistant, and she has turned the job of preparing the cash budget over to you. You must meet with her and Dan Culbreth on Sunday night to review the budget prior to Dan's meeting with the bankers on Monday. You recall the cash budgeting process from your recently completed finance course, and you plan to use the format shown in Table 1 as a guide to prepare a monthly cash budget for Toy World for January through June 1996. Based on information obtained from the firm's credit department, Grace suggests that the following assumptions be used to prepare the budget. Initially, disregard both interest payments on short-term bank loans and interest received from investing surplus funds. Also, assume that all cash flows occur on the 15th of each month. Finally, note that collections from sales in November and December of 1995 will not be completed until January and February of 1996, respectively.

Grace is extremely concerned about the peak funds shortfall during the 6-month planning period. She is hoping that a $500,000 line of credit will be sufficient to cover any expected cash shortfall. There has been talk in the industry about changes under which suppliers would bill on terms requiring payments early in each month and, separately, customers would pay toward the end of the month. If these changes are made, competition would force Toy World to adapt to them. Therefore, Grace would also like to know how the cash budget would be affected if Toy World's cash outflows start to cluster at the beginning of the month, while collections become heaviest toward the end of the month.

At the last minute, Grace decided that a daily cash budget for the month of January should also be developed (Table 2 is provided as a guide). She obtained the following information from Toy World managers for use in developing the daily cash budget:

1. Toy World normally operates 7 days a week.
2. Sales generally occur at a constant rate throughout the month; that is, 1/31 of the January sales are made each day.
3. Daily sales typically follow the 35 percent, 60 percent, 5 percent collection breakdown.
4. Discount purchasers take full advantage of the 15-day discount period before paying, and "on time" purchasers wait the full 30 days to pay. Thus, collections during the first 15 days of January will reflect discount sales from the last 15 days of December plus "regular" sales made in earlier months. Also, on January 31, Toy World will begin collecting January's net sales and December's late sales.
5. The lease payment is made on the first of the month.
6. Fifty percent of both labor costs and general and administrative expenses are paid on the first and 50 percent are paid on the 15th.
7. Materials are assumed to be delivered on the first and paid for on the fifth.
8. Miscellaneous expenses are incurred and paid evenly throughout the month, 1/31 each day.
9. Required interest payments are made on the 15th.
10. The target cash balance is $450,000, and this amount must be in the bank on each day. This balance is higher than the firm would otherwise keep, but it is required as a compensating balance under terms of the firm's bank loan agreement. However, the bank may be willing to renegotiate this provision.

Dan has expressed some concern about the efficient use of his firm's cash resources. Specifically, he has questioned whether or not seasonal variations should be incorporated into the firm's target balance. In other words, during months when cash needs are greatest, the target balance would be somewhat higher, and the target would be set at a lower level during slack months. He asked you to consider this situation and to run some numbers to demonstrate the effect of using different target balances. Of course, this requires a modification to the bank loan agreement.

Grace noted that the only receipts shown in Toy World's cash budget are collections. She notes that Toy World pays a 7 percent interest rate on the short-term bank loan and would probably earn 5 percent on surplus cash. She wants to know how these new items could be incorporated into the cash budget. Additionally, she would like your views on an investment strategy for Toy World to invest any surplus funds. Toy World's policy has been to invest only in securities that provide liquidity and safety, yet offer a reasonable rate of return. Grace has heard about securities called "derivatives" that are backed by U.S. Treasury bonds yet offer higher returns than T-bonds, and she wonders if they should be used.

Dan Culbreth is an astute businessman, so he realizes that the cash budget is a forecast, and that many of the cash flows shown are expected values rather than amounts known with certainty. If actual sales, hence collections, are different from forecasted levels, the forecasted surpluses and deficits would be incorrect. He is interested in knowing how various changes in the key assumptions would affect the firm's cash surplus or deficit. It would be particularly bad to obtain a $500,000 line of credit and then find that, because of incorrect assumptions, the actual loan requirement is $700,000. Labor costs and many other expenses are set by contract at the start of the 6-month forecast period on the basis of the original expected sales. Therefore, many of the outflows cannot be adjusted downward during the planning period even if sales decline below the forecasted levels. Therefore, Dan sent Grace a memo requesting that the following three scenarios be specifically considered: (1) What would be the impact on the monthly net cash flows from January to June 1996 if actual sales for November through June were 20 percent below the forecasted amounts? (2) What if actual sales were only 50 percent of the forecasted level? (3) Even if sales are as expected, what would happen if customers changed their payment patterns and began paying more slowly, such as 25 percent in the month of sale, 55 percent in the following month, and 20 percent in the second month versus the old 35-60-5 pattern?

Based on an analysis of the situation, recommend the size of the credit line Toy World should seek. Think about any other related issues that Grace, Dan, or the bankers might raise concerning the budgets. In particular, be prepared to explain the sources of all the numbers and the effects on the company's cash requirements if any of the basic assumptions turn out to be incorrect. It would be useful to do some sensitivity analyses and to be prepared to answer various "what if" questions Dan might ask. Be prepared to discuss the tradeoff between a high credit line with a high commitment fee versus a low credit line with a low commitment fee. Finally, Grace knows that Dan has been thinking about altering the production process to produce at a level rate all year rather than producing 1 month based on sales expected in the next month. How might such a change affect loan requirements?

**Table 1**

*Monthly Cash Budget Worksheet*

| | November | December | January | February | March | April | May | June | July | August |
|---|---|---|---|---|---|---|---|---|---|---|
| I. Collection and Payments | | | | | | | | | | |
| Gross Sales (expected) | $800,000 | | | | | | $200,000 | $250,000 | $350,000 | $400,000 |
| Gross Sales (realized) | $800,000 | | | | | | $200,000 | $250,000 | $350,000 | $400,000 |
| Collections | | | | | | | | | | |
| Month of Sale | $274,000 | $317,275 | | | | | 68,600 | $ 85,750 | | |
| 1 Month After Sale | | | | | 180,000 | 168,000 | 135,000 | 120,000 | | |
| 2 Months After Sale | | | | | 25,000 | 15,000 | 14,000 | 11,250 | | |
| Total Collections | | | $766,500 | $449,150 | | | | | | |
| Purchases | $150,000 | | | | $ 60,000 | $75,000 | $105,000 | $120,000 | | |
| Payments: | | | | | | | | | | |
| 2 Months Before Sale | 90,000 | 54,000 | 50,400 | | | | | | | |
| 1 Month Before Sale | | 60,000 | 36,000 | 33,600 | | | | | | |
| Total Payments | | | $ 86,400 | | | | | $114,000 | | |
| II. Cash Gain (Loss) For Month | | | | | | | | | | |
| Collections | | | $766,500 | | | | | | | |
| Payments | | | | | | | | | | |
| Purchases | | | | | | | | $114,000 | | |
| Labor | | | | | | | | | | |
| 2 Months Before Sale | | | 56,000 | | | | | 80,000 | | |
| 1 Month Before Sale | | | 60,000 | $ 56,000 | $ 45,000 | $40,000 | $ 50,000 | 70,000 | | |
| General/Admin. Exp. | | | 95,000 | | | | | | | |
| Lease | | | 60,000 | | | | | | | |
| Miscellaneous Exp. | | | 40,000 | | | | | | | |
| Taxes | | | | | 90,000 | | | 90,000 | | |
| Interest (on bonds) | | | 80,000 | | | | | | | |
| New Equipment | | | | | | | | 100,000 | | |
| Total Payments | | | $477,400 | | | | | | | |
| Net Cash Gain (Loss) | | | $289,100 | $ 79,050 | | | | | | |
| III. Cash Surplus or Loan Requirement | | | | | | | | | | |
| Cash at Start (no borrowing) | | | $450,000 | $739,100 | | | | | | |
| Cumulative Cash | | | $739,100 | | | | | | | |
| Target Cash Balance | | | $450,000 | | | | | | | |
| Surplus Cash or Total Loans Outstanding to Maintain Target Cash Balance | | | $289,100 | | | | | | | |

**Table 2**

*Daily Cash Budget Worksheet*

| Day: | 1 | 2 | ••• | 5 | ••• | 10 | ••• | 15 | 16 | ••• | 28 | 29 | 30 | 31 |
|---|---|---|---|---|---|---|---|---|---|---|---|---|---|---|
| I. Collections and Payments | | | | | | | | | | | | | | |
| Gross Sales | $ 16,129 | | ••• | $ 16,129 | ••• | $ 16,129 | ••• | $ 16,129 | $ 16,129 | ••• | | | $ 16,129 | $ 16,129 |
| Collections: | | | | | | | | | | | | | | |
| Discount Payers | $ 10,235 | | ••• | | ••• | | ••• | | $ 5,532 | ••• | | | $ 5,532 | $ 5,532 |
| Net Payers | 17,903 | | ••• | | ••• | | ••• | | 17,903 | ••• | | | 17,903 | 9,677 |
| Late Payers | 1,333 | | ••• | | ••• | | ••• | | 1,333 | ••• | | | 1,492 | 1,492 |
| Total Collections | $ 29,471 | $ 29,471 | ••• | $ 29,471 | ••• | $ 29,471 | ••• | $ 29,471 | $ 24,768 | ••• | $ 24,768 | $ 24,768 | $ 24,927 | $ 16,701 |
| Purchases | $ 84,000 | | | | | | | | | | | | | |
| Payments: | | | | | | | | | | | | | | |
| 2 Months Before Sale | | | | | | | | | | | | | | |
| 1 Month Before Sale | | | | $ 36,000 | | | | | | | | | | |
| Total Payments | $0 | $ 0 | ••• | $ 86,400 | ••• | $0 | ••• | $0 | $0 | ••• | $0 | $0 | $0 | $0 |
| II. Cash Gain (Loss) For Day | | | | | | | | | | | | | | |
| Collections | $ 29,471 | $ 29,471 | ••• | $ 29,471 | | $ 29,471 | | $ 29,471 | $ 24,769 | ••• | $ 24,769 | $ 24,769 | $ 24,927 | $ 16,702 |
| Payments: | | | | | | | | | | | | | | |
| Purchases | | | | $ 86,400 | | | | | | | | | | |
| Labor | | | | | | | | | | | | | | |
| 2 Months Before Sale | $ 28,000 | | | | | | | $ 28,000 | | | | | | |
| 1 Month Before Sale | 30,000 | | | | | | | 30,000 | | | | | | |
| General/Admin. Exp. | 47,500 | | | | | | | 47,500 | | | | | | |
| Lease | | | | | | | | | | | | | | |
| Miscellaneous Exp. | 1,290 | | | 1,290 | | 1,290 | | 1,290 | 1,290 | | 1,290 | 1,290 | 1,290 | 1,290 |
| Taxes | | | | | | | | | | | | | | |
| Interest (on bonds) | | | | | | | | 80,000 | | | | | | |
| Total Payments | $106,790 | $ 1,290 | | $ 87,690 | | $ 1,290 | | $186,790 | 1,290 | | $ 1,290 | $ 1,290 | $ 1,290 | $ 1,290 |
| Net Cash Gain (Loss) | ($177,319) | | ••• | ($ 58,219) | ••• | $ 28,181 | ••• | (157,319) | $ 23,479 | ••• | $ 23,479 | $ 23,479 | $ 23,637 | $ 15,412 |
| III. Cash Surplus or Loan Repayment | | | | | | | | | | | | | | |
| Cash at Start (no borrowing) | $450,000 | $312,681 | | $397,224 | ••• | $451,728 | ••• | $592,633 | $435,314 | ••• | $717,056 | ______ | $764,013 | $787,650 |
| Cumulative Cash | $312,681 | 340,862 | | $339,005 | | 479,909 | | | $458,792 | | | | $787,650 | $803,061 |
| Target Cash Balance | 450,000 | 450,000 | | 450,000 | | 450,000 | | ______ | 450,000 | | ______ | ______ | 450,000 | 450,000 |
| Surplus Cash or Total Loans Outstanding to Maintain Target Cash Balance | ($137,319) | ($109,138) | ••• | ($110,995) | ••• | $ 29,909 | ••• | $ 8,792 | ______ | ••• | $290,534 | $314,013 | $337,650 | $353,061 |

PART 5

# Short-Term Investment and Financing

With a cash flow forecast and a financial planning model, the financial manager is now ready to develop an investment and financial strategy. Chapter 14 introduces the basics of the money market, the financial environment in which investment and financing strategies are developed. Chapter 15 then introduces a portfolio approach to investment decision making. Chapter 16 provides a broad overview of short-term financing and how to compare effective costs of bank financing with direct financing. Finally, in Chapter 17, we indicate how to manage cash flows within a multinational firm where cash flows involve one or more non-domestic currencies.

CHAPTER

14

# The Money Market

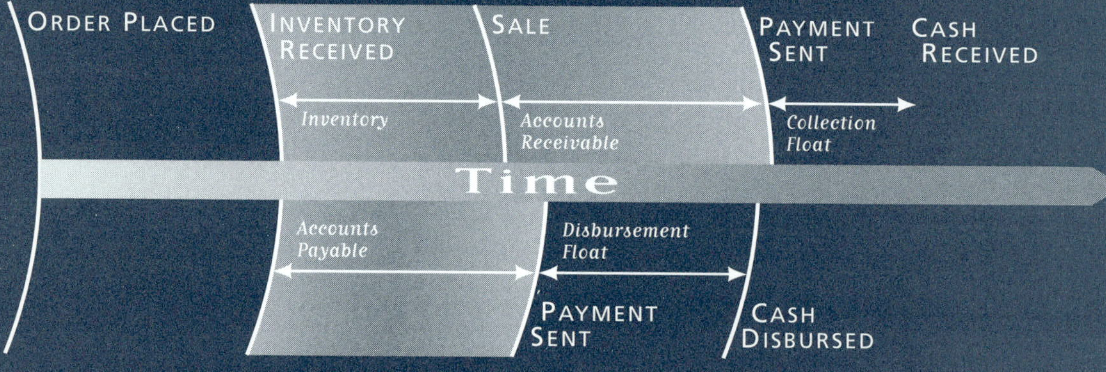

# OBJECTIVES

## *After studying this chapter, you should be able to:*

- specify the important features of money markets.
- define the various money market instruments by category: bank, corporate, federal government, and state and local government.
- calculate taxable-equivalent yield, yield from dividend capture, discount yield, coupon-equivalent yield, and effective annual yield.
- specify types of investment risk and their effect on yields.
- indicate the importance of yield curves and theories that explain the shape of an empirical yield curve.

Toyota Motors, called Toyota Bank by some, piled up cash and securities surpluses amounting to more than $27 billion in 1996, and in early 2003, it still had $13.7 billion in cash and equivalents and another $5 billion in short-term investments. Primarily resulting from a surplus of operating cash flow awaiting long-term reinvestment coupled with a meager 6-percent dividend payout ratio, these funds must be invested carefully. Otherwise, stockholders could justifiably demand that Toyota simply pay large cash dividends and later issue new shares of stock if profitable capital investments became available. General Motors once amassed liquid assets of $9 billion before acquiring Electronic Data Systems (EDS) and Hughes Aircraft for a combined $7.6 billion. Similarly, in the late 1980s, Ford accumulated more than $12 billion, mostly in the form of short-term and very liquid long-term securities. At the time, this was equivalent to approximately $40 per share—40 percent of the market value of Ford's common stock—leading one securities analyst to christen the company Fort Knox. Some of this cash was used to repurchase common stock.[1]

Knowing the available investment options and how to evaluate them is important for three major reasons. First, the company that has worked hard to improve its cash management and forecasting ability has done so to no avail if it cannot increase interest income or reduce interest expense. It makes no sense to leave freed-up cash idle. Second, even when the company is a net borrower during much of the year, it still needs a liquidity reserve—and not all of this would be in the form of cash or untapped short-term borrowing. Recall that cash flows are unsynchronized, uneven, and uncertain. If cash receipts and disbursements (including capital investments and dividends) were perfectly synchronized and even, there would be a much smaller money market. Third, the corporate treasurer must understand the money markets because each investment represents someone else's borrowing. Learning about potential investments implies understanding when and how each security could be used as a way to borrow funds. We develop the borrowing aspects of the money market instruments in Chapter 16.

Short-term investment and borrowing decisions require a mastery of money market concepts, as the following Financial Dilemma illustrates.

[1] For an interesting diagnosis of what Shell should do with its $12.4 billion of cash and short-term securities, see "The $12.4 Billion Problem," *Fortune* (August 4, 1997), p. 125.

## FINANCIAL DILEMMA

### Selecting an Investing Maturity

Dave's workday was just interrupted by a telephone call from his relationship banker recommending that Dave look into longer maturities for his company's investments. Dave has been investing the surplus cash exclusively in overnight repurchase agreements (RPs). He thought he was doing well with his overnight investments considering the bank's earnings credit rate was a miniscule one-half of 1 percent the last he checked. But the banker insists that monies the company will not need for six months will receive higher interest with certificates of deposit (CDs). The normal "premium" for "extending maturities" in this fashion is about 1.4 percent. In fact, the banker suggested that if the company later needs the money on short notice, it could use the CDs as collateral. Dave cannot understand why 6-month CDs should offer a higher yield than overnight investments and wonders what the banker meant by the expression "riding the yield curve." A thought crosses Dave's mind: "Maybe this banker's just trying to sell some of the bank's CDs."

In this first of two investments chapters, we examine the short-term investment alternatives and the risks that account for different yields on specific investments. These risks are related to differences in maturities, default risk, interest rate risk, and other factors. We also discuss the growing focus on event risk, which is prominent in the minds of investors since the September 11 tragedy. In Chapter 15, we show how the investments manager puts information about alternatives and their risks together in assembling a securities portfolio.

## NATURE OF THE MONEY MARKET

The **money market** is composed of all securities maturing in one year or less. It is not a single unified market, but a collection of markets for various short-term securities. Two words for investment alternatives, security and **instrument**, are often used interchangeably, but we will distinguish between them. We define a security as a specific investment issued by a given issuer.[2] An example is the Student Loan Marketing System's $650 million issue of short-term floating rate notes on March 12, 2001, with an interest rate reset each week on the day following the U.S. Treasury bill auction, with the repayment of the notes due (maturing) on September 20, 2001. Each security belongs to a class of similar investments that we define as an instrument. Examples of instruments are agency notes, commercial paper (CP), Treasury bills, CDs, bankers' acceptances (BAs), and RPs. The investment process thus involves selecting an instrument before choosing among all the different issuers' securities for that instrument.

[2] Technically, a security is distinguished by the qualities of marketability and negotiability, but with rare exception, all the money market instruments corporate investors might consider for investment purposes have these qualities.

## Primary and Secondary Markets

The money market does not exist merely in a single location. Rather, there are several key locations where much of the security issuance occurs. The **primary market**, or new issue market, is centered in money centers such as New York City, London, Frankfurt, Singapore, and Hong Kong. Investors can access this over-the-counter market from anywhere because the market consists of telephone and computer hookups among all participating dealers and brokers. It is in the primary market that investment bankers arrange for the marketing and pricing of new issues of money market securities.

Sometimes a group of investment banks, called a syndicate, works together on the marketing and shares the risk involved with bringing a new issue to market—which may or may not be acceptable at the predetermined price. Alternatively, the investment banker may arrange a **private placement**, in which a large institution such as a retirement fund or insurance company buys the entire issue. To distinguish the money market from capital markets, only securities with a current maturity of one year or less are included. When first issued, a 5-year Treasury note has an *original maturity* of five years; one year later, it has a current maturity of four years. Four years after its issue, it has a *current maturity* of one year and changes from a capital market security to a money market security. If traded, it is not considered part of the primary market.

Investors holding the investment to maturity will receive the face value of that investment from the issuer. Not every investor holds the security to maturity, however, necessitating a well-functioning secondary market (in which outstanding issues are traded) for resale. Securities with a current maturity of one year or less bought and sold on the secondary market are considered part of the money market. The **secondary market**, even more so than the primary market, is best thought of as a global network of telecommunication hookups between all potential buyers and sellers. Primary and secondary markets are interrelated because the larger the volume on the resale market, the less risk involved with buying the security on the primary market. Treasury bills and other instruments with smoothly functioning secondary markets can offer a slightly lower interest rate when originally issued, corresponding to this lower risk. Rates on a given instrument with identical maturities and the same issuers can vary depending on whether the quote is on a new issue or a resale. These differences are mainly a result of differences in an instrument's liquidity. An instrument is liquid if it can be sold quickly at or very close to the present market price. An instrument will normally be quite liquid if it has high degrees of *secondary market* breadth, depth, and resiliency. Market **breadth** refers to the number and size of parties that are potential buyers of the instruments. Thus, a **thin market** is one with little participation by buyers and/or sellers. The **depth** of a market is its ability to absorb a large quantity of a security without a major change in the security's price or yield. **Resiliency** exists if many new orders enter the market in response to a temporary imbalance in buy or sell orders that has pushed the price away from its equilibrium level. In a later section of this chapter, we note the instruments whose marketability is compromised by lack of market breadth and depth.

## Wholesale and Retail Markets

Another common way of dividing the money market is into wholesale and retail markets. The **wholesale market** is for large-dollar transactions between large investors. The transaction amount may be large because a group of securities is being sold or because one large denomination security is involved. The **denomination** of a security refers to its **face value**. Much of the dollar volume in the money market is characterized by such trades, in which typical "round lots" are $1 million or more. In contrast, individuals might purchase $500 CDs from their local banks as part of the small-dollar **retail market**. The money market is largely a wholesale market, and we are exclusively interested in that segment because most businesses take part in it. Corporate investors are sometimes labeled institutional investors, along with other large, nonpersonal investors such as pension funds, governments, mutual funds, and insurance companies. Because fixed costs are involved in preparing securities for sale and selling them, the issuer offers a lower yield on retail securities. The growing popularity of money market mutual funds, as an investment both for individuals and businesses, arises from the fact that investors can achieve the higher wholesale market interest rates by pooling their funds with other investors until the fund has large enough sums to invest in large-denomination securities.

## Money Market Interest Rates

Interest rates on money market securities typically move in unison. Rates (or yields, when considered from the perspective of the investor) are only partly the result of supply and demand conditions in the instrument's market. The various instruments are close substitutes for one another, particularly for the short-term investor. Therefore, the major investor(s) and borrower(s) in one instrument's market influence yields in all other markets. The most important common influences arise from the activities of the U.S. Treasury, the Federal Reserve, and daily CD or CP issuers such as Citicorp and General Motors Acceptance Corporation.

The Treasury conducts weekly auctions of Treasury bills, as well as less frequent auctions of notes and bonds, as a means of financing the huge federal debt. These multibillion dollar issues exert tremendous influence on all money markets because of their size and also because Treasury securities constitute an investment alternative for most investors. There is essentially no risk of the Treasury not paying interest and repaying principal on its securities, so risk premiums on corporate or other government securities are priced relative to Treasury securities.

*ROLE OF THE FEDERAL RESERVE* Short-term interest rates in the United States are largely influenced by the Federal Reserve's monetary policy. The Federal Reserve (Fed) directly and indirectly influences interest rates as it carries out its monetary policy. The open-market buying of Treasury securities influences demand and supply conditions. The Fed also sets the discount rate and the Fed funds rate. The **discount rate** is the rate charged depository institutions when they borrow reserves from the Fed to meet their reserve requirements. The **Fed funds rate** is the rate charged on reserve borrowings, mostly overnight, transacted between banks. Whereas the discount rate is not changed often, the Fed funds rate may vary widely even within one day's trading. Alternate Wednesdays experience the most volatile rate swings, as banks jockey to get their reserves up to required levels for Federal Reserve reporting purposes. Except when affected by these technical conditions, Fed funds rate movements tend to underlie movements in all money market rates.

*CORRELATION OF SHORT-TERM INTEREST RATES* Studies find a very high correlation between short-term rates; underlying these rate movements are movements in the Fed funds rate. Rates on the investments that represent close substitutes for the investor—Treasury bills, domestic CDs, CP, and Eurodollar CDs—track very closely with each other, with correlations between these securities all being 0.99 when studied over recent years in the United States (compared with a perfect positive correlation of 1.00). This does not mean that the rates are identical, but that the differences between them tend to persist as rates move up and down together. Some astute corporate investors will watch for temporary divergences between the rates and buy the attractively priced securities. In Exhibit 14–1, you can see the correlation between the Fed funds rate and various short-term interest rates such as the rate for Eurodollar deposits (LIBOR, discussed later), the Prime lending rate, commercial paper, and T-bill rates.

**Exhibit 14–1**

*Correlation between Short-Term Interest Rates and the Fed Funds Rate*

| Index | Correlation with Fed Funds Rate |
|---|---|
| 1-month LIBOR | 0.9921 |
| 3-month LIBOR | 0.9863 |
| Prime rate | 0.9795 |
| 30-day commercial paper | 0.9742 |
| 6-month LIBOR | 0.9722 |
| 60-day commercial paper | 0.9712 |
| 90-day commercial paper | 0.9655 |
| 3-month T-bill | 0.9628 |
| 6-month T-bill | 0.9201 |
| 1-year T-bill | 0.8818 |

Note: These correlations are from monthly data over the period October 1, 1992 to September 30, 2002, as determined by Standard & Poor's.
*Source:* Corporates Department, 2003 Money Market Fund Ratings Criteria, "Correlation of Various Indices," p. 10. Reproduced with permission of Standard & Poor's, a division of the McGraw Hill Companies. Copyright © 2003.

## Tax Status

Money market instruments can also be divided into taxable and tax-advantaged categories. **Taxable instruments** include CP, domestic and Eurodollar certificates of deposit, bankers' acceptances, repurchase agreements, and money market mutual funds invested in these instruments. Interest is fully taxable, as are capital gains.

**Tax-advantaged instruments** are those on which part or all of the income is exempted from taxation or on which the tax is deferred. In most states, there is no state income tax liability for interest income on Treasury securities. Corporations buying another company's stock may exclude 70 percent of the dividends received from taxable income. Municipal obligations, or munis, pay interest that is not taxable for federal income tax purposes. Additionally, interest on munis is often exempted from tax for residents of the state in which the issuer is located. Capital gains on Treasury bills or munis are fully taxable, however.[3] The differential tax treatment of some securities implies that the investor must adjust both taxable and tax-advantaged yields to a common basis for comparison. We will illustrate this adjustment in a later section.

## Market Mechanics and Intermediaries

The **market microstructure** consists of the participants and mechanics involved in making transactions. Other than the buyers and sellers, the key actors in money markets are dealers and brokers. Sales agents and traders also play a role.

**Dealers** typically "take a position" in the security instrument(s) that they trade, meaning they hold an inventory of securities. Independent securities dealers, investment banks, and large commercial banks commonly have individuals that perform the dealer role. Like car dealers, money market dealers profit from the difference between what they pay for

[3] An additional complication is posed by the alternative minimum tax, which applies to individuals and corporations claiming an unusually large number of deductions in a given year. Items normally not taxed may be assessed under the alternative minimum tax.

## FOCUS ON PRACTICE

### *How Important Are Ethics and Trust in the Money Market?*

If power corrupts, and absolute power corrupts absolutely, the classic example is the Salomon Brothers' manipulation of Treasury security issues in the early 1990s. Seizing a large proportion of a given issue in the preliminary trading of these securities, Salomon tacked on abnormally large spreads before reselling the securities. Other dealers among the more than 40 then authorized to deal in government securities subsequently were squeezed because they had already committed to supply securities to their customers at agreed-on prices. None of this would have created a furor except that Salomon went well beyond the legal maximum amount for which a dealer is permitted to bid, in effect cornering the market. Mostly, this was done through fictitious orders placed on behalf of Salomon's customers. The stir was so great that the government opened Treasury security bidding to all parties, not just approved dealers and commercial banks. Additionally, some of Salomon's biggest customers, including the World Bank, quit doing business with the company for three months or more. And this was not a matter of confusion regarding gray areas: A senior U.S. Treasury official was quoted in *The Wall Street Journal* as saying the traders "broke lessons you learned in Sunday School in second grade." Possibly, the difference between primary and secondary market yields will be smaller because of the elimination of fraud and the newly intensified competition.

the security and what they sell it for. At any time, a dealer's profit margin is revealed by the spread between his or her quoted bid (buy) and offer (sell) prices. The spread in large CDs is approximately five basis points (one basis point is 1/100 of 1 percent, so 100 basis points equate to 1 percent), and on CDs issued frequently in large volumes, the spread may even be lower.

Dealers finance this inventory of securities mainly by borrowing funds on an overnight basis. Dealers are exposed to **interest rate risk**—the possibility that interest rates will increase—which causes the prices of existing fixed income securities to drop. This motivates dealers to sell off and replenish their inventory as quickly as possible.[4] When dealers have relatively small supplies of securities and customer demand for those securities increases, dealers may drive prices up and interest rates down as they enter the markets to fill demand, as happened in late 1993.

Trust plays a vital role in transacting business, as most trades are agreed on by telephone, with no written contract. Because the money markets are so dependent on integrity, particularly on the part of dealers, the Salomon Brothers scandal in 1990 and 1991 rocked the markets.

**Brokers** also are middlemen, but they do not inventory the securities; they arrange transactions. When receiving an order, they check around for the security; when located, the brokers execute the trade. They are paid a commission for their services, which may be as small as $1 per $1 million on Fed funds trades. Dealers often work through brokers when trading with other dealers, to hide their identity.

Dealers function as brokers in their role as **sales agents** for banks (bank deposit notes and bank notes) and CP issuers. For a commission, the agent locates buyers for the institution's securities; again, this is without risk because the agent does not have to buy and resell the securities.

---

[4] Generally, this is the case because of financing costs and interest rate risk. However, sometimes the dealer speculates on interest rate movements in the role of a trader.

In addition to their middlemen roles, brokers and dealers sometimes participate as **traders**, trying to profit on anticipated interest rate or currency movements. Here, they are "positioned" in securities not as intermediaries but as traders for their company's own account. When traders guess right, their trading profits add to the revenues gained from brokerage commissions and bid-ask spreads. However, trading is extremely risky when interest rates are volatile.

In their roles as dealers, brokers, sales agents, and traders, money market intermediaries provide market breadth and depth. The result is greater marketability and smaller bid-ask spreads for investors, reducing securities' liquidity risk.

## MONEY MARKET INSTRUMENTS

Treasury professionals invest in a wide array of short-term securities to earn a high yield while preserving the invested capital. Capital preservation guidelines in most companies' investment policies dictate that safety and liquidity be preeminent in investment selection decisions. Security safety implies a very low **default risk** (or credit risk), the possibility that the issuer will not meet contractual obligations to pay interest or repay principal. It also implies that securities with low interest rate risk be selected.

**Liquidity risk** is tied to the marketability of a security—the ability to sell quickly at or very near the current market price. Money market securities are generally both safe and liquid, but there is some variation across the spectrum of instruments. We complete our discussion of risk attributes after surveying the major classes of short-term instruments: bank, corporate, federal government, state and local government, and mixed.

### Bank Instruments

The most convenient method of investing for corporations is to leave the excess cash at the bank. Although corporations cannot legally be paid interest on demand deposit accounts, surplus funds can be swept into overnight investments or invested in the bank's CDs or the parent bank holding company's CDs, other time deposits, or CP. Large banks also offer for corporate investors part or whole interests in loans, known as **loan participations**, and securities backed by credit card receivables or auto loans. These forms of asset securitization have become prevalent in the United States because of the need for banks to increase their capital-to-assets ratio. Banks, especially those with sizable problem loan portfolios, have had difficulty selling new capital stock, necessitating asset sales and slowed loan growth.

*CERTIFICATES OF DEPOSIT* Large-dollar CDs were formerly the favorite instrument of corporate investors, but many money center banks have recently turned to other time deposits to raise additional funds. First offered in 1961 by Citibank, a **certificate of deposit (CD)** is an interest-bearing account having a specific denomination and a specific maturity. Most CDs impose a substantial penalty for early withdrawal, usually three months of interest. To avoid this, a business might invest in a large-dollar **negotiable CD**, which comes in $100,000 and larger denominations. Negotiability means the security can be legally sold and exchanged between investors, circumventing the early withdrawal penalty charged by the issuing bank. On approximately 40 of the largest money centers and super-regional banks' negotiable CDs, there is very good liquidity because of an active secondary market centered in New York City. Investors buy and sell round lots of $1 million or more. Basic information regarding negotiable CDs and other bank-issued instruments, including typical denominations and maturities and major risk attributes, is presented in Exhibit 14–2. The size of the large-dollar CD market is evidenced by the

**Exhibit 14–2**

*Bank Instruments*

| Instrument | Purpose Issued | Denomination | Maturity | Risk Aspects |
|---|---|---|---|---|
| Certificates of deposit | Raise funds to make new loans. | Primary market: $100,000 + (mostly $1 million).<br>Secondary market: round lot is $2–$5 million. | Range: 7 days to 8 years.<br>Typical: 1, 2, 3, 6 months. | Default risk:<br>• only first $100,000 guaranteed by FDIC.<br>• amount of premium not guaranteed if buying on secondary market at premium. |
| Time deposits | Raise funds to make loans. Interbank deposits for domestic correspondent banks and other banks in eurodollar market. | Any amount, except when minimum amount set by bank. | Range: 1 day to 3 months when purchased for short-term investments portfolio. | Liquidity risk:<br>• usually non-negotiable.<br>• fixed maturity.<br>Political risk:<br>• eurodollar time deposits at branches may be vulnerable to expropriation by government. |
| Bankers' acceptances | Finances import or export by having bank accept a time draft drawn on buyer, usually linked to the bank's letter of credit. | Mostly $500,000 to $1 million. | Range: Up to 270 days, with most being 1 to 6 months.<br>Typical: 3 months. | Default risk:<br>• negligible because buyer and bank obliged to pay draft.<br>Liquidity risk:<br>• active secondary market implies little liquidity risk. |
| Loan participations | Risk sharing strategy of lender; also allows bank to relend part or all of loan principal. Substitutes for commercial paper, which banks are prohibited from underwriting. | Varies. | Range: 1 day to 3 months. | Default risk:<br>• investor takes part or all of the default risk when buying part or all of the loan participation. Some issuers are not creditworthy enough to issue commercial paper. Most participations have guarantor.<br>Liquidity risk:<br>• not liquid, no secondary market; whole loans have secondary market. |
| Securitized assets: auto loans, credit cards, other | To take existing assets off the books of the bank while retaining servicing fees. Allows banks to reloan the money. | Varies. | Range: 1–3 years for securities backed by auto loans and credit card receivables. | Default risk:<br>• depends on credit enhancement. Partly mitigated by the portfolio effect of pooling many loans. |

amount of large-denomination deposits outstanding, which totaled about $1.1 trillion at the end of March, 2004.

The **Eurodollar CD** market has grown rapidly, eclipsing the domestic CD market for institutional investors. Eurodollar securities are dollar-denominated deposits held in banks or bank branches outside the United States or in international banking facilities (which can offer Eurodollar deposits only to non-U.S. residents) within the United States. Most Eurodollar deposits are in London-based branches of U.S. or foreign banks, but volume is increasing in Frankfurt and non-European locations such as Hong Kong and Singapore. Eurodollar CDs and other time deposits range from overnight to five years in maturity, but most are six months or shorter. They are mainly used to make dollar-denominated loans to U.S. multinational corporations, to foreign corporations and governments wishing to borrow in dollars, and to domestic banks. The banks borrow funds in the euro market as a substitute for Federal Reserve funds borrowing so that interest rates track fairly closely with the Fed funds rate (refer back to Exhibit 14–1). Eurodollar deposits are not assessed a Federal Deposit Insurance Corporation (FDIC) premium, nor are they required to have reserves held against them. The lower costs to issuers imply higher yields than domestic CDs for the investor. Eurodollar CDs yield slightly less than the **London Interbank Offer Rate (LIBOR)**, the rate at which banks offer term Eurodollar deposits to each other. Liquidity risk is minimal because of an active secondary market.

*OTHER TIME DEPOSITS* Corporate investors rarely invest in domestic time deposits other than CDs because they are illiquid until the principal is repaid at the end of the fixed term. The flexibility of Eurodollar time deposits, which may be structured for the individual company's specific cash needs, makes these attractive investments. Three factors make the Eurodollar time deposits less attractive than other alternatives such as domestic CDs. First, there is no FDIC guarantee. Second, the investor bears the risk that the host country where the deposit is issued may seize foreign investors' funds or at least block dollar outflows. Third, if the investor is basing the maturity decision on a flawed cash forecast, illiquidity is problematic. As with nonnegotiable CDs, the investor can get around the illiquidity of time deposits by arranging beforehand for the option to make a deposit-collateralized loan. Furthermore, many bank **sweep accounts**, in which surplus funds are moved out to investments on an overnight basis, move funds to 1-day Eurodollar deposit accounts. Bookkeeping entries move the funds out and back into the company's domestic account.

Two unique time deposits that have recently appeared and grown rapidly in the domestic money market are bank deposit notes and bank notes. **Bank deposit notes** range from nine months to 30 years in maturity and have an active secondary market. The issuing bank's credit quality is the key for assessing default risk, but the first $100,000 is federally guaranteed. Not so for **bank notes**, which technically are not deposits and therefore avoid FDIC insurance premiums (and also forfeit deposit insurance coverage). Corporate investors invest mainly in top-rated bank deposit notes and bank notes.[5] Suntrust Banks had to pay eight basis points above the 3-month LIBOR (about 50 basis points above a 3-month Treasury bill) on its 5-year A1-rated floating rate bank notes, issued in the late 1990s. Maturities range from one month to 15 years, with a minimum denomination typically being $250,000.

*BANKERS' ACCEPTANCES* Corporate time drafts that are accepted, or guaranteed, for payment by the issuer's bank are called **bankers' acceptances (BAs)**. Acceptances mainly are used to finance international trade but also have been used in domestic transactions.

---

[5] See the brief discussion of these securities in Alan Seidner's *1990 Supplement*, cited in the end-of-chapter references.

They arise mainly from the difficulty businesses in the exporting country have in assessing the creditworthiness of importers. Having the importer's bank guarantee payment implies two parties are liable for the importer's time draft: the importer and its bank. The creditworthiness of the accepting bank is substituted for that of the importer, leading exporters to request guarantee by an AAA-rated bank.

A BA often is issued consequent to a bank letter of credit (LOC), which states that the bank will pay the amount owed if the buyer defaults. Once the exporter receives the accepted draft from the importer's bank, it can endorse and sell it to receive immediate cash because acceptances are negotiable instruments. The difference between the discounted price at which the acceptance is sold and its face value paid at maturity is the interest return to the investor. Liquidity is good because of an active secondary market. Since their inception in the 1920s in the United States, there never has been a default on a BA, except when a counterfeit acceptance was executed. Bankers' acceptances yield 0.5 to 2 percent more than Treasury bills of the same maturity. Details regarding denominations, maturities, and default risk are provided in Exhibit 14–2.

*LOAN PARTICIPATIONS* After a bank or syndicate of banks arranges a large loan, part or all of the loan may be sold off in the form of a loan participation. Banks may sell loans to other banks or corporate investors. The bank arranging the loan receives fees from loan originating (setting up the documentation and payment structure) and servicing (processing interest payments and principal repayment and passing correct proceeds to loan participants). The bank thereby maintains its capital-to-assets ratio while increasing profits. Although the originating bank is charged with ensuring that the borrower adheres to the payment structure, the investor(s) assumes the loan's default risk. Many times, the borrowers are companies that are not creditworthy enough to issue securities directly, suggesting that the corporate investor buying a participation must do an extensive analysis of the borrower's financial statements. Correspondingly, yields are higher than CD or CP yields. Aggressive cash managers, such as those at Chrysler, invest in 30-day loan participations for the 1/8 percent additional yield they provide above standard overnight investments such as RPs. The lack of marketability makes participations illiquid. On the positive side, studies done by rating agencies such as Moody's and Fitch indicate that *post-default* loan recoveries are much higher (70 percent to 92 percent on secured bank loans) than on subordinated, unsecured corporate bonds (about 34 percent). The recovery rates are highly variable, depending on the quality of collateral and other loan covenants. Other features of participations are included in the bank instrument exhibit.

*SECURITIZED ASSETS* Credit card receivables and automobile loans also have become candidates for corporate investors by being transformed into asset-backed securities. Corporate investors may then buy these securities, which are backed by pools consisting of the original loans or other assets. As with loan participations, the effect is to improve capital ratios and enhance bank liquidity because of the transformation of a future stream of cash flows to a lump-sum present receipt. The captive finance subsidiaries of automobile manufacturers and other manufacturers' leasing subsidiaries also offer securitized loans, some backed by leases.[6] Additionally, receivables of all types such as insurance and mutual fund receivables and even trade receivables are being securitized: excluding mortgage-backed and home equity loan-backed securities, the amount of asset-backed securitizations grew from $108 billion in 1995 to $348 billion at the beginning of 2004. These asset-backed securities (ABS) are not held by most short-term investors because of the maturities. The

---

[6] See Moody's Investor Service, "Securitization and Its Effect on the Credit Strength of Financial Services Companies: Moody's Special Comment" (November 1996). Moody's Chief Credit Officer Kenneth J. H. Pinkes and senior analyst Eric Goldstein note that the coupling of securitization and information technology is fundamentally altering the structure and competitive environment of financial services.

maturities range from one to three years on automobile loan securities and one and a half to two years on credit card receivables, subjecting the short-term investor to interest rate risk. The securities are quite often overcollateralized in the sense of having more receivables or loans than the aggregate face value of the securities issued. The issuer (if a bank) or a bank (through a LOC) also may guarantee security interest and principal payments. Both credit enhancement measures effectively reduce default risk, allowing AAA-rated securities to be issued in 2003 for as little as 52 basis points (AAA credit card-backed securities) or 38 basis points (AAA auto loan-backed securities) above Treasury securities with comparable maturities. The inclusion of many loans or credit card accounts in a pool, which in turn backs the individual securities, diversifies the default risk of individual accounts.

## Corporate Instruments

Next to bank deposits and securities, the most popular securities for corporate investors are instruments issued by other corporations. One reason for this is that CP is now widely available for overnight investing. Corporate short-term instruments traditionally have been issued to raise funds to finance seasonal working capital needs, but increasingly they fund permanent current asset and fixed asset investments. The latter may occur as the borrower awaits lower long-term interest rates, or a higher stock price. When this comes about, the short-term borrowing will be retired as bonds or stock, or both, are issued. Medium-sized and larger corporations commonly issue three securities that appeal to corporate investors: CP,[7] floating-rate notes, and common or preferred stock with high dividend yields.

*COMMERCIAL PAPER* Banks have lost much of their prime corporate lending business to the issuers of CP. Total dollar volume outstanding has exploded from $120 billion in 1981 to $1.4 trillion in 2004—exceeding every other money market instrument including Treasury bills. Historically, almost all CP was unsecured, meaning there was no collateral backing it up in the event of a default. High-quality issuers have always been able to issue CP, but the market now includes medium-quality issuers offering credit enhancement in the form of collateral (over $760 billion of asset-backed CP outstanding in 2004) or a backup line of credit from their banks. Often used in conjunction with a letter of credit, which guarantees the investor of principal repayment, the use of backup bank financing allows the bank's credit rating to be substituted for the issuer's credit rating. Most CP is issued by companies in the financial sector, including bank holding companies, but nonfinancial issuers now issue about $170 billion of unsecured paper. The average maturity of CP issued in the United States as of year-end 2003 was 45 days. Typical denomination, maturity, and risk attributes are provided in Exhibit 14–3. Some paper is issued "direct," in which the borrower sells it to the investor without a dealer being involved. The GE Capital Corporation issues in Exhibit 14–4 (pages 493–496) illustrate this. Most industrial paper, which can be bought in denominations as small as $1,000, is sold through dealers. Some of the basic questions you may have about GE's commercial paper issuance are addressed in Exhibit 14–5 (page 497). Yield calculations and risk ratings are discussed later in the chapter. Commercial paper investment decision making is also illustrated later in the chapter and is covered in greater detail in Chapter 16 because of the importance of this instrument to corporate borrowing.

A hybrid instrument related to CP is being issued with increasing frequency: the master note. **Master notes** are open-ended CP, allowing investors to add or withdraw monies on a daily basis, up to a specified maximum amount. The interest rate paid is tied to the CP rate, and the investor is notified of the newly revised rate daily. Investors determine the

[7] CP is issued by bank holding companies, as well as finance companies and other nonbank issuers.

**Exhibit 14–3**

*Corporate Instruments*

| Instruments | Purpose Issued | Denomination | Maturity | Risk Aspects |
|---|---|---|---|---|
| Commercial paper | Typically unsecured borrowing to support working capital, especially seasonal needs. Sometimes used as bridge borrowing until long-term rates are more favorable. Issued mainly by finance companies, bank holding companies, and insurance companies but also by large and some mid-sized non-financial companies. | Primary market: As low as $1,000 but almost always $100,000+ and commonly $1 million.<br>Secondary market: round lot is $5 million. | Range: 1 day to 270 days.<br>Typical: 5–45 days, 30 days most common. | Default risk:<br>• usually low because of credit quality of typical issuers or of bank providing backup letter of credit.<br>Liquidity risk:<br>• dependent on quality of issuer, but higher than on Treasuries because individual issues are too disimilar to assemble into large blocks for secondary market trading.<br>• very large issuers such as GMAC are exceptions, offering excellent liquidity. |
| Floating-rate notes | Raise funds to make loans. Mostly issued by finance companies and banks. | Primary market: $1,000–$100,000.<br>Secondary market: $5 million is round lot. | Range: 9 months to 30 years. 20% are 9 months to 2 years, 60% are 2–5 years, and 20% are more than 5 years. However, interest rate resets may be as often as weekly. | Default risk:<br>• can be high, depending on issuer.<br>Event risk:<br>• as with bonds, investor is concerned about subsequent issues of bonds or preferred stock, which imply lower coverage ratios on existing notes.<br>Liquidity risk:<br>• depends on dealer's willingness to buy back from investor. |
| Common or preferred stock with high dividend yield<br>OR<br>Adjustable-rate preferred stock | As with all common or preferred stock, issued to raise long-term funds in support of capital projects and permanent working capital. The issues of special interest to corporate investors are those with high dividend yields, including those whose yields adjust to prevailing interest rate conditions. Utilities account for many of these issues. | No typical price. | Permanent financing unless later repurchased.<br>Rates on adjustable issues typically reset every 49 days because corporate investors must hold at least 46 days to qualify for 70% dividend exclusion. | Default risk:<br>• varies greatly, depends on issuer. Utilities have small bankruptcy risk, with some exceptions.<br>Risk of declining stock price:<br>• on issue without periodic reset, exposure to stock price decline often hedged with put options. Always a big concern for stock investors, regardless of issue type or issuer.<br>Event risk:<br>• can be a major concern on utility issuers or other capital-intensive issuers, because of possibility of subsequent bond and stock issues reducing coverage ratios. On utilities, additional concerns are accidents at nuclear generating plants and the possibility of cost hikes or of rate hike proposals being turned down by state energy commissions. |

## Exhibit 14–4

*Money Rate Table*

**MONEY RATES**

Thursday, January 22, 2004

| **Prime Rate:** The base rate on corporate loans posted by at least 75% of the nation's 30 largest banks. | **Rate** | **Effective Date** |
|---|---|---|
| | 4.00% | 06/27/03 |

| **Discount Rate:** The charge on loans to depository institutions by the Federal Reserve Banks. | **Rate** | **Effective Date** |
|---|---|---|
| | 2.00% | 06/25/03 |

| **Federal Funds:** Reserves traded among commercial banks for overnight use in amounts of $1 million or more. FOMC target rate effective 06/25/03. | **Rate** | |
|---|---|---|
| | 1.0000% | FOMC target rate |
| | 1.0313% | High |
| | 1.0000% | Low |
| | 1.0000% | Near Closing Bid |
| | 1.0625% | Offered |

*Source:* Prebon Yamane (U.S.A.) Inc.

| **Call Money:** The charge on loans to brokers on stock exchange collateral. | **Rate** | **Effective Date** |
|---|---|---|
| | 2.75% | 06/25/03 |

*Source:* Reuters

| **Commercial Paper:** Commercial paper placed directly by General Electric Capital Corp. | **Rate** | **Period** |
|---|---|---|
| | 1.02% | 30 to 62 days |
| | 0.80% | 63 to 73 days |
| | 1.03% | 74 to 153 days |
| | 0.80% | 154 to 167 days |
| | 1.06% | 168 to 202 days |
| | 1.07% | 203 to 227 days |
| | 1.10% | 228 to 270 days |

*continued*

**Euro Commercial Paper:**
Commercial paper placed directly by General Electric Capital Corp.

| Rate | Period |
|---|---|
| 2.03% | 30 days |
| 2.03% | Two Months |
| 2.04% | Three Months |
| 2.04% | Four Months |
| 2.05% | Five Months |
| 2.05% | Six Months |

**Dealer Commercial Paper:**
High-grade unsecured notes sold through dealers by major corporations.

| Rate | Period |
|---|---|
| 1.03% | 30 days |
| 1.03% | 60 days |
| 1.04% | 90 days |

**Certificates of Deposit:**
Typical rates in the secondary market.

| Rate | Period |
|---|---|
| 1.04% | One Month |
| 1.05% | Three Months |
| 1.11% | Six Months |

**Banker's Acceptances:**
Offered rates of negotiable, bank-backed business credit instruments typically financing an import order.

| Rate | Period |
|---|---|
| 1.03% | 30 days |
| 1.03% | 60 days |
| 1.04% | 90 days |
| 1.05% | 120 days |
| 1.06% | 150 days |
| 1.08% | 180 days |

**London Late Eurodollars:**

| Rate | Period |
|---|---|
| 1.00 - 1.03% | One Month |
| 1.03 - 1.06% | Two Months |
| 1.04 - 1.07% | Three Months |
| 1.05 - 1.09% | Four Months |
| 1.08 - 1.10% | Five Months |
| 1.09 - 1.12% | Six Months |

**London Interbank Offered Rates Rate Period (LIBOR):**
In the London market based on quotations at 16 major banks. Effective rate for contracts entered into two days from date appearing at top of this column.

| Rate | Period |
|---|---|
| 1.10000% | One Month |
| 1.12000% | Three Months |
| 1.17000% | Six Months |
| 1.37000% | One Year |

| **Euro Libor:** British Banker's Association average of interbank offered rates for euro deposits in the London market based on quotations at 16 major banks. Effective rate for contracts entered into two days from date appearing at top of this column. | Rate | Period |
|---|---|---|
| | 2.07050% | One Month |
| | 2.07125% | Three Months |
| | 2.08875% | Six Months |
| | 2.17063% | One Year |

| **Euro Interbank Offered Rates Rate Period (EURIBOR):** European Banking Federation-sponsored rate among 57 Euro zone banks. | Rate | Period |
|---|---|---|
| | 2.074% | One Month |
| | 2.075% | Three Months |
| | 2.095% | Six Months |
| | 2.175% | One Year |

| **Foreign Prime Rates:** These rate indications aren't directly comparable; lending practices vary widely by location. | Rate | Country |
|---|---|---|
| | 4.250% | Canada |
| | 2.000% | Germany |
| | 1.375% | Japan |
| | 2.130% | Switzerland |
| | 3.750% | Britain |

| **Treasury Bills:** | Rate | Period |
|---|---|---|
| Results of the Monday, January 19, 2004, auction of short-term U.S. government bills, sold at a discount from face value in units of $1,000 to $1 million: | 0.875% | 13 Weeks |
| | 0.950% | 26 Weeks |
| For results of Tuesday, January 20, 2004 auction: | 0.800% | 4 weeks |

| **Overnight Repurchase Rate:** Dealer financing rate for overnight sale and repurchase of Treasury securities. | Rate |
|---|---|
| | 0.99% |

*Source:* Reuters

| **Freddie Mac:** Posted yields on 30-year mortgage commitments. | Rate | |
|---|---|---|
| | Standard Conventional Fixed-Rate Mortgages | |
| | 5.250% | Delivery within 30 days |
| | 5.330% | Delivery within 60 days |
| | One-Year Adjustable Rate Mortgages | |
| | 3.38% | 2% Rate Capped |

*Source:* Reuters

*continued*

| **Fannie Mae:** Posted yields on 30 year mortgage commitments (priced at par). | **Rate** | |
|---|---|---|
| | Standard Conventional Fixed-Rate Mortgages | |
| | 5.350% | Delivery within 30 days |
| | 5.440% | Delivery within 60 days |
| | One-Year Adjustable Rate Mortgages | |
| | 2.95% | 2% Rate Capped |

*Source:* Reuters

| **Merrill Lynch Ready Assets Trust:** Annualized average rate of return after expenses for the past 30 days; not a forecast of future returns. | **Rate** |
|---|---|
| | 0.52 % |

*Source:* Reuters

| **Consumer Price Index:** Bureau of Labor Statistics. For Month of: December | **Index** | **% Chg*** |
|---|---|---|
| | 184.3 | 1.9 % |

* Percent change from year earlier



dollar amount their companies wish to invest at that rate. Most of the master note arrangements are offered by super-regional bank holding companies, as opposed to nonfinancial companies. Master note arrangements are brokered by firms such as Merrill Lynch.

*FLOATING-RATE NOTES* Medium-term notes are unsecured promissory instruments issued by corporations in maturities of 270 days to 10 years. These notes are distinguished by the fact that they are continuously offered to investors. Securities with original maturities greater than 270 days must be registered with the Securities and Exchange Commission (SEC), so issuing corporations must be willing to accept the delays and costs involved.[8] These notes are generally **noncallable**, implying that the investor need not worry about the issuer forcing a buyback of the securities if interest rates rise subsequent to issuance. A total of $516 billion in medium-term notes was outstanding in the United States at the end of 2002.

[8] Fixed costs associated with SEC registration are reduced somewhat if the company executes a *shelf* registration, whereby it is approved for an ongoing, multiyear issuance program. One estimate places the legal, investment banking, documentation, and SEC registration costs at between 0.8 and 1 percent ($800,000 to $1 million for a typical $100 million medium-term note offering, issued by a creditworthy issuer). Savings from fewer registrations can therefore be significant. Merrill Lynch underwrites most medium-term notes, and more information on these notes is available in the occasionally issued *Medium-term notes: An investment opportunity*. New York: Merrill Lynch Money Markets.

**Exhibit 14–5**

*Frequently Asked Questions Regarding the Largest Commercial Paper Issuer*

Frequently Asked Questions—U.S. Dollar Commercial Paper

**Where can I find rate information?**
Our rates are available electronically:

| Source | Page |
|---|---|
| Bloomberg | GECP or DOCP |
| Bridge/Telerate | 25 and 33 |
| Reuters | GECP 1 |
| Internet | cpmarket.com |
| Wall Street Journal | Section C-Money Rates |
| Or call GE Capital | (800) 525-5471 |

**Is there a minimum investment amount?**
Yes. $100,000 for transactions of seven days or more. For one to six days, the minimum amount is $500,000.

**What is the range of maturities?**
From 1 to 270 days.

**Are there any fees?**
No. GE Capital issues commercial paper directly. When sold this way to an institutional investor, there is no fee, spread or commission paid to GE Capital.

**Do I need a custodial account?**
Yes. GE Capital settles its commercial paper transactions through the Depository Trust Company (DTC). DTC will deliver the commercial paper transaction in book entry form to your custodian.

**How do I place a transaction?**
Transactions can be completed by phone via a sales representative. Alternatively, an institutional investor may place a transaction online through Bloomberg (GECP) or through the Internet at cpmarket.com.

**How do I get started or get more information?**
Call (800) 525-5471 or e-mail cpdirect@ge.com.

**Can I buy commercial paper as an individual investor?**
Not directly. GE Capital sells its commercial paper directly to institutional investors only. There are other investment options available to the individual investor in the Investment Opportunities section of this Web site.

> Corporate Home > Products & Solutions > Financial Services > Our Commitment > Our Company > FAQs > Contact Us > Privacy Policy > Accessibility Statement > Terms and Conditions

*Source:* © 2004 General Electric, **http://www.ge.com/en/company/investor/fixed_income/fixed_income_faqs.htm.** Accessed online 1/24/04.

Short-term investors are most attracted to one form of medium-term notes, the **floating-rate note**. The interest rate on these notes is reset either daily, weekly, monthly, quarterly, or semiannually. Yields are pegged to either the Treasury bill rate, prime rate, LIBOR, or a composite CP rate. Except during the period between interest rate resetting, the investor is shielded against interest rate risk. An example is the Student Loan Marketing Association's (Sallie Mae) short-term floating-rate notes mentioned earlier, which are priced at a spread (or some amount above) of the 91-day U.S. Treasury bill. The interest rate is reset each week on the calendar day following that week's Treasury bill auction. Investors can add to their holdings of these notes each month because of the regularity of Sallie Mae issues of short-term floating-rate notes.

*HIGH DIVIDEND YIELD STOCK* When money market interest rates drop to historically low levels, as in the early 2000s, Treasury professionals look to dividend capture and other strategies to maintain attractive yields. Dividend capture simply means buying a common or preferred stock shortly before it pays its dividend or buying a preferred stock having an adjustable dividend payment.[9] Utilities and some banks pay large dividends relative to their common stock's price, and almost all preferred stock is high in yield. High yields attract income-oriented investors who by choice or necessity cannot wait for capital gains. Corporate treasurers investing surplus funds are willing to take the risk that the stock might drop in price because of the high yield that can be captured. This strategy is enhanced if the investor can invest large-dollar amounts, because the 3- to 5-percent commission on a small purchase (and paid again on the subsequent resale) would negate stocks' typical yield advantage over safer investments. The federal income tax deduction of 70 percent of intercorporate dividends (if the stock is held at least 46 days) makes dividend-paying investments even more attractive. Because only 30 percent of the income is taxable, the investor in the 34-percent tax bracket retains 89.8 percent [100% − (30% × 0.34)] of its income instead of only 66 percent of it (100% − 34%). Put another way, it pays tax on the dividend income at a rate of only 10.2 percent if it is in the 34-percent tax bracket. We illustrate the dividend capture yield and the taxable equivalent yield from dividend capture in a later section.

In some market eras, investors earn substantial returns using dividend capture. Illustrating, corporate investors willing to endure the price risk on a diversified portfolio of adjustable-rate preferred stock were rewarded with a 1991 total return of almost 20 percent, even after subtracting transaction costs. By contrast, Treasury bill yields averaged only 5 percent in 1991. The two dividend capture strategies that can be used are short-term captures of dividends paid on high-yield common or preferred stock and purchase and long-term holding of preferred stock whose dividends are adjusted to prevailing money market interest rates. Some of the largest users of high-yield captures in the 1980s were Japanese insurance companies, which at the time were required to invest most of their premiums in income-producing investments. Japanese regulators relaxed the mandate in 1987, however, and the insurers largely abandoned the practice. We return to this form of dividend capture in Chapter 15, in which we evaluate portfolio strategies, because it represents an important active strategy.

Preferred stock on which the dividend is reset quarterly [**adjustable-rate preferred stock (ARPS)**] or every 7, 28, 35, or 49 days through an auction bidding process [**auction preferred stock (APS)**] emerged in the early 1980s as a vehicle to gain dividend income. Although both types of preferred stock protect against interest rate risk, only the APS has survived as a viable investment. All purchases and sales are made at the original issue price (par), insulating the investor from price fluctuations related to interest rate changes. About 10 percent of outstanding preferred stock is APS, but more noteworthy is the fact that about 60 percent of new issues are of this form. Yields move within range of a maximum

[9] Dividend yield is computed as the annual dividend per share divided by the current stock price.

of 100 percent and a minimum of 59 percent of the 60-day CP rate but may be higher or lower depending on the issuer. The APS offers some liquidity, because investors can sell their $100,000 units at each auction. Illiquidity can still be a problem, however. If insufficient bids are offered at an auction for the amount of stock present investors wish to sell, the auction is said to have failed, and the issuer must pay a penalty in the form of a higher dividend rate—typically 100 to 120 percent of CP rates. The investor is stuck with an illiquid investment until the next auction. The way around this problem is to diversify across issuers by investing in a mutual fund holding APS.

### Federal Government Instruments

Because corporate investors wish to preserve their principal when investing surplus cash, securities issued by the U.S. Treasury or by federal government agencies are very attractive. Treasury securities have the lowest default risk of any security available worldwide.

*U.S. TREASURY SECURITIES* Investors seeking the highest degree of safety possible prefer bills, notes, and bonds issued by the U.S. Treasury. Backed by the full faith and credit of the federal government, default risk on these securities is considered to be almost nonexistent. Maturing securities can be paid off with tax revenues, through money creation (through Fed purchase of the securities, which expands reserves and ultimately the money supply), or by rolling over the borrowing by replacing the maturing securities with newly issued securities. Liquidity of Treasury securities is also unequaled, because the secondary markets experience daily volumes that dwarf the stock market. In addition to the high degree of safety and liquidity, interest income from Treasury securities is exempted from state and local income taxes. Treasury bills are offered in an auction held usually every Tuesday for 4-week, and every Monday for 3-month and 6-month maturities.[10] Notes and bonds are sold monthly and quarterly (technically, on an as-needed basis), with notes having original maturities of two, three, five, and 10 years, and bonds having original maturities beyond 10 years. The Treasury recently started issuing "Inflation Index Notes" with maturities of five and 10 years. The Treasury issues these quarterly on the 15th of January, April, July, and October. Exhibit 14–6 profiles the typical Treasury auction schedule

**Exhibit 14–6**

*U.S. Treasury Auction Schedule*

| Treasury Security | Maturities | Expected Schedule | Minimum Face Value |
|---|---|---|---|
| Treasury bills | 4 weeks, 3 and 6 months | Weekly | $1,000 |
| Treasury notes | 2 years | Monthly | $5,000 |
| | 3 years, 5 years | Quarterly: Feb., May, Aug., Nov. | $1,000 |
| | 10 years | Quarterly: Feb., May, Aug., Nov. | $1,000 |

*Sources:* (1) **http://www.publicdebt.treas.gov/of/ofsectable.htm** (2) Fidelity Investments.

[10] On occasion, the Treasury also sells short-term "cash management bills" that provide interim financing in anticipation of tax collections and have maturities up to two months.

along with maturities and minimum face values. The treasurer investing for the short-term generally considers notes and bonds when their current maturities are one year or less but may extend maturities for the normally higher yield.

Investors may make two types of bids when buying new issues of Treasury securities in the primary market. **Competitive bids** are mainly entered by financial institutions, including dealers such as Salomon Brothers. Competitive bidding is preceded by close watching of the secondary market for existing securities, right up to the time of the new issue. Competitive bidders hope to receive the highest yield possible, while still being awarded some of the securities. Investors willing to accept the yield of accepted competitive bids enter a **noncompetitive bid.**[11] Investors may bid directly through a "tender offer" to the nearest Federal Reserve District Bank or through a broker or commercial bank. Investors not wishing to participate in the new issue auction may defer until a short time after the auction and purchase the security in the secondary market. Refer to Exhibit 14–7 for additional details on Treasury securities.

*AGENCY INSTRUMENTS* For a slightly higher default risk and less liquidity, investors can gain higher yields on federal agency securities than on Treasury securities with similar maturities. **Agencies** are securities issued by governmental agencies and several private financing institutions that have governmental backing. The securities' proceeds are used to support lending to farmers (Farm Credit Administration), savings and loan associations (Federal Home Loan Bank), mortgages (Federal Home Loan Mortgage Corporation, or Freddie Mac; Federal National Mortgage Association, or Fannie Mae; and the Government National Mortgage Association, known as Ginnie Mae), and federally guaranteed student loans (Student Loan Marketing Association, or Sallie Mae). Freddie Mac and Ginnie Mae typically buy mortgages from the originating lenders, pool them, and then package them into small-denomination pass-through certificates.

Mortgage-backed securities, although the most prominent of agency securities, are not normally well suited to the corporate short-term investor because of uneven cash flows, interest rate risk, and prepayment risk. Uneven cash flows result from the fact that part of the principal is returned each month along with interest. Interest rate risk applies because these are mostly fixed-income securities; they are backed by fixed-rate mortgages (although adjustable-rate mortgages also are available). Prepayment risk refers to a return of principal whenever a mortgage in the pool is paid off because of homeowner relocation or a drop in general interest rates, which triggers refinancing.

Discount notes and short-term coupon securities are appropriate for the money market portfolio. Although not exempted from state and local income taxes, they are considered to be very low in default risk because of the belief that they are a moral obligation of the federal government on which Congress and the President would never allow a default. The liquidity of agency securities can be quite good, but this is predicated on the willingness of the dealer from which they were purchased to buy them back. The combination of these risk factors causes agency yields to rise slightly above comparable-maturity Treasury securities. Consult Exhibit 14–7 for further details on agencies.

## State and Local Instruments

Municipal securities (munis) are issued by any governmental authority below the federal level: states, counties, localities, and school districts. They generally fund water treatment, sewage, pollution control, bridges, or turnpikes, but at times will fund projects such as

[11] Treasury securities are now sold at "single-price auctions." According to the Bureau of Public Debt, "In a single-price auction, all successful competitive bidders and all noncompetitive bidders are awarded securities at the price equivalent to the highest accepted rate or yield of accepted competitive tenders." **http://www.publicdebt.treas.gov/sec/secfaq.htm**.

## Exhibit 14–7

*Federal Government Instruments*

| Instruments | Purpose Issued | Denomination | Maturity | Risk Aspects |
|---|---|---|---|---|
| Treasury bills | U.S. Treasury raises money to finance U.S. debt and current year's deficit spending. | Primary market: $1,000+, in multiples of $1,000.<br>Secondary market: round lot is $1 million. | Range:<br>3 months<br>6 months<br>1 year | Default risk:<br>• none, because of taxing and money creation abilities of the issuer.<br>Liquidity risk:<br>• none if have $1 million block for secondary market resale.<br>Interest rate risk:<br>• insignificant on 3-month, small on 6-month, of concern on 1-year. |
| Treasury notes and bonds | U.S. Treasury raises money to finance U.S. debt and current year's deficit spending. | Primary market:<br>Notes:<br>• 2-year notes have minimum of $5,000, then multiples of $5,000.<br>• 3-, 5-, 7-, and 10-year notes have $1,000 minimum, then multiples of $1,000.<br>Bonds: same as longer-term notes.<br>Secondary market: $1 million is round lot. | Notes: 2–5, 7, 10 years.<br>Bonds: >10 years, mainly 20 or 30 years. | Default risk:<br>• none, for same reasons as on Treasury bills.<br>Liquidity risk:<br>• secondary markets do not have same breadth or depth as Treasury bill market.<br>Interest rate risk:<br>• substantial except on seasoned issue with short current maturity. |
| Government agencies:<br>• Discount notes<br>• Coupon securities | U.S. government agency securities issued by the Farm Credit System, Federal Home Loan Banks, and the Federal National Mortgage Association. Provide bridge financing until agency can issue longer-term securities or when the rate on long-term securities is relatively high and agency does not want to lock in that rate. | Primary: $1,000 minimum.<br>Secondary:<br>Discount Notes:<br>mainly $5–$10 million but up to $50 million.<br>Coupon Securities:<br>mainly $500,000 but up to $10 million. | Discount: most <6 months, with 3 months most common.<br>Coupon: range is from overnight to 360 days. | Default risk:<br>• low, but difficult to estimate because of uncertainty over whether government will honor in event of default.<br>Liquidity risk:<br>• sporadic liquidity, based on dealer's willingness to rebuy.<br>Interest rate risk:<br>• low on discount notes and short-term coupon securities. Significant on longer-term agencies, such as those issued by the Government National Mortgage Association (Ginnie Mae).<br>Event risk:<br>• can be a major concern on mortgage-backed securities because of the prepayment risk involved. On shorter-term notes, the major concern is changing regulation or legislation affecting governmental agencies. |

baseball stadiums, dormitories, or even private-purpose projects for nonprofit organizations or businesses. Munis are exempt from federal income tax, except for private-purpose projects. Tax-exempt securities appeal to corporations that are in the higher federal income tax brackets, because the **taxable-equivalent yield** makes these securities yield more on an after-tax basis than comparable taxable securities. The taxable-equivalent yield is the nominal (stated) yield divided by (1 − corporation's marginal tax rate).

Most municipal securities are **general obligation securities**, meaning the backing for the interest and principal payments is simply future general revenues and the issuer's capacity to raise taxes. Examples are **tax anticipation notes, revenue anticipation notes**, and **bond anticipation notes**, which provide working capital financing for states and localities as they await anticipated revenues from tax collections, other sources of revenue, or upcoming bond issuance, respectively. Exhibit 14–8 describes the essential features of municipal instruments of interest to corporate short-term investors.

Municipal securities also may be **revenue securities**, which tie security cash flows to pledged revenue from the facilities being financed: for example, rental revenue from a convention center or tolls from a bridge or toll road.

Longer-term bonds also found in some corporate portfolios because of their periodically reset interest rates are known as **variable-rate demand notes**. If investors do not prefer the reset interest rate, which is a function of supply and demand factors in this specialized market, they can put (sell) the bond back to the issuer at par. Between reset dates, the securities are very illiquid, however, as a result of a thin secondary market. The interest rate reset and put feature imply that 20- or 30-year maturities do not pose much interest rate risk. These notes are often backstopped by a bank line of credit, which guarantees the securities if the issuer defaults or if put-back securities cannot be resold to new investors. They are often issued to support construction of educational facilities, hospitals, and sewage projects. They will continue to be popular because of the inadequate supply of anticipation notes available to buyers of tax-exempt securities.

States and localities also issue some **tax-exempt CP**. The risks are very similar to those of anticipation notes. These securities are very illiquid because of the absence of a secondary market.

We have covered the major money market instruments offered by banks, corporations, the U.S. government, and state and local governments. We now conclude our discussion of short-term alternatives by looking at some creative hybrids that may invest in a cross section of instruments. The repackaging involved in what we term *mixed instruments* offers tailoring to the specific desires of the investor.

## Mixed Instruments

We address three popular mixed instruments: money market mutual funds, RPs, and sweep accounts. One similarity that they share is the ability to invest surplus cash on an overnight (actually 1-day) basis. Basic features are provided in Exhibit 14–9.

*MONEY MARKET MUTUAL FUNDS* A **money market mutual fund** is a company that invests in short-term securities with funds pooled from numerous individuals or institutions. A 1999 survey by Treasury Strategies, Inc., found that 8 percent of all liquid funds (demand deposits plus other short-term investments) was placed in money funds (for nonfinancial companies having revenues in excess of $100 million). Smaller companies find this vehicle relatively more attractive because of the lack of in-house time and expertise. The advantages of pooling monies before investing are:

- *Professional money management.* Professional money managers make the investment decisions and oversee the securities in the funds.

**Exhibit 14–8**

*State and Local Government Instruments*

| Instrument | Purpose Issued | Denomination | Maturity | Risk Aspects |
|---|---|---|---|---|
| Anticipation notes | State and local governments issue securities to get "cash in advance" of anticipated revenues from taxes, bridge or toll road user fees, or bond issues, for example. | Primary market: $5,000 minimum.<br>Secondary market: round lot is $100,000 minimum. | Range: few weeks to several years. | Default risk:<br>• low, because of taxing and reborrowing abilities of the issuer. Depends on municipality offering—default is possible in certain circumstances.<br>Liquidity risk:<br>• depends on lead dealer's willingness and ability to buy back at market prices, which is hard to estimate.<br>Interest rate risk:<br>• insignificant on shorter maturities, of concern on several-year maturity. |
| Variable rate demand notes (VRDNs, also called "7-day floaters") | Securities issued by states and localities in long-term maturities, but with put feature enabling investor to liquidate if periodically reset interest rate (interest usually paid monthly or quarterly) is not acceptable. | Primary market: $5,000–$100,000.<br>Secondary market: $100,000 minimum is round lot. | Bond maturity up to 15 years, but with put feature. Interest rate is reset periodically, when period could be 1–90 or 180 days. | Default risk:<br>• same as anticipation notes, except for longer maturity, implying greater uncertainty about future tax base and financial condition of issuer; backed by irrevocable letter of credit from bank.<br>Liquidity risk:<br>• same as anticipation notes.<br>Interest rate risk:<br>• insubstantial because of periodic reset of coupon. |
| Tax-exempt commercial paper | Same as for anticipation notes, and possibly to finance seasonal needs. | Primary: $50,000–$100,000.<br>Secondary: $100,000 minimum is round lot. | Range: from few days to several years, most commonly 30 days. | Default risk:<br>• same as anticipation notes.<br>Liquidity risk:<br>• same as anticipation notes. |

**Exhibit 14–9**

*Mixed Instruments*

| Instrument | Purpose Issued | Denomination | Maturity | Risk Aspects |
|---|---|---|---|---|
| Money market mutual funds (MMMFs) | Fund administrator collects money from investors, pools to enable purchase of diversified large-dollar denominations. Mostly invest in commercial paper, but also in negotiable certificates of deposit, bankers' acceptances, Treasuries, and repurchase agreements (see below). | $10,000 usual minimum for institutional account. | Range: 25–60 days for weighted average maturity. | Default risk:<br>• unlike MMDAs, no FDIC guarantee. Risk is comparable to commercial paper because of its heavy weighting in most MMMF portfolios. Some MMMFs are insured by third-party, private insurer.<br>Liquidity risk:<br>• no risk because of daily access through wire transfers or check-writing privileges.<br>Interest rate risk:<br>• on pure money fund, net asset value is kept at $1.00, and short maturities eliminates risk. For new funds that are invested in maturities >65 days, slight risk. |
| Repurchase agreements (RPs) | Bank or security dealer uses to raise money to finance investments or loans. Financing occurs because originator "sells" portfolio of investments with an agreement to repurchase them shortly at a slightly higher price. | Can be under $100,000, but typically $1 million. Term, as opposed to overnight, repurchases may be over $25 million, but are typically $10 million. | Mostly overnight. Term RPs are 7 to 30 days, with some up to 1 year. | Default risk:<br>• higher when institution initiating RP is an aggressive trader of securities.<br>• linked to risks of underlying securities (collateral), whether the securities are, in fact, considered to be collateral and whether the investor's custodian takes possession of the collateral.<br>Liquidity risk:<br>• overnight RPs are obviously liquid, but term repos also offer some flexibility for post-agreement alteration of maturity to provide for early resale.<br>Event risk:<br>• investor must guard against fraud and valuation mistakes, particularly when dealing with unregistered, nonprimary government securities dealers. |
| Sweep accounts | Deposit account in which excess balances are automatically transferred, on overnight basis, into interest-bearing investment. Sweep may be initiated by bank or broker; if by broker, monies are moved via wire transfer. Offered mainly as customer convenience but may fund loans or investments much like repurchase agreement. | Bank sweep account: amount of surplus balance, above compensating balance.<br>Broker sweep account: amount large enough to make the interest exceed the wire transfer costs. | Overnight | Default risk:<br>• linked to the instrument invested in. Primarily, these are invested in mutual funds offered by the bank's parent bank holding company or the brokerage house. These might be invested in one or more of the following: commercial paper, Treasury bills, Euro time deposits, or tax-exempt securities. |

- *Diversification of default risk.* Many issuers' securities, and possibly even securities from issuers in various countries, are included in the pool.
- *Higher yields.* Investment in much larger denominations than would be possible for any single investor increases overall yield.
- *Enhanced liquidity.* As some investors withdraw funds, others are reinvesting; individual securities do not have to be sold to fund withdrawals.
- *Greater flexibility.* Any combination of securities can be assembled—by maturity, issuer type, issuer geographic location, or other mixes investors might desire.

Money funds have parlayed the enhanced liquidity into an even greater feature by allowing investors to write checks (minimum of $100 for institutional funds offered to corporate investors), wire transfer, or telephone transfer among the same provider's funds. Interest rate risk is eliminated because the price[12] of the money fund is kept constant at $1.00, regardless of changes in interest rates. This is possible because the funds' average maturity of 24 to 48 days combined with the practice of buying and holding securities until maturity insulates the funds' values from interest rate movements. Management fees are as low as 0.26 percent, which is achieved by Vanguard's Prime Portfolio Money Market Fund. Business corporations have increased their investments in money market funds markedly in recent years, growing from $142 billion in 1995 to about $1.13 trillion at the beginning of 2004. iMoneyNet data indicate that the average maturity of money funds' portfolios at year-end 2003 was 54 days. In Chapter 15, we will weigh the advantages of having an outside entity make almost all the treasurer's short-term investment decisions.

Several other types of mutual funds are not technically money funds but may be used in their place. Short-term government bond funds or short-term municipal bond funds, holding portfolios with average maturities of two to three years, and APS funds are options for the investor willing to take more interest rate risk or even some price risk (on the preferred stock).

*Repurchase Agreements* A **repurchase agreement** (RP, or "repo") is the sale of a portfolio of securities with a prearranged buyback one or several days later. The difference in sale price and repurchase price constitutes the interest yield. Banks and securities dealers needing to finance inventories of loans or securities on a short-term basis may do so by engaging in RPs. Until the 1980s, RPs were the only means for most corporate investors to gain a 1-day return on surplus cash, so they were very popular. Although RPs still are widely used (about 11 percent of liquid funds are placed there according to the 1999 Treasury Strategies survey), other instruments such as overnight CP, muni notes, Eurodollar time deposits, and sweep accounts (our next topic) are replacing them. Repurchase agreements must be structured carefully so that the underlying securities count as collateral. Investors should take the precaution of having a custodian bank take possession of these securities. Because of this collateral, overnight repo rates are typically five to 15 basis points below the Fed funds rate. Borrower defaults are not a serious concern, because the investor can sell the underlying securities, which are generally Treasury bills or government agency notes. **Term repos** can be arranged for several days up to several weeks for the company having an investment horizon longer than one day.

*Sweep Accounts* Banks and brokerage firms offer sweep accounts in which excess funds are automatically, or at the cash manager's request, transferred (swept) from the

---

[12] Technically, price is a misnomer, and net asset value is quoted, which equals [(Sum of market values of securities − Liabilities)/Number of shares]. Liabilities would consist of accrued expenses for commissions or management fees.

demand deposit account into an interest-bearing overnight investment. Treasury Strategies did a survey in 1999 and found that the popularity of sweeps continues to grow. Surprisingly, in the follow-up 2003 survey, corporate investors actually showed more conservatism in their investing, despite the much lower interest rates. Banks offer the convenience of one-stop shopping, automatic transfers of amounts above the compensating balance level, choices of several pooled investments to select from, and perhaps even an optional credit line paydown instead of investing the surplus. Brokerage houses have the money wired out into a money fund or some other short-term investment. It is conceivable that future regulations will hamper banks' ability to avoid also wiring funds out of deposit accounts (at present, they simply make a bookkeeping entry to sweep monies) because of Federal Reserve concern that they are circumventing reserve requests by reporting lower transaction account balances because of the sweep accounts.[13] Banks will undoubtedly contest any proposed change vigorously, because they need to offer sweep accounts to have a competitive product for corporate overnight investments.

Our survey of short-term investment instruments has highlighted key features, including the major risk attributes of the various instruments. We will be prepared to consider security risk-return tradeoffs and all types of investment risk after presenting the essential money market yield calculations.

## MONEY MARKET CALCULATIONS

The short-term investor must master several essential calculations, all dealing with various yields. Yield calculations depend on whether the security is a tax-advantaged or fully taxable security. Then, for fully taxable securities, the proper calculation depends on whether the security is a **discount security** or an interest-bearing, or coupon, security. Calculations of money market yields are based on simple interest—as if interest is paid once a year, at year's end. We go beyond the standard calculations to demonstrate how to calculate an effective annual yield from a nominal yield.

### Yields on Tax-Advantaged Securities

Recall from our earlier discussion that municipal securities are usually tax exempt, meaning that investors do not have to pay federal income tax on the interest received. When comparing munis to fully taxable securities, the investor may calculate a taxable-equivalent yield on the municipal security. This is the yield that a fully taxable security must provide to leave the investor with the same after-tax yield as he or she is getting on the muni.

*Taxable-Equivalent Yield on Municipal Security* Assuming the security is selling at par, the taxable-equivalent yield is calculated as shown in Equation 14.1.

$$\textit{Taxable-equivalent yield} = \frac{\textit{Nominal yield}}{(1 - T)} \tag{14.1}$$

Illustrating, a company in the 34-percent tax bracket would have to get 6.06 percent [4%/(1 − 0.34)] from a taxable security to match a municipal security's 4-percent non-

[13] The Fed has prohibited multiple savings accounts, in which one of the accounts is used for incoming transfers from demand deposit accounts, and requires that banks assess early withdrawal penalties to any withdrawal from a corporate time deposit made within six days of the most recent deposit to the account. See "Sweep Account Loopholes Closed in Federal Reserve Requirement Rule," *The Regulatory Compliance Watch* (American Banker Bond Buyer newsletter) (April 12, 1991), pp. 1–2.

taxable yield. The fact that municipal securities are generally exempted from state and local income taxes in the state where issued means the treasurer might want to use an overall combined income tax rate instead of the federal rate.[14]

**YIELD ON DIVIDEND CAPTURE** The annualized yield for the dividend capture, $y_{cap}$, ignoring commissions and compounding, is given in Equation 14.2.

$$y_{cap} = \frac{D}{P} \times \frac{365}{n} \tag{14.2}$$

Where:

$D$ = Dollar amount of dividend

$P$ = Price (amount invested)

$n$ = Holding period

Illustrating, if you buy a stock for $20 per share, receive a $0.20 dividend, and sell the stock after 47 days, the annualized yield is:

$$\begin{aligned} y_{cap} &= \frac{\$0.20}{\$20} \times \frac{365}{47} \\ &= 0.07766 \ \textit{or} \ \underline{\underline{7.77\%}} \end{aligned}$$

The federal income tax deduction of 70 percent of intercorporate dividends (if the stock is held at least 46 days) makes dividend-paying investments even more attractive. Because 30 percent of the income is not taxed, the investor in the 34-percent tax bracket retains 89.8 percent [100% − (30% × 0.34)] of its income instead of only 66 percent (100% − 34%). Put another way, it pays a tax rate on the dividend income of only 10.2 percent if it is in the 34-percent tax bracket. To compare the yield with fully taxable securities' yields, we need to compute a taxable-equivalent yield from the dividend capture. We can use this relationship to calculate Equation 14.3, $y_{cap-te}$, the taxable-equivalent yield of the dividend capture.

$$y_{cap-te} = \frac{y_{cap}\,[1 - (0.30 \times T)]}{(1 - T)} \tag{14.3}$$

Where:

$y_{cap}$ = Annualized yield for dividend capture

$T$ = Investor's marginal tax rate

Continuing with our example, with a dividend capture yield of 7.77 percent and assuming your company is in the 34-percent marginal tax bracket, to do as well with a fully taxable security, you would have to find one yielding:

$$\begin{aligned} y_{cap-te} &= \frac{7.77[1 - (0.30 \times 0.34)]}{(1 - 0.34)} \\ &= \underline{\underline{10.57\%}} \end{aligned}$$

---

[14] The taxable-equivalent yield when taking into account state income taxes, assuming the state allows deductibility of the interest and the issuer is located in the same state, involves a change in the denominator of Equation 14.1. Distinguishing between $T_F$ (the corporation's marginal federal tax rate) and $T_S$ (the corporation's marginal rate on the state income tax), the denominator becomes:

$$\text{Taxable-equivalent yield} = \frac{\textit{Nominal yield}}{\{1 - [T_F + T_S(1 - T_F)]\}}$$

For details on the adjusted formula, see John R. Walter, "Short-Term Municipal Securities," *Federal Reserve Bank of Richmond Economic Review* (November/December 1986), pp. 25–34.

As we cautioned earlier in the chapter, recognize that you are taking the risk that the stock price will drop during the holding period unless some type of hedging is done. Any commissions paid will reduce the dividend capture yield and the taxable-equivalent yield of the dividend capture.

## Discount Yield

Treasury bills, CP, BAs, agency discount notes, and some RPs are discount securities, meaning they are bought at a price below their face or par value and the investor receives face value at maturity. The difference is the interest return on the security. We can apply Equation 14.4 to calculate a Treasury bill **discount yield**, $y_d$.

$$y_d = \frac{FACE - P}{FACE} \times \frac{360}{n} \qquad (14.4)$$

Where:

$y_d$ = Discount yield

$FACE$ = Face value (or par)

$P$ = Price

$n$ = Number of days until maturity

Notice that this is a nominal yield, not an effective annual yield. We illustrate the discount yield calculation with the actual results of a Treasury bill auction, shown in Exhibit 14–10.

The 13-week (3-month) bill had $36.98 billion in public bids for the $17.78 billion offered for sale (the Fed's rollover of maturing Treasury bills and foreign and international monetary authority [FIMA] purchases are in addition to these totals). The Treasury auctions bills using a single-price format. Starting with the highest price (lowest yield, or cost) bids, it sums up bid dollar amounts until all of the auctioned securities are accounted for. The price (yield) at which the last Treasury bill would have to be sold to complete the amount offered becomes the single price (yield) at which all successful bids are transacted. In Exhibit 14–10, that price (yield) is the "Dollar price" listed: $99.779. The "high discount rate" associated with this price, or the discount yield for this particular auction, is 0.875 percent. We can see how this is calculated on these $1,000 minimum denomination bills by plugging into Equation 14.4 the $1,000 face amount, the price (found by taking the Dollar price/$100, or $99.779/$100, times the face amount of $1,000), and a factor to annualize the period rate (360/Number of days).

$$y_d = \frac{\$1{,}000 - (0.99779 \times \$1{,}000)}{\$1{,}000} \times \frac{360}{91}$$

$$= 0.0087, \text{ or } \underline{\underline{0.87\%}}$$

As stated, this is the high discount rate shown for the auction.

## Coupon-Equivalent Yields

Notice, in the 3-month Treasury auction detail, the coupon-equivalent yield ("investment rate") of 0.89 percent. This yield is calculated based on a 365-day year instead of 360 days and assuming that interest owed is based on the actual number of days elapsed. For a discount security maturing within one year, the **coupon-equivalent yield** also is adjusted to account for the fee that the price paid is less than the face value, which increases the true yield, as shown in Equation 14.5. The coupon-equivalent yield on a discount security, $y_{ce}$, would be:

$$y_{ce} = \frac{FACE - P}{P} \times \frac{365}{n} \qquad (14.5)$$

## Exhibit 14–10

*Treasury Auction Information*

January 20, 2004 202-691-3550

RESULTS OF TREASURY'S AUCTION OF 13-WEEK BILLS

| | |
|---|---|
| Term: | 91-Day Bill |
| Issue Date: | January 22, 2004 |
| Maturity Date: | April 22, 2004 |
| CUSIP Number: | 912795PV7 |

High Rate: 0.875% Investment Rate 1/: 0.891% Price: 99.779

All noncompetitive and successful competitive bidders were awarded securities at the high rate. Tenders at the high discount rate were allotted 22.79%. All tenders at lower rates were accepted in full.

AMOUNTS TENDERED AND ACCEPTED (in thousands)

| Tender Type | Tendered | Accepted |
|---|---|---|
| Competitive | $35,647,482 | $16,447,452 |
| Noncompetitive | 1,327,555 | 1,327,555 |
| FIMA (noncompetitive) | 225,000 | 225,000 |
| SUBTOTAL | 37,200,037 | 18,000,007 |
| Federal Reserve | 6,771,484 | 6,771,484 |
| TOTAL | $43,971,521 | $24,771,491 |

Median rate 0.865%: 50% of the amount of accepted competitive tenders was tendered at or below that rate. Low rate 0.855%: 5% of the amount of accepted competitive tenders was tendered at or below that rate.

Bid-to-Cover Ratio = 37,200,037 / 18,000,007 = 2.07

1/ Equivalent coupon-issue yield.
2/ Awards to TREASURY DIRECT = $1,087,632,000

*Source:* **ftp://ftp.publicdebt.treas.gov/of/ofh30120041.pdf**. Accessed online 1/24/04.

Substituting the figures for the 13-week Treasury bill, we get the following nominal yield:

$$y_{ce} = \frac{\$1{,}000 - (0.99779 \times \$1{,}000)}{(0.99779 \times \$1{,}000)} \times \frac{365}{91}$$

$$= 0.0089 \text{ or } \underline{\underline{0.89\%}}$$

The coupon-equivalent yield is always higher than the discount yield, with the gap widening at higher interest rates.

On coupon securities, such as Treasury notes and bonds, short-term CDs, muni and corporate notes, Eurodollar CDs and time deposits, and money market mutual funds, the quoted coupon rate is already comparable with the above coupon-equivalent yield. For a 10-percent note, the simple interest calculation implies that every \$100 of principal will be paid \$10 (0.10 × \$100) of interest each year.[15]

### Annual Effective Yield

Neither of the yields considered up to this point accounts for the compounding of interest earned on a short-term security. To get an effective annual yield ($y_{eff}$), we adjust for the fact that the investor has only invested *P* (the price), a 365-day year, and the ability of the investor to earn compounded interest until year's end. This is shown in Equation 14.6.[16]

$$y_{eff} = \left[1 + \left(\frac{FACE - P}{P}\right)\right]^{365/n} - 1 \qquad (14.6)$$

Illustrating with the 13-week Treasury bill again, we have:

$$y_{eff} = \left[1 + \left(\frac{\$1{,}000 - \$997.79}{\$997.79}\right)\right]^{365/91} - 1$$
$$= 0.0089, \text{ or } \underline{\underline{0.89\%}}$$

Because of the compounding of intrayear interest, the equivalent annual yield exceeds the coupon-equivalent yield as well as the discount yield. In our example, the low interest rates mask the difference. Assuming we can reinvest interest and principal at the coupon-equivalent rate or higher, this measure gives us a more accurate picture of the increase in portfolio value that occurs over time.

The return calculations have prepared us to take a closer look at how to analyze individual security risks and evaluate the risk-return tradeoff. Portfolio aspects of having numerous securities to evaluate at one time are covered in Chapter 15.

## YIELD AND RISK ANALYSIS

The magnitude of securities available to the corporate investor can be overwhelming unless some technique for narrowing candidates is implemented. Comparing yields is helpful, but return is only half the picture. Knowledge of the risks involved and how they affect yield facilitates comparisons. Corporate investors lacking the time or expertise to conduct formal risk analysis may minimize certain of these risks (e.g., diversify away much of the default risk by investing in a large managed portfolio of securities) or delegate risk management (e.g., by assessing default risk through reliance on third-party rating services). However, not all risks can be simultaneously minimized, and lowered risks generally entail lowered returns.

We classify risks in relation to how they determine security yields: risk factors influencing return differences for different maturities, and risk factors that drive yields for securities with identical maturities. Yield relationships in the first category are generally characterized as the term structure of interest rates, and we define the second category as the risk structure of interest rates. We use an additive risk factor model (Equation 14.7) to show the overall yield-risk relationship.

---

[15] The fact that half the interest is paid every six months on most coupon securities implies a higher effective yield, however. We note in Chapter 3 that the effective yield is $[(1 + i/2)^n - 1]$. For the 10-percent note, the effective yield is $[(1 + 0.10/2)^2 - 1 = 0.1025]$, or 10.25 percent. The effective yield of the Treasury bill can be annualized in a similar fashion if no change in the 91-day yield for the remainder of the year is assumed.

[16] Another way to get to the same result is: $y_{eff} = (\text{FACE}/\text{P})^{365/n} - 1$.

$$k_s = k_{rf} + k_{tm} + k_{rp} \tag{14.7}$$

Where:

$k_s$ = Interest rate for security $s$

$k_{rf}$ = Risk-free interest rate

$k_{tm}$ = Term premium

$k_{rp}$ = Risk premium for security $s$

The risk-free rate is determined primarily by investors' collective time preferences, the rate of inflation expected over the maturity period, and demand-side influences such as economic productivity. It is apparent that there is no default risk or liquidity risk incorporated in the risk-free rate, which explains why Treasury bill or Treasury bond rates are used to proxy for this unobservable rate. If the security being evaluated with the model is a municipal note or bond, the risk-free rate used must be for a tax-exempt security without default risk. The **term spread** ($k_{tm}$) captures the component of a security's return that is necessary to induce investors to bear risks linked to maturity. The **risk spread** ($k_{rp}$) is the added yield necessary to compensate for other risk factors such as default risk (which, technically, gives rise to the default spread or credit spread) and liquidity risk that make up the risk structure of interest rates. Inadequate term or **risk premiums** do not persist in the **efficient money market**, because investors will sell (or at least not buy) securities with inadequate yields, leading to lower prices and correspondingly higher yields.

## Term Structure of Interest Rates

One of the most important determinants of a security's yield is its maturity. Securities issued by the same issuer offer varying yields-to-maturity for different maturities. The tendency for the maturity-yield relationship to hold across all issuers in a systematic way is called the **term structure of interest rates**. A graph of the term structure, showing current maturities on the horizontal axis and yield-to-maturity on the vertical axis, is known as the **yield curve**. Usually, Treasury securities are plotted to not confuse default risk or liquidity risk effects with maturity effects on yields. Yield comparability is achieved by expressing Treasury bill yields on a coupon-equivalent basis or by using only zero-coupon Treasury notes and bonds. Typically, the curve is upward-sloping, because 30-year Treasury bonds yield more than 3-month bills. Exhibit 14–11 shows the early 2004 yield curve.

**Exhibit 14–11**

*Yield Curve*

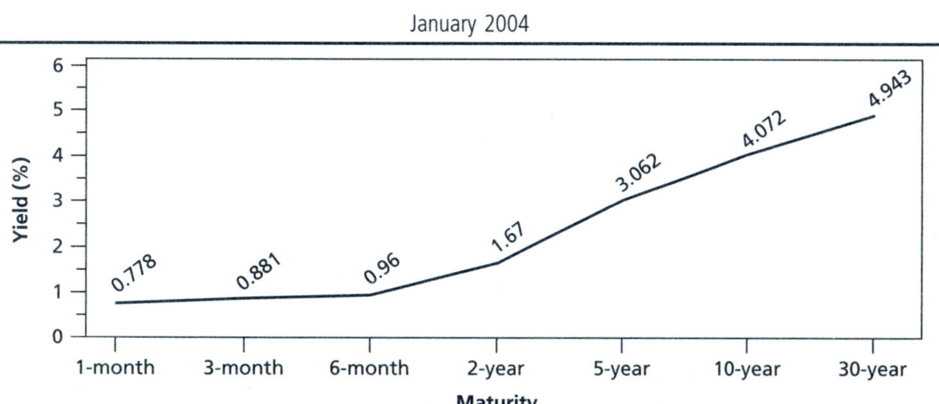

Note the steep upward slope of the curve, and that the investor can double his or her yield from 0.78 percent to 1.67 percent by investing his or her money for two years instead of for one month. The **normal yield curve** is generally upward-sloping, with longer-term maturities yielding more than short-term, for several reasons.

- Liquidity risk may be similar because all Treasury securities have active secondary markets, but Treasury bond investors are committing their principal for a much longer period—especially for the institutional investors that buy and hold to maturity—and some yield inducement is appropriate to cover the possibility that interest or principal payments might be late or missed.
- Longer maturities involve higher probabilities of capital losses because of their greater interest rate risk (the possibility that interest rates will increase, leading to capital losses for existing securities) combined with the fact that investors may have to sell before maturity.
- **Purchasing power risk** is related to interest rate risk but is distinct: for long-term investors, unexpected economy-wide price increases cut into the purchasing power of interest and principal cash flows and tend to drive prevailing interest rates up, feeding back into interest rate risk.
- On foreign securities, another risk that is greater for longer time horizons is the exchange rate risk, in which adverse changes in exchange rates cut into the dollar value of interest and principal returns when converted out of the foreign currency.

The yield curve is also affected by future interest rate expectations, however, leading at times to a **flat yield curve** and less often to a downward-sloping or **inverted yield curve**. We require a deeper understanding of what factors lie behind the makeup of a yield curve to explain flat and inverted curves.

*TERM STRUCTURE THEORIES* There are four prominent explanations for the interest rate term structure. Ideally, an explanation for the shape of the yield curve will be able to interpret the interrelationships of a security's issues across the maturity spectrum.

The oldest and most important explanation is the **unbiased expectations hypothesis**. This theory posits that the prevailing yield curve is mathematically derived from the present short-term rate and expectations for rates that will exist at various points in time in the future. Existing interest rates in today's markets are called **spot rates**; rates that the market collectively forecasts today for future years are called **forward rates**. Combining the shortest-term spot rates with the forward rates being forecasted by the market, we can derive today's spot rates for medium- and long-term securities. If we assign the spot rate the symbol ${}_tR_n$, in which the preceding subscript refers to the point in time when it occurs and the following subscript refers to the maturity, we have the following rather elaborate expression:

$$(1 + {}_tR_n) = [(1 + {}_tR_1)(1 + {}_{t+1}r_{1,t}) \times \cdots \times (1 + {}_{t+n-1}r_{1,t})]^{1/n} \quad (14.8)$$

Where: ${}_tR_n$ = Spot rate for 1-year security as of time period $t$

${}_{t+1}r_{1,t}$ = Forward rate, the rate the market thinks will exist at period t + 1, for 1-year security, predicted as of period $t$

$1/n$ = $n^{th}$ root of entire expression

If we subtract 1 from both sides of Equation 14.8 (after taking the root on the right-hand side) and $t$ is set equal to 0, we have formulated the expression we need for linking today's 1-year rate, $({}_0R_1)$, to longer-maturity rates. Let's look at an example.

If the 1-year Treasury bill coupon-equivalent yield is 5.50 percent and the 2-year rate is 5.80 percent, what 1-year rate did the money market expect to exist at the end of the first year?

**Solution.** First, recognize that the observed current rates are spot rates ${}_0R_1$ and ${}_0R_2$, respectively, and the solution that we are seeking is a forward 1-year rate. Here, $t = 0$ and $n = 2$; we plug the values into Equation 14.8 to solve for ${}_{t+1}r_{1,t}$. Because $t = 0$, we are solving for ${}_1r_{1,0}$.

$$(1 + 0.0580) = [(1 + 0.0550)(1 + {}_1r_{1,0})]^{1/2}$$
$$1.0580 = [(1.0550)(1 + {}_1r_{1,0})]^{1/2}$$

Because raising an expression to the ½ power is the same as taking the square root, we must square both sides to get rid of the square root on the right.

$$1.119364 = (1.0550)(1 + {}_1r_{1,0})$$

Dividing by 1.0550 and subtracting 1 from both sides, we have

$$0.06101 = {}_1r_{1,0}$$
$$6.10\% = {}_1r_{1,0}$$

Interpreting our example, the expectations theory states that the year-ahead 6.10 percent forward rate for a 1-year security, when combined with the spot 1-year rate of 5.50 percent, causes the market to require 5.80 percent (spot rate) from the 2-year security to be in equilibrium. Investors with a 2-year investment horizon are assumed to be indifferent to holding one 2-year security or two consecutive 1-year securities and will engage in arbitrage (a sale of the 2-year security and purchase of the 1-year, or vice versa) until the equilibrium relationship holds. Although we worked backward to reveal the unobservable forward rate (you will not find forward rates in *The Wall Street Journal*), we could just as easily have polled market participants for their year-ahead forecast for a 1-year security, plugged that in, and solved for the theoretical 2-year spot rate, ${}_0R_2$.[17] Study Exhibit 14–12, in which you will see the unbiased expectations explanation for empirically observed U.S. yield curves (second column).

The second explanation for a yield curve's shape is the **liquidity preference hypothesis**. Recall our earlier argument about the higher yields necessary to induce investors to tie their funds up for long periods (i.e., to be illiquid) in light of the increasing default probability and interest rate risk. Preference for liquidity is thought to characterize enough investors that the yield curve (in the absence of expectations or other influences on other than the short-term securities) should slope upward from left to right—yielding a "liquidity premium." The longer the maturity, the larger the liquidity premium that must be offered to attract investors. Liquidity preference, as a sole explanation for the yield curve, is unable to explain flat, humped, or inverted yield curves.

The **market segmentation hypothesis** contends that instead of being close substitutes, securities with short, medium, and long maturities are seen by investors (funds suppliers) and issuers (funds demanders) as being quite different. The implication is that the term structure for a given issuer or group of similar issuers must be assembled by looking at separate supply and demand conditions in each segment of the maturity spectrum. Proponents point out that banks issue mainly short-term securities and utility companies mainly deal in long-term securities, whereas on the investing side money funds invest only in short-term securities and insurance companies almost exclusively in long-term securi-

[17] We are portraying one of five versions of the expectations hypothesis; see the McEnally and Jordan citation in the end-of-chapter references for an exposition of the others.

## Exhibit 14–12

*Alternative Classic Yield Curves and Their Explanations*

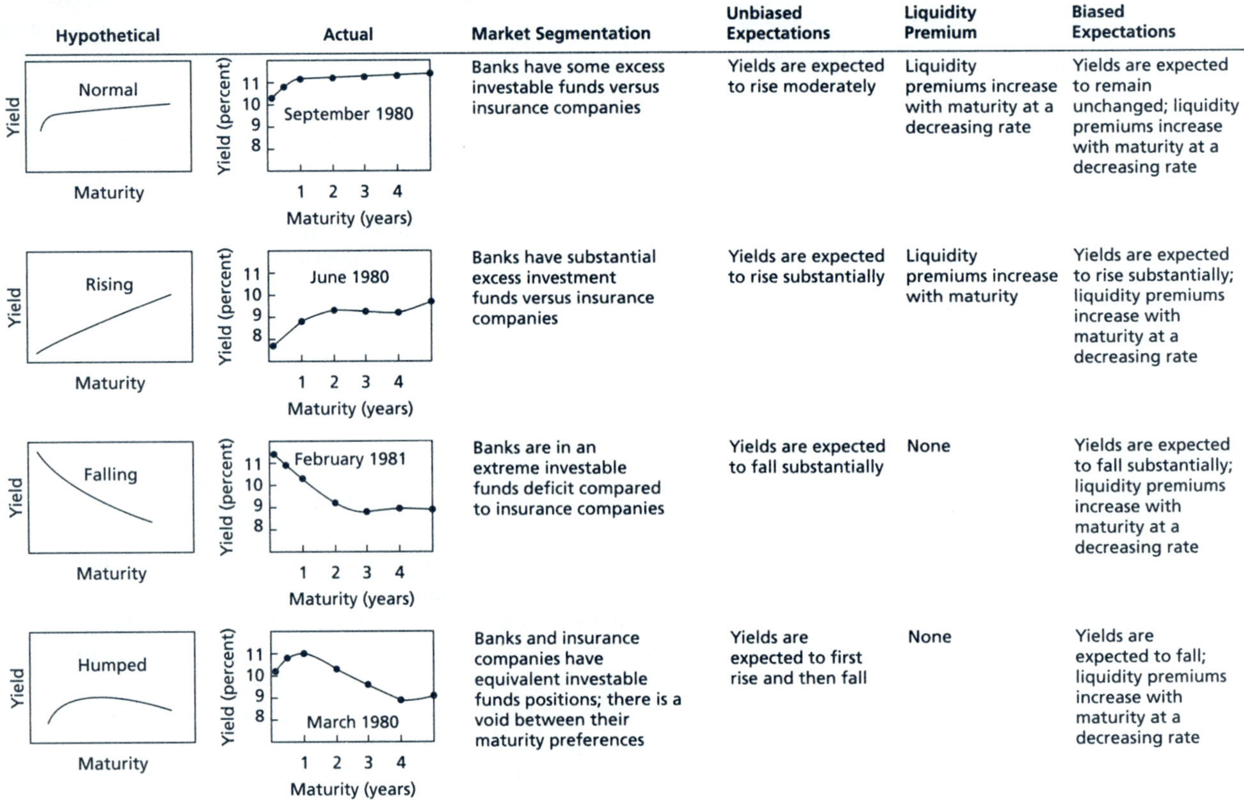

| Hypothetical | Actual | Market Segmentation | Unbiased Expectations | Liquidity Premium | Biased Expectations |
|---|---|---|---|---|---|
| Normal | September 1980 | Banks have some excess investable funds versus insurance companies | Yields are expected to rise moderately | Liquidity premiums increase with maturity at a decreasing rate | Yields are expected to remain unchanged; liquidity premiums increase with maturity at a decreasing rate |
| Rising | June 1980 | Banks have substantial excess investment funds versus insurance companies | Yields are expected to rise substantially | Liquidity premiums increase with maturity | Yields are expected to rise substantially; liquidity premiums increase with maturity at a decreasing rate |
| Falling | February 1981 | Banks are in an extreme investable funds deficit compared to insurance companies | Yields are expected to fall substantially | None | Yields are expected to fall substantially; liquidity premiums increase with maturity at a decreasing rate |
| Humped | March 1980 | Banks and insurance companies have equivalent investable funds positions; there is a void between their maturity preferences | Yields are expected to first rise and then fall | None | Yields are expected to fall; liquidity premiums increase with maturity at a decreasing rate |




*Source:* Adapted from Exhibit 56–7 in Richard W. McEnally and James V. Jordan, "The Term Structure of Interest Rates," in Frank J. Fabozzi (ed.): *The Handbook of Fixed Income Securities, 3rd ed.* Homewood, IL: Business One Irwin (1991), p. 1268.

ties. Also, recall the role of the Fed in controlling the money supply, which mainly involves open market purchases and sales of Treasury bills as opposed to notes or bonds. The markets are thus separated, or segmented, by the self-limiting behavior of institutions staying within their preferred habitats. Arbitrage across maturities that makes investors indifferent to which maturity they select, as perceived by advocates of the unbiased expectations hypothesis, is thought to be nonexistent by the market segmentation school. This view implies that investors should try to beat the market by searching out attractive risk-return tradeoffs in overlooked maturity segments.

A fourth hypothesis merges unbiased expectations and liquidity preference into the **biased expectations hypothesis.** Basically, this hypothesis reflects expectations modified by some degree of liquidity preference (see Exhibit 14–12, right column). Many market observers find the biased expectations hypothesis to be the most plausible of the four explanations. They use the forward rates, which are implied interest rate forecasts, as a tool for discerning the market's collective interest rate forecast. Investors then use that information to decide when to take advantage of the higher yields available on longer-term securities during normal yield curve eras. We develop the mechanics of this "riding the yield curve" strategy in our resolution of the chapter's opening Financial Dilemma after commenting on the empirical evidence supporting the four explanations.

The best supported explanation for yield curve configurations is the biased expectations hypothesis. Although the market segmentation hypothesis clearly applies to some markets at certain times (e.g., when the Fed is actively increasing or draining credit) and provides a rational explanation for humped yield curves (refer to Exhibit 14–12), studies fail to find consistent support. Yet, there are some puzzles remaining to be solved, such as why Treasury bill rates on recently issued securities behave oddly when a new auction approaches (changing the yield curve from what unbiased expectations would predict). The chapter references provide citations for the major studies that have been conducted on the different theories. We close our survey of the term structure of interest rates by resolving the Financial Dilemma.

## FINANCIAL DILEMMA REVISITED

The banker advising Dave is basing his recommendation to move from overnight investments into 6-month CDs on a normal yield curve. Dave may want to first investigate the reason(s) for the forecasts of higher future rates to better evaluate the interest rate risk he would be facing. Although he anticipates not needing the funds for six months, his cash flow forecast may be in error. This would force him to liquidate the CD early and accept the associated penalty. After you explain to Dave about the higher yield for longer maturities, he decides to consider a 1-year maturity. He decides that he does not want to deal with early withdrawal penalties and insists he will only invest in 6-month CDs with active secondary markets—otherwise, he will stay with overnight investments.

We can help Dave by simulating his total return for the two alternatives in which he is interested: buying a 6-month CD and holding it to maturity or buying a 1-year CD and selling it in the secondary market after six months. The first alternative does not subject Dave to any interest rate risk, but the second clearly does. Dave's enthusiasm for riding the yield curve by investing in a maturity longer than his investment horizon may wane if we show him two scenarios: one in which the yield curve remains stable (scenario 1) and the other in which it shifts upward or steepens in slope (scenario 2). Six-month CDs presently yield 6 percent, and 1-year CDs yield 6.5 percent, so the market has "built in" a 7 percent forward CD rate for that second 6-month period. We will assume a $1 million negotiable CD is to be bought.

***Scenario 1: Stable Yield Curve*** Labeling the 6-month alternative as option A and the purchase and resale of the 1-year CD as option B:

Option A: Total return is simply the 6-percent yield received on the 6-month CD.

Option B: Total return is the sum of a half-year's interest on the 1-year CD, plus the capital appreciation that will occur as the 1-year CD moves down the yield curve and becomes a lower-yielding 6-month CD. The adjustment process involves an increase in the CD's price, because the coupon is fixed. The interest return received in the first six months is $32,500.

$$\text{Interest return} = \tfrac{1}{2}\,(0.065) = 0.0325 \times \$1{,}000{,}000 = \$32{,}500$$

The 6.5-percent coupon on the $1 million CD means the dollars of interest per year would be $65,000 (0.065 × $1 million). Of this, half of the year's interest, or $32,500, has been paid at the end of six months, leaving $32,500 to be paid in the last half of the year. That amount will help determine the change in price that occurs during the first six months.

That change in price provides the second portion of total return, which we label capital gain or loss.

$$\text{Capital gain (loss)} = \text{Sales price} - \text{Buy price}$$

The sales price is based on the CD yielding 6 percent (annualized) after the first six months. The buyer will be willing to pay a price that provides him with a 6-percent return, which is a dollar return of $30,000 = (0.06/2) × $1,000,000. That price will be slightly over $1 million, taking into account the $32,500 interest, which is greater than the $30,000 return required. Let's express it as a formula to make the calculation easier.

$$\text{Sales price} = \$1{,}000{,}000 + (\text{Interest promised} - \text{Interest required})$$

Thus, we have:

$$\text{Sales price} = \$1{,}000{,}000 + (\$32{,}500 - \$30{,}000)$$
$$\text{Sales price} = \$1{,}000{,}000 + \$2{,}500$$
$$\text{Sales price} = \$1{,}002{,}500$$

For the seller, then, the capital gain is the difference between his original buy price and this sell price.

$$\text{Capital gain return} = \$1{,}002{,}500 - \$1{,}000{,}000 = \$2{,}500$$

Finally, we add the interest and capital gain returns together to arrive at the original investor's option B "riding the yield curve" total return.

$$\text{Total return for B} = \$32{,}500 + \$2{,}500 = \$35{,}000$$

On a percentage basis, we find the annualized 6-month total return to be 7 percent [2 × ($35,000/$1,000,000)]. Dave's pretty happy with that thought.

Riding the yield curve is relatively profitable if this upward-sloping yield curve remains stable. You warn Dave that the reason he might get this attractive return is because the money market investors collectively expect short-term rates to move sharply higher in the near future. Dave immediately asks what his risk exposure would be, so you show him a second scenario that is predicated on a higher 6-month forward rate.

**SCENARIO 2: YIELD CURVE SHIFTS OR TILTS UPWARD** If the new 6-month rate when Dave sells the CD six months from now is higher than 6.5 percent, then the price of his 1-year CD would have had to drop accordingly to make it attractive to a buyer six months from now. Let's predict the new 6-month CD rate to be 7 percent, which (ignoring compounding) is what the yield curve is signaling; the unchanged 6-month CD (option A) return of 6 percent would now be compared with a worse option B riding the yield curve result.

Option B: The interest return is still 3.25 percent, or $32,500.

$$\text{Capital gain (loss)} = \text{Sales price} - \text{Buy price}$$

The sales price is now based on the CD yielding 7 percent (annualized) after the first six months. The buyer will be willing to pay a price that provides him with a 7-percent annualized return, which is a dollar return of $35,000 = [(0.07/2) × $1,000,000]. That price will be slightly under $1 million, taking into account that the $32,500 interest is now less than the $35,000 return required. Let's again express it as a formula to make the calculation easier.

$$\text{Sales price} = \$1{,}000{,}000 + (\text{Interest promised} - \text{Interest required})$$

Thus, we have:

$$\text{Sales price} = \$1{,}000{,}000 + (\$32{,}500 - \$35{,}000)$$
$$\text{Sales price} = \$1{,}000{,}000 + (-\ \$2{,}500)$$
$$\text{Sales price} = \$997{,}500$$

For the seller, now, the capital loss is the difference between his original buy price and this sell price.

$$\text{Capital loss return} = \$997{,}500 - \$1{,}000{,}000 = -\$2{,}500$$

Finally, we add the interest and capital gain returns together to arrive at the original investor's option B riding the yield curve total return for the six months.

$$\text{Total return for B} = \$32{,}500 + (\$2{,}500) = \$30{,}000$$

On a percentage basis, we find the annualized 6-month total return to be 6 percent [2 × ($30,000/$1,000,000)]. Dave has broken even. He chuckles, thinking this is great: "Heads I win, tails I break even"—riding the yield curve does better in Scenario 1 (rates stable or dropping) and no worse in Scenario 2 (rates rise as yield curve predicts). He then remembers another sobering thought: None of this takes into account any transaction costs for the riding the yield curve strategy. If he buys a 6-month CD and it matures (option A), he doesn't pay a commission to sell the CD early. If he rides the yield curve and cashes out of the 1-year CD while it still has six months to go before maturity, he'll have to pay a commission. "Maybe this isn't such a great strategy after all—especially in that my Scenario 1 idea is based on my interest rate forecast being different from the market's." He decides to think some more about what to do to gain yield on his short-term investments portfolio and concludes that a more accurate cash forecast will be necessary before he is ready to move his money out of overnight sweep account investments. "Oh yes," he remembers, "our short-term investment policy says something about not taking unnecessary risks related to interest rate changes. I'd better sit tight with my overnights."

### Risk Structure of Interest Rates

Securities that have the same maturity but were issued by different issuers and with different issue characteristics are priced to reflect risk differences. The major risk factors accounting for this risk premium are default risk, liquidity risk, reinvestment rate risk, purchasing power risk, and event risk. With foreign securities, the analyst also must consider exchange rate risk and political risk. Even interest rate risk can influence identically termed securities. Differing durations (a measure closely linked to the security's maturity) account for most of the difference.

Default risk and liquidity risk, defined earlier, obviously vary depending on the creditworthiness of the issuer and the depth and breadth of the security's secondary market, respectively. One other concern, which is specific to the *investor*, is the probability that the security will have to be sold before maturity. When riding the yield curve, by definition the security will be sold prematurely. When the corporate investor is matching the maturity to his or her best estimate of when the proceeds will be needed, the liquidity risk (and interest rate risk) is partly linked to the certainty of the investor's cash flows and the accuracy of the cash forecast. The more certain the company's cash flow and the more accurate its cash forecast, the less of a concern liquidity risk is. Again, if the corporate investor is riding the yield curve—buying maturities in excess of the investment horizon—the company is knowingly exposing itself to liquidity risk as well as interest rate risk. Exhibit 14–13 has been developed to help focus on the primary questions an investment analyst would address when evaluating each type of risk. For example, the worse the outlook for the economy and the higher the probability that a particular issuer's security interest coverage will be inadequate as a result of that company's business and financial risk, the higher the default risk and the larger the required risk premium for that security.

**Reinvestment rate risk** is the possibility that the investor will have to invest cash proceeds at a lower interest rate for the remainder of the predetermined investment horizon. Reinvestment rate risk is borne when the maturity is less than the investment horizon or

Exhibit 14–13

*Risk Structure of Interest Rates*

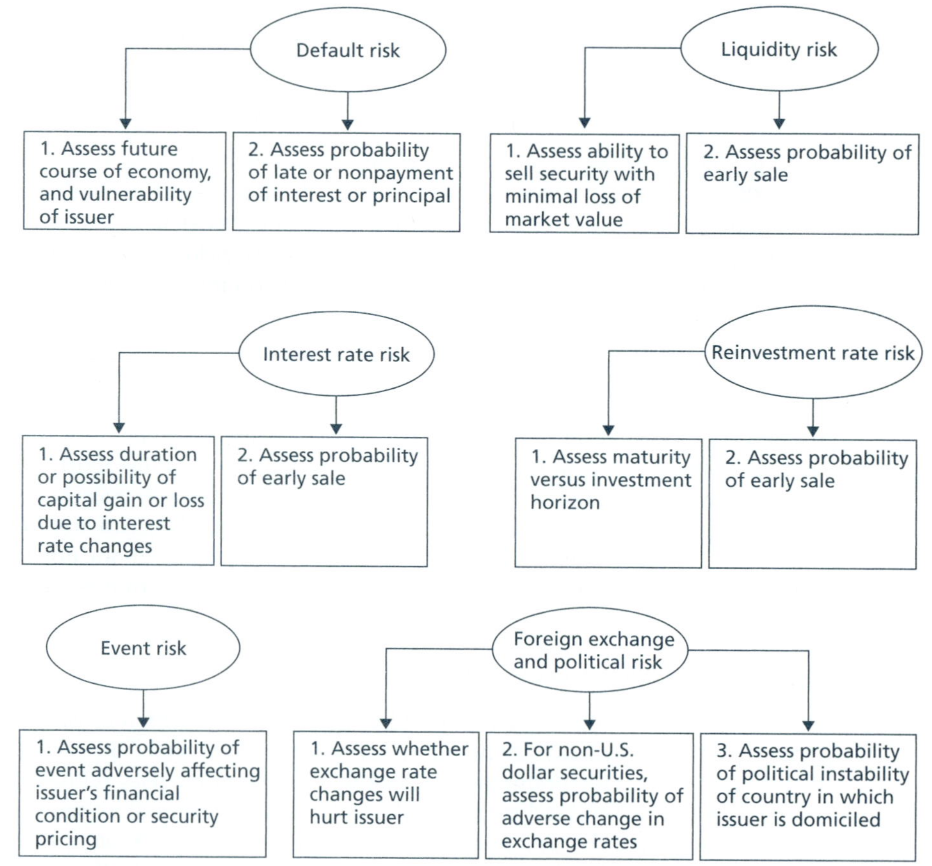


*Source:* Adapted from Exhibit 56–7 in Richard W. McEnally and James V. Jordan, 1991, "The Term Structure of Interest Rates." In Frank J. Fabozzi (ed): *The Handbook of Fixed Income Securities, 3rd ed.* Homewood, IL: Business One Irwin, p. 1268. Used by permission of Business One Irwin, Homewood IL. © Richard D. Irwin, Inc., 1983, 1987, 1991.

the company invests in a **coupon security** that pays one or more interest payments before the end of the investment horizon. Accrued interest, which is interest earned but not yet paid out in cash, is not a problem because it does not need to be reinvested yet. Recognize that, like interest rate risk, reinvestment rate risk cuts both ways. The treasurer may find that rates have gone up, and cash proceeds from maturing investments can be reinvested at higher yields than were achieved earlier.

**Event risk** includes any security feature or possible event that subjects the investor to a disruption to or reduction in the expected yield. Outstanding RJR-Nabisco bond prices dropped more than 20 percent within 48 hours of an announcement that the company was going to be taken private by using massive amounts of debt. This is a type of **financial restructuring**. Also of concern is **operational restructuring**, in which the company changes its product lines or use of assets with heavy fixed operating costs and alters the company's business risk. Call features, prepayment risk on mortgage-backed securities, problems affecting the guarantor of an issuer's securities, the default of a major issuer in the instrument's market, and unforeseen regulatory changes are other events that hurt investors and should be compensated for in the form of higher yields. The most common event risk in the twenty-first century is litigation.

On foreign securities, such as CP issued by a U.S. manufacturer that is issued in France and denominated in euros, the investor should be alerted to foreign exchange risk and political risk. We illustrated foreign exchange risk earlier and merely point out here that although the French government might not seize the U.S. company's French operations or block the outflow of investment proceeds, other countries have and will continue to initiate such actions.

Although not a major factor in the U.S. money market during the early twenty-first century, and therefore not included in our diagram of risk factors, purchasing power risk also can affect yields. Anticipated inflation is built into the risk-free interest rate, but investors still are vulnerable to losses in purchasing power from unanticipated inflation. This risk is especially problematic for investments made in foreign securities issued in countries with high and volatile inflation rates. In fact, this is a major reason for the extreme foreign exchange risk evident in many less-developed countries.

We conclude our analysis of individual money market security risk-return evaluation by providing an analysis of how default risk and liquidity risk can be assessed. These are the main determinants of investment safety, which is consistently ranked as the key attribute for treasurers in their security selection.

## Risk-Return Assessment in Practice

How are the safety and risk-return features of an issuer of short-term securities evaluated? We provide the details of CP evaluation to illustrate a process that is similar for all money market securities. Treasury professionals apply two main approaches to evaluating a bank's safety: yield spread analysis and third-party safety ratings.

*Yield Spread Analysis* Yield spread analysis involves calculating or plotting the differential between CP yields and Treasury bill or federal funds yields; the differential is often, but not always, a risk premium. For example, the analyst might compare Ford Credit's CP yield with an identical maturity Treasury bill, implicitly assuming that the yield difference is due to default risk differences. Exhibit 14–14 illustrates this approach with a yield comparison of the largest issuer of CP, General Electric Capital Corporation (GECC), and the Fed funds rate over the same periods.

Such yield comparisons are inadequate for risk evaluation purposes, however. First, yield premiums are constantly changing. For example, as money market rates move up, bank CD yields may noticeably lag behind Treasury bill rates. Second, there are important risk factors, other than default or marketability risk, that influence yield spreads.

- The supply and demand of loanable funds in a specific issue type market—CP issuance tends to be relatively lower as the economy heads into a recession and as potential buyers perceive even slight default risk.
- The negative "halo effect" of a default, such as that by Penn Central in the early 1980s and the two large southern California utilities in early 2001.
- Current money market conditions (especially in the federal funds and CP markets) that affect Fed funds rates and CP yields differently at various points.

Finally, trying to implement this approach to risk analysis is complicated. The treasurer must analyze instrument average premiums (CDs versus Treasury bills, CDs versus CP, CP versus Fed funds, and so on) as well as issuer characteristic premiums (e.g., financial CP issuers vs. nonfinancial CP issuers, domestic CP issuers vs. euro-CP issuers), which are very difficult to segregate from the yield figures. Furthermore, some empirical evidence regarding using yield spreads in other sectors of the market indicates that the investor may have to wait at least six months before spreads return to normal and the

Exhibit 14–14

*Yield Spreads for CP and the Fed Funds Rate*

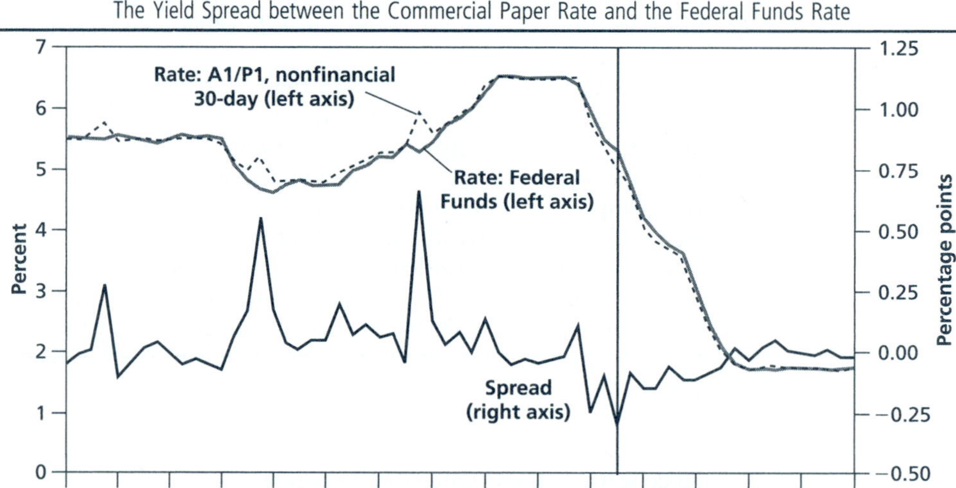


Note: The vertical bar indicates the start date of the most recent recession.
*Sources:* Federal Reserve Board of Governors and author's calculations. Pu Shen, "Why Has the Nonfinancial Commercial Paper Market Shrunk Recently?" *Federal Reserve Bank of Kansas City Economic Review* (First Quarter 2003), p. 72.

above-average return is earned.[18] In summary, using yield premiums to accurately infer default risk is tremendously difficult.

*CREDIT RATINGS* Another approach to risk-return assessment is to get help from third-party rating services that have specialized expertise in risk evaluation. Several agencies presently rate corporate issuers for performance and creditworthiness: Standard & Poor's (S&P); Moody's Investors Services (Moody's); and Fitch/IBCA (Fitch). Exhibit 14–15 describes Standard & Poor's commercial paper rating criteria.

One benchmark, useful in selecting CP as an investment as well as evaluating realized returns from CP investments recently made, is to compute risk-adjusted yield premiums. This simply involves subtracting Treasury bill rates or the Fed funds rates from a market CP quote and assessing the difference in light of the issuer's CP rating. A novel approach to investment vehicle selection might be suggested here: Assuming the approved list already has been generated, the treasurer might switch from Treasury bills to CP whenever the CP yields exceed the Treasury bills (or the Fed funds rate) by a certain number of basis points, with the exact spread depending on which rating class the issuing institution is in. To illustrate, refer back to Exhibit 14–14 and note when the yield spreads get wider: late in 1997, 1998, 1999, and 2000, we see this pattern repeated. There may be other times within a year when spreads increase, presenting buying opportunities for corporate investors. Research done on these events finds that the spread increases are not the result of higher risk, but from such things as widely reported corporate scandals, and more consistently, from seasonal fluctuations such as those noted here.[19]

[18] This is documented in Fridson and Bersh (1994). See the end-of-chapter references.

[19] This is documented in Shen (2003), cited in the end-of-chapter references. Shen notes that rather than the CP rate going up as creditworthiness declines, investors shun the issuer altogether, leading the issuer to an "orderly exit" from the CP market.

## Exhibit 14–15

*Standard & Poor's Commercial Paper Rating Criteria*

Evaluation of an issuer's commercial paper (CP) reflects Standard & Poor's opinion of the issuer's fundamental credit quality. The analytical approach is virtually identical to the one followed in assigning a long-term corporate credit rating, and there is a strong link between the short-term and long-term rating systems. Indeed, the time horizon for CP ratings extends well beyond the typical 30-day life of a CP note, the 270-day maximum maturity for the most common type of CP in the U.S., or even the one-year tenor used to distinguish between short-term and long-term ratings in most markets. CP ratings are intended to endure over time, rather than change frequently. In effect, to achieve an 'A-1+' CP rating the firm's credit quality must be at least the equivalent of an 'A+' long-term corporate credit rating. Similarly, for CP to be rated 'A-1', the long-term corporate credit rating would need to be at least 'A-'. (In fact, the 'A+'/'A-1+' and 'A-'/'A-1' combinations are rare. Typically, 'A-1' CP ratings are associated with 'A+' and 'A' long-term ratings.)

Conversely, knowing the long-term rating will not fully determine a CP rating, considering the overlap in rating categories. However, the range of possibilities is always narrow. To the extent that one of two CP ratings might be assigned at a given level of long-term credit quality (e.g., if the long-term rating is 'A'), overall strength of the credit within the rating category is the main consideration. For example, a marginal 'A' credit likely would have its CP rated 'A-2', whereas a solid 'A' would almost automatically receive an 'A-1'. Occasionally, the CP rating may focus more intensely on the nearer term. For example, a company may possess substantial liquidity—providing protection in the near or intermediate term—but suffer from less-than-stellar profitability, a longer-term factor. Or, there could be a concern that, over time, the large cash holdings may be used to fund acquisitions.

Conversely, following a major acquisition, confidence that the firm can restore financial health over the next couple of years may be factored into its long-term ratings, while the financial stress that dominates the near term may lead to a relatively low CP rating. Having different time horizons as the basis for long- and short-term ratings implies that either one or the other rating is expected to change.

**Backup Policies**

Ever since the Penn Central bankruptcy roiled the commercial-paper market and some companies found themselves excluded from issuing new commercial paper, Standard & Poor's has deemed it prudent for companies that issue commerical paper to make arrangements in advance for alternative sources of liquidity. This alternative, "backup" liquidity protects them from defaulting were they unable to roll over their maturing paper with new notes—due to a shrinkage in the overall commercial-paper market or some cloud over the company that might make commercial-paper investors nervous. Many developments affecting a single company or group of companies—including bad business conditions, a lawsuit, management changes, a rating change—could make CP investors flee the credit.

(Given the size of the CP market, backup facilities could not be relied on with a high degree of confidence in the event of widespread disruption. A general disruption of CP markets cold be a highly volatile scenario, under which most bank lines would represent unreliable claims on whatever cash would be made available through the banking system to support the market. Standard & Poor's neither anticipates that such a scenario is likely to develop, nor assumes that it never will.) Having inadequate backup liquidity affects both the short- and long-term ratings of the issuer because it could lead to default, which would untimately pertain to all of the company's debt. Moreover, the need for backup applies to all confidence-sensitive

*continued*

**Exhibit 14–15** *(continued)*

*Standard & Poor's Commercial Paper Rating Criteria*

obligations—not just rated CP. Backup for 100% of rated CP is meaningless if other debt maturities—for which there is no backup—coincide with those of CP. Thus, the scope of backup must extend to Euro CP, master notes, and short-term bank notes.

The standard for industrial and utility issuers has long been 100% coverage of confidence-sensitive paper for all but the strongest credits. Backup is provided by excess liquid assets or bank facilities in an amount that equals all such paper outstanding. (While the backup requirement relates only to outstanding paper—as opposed to the entire program authorization—a firm should anticipate prospective needs. For example, it may have upcoming maturities of long-term debt that it may want to refinance with commercial paper, which would then call for backup of greater amounts.)

Available cash or marketable securities are ideal to provide backup. (Of course, it may be necessary to "haircut" their apparent value to account for potential fluctuation in value or tollgate taxes surrounding a sale. And it is critical that they be immediately saleable.) Yet the vast majority of commercial paper issuers rely on bank facilities for alternative liquidity. (This high standard has provided a sense of security to the commercial-paper market—even though backup facilities are far from a guarantee that liquidity will, in the end, be available. For example, a company could be denied funds if its banks invoked "material adverse change" clauses. Alternatively, a company in trouble might draw down its credit line to fund other cash needs, leaving less-than-full coverage of paper outstanding, or issue paper beyond the expiration date of its lines.)

Companies rated 'A-1+' can provide 50%–75% coverage. The exact amount is determined by the issuer's overall credit strength and its access to capital markets. Current credit quality is an important consideration in two respects. It indicates:

1) The different likelihood of the issuer's ever losing access to funding in the commercial-paper market; and

2) The time frame presumed necessary to arrange funding should the company lose access. A higher-rated entity is less likely to encounter business reverses of significance and—in the event of a general contraction of the commercial-paper market—the higher-rated credit would be less likely to lose investors. In fact, higher-rated firms could actually be net beneficiaries of a flight to quality.

---

*Source:* **http://www2.standardandpoors.com/spf/pdf/fixedincome/CorpCrit2004.pdf**, pp. 83–84. Accessed online April 10, 2004.

CDs and CP issued by bank holding companies are popular investments for corporate treasurers. Corporate investment analysts may decide to do their own financial evaluation of the issuing bank to determine if a risk-return tradeoff is attractive. This can supplement yield spread analysis and a third-party rating or be used as the sole means of investigation. Whatever approach is used can be applied to evaluation of CDs, CP, and government securities, as well as other bank securities such as time deposits.

*Assessing Liquidity Risk* The liquidity risk assessment of securities is more problematic than default risk appraisal. The differences in various instruments' liquidity are so intangible that treasury professionals have struggled with liquidity evaluation. Individual security liquidity assessment has been slightly easier, at least for issuers that have issued securities for several years and for which a secondary market activity track record has been established. Alan Seidner of Seidner & Associates (Pasadena, CA) has developed a subjective rating system for instrument liquidity, which is adapted in Exhibit 14–16.

**Exhibit 14–16**

*Instrument Liquidity Ratings*

| Instrument | Liquidity (0 Low to 10 High) |
|---|---|
| United States Treasury bills | 10 |
| United States Treasury notes | 9 |
| United States Treasury bonds | 8+ |
| Agency discount notes | 9 |
| Municipal notes | 7 |
| Municipal commercial paper (tax-exempt) | 7 |
| Municipal floating-rate notes | 9+ |
| Bankers' acceptances | 8 |
| CDs issued in United States: | |
| United States bank | 8 |
| Foreign bank | 7 |
| Savings and loan | 5 |
| Eurodollar CDs: | |
| United States bank | 7 |
| Foreign bank | 5 |
| Eurodollar time deposits | 0 |
| Commercial paper | 8 |
| Corporate notes | 6 |
| Preferred stock | 5 |
| Term repurchase agreements | 0 |

*Source:* Reprinted from Alan G. Seidner, *Corporate Investments Manual.* New York: Warren, Gorham, & Lamont, 1990.

## SUMMARY

We have surveyed the menu of short-term investment alternatives and indicated popular choices within bank, corporate, U.S. government, state and local, and mixed investment categories. Typical denominations for many of these exclude small businesses and individuals, who must turn to money market mutual funds for the high yields offered to "wholesale quantity" investors. The money market is a global web of telecommunication ports, with dealers and brokers playing a vital role in coordinating investment purchases and sales.

Surveys indicate that the major concern of corporate treasury personnel is investment safety, with the related notion of liquidity second and yield third. Sweep accounts and money market funds continue to grow in importance especially for small and mid-sized organizations. This approach also fits with the "do more with less" pressure in corporate America that has led many firms to outsource nonoperational activities such as short-term investing. The slight differences in many money market instruments, as far as safety and liquidity are concerned, imply that yield shopping is more frequent than it would seem. Safety particularly means default risk, whereas liquidity translates into marketability. We investigated the safety evaluation of CD in detail, noting that creditworthiness of CDs and other types of instruments might be similarly appraised. Safety also relates to interest rate risk, which we analyzed by drawing a yield curve and estimating price changes that occur for given changes in market interest rates. Longer maturities imply larger price swings on existing securities when prevailing money market interest rates change. We noted the four major explanations for a given yield curve.

In the next chapter, we will look at risk and return from the portfolio manager's perspective. Individual security risks are still important in that context, but the manager also must attend to the interrelationships in security risk.

## USEFUL WEB SITES

| | |
|---|---|
| BanxQuote.com Yield Data | **http://www.banxquote.com/** |
| Bloomberg fixed income resources | **http://www.bloomberg.com** |
| Fidelity Investments | **http://www.fidelity.com** |
| Treasury securities listing | **http://www.publicdebt.treas.gov/of/ofsectable.htm** |
| Treasury securities FAQ | **http://www.publicdebt.treas.gov/sec/secfaq.htm** |
| SEI Investments services and market views | **http://www.seic.com/institutions/** |
| Standard & Poor's Corporate Ratings Criteria *(requires free registration)* | **http://www2.standardandpoors.com/NASApp/cs/contentserver?pagename=sp/P-yclhomepg** |
| Standard & Poor's Money Fund Ratings Criteria | **http://www2.standardandpoors.com/spf/pdf/funds/MMFCriteria.pdf** |
| TreasuryPoint Listing of Institutional Money Funds | **https://www.trading.treasurypoint.com/research/fundlist.asp** |
| Treasury Strategies, Inc., consulting firm | **http://www.treasurystrat.com** |

## QUESTIONS

1. Why is knowledge of the money market important for carrying out of value-maximizing short-term financial management? What are the opportunity costs of not taking into account the risk-return tradeoffs of the various short-term instruments?
2. What is the difference between a primary and a secondary market? Why does a primary market's functionality depend on the secondary market?
3. "Interest rates moved up today in the money market." Comment on why this statement can be made without detailing the rates on each different type of money market instrument.
4. How do the roles of money market dealers and brokers differ?
5. Define the following:
   **a.** default risk
   **b.** liquidity risk
   **c.** reinvestment rate risk
   **d.** interest rate risk
   **e.** prepayment risk
6. Why do Eurodollar CDs generally yield more than domestic negotiable CDs?
7. Given that the major concern of short-term corporate investing is safety of principal, why are corporate investors buying unsecured CP?
8. Why would corporate investors use a dividend capture strategy? What is the major risk involved?

9. Are agency securities as creditworthy as Treasury securities? Explain.
10. Explain the mechanics of interest rate resetting on variable rate demand notes.
11. List and explain briefly the advantages of pooling investors' monies in a money market mutual fund.
12. Explain how an RP works, and distinguish it from a sweep account.
13. Why are sweep accounts done with a company's deposit bank the most convenient method of investing surplus cash balances? Why do large companies not use them as commonly as small companies?
14. Distinguish between discount securities and coupon securities.
15. In Exhibit 14–10, note the coupon-equivalent rate for the 13-week Treasury bills. Assume that the coupon equivalent rate for 26-week bills at the time was 0.96%. Use the models of term structure from Exhibit 14–12 to explain what might account for the relationship between the two rates.
16. What is the mathematical relationship between the discount yield and the coupon-equivalent yield?
17. Summarize the theories regarding the term structure of interest rates.

## PROBLEMS

1. Reggie White, a corporate treasurer, is trying to decide which of two 1-year securities to purchase: a negotiable CD with a nominal yield of 6 percent or a municipal security with a nominal yield of 4.25 percent. The issuing municipality is not in the same state as Reggie's company, but he recognizes that the muni's interest is exempt from federal income taxation. His company's marginal federal tax rate is 39 percent. Which security should the treasurer select, assuming the securities have equal default risk?
2. Jacqui Velasquez, a treasury assistant, is considering the purchase of municipal notes but needs to compare their tax-advantaged yield with the yield on taxable securities. The company's marginal federal tax rate is 34 percent.
   **a.** What advice would you give Jacqui about comparing these securities?
   **b.** If she is considering a muni that is yielding 5 percent, how high must the taxable rate be to provide a higher after-tax yield on the taxable security?
3. Heather Bell, the new cash manager at Centron, a small electronics firm, is excited about the possibilities of investing in high dividend yield stocks. She found one, a stable nuclear electrical utility, whose stock is yielding 8 percent. Centron's marginal federal income tax rate is 34 percent.
   **a.** What would be the dividend capture yield to Centron?
   **b.** How much would CP have to yield to be equivalent (on an after-tax basis) to the stock's yield?
   **c.** Of what types of risk should Heather be made aware? Are there extra return possibilities to offset this risk?
4. Cash manager Ken Johnson just picked up the financial newspaper and is having trouble understanding the jargon. He notices that at a recent Treasury auction of 13-week Treasury bills, the lowest price bid for $10,000 bills was 97.569 percent of par. Can you help Ken understand the various yield calculations?
   **a.** What is the discount yield on these securities?
   **b.** What is the coupon-equivalent yield on the Treasury bills?
   **c.** What is the annual effective yield on the Treasury bills?
   **d.** Comment on the relationship between the results you got in **a** through **c**.
5. CP is a discount security whose nominal yield is very similar to the coupon-equivalent yield of Treasury bills. The CP nominal yield (CPNY) formula uses a 365-day basis.

$$\text{CPNY} = (\text{Dollar discount/Purchase price}) \times (365/\text{Days to maturity})$$

In which: Dollar discount = Face value − Purchase price

Use this relationship to find the nominal yields of the following securities:

**a.** A 45-day, $100,000 CP issue selling at a price of $98,950.

**b.** A 30-day, $1 million CP issue selling at a price of $990,450.

**c.** Compare the results you got in **a** and **b** with those obtainable from GE Capital Fixed Income Investing's online calculator, located at **https://www.gedirectcp.com/cpdirect2/source/InterestYieldCalc.asp**

Recognize that, for **a**, the amount of the investment is the face value, and you will need to convert the 45-day rate to a 360-day rate of interest, and then put it into the online calculator as a whole number (the instructions say "decimal," but intend for this to be a whole percent discount rate). Once you have the numbers, interpret the ones labeled "% on 365-day basis."

**6.** If the 1-year Treasury bill coupon-equivalent yield is presently 5.25 percent and the 2-year Treasury note is yielding 5.95 percent,

**a.** What is the implied 1-year forward rate?

**b.** Should a corporate investor buy two consecutive 1-year securities or buy and hold the 2-year security if his or her forecast for the 1-year forward rate is 7 percent (assuming that he or she trusts the reliability of the forecast)?

## REFERENCES


N. Arshadi, "Capital Structure, Agency Theory, and Banks," *Financial Review* 24 (1989), pp. 31–52.

W. Brian Barrett, "Term Structure Modeling for Pension Liability Discounting," *Financial Analysts Journal* 44 (1988), pp. 63–67.

W. Brian Barrett, Thomas F. Gosnell, and Andrea J. Heuson, "Yield Curve Shifts and the Selection of Immunization Strategies," *Journal of Fixed Income* (September 1995), pp. 53–64.

Brian Belt and Keith V. Smith, "Working Capital Management in Practice: An Update," *Working Paper 951*, West Lafayett, IN: Krannert Graduate School of Management, Purdue University (1989).

John Y. Campbell, "A Defense of Traditional Hypotheses About the Term Structure," *Journal of Finance* 41 (1986), pp. 183–193.

Timothy Q. Cook and Timothy D. Rowe, eds., *Instruments of the Money Market*, 7th ed. Richmond, VA: Federal Reserve Bank of Richmond (1993).

John Cox, Jonathan E. Ingersoll, Jr., and Stephen A. Ross, "A Reexamination of Traditional Hypotheses About the Term Structure of Interest Rates," *Journal of Finance* 36 (1981), pp. 769–799.

John M. Culbertson, "The Term Structure of Interest Rates," *Quarterly Journal of Economics* 71 (1957), pp. 485–517.

Steven W. Dobson, Richard C. Sutch, and David E. Vanderford, "An Evaluation of Alternative Empirical Models of the Term Structure of Interest Rates," *Journal of Finance* 31 (1976), pp. 1035–1065.

Michael E. Echols and J. W. Elliott, "A Quantitative Yield Curve Model for Estimating the Term Structure of Interest Rates," *Journal of Financial and Quantitative Analysis* 11 (1976), pp. 87–114.

J. W. Elliott and Michael E. Echols, "Market Segmentation, Speculative Behavior and the Term Structure of Interest Rates," *Review of Economics and Statistics* 59 (1976), pp. 40–49.

Frank Fabozzi, ed., *The Handbook of Fixed Income Securities*, 3rd ed. Homewood, IL: Business One Irwin (1991).

Eugene F. Fama, "The Information in the Term Structure," *Journal of Financial Economics* 13 (1984), pp. 509–528.

Eugene F. Fama, "Term Premiums and Default Premiums in Money Markets," *Journal of Financial Economics* (September 1986), pp. 175–196.

Irving Fisher, *The Theory of Interest*," New York: Macmillan (1930).

Martin S. Fridson and Jeffrey A. Bersh, "Spread versus Treasuries as a Market-Timing Tool for High-Yield Investors," *Journal of Fixed Income* (June 1994), pp. 63–69.

Craig H. Furfine and Eli M. Remolona, "What's Behind the Liquidity Spread? On-the-Run and Off-the-Run, U.S. Treasuries in Autumn 1998," *BIS Quarterly Review* (June 2002), pp. 51–58.

Michael J. Hamburger and Elliot N. Platt, "The Expectations Hypothesis and the Efficiency of the Treasury Bill Market." *Review of Economics and Statistics* 57 (1975), pp. 190–199.

M. K. Lewis and K. T. Davis, *Domestic & International Banking*, Cambridge, MA: MIT (1987).

Dana Lieberman and Lea V. Carty, "Commercial Paper Defaults and Rating Transitions, 1972–1995," *Journal of Risk Finance* 1 (1999), pp. 87–105.

Miles Livingston, "A Theory of Humpbacked Bond Yield Curves," *Journal of Finance* 32 (1977), pp. 1747–1751.

Burton G. Malkiel, *The Term Structure of Interest Rates*, Princeton, NJ: Princeton University (1966).

J. Huston McCulloch, "An Estimate of the Liquidity Premium," *Journal of Political Economy* 83 (1975), pp. 95–119.

Richard W. McEnally and James V. Jordan, "The Term Structure of Interest Rates," in Frank J. Fabozzi (ed.): *The Handbook of Fixed Income Securities*, 3rd ed. Homewood, IL: Business One Irwin (1991), pp. 1245–1295.

David Meiselman, *The Term Structure of Interest Rates*, Englewood Cliffs, NJ: Prentice-Hall (1962).

Charles R. Nelson, *The Term Structure of Interest Rates*, New York: Basic Books (1972).

Andrew Osterland, "Commercial Paper Chase," *CFO* (June 2002), pp. 83–85.

Vincent Reinhart and Brian Sack, "The Changing Information Content of Market Interest Rates," *BIS Quarterly Review* (June 2002), pp. 40–49.

Mary Jean Rivers and Barbara M. Yates, "City Size and Geographic Segmentation in the Municipal Bond Market," *Quarterly Review of Economics and Finance* 37 (1997), pp. 633–645.

Richard Roll, *The Behavior of Interest Rates: An Application of the Efficient Market Model to U.S. Treasury Bills*, New York: Basic Books (1970).

Alan G. Seidner, *Corporate Investments Manual: Short- and Intermediate-Term Fixed-Income Securities*, New York: Warren, Gorham, & Lamont (1989).

Alan G. Seidner, *Corporate Investments Manual: Short- and Intermediate-Term Fixed-Income Securities 1990 Cumulative Supplement*, New York: Warren, Gorham, & Lamont (1990).

Pu Shen, "Why Has the Nonfinancial Commercial Paper Market Shrunk Recently?" *Federal Reserve Bank of Kansas City Economic Review* (First Quarter 2003), pp. 55–76.

Andrew F. Siegel and Charles R. Nelson, "Long-Term Behavior of Yield Curves," *Journal of Financial and Quantitative Analysis* 23 (1988), pp. 105–110.

Manoj K. Singh "Estimation of Multifactor Cox, Ingersoll, and Ross Term Structure Model: Evidence on Volatility Structure and Parameter Stability," *Journal of Fixed Income* 8 (1995), pp. 10–28.

Venkat Srinivasan, Paul J. Bolster, and Ronald A. Johnson, "Sovereign Debt Ratings: A Judgmental Model Based On the Analytic Hierarchy Process," *Journal of International Business Studies* 21 (1990), pp. 95–117.

M. L. Stigum, *The Money Market,* 3rd ed. Homewood, IL: Dow Jones-Irwin (1990).

M. L. Stigum and R. O. Branch, *Managing Bank Assets and Liabilities: Strategies for Risk Control and Profit*, Homewood, IL: Dow Jones-Irwin (1983).

Duane Stock, "Price Volatility of Municipal Discount Bonds," *Journal of Financial Research* 8 (1985), pp. 1–13.

Suresh Sundaresan, "An Empirical Analysis of U.S. Treasury Auctions: Implications for Auction and Term Structure Theories," *Journal of Fixed Income* (September 1994), pp. 35–50.

Susan Woodward, "The Liquidity Premium and the Solidity Premium," *American Economic Review* 73 (1983), pp. 348–361.

Michael Zaretsky, "Generation of a Smooth Forward Curve for U.S. Treasuries," *Journal of Fixed Income* (September 1995), pp. 65–69.

John T. Zietlow, "Evaluating the Risk in Negotiable CDs," *Journal of Cash Management* (November/December 1990), pp. 39–41, 43, 45–46.

CHAPTER

15

# Short-Term Investment Management

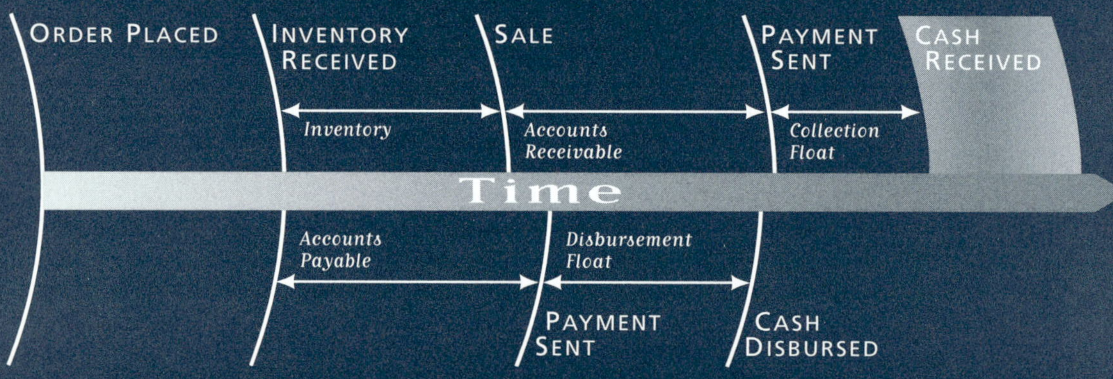

## OBJECTIVES

*After studying this chapter, you should be able to:*

- define an investment policy, and indicate what inputs are used to develop the policy.
- describe the cash and securities allocation decision.
- describe the short-term investment decision-making process.
- calculate portfolio return for the purpose of evaluating portfolio performance.
- indicate how a portfolio manager might assess risk and return tradeoffs involved with assembling a short-term investment portfolio.

Investment is one of the most exciting areas in finance. Deciding which investments to include in the corporate marketable securities portfolio and in what amounts is an intriguing part of the treasury management process. Shareholder value is enhanced by decisions that properly balance risk and return in the short-term portfolio in light of the liquidity position of the firm and its forecasted cash flows.

In the previous chapter, we presented the major short-term investment alternatives and their chief characteristics. We now turn our attention to how the investments manager can select from among those alternatives to assemble a portfolio that meets the company's investment objectives. We consider the factors driving an investment policy, what that policy might include, and how the company decides on the size of its cash and securities holdings. Additionally, we propose the major advantages and disadvantages of external and internal portfolio management and indicate how the portfolio performance might be monitored and evaluated. Part of our discussion focuses on active management strategies such as investing in securities with longer maturities to attain a higher yield. The Financial Dilemma illustrates a typical decision facing the investment manager pursuing an active strategy.

### FINANCIAL DILEMMA

#### Evaluating Interest Rate Risk

Margaret Becker, fresh out of business school, has begun working in the cash management area of her company as part of the management development program. The company pursues an active portfolio management strategy that attempts to gain extra yield by taking measured risks. Margaret has $1,000,000 to invest, and it appears from the cash forecast provided to her by the previous analyst that the company will not need the money for 90 days. She notices that the investment policy recommends choosing either 3-month or 1-year Treasury bills for any investment horizon in excess of 30 days. Margaret is more than a little nervous about the prospect of botching her very first assignment, and she does not know how to compare the risks involved with 3-month and 1-year bills.

## SHORT-TERM INVESTMENT POLICY

The sheer number of alternative investments, available in varying denominations and maturities—each with slightly different risk-return dimensions—presents a major challenge to the investment manager. Increased complexity results from the manager's own view of risk and his or her desire to reflect shareholders' risk preferences in portfolio decisions. Managers have found that a prerequisite for screening investment alternatives is to formulate an **investment policy**. Unfortunately, the 2000 Liquidity Survey conducted by Treasury Strategies found that only about 45 percent of companies have an active, up-to-date investment policy. The investment policy defines the company's posture toward risk and return and specifies how it is to be implemented. A common risk perspective is the evaluative criteria of "safety, liquidity, and yield," implying that risk aspects take precedence over return because of the importance of preserving the principal invested. Specific policy directives might address potential investment eligibility standards such as:

- the minimal acceptable security rating
- limits to dollar amounts or percent of portfolio invested in any one issuer's securities, industry, geographic area, or instrument
- whether a "buy and hold" strategy will be used
- absolute or relative portfolio return (yield) targets
- whether the company will invest through investment company brokers, dealers, or bank traders
- maturity limits
- procedures and controls, including authorized individuals and approvals
- how portfolio performance will be monitored and evaluated

Before the policy can be developed, the treasury department should assess the company's liquidity, its tolerance for risk, and whether any external third-party restrictions limit investment policy. Exhibit 15–1 diagrams these inputs into the policy-making decision, which is one of the first decisions a business must make regarding its investing strategies.

Liquidity assessment can be done using the tools presented in Chapter 2. Dynamic liquidity indicators such as lambda and the net liquid balance can be calculated and evaluated, and the analyst should project both a monthly cash budget for the next six to 12

**Exhibit 15–1**

*Short-Term Investment Process*

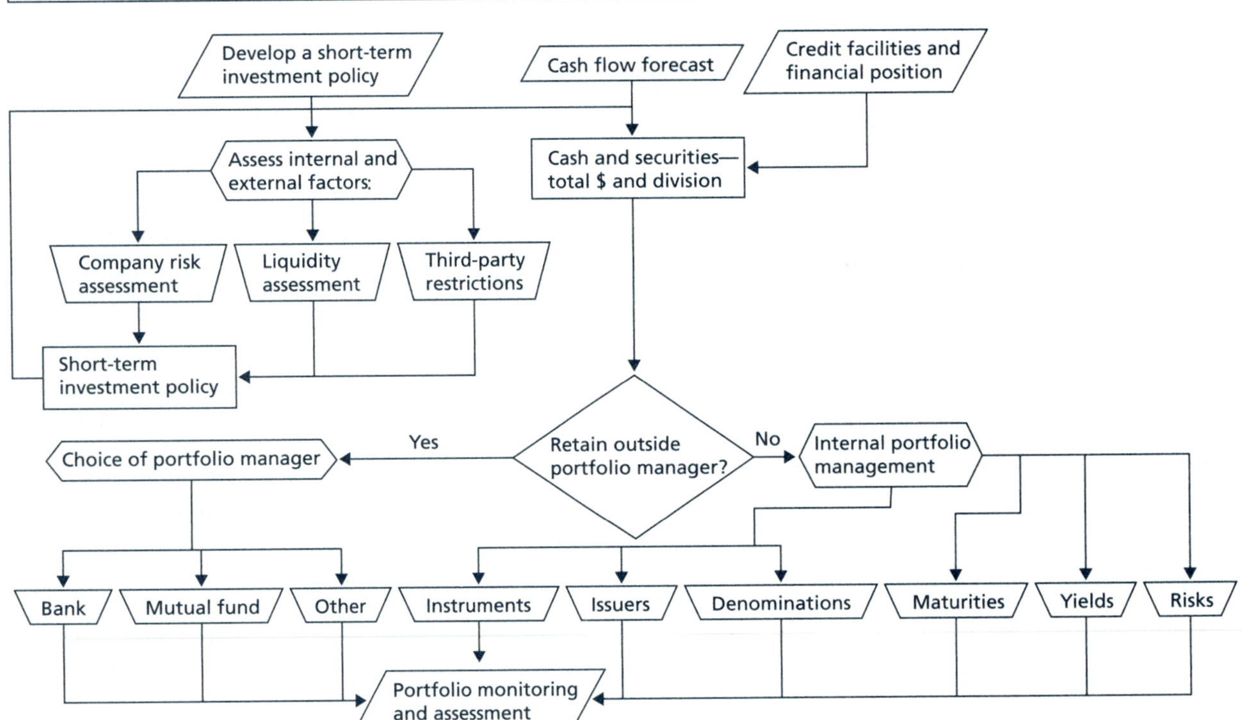

## FOCUS ON PRACTICE

### *Short-Term Investment Policies*

State, county, and city treasurers often work within the most restrictive investment policies. State laws in Idaho and Missouri, for example, prohibit public funds from being invested in commercial paper or bankers' acceptances. In many states, federal agency obligations are also off limits, despite their relative safety. One way to increase yield, given these constraints, is to carefully segment the investable funds into an amount that must be available at short notice and another amount that can be tied up for longer periods and therefore invested in longer-term securities with greater yields. That is exactly what has been done in Missouri, where the total short-term investment portfolio of $3.6 billion was divided into $2.6 billion "short notice" funds (average maturity of five months) and $1 billion in intermediate term investments (average maturity of about two years). However, the investment policy group decided to play it safe—the economy might slow down and tax receipts decline—and put only $500 million of the latter amount into the 2-year portfolio. Because Missouri was the only one of nine states with the top AAA credit rating that was not permitted to buy commercial paper (39 states have investment policies allowing commercial paper as an eligible investment), a ballot proposal was put together to liberalize the state's investment policy.

*Source:* Richard Gamble, "Cash Rich with Few Freedoms," *Treasury & Risk Management Magazine* (November/December 1998).

months and a statement of cash flows for each of the next several years. Most important, at a minimum, the variability and pattern of cash flows (including trend, cyclical, and seasonal components) should be identified. Finally, stocks of liquid assets—particularly of cash and securities—and unused short-term borrowing capacity should be incorporated into the comprehensive liquidity analysis.

The risk tolerance of both the management team and the stockholders also enters into the investment policy formulation, as noted in the Focus on Practice box. The management team has the best grasp of the overall risk attributes of the company. This includes **business risk**, the possibility that the company will not be able to meet ongoing operating expenditures[1]; and **financial risk**, the possibility that the company will not be able to cover financing-related expenditures such as lease payments, interest, principal repayment, and preferred stock dividends. A different perspective on risk characterizes the company's investors who are well diversified, meaning that they own stock in other companies as well. Risk that is relevant to them is **systematic risk**, which is the degree of sensitivity of the company's stock returns to marketwide returns. To the degree that the company's business and financial risk are company-specific, and therefore the overall business and financial risk are in excess of the systematic (market-related) risk, there is a divergence of risk perceptions. This is an example of an **agency problem**, in which the interests of the principals (stockholders) do not coincide with those of the agents (managers). Stockholders

[1] The major determinants of a company's business risk are the vulnerability of sales to recession, input price variability, output price variability and flexibility, degree and size of competition, and degree of operating leverage (preponderance of fixed operating costs such as depreciation, taxes, insurance, and utilities). For a lucid discussion of operating leverage measurement, see Thomas J. O'Brien and Paul A. Vanderheiden, "Empirical Measurement of Operating Leverage for Growing Firms," *Financial Management* 6 (Summer 1987), pp. 45–53.

## FOCUS ON PRACTICE

### Short-Term Investment Management Out of Control

Archer Daniels Midland, better known as ADM, is a large food processing company headquartered in Decatur, Illinois. ADM's monthly purchases of corn and other grains average several hundred million dollars, and ADM hedges its exposure to higher crop prices by using commodity futures. Somehow, things got out of hand in 1989. Having gained futures market experience through ultraconservative hedging, one or more finance personnel started betting on interest rates by buying financial futures. As sometimes happens to gamblers, they bet wrong. ADM had to take a $6.5 million charge to 1992 fiscal year profits because of large losses that the traders suffered. The treasurer quietly left the company a short while later, primarily because of the trading loss, which was discovered by auditors two years after it occurred.

may elect to introduce monitoring, incentive, and control mechanisms such as stock option plans to realign managerial and stockholder interests.[2]

Lender, bank, and regulatory restrictions compose the third area of influence on short-term investment policy. Loan covenants may restrict the types or amounts of securities in which companies may invest. Bank compensating balances limit the amount of surplus funds that can be invested, lowering the overall rate of return on cash and securities because of the lower-than-market earnings credit rate that banks apply. Regulators restrict the types of investments that utilities, insurance companies, and banks can make.

Taking the historical liquidity assessment, company risk tolerance, and third-party restrictions into account, company personnel are able to devise an appropriate investment policy. The remainder of this chapter addresses portfolio decision making with the implicit understanding that the investment manager is making decisions consistent with that policy. Although not all organizations have policies and those that do may have ambiguous policies, investment decisions are generally made with greater ease and consistency when guided by such a policy. We conclude this section with an example of what can happen when a company has either not formulated a policy or is careless in implementing its policy (see the Focus on Practice box).

## CASH AND SECURITIES ALLOCATION DECISION

The first two investment decisions that a company makes, sometimes unconsciously, are to allocate a portion of total assets to cash and securities and then to allocate funds between cash and securities. The first decision is closely related to the working capital investment decision, and the outcome is usually linked closely to the company's risk posture. The **working capital investment decision** refers to the proportion of total assets held in current asset accounts. The second decision, determining the proportion of the company's most liquid assets to be held in cash versus short-term investment securities, is usually approached by viewing cash as a necessary evil. Cash is viewed as a stock of liquidity needed to meet upcoming disbursements. Aside from any earning credits applied to demand de-

[2] The classic reference on agency problems and their correctives is Amir Barnea, Robert A. Haugen, and Lemma Senbet, *Agency Problems and Financial Contracting* (Englewood Cliffs, NJ: Prentice-Hall, Inc., 1985).

posit balances by the company's bank, the cash balance can be seen as an inventoried, nonearning asset, which is necessary to offset unsynchronized cash receipts and disbursements. The objective of managing cash is to minimize total cost, which is the sum of transaction costs (for funds transfers and brokers' commissions) and the opportunity cost of forgone interest. Cost is minimized just like it would be in the EOQ model for inventories when using the most basic of cash management models. In fact, the early attempts at modeling decisions involving cash and securities were based closely on the EOQ inventory model.

## Aggregate Investment in Cash and Securities

The manager may select from three generic strategies when deciding what quantity of total assets to hold in the form of cash and securities: a low-liquidity, moderate-liquidity, or high-liquidity strategy. The lower the liquidity, the riskier the strategy, and the higher the strategy's expected profitability.

The **low-liquidity strategy** entails driving the investment in cash and securities to a minimum. Therefore, cash and securities are a very small proportion of total assets. Assuming that the company does not subsequently overinvest in inventories and receivables, this approach should enhance profitability while also increasing business risk. Lesser amounts invested in cash and securities implies larger amounts invested in receivables, inventories, and higher-return fixed assets.[3] This comes at the expense of greater default and bankruptcy risk, however, because the company has a smaller liquidity cushion with which to weather unexpected and business cycle-related downturns in operating revenues. Obviously, other sources of liquidity—salability of inventories and receivables (or the ability to securitize these), available credit lines, and other sources of untapped debt capacity—affect the riskiness (and therefore the advisability) of the low-liquidity strategy. Companies following the low-liquidity strategy justify it on the basis of untapped credit lines, which we included in the definition of the liquid reserve (see Chapter 2 section on lambda).

The **moderate-liquidity strategy** implies a somewhat greater investment in cash and securities, with correspondingly less risk. This strategy may be premised on a matching philosophy: the higher the level of near-term current liability obligations, the greater the proportion of assets the company should hold in cash and securities. The many defunct savings and loan associations are sober reminders of what can happen to organizations whose assets and liabilities are substantially mismatched.[4]

The **high-liquidity strategy** prescribes a higher proportion of assets to be held in cash and securities. Risk of default on securities and the risk of bankruptcy are reduced because of the greater liquidity cushion, but profitability is lower as well. Companies with significant business risk or financial risk might implement this strategy. Automakers and Microsoft justify their high-liquidity strategies because of unknown future capital investment opportunities, such as newly developed technologies. Again, the company's posture toward risk and the availability of other potential sources of liquidity should be analyzed before adopting a particular cash and securities strategy.

The company's present financial situation may lead it to temporarily deviate from its chosen strategy. It may invest either more or less in cash and securities than the chosen strategy indicates. The current cash flow forecast, in connection with the amount of borrowing, the amount of untapped short-term credit lines, and the financial position of the

[3] Fixed asset investments are generally property, plant, and equipment expenditures made in support of new products and market expansion, which presumably have positive net present value, thus enhancing shareholder value.

[4] In fact, the best way to gain an appreciation of the importance and mathematics behind maturity matching is to consult sources on bank asset and liability management regarding a measure of the degree of mismatch known as "duration gap." Bank management textbooks provide a formula and discussion of this topic.

company, might be taken into consideration. The cash and securities balance might be augmented if the cash forecast shows net cash outflows or increased uncertainty in the cash forecast and a lack of alternate sources of liquidity. The treasurer also may take other precautions, such as engaging in hedging transactions if the cash flow uncertainty stems from future movements in interest rates or commodity input prices. Finally, the decision maker should consider what fraction of the total will be held in cash and what fraction will be held in securities when determining the company's aggregate investment in cash and securities.

Empirical evidence on the use of the various strategies provides some clues about the effects of the operating and financial motives just mentioned.[5] Although based on the ratio of current assets to total assets, the 10-industry, 10-year study by Weinraub and Visscher (1998) indicated that industry has a very large effect on which strategy is adopted (which we note may link to business risk differences) and low-liquidity strategies are often offset by low-risk current liability postures (relatively more permanent financing). Kim, Mauer, and Sherman, using a large panel of U.S. industrial firms spanning 1975 to 1994, found that more cash and short-term securities are held by firms facing higher costs of external financing, having more volatile earnings (and presumably, more business risk), and having lower returns on physical assets *relative* to returns available on financial securities. They also found that companies build liquidity when anticipating profitable future investment opportunities. However, Opler, Pinkowitz, Stulz, and Williamson (1999) found that many firms seem to hold too much cash (moderate-liquidity or high-liquidity strategies, in our framework) and they do so for extended periods. Pinkowitz extended that study and found that, despite the agency problems associated with leaving discretionary cash with managers over long periods, the market for corporate control is unable to exert a monitoring effect on cash (and short-term security) holdings. This is so even for those firms that appear to hold "too much cash" based on several measures of excess cash holdings. Weak control is also true, Pinkowitz found, for firms with poor capital investment opportunities. Ironically, firms reduce their cash holdings shortly after states pass anti-takeover legislation. It appears, then, that agency problems motivate some of the firms opting for moderate- or high-liquidity strategies, and that such strategies are not linked only to business risk or financial concerns. However, the same study did note a negative correlation between the ratio of cash flow to total assets and the ratio of cash and securities to total assets. Reflecting on the current liquidity index and lambda, in our Chapter 2 discussion of "how much liquidity is enough," this is exactly what we would expect for managers targeting some level of liquidity based on their business and financial risks. A recent study by Williamson and Pinkowitz (2002)[6] found that high-liquidity firms add value for stockholders, in that they bring higher market-to-book ratios. The value of the marginal dollar of cash is $1.20, with firms having great capital project investment opportunities seeing higher valuations of cash and valuations being widely variable across firms and industries. They also found, in support of the liquidity analysis we presented in Chapter 2, that firms facing the prospect of financial distress have each $1 of cash holdings valued at less than $1. Harford (1999) also documented that "strategic cash reserves" can be problematic for firms, in that monies are often poorly invested in value-decreasing acquisitions.

## Cash and Securities Mix

The proportional breakdown of cash and securities may be termed the **cash and securities mix decision**. This mix decision may or may not be the result of a well thought out

[5] Excellent background information on the theoretical issues involved in determining optimal and excess liquidity may be found in Tsetsekos (n.d.), Ang (1991), John (1993), and Haubrich and dos Santos (1997), cited in the end-of-chapter references.

[6] Working paper, located at **http://payers.ssrn.com/sol3/papers.cfm?abstract_id=355840#paperdownload**.

strategy. When it is not consciously planned, it is simply the end result of the current operating, investing, and financing practices of the company. There is much confusion about this mix decision and the actual or potential use of cash management models in selecting the mix. For clarification, we distinguish between two interrelated decisions: setting the target mix, and managing the cash and securities balances as they deviate from the target mix.

The "target mix" simply refers to the average or ideal mix of cash and securities. The treasurer might set the target mix based on historical averages or on some type of a financial model or simulation.[7] It may be helpful to view this as an equilibrium value that the treasurer strives toward but may not attain—at least not for long. Cash flows are dynamic, pushing the cash position away from the target level as quickly as it has been attained.

When formal cash optimization models are used, they primarily address the management of the cash and securities balances over time. To some degree, this is uncontrollable because the aggregate position changes in response to outside forces, as mentioned earlier. However, the cash manager wants to maintain control over how much is kept in cash because although cash is the most liquid asset, it incurs opportunity costs in the form of forgone investment interest income or increased interest expense, and there are transaction costs associated with security purchases, sales, and the related funds transfers. If there are no brokerage commissions or other transaction costs and one can find investments (paying competitive interest rates) that might be easily sold and quickly converted to cash, then the decision rule simplifies to cash balance minimization. Practically, this translates into holding the minimal balances in transaction accounts to pay one day's disbursements or meet the bank's compensating balance requirements. Money markets are characterized by imperfections such as transaction costs, however, and the manager must determine how large a cash balance to hold to minimize the costs of cash management.

Three main cash management models, each with different assumptions, can be used to reallocate the cash and securities mix through time. Each views cash as an inventoried asset, with the transaction motive driving a company's allocation of resources to cash held in the form of transaction account balances.[8] Given the total disbursements for a period, each model can specify the number and timing of securities-cash transfers. The larger the per-transfer cost and the higher the interest rate being earned on securities, the fewer and more delayed the sales of securities. These models are profiled in the chapter appendix.

## INVESTMENT DECISION-MAKING PROCESS

Once the total amount of cash and securities has been determined, along with a target amount for each, the investment manager is ready to engage in the most exciting aspect of portfolio management—selecting the investments to be included in the portfolio. Some companies shy away from doing this internally. Many times, the treasury staff is just too small, resulting in a shortage of time or lack of expertise. For smaller companies, the company's short-term investments portfolio also may be too small to make internal management economically desirable.

---

[7] An illustrative simulation, based on historical analysis of actual cash flows, is presented in Daellenbach, cited in the end-of-chapter references.

[8] Although the models tend to focus on the transactions motive for holding cash, the addition of a safety stock buffer enables the models to also incorporate the precautionary and speculative motives for holding cash. The precautionary balance is kept to protect against unforeseen shortages in cash flow, perhaps related to unexpected sales declines. See the discussion of the EOQ model and safety stock considerations in Chapter 4.

## Outside Management

The decision-making emphasis when portfolio management is delegated to an outside party centers on selection of the manager and performance evaluation. Specific portfolio-related decisions retained internally are how much to invest, allocation among outside parties when using more than one, and perhaps specification of the maturities of securities selected by the outside portfolio manager.

*Selecting the Portfolio Manager* The company using an outside investment manager must first decide what type of manager to use. Selections can be made from among brokerage houses, banks, and money market mutual funds (refer to Exhibit 15–1 for a schematic representation of this decision).[9] Brokerage houses specialize in investments, and they are really the department stores of financial services. They are the first to offer innovative products such as the master note commercial paper and online commercial paper programs offered by Merrill Lynch. Brokers offer slightly higher yields than banks on comparable securities, and they have been more aggressive in introducing customer conveniences such as before- or after-hours order initiation and computerized order transmission and confirmation. An example of one such brokerage product works as follows. Idle balances, awaiting reinvestment, automatically are swept into the account. Clients wishing to invest funds on an overnight basis can contact the broker with the dollar figure, and the broker automatically initiates a wire drawdown to transfer the funds from the client's bank account. The balances earn a competitive rate that is revised on a daily basis, and if clients desire, the funds are invested in a tax-free account. Hypothetical, but realistic, rates are provided in Exhibit 15–2. The rates on the taxable account might be in the range of 5–10 basis points above the current average of money market mutual fund interest rates.

Banks may offer the corporate investor bank-issued certificates of deposit, money market deposit accounts, or the parent holding company's commercial paper as ways of funding the bank's operations. Security traders in the parent company also compete for corporate clients but trade for their own accounts. As is the case when the customer is buying from a brokerage dealer, a potential conflict of interest is inherent in this latter arrangement. It is difficult to know if the interest rate quoted to the investor is a competitive market rate or if it is artificially low because the trader wants to pocket a slightly larger profit.[10]

**Exhibit 15–2**

*Hypothetical Brokerage Interest Rates for Sweep Mutual Fund*

Daily Interest Rate (1 Q 2004)

| Investment Vehicle | Rate |
|---|---|
| Taxable sweep fund | 0.60% |
| Tax-free sweep fund | 0.48% |

[9] We identified three major classes of outside advisors in Exhibit 15–1: brokers, banks, and others. Although the most popular other advisor is a money market mutual fund, other options such as insurance company-based advisors are available.

[10] Dealers sell securities from their inventories. They have purchased these at some rate, say, 5 percent, and they profit by reselling them at a lower rate. The difference in interest rates comprises dealers' total return on the transactions.

Investing through the bank has three main advantages. First, as long as the bank's securities are invested (other than in commercial paper), the customer has deposit insurance coverage up to $100,000 of total balances. Second, the ultimate in convenience is afforded when the bank where the company invests is the same one it disburses from and concentrates to. Either an automated sweep account can be opened, or the bank can open a **custody account**, in which it holds securities, automatically reinvests interest and other investment-related cash receipts, transfers funds per corporate instructions, monitors issuers actions such as calls and refundings, and provides a monthly statement on all account transactions. This is provided by the larger banks for a fee that ranges from two to 10 basis points, depending on the size of the account. If immediate reinvestment saves even one day of interest on a 30-day investment yielding 6 percent, this service prevents an annual 20-basis-point reduction in yield. We note that some banks now offer a "late-day sweep" (so 100 percent of end-of-day balances can be invested), and even a "next-day sweep" (so early-morning investment of balances computed during the off hours are invested that may pay dividends on day 1, by the bank having taken an anticipated position in a fund prior to the cutoff). Finally, a third advantage to investing with the bank is that the securities portfolio can serve as collateral for a loan, providing greater liquidity for the corporation. At a minimum, a better rate might be possible for existing credit arrangements if the company can offer a portfolio of securities as collateral.[11]

We have alluded to the rapid growth of money market mutual funds in earlier chapters, and for many companies, this seems to be the best way to go. Exhibit 15–3 profiles the largest institutional money funds as of early 2004. The economies of scale and benefits of specialization that accrue to these mutual funds have enabled them to offer extremely competitive yields. Additionally, the company can write checks for amounts of $500 or more from the fund account, allowing the fund to be used partly for disbursing. Perhaps the major attraction is the ability of the funds to diversify the company's monies by pooling them with other investors' funds and then investing them in many different securities from various issuers. The large dollar amounts of such investments provide an additional bonus to fund investors: higher yields than they would be able to get on their own. The professional management of the money funds allows the corporate cash manager to concentrate on other issues. In response to the market share gains of the money funds, brokerage houses and banks are beginning to offer their own money funds—which, for the banks, is a tacit admission of the eroding attractiveness of money market deposit accounts. Exhibit 15–4 draws our discussion up to this point into focus, with practical considerations of active-versus-passive and external-versus-internal investment management approaches contrasted.

*EVALUATING PORTFOLIO PERFORMANCE* A 2000 Liquidity Management survey by Treasury Strategies reported that only about one-third of companies are measuring their short-term investment performance against a benchmark. Four main benchmarks can be used to evaluate portfolio performance: U.S. Treasury instruments, other money market instruments, money market mutual funds[12] (particularly when evaluating a bank or brokerage), and a synthetic composite. Because of yield curve relationships, the evaluator must be careful to match the maturities of the benchmark as closely as possible to the average maturity of the company's portfolio. Money market mutual funds publish their average maturities along with their 7-day and 30-day yields. The **synthetic composite** is an artifi-

[11] An excellent discussion of the interface of short-term investing with banking considerations is found in Nuttall on which much of this section is based. See the end-of-chapter references for complete citation.

[12] iMoneyNet (**http://www.imoneynet.com**) summarizes the performance of many money market funds, with some information about each. *Pension & Investment Age* now reports on an index of short-term investment yields, the Yanni-Bilkey CA$H™ Universe (provided by Yanni Partners). The CA$H™ data profiles managers of short-term liquid money market instruments. Finally, several organizations will do more focused or even customized indices, with Decision Analytics (San Francisco) being a primary provider.

## Exhibit 15–3

*Largest Institutional Money Market Mutual Funds*

**Largest Institutional MMFs** data as of January 20, 2004

| Fund Name | 7-Day Yield (%) | WAM | Assets ($mils) | Minimum Investment |
|---|---|---|---|---|
| Merrill Lynch Premier Instit Fund (800) 637-7455 | 1.03% | 67 | $54,285.1 | $10,000,000 |
| One Group Instit Prime MMF/Cl I (877) 691-1118 | 0.98 | 54 | 27,185.4 | 1,000,000 |
| Nations Cash Reserves/Capital Cl (800) 626-2275 | 0.95 | 60 | 25,721.0 | 1,000,000 |
| JPMorgan Prime MMF/Instit (800) 766-7722 | 0.95 | 50 | 25,037.7 | 20,000,000 |
| BlackRock Provident:TempFund Inst (800) 821-7432 | 0.95 | 50 | 24,461.7 | 3,000,000 |
| Citi Instit Liquid Reserves (800) 331-1792 | 0.97 | 46 | 23,126.2 | 1,000,000 |
| Goldman Sachs FS Prime Oblig/Inst (800) 621-2550 | 0.94 | 47 | 19,961.5 | 10,000,000 |
| Federated/Prime Oblig Fund/Instit (800) 341-7400 | 0.95 | 46 | 18,333.1 | 1,000,000 |
| Fidelity Instit MMF I ⓘ (800) 544-6666 | 1.01 | 82 | 18,132.4 | 1,000,000 |
| AIM STIC Liquid Assets/Instit (800) 659-1005 | 0.99 | 44 | 16,964.5 | 10,000,000 |

E-mail iMoneyNet: info@imoneynet.com



*Source:* **http://www.imoneynet.com/institutionalLargestMMF.htm**. Accessed 1/24/2004.

cial security that is devised to mirror the portfolio's average coupon interest rate, maturity, and risk rating.[13] This single composite then serves as a benchmark for an entire portfolio. The composite could be maturity of 63 days, yield of 1.75 percent, and a rating equivalent of A-1/P-1 commercial paper, which represents the safest issuers. This composite cannot only be used to calculate the interest rate risk of the company's portfolio, but its yield can be compared with Treasury bills to see how much of a risk premium should be received on that portfolio. Every time the company's portfolio changes, the eval-

[13] The synthetic composite idea was formulated by Lee Epstein in his "Basis Points" column, *Corporate Cashflow* (May 1989), pp. 56–57. For more on all four of the evaluation benchmarks, see the excellent presentation by Richard Bort in *Corporate Cash Management Handbook*, 1991 Cumulative Supplement, Chapter 21.

**Exhibit 15–4**

*Short-Term Investment Management Alternatives*

| Investment Management Approach | Features | Advantages | Disadvantages |
|---|---|---|---|
| **Bank sweep accounts** | The most passive option. Automatic movement of excess funds into overnight investments (deposit in bank's offshore affiliate, money market mutual fund managed by outside firm, or family of funds managed by nonbank affiliate). Money funds account for 44 percent of sweep investments,* with 15 percent of that amount being outside firm funds and 85 percent being bank proprietary funds. Involve monthly sweep fee and perhaps per-transfer fee. | • Easy to implement<br>• Require little staff time<br>• Reduce idle balances<br>• Approvable in almost all short-term investment policies | • Money swept not covered by FDIC insurance unless put in another deposit account<br>• Money swept out of bank is no longer a bank liability, no longer under FDIC's domain if problems arise<br>• Offshore bank affiliate is subject to the authority of a foreign central bank, may institute exchange controls<br>• Sweep fees may exceed interest income |
| **Money market funds** | Mutual fund of various short-term securities, typically with about two-thirds of the allocation to commercial paper. Maximum weighted average maturity of 90 days, no more than 5 percent can be invested in securities falling below the top rating as assigned by a nationally recognized rating agency such as Standard & Poor's or Moody's. | • Professionally managed, well-diversified portfolio<br>• Flexibility of yield and market risk depending on the fund's asset quality, tax status, and average maturity<br>• Management fees low due to competition<br>• Report yield and average maturity using uniform standards, giving ease of comparison | • Hard to know exactly what the fund is investing in between quarterly reporting dates (prospectus has general statement of intent)<br>• Fund may postpone returning cash up to seven days in volatile market conditions, threatening liquidity when it may be most needed by investor |
| **Using an outside manager** | Logical outsourcing move for cash manager, in which external party does the investment decision making, monitoring, and reporting. This taps into the expertise of an outside specialist while freeing up treasury department time for other activities. Outside manager can match company's policy with a customized investment portfolio and strategy. | • More control and transparency than a sweep or mutual fund<br>• Flexible, going from very conservative Treasury-only strategy to "yield enhancement strategy" with high exposure to market risk<br>• Treasurer can change investment guidelines easily<br>• Monitoring is done daily, both for performance and mark-to-market values | • Possibly high fixed costs<br>• May require internal negotiation to "sell" the idea and justify the cost allocation<br>• Outside manager may not be as large as mutual fund or bank, possibly meaning a lower level of capital in the management firm |

*continued*

**Exhibit 15–4**

*Concluded*

| Investment Management Approach | Features | Advantages | Disadvantages |
|---|---|---|---|
| **In-house investing** | The most labor-intensive option. Individual or staff uses its expertise to assess money markets, credit risk and interest rate risk of individual securities, portfolio effects, negotiates with the security dealers' sales forces, and keeps track of account values and account reconciliations. | • Firm has maximum control over the quality, liquidity, and yield of investments<br>• Firm has no outside management fees, retaining the gross interest on investments | • Firm must invest in a dealing screen and market data service such as Bloomberg<br>• Fees for executing transactions and from holding securities in custody accounts<br>• High cost of hiring and training individuals with the necessary expertise, implying a minimum short-term portfolio of \$50–\$75 million |

*Treasury Strategies, Inc. (2002), *Treasury Strategies Commercial Bank Sweep Survey.*

*Source:* Adapted from Eric A. Bloom, "More Reward with Less Risk: Investment Options for Corporate Treasurers," *AFP Exchange* (Spring 2000), pp. 18–21.

uator must alter the synthetic composite accordingly. Proactively, the synthetic composite can be used as a target that the manager tries to match with respect to portfolio interest rate, maturity, and risk rating.

## Internal Portfolio Management

If the company manages the portfolio itself, many more decisions must be made. As investable funds become available, the investment manager must decide from among options available for each of the following:

- *Instruments*—foreign or domestic, and what category, such as money market securities (and within that category, what type: Treasury bills, commercial paper, etc.), preferred stock, common stock, or bonds (refer to Chapter 14).
- *Issuers*—Treasury, federal agency, municipality, corporate (including sectors within any of these that would be unacceptable in any situation).
- *Denominations*—generally larger denominations (the face value dollar amounts) are chosen when feasible because of their higher yields and the fact that some of these are negotiable.
- *Maturities*—will the time when the face value is repaid by the issuer be matched to the investment horizon, and if not, how will the additional risk be weighed?
- *Yields*—although safety and liquidity often come before yield[14] on short-term investments, the manager must determine when, if ever, the company will be more aggressive and reach for yield.

[14] This ranking has been documented in two surveys: (1) a survey of 46 companies conducted by the National Association of Accountants ["Performance Measurement of Short-Term Investments," *Management Accounting* (August 1983), p. 20] and (2) a survey of the Fortune 500 by Keith V. Smith and Brian Belt ["Working Capital Management in Practice: An Update," Krannert Graduate School of Management Working Paper 951 (March 1989), Exhibit 19].

- *Risks*—the probability of issuer default and bankruptcy, of a capital loss resulting from higher interest rates, and other aspects of overall investment risk must be traded off.

Some of these decisions must be tailor made to the particulars of an individual situation, and although some of these decision realms are most likely addressed in the company's investment policy, the policy may be purposefully vague to retain latitude for the manager. Blanket statements such as "invest in the largest denomination possible" prevent the manager from selectively making exceptions to take advantage of market situations, such as a very attractive yield on a Eurodollar certificate of deposit sold by Chase Bank in the London market.

Internal portfolio management does not eliminate the need for performance monitoring. The company again might measure itself against an external passive index, a benchmark security, a managed portfolio, or the performance of a peer manager at a similar company (if available). Management accounting principles suggest that the investment manager's area within the company be treated as an "investment center," meaning that he or she must earn an adequate return given the resources allocated to that area.[15] Otherwise, the activity should be outsourced. One additional complication that may be encountered when evaluating internal-versus-external portfolio performance is the difficulty of calculating realized portfolio yield for a period. Although the calculation is straightforward for an individual security with a lump-sum end-of-period payout, it is more complex when considering an account in which monies were added (as with intermediate interest payments) or withdrawn from time to time. The calculation is likewise more complicated when there is a succession of shorter periods making up the period of comparison, which we demonstrate later in the chapter in our discussion of the structure of interest rates. Furthermore, transaction costs and taxes affect the realized yield earned on investments.[16] The following example illustrates portfolio return calculations for the simple case in which the entire amounts invested in each security are left invested throughout the period and there are no transaction costs or taxes.

Generally, the portfolio rate of return is the weighted average of the individual security returns. Assume that the manager bought (or already held) each of the securities at the beginning of the period. We simply multiply the dollar amounts invested in each by the security return, add the products together, and divide by the total amount invested in the portfolio.

| Security | Dollar Amount Invested | Rate of Return | Dollar Return |
|---|---|---|---|
| Treasury bill | $100,000 | 6.05% | $ 6,050 |
| Commercial paper | 250,000 | 6.75 | 16,875 |
| Certificates of deposit | 100,000 | 6.65 | 6,650 |
| Total | $450,000 | | $29,575 |

[15] This is not as easy as it might seem. For one thing, a decision must be made about whether resources should be calculated on a direct cost or fully allocated cost basis. The investment area may share resources with other areas in the company, meaning that subcontracting investment services may not reduce costs as much as it would appear. The existence of shared costs suggests the company is enjoying *economies of scope*, which are difficult to estimate. For help with cost allocations, see Edward Blocher, Kung Chen, Gary Cokins, and Thomas Lin, *Cost Management: A Strategic Emphasis, 3rd ed.* (New York: McGraw-Hill/Irwin, 2005); investment centers are dealt with in detail in Robert N. Anthony, John Dearden, and Vijay Govindarajan, *Management Control Systems, 7th ed.* (Homewood, IL: Richard D. Irwin, 1992).

[16] It is not enough to simply adjust pretax returns by multiplying them by (1 − marginal tax rate). Unlike individuals, corporations are not permitted to use capital losses to offset ordinary income. Instead, they must net capital losses against capital gains. Consequently, if a corporation has a tax loss carryforward, it would prefer to receive investment income in the form of capital gains. Treasury bill income is not taxable in most states and localities. Transaction costs, if explicit, are more easily handled. The cost would be subtracted from the investment income; if it is charged at the beginning of the investment period, it should also be added to the amount invested.

The portfolio return is determined by dividing the total dollar return by the aggregate investment. In this case, the return is 6.57 percent ($29,575/$450,000).

If we already know the ending dollar figure for the portfolio, the process is much simpler. We simply solve for the interest rate that equates the ending portfolio balance with the beginning balance. The $450,000 invested in our example grew to $479,575. Thus, $479,575 = $450,000 $(1 + i)^t$, in which $t$ represents the time during which the money was invested. If $t = 1$ year, $i = [(\$479{,}575/\$450{,}000) - 1] = 6.57$ percent, as we just saw.

In reality, money is alternately withdrawn and added to the investments account throughout the period. Calculating the portfolio return is more complex in this case. We develop the appropriate formula in the context of the following example.

At the beginning of a year, $500,000 is invested. The company pulls out $45,000 at the end of the first quarter, $55,000 at the end of the second quarter, and $35,000 at the end of the fourth quarter. If the company invested an additional $100,000 at the end of the third quarter and has $535,000 still invested at the end of the year, what rate of return did the portfolio earn? Assume that the company earned $20,000 of interest during the first quarter, $15,000 in the second quarter, $20,000 in the third quarter, and $15,000 in the fourth quarter.

SOLUTION We need an equation that converts intrayear rates of return to their annual equivalent rate. Equation 15.1 indicates that to do so, we must add 1 to the period rate of return, then take the product of all periods' returns. Finally, 1 is subtracted from the result to get the decimal equivalent of the annualized rate of return.

$$K = \prod_{t=1}^{N} (1 + i_t) - 1 \tag{15.1}$$

Where:

$K$ = Annual effective rate of return

$t$ = Time period

$N$ = Total number of time periods

$i_t$ = Interest rate earned during a period

The number of time periods for which $i_t$ must be calculated depends on the frequency with which the manager either invests new money or withdraws new money from the investment account. In our example, this is quarterly, but managers investing varying amounts overnight must do this each day. The formula says to calculate the rate of return for each period and then add 1 to each period return. After this has been done for each period, the product of all $(1 + i)$'s is calculated. Finally, 1 is subtracted from this product to arrive at the decimal equivalent of the annualized return. Note in the table that we used a shortcut (ending value/beginning value) to get $(1 + i)$. The end-of-year withdrawal shown at the bottom of the table is irrelevant for computing the year's return. For the quarterly activity in our example, the annualized return is 15.25 percent.

| (1) Quarter | (2) Beginning of Period Investment/(Withdrawal) | (3) Beginning Value | (4) Interest | (5) End of Period Value [(3) + (4)] | (6) $1 + r_t$ [(5)/(3)] |
|---|---|---|---|---|---|
| 1 | $500,000 | $500,000 | $20,000 | $520,000 | 1.0400 |
| 2 | (45,000) | 475,000 | 15,000 | 490,000 | 1.0316 |
| 3 | (55,000) | 435,000 | 20,000 | 455,000 | 1.0460 |
| 4 | 100,000 | 555,000 | 15,000 | 570,000 | 1.0270 |
| 5 | (35,000) | | | | |
| | | | | Annual rate of return: | 0.1525 or 15.25% |

We have now worked through the development of the short-term investment policy and how companies can make the aggregate cash and securities allocation. We have briefly developed the nature of the decision about whether to manage the portfolio internally or externally, along with several of the implications of that decision. We now move into a presentation of the principles involved in assembling a portfolio, whether done by an outside advisor or the company's investment manager.

## ASSEMBLING THE PORTFOLIO

Three principles govern the portfolio selection process. First, the basic objective is to balance risk and return within the parameters set by the company's investment policy. Second, unlike stock or bond portfolio management, safety predominates in the short-term portfolio. The securities portfolio represents a vital part of the company's liquidity, so security defaults or capital losses jeopardize the holder's financial health. Third, the investment manager must learn how to make security selection and disposition (abandonment) decisions efficiently. A bewildering array of choices confronts the manager, who must learn to economize on the information processing involved. These three principles can be implemented if the manager understands the underlying factors driving risks and returns, how the individual risk factors fit together in the portfolio context, and several approaches to trading off risk with expected returns.

### General Risk-Return Factors

In the money markets, a very high degree of correlation exists between the returns on various instruments. Generally, as the federal funds rate moves up or down, the Treasury bill rate, commercial paper rate, or certificate of deposit rate moves correspondingly (as noted in the previous chapter). Technical factors such as an imbalance of supply and demand, especially in the federal funds market, can cause temporary deviations from the overall pattern. Our present focus, however, is on what common factors cause the rates on all of these instruments to change. Most movements in securities' interest rates can be linked to three common factors: changes in gross domestic product (GDP), an industry-specific factor, and an underlying interest rate trend factor (which subsumes all other influences on the supply or demand for near-maturity loanable funds). Ideally, the investment manager obtains or conducts forecasts of each of these factors.

*GDP* GDP movements give insight into the present and future demand for credit. Real interest rates are affected by the prospects for making positive net present value investments, which in turn affect GDP and are reflective of GDP trends. Money is said to be "tight" when GDP is increasing, especially as inflation rates begin an upsurge and the Federal Reserve (Fed) curtails money supply growth.

*INDUSTRY-SPECIFIC EVENTS* The industry a company is in may have even more influence on that company's fortunes than overall GDP. Not only does industry membership affect a company's stock returns, but it also has an effect on its business risk and therefore the default probability of its borrowings. This translates into changes in the interest rate that investors require for that issuer.

*INTEREST RATE TRENDS* Interest rate trends are best divided into shifts in the yield curve and changes in the slope of an existing yield curve. By looking at a Treasury yield curve, we can eliminate default risk. In this way, we will not confuse changes in default risk with overall interest rate trends.

Any catalyst that changes all interest rates, both short-term and long-term, can be analyzed to arrive at a forecast for yield curve shifts. Either an increased risk aversion on the part of investors or an increase in inflation expectations will shift the entire curve. Although risk aversion is unobservable, various surveys of economists and market participants give insight into inflation expectations. Many of the same techniques used for cash forecasting (in Chapter 12) can be used to forecast overall interest rate trends. It is doubtful, however, whether analysts can consistently outperform market consensus estimates, as we noted in our earlier Focus on Practice box (page 532) profiling Archer Daniels Midland.

Shifts in the yield curve relate primarily to Fed policy actions. The Fed's open market operations, in which it buys or sells Treasury bills to achieve reserve targets, greatly influence short-term rates. Adherents to the market segmentation theory also appraise relative supply and demand in each maturity spectrum to arrive at a yield curve forecast. Political or economic instability, whether in the United States or another country, many times leads to a massive inflow of funds into the Treasury bill market, pushing prices up and yields down. Finally, market participants might anticipate an upsurge in inflation that begins at some point in the future, affecting medium- and long-term securities much more than short-term securities.

## Risk Factors Revisited

In the previous chapter, we developed several types of individual security risk: default risk, interest rate risk, reinvestment rate risk, liquidity risk, and event risk. In this section, we further our analysis by noting the interrelationships between two or more of these risk elements. We also indicate why the risk estimates themselves are subject to uncertainty and how to bring that uncertainty into the analysis. Our goal throughout is to enable the investment manager to determine whether the company will be adequately compensated for risk for any given security alternative and what the appropriate level of risk is for the company's short-term portfolio. Although exact answers to these questions sometimes elude the manager, a fundamentally sound approach can at least narrow the menu of choices.

*Interrelationships among Risk Types* We can analyze the important security risks jointly by conceptualizing that portfolio risk is a function of several risk factors, as shown in Equation 15.2.

$$\text{Portfolio risk} = f(\text{default risk, liquidity risk, interest rate risk, reinvestment rate risk, event risk}) \quad (15.2)$$

Portfolio risk, evaluated for a given investment horizon, is seen to be a function of default risk, liquidity risk, interest rate risk, reinvestment rate risk, and event risk. Of these risk determinants, default risk stands out as the most important single factor. Most analyses of portfolio risk, however, do not consider the interactions of these risk factors with one another or with outside variables. No operational approach exists at present to quantify and trade off the interrelationships among these risk factors. Managerial judgment regarding the relative importance of each risk as it occurs in the portfolio must be applied instead.

A good example of risk interaction is the decision to match the maturity of the investment to the investment horizon. This strategy greatly reduces interest rate risk and liquidity risk, but at the expense of greater reinvestment rate risk. To see this, recognize that by focusing only on the investment horizon, the decision process is limited to a single period. However, the strategy that is optimal in the long run should be pursued, and the long run is simply a series of short runs. A technical way of saying this is that single-period optimization may result in multiperiod suboptimization. Only if we had perfect certainty about future cash flow needs and were forced into investing in securities equal to a given horizon could we overlook the reinvestment rate implications of our investment strategy—and then only if we invested solely in Treasury bills or other discount securities.

Risk factors also are linked to other company attributes. Liquidity, interest rate, and reinvestment rate risks are inextricably tied to the accuracy of the company's cash flow forecast. If the manager is absolutely certain that the period-beginning excess cash will not be needed until the end of the horizon, then liquidity and interest rate risk take on much less importance because the vulnerability of the company to premature sale of securities is eliminated. The accuracy of the cash flow forecast, in turn, is a function of the amount expended on developing the forecast and the variability (e.g., standard deviation) of those flows. Ideally, all variables affecting the individual risk factors, as well as their interactions, are incorporated into the portfolio risk assessment.

A sober example of event risk is the September 11 attacks on the World Trade Center. Cantor Fitzgerald, the principal inter-dealer broker in the U.S. Treasury bond market, suffered the tragedy of losing 657 of its 1,000 personnel housed on the top floors of the north tower. Cantor staff in London worked around the clock and got the eSpeed software systems back online on September 13. So investors were unable to trade for two days, and the event repercussions snowballed in the following days and months as corporate securities' yield spreads increased immediately by as much as 100 basis points relative to same-maturity Treasury securities.[17]

*Uncertainty of Risk Estimates* The uncertainty of risk estimates refers to the fact that our risk estimates are subject to error. For example, we do not know exactly how much variability characterizes the return distribution at present. Does the distribution of certificate of deposit rates still have a standard deviation of 4 percent if that is our most recent estimate? Our estimate may be based on a historical distribution of certificate of deposit returns, but we realize that changes in bank regulation or in the certificate of deposit market may invalidate this sample estimate. Each risk component is likewise estimated subject to error. An estimate of interest rate risk depends on our forecast for the probabilities of rates increasing, staying the same, or decreasing. Our probabilities, and thus the entire probability distribution, again are just estimates, subject to error. Similar difficulties attend default, liquidity, and reinvestment rate estimates. Just as crucial, the importance of liquidity risk or interest rate risk is tied to the future possibility of premature liquidation, signaling the need to bring the cash forecast uncertainty into the portfolio selection process.

Incorporating uncertainty into portfolio risk-return evaluations can be done in several ways. First, sensitivity analysis can be used. Recall that sensitivity analysis involves varying key inputs, one at a time, and observing the effect on the decision criterion. This can be done with arbitrary ranges of values, such as −15 percent to +15 percent in 5-percent increments, or in conjunction with realistic scenarios (e.g., recession, stable economy, moderately growing economy) guiding the choice of what input values to use. Either way, a judgment call is required of the portfolio manager regarding the cutoff point in the decision criterion that results in one alternative being selected over another. Some analysts stress test their investment alternatives under several adverse scenarios and attempt to find an alternative that does relatively well (compared to the other alternatives) even when the cash forecast is wrong.

A second, and preferred, approach to incorporating uncertainty is simulation. Simulation begins with calculation of the expected value and standard deviation of the input variables, then uses iterative draws from each variable's probability distribution to draw up a probability distribution for the decision criterion. Many theoretical distributions, including the normal distribution, can be modeled using computer simulation software such as @RISK or Crystal Ball, add-in software packages for Microsoft Excel. Even before spreadsheet-based packages became available, roughly half of all large companies reported

[17] Standard & Poor's, "Corporate Defaults Climb After Terrorist Attacks," October 26, 2001.

using simulation for uncertainty modeling in financial decisions. Microcomputer-based software makes simulation accessible to even the smallest organization.

*PORTFOLIO RISK AND THE RISK-RETURN TRADEOFF* Modern portfolio theory informs us that when we invest in more than one security, the portfolio's risk is generally lower than the average of the individual securities' risks. Although a detailed explanation is beyond our scope, we point out that the lower the correlation between two securities' returns through time, the greater the reduction in risk that is achieved by combining them in a portfolio.[18] Unfortunately, the interest rates of most domestic money market securities are so closely associated that this type of risk reduction is limited. Two determinants of individual security risk, default risk and event risk, are reducible through adding numerous securities to the portfolio, because of the diversification effects of having multiple securities in a portfolio. Put simply, the more securities one has in the portfolio, the less effect an individual security default will have on overall performance. With equal dollar amounts invested in 100 securities, even if the investor loses his or her entire investment in a given security, 99 percent of the capital is still intact.

*ASSESSING THE RISK-RETURN TRADEOFF* One of the most underexplored areas in treasury management is how to determine when a security or portfolio offers an acceptable return for its risk characteristics. In the absence of an established theoretical framework, for money market securities we offer a 3-step approach:

1. Account for the contextual variables affecting the present investment decision.
2. Evaluate the individual security risks for a set of potential investments, sifting out only those that appear ideal (dominant) on an individual basis.
3. Redo the risk analysis while additionally considering the interactions of the securities' risk elements and portfolio effects.

Exhibit 15–5 depicts the three decisions in a flow chart format.

Contextual parameters include the current cash flow forecast, existing short-term borrowings and investments, the investment horizon, and the investment policy. There are some obvious overlaps here: The cash flow forecast helps define the investment horizon, for example. Short-term borrowings are relevant because they indicate one of the components of financial risk and because untapped short-term debt capacity can be drawn on (instead of prematurely liquidating securities) if the cash forecast turns out to be overoptimistic. We do not want to overexpose the company to a single type or issuer of securities, implying the need to inspect present security holdings. The horizon also is important. If the horizon is a day or several days, the company will probably want to minimize interest rate and liquidity risk by relying on overnight investments such as commercial paper, repurchase agreements, or sweep accounts (which usually direct investment into either commercial paper, repurchase agreements, or money market mutual funds). Finally, the investment policy may specify risk-oriented limits on instruments, guarantors, issuers, and

---

[18] This is especially true if foreign money market securities are included in the portfolio. Salomon Brothers data indicate that the monthly return correlation (in terms of U.S. dollars) between the United States and non-U.S. money markets for the period from January 1985 to June 1990 was only 0.07. Non-U.S. money markets underperformed the U.S. market for the period 1978–1985 but returned 17.9% per year from 1985 to mid-1990, versus a U.S. money market return of 7.9% per year. The standard deviation for the non-U.S. markets' monthly returns was about twice that of the U.S. market: 1.4% versus 0.7%. Investing internationally requires a careful analysis of hedging the currency risk, however. See Duen-Li Kao, "Global Short-Term Investments and Currency Hedging Strategies," *Journal of Cash Management* (September/October 1990), pp. 55–57. Also see Ahmad and Sarver, cited in the end-of-chapter references, who document that international money markets are less interdependent than equity markets and changes in the U.S. market are less dominant in affecting other markets.

**Exhibit 15–5**

*Risk-Return Evaluation for Short-Term Investments*

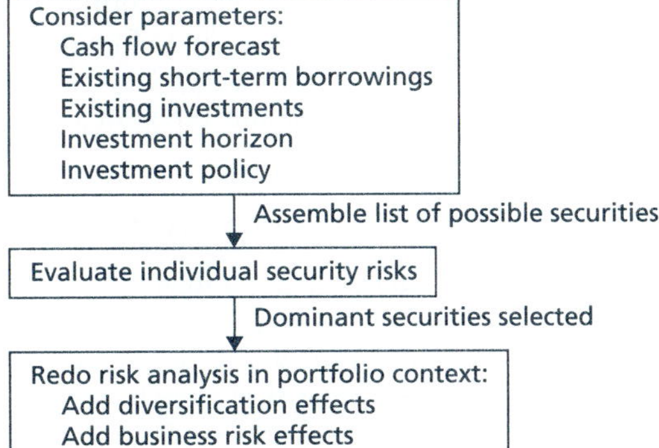


currencies. It also may specify the management perception of what is appropriate risk taking, which ideally should reflect shareholder preferences.

Individual security risk-return tradeoffs can be evaluated statistically or graphically. To assess the variability of a security's returns, vis-à-vis the return itself, the analyst can compute the coefficient of variation. The **coefficient of variation** is the standard deviation of a return distribution divided by the expected return.

Another approach is to plot the risk-return relationships for a manageable list of potential securities on the same graph and to pick those with the best return for a given risk. Those securities that provide a higher expected return for a given amount of risk are said to be **dominant.**

If the analyst wishes to focus primarily on default risk, a listing of securities' returns by rating class is a workable approach. To get a broader picture of risk, which encompasses default as well as liquidity risks, the analyst can compare the difference between a security's return and the return on a Treasury bill of the same maturity. The difference, expressed as a percentage, is one type of **yield spread**. As we saw in the previous chapter, however, this approach also has some limitations. Probably the best approach for jointly assessing risk and return is to conduct a simulation or sensitivity analysis. We present a sensitivity analysis a bit later when discussing riding the yield curve.

Once the individual security evaluations are complete, the analyst should have a listing of dominant securities based on the criteria the company applies to candidate investments. At this point, the risk analysis is redone, but from a portfolio vantage point. Diversification effects and risk interactions, discussed earlier, are of primary interest. Diversification objectives may address any or all of the following categories:

- instruments
- issuers, both within and across different instruments
- industries
- markets (geographic and currencies)

In addition, the analyst considers management's target values for the size and composition of cash accounts and securities purchases. There may also be ad hoc standards for the company's portfolio, such as "no more than 15 percent of short-term investments may be held in securities rated below A-1/P-1" (the highest rating class for short-term securities, signifying the least default risk). Although it is futile to search for the best possible set of securities, because of the large number that exists from which to choose, selecting from a carefully limited field can bring about near-optimal results. The company's willingness to take risks, the size of its portfolio, and the resources it can dedicate to portfolio management direct the company's decision on whether it will use an active or passive portfolio management strategy.

A very recent development, a comprehensive treasury department risk report card, is being used by companies such as Freddie Mac—otherwise known as the Federal Home Loan Mortgage Corporation (Smith and Miles, 1997). This approach, although somewhat subjective, gives a global and integrated picture of an organization's financial risks.

## Short-Term Investment Strategies

Many possible investment strategies can be used. Generically, we divide them into passive strategies and active strategies. A **passive investment strategy** involves a minimal amount of oversight and very few transactions once the portfolio has been selected.

An **active investment strategy** involves more trading and active monitoring of the portfolio and may be motivated by a philosophy that the investor can "beat the market." In the money markets, this generally means earning higher-than-normal yield spreads and/or capital gains as a result of accurate anticipation of interest rate movements.

*Passive Strategies* A popular passive strategy is the **buy-and-hold strategy**. Quite often, this is part of a "maturity matching" approach to investing that prescribes investing in a security that will mature at the end of the investment horizon. The horizon is based on how long the company can tie up the investable funds. This eliminates interest rate risk if the company does hold the security to maturity as planned, because it will receive the face value of the security at that time. The buy-and-hold strategy may be implemented by investing part or all of the portfolio in an index fund, which is a managed portfolio assembled to mirror a particular money market composite. The composite serves as an index because it is calculated by averaging the yields of a broadly based basket of securities. A **modified buy-and-hold strategy** might be used when the investor wishes to take advantage of favorable interest rate movements, should they occur. If rates come down and the portfolio report shows a paper capital gain, the investor may sell or swap for another security to capture the gain.

*Active Strategies* There are numerous active strategies. One strategy is to try to spot inefficiencies in the way securities are priced at present and to buy those that are underpriced (have higher yields than warranted by their riskiness). These are then held to maturity or sold at a capital gain when the market recognizes the mispricing and corrects it by bidding up the price. One way of implementing this strategy is to study yield spreads.

**Historical yield spread analysis** suggests other profitable trading strategies. For temporarily underpriced securities, the yield offered will be higher than warranted by the underlying risks. Market overreactions to events such as credit rating changes (part of the event risk phenomenon) may open up some attractive yield opportunities. The historical yield spreads, computed as the difference between a given security and short-term Treasury bills on the top-quality securities for each instrument, have been determined by consultant Alan Seidner (Exhibit 15–6). The analyst compares the current yield spread for the instrument type (or given rating class) or for an individual security within that type to see if abnormally large spreads exist.[19] An aggressive investor might research the largest spreads available, seeking to determine why they exist; if there is no exceptional default, liquidity, or event risk associated to account for the spread, then a purchase would be made. Little research has been done on spreads for short-term securities. However, it is interesting to

[19] Yield spread analysis is covered in D'Amato and Remolona, Irving and Raney, Zietlow, and Khaksari. Full citations appear in the end-of-chapter references.

**Exhibit 15–6**

*Historical Average Yield Spreads Instrument versus Treasury Bills (Basis Points)*

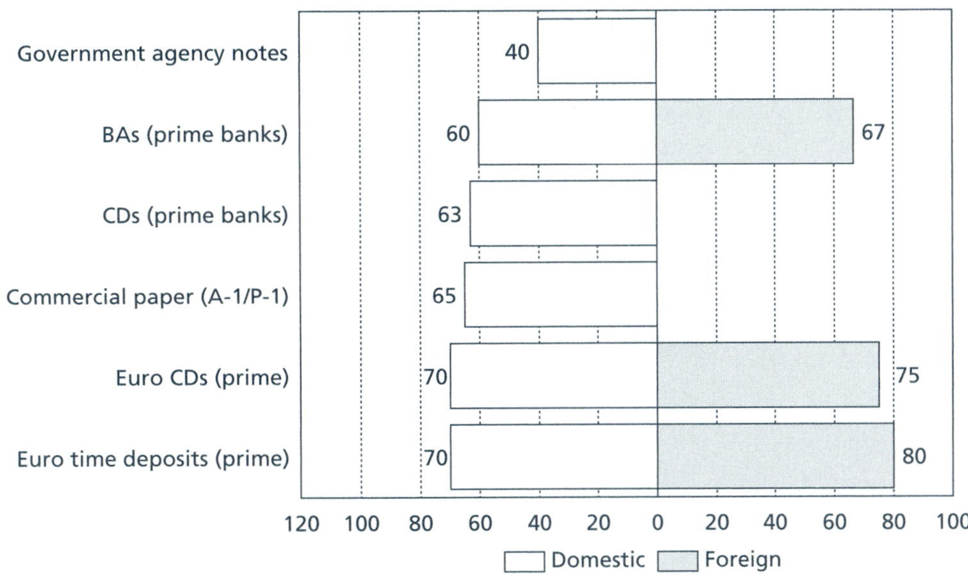


*Source:* Reprinted from Alan Seidner, *Corporate Investments Manual,* New York: Warren, Gorham & Lamont (1990), Research Institute of America. Used with permission.

note that very recent evidence indicates that corporate bond spreads for 1- to 3-year (current) maturities are about 50 basis points, but the expected loss related to default is 1/16 of one basis point. Taxes, liquidity risk, and uncertainty about default risk account for much of the remaining spread, but there appears to be a yield pickup that the buy-and-hold investor can earn that exceeds what one would expect by looking at the typical risk factors (D'Amato and Remolona, 2003). It also appears that investors have difficulty diversifying away unexpected losses in their bond portfolios because it would take very large portfolios to diversify the returns of bonds that are highly negatively skewed.

A second, and also a very popular, active strategy is **riding the yield curve.** This involves buying securities with maturities longer than the investment horizon, fully intending to liquidate the position early. If the yield curve is stable, meaning it neither shifts nor changes slope during the holding period, the investor can generally outperform a maturity matching strategy. This occurs because the normal yield curve is upward-sloping, giving higher interest rates for longer-maturity instruments. Domian, Maness, and Reichenstein (1998) documented the very attractive return-risk tradeoff available to treasurers willing to stretch 3-month Treasury bill investments out to six months, one month, or one year.

## FINANCIAL DILEMMA REVISITED

Returning to the chapter's opening Financial Dilemma, assume that an investor with a 3-month horizon has available a 3-month Treasury bill yielding 1.61 percent and a 1-year bill yielding 2 percent. Not only will the investor gain additional interest for buying the 1-year bill, but he or she will also earn a capital gain as the 1-year bill increases in price until it yields 1.87 percent at the end of the 3-month horizon (the current maturity is then nine months). To evaluate this strategy, an investor might use sensitivity analysis. Exhibit 15–7 profiles the advantage to the 1-year bill in terms of its yield differential over the 3-month bill. Each entry in the table represents the total return for the 1-year bill (interest +/− capital gain or loss) less the total return for the 3-month bill (interest +/− capital gain or loss), adjusted for transactions costs, if any. This is calculated while varying two important assumptions: what happens to interest rates over the holding period (each row represents a possible change, with the middle row showing the baseline no-change forecast) and the holding period (starting with liquidation after one week, implying 12 weeks are left in the period, etc.).[20] Note that the advantage to the 1-year bill increases with general interest rate reductions (the first four rows in the table) and with longer holding periods (as we move rightward in the table). This makes sense because the 1-year bill has a larger interest rate risk than the 3-month bill, implying capital gains when rates fall and capital losses when rates rise.

Because the transaction cost for early sale is only 2 basis points ($2,000/$1,000,000), the 1-year outperforms the 13-week, even when the 13-week is held to maturity and interest rates go up 20 basis points in the next week or next 13 weeks.

## Exhibit 15–7

*Sensitivity Analysis: Riding the Yield Curve*

Spreadsheet table for evaluating riding the yield curve; relative advantage (in terms of increased rate of return) to a 1-year Treasury bill over a 3-month Treasury bill. The middle row in the table is a "no change" interest rate scenario, and rows above (below) are 5 basis point decreases (increases) in all interest rates. The right column indicates that the investor held the entire holding period; other columns are early sales.

INPUTS:

| | |
|---|---|
| Amount invested | $1,000,000 |
| 3-month rate, annualized | 0.0161, or 1.61% |
| 1-year rate | 0.02, or 2.00% |
| Investment horizon | 13 weeks |
| Most likely change in rates | 0, or no change |
| Transaction cost if sell early | $2,000 |
| Yield curve slope | Upward, 1 basis point per week |

| | Number of Weeks Left Within Horizon When Cash Flow Situation Causes Premature Liquidation | | | | | | |
|---|---|---|---|---|---|---|---|
| Change in Short-Term Interest Rates | 12 | 10 | 8 | 6 | 4 | 2 | 0 |
| −0.0020 | 0.010690 | 0.010906 | 0.011122 | 0.011337 | 0.011552 | 0.011767 | 0.009973 |
| −0.0015 | 0.010559 | 0.010776 | 0.010991 | 0.011207 | 0.011423 | 0.011638 | 0.009844 |
| −0.0010 | 0.010428 | 0.010645 | 0.010861 | 0.011077 | 0.011293 | 0.011508 | 0.009716 |
| −0.0005 | 0.010298 | 0.010514 | 0.010731 | 0.010947 | 0.011163 | 0.011379 | 0.009587 |
| 0.0000 | 0.010167 | 0.010384 | 0.010601 | 0.010817 | 0.011034 | 0.011250 | 0.009458 |
| 0.0005 | 0.010036 | 0.010253 | 0.010471 | 0.010687 | 0.010904 | 0.011121 | 0.009329 |
| 0.0010 | 0.009905 | 0.010123 | 0.010340 | 0.010558 | 0.010775 | 0.010991 | 0.009200 |
| 0.0015 | 0.009774 | 0.009992 | 0.010210 | 0.010428 | 0.010645 | 0.010862 | 0.009071 |
| 0.0020 | 0.009643 | 0.009862 | 0.010080 | 0.010298 | 0.010515 | 0.010733 | 0.008942 |

[20] The analysis is performed using a financial spreadsheet (e.g., two-variable Data Table in Microsoft Excel™). The advantage to the longer-term investment is calculated as the difference in yield over the holding period, plus (minus) the capital gain (loss) difference, minus early sale transactions costs, when selling either or both of the securities before their maturity dates. No transaction cost on 3-month if able to hold entire horizon.

In conjunction with the uncertainty surrounding the cash flow forecast and the short-term borrowing situation, the investment manager can decide whether the risk merits selecting the longer maturity. Empirical evidence about the relative advantage of riding the yield curve is mixed, indicating an advantage to the strategy for periods of generally declining rates, and reduced portfolio performance when the yield curve flattens out or shifts upward.[21] This confirms the finding of our sensitivity analysis in Exhibit 15–7.

Even more explicit in its reliance on interest rate forecasts is an active **trading strategy** based on augmenting yields with capital gains. When the analyst forecasts a change in interest rates, trading strategies can be devised to enhance investment profits. This approach is very risky and is little used for short-term portfolios, as pointed out earlier in our portrayal of ADM.

An active strategy that became popular in the 1980s is the **dividend capture strategy**. Because intercorporate dividends have been largely excludable for income tax purposes (presently, there is a 70-percent exclusion), corporate investors decided to buy a stock with a high dividend yield,[22] hold until just after the record date for payment, and then sell the stock. This strategy is sometimes termed a **dividend roll**. For a company in the 34-percent tax bracket, the tax rate on dividends is reduced to 10.2 percent [34%(1 − 0.70)]. Thus, the after-tax yield is 89.8 percent of the pretax yield, whereas on taxable commercial paper or certificates of deposit, it would only be 66 percent of the pretax yield. By law, the company must hold the stock for at least 46 days to qualify for the 70-percent exclusion. The obvious risk of the strategy is the possibility of the stock price declining during the holding period, which might be hedged by buying a put or selling a covered call.[23] The Japanese insurance industry is one of the main investor groups pursuing this strategy because of its unique regulatory and tax situation. The dividend capture strategy has become less popular for U.S. companies because of the availability of the auction rate preferred stock mentioned in Chapter 14. However, Murphy (2001) demonstrated that, even after hedging costs, a preferred stock portfolio combined with money market assets may have no material chance of loss but will have average after-tax returns greater than those on money market investments alone.

Active strategy managers also use **swap strategies**, particularly when a position has already been taken but a new, better opportunity arises. There are numerous types of swaps, but we limit our discussion to two popular types: a **maturity extension swap** and a **yield spread swap**. In each swap arrangement, the present holding is sold and replaced with another security that will increase the yield or dollar return while minimally affecting credit risk. The maturity extension swap is executed when the manager wishes to ride the yield curve, but instead of investing a recent cash inflow, he or she must liquidate another security to make the investment. Surprisingly, only 14 percent of larger companies surveyed in 2003 by Treasury Strategies had lengthened their maturities in light of the very low 1-percent yield on short-term institutional money market mutual funds (and 11 percent had actually shortened maturities, while the remaining companies had not changed maturities). Microsoft, with its $49 billion in cash and short-term investments in late 2003, invested only $6.4 billion in maturities of one year or less, with the remainder being in the 1- to 3-year maturity range.[24] The higher yield in that second portion of the portfolio would have come with significantly higher risk had not Microsoft been confident in its ability to buy and hold the securities to neutralize the effects of interest rate risk. Yield

---

[21] See Ed A. Dyl and Michael D. Joehnk, "Riding the Yield Curve: Does It Work?" *Journal of Portfolio Management* (Spring 1981), pp. 13–17.

[22] Dividend yield is the year's cash dividend divided by the current stock price.

[23] For the dynamics and advantages to these risk-reduction strategies, see Krause. An excellent risk-return model for evaluating hedged and unhedged capture strategies is contained in Duen-Li Kao and Mark A. Zurack. Atchison and Kling present a good review of previous simulations and original results of their simulation of the dividend roll strategy. See the end-of-chapter references for full citations.

[24] Reuters, "Microsoft: What Do You Do With $49 billion?" (July 21, 2003). Accessed online at **http://zdnet.com.com/2100-1104-5047534.html** on 1/12/04.

spread swaps are similar to maturity extension swaps, except the motivation is to take advantage of a mispriced security based on historical spread analysis.

*Strategy Implementation* Whether a company uses a passive or active strategy, it may implement the strategy itself or rely on an outside advisor or money market mutual fund to carry the strategy out. The company might evaluate these alternatives by conducting a make-versus-buy analysis. The relative costs are more easily estimable than the potential gains of going outside.

*Survey Evidence on Strategies* Evidence regarding short-term investment practices represents most companies as applying many of the principles we have developed in this chapter. One of the most revealing summaries of portfolio management, although somewhat dated, is a *Fortune 1000* survey conducted in the mid-1980s by Frankle and Collins.[25] Although they asked the highest-ranking financial officers about their approach to cash management strategy, not specifically their investment strategy, the concepts should overlap greatly. Aggressive cash managers are more likely to use active strategies, and passive managers probably use the buy-and-hold approach more often. Respondents labeled themselves as aggressive (47 percent), moderate (34 percent), conservative (17 percent), and passive (2 percent). As might be expected, the division of cash and securities was weighted toward investments for the aggressive (74 percent of aggressive managers had 75 percent or more of the excess cash invested, on average) and lowest for the passive (50 percent invested). Rate of return was deemed to be the most important attribute of potential investments to the aggressive strategist, whereas moderate and conservative strategists ranked default risk the highest (the passive strategists did not rank any attribute as very important, possibly because they had less funds invested). Aggressive strategists used the "riding the yield curve" strategy much more often (30 percent usage rate) than moderate (24 percent) or conservative (9 percent) strategists. In the era studied, Eurodollar certificates of deposit and time deposits ranked as the favorite instrument, followed by repurchase agreements (moderate and conservative managers) or commercial paper (aggressive managers).

In the *Fortune 500* survey by Smith and Belt,[26] additional evidence on two of these issues is provided. First, the determination of how much to transfer between cash and securities was only made with cost balancing models by 10 percent of the respondents (these models are discussed in the chapter appendix); 42 percent used subjective judgment, and 23 percent used established guidelines (the remainder specified "other" as their approach). Second, the buy-and-hold portfolio management strategy was the most popular strategy used by the *Fortune 500* companies.

*Critique of Strategies* Active portfolio management strategies, much more than passive strategies, rely on the ability of the investment manager to forecast interest rates. The extensive literature on money market pricing efficiency and interest rate forecasting is conclusive in its findings: Pricing is rapid and mainly unbiased, and most forecasters cannot forecast more accurately than either a naive "no change from last period" forecast or a forecast based on the futures market.[27] Unless the forecaster knows something about

---

[25] See the end-of-chapter references for full citation.

[26] See the end-of-chapter references for full citation.

[27] A good but somewhat dated review of the literature on interest rate forecasting accuracy is contained in R. W. Hafer and Scott E. Hein, "Comparing Futures and Survey Forecasts of Near-Term Treasury Bill Rates," Federal Reserve Bank of St. Louis *Review* (May/June 1989), pp. 33–42. Investment textbooks generally support money market efficiency; however, some counterevidence is presented in Marcia Stigum, *The Money Market*, 3rd ed. (Homewood, IL: Dow Jones-Irwin, 1990), pp. 511–512, 527–533. For more recent studies, see Sarno, Thornton, and Valente (2002), Diebold and Li (2003), and Owens and Webb (2001), all cited in the end-of-chapter references.

the pricing of securities or the future course of interest rates that is not known by other market participants, passive portfolio management strategies should be used.

## SUMMARY

Short-term investment management is a challenging and rapidly changing area of financial management. The number of securities from which the investment manager can select and the stream of innovative new securities that must be evaluated present a unique opportunity to conduct risk-return analysis. Not only must individual security risks be appraised, but interdependencies and risk in a portfolio context must also be managed.

The investment manager begins the portfolio selection by considering the cash forecast, the company's financial position, and the investment policy. The investment policy limits the types of securities to be included and perhaps gives guidelines to follow in assembling the portfolio. This information is combined with an understanding of the company's posture on the total amount invested in cash and securities and the cash-securities mix. The Baumol, Miller-Orr, and Stone models covered in the chapter appendix may be consulted for help in determining how and to what extent funds should be reallocated from securities to cash. These models should be used only as part of a more comprehensive analysis of liquidity and current asset investment, so that shareholder wealth is maximized. The financial manager is attempting to maximize the present value of cash flows, not merely to minimize the company's costs.

If the company decides to have an outside investment manager, the next step is selecting the manager(s) to be used. A common choice for such firms is to wire money to a money market mutual fund, which provides daily interest and immediate access to funds. If done internally, corporate personnel are faced with sifting through a set of potential securities to evaluate their risk and risk-return tradeoff. After doing individual security risk analysis, the manager should have a shorter list of potential investments, which are then re-evaluated from a portfolio perspective. Regardless of whether decision making is done externally or internally, the results must be monitored and evaluated. The common benchmarks are Treasury bill rates, money market mutual fund rates, indexes, or synthetic composites.

The chapter concluded with profiles of passive and active investment strategies. Passive strategies, such as the buy-and-hold strategy, typify the approach taken by many companies when investing surplus cash. Active strategies usually imply an interest rate forecast, but the analyst may be wrong more often than right unless the forecaster possesses special analytical ability or more rapid access to critical information. The predominant concerns for most managers are safety and liquidity, not yield. The possibility of yield enhancement may be viewed as too risky for the short-term securities portfolio.

## USEFUL WEB SITES

| | |
|---|---|
| AFP | **http://www.afponline.org** |
| International Treasury Management Benchmarking Consortium | **http://www.itmbc.com/** |
| Institutional Investor Magazine and other magazines | **http://www.institutionalinvestor.com/** |
| Merrill Lynch WCMA | **http://www.businesscenter.ml.com/pdf/200240913_Insert_OBS.pdf** |

## QUESTIONS

1. What is an investment policy? What are the key inputs that a company might use in developing the policy?
2. How can a liquidity assessment be conducted? Why is this an important prerequisite to determining the target mix of cash and marketable securities?
3. Contrast business risk and financial risk. Of what relevance is either type of risk to the risk posture a company might take regarding short-term investments?
4. Agency problems occur when managerial interests deviate from those of shareholders. Given that managers may be more interested in business and financial risk than systematic risk:
   **a.** How might this affect the short-term investments policy?
   **b.** What effect will this have on the investment returns earned?
5. Compare and contrast the low-liquidity, moderate-liquidity, and high-liquidity strategies. Include the following in your answer:
   **a.** Regardless of which strategy is used, what specifically is being determined?
   **b.** The riskiness of each strategy.
   **c.** The likely profitability (or return) effects of each strategy.
   **d.** Which strategy would you recommend to a stable consumer goods company that is not currently facing any strong competition for its market position and is not likely to face strong competition in the near future?
   **e.** What additional information about the company mentioned in **d** would you collect if you were actually making this decision?
6. What is the difference between the target mix decision and the management of cash and securities balances as they deviate from the target mix?
7. What steps should a portfolio manager follow when selecting individual securities for inclusion in the company's short-term securities portfolio?
8. What are the pros and cons of using outside advisors to manage the company's short-term portfolio?
9. List and define briefly the four major benchmarks that can be used for evaluating portfolio performance.
10. List the decisions the portfolio manager must make when the short-term investments portfolio is managed internally.
11. "The short-term portfolio performance can be assessed by taking the year-end account value and dividing it by the year-beginning value, then subtracting 1 from the quotient." When is this statement invalid for assessing actual performance?
12. Because the returns on most money market instruments are highly correlated, why does it make sense to spread a portfolio's allocation across various instruments and securities?
13. What types of risk are reduced by diversification?
14. "Risk factors are interrelated." Explain.
15. What does it mean to say that risk estimates are uncertain?
16. Summarize the approach given for assessing the portfolio risk-return tradeoff.
17. Contrast passive and active investment strategies, giving an example of each.
18. Summarize the survey evidence given regarding real-life cash balance and investment portfolio management. Are any of the findings surprising?

## PROBLEMS

1. A company invests $1,000,000 at the beginning of the year. It adds another $250,000 at the end of the first quarter, withdraws $350,000 at the end of the second quarter, adds $145,000

at the end of the third quarter, and withdraws $450,000 of the remaining funds at the end of the year. It earns $20,000 of interest in the first quarter, $17,000 in the second quarter, $12,000 in the third quarter, and $29,000 in the fourth quarter.

**a.** What is the annual effective rate earned on the investments portfolio?

**b.** What rate of return would have been calculated if one only looked at the ending portfolio value as compared with the beginning $1,000,000 investment?

**2.** One way of enhancing short-term investment portfolio returns is to "reach for yield." As a small business owner, with no time or expertise to select or evaluate investments, an alternative to a money market mutual fund is an "ultra short-term bond fund." Such a mutual fund invests primarily in very short-term, investment grade debt obligations, with an average effective maturity on the portfolio of one year or less. Here are the starting (time of the fund's inception) and ending portfolio values, assuming reinvestment of all dividends and capital gains, for one such fund and two benchmark indexes.

| Portfolio/Index | Beg. Value (11/25/88) | End. Value (2/28/97) |
|---|---|---|
| Strong Advantage Ultra Short Bond Fund | $10,000 | $18,331 |
| Salomon 1-Year Treasury Index | 10,000 | 16,842 |
| Lipper Ultra Short Obligation Avg. | 10,000 | 16,084 |

As of 2/28/97, the Strong Advantage bond fund had an average effective maturity of 0.74 year. Its portfolio composition was as follows:

| Asset Type | Percent of Net Assets |
|---|---|
| Corporate Debt Securities | 63.8% |
| Non-Agency Mortgage & Asset-Backed Securities | 26.4 |
| Short-Term Investments | 7.5 |
| Preferred Stocks | 1.4 |
| U.S. Government and Agency Issues | 0.9 |
| Total | 100.0% |

Most of the corporate debt consisted of subordinated notes and floating rate notes. Almost 83 percent of the net assets were investments in U.S. issuers' securities.

**a.** What is the annualized rate of return for the bond fund and each index for the $8\frac{1}{4}$-year period? Should the fund manager be proud of this performance (why or why not)?

**b.** What risks are taken by the bond fund that might explain some of the performance differences in **a**?

**c.** Comment on the diversification reflected in the bond fund's portfolio composition. What is the relationship between degree and type of diversification and your evaluations in **a** and **b**?

**d.** Assume that the typical money market fund has an average effective maturity of $1\frac{1}{2}$ months. What is the difference in price change for the bond fund relative to the typical money fund, if interest rates were to immediately increase by 1 percent? (Assume the small business owner considering this investment has $35,000 invested in either of the two types of funds at the time.)

**e.** Assuming that the bond fund earns an average annual return that is 1.2 percent above the typical money fund, how long will it take before the additional interest earned recouped the incremental price change you calculated in **d**?

## REFERENCES

Syed M. Ahmad and Lee Sarver, "The International Transmission of Money Market Fluctuations," *The Financial Review* (August 1994), pp. 319–344.

Michael J. Alderson, Keith C. Brown, and Scott L. Lummer, "Dutch Auction Rate Preferred Stock," *Financial Management* (Summer 1987), pp. 68–73.

James S. Ang, "The Corporate-Slack Controversy," in Yong Kim and Venkat Srinivasan, V., (eds.), *Advances in Working Capital Management*, Vol. 2, Greenwich, CT: JAI Press (1991), pp. 3–14.

Michael D. Atchison and John L. Kling, "How Good Are Preferred Dividend Capture Plans?" *Journal of Cash Management* (November/December 1988), pp. 71–74.

Bruce D. Bagamery, "On the Correspondence Between the Baumol-Tobin and Miller-Orr Optimal Cash Balance Models," *The Financial Review* (May 1987), pp. 313–319.

Eric A. Bloom, "More Reward with Less Risk: Investment Options for Corporate Treasurers," *AFP Exchange* (Spring 2000), pp. 18–21.

Morris Budin and A. T. Eapen, "Cash Generation in Business Operations: Some Simulation Models," *Journal of Finance* 5 (1970), pp. 1091–1107.

Dimitris N. Chorafas, *Liabilities, Liquidity, and Cash Management*, New York: John Wiley & Sons, Inc. (2002).

Agnes T. Crane, "Stocks Steal Bond Funds' Thunder," *The Wall Street Journal* (January 2004), p. R9.

Hans G. Daellenbach, "Are Cash Management Optimization Models Worthwhile?" *Journal of Financial and Quantitative Analysis* (September 1974), pp. 607–626.

Jeffery D'Amato and Eli M. Remolona, "The Credit Spread Puzzle," *BIS Quarterly Review* (December 2003), pp. 51–63.

Francis X. Diebold and Canlin Li, "Forecasting the Term Structure of Government Bond Yields," NBER Working Paper No. w10048 (October 2003).

Dale L. Domian, Terry S. Maness, and William Reichenstein, "Rewards to Extending Maturity," *Journal of Portfolio Management* (Spring 1998), pp. 77–92.

Mark Fisher, "Forces that Shape the Yield Curve," *Federal Reserve Bank of Atlanta Economic Review* (First Quarter 2001), pp. 1–15.

Mark Fisher and Christian Gilles, "Around and Around: The Expectations Hypothesis," *Journal of Finance* (February 1998), pp. 365–383.

Alan W. Frankle and J. Markham Collins, "Investment Practices of the Domestic Cash Manager," *Journal of Cash Management* (May/June 1987), pp. 50–53.

Richard Gamble, "Dividing Head First into the Liquidity Pool," *Treasury & Risk Management* (December/January 2002), pp. 31–32.

Larry Gitman and M. D. Goodwin, "An Assessment of Marketable Securities Management Practices," *Journal of Financial Research* (Fall 1979), pp. 161–169.

Larry Gitman, Edwin A. Moses, and I. T. White, "An Assessment of Corporate Cash Practices," *Financial Management* (Spring 1979), pp. 32–41.

Robin Grieves, Steven V. Mann, Alan J. Marcus, and Pradipkumar Ramanlal, "Riding the Bill Curve: This Effective Strategy Is as Simple as It Is Well Known," *Euromoney* (Spring 1999), pp. 74–83.

Joseph G. Haubrich and Joao Cabral dos Santos, "The Dark Side of Liquidity," *Federal Reserve Bank of Cleveland Economic Commentary* (September 15, 1997).

Michael Hunstad, "2003 Corporate Treasury Response to Low Interest Rates." Available online at http://www.treasurystrategies.com. (2003) Accessed 1/23/2004.

iMoneyNet, "Short-Term Alternatives Stand to Gain From Depressed MMF Yields," (May). Available online at: http://www.imoneynet.com. (2002) Accessed 1/24/2004.

Sara A. Irving and Timothy G. Raney, "Use Yield Spreads to Score Birdies," *Corporate Cashflow* (September 1991), pp. 37, 40, 42–44.

Teresa A. John, "Accounting Measures of Corporate Liquidity, Leverage, and Costs of Financial Distress," *Financial Management* (Autumn 1993), pp. 91–100.

Ravi R. Kamath, Shahriar Khaksari, Heidi Hylton Meier, and J. Winklepeck, "Management of Excess Cash: Practices and Developments," *Financial Management* (Autumn 1985), pp. 70–77.

Duen-Li Kao and Mark A. Zurack, "Investment Risks of Dividend Capture Programs," *Journal of Cash Management* (January/February 1988), pp. 46–49.

Shahriar Khaksari, "Analyzing Yield Spreads Between Eurodollar and Domestic Rates," *Journal of Cash Management* (March/April 1990), pp. 50–52.

Chang-Soo Kim, David C. Mauer, and Ann E. Sherman, "The Determinants of Corporate Liquidity: Theory and Evidence," *Journal of Financial and Quantitative Analysis* (September 1998), pp. 335–359.

David S. Krause, "The Covered Call Dividend Capture Strategy," *Journal of Cash Management* (March/April 1988), pp. 22–25.

Merton Miller and Daniel Orr, "A Model of the Demand for Money by Firms," *The Quarterly Journal of Economics* (August 1966), pp. 413–435.

Austin Murphy, "Hedging Fixed-Rate Preferred Stock Investments," *Journal of Applied Corporate Finance* (Spring 2001), pp 80–90.

Preston Nuttall, "Keep Short-Term Investments on the Right Track," *Corporate Cashflow* (October 1991), pp. 56, 58, 60, 62.

Tim Opler, Lee Pinkowitz, Rene Stulz, and Rohan Williamson, "The Determinants and Implications of Corporate Cash Holdings," *Journal of Financial Economics* 52, (1999), pp. 3–46.

Raymond E. Owens and Roy H. Webb, "Using the Federal Funds Futures Market to Predict Monetary Policy Actions," *Federal Reserve Bank of Richmond Economic Quarterly* (Spring 2001), pp. 69–77.

Lee Pinkowitz, "The Market for Corporate Control and Corporate Cash Holdings," Washington, DC: Georgetown University, Working Paper.

Lucio Sarno, Daniel L. Thornton, and Giorgio Valente, "Federal Funds Rate Prediction," *Federal Reserve Bank of St. Louis Working Paper 2002–005B* (November 2002).

Alan G. Seidner, *Corporate Investments Manual*, Boston, MA: Warren, Gorham & Lamont. (1989)

Alan G. Seidner, "*Corporate Investments Manual 1990 Supplement*, Boston, MA: Warren, Gorham & Lamont. (1990)

Cynthia Smith and Sandra Miles, "The Risk Report Card: A Risk Management Tool at Freddie Mac," *TMA Journal* (May/June 1997), pp. 26–28, 30.

Keith V. Smith and Brian Belt, "Working Capital Management in Practice: An Update," West Lafayette, IN: Purdue University—Krannert Graduate School of Management, Working Paper 951.

Bernell K. Stone, "The Use of Forecasts and Smoothing in Control-Limit Models for Cash Management," *Financial Management* (Spring 1972), pp. 72–84.

George P. Tsetsekos, "Liquidity Balances and Agency Considerations," Washington, DC: The American University, Working Paper.

Herbert J. Weinraub and Sue Visscher, "Industry Practice Relating to Aggressive/Conservative Working Capital Policies," *Journal of Financial and Strategic Decisions* (Fall 1998), pp. 11–18.

Kaja Whitehouse, "Corporate Money Funds Offer an Alternative Savings Method," *The Wall Street Journal* (January 21, 2004), p. D2.

John T. Zietlow, "Evaluating the Risk in Negotiable CDs," *Journal of Cash Management* (September/October 1990), pp. 39–41, 43, 45–46.

John T. Zietlow and David Scheidt, "Benchmarking Investment Performance: A Case Study Using AFP Investment Benchmarks," (November 4, 2003). Presentation to the Association for Financial Professionals Annual Conference, Orlando, FL.

# APPENDIX 15A

## Cash Management Models

We noted in Chapter 15 that when cash optimization models are used, they primarily address the management of the cash and securities balances over time. The cash manager wants to maintain control over how much is kept in cash, because although cash is the most liquid asset, it incurs opportunity costs in the form of forgone investment interest income or increased interest expense, and there are transaction costs associated with security purchases, sales, and the related funds transfers. If there were no brokerage commissions or other transaction costs, and investments (paying competitive interest rates) that might be easily sold and quickly converted to cash could be found, then the decision rule would simplify to cash balance minimization. Practically, this translates into holding the minimal balances in transaction accounts to pay one day's disbursements or meet the bank's compensating balance requirements. Money markets are characterized by imperfections such as transaction costs, however, and the manager must determine how large a cash balance to hold to minimize the costs of cash management.

Three main cash management models, each with different assumptions, can be used to reallocate the cash and securities mix through time. Each model views cash as an inventoried asset, with the transaction motive driving a company's allocation of resources to cash held in the form of transaction account balances.[28] Given the total disbursements for a period, each model can specify the number and timing of securities-cash transfers. The larger the per-transfer cost and the higher the interest rate being earned on securities, the fewer and more delayed the sales of securities. The models are the Baumol model, the Miller-Orr model, and the Stone model.

[28] Although the models tend to focus on the transactions motive for holding cash, the addition of a safety stock buffer enables the models to also incorporate the precautionary and speculative motives for holding cash. The precautionary balance is kept to protect against unforeseen shortages in cash flow, perhaps related to unexpected sales declines. See the discussion of the EOQ model and safety stock considerations in Chapter 4.

## THE BAUMOL MODEL

The earliest model, an adaptation by William Baumol of the EOQ model, was developed to explain how companies may minimize the total costs involved with transferring funds out of securities into cash during a given time period. The company is attempting to minimize total costs, composed of transaction costs to replenish cash by selling securities and opportunity costs of forgone interest resulting from holding demand deposit balances. The Baumol model assumes that:

- The company receives funds periodically but must disburse monies at a continuous, steady rate.
- The company's cash needs are anticipated with perfect accuracy (complete certainty).
- When the initial cash balance is drawn down to zero (or to a small "safety stock" level), the balance is replenished by a sale of securities identical in size to the initial cash balance, denoted as $Z^*$.

Diagrammatically, the cash transfer sequence is identical to that shown in the EOQ presentation in Chapter 4 (see Exhibit 4–2). The model allows the analyst to solve for the optimal number of transactions that should be made to invest in securities or to transfer invested monies into cash (the disbursement account). For example, two transactions are implied by a strategy that invests one-half of the funds received until needed, at which time the other half is sold and the proceeds deposited into the disbursement account.

In symbol form, the total costs incurred over a period of time are summed up as shown in Equation 15.1A.

$$\text{Period cost} = F(TCN/Z) + i(Z/2) \qquad (15.1A)$$

Where: $F$ = Fixed transaction cost, per security purchase or sale

$TCN$ = Total cash needs during period

$Z$ = Cash balance starting and return point

$i$ = Interest rate, per period, on marketable securities (opportunity cost for holding cash balances)

The first term gives us the aggregate transaction cost, because $TCN/Z$ is the number of transactions made and $F$ is the fixed cost per security purchase or sale.[29]

Commissions charged by brokers are an obvious component of securities transaction costs, but there may be other costs such as the cost of communicating the transaction instructions and clerical time necessary for record keeping. $Z/2$ is the average cash balance, which can be multiplied by the interest rate per period ($i$) to give us the dollar opportunity cost for having funds tied up in interest-bearing disbursement accounts.

Using the derivative of the period cost, which is a total cost function, we can solve for the cost-minimizing number of transactions and the optimal transaction size, $Z^*$:

$$Z^* = \sqrt{\frac{2(F)(TCN)}{i}} \qquad (15.2A)$$

Thus, $Z^*$ is the optimal dollar amount of securities that should be sold to replenish cash when the disbursement account has been drawn down. It also can be thought of as the optimal return point for the cash balance. Equation 15.2A should look familiar because it is simply a restatement of the EOQ formula. Economies of scale in cash management are implied by the model because a given percentage increase in the total cash needs ($TCN$) leads to a smaller than proportional increase in $Z^*$. Based on the cash balance specified, we can further calculate the average cash balance ($Z/2$), the frequency of transactions ($TCN/Z$, rounded to the nearest integer), and when substituting $Z^*$ into Equation 15.1A for $Z$, the total cost of following the EOQ-based reallocation rules. The following example illustrates use of the Baumol model.

Joe Nevada, entrepreneur and one-time football great, recently started a business that is enjoying unexpectedly rapid growth. Profits have been adequate, but Joe is concerned about maintaining adequate liquidity so he does not get tackled by his banker. Specifically, he is having trouble deciding how to allocate his transaction liquid assets between cash and marketable securities. He figures that his company has disbursements of $1 million per year. His broker charges $65 each time Joe wants to pass money from securities to his cash disbursement account. Short-term interest rates on potential investments are now approximately 7 percent. Not having skill with numbers (other than calling signals at the line of scrimmage), Joe asks your advice. What should Joe do?

### Solution

Applying the Baumol model, we solve for the optimal initial and return level for cash by using Equation 15.2A:

$$Z^* = \sqrt{\frac{2(F)(TCN)}{i}}$$

$$= \sqrt{\frac{2(\$65)(\$1{,}000{,}000)}{0.07}}$$

$$= \$43{,}095$$

The average cash balance, $Z/2$, is $21,548 ($43,095/2). Joe's company would transfer money ($TCN/Z$) times a year by selling securities, which is 23 transfers in this case ($1,000,000/$43,095).

The major shortcoming of the Baumol model is the unrealistic assumptions underlying the equation. It is impossible to know if the model $Z^*$ is really cost minimizing unless the assumptions are guaranteed to hold. The model's simplicity comes at the expense of oversimplifications such as the following:

- known, certain future disbursements ($TCN$) that implicitly depend on perfect accuracy in cash forecasting
- transaction costs ($F$) that do not vary with the dollar size of the securities transaction (an assumption that is obviously violated for companies with money market accounts or sweep accounts that do not charge for transactions on a per-transfer basis)
- lumpy periodic cash receipts but a continuous disbursing rate, which fits mortgage bankers and apartment rental businesses and health care providers or governmental agencies receiving lump-sum reimbursements or budget allocations[30]

[29] Two strategies may help us understand this process. If the entire beginning-of-period cash receipt is deposited into the cash disbursement account, there are no transactions because no securities would need to be purchased or sold during the period. If one-half of the receipt is put in securities, which are sold halfway through the period to fund remaining disbursements, we have $TCN/Z = 2$. The two transactions involved are the original purchase of securities and subsequent sale to fund the cash account.

[30] A model that assumes continuous cash receipts and lumpy disbursements has been developed in William Beranek, *Analysis for Financial Decisions* (Homewood, IL: Richard D. Irwin, 1963), Chapter 11. In situations in which cash accrues and is then paid out in a lump sum (e.g., a quarterly dividend), this model would be appropriate. This model, like the Baumol model, assumes perfect certainty of future cash flows. In companies for which cash receipts are highly predictable, the Beranek model may be used to give guidance on how often to sweep monies from many collection accounts into a concentration account.

Despite such oversimplifications, the Baumol model is instructive. First, the model shows the decision maker the extent of suboptimization, in the form of higher cash-related costs, when the initial and return level of cash is set very low or high. Exhibit 15–1A depicts the data used in our earlier example and graphically portrays the cost penalties of extreme cash positions. We can visualize how the company incurs large transaction costs when $Z$ is too low, because of numerous transactions, and loses considerable interest revenue or incurs considerable interest expense when $Z$ is too large. Second, rapid updating, or rerunning the model, is a way to get around the lumpy receipt oversimplification: the period modeled can be shortened to a month or week and rerun as new data become available.

Whether or not a company sets actual transaction cash balances to the model's prescribed $Z^*$, sensitivity analysis using the model can show how to revise the cash replenishment. We can vary the interest rate ($i$) and the transaction cost ($F$) up and down 5 to 15 percent from the present levels and calculate the revised values for $Z^*$. This analysis enables the manager to anticipate the revision to the cash balance necessary if and when either of these two critical inputs change and to devote more time and effort to getting accurate data on the cost item that affects the cash balance the most. We hold all other variables constant when changing the value of one input variable. In our example, the interest rate forecast is the most critical variable in the analysis of factors causing an increase in cash balances. The same kind of analysis can be performed for an increase in the interest rate and a decrease in the fixed transaction costs. Additionally, as actual interest rates change, cash balances can be rapidly adjusted to the new optimal level prespecified by this sensitivity analysis.

## THE MILLER-ORR MODEL

The **Miller-Orr model** varies from the Baumol model in two ways. First, it allows for unpredictable fluctuations in the cash balance instead of assuming perfect cash forecasting ability. The model accomplishes this by incorporating the variance of the company's daily net cash flows. Second, it permits both upward and downward movements in the cash balance subsequent to replenishment, as opposed to the supposition that the company experiences a one-time cash infusion each period, which is subsequently depleted at a continuous rate. Miller and Orr handled this by including two trigger points instead of one in the model. These trigger points, which signal a purchase or sale of securities, are termed **control limits**. The **upper control limit (UCL)** triggers a purchase of securities large enough to reduce excess cash balances to the return point $Z^*$ (Exhibit 15–2A). When the cash bal-

Exhibit 15–1A

*Period Cost When Varying Level of Cash*

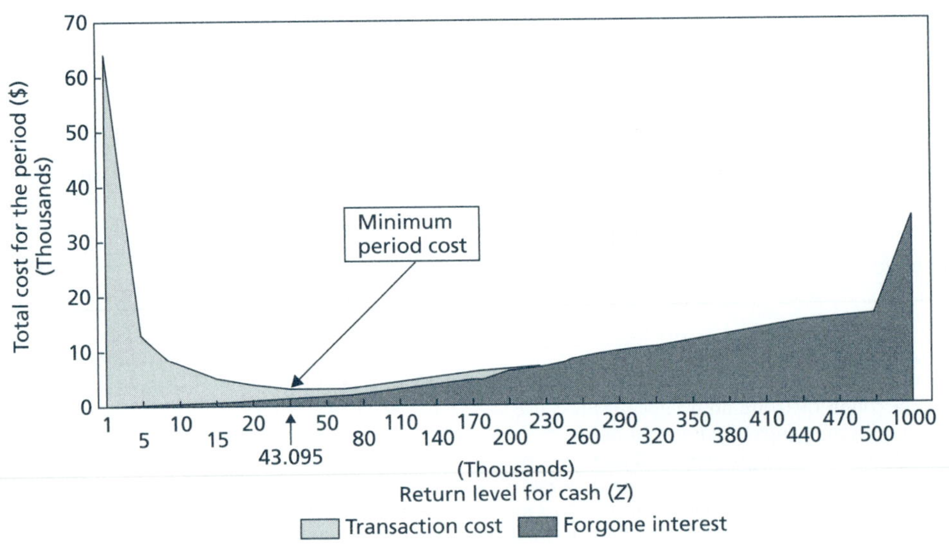

Shaded areas indicate cost composition

ance dips down to the **lower control limit** (LCL), a sale of securities sufficient to return the cash balance to $Z^*$ is initiated. Notice that as long as the cash balance drifts along within the two control limits, no securities trades are triggered. In that case, the stream of cash receipts and disbursements must have been at least moderately synchronized—but the assumption of the model is that cash flows are unpredictable (random), meaning that next period's flows may be totally asynchronous.

The formula underlying the Miller-Orr model is presented as Equation 15.3A.

$$Z^* = \sqrt[3]{\frac{3F\sigma^2}{4i}} \qquad (15.3A)$$

Where: $Z^*$ = Optimal transfer amount

$F$ = Fixed transaction cost

$\sigma$ = Variance of daily net cash flows

$i$ = The daily interest rate

Like the Baumol model, $Z^*$ minimizes the sum of transactions and forgone interest costs, except here we are actually balancing the expected value of a probability distribution of costs because of the uncertainty in the future cash flows. Be careful about the interpretation of $Z^*$. If the company sets the LCL limit at any value other than zero, then $Z^*$ is no longer the return point for cash. Instead, the return point is $Z^* + LCL$. Because we are addressing the disbursement account balance, the company might need to set LCL above zero to meet compensating balance requirements. Or LCL could represent a safety stock of liquidity, with the exact level dependent on management's target for this component of the company's liquidity. While the LCL is set at zero or some arbitrary low value, the optimal value of UCL (derived using stochastic calculus) specified by the model is $3Z^* + LCL$. Miller and Orr solved for an average cash balance of $4/3(Z^*) + LCL$. The return point is $Z^* + LCL$. We can illustrate the computations by returning to our example.

After being presented with your recommendations based on the Baumol model, Joe Nevada asks for some background information about the model and what it is based on. You warn Joe that the model assumes his forecasts of cash needs are perfectly accurate, at which point he becomes visibly uncomfortable. "Our cash flows jump all over the place," he grumbles. "Can we adjust the model?" You reply that there might be a better way, as you think about the less demanding assumptions behind the Miller-Orr model, while hoping Joe will not ask you what variance means. Your thoughts are interrupted by Joe's insistence that you let him know right away how the cash balances will change "if reality is incorporated into the analysis."

**Exhibit 15–2A**

*Cash Movements in the Miller-Orr Model*

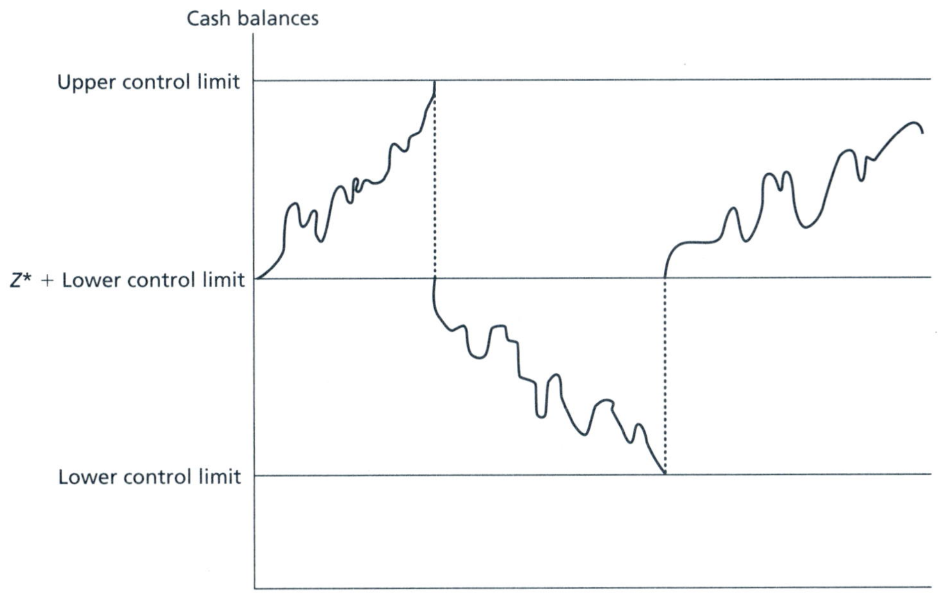

## Solution

You first analyze the historical net cash flows of Joe's business and compute the variance of the flows to be $1,000,000. Using the example values for $F$ of $65 and converting $i$ to a daily rate of 0.0001918 (0.07/365), you can use Equation 15.3A to compute $Z^*$:

$$Z^* = \sqrt[3]{\frac{3F\sigma^2}{4i}}$$

$$= \sqrt[3]{\frac{3(65)(\$1{,}000{,}000)}{4(0.0001918)}}$$

$$= \$6{,}334$$

When asked, Joe declares that he would never want the cash balance going below $5,000, because this represents the compensating balance requirement part of his overall bank compensation. Recognizing this value as LCL, we know the return point is:

$$Z^* + LCL = \$6{,}334 + \$5{,}000$$

$$= \$11{,}334$$

The $UCL$ is then $3Z^* + LCL$:

$$UCL = 3\ (\$6{,}334) + \$5{,}000$$

$$= \$24{,}002$$

The average cash balance is $13,445 [4/3($6,334) + $5,000].

You advise Joe that if his company's cash flows are completely unpredictable with the specified variance, he should start with $11,334 in his business checking account. If and when cash builds up to $24,002, he should invest $12,668 ($24,002 − $11,334) in securities. Anytime the cash account is drawn down to $5,000, he should sell $6,334 of securities to return to the $11,334 target.

The Miller-Orr model has two main appeals. First, it presumes that the company's cash flows are random, or entirely unpredictable. Although many disbursements are predictable, for most companies unpredictability of cash flows is closer to reality than the perfect certainty of the Baumol model. Second, it allows the cash manager to manage the cash position between limits of excessive cash and insufficient cash, triggering responses on the manager's part only when the position gets out of bounds. This is intuitively appealing to the manager, and it constitutes an efficient approach because it adheres to a "management by exception" philosophy.

Restrictive assumptions about the statistical nature of cash flows plague this model, however. Cash flows are assumed to be unpredictable, normally distributed with a constant variance, and uncorrelated (independent) across successive time periods. Cash managers recognize that they can predict some elements such as salaries and loan payments. Tests of companies' actual cash flows have revealed nonnormality[31] or shifting cash flow distributions that are correlated through time.[32] There may be some companies with normal distributions of a large number of small receipts, but these are likely to follow some pattern over time—which the Miller-Orr model does not incorporate. The most damaging shortcoming of the Miller-Orr model, however, is the insignificance of the improvement brought about by its use in realistic situations. Because cash managers do have some forecasting ability, they can easily outperform the model-driven strategies.

The two main uses of the model's prescriptions, then, might be to provide a starting point for the manager who is deciding where to set the target cash balance and as an after-the-fact benchmark with which to evaluate realized performance. One comparison is the cash balances actually held relative to the model's prescription. As opposed to the Baumol model's complete certainty, the Miller-Orr model assumes complete uncertainty, implying larger cash balances if the variance of net cash flows ($\sigma^2$) is large relative to the company's total cash needs ($TCN$). In reality, no company is faced with complete uncertainty (e.g., payroll amounts are easily forecasted), and if the historic cash balances exceed the Miller-Orr recommendation, this signals excessive cash balances and excess costs. A second comparison is to assess the incremental improvements brought about by the cash manager's forecasting and investment abilities. The interest income for a given period, had the model's recommendation been used, would be compared with the actual interest income. Some type of risk adjustment should be made to the realized results to ensure high (low) returns were not simply the product of greater (lesser) risk taking.

Both the Baumol and Miller-Orr models are forms of "automatic pilot" reallocation strategies. But why should an investment manager mindlessly sell securities when the cash balance approaches a lower limit if the company knows it will receive next-day availability on a sizable automated clearinghouse (ACH) collection initiated today? Bernell Stone has developed a model that allows managerial foresight to change model pre-

[31] Detected by Miller and Orr in the Union Tank Car data that they modeled and by others who have analyzed actual company cash flows. See full citation in the end-of-chapter references.

[32] Gary Emery, "Some Empirical Evidence on the Properties of Daily Cash Flow," *Financial Management* (Spring 1981), pp. 21–28.

scriptions and that operates under much less restrictive assumptions regarding cash flow patterns.

## THE STONE MODEL

The **Stone model** improves on the realism of the Miller-Orr optimization process by allowing the cash manager's knowledge of imminent cash flows to permit him or her to selectively override model directives.[33] This "look-ahead" model promises larger cost savings because there are times that the manager will see a large receipt coming and not have to sell securities, and at other times cash disbursements are large enough to pull the cash balance back within the UCL. Stone's formulation permits cash managers to look ahead up to $K$ (generally three to 12) days, with the value selected for $K$ being larger when company's cash forecasts are relatively accurate. Additionally, the model recognizes that the penalties for being outside the control limits for one or several days are quite small. Therefore, the manager does not need to buy (sell) securities as long as the cash balance will be within the upper (lower) control limit (possibly modified by a safety stock cushion) within $K$ days. A security transaction only occurs when the cash balance is both out of bounds today and will still be out of bounds $K$ days from now. This makes sense because businesses rarely are faced with inviolable minimums (except perhaps zero, which represents an overdraft threshold), and compensating balance requirements are based on month-average balances. A numerical example provides a better understanding of how to apply the Stone model.

Advanced Software, Inc., (ASI) has been unsuccessfully trying to use cash management models for several years. Ed, the cash manager, has just returned from a training seminar at which he heard about the Stone model, and he is excited about applying it. The seminar instructor told Ed to use the same control limits that he has been using but to modify the decision rules. First, transfers between cash and securities will not take place unless the cash position gets very high or low and it looks like it will stay that way for another three days. This implies that Ed must make decisions based on the anticipated cash position, which is the sum of today's cash position and the next three days' forecasted cash flows ($K = 3$). Second, to adjust partially for forecasting errors, the trigger points will be modified. The control limits will be adjusted by a 3-percent safety stock cushion. This effectively shrinks the range of values the forecasted cash position can move within before a transaction is triggered.

ASI's control limits are $50,000 (LCL) and $125,000 (UCL), and the return point is $75,000. The present cash balance is $105,000. The next seven days' net cash flows are projected to be:

| Day | Cash Flow Forecast |
|---|---|
| 1 | $ 45,000 |
| 2 | (20,000) |
| 3 | 25,000 |
| 4 | 5,000 |
| 5 | 10,000 |
| 6 | (35,000) |
| 7 | (45,000) |

What transactions should Ed make during the next three days, if any?

### Solution

First, add two columns to the problem data to show the new cash position, assuming no transactions are made. "Cash Flow Balance" shows the daily anticipated balance. "Period Cash" is the anticipated balance $K$ days hence:

| Day | Cash Flow Forecast | Cash Flow Balance | Period Cash (Cash Balance + $K$ Days' Cash Flows) |
|---|---|---|---|
| 0 (present) | — | $105,000 | $155,000 |
| 1 | $ 45,000 | 150,000 | 160,000 |
| 2 | (20,000) | 130,000 | 170,000 |
| 3 | 25,000 | 155,000 | 135,000 |
| 4 | 5,000 | 160,000 | 90,000 |
| 5 | 10,000 | 170,000 | |
| 6 | (35,000) | 135,000 | |
| 7 | (45,000) | 90,000 | |

Next, we compute modified trigger points for security purchase or sale. The LCL adjusted for the 3-percent safety stock cushion is:

$$\$50{,}000 + (0.03)(\$50{,}000) = \$51{,}500$$

The UCL adjusted for the safety cushion is $121,250 (found by subtracting 3 percent from $125,000). Third, we check to see if the cash balance ever gets outside the original control limits of $50,000 and $125,000. If the

[33] Statistically, the Stone model relaxes assumptions about cash flow normality, independence, and variance constancy. Whether or not these assumptions fit a company's cash flows, a manager who is actually not technically oriented should be more comfortable with the Stone model.

cash flow balance gets outside the original control limits at any time, an analysis of whether to initiate a transaction is triggered. But no action is taken unless the period cash will be below (above) the modified LCL (UCL) limit *at the end of the look-ahead period*. We notice when visually scanning the cash balances in our table that the UCL is penetrated on day 1. We add the cash balance at that time, $150,000, to the sum of the next three days' cash flows—or simply scan down three rows in the table—and then compare this figure with the modified control limit. Because the projected period cash of $160,000 three days hence is obviously greater than the modified UCL, we advise Ed to plan on buying securities on day 1. The dollar amount of the purchase should be sufficient to return the *expected* cash balance in $K$ days to the return point of $75,000. This implies a day 1 transaction of $85,000 ($160,000 − $75,000). One caution: If tomorrow's actual cash flow is $5,000 instead of the forecasted $45,000, the upper limit will not be penetrated during the planning horizon, and Ed can relax instead of worrying about which securities to buy. He will need to redo the table, however, to incorporate the actual cash position in the updated forecast.

Given a choice, this model should be the clear favorite of practicing cash managers. First, it fits well with the decision-making approach used by cash managers. Recall from our discussion of cash forecasting that the scheduling, or receipts and disbursements method, predominates as the preferred forecasting method for daily cash forecasting. This involves laying out cash flows for several days ahead to see if the cash position will be short or in surplus. The Stone approach uses these forecasts as inputs, and thus, fits extremely well into the operating mode of managers. Second, the Stone model has minimal statistical and data requirements. In our example, we used the Miller-Orr control limits, but there is no need to do this. The cash manager uses his or her own best estimate of what the upper and lower limits or modified limits should be. One alternative approach is to use simulation of the company's cash flows to estimate the probability of running short on cash for any particular limit.

If control limits, modified limits, or the return level are established subjectively, this may reduce the attractiveness of model use, however. For the Miller-Orr model when the assumptions are valid, an optimal cost-minimizing strategy is provided. There is no such assurance with the Stone model. In our view, this is not a major objection. We advocate a 3-step approach: using the Miller-Orr limits to get starting values for the permissible cash balance range, lowering them for companies in which the cash flow variability is small, and then managing the cash position using Stone's approach. The cash manager can demonstrate the cost reductions under this approach by conducting a comparative simulation with historical data. The model's recommendations can be back-tested against what was actually done by the cash manager. Relative improvements from model use can be established in this fashion, giving confidence for future use. The key to approaching optimality is having a good understanding of the company's cash forecasting ability. If overly confident, the manager might set $K$ too low or the modified control limits too close to the Miller-Orr control limits. The result(s) would be to undershoot in maintaining compensating balances, overdraft the account, or forego significant interest income.

## Recap on Optimization Models

Optimization models are best suited for cash and securities decisions involving very short planning horizons and/or small aggregate cash balances. The net result of either of these situations is to elevate the relative importance of transaction costs such as brokerage commissions. When companies have longer planning horizons (implying the possibility of substantive changes in interest rates during the period), have large investable balances (implying low relative transaction costs and possibly volume discounts on commissions), or are assessed fixed per-year fees to maintain automated investment accounts (implying low or nonexistent per-transaction costs), optimization models are of limited value. The Stone model could still be used, but the limits would have to be set arbitrarily, and the cash manager might do so without the help of the model. The objective switches to yield maximization[34] when transaction costs are low or nonexistent. At a minimum, the philosophy of carefully managing the cash position to avoid having too much or too little of this nonearning asset can be implemented by all organizations.

Cash management models share another common shortcoming: They are partial equilibrium models that address cash management costs but ignore the other current asset accounts. Recall that the target cash balance decision precedes the management of cash balances through time. The former decision should be carefully tied to the company's liquidity objectives, in the light of its investment in receivables and invento-

---

[34] Yield maximization is equivalent to minimizing the foregone investment income of the cash management strategy, within the risk posture stipulated in the investment policy.

ries. Only in this way can the manager ensure that the limited cash management focus of the models does not interfere with shareholder wealth maximization.

## QUESTIONS

**15A-1.** What are the assumptions for each of the three major cash management models? What are some of the characteristics of companies for which each would be most appropriate?

**15A-2.** What are the two components of the total period cost addressed in the Baumol model? Why does one cost component increase as the other decreases?

**15A-3.** The total cash needs of Alpha Grocery are twice that of Beta Grocery. Would Alpha's optimal cash balance be twice that of Beta, according to the Baumol model?

**15A-4.** How can sensitivity analysis be performed on the results of a Baumol model calculation? How might the results of that sensitivity analysis be used?

**15A-5.** Because no company has completely unpredictable cash flows, why should any cash manager use the Miller-Orr model?

**15A-6.** Why is the Stone model so appealing to practicing cash managers? Are there any weaknesses inherent in the model?

**15A-7.** When does the cash manager take action to sell or buy securities when using the Stone model? How much is bought or sold?

## PROBLEMS

**15A-1.** The assistant treasurer of Monroe Tires, Inc., is trying to determine what the appropriate cash return level should be. The company's cash balances have been fluctuating wildly because of unpredictable and wide-ranging receipts and disbursements. The best estimate of annual disbursements is $5,000,000. The investment broker charges $75 per securities transaction. Short-term investment interest rates are 12 percent. The company does not mind a $0 cash balance but does not want the balance to be negative.

a. What should the cash return level be, according to the Baumol model?

b. What will the average cash balance be if the company's cash outflows fit the assumptions of the Baumol model?

c. How many security sales will Monroe have in a year, assuming the model's assumptions are valid?

d. What will the total period costs be for a year?

e. Do you recommend that Monroe use the Baumol model? Why or why not?

**15A-2.** Conduct sensitivity analysis on your results from Problem A-1. What conclusions do you reach based on your analysis? How might Monroe use this information?

**15A-3.** Monroe's assistant treasurer (see Problem A-1) estimates the variance of daily net cash flows to be $5,000,000. Again, using a LCL of $0:

a. What should the cash return level be, using the Miller-Orr model?

b. What is your estimate of the average cash balance if the Miller-Orr calculation is used to set the cash return level?

c. How do you explain your finding in **a** to the assistant treasurer, who wants to know how to use the information provided by the model?

d. If the variance of daily net cash flows is $10,000,000 instead of $5,000,000, how does this change the answer determined in **a**? Is the cash return level double your earlier result? How do you interpret this?

e. (Optional) How does your result in **a** compare with the Baumol model prescriptions found in Problem A-1?

**15A-4.** Conduct a Miller-Orr analysis using the data in Problems A-1 and A-3 but with a lower cash limit of $5,000.

a. What should the cash return level be, using the Miller-Orr model?

b. What is your estimate of the average cash balance if the Miller-Orr calculation is used to set the cash return level?

c. How do you explain your finding in **a** to the assistant treasurer, who wants to know how to use the information provided by the model?

d. If the variance of daily net cash flows is $10,000,000 instead of $5,000,000, how does this change the answer determined in

**a**? Is the cash return level double your earlier result? How do you interpret this?

e. (Optional) How does your result in **a** compare with the Baumol model prescriptions found in Problem A-1?

**15A-5.** Megamedia Enterprises wishes to apply the Stone model to its cash position management situation. It has never used a cash management model before. Its control limits are $20,000 (lower) and $75,000 (upper). The company wishes to try the model out with a 2-day look ahead, as well as a 3-day look ahead. In other words, transfers between cash and securities will not take place unless the cash position gets very high or low and it looks like it will stay that way for another two days in the first analysis and three days in the second analysis. This implies that the cash manager must make decisions based on the anticipated cash position, which is the sum of today's cash position and the next two or three days' forecasted cash flows ($K = 2$ or $K = 3$). Second, to partially adjust for forecasting errors, the trigger points will be modified. The control limits will be adjusted by a 5-percent safety stock cushion. This effectively shrinks the range of values within which the forecasted cash position can move before a transaction is triggered. The company has been using a return point of $50,000, and the present cash balance is $45,000. The next seven days' net cash flows are projected to be:

| Day | Cash Flow Forecast |
|---|---|
| 1 | $ 35,000 |
| 2 | (50,000) |
| 3 | (25,000) |
| 4 | 5,000 |
| 5 | (10,000) |
| 6 | 25,000 |
| 7 | 45,000 |

a. What transactions should the cash manager make during the next two days, if any, under the 2-day look ahead?

b. What transactions should the cash manager make during the next three days, if any, under the 3-day look ahead?

c. What general advice do you have for the cash manager, given what you know about the Stone model and the fact that the company has never before used a cash management model?

CHAPTER

16

# SHORT-TERM FINANCING

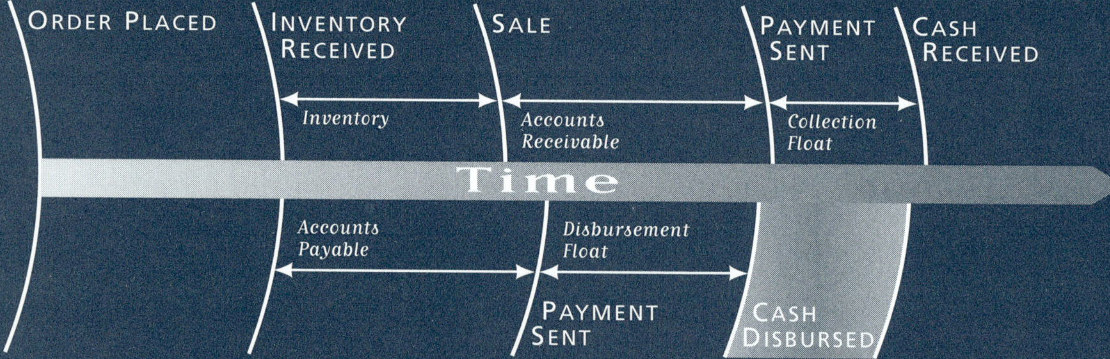

## OBJECTIVES

*After studying this chapter, you should be able to:*

- formulate a short-term financing strategy.
- choose the appropriate financing instrument from among the array of financing instruments available.
- compute the effective cost of short-term financing alternatives when commitment fees and compensating balances are involved.

A business firm in need of additional short-term funds beyond what its spontaneous payables and accrual sources provide can choose among a myriad of alternatives. This chapter will introduce the more common short-term discretionary sources of financing. The sum of these sources on any one balance sheet is typically smaller than the funds provided by accounts payable and accruals. However, these alternative short-term funding sources are an important part of a firm's liquidity reserve and tend to complement payables and accruals.

Short-term borrowing instruments are different from the spontaneous sources in several important respects. First, the firm is actually acquiring the use of dollars directly rather than goods or services as in the case of payables and accruals. Second, these sources are the result of choices made by the financial manager and must be deliberately acquired rather than being spontaneously generated by operations. Third, these funds have an explicit cost as represented by the interest rate and commitment fee charged.

The chapter begins by outlining three strategies that represent the choices financial managers have in managing the maturity structure, the balance between long- and short-term financing sources, of the balance sheet. Then, the array of the more popular short-term financing instruments is discussed with each financing alternative reviewed in detail. The chapter concludes with a section discussing the effective cost of short-term financing.

### FINANCIAL DILEMMA

When Is Prime Not Prime?

The treasurer at Beco, Inc., was arranging for a line of credit with the firm's bank for 2005, the new fiscal year. Beco's lending officer indicated that the rate on borrowed funds would be 10 percent, the bank's current prime rate which it offers to its "best" customers. The treasurer was proud of Beco being labeled a "prime rate borrower." In addition to the interest rate of 10 percent, the lending officer went on to say that the line carried a 25-basis point commitment fee to guarantee the availability of funds and that Beco would need to leave a 20-percent compensating balance on funds borrowed. While the treasurer felt good about getting the prime rate, he was curious as to the impact the commitment fee and compensating balance requirements would have on the overall financing cost of the line.

## FINANCING AND THE CASH FLOW TIMELINE

At this point, we have reached a position on the company's cash flow timeline at which cash has been collected and disbursed, resulting in a daily ending cash position that may be positive or negative. If the daily cash position is positive, then the cash manager faces an investment opportunity (discussed in the previous chapter). If the daily cash position is negative, then the cash manager faces a dilemma on how to fund the cash deficit.

A deficit cash position may be the result of inefficient or inappropriate working capital policies. As seen in earlier chapters, excess accumulation of inventory, slow collections, and/or quick disbursements may lead to cash being disbursed prior to cash collection. Thus, the financial manager should re-evaluate the company's working capital policies in order to ensure the most efficient stream of cash flow resulting from operations.

Even the most efficient working capital policies, however, may result in a deficit cash position at different times during the working capital cycle. This is especially true during periods of rapid growth and the early phase of the working capital cycle. At this point, the manager must have a well-developed plan for financing short-term cash deficit positions.

## FINANCING STRATEGIES

Over the course of its operating cycle, a firm's assets tend to fluctuate, rising as operations gear up for seasonal peak sales and then subsiding as sales fall. Exhibit 16–1 demonstrates this trend for a firm that is growing and adding to its fixed assets base. In the exhibit, assets begin to grow as time moves from the left to the right with inventory build-up in anticipation of future sales. As sales pick up, inventory is maintained for a period of time by increased production, and receivables begin to accumulate as inventory is sold. As sales

**Exhibit 16–1**

*The Firm's Fluctuating Assets Over Its Operating Cycle*

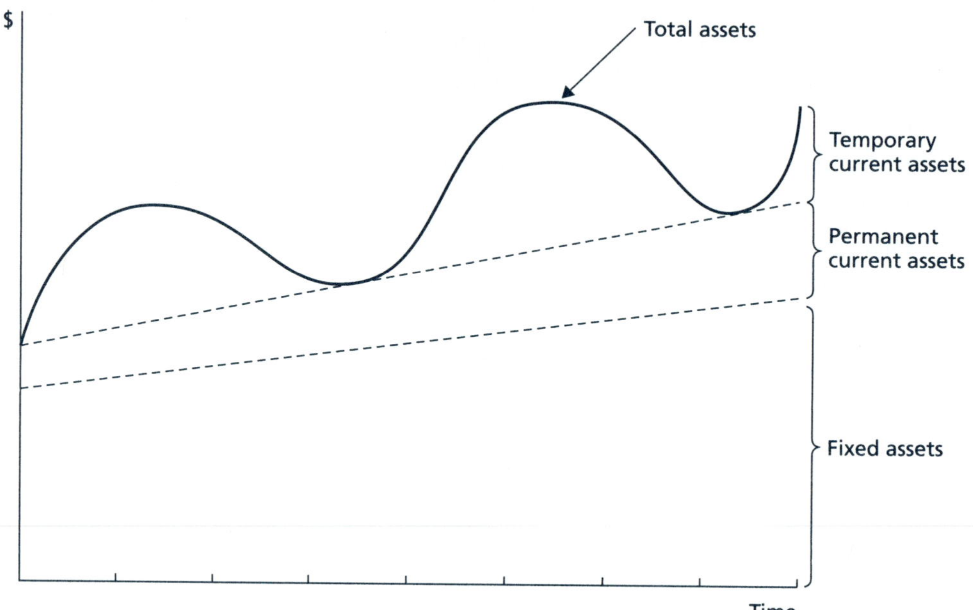

level off, production is reduced resulting in a drop in inventory. Receivables also begin to fall as collections exceed the creation of new receivables. As receivables are collected, the cash received is used to pay off accounts payable and short-term loans used to finance the earlier accumulation of inventory and receivables. This cycle then repeats itself as the firm approaches a new operating period.

In Exhibit 16–1, you may have noticed the decomposition of total current assets into two parts, a level of **permanent current assets** and a level of **temporary current assets**. It may seem strange to refer to current assets as permanent, but firms always have some minimum or permanent amount of inventory and receivables on their books. Although the products in inventory and the specific accounts held as receivables do turn over, a minimum amount of resources is always invested in these accounts. This minimum level of ongoing inventory and receivables is what is referred to as permanent current assets.

The temporary component of total current assets, then, represents the accumulation of inventory in anticipation of the peak selling season and the resulting receivables generated by the increasing sales. This bulge in inventory and receivables then subsides as the firm passes through its peak selling season.

The financial manager can choose from three basic strategies as financing is sought to support the firm's asset needs over its operating cycle. The three strategies include (A) the aggressive strategy, (B) the conservative strategy, and (C) the moderate strategy. These three financing strategies are illustrated in Exhibit 16–2. You may wish to refer to this exhibit as each of the strategies is discussed.

## Aggressive Strategy

The **aggressive financing strategy** is basically a maturity matching strategy. Using this strategy, the financial manager chooses to match the maturity of the source of financing with the duration of the need of cash. In the exhibit, the wavy line represents the total assets of the firm over time. Over the course of the firm's operating activities, total assets rise and fall due primarily to fluctuations in receivables, inventory, and payables over the working capital cycle. The wavy line will exhibit an upward trend if the firm is growing and adding to its fixed assets base. In Panel A of Exhibit 16–2, the firm is maximizing its reliance on short-term financing and minimizing its reliance on permanent or long-term financing. The corporation's net working capital position, as a result, is minimal because of the heavy reliance on short-term financing, and therefore the solvency position of the

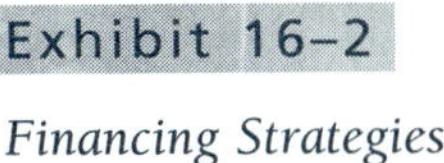


*Financing Strategies*

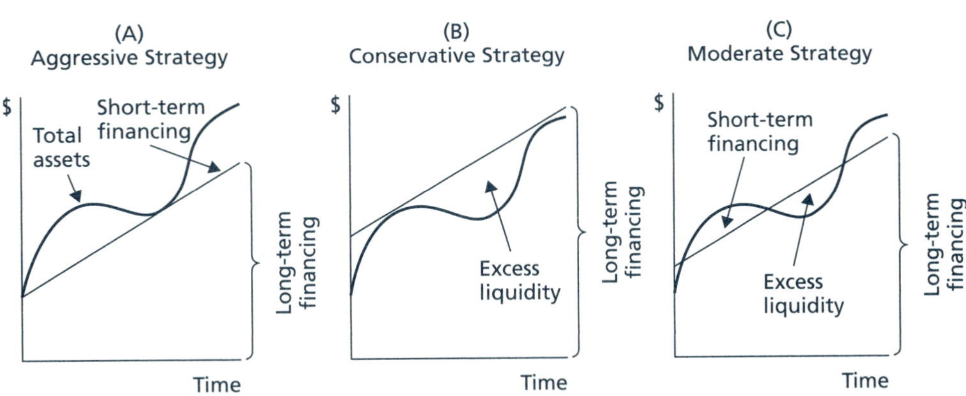

firm, as measured by the current ratio, will suffer. This strategy has an advantage in that during normal financial conditions, short-term sources of financing cost less than longer-term sources. For example, on June 27, 2003, 90-day Treasury bills yielded 0.88 percent while 5-year Treasury notes yielded 2.36 percent. Therefore, there is normally a tradeoff of a lower financing cost at the expense of a reduced solvency level.

Some evidence suggests that firms use a maturity matching strategy as reported by Beranek, Cornwell, and Choi. In their research, they found that firms do not emphasize external short-term sources in the financing of capital expenditures, nor do they use the bulk of long-term external financing in a given period to finance the acquisition of short-lived assets. Thus, firms generally act as if they seek to match the maturity of their external financing with the life of their acquired assets.

### Conservative Strategy

The **conservative financing strategy** uses only long-term sources to fulfill all the corporation's financing needs as demonstrated in Panel B of Exhibit 16–2. As total assets increase as a result of a build-up of inventory and receivables, the firm draws down its excess liquidity stored in short-term investments. Then as inventory is sold and receivables are collected, excess cash is reinvested in short-term investments. Thus, over a part of its working capital cycle, the corporation has an excess solvency position, as indicated by a relatively high current ratio. Because the corporation uses no short-term financing, it would have substantial financing flexibility in acquiring new short-term sources of financing if it underestimated its actual future cash needs. Under normal financial market conditions, this strategy would be relatively expensive because long-term financing sources are generally more expensive than short-term sources. However, the reliance on longer-term sources does provide a greater solvency position as measured by the current ratio.

### Moderate Strategy

The **moderate financing strategy**, Panel C of Exhibit 16–2, is a blend of the aggressive and conservative strategies. The exact blend of short- and long-term sources depends on the risk preferences of the corporation as well as the current financial market conditions.

## SHORT-TERM FINANCING ALTERNATIVES

Business borrows short term for seasonal working capital, to cover abrupt changes in payment patterns or unexpected expenses, and when short-term profitability is not adequate to support continued operations. Banks have traditionally provided most of the short- and medium-term loans for businesses; however, in more recent times, financing alternatives such as commercial paper have eroded this once prominent role played by commercial banks. As of the second quarter of 2003, bank loans supplied approximately 16 percent of total nonmortgage credit market debt for nonfinancial businesses.[1] Generally, about half of short-term bank loans is **unsecured** (usually in the form of a line-of-credit arrangement) and the other half is secured (meaning that collateral is required to ensure an adequate secondary source of repayment).

Increasingly, banks are moving away from a direct finance role to a risk-sharing role, in which they guarantee the payment of a corporation's commercial paper borrowings at

[1] Statistics based on Federal Reserve data.

maturity. Banks collect fees for providing the guarantee, and the issuer receives a better credit rating with a correspondingly lower interest rate.

The financial manager has a wide assortment of bank and nonbank short-term financing sources from which to choose. Although this section does not attempt to be exhaustive, the primary short-term financing alternatives are discussed.

### The Role of the Internet in Obtaining Credit

Internet usage is having a dramatic impact on how financial managers seek information regarding credit alternatives as well as making actual transactions. According to a survey conducted by the Association for Finance Professionals, four out of five respondents reported they are likely to use the Internet to obtain information, communicate with service providers, and actually transact business.[2] Two years earlier, less than 20 percent of the respondents indicated that they made credit transactions over the Internet. Approximately 70 percent indicated that they currently make credit transactions over the Internet, with 90 percent indicating that they anticipate doing this over the coming 2-year period. For example, Norwest Bank (now Wells Fargo) was one of the first institutions to offer their customers in the United States and Asia the ability to initiate letters of credit on the Internet. As you will learn in a later section, letters of credit are one of the payment vehicles U.S. importers obtain from financial institutions to ensure timely delivery of their overseas purchases.

The International Trade Administration (ITA) recently unveiled a new Web site that enables exporters to find firms that can finance their sales to overseas buyers. Historically, it took days, weeks, and even months for exporters, especially smaller businesses, to find the right financing to support their export business. However, thanks to this new Web site, exporters are able to find firms that can finance their foreign sales almost instantaneously. Once the application is submitted, the Export Finance Matchmaker (EFM) Web site searches its database for a financial institution that matches the loan needs of the company. Upon completion of the search, the exporter is provided the contact information for all matches.

### Credit Lines

A **line of credit** is a short-term source of funds in that it represents a sum of funds that a bank stands ready to lend a corporate client upon demand at any time during a given period, generally a year. Most banks require customers using credit lines to "clean up" any outstanding balances for a period of a few weeks each year to demonstrate the line is used for short-term purposes only. The length of the cleanup period is a feature that can be negotiated by the firm.

Banks usually require a **compensating balance** on the line of credit so the firm does not have full use of the line. For example, if a bank required a compensating balance of 20 percent on the amount borrowed, then the corporation could only avail itself to 80 percent of the line of credit. In a later section, we will address how such required balances affect the effective cost of credit lines.

Credit lines come in two basic forms, committed lines and uncommitted lines. A **committed line of credit** is a formal, written agreement contractually binding the bank to provide the funds when requested. Such agreements require a **commitment fee** paid to the bank to ensure the availability of funds. Also, committed lines generally have covenants to ensure that the borrower adhere to certain basic conditions generally specifying limits on a variety of financial ratios.

---

[2] "Survey Results: Changes in the Short-Term Credit Market," *Association for Financial Professionals* (December 21, 1999).

## FOCUS ON PRACTICE

### *How Credit Lines Are Structured*

A Midwestern utility supplies the electrical power for much of the state of Indiana. The primary purposes of its credit line bank borrowings are to provide funds for periods of cash shortage and to act as an emergency source of funds. The first need is met by either committed, formal lines of credit (totaling $106 million) or commercial paper—whichever is less expensive at the time funds are required. The utility has established committed lines of credit with 12 banks, six domestic and six foreign. The foreign banks have higher credit ratings from agencies such as Moody's Investor Services and Standard & Poor's, which rate the creditworthiness of banks, indicating greater soundness and that "they'll be there when you need them." Most foreign banks also have fiscal years ending in March instead of December, making them more willing to lend at the end of December when the utility generally needs funds. The utility pays a commitment fee averaging 3/16 of 1 percent on unused portions of these credit lines, and on amounts borrowed it is charged a floating interest rate typically 1 or 2 percent below the prime interest rate. These rates are based on the Federal funds rate, or the London Interbank Offered Rate (LIBOR). In the past few years, it used committed lines of credit rarely, usually around the date of its quarterly dividend payment or when paying for a major coal shipment.

The utility also has established uncommitted, informal credit lines totaling $123 million with five banks. It has never used any of these funds. The rate charged on these lines, if used, is higher than on the committed lines. No fee is paid on unused balances.

An **uncommitted line of credit** is technically not binding on the bank, although it is almost always honored.[3] These informal arrangements are appealing to companies that only rarely need to draw down the credit line, maintain a consistently strong financial position, and like the fact that uncommitted credit lines do not require a fee to be paid on unused balances. The only charge is interest on amounts borrowed. Banks like the flexibility offered by such arrangements, which free the bank from providing funds in the event of financial deterioration by the borrower or due to capital restrictions being imposed on the bank by regulators.

A noteworthy trend regarding credit lines is the rapid growth of **the standby letter of credit**, which guarantees that the bank will make funds available if the company cannot or does not wish to meet a major financial obligation. This constitutes one form of guarantee a bank can provide for borrowers.[4]

### Letter of Credit

A **letter of credit (LOC)** is a promise, generally by a bank, to make payment to a party upon presentation of a draft provided that the party complies with certain documentary

---

[3] The banks give themselves the flexibility to deny some borrowers credit if many requests are received at the same time. Thus, total credit lines for a given bank exceed its ability to finance them simultaneously. Furthermore, material changes in the potential borrower's financial condition might result in the bank's denial of credit for an uncommitted line, although this is rare.

[4] Commitments and contingent claims that banks make include financial guarantees and trade finance instruments. Financial guarantees include standby letters of credit, lines of credit, revolving loan commitments, note issuance facilities, and no recourse securitization. Trade finance services offered by banks include commercial letters of credit and acceptance participations. These are profiled briefly in George H. Hempel, Alan B. Coleman, and Donald G. Simonson, *Bank Management, 3rd. ed.* (New York: John Wiley & Sons, 1990), pp. 46–47, and in some depth in M. K. Lewis and K. T. Davis, *Domestic and International Banking* (Cambridge, MA: The MIT Press, 1987), Chapters 4 and 8.

FOCUS ON PRACTICE

## Managing the Maturity Structure of Loans

Denny's Corporation announced in September 2003 that it had amended its $125 million **revolving credit facility** to include a new $40 million term loan increasing its aggregate commitments to $165 million. The new term loan bears interest at a fixed rate of 11 percent and will not amortize prior to maturity. Denny's said that it used the $40 million term loan proceeds to pay down outstanding revolving loans to enhance its current liquidity position. The aggregate commitments now consist of outstanding term loans of $40 million, outstanding letters of credit of $38 million, and outstanding advances under the revolver of $22 million, leaving a net availability of $65 million.

*Source:* Company press release, September 26, 2003, 5:44 P.M. ET.

requirements as stated in the LOC agreement. The net effect of the LOC is to trade the credit of a well-known bank for that of a perhaps less-known corporate borrower. LOCs are generally a required feature of international borrowing.

### Bankers' Acceptances

**Bankers' acceptances** are time drafts drawn against a deposit in a commercial bank but with payment at maturity guaranteed by the bank. The original time draft usually is a result of international transactions between importers and exporters.

For example, a U.S. importer wishing to import goods from abroad may request its bank to issue a letter of credit on its behalf in favor of the foreign seller. If the bank finds the importer's credit standing satisfactory, it will issue such a letter, authorizing the foreign exporter to draw a time draft upon it in payment for the goods delivered. Equipped with this authorization, the exporter can discount the time draft with its bank when it ships the goods, thereby receiving payment immediately; the foreign bank then forwards the time draft, along with the shipping documents, to its correspondent bank in the United States. Generally, the U.S. correspondent bank will present the time draft for "acceptance" at the importer's bank, which forwards the shipping documents to the importer, who now may claim the shipment. Once accepted by the importer's bank, the time draft becomes a negotiable money market security, referred to as a bankers' acceptance, that trades in the money market until the maturity date of the time draft.

### Reverse Repurchase Agreement

Repurchase agreements were discussed in Chapter 15 as a short-term investment alternative. In essence, a **reverse repurchase agreement** (a reverse repo) is the other side of the repurchase agreement transaction. In this case, a corporate investment manager may negotiate with its bank to sell to the bank a specific dollar amount of marketable securities currently held in the firm's investment portfolio at a specified price. Thus, the party currently holding the securities initiates reverse repos. In addition, the contract would stipulate that the selling corporation would agree to repurchase the designated securities at the same price plus a stipulated amount of interest in an agreed upon number of days in the future. Most repos or reverse repos are overnight or 1-day contracts.

This type of an agreement might be used to obtain a quick infusion of cash to offset the delay of forecasted cash receipts without actually liquidating a portion of the firm's investment portfolio. Such transactions can also be useful for end-of-year financial statement window dressing.

## Commercial Paper

**Commercial paper** is a short-term promissory note issued by a corporation for a fixed maturity at a fixed yield. It is usually issued in bearer form with a minimum denomination of $100,000. Historically, commercial paper was unsecured. However, since the failure of the Penn Central Transportation Company in 1970, firms have had to support new issues of commercial paper through dealer networks with bank lines of credit or letters of credit. Maturities can be tailored to fit the need of the issuing corporation and range from one day to 270 days. Securities with maturities greater than 270 days must be registered with the Securities and Exchange Commission, a relatively expensive and time consuming exercise. Most commercial paper issues carry an original maturity of less than 180 days, and the average is about 30 days.

Commercial paper can be issued directly by the borrower itself or through a dealer network. Generally, commercial finance companies such as GMAC and bank holding companies directly issue their paper, while most nonfinancial firms use commercial paper dealers to facilitate the issue of new commercial paper. Dealers act very much like investment banking underwriters. They not only distribute the paper, but they may also advise their clients regarding the paper's price and maturity.

There are two pricing formats for commercial paper. Most commercial paper is sold on a **discount basis**, similar to Treasury bills. The paper is sold at a price less than its face value or maturity value. The interest paid to the investor is thus the difference between the proceeds of the issue and the dollar amount of the face value. Discounted commercial paper is by far the more popular pricing format. An alternative, and less popular, pricing format is commercial paper that is **interest bearing**. In this case, the paper has a face value, and the interest paid is based on a quoted rate based on the face value. At maturity, the issuer repays the face value along with the appropriate amount of interest.

Yields offered by commercial paper exceed those on comparable maturity Treasury bills because of the credit risk associated with the issuer. Although only the most creditworthy firms can issue commercial paper, some credit risk remains. However, the yields on commercial paper are generally less than the effective cost of bank lines of credit, which explains why banks have lost a portion of its short-term lending to those firms that can access the commercial paper market. However, recently corporations have been issuing more corporate bonds in order to lock in historically low interest rates as shown in Exhibit 16–3.

Four different agencies, including Standard & Poor's, Moody's, Fitch Investor Services Corporation, and Canada's Dominion Bond Rating Service Ltd., rate credit market instruments. Standard & Poor's ratings range from A, for the most creditworthy, to D, the least creditworthy. Within the A category, the agency further refines the rating with a 1, 2, or 3. The A-1 rating, for example, "indicates that the degree of safety regarding timely payment is either overwhelming or strong," with the 2 and 3 designations indicating slightly less strength. Finally, the agency adds a "+" to the A-1 rating for the financially strongest companies. So the highest rated company would carry a rating of A-1+. Ratings are important because the better the rating, the lower the borrowing cost.

A good example demonstrating the intricacies of commercial paper is the Salomon Brothers' situation in 1991. Salomon Brothers, like most other major investment banking firms, utilized a back-up line of credit to support its outstanding commercial paper. During 1991, Salomon had a $2 billion credit line at its disposal for this purpose. The credit line generally covered a quarter of the total paper outstanding with unen-

**Exhibit 16–3**

*Three Major Financing Sources (billions of $)*

| Source | 1998 | 1999 | 2000 | 2001 | 2002 | 2003 2nd QTR |
|---|---|---|---|---|---|---|
| Commercial paper | $193 | $230.3 | $278.4 | $190.1 | $126.0 | $107.0 |
| Percent of total | 5.49% | 5.97% | 6.63% | 4.33% | 2.86% | 2.38% |
| Bank loans | $764.7 | $825.5 | $887.9 | $816.5 | $746.6 | $713.8 |
| Percent of total | 21.77% | 21.40% | 21.13% | 18.61% | 16.94% | 15.87% |
| Corporate bonds | $1,846.0 | $2,063.9 | $2,225.1 | $2,565.6 | $2,698.2 | $2,820.3 |
| Percent of total | 52.54% | 53.50% | 52.96% | 58.48% | 61.24% | 62.72% |

*Source:* Federal Reserve, B.103 Balance Sheet of Nonfarm Business.

cumbered securities guaranteeing the balance. For Salomon to have a guarantee of the funds available, it had to pay an annual commitment fee of between 10 and 15 basis points on the credit line and an interest rate of 25 basis points above LIBOR on funds drawn down. Salomon was required to renew $500 million of the $2 billion line every three months.

During the fall of 1991, after Salomon's disclosure of its illegal bidding tactics in the government bond auction, Salomon's financial prospects changed dramatically. There were three basic responses to the Salomon situation. First, Salomon began to consider reducing the size of its credit line. This was partly in response to its reduced need for commercial paper since Salomon's business activities were shrinking as a result of its illegal activities. Second, the rating agencies were re-evaluating Salomon's liquidity situation and its ability to fund its commercial paper to determine whether or not a rating change was needed. Finally, the banks that held Salomon's credit lines were reassessing the appropriate premium to charge as well as renegotiating the bank **syndicate** arrangement offering the line.[5]

Many top rated U.S. corporations are taking advantage of placing euro commercial paper. Issuing commercial paper to foreign investors has many advantages. First, as long as commercial paper is targeted for foreign investors, it is not subject to several Securities and Exchange Commission requirements. This generally results in some cost and paperwork savings. Second, the euro commercial paper (CP) market is name oriented, and it is uncommon for euro commercial paper to be rated. For those companies that have international name recognition, this offers additional cost savings since rating agencies charge for their services. Finally, although domestic issues require a back-up credit facility, euro CP programs generally require no such collateral.

The euro market differs from its U.S. counterpart in that the maturities of **euro CP** are generally longer than domestic CP maturities. Euro paper generally carries maturities that average in the 60- to 90-day range, while the average maturity for U.S. domestic CP is in the 30-day range. In addition, U.S. companies are effectively limited to issuing euro CP for a maximum of 183-day maturities because of U.S. withholding tax considerations.[6] Thus, financial managers at large multinational U.S. corporations can compare effective rates domestically against their euro CP counterpart to trim additional basis points from the cost of their short-term financing strategies.

[5] For additional information on the Salomon credit line, see Steven Lipin, "Salomon Reduces Bank Credit Line," *The Wall Street Journal* (September 23, 1991), p. C1.
[6] Alan Taylor, "Euro CP," *CASHFLOW* (October 1986), p. 50.

## FOCUS ON PRACTICE

The main markets for commercial paper include the domestic U.S. market, the domestic Japanese market, the domestic French market, and the international market based in Europe referred to as the euro commercial paper market. While U.S. commercial paper is the largest and most mature of the commercial paper markets, euro-denominated commercial paper issued in the euro commercial paper market has exhibited enormous growth since the single currency's introduction. In fact, such issues now outnumber new euro commercial paper denominated in U.S. dollars.

*Source:* Philippe Laurensy, "The Rise and Rise of Commercial Paper in Europe," *Euroclear* (August 12, 2003), **http://www.GTNews.com.**

### Asset-Based Loans

**Asset-based loans** represent a source of financing obtained from a bank or commercial finance company secured by accounts receivable or inventory. Some of the more prominent commercial finance companies include CIT Group, Fleet Capital, and GE Capital Services. Asset-based loans are generally more expensive than unsecured financing as a result of the transaction costs of monitoring the collateral, and the fact that such collateral has been pledged indicates that the loan has some degree of risk of nonrepayment. For example, the company may have already borrowed all of the unsecured funds it can get and is now turning to secured financing sources.

*RECEIVABLES FINANCING* The first asset-based financing source to be discussed is the **pledging of receivables**. This is a situation in which a lender, such as a commercial bank or a commercial finance company, makes a loan protected by a lien placed on a certain portion of the firm's receivables. In those cases where receivables represent a major portion of financing need, this represents an effective method of financing.

This type of financial arrangement has three basic drawbacks. First, a receivable does not represent a tangible piece of property, and the lending institution will rarely lend 100 percent of the book value of the receivables. Indeed, the ratio of loan value to collateral value may not be higher than 50 percent, depending on the perceived quality of the receivables. Second, the lender requires the borrower to keep detailed records of any change in the status of the pledged receivables. Finally, risk remains with the borrower. If the receivable is not collected, the borrower must still repay the lending institution.

Loans based on pledging receivables are typically obtained from both commercial banks and commercial finance companies. The main difference between these two types of lending institutions, from the borrower's standpoint, is that commercial finance companies usually allow a greater loan to collateral ratio but, in so doing, charge a higher rate of interest on the loan (about five percentage points above prime).

The second receivables financing technique is **factoring**. A factor is a corporation that participates as an original party to the sale of a product on credit, making the decision involving approval of the buyer's creditworthiness. In this situation, the seller of the product never becomes the creditor and is not held responsible for any bad debts. In this capacity, the factor acts as a substitute for an internal credit department for the seller. The seller receives its money in a stated number of days after the end of the credit period. This, in itself, is not a financing arrangement in the strict sense of the word. Rather, it is a process in which a company can sell on credit without establishing a credit department.

## FOCUS ON PRACTICE

### *Commercial Paper Usage Compared to Bank Credit*

According to a survey administered December 9–16, 1999, by the Association for Financial Professionals, large and mid-sized corporations looking for short-term credit will turn increasingly away from commercial banks and toward the commercial paper market. For these firms, bank credit accounted for approximately 43 percent of their total corporate borrowings. This is expected to drop to 37 percent in the coming 2-year period, which is a continuation of a trend that saw bank credit accounting for over 50 percent of corporate borrowings two years earlier. Over this 4-year period, the utilization of commercial paper is expected to increase from 13 percent of borrowings to 18 percent. The survey was administered to senior-level financial professionals at companies with revenues of $100 million or more.

*Source:* "Survey Results: Changes in the Short-Term Credit Market," *Association for Financial Professionals* (December 21, 1999).

What if the seller needs its money earlier than at the end of the credit period? The seller is basically holding only one receivable called due from factor rather than a multitude of receivables from many different customers. This receivable can effectively be pledged as collateral for a short-term loan from the seller's commercial bank. The bank finds it much easier to evaluate the creditworthiness of a large, nationally known factoring company than a multitude of individual customers spread throughout the nation.

Some factors actually "buy" receivables from companies for cash—usually at a stated discount from face value of the receivables. It is important for the seller to know whether the receivables are sold with or without recourse. If the receivables are sold **with recourse**, then the factor can demand that funds be returned for uncollected receivables. If the receivables are sold **without recourse,** then the seller is not liable for uncollected receivables.

Examples of nonrecourse factoring arrangements are the MasterCard and Visa credit card operations. The customer purchases an item from a particular retail outlet but pays the factor, either Visa or MasterCard. These companies provide the credit checking for the selling company and an established payment pattern usually for a fee of around 3 percent. The company selling the product receives payment from the credit card company, and the credit card company is at risk if the customer defaults on the payment.

*INVENTORY FINANCING* **Inventory financing** is an extremely critical component of the total financial plan of most corporations. This is because, historically, inventory has generally represented a significant portion of the corporation's total working capital, and as we have seen, inventory represents a resource commitment which has yet to release cash and will not do so until the item is sold and cash collected. In terms of volume, total business inventory is in the hundreds of billions of dollars. Inventory financing can take several different forms.

*FLOATING LIEN* A **floating lien** is very general in nature. Basically, under this type of arrangement, the borrower pledges its inventories "in general" without any particular specification. Under this type of arrangement, the lender would typically only lend a relatively small fraction of the total value of the inventory.

*TRUST RECEIPTS* A **trust receipt loan** is just the opposite of a floating lien. In this situation, a serial number or some other readily identifiable mark notes the collateralized in-

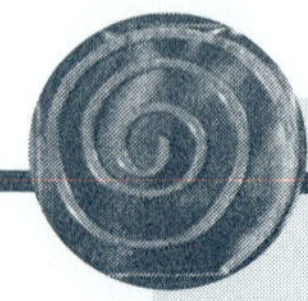

## FOCUS ON PRACTICE

### Asset-Based Financing

The importance of asset-based financing is underscored by the example of an importer and distributor of lawn equipment as cited by James Connolly, chief executive officer of Fleet Capital. According to Mr. Connolly, this company with over $200 million in annual revenues could receive up to 60-percent financing on the strength of its $25 million in inventory and $25 million in receivables.

*Source:* Paul Sweeny, "Capital Structure: Credibility and Flexibility Rule," *Financial Executive* (September 2003), **http://www.fei.org/mag/articles/9-2003_cover.cfm.**

ventory items. Thus, the lender has a direct lien on a specific inventory item. This type of arrangement is suitable for relatively expensive and low turnover items such as automobiles, consumer durables, and industrial machinery and equipment. Because the inventory is easily identifiable by serial number, the lender allows it to remain on the borrower's premises. As the inventory is sold, the borrower remits payment on the loan along with accrued interest. The lender then releases the lien and the appropriate item.

Commercial banks, commercial finance companies, and **captive finance companies** issue receipt loans. For example, General Motors Acceptance Corporation (GMAC), a captive finance company of General Motors Corporation, makes these types of loans to GM's dealers also known as **floor planning**.

*Warehouse Receipts* From a lending institution's viewpoint, the main inventory financing problem is the securing of the collateral—the inventory item.

One method of inventory financing is called field warehousing. This technique results in advances being issued against field warehouse receipts. Essentially, a **field warehouse** may be nothing more than a segregated area of the borrower's facility which houses the pledged inventory. A third-party firm is responsible for issuing the receipts, which ensures that the pledged items are physically located on the premises. These warehouse receipts are viewed by lending institutions as acceptable collateral for the basis of a loan. In a sense, the pledged inventory items are in the possession of the field warehouse firm—not the borrower.

The problem with this financing technique is that it is rather inflexible. The pledged inventory items must be segregated and stored in a mutually acceptable location. In addition, this type of arrangement is not really feasible for small inventory items that have a frequent turnover. The reason is that before the field warehousing firm can release the item, it must receive approval to do so from the lending institution.

A **terminal warehouse agreement** is similar to a field warehouse agreement except that, in this case, the inventories pledged as collateral are moved to a public warehouse that is physically separated from the borrower's premises. This agreement gives the lender more security for the pledged inventory items.

*Securitization* **Securitization** involves issuing debt securities collateralized by a pool of selected financial assets such as mortgages, auto loans, or credit card receivables, to name a few. Banks and large finance companies have issued increasingly larger amounts of commercial paper securitized in such a fashion. It is not uncommon for financing rates on such paper to be cheaper than rates obtained on more conventional bank financing.

### Trends in Lending Services

Many banks are going after smaller companies as part of their client bases. For example, Wells Fargo has begun offering small businesses a credit card that acts as a committed line of credit. For larger corporations, lending services are more extensive. Where the loan principal is very large, a group (syndicate) of banks will jointly make the loan, thus spreading the risk. This adds complexity to attempted restructuring, as in the case of Trans World Airlines' efforts at negotiating with a syndicate of 92 banks during its financial crisis in the late 1990s. **Participations** involving other nonfinancial corporations also have appeared, offering a substitute for commercial paper borrowings.

### Comparing Short-Term Financing Rates

Exhibit 16–4 displays comparative yields on various money market yields including the prime rate offered by commercial banks, 90-day commercial paper, and 90-day Treasury bills.

## THE EFFECTIVE COST OF SHORT-TERM FINANCING

Short-term financing arrangements have several features that cause the stated interest rate on the financing to be different from the **effective interest rate**. A very general formula that will form the basis for our discussion is shown in Equation 16.1.

**Exhibit 16–4**

*Comparison of Average Weekly Short-Term Financing Yields for 1999–2003*

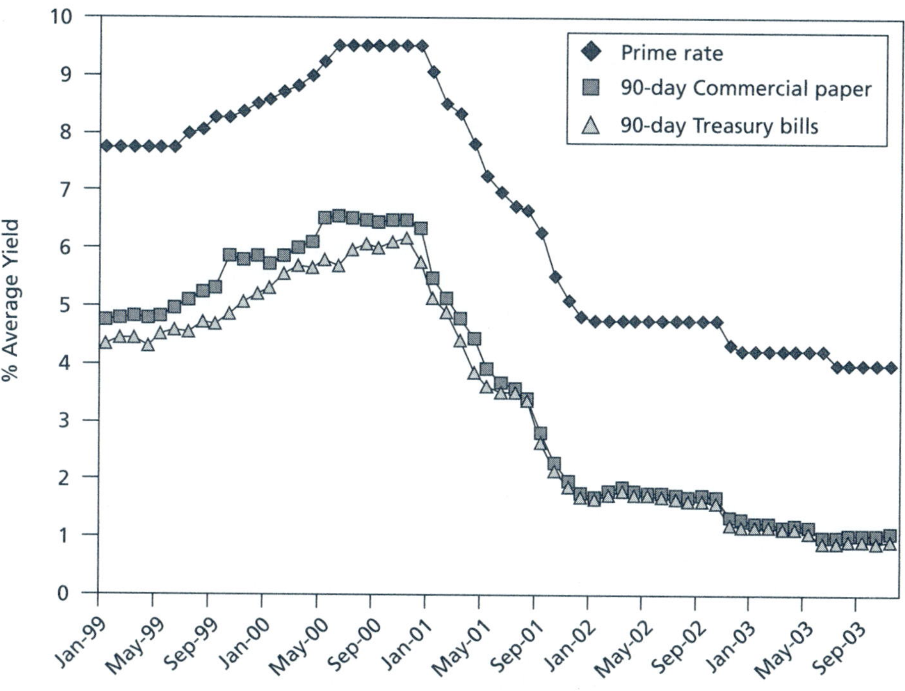

$$\text{Effective rate} = \frac{\text{Out-of-pocket expenses}}{\text{Usable funds}} \times \frac{365}{M} \tag{16.1}$$

**Out-of-pocket expenses** include interest expense and fees. Interest expense is based on the stated interest rate and the amount borrowed over the funding period. Fees include commitment fees charged by the bank for the total amount of funds the bank stands ready to lend to the firm through a line of credit or a letter of credit facility, letter of credit fees, or commercial paper dealer fees. **Usable funds** represent the net proceeds the firm receives from the financing vehicle. If funds are received through a credit line, then the amount received may be less than the amount borrowed if the bank requires the firm to leave compensating balances as a percent of the amount borrowed. If funds are received through an issue of commercial paper, then the amount received is reduced by the discounted interest paid.

The final part of Equation 16.1 annualizes the length of the borrowing period, *M*, assuming that it is one year or less. The effective rate thus calculated is the annualized effective simple interest rate on the financing arrangement. This equation is applied to commercial paper and a bank credit line facility in the following sections.

### Effective Cost of Commercial Paper

The treasurer at Consolidated Trailways, Inc., is preparing a new issue of commercial paper through a dealer network. Commercial paper is a typical source of financing for Consolidated, and the firm generally has several million dollars of paper outstanding throughout the year. In discussing the new issue with its commercial paper dealer, Consolidated learned that new 30-day issues in the range of $1 to $5 million could be priced to sell at a 9-percent discount rate. The dealer's fee will be an annual rate of 1/8 of 1 percent, and the commitment fee on a back-up line of credit will be an annual rate of 0.25 percent. The treasurer wants to know what the effective rate of issuing $3 million of commercial paper will be.

*OUT-OF-POCKET COSTS* To apply Equation 16.1, the treasurer needs to determine the value of two variables, out-of-pocket costs and usable funds. Let's start with out-of-pocket costs. First, the major component of out-of-pocket costs is the interest that Consolidated will have to pay. The commercial paper will be issued on a discount basis; the difference between the face amount and the discounted price is the interest that the firm pays. The face amount is the $3 million stated earlier. The discounted price is the face amount less 30 days' interest, 30 days being the maturity of the paper. The discount price is $2,977,500 {$3 million − [0.09 × (30/360) × $3 million]}. The interest paid is thus $22,500. Note that the interest computation uses a 360-day year, which is the convention with discount rates. The dealer's fee is 0.125 percent, which costs the firm $312.50 [$3 million × 0.00125 × (30/360)]. The commitment fee for the back-up line of credit is $625 {$3 million × [0.0025 × (30/360)]}. The total out-of-pocket cost is the sum of the interest expense, dealer's fee, and bank commitment fee, which totals $23,437.50 ($22,500 + $312.50 + $625).

*USABLE FUNDS* Next, the dollar amount of usable funds must be determined. The treasurer has determined that the discount price of the $3 million issue will result in proceeds of $2,977,500, which is equal to the face value less the discount interest at the asked rate.

*EFFECTIVE INTEREST RATE* Plugging the values for the out-of-pocket costs and usable funds into Equation 16.1 results in the effective annualized interest rate for the 30-day commercial paper.

$$\text{Effective rate} = \frac{\$23{,}437.50}{\$2{,}977{,}500} \times \frac{365}{30}$$

$$\text{Effective rate} = 0.0958, \text{ or } 9.58\%$$

The effective cost of the paper is 58 basis points above the stated asked discount rate of 9 percent. Note the money market convention that effective rates are based on a 365-day year rather than a 360-day year.

Had Consolidated not been a regular issuer of commercial paper, using a line of credit as a back-up facility might not be appropriate. Credit lines are not generally set up for periods less than one year. Therefore, the annual cost of the credit line would have to be allocated to the 30-day financing period and then annualized. This would result in an out-of-pocket cost of $30,312.50 ($22,500 + $312.50 + $7,500). The $7,500 is the annual cost of the credit line commitment fee and must now be allocated in total to the 30-day financing period. Usable funds would remain unchanged. The effective rate then becomes 12.39 percent. In this case, the use of a letter of credit rather than a line of credit as a back-up facility would be more appropriate. A letter of credit can be designed to be in effect for any length of time necessary.

## FINANCIAL DILEMMA REVISITED

As indicated in the Financial Dilemma presented at the beginning of the chapter, the treasurer at Beco, Inc., arranged for a line of credit with the firm's bank. The line is for $100,000, which could be drawn down at any time during the year, but the line had to be fully repaid by the end of the year. The stated rate on funds borrowed was set at 10 percent, and the bank assessed a fee of 1/4 of a percent on the unused portion of the line. Beco is required to maintain a compensating balance of 20 percent of the funds borrowed. Beco's cash management system keeps all current balances fully invested so it essentially must borrow the balances required for compensation. Over the course of the year, Beco borrows an average of $60,000. The interest paid is $6,000 ($60,000 × 0.10), and the commitment fee paid is $100 [($100,000 − $60,000) × 0.0025]. Although Beco borrows an average of $60,000, $12,000 ($60,000 × 0.20) of that must remain at the bank as a compensating balance, leaving $48,000 of usable funds. Applying Equation 16.1, Beco's effective rate of interest for the year is:

$$\text{Effective rate} = \frac{\$6{,}000 + \$100}{\$48{,}000} \times \frac{365}{365}$$

$$\text{Effective rate} = 0.1271, \text{ or } 12.71\%$$

Beco is effectively borrowing at a rate of 12.71 percent rather than the stated interest rate of 10 percent. The effective rate is 271 basis points higher than the stated rate because of the fee and more importantly because of the compensating balance requirements reducing the usable amount of funds.

Suppose that Beco had been carrying idle balances at the bank that could be used as compensating balances. Because the firm received the use of only $48,000, we recalculate the effective rate assuming Beco borrows $48,000 and the compensating balances are covered by existing cash balances at the bank. The interest expense is $4,800 ($48,000 × 0.10), and the fee is $130 [($100,000 − $48,000) × 0.0025]. The dollar amount of usable funds in this case is equal to the $48,000 borrowed. The effective rate is:

$$\text{Effective rate} = \frac{\$4{,}800 + \$130}{\$48{,}000} \times \frac{365}{365}$$

$$\text{Effective rate} = 0.1027, \text{ or } 10.27\%$$

In this case, the effective rate is only 27 basis points above the stated rate of 10 percent solely because of the commitment fee. The commitment fee can be reduced if the firm reduces the size of the credit line to an amount closer to the amount borrowed. However, remember that the $48,000 borrowed is an average and the firm may actually need to borrow as much as $100,000 at some point during the year. The point here is that setting a credit line for an excessive amount is expensive, and effective cash forecasting should be used to estimate the maximum borrowings needed.

## SUMMARY

The short-term financing alternatives discussed in this chapter differ from spontaneous financing provided through trade credit and accruals as covered in Chapter 7. The financing sources discussed in this chapter are discretionary, the use of which must be explicitly sought.

The chapter began with a discussion of financial strategy and focused on the maturity decision. The question of managing the maturity structure of the firm's financing sources is difficult, but three different strategies to mitigate this difficulty were described: the aggressive strategy, the conservative strategy, and the moderate strategy.

Our attention then turned to the major forms of available short-term financing. Each of the major short-term sources was described and the basic characteristics outlined.

The chapter concluded with a discussion of calculating the effective rate of interest on two popular forms of short-term financing: a bank credit line and commercial paper. Commercial paper was chosen because it offered a good example of nonbank financing and the inclusion of dealer spreads and commitment fees. The bank credit line financing source was chosen because it includes factors, such as compensating balances, that are not a part of commercial paper issues.

Short-term financing is an important component of maintaining the firm's liquidity. The financial manager should forecast the firm's cash position on a regular basis and then have in place contingency financing sources to handle forecasted as well as unexpected cash needs. Effective financing of the firm's short-term financing position impacts the firm's liquidity position and, as such, ultimately affects its value.

## USEFUL WEB SITES

| | |
|---|---|
| Integral Development Corporation | **http://www.integral.com** |
| Export Financing Matchmaker | **http://www.ita.doc.gov/td/efm** |
| Commercial Finance Association | **http://www.cfa.com** |
| KPMG LLP | **http://www.kpmginsiders.com** |

## QUESTIONS

1. How do cash forecasting and short-term borrowing strategies relate?
2. Compare and contrast the three short-term borrowing strategies. Which strategy would generally result in the lowest borrowing cost? The highest borrowing cost? The most liquidity? The least liquidity?
3. How does the amount of buffer that a treasurer decides to use when establishing a line a credit affect the effective cost of the credit line?

4. What factors cause the nominal rate on a credit line to differ from its effective rate?
5. What factors cause the nominal rate on commercial paper to differ from its effective rate?
6. How does a firm's short-term financing strategy impact its liquidity?

## PROBLEMS

1. You are provided the following 10 years of asset data for Smacker's Candy Company:

| Year | Current | Fixed | Total |
|---|---|---|---|
| 2001 | $100 | $100 | $200 |
| 2002 | 130 | 110 | 240 |
| 2003 | 150 | 120 | 270 |
| 2004 | 140 | 130 | 270 |
| 2005 | 170 | 140 | 310 |
| 2006 | 190 | 150 | 340 |
| 2007 | 180 | 160 | 340 |
| 2008 | 210 | 170 | 380 |
| 2009 | 230 | 180 | 410 |
| 2010 | 220 | 190 | 410 |

   a. Draw a simple graph of the data with assets on the vertical axis and time on the horizontal axis.
   b. Graphically depict what might be considered to be the level of permanent current assets.
   c. Suppose that Smacker uses the aggressive strategy to finance these assets. Indicate this financing strategy on your graph, and discuss the financial implications of using this particular strategy.
   d. Suppose that Smacker employs the conservative strategy to finance its assets. Indicate this financing strategy on your graph and discuss its implication.
   e. Suppose that Smacker decides to employ the moderate strategy to finance its assets. Indicate this strategy on your graph and discuss its implication.

2. Gilmore, Inc., builds recreational equipment. Its sales are very seasonal with most of its sales occurring in the February to August time period. The following data contain some working capital to sales ratios as well as a sales projection for the next four quarters:

$$\frac{\text{Cash} + \text{Mkt. sec.} + \text{A/R} + \text{Inventory}}{\text{Sales}} = 0.30$$

$$\frac{\text{Accounts payable}}{\text{Sales}} = 0.15$$

(In the table below, dollar amounts are in millions.)

| | Jan.–Mar. | Apr.–June | July–Sept. | Oct.–Dec. |
|---|---|---|---|---|
| Sales | $ 5.00 | $50.00 | $30.00 | $5.00 |
| Purchases | 22.50 | 13.50 | 2.25 | 2.25 |

Gilmore's level of net fixed assets is $1,500,000, and its capital structure consists of $1,500,000 of shareholders' equity. Current liabilities consist solely of accounts payable. Net income as a percentage of sales is forecasted to be 7.5 percent for the coming year. Dividends equal to net income are paid out.

   a. Calculate Gilmore's balance sheet for each of the four projected quarters. Use the following form:

| | |
|---|---|
| Cash + Mkt. sec. + A/R + Inventory | Accounts payable |
| Net fixed assets | New loans |
| | Shareholders' equity |

Force the balance sheets to balance by putting new financing needs in the new loans account.

**b.** Calculate the current ratio for Gilmore at the end of each quarter for each of the three financing strategies: aggressive, conservative, and moderate (using half long-term and half short-term financing).

**c.** Discuss your results in **b** regarding the impact that financing strategy has on Gilmore's liquidity.

**d.** What options are open to Gilmore if it did not want to increase its borrowing?

**3.** Sara, treasurer for SAFECO Instruments, Inc., updated her firm's short-term cash forecast only to discover that the firm will suffer a cash shortage of $9 million for a period of two months or 60 days. SAFECO issues commercial paper sporadically and currently has none outstanding. One alternative is to liquidate a portion of her marketable securities portfolio, but with interest rates up, this is not a good alternative. She just learned from one of her commercial paper dealers that paper in the 60-day range is in demand by investors and that the asked discount rates are comparably good at about 4.5 percent. The dealer's annual fee is 12 basis points, and the annual commitment fee on a back-up line of credit is 20 basis points. Estimate the effective cost of the commercial paper assuming this is the only commercial paper issue she would make during the year.

Sara was also approached by a bank, wanting her company's business, offered a letter of credit back-up facility with an annual fee of 50 basis points rather than a line of credit. Sara wondered how this would affect the cost of the commercial paper issue, as the fee seemed a little high.

**4.** Ralph, treasurer for M & M Products, Inc., recently updated his firm's short-term cash forecast only to discover that the firm will suffer a cash shortage of $15 million for a period of 30 days. One alternative is to liquidate a portion of his marketable securities portfolio, but with interest rates up, this is not a good alternative. Ralph just learned from one of his commercial paper dealers that paper in the 30-day range is in demand and that asked discount rates are comparably good at about 3.7 percent. The dealer's annual fee is 10 basis points and the annual commitment fee on a back-up line of credit is 25 basis points.

**a.** Estimate the effective cost of the commercial paper assuming that this is the only commercial paper issue planned for the year.

**b.** Estimate the effective cost of the commercial paper assuming that there will be recurring issues of commercial paper all year long.

**5.** You recently approached your bank about establishing a credit line facility. The terms offered by your bank include a nominal rate of prime + 1.5 percent (prime is currently 5 percent) on the amount borrowed, a commitment fee of 25 basis points on the unused portion of the credit line, and a compensating balance of 10 percent on the amount borrowed.

You decide to establish the line for $75 million. Over the course of a year, you anticipate the average amount borrowed to be $55 million. Your firm keeps no balances at the bank and pays fees for all cash management services.

**a.** Estimate the cost of the credit line.

**b.** Assume that the firm did have cash balances to cover the required compensating balances resulting from the credit line borrowings. Estimate the effective cost of the credit line.

**6.** As treasurer of your firm, you wish to establish a credit line facility to cover an expected average annual borrowing of $65 million. You have asked two banks to submit proposals for a credit line of $80 million. Based on the credit line of $55 million, Bank of the West proposes a nominal rate of 6 percent, a commitment fee of 0.25 percent on the unused portion of the credit line, and a 20-percent compensating balance on the amount borrowed. Bank of the East offers a rate of 5.75 percent if the size of the credit line is $95 million. In addition, the commitment fee on the unused portion of the credit line is 20 basis points, and compensating balances of 25 percent will be required on the amount borrowed.

Calculate the effective cost of both proposals, and indicate which proposal should be accepted.

## REFERENCES

William Beranek, Christopher Cornwell, and Sunho Choi, "External Financing, Liquidity, and Capital Expenditures," *The Journal of Financial Research,* Vol. XVIII, No. 2, (Summer 1995), pp. 207–222.

S. H. Griffiths and N. J. Robertson, "Global Cash: Short-Term Investing and Borrowing Overseas," *Journal of Cash Management* (March/April 1987), pp. 52–56.

B. W. Harries, "How Corporate Bonds and Commercial Paper Are Rated," *Financial Executive* (September 1971), pp. 30–36.

N. C. Hill, W. L. Sartoris, and S. L. Visscher, "The Components of Credit Line Borrowing Cost," *Journal of Cash Management* (October 1983), p. 47ff.

J. C. T. Mao, "Application of Linear Programming to the Short Term Financing Decision," *Engineering Economist* (1968), pp. 221–241.

K. L. Stock, "Asset-Based Financing: Borrowing and Lender Perspectives," *Journal of Commercial Bank Lending* (December 1980), pp. 31–46.

O. Williamson, "Corporate Finance and Corporate Governance," *Journal of Finance* (July 1988), pp. 567–592.

J. D. Stowe, C. J. Watson, and T. D. Robertson, "Relationships Between the Two Sides of the Balance Sheet: A Canonical Correlation Analysis," *Journal of Finance* (September 1980), pp. 973–980.

FOCUSED CASE

# Jones Salvage and Recycling, Inc. (B)

Note: This is a continuation of the Jones Salvage and Recycling, Inc. (A) case found immediately following Chapter 13. That case concluded with a monthly forecasted income statement, cash budget, and balance sheet for the first 6 months of the new year. Jones (B) will use that information to determine the financing and investment strategy that is best for Jones to use.

Mr. Jones was very impressed with the ability of Carl Malone, the company's financial manager, to forecast the company's cash position for the coming 6 months and felt that this would put the company in a great position to prevent the recurring liquidity crises the company has faced each spring. Historically, although the company has always been able to get the needed financing, it was obvious that "eleventh hour" nature of its loan requests were very frustrating to the company's bank. Armed with the projected financial statements, Jones asked Malone to approach the bank and develop a financing strategy in anticipation of the coming 6 months.

During the discussions with the bank's lending officer, Malone asked for and received the following interest rate projections that the bank uses for its planning purposes. One thing that was painfully obvious to Jones was the dramatic jump in interest rates expected to occur in January. In addition, it appeared that interest rates would continue to rise for the next several months. Mr. Malone confirmed this and observed that the current Fed chairman was a real inflation hawk and was taking a very aggressive approach to controlling inflation by tightening up bank credit. The raw data comes from an economic forecasting service and then the bank adjusts the raw data to arrive at its projected lending rates for loans of various maturities for the local market. A table of the interest rate data follows:

| Month | MS (30 day) | MS (90 day) | NP (30 day) | NP (90 day) | NP (180 day) | LTD |
|---|---|---|---|---|---|---|
| January | 6.00% | 6.75% | 8.00% | 8.50% | 9.50% | 10.00% |
| February | 7.00% | 7.00% | 9.50% | 9.50% | 9.50% | 9.50% |
| March | 8.00% | 7.50% | 10.50% | 10.00% | 9.50% | 9.00% |
| April | 7.50% | 7.50% | 12.00% | 10.00% | 9.50% | 9.00% |
| May | 7.00% | 7.00% | 10.00% | 10.50% | 10.00% | 9.50% |
| June | 6.00% | 6.00% | 9.00% | 10.00% | 11.00% | 12.00% |

The company has limited investment and financing opportunities. Investments can only be made in 30-day and 90-day marketable securities (MS). Mr. Malone's discussions with the bank lending officer centered on 30-day, 90-day, and 180-day loans. Although long-term financing is a possibility, Mr. Malone will only consider it for the month of January, which is also the case for the 6-month loan.

The financial planning model Jones uses assumes that investments and financing are done at the end of the month, which means no interest is earned or paid until the following month. Interest is received and paid on a monthly basis. The current mortgage loan is carrying an interest rate of 8 percent and no principal payments will be made until December. The current 30-day note payable is carrying an interest rate of 6 percent. Note the following restrictions: 180-day and long-term financing can only be taken out in January; 90-day notes cannot be taken out nor can 90-day MS be invested in during May or June; no financing is available during the month of June.

## REQUIRED

1. Develop a financing and investment plan that will maximize the sum of net interest income of the 6-month planning period.
2. Develop a financing plan that is consistent with a conservative financing strategy as defined in Chapter 16. You should plan to keep all surplus cash over $1,000 invested.
3. Develop a financing plan that is consistent with the aggressive strategy as defined in Chapter 16. You should plan to keep all surplus cash over $1,000 invested.
4. Compare the month current ratio and net profit margin for each strategy. Discuss the trade-offs that the financial manager must consider when deciding on a strategy.

# APPENDIX 16A

## The Effective Cost of Credit Lines

This appendix will develop a much more explicit and detailed model, based on the Hill, Sartoris, and Visscher approach, for estimating the effective cost of bank credit lines when compensating balances and commitment fees are present. The advantage of this model is that it can account for the exact timing and amount of borrowing over a year rather than just assume an average borrowed amount, as does the model discussed in the chapter.

The effective rate on a bank credit line is impacted by the nominal interest rate charged, the commitment fee, the structure of the compensating balance requirements, the seasonality of borrowing, and the difference between the maximum amount borrowed and the size of the credit line. The critical relationships are presented in Equations 16.1A through 16.4A.

Equation 16.1A states that the dollar amount of required compensating balances for month *t* is equal to the proportion *a* of the amount borrowed during the month plus the proportion *b* of the dollar level of the credit line established.

$$CMP_t = aTLOAN_t + bCRLN \qquad (16.1A)$$

Where: CMP = The dollar amount of compensating balance required during month *t*

TLOAN = The total loan borrowed during month *t*

CRLN = The dollar amount of the credit line

a = The percentage compensating balance required on the total amount borrowed

b = The percentage compensating balance required on the size of the credit line

Equation 16.2A states that the total loan during month *t* is equal to the total cumulative cash needs plus the dollar amount of compensating balances that must also be borrowed. If the firm has enough idle cash balances at the bank to offset the compensating balance requirement, then the total loan for the month would equal just the total cumulative cash needs.

$$TLOAN_t = TCCN_t + aTLOAN_t + bCRLN \qquad (16.2A)$$

Where: TCCN = total cumulative cash needs

Equation 16.3A calculates the size of the credit line. The credit line is equal to the maximum cumulative cash needs times one plus the buffer percentage plus the dollar amount compensating balances based on the maximum borrowing level which would equal the size of the credit line.

$$CRLN = (1 + B)\max(TCCN_t) + aCRLN + bCRLN \qquad (16.3A)$$

Where: B = The percentage amount of desired credit line buffer over the maximum total cumulative cash needs forecasted without considering the additional amount borrowed to satisfy compensating balance requirements

Equation 16.4A calculates the annual effective rate of interest based on the calculated out-of-pocket expenses and the dollar amount of usable funds.

$$I = \frac{\Sigma\, i_t \times TLOAN_t + f \times CRLN}{\Sigma\, TCCN_t/12} \qquad (16.4A)$$

Where: f = The annual commitment fee rate based on the size of the credit line

$i_t$ = The monthly interest rate for each month *t*

I = The annual effective rate of interest

The information required to implement the model includes a monthly forecast of the firm's cumulative cash needs, the nominal or stated interest rate on funds borrowed though the credit line, compensating balance parameters, and finally the percentage commitment fee. For demonstration purposes, assume the following forecast of a firm's total cumulative cash needs and credit line parameters provided by its bank.

**Total Cumulative Cash Needs, $TCCN_t$**

| | | | |
|---|---|---|---|
| January | $50,000 | July | $ 0 |
| February | 75,000 | August | 100,0000 |
| March | 75,000 | September | 150,0000 |
| April | 25,000 | October | 75,0000 |
| May | 0 | November | 50,0000 |
| June | 0 | December | 0 |

a = 0.05
b = 0.05
f = 0.005
i = 0.10/12
B = 0.20

The solution begins by solving for the size of the credit line, *CRLN*, using Equation 16.3A. Note, that in this equation, *CRLN* is substituted for *TLOAN* with the parameter *a* because we are solving for the size of the credit line consistent with our maximum borrowing which would be where *TLOAN* = *CRLN*. Plugging in the values for the variables in Equation 16.3A results in a credit line of $200,000, as shown below.

$$\text{CRLN} = (1 + 0.20) \times (\$150{,}000) + 0.05 \times \text{CRLN} + 0.05 \times \text{CRLN}$$

$$\text{CRLN} = \$200{,}000$$

Once *CRLN* is determined, the monthly total loan, $TLOAN_t$, can be solved using Equation 16.2A. This equation is shown below in a form which can directly solve for the dollar amount of the total loan for each month.

$$\text{TLOAN}_t = \text{TCCN}_t + \text{aTLOAN}_t + \text{bCRLN}$$
$$(1 - \text{a})\text{TLOAN}_t = \text{TCCN}_t + \text{bCRLN}$$
$$\text{TLOAN}_t = \text{TCCN}_t/(1 - \text{a}) + \text{bCRLN}/(1 - \text{a})$$

| Month | TCCN | TLOAN |
|---|---|---|
| January | $ 50,000 | $ 63,158 |
| February | 75,000 | 89,474 |
| March | 75,000 | 89,474 |
| April | 25,000 | 36,842 |
| May | 0 | 10,526 |
| June | 0 | 10,526 |
| July | 0 | 10,526 |
| August | 100,000 | 115,789 |
| September | 150,000 | 168,421 |
| October | 75,000 | 89,474 |
| November | 50,000 | 63,158 |
| December | 0 | 10,526 |

Finally, having solved for the monthly *TLOAN* and the size of the credit line, *CRLN*, we have all the numbers necessary to solve for the annual effective rate of interest using Equation 16.4A. The effective interest rate paid on the credit line is 14.63 percent, a rate that is 463 basis points above the stated 10-percent rate. The additional basis points paid result from the 20-percent buffer, the compensating balance requirements, and the commitment fee charged.

The usefulness of such a model can readily be seen when different banks offer different terms and you are trying to determine those terms, which are most cost effective. Alternatively, you can perform sensitivity analysis by varying the terms so that you can offer an alternative set of terms for your bank to consider. In fact, in the Hill et al. article, the authors show how to solve for the incremental impact that the compensating balance terms, buffer size, and seasonality have on the effective rate.

## PROBLEMS

**16A-1.** The treasurer at AFC Videos, Inc., has established a credit line with its bank. AFC's estimated seasonal cumulative borrowing needs are as follows:

| | | | |
|---|---|---|---|
| January | $100,000 | July | $ 75,000 |
| February | 40,000 | August | 300,000 |
| March | 10,000 | September | 225,000 |
| April | 0 | October | 100,000 |
| May | 0 | November | 50,000 |
| June | 0 | December | 0 |

AFC's bank indicates the stated rate on the line would be 8 percent with a 0.5-percent commitment fee on the unused balance and 15-percent compensating balances on the amount borrowed. AFC's treasurer would like to establish the line with a 20-percent buffer. That is, the size of the credit line would be 20 percent above the maximum estimated amount borrowed. Estimate the effective annual rate of the credit line.

**16A-2.** Redo Problem A-1 except assume that the percent buffer is zero rather than the stated 20 percent. How much does the 20-percent buffer contribute to the effective cost of the credit line?

**16A-3.** Redo Problems A-1 and A-2 except assume that AFC maintains an average idle cash balance at its bank of $3,000 throughout the year. Re-estimate the effective cost of the credit line.

**16A-4.** The treasurer at Fun Corporation of the USA, Inc., just established a credit line with its bank for the coming fiscal year. Fun Corp.'s estimated seasonal cumulative borrowing needs are as follows:

| | | | |
|---|---|---|---|
| January | $ 0 | July | $200,000 |
| February | 0 | August | 100,000 |
| March | 0 | September | 25,000 |
| April | 50,000 | October | 0 |
| May | 100,000 | November | 0 |
| June | 300,000 | December | 0 |

Fun Corp.'s loan officer indicates the stated rate on the line would be 4.5 percent with a 0.15-percent commitment fee on the unused credit line and 25-percent compensating balances on the amount borrowed. The treasurer would like to establish the line with a 20-percent buffer. That is, the size of the credit line would be 20 percent above the maximum estimated amount borrowed. Estimate the effective annual rate of the credit line.

**16A-5.** Redo Problem A-4 except assume that the percent buffer is zero rather than the stated 20 percent. How much does the 20-percent buffer contribute to the effective cost of the credit line?

**16A-6.** Redo Problems A-4 and A-5 assuming that the treasurer maintains an average idle cash balance at its bank of $40,000 throughout the year. Re-estimate the effective cost of the credit line.

CHAPTER

17

# Managing Multinational Cash Flows

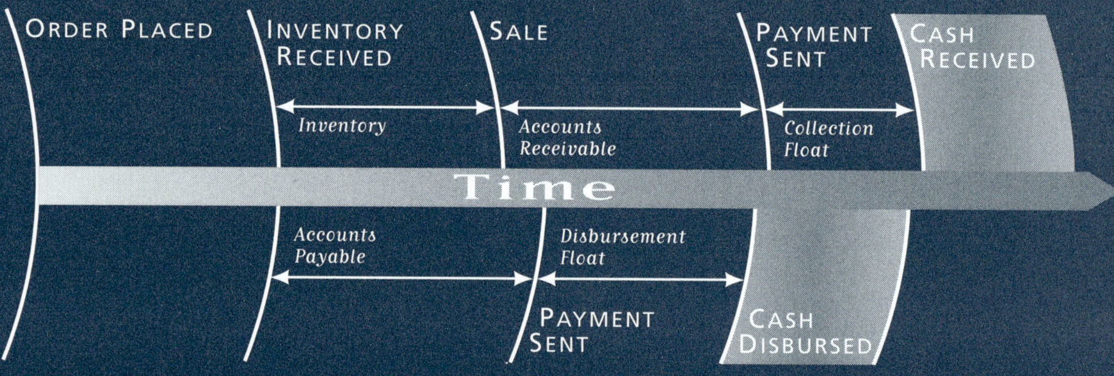

## OBJECTIVES

*After studying this chapter, you should be able to:*

- have an appreciation of the development of the current exchange rate system.
- understand the basic driving forces causing exchange rates to fluctuate.
- gain a basic understanding of the various means by which firms can create internal structures to manage exchange rate fluctuations.
- have an appreciation for the differences between the U.S. and foreign banking systems.

Throughout this book, we have attempted to integrate the international aspects of short-term financial management decisions. This chapter will present an overview and synthesis of many of these areas, but more importantly, the chapter will also introduce some of the features that are unique to managing international cash flows, in particular managing the firm's exposure to movements in foreign currency exchange rates. The fact that managing international cash flows is different from managing domestic cash flows is highlighted by the fact that most large corporations have financial managers who specialize in domestic cash management and a different set of financial managers responsible for the international dimension of the firm's business.

This chapter focuses on the management of cash flows created through international transactions. For example, suppose an exporting firm sells to various countries and receives foreign currencies at a future date for the products sold. The exporter is exposed to exchange rate movements between the foreign currency received and the exporter's domestic currency. We will develop a variety of strategies to manage these types of foreign exchange problems.

### FINANCIAL DILEMMA

What Can Be Done about Uncertain Currency Exchange Rates?

A mid-size family-owned business in the pharmaceutical industry is based in Basel, Switzerland. The company's currency structure includes 60 percent of sales in Swiss francs, 23 percent of sales invoiced in euros, 15 percent invoiced in U.S. dollars, and the remainder in various other currencies. It has 11 bank accounts in Switzerland, Austria, and Germany, with non-interest-bearing checking accounts and a high interest line of credit accounts.[1]

[1] Regula Spottl, "Reorganizing Cash Management and Foreign Exchange in an Industrial Company," **http://www.gtnews.com** (July 21, 2000).

## EXCHANGE RATES

When a domestic corporation does business in a foreign country, currency exchange problems occur. For example, a U.S. financial manager may buy products from a German supplier. If the German corporation decides to export, should it demand payment at the end of the stated credit terms in dollars or in euros? If it accepts payment in dollars, the U.S. importer is able to transfer all currency exchange risk to the German supplier because when the German exporter receives dollars, it then must convert them to euros. If, instead, the German exporter demands payment in euros, then it transfers all currency exchange risk to the U.S. importer. The importer must exchange dollars for euros and remit the invoice price in euros.

Exhibit 17–1 displays a comprehensive list of exchange rates for the world's major currencies stated in terms of U.S. dollars per unit of foreign currency and unit of foreign currency per U.S. dollar. A **foreign exchange rate** is the price of one currency stated in relation to the price of another currency. For example, according to Exhibit 17–1, on Friday, January 9, 2004, one euro was valued at $1.2843, or 0.7786 euros were worth one U.S. dollar.

**Exhibit 17–1**

*Exchange Rate Quotes for Selected Currencies*[2]

| Country | Currency | U.S. $ per Unit of Foreign Currency | Unit of Foreign Currency Per U.S. $ |
|---|---|---|---|
| Australia | Dollar | 0.7765 | 1.2878 |
| Brazil | Real | 0.3530 | 2.8329 |
| Britain | Pound | 1.8486 | 0.5409 |
| Canada | Dollar | 0.7867 | 1.2711 |
| China | Renminbi | 0.1208 | 8.2781 |
| India | Rupee | 0.02201 | 45.434 |
| Israel | Shekel | 0.2283 | 4.3802 |
| Japan | Yen | 0.009401 | 106.37 |
| Saudi Arabia | Riyal | 0.2667 | 3.7495 |
| Switzerland | Franc | 0.8195 | 1.2203 |
| Thailand | Baht | 0.02565 | 38.986 |
| | Euro | 1.2843 | 0.7786 |

[2] Quotes for Friday, January 9, 2004, from *The Wall Street Journal* (January 12, 2004).

## Fixed versus Floating Exchange Rates

The exchange rate quotes shown in Exhibit 17–1 indicate the relative price of the various currencies at a particular point in time, specifically, January 9, 2004. Currently, exchange rates are free to change on a daily basis depending on the relative supply and demand for the currencies. However, this has not always been the case.

Before World War I, a gold standard existed in which all currencies were priced relative to gold and each country attempted to maintain the price relationship. Because of the disruption caused by the war, the gold standard was abolished and all currencies were allowed to float; that is, their exchange rates were allowed to fluctuate based on the supply and demand conditions for the currency relative to other currencies.

Following the depression and World War II, the major trading countries met in Bretton Woods, New Hampshire, and signed the **Bretton Woods Agreement**. This agreement essentially returned the world economy to a type of gold standard. The United States fixed the price of an ounce of gold at $35. Each country then fixed its currency in relation to the dollar. Only the U.S. dollar was convertible into gold at a fixed price of $35 per ounce. Each country agreed to maintain its rate of exchange into the dollar within 1 percent of this established price. This agreement essentially returned the world economy to a system of fixed foreign exchange rates.

The foreign exchange system created by the Bretton Woods Agreement worked well initially. However, by the late 1960s, problems were developing as evidenced by large balance of payment deficits in the United States and other major trading countries. Inflation was increasing, and in the 1970s, the Organization of Petroleum Exporting Countries (OPEC) began to cause serious disruptions in the world economy through oil price shocks and oil embargoes. By this time, the fixed exchange rate system had already evolved into a system of "managed" floating rates where exchange rates were allowed to float within boundaries wider than the 1-percent band determined at Bretton Woods.

The world economy continued to struggle due to rising rates of inflation, continuing balance of payment problems, and shocks created by OPEC. In particular, currency decisions made by the newly rich OPEC countries became a key to the stability of the world's currencies. As a result, the exchange rate boundaries were continually tested, and by 1976 the **Jamaica Agreement** was signed by the major trading nations which created a system of floating exchange rates and the demonetization of gold.

Since the Jamaica Agreement, the only major change in the structure of the foreign exchange markets has been the development of **currency blocs** where major European trading partners, members of the European Economic Community (**EEC**), have created a subset of controlled exchange rates between the currencies of the partners referred to as the European Monetary System (**EMS**). The outgrowth of the EMS is the creation of a new currency unit known as the **euro** that represents a basket of currencies of the participating countries. The whole system, though, is then allowed to float relative to the currencies of those countries not included in the system. Thus, the foreign exchange market is evolving into a system of floating currency blocs.

## Spot Rates

**Spot currency rates** are exchange rate quotes based on immediate delivery of the currency being traded. Generally, a corporation needing to purchase foreign currency will contact its bank. The bank will purchase the desired currency through the interbank market; that is, spot exchange rate quotes are received from other banks wishing to sell the currency. Settlement of the interbank market transaction will generally take one to two days. The settlement date is referred to as the value date.

## Forward Rates

A **forward currency rate** is an exchange rate between currencies that is contracted to exist at a future value date. The exchange rate is established at the time the forward contract is created, but payment and delivery do not occur until the maturity date of the forward contract, generally, 30, 90, or 180 days in the future.

Exhibit 17–2 shows spot and forward rates that existed on Friday, January 9, 2004, for selected foreign currencies as reported by *The Wall Street Journal.* According to the exhibit, a financial manager wishing to purchase British pounds sterling on the spot market can buy them at an exchange rate of $1.8486 per pound sterling. However, if the foreign currency was needed in 180 days, it could be purchased at an exchange rate of $1.8219.

**Exhibit 17–2**

*Selected Spot and Forward Exchange Rates*

| Country (Currency) | U.S. $ Equivalent |
|---|---|
| Britain (Pound) | 1.8486 (Spot) |
| 1-month forward | 1.8443 |
| 3-month forward | 1.8355 |
| 6-month forward | 1.8219 |
| Japan (Yen) | 0.009401 (Spot) |
| 1-month forward | 0.009411 |
| 3-month forward | 0.009428 |
| 6-month forward | 0.009455 |
| Switzerland (Franc) | 0.8195 (Spot) |
| 1-month forward | 0.8202 |
| 3-month forward | 0.8213 |
| 6-month forward | 0.8230 |

### Futures Rates

A **futures exchange rate** is similar in concept to a forward rate. It reflects the exchange rate at which currencies can be traded at a future date. Chapter 18 goes into more detail regarding futures contracts. The primary difference between a futures contract and a forward contract is standardization. A **futures contract** is standardized and is traded on a national market and a clearinghouse guarantees each trade. Thus, a financial manager could purchase a foreign currency contract on one day and sell it on any day prior to the expiration of the contract. A **forward contract** is a contract negotiated between the financial manager and a bank. It is not a negotiable instrument and must be held to maturity.

Another important difference between these two types of contracts is that **margin** must be posted when a futures contract is bought. This margin is generally only a fraction of the total value of the contract, but if the value of the contract falls, additional margin may be requested. A forward contract, on the other hand, requires no margin, and no cash is exchanged until the forward value date.

## FACTORS AFFECTING EXCHANGE RATES

If demand for a particular currency exceeds the supply of that currency, then the relative value of that currency increases. Movements in the exchange rate between two currencies basically demonstrate the change in the relative values of the two currencies. For example, suppose the current exchange rate between British pounds and dollars is $1.65 per pound sterling and then increases to $1.80. This indicates that it takes more dollars to equal the value of a pound sterling resulting in a depreciation of the dollar and an appreciation of the pound relative to the dollar.

Several factors can cause exchange rates between any two currencies to change. One important factor is the relative level of interest rates that exist between the two countries. A country that has high interest rate levels relative to another country may experience excess demand for its currency as global investors purchase the currency to invest in that country's financial markets taking advantage of the relatively high interest rates. The **interest rate parity hypothesis** suggests that exchange rates will adjust to offset the interest rate differential.

A second factor is the relative rate of inflation in one country compared with another. The **purchasing parity hypothesis** suggests that exchange rates between two countries will adjust to offset the relative rates of inflation between two countries. As one country experiences inflation at a rate greater than another country, its currency will be devalued relative to the currency of the country with the lower inflation rate.

A third factor affecting exchange rates is the reaction of the respective government's central bank to changes in exchange rates caused by economic circumstances such as inflation. Historically, central banks have stepped in to purchase their currency when it begins to lose value relative to other currencies. It does this to reduce the supply of the currency, since a currency that is being devalued in the currency markets is one where supply of the currency exceeds the demand for it. On the other hand, a currency's appreciation means that the respective currency is becoming more valuable relative to other currencies. The central bank might begin to sell its currency in the currency markets to increase supply in order to stabilize the exchange rate. An appreciating exchange rate will make that country's products more expensive overseas and will therefore hurt exports.

Economic and political factors generally change the supply and demand balance of the world's currencies. For example, during the period 1979 to 1986, the United States experienced relatively high interest rates, drawing a large increase of foreign investment to the U.S. financial markets. Foreign investors must obtain the domestic currency before investing in domestic financial markets. Consequently, the U.S. dollar appreciated dramatically compared to most other major currencies.

The role that politics plays with exchange rates was evident when France shifted to a socialist government in 1981. France's major industries perceived this socialist government as a threat because they feared that the new government would nationalize industry. Consequently, the French franc was devalued dramatically in the currency markets by the flight of capital from francs into other currencies.

## FOREIGN EXCHANGE EXPOSURE

Because exchange rates between currencies do change, the multinational corporation faces risks not experienced by a corporation doing all its business domestically. These risks associated with floating exchange rates include economic exposure, transaction exposure, and translation exposure.

### Economic Exposure

**Economic exposure** is the possibility that the long-term net present value of a firm's expected cash flows would change due to unexpected changes in exchange rates. For example, a U.S. exporter gains international sales and cash flows when the dollar depreciates against world currencies. This makes U.S. goods cheaper relative to foreign goods, and demand for U.S. goods increases.

### Transaction Exposure

**Transaction exposure** relates to the gains or losses associated with the settlement of business transactions denominated in different currencies. For example, the transaction between the U.S. importer and German exporter discussed earlier is an example of transaction exposure. Suppose the importer entered into a contract to purchase goods denominated in euros with payment due in 90 days. The U.S. importer faces transaction exposure because it must obtain euros in 90 days to honor the contract. Although the contract is fixed in terms of euros, it is not fixed in terms of U.S. dollars, which the importer will use to purchase the euros.

### Translation Exposure

**Translation exposure** results when the balance sheet and income statement of a foreign subsidiary are translated into the parent company's domestic currency for consolidated financial reporting purposes. If exchange rates have changed during the financial reporting period, then a translation gain or loss will occur affecting the consolidated financial position of the parent company. For example, the assets of a foreign subsidiary of a U.S. multinational corporation will experience a translation loss if the foreign currency depreciates relative to the currency in which the parent company's assets are denominated. Suppose the subsidiary is based in London and the subsidiary's assets are valued at 100 million pounds sterling. Now assume that the exchange rate changes from $1.60 per pound to $1.10 per pound over the accounting period. At the beginning of the accounting period, the 100 million pounds were worth $160 million; but at the end of the accounting period, the assets are only worth $110 million. The subsidiary's assets experienced a translation loss of $50 million. The important impact of translation exposure was noted by the shareholders of Kodak when, from 1999 to 2001, about one-third of their decline in shareholder equity was due to currency translation losses that weren't offset by the company's hedging program.[3]

---

[3] Ronald Fink, "Natural Performers," *CFO* (June 2003), p. 39.

The currency translation process for consolidating financial statements for a corporation with foreign subsidiaries is governed by the Financial Accounting Standards Board's Statement Number 52 (FAS 52). Under this ruling, translation exposure is based on the dollar value of all assets denominated in a foreign currency less the dollar value of all liabilities denominated in that currency. A translation gain or loss is then posted to a reserve account on the balance sheet rather than running it through the income statement as was done under FAS 8 prior to 1981.

## CORPORATE STRUCTURE FOR GLOBAL LIQUIDITY MANAGEMENT

To centralize or decentralize...that is no longer the question. From all indications, global corporations have moved their treasury management function to a more centralized structure. In order to achieve global liquidity management, financial executives are doing three things. First, they are building global liquidity pyramids that consolidate net cash positions at the national level, then at the broad regional level, and finally at the enterprise level. Second, they are leveraging the capacity of their companies' enterprise resource planning (ERP) systems and treasury work stations to get more complete and timely cash balance reports. Third, they are reducing the number of banks in their system.[4] So global corporations are making a big push to centralize their treasury operations in order to mobilize the enterprise's liquid resources for the best use possible.

A recent survey by Treasury Strategies showed the extent of centralization. The survey polled a group of primarily U.S.-based corporations from a range of industries with revenues ranging from just under $1 billion to over $25 billion.[5] They found that most companies have centralized their treasury structures with 30 percent of the responding companies having fully centralized their treasury functions at headquarters and 62 percent centrally coordinating treasury functions from headquarters. Among the respondents that envisioned their treasury structure changing in the future, two-thirds anticipated their structure becoming more centralized. A good example of this direction of change occurred recently at EDS Corporation. Treasury was given the mandate to consolidate, and, as a result, treasury offices in four foreign locations—São Paulo, Hong Kong, Mexico City, and London—were consolidated into the corporation's Plano, Texas, location. Everything with regard to global liquidity management was centralized including all cash, all foreign exchange, all debt, and all investment activities. The benefits have been enormous with the amount of idle cash reduced by 75 percent, foreign exchange trading costs reduced by 60 percent, and staff and associated costs reduced by over 40 percent.[6]

While the debate seems to swing back and forth regarding centralization versus decentralization for many management areas, there currently appears to be little doubt that centralization of the treasury function, especially in the global arena, is the right choice. Certainly, the increasing sophistication of information technology and implementation of ERP systems support the ability of treasurers to gather information enterprise-wide on a global basis where this was not really practical before.

## MANAGING FOREIGN EXCHANGE EXPOSURE

A corporation that deals in one or more currencies other than its own domestic currency must be concerned about its exposure to **exchange rate risk**. This section addresses sev-

---

[4] Richard Gamble, "Now, the Only Choice Is to Go Global on Cash," *Treasury & Risk Management* (December/January 2003), p. 32.

[5] "Global Treasury Management Survey Results—2002," *Treasury Strategies.*

[6] Harvey D. Shapiro, "Centralize This," *Treasury & Risk Management* (February 2002), p. 13.

eral different techniques for managing this risk exposure other than using exchange-traded instruments such as futures, options, and swaps discussed in Chapter 18. Most firms will first implement these internal strategies prior to using the kinds of strategies discussed in the next chapter.

### Avoidance

Perhaps the simplest way to manage the exposure is to employ a strategy referred to as **avoidance**. Invoices can be stated in such a way that only the selling firm's domestic currency will be accepted for payment of goods and services or purchases paid for in the firm's domestic currency. However, this may cause ill will and loss of international business. In addition, this may be a costly strategy in that suppliers who have to sell their products in a currency other than their own domestic currency are likely to build into their pricing structure their own currency hedging costs effectively raising the price of the product. One way around this pricing problem is to require purchasing managers to request price quotes in the domestic currency as well as the foreign currency. Finally, though, doing business in a single domestic currency may not be realistic for larger firms with multinational subsidiaries.

### Leading and Lagging

Because exchange rates do fluctuate, one tool to manage fluctuating exchange rates is to try and take advantage of these changes by leading and lagging cash flows related to collections and payments in foreign currencies. **Leading** is the practice of accelerating collections or payments, and **lagging** is the practice of delaying collections or payments. Why would a firm wish to lag collections or lead payments? This seems to be the opposite of sound financial practice given what we know about the time value of money. It all depends on the anticipated change in future exchange rates. Lagging collections denominated in a foreign currency that is appreciating or accelerating payments of a currency that is expected to depreciate is a very sound financial policy.

An example will help demonstrate this strategy. Suppose a U.S. importer has an invoice for 100,000 British pounds sterling. The payment is due in 60 days. However, the dollar is expected to continue to depreciate from the current $1.50 per pound to $1.65 in 60 days. The U.S. importer can speed up payment by buying pounds sterling in the near future for $1.50 and pay the invoice costing $150,000. Waiting and buying pounds later when the dollar has depreciated results in the U.S. importer paying $165,000 or an increase in cost of $15,000 over the 60-day credit period. Of course, a leading or lagging strategy is only effective if the firm guesses correctly about the direction of exchange rate movements. Thus, when a firm anticipates that the domestic currency will appreciate, it should lead collections and lag payments. When it anticipates that the domestic currency will depreciate, it should lag collections and lead payments.

### Netting

The first line of defense in managing foreign exchange exposure is to develop an internal company information system that allows the firm to track its current and expected daily cash flows in all currencies in which it does business. This allows the cash manager to net outflows in one currency against inflows of the same currency reducing foreign exchange exposure to only the net difference. For example, payment of an invoice for 10,000 pounds sterling payable in 20 days might be covered by receipt of 10,000 pounds sterling in 20 days as a result of selling activities in Great Britain. The firm therefore would not need to purchase sterling, since that currency would be generated by the firm's multinational operations. This process is known as **netting**.

# FOCUS ON PRACTICE

## The Multilateral Netting System at Nokia

Setting up a multilateral netting system at Nokia allowed the treasury department to get a handle on the multicurrency cash flows throughout this far-flung enterprise in a noninvasive way. It was noninvasive in that setting up such a system did not require any system changes at the various operating units, but it did provide very valuable information flows to the treasury organization. The netting system created a situation where all internal cash flows between the various units occurred once a month on the netting date. Thus, all intercompany funding was synchronized on the monthly netting date; likewise, all foreign exchange hedging was focused on the netting date. This maximized the opportunities for natural exposure offset where only the net differences required hedging.

*Source:* David Blair, "Providing the Right Links," *The Treasurer* (May 20, 2003).

**Bilateral netting** is a system set up between two subsidiaries of the same company that transact between each other in different currencies. At the end of each month, typically, the transactions are netted against each other and the net difference is transferred.

Firms with more than two subsidiaries dealing in different currencies may use a **multilateral netting system.** Exhibit 17–3 demonstrates the basic structure of a multilateral netting system. Each subsidiary informs the central treasury management center, or in some cases its financial institution that manages its foreign exchange exposure, of all planned cross-border payments. To determine the netting transactions, payments are converted into a common reference currency and then payments are combined resulting in fewer and larger currency transactions. Prior to the settlement date, each subsidiary is informed of the net amount to pay or to be received in its own currency.

### Reinvoicing

A **reinvoicing center** can be used to centralize the monitoring and collecting of accounts receivable and for managing foreign exchange exposure. This is a more invasive ap-

Exhibit 17–3

*A Typical Multilateral Netting System*

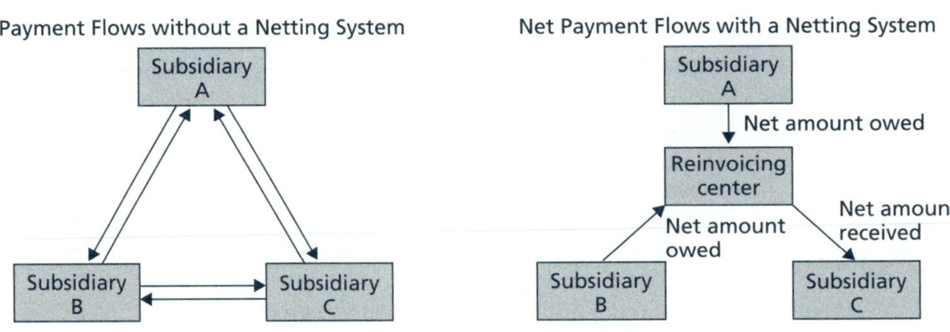

proach in that the corporate structure must change. It requires setting up a company-owned subsidiary that buys goods from an exporting subsidiary in that subsidiary's currency and sells those goods to an importing subsidiary in its own currency. At the center of the system is a reinvoicing center that receives all the invoices from all the firm's subsidiaries reinvoicing only the net difference owed to each subsidiary. It is also common for the reinvoicing center to manage the firm's foreign currency exposure that results from the netting process. Although actual delivery of the goods occurs between the exporting and importing subsidiaries, it is common for the title to flow through the reinvoicing center. Both the netting system and the reinvoicing system can be used to implement a leading and lagging cash flow management system that can be effective in managing the liquidity of the organization by timing the cash inflows and outflows within the system.

## Hedging

In most cases, some exposure to foreign exchange movements will remain after the firm has netted and/or reinvoiced all possible cash flows. The financial manager may wish to consider hedging the remaining exposure through the use of forward, futures, option, or swap contracts. In this section, we will discuss the use of forward contracts, while hedging through the use of futures, options, and swaps is discussed in Chapter 18.

A forward currency contract represents an agreement to buy or sell a specified amount of a stipulated foreign currency at a specified price on a specified date. The forward contract terms dealing with the amount, currency, and maturity are negotiable. There are, however, standard maturities for these contracts including 30-, 90-, and 180-day forward contracts, and the forward exchange rates on these contracts are reported in *The Wall Street Journal* as was shown in Exhibit 17–2.

According to this exhibit, the 90-day forward rate that could be obtained on Friday, January 9, 2004, for the British pound was shown to be $1.8355 per pound. If a U.S. importer needed British pounds to pay for an invoice in 90 days, the importer could contract today to purchase those pounds 90 days in the future at a rate of $1.8355 per pound. Suppose that the U.S. importer purchased goods from a British exporter valued today at 500,000 pounds sterling. The U.S. importer could do nothing now and simply purchase pounds sterling on the spot market in 90 days to pay the exporter. However, given any movement in the exchange rate for sterling over the next 90 days, the importer's dollar cost will fluctuate. One technique to lock in the dollar cost of the order is to place an order now to purchase pounds sterling in the forward market. Given the quote mentioned earlier, the exporter could contract with a bank to purchase pounds sterling in 90 days at a guaranteed price of $1.8355 per pound no matter if the dollar appreciated or depreciated against sterling over the 90-day period. Thus, the importer has stabilized the cost of the order at $917,750 (500,000 × $1.8355). Of course, the importer gives up the opportunity to effectively pay less if the dollar appreciates relative to sterling but is now protected from paying more if the dollar depreciates against sterling. Hedging, therefore, is a risk reducing strategy that allows the manager to better forecast cash flows in the future and to protect current profit margins. A hedging strategy does not require attempting to forecast the future direction of exchange rates; it simply requires the financial manager to be willing to accept the current exchange rate structure.

This forward currency exchange market is primarily an interbank market because most of the volume of these contracts is comprised of currency transactions between banks. The corporation wanting to purchase a forward contract would either contact a dealer or deal directly with its bank's foreign exchange department. Additional hedging strategies are developed in Chapter 18.

## FOCUS ON PRACTICE

### *Survey Results Concerning Global Management Issues*

Financial executives at four major Finnish corporations respond to four questions concerning global management issues.

| | **Outokumpu** (A metals company) | **Norske Skogindustrier** (Newsprint maker) | **Fortum** (Oil and gas producer) | **Stora Enso** (Paper and board maker) |
|---|---|---|---|---|
| **How do you manage currency exposure?** | Use currency forwards. | Hedge 50–100% of expected cash flow using forwards and options. | Use forwards or options. | After natural hedges (match currency of expenses and revenues), they cover half of net cash flow with forwards. |
| **How have you changed your banking system recently?** | Reduced number of key bank accounts to reduce float and streamline liquidity management. | Reduced number of bank accounts. | | Reduced number of bank accounts. Emphasis on reducing receivables. |
| **What is your corporate treasury structure?** | Centralized to a great extent. | Fully centralized. | Centralized. | Centralized. |
| **What are your key risk management priorities?** | Understanding and managing key market price risk such as euro/USD, price of zinc, price of Scandinavian electricity, and level of short-term interest rates. | Two: Financial risk (foreign exchange, liquidity risk, forecasting, asset and liability management) and operating risk management using typical insurance products. | Interest rate risk. | |

*Source:* Adapted from "Together We Stand—The Nordic Conundrum," © GTNews.com, June 2, 2003. **http://www.gtnews.com/article/5017.cfm.**

## FINANCIAL DILEMMA REVISITED

The company hired a consultant who offered the following recommendations.

- Institute a "macrohedge" by using a multilateral system netting required foreign currencies for imports against incoming foreign currencies from exports.
- Institute the use of "microhedges" using foreign currency option contracts related to large single transactions of goods for the purpose of securing an exchange rate guarantee.

- For foreign currency purchases and sales, the consultant recommended a time frame no longer than six months to avoid locking in prices for export markets which could result in loss of revenues or market share.
- The consultant negotiated new conditions on bank account debit and credit interest rates. The number of U.S. dollar and euro accounts was reduced from 11 down to four accounts at banks in Switzerland, one in Austria, and one in Germany. As a result, the daily cash report immediately improved in quality and saved time in executing bank and account transfers.
- As a result, charges on term loans were reduced by up to 30 percent and the interest paid on overdrawn accounts reduced to zero.

## FEATURES OF NON-U.S. BANKING SYSTEMS

Non-U.S. banking systems are quite different from their U.S. counterparts. This section will present an overview of some of the more important differences between the U.S. and foreign banking systems.

### Check Clearing

It is common practice in non-U.S. banking systems to value date checks. Checks deposited are granted a **forward value date** which is the date that good funds will be credited to the account (this is actually similar to the availability schedules used in the United States). Cleared checks may be assigned a **back value date**, in essence drawing funds out of the account before the check actually arrives. Back-value dating is not generally done in the United States. Foreign banks value date to enhance the compensation for their clearing services beyond the fees charged.

Because most non-U.S. banking systems have far fewer banks than in the United States, the clearing of domestic checks within these countries is more straightforward than it is in the United States. However, the clearing of checks denominated in one currency drawn on a bank in another country that uses another currency is more complicated as the check generally has to travel between several correspondent banks in order to finally clear. A check denominated in a foreign currency and deposited in a U.S. bank, for example, must be transported back to the country of origination, the currency converted and exchanged for a dollar-denominated check drawn on a U.S. bank. The process can take from a couple weeks to a month, compared to only a few days for the clearing of domestic checks.

### Interest on Demand Deposits

To compensate for the uncertainties created by the value dating system, it is common practice for non-U.S. banks to pay interest on corporate demand deposit balances and to charge interest on overdrafts. The fact that interest is earned on balances and that **overdraft facilities** exist lessens the need for daily cash balance reporting which is not always available internationally.

### Pooling

Pooling systems in international banking structures are somewhat similar to concentration systems in the United States and are useful for those corporations that may have a number of operations and bank accounts in the same country. Some of those accounts may have positive balances that earn interest, while others may be in an overdraft status and assessed an interest charge. When pooling is available, the bank looks at all of the company's accounts as one balance and pays interest on the net balance if positive and assesses interest if the balance is in a deficit.

**Pooling** may occur by actually having the funds transferred to a concentration account each day within the banking system or notional pooling may occur. With notional pooling, funds are not literally transferred. Rather, the bank's accounting system that tracks the account balances basically sums up the balances and pays interest on the net balance if positive and assesses interest if the net balance is negative.

### Governmental Policies and Restrictions

Several potential problems are related to the movement of funds across country borders. For example, some countries tax international funds that transfer across their borders. This is why netting systems, discussed earlier, are so important because they reduce the number and amount of transfers. Some countries that stringently control cross-border cash flows (e.g., many countries in South America) have gone so far as to make netting systems illegal.

### Cash Management Services

The banking system in the United States is relatively unique in that nationwide branching prior to 1997 was illegal. As a result, independent or unit banks dominated the system. The cash management services that are so common in the United States, for example, lockboxes, controlled disbursement systems, concentration systems, and balance reporting, have developed to provide the financial manager of a company selling nationwide an efficient means of consolidating cash resources given the fragmented banking structure.

Such services are not as essential in non-U.S. banking systems, and in some cases not available, because most countries have far fewer independent banks each with a multitude of branches. Companies that use the same bank in a foreign country can utilize the branches of the bank for collection services negating the need for lockbox and concentration systems since the funds are in the same bank. In fact, it is common to find the banks offering pooling services that allow a firm's excess balances to spread across its bank branches to offset corporate deficit balances in other branches of the same bank. In essence, the bank can treat all the accounts for a firm in its branches as one account, thereby allowing the firm to avoid interest charges at those branches where deficit balances are occurring.

One collection system for consumer payments that is commonplace in Europe is the **giro system**, which is similar in nature to the automated clearinghouse (ACH) system in the United States. The invoice that a seller sends to its customers includes a payment stub encoded with the seller's bank account number. The customer signs the stub and then takes it to a giro processor such as the local post office. The processor delivers the stub to the nearest giro bank, which in turn debits the customer's account and credits the seller's account.

## SUMMARY

Although managing cash flows domestically in the United States is somewhat complicated by the number of banks and other regulations that exist, managing international cash flows is even more complex. Some of the factors that contribute to the additional complications in managing multinational cash flows include different banking systems, structures, and regulations that exist in each country; the restrictions imposed on data and funds flows across borders; value dating systems; and the fluctuating values of currencies.

This chapter began by providing a brief history of the exchange rate system that exists and a description of the different forms of currency quotations including spot rates, forward rates, and futures rates. Given the fluctuating values of exchange rates, managing the firm's foreign currency exposure is one of the more important aspects of managing international cash flows. Three types of foreign exchange exposure were introduced. A variety of techniques for managing foreign currency exposure were described. The chapter concluded with a discussion of the characteristics of non-U.S. banking systems.

## USEFUL WEB SITES

| | |
|---|---|
| Futures Magazine, Inc. | **http://www.futuresmag.com/** |
| Society for Worldwide Interbank Financial Transactions (SWIFT) | **http://www.swift.com** |

## QUESTIONS

1. When would a company get foreign exchange in the spot rate, and when should the company use the forward market to get foreign exchange?
2. What is the difference between transaction exposure and translation exposure?
3. How does a multilateral netting system help manage foreign currency exposure?
4. How is transaction exposure different from economic exposure?
5. Identify some of the key differences between the U.S. banking system and foreign banking systems.

## PROBLEMS

1. Convert the following exchange rates expressed as U.S. dollars per unit of foreign currency into the number of units of foreign currency per U.S. dollar.

| Country | U.S. $ per Unit of Foreign Currency | Unit of Foreign Currency per U.S. $ |
|---|---|---|
| Australia | 0.44 | ________ |
| Britain | 1.67 | ________ |
| Japan | 0.010 | ________ |
| Thailand | 0.03 | ________ |

2. A multinational company has three subsidiaries located in the United States, Switzerland, and Great Britain. The company recently set up a multilateral netting center to help manage its foreign exchange exposure. Listed below are the average monthly invoices sent from each country to each of the other subsidiaries with which it does business. Calculate the net flows that will occur as a result of the new netting system. The company uses the U.S. dollar as the common referencing currency.

   Existing Exchange Rates:

   Swiss franc (SF) = $0.13
   Pounds sterling (PS) = $1.45

| | | | | |
|---|---|---|---|---|
| U.S. | To | Switzerland | $ | 100 |
| | To | GB | $ | 250 |
| Switzerland | To | U.S. | SF | 300 |
| | To | GB | SF | 150 |
| GB | To | Switzerland | PS | 200 |
| | To | U.S | PS | 100 |

3. You are concerned about your transaction exposure on a recent purchase from an exporter in Great Britain. The invoice, just received, is for 275,000 pounds sterling payable in 90 days, which will be about mid-June. The current exchange rate is $1.35 per pound sterling, and you fear that the dollar will depreciate against the pound due to the relatively low interest rates currently prevailing in the United States. The following forward rate is $1.38.
   a. What is the cost of the invoice in dollars at the current spot rate?
   b. If a forward contract is purchased, what will be the cost of the invoice in dollars at the forward rate?
   c. What are the advantages and disadvantages of hedging the transaction with a forward contract?
4. You are concerned about your transaction exposure on a recent purchase from an exporter in Germany. The invoice, just received, is for 950,000 euros payable in 60 days, which will be about mid-September. The current exchange rate is $1.10 per euro, and you fear that the dollar will depreciate against the euro due to the relatively low interest rates currently prevailing in the United States. The following forward rate is $1.12.
   a. What is the cost of the invoice in dollars at the current spot rate?
   b. If a forward contract is purchased, what will be the cost of the invoice in dollars at the forward rate?
   c. What are the advantages and disadvantages of hedging the transaction with a forward contract?
5. You are a U.S. exporter concerned about your transaction exposure on a recent sale to an importer in Germany. The invoice, just sent, is for 500,000 euros payable in 60 days, which will be about mid-February. The current exchange rate is $1.00 per euro, and you fear that the dollar will appreciate against the euro due to the rebound in the domestic economy and the improvement in the economy with potentially increasing interest rates. The 60-day forward rate is $0.99.
   a. What is the value of the invoice in dollars at the current spot rate?
   b. If a forward contract is sold, what will be the value of the invoice in dollars at the forward rate?
   c. What are the advantages and disadvantages of hedging the transaction with a forward contract?

## REFERENCES

K. Alec Chrystal, "A Guide to Foreign Exchange Markets," *Review*, Federal Reserve Bank of St. Louis (March 1984), pp. 5–17.

William R. Folks, Jr., and Raj Aggarwal, *International Dimensions of Financial Management*, (Boston: PWS-Kent Publishing Company, 1988).

Susan Griffiths, "International Pooling—Getting the Story Straight," *Journal of Cash Management* (November/December 1992), pp. 26–34.

Neil A. Leary, "The Basics of Doing Business Overseas: An Overview of International Treasury Management," *The Journal of Cash Management* (March/April 1993), pp. 33–38.

Cecilia Wagner Ricci and Gail Morrison, "International Working Capital Practices of the Fortune 200," *Financial Practice and Education* (Fall/Winter 1996), pp. 7–20.

# INTEGRATIVE CASE—PART 5

## *Jones Salvage and Recycling, Inc. (C)*

**Note:** This is a continuation of the Jones Salvage and Recycling, Inc. (A) case found immediately following Chapter 13 and Jones (B) found immediately following Chapter 16. Jones (A) concluded with a monthly forecasted income statement, cash budget, and balance sheet for the first 6 months of the new year. Jones (B) used that information to determine the financing and investment strategy that is best for Jones to use. Jones (C) focuses on solving the company's liquidity needs by changing its working capital policies.

Mr. Jones was impressed with the financial strategy created by the lending officer and the company's financial manager. However, Mr. Jones had heard and read a lot about the reengineering efforts that companies were employing in their working capital management with what seemed to be great successes. In fact, he was aware that some companies were striving for zero working capital, a concept foreign to him. He always considered working capital an asset, something that created value on the balance sheet.

In his discussions about this with Carl Malone, his bank's relationship manager, he learned that indeed there was an industry trend toward zero working capital and that this should really be investigated. Zero working capital basically means that the sum of the accounts receivable and inventory equal the sum of accounts payables and operating accruals. In other words, the working capital is self-financed, an intriguing idea, Mr. Jones thought. All of a sudden he realized that this could mean a drastic reduction in the need for bank financing, and consequently, less interest to be paid. Being a pragmatist, however, he quickly realized that this could not be achieved without some kind of cost involved. He just wasn't sure what those costs might be and immediately asked Bob Jones, his business manager, to study the issues and submit a report in a week.

### Accounts Receivable

Obviously, one part of the solution would be to tighten up on collections or even change the company's credit terms. Tightening up on the existing credit terms could only be done by spending additional sums of money on credit investigation and collection efforts. Bob estimates that this would not cause any noticeable change in sales but would increase operating expenses by $2,000 per month. The benefit would be that the collection fractions might improve to 20 percent for the month of sale, 70 percent for the month after sales, and 10 percent for 2 months after sale.

Giving shorter credit terms would probably cause a decrease in sales and invoke some type of reaction from the company's competitors and Bob preferred to not touch this approach at this time.

### Inventory

As discussed earlier, the company's current inventory policy is to end each month with ending inventory equal to the following month's cost of sales. This is a relatively conservative policy and the company has never stocked out in the past, a fact that Mr. Jones was rather proud of. However, Bob used this opportunity to suggest that this policy was simply too conservative and costly for the firm in light of the projected financing needs of the company. Carl felt that with a closer coordination with their commercial suppliers of scrap as well as better information from their commercial customers, the company could afford to turn their inventory over at a faster pace. His estimate is that by incurring an additional $1,000 per month of personnel time and communication costs, they could reduce their ending inventory needs to only a quarter of what they were currently.

### Accounts Payable

After calling several suppliers, Bob discovered that they indeed were already getting the best credit terms available and did not see much opportunity to improve in this area. He briefly considered stretching payables by simply not paying within terms but quickly dismissed this idea.

### The Proposed Plan

Bob Jones put the plan together and had it on Mr. Jones' desk at the end of the following week. The plan consisted of the components as discussed above. Mr. Jones was intrigued with the idea but was concerned about the trade-offs and wasn't sure if the reduced inventory and receivables would contribute enough to offset the increased costs. He also wasn't sure how to compare this alternative with the best financing strategy.

## REQUIRED

1. Input the suggested working capital management plan into the financing planning model from Jones (A) and discuss the impact it has on the projected cash flow of the company.
2. Given the results in part 1, invest any monthly surplus cash or borrow to fund any deficit so that the minimum cash balance of $1,000 is maintained.
3. Compare the result you arrive at in part 2 with your conclusions drawn from Jones (B). Which strategy would you recommend and why?

PART

6

# Special Topics

Part 6 includes two chapters that offer additional insight and detail into two very important short-term financial management topics. Chapter 18 studies the management of financial risk including interest rate as well as exchange rate risk by hedging with a variety of financial derivative instruments. Another critical area impacting short-term financial management is the area of managing information flows. Although a variety of information management issues were discussed at appropriate places in the text, Chapter 19 cohesively brings together some of the more critical aspects of the problem for a more complete treatment of this emerging and very important topic.

CHAPTER

# 18

# Managing Financial Risk with Derivatives

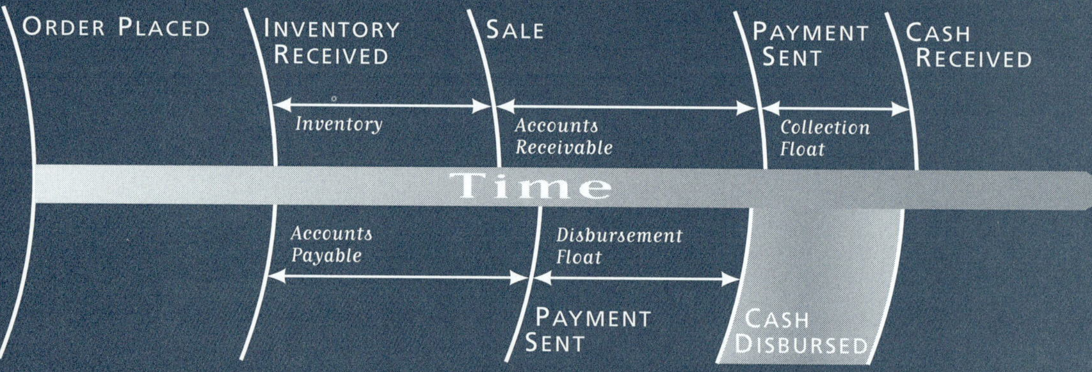

## OBJECTIVES

*After studying this chapter, you should be able to:*

- understand the basic difference between hedging and speculating.
- discern between hedging instruments including futures, options, swaps, and products such as interest rate caps, floors, and collars.
- develop appropriate hedging strategies using futures, options, swaps, caps, floors, and collars.

In earlier chapters, various strategies such as balance sheet matching to manage **interest rate risk** or netting to manage exchange rate risk where discussed. However, even after these strategies are used, some exposure to interest or exchange rate movements may remain. This chapter focuses on using financial derivatives such as futures, options, and swaps to manage uncertain cash flows resulting from movements in market interest rates and exchange rates. We will first discuss the characteristics of these contracts and then develop appropriate strategies for the different types of contracts as they apply to managing the variability of cash flows.

In Chapters 14 and 15, we discussed the various types of money market investment strategies useful for investing short-term funds. The basic purpose of short-term investments is to earn a reasonable rate of return until the funds need to be redeployed back into the operations of the firm. Thus, the decision of whether to invest or not and the maturity decision had to weigh transaction costs against the opportunity cost of idle funds. Some of the strategies left the firm exposed to interest rate risk. For example, a "riding the yield curve" strategy forces the firm to sell the security before it matures exposing the firm to an uncertain selling price which is dependent on the interest rate structure that exists at the time the security is sold. Chapter 16, dealing with short-term financing decisions, related similar types of problems from the financing or liability management side. Finally, when firms do business with foreign corporations as discussed in Chapter 17, financial risk is created due to the differences in the currencies used by the two firms. This chapter will discuss a variety of strategies useful in managing risk associated with uncertain movements in interest and foreign exchange rates.

### FINANCIAL DILEMMA

What Can Be Done about Uncertain Interest Rates?

Mark Thompson wondered what he should do. His most recent cash flow forecast indicated that in 30 days he would need to borrow $3 million for approximately three months. While he currently enjoyed a healthy liquid asset balance of marketable securities, those funds would be drawn down in the near term resulting in needed external financing to fund the firm's seasonal working capital needs.

His concern was over the future direction of interest rates. The current yield curve was relatively flat with short-term borrowing rates at 9.75 percent. He felt that this level represented a reasonable borrowing cost and wished he could lock in that rate today as his financing cost in 30 days. While rates could go lower, he was more worried about them rising over the next month.

## HEDGING COMPARED TO SPECULATING

The same financial contracts that allow a financial manager to hedge movements in interest rates can also be used to speculate on the future direction of these rates. Although both hedgers and speculators use the same financial contracts, the ways they are used is quite different.

A **hedger** has a cash position or an anticipated cash position that he or she is trying to protect from adverse interest or exchange rate movements. A **speculator**, on the other hand, has no operating cash flow position to protect and is trying to profit solely from rate movements.

An example may help to more clearly differentiate hedging strategies from speculative strategies. Suppose a financial manager forecasts a temporary surplus of funds for a brief period of time beginning 30 days from today. The plan is to invest these funds in a short-term money market instrument, but the future interest rate environment is relatively cloudy. The current level of interest rates is reasonable, and the financial manager would not mind getting today's rates 30 days from now. In essence, the financial manager would like to hedge against future movements in interest rates and lock in today's rate if possible.

Contrast this hedging situation with a local floor trader on the Chicago Mercantile Exchange's International Monetary Market where Treasury bill futures are traded. The local floor trader purchased a seat on the exchange some years ago and earns a living by trading interest rate futures contracts. If the trader senses that interest rates are rising, then he or she will sell a futures contract short and buy it back at a lower price after rates have risen.[1] If the trader senses that rates are falling, then he or she will purchase futures contracts and then sell them at a higher price after interest rates have fallen. Thus, a speculator trades to profit from changes in interest rates or exchange rates. A hedger, on the other hand, trades futures contracts in order to protect a cash position from changes in interest or currency exchange rates.

Speculators serve a very important function by providing liquidity in the futures markets through their continual trading of contracts. This liquidity provides assurance to hedgers that they can liquidate their hedging contracts whenever necessary.

## HEDGING WITH FINANCIAL FUTURES

The first hedging strategy we will develop uses a futures contract. The next section provides background on futures contracts and then develops the basic hedging strategies for managing interest and exchange rate risk for a variety of cash positions.

### Introduction to Futures Contracts

A **futures contract** is a standardized contract that carries with it a performance obligation at the expiration of the contract. For example, the buyer of a 90-day Treasury bill futures contract first purchases the futures contract by putting up margin, a small percentage of the contract price, rather than paying the price of the contract. At expiration, the buyer pays the contract price, less the dollar amount of funds in the margin account, and receives the cash market instrument, which in this case is a Treasury bill with 90 days to maturity.

A unique feature of a futures contract is the **margin account**. The margin account, created as a part of the futures contract transaction, is **marked-to-market** daily with the

---

[1] As interest rates rise, the price of a futures contract falls.

positive changes in the market price of the contract credited to the buyer's margin account and debited from the seller's margin account. Negative changes in the price of the contract would have just the opposite transactions with the margin account for the buyer and seller. Margin calls occur if the margin account falls below some predetermined level.

For example, assume that a treasurer purchased a Treasury bill futures contract with an initial margin of $2,000. The treasurer would give his or her broker $2,000 and as a result would own a Treasury bill futures contract. Assume the contract is initially priced at $950,000. The next day, interest rates fall and as a result the contract price increases by $625. The financial manager now owns a contract worth $950,625, and at the close of business that day his or her margin account would be worth $2,625. Exhibit 18–1 carries this example on for several more days showing how the margin account varies in relation to the change in the price of the futures contract.

On day 5, the financial manager would receive a margin call from his or her broker requesting the financial manager to deposit enough cash that day to bring the margin account back to a level referred to as the **maintenance margin**. The margin call would be for at least $175, bringing the margin account to zero and then an additional amount to return the account to the maintenance level.

The first financial futures contracts began trading in 1972 and were on foreign currencies. In that year, the Chicago Mercantile Exchange organized the International Monetary Market in order to trade the newly developed financial futures instrument. Exhibit 18–2 shows the more popular exchange rate futures contracts including the Japanese yen, the British pound, and the euro. To better understand the information presented in the table, let's take the British pound quote from Exhibit 18–2 as an example. One contract month is reported. Contracts expire the third Wednesday of the contract month. The British pound contract is for 62,500 pounds sterling, and the March 2004 contract price closed on Monday, January 12, 2004, at a price of $1.8373 per pound. Thus, one contract could have been purchased on that day, and if held to expiration, the buyer of the contract would receive 62,500 pounds sterling in exchange for $114,831.25 (62,500 × $1.8373). To purchase the futures contract, the buyer would have to post initial margin of approximately 1 to 2 percent of the contract price and pay the contract price at expiration of the contract.

In 1975, a futures contract on a Government National Mortgage Association (GNMA) pass-through security began trading followed by trading in 90-day Treasury bill futures contracts in 1976. Since that time, numerous types of futures contracts have been created. Exhibit 18–3 displays the interest rate futures contracts reported by *The Wall Street Journal.*

One of the more popular interest rate futures contracts is the eurodollar contract that is a futures contract on a 90-day eurodollar deposit. Because we will use the eurodollar futures contract in later examples, let's discuss the information about that contract as highlighted in Exhibit 18–3. The eurodollar futures contract is for a $1 million face value 90-day eurodollar deposit. Multiple contract months are reported in the exhibit including

**Exhibit 18-1**

*Variations in the Margin Account as a Result of Future Contract Price Changes*

| Day | Contract Price Change | Margin Account |
|---|---|---|
| 0 | | $2,000 |
| 1 | $ 625 | 2,625 |
| 2 | 100 | 2,725 |
| 3 | −900 | 1,825 |
| 4 | −1,500 | 325 |
| 5 | −500 | −175 Margin Call |

## Exhibit 18–2

*Foreign Currency Futures Contracts*

### Currency Futures

| **Japanese Yen** (CME)-¥12,500,000; $ per ¥ | | | | | | | | |
|---|---|---|---|---|---|---|---|---|
| Mar | .9395 | .9417 | .9386 | .9392 | −.0025 | .9464 | .8240 | 150,635 |
| June | .9428 | .9442 | .9416 | .9420 | −.0026 | .9500 | .8496 | 7,452 |

Est vol 8,882; vol Fri 39,782; open int 158,147, −839.

| **Canadian Dollar** (CME)-CAD 100,000; $ per CAD | | | | | | | | |
|---|---|---|---|---|---|---|---|---|
| Mar | .7844 | .7862 | .7809 | .7823 | −.0017 | .7863 | .6150 | 77,112 |
| June | .7796 | .7820 | .7785 | .7801 | −.0017 | .7850 | .6201 | 2,683 |
| Sept | .7768 | .7800 | .7768 | .7782 | −.0017 | .7805 | .6505 | 1,410 |
| Dec | .7748 | .7781 | .7748 | .7763 | −.0017 | .7785 | .6940 | 676 |

Est vol 5,821; vol Fri 19,208; open int 81,945, +215.

| **British Pound** (CME)-£62,500; $ per £ | | | | | | | | |
|---|---|---|---|---|---|---|---|---|
| Mar | 1.8388 | 1.8488 | 1.8352 | 1.8373 | −.0003 | 1.8488 | 1.5654 | 61,326 |

Est vol 7,022; vol Fri 18,252; open int 61,759, −328.

| **Swiss Franc** (CME)-CHF 125,000; $ per CHF | | | | | | | | |
|---|---|---|---|---|---|---|---|---|
| Mar | .8215 | .8249 | .8150 | .8159 | −.0041 | .8249 | .7060 | 48,714 |
| June | .8215 | .8248 | .8168 | .8175 | −.0041 | .8248 | .7117 | 197 |

Est vol 4,708; vol Fri 8,378; open int 49,013, −1,329.

| **Australian Dollar** (CME)-AUD 100,000; $ per AUD | | | | | | | | |
|---|---|---|---|---|---|---|---|---|
| Mar | .7710 | .7745 | .7690 | .7715 | .0008 | .7745 | .5193 | 62,687 |
| June | .7660 | .7660 | .7609 | .7631 | .0008 | .7660 | .5645 | 620 |

Est vol 3,380; vol Fri 7,078; open int 63,446, −702.

| **Mexican Peso** (CME)-MXN 500,000; $ per MXN | | | | | | | | |
|---|---|---|---|---|---|---|---|---|
| Mar | .09172 | .09217 | .09140 | .09192 | 00015 | .09330 | .08600 | 34,364 |
| June | .09050 | .09100 | .09050 | .09087 | 00015 | .09100 | .08495 | 417 |

Est vol 5,001; vol Fri 8,373; open int 35,158, +2,040.

| **Euro/US Dollar** (CME)-€125,000; $ per € | | | | | | | | |
|---|---|---|---|---|---|---|---|---|
| Mar | 1.2827 | 1.2875 | 1.2711 | 1.2729 | −.0089 | 1.2875 | 1.0425 | 121,543 |
| June | 1.2800 | 1.2837 | 1.2686 | 1.2700 | −.0089 | 1.2837 | 1.0570 | 885 |
| Sept | 1.2747 | 1.2776 | 1.2675 | 1.2673 | −.0090 | 1.2780 | 1.0500 | 90 |

Est vol 26,535; vol Fri 67,095; open int 122,704, −7,934.

| **Euro/US Dollar** (FINEX)-€200,000; $ per € | | | | | | | | |
|---|---|---|---|---|---|---|---|---|
| Mar | 1.2820 | 1.2841 | 1.2841 | 1.2729 | −.0067 | 1.2841 | 1.1472 | 417 |

Est vol 283; vol Fri 255; open int 419, +4.

| **Euro/Japanese Yen** (FINEX)-€100,000; ¥ per € | | | | | | | | |
|---|---|---|---|---|---|---|---|---|
| Mar | 136.40 | 136.44 | 135.92 | 135.52 | −.59 | 136.44 | 130.45 | 12,790 |

Est vol 488; vol Fri 4,414; open int 12,790, +2,851.

| **Euro/British Pound** (FINEX)-€100,000; £ per € | | | | | | | | |
|---|---|---|---|---|---|---|---|---|
| Mar | .6975 | .6945 | .6929 | .6928 | −.0049 | .7094 | .6929 | 3,615 |

Est vol 544; vol Fri 169; open int 3,615, unch.

*Source:* "Futures," *The Wall Street Journal*, January 13, 2004, p. C-15.

January 2004 through July 2009 expiration dates. The contracts trade on the Chicago Mercantile Exchange (CME), and the March contract closed or settled on Monday, January 12, 2004, priced at an annualized rate of 1.17 percent. If someone purchased the March contract on this day and held it to expiration, they would receive $1 million face value Eurodollar deposit earning a 1.17-percent return. Characteristic of all futures contracts, at the time the contract was purchased, only a small margin had to be posted with cash settlement of the contract price at contract expiration. Although not shown in the data reported in *The Wall Street Journal*, the initial margin for many of the $1 million interest rate futures contracts is approximately $2,000 per contract.

The numbers under the headings of Open, High, Low, and Settle in the body of the table for the futures contracts represent an index number that is calculated by taking the annual discount rate from 100. While this index does not represent the price of the contract, it does reflect direction of price movement when interest rates change. For example, if interest rates rise, the dollar price of a futures contract will fall, just like any other fixed price financial contract. The higher the interest rate, the lower the financial futures contract index.

This "price" index was developed when the interest rate futures contracts were first developed in the 1970s. The price index helped futures traders, used to trading commod-

## Exhibit 18-3

*Interest Rate Futures Contracts*

### Interest Rate Futures

**Treasury Bonds** (CBT)-$100,000; pts 32nds of 100%

| | | | | | | | | |
|---|---|---|---|---|---|---|---|---|
| Mar | 111-13 | 112-00 | 110-31 | 111-10 | 1 | 116-23 | 101-05 | 455,359 |
| June | 109-22 | 110-17 | 109-18 | 109-28 | 1 | 116-15 | 104-00 | 15,159 |

Est vol 210,741; vol Fri 265,844; open int 470,917, +19,888.

**Treasury Notes** (CBT)-$100,000; pts 32nds of 100%

| | | | | | | | | |
|---|---|---|---|---|---|---|---|---|
| Mar | 13-295 | 114-12 | 13-215 | 113-31 | 1.5 | 116-10 | 106-29 | 1,048,043 |
| June | 112-08 | 112-25 | 12-045 | 12-125 | 1.5 | 112-25 | 107-13 | 29,915 |

Est vol 624,377; vol Fri 803,109; open int 1,077,958, +47,559.

**10 Yr. Agency Notes** (CBT)-$100,000; pts 32nds of 100%

| | | | | | | | | |
|---|---|---|---|---|---|---|---|---|
| Mar | ... | ... | ... | na | ... | ... | ... | 0 |

Est vol na; vol Fri na; open int na, .

**5 Yr. Treasury Notes** (CBT)-$100,000; pts 32nds of 100%

| | | | | | | | | |
|---|---|---|---|---|---|---|---|---|
| Mar | 12-245 | 13-025 | 12-205 | 112-26 | 1.0 | 19-215 | 09-145 | 827,502 |

Est vol 238,098; vol Fri 343,718; open int 840,286, +2,487.

**2 Yr. Treasury Notes** (CBT)-$200,000; pts 32nds of 100%

| | | | | | | | | |
|---|---|---|---|---|---|---|---|---|
| Mar | 107-14 | 107-17 | 07-125 | 07-142 | ... | 107-17 | 106-02 | 160,879 |

Est vol 19,545; vol Fri 18,841; open int 160,879, +5,361.

| | OPEN | HIGH | LOW | SETTLE | CHG | LIFETIME HIGH | LIFETIME LOW | OPEN INT |
|---|---|---|---|---|---|---|---|---|
| **30 Day Federal Funds** (CBT)-$5,000,000; 100 - daily avg. | | | | | | | | |
| Jan | 99.005 | 99.005 | 99.005 | 99.005 | ... | 99.240 | 98.660 | 48,863 |
| Feb | 99.00 | 99.01 | 99.00 | 99.00 | .01 | 99.99 | 98.70 | 76,188 |
| Mar | 99.00 | 99.00 | 99.00 | 99.00 | ... | 99.16 | 98.74 | 45,587 |
| Apr | 99.00 | 99.00 | 98.99 | 99.00 | ... | 99.17 | 89.96 | 75,586 |
| May | 98.97 | 98.98 | 98.97 | 98.97 | ... | 99.79 | 98.40 | 29,226 |
| June | 98.97 | 98.97 | 98.96 | 98.96 | ... | 98.97 | 98.38 | 18,831 |
| July | 98.91 | 98.92 | 98.91 | 98.91 | ... | 98.92 | 98.20 | 18,375 |
| Est vol 16,669; vol Fri 68,235; open int 315,863, +11,383. | | | | | | | | |
| **10 Yr. Interest Rate Swaps** (CBT)-$100,000; pts 32nds of 100% | | | | | | | | |
| Mar | 111-11 | 111-31 | 111-08 | 111-18 | 4 | 111-31 | 107-20 | 37,944 |
| Est vol 464; vol Fri 817; open int 37,945, +222. | | | | | | | | |
| **10 Yr. Muni Note Index** (CBT)-$1,000 x index | | | | | | | | |
| Mar | 104-11 | 104-28 | 104-10 | 104-15 | ... | 104-28 | 99-21 | 2,294 |
| Est vol 69; vol Fri 424; open int 2,294, +203. | | | | | | | | |
| Index: Close 105-03; Yield 4.366. | | | | | | | | |

| | OPEN | HIGH | LOW | SETTLE | CHG | YIELD | CHG | OPEN INT |
|---|---|---|---|---|---|---|---|---|
| **13 Week Treasury Bills** (CME)-$1,000,000; pts of 100% | | | | | | | | |
| Jan | ... | ... | ... | n.a. | ... | ... | ... | 0 |
| Est vol n.a.; vol Fri 0; open int 0, unch. | | | | | | | | |
| **1 Month Libor** (CME)-$3,000,000; pts of 100% | | | | | | | | |
| Jan | 98.89 | 98.90 | 98.89 | 98.90 | ... | 1.10 | ... | 20,310 |
| Feb | 98.89 | 98.89 | 98.88 | 98.89 | ... | 1.11 | ... | 25,482 |
| Mar | 98.87 | 98.87 | 98.87 | 98.87 | ... | 1.13 | ... | 8,521 |
| May | 98.83 | 98.84 | 98.83 | 98.84 | ... | 1.16 | ... | 804 |
| June | 98.79 | 98.82 | 98.79 | 98.81 | ... | 1.19 | ... | 5,164 |
| Est vol 3,475; vol Fri 14,346; open int 71,573, –6,191. | | | | | | | | |
| **Eurodollar** (CME)-$1,000,000; pts of 100% | | | | | | | | |
| Jan | 98.87 | 98.87 | 98.87 | 98.87 | .01 | 1.13 | –.01 | 95,686 |
| Feb | 98.85 | 98.86 | 98.85 | 98.85 | ... | 1.15 | ... | 27,948 |
| Mar | 98.84 | 98.84 | 98.83 | 98.83 | ... | 1.17 | ... | 835,463 |
| Apr | 98.81 | 98.81 | 98.81 | 98.81 | .01 | 1.19 | –.01 | 17,054 |
| May | 98.78 | 98.78 | 98.77 | 98.77 | .01 | 1.23 | –.01 | 10,986 |
| June | 98.73 | 98.75 | 98.70 | 98.72 | .01 | 1.28 | –.01 | 765,368 |
| Sept | 98.46 | 98.52 | 98.45 | 98.47 | ... | 1.53 | ... | 677,848 |
| Dec | 98.12 | 98.18 | 98.09 | 98.11 | ... | 1.89 | ... | 586,844 |
| Mr05 | 97.72 | 97.79 | 97.68 | 97.71 | ... | 2.29 | ... | 379,410 |
| June | 97.29 | 97.38 | 97.27 | 97.30 | .01 | 2.70 | –.01 | 288,151 |
| Sept | 96.93 | 97.02 | 96.91 | 96.95 | .01 | 3.05 | –.01 | 230,827 |
| Dec | 96.63 | 96.72 | 96.61 | 96.65 | .02 | 3.35 | –.02 | 172,983 |
| Mr06 | 96.37 | 96.47 | 96.36 | 96.41 | .03 | 3.59 | –.03 | 149,898 |
| June | 96.14 | 96.24 | 96.12 | 96.17 | .03 | 3.83 | –.03 | 128,501 |
| Sept | 95.90 | 96.02 | 95.90 | 95.96 | .04 | 4.04 | –.04 | 108,530 |
| Dec | 95.67 | 95.79 | 95.67 | 95.74 | .05 | 4.26 | –.05 | 100,374 |
| Mr07 | 95.49 | 95.61 | 95.49 | 95.56 | .05 | 4.44 | –.05 | 76,735 |
| June | 95.31 | 95.43 | 95.31 | 95.39 | .05 | 4.61 | –.05 | 65,530 |
| Sept | 95.15 | 95.27 | 95.15 | 95.22 | .05 | 4.78 | –.05 | 66,410 |
| Dec | 94.99 | 95.11 | 94.99 | 95.06 | .05 | 4.94 | –.05 | 54,167 |
| Mr08 | 94.86 | 94.99 | 94.86 | 94.94 | .05 | 5.06 | –.05 | 46,961 |
| June | 94.74 | 94.87 | 94.74 | 94.82 | .05 | 5.18 | –.05 | 47,998 |
| Sept | 94.63 | 94.75 | 94.62 | 94.70 | .05 | 5.30 | –.05 | 31,313 |
| Dec | 94.51 | 94.64 | 94.51 | 94.59 | .05 | 5.41 | –.05 | 21,772 |
| Ju09 | 94.37 | 94.44 | 94.37 | 94.42 | .04 | 5.58 | –.04 | 9,414 |
| Est vol 1,169,801; vol Fri 1,961,007; open int 5,057,519, +89,292. | | | | | | | | |

*Source:* "Futures: Interest Rate Futures," *The Wall Street Journal*, January 13, 2004, p. C-15.

ity contracts based on quoted prices, make a smooth transition to the interest rate futures markets where information is quoted based on interest rates and prices move inversely to interest rates. The exhibit shows the "price" index on January 12 at the opening of trading, the high, the low, and the settlement index. The settlement index is basically the index of the last trade and is the basis by which margin accounts are adjusted at the end of the day.

Finally, Exhibit 18–3 reports the number of outstanding contracts at the close of trading for each day. This is termed open interest. Nearby contracts generally have the greatest number of contracts outstanding with the amount of contract activity quickly dwindling the further out the expiration date of the contract.

### Type of Hedge: Buy versus Sell

A financial manager can create a hedge by either initially buying a futures contract, referred to as a **buy hedge**, or issue a futures contract, referred to as a **sell hedge**. The type of hedge desired depends on the hedger's cash flow position that is being hedged, not on the anticipated direction of interest rates. Generally, the financial manager places a hedge that, in effect, acts as a temporary substitute for the cash transaction that will take place.

Suppose that a financial manager's cash budget indicates a cash surplus will occur in two months. The financial manager cannot invest today but will have available funds in the near future. How can the financial manager reduce the uncertainty of the future investment rate? The proper hedge in this situation is a buy hedge. The financial manager should buy an appropriate futures contract now to act as a substitute for the future investment of cash in two months. If the contract expires in two months, then the financial manager could use the futures contract to receive the money market instrument underlying the futures contract. If expiration of the futures contract occurs beyond two months, then the contract would be sold in two months. The gain or loss incurred by the futures contract could then be used to offset the opportunity loss or gain incurred in the cash market resulting from interest rate movements over the 2-month period.

Whether a hedge is created by issuing a futures contract or by purchasing a futures contract is dependent on the cash position being hedged. Exhibit 18–4 presents several different cash flow positions and the type of hedge that is appropriate for each one. The guiding principle in determining whether to form a buy hedge or a sell hedge is to use the type of hedge that will allow the cash instrument to be delivered through the futures contract if it were held to expiration. For example, a sell hedge would allow the financial manager to issue a liability at a predetermined price by delivering it through the futures contract if the contract was held to expiration.

### Choosing the Proper Futures Instrument

As Exhibits 18–2 and 18–3 show, a wide variety of futures contracts is available. The basic principle guiding the choice of the type of futures contract is that price movements of

**Exhibit 18–4**

*Cash Position and the Corresponding Futures Position*

| Cash Position | Futures Position |
|---|---|
| A future investment | Buy hedge |
| Retire liability prior to maturity | Buy hedge |
| A future issue of a liability | Sell hedge |
| Current investment that will be sold prior to its maturity | Sell hedge |

the futures contract and the cash market instrument should have a high correlation. A **direct hedge** is a hedge in which the underlying instrument of the futures contract and the cash market instrument being hedged are the same. If the underlying instrument of the futures contract is different from the cash position being hedged, then this is referred to as a **cross hedge**. For example, because there is not an actively traded commercial paper futures contract, investments in and issuance of commercial paper might be hedged with a Treasury bill, Eurodollar futures contracts, or some other closely related contract.

## Choosing the Proper Expiration Date

The choice of the proper expiration date is relatively simple. A quick reference to Exhibit 18–3 and the Eurodollar futures quotes indicates that there are many possible contracts from which to choose. The contracts generally expire before the end of the expiration month.

The guiding rule for the choice of the contract expiration month is to choose the contract expiration date that occurs nearest to, but after, the date of the cash market transaction to be hedged. This contract is referred to as the **nearby contract**. That is, if the cash position to be hedged is to take place in February, then the March contract should be chosen. The closer the price movements of the futures contract follow the price movements of the cash position being hedged, the more effective is the hedge. The more distant the contract expiration month is from the date of the cash position, the less correlation will exist between the current cash and futures price movements. Because there are only discrete expiration dates during the year for the futures contracts, it is likely that the expiration date will not match up exactly with the cash position date to be hedged. Thus, the best that can generally be accomplished is to hedge with the futures contract whose expiration date is past but nearest to the cash transaction date.

## Choosing the Number of Contracts

The choice of the number of futures contracts to use is a function of two variables. The first variable, the denomination of the contract, is fairly obvious. The 90-day eurodollar futures contract, shown in Exhibit 18–3, has a denomination of $1 million. If the financial manager needed to hedge a $3 million cash position, then three futures contracts are needed based solely on the differences between the hedger's cash position and the dollar size of the futures contract. Contract denomination is the sole variable that determines the number of contracts for currency futures.

Hedging with interest rate futures, however, requires a second variable to determine the number of contracts. This second variable is the maturity of the cash market instrument relative to the maturity of the instrument underlying the futures contract.[2] For example, suppose the financial manager planned to make a future investment in 180-day Treasury bills and wanted to hedge the future investment with a 90-day Eurodollar contract. The longer the maturity of a financial instrument such as a Treasury bill, the greater the price movement for a given movement in interest rates. For example, the price of a $1 million face value 90-day Eurodollar deposit will change $25 for each basis point change in interest rates.[3] The price change of a $1 million face value 180-day Treasury bill will

---

[2] Actually, the ratio of the maturities of the cash and futures instruments is only an approximation. The actual variable is a sensitivity factor or a type of beta coefficient that would measure the degree of sensitivity of the price of the cash instrument and the price of the futures contract to changes in interest rates. The ratio of maturities only approximates this sensitivity factor but is a reasonable approximation for our purposes.

[3] A basis point is 1/100 of 1 percent. Value of 1 basis point is Principal × (0.0001) × (Days/360). For the Eurodollar futures contract, the contract principal is $1 million and days is 90 days. Thus, the dollar value of one basis point is $25 [$1,000,000 × 0.0001 × (90/360)].

change \$50 for each basis point change in interest rates. Thus, for the financial futures contract to effectively hedge a cash position, the maturities of the cash and futures instruments should be the same, or the number of futures contracts can be adjusted in order to equal the dollar price change per basis point. In our example, the cash position will be an investment in a 180-day Treasury bill. Since the price movement of a 90-day instrument, which is the futures contract, will be only half that of the cash instrument per basis point change, it will take two contracts to equal the price volatility of the cash instrument. An equation that calculates the proper number, *N*, of futures contracts based on these two variables is presented in Equation 18.1.[4]

$$N = \frac{\text{Size of cash market position}}{\text{Futures contract denomination}} \times \frac{\text{Maturity of cash market instrument}}{\text{Maturity of futures contract instrument}} \tag{18.1}$$

## Evaluating the Performance of an Interest Rate Hedge

Having discussed all the component parts of a hedge, it is now time to learn how to properly assess the performance of the hedge.

The first part of the performance analysis is to evaluate the change in the cash market instrument from the time the hedge is placed, at time period 0, to the time the hedge is lifted, at time period 1. The spot rates, $SR_0$ and $SR_1$, are annual interest rates related to the cash market instrument and must be de-annualized using the factor, $MAT_c/360$. $MAT_c$ represents the number of days to maturity for the cash market instrument. Equation 18.2 computes the change in the value of the cash instrument over the hedge period resulting from a change in interest rates and would be an estimate of the gain or loss that would occur if a hedge were not placed. Face value cash should be a negative number if investing cash (this is equivalent to disbursing cash) and a positive number if issuing a liability or selling an asset (this is equivalent to receiving cash).

$$\text{Cash position} = \text{Face value cash} \times (SR_0 - SR_1) \times \frac{MAT_c}{360} \tag{18.2}$$

Equation 18.3 is an expression for the gain or loss that occurs in the futures contract over the hedge period. Since the futures rates, $FR_0$ and $FR_1$, are annualized rates, the factor, $MAT_f/360$, de-annualizes the impact of the change in interest rates so that the value change is just for the hedge period. To make this expression work appropriately, the variable, *Face value futures*, should be a positive number for a buy hedge (a buy hedger first buys the futures contract to place the hedge but then sells the contract at the end of the hedge period so the positive number represents the selling aspect of the hedge at the time the hedge is unwound) and a negative number for a sell hedge (a sell hedger first issues a futures contract but then buys it back at the end of the hedge period).

$$\text{Futures position} = \text{Face value futures} \times (FR_0 - FR_1) \times \frac{MAT_f}{360} \tag{18.3}$$

In Equation 18.3, $MAT_f$ represents the maturity of the instrument underlying the futures contract.

---

[4] Note that if this equation is used to calculate the number of contracts for a riding the yield curve hedge, the maturity of the cash instrument changes each day. Therefore, the number of contracts should be adjusted over the duration of the hedge. For simplicity, we will ignore this adjustment process.

Next, there are commission rates for buying and selling financial futures. A ballpark cost figure for the round trip commission charge for one financial futures contract is \$60.[5] Equation 18.4 can be used to compute the financial futures commission costs.

$$\text{Commission cost} = N \times \text{Commission rate per contract} \tag{18.4}$$

The final consideration involves the opportunity cost of the initial margin. Margin, *MRG,* of approximately \$2,000 per contract must be used to set up the margin account. The initial margin may differ among various types of futures contracts. However, \$2,000 is a reasonable estimate of the initial margin for one 90-day Treasury bill futures contract or eurodollar contract. These funds do not earn interest while in the margin account and thus incur an opportunity cost. This is computed in Equation 18.5. In this expression, $D$ represents the number of days the hedge is maintained, and $k$ is the annual opportunity cost of corporate idle cash balances.

$$\text{Margin cost} = N \times MRG \times (D \times k/360) \tag{18.5}$$

It is now time to put Equations 18.2 through 18.5 together to compute the net gain or loss resulting from the hedge. Equation 18.2 will either be an inflow or an outflow depending on the direction of the interest rate change and the type of cash market transaction that is being made. For example, issuing a liability with interest rates falling will result in a gain. Investing with interest rates falling will result in a loss. The same is true for Equation 18.3. A buy hedge with interest rates falling results in a gain, while a buy hedge with interest rates rising results in a loss. A sell hedge with interest rates falling results in a loss, and a sell hedge with interest rates rising results in a gain. Equations 18.4 and 18.5 will always be outflows.

## FINANCIAL DILEMMA REVISITED

Let's apply these equations to analyze Mark Thompson's dilemma as given at the outset of the chapter. You may remember that the current short-term borrowing cost was 9.75 percent. Mark plans to issue 90-day commercial paper in 30 days. He plans to hedge the commercial paper issue with a 90-day Eurodollar futures contract given the high degree of liquidity of the contract and its high degree of correlation with commercial paper rates. The interest rates on the spot commercial paper and the Eurodollar futures contract at the time the hedge was created and then lifted are shown below:

| | Today | 30 Days from Now |
|---|---|---|
| 90-day commercial paper rates | 9.75% | 11.25% |
| 90-day Eurodollar deposit | 9.60% | 11.00% |
| Cash position: | \$3,000,000 × (0.0975 − 0.1125) × (90/360) = | −\$11,250.00 |
| Futures position: | −\$3,000,000 × (0.0960 − 0.1100) × (90/360) = | 10,500.00 |
| Commission: | −3 × \$60 = | −180.00 |
| Margin: | −3 × \$2,000 × 30 × (0.0975/360) = | −48.75 |
| Net position from the hedge | | −\$ 978.75 |

Had Mark not hedged, the increase in interest rates would have cost him an additional \$11,250 of interest on the commercial paper. The hedge resulted in a gain in the futures contract of \$10,500. However, with costs of \$180 in commissions and \$48.75 in opportu-

[5] The term "roundtrip" with respect to hedging reflects the creation and then unwinding of the hedge position.

nity cost of the initial margin, a net loss of only $978.75 occurred as a result of the hedge. This represents a saving of $10,271.25 on this one transaction. Although the hedge did not offset the increase in interest rates perfectly, it did so substantially.

## Evaluating the Performance of a Currency Futures Hedge

Now let's explore how futures contracts can be used to hedge exchange rate risk. The basic principles are the same as hedging interest rate risk presented earlier. A buy hedge is used to hedge the purchase of foreign currency in the future, and a sell hedge is used to hedge the selling of foreign currency in the future. To illustrate, assume a U.S. importer just received invoices to pay a British exporter 62,500 pounds sterling in two months. The U.S. importer has several options. First, the importer could do nothing now and then buy pounds sterling in two months in the spot market. Or, the importer could buy pounds sterling now and hold them for two months. Another option would be to buy a futures contract that allows the U.S. importer to receive pounds sterling in the future at an exchange rate determined today.

The four transaction cash flows (cash position, futures position, commission, and margin) related to a foreign exchange futures contract are shown below and are similar to those for an interest rate futures contract developed earlier. CX stands for cash market exchange rate, and FX stands for futures market exchange rate. The subscripts 0 and 1 stand for the current period and future period, respectively. In the following example, assume that the cash exchange rate now is $1.73 per pound sterling and will be $1.83 in 60 days. The futures exchange rate now is $1.75 and will be $1.84 in 60 days. One futures contract carries a roundtrip commission rate of $60, and each contract requires an initial margin of $1,500. Assume that the current money market interest rate is 9 percent.

Spot Market Position:

$$\text{Pounds sterling} \times (CX_0 - CX_1) = \text{Gain(Loss) on spot}$$
$$62{,}500 \times (\$1.73 - \$1.83) = -\$6{,}250.00$$

Futures Market Position:

$$\text{Pounds sterling} \times (FX_0 - FX_1) = \text{Gain(Loss) on futures}$$
$$-62{,}500 \times (\$1.75 - \$1.84) = +\$5{,}625.00$$

Commission Cost:

$$\text{Number of contracts} \times \text{Commission} = \text{Commission cost}$$
$$-1 \times \$60 = -\$60.00$$

Opportunity Cost of Margin:

$$\text{Number of contracts} \times \text{Margin} \times \text{Days} \times \text{Rate} = \text{Margin cost}$$
$$-1 \times \$1{,}500 \times 60 \times (0.09/360) = \underline{-\$\ 22.50}$$

Net position from the hedge $\underline{\underline{-\$707.50}}$

Some explanation of the positive and negative signs is warranted at this point. In the cash position, the pounds sterling is positive because pounds are received or purchased. Pounds sterling has a negative sign in the futures position line because a pounds sterling futures contract was initially bought and then sold in 60 days, thus getting rid of pounds sterling.

In this example, the U.S. importer loses a net $707.50 as a result of the hedge, but would have lost $6,250 if pounds sterling had been purchased in the open market 60 days after receiving the invoice. Thus, the hedge saved the importer $5,542.50 ($6,250 − $707.50) relative to waiting to buy pounds sterling in 60 days. Of course, the importer could have purchased pounds sterling at the time the invoice was received, but this would have negated the credit terms allowing 60 days to pay since the importer would have to use dollars now to buy the pounds sterling. The hedge nearly accomplished the same result without having to commit dollars (with the exception of the margin) immediately.

### Why Hedges Are Not Perfect

A perfect hedge is one where the gain (loss) on the cash position is exactly offset by the loss (gain) related to the futures contract. In Mark Thompson's case, the hedge was imperfect as evidenced by the net loss of $978.75. Several factors can impact the financial result from the hedged position. First, as was the case in the Mark Thompson example, the interest rates on the cash instrument and on the futures instrument were not perfectly correlated so the price movements of the two instruments did not exactly match. Second, futures contracts are for only one contract size, and they expire on only a very limited number of dates. For example, the 90-day Eurodollar futures contract is for $1 million and expires on discrete dates during the year. If you wish to hedge a $1.5 million cash market Treasury bill position on March 1, the hedge will be imperfect because the exact dollar amount cannot be hedged. In addition, only a nearby contract expiration date can be chosen such as the March contract since the February contract would have already expired. Finally, a hedge may be imperfect because a futures contract for the exact cash market instrument to be hedged may not be available. In this case, the cash market position would be cross-hedged with a futures contract that is as similar as possible to the cash instrument.

## HEDGING WITH OPTIONS

Options provide an alternative hedging tool to financial futures contracts. This section develops a hedging strategy using option contracts.

### Introduction to Option Contracts

An **option contract** gives the option buyer the right but not the obligation to purchase the underlying asset at a specific price, referred to as the **striking price**, over a specific span of time. This type of option is known as a **call option**. The option buyer pays a **premium** for this right. If the option buyer does not exercise the option by the expiration date, it expires worthless.

A **put option** allows the owner of the option to *sell* the *underlying asset* at a specific price over a specific span of time. The purchaser pays a premium for the right, but not the obligation to sell at a predetermined price. Thus, options are fundamentally different from futures contracts in that there is no performance obligation. If the option is not exercised by the expiration date, then it simply expires worthless.

Option contracts were initially developed for common stocks, but now there are option contracts on futures contracts, or as reported in *The Wall Street Journal,* futures options. These options on futures provide a more palatable alternative to futures contracts since options are purchased by paying a premium rather than purchased on margin. Consequently, hedging with options does not incur the potential for margin calls but still provides interest or exchange rate protection.

**Futures options** give the holder the right to buy (call option) or sell (put option) a single standardized futures contract for a specified period of time at a specified striking price. Exhibit 18–5 lists several of the more heavily traded interest rate futures options.

Take the Eurodollar futures option in Exhibit 18–5 for example. This contract is based on a $1 million 90-day Eurodollar deposit. The premium for the March call option with a striking price of 9850[6] is reported as 3.37 points of 100 percent or 3.37 basis points.

---

[6] The 9850 quoted in *The Wall Street Journal* represents the striking price quoted as an index. So, 9850 represents an index value of 98.50, which is related to a 1.50-percent annualized interest rate.

**Exhibit 18–5**

*Exchange Traded Interest Rate Futures Options*

## FUTURES OPTIONS PRICES

| STRIKE | CALLS-SETTLE | | | PUTS-SETTLE | | |
|---|---|---|---|---|---|---|
| **T-Bonds (CBT)** | | | | | | |
| $100,000; points and 64ths of 100% | | | | | | |
| Price | Feb | Mar | Apr | Feb | Mar | Apr |
| 109 | 2-29 | 3-01 | 2-44 | 0-09 | 0-45 | 1-52 |
| 110 | 1-40 | 2-20 | 2-10 | 0-20 | 1-00 | 2-18 |
| 111 | 0-61 | 1-46 | 1-44 | 0-41 | 1-26 | ... |
| 112 | 0-30 | 1-15 | ... | 1-10 | 1-59 | ... |
| 113 | 0-12 | 0-54 | 0-62 | 1-57 | 2-34 | ... |
| 114 | 0-05 | 0-35 | 0-47 | 2-49 | 3-15 | ... |
| Est vol 70,379; | | | | | | |
| Fr vol 49,285 calls 39,995 puts | | | | | | |
| Op int Fri 357,645 calls 307,103 puts | | | | | | |
| **T-Notes (CBT)** | | | | | | |
| $100,000; points and 64ths of 100% | | | | | | |
| Price | Feb | Mar | Apr | Feb | Mar | Apr |
| 112 | 2-04 | 2-28 | 1-53 | 0-06 | 0-30 | 1-28 |
| 113 | 1-14 | 1-46 | 1-20 | 0-16 | 0-48 | 1-59 |
| 114 | 0-37 | 1-08 | 0-58 | 0-39 | 1-10 | ... |
| 115 | 0-13 | 0-43 | 0-39 | 1-15 | 1-45 | ... |
| 116 | 0-03 | 0-24 | 0-25 | 2-05 | 2-26 | ... |
| 117 | 0-01 | 0-12 | ... | ... | ... | ... |
| Est vol 183,185 Fr 271,246 calls 163,461 puts | | | | | | |
| Op int Fri 842,072 calls 772,725 puts | | | | | | |
| **5 Yr Treas Notes (CBT)** | | | | | | |
| $100,000; points and 64ths of 100% | | | | | | |
| Price | Feb | Mar | Apr | Feb | Mar | Apr |
| 11200 | 0-61 | 1-16 | ... | 0-09 | 0-28 | ... |
| 11250 | 0-37 | 0-59 | ... | 0-17 | 0-39 | ... |
| 11300 | 0-19 | 0-42 | 0-29 | 0-31 | 0-54 | ... |
| 11350 | 0-08 | 0-27 | ... | ... | ... | ... |
| 11400 | 0-03 | 0-18 | ... | ... | ... | ... |
| 11450 | 0-01 | 0-11 | ... | ... | ... | ... |
| Est vol 32,825 Fr 27,795 calls 68,403 puts | | | | | | |
| Op int Fri 98,109 calls 300,838 puts | | | | | | |
| **30 Day Federal Funds (CBT)** | | | | | | |
| $5,000,000; 100 minus daily average | | | | | | |
| Price | Jan | Feb | Mar | Jan | Feb | Mar |
| 988750 | ... | .127 | .125 | ... | .002 | .005 |
| 989375 | ... | .062 | .065 | ... | .005 | .007 |
| 990000 | .010 | .007 | .010 | .005 | .007 | .015 |
| 990625 | ... | ... | .005 | ... | ... | ... |
| 991250 | .002 | .002 | .002 | ... | ... | ... |
| 991875 | ... | ... | ... | ... | ... | ... |
| Est vol 6,113 Fr 1,685 calls 250 puts | | | | | | |
| Op int Fri 102,605 calls 134,117 puts | | | | | | |
| **Eurodollar (CME)** | | | | | | |
| $ million; pts. of 100% | | | | | | |
| Price | Jan | Feb | Mar | Jan | Feb | Mar |
| 9825 | 5.85 | ... | 5.87 | 0.00 | 0.00 | 0.02 |
| 9850 | 3.35 | ... | 3.37 | 0.00 | 0.02 | 0.02 |
| 9875 | 0.90 | 0.92 | 1.02 | 0.05 | 0.07 | 0.17 |
| 9900 | 0.00 | ... | 0.05 | ... | ... | 1.70 |
| 9925 | ... | ... | 0.00 | ... | ... | 4.15 |
| 9950 | ... | ... | 0.00 | ... | ... | 6.65 |
| Est vol 326,684; | | | | | | |
| Fr vol 410,963 calls 298,807 puts | | | | | | |
| Op int Fri 3,739,820 calls 3,858,264 puts | | | | | | |

*Source:* "Futures Options Prices: Interest Rate," *The Wall Street Journal*, January 13, 2004, p. C-15.

The biggest difference between the futures option and a futures contract is that the option limits the loss exposure to the option premium. The premium paid for the option is the most that can be lost, whereas the theoretical loss on a futures contract is unlimited. We discuss hedging strategies with futures options in a later section.

### Type of Hedge: Write or Purchase, Call or Put

As we saw with financial futures hedging strategies, a financial manager who will be investing funds in the near future can buy a futures contract as a temporary substitute for the anticipated cash position. As an alternative, a hedger could form a buy hedge with futures options by purchasing a call option on a futures contract. That way, if interest rates fall, the price of the futures will rise, and the price of the futures option will likewise rise.[7] A call option used in this way provides protection against falling interest rates, or put another way, rising prices on the anticipated cash investment instrument. Thus, the purchase of a call futures option is used to hedge the future investment of cash or retiring liabilities prior to maturity.

A put option is used to protect against lower prices or correspondingly higher rates. Therefore, put options are useful in hedging the future issue of liabilities or the future liquidation of financial assets where the financial manager is afraid that interest rates may rise. Exhibit 18–6 summarizes the four types of cash positions and their related futures options transactions.

Should a hedger ever write option contracts? The primary reason for writing or issuing call and put options is to earn the option premium that is really not related to any hedging motive. Thus, hedgers will normally either buy a call or buy a put, depending on the cash position they are trying to protect.

Another reason that hedgers don't write options is that writers of futures options contracts are required to post margin. This is required since option writers face similar risks as participants in the futures markets. The exercise of an option is up to the option buyer. Hence, the call option writer may have to issue a futures contract that will result in the same financial risk as having originally sold a futures contract. Therefore, the option writer is required to post margin to demonstrate ability to meet potential contract obligations and the option writer's position is marked-to-market daily.

## Number of Contracts

The number of options that need to be purchased is based directly on the number of futures contracts needed. For example, we saw earlier that one eurodollar futures option is for $1 million face value futures contract. Thus, if a futures hedging program called for 10 futures contracts, an equivalent futures option hedging strategy will require 10 futures options.

## Evaluating the Performance of the Interest Rate Option Hedge

Returning to Mark Thompson's dilemma, suppose that Mark considered using a futures option rather than the futures contract as used earlier and the following interest rates exist today along with the expected rates to occur in 30 days.

**Exhibit 18–6**

*Cash Positions and Related Futures Options Transactions*

| Cash Position | Futures Options Transaction |
|---|---|
| A future investment | Buy a call |
| Retire liability prior to maturity | Buy a call |
| A future issue of a liability | Buy a put |
| Current investment that will be sold prior to its maturity | Buy a put |

[7] The price of a call option will always increase as the price of the underlying asset of the option increases because the call option gives the holder the right to purchase the underlying asset at a fixed price. Thus, as the price of the underlying asset rises, the call option becomes more valuable.

| | Today | 30 Days from Now |
|---|---|---|
| Cash rates | 9.75% | 11.25% |
| 90-Day eurodollar futures rates | 9.60% | 11.00% |
| 90-Day eurodollar, $1 million contract futures option (put, pts. of 100%) | | |
| striking price | Points of 100% | |
| 8875 | 0.00009 | 0.0001 |
| 8900 | 0.0005 | 0.01 |
| 8925 | 0.0009 | 0.25 |
| 8950 | 0.003 | 0.50 |
| 8975 | 0.007 | 0.75 |
| 9000 | 0.009 | 1.00 |
| 9025 | 0.01 | 1.25 |
| 9050 | 0.10 | 1.50 |

Mark could have purchased three 90-day eurodollar put futures options with a striking price of 9050 for $750 [$3,000,000 × (0.10/4)/100]. Note that the stated premium is based on annualized rates of interest and must be de-annualized by dividing it by the number of periods in a year. Because this is an option contract on a 90-day futures instrument, the premium is divided by 4 because there are four 90-day periods in a 360-day year. In 30 days, according to the data for this example, the 90-day eurodollar futures contract interest rate rises to 11 percent. As a result, the option with a striking price of 9050 will be priced at 1.50 points per 100 percent, according to the example data provided, or three options will be worth $11,250 [$3,000,000 × (1.50/4)/100]. The three options can be sold for that amount, netting Mark a gain of $10,500 ($11,250 − $750), which offsets most of the $11,250 loss in cash market position resulting from the rise in interest rates.

A major advantage of this option strategy is that the treasurer established an interest rate ceiling, but not an interest rate floor. Had interest rates fallen, the value of the put option would have fallen and Mark could have let the option simply expire or even sold it and then issued the commercial paper at the new lower rates. The only loss would have been the original premium paid for the three options at a cost of $750. But, since rates rose, the option became more valuable as interest rates rose to higher levels. Rising interest rates drive the market price of a futures contract down. Given the fixed striking price, the put option, which allows the owner to sell at the fixed striking price, gains in value offsetting the increasing level of interest rates.

## Evaluating the Foreign Currency Option Hedge

Two types of foreign currency options are available. Hedgers can trade options directly on the foreign currency, or they can trade options on foreign currency futures contracts. We will first explore options on currencies and then options on futures contracts.

*Foreign Exchange Options* Exhibit 18–7 reports pricing data for options on a variety of foreign currencies. The data presented, all expressed in cents per unit of foreign currency, include the various striking prices for which options are being traded in the first column from the left and the premiums for the various call and put options. For example, the March 2004 call option on the British pound with a striking price of 1900, or $1.90, has a premium of 1.36 cents per pound. The option contract is for 31,250 pounds sterling; so, one option would cost $425 (31,250 × $0.0136).

Let's now look at an example of using currency options to hedge the future purchase of a foreign currency. Suppose that an American importer will have a cash outflow in late

## FOCUS ON PRACTICE

### Microsoft's Real Hedge

Microsoft was experiencing a dilemma with its Brazilian subsidiary as a result of offering its price list only in U.S. dollars. If its Brazilian customers thought the Brazilian real would appreciate, they would delay purchases; if the real was anticipated to depreciate, they over-ordered. Thus, hitting revenue targets for Microsoft became a much more uncertain venture. After unsuccessfully attempting to convert the price list to reals, treasury developed a program of hedging invoices in dollars with options.

In essence, treasury fixed a hedge cost for the Brazilian subsidiary as a percent of the U.S. dollar price list for a specified time period. The subsidiary then budgeted the cost, changing dollar prices as needed. By using options, Microsoft gave itself the choice not to exercise, taking advantage of the upside in the market.

*Source:* "For Microsoft, It's the Real Thing," *Treasury & Risk Management* (October 2003), p. 46.

**Exhibit 18–7**

*Foreign Currency Options*

| | | CALLS | | PUT | |
|---|---|---|---|---|---|
| | | VOL | SETTLE | VOL | SETTLE |
| Bpound | MAR04 | | | | |
| 31,250 Brit. Pound-cents per unit | | | | | |
| 1880 | | 235 | 2.24 | 11 | 1.76 |
| 1900 | | 51 | 1.36 | 5 | 2.88 |
| Japanese Yen | MAR04 | | | | |
| 9500 | | 6 | .680 | 5 | .700 |
| 9600 | | 10 | .350 | 5 | 1.370 |
| Canadian Dollar | MAR04 | | | | |
| 7500 | | 5 | 1.900 | 15 | .410 |
| 7600 | | 26 | .570 | 5 | .850 |
| Euro | MAR04 | | | | |
| 1260 | | 41 | .02560 | 46 | .00730 |
| 1270 | | 10 | .01920 | 67 | .01090 |

*Source:* Chicago Mercantile Exchange, settle prices as of 2/12/2004.

March 2004 of British pounds. The importer would like to protect against a deteriorating dollar, that is, having to pay more U.S. dollars to purchase the same number of units of pounds sterling in January, and thus buys one 1900 call option at $0.0136 per pound.[8] The importer has guaranteed an exchange rate of $1.9136 ($1.90 + $0.0136), which is the 1900 striking price plus the $0.0136 premium. If the dollar weakens (i.e., the dollar price of pounds sterling increases), then the importer will exercise the option to purchase pounds at an effective cost of $1.9136. If the dollar strengthens (i.e., the dollar price of pounds sterling decreases), then the importer will simply purchase pounds in the spot market and let the option expire. The cost of the option is $425 (31,250 × $0.0136) for the option to acquire 31,250 pounds sterling which has a dollar value at the striking price of $59,375

[8] These quotes are taken from Exhibit 18–7 for currency options shown earlier.

(31,250 × \$1.90). Thus, the option premium represents approximately 0.716 percent of the dollar price of the contract or 0.00716 (\$425/\$59,375).

*Futures Options* Buying call or put options on foreign currency futures contracts is also possible. These contracts are referred to as futures options, and Exhibit 18–8 displays quotes for a variety of these contracts. Futures options work the same way that options work—the only difference is that the option is on a futures contract rather than on the foreign currency itself.

For example, in Exhibit 18–8, the March call British pound futures option with a striking price of 1850 or \$1.85 can be purchased for a premium of \$0.0226 per pound sterling. The contract denomination is 62,500 pounds. The cost of the March call option is therefore \$1,412.50 (62,500 × \$0.0226).

The buyer of a call option can exercise the option anytime before it expires in March and receive a futures contract on the pounds sterling. A financial manager wishing to hedge the future purchase of a foreign currency should buy a call; if a foreign currency were to be sold in the future, then buying a put option would be appropriate.

**Exhibit 18–8**

*Foreign Currency Futures Options*

| STRIKE | CALLS-SETTLE | | | PUTS-SETTLE | | |
|---|---|---|---|---|---|---|
| **Currency** | | | | | | |
| **Japanese Yen** (CME) | | | | | | |
| 12,500,000 yen; cents per 100 yen | | | | | | |
| Price | Feb | Mar | Apr | Feb | Mar | Apr |
| 9300 | 1.32 | 1.68 | ... | 0.40 | 0.76 | ... |
| 9350 | 1.01 | 1.40 | ... | 0.59 | 0.98 | ... |
| 9400 | 0.76 | 1.16 | ... | 0.84 | 1.24 | ... |
| 9450 | 0.56 | 0.96 | ... | 1.14 | 1.54 | ... |
| 9500 | 0.41 | 0.79 | ... | ... | 1.87 | ... |
| 9550 | 0.30 | 0.65 | ... | 1.88 | ... | ... |
| Est vol 1,080 Fr 880 calls 1,245 puts | | | | | | |
| Op int Fri 18,200 calls 15,868 puts | | | | | | |
| **Canadian Dollar** (CME) | | | | | | |
| 100,000 Can.\$, cents per Can.\$ | | | | | | |
| Price | Feb | Mar | Apr | Feb | Mar | Apr |
| 7700 | 1.55 | 1.83 | ... | 0.32 | 0.60 | ... |
| 7750 | ... | 1.51 | ... | 0.47 | 0.78 | ... |
| 7800 | 0.89 | 1.23 | ... | 0.66 | 1.00 | ... |
| 7850 | 0.65 | 1.00 | ... | ... | 1.27 | ... |
| 7900 | 0.47 | 0.81 | ... | 1.24 | 1.58 | ... |
| 7950 | ... | 0.65 | ... | ... | ... | ... |
| Est vol 253 Fr 1,472 calls 315 puts | | | | | | |
| Op int Fri 11,322 calls 6,873 puts | | | | | | |
| **British Pound** (CME) | | | | | | |
| 62,500 pounds; cents per pound | | | | | | |
| Price | Feb | Mar | Apr | Feb | Mar | Apr |
| 1820 | 2.83 | 3.73 | ... | 1.10 | 2.00 | ... |
| 1830 | 2.20 | 3.19 | ... | 1.47 | 2.46 | ... |
| 1840 | 1.72 | 2.68 | ... | 1.99 | 2.95 | ... |
| 1850 | 1.40 | 2.26 | ... | ... | ... | ... |
| 1860 | 1.08 | 1.84 | 1.76 | 3.35 | ... | ... |
| 1870 | ... | 1.47 | 1.44 | ... | 4.73 | ... |
| Est vol 919 Fr 1,001 calls 152 puts | | | | | | |
| Op int Fri 3,761 calls 2,968 puts | | | | | | |
| **Swiss Franc** (CME) | | | | | | |
| 125,000 francs; cents per franc | | | | | | |
| Price | Feb | Mar | Apr | Feb | Mar | Apr |
| 8050 | 1.66 | 2.07 | ... | 0.57 | 0.98 | ... |
| 8100 | ... | 1.77 | ... | ... | 1.18 | ... |
| 8150 | 1.08 | 1.51 | ... | 0.99 | 1.42 | ... |
| 8200 | 0.85 | 1.28 | ... | 1.26 | 1.69 | ... |
| 8250 | ... | ... | ... | ... | ... | ... |
| 8300 | 0.51 | 0.90 | ... | ... | ... | ... |
| Est vol 107 Fr 119 calls 16 puts | | | | | | |
| Op int Fri 1,151 calls 1,359 puts | | | | | | |
| **Euro Fx** (CME) | | | | | | |
| 125,000 euros; cents per euro | | | | | | |
| Price | Feb | Mar | Apr | Feb | Mar | Apr |
| 12650 | 1.90 | 2.56 | ... | 1.11 | 1.77 | ... |

*Source:* "Futures Options Prices: Currency," *The Wall Street Journal*, January 13, 2004, p. C-15.

FOCUS ON PRACTICE

*How Corporations Use Derivatives*

Based on survey results presented by Bodnar, Hayt, Marston, and Smithson (1995), there appears to be a reasonably high degree of use of derivatives by nonfinancial firms in an attempt to manage financial risk. Of the 530 firms that responded to the survey, 35 percent indicated that they use derivatives (forwards, futures, options, or swaps). However, when the sample is stratified by size and industry, some interesting disparities are discovered. While 65 percent of the large firms reported using derivatives to manage financial risk, only 30 percent of mid-sized firms and 13 percent of small firms reported doing so. The predominant industry group users were commodity-based industries such as agriculture, refining, and mining with 50 percent of this group reporting using derivatives as a risk management tool. Manufacturing firms were the second most frequent users of derivatives, and services firms were the least frequent users.

Nonfinancial firms use derivatives to manage four general types of exposure including foreign exchange, interest rate, commodity price, and equity price. The survey indicated that swaps were the most prevalent instrument for managing interest rate risk, while forward contracts followed by options and then swaps were used for managing foreign currency risk.

Finally, the survey made it very clear that the predominant use of derivative securities by nonfinancial firms is for hedging purposes and not for speculation. The most common type of hedging was for well-defined exposures arising from firmly committed transactions or anticipated transactions less than a year away. Only 9 percent of the firms reported commonly using derivatives to take position on the direction of market prices or interest rates.

## HEDGING WITH SWAPS

A **swap** is an agreement between two different institutions or firms, generally referred to as **counterparties,** to swap cash flows between themselves. Often, an intermediary institution acts as a market maker through which the payments flow. In 1982, the combined dollar volume of currency and interest rate swaps was only about $5 billion. More recently, the interest rate swap market alone had grown to exceed $3 trillion. Manufacturers, retailers, transportation companies, financial services firms, governmental agencies, and many others now use swaps. The typical swap deal involves $25 to $100 million with maturities ranging from two to 10 years.

### Introduction to Interest Rate Swaps

In its simplest form, a **financial swap** represents an exchange of periodic cash flows between two parties. The two basic types of financial swaps involve the exchange of different currencies, known as a **currency swap**, and a swap of interest flows, generally referred to as an **interest rate swap**. The swap agreement specifies the currencies to be swapped; the applicable interest rates to be used; an agreed-upon **notional amount,** which is the agreed upon face amount on which exchange rates or interest rates are to be applied to calculate the cash flows; and the timing of the payment of the cash flows.

The most common type of interest rate swap is a **fixed-for-floating rate swap**, as shown in Exhibit 18–9. In it, Party A, with floating-rate debt, agrees to pay to Party B, who has fixed rate debt, a fixed rate interest payment based on the notional amount stated in the agreement, in exchange for receipt of a floating-rate interest payment. The receipt of the floating-rate payment can be used to cover the cost of the floating-rate liability leaving

Exhibit 18–9

*Fixed-for-Floating Interest Rate Swap*

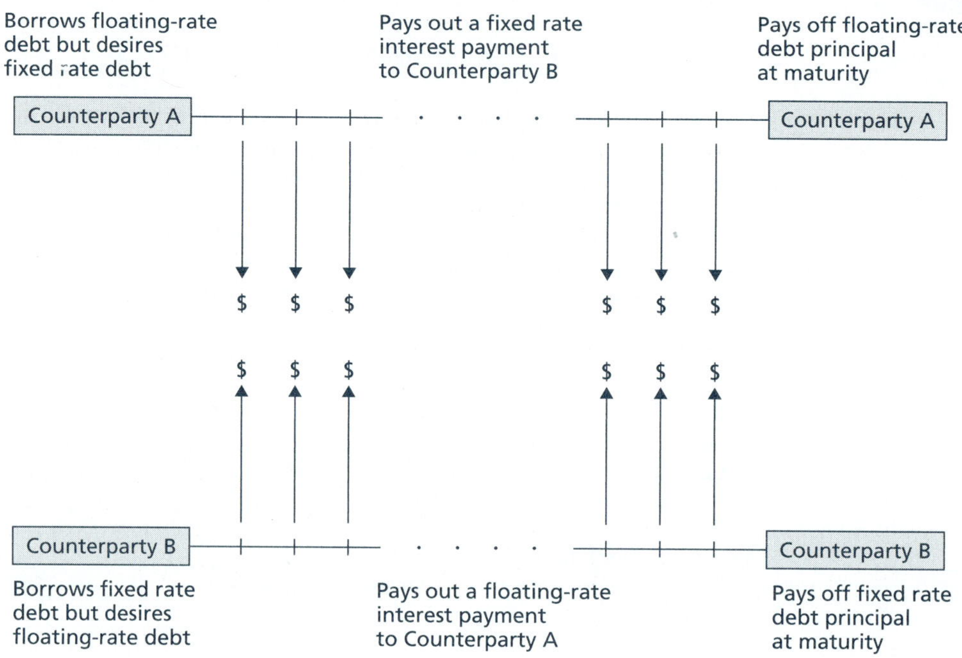


Party A paying, effectively, a fixed rate of interest. Party B can apply the receipt of the fixed rate interest payment to the interest due on its fixed rate liabilities effectively leaving it paying a floating rate of interest. Thus, swaps have become a very effective way for firms to manage their interest rate exposure.

One of the main characteristics of an interest rate swap is that the principal amount does not change hands. Rather, only interest payments are swapped, and the payments are based on an agreed upon notional amount of principal.

## Why Swaps Work

Swaps work because of the ability to share the comparative advantage counterparties may have in their own respective market places. The theory of comparative advantage was originally advanced in the international trade area and explained how two countries could both be better off by specializing in those products in which they had a comparative advantage and then trading among themselves to acquire those products they individually did not produce.

The same concept works for corporations in the capital markets. For example, suppose two companies have the same credit rating such as AAA or AA. One may receive a slightly lower borrowing rate in the short-term market because it may tap the short-term market more often and therefore be more familiar to investors. The other firm may tap the longer-term market more often and thus receive a slightly preferential borrowing rate with longer maturities.

These pricing discrepancies create opportunities for corporations to take advantage of these variations and share the cost savings. Because each firm borrows in the market it has a comparative advantage, it can trade a portion of that advantage with a counterparty and both companies can reduce their borrowing costs or enhance their investment returns.

We now discuss two basic categories of interest rate swaps including asset or investment swaps and liability or financing swaps.

### Interest Rate Asset Swap

Suppose that an institution such as a thrift or savings and loan association has a portfolio of fixed rate investments such as mortgages. Further, assume that the institution's primary source of financing carries a variable rate or has such a short maturity relative to the maturity of the investment portfolio of mortgages that the interest expense is essentially variable. The institution has a problem if interest rates begin to rise, because the interest receipts from the mortgage portfolio are fixed but the interest that must be paid on its liabilities increases as market rates rise.

The institution's problem would be solved if it could pay out, or *swap* the fixed rate interest receipts in exchange for a receipt of variable rate interest payments. This type of swap is referred to as a fixed-for-floating swap and was one of the first types of interest rate swaps to be developed. These swaps have three basic cash flows to consider. First, the institution has the investment rate, *ir*, that is being received from the original investment. Second, there is the swap outflow, *so*, which is the interest rate that the institution agrees to pay to the other party, the counterparty. Finally, there is the swap inflow, *si*, which is the interest rate that will be received from the counterparty. If *ir* is fixed, as in our example, the *so* is also fixed because the institution is merely passing the interest received, or some portion of it, on to the counterparty. Further, *si* is a variable rate payment from the counterparty. As a result, the institution is essentially receiving a variable rate of interest.

Exhibit 18–10 presents a summary of these transactions. In this example, Counterparty A has a comparative or relative advantage in fixed rate investments and Counterparty B has a comparative advantage in floating-rate investments. Counterparty A takes advantage of its higher fixed rates and passes those rates on to Counterparty B. Counterparty B takes advantage of its higher floating rates and passes that advantage on to Counterparty A.

The effective rate from the swap, $k_{swap}$, is equal to the original *ir* minus the *so* plus the *si*. The effective rate from the swap can then be compared to the alternative rate in each institution's respective market to verify that indeed the swap was able to yield a better return than could be obtained otherwise. Note that the swap expression, $k_{swap}$, also deducts for any fee percentage that the clearing bank or institution may charge for helping to manage the swap flows. In this example, as long as the fee is less than 0.5 percent per year, the swap is advantageous to both parties.

### Interest Rate Liability Swap

A **liability swap** is similar in structure to the **asset swap** just discussed except that the counterparties are trying to manage the interest rate risk of their liabilities rather than their

**Exhibit 18–10**

*The Basic Structure of an Asset Swap*

| | Alternative Interest Rates in the Home Market | |
|---|---|---|
| | Counterparty A | Counterparty B |
| Fixed: | 9% | 8% |
| Variable: | LIBOR | LIBOR + 0.5% |
| ir: | 9% | LIBOR + 0.5% |
| so: | 9% | LIBOR + 0.5% |
| si: | LIBOR + 0.5% | 9% |
| | $k_{swap}$ = ir − so + si − fee | ir − so + si − fee |
| | $k_{swap}$ = LIBOR + 0.5% − fee | 9% − fee |

assets. To see how a liability swap is structured, assume that Counterparty A can finance at relatively low variable rates compared to Counterparty B, but its fixed rates are relatively higher. Further assume that Counterparty A desires to finance using fixed rate financing.

The institution's problem will be solved if it issues the relatively cheaper variable rate liabilities and receives variable rate payments from the counterparty in exchange for fixed rate payments. Just like the asset swaps discussed earlier, liability swaps also have three basic cash flows to consider. First, there is the financing rate, *fr,* that is being paid on the original liability. Second, there is the swap outflow, *so,* which is the interest rate that the institution agrees to pay to the other party, the counterparty. Finally, there is the swap inflow, *si,* which is the interest rate that will be received from the counterparty. If the *fr* is variable, as in our example, the *si* will also be variable since this is the cash flow that the firm will use to pay the interest payment on the original debt, and the *so* will be fixed because Counterparty A desires to net out fixed rate financing. As a result, the firm is essentially paying a fixed rate of interest.

Exhibit 18–11 presents these transactions for a liability swap. In this example, Counterparty A has a comparative advantage in floating-rate liabilities, while Counterparty B has a comparative advantage in fixed rate liabilities. Counterparty A takes advantage of its lower variable rate financing and passes this rate on to Counterparty B. Counterparty B takes advantage of its lower fixed rate financing and passes that advantage on to Counterparty A.

The effective rate from the swap, $k_{swap}$, is equal to the original *fr* plus the *so* minus the *si.* The effective rate from the swap can then be compared to the alternative rate in each institution's respective market to verify that indeed the swap was able to yield a better financing cost than could be obtained otherwise. Note that $k_{swap}$ also accounts for any fee percentage that the clearing bank or institution may charge for helping to manage the swap flows. In this case, the fee rate represents an addition to the cost of financing.

### Exhibit 18–11

*The Basic Structure of a Liability Swap*

| | Alternative Interest Rates in the Home Market | |
|---|---|---|
| | Counterparty A | Counterparty B |
| Fixed: | 9% | 8% |
| Variable: | LIBOR | LIBOR + 0.5% |
| fr: | LIBOR | 8% |
| so: | 8% | LIBOR |
| si: | LIBOR | 8% |
| | $k_{swap}$ = fr + so − si + fee | fr + so − si + fee |
| | $k_{swap}$ = 8.0% + fee | LIBOR + fee |

## FINANCIAL DILEMMA

What Can Be Done about Uncertain Currency Exchange Rates?

The Body Shop, Ltd., is a retail operation focusing on body care products produced from natural sources. The company was founded in the United Kingdom and found quick success with the consumer public. The company began expansion in the U.S. consumer skin care market during the early 1990s. To fund the expansion, the company should attempt to find dollar-based financing since its earnings will be in dollars but the company is not well-known outside the U.K. If it borrows in the United Kingdom, it will face exchange rate exposure converting its dollar earnings to pounds sterling to service its sterling debt. How can the company manage the exchange rate risk of expansion into the U.S. market?

## Foreign Currency Swap

A **currency swap** is an agreement between two parties to exchange different currencies and then to re-exchange them at a future date at the same exchange rate. Periodic interest payments are made during the term of the swap.

A currency swap involves three distinct cash flows, as shown in Exhibit 18–12. First, there is the initial exchange of principal amounts. Second is the exchange of interest payments over the course of the borrowings. Third is the final exchange, or re-exchange, of principals in their respective currencies.

For example, suppose a U.K. retailer wants to expand its operations in the U.S. market. It will sell its products in the United States for dollars and thus wants to borrow dollars to fund the expansion. Although it may be a well-known credit in the United Kingdom, the firm may be a relative unknown in the U.S. financial markets and thus borrowing may be at relatively high rates. The U.K. retailer may therefore borrow in pounds sterling in the United Kingdom, where it is a better known credit, and exchange the pounds sterling for U.S. dollars borrowed by a U.S. firm that was looking to borrow pounds sterling. The two firms initially swap currencies, generally through an intermediary, at the current exchange rate. Over the life of the swap agreement, the U.S. firm pays the U.K. firm's interest payments in pounds sterling, and the U.K. firm pays the U.S. firm's interest payments in dollars. At the end of the swap agreement period, the two firms re-exchange principals at the original spot exchange rate.

## FINANCIAL DILEMMA REVISITED

Recall the Body Shop dilemma described earlier A currency swap arrangement is an ideal exchange rate risk management vehicle for the firm to consider. First, the financial manager at the Body Shop borrows pounds sterling in the United Kingdom. The pounds sterling can then be swapped for dollars with a counterparty in the United States. The two firms then agree to pay each other's interest payments and finally agree to swap back the principal amounts at the same exchange rate that existed at the time of the swap origina-

Exhibit 18–12

*Cash Flows of a Currency Swap*

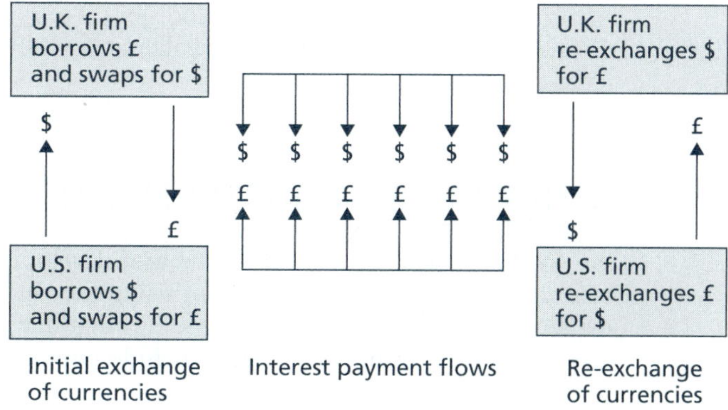

## FOCUS ON PRACTICE

### *What Derivatives Are Used in Practice?*

The following derivative usage was compiled by Treasury & Risk Management's 2001 Derivatives Survey:

| Derivative Type | Used by X% of Respondents |
|---|---|
| Interest rate swaps | 69% |
| Foreign exchange forwards | 67 |
| OTC foreign exchange options | 39 |
| OTC interest rate options | 32 |
| Exchange traded interest rate futures or options | 22 |
| Energy derivatives | 18 |
| Exchange traded FX futures or options | 18 |
| OTC equity swaps or options | 16 |
| Credit derivatives | 14 |
| OTC commodity swaps or options, other than energy derivatives | 13 |

*Source:* Lewis Knox, "Life Under the Thumb of FAS 133," *Treasury & Risk Management* (October 2001), pp. 49–52.

tion. The Body Shop uses its dollar earnings in the United States to service the dollar interest payment flows.

Let's now put some numbers to this example to better see how it works. Suppose that the Body Shop can borrow pounds at 10 percent and borrow dollars in the United States at 12 percent because of its lack of exposure in the U.S. market. Further assume that its U.S. counterparty can borrow dollars at 11 percent. The current exchange rate is $1.70 per pound sterling. The principal amount involved is $25 million or 14,705,882 pounds sterling. The Body Shop borrows the 14.7 million pounds sterling and swaps it for the $25 million, which is the dollar amount of funding it needs for the U.S. expansion effort. The Body Shop agrees to pay the 11-percent interest in dollars, while the U.S. counterparty agrees to pay the 10-percent interest in pounds. At the end of the swap period, the two firms exchange principal; the Body Shop receives 14.7 million pounds sterling and the U.S. counterparty receives $25 million. The advantage to the Body Shop is that it effectively borrowed dollars at 11 percent rather than the 12 percent available to it through the traditional U.S. credit market. In addition, it can now use its dollar earnings to service dollar-denominated debt, thus neutralizing its foreign currency exposure related to its financing needs.

## OTHER HEDGING INSTRUMENTS

You will probably agree by this time that developing appropriate hedging strategies can be a very complex task. Rather than using futures and options directly, some corporate treasurers take advantage of new products that have been developed from options but are not as complex. Examples of these include interest rate caps, interest rate floors, and interest rate collars.

## Interest Rate Caps

An **interest rate cap** is marketed by institutions such as commercial banks, which stand ready to buy and sell interest rate caps. The interest rate cap contract specifies:

- the reference rate (such as the Treasury bill, LIBOR, eurodollar, commercial paper, or even the certificate of deposit rate),
- the strike rate (the rate level at which payments begin to be made to offset adverse rate movements),
- a notional amount of principal (the dollar amount on which the rate is based), and
- the term (generally from one to 10 years, but can be as short as three months).

The purchaser of a rate cap pays a premium up front, much like an option, and will receive cash payments from the rate cap seller whenever the reference rate exceeds the strike rate. The calculation for the cash payment is relatively simple as shown in Equation 18.6.

$$\text{Cap payment} = (\text{ref} - \text{strk}) \times \text{NP} \times \text{L} \tag{18.6}$$

Where:

$$\begin{aligned} \text{ref} &= \text{Reference rate} \\ \text{strk} &= \text{Strike rate} \\ \text{NP} &= \text{Notional principal} \\ \text{L} &= \text{Length of the payment period} \end{aligned}$$

For example, suppose a bank investment officer wishes to purchase a rate cap that limited the bank's exposure to interest rate increases on its variable rate certificates of deposit (CDs). Assume that the reference rate is an index of CD rates that now stands at 10 percent. Further, assume that the strike rate is 9.50 percent and the notional principal is $10 million. Assuming the payment period is for six months (half a year or $L = 0.5$), the cash payment received from the rate seller is:

$$\begin{aligned} \text{Cash payment} &= (0.10 - 0.0950) \times \$10{,}000{,}000 \times 0.5 \\ \text{Cash payment} &= \$25{,}000 \end{aligned}$$

Ocean Spray Cranberries, Inc., traditionally uses short-term financing to finance its seasonal working capital needs. During its peak season in the fall, Ocean Spray finances its expanding working capital with seasonal borrowings until it sells the bulk of its products during the Thanksgiving season. Its receipts are then used to pay off its seasonal financing. However, during the late 1980s, the company was hit hard by rising short-term rates. The company decided to protect itself against adverse rate movements by using interest rate caps. Ocean Spray hedged half of its estimated seasonal borrowing needs by purchasing a 2-year interest rate cap at a 10.5-percent maximum rate, the strike rate in Equation 18.6, to cover a 2-year operating period.[9]

Ocean Spray chose to use a cap rather than an interest rate floor or collar, which will be discussed later, because the company simply wanted insurance against upward rate spikes, not an assurance of a specific or set rate.

## Interest Rate Floor

An **interest rate floor** works in a similar fashion to a rate cap except that it is used to place a lower limit on the selected interest rate. The rate floor purchaser will pay a premium for

[9] For additional details, see Peter D. Hanson, "How Ocean Spray Trims the Risks of Seasonal Borrowing," *CORPORATE CASHFLOW* (May 1990), p. 58.

the rate floor contract and then receive from the rate floor seller a cash payment whenever the reference rate falls below the striking rate. The calculation for the cash payment is the same as for the rate cap with the variables *ref* and *strk* reversed as shown in Equation 18.7.

$$\text{Floor payment} = (\text{strk} - \text{ref}) \times \text{NP} \times \text{L} \tag{18.7}$$

### Interest Rate Collar

Rate caps and floors can be combined to form what are called **interest rate collars.** To create a rate collar, the user would purchase a rate cap and sell or issue a rate floor. The premium received from issuing the rate floor is used to offset the cost of the rate cap. If the reference rate exceeds the strike rate on the cap, then a cash payment is received. If the reference rate falls below the strike rate on the floor, then a cash payment is made to the purchaser of the floor. Thus, the effective interest rate is managed within a narrow bound determined by the strike rate on the cap and floor contracts.

Exhibit 18–13 demonstrates how a collar works over a range of interest rates. Assume that the financial manager of a large financial institution wished to form an interest rate collar on its CD cost essentially forming a maximum borrowing rate of 9.5 percent and a minimum borrowing rate of 9 percent. In the exhibit, the strike rate for the interest rate cap is 9.5 percent, and the strike rate for the interest rate floor is 9 percent. The notional amount on which the cash payments are based is $1 million, and the period is one year. If the reference rate is 8 percent, then the financial manager makes a cash payment to the floor purchaser of $10,000. No cash payments are made if the reference rate is between 9 percent and 9.5 percent. If the reference rate rises to 10 percent, then the financial manager receives a $5,000 cash payment from the cap seller. The cash payments received compensate the financial institution for the rates rising above the strike rate and essentially capping the effective cost of its CDs at 9.5 percent. The cash payments paid by the financial institution in essence keep the effective rate of the CDs at a minimum rate of 9 percent.

One example of a business application involving an interest rate collar was a transaction involving the business background music company Muzak, Inc. The company decided to take advantage of an interest rate collar to lock in or stabilize its borrowing rate

**Exhibit 18-13**

*An Example of the Cash Payments Related to an Interest Rate Collar*

Cap strike rate = 9.5%
Floor strike rate = 9.0%
Notional amount = $1,000,000
Period = 1 year

| REF | Cap Payment | Floor Payment | Effective Rate |
|---|---|---|---|
| 0.0800 | $ 0 | $10,000 | 0.0900 |
| 0.0850 | 0 | 5,000 | 0.0900 |
| 0.0900 | 0 | 0 | 0.0900 |
| 0.0950 | 0 | 0 | 0.0950 |
| 0.1000 | 5,000 | 0 | 0.0950 |
| 0.1050 | 10,000 | 0 | 0.0950 |
| 0.1100 | 20,000 | 0 | 0.0950 |

Effective Rate = REF + [(Floor payment − Cap payment)/Notional amount]

over the coming two years.[10] The treasury officials at Muzak mainly wanted protection from rising rates but decided to utilize a collar in order to reduce the effective cost of the cap. They paid an up-front premium to purchase the cap but received a premium by selling or issuing an interest rate floor. As a result, Muzak was protected from rate increases over the negotiated strike rate and was willing to forego the benefits if rates declined in order to reduce the up-front cost of the transaction.

These interest rate management contracts have gained due to the reduced complexities they offer the financial manager.

## REGULATORY ISSUES

FAS 133 and its amending statement, FAS 138, went into effect for all companies with fiscal years beginning after June 15, 2000. This will be followed by the introduction of International Accounting Standard (IAS) 39 in January 2005. These guidelines require hedges to be marked-to-market instead of reported at historical cost and that gains and losses on the derivatives be included in earnings when they cannot be shown to effectively hedge an exposure. The problem for the corporation is that these changes are recorded without offsetting changes to the value of the currency being hedged *unless* the transaction can be defined to be a qualifying hedge. For nonqualifying hedges, this exposes the company's financial statements to potential volatility. As a result, many financial managers are reassessing their hedging strategies. Four key rules form the backbone of FAS 133:[11]

- All stand-alone and qualifying embedded derivatives must be marked-to-market and reported on the balance sheet.
- The gain or loss on changes in the value of the derivative must be reported immediately in earnings unless the derivative is part of a qualifying hedge. To qualify, the hedge must satisfy rigorous criteria regarding its effectiveness.
- If the hedge passes the qualifying test but is not 100 percent perfect, the amount by which it is not perfect must be reported on the income statement.
- Companies must fully describe their derivative and hedging activities in the footnotes to their financial statements.

Treasurers have three alternatives to choose from in reacting to these new reporting requirements. First, they may elect to simply not hedge. Of course, this should be a strategic decision that considers potential competitive implications of their firm versus the industry. Second, treasurers may elect to continue to hedge but simply not use hedge accounting. They would therefore avoid the costs associated with compliance but likely suffer increased earnings volatility due to the necessity to mark-to-market the price changes of the derivative instruments without being able to offset this with price changes in the underlying instrument being hedged. Finally, the treasurer may use hedge accounting to reduce earnings volatility while incurring the compliance cost.

Prior to FAS 133, accounting for foreign exchange hedging activities was based on a series of accounting standards such as FAS 52 and 80. As a result, hedge accounting practices were widely varied and derivative losses could easily be hidden.

Because of the complexity of complying with the FAS 133 guidelines, several software vendors and consulting firms have established Web sites that provide help for corporate treasurers. For example, PricewaterhouseCoopers formed a business in

[10] For additional details on the Muzak transaction, see Lori Kuo Dillon and Marshall A. Blake, "How Muzak Stays in Tune with Interest Rate," *CORPORATE CASHFLOW* (March 1990), p. 41.

[11] Jeffrey Wallace, "Foreign Exchange Hedging under FAS 133," *AFP Exchange* (Fall 2000), pp. 50–59.

partnership with Gifford Fong Associates. They offer their clients an Application Service Provider tool that gives companies the ability to document hedges, allows one-to-one and many-to-many hedge relationships, archives historic market values and effectiveness, flags hedge types at inception, marks derivatives hedges to market, assesses the prospective effectiveness of derivatives, measures actual effectiveness, and prepares compliant FAS 133 reports.[12]

In 2002, the Association for Financial Professionals (AFP) conducted a survey of its members to determine the impact that this new accounting standard was having on the hedging practices of corporations.[13] A summary of the primary conclusions include:

- While over 60 percent of the respondents indicate they use derivatives to hedge interest rate and currency exposure, only a third of the respondents indicated they hedge commodity prices.
- While 70 percent of the respondents indicated their use of derivatives had not changed as a result of FAS 133, the survey did note lower levels of hedging activity for most of the derivative tools and strategies compared to an earlier survey.
- Nearly half of the respondents indicated that complying with FAS 133 rules is excessively burdensome even though there is a strong preference for the use of the simplest types of hedges.
- While companies generally use hedge accounting, a significant minority indicated they have forgone hedge accounting on significant portions of their derivative positions.

## SUMMARY

This chapter discussed several different approaches to managing exposure to changes in interest rates and currency exchange rates. These include futures contracts, options, swaps, caps, floors, and collars. Each of the alternative contracts has their own advantages and disadvantages. Thus, the financial manager needs to be aware of all possible alternatives and choose that strategy which best matches the needs and situation of the firm.

Financial risk management is one area that is constantly changing with new strategies and contracts being created continuously. It is imperative that the financial manager stays abreast of the latest developments to best manage the firm's exposure to changes in interest rates and exchange rates.

## USEFUL WEB SITES

| | |
|---|---|
| Chicago Mercantile Exchange | **http://www.cme.com** |
| Futures Magazine, Inc. | **http://www.futuresmag.com** |
| The Publisher of International Treasurer | **http://www.fas133.com** |
| The Gifford Fong Associates | **http://www.solution133.com** |

---

[12] Steve Bergsman, "133 Help on the Web," *Treasury & Risk Management* (December/January 2001), p. 15.

[13] "The Impact of FAS 133 on the Risk Management Practices of End Users of Derivatives," *Association for Financial Professionals* (September 2002). Also see "Natural Performers," *CFO* (June 2003), pp. 37–39.

## QUESTIONS

1. Explain the difference between a speculator and a hedger.
2. Explain in your own words what is meant by hedging.
3. How are futures options different from futures contracts? What are the relative advantages and disadvantages?
4. Why don't hedgers write options on futures?
5. Why should a hedger using futures contracts generally use the nearby contract?
6. What risks are assumed by the counterparties in a swap transaction?
7. Explain the transactions required to create an interest rate collar. Explain how a collar can stabilize the firm's borrowing rate.
8. Explain how a collar stabilizing an investment rate would be different from a collar designed to stabilize a financing rate.
9. How is a forward contract like a futures contract and how is it different?
10. Compare and contrast futures contracts, futures options, and options.

## PROBLEMS

1. As treasurer of CCM, Inc., part of your job is to invest short-term funds. Your cash budget forecast indicates the firm will generate $10 million of surplus funds in two months which is March 1. The funds can be invested for 90 days. The current cash market 90-day rate on Treasury bills is 5.50 percent, and the current futures rate on 90-day Treasury bills is 5.70 percent. Your investment company requires $2,000 of initial margin per $1 million contract and the roundtrip commission rate is $100.
   a. Assume that in two months, the 90-day cash rate rises to 6 percent and the 90-day futures rate rises to 6 percent. What is the net position from the hedge?
   b. Assume that in two months, the 90-day cash rate falls to 5 percent and the 90-day futures rate falls to 5 percent. What is the net position from the hedge?
   c. Rework **a** and **b** assuming that the denomination of the futures contract is $1 million but you plan to invest $10 million and that the only futures contract available is for 180-day Treasury bills. Substitute 180-day futures for 90-day futures in **a** and **b**, and use the same rates as before.
2. Your firm has been a net borrower of commercial paper for several months. You are preparing a new $20 million issue of 180-day commercial paper, and the current cash market rate is 5.5 percent. The futures rate on a comparable instrument is 5.75 percent. You plan to issue the paper in two weeks, but given the recent volatility in the money market, you are uncertain of the rate the paper will be priced at upon issuance. Assume that margin is $1,500 per futures contract, the contract denomination is $0.5 million, and the roundtrip commission rate is $100 per contract.
   a. Assume that cash rates are 6.5 percent at issuance in two weeks and the futures contract rate is 6.75 percent. What is the net position of the hedge?
   b. Assume that cash rates are 5 percent at issuance in two weeks and the futures contract rate is 5.25 percent. What is the net position of the hedge?
3. You have been pursuing some rather risky money market investment strategies, and as a result, have been burned more than once. You recently came across an article describing hedging techniques using financial futures contracts and wondered how these might apply to a riding the yield curve strategy.

   Suppose that the current cash rate on 180-day Treasury bills is 5.30 percent and 5.00 percent on 90-day bills. The futures rates on 90-day Treasury bills is currently 5.20 percent. You invest in a 180-day bill today and sell it in 90 days when it becomes a 90-day bill. Rates on

90-day cash bills are 5.25 percent at the time of sale. Assume that the rate on a 90-day Treasury bill futures contract is 5.30 percent in 90 days. If you invest $1 million and the futures contract denomination is $1 million, the commission rate is $100, and the margin is $2,000 per contract, then what is the net position resulting from the hedge? How does this result compare if you had not hedged? How does the original result compare to having invested in a 90-day cash T-bill?

**4.** The treasurer of ABCO, Inc., is making plans to invest in $12 million, face value, of 90-day Treasury bills on June 1, 30 days from today. The current cash rate on 90-day bills is 4.38 percent, and the June 90-day futures contract settled at a discount rate of 4.58 percent. She would like to hedge her 30-day exposure until she can make the investment and chooses to use a 90-day Treasury bill futures option. The contract size is $1 million. The striking price she chooses for the June call option is 9400, and the premium is stated as 0.50 pts. per 100 percent.

**a.** Assume that rates on 90-day cash bills increase to 5.70 percent by June 1. At the same time, assume that the futures rate increased to 5.79 percent and the premium on the options contract falls to 0.21. What would be the net result of the hedge?

**b.** Assume that rates on 90-day cash bills fall to 5.00 percent by June 1. At the same time, assume that the futures rate falls to 5.09 percent and the premium on the options contract rises to 91 basis points. What would be the net result of the hedge?

**5.** The treasurer of COMCO, Inc., is making plans to issue $5 million of 90-day commercial paper on June 1, 30 days from today. The current cash rate on 90-day paper is 5.38 percent, and the June 90-day futures contract settled at a discount rate of 5.47 percent. She would like to hedge her 30-day exposure until she can make the investment and chooses to use a 90-day Treasury bill futures option. The contract size is $1 million. The striking price she chooses for the June put option is 9500, and the premium is stated as 0.47 pts. per 100 percent.

**a.** Assume that rates on 90-day paper increase to 5.70 percent by June 1. At the same time, assume that the futures rate increased to 5.79 percent and the premium on the options contract rises to 0.79. What would be the net result of the hedge?

**b.** Assume that rates on 90-day paper fall to 5.3 percent by June 1. At the same time, assume that the futures rate falls to 5.39 percent and the premium on the option contract falls to 0.39. What would be the net result of the hedge?

**6.** OSO, Inc., is concerned about its long-term interest rate exposure. Its bank has just proposed entering into a swap arrangement with ESSEX, Inc., who also has an unfavorable exposure to interest rate risk. OSO desires floating-rate financing, while ESSEX is looking for fixed rate financing. The following table presents the interest rate opportunities available to each company in their own market places.

| | OSO, Inc. | ESSEX, Inc. |
|---|---|---|
| Fixed rate | 8% | 9% |
| Floating rate | LIBOR + 1.5% | LIBOR + 1.75% |

The bank recommends that OSO arrange fixed rate financing at the 8-percent rate, while ESSEX arranges floating-rate financing at its LIBOR + 1.75 percent. Then OSO pays LIBOR + 0.5 percent to ESSEX, and ESSEX pays 7.5 percent to OSO. Assume the notional amount is for $100 million.

**a.** What is the effective annual rate from the swap for each company?

**b.** How much of a fee could the bank charge each party for the swap to just break even (assume the fee rate must be the same to each firm)?

**7.** You are currently in the midst of a swap contract negotiation with a counterparty. You need variable rate financing, and the counterparty is looking for fixed rate financing.

| | Your Market | Counterparty's Market |
|---|---|---|
| Fixed rates | 7% | 8% |
| Floating rates | T-bill + 1% | T-bill + 0.5% |

Please provide the following:

**a.** What type of financing rate should you lock in at the current time (fixed or floating)? Explain why.

**b.** What type of swap outflow rate should you agree to (fixed or floating)? Explain why.

**c.** What type of swap inflow rate should you agree to (fixed or floating)? Explain why.

**8.** Rail Transport, Inc., is concerned about its interest rate exposure. Its investment bank has just proposed entering into a swap arrangement with Agriproducts, Inc., who also has an unfavorable exposure to interest rate risk. Rail Transport desires a floating investment rate, while Agriproducts is looking for fixed rate investments. The following table presents the interest rate opportunities available to each company in their own market places.

| | Rail Transport, Inc. | Agriproducts, Inc. |
|---|---|---|
| Fixed rates | 7% | 6.3% |
| Floating rates | T-bill +1.5% | T-bill + 1.75% |

The investment bank recommends that Rail Transport invest in the fixed rate instrument at 7 percent, while Agriproducts invest at its current floating rate of T-bill + 1.75 percent. Then Rail Transport should pay 7 percent to Agriproducts, and Agriproducts should pay T-bill + 1.75 percent to Rail Transport. Assume the notional amount is for $50 million. What is the effective annual rate from the swap?

**9.** XYZ, Inc., is concerned about its long-term interest rate exposure to its fixed rate bond portfolio. Current rates are historically low, and the firm anticipates that they will rise. XYZ could go liquid by simply selling the bonds. However, the firm's investment banker recently introduced the idea of an interest rate swap. XYZ purchased the 7-year fixed rate bonds as a new issue three years ago priced at par with a coupon rate of 12 percent. The current year bid rate on 4-year bonds is 11 percent.

The investment bank has indicated that a swap is possible with an unidentified counterparty for XYZ to pay an 11-percent fixed rate to the counterparty and receive a variable interest payment of LIBOR. What is the effective annual rate XYZ would receive from the swap? What benefits are provided by the swap arrangement?

**10.** TRKY, Inc., is a firm that grows and sells turkeys. The business is highly seasonal with 80 percent of its revenues generated during the Thanksgiving season. The firm relies heavily on commercial paper to finance its seasonal working capital needs. The financial manager of TRKY, Inc., is considering the use of an interest rate cap to protect the firm from an increase in borrowing costs. The notional amount is $10 million, and the strike rate is set at 10 percent over an effective period of six months.

Estimate the cash payments for reference rates of 9 percent, 10 percent, and 11 percent.

**11.** The financial manager of Floor-Mart finds the company in a $10 million cash surplus position and wishes to protect its short-term investment portfolio from dropping interest rates. The financial manager would like to create an interest rate floor on the firm's commercial paper investments. Assume the strike rate is 7.5 percent and the notional amount is $10 million. The protection period is set for six months.

Estimate the cash payments related to the floor for reference rates of 7 percent, 8 percent, and 9 percent.

**12.** Suppose the financial manager of ACE, Inc., wished to form an interest rate collar. Explain the transactions that ACE's financial manager could negotiate with the firm's bank assuming that she did not want her effective borrowing rate to range outside of a 1-percent band with a high of 9.5 percent and a low of 8.5 percent.

**13.** You recently sold some goods to an importer in Switzerland and during the negotiations you agreed to invoice the goods in francs, knowing that you will need to convert the francs to dollars upon receipt. The current exchange rate is $0.60 per franc, and the invoice will be for 250,000 francs. Payment is due in 60 days. You decide to hedge your exposure using futures contracts.

**a.** How many futures contracts will you need?

**b.** Will you create a buy hedge or a sell hedge?

**c.** What will your spot market position be if the spot exchange rate is $0.70 in 60 days?

**d.** What will your futures contract gain or loss be if the futures rate, which is currently $0.63, increases to $0.71?

**e.** Assume that one futures contract has a commission rate of $25 and the margin is $1,000 per contract. The current money market interest rate is 7 percent. What is the net position resulting from the hedge, and how does the hedged position compare with an unhedged position?

**14.** As manager of a U.S. domestic company, you are concerned about the foreign currency exposure of your firm's sales to the United Kingdom. You currently export $10 million of products to the United Kingdom annually and receive payment in pounds sterling. You send two large shipments each year valued at $5 million each. The invoice carries net 90-day terms. Thus, from the invoice date, your company is exposed to currency exchange risk for a period of 90 days.

You are considering the possibility of using futures, options, or futures options as possible hedging tools. Your broker recently sent you the following data on the various hedging contracts available for your June 1 invoice with payment due September 1.

Current exchange rate (June 1) $1.67 per pound

Assumed spot exchange rate on September 1 is $2.00

90-day forward rate as of June 1: $1.65

Options (31,250)

| Striking price | June 1, September Call Premium | Call Premium September 1 |
|---|---|---|
| 165.0 | 4.35 | 35.00 |
| 170.0 | 2.40 | 30.00 |
| 175 | 1.20 | 25.00 |

Futures options (62,500)

| Striking Price | June 1, September Call Premium | Call Premium September 1 |
|---|---|---|
| 1650 | 4.12 | 33.00 |
| 1700 | 2.20 | 27.00 |
| 1750 | 1.06 | 22.00 |

Futures (62,500)

| | June 1 Settle | September 1 Settle |
|---|---|---|
| September | 1.6496 | 2.055 |

**a.** Assume you don't hedge. Calculate the dollar loss occurring from the change in exchange rates from June 1 to September 1.

**b.** Assume you hedge with an options contract. Calculate the net result from the change in the exchange rate from June 1 to September 1. Assume commission fees equal $60.

**c.** Assume you hedge with a futures option contract. Calculate the net result from the change in the exchange rate from June 1 to September 1. Assume commission fees equal $60.

**d.** Assume you hedge with a futures contract. Calculate the net result from the hedge assuming that margin for one contract is $1,000 and roundtrip commission fees equal $60.

**e.** Assume you enter into a 90-day forward rate agreement. Calculate the net result from the hedge assuming that the fee for the agreement is $150.

## REFERENCES


Raj Aggarwal, "Assessing Risks in Interest-Rate Swaps: The Role of Legal and Institutional Uncertainties," *Journal of Cash Management* (May/June 1991), pp. 15–18.

Raj Aggarwal and Luc A. Soenen, "Corporate Use of Options and Futures in Foreign Exchange Management, *Journal of Cash Management* (November/December 1989), pp. 61–66.

Robert Baldoni and Gerhard Isele, "A Simple Guide to Choosing Between Futures and Swaps," *INTERMARKET* (October 1986), pp. 15–22.

James Bicksler and Andrew H. Chen, "An Economic Analysis of Interest Rate Swaps," *The Journal of Finance* (July 1986), pp. 645–655.

Stanley B. Block and Timothy J. Gallagher, "The Use of Interest Rate Futures and Options by Corporate Financial Managers," *Financial Management* (Autumn 1986), pp. 73–78.

Theodore Brauch, "An Interest Rate Swap Primer," *Journal of Cash Management* (July/August 1993), pp. 8–14.

*Commodity Trading Manual*, Chicago Board of Trade (1989).

Mark Cook, "Foreign Exchange Management at Blount, Inc." *TMA Journal* (January/February 1995), pp. 30–32.

Richard Filler, "Credit Risks and Costs in Interest Rate Swaps," *Journal of Cash Management* (January/February 1993), pp. 38–41.

Brian Genreau, "Interest-Rate and Currency Swaps," *Commercial Lending Review* (Vol.4/No.4), pp. 47–54.

Benoit J. Jadoul and Charles M. Seeger, "Hedging Currency Risk," *TMA Journal* (November/December 1994), pp. 38–44.

Ira G. Kawaller, "How and Why to Hedge a Short-Term Portfolio," *Journal of Cash Management* (January/February 1985), pp. 26–30.

Ira G. Kawaller, "Interest Rate Swaps: A Primer . . . and a Caution," *AFP Exchange*, (March/April 2003), pp. 50–53.

Ira G. Kawaller, " What Every Treasurer Needs to Know About Interest Rate Risk," *TMA Journal* (September/October 1994), pp. 14–20.

Eileen Klecka, "Understanding Financial Futures," *TMA Journal* (July/August 1994), pp. 49–53.

John F. Marshall and Kenneth R. Kapner, *Understanding Swap Finance* (Cincinnati, OH: South-Western Publishing Co., 1990).

A. S. Mello and J. E. Parson, "Maturity Structure of a Hedge Matters: Lessons From the Metallgesellshaft Debacle," *Journal of Applied Corporate Finance* (Spring 1995), pp. 106–118.

D. R. Nance, C. W. Smith, and C. W. Smithson, "On the Determinants of Corporate Hedging," *Journal of Finance* (March 1993), pp. 267–284.

Anita B. Pasmantier, "Hedging Foreign Exchange Exposure," *Journal of Cash Management* (November/December 1993), pp. 36–43.

A. L. Phillips, "1995 Derivatives Practices and Instruments Survey," *Financial Management* (May 1995), pp. 115–125.

Robert Richardson, "Developing and Implementing Corporate Foreign Exchange Policies and Procedures," *TMA Journal* (July/August 1994), pp. 18–21.

Donald J. Smith, "The Arithmetic of Financial Engineering," *Journal of Applied Corporate Finance* (Winter 1989), pp. 49–58.

Alan L. Tucker, *Financial Futures, Options, and Swaps* (West Publishing Company, 1991).

Stuart M. Turnbull, "Swaps: A Zero Sum Game?" *Financial Management* (Spring 1987), pp. 15–21.

CHAPTER

# 19

# Treasury Information Management

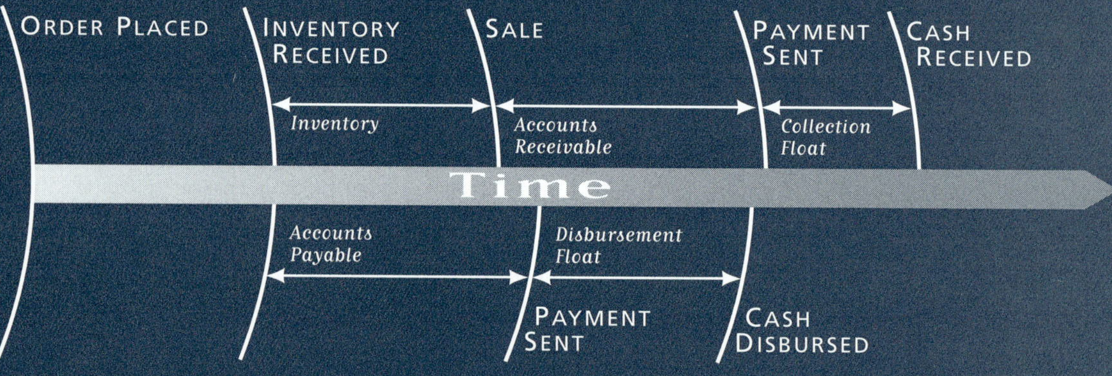

## OBJECTIVES

*After studying this chapter, you should be able to:*

- appreciate the benefits of e-commerce.
- understand what EDI is and the issues involved in its implementation.
- understand the benefits of applying the Internet to e-commerce.
- understand how treasury managers use information technology to make better financial decisions.
- understand the benefits of process outsourcing and benchmarking.

The management of information flows to create shareholder value is our final topic. The previous 18 chapters developed models for making financial decisions in all areas of short-term financial management including inventory, receivables, payables, cash, short-term investing, and short-term financing. Technology advances in information processing and analysis impact the management of all of these areas.

This chapter begins by outlining the basic information flows dealing with short-term financial management. We then turn to a discussion of electronic data interchange (EDI) and electronic commerce (EC). The continued development of information technology, along with the benchmarking and process outsourcing it enables, promises to have a greater impact on all phases of short-term financial management than did the level and volatility of interest rates from the mid-seventies to the mid-eighties. The impact of information technology will be long-term and process changing. The Focus on Practice box shows how companies such as Dreyer's Grand Ice Cream have benefited from integrated, electronic, automated information systems. We will see the cash flow timeline benefits at several points throughout this chapter. The chapter concludes with a section providing checklists auditing a company's financial information system and a brief discussion of treasury work stations and enterprise resource planning systems such as that used by Dreyer's.

## KEY INFORMATION FLOWS

Exhibit 19–1 shows the three levels of information needs in the financial management of the company. The first level is an operations level and deals with routine daily operations and cash management activities. These are daily information flows dealing with sales, receivables, inventory, and payables. In addition, the company's cash management area processes daily information regarding the reporting and verification of bank balances, cash concentration activities, reconciliation of outstanding payments and receivables with information received from the bank balances, development of the daily cash position, bank account analysis, and investment and financing portfolio transaction settlement and accounting.

This level of information flow is extremely important because it serves three critical functions:

- the updating of the company's general ledger accounts and a variety of sub-ledger systems;
- the receipt of timely information from the company's customers, suppliers, and the banking system; and
- verification of the information with the company's existing records.

The second level of information need is the management level. Rather than being primarily transaction oriented, the management level focuses on analysis and decision support. These information flows include the analysis of working capital accounts (receivables, inventory, and payables), finalizing the daily cash position, cash flow and cash balance forecasting, investment portfolio interest rate sensitivity and developing

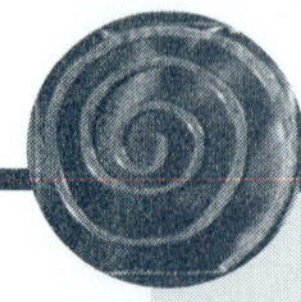

## FOCUS ON PRACTICE

### *Spoonful of Ice-Cold Sugar Helps the Automated Information Flow Down*

Dreyer's Grand Ice Cream, headquartered in Oakland, sold nearly $1.4 billion in premium and superpremium ice cream in 2001. Keeping track of the sales and expenses and all the purchasing, production, inventory, invoices, payments, marketing, accounting, finance, human resource, and other data flows that are necessary to make this ice cream is a monumental task liable to send chills down an Eskimo's spine. Dreyer's turned to its bank and software company, Oracle, to help it with these tasks. It implemented an enterprise resource planning (ERP) system as the main means of integrating its data flows. This spawned another problem: how to ensure that the bank lockbox personnel would properly interpret and key remittance advices so that payments would automatically apply in the ERP receivables software module. Attention to detail was the key—including carefully prepared detailed instructions, samples of the more complex invoices that might come to the bank, and personal training of bank lockbox clerks regarding how to interpret and code the invoices. The whole process worked extremely well according to a Dreyer's manager who commented, "...it also helps that we occasionally send ice cream gift certificates to the bank personnel who key in our remittances."

Dreyer's and other companies who have braved the challenges of automating and integrating electronically transmitted information have achieved at least four benefits: (1) automated cash application, avoiding rekeying of remittance data and having to manually match invoices to payments due to a "hit rate" as high as 91 percent of remittances; (2) improved liquidity management (rapid and accurate determination of the company's global cash position, due to more timely balance information—Nike's system automatically generates a 2-year cash forecast!); (3) improved productivity; and (4) reduced inventory (viewing customer payments online within hours of receipt allows orders to be released for shipment more quickly when customers are up against their credit limits).

---

*Source:* Bank of America, "ERP Solutions in a Working Capital World" (2002). Located online at **http://corp.bankofamerica.com/portal/portal/controller/controller.jsp?path=wcm/treas_srvcs/feat_art/content.xml.** Accessed 1/24/04.

new portfolio investment strategies or adjusting the current portfolio based on the assessed market trends.

Once the company's databases have been updated with new daily information, the company's forecasting model should be updated such that the current day's forecast can be audited and the variance between actual and forecast can be assessed. Then a new forecast for the future period can be generated. Investment and borrowing strategies can be tested on a what-if basis for different interest rate environments.

The third level of information flows is an executive level. The primary objective here is to provide senior management with timely information regarding the company's debt/investment management, the company's relationship with its banks, and its liquidity position.

While all three levels of information flow are important, this chapter will focus on the development of those systems that primarily affect the company's operations or Level 1 information flows. In the past, the majority of Level 1 information flows, including payments, were exchanged between companies using paper-based documents. Today, it is more common for these information and payment flows to be done electronically, a process

Exhibit 19–1

*Three Levels of Information Needs*

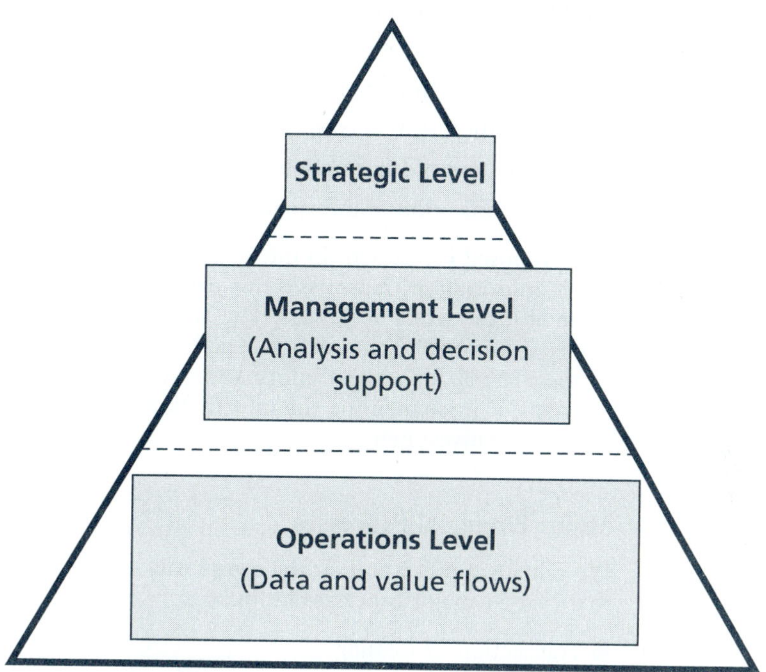


referred to as electronic commerce or **e-commerce.**[1] A subset of e-commerce, electronic data interchange (EDI) was initially created to apply electronic technology to create efficiencies in the movement of business information and payments. This system initially utilized proprietary systems of structured data formats to communicate between trading partners as well as with financial institutions. Now, the Internet is being utilized in an open system to create new and more efficient ways of transmitting information and payments. The label e-commerce will be used in a broad sense in this chapter to include EDI and electronic payments.

---

[1] There are various interpretations of these terms in industry. Some analysts use the term "e-commerce" to apply only to B2C or only to Web-based sales and related transactions, applying the term "e-business" to either B2B transactions or to the broader scope of electronic documents, trade data, and payments. A technical definition of e-business includes these items: "(1) E-business involves company-to-company trading activity and data exchange; (2) E-business activity often involves many line items per order, each with specific delivery confirmation dates, quantities, delivery points, and shipping methods; (3) E-business uses an interface that may provide user-selected information type/content/scope and associated interaction tools, reflecting the system's greater scale, scope, and depth of functionality; (4) E-business uses PO numbers, releases against blanket POs, and involves invoicing and payment methods; (5) E-business includes transactions using any or all EDI (electronic data interchange) protocols, Web-based screens, thin-client networks, browser screens presenting system displays and interaction, faxing, and automatic interception of electronic servicing by customer response teams; (6) E-business offers internal employee services, such as self-service access to personnel records, travel and expense reporting, and nonproduction procurement." Dave Monroe, Plant-Wide Research Group, quoted in Janet Gould. "What's the Difference Between E-Commerce and E-Business? And Why Should You Care?" *SCS Magazine* (November 1999). Located online at **http://www.scs-mag.com/reader/1999_11/what1199/what1199.htm**. Accessed 1/31/04.

## TREASURY INFORMATION MANAGEMENT OBJECTIVES

We propose six treasury information management "value drivers":

1. Information availability
2. Information accuracy
3. Information timeliness
4. Information system cost
5. Automation of information generation, transmission, analysis, and decision making
6. Electronification of information and payment systems

Any proposed investment in information technology, automation, or conversion to electronic information transmission or electronic payment may be valued based on one or more of these six value drivers. The last two suggest that companies create value by the electronification and automation of activities across the cash flow timeline. The value added by these items, for a given information system decision alternative, may be compared to the costs of implementing the information system solution to determine whether it is a worthwhile investment.

### Major Financial Processes

We gain an appreciation for the complexity of information management when we see that there are 31 major processes in finance:

- Transaction Processing
  A/P, A/R, credit, collections, accounting, billing, payroll, etc.
- Control and Risk Management
  Budgeting, forecasting, cash and treasury management, risk management, tax planning, etc.
- Decision Support
  Business performance analysis, new business analysis, strategic planning support, management of finance function, etc. (See Alfonsi and Ball in end-of-chapter references.)

With many treasury departments downsized or staffed at a constant level while sales grew and the companies made acquisitions, finance professionals have struggled with maintaining oversight and control of these disparate processes and the information flows describing them. Our particular focus topics in this chapter are accounts payable, travel and expense, accounts receivable, credit, collections, customer billing, tax filing and reporting, and payroll in the "Transaction Processing" category; cash budgeting, interim forecast, business performance reporting, cash management, treasury management, and risk management in the "Control and Risk Management" category; and business performance analysis and finance function management in the "Decision Support" category. The cash management adage pertains here: "it's not enough to have the cash, you have to know you have the cash" in order to benefit from improved treasury management.

## ELECTRONIC COMMERCE

Treasury professionals now perceive their need for corporate-wide information in real time. Two of the four major trends identified for treasury departments in the new millennium are knowledge management applications. Significant obstacles face the financial manager in reaching the six objectives we proposed earlier. Centralized and automated information management is elusive. Infosys Technologies, Ltd. (India) has found some multinational banks having as many as 150 different portals (individualized entrance points for corporate clients) as well as many different software formats accumulated from merged and acquired banks.[2] Additionally, the much-heralded "checkless" and "paperless" economy remains elusive in the United States and many other nations. It was estimated in 1991 that only 1 percent of all corporate trade payments were made electronically. While the growth rate of electronic payments is impressive, even today at least 80 percent of U.S. corporate trade payments remain paper-based. In this section, we will survey the area of electronic communications between companies and between companies and their banks.

Electronic data interchange is "the computer-to-computer exchange of normal business transactions including payments, information exchange and purchase order requests."[3] Note that this definition is broader than the older definitions used for EDI, such as this standard one: "the intercompany, computer-to-computer exchange of business documents in standard formats."[4] The electronic transmission of purchase orders and invoices would be just two examples of EDI information flows. EDI also may include transmission of financial information (formerly called financial EDI, or FEDI). EC includes all of these types of EDI exchanges, as well as electronic funds transfer (EFT).

## EDI and the Current System

To better understand the improvements that EDI makes in the data sharing between companies or a company and one of its banks, let's take a look at the way product ordering and delivery systems worked traditionally. A sales representative visits a customer, and an order is consummated. The sales representative may phone in the order to the regional headquarters or field office or may hand deliver a purchase order upon return to the field office. The order is processed internally. The customer's credit limit is manually checked, and an invoice is created. The order is processed for delivery. Inventory availability is verified, and the units ordered are manually tabulated into the company's inventory control and management system. The order is prioritized, and delivery is scheduled. Product shipment is initiated with an enclosed invoice. The customer, upon receipt of the shipment, checks for quality and quantity discrepancies. The customer then processes the invoice received scheduling payment based on the credit terms and the company's policy regarding payment. A check is then mailed on the date scheduled and from the administrative office dictated by the company's payment policy. Throughout this process flow, information is manually copied from one source to another source creating inefficiencies and potential errors.

Contrast this traditional system with a fully implemented EDI system. The customer or sales representative places an order electronically from the customer's location to the supplier's appropriate field or regional office. For example, at Johnson & Johnson's Hospital Services subsidiary, customers can place an order by phone, remote terminal, or computer-to-computer connection. Additionally, some field representatives use laptop computers to send and receive real-time reports on shipment status, back-orders, and sales

---

[2] Infosys, "Cash Management IT: Managing the Technology Evolution," *HSBC's Guide to Cash and Treasury Management in Asia Pacific* (2003), p. 148.

[3] dmreview.com (2004), **http://www.dmreview.com/resources/glossary.cfm**.

[4] Kathleen Conlon Hinge, *Electronic Data Interchange: From Understanding to Implementation*, New York: American Management Association (1988), p. 9.

volume.[5] The supplier's computers receive the order and feed the information electronically to its inventory and shipping area as well as the credit department. Without re-keying any additional data, the shipment is confirmed and upon shipment, an invoice is electronically transmitted to the customer. The supplier then initiates payment instructions to its bank based on a previously agreed upon date. Payment instructions are then transmitted to the customer's bank, and the customer's bank account is debited while the supplier's bank account is credited. No paper documents have been transmitted; there is no redundant re-keying of data, and, as a result, processing times, transmittal times, and clerical costs are minimized.

*BENEFITS AND COSTS OF EDI* EDI systems and other EC investments such as those described above have several advantages. Companies are discovering that past-due receivables can be drastically reduced, effectively reducing days sales outstanding (DSO) and thereby reducing funds invested in receivables. CompUSA used dispute collection and dispute resolution software from GetPaid Corp. to cut its past-due receivables by 75 percent (from $8 million to $2 million) and its DSO from 52 days to 46 days within six months. CompUSA recorded a payback period of six months on the software investment, reducing its collections staff by 39 percent during its implementation period.[6] It is not uncommon to experience significant reductions in bad debt write-offs. In addition, banks will often allow for increased credit lines because of the enhanced asset control provided by such EDI systems.[7] The reduction in a company's working capital cycle brought about by the implementation of these systems can be significant and allow for a competitive advantage in reduced financing costs, effectively enhancing profit margins. Companies embracing Internet technology have seen their overall financial transaction costs drop as much as 40 percent compared to average firms.[8] Even more impressive, companies that move from paper to electronics in payables areas including supplier invoicing to vendor payments experience cost reductions of up to 90 percent, according to Hackett Group research. Comparing top-quartile cost to bottom-quartile cost companies, and factoring in their sizes, this constitutes a $590,000 savings per $1 billion in sales.[9] EDI can also improve forecasts, service quality, and employee productivity.

The major costs associated with EC are hardware and software related. Companies must invest in the required computer communications systems including the ability to handle various data transmission format standards.

## Company-to-Bank EDI

EDI includes the exchange of electronic business information between a company and its bank, such as electronic account analysis statements.[10] This is not to be confused

[5] Janet W. Mills and Edward K. Freitas, "EDI at Johnson & Johnson," *Journal of Cash Management* (September/October 1989), pp. 14–16.

[6] Kathie O'Donnell, "Making Sure 'The Check Is in the Mail,'" *Treasury & Risk Management* (December/January 2004), p. 19.

[7] For an example of the impact that EDI has on MicroAge, Inc., see Jeffrey L. Masich, "Improving Cash Flow and Streamlining Operations Through EDI," *Journal of Cash Management* (January/February 1991), pp. 13–16.

[8] Jeffrey S. Rosengard, "Transforming Finance into a Competitive Weapon," *Financial Executive (fe) Magazine* (July/August 2000), pp. 51–52.

[9] Treasury & Risk Management Express e-mail listserv, "Looking for Savings? Try Getting Out of the Paper Business When It Comes to Accounts Payable" (November 17, 2003).

[10] The "ANSI 822" electronic account analysis statement can now be constructed and delivered electronically by corporate customers by more than 80 North American banks.

with the term electronic funds transfer, which refers to payment instructions between banks. Other examples of EDI transmissions from banks to companies include lockbox information reports and daily balance reports. Due to the fact that EDI permits the exchange of extensive information about each payment, companies are able to improve their cash application and accounts payable processes. Consequently, buyers and sellers make fewer follow-up calls to complete the payment process and therefore reduce related manual operations.[11] To understand how this process works, let's return to a topic we introduced in Chapter 11: comprehensive, or integrated, payables. This process allows a company to outsource its vendor payments, payroll, and miscellaneous payments to a bank or other third party. Exhibit 19–2 depicts the process and the steps involved, using Mellon Bank's RemEDI® service to illustrate. Companies large enough to make this cost beneficial have reaped large returns from outsourcing some or all of their payables function.

Treasury workstations were developed during the mid-1980s to facilitate financial aspects of EDI. A treasury workstation is an automated system of software modules de-

EXHIBIT 19–2

*How Mellon RemEDI® Comprehensive Disbursements Works*

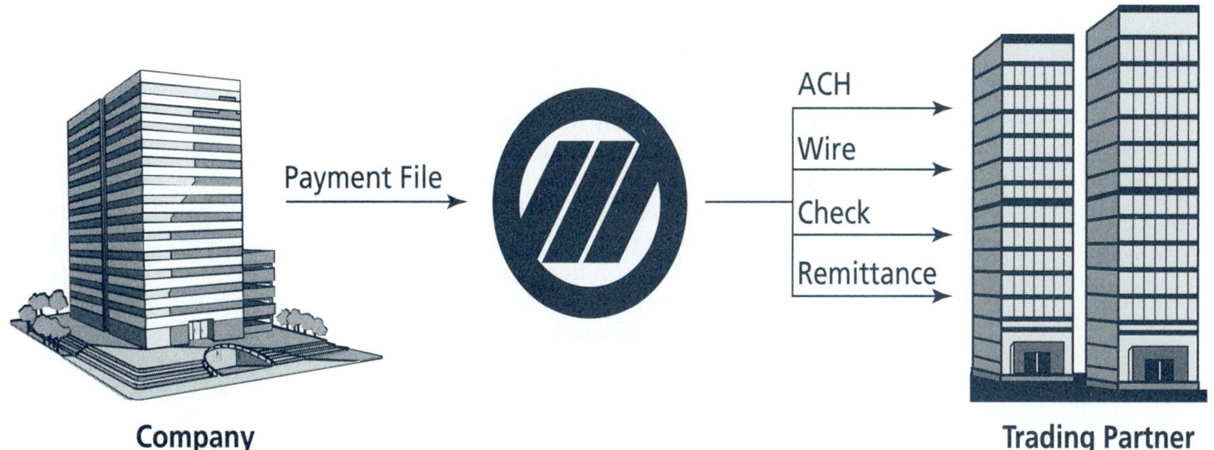


1. Your company delivers a single standards-based file containing payment and remittance information for all your payment types.
2. Mellon Rem*EDI* converts your payment instruction file into the required format for all payment applications, including automated clearinghouse (ACH), check, and wire transfer.
3. Your trading partner is paid and remittance detail is forwarded to your trading partner according to your instructions.

*Source:* Mellon Financial Corporation, **http://www.mellon.com/cashmanagement/payables/edidisbursements-work.html**. Accessed 1/29/04.

[11] Susan Rapp, "Successful Financial EDI Implementation Among Trading Partners," *The Journal of Cash Management* (January/February 1993), p. 10.

signed to support treasury management operations. Various hardware and software vendors, as well as many commercial banks, developed systems utilized by corporate cash managers and treasurers to facilitate the transmission of data and payment requests between the company and its bank(s). Data transmissions include account balance information from controlled disbursement accounts and lockbox deposit accounts and account analysis statements. Treasury workstations were also designed so that cash managers could initiate wire transfers and ACH credits and debits for cash mobilization and payment purposes.

Along with the EDI systems packaged with the workstations, most treasury workstations also include software to aid in the management of the company's investment and debt portfolios. Such modules track maturing securities so that the company's short-term cash forecasting system is regularly updated and even allow the user to initiate and confirm investment transactions. SunGard Financial Networks has an online money market trading site (SunGard Transaction Network Money Markets) that has commercial paper, certificates of deposit, and more than 100 money market funds offered by 25 mutual fund families—and already has more than 400 customers, including money managers, insurers, and corporate treasurers.[12] Most treasury workstation systems include the ability to track target required bank balances so that the company's banks are properly compensated for the services performed. We will return to this topic later in the chapter.

## Electronic Funds Transfer (EFT)

**Electronic funds transfer** primarily deals with the actual electronic transfer of payments, or value, between trading partners involving the partners' financial institutions. Contrast EFT to EDI, which primarily deals with the electronic transfer of information or data between trading partners, and to communications between the company and its bank. At its inception, EFT was initiated only after paper-based invoices were received. Today, EDI and EFT are merging so that the processing of electronic payment requests can be linked to order initiation and completion of the payment. While EFT primarily takes care of dollar float, EDI impacts information float.

Two decades ago, it appeared imminent that EFT would replace the paper-based payment system. Today, the use of checks by consumers as well as corporations is actually still only declining slightly. The typical routine use of EFT includes consumer bill payment collection through the ACH, cash concentration with wire transfers or the ACH, origination of state tax payments through the ACH, employee expense reimbursements, and direct deposit of payrolls. The two major applications of electronic payments include direct payroll deposit activities and the collection of preauthorized checks.

The early 1960s witnessed many insurance companies developing the use of preauthorized checks to collect insurance policy premiums. Originally, this was a paper-based system. The system involved obtaining approval from the company's customers to allow the insurance company to automatically debit the customer's bank account on a particular day each month or some other stipulated payment interval. Now this is done using ACH debits.

There are numerous advantages of using EFT over a paper-based system for collecting customer payment including improved cash forecasting, lower costs per item, and more efficient return item processing.[13] In addition, studies of historic payment trends indicate

[12] Susan Kelly, "Sungard Expands Money Market Offering," *Treasury & Risk Management* (December/January 2004), p. 17.

[13] Robert J. DalSanto, A. Post Howland, and Sharon Morton, "What's New in EFT?" *Journal of Cash Management* (May/June 1991), p. 40.

that policyholders paying with preauthorized payments have a much higher payment rate than policyholders that pay after receiving an invoice for payment.

Another major application of EFT is the direct deposit of payrolls and other payments such as dividends, annuities, and Social Security checks. The paying corporation collects the payees' bank account information and prior to the payment date initiates an ACH transaction that effectively moves funds from the payor's payroll account, or other appropriate expense account, to the payees' accounts. Social Security direct deposit represents one of the most successful applications of direct deposit. In 1989, almost half of the eligible recipients received their monthly Social Security benefits deposited directly to their bank account though the ACH system. By 2004, over 80 percent did so. The benefits of such a system include substantial processing cost savings and a more predictable cash disbursement for the payor: it costs the government 42 cents for processing and mailing a Social Security check, versus 2 cents for a direct deposit. The negatives include a loss of float for the payor, but the success of the system indicates that the cost savings more than offset the opportunity cost of the float loss.

## EDI Communication Formats

A large percentage of one company's output is another company's input. As such, effective EDI can significantly reduce the amount of re-keying of the order, shipping, and invoicing data and instructions. However, such improvements were stymied by the lack of standardized document formats. Correspondingly, the Accredited Standards Committee (ASC) of the American National Standards Institute has developed document standards for electronic communication referred to as ASC X12 Standards. Some of the more common standards, which are referred to as **transaction sets**, developed thus far to facilitate the electronic communication between trading partners and financial institutions include the following:

| | |
|---|---|
| 810 | Invoice |
| 820 | Payment order/remittance advice |
| 821 | Financial information reporting |
| 822 | Customer account analysis |
| 823 | Lockbox information |
| 824 | Application advice |
| 828 | Debit authorization |
| 832 | Price/sales catalog |
| 835 | Health care claim payment/advice |

These transaction sets are developed for the transmission of data only, not actual payments.

In addition, many countries have developed EDI standards. This process led to the development of United Nations EDI for Administration, Commerce and Transportation (UN/EDIFACT) rules, which are simply a set of standards for electronic interchange of structured data between computerized information systems in different countries.

Finally, with the popularity of the Internet, developers have created Web-based EDI Internet sites using eXtensible Markup Language (XML). Standard EDI transaction sets are converted with this form of protocol either to or from Web-based forms in order to transfer information between large EDI hubs.

Distinct from the ASC standards presented earlier, which have to do with the transmission of *information*, the National Automated Clearing House Association (NACHA) has developed format options that allow the electronic movement of *funds*, each with varying amounts of data. We presented several of these payment formats earlier in Chapter

11, and we repeat these below as a review. We have added the new ARC, POP, WEB, and TEL codes as well.[14] Early evidence of fraud, linked to unauthorized users initiating ACH debits of others' checking accounts, has caused some concern in credit card and utility companies.

PPD: Direct deposit of payroll—automatic utility or loan bill paying services. Settles in two days and used for crediting or debiting consumers' accounts.

CCD: Cash concentration and disbursement format—minimal data with payment details submitted separately created for next-day settlement. Most banks can process this format.

CCD+: A cash concentration and disbursement format with addendum space for payment details attached. Banks may not be able to capture and relay the addenda information.

TXP: A special provision of the CCD+ for the express purpose of electronic payment of taxes to state and federal governments.

CTX: Corporate trade X12 format—variable data fields as developed by ASC X12. The ability to include variable data fields allows the remittance of information contained in transaction sets such as ASC X12 820, 823, or 835 to move through the ACH network together with the payment rather than having to be separated and sent through a third party.

RCK: Represented check entries format—used to transmit ACH debit entries related to paper checks written by consumers of less than $2,500 that were returned to the depositor's bank for insufficient funds. These may be resubmitted around the first of the month when many workers get paid and should have adequate funds in their checking accounts. Originators may transmit an RCK no more than twice after the first return of a paper item, and no more than once after the second return of a paper item.

ARC: Allows payees ("originators") to use the PPD format to truncate consumer checks that were received through the U.S. mail (not at retail point-of-purchase) in payment for goods or services, thereby collecting those checks via the ACH network. Must prenotify consumers before first check is truncated, but may inform customers that if they do not notify payee of their refusal to allow checks to be truncated, practice will be permissible. Not allowable for business checks at this time.

POP: A point-of-purchase (POP) transaction that is a one-time ACH debit initiated by payee (originator) as a replacement to a check or share draft payment for goods or services purchased in person. The customer presents a check or share draft to initiate the point-of-purchase entry, and the payee uses a check reading device to capture the MICR information from the check (transit routing number, checking account number, and check serial number); a voucher is signed by the payor authorizing the ACH debit, and the MICR information is then used by the payee to transmit the electronic debit to the consumer's account. The check is voided, so this is not considered to be a form of check truncation. Not allowable for business checks at this time.

TEL: An ACH debit initiated by a company (originator) upon a consumer's oral authorization, which includes the consumer's banking information, received via a telephone, to transmit a one-time ACH debit to his or her account to collect payment for goods or services. Payee cannot originate credit entries, except for reversals, to the consumer's account. Must have an ongoing relationship with the consumer, or the consumer must have initiated the phone call. Often used by credit card companies to collect late payments.

---

[14] Based on information provided by National EFT, available at **http://www.nationaleft.com/faqarct.html**. Accessed 2/01/04.

## FOCUS ON PRACTICE

### *How Transaction Sets and Payment Formats Are Used at GM*

General Motors' divisions transmit remittance instructions using the ASC X12 820 format to their banks. The banks convert the 820 transmission into the CTX format, which includes payment instructions, dollars, and invoice remittance data. If the supplier's bank cannot handle such a format, GM's bank will send the payment instructions in a CCD format and will then route a printed report of the remittance data to the supplier.

*Source:* Robert D. Edward and Craig S. Saxer, "EDI Payment Development: The Dollars and Data Issue," *Journal of Cash Management* (January/October 1990), p. 21.

WEB: May be called an "online electronic check," (but not the same as electronic check conversion) an ACH debit initiated by having the consumer key his or her bank account information into an Internet form, authorizing payee to create the electronic ACH debit to the consumer's account.

The existence of various data formats has led to the creation of **value added networks** or VANs. A VAN is a third-party service company that receives data transmissions in one format, restructures the data into an alternative format, and then retransmits the data in a revised format to its final destination. Subscribing to a VAN service is one alternative to solving the multiple format problem allowing different trading partners to electronically communicate with each other without having to alter their own systems.

### Benefits of and Problems with EDI [15]

Several benefits will accrue to companies as the use of EDI proliferates. First, EDI improves quality of services offered to customers. Orders move faster with fewer errors because communication time is reduced and redundant data keying is eliminated. Customer queries about the status of their order or even payment can also be handled more accurately. Second, employee productivity is enhanced because redundant data keying is reduced or eliminated. Paper handling is also reduced and fewer errors are made. Third, operations are streamlined by shortening the processing timeline, controlling and reducing inventory, and improving production forecasting. Fourth, EDI provides a means for more effective asset management. Receivables and inventories can be converted into cash more quickly, and payments can be applied more rapidly. Fifth, effective use of EDI can even improve the payables area. In the past, most companies have been reluctant to pay electronically. However, General Motors in the mid-eighties realized that the cost of paying by paper was increasing at a high rate due to the escalating costs of paper, the costs of employee time, and bank processing and clearing costs. GM contrasted this with declining costs for computer hardware and software and made a strategic decision to move away from paper-based transactions. The sixth benefit is to the company's cash management area. The costs

[15] The benefits as outlined in this section were introduced in Victor N. Azar and Tom R. Tabor, "Business Justification for Electronic Data Interchange," *Journal of Cash Management* (July/August 1988), pp. 15–19 and Christopher Skaar, Jr., "Moving Toward Electronic Data Interchange," *Journal of Cash Management* (July/August 1986), pp. 16–20.

of cash management will be reduced because the number of bank relationships will generally fall as more payments are processed electronically. Cash flow forecasting is also improved. Finally, as companies move to EDI, banks are generally responding by allowing greater credit lines because of the increased asset control provided by the EDI systems.

Most of the improvements that result from EDI implementation affect information float more than dollar float. In fact, the improvements made in the payment system over the last decade have left opportunities for only marginal improvements to be made by improving EFT capabilities. The real opportunities that are open are in the area of process and information flow improvement internally and between trading partners. Thus, it should be obvious that many benefits accrue to the company as paper-based transactions and payments are replaced with their electronic equivalents.

So, with all of these benefits favoring EDI, why do we still find ourselves in the infancy of its application? One problem is the development and acceptance of standards for data transmission. Second are concerns about data communication security and authorization. Third are legal issues dealing with liabilities resulting from failure of various components of the system over which an individual company has no control. Most of our laws dealing with commercial transactions are based on the premise of paper documents. So, new interpretations are needed, and in some cases, new laws enacted. Finally, some suppliers have been reluctant to negotiate different credit terms for electronic collection of funds owed. The legal issues surrounding changing credit terms based on EDI are not yet clear. The Robinson-Patman Act makes it illegal to offer different credit terms to different customer groups unless justified by the product sold, the quantity sold, or the delivery costs incurred. Since EDI does not neatly fit in any of these categories, suppliers have been slow to offer credit terms for EDI transactions that differ from the credit terms offered to their non-EDI customers.

These are just a few of the many issues that have slowed and continue to impede progress of EDI implementation. However, each new year shows increased use of EDI in the United States.

## E-COMMERCE AND THE INTERNET

The traditional EDI model we discussed earlier is being enhanced by a newer and more flexible model—electronic commerce over the Internet. "Surfing the net" is no longer an activity reserved for computer geeks. Dow Chemical now makes 15 percent of its selling transactions over the Internet—an almost 5-fold increase since 2000. All told, U.S. businesses spent about $482 billion online in B2B purchases in 2002.[16] It seems as though everyone is on the Net. More and more individuals, companies, interest groups, and nonprofit organizations are creating their own Web pages as a means of communication and increasingly as a way to sell products and services and to transact business information. Kathleen Hagen put forth the following vision of how financial managers may tap into the power of the Internet.

> Working from her "virtual office" at home, Jane Smith begins to prepare the daily cash position for her company. Using a treasury management work station that provides an automatic Internet link, she clicks on the company logo icon to access the company's internal Web site and downloads all of the investment transactions from the previous business day. The file is stored on her hard drive, and the work station is immediately updated.
>
> To retrieve the details of yesterday's accounts receivable payments, she selects the VAN DOWNLOAD button, which accesses the FTP (file transfer protocol) server

[16] Julia Angwin, "Renaissance in Cyberspace," *The Wall Street Journal* (November 20, 2003), p. B1.

of the VAN that processes their EDI transactions. Clicking on an "Update" icon, the receivable information is now copied to the company FTP server and then to the cash position worksheet. Later, the accounts receivable department will access the FTP server to update the receivables system.

To retrieve a list of internal payment requests, Jane clicks the "Today's Payments" button, which automatically accesses the accounts payable information posted on the Web site and downloads the payment requests for the day. The files are "signed" with digital signatures so that Jane can verify that they have been properly authorized. Jane reviews the payment requests, and the file automatically updates the daily cash position worksheet. Before finalizing the daily cash position, Jane verifies the target balances calculated by the workstation. She can increase or decrease the amounts with a click of the mouse. Having completed this, she selects the "Create Payments File" button, and a transfer file is created to send the payment instructions to the bank.

Before the file can be sent to the bank, it must first be signed by the treasurer. Jane attaches the file to an e-mail message, which she digitally signs. When the treasurer opens his e-mail, he will review the wire instructions, encrypt the file, and forward it on to the bank by uploading it to the bank's FTP server.[17]

As we will see later, the role of value added networks (VANs) is being supplanted by Internet linkups that are part of treasury workstations or enterprise resource planning software. The following sections provide some examples of e-commerce applications that have been developed through the use of the Internet.

## Information Reporting

In the 2003 Cash Management Services (CMS) survey,[18] Ernst & Young reported that 98 percent of the respondent banks were offering information reporting services to corporate customers over the Internet. The sample of respondents includes virtually all of the nation's largest banks. This compares to offerings by only about 5 percent of the responding banks in 1997 and 25 percent in 1999. Companies in the United States and in the United Kingdom reported this as their top Web-based banking activity[19] (refer back to the online banking discussion in Chapter 8).

## Transaction Initiation

In 1997, the CMS survey reported that less than 5 percent of the respondents reported offering any form of transaction initiation via the Internet. By 2003, 97 percent of the responding banks offered Internet-initiated funds transfers between accounts within the bank, over 90 percent offered ACH initiation, and 82 percent offered wire transfer capability over the Internet, compared to 20 percent of the banks in 1997.

---

[17] Kathleen A. Hagen, "Banking in Cyberspace—A New Frontier for Treasury Professionals," *TMA Journal* (March/April 1996), p. 45.

[18] Lawrence Forman, et al. Ernst & Young 20th Annual Cash Management Survey: 2003 Executive Summary. Available online at **http://www.ey.com**. Accessed 2/1/2004. Also see, for comparison, an earlier study at Lawrence Forman and David L. Shafer, "From Doubt to Adoption . . . Internet Delivery of Cash Management Services Is Changing the Marketplace," AFP Exchange, Volume 20, Number 4 (Fall 2000), pp. 104–107.

[19] Debbie M. Smart, "Web-Based Treasury Management: Now That It's Here, What Does It Mean to You?" *Business Credit* (January 2003), pp. 43–44; A Greenwich Associates survey of large European corporates found that 66% use account information Web services, 58% use foreign exchange, 50% use disbursement services, and about 40% say they would prefer to use the Internet extensively to replace traditional banking methods; cited in ABN AMRO's Global Transaction Services, "'E' is Just Technology: The Core Treasury Role Continues," *Business Credit* (October 2002), pp. 47–48.

## Image Access

In the 2003 CMS survey, 58 percent of the bank respondents offered issued item images, mainly associated with positive pay services, and lockbox item images are offered by 61 percent of the banks. Images of deposited items are now offered by about one-fourth of the banks.

## E-Procurement

Procurement over the Internet offers immediate savings in processing costs and even more significant savings from strategic sourcing.[20] Generating a paper-based purchase order is estimated to cost $150, on average. However, those companies who automate this function incur an average cost of only $30. In addition, three additional benefits that companies gain include:

- a 5 to 10 percent price savings generated by e-procurement,
- an improvement in the purchase and fulfillment cycle that drops from over seven days to about two days, and
- reduction of 25 to 50 percent in inventory costs due primarily to reduction in inventory.

Perhaps one of the greatest benefits, however, is that purchasing managers no longer are simply executing transactions. They now have the time to devote to supplier negotiations and evaluations that is more strategic with a more direct consequence on company profitability. E-procurement solutions are migrating to supply chain management solutions that enable greater collaboration among trading partners, greater customization of product and service, and better management of demand and delivery. Corporate cards are now being used to streamline purchases of goods and services by companies of all sizes, providing (1) better information for analyzing suppliers; (2) volume discounts and better pricing; (3) stronger controls of purchasing and travel expenditures; (4) better information and reports; (5) lower per-transaction fees; (6) less time spent on overseeing small-dollar purchases; (7) better relations with suppliers; and arguably of greatest importance, (8) more time for focusing management attention on core business functions.[21]

## Internet Invoicing and Payment[22]

While the supplier may benefit if the revenue cycle accelerates, the buyer may expect to also gain by taking more trade discounts or better manage its trade credit due to more prompt receipt and processing of invoices. Web-based invoicing and payment provide an opportunity for the trading partners to renegotiate current trade and payment terms. When applied to B2B invoicing and electronic payment, it is termed **Electronic Invoicing Presentment and Payment (EIPP)**; electronic consumer billing and payment is **Electronic Bill Presentment and Payment (EBPP)**. While there have been almost two decades of EDI experience proving significant financial and process benefits, the ubiquitous and nonproprietary nature of the Internet suggests that those benefits may even be more significant. For example, some consultants estimate that there are potential cost savings of up to 50 percent in the generation, delivery, and processing of invoices and payments when moving from a paper-based system to an electronic system. Consultant Gartner, Inc., estimates the average B2B seller could save $10 million per year if it would automate the delivery of

[20] Jane McAllister, "Avoiding Online Chaos," *AFP Exchange*, Vol. 20, Number 4 (Fall 2000), pp. 84–87.

[21] Fay Hansen, "Global E-Commerce Growth," *Business Credit* (October 2003), pp. 58–60.

[22] McAllister, supra note 17.

all bills over the Internet (EIPP), automate all disputes and payments, and convert all dispute phone calls to Web-based self-service.[23]

### Digital Marketplaces [24]

By bringing together numbers of buyers and sellers, Internet marketplaces create access to broader markets for sellers and a greater selection for buyers. However, the Federal Trade Commission is taking an active interest in these marketplaces to ensure that business will be conducted in an environment of collaboration, not collusion. Currently, the largest online exchange for chemical trading, ChemConnect Inc., is still not profitable even though it saw a volume of $8.8 billion in 2002 and is used by 44 percent of the industry.[25]

### Future Role of the Internet

As noted earlier, the Internet is providing a less expensive and easier to use electronic system compared to the initial EDI applications. A survey conducted by *Business Finance* magazine and JPMorganChase found that about 80 percent of finance professionals surveyed stated that the Internet had a significant impact on treasury function over the past year. Benefits cited by respondents included better access to real-time bank information, wider access to bank data, self-service bank account inquiry abilities, ability to work remotely, and lessened the need for treasury staff training. Respondents believe the Internet will continue to make their treasuries more efficient.[26] Thus, we are witnessing a much more rapid implementation. As Web-based systems allow more and more daily processes to be automated, the role of the treasury function will continue to evolve. Treasury will be able to deal with an increasing volume of more complex transactions. This will provide the opportunity for treasury to focus on more significant value adding activities such as risk management, financial analysis, and investing/borrowing strategies and more effective management of global financial flows. A nagging concern is security, especially as some applications migrate to wireless access.[27]

## AUDITING THE STFM INFORMATION SYSTEM

We have witnessed and will continue to witness improvement in the integration of the management of information flows and dollar flows along the entire path of the cash flow timeline. Better management of the information flows yields faster cash collections and better control over cash disbursements enhancing the company's liquidity position. An obvious question now is to what extent are companies using electronic information systems as a part of their strategic business plan.

### Survey Results

Ahmad Salam conducted an EDI implementation survey of the Fortune 500 manufacturing firms in 1992.[28] This insightful study found five important reasons explaining why

---

[23] Hansen, supra note 18.
[24] McAllister, supra note 17.
[25] Julia Angwin, "Top Online Chemical Exchange Is Unlikely Success Story," *The Wall Street Journal* (January 8, 2004), pp. A15, A20.
[26] Richard H. Gamble, "Treasury's Net Gains," *Business Finance* (October 2003), p. 37.
[27] See Long, Yuan, and Whinston (2003), cited in the end of chapter references.
[28] Ahmad W. Salam, "Electronic Data Interchange and Corporate EFT: A Survey," *TMA Journal* (May/June 1994), pp. 59–61.

firms implemented EDI including being part of an industry group that uses EDI, it was required for implementation of JIT, to reduce inventory, certainty of payment date, and the encouragement of senior management. The survey respondents reported a number of quantifiable benefits derived from the use of EDI. These ranged from the reduction of clerical costs and cost savings of reduced paper and forms to resulting reductions in inventory and labor savings through improved scheduling.

Relatively few companies had implemented EDI in their international operations, and Salam points to a lack of acceptable worldwide standards as a major factor in this result, as well as existing legal issues regarding cross-border EDI transactions. With the economic unification of Europe, both issues are being addressed in the 2000s.

Another valuable survey of EFT and EDI usage was conducted by Gilbert and Reichert in 1996. They found that, for 146 responding Fortune 500 firms, 53 percent frequently used EDI to interface with their customers, while 46 percent did the same with their suppliers. Interestingly, size was not found to be a significant factor in EDI use in the 1996 survey, unlike a similar survey done by the same authors in 1991 in which large firms showed higher usage than smaller (but obviously still fairly large) Fortune 500 firms.[29]

Switching our focus to the use of technology to run the treasury function itself, Treasury Strategies, Inc., found in their 2003 survey that 65 percent of corporations use a treasury management system, with size being a strong predictor of use: 35 percent of companies with less than $1 billion in sales use a system, versus 100 percent of companies over $25 billion. Only 28 percent of the systems used were Web-enabled, but companies were hampered by banks' or other third parties' inability to provide these systems: when available, these features were used by 75 percent of companies.[30]

The next section highlights the major cash flow timeline events as well as the information and dollar variables that are related to each of those events. We then turn to a more detailed look at two types of electronic information systems available for the corporate cash management function.

## Cash Flow Timeline Events

In this section, we are concerned about identifying the major business events along the cash flow timeline, the information required for each event, and some of the relationships involved for each event.[31]

*PURCHASING* The applicable information here is the status of the purchase order. The manager should be concerned with purchase projections and variances from the projection. Discount policies, vendor relations, and bank services expediting the order process are important.

*ACCOUNTS PAYABLE* The company's cash disbursement ledger is the critical piece of information here, and disbursement policy related to cash discounts and the available bank services for finalizing payment are also of concern.

A computerized disbursement system with necessary links to intracompany data allows the treasurer to improve cash flow forecasting by having better cash disbursement

---

[29] Gilbert and Reichert (1997), cited in the end-of-chapter references.

[30] Treasury Strategies, Inc. (2003), "The 2003 Corporate Treasury Survey," p. 11. Online at **http://www.treasurystrategies.com**. Accessed 1/24/2004. The survey also documented that the treasury work station market share (for respondents) was third-party provided (56%), bank-provided (36%), ERP treasury module (5%), or other, including homegrown (11%).

[31] The concept of the information requirements for each stage in the cash flow cycle is from Aviva Rice, "Improving Cash Flow Control Throughout the Corporation," *Journal of Cash Management* (November/December 1985), pp. 48–53.

information. In addition, the use of cash discounts can be optimized, and the treasurer can more precisely time the actual disbursement of cash with cash receipts thus optimizing investment opportunities and reducing borrowing costs. Even companies with good information systems have difficulty anticipating when one subsidiary's remittance will be received at another subsidiary or at corporate headquarters in another country.

*INVENTORY* Obviously, inventory summaries and shipping schedules are important here along with systems for monitoring inventory. It is critical that inventory and sales systems communicate with each other so that information regarding changing sales patterns translates into appropriate ordering and inventory levels.

*SALES* Sales forecasts and customer billing data are critical pieces of information at this stage in the cash flow cycle. Proper systems allow a seller to capture sales data, promptly invoice customers, track customer buying patterns, and update forecasts.

*RECEIVABLES* At the time that an order is placed on credit, the credit department should be immediately notified so that delays related to the credit decision can be minimized. Once credit is granted, then credit and collection statistics should be maintained and customer profiles established. Payment terms and policies should be adhered to and procedures established for handling overdue accounts.

*TREASURY* The treasury function is extremely important in coordinating cash collection, cash mobilization, and cash disbursements. The treasurer should maintain accurate information related to the company's cash position and constantly update the daily cash forecast. With this information, the treasurer can make informed decisions regarding investment and financing decisions. Concern here is with properly managing the liquidity level of the company.

*FINANCIAL ADMINISTRATION* Effective financial administration requires the creation of budgets, variance analysis, long-term planning and financial forecasting, and an assessment of long-term capital needs and funding strategies.

## Assessment of a Firm's Cash Management Practice

There are four basic cash management areas that need to be assessed including cash positioning/mobilization (Chapters 9, 10, and 11), bank relationship management (Chapter 8), short-term investement/borrowing (Chapters 15 and 16), and treasury systems management (Chapter 19).[32] Each of the four basic cash management areas should be assessed based on six key elements. First, does the area exhibit a high level of productivity resulting from efficient automation of routine functions allowing staff to be reduced to the minimum? Second, are advanced strategies utilized such as advanced cash management strategies and fully integrated treasury/financial systems? Effectively, implemented and integrated EDI systems would satisfy these first two elements. A third key element is the effectiveness of internal controls performed by individuals outside the areas reviewed as well as the existence of current documented policies and procedures. The fourth element is the level of performance of each of the four areas as measured against internal goals or industry benchmarks. Fifth, each of the four areas should be assessed as to the level of integration of cash-related decision making company-wide. The sixth and final assessment

---

[32] Joseph J. Bonocore and Jeffrey S. Rosengard, "Managing the Effectiveness of Your Cash Management Function," *Journal of Cash Management* (January/February 1991), pp. 32–36.

areas is based on industry reputation. That is, to what extent are each of the four areas known in the industry as being innovative?

### Assessing the Treasury Management Workstation

One of the major technological innovations that developed during the 1980s was the **treasury management workstation**. The following modules and functions would generally be provided by a sophisticated workstation.[33] Indeed, this checklist can be used as a basis on which to judge the capabilities of a particular system. By reading through the checklist, you may get a sense of the power and the necessity of such systems if a company is going to improve its information and dollar-flow management.

Balance Reporting Module

- Balance reporting
- Target balance
- Exception reporting
- Balance history
- Previous day's credit/debit
- Intraday debit/credit
- Intracompany funds flow analysis

Bank Information

- Account analysis/earnings credit
- Bank relationship manager
- Signature control
- Access to external databases
- Daily events reminder

Cash Mobilization

- Prespecified (line) wires
- Free-form wires
- Automated ACH
- Automated corporate trade payments

Consolidation of Information

- Automated cash ledger update
- General ledger interface
- Cash forecasting & variance analysis

General Investment Module

- Investment portfolio monitoring
- Multiple portfolios
- Position tracking
- Margin reporting and broker status
- Adjusted book versus market analysis

---

[33] This listing is adapted from Joseph Saturnia, Raymond Houlihan, and Timothy F. Coluccio, "How to Evaluate Treasury Workstations," *Journal of Cash Management* (November/December 1986), pp. 46–50.

- Track pending trades
- Portfolio performance history

General Debt Module

- Tracking and monitoring
- Swap analysis
- Multiple debt portfolio analysis

Communication & System Features

- Internet access
- Unattended auto-dial
- Parsing of balance report information
- Acceptance of BAI-formatted information
- Data back-up capabilities
- Communications capability
- Multi-tiered security screen
- Unique preformatted screens
- Electronic mail
- Electronic worksheet capability
- Graphics capability
- Word processing
- Hardware discounts
- Trade-in on old hardware
- Trade-in on old software

Vendor Services and Support

- Turnkey package
- Software customization
- Training on-site
- Customer references
- Nationwide and international coverage
- Trial period
- System test
- Free installation
- Published down-time statistics
- Date of first system installation
- Purchase-to-installation timeframe

A key to success is careful and proactive risk management during the workstation implementation. The five major risks identified by a consultant and a vendor are:[34]

1. **Misplaced expectations**—Make sure to state unique requirements and clearly articulate and document expections.

---

[34] Ari Morris, Syung W. Oh, and Ron Chakravarti, "Exceeding Expectations: Treasury Technology Implementation Best Practices" (April 18, 2002). Online at **http://www.treasurypoint.com**. Accessed 8/13/2003.

2. **Ineffective practices**—Be careful to not computerize and automate processes that are inefficient and ineffective prior to placing them in your information system.
3. **Unmotivated participants**—Banks, your information technology group, and accounting must cooperate, even though they may not wish to, but the only real stakeholders may be the treasury department and outside consultants.
4. **Inadequate resources**—Any technology implementation needs resources and follow-through, so specify who, what responsibilities, and time allocations.
5. **Scope creep**—Don't let a mushrooming wish list deep-six your project, as your staff needs a feeling of success to perform at a high level.

A treasury management workstation may be sold by a third-party vendor (e.g., Sungard, Selkirk, Wall Street Systems, and XRT) or by the company's bank. While not all treasury management workstations may provide all the modules and services listed earlier, the list should allow the financial manager to make a comparative assessment of competing systems and choose the system providing the modules and services that the company needs.

## Assessing the Enterprise Resource Planning (ERP) System

According to one authority, "ERP systems are comprised of software programs which tie together all of an enterprise's various functions—such as finance, manufacturing, sales and human resources."[35] Originally, these systems were used for human resource management and to tie customer relationship management together with accounting systems. Now, however, they promise the ability to seamlessly, automatically, and electronically tie together almost every facet of a company's operations and financial data. Timely and accurate reports (such as hourly bank statements) are produced by some of these systems. "End-to-end business processing" from A/P and A/R through inventories, orders, working capital, currency, and risk forecasting are all available with a properly implemented ERP system that has the full set of modules. This software also provides for the analysis of the data from these areas to plan the company's production, forecast its sales, and even analyze quality. Unfortunately, these systems are extremely expensive to purchase and require even more money to properly train personnel and to get the system to work with the treasurer's needs. One company reportedly spent $25 million and then abandoned its ERP implementation.[36] The new competitor for ERP systems are ASP, or application service provider offerings. These are either (1) Web-based treasury information services offered through the Internet, promising implementation times of only a few days and low monthly payments with no front-end license costs (ERP systems can easily run $150,000 for a basic package); or (2) a "hosted" Treasury Management System (TMS), which has the flexibility, integration, and cost structure of an installed ERP system but also charges a monthly hosting cost (as the package resides on the host's computer, not on the user's computer).[37] Smaller and middle-market companies are adopting ASP solutions in large numbers, primarily because they see the advantages of having ERP abilities but heretofore could not afford the large initial investment.

---

[35] WSReview.com (formerly *EDI World Magazine*). Located at **http://www.dmreview.com/resources/glossary.cfm**. Accessed 1/31/04.

[36] Michele Allman-Ward and James Sagner, *The Essentials of Managing Corporate Cash* (New York: John Wiley & Sons, 2002).

[37] Andrew Bateman (2003), "Is ASP a Viable Alternative in the Treasury Software Market?" Available online at **http://www.gtnews.com**. Accessed 1/31/2004.

## SUMMARY

This chapter had a dual focus. First, the chapter discussed the application of e-commerce through the electronic data interchange format and EFT. While business process EDI impacts the entire business information process system, financial communications EDI (primarily bank-to-company) and EFT are primarily in the domain of the corporate cash manager. We then documented the dramatic effects of the recent application of the Internet as a system used in e-commerce and internal treasury information applications.

The chapter concluded with a section providing a variety of checklists for auditing the company's short-term financial management system. First, a checklist for auditing the company's cash flow timeline was introduced. One important aspect of this checklist involves the degree of automation utilized along the cash flow timeline. Results from two surveys were reported to indicate the status and causal factors behind the implementation of EDI. The second checklist focused specifically on the company's cash management activity. The third and final checklist pertained to the treasury management workstation, an essential tool for value-maximizing electronic commerce.

Effective cash flow management requires an assessment of the company's cash flow timeline and effective implementation of the appropriate component parts of electronic commerce, including various facets of EDI, EFT, and treasury information systems. Benchmarking and outsourcing continue to make treasury and working capital management more efficient. And, since "good governance comes with good information," companies will invest in better information systems and more electronic and automated processes to help meet the control requirements of the Sarbanes-Oxley Act of 2003.[38]

## USEFUL WEB SITES

| | |
|---|---|
| Bank of America Treasury articles | **http://corp.bankofamerica.com/portal/portal/controller/controller.jsp?path=wcm/treas_srvcs/feat_art/content.xml** |
| PNC Bank E-business | **http://www.treasury.pncbank.com/ecommerce/productecomm.html** |
| Wells Fargo bank portal | **http://wellsfargo.com/com/ceo** |
| Global Treasury News | **http://www.gtnews.com** |

## QUESTIONS

1. What are the three information level needs in the short-term financial management area?
2. What is electronic data interchange?
3. How does EC differ from EDI?
4. Outline the benefits and problems with EDI.
5. Summarize the major activities that a treasury workstation facilitates.
6. Describe and summarize the advantages of an enterprise resource planning system.

---

[38] Amy Cortese, "It's Not Exactly Christmas, but It's Better than a Lump of Coal," *Treasury & Risk Management* (December/January 2004), pp. 49–50, 52.

## REFERENCES

Michael J. Alfonsi and Gail Ball, "Treasury Workstation? ERP? Both, Either, or Neither?" *AFP Virtual Education Web Seminar* (March 3, 2003).

Joseph J. Bonocore and Jeffrey S. Rosengard, "Managing the Effectiveness of Your Cash Management Function," *Journal of Cash Management* (January/February 1991), pp. 32–36.

Business International, *Automating Global Financial Management* (John Wiley & Sons/New York, 1988).

Robbie Downing and Ross McKean, "Digital Signatures: Addressing the Legal Issues," *Business Credit* (May 2001), pp. 44–47.

Lawrence Forman and David L. Shafer, "From Doubt to Adoption . . . Internet Delivery of Cash Management Services Is Changing the Marketplace," *AFP Exchange*, Vol. 20, No. 4 (Fall 2000), pp. 104–107.

J. A. Gentry, "Management of Information, Competitive Advantages and Short-Run Financial Management Systems," in *Advances in Working Capital Management*, Y. H. Kim (ed.) (Reading, MA: Addison-Wesley Publishing Company, 1988).

Erika Gilbert and Alan Reichert, "Trends in the Use of EFT and EDI Among Large U.S. Firms," *TMA Journal* (May/June 1997), pp. 49–54.

Ju Long, Michael J. Yuan, and Andrew B. Whinston, "Securing a New Era in Financial Services," *IT Pro* (July/August 2003), pp. 49–55.

Jane McAllister, "Avoiding Online Chaos," *AFP Exchange*, Vol. 20, No. 4 (Fall 2000), pp. 84–87.

Ahmad W. Salam, "Electronic Data Interchange and Corporate EFT: A Survey," *TMA Journal* (May/June 1994), pp. 59–61.

John F. Wilson and Hugh S. McLaughlin, "Developing an Information Strategy for Treasury Operations," *Journal of Cash Management* (January/February 1992), pp. 40–44.

# INTEGRATIVE CASE—PART 6

## *General Motors—Europe: The Regional Treasury Center International Finance*

In the fall of 1988, Ellen Stanley transferred to the Regional Treasury Center (RTC) of General Motors—Europe in Belgium after a two-year stint in the Treasury Department of General Motors in Detroit. She was generally well versed in the responsibilities of the treasurer of a large domestic industrial firm, but this assignment was her first in dealing with the international and foreign exchange issues of her firm.

Stanley was spending about four months in the various areas of the RTC in Brussels to familiarize herself with its primary responsibilities. By the time she completed her rotation, she would cover the three areas within the RTC: financing and investment, trading, and accounting.

In the current portion of her training she was trying to quantify the exposure of GM to the currencies of the various countries in which GM operates throughout Western Europe. Second, she needed to assess how the firm had lessened or should attempt to lessen its exposure to these major currencies.

### Development of General Motors' RTC

During her training, Stanley learned that General Motors was but one of 200 companies that had set up regional coordinating centers within the small Western European country of Belgium. The king of Belgium in 1982 made a conscious decision to provide substantial tax breaks to multinational corporations that set up coordination centers within its country. These tax benefits included exemption from corporate taxes for 10 years. In addition, the centers were exempt from withholding taxes (currently 25 percent) on all payments of dividends, interest, and royalties. Also, the centers were provided a tax credit of 25 percent for interest paid by the centers. The idea behind this credit was to enable banks to finance investment projects through the centers at a much lower rate than would be available in other European countries. Likewise, the coordination centers were permitted to receive leasing income free of income taxes.

Other tax benefits included the absence of a registration tax on capital and a tax on real estate owned by the coordination center; exemption from foreign exchange regulations; and tax concessions for expatriate employees. In brief, Belgium created an excellent environment for General Motors, Levi Strauss, Phillips Petroleum, Dow Corning, and many other businesses to carry out the treasury function of their organizations, including their foreign exchange activities.

*Source:* Cases in Financial Management, © 1992 by Joseph M. Sulock and John S. Dunkelberg, New York: John Wiley & Sons, Inc.

### Current Situation for General Motors in Europe

Although the General Motors' RTC could be instrumental in helping the firm acquire funds at a reasonable cost as well as managing its foreign exchange exposure, the firm's major task was building automobiles within the highly competitive European market. Volume leaders in Europe were as follows:

| MANUFACTURER | HOME COUNTRY |
|---|---|
| Volkswagen/Audi | Germany |
| Fiat | Italy |
| Peugeot/Citroen | France |
| Ford | U.K. |
| Opel/Vauxhall (GM) | Germany |
| Renault | France |

The market shares for these six producers ranged from 10.1 percent to 14.6 percent. As the value of each country's currency changed, the competitive position of each manufacturer was helped or hurt. Depreciation in currencies improved the competitiveness of the domestic producer(s) within those countries. Appreciation in currencies impaired competitiveness by raising costs and prices relative to other nondomestic producers. At the present time the Italian, British, and German currencies have been relatively strong. Most of General Motors' assembly operations are done in Germany.

In order to cope with the strong currencies in their home countries, both Ford and General Motors adopted a similar strategy. First, to balance their foreign exchange exposure, they diversified their production locations. However, because of economics of scale, the carmakers eventually found it prohibitively expensive to have multiple assembly locations. Instead of multiple assembly plants, the firms relocated the plants that produced such components as brakes, radiators, and transmissions. As Stanley learned, with these relocations the firms were able to benefit from lower wage scales as well as the weaker currency environments. However, it was important for both firms to balance higher shipping costs against gains that might be realized from lower wage rates and weaker currencies than the British or German currencies.

A second strategy for both General Motors and Ford was the diversification of their supply bases into weak-currency and low wage countries. This end was accomplished by purchasing tires, plastics, and glass in France and Italy, the home of some of their major competitors. Some of their government-owned competitors, like Volkswagen and Renault, had a difficult time employing this multicountry supplier diversification because of political resistance to foreign purchases by government corporations. The situation provided Ford and General Motors with a significant competitive advantage over Volkswagen and Renault.

## The Foreign Currency Situation for GM—Europe

Even with all of General Motors' attempts to balance and diversify its foreign exchange, Stanley was amazed to find that the company still had significant imbalances in its relationship between purchases and sales. Stanley's main assignment for this phase of her training rotation was to identify the magnitude of the firm's exposures in the various key currencies. In addition, since she was new on the job, she was asked to suggest strategies that the firm might use to soften the effect of these exposures. For a veteran in the RTC, this assignment could have been done almost intuitively, but for a rookie, there were some serious questions that needed to be answered.

## Questions

1. What is the magnitude of the foreign exchange exposure for each of the currencies in Exhibit 1? Note: this case predates the introduction of the euro, so consider each country's exposure as a separate exposure.
2. Does the exposure to German currency help or hinder the competitive performance of General Motors?
3. How would the parent company in Detroit view the situation if the gross buys and gross sales in Germany were reversed?
4. The data in the case address the currency flows for General Motors—Europe that are tracked by the Regional Treasury Center in Brussels. However, another issue involves the stock of assets that the firm has in Europe. Speculate on what you think might be happening to the value of GM's investment in Europe in light of the various currency appreciations and depreciations, especially the German currency.
5. What techniques and financial instruments might the RTC employ to control its currency exposure? Explain these techniques in light of the French currency situation.
6. What financial benefits, if any, does General Motors have from locating its treasury function in Belgium? What benefits, if any, accrue to Belgium?
7. What parties, if any, might be harmed by the existence of regional treasury functions like GM's?

**Exhibit 1**

*Annual Currency Flows ($ millions)*

| COUNTRY | GROSS BUYS | GROSS SALES |
|---|---|---|
| Germany | $ 5,845 | $ 2,400 |
| U.K. | 440 | 2,245 |
| Spain | 1,395 | 1,340 |
| France | 380 | 920 |
| Holland | 55 | 750 |
| Belgium | 705 | 560 |
| Italy | 180 | 530 |
| Austria | 485 | 465 |
| Sweden | 0 | 255 |
| U.S. | 255 | 140 |
| Japan | 455 | 0 |
| Australia | 195 | 0 |
| Other | 0 | 785 |
| | $10,390 | $10,390 |

# Appendix A

## Time Value of Money Calculations

Any decision having a quantifiable financial impact lasting beyond the current year should be evaluated using **discounted cash flow** techniques. When companies are making decisions with sizable financial impacts, several alternative proposals typically are considered. Discounted cash flow techniques properly account for the timing of all cash inflows and cash outflows attributable to a given alternative by converting those flows to their value at an identical point in time. In most cases, that point in time is at the time of the initial cash outlay related to that alternative. For example, when evaluating the purchase of a machine, the first cash flow would be the purchase of that machine. Failure to consider the timing of cash flows results in poor decisions, reducing the value of the company's stock.

In this appendix, we will first present the necessary discounting and compounding equations. Then, we will illustrate a simple discounted cash flow calculation. Almost all of the computations made in this textbook are discounting calculations so we will conclude with a brief discussion of the appropriate discount rate for determining present values.

In our discussion, we will assume that the annual interest rate is a **nominal rate**. Also called the quoted rate or stated rate, this rate is best understood by distinguishing it from an **effective annual rate**. The effective annual rate takes into account the frequency of compounding, or how often interest is credited to the account. If **simple interest** is paid, interest is only added one time to the account, at the end of the investment period. For an investment paying simple interest, the nominal rate would be identical to the effective annual rate. For an investment paying **compound interest**, the investor earns "interest on interest." The investment grows in value more quickly because not only is interest paid on the original amount invested (the **principal**) but also on intrayear interest. The distinction is an important one, because with compound interest, the effective annual rate is greater than the nominal rate. In each of the formulas, we will be working with nominal interest rates and simple interest, unless otherwise specified.

## DISCOUNTING AND COMPOUNDING

The determination of a present dollar equivalent of a cash flow to be received in the future is called **discounting**, whereas compounding involves determining what a dollar amount invested today would be worth at some specified point in the future. Present value effects of financial decisions are assessed through time value calculations.

### Discounting and Compounding Single Sums

The simplest discounted cash flow calculations involve translating a single dollar amount to its value at a different point in time. We begin with the calculation that is used the most throughout this textbook, discounting a future sum to determine its present dollar equivalent. Calculation of the present value is best illustrated by an example.

Sandy is wondering how much money she needs to invest today to have $10,000 available to pay the first tuition payment for her M.B.A. program, due one year from today. She plans to invest the money in a 1-year certificate of deposit, which currently yields 9 percent. To determine the present dollar equivalent of $10,000, she can use Equation A.1:

$$PV = \frac{FV_n}{(1 + k)^n} \qquad \text{(A.1)}$$

Where: $FV_n$ = Cash flow received in period $n$

$k$ = Interest rate earned

$n$ = Number of time periods from now

*Solution.* Substituting the appropriate values into the equation:

$$PV = \frac{\$10{,}000}{(1 + 0.09)^1}$$

$$PV = \$9{,}174.31$$

As illustrated in the example, the cash flow timing is recognized via the number of days or years over which we are discounting.

Finding the future value of a single dollar amount being invested today is accomplished by a technique called **compounding**. Equation A.2 states the formula for determining the compounded future value of a known present amount:

$$FV_n = PV(1 + k)^n \qquad \text{(A.2)}$$

Where: $FV_n$ = Future dollar value at end of $n$ years

$PV$ = Present dollar amount

$k$ = Annual interest rate quoted

$n$ = Number of years

The following example shows how this is done. Notice that it is exactly the opposite of discounting.

> Larry has just talked with his bank's trust officer, who offered him a 5-year certificate of deposit paying 12 percent, compounded annually. Larry forgot to ask the officer what his $10,000 would be worth at the end of the five years. Can you help him?

SOLUTION. Substituting the numbers for Larry, we have:

$$FV_5 = \$10{,}000(1 + 0.12)^5$$

$$FV_5 = \$17{,}623.42$$

## Compounding and Discounting Periods Other than Annual

If the time period involves less than one year and compound interest is paid on the account (interest is credited more frequently than once a year), in order to modify Equation A.2, both $k$ and $n$ must be adjusted. Before showing the future value formula, we'll show how to calculate a period interest rate for a partial year. The general formula we use is shown in Equation A.3:

$$i = \left(1 + \frac{k}{m}\right)^{m \times n} - 1 \qquad \text{(A.3)}$$

Where: $i$ = Interest rate per period

$k$ = Nominal interest rate

$m$ = Number of times per year compounding occurs

$n$ = Number of years

Be careful in selecting the value for $n$ when the compounding occurs over a period less than one year. For example, for daily compounding ($m = 365$) over a period of 270 days, $n$ would be 270/365. Illustrating, if the nominal interest rate is 10 percent, we would get a period interest rate ($i$) of 0.0767664:

$$i = \left(1 + \frac{0.10}{365}\right)^{365 \times (270/365)} - 1$$

$$= (1.000273973)^{270} - 1$$

$$= 0.0767664$$

This revised value for $i$ would then be used in the discounting formula to calculate present values. Illustrating, the present value of $1,000 received 270 days from now, assuming daily compounding, is $928.71 [$1,000/(1 + 0.0767664)].[1] Recognize that this implies that the firm is earning a higher effective annual rate than the 10-percent nominal rate.

The future value formula makes use of the same adjustment, as we see in Equation A.4:

$$FV = PV\left(1 + \frac{k}{m}\right)^{m \times n} \qquad \text{(A.4)}$$

Again, if the cash flow is received less than one year later, $n$ would need to reflect that fact. Illustrating, a cash flow received 180 days from now would be handled by using $n = (180/365)$.

### Simple Interest

*If compound interest is not earned*, implying that interest is paid only at the end of the investment period based on the beginning principal, the account holder is receiving *simple interest*. Simple interest compounding and discounting calculations merely involve multiplying $n$/365 by the annual interest rate. Equation A.1 would have to be reformulated as shown in Equation A.5:

$$PV = \frac{FV_n}{1 + [k(n/365)]} \qquad \text{(A.5)}$$

Adjustments also would have to be made for partial year interest rate calculations. Returning to our earlier example, with a nominal interest rate of 10 percent and a 270-day period, the 270-day interest rate under compounding, 0.0767664, differs from the rate based on simple interest. With simple interest,

$$i = 0.10 \times (270/365) = 0.0739726.$$

---

[1] The keystrokes for a Hewlett-Packard 10BII calculator are as follows:

365 ■ [P/YR]
1000 [FV]
270 [N]
10 [I/YR]
Press [PV] to get $928.71.

### Continuous Compounding

Sometimes, you will read an advertisement for a bank account paying interest **continuously compounded**. This means that compounding is done every instant, and the results turn out to be almost the same as with daily compounding. The formula for continuous compounding of a lump sum involves raising *e* (approximately 2.7183) to the *kn* power as shown in Equation A.6:

$$FV_n = PV(e^{kn}) \qquad \text{(A.6)}$$

Illustrating, based on an annual interest rate of 6 percent and three years, the future value of $100 would be $119.72 {$100[$e^{(0.06)(3)}$]}.

## DISCOUNTING CASH FLOW STREAMS: ANNUITIES AND PERPETUITIES

Two other calculations that are especially useful for evaluating financial decisions that will have an ongoing, multiyear or even permanent effect on a corporation's cash flows are the annuity and perpetuity discounting formulas. To better understand how these work, we must distinguish between an annuity and a perpetuity. A constant dollar amount received over a *finite* number of time periods is called an **annuity**. If that cash flow stream will last *indefinitely* into the future, it is termed a **perpetuity**.

### Annuity Discounting

We first illustrate how an annuity is discounted. Assuming that the cash flows occur at the *end* of each time period, Equation A.7 can be used as follows:

$$PV = PMT\left(\frac{1 - [1/(1+k)^n]}{k}\right) \qquad \text{(A.7)}$$

Where: $PV$ = Present dollar equivalent of the series of cash flows

$PMT$ = Dollar amount of *each* period's cash flows

$k$ = Discount rate per period, in decimal form

$n$ = Number of periods

When provided with an annual discount rate, one must be careful to convert that rate to the rate *per period*, expressed in decimal form. The following example illustrates use of the annuity discount formula.

Concorde Corp. provides electronic check authorization systems to retailers, primarily grocers. It has been offered a 9-year contract to supply check authorization to a grocery chain, where it figures that the net cash flows arising from the contract would be $350,000 per year. Concorde would have to utilize an annuity present value formula to evaluate the present dollar equivalent of that cash flow series. Assuming the discount rate on similar risk projects is 10 percent, how much is the contract worth to the company in present dollar terms (ignoring any necessary initial investment outlays)?

*SOLUTION.* In terms of the above formula (Equation A.7),

$$PMT = \$350{,}000$$
$$k = 10\%$$
$$n = 9 \text{ years}$$

Substituting these into our formula,[2]

$$PV = \$350{,}000\left(\frac{1 - [1/(1+0.10)^9]}{0.10}\right)$$
$$= \$2{,}015{,}658.34$$

Concorde could compare this present value to the initial investment in order to determine whether the contract offered would be attractive.

The above approach is preferable to the use of financial tables, because most short-term financial management decisions involve time periods of less than one year, and standard tables do not include the necessary values.

To resolve financial decision-making situations such as that provided in the above example, we calculate the difference between the present value revenues and the present value costs. This difference is termed **net present value**. If the net present value is positive, the proposal would add value to the company and should be adopted. If there are several proposals that constitute competing or alternative ways of accomplishing an objective, we call them **mutually exclusive** projects, and we select the alternative having the highest net present value. In our example problem, the investment represents an independent project, which

[2] The keystrokes on a Hewlett-Packard 10BII calculator are as follows:
1 ■ [P/YR]
350000 [PMT]
10 [I/YR]
9 [N]
Press the [PV] button.

stands or falls on its own merits. The net present value is determined as shown in Equation A.8:

$$NPV = PV_{net\ cash\ flows} - Initial\ investment \quad (A.8)$$

Recall the electronic check authorization system that Concorde Corp. is considering providing to a grocery chain. Assuming the initial investment for Concorde is \$1,500,000, should Concorde proceed with it?

$$\begin{aligned} NPV &= PV_{net\ cash\ flows} - Initial\ investment \\ &= \$2{,}015{,}658.34 - \$1{,}500{,}000 \\ &= \$515{,}658.34 \end{aligned}$$

From a financial perspective, this is attractive to Concorde.

### Perpetuity Discounting

The perpetuity discounting formula is derived in a straightforward fashion from Equation A.7. First, we move the denominator $k$ outside the brackets:

$$PV = \frac{PMT}{k}\left(1 - \left[\frac{1}{(1+k)^n}\right]\right)$$

Second, notice what happens when $n$ goes to infinity: the expression inside the brackets converges on 1. We are left with $PMT/k$, as shown in the perpetuity formula illustrated below (Equation A.9). It illustrates how the total value effect of a project can be determined when one anticipates a permanent, ongoing stream of cash flows expected to start next period and continue indefinitely. Symbolically, we have $CF_1, CF_2, \ldots CF_\infty$. For annual net cash flows, we can use Equation A.9.

$$PV = \frac{CF}{k} \quad (A.9)$$

Where: $k$ = Discount rate

$CF$ = Dollar amount of perpetual cash flow stream

Many times, we will be working with daily cash flows, however. We can still use Equation A.9, but instead of $k$, we will use the daily discount rate $i$. For example, the present value of a perpetual stream of \$100 daily cash receipts, if the nominal rate is 10 percent, would be \$365,000 if we assume simple interest [\$100/(0.10/365)].[3]

Where the company is not paid daily interest (i.e., a daily average balance for the investment period is computed and the interest is posted at the end of the period), simple interest is earned on freed-up cash, and we would compute PV by taking the average account balance for the year and dividing by $k$ (or if we get monthly interest compounding, determine the average balance for the month and divide by the monthly interest rate $i$). For example, if the company gets paid interest annually, a simple interest situation, we may average the account balance over a year's time and then determine the present value of this perpetuity by dividing the balance by the nominal annual rate.

When receiving daily compound interest, first determine the daily rate using Equation A.3, then use this daily rate in Equation A.9.

## RISK AND CORPORATE DECISIONS

Risk is brought into the picture by selecting an appropriate discount rate. The rate used should be one that reflects the rate of return that could be earned on another investment of similar risk—where risk refers to the uncertainty of the cash flows. For long-lived capital projects, the company's cost of funds is typically used as the discount rate. Mathematically, discounting at the company's cost of capital enables the analyst to determine whether the project's cash flows are adequate to cover financing costs; when net present value equals 0, the net cash flows just cover the financing costs. For capital projects whose cash flows are more or less risky than the company's typical project, some adjustment must be made to the cost of capital to arrive at an appropriate discount rate. Coming up with the appropriate discount rate is often also a difficult task when evaluating working capital decisions. In this appendix, we necessarily limit our focus to the mathematics of time value. In the appendix to Chapter 3, we presented the capital asset pricing model, which is one approach that can be used to determine risk-adjusted discount rates.

## PROBLEMS

1. Jim is confused about the difference between simple interest and compound interest. He wants to know the daily interest rate equivalent to an 8-percent nominal rate, assuming:
   a. Simple interest is credited to his account.

[3] Again, we are assuming that $k$ is specified as a nominal or stated interest rate, on an annual basis. If we were presented with an annual effective rate, then we would have to use a slightly different formula:

$$i = (1 + k)^{n/365} - 1$$

where $k$ is the annual effective rate and $n$ is the number of days, which for a perpetual stream of daily cash flows would be 1.

**b.** Compound interest is credited to his account daily.

**c.** Compound interest is credited to his account on a continuous basis.

**2.** How much money would Jim have in his account (see Problem 1) if he starts out with $1,000 and leaves the money in the account for six months, for each of the situations given in **a–c**? Comment on the differences from the results in Problem 1, indicating why they arise.

**3.** Barbara has inherited a 5-year annuity of $2,000 per year. She wishes to know how much this is worth in today's dollars, assuming the discount rate is 11 percent.

**4.** How much would Barbara's inheritance (from Problem 3) have been worth if she (and her heirs) had received the $2,000 as a perpetuity instead of an annuity?

**5.** Diamond Grocers is considering a 1-year lease on an automated warehousing system. It estimates the company would save $400,000 from the system, which would have a lease cost of $360,000. Ignoring tax effects, would the system add value for Diamond, if Diamond's cost of capital is 10 percent per year?

**a.** Assume the $400,000 savings and $360,000 lease payment both occur at the end of the year.

**b.** Assume the savings and lease expense both occur evenly throughout the year and with equal amounts realized at the end of each month.

# Glossary

## A

**account analysis statement** monthly listing which banks provide corporate customers indicating the services used and the charges assessed the company. The statement provides in-depth balance information, a 12-month balance history, a detailed listing and pricing of services used, and the degree to which the company's actual balances offset fees charged for the services used.

**account parameters and records** credit customer identifiers such as name, address, and the customer's bank transit routing number. These items are included in the customer's credit file.

**account reconciliation** a disbursement-related service in which the bank develops a detailed report of checks paid as well as miscellaneous debits and stopped payments. In a full account reconciliation, the company also provides the bank with a record of checks drawn, and the bank informs the company of which checks remain outstanding.

**accounts payable** a liability that is generated by purchasing a good or service on credit.

**accounts receivable turnover** computed by dividing days' sales outstanding into the number of days in the calculation period, which is usually 365. Indicates how many times per year the seller's investment in accounts receivable "turns over" into sales, which is an efficiency measure giving the same signal as days sales outstanding.

**accrual** a liability account that results from expenses incurred during the operating process that are not yet paid.

**ACH credit** payment order transmitted through the automated clearing house system and originated by the payor. The routing bank (originating institution) in this case is the payor's disbursement bank.

**ACH debit** payment order for payment through the automated clearing house system and originated by the payee, based on the prior authorization by the payor. This order is routed through the payee's bank (originating financial depository institution, or OFDI). Another name for an electronic depository transfer.

**active investment strategy** an approach to investing which involves relatively more trading and active monitoring of the portfolio, and many times is motivated by a philosophy that the investor can "beat the market." Active strategy managers would rarely buy a security with the intention of holding it to maturity. For example, when an analyst forecasts a change in interest rates, trading strategies can be devised to enhance investment profits.

**adjustable-rate preferred stock (ARPS)** preferred stock on which the dividend is reset quarterly.

**adjusted $r^2$** a measure for a statistical model's goodness of fit which compensates for the upward bias in goodness-of-fit resulting from the inclusion of additional predictor variables.

**advised line** a standard lending service used abroad, which is very similar to credit lines in the United States. The advised line involves unsecured lending of up to one year maturity, available on short notice to the borrower.

**advisory services** include all specialized and general financial management consulting banks might provide to corporations.

**agencies** securities issued by governmental agencies and several private financing institutions that have governmental backing.

**agency problem** a conflict that arises when the interests of the principals (stockholders) do not coincide with those of the agents (managers).

**aging schedule** shows a percent breakdown of present receivables, with the categories shown typically as follows: current, 0–30 days past due, 31–60 days past due, and over 90 days past due.

**aggressive financing strategy** a strategy that minimizes the amount of long-term financing used. This strategy generally results in a lower current ratio and higher but more volatile profitability during periods of normal yield curves.

**ANSI** the American National Standards Institute.

**annuity** a constant dollar amount received over a finite number of time periods.

**anticipation rule** this transfer rule initiates a cash transfer before the related deposit is made.

**asset-based loans** a form of collateralized lending which has a claim on an asset or group of assets, ordinarily receivables or inventory, which could be easily sold if the borrower defaults on the loan.

**asset securitization** has become prevalent in the United States because of the need for banks to increase their capital-to-assets ratio.

**asset swap** a swap created to hedge cash flows related to assets or investments.

**auction preferred stock (APS)** preferred stock on which the dividend is reset every 49 days through an auction bidding process.

**automated clearing house (ACH)** a quick and relatively inexpensive means of electronically processing large numbers of routine transactions. The electronic equivalent of the paper check clearing system.

**availability float** the delay from the time a check is deposited until the time when funds are available to be spent. This time lag may not always coincide with the amount of time it takes the check to actually clear, but generally the two are closely linked. Delays in collecting checks caused by delays in the check clearing process after the check has been deposited.

**availability schedule** listing of how long after deposit checks will become "good funds" for spending by the depositor. Prior to recording available funds, the bank will credit the depositor's ledger balance, but the portion of the total deposit available as "good funds" ready to be spent varies according to the bank's schedule.

**average collection period** how long the typical customer is taking to pay its bills. Alternately, how long, on average, the seller is taking to collect its receivables. It is computed by dividing accounts receivable by daily sales. Also known as days sales outstanding.

**avoidance** the pricing of invoices in the seller's currency.

## *B*

**back value date** the date that cleared checks are assigned and may cause funds to be drawn from an account before the check actually arrives at the drawee bank.

**balance fractions, inventory** the percent of an inventory purchase order that remains as inventory over succeeding months.

**balance fractions, payables** the dollar amount remaining to be paid in succeeding months as a percent of the original accounts payable balance.

**balance reporting services** means by which the treasurer may inquire by phone or PC hook-up about the balance positions in many different accounts and about transactions affecting the accounts.

**bank deposit notes** short-term debt securities issued by banks, which range from 9 months to 30 years in maturity, and have an active secondary market.

**Bank Holding Company Act of 1956** prohibited further acquisitions by bank holding companies unless specifically allowed by state law in the state of the proposed acquisition.

**bank notes** technically not deposits, these bank debt obligations thereby avoid FDIC insurance premiums which also forfeits deposit insurance coverage.

**bank relationship policy** document which establishes the company's objectives, compensations, and review process for the banks with which it has a relationship.

**bank selection process** involves assembling a system of banks to serve all of a company's cash management and related needs.

**banker's acceptance (BA)** a corporate time draft drawn on the buyer, whose bank agrees to pay ("accepts") the amount if the buyer does not. Related to this, a short-term acceptance facility allows the selling firm to initiate drafts (called bills of exchange) against the buyer's bank instead of against the buyer, which can be discounted at the bank. A time draft drawn against a deposit in a commercial bank but with payment at maturity guaranteed by the bank.

**biased expectations hypothesis** a theory of the term structure of interest rates in which market expectations are modified by some degree of liquidity preference.

**bilateral and multilateral netting systems** are centralized bookkeeping entries made to eliminate ("net out") offsetting amounts owed by divisions or subsidiaries within a company.

**Board of Governors** the main Federal Reserve System's policy-making body, which is comprised of seven members. Governors are appointed by the President and confirmed by the U.S. Senate. The Board of Governors supervises the district Federal Reserve banks, limiting to some extent the powers and privileges of their stockholders.

**Bond Anticipation Notes** short-term debt instrument which provides working capital financing for states and localities as they await anticipated revenues from upcoming bond issuance.

**Box-Jenkins model** a type of time-series forecasting technique. Named after two pioneers in the field of time series modeling, this approach lets the data specify the best model.

**breadth** refers to the number and size of parties which are potential buyers of the instruments in a market.

**Bretton Woods Agreement** an agreement signed by the major trading countries following World War II which returned the world economy to a type of gold standard. The U.S. dollar was pegged to gold at $35 per ounce. Currencies of all other countries were then fixed in price to the dollar and the countries agreed to maintain the established exchange rate within 1 percent.

**brokers** middlemen which do not inventory the securities they arrange transactions for.

**business risk** the possibility that a company will not be able to meet ongoing operating expenditures.

**buy hedge** a hedge created by purchasing a futures contract.

**buy-and-hold strategy** an approach to investing which involves holding until maturity securities purchased. Quite often, this is part of a "maturity matching" approach to investing that prescribes investing in a security that will mature at the end of the investment horizon.

**call option** a contract that allows the owner to purchase the underlying asset at a specific price over a specific span of time.

**capital asset pricing model (CAPM)** a mathematical representation of the relationship between a stock's risk and its expected market return. The CAPM is also used to give the analyst an estimate of the effect of a project's risk on its required rate of return.

**captive finance companies** a financing subsidiary of a corporation that facilitates arranging financing for customers of the firm's products.

**cash and securities mix decision** the proportional breakdown of cash and securities held by a company as part of its current asset holdings.

**cash application** crediting the account upon payment for a credit sale, this process frees up that amount of the credit limit for additional orders from this customer.

**cash budget** forecast showing cash receipts and disbursements on a monthly basis for a minimum horizon of one year, typically assembled before the beginning of a new fiscal year.

**cash collection system** a management designed system that converts checks to cash and considers mail float, processing float, and availability float.

**cash concentration** the process of moving dollar balances from deposit banks to concentration banks.

**cash conversion period** a liquidity measure that takes a going-concern approach. It measures the difference in time from when cash is received from credit customers and when cash is paid to suppliers. The length of time from when cash is paid out for purchases and when cash is received from collections on credit sales.

**cash cycle** the time that elapses from the purchase of raw materials until cash is received from the sale of the final product.

**cash discount** the percentage amount that can be subtracted from the invoice if the customer pays within a stated period of time.

**cash flow from operations** one of the most direct measures of liquidity found by subtracting operating cash disbursements from operating cash receipts.

**cash flow timeline** the cash cycle displayed along a time dimension.

**cash items** deposited checks given immediate, provisional credit by the bank.

**cash letter** the accompanying listing of checks that are bundled by the deposit bank for routing through the check clearing process.

**causal distributions** a set of outcomes characterized by situations where a predictor variable has changed from what was expected, causing the forecast variable to deviate from what was expected.

**causal techniques** forecasting methods linking the forecast values of an effect variable to one or more hypothesized causes.

**centralized disbursing** an organizational structure which disburses corporate cash from a central area, allowing the corporate headquarters' staff to check each disbursement and possibly initiate each payment as well.

**centralized processing system** a cash collection system where corporate headquarters receives all customer remittances.

**centralized transfer initiation** the timing and amount of the transfer is centered either at the concentration bank or corporate headquarters.

**certificate of deposit (CD)** an interest-bearing account which evidences (certifies) that a certain amount of money has been deposited at the bank for a pre-specified period of time, and that will be redeemed with interest at the end of that time (maturity).

**Check Clearing for the 21st Century Act** also called "Check 21," encourages banks to transmit check images electronically to print centers located near the paying banks, where substitute checks are created from the images of the original checks and the MICR information. These substitute checks (Image Replacement Documents, or IRDs) function as the legal equivalent of the original checks and are then presented to the banks for payment, speeding presentment while reducing risk.

**check imaging** digital capture of the front of a check, the back of a check, or both. Used extensively in positive pay services and in lockbox operations.

**check processing float** delays in collecting cash caused by delays between the time a check is received and when it is deposited in the banking system.

**check truncation** involves expediting clearing by scanning the data on the check's MICR line, and then processing only that data back to the payee's bank.

**CHIPS** short for Clearing House Interbank Payment System, the institution which was established in 1970 to handle interbank transactions needed to settle international transactions. CHIPS is a private association of banks that operates through the New York Clearinghouse Association.

**clearing agent** often a Federal Reserve bank, branch, or RCPC, an entity which uses the information printed at the bottom of the check to process the check.

**clearing bank(s)** when checks are deposited, the bank(s) used for processing those checks into the clearing system. Sometimes called deposit bank(s).

**clearing float** sometimes called "availability float," the delay in availability incurred after deposit. The length of this component of float is linked to the bank's availability schedule in connection with the location of the payor's bank.

**clearinghouse** a central location where representatives of area banks meet, and each bank settles its balances with one institution (the clearing house) instead of with each bank individually.

**coefficient of determination ($r^2$)** gives the goodness-of-fit for a fitted regression equation. It indicates the proportion of the total variance of the forecasted variable that is accounted for, or "explained," by the fitted regression equation.

**coefficient of variation** the standard deviation of a variable divided by the mean or expected value of that variable.

**coin & currency services** procedures provided by banks which include receiving of bulk cash deposits sent by armed courier, sorting of deposit items, same day verification of the total deposit if received by the bank's cutoff time, and supply of coins and currency for the company's cash payment needs.

**collected balance** sometimes called the available balance, this amount represents how much of a deposit balance is immediately spendable. It may be somewhat less than the ledger balance because of availability delays applied to the checks by the bank.

**collection bank** the bank of deposit that encodes the dollar amount of the check in magnetic ink on the bottom right side of the check and then routes the check through the clearing process.

**collection float** the sum of the delays in collecting cash from customers caused by mail, process, and availability delays.

**collection procedures** detailed statements regarding when and how the company will carry out collection of past due accounts. These policies specify how long the company will wait past the due date to initiate collection efforts, the method(s) of contact with delinquent customers, and whether and at what point accounts will be referred to an outside collection agency.

**commercial paper** an unsecured IOU issued mainly by financial companies such as banks, their parent holding companies, and consumer or commercial finance companies. A short-term promissory note issued by a corporation for a fixed maturity generally in the 30 day range but can be as much as 270 days.

**commitment fee** an annual fee of between one-quarter and one-half percent of the size of the credit line a firm pays to a bank to guarantee access to the line.

**committed line of credit** a line of credit where the firm pays a commitment fee that obligates the bank to provide funding for the credit line with a formal written agreement.

**company processing center** an administrative office or area within the corporation that processes payments received from customers.

**compensating balances** amounts held in a deposit account which the company holds to offset bank-provided cash management and/or lending services. When held in support of lending, these balances are not considered to be transaction balances, and are not subject to the Fed's required reserve ratio.

**competitive bids** offers to buy securities at a given price or yield. In the Treasury auctions, these are mainly entered by financial institutions, including dealers.

**Competitive Equality Banking Act of 1987** allows existing nonbank banks to continue to operate, but prohibits the establishment of new nonbank banks.

**complete enumeration** a lockbox model that analyzes all possible lockbox sites to determine the optimal combination that maximizes shareholder wealth.

**compound interest** interest paid on interest.

**compounding** the future value of a single dollar amount being invested today.

**comprehensive payables** is the outsourcing of part or all of the accounts payable and/or disbursement functions.

**concentration accounts** deposit account into which funds are pooled at the endpoint(s) of a company's collection system.

**concentration bank** a bank that receives balance transfers from several deposit or gathering banks.

**conservative financing strategy** a strategy that uses a majority of long-term sources to fulfill its financing needs. This strategy results in a higher current ratio but a lower but more stable level of profitability during periods of normal yield curves.

**consignment** an arrangement whereby a retailer obtains an inventory item without obligation. If not sold, the inventory can be returned.

**contingency plans** actions that can be taken if and when necessitated by deteriorating conditions.

**continuously compounding** when compounding is done every instant.

**contracting cost motive** theoretical motive for trade credit extension in which the buyers' sales contracting costs are reduced in that they can inspect the quantity and quality of the goods prior to payment due to the delayed payment offered.

**control limits** trigger points, which signal a purchase or sale of securities, and are part of the decision-making apparatus in the Miller-Orr cash management model.

**controlled disbursement account (CDA)** a checking account for which the bank provides early morning presentment information via a phone call, Web site, or computer message to the cash manager. Notification for controlled disbursement accounts involves informing the company of the total dollar amount of checks that will be presented later that day, so that sufficient funds can be transferred into the account. Accounts at banks in small towns that only receive cash letters once a day. The bank can inform the financial manager of the dollar amount of check clears that will be charged against the account early in the day.

**corporate agency services** security-related services, some of which are related to short-term borrowing and investing, offered by financial institutions to publicly held corporations.

**counterparties** the two entities involved on either side of a swap agreement.

**country risk** the possibility of loss of assets due to political, economic, or regulatory instability in a nation in which business is being conducted.

**coupon-equivalent yield** interest return figure calculated based on a 365-day year instead of 360 days. For a discount security maturing within one year, it is also adjusted to account for the fact that the price paid is less than the face value, which increases the true yield.

**coupon security** one which pays interest periodically prior to maturity.

**credit administration** the establishment of credit policy and planning, organizing, directing, and controlling all aspects of the credit function.

**credit decision process** sequence beginning with the marketing contact with potential customers and ending with the credit extension decision. Includes credit investigation, customer information contacts, written document preparation, credit file establishment, and financial analysis.

**credit extension** the decision to sell on credit to a customer.

**credit interchange bureaus** departments of local credit associations that provide information on the credit history of local businesses and individuals.

**credit limit** where credit is extended, the maximum dollar amount that cumulative credit purchases can reach for a given customer. Also known as the credit line.

**credit period** the length of time allowable for payment of the invoice amount.

**credit policy** a company's credit standards, credit limits, approach to credit investigation, credit terms, and collection activity.

**credit reporting agencies** sources of business credit information, such as Dun & Bradstreet.

**credit scoring models** evaluation approach which weights variables depending on their helpfulness in discriminating between "good" and "bad" applicants, based on past payment histories. These models are developed with the assistance of computerized statistical techniques such as multiple discriminant analysis.

**credit standards** the minimally acceptable creditworthy customer, from the perspective of the company extending credit.

**credit terms** specification of when invoiced amounts are due and whether a cash discount can be taken for earlier payment.

**credit-granting decision** determination of whether and how much credit to give customers, a process which involves four distinct steps: development of credit standards, getting necessary information about customers, application of credit standards, and setting credit limits.

**cross hedge** a hedge that uses a futures contract that has a different underlying instrument from the cash market instrument being hedged.

**currency blocs** a subset of controlled exchange rates between currencies of the included countries.

**currency swap** an agreement between two parties to exchange different currencies and then to reexchange them at a future date at the same exchange rate. Periodic interest payments are made during the term of the swap.

**current liquidity index** a cash coverage ratio found by adding beginning of period balance of cash assets and the cash flow from operations during the period and then dividing this sum by the sum of beginning of period notes payable and current maturing debt.

**current maturity** the length of time remaining until a security matures. When first issued, a five-year Treasury note has an original maturity of five years; one year later it has a current maturity of four years.

**current ratio** the ratio of current assets to current liabilities used to measure the degree of coverage available to short-term lenders.

**custody account** specialized account in which financial institution holds securities, automatically reinvests interest and other investment-related cash receipts, transfers funds per corporate instructions, monitors issuers actions such as calls and refundings, and provides a monthly statement on all account transactions.

**cutoff time** deposit deadline for receiving a given day's stated availability.

**daily NPV** the difference between the present value of a project's daily inflows and the present value of its daily outflows.

**daily transfer rule** the simplest and most common transfer rule that initiates a daily transfer from the deposit bank to the concentration bank in the amount of the daily deposit.

**daylight overdrafts** bookkeeping negative account balances which occur when a bank's Federal Reserve account book balance is negative during the day or it sends more funds via Fedwire than it receives, prior to final end-of-day settlements. Many of the overdrafts occur because of international funds transfers of government securities transactions.

**days inventory held (DIH)** the average number of days a firm holds inventory found by dividing average daily cost of goods sold into the balance sheet inventory account.

**days payables outstanding (DPO)** the average number of days the firm takes to pay for its purchases found by dividing average daily purchases into the balance sheet accounts payable balance.

**days sales outstanding (DSO)** measure of how long a company is taking to collect receivables. Also known as average collection period. It is computed by taking the latest period's accounts receivables and dividing it by daily credit sales. Daily credit sales, in turn, are computed by taking the period's sales and dividing by the number of days in the period—365 when computing DSO over a yearly period. The average number of days credit customers take to pay for their purchases found by dividing average daily sales into the accounts receivable balance.

**dealers** market participants which typically "take a position" in the security instrument(s) they trade, meaning they hold an inventory of securities.

**debit cards** similar to credit cards except the transaction amount is immediately (or within two business days) charged against the user's checking account balance. These cards allow consumers to pay grocery and other bills through an electronic charge to their bank accounts.

**decentralized disbursing** corporate arrangement which allows payments to be made by divisional offices or individual stores, usually from accounts held at nearby banks.

**decentralized processing system** a collection system that has the company's various field offices or stores receive payments from the company's customers.

**decentralized transfer initiation** the cash transfer decision initiated by the field office manager.

**decomposition method** analysis of collection experience which involves segregating the period-to-period changes in receivables into three effects: the collection effect, the sales effect, and the interaction effect.

**default risk** the possibility that the issuer will not meet contractual obligations to pay interest or repay principal or will violate a covenant in a debt agreement.

**demand deposit account (DDA)** non-interest bearing checking accounts. This account is the foundation for all other cash management services the bank might offer to the corporate client.

**demand flow** an inventory system similar to the just-in-time system, but more encompassing.

**denomination** refers to a security's dollar amount or face value.

**deposit reconciliation** one type of account reconciliation, this service minimizes the number of depository accounts a company must have while offering the added advantage of convenience.

**deposit reporting service** information on account balances offered by a bank or third-party vendor, which enables the treasury staff to know when and where the company's operations have deposited money into bank accounts.

**Depository Institution Deregulation and Monetary Control Act of 1980** landmark legislation which enabled savings and loans, mutual savings banks, and credit unions to operate more like commercial banks. Also established reserve requirement ranges for various deposit accounts.

**depository transfer checks (DTC)** non-negotiable, unsigned checks used by firms to move funds from one account to another. They are often used to move (concentrate) monies collected in many different locations into a pooled account in a "concentration bank," where the money can be invested as a single large amount.

**depth** a characteristic of a market in which a very large dollar amount of securities can be easily absorbed without large changes in the market price.

**deterministic model** data input for deterministic models are single point estimates.

**direct deposit** service in which the employer's bank automatically deposits employees' wages and salaries. The bank sorts out the on-us checks for employees having checking accounts at that bank, and credits their accounts. Employees banking elsewhere are paid through the local clearing house or ACH-initiated transactions. Direct deposit of payroll is easily the most popular electronic payment application.

**direct hedge** a hedge using a futures contract that is of the same type as the cash market instrument being hedged.

**direct presenting** situation in which checks are sent to the drawee bank or its local clearinghouse via courier. Direct presenting is mainly used for large checks.

**disbursement float** the delay between the time when the company writes the check and the time when its bank charges the checking account for the amount of the check.

**disbursement policy** whether an informal strategy or a formal written document, specifies which payment mechanism to utilize for a given disbursement, when to pay a given invoice, and the setup of guidelines regarding the disbursement system (including which bank(s) might be involved).

**disbursement system** a company's payment methods, disbursement banks, and disbursing locations.

**disbursing bank** bank used to pay from.

**discount basis** when the selling price of a financial instrument is less than its face value or value at maturity.

**discount rate** in a capital project evaluation, it is the opportunity cost of the use of funds, which is used to determine the present value of cash flows.

**discount rate (Fed)** the rate charged depository institutions when they borrow reserves from the Fed in order to meet their reserve requirements or meet unusual loan demand.

**discount security** one which does not pay regular interest payments, but compensates the investor for implied interest by returning at maturity a principal amount greater than the purchase price.

**discount yield** the difference between the maturity cash flow and the purchase price on a discount (non-interest bearing) security, expressed as a percentage of the purchase price.

**discounted cash flow** capital budgeting approach to making financial decisions that involves determining the present value of all cash inflows then subtracting the present value of cash outflows. Typically, this process results in the calculation of an investment's net present value, but internal rate of return is also a discounted cash flow technique.

**discounting** the determination of a present dollar equivalent of a cash flow to be received in the future.

**distribution method** a regression-based cash forecasting approach which spreads, or "distributes," a monthly total across the weeks or days within that month. This method has also been used to model payroll-related cash disbursements by relating cash outflows to how many business days have elapsed since payroll checks have been issued.

**dividend capture strategy** corporate investment strategy involving buying a common or preferred stock shortly before it pays its dividend, or buying a preferred stock having an adjustable dividend payment. Because intercorporate dividends have been largely excludable for income tax purposes (presently there is a 70% exclusion), corporate investors buy stocks with high dividend yields, hold them at least 49 days (until the record date for payment), and then sell.

**dividend roll** an investment approach which involves buying stocks with high dividend yields, holding them at least 49 days to collect the dividend, and then selling the stocks.

**dollar-day float** a measure of delay that considers both the dollar amount and the time lag.

**dominant** securities which provide a higher expected return for a given amount of risk than other securities.

**double counting** this can either occur when a bank counts the same balances as compensation for a loan and as compensation for cash management services, or if the company has written a depository check for which it has been granted availability at the concentration bank, but has not had its checking account debited.

**draft** a written order to make payment to a third party, where the entity ordered to pay the draft is usually a bank. Any party holding a credit balance for the person writing the draft may have a draft drawn on it.

**drawee bank** the bank on which a check or draft was written ("drawn").

**driving variable** a key variable in most financial planning models to which most relationships are tied. Sales is generally such a variable in many financial planning models.

**dual balance** the same dollar balance that is temporarily on deposit at two different banks.

**dummy variables** variables included in the regression equation when modeling seasonal or monthly effects. The number included is one less than the number of seasons. Each dummy variable that is included as an independent variable takes on a value of 1 only when the season it represents is the season for which the forecast is being made, and 0 at all other times.

**duration** a tool for evaluating the interest rate risk of interest-bearing notes and bonds. It is defined as the weighted average time until the investor receives an investment's discounted cash flows.

## E

**earnings credit rate (ECR)** a rate that banks credit collected balances with as compensation for leaving the balances in the account.

**e-commerce** involves transmitting information and payment flows electronically, a process that includes EDI and electronic payments.

**economic exposure** refers to the possibility that the long-term net present value of a firm's expected cash flows will change due to unexpected changes in exchange rates.

**economic order quantity (EOQ)** the order quantity that minimizes the total cost of managing inventory.

**EEC** the European Economic Community.

**effective annual rate** incorporates the compounding of interest through time to give a more accurate reflection of the increase in wealth gained by holding a security. Whenever the interest is compounded more than once a year, the effective annual rate will exceed the nominal rate. On loan agreements, the effective rate is the annualized effective simple interest rate on the financing arrangement considering all out of pocket costs relative to the dollar amount of usable funds received.

**effective interest rate** the rate of interest that is equal to or greater than the stated interest rate because of out-of-pocket expenses and usable funds that are less than the face value of the loan.

**efficient markets** where prices change freely and instantly in response to supply and demand, and are not significantly affected by poor information or tax code barriers.

**Electronic Bill Presentment and Payment** Web-based B2C invoicing and electronic payment.

**electronic check presentment (ECP)** an arrangement in which the image of the MICR line of a check is presented to the paying back, instead of presenting the physical check, shortening clearance float.

**electronic corporate trade payment** an arrangement between two corporations (a buyer and a seller) and the banks of the two parties so that payment is effected without a paper check being issued.

**electronic data interchange (EDI)** the electronic transmission of purchase-related data such as orders, shipping notices, invoices, credits and other adjustments, and payment notices.

**electronic depository transfer checks (EDT)** payment process in which a local or regional account is debited electronically and the amount sent through an automated clearing house to the concentration bank account. Also known as an ACH debit, is an electronic equivalent to the paper DTC. The electronic transaction provides quicker availability in the concentration account for the company.

**electronic funds transfer (EFT)** the actual electronic transfer of payments, or value, between trading partners.

**Electronic Invoicing Presentment and Payment** Web-based B2B invoicing and electronic payment.

**electronic lockbox** collection system offered by banks for companies to receive payments, via wire transfers or ACH, from customers.

**EMS** members of the EEC created a subset of controlled exchange rates between their respective currencies, which is referred to as the European Monetary System.

**enterprise resources planning (ERP)** accounting-oriented information systems used for identifying and planning the enterprise-wide resources needed to take, make, ship, and account for customer orders.

**error distribution** the shape or pattern of the array of forecast errors.

**Euro** a new currency that represents a basket of currencies of the participating countries in the European Monetary System.

**euro cp** similar in concept to domestic commercial paper except issued in the Euro-market which has fewer restrictions, is unrated, and generally has a longer maturity averaging from 60 to 90 days.

**Eurodollar CDs** dollar-denominated deposits held in banks or bank branches outside the U.S. or in International Banking Facilities (IBFs, which can offer Eurodollar deposits only to non-U.S. residents) located within the United States.

**Eurogiro** an electronic payment network established to enable European financial institutions to exchange transactions. Eurogiro is tailored toward making cross-border transactions for small currency amounts.

**evaluated receipt settlement (ERS)** an electronic payment process in which receipt of shipment (not receipt of invoice) triggers payment by the purchasing company.

**event risk** includes any security feature or possible event that subjects the investor to a disruption to or reduction in the expected yield.

**exchange-rate risk** the risk that a firm faces when buying or selling in one or more currencies different from its domestic currency.

**expedited check processing** speedier check clearing provided by the clearing bank if the depositor is willing to perform extra tasks or pay the bank the extra charge involved.

**Expedited Funds Availability Act of 1987** required that shorter availability schedules be put in place to reduce arbitrarily long holds on deposited checks.

**expert systems** computerized decision-making procedure based on a mimicking of what experienced human decision makers have done in many similar situations.

**exponential smoothing** statistical forecasting technique similar to a moving average, but overcoming the slowness of adaptation to changing patterns inherent in the moving average by allowing a greater weighting for more recent data.

**face value** investors holding an investment to maturity will receive this amount back from the issuer. Also called the investment's principal.

**factoring** the process of selling receivables and receiving funds before payment of the receivables is made by the customers.

**factors** companies that buy receivables from the selling firm at a discount from face value, possibly giving the selling firm a cash advance on the anticipated collections. Usually the receivables are bought on a nonrecourse basis, meaning that the factor bears the risk of nonpayment.

**FASB Statement 95** the accounting standard that created the Statement of Cash Flows. Provides a set of guidelines to help classify cash receipts and disbursement according to type of activity.

**Fed float** part of the clearing float for a mailed check, it arises because the Fed may grant availability to the clearing bank before it presents the check to (and debits the account of) the payee's bank. Fed float has been greatly reduced since 1980, because the 1980 Monetary Control Act mandated that the Fed eliminate or charge for Fed float.

**fed funds rate** the rate charged on reserve borrowings, mostly overnight, transacted between banks.

**Federal Advisory Council** is a group of prominent commercial bankers which gives input into Fed decision making.

**Federal Deposit Insurance Corporation Improvement Act of 1991** requires the FDIC to give acquiring banks the choice of whether to bid for all of a failed bank's deposits or just the insured deposits, signaling a reduction in coverage for uninsured deposits.

**Federal Open Market Committee (FOMC)** the seven members of the Board of Governors are also members of this group, which makes most of the monetary policy for the U.S. in its eight regularly scheduled meetings per year. The FOMC effects changes in the money supply by buying and selling Treasury securities (open market operations), which affects the reserve position of banks, and ultimately the money supply.

**Federal Reserve Act (1913)** established the Federal Reserve System to oversee and regulate the national money and credit system.

**Federal Reserve Banks (FRBs)** 12 district banks, which together with branches and regional check processing centers, make up the banking portion of the Federal Reserve System. These are private organizations with a corporate structure very similar to that of a commercial bank. Each Reserve Bank issues stock and has a board of directors that elects the bank's officers and oversees the bank's operations.

**Federal Reserve member banks** see member banks.

**Federal Reserve System (Fed)** the nation's central bank, this organization oversees the national money and credit system by acting as lender of last resort, lending money to banks through the "discount window," facilitating the payments mechanism, and is one of several national bodies that supervises and regulates banks.

**Fedwire** a linked network of the twelve Fed district banks which transfers funds for banks (and by extension their customers) by debiting or crediting the banks' reserve accounts. It is a major part of the Federal Reserve System's payment system involvement.

**field warehouse agreement** inventories pledged as collateral and physically segregated from other inventory generally on the borrower's premises.

**financial EDI (FEDI)** the exchange of electronic business information such as lockbox information reports, daily balance reports, and monthly account analysis reports between a firm and its bank. In the context of payments, financial EDI refers to electronic data interchange combined with payment instructions. This allows customers to include invoice data and payment instructions in the same payment order.

**financial flexibility** the ability of the firm to augment its future cash flows to cover any unforeseen needs or to take advantage of any unforeseen opportunities.

**Financial Institutions Reform, Recovery, and Enforcement Act (1989)** allowed bank holding companies to buy healthy savings and loan associations.

**financial motive** one of the theoretical motives for trade credit extension, applies where the seller has a lower cost of capital than the buyer and is able to pass along some of the difference.

**financial restructuring** situation in which the company changes its relative use of debt financing—altering the company's financial risk.

**financial risk** the possibility that a company will not be able to cover financing related expenditures such as lease payments, interest, principal repayment, and preferred stock dividends.

**Financial Services Modernization Act of 1999** also known as the Gramm-Leach-Bliley Act, this law repealed the 1933 Glass-Steagall Act's prohibition on bank-investment company affiliations.

**financial statement approach** utilizes profitability analysis along with a balance sheet evaluation of what the effect of a proposed course of action would have on the company's liquidity and cash position. Approximate timing of financial effects can be seen through the use of pro forma, or projected, financial statements.

**financial swap** an exchange of periodic cash flows between two parties.

**financing activities** defined as cash flows resulting from proceeds of issuance of securities, retirement of debt, and payments of dividends or other distributions to shareholders.

**finished goods inventory** inventory of the finished product ready for sale.

**first differencing** a means of correcting a data series for autocorrelation, which is accomplished by subtracting the previous value for the dependent variable from the current value, and then using the differences as the dependent variable (in lieu of the original values of the dependent variable).

**five C's of credit** traditional means of evaluating a corporate credit applicant by investigating character, collateral, capacity, conditions, and capital. Character is thought to be the single most important aspect in this approach.

**fixed costs** expenses which do not change with changes in activity or sales volume, such as rent or insurance.

**fixed-for-floating rate swap** in this type of swap, Party A, with floating rate debt, agrees to pay Party B, who has fixed rate debt, a fixed-rate interest payment based on the notional dollar amount stated in the agreement, in exchange for receipt of a floating-rate interest payment.

**flat yield curve** horizontally shaped graph of the yields to maturity of securities with various maturities, implying a "no change" forecast of future interest rates.

**float** the delay between the time a payment is initiated and the time when the payment is debited to the payor (disbursement float) or credited to the payee (collection float). Within ethical limits companies try to maximize it on payments or minimize it on collections, and float continues to be an important fact of life that must be coped with.

**floating lien** a financing arrangement where a borrower's inventory in general is pledged as collateral for a loan.

**floating-rate note** type of loan in which the interest rate is reset either daily, weekly, monthly, quarterly, or semi-annually.

**floor planning** the common name used for trust receipt loans made to automobile dealerships.

**forecast bias** tendency for a forecasting model to systematically over- or under-predict the variable of interest. It can often be detected on a graph of forecast errors over time or across values of an important predictor variable.

**forecast horizon** how far ahead the cash balance is being projected.

**forecast interval** the units the horizon is segmented into, such as months in a year-ahead forecast.

**foreign exchange rate** the price of one currency stated in relation to the price of another currency.

**foreign exchange risk** the possibility that exchange rates will move adversely, causing results of foreign business activities to have a reduced value when converted into the company's home currency.

**forward contract** a contract negotiated between a financial manager and a bank for the future delivery of a foreign currency.

**forward rates** prices or yields which the market collectively forecasts today for future periods. In foreign exchange markets, forward rates refer to exchange rates between currencies which are contracted to exist at a future value date.

**forward value date** the date that good funds will be credited to the account (similar to availability schedules in the U.S.).

**full reconciliation** service which provides detailed checks outstanding information along with the checks paid data from company-supplied check issue detail.

**futures contract** a standardized contract that obligates the buyer (issuer) to purchase (sell) a specified amount of the item represented by the contract at a set price at the expiration of the contract.

**futures option** an option contract that gives the buyer (issuer) the right to purchase (sell) the futures contract underlying the options contract.

**futures exchange rates** an exchange rate at which currencies can be traded at a future date. Futures differ from forwards in that the futures contract is standardized and traded on a national exchange.

## G

**Garn-St. Germain Depository Institutions Act of 1982** enacted alterations allowing: (1) depository institutions to pay interest on money market deposit accounts in order to compete with money market mutual funds and (2) savings and loans associations to lend to businesses.

**general obligation securities** the backing for the interest and principal payments of these securities is simply future general revenues and the issuer's capacity to raise taxes.

**giro acceptance** foreign payment method in which computer-processable stub card is signed by the customer, who then takes it to the post office. The bill mailed to the customer has a stub attached to it that includes the seller's bank and account number.

**giro systems** a collection system for consumer payments that is commonplace in Europe. Sellers send customers an invoice with a payment stub encoded with the seller's bank account number. The customer signs the stub and then takes it to a GIRO processor. The processor delivers the stubs to the nearest GIRO bank which then debits the customer's account and credits the seller's account.

**government warrant** essentially a payable-through-draft issued by a government agency.

## H

**hedger** a person who has a cash position or an anticipated cash position that he or she is trying to protect from adverse interest rate or exchange rate movements.

**high dollar group sort** a special expediting of large dollar amounts through the clearing system, with the Fed granting the depositing bank immediate credit if it deposits the check early in the morning.

**high liquidity strategy** current asset allocation strategy which prescribes a high proportion of assets to be held in cash and securities in order to reduce the chance of running out of cash.

**historical yield spread analysis** study of risk-related and maturity-related interest rate differences, motivated by a desire to detect profitable trading strategies.

**holding costs** the costs associated with the storage of inventory.

## I

**imaging** digitizing documents, such as invoices and checks.

**index fund** a managed portfolio assembled to mirror a particular financial market composite.

**initial investment** expenses necessary to implement a capital budgeting proposal must be determined. This may include set-up costs, physical asset acquisition or disposition costs, permanent increases in the company's investment in cash, receivables, and inventories, and other cash outflows incurred at the time the project is initiated.

**in-sample validation** involves gauging forecast errors by using the data set on which the model is fitted. This gives an upward bias to forecast accuracy.

**instrument** a class of similar investments. Examples are agency notes, commercial paper, Treasury bills, certificates of deposit (CDs), banker's acceptances, and repurchase agreements.

**interdistrict transportation system** redesign of the Federal Reserve's routing modes and techniques to shorten delays and minimize system-wide float.

**interest bearing** when the interest paid is based on a quoted rate based on the face value of the financial instrument.

**interest rate cap** a financial contract which limits the rise in a selected interest rate.

**interest rate collar** a financial contract which restricts the movement of a selected interest rate within a narrow band referred to as a collar. It is essentially a combination of an interest rate floor and cap.

**interest rate floor** a financial contract which limits the decline in a selected interest rate.

**interest rate parity hypothesis** a theory suggesting that exchange rates will adjust to offset the interest rate differential that exists between two countries.

**interest rate risk** the possibility that interest rates will increase, causing the prices of existing fixed-income securities to drop.

**interest rate swaps** an agreement between two different institutions or firms, generally referred to as counterparties, swapping cash flows between themselves.

**Interstate Banking and Branching Efficiency Act (IBBEA) (1994)** permitted interstate bank acquisitions, mergers, and branching.

**inventory control systems** an information system employed to help control inventory.

**inventory financing** a very important component of the total financial plan of most corporations because inventory makes up a significant portion of total working capital.

**inventory turnover ratio** a measure of inventory usage that is found by dividing cost of goods sold by either the year-end inventory balance or by the average inventory balance.

**inverted yield curve** downward-sloping graph of yields to maturity of securities with different maturities. Given the possibility to engage in arbitrage (simultaneously buy and sell otherwise identical securities having different maturities), this slope implies that the market collectively anticipates future shorter-term interest rates to decline.

**investing activities** on the statement of cash flows items that are defined as receipts of cash from loans, sale of property, and cash disbursed for loans to other business entities and payments for property, plant, and equipment.

**investment policy** defines the company's posture toward risk and return and specifies how that posture is to be implemented.

## *J*

**Jamaica Agreement** as a result of the inflation and balance of payment problems after World War II, causing many countries great difficulty in maintaining their appropriate exchange rate, the major trading nations signed the Jamaica Agreement in 1976 to demonetize gold and create a system of floating exchange rates.

**judgmental approach** relies heavily on intuition to adjust what is known about upcoming cash flows to arrive at the cash forecast.

**just-in-time inventory management system** a system focused on redesigning the production process to streamline the ordering process and eliminate waste errors, thereby improving the quality of the production process.

**just-in-time inventory system** an inventory system designed to reduce the levels of inventory kept at the manufacturing site increasing quality in the production process and by shifting the inventory burden to the supplier.

## *L*

**lagged regression analysis** a quick and relatively inexpensive way of determining a company's collection experience by determining a mathematical equation relating cash collections to the sales that gave rise to them.

**lagging** the practice of delaying collections or payments.

**lambda** a liquidity measure from a function of the likelihood that a firm will exhaust its liquid reserve. The measure's numerator is the sum of the firm's initial liquid reserve and total anticipated net cash flow during the analysis horizon and the denominator is the standard deviation of the net cash flow during the analysis horizon.

**later presentments and deposit deadlines** a second, mostly electronic, presentment of checks later in the morning to supplement the Fed's standard early morning presentment, and it also allowed banks to deposit checks as late as 2:30 A.M. (instead of at midnight) for some items that will be processed through RCPCs. It charges an extra fee to banks using the later deposit deadline.

**leading** the practice of accelerating collections or payments.

**ledger balance** reflects all credits and debits posted to an account as of a certain time, but this balance may not be entirely spendable.

**letter of credit (LOC)** a promise by a bank to make payment to a party upon presentation of a draft provided that the party complies with certain documentary requirements. This guarantees the investor of principal repayment, and the use of backup bank financing allows the bank's credit rating to be substituted for the issuer's.

**liability swap** a swap created to hedge cash flows related to liabilities.

**LIBOR** the London Interbank Offer Rate which is commonly used internationally as a reference rate for variable rate loans.

**line of credit** short term lending arrangement which allows the company to borrow up to a pre-arranged dollar amount during the one-year term.

**liquidity** the ability to sell an asset quickly, at or very close to the present market price. For a company, the ability of the firm to pay its bills on time.

**liquidity preference hypothesis** theoretical explanation for the term structure of interest rates that hypothesizes that higher yields will be necessary to induce investors to tie their funds up for long time periods (in other words, to be illiquid) in light of the increasing interest rate risk. Preference for liquidity is thought to characterize enough investors that the yield curve (in the absence of expectations or other influences on other than the shortest-term securities) should slope upward from left to right. The longer the maturity, the larger the liquidity premium must be to attract investors.

**liquidity risk** the inability to sell quickly at or very near the current market price, which is tied to the marketability of a security.

**lockbox** a special post office arrangement where customers are instructed to mail their remittances.

**lockbox collection system** a cash collection system that intercepts customer remittances close to the sending location and deposits the checks in the banking system prior to the company receiving notification.

**lockbox consortium** a system composed of several independent banks operating under a contractual agreement to provide lockbox services for each other's customers.

**lockbox optimization model** a set of variables, relationships, and rules that determine the optimal number of lockboxes, their locations, and the customer allocations to the selected lockbox sites.

**lockbox services** a collection service offered by banks, with the emphasis being to reduce collection float. Banks receiving one million or more pieces of mail per year can have a unique zip code set up for them, saving one or more sorts by post office personnel.

**lockbox study** a study usually conducted by a bank consulting group to help a corporation decide the structure of its collection system.

**log-linear regression** is an approach to estimating a variable's growth rate, which takes into account all of the variable's observed values.

**London Interbank Offer Rate (LIBOR)** the rate at which banks offer term Eurodollar deposits to each other.

**low-liquidity strategy** aggressive current asset allocation strategy which entails driving the company's investment in cash and securities to a minimum.

**lower control limit (LCL)** in the Miller-Orr cash management model, this would be the low point in the cash position, and the point at which a sale of securities sufficient to return the cash balance to the cash return point is initiated.

## M

**magnetic ink character recognition (MICR) line** the clearing agent, often a Federal Reserve bank, branch, or RCPC, uses the information printed at the bottom of the check to process the check. This information can be read by scanning machines and indicates several items about the drawee bank.

**mail float** the time that elapses from the point when the check is written until it is received by the payee. It may range from a day for local checks immediately mailed out to 10 days for a check sent to New York from Rome, Italy.

**maintenance margin** the level that the margin account returns to after a margin call.

**managing about a target rule** rather than make daily transfers, this transfer rule makes only one transfer for several days of deposits and the amount transferred takes into consideration a desired target balance that is to be left at the deposit bank.

**manufacturing resource planning systems (MRP II)** systems that are made up of a variety of functions that are linked together including business planning, sales and operations planning, production planning, master production scheduling, material requirements planning, capacity requirements planning, and the execution support systems for capacity and materials.

**margin** a small percentage of the contract price that is put up rather than paying the full price of the contract.

**margin account** the holding account that keeps track of the daily changes in the price of a futures contract where the positive changes in the market price of the futures contract are credited to the buyer's margin account and debited from the seller's margin account.

**marked-to-market** when changes in the market price of the futures contract impact the margin account on a daily basis.

**market microstructure** consists of the participants and mechanics involved in making transactions.

**market segmentation hypothesis** a theoretical explanation of the term structure of interest rates which contends that instead of being close substitutes, securities with short, medium, and long maturities are seen by investors (fund suppliers) and issuers (funds demanders) as quite different. Thus, interest rates for securities with different maturities are set by diverse supply and demand conditions.

**Markov chain analysis** an elaborate means of identifying changes in the collection experience. It is related to the uncollected balance percentages.

**master note** open-ended commercial paper, which allow the investor to add or withdraw monies on a daily basis, up to a specified maximum amount.

**material requirements planning (MRP)** an inventory planning system that focuses on the amount and timing of finished goods demanded and translates this into the derived demand for raw materials and subassemblies at various stages of production.

**maturity extension swap** situation where a security is sold and replaced or exchanged with another security which will increase the yield or dollar return, while affecting credit risk minimally. The swap is executed when the manager wishes to ride the yield curve, but to make the investment, he must liquidate another security.

**McFadden Act (1927)** limited branch banking by national banks to the same areas in which state-chartered banks in that state were permitted to branch, effectively prohibiting interstate branching.

**mean absolute error (MAE)** measure of forecast error calculated by adding up the absolute values of the difference between forecasted and actual values, and then dividing by the number of forecasts.

**mean square error (MSE)** weights large errors more than small ones, and thus favors forecasting models that rarely, if ever, miss by a large amount.

**member banks** commercial banks which belong to the Federal Reserve System. Being a member of the Federal Reserve System has historically been a requirement of all national banks, and many state-chartered banks joined voluntarily. Subsequent to the 1980 Monetary Control Act, membership has been much less important, in that all depository institutions must adhere to reserve requirements and can now borrow from the Fed.

**Miller-Orr model** cash management model which has two important characteristics: (1) it allows for unpredictable fluctuations in the cash balance instead of assuming perfect cash forecasting ability; and (2) it permits both upward and downward movements in the cash balance subsequent to replenishment, as opposed to the assumption that the company experiences a one-time cash infusion each period, which is subsequently depleted at a continuous rate.

**mixed approach** when applied to forecasting, involves the use of both quantitative and judgmental approaches.

**mixed instruments** specialized investment instruments which offer tailoring to the specific desires of the investor.

**model audit** the monitoring of an existing model to ensure its continued validity.

**model estimation** includes the selection of an appropriate forecasting technique and model calibration.

**modeling** the process of establishing a relationship between a set of independent variables in order to produce an estimate of a dependent variable.

**moderate-liquidity strategy** an approach to liquidity management which implies an intermediate concentration of current assets in the form of cash and securities, with corresponding intermediate levels of risk. This strategy falls between and should be contrasted with conservative and aggressive liquidity strategies.

**moderate financing strategy** in short-term financing, a strategy that is a blend of the aggressive and conservative financing strategies.

**modified accrual method** sometimes called the "accrual add-back technique" or "adjusted net income technique," this cash forecasting approach begins with accounting reports or the operating budget and then adjusts these number to reflect the timing of cash flows related to these transactions.

**modified buy-and-hold strategy** an approach to investing in which the investor plans to hold the security to maturity, but will selectively sell securities on which capital gains might be realized. This strategy might be utilized when the investor wishes to take advantage of anticipated favorable interest rate movements.

**money market** arena in which buyers and sellers of all securities maturing in one year or less interact; trading does not take place in any one physical location, but mainly by phone and computer communications. To distinguish the money market from capital markets, only securities with an original maturity of one year or less are included.

**money market deposit accounts (MMDAs)** savings accounts offered by depository institutions which pay interest. These were introduced to give depository institutions an account to compete with money market mutual funds.

**money market mutual fund** an investment vehicle which invests in short-term securities with funds pooled from numerous individuals or institutions. The money market mutual fund was first introduced in 1972 and became very popular in the high-interest era of late 1981.

**moving average** statistical forecasting technique which evens out temporary ups and downs by taking the mean of the most recent observations.

**multicollinearity** presence of moderate or high correlation between predictor variables in a regression equation. This condition is a violation of one of the assumptions of ordinary least squares regression modeling, the most common form of regression analysis.

**multilateral netting system** a netting system resulting from a corporation having subsidiaries in a number of different countries.

**multiple-drawee checks** negotiable payment order having more than one bank listed on the face of the check, with one of the banks being a bank located near the disbursing location, for which the check is an "on us" item.

**multiple processing centers** processing centers established around the country to pick up lockbox mail and do the processing while the processed checks are deposited in accounts at correspondent banks in the company's name. Cash is then concentrated in the company's account at the lockbox bank's headquarters.

**multiple regression** statistical model incorporating two or more predictor variables to explain the movement in the variable of interest. The form of a multiple regression model having two predictor variables is generally of the form: $Y = a + b_1X_1 + b_2X_2$.

**multivariate models** description of the relationship between three or more variables, typically with one of the variables being explained as the influence of two or more predictor variables.

**municipal obligations** securities issued by governmental authorities, governments, or government-authorized entities at other than the federal level. These securities, sometimes called "munis," pay interest that is not taxable for federal income tax purposes and usually not taxable for state income tax purposes in the state in which the issuer is located. Examples of issuers would be states, counties, localities, and school districts.

**mutually exclusive** competing investments, in which selection of one excludes the other from consideration.

**NACHA** the National Automated Clearing House Association. NACHA has been involved in developing format options that allow the movement of funds electronically, each with varying amounts of data.

**nearby contract** the futures contract with a maturity date that occurs nearest to, but after, the date of the cash market transaction that is to be hedged.

**negotiable certificate of deposit** bank deposits which come in $100,000 and larger denominations. Negotiability means the security can be legally sold and exchanged between investors, circumventing the early withdrawal penalty charged by the issuing bank. Only the first $100,000 is insured by the Federal Deposit Insurance Corporation, however.

**negotiated order of withdrawal (NOW) account** this checking with interest account has been offered by banks in the U.S. since early 1981 to individuals, sole proprietorships, and nonprofit organizations. Like a demand deposit account, it obligates the bank on which the item is drawn to honor requests for withdrawals on demand. Credit unions call these accounts share draft accounts.

**net liquid balance** cash and marketable securities less notes payable and current maturities of long-term debt.

**net present value (NPV)** a measure of the present dollar equivalent of all cash inflows and outflows flowing from a capital investment proposal. To compute net present value, each cash inflow and outflow must be converted to its dollar value at a standard point in time. Calculation of NPV involves discounting all cash flows to the beginning of the cash flow timeline, then subtracting the present value of the outflows from the present value of the inflows.

**net working capital** current assets less current liabilities.

**netting** receipts denominated in a currency are netted against expenses due to be paid in the same currency in order to reduce the total volume of foreign currency transactions.

**nominal interest rate** the stated interest rate for an investment or borrowing opportunity, ignoring the effect of the frequency of compounding. In order to compare various investments, the nominal rate is usually converted to an effective annual rate.

**nonbank banks** make loans or accept deposits, but not both.

**noncallable** a feature of a security which stipulates that the investor need not worry about a forced buyback of the security if interest rates fall subsequent to issuance. The absence of a call feature allows the issuer to pay a slightly lower interest rate due to the lower risk to the investor.

**noncompetitive bid** bids which are entered directly through a tender offer to the nearest Federal Reserve district bank or through a broker or commercial bank. Investors willing to accept the average yield of all accepted competitive bids enter a noncompetitive bid.

**nonrecourse or without recourse** when a factor buys receivables and the selling firm is not ultimately responsible for final payment.

**normal distributions** in forecasting, an array of forecast errors which occur in seemingly random fashion above and below forecasted values and graph as a symmetrical, bell-shaped curve.

**normal yield curve** upward-sloping graph of yields to maturity for securities with various maturities, with longer-term maturities yielding more than shorter-term.

**notional amount** the agreed upon face amount of the swap contract to which exchange rates or interest rates are to be applied to calculate the cash flows which are to be swapped.

**number of days of purchases outstanding (DPO)** a payables activity measure found by dividing the payables balance by average daily purchases (alternatively, average daily cost of goods sold can be used in the denominator).

**omitted variables** independent variables which should have been included in a regression model and that could have helped the analyst predict the variable of interest. If important, omission may give rise to a violation of ordinary least squares assumption.

**ongoing validation** involves continually checking a model's forecast accuracy by monitoring each period's forecast error and comparing it to past forecast errors.

**on-us** when the payee deposits the check in the bank on which it is drawn.

**open account** (or **open book account**) once approved for credit, a customer can make repeated purchases as long as the total amount owed at any one time is less than some predetermined ceiling.

**operating activities** those cash flows that are not classified as either investing or financing activities. Generally operating cash flows are related to cash collected from sales and cash disbursed to supplies, workers, management, and taxes.

**operating cycle** the process of funds flowing from inventory to receivables to payables.

**operating motive** theoretical motive for trade credit extension in which the seller responds to variable and uncertain demand by altering its trade credit availability.

**operational restructuring** when a company changes its product lines or use of assets with heavy fixed operating costs and alters the company's business risk.

**opportunity cost** what is given up in order to pursue a course of action. Conceptually, the discount rate chosen in capital budgeting evaluations should reflect the interest rate one could earn on the next best investment opportunity of about equal risk. Correspondingly, the discount rate used for making long-lived capital budgeting decisions is the company's weighted average cost of long-term capital.

**option contract** a financial contract that gives the right but not the obligation to purchase or sell the underlying asset at a specific price over a specific span of time.

**order handling** disposition of orders that are within credit limits and handling of orders which violate limits.

**ordering costs** costs associated with the inventory ordering process.

**original maturity** length of time until principal is repaid, measured at the time the security is first sold.

**originating ACH** the automated clearing house contacted by the bank initiating the transaction. The originating ACH must then transmit the payment order to the receiving institution's ACH (termed the receiving ACH).

**originating depository financial institution (ODFI)** bank which is contacted by the ACH payment initiator.

**out-of-pocket expenses** financing expenses that include interest and bank commitment fees.

**out-of-sample validation** using a new data set to assess a forecasting model's forecast accuracy.

**outsourcing** contracting with outside companies to conduct certain business functions, such as check issuance.

**overdraft credit lines** whether uncommitted or committed, have the added feature of being automatically drawn down whenever the company writes a check for which it does not have the sufficient funds to cover when it clears. Used extensively in foreign countries.

**overdraft facility** a banking service that allows a firm to overdraw its account. The overdraft is then charged interest as if it were a loan.

# P

**paid-only reconciliation** bank-provided demand deposit report which indicates all paid checks by check number, with check number, dollar amount, and date paid.

**participation** after a bank or syndicate of banks arranges a large loan, part or all of the loan may be sold off to corporate or other institutional investors, as well as to other banks.

**passive investment strategy** involves a minimal amount of oversight and very few transactions once the portfolio has been selected.

**payable through draft (PTD)** gives the payor 24 hours to decide whether to honor or refuse payment after it has been presented to the payor's bank. They are used for claim reimbursement by insurance companies, which use the 24-hour period to verify the signature and endorsements.

**payables turnover ratio** found by dividing purchases over a given time period by the year-end or average payables balance. Indicates the firm's payment behavior.

**paying agent** the bank performing this function makes interest and dividend payments to bondholders and shareholders, respectively, and repays the bond principal at maturity.

**percent of sales** forecasting model in which an expense or balance sheet amount is expressed as some fraction of sales.

**permanent current assets** the minimum amount of funds that are invested in current assets over the firm's operating cycle.

**perpetuity** a cash flow stream of equal dollar amounts that will last indefinitely into the future.

**piggyback** situation in which a bank is permitted to add a check or checks it is clearing and an accompanying listing to whatever checks the local Fed district bank is sending to the distant Fed office. This way the clearing bank can miss the local Fed's cutoff time but still meet the distant Fed's cutoff.

**pledging of receivables** a lender makes a loan protected by a lien placed on a certain portion of the firm's receivables.

**pooling** a banking service offered by many banking systems outside the U.S. which allows a firm's excess balances spread across its bank branches to offset corporate deficit balances in other branches of the same bank.

**positive float** the time period between receipt of the goods or services and the date on which cash payment is made.

**positive pay** a company sends its daily check issue file to its disbursing bank. Before the bank honors incoming checks, it refers to the issue file to see if the payee and check amounts match up.

**preauthorized debits** arrangement in which a customer agrees to allow his bank to automatically charge his checking account balance to make a fixed or variable payment each month.

**preauthorized draft** payment order initiated by the payee, who has been authorized to draw against the payor's account. Banks sometimes collect mortgage payments this way, and most automobile dealerships now make payments to Ford, GM, and Chrysler by these drafts.

**preauthorized payment** the seller and buyer agree to a payment date and the seller initiates a request to the buyer's bank for payment of the predetermined amount.

**precautionary motive** additional inventory held as a cushion for an unexpected increase in demand.

**premium** the amount paid for purchasing an option or received from writing (selling) an option.

**presentment** step seven in the check clearing process, when the check is returned to the drawee bank for payment.

**pricing motive** theoretical motive for trade credit extension in which sellers unable to change prices, perhaps due to market conditions or regulation, alter trade credit instead in order to charge varying amounts to buyers.

**primary market** also called the original issue market, is centered in money centers such as New York City, London,

Frankfurt, Singapore, and Hong Kong. Investors can access this "over-the-counter" market from anywhere, as the market consists of phone and computer hook-ups among all participating dealers and brokers.

**principal** the original amount invested or borrowed.

**private placement** security issuance transaction in which a large institution such as a retirement fund or insurance company buys the entire issue.

**pro-forma balance sheet approach** method of generating a cash forecast which involves determination of the amount of cash and marketable securities by computing the difference between projected assets (excluding cash and marketable securities) and the sum of projected liabilities and owner's equity.

**processing float** the amount of time that transpires from the point of receipt of the check at a lockbox or company mail room and the time when the check is deposited at the bank.

**prox** payment due on a specific day in the following month.

**purchase order with payment voucher attached** a draft coupled with a purchase order, which eliminates the need for a supplier to issue an invoice and for a customer to process the invoice and issue a check.

**purchase terms** terms of credit offered by suppliers.

**purchasing cards** credit cards used by businesses to make small dollar purchases of maintenance, repair, and operating supplies. Use of purchasing, or procurement, cards greatly reduces the number of purchase orders and invoices processed and payments made.

**purchasing parity hypothesis** a theory suggesting that exchange rates between two countries will adjust to offset the relative rates of inflation between the two countries.

**purchasing power risk** the possibility that an investment's proceeds will not be worth as much as anticipated due to general price level increases in the economy. Anticipated inflation is built into the risk-free interest rate, but investors are still vulnerable to losses in purchasing power from unanticipated inflation and will require a higher yield when price levels are volatile.

**put option** a contract that allows the owners to sell the underlying asset at a specific price over a specific span of time.

## *Q*

**quantitative approach** any forecasting technique which involves the use of a numerical model to forecast; the technique is usually implemented on a computer.

**quantity discounts** a reduction in the cost per order based on the quantity ordered.

**quick ratio** the ratio of current assets less inventory to current liabilities. Also referred to as acid-test ratio.

## *R*

**range reconciliation** provides subtotals of all checks within a range of check serial numbers. This is especially useful for identifying disbursements from the same account but from several locations.

**raw material inventory** inventory of the raw material of production.

**receipts and disbursements method** a commonly used cash forecasting approach which involves determining upcoming sources of cash inflows and outflows, then laying these out on a schedule to see the aggregate effect.

**receiving ACH** if the originating bank in an ACH transaction is serviced by a different ACH operator than that servicing the receiving bank, the receiving bank's operator is called the receiving ACH. The Fed may be the originating ACH and a private sector operator may be the receiving ACH, or vice versa.

**receiving depository financial institution (RDFI)** ACH payee's bank in an ACH credit transaction.

**recursive least squares (RLS) regression model** in the context of receivables monitoring, a regression model which allows the estimated receivables collection fractions (the regression coefficients) to change over time.

**Regional Check Processing Centers (RCPCs)** Fed offices set up to help clear checks.

**registrar** bank which keeps records of the number of shares of stock authorized, issued, and redeemed, and ensures that the number of share issued does not exceed those authorized.

**Regulation CC** effective September 1990, this ruling stipulates that from the day of deposit local checks must be given availability within two business days, and nonlocal checks within five days.

**Regulation Q** a Federal Reserve regulation that restricts banks from paying interest on demand deposit accounts.

**reinvestment rate risk** the possibility that the investor will have to invest cash proceeds at a lower interest rate for the remainder of a predetermined investment horizon.

**reinvoicing center** an entity which buys raw materials and final products from producing units of the same company, then rebills ("reinvoices") those items to foreign selling subsidiaries and non-company customers. The center is a separate operation of a corporation where the firm's different subsidiaries dealing in different currencies send their invoices and the center reinvoices only the net difference owed to each subsidiary. As a result, this center is generally responsible for managing the corporation's foreign exchange exposure. The costs of setting up a center are offset by economies of scale in purchasing and centralized exchange rate risk management.

**relationship approach** one view of the corporation's link to its banks, in which the corporation chooses its bank services primarily based on preexisting business dealings. Loyalty to prior arrangements is considered to be more important than price when selecting banks for cash management or lending services. Usually implies that credit and cash management services will both be handled by the same bank or network of banks.

**remittance advice** a document which usually accompanies payment, indicating customer, account number, date, and invoice(s) being paid.

**reorder point** the inventory level at which an order should be placed.

**repurchase agreement (RP)** the sale of a portfolio of securities with a prearranged buyback one or several days later. A repurchase agreement, or "repo" as it is often called, involves the bank "selling" the investor a portfolio of securities, then agreeing to buy the securities back (repurchase) at an agreed-upon future date.

**required rate of return** the percent return necessary to compensate investors for the risk borne when holding a company's securities. For a company as a whole, risk is a function of the variability of the average project undertaken. This, in turn, heavily influences the required returns on the company's equity and debt securities. For all capital taken together, the required rate of return translates into the company's cost of capital. For projects of lesser (greater) risk than the company's average capital project, the required return will be lower (higher) than the average cost of capital.

**resiliency** condition of a market in which new orders enter when a temporary imbalance of buy or sell orders push the price away from its equilibrium level.

**retail lockbox** is set up for a business receiving a large volume of relatively small dollar checks. Processing costs must be considered here along with collection float, and optically scannable invoices are read by machine to minimize human processing.

**retail lockbox system** a lockbox system structured to handle a large volume of standardized invoice materials where the remittance checks have a relatively low average dollar face value.

**retail market** an exchange situation where the buyers and/or sellers are primarily small entities, especially individuals.

**return items** checks that bounce, leading to their return to the bank of first deposit through each bank involved in the forward presentment.

**Revenue Anticipation Notes** short-term debt instruments which provide working capital financing for states and localities as they await anticipated revenues from other sources of revenue.

**revenue securities** issues which tie cash flows to pledged revenue from the facility(ies) being financed: rental revenue from a convention center, or tolls from a bridge or toll road.

**reverse positive pay** the disbursing bank sends the check presentment file to the company to see if all the items should be honored.

**reverse repurchase agreement** the other side of a repurchase agreement. In this case, a firm needing a temporary source of cash for a few days can negotiate with its bank to temporarily sell securities with an agreement to repurchase them at the end of the specified period.

**revolving credit facility** allows the borrower to continually borrow and repay amounts up to an agreed-upon limit. The agreement is annually renewable at a variable interest rate during an interim period of anywhere from one to five years.

**riding the yield curve** investing strategy which involves buying securities with maturities longer than the investment horizon, fully intending to liquidate the position early.

**risk classes** an approach to risk adjusting potential capital projects by developing discount rates based on anticipated variability in the projects' cash flows. Proposals with longer time horizons, or permanent effects on the firm's cash flows, or those with a short time horizon that might result in a very large range or standard deviation of outcomes would be assigned a higher discount rate.

**risk premium** securities with the same maturity but issued by different issuers and with different issue characteristics are priced to reflect risk differences. The major risk factors accounting for this are default risk, liquidity risk, reinvestment rate risk, purchasing power risk, and event risk. On foreign securities, one must also consider exchange rate risk and political risk.

**risk spread** the added yield necessary to compensate for risk factors other than maturity differences, such as default risk and liquidity risk.

**risk structure of interest rate** set of interest rate differences between various securities which arise due to any factor other than a different maturity. The main risk factors giving rise to this structure are default risk, reinvestment rate risk, and purchasing power risk.

**risk-adjusted discount rate** higher (lower) interest rate used in present value calculations when the project is of greater (lesser) risk than the average capital budgeting project invested in by the company.

**risk-free rate** is determined primarily by investors' collective time preferences, the rate of inflation expected over the maturity period, and demand-side influences such as economic productivity.

**root mean square error (RMSE)** has become increasingly popular in business and economic applications. It simply involves taking the square root of the mean square error (MSE).

## S

**safety stock** an extra inventory balance that acts as insurance against inventory stock outs.

**sales agents** dealers sometimes function as brokers in their role, as for banks and other issuers of short-term securities. For a commission, the agent will locate buyers for the institution's securities, again without risk, because the agent does not have to buy and resell the securities.

**same-day settlement (SDS)** presentment of a check to the paying bank by 8:00 A.M. local time, with payment of the check required by Fedwire by the close of business day. This Fed initiative was enacted to reduce arbitrary holds or fees used by disbursing banks to slow check clearing.

**seasonal dating** allows customers to purchase inventory before the peak buying season and defer payment until after the peak season.

**secondary market** exchange arena for securities subsequent to their original issue. Not every investor holds the security to maturity, necessitating a well-functioning market for resale.

**securitization** involves issuing debt securities collateralized by a pool of selected financial assets such a mortgages, auto loans, or credit card receivables.

**security** a specific investment offered by a given issuer.

**sell hedge** a hedge created by selling a futures contract.

**sensitivity analysis** means of incorporating risk in financial outcomes which involves varying key inputs, one at a time, and observing the effect on the decision variable(s). For example, the analyst might vary the sales level and observe the effect on the company's cash forecast.

**serial correlation** the existence of correlated errors in a regression model of a time series of data points.

**shareholder value maximization** presumed goal of publicly held companies, in which decisions are made which will lead to the greatest anticipated increase in the value of the financial claims on the company. In practice, the company's stock price is utilized as a measure of the value of all financial claims.

**sight draft** a formal, written agreement whereby an importer (drawee) contracts to pay a certain amount on demand ("at sight") to the exporter. The bank is not extending credit, but simply helping in the payment process by receiving the draft and presenting it to the drawee. Sight drafts often must have documentation attached to verify that conditions for payment (receipt, or "sight" of goods) have been met.

**simple interest** arrangement in which interest is only added to the account at maturity. Because no compounding occurs, the nominal interest rate is also the annual effective rate.

**simple interest approximation formula** simple interest formula to approximate the present value effect of a financial decision. The simplicity of this approach makes its use desirable where the effect of ignoring cash flow compounding would not have a significant effect on the valuation of those flows.

**simple regression** a statistical model in which the equation used to predict the value of the variable of interest (dependent variable) involves just one predictor (independent) variable.

**simulation** statistical technique for modeling uncertainty which begins with calculation of the expected value and standard deviation of the input variables, then uses iterative draws from each variable's probability distribution to draw up a probability distribution for the decision variable. For example, the analyst might simultaneously vary sales and a key input price, and observe the effect on the forecasted cash position.

**solvency** a firm is solvent when the dollar level of its assets exceed the dollar level of its liabilities.

**speculative motive** additional inventory held to take advantage of unique business opportunities such as future shortages.

**speculator** a person who has no operating cash flow position to protect and is trying to profit solely from interest rate movements.

**spontaneous financing** those financing sources such as accounts payables and accruals that are generated as a part of the operations of the firm.

**spot rates** existing prices or interest rates in today's markets. In foreign exchange, the spot rate is an exchange rate quote based on immediate delivery of the currency being traded.

**spurious correlation** chance association between two variables, which the analyst should watch for because it might account for a high coefficient of determination.

**stable distribution** pattern of outcomes which characterizes a variable with a well-defined, consistent trend or seasonal component.

**standard check processing** when the deposit bank verifies the depositor's cash letter—which lists the checks and their amounts—and then encodes the dollar amount on the MICR line and sends the checks to a correspondent bank or the nearest Federal Reserve facility to be cleared back to the disbursing bank on which the check was written.

**standby letter of credit** document which guarantees that the bank will make available necessary funds to meet a financial obligation if the responsible company cannot or does not wish to meet a major financial obligation.

**Statement of Cash Flows** a statement created by the Financial Accounting Standards Board, No. 95, showing the change in the cash balance as a result of cash flows from operating activities, cash flows from investing activities, and cash flows from financing activities.

**statistical decomposition** a complex forecasting technique which uses the past observations of a variable to forecast future values. Sometimes called Census X-11 decomposition (after the computer software developed by the Census Bureau), this approach is especially useful for forecasting variables which have trend, seasonal, and cyclical variations.

**stochastic model** data input for stochastic models represent probability distributions for one or more of the variables.

**Stone model** optimization process similar to Miller-Orr but allows the cash manager's knowledge of imminent cash flows to permit him to selectively override model directives.

**striking price** the price that an option contract allows the buyer to purchase a security at or a seller to sell a security at.

**Super-NOW accounts** while banks continue to set higher minimum balance requirements for NOW accounts, in 1986 regulators removed interest rate distinctions between the accounts by eliminating the maximum NOW rate of 5 1/4%.

**supply chain management** the process by which companies move materials and parts from suppliers through the production process and on to the consumers.

**sustainable growth rate** the rate of sales growth that is compatible with a firm's established financial policies including asset turnover, net profit margin, dividend payout, and debt to equity ratio and assumes that new equity is derived only through retained earnings, not new common stock.

**swap** exchange of securities between two parties, often with the assistance of an intermediary known as a swap dealer. In its simplest form, a company engaging in a swap exchanges a fixed interest rate obligation for one that has a variable, or floating interest rate.

**swap strategies** see for example, maturity extension swap and yield spread swap.

**sweep accounts** special accounts whereby excess funds are automatically or at the cash manager's request transferred ("swept") from the demand deposit account into an interest-bearing overnight investment.

**SWIFT** the Society of Worldwide Interbank Financial Telecommunications, is a communication network for relaying payment instructions for international transactions. It boasts many member banks in many different countries, and thousands of banks are connected to the network.

**syndicate** sometimes a group of investment banks works together on the marketing and shares the risk involved with bringing a new issue to market, which may or may not be acceptable at the predetermined price. This grouping is called a syndicate.

**synthetic composite** an artificial security which is devised to mirror the portfolio's average coupon interest rate, maturity, and risk rating.

**systematic risk** is the degree of sensitivity of the company's stock returns to market-wide returns.

## *T*

**Tax Anticipation Notes** short-term debt instruments which provide working capital financing for states and localities as they await anticipated revenues from tax collections.

**tax-advantaged instruments** those on which part or all of the income is exempted from taxation, or where the tax is deferred.

**tax-exempt CP (commercial paper)** states and localities issue some of these items. The risks are very similar to those of anticipation notes.

**taxable instruments** security types which are not given preferential tax treatment, including commercial paper, domestic and Eurodollar certificates of deposit, banker's acceptances, repurchase agreements, and money market mutual funds invested in these instruments.

**taxable-equivalent yield** the yield of a tax-exempt security on an after-tax basis, which facilitates comparison with the yield of taxable securities. The taxable-equivalent yield is the nominal (stated) yield divided by (1 − corporation's marginal tax rate).

**temporary current assets** the accumulation of inventory in anticipation of the peak selling season and the resulting receivables generated by the increased sales. This bulge then subsides as the firm passes through its peak selling season.

**term loan** a loan made with an initial maturity of more than one year.

**term repos** repurchase agreement which is arranged with a maturity of several days to several weeks, making them well-suited for the investor having an investment horizon longer than one day.

**term spread** the component of a security's return that is necessary to induce investors to bear risks linked to maturity.

**term structure of interest rates** the tendency for the maturity-yield relationship to hold across all issuers in a systematic way. The graph of the term structure existing at a particular point in time is called a yield curve.

**terminal warehouse agreement** inventories pledged as collateral are moved to a public warehouse that is physically separated from the borrower's premises.

**thin market** one with little participation by buyers and/or sellers.

**third-party information vendor** an information service that receives deposit information from field offices and transmits that information to the appropriate concentration banks and to corporate headquarters.

**time draft** involves a credit element, because the payment obligation agreed to by the drawee is designated as due at a specified future date. Time drafts are usually dated after verification of a shipment of goods.

**time series regression** a naive modeling approach in the sense that the mere passage of time generally does not cause the variable to change in value.

**time-series techniques** forecasting methods which predict future movements in the forecast variable based on patterns revealed in historical movements of that same variable.

**trade credit** permission to delay payment which arises when goods are sold under delayed payment terms.

**trade discount** percent reduction to quoted price offered to all customers, and not linked to early payment. This discount is typically offered to all customers, and the seller expects all customers to pay at the discounted price within the agreed-upon period. One example is a quantity discount, a price break given for a large purchase.

**traders** market participants which try to profit on anticipated interest rate or currency movements. They hold securities not as intermediaries, but as investors attempting to gain profits for their company's own account.

**trading strategy** an active strategy that relies on interest rate forecasts to augment yields with capital gains. When the analyst forecasts a change in interest rates, trading strategies can be devised to enhance investment profits. This approach is very risky and is not commonly used for corporate short-term portfolios.

**transaction approach** an approach to bank selecting in which there is a decoupling or "unbundling" of services, meaning the company will not necessarily borrow from the bank(s) it utilizes for cash management services. In this approach the treasurer selects the bank(s) that can best provide a specific service or can provide it at the best price.

**transaction exposure** related to the gains or losses associated with the settlement of business transactions denominated in different currencies.

**transaction motive** inventory held in relation to the level of operating activity expected by the firm.

**transaction sets** a set of standards for EDI information flows developed by the ANSI X12 committee to facilitate the electronic communication between trading patterns.

**transfer agent** the financial institution which takes care of updating the records for the corporation's stock and registered bonds.

**transit items** are checks drawn on banks that do not participate in a deposit bank's local clearinghouse or exchange, these are sometimes called "out-of-town" checks.

**transit routing number** also called the FRD/ABA (Federal Reserve District/American Banker's Association) bank ID number, a number imprinted on checks which identifies the payee's bank. This number is used by the deposit bank to determine how best to clear the check.

**translation exposure** this type of exposure occurs when the balance sheet and income statement of a foreign subsidiary are translated into the parent company's domestic currency for consolidated financial reporting purposes.

**treasury workstation** a computer system that provides a means for the treasury manager to efficiently manage cash concentration, account balances at banks, cash transfers, and the short-term investment and borrowing portfolio. These are sold by banks and some specialized vendors.

**trust receipt loans** a financing arrangement where the collateralized inventory items are noted by serial number or some other readily identifiable mark.

**trust services** safekeeping, record keeping, and perhaps investing of corporate or individual pension or profit-sharing plans. For a corporate pension, the trustee institution receives the payments, invests them, maintains record for each of the employees, and pays the pensioners after they retire.

**trustee under indenture** the third-party financial institution charged by investors with the responsibility of monitoring the issuing corporation to ensure that it abides by all provisions of the bond agreement, called indenture.

## *U*

**unbiased expectations hypothesis** a theory of interest rate determination which posits that the prevailing yield curve is mathematically derived from the present short-term rate and expectations for rates that will exist at various points in time in the future.

**uncollected balance percentages** a proportional break-down of the present accounts receivable balance, with the proportions based on the month the credit sales originated. The pitfalls of DSO, accounts receivable turnover, and the aging schedule have led to the development of this improved measure, in which the receivables balance is broken down, and the monthly components are divided by the credit sales in the month in which the receivables originated. Sometimes called the "payments pattern approach," the uncollected balance percentages accurately depict a company's collection experience, even when sales are changing.

**uncommitted lines of credit** short-term lending agreements which are not technically binding on the bank, although they are almost always honored. Uncommitted lines are usually renewable annually if both parties are agreeable. A less formal agreement than a committed line and the availability of funds may be in question if the general economic or bank internal liquidity position slips.

**unique ZIP code** used by banks to increase the efficiency of their lockbox operations.

**unsecured** lending arrangement in which there is no collateral backing up the loan in the event of a default.

**upper control limit** (UCL) cash balance which triggers a purchase of securities large enough to reduce excess cash balances to a predetermined return point.

**usable funds** the net proceeds the firm receives from the financing sources. This represents the amount borrowed less compensating balances, in the case of credit lines, and the bid-ask spread in the case of commercial paper.

**usage rate** the daily rate of drawing down the inventory balance. Calculated by dividing the total inventory needs by the number of days in the production planning period.

**valuation** the determination of the present dollar value of a series of cash flows.

**valuation approach** method of financial decision-making in which the anticipated shareholder value effect determines which alternative is chosen. The present values of cash inflows and outflows are compared for each alternative.

**value added network (VAN)** a computer system that receives EDI information from one firm in one format and transmits to another firm or bank in a different format. The system transmits messages and data from point of origination to prespecified endpoints, and which may offer one or more auxiliary services.

**value dating** involves forward movement of the amount of a deposited check and back dating of a presented check. This is a common practice by some European banks.

**variable costs** expenses which increase or decrease with the level of production or sales, such as direct labor or raw materials.

**variable identification** involves determining what items need to be forecasted and how best to measure those items.

**variable-rate demand notes** medium-term debt instruments issued by municipalities, which are found in some corporate short-term investments portfolios because their interest rates are periodically reset.

**variance** the amount by which the actual amount is over or under the forecasted or budgeted amount.

**variance analysis model** receivables control technique which builds on the decomposition model, and compares actual receivables performance to the budgeted amounts. If the budget captures the unique conditions and sales levels a company is experiencing, or is so adjusted after the period is over ("flexible budgeting"), then one can discern the true reason(s) for changes in receivables levels.

**WCR/S** working capital requirements divided by sales.

**weekend balances** a concern in making cash transfers that takes into account weekend balances, since deposit accounts in the U.S. do not earn interest, and also considers weekend deposits that will be credited to the deposit account on Monday.

**weighted-average cost of capital** the summed product of the proportion of each type of capital used and the cost of that capital source. This "hurdle rate" for capital investments is usually based on a company's long-term financing sources.

**wholesale lockbox system** special arrangement for collecting mailed payments, established for collecting relatively few large dollar remittances. Because the dollar amounts per check are larger (perhaps $1 million or more), the received checks are processed more often and checks are processed for deposit more rapidly by bank than by company personnel.

**wholesale market** investment supply and demand interaction for large dollar transactions between large investors (such as the money market).

**wire drawdowns** wire transfers which are initiated by the receiving party, instead of the sender or payor.

**wire transfers** bookkeeping entries that simultaneously debit the payor's account and credit the payee's account. The best way to quickly move money from one place to another is with a wire transfer. A real-time transfer of account balances between banks.

**with recourse** when a factor buys receivables with recourse, the selling firm is ultimately responsible for payment if the customer defaults.

**without recourse** the seller is not liable for uncollected receivables.

**work-in-process inventory** inventory of items beyond the raw material stage but not yet at the completed product state.

**working capital cycle** the continual flow of resources through the various working capital accounts such as cash, accounts receivables, inventory, and payables.

**working capital requirements** the difference between current operating assets (receivables, inventory, and prepaids) and current operating liabilities (accounts payable and accruals).

**yield curve** a graph of the yields to maturity of an issuer's securities having several different maturities, showing current maturities on the horizontal axis and yield-to-maturity on the vertical axis. This curve provides a graphical depiction of the existing term structure of interest rates.

**yield spread** the difference between two interest rates, expressed as a percentage difference.

**yield spread swap** exchange of one debt security for another, usually with the motivation of taking advantage of a mispriced security, based on the investor's study of historical interest rate differences.

**zero balance account (ZBA)** a corporate bank account which maintains a zero dollar balance because the total presented against it each day is automatically funded by another of the company's accounts, usually the "master" or concentration account.

# Index

# *D*

## G



## H

## I

## J

# K



# L



# M

## P

# PHYSICAL GEOGRAPHY

E. Willard Miller
The Pennsylvania State University

# PHYSICAL GEOGRAPHY

## EARTH SYSTEMS AND HUMAN INTERACTIONS

Charles E. Merrill Publishing Company
A Bell & Howell Company
Columbus Toronto London Sydney

Published by
Charles E. Merrill Publishing Company
A Bell & Howell Company
Columbus, Ohio 43216

This book was set in Italia.
The administrative editor was Kathy Nee.
The production editor was Rebecca Money Bobb.
Text design by Cynthia Brunk
Cover design by Cathy Watterson
Cover photograph of Dunnigan Hills, California, by William Garnett



Library of Congress Catalog Card Number: 84–71918
International Standard Book Number: 0–675–20143–8
2 3 4 5 6 7 8 9–90 89 88 87 86
Printed in the United States of America

Photo credits: p. 1, Washington State Travel Photo; p. 5, Michigan Department of Natural Resources; p. 7, Courtesy of NASA; pp. 19, 97, Courtesy of NOAA; p. 33, Strix Pix; p. 53, Linda Ammons; p. 77, Finland National Tourist Office; p. 125, Wyoming Travel Commission Photograph; p. 145, USDA—Soil Conservation Service photo by H. E. Alexander; p. 163, New York State Department of Environmental Conservation photo by J. Goerg; p. 165, USDA photograph; pp. 189 and 343, Paul M. Schrock; p. 215, Swiss National Tourist Office; p. 217, U.S. Geological Survey; pp. 255, 277, 311, Tad Nichols; pp. 297, 325, © Peter Kresan.

# PREFACE

To the uninitiated, the world appears as a jumble of places. The study of geography helps us recognize the inherent orderliness of space on the earth. We become able to organize the physical world into systems of climates, soils, vegetation, and landforms. To create these orderly systems, the field of physical geography relies on knowledge from the systematic disciplines, especially meteorology, hydrology, pedology, botany, and geology.

*Physical Geography* is a broad and nonmathematical survey at the introductory level. It does not emphasize abstract facts or theoretical concepts; instead, it encourages students to analyze and interpret geographical phenomena in the real world. The initial chapter lays the foundation for this study. The next seven chapters introduce the atmospheric processes that form the basis for a world climatic classification system. Chapter 9 considers climatic change from both a geologic and a modern perspective. The next two chapters analyze the regional distribution of soils and natural vegetation. The final six chapters cover landforms. Their origins are explored, as are the forces—water, ice, and wind—that shape them. The discussion of landforms, like those on climate, soils, and natural vegetation, concludes by presenting a classification system.

While physical geography is one of the oldest branches of the discipline, it has experienced remarkable growth in recent decades. This text introduces some of the latest advances to the student. New knowledge on the dynamics of the upper atmosphere, for example, provides us with changed perspectives on the movement of middle-latitude cyclones and their fronts. Progress in the soil sciences has made possible a modern soil classification system. The study of plate tectonics has established scientific proof of continental drift and has revolutionized the concepts of the origin of second-order landforms. Even though William Morris Davis proposed the geographical cycle of erosion early in the twentieth century, the study of the forces that shape the third-order landforms continues to spawn new theories.

This book also investigates how nature and people interrelate. With the world's growing population, how do we keep the earth a satisfactory place on which to live? This text demonstrates the magnitude and seriousness of this question. Students who gain an understanding of the complexity of environmental problems will realize that they require our greatest efforts to solve.

Knowledge of physical geography not only helps us deal with global environmental problems, but also enriches the lives of individuals. We must understand the physical world to fully appreciate its beauty. The pleasures of travel are greatly enhanced, for example, when we realize that the landscape is constantly changing. It is my hope that students will learn that they are a part of the natural environment and that learning about it can be an exciting experience.

Data pertaining to space on the earth can be comprehended more easily by looking at maps rather than tables or charts. The map is a fundamental tool in geographic study, and is at times essential. Maps are thus an integral part of this volume.

## ACKNOWLEDGMENTS

I wish to make several specific acknowledgments. An invaluable contribution has been made by my students, who challenged me to pursue this study. I am greatly indebted to my colleagues, scattered throughout the world, who have provided intellectual stimulation. I have benefitted greatly from the constructive comments of those who reviewed the manuscript: Joseph Bencloski of the University of Georgia, David Butler of Oklahoma State University, Richard Jarvis of the State University of New York at Buffalo, Edward Lyon of Ball State University, George McCleary of the University of Kansas, Scott Morris of the University of Idaho, Rawhide Papritz of Green River Community College, Charles Rosenfeld of Oregon State University, Richard Stephenson of East Carolina University, Tom Templeton of Mesa Community College, and John Vitek of Oklahoma State University.

The maps and graphs were prepared in the George F. Deasy GeoGraphics Laboratory of The Pennsylvania State University, under the direction of Ronald Abler and staff cartographer Abby Alexander Curtis, with the assistance of Nancy Anderson and Dorn Van-Dommelen. I am indebted to many people at the Charles E. Merrill Publishing Company, but special thanks are due to Kathy Nee, geography editor, and Rebecca Money Bobb, production editor. To my secretaries, Nina McNeal and Joan Summers, I owe a debt of gratitude for their invaluable assistance and seemingly endless typing and retyping of the manuscript. Finally, I dedicate this book to my wife, Ruby Skinner Miller, not only for her able assistance, but also for her inspiration.

*E. Willard Miller*

# CONTENTS

## PART II SOILS AND NATURAL VEGETATION



## PART III LANDFORMS

# 1
# GEOGRAPHY: THE ANALYSIS OF AREA

Geography has evolved over scores of centuries. An awareness of place became important to our earliest human ancestors as soon as they recognized that their food sources were widely distributed. By the time of the ancient Greeks a vast body of geographical knowledge had been accumulated. These early philosophers recognized that the cataloging of places was not sufficient: They also sought explanations for the variations in the earth's features. For example, to help them understand the world's climates, they devised a regional system that divided a portion of the earth into heat belts corresponding to zones of latitude. Possibly the Greeks' most lasting contribution to geography was their study of cartography. The maps they made were the standard sources of geographical information for more than a thousand years.

The advancement of geographic knowledge has not been steady. During the Middle Ages there was a long period of intellectual stagnation in Europe. Not until the Age of Exploration (fifteenth to nineteenth centuries) was geographical information once again sought. While European explorers ventured to more distant places, the scientists of the day recognized that geographical information had to be placed in a scientific framework. Through the work of Bernhardus Varenius (1622–1650), a new structure for ordering geographic knowledge evolved. He recognized that one branch of geography deals with the purely physical world, including the atmosphere, the hydrosphere, and the lithosphere, while the other branch considers the social and cultural patterns of the world. At this early stage of evolution of the geographic field, Varenius recognized the interrelationship between people and the physical world.

While Varenius laid the foundation for the scientific structure of geography, it remained for Immanuel Kant

(1724–1804) to determine geography's place among the sciences. According to Kant, knowledge can be organized three different ways. One way is to classify the facts according to the kinds of things studied. The resulting disciplines, including chemistry, geology, zoology, botany, and many others, are known as the systematic fields. The second method, known as the historical approach, studies relationships through time. The third way to organize knowledge is to study how places are associated. This is the realm of geography.

## THE FIELD OF MODERN GEOGRAPHY

Kant's philosophic framework enabled geography to assume a respected place among the disciplines. From Kant onward, the purpose of geographic study has been to describe, analyze, and interpret spatial patterns, and to compare and contrast these patterns.

A student may approach the study of geography with three basic questions in mind: *Where* are the earth's features located? *Why* are they located there? and *What* are the consequences of their location? Although the first question is fundamental to the geographic approach, scholars recognized centuries ago that *where* simply defines the location to be analyzed and interpreted. If the study ends there, geography becomes a sterile field of memorization. The vitality of the discipline lies in the attempt to explain the existence of incredibly complex geographic patterns. The answers are rarely obvious, but seeking to solve these puzzles makes the geographic approach exciting.

## THE SCOPE OF PHYSICAL GEOGRAPHY

Physical geography studies the patterns of weather and climate, soils, vegetation, and landforms, and the interrelationships of these patterns with human activities. Each of these areas of study has a counterpart in the systematic sciences; thus, to understand physical geography a basic knowledge of each of these systematic fields is necessary. For example, meteorology and climatology define the processes that are used by geographers to analyze atmospheric phenomena. In the same way, soil sciences and botany provide other constituents of physical geography. The science of geomorphology, which studies the origin and systematic development of landforms, provides fundamental information for the study of the distribution of landforms, the traditional core of physical geography.

The purpose of studying physical geography is to acquire an understanding of how the earth's physical patterns developed. To help students achieve this goal, this text begins by analyzing earth processes and then proceeds toward patterns. This approach results from the belief that learning about processes is necessary for understanding the development of regional patterns. Both process and patterns are therefore emphasized.

Physical geography traditionally was limited to the study of the natural world. This narrow approach failed to recognize that the natural environment is a part of all human experience. Modern physical geography cannot ignore the effects of people on the environment and the effects of the environment on people. As the population of the world increases and as technology becomes more sophisticated, we become more able to alter the environment. We can pollute the atmosphere, modify landforms, and destroy the soil and vegetational covering.

The variety, intensity, and geographical extent of these environmental changes are increasing. The consequences of these alterations are extremely difficult to evaluate. It must be remembered that we can change the environment to our advantage (as when we level hills and fill in valleys to produce a level-grade highway), or to our disadvantage (as when we use streams to dispose of toxic chemicals).

We are only beginning to realize that we must live in harmony with the natural environment if we are to exist on this earth. The study of the physical world is not sufficient. We must include ourselves in the study of modern physical geography.

## THE EARTH'S NATURAL SYSTEMS

In the past, science tried to explain observable phenomena by reducing them to elementary units that could be investigated independently of each other. This approach neglects the interrelationships that produce natural systems which are collections of interacting phenomena. The earth itself can be viewed as a single system. In this system, however, so many phenomena interact together that understanding the complete system becomes extremely difficult. In order to simplify the study of the earth, the total system can be divided into subsystems such as climate, soils, vegetation, and landforms.

Because all systems have many common features, the systems approach is an effective way to organize knowledge. Systems are classified as open or closed. Nearly all systems on the earth are considered open systems because they exhibit several basic characteristics. First, fundamental to open systems are an input of energy and materials from outside their boundaries and an output of energy and materials from within. For example, in the atmospheric subsystem, energy originates primarily from the sun and is returned to space and to the earth. This cycle has been named the heat balance or heat budget of the earth. A second characteristic of open systems is that energy entering the system from the outside, although it may remain constant for awhile, eventually creates changes in the system. Third, any change in the system is reflected by either *positive* or *negative* feedback. A *positive feedback* accelerates the changes while a *negative feedback* slows the rate of change. Finally, most open systems tend toward a state of equilibrium in which input is equal to output. In the heat balance example, the energy input of the atmosphere is equal to the output of energy. If it were not, the earth would become either warmer or colder.

In contrast to the open system, the closed system has neither inputs nor outputs, but is affected only by other elements in the system. Conventional physics deals only with closed systems; that is, the physical systems that are considered to be isolated from their environment. Although a closed system is rare on the earth, it does exist. The lithosphere is an example, because, with the exception of meteorites, no material enters or leaves the earth's surface.

A study of the earth's subsystems will reveal that they depend greatly upon one another. For example, there is a strong relationship between the climatic subsystem and the soil subsystem on the earth. In the rainy tropical areas the type of soil developed is directly related to atmospheric conditions. The heavy precipitation and the continuously high temperatures are major factors in the leaching process that produces oxisols, the characteristic soils of the wet tropics. Further, the atmospheric conditions produce luxuriant forests, but because the vegetation decomposes rapidly, the soils are poor in humus materials. Thus the climate, soils, and natural vegetation are interrelated. Ultimately all subsystems of the earth are so linked. The activity of one subsystem is a response to the output of another subsystem.

When we study a subsystem of the earth such as climate, we discover that its elements—energy and water, for example—are not equally distributed throughout the earth. This unequal distribution from area to area forms the basis for classification systems, such as climate or landform classifications that recognize regional variations.

As a regional classification evolves, similarities within areas as well as differences between them become evident. For example, the Tropical Rainforest climate is found not only in the Amazon Basin of Brazil but also in similar latitudes around the world. Mollisol soils are related to subhumid climates in the United States and also in the Soviet Union. As a general rule, systems that have similar inputs and processes respond in a similar manner. These inputs and processes are reflected in definite outputs and related regional patterns on the earth.

## OBJECTIVES OF THE STUDY OF PHYSICAL GEOGRAPHY

The beginning student may wonder, Why study physical geography? The answer to this question lies in the fact that the geographic approach is fundamentally unique in the fields of science. No other discipline places the analysis of area at its core. Basic objectives in the study of physical geography are (*a*) to acquire an appreciation of the scientific approach through geography's unique perspective, (*b*) to understand the associations between the physical features of the earth's different areas, and (*c*) to explore interrelationships between human activities and the physical world.

The geographic approach is equally appropriate for those who want to pursue professional careers in geography as well as for those who want to be informed citizens. Critical decisions are now being made and will continue to be made as to how our activities will affect the natural environment. The quality of these decisions depends upon our ability to assess and evaluate pertinent geographic factors.

# I

# WEATHER AND CLIMATE

# 2
# EARTH IN TIME AND SPACE

## KEY WORDS

Antarctic Circle
aphelion
Arctic Circle
axis
circle of illumination
ellipse
equator
equinox
inclination
insolation
international date line
latitude
longitude
meridians
oblate spheroid
orbit
parallelism of the axis
parallels
perihelion
prime meridian
revolution
rotation
solar radiation
solstice
standard time
suntime
Tropic of Cancer
Tropic of Capricorn

The earliest written records, dating before 3000 B.C., reveal the human fascination with finding our place in the universe. People have always watched celestial phenomena and wondered about the size of the universe. We have never been able to comprehend its vastness, for it is everything that is: space, galaxies, stars, the solar system, Earth, and all the things on it, including you and me.

Only a few hundred years ago, the earth was thought to occupy a privileged position as the center of the universe. The celestial sphere, our view of the sky from the earth, is one of nature's greatest illusions. The earth appears to be stationary while the sky seems to turn. Celestial objects appear to rise in the east, cross the sky, and set in the west. The sky seems to be curved, with all the objects in it the same distance from us. The sun also seems to shift northward and southward in the course of a year. All of these phenomena are optical illusions. In the sixteenth century, Copernicus began to challenge the false concept of a celestial sphere. His observations laid the foundation for the sun-centered theory of the solar system. He explained the motion of celestial bodies by assuming that the earth and other planets revolved around the sun. This revolutionary concept transformed the human understanding of our relationship to the universe. Since the time of Copernicus our universe has been widened immeasurably. Most of what we know about the universe has been learned by inference, using imprecise mathematical calculations to visualize the characteristics of unattainable places. The most fruitful measurements are those that attempt to determine masses and motions of faraway objects, their distance from Earth, and the different hues of light the objects emit. Increasingly powerful telescopes continue to probe deeper into the universe, adding to the magnificent picture of immensity that has gradually evolved.

The first investigations of space concerned the solar system. Astronauts have already landed on the moon; in the future they will visit the planets themselves. Satellites, such as the one that passed Jupiter in 1980, are providing startling new information. It is now known that the *solar system* consists of 1 sun, 9 planets—Mercury, Venus, Earth, Mars, Jupiter, Saturn, Uranus, Neptune, and Pluto, in order from the sun—more than 30 moons, some 30,000 asteroids, and on its perimeter about 100 billion comets, plus innumerable dust specks, gas molecules, and atoms. Of the total matter in the solar system, the sun possesses 99.86 percent. The sun is the fundamental source of energy to Earth, converting over 4 million tons of its mass into radiant energy each second. Because of the smallness of Earth and its distance from the sun, the planet intercepts less than 1/200,000,000,000 part of the solar output. Yet, all life on Earth and many of its physical processes are controlled by the sun's radiant energy. This radiant energy, transmitted in the form of short waves and traveling at a speed of 299,460 kilometers (186,000 miles) a second, is called *solar radiation* or *insolation.*

Although the solar system is 50 billion times as large as Earth itself, it is still only a tiny speck in the universe. The solar system, which extends for more than 16 billion kilometers (10 billion miles) in space, is a part of a *galaxy* known as the Milky Way. This galaxy has more than 100 billion stars. If you were to begin to count the stars in this single galaxy at the rate of 1 per second, it would take more than 3,000 years of steady counting. One of the great unanswered questions is, How many planets similar to our own exist in this single galaxy? Because the Milky Way is disk-shaped, we can see these stars as a bright band of light in the night sky. The phrase *Milky Way dust* is commonly applied to this phenomenon.

The great adventure of twentieth-century astronomy has been the exploration of the universe beyond the Milky Way. Telescopes continue to probe farther and farther into the universe, and despite the fact that the more distant galaxies appear fainter and fainter, still more of them are found. Questions that intrigue astronomers are, How far do galaxies reach into space? How many are there? It has been observed that the farther a galaxy is from Earth, the faster it is moving away. The best known method for determining distance requires the astronomer to observe individual stars in galaxies. When individual stars cannot be seen through a telescope, it is then necessary to use less exact methods that depend on the average apparent size and brightness of galaxies in clusters. By this method the average distance to a cluster of galaxies can be determined.

Today's astronomer frequently views more galaxies than stars through modern telescopes. The stars, of course, belong to our own Milky Way galaxy. Ours is only one of billions of galaxies in the universe, and the sun is but one star out of billions and billions of stars in that one galaxy. It is thus beyond human comprehension to imagine how many Earth-like planets are found in the universe.

## EARTH MOTIONS AND POSITIONS

The earth is part of a universal system that is held in space by gravitational forces. These forces control its motions. The two primary motions that affect the earth's inhabitants are *rotation* and *revolution* (Figure 2.1).

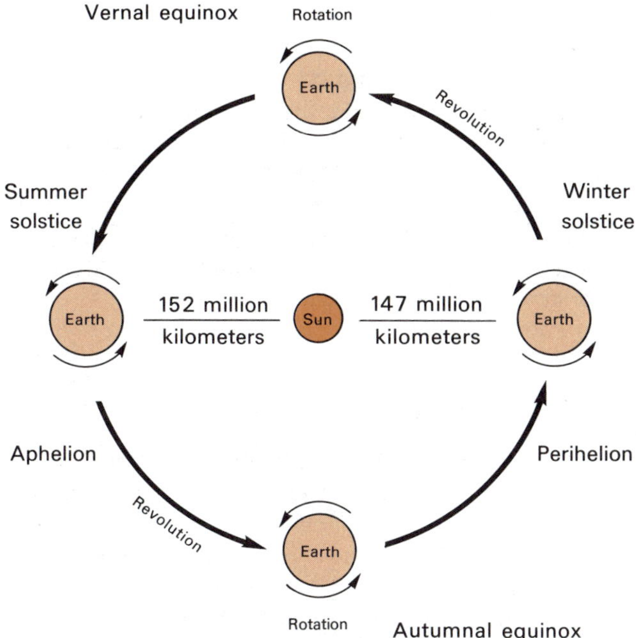


**FIGURE 2.1**
Earth motions and positions. Rotation of the earth on its imaginary axis creates daily changes. Revolution of the earth around the sun creates seasonal changes.

## ROTATION

Rotation is the turning of the earth on its axis. The earth's *axis* is defined as an imaginary line extending through the earth from pole to pole. Direction of rotation is from west to east, or, in other words, opposite to the sun's apparent movement from east to west. The earth rotates approximately once in 24 hours, and this fact determines the length of a day on earth. Speed of rotation for points along the equator is slightly over 1,600 kilometers (1,000 miles) per hour. In spite of this rapid movement, we have no sensation that the earth is moving, because the movement is virtually uniform and because heavenly bodies such as the moon and sun are too distant for us to use them as stationary reference points.

Rotation is responsible for many of the conditions that exist on the earth's surface. For example, if the rotation ever slowed so that the earth completed only one rotation, instead of 365.25 rotations, each year, the same face of the earth would always be turned toward the sun. As a result, one half of the earth would have constant daylight, and the other half constant darkness. The moon exhibits this characteristic because it rotates once while it completes its revolution around the earth. If the earth rotated only once during its revolution around the sun, one side of the earth would be extremely hot, and the other extremely cold, as is the situation on the moon. If, on the other hand, the earth rotated more rapidly, our periods of daylight and darkness would be shorter. The rotation of the earth also influences such important features as the direction of winds and ocean currents.

## REVOLUTION

Revolution is the movement of the earth around the sun. The path followed by the earth is known as its *orbit.* This orbit is not a perfect circle, but an *ellipse.* As a consequence the distance from the earth to the sun varies during the year. In July, when the earth is farthest from the sun at a distance of 152,145,000 kilometers (94,500,000 miles), it is in the *aphelion* position. In contrast, at the *perihelion* position in January, the earth is nearest the sun at a distance of 147,315,000 kilometers (91,500,000 miles).

The earth completes one journey around the sun in approximately 365.25 days. The speed of this journey averages 29.8 kilometers (18.5 miles) per second. As is the case with rotation, the near uniformity of movement obliterates the feeling of rapid movement. The calendar year is determined by the earth's revolution. The extra quarter-day is saved for four years and is then added to the year, making a 366-day year, or leap year.

Because half of the earth faces the sun at any one time, one half of the earth has light and one half of the earth has darkness. The side of the earth that is emerging from darkness is experiencing dawn, and the side of the earth approaching darkness is experiencing twilight. Because the earth's rotation is uniform, the line between light and darkness is continuously moving. This line is known as the *circle of illumination.* The circle of illumination does not pass through the poles during most of the year, so the length of light and darkness varies from place to place (Figure 2.2).

This variation in length of the day is caused by the fact that the earth's axis does not stand perpendicular to the plane formed by the earth's orbit. Rather, the axis of the earth is inclined away from the perpendicular at an angle of approximately 23°30′. This angle is called *inclination.* Further, at all points in the earth's orbit, all positions of the axis are parallel to each other. This phenomenon is known as *parallelism of the axis.* Because of the inclination and parallelism of the earth's axis, the circle of illumination is ever shifting its position relative to the poles. Only twice in a single revolution of the earth does the circle pass through the two poles, cross the parallels of latitude at right angles, and lie in the same plane as the meridians. These points in the earth's revolution occur on March 20 or 21 and Sep-

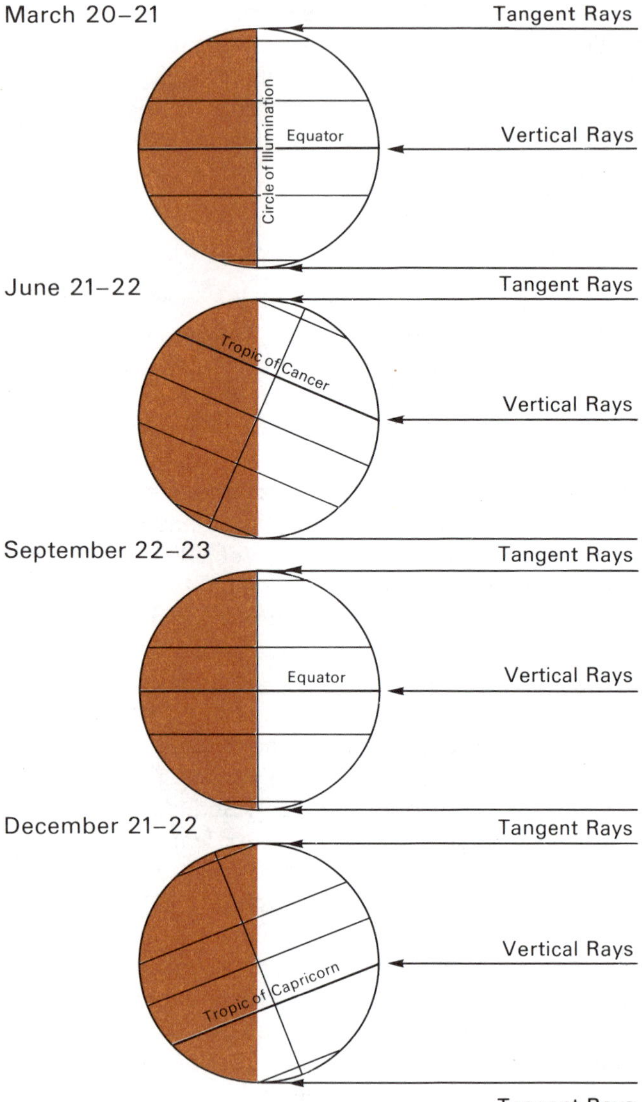


**FIGURE 2.2**
Location of the circle of illumination with respect to the earth's axis. Because of the inclination and parallelism of the axis, the lengths of day and night vary at different latitudes during the year. On March 20–21 and September 22–23 the sun is directly overhead at the equator, and the circle of illumination passes through the poles, bisecting all parallels equally. Day and night are the same length at all locations on these dates. On June 21–22 and December 21–22 the circle of illumination cuts all parallels, except the equator, unequally. Days and nights are therefore unequal in length except at the equator.

tember 22 or 23, the two dates of the year when the sun lies directly overhead at the equator.

Physical phenomena on the earth's surface are produced by the unique combination of factors just discussed: the speed of the earth's rotation, the period of the earth's revolution around the sun, the degree of inclination of the axis, and the parallelism of the axis. These factors combine with others, such as the elliptical shape of the earth's orbit and the oblate (flattened) shape of the earth itself, to form the basis for the development of the earth's weather and climate. The motions and positions of the earth in space are thus vital to all life on the surface.

## MARCH OF THE SEASONS

The variation in the amount of insolation at any latitude on the earth's surface, in large part, determines the seasons. In order to understand the cycle of the seasons, imagine the position of the earth in its revolution around the sun on March 20 or 21, June 21 or 22, September 22 or 23, and December 21 or 22. On each of these dates the vertical rays of the sun (those rays that strike the earth at a 90° angle) are in a particular position on the earth (Figure 2.3).

The first of these dates in the calendar year is March 20 or 21. On this date the earth is in such a position in its orbit that the sun's rays are vertical along the equator and tangent at the poles (Figure 2.4). This date is called the *vernal* or *spring equinox* in the Northern Hemisphere and the *autumnal equinox* in the Southern Hemisphere. *Equinox* means equal day and equal night. On this date day and night are each twelve hours long everywhere in the world. The circle of illumination, which is the dividing line between day and night, cuts all the parallels exactly in half at all latitudes. The Northern Hemisphere receives exactly the same amount of insolation as the Southern Hemisphere.

By June 21 or 22 the earth has completed another quarter of its orbit around the sun. Because of inclination and parallelism of the axis, the earth is now positioned so that the sun's rays are falling vertically on the parallel 23½ degrees north of the equator, the *Tropic of Cancer.* At the same time the sun's rays are tangent on the Antarctic Circle on the side nearest the sun, and all of the area within the Antarctic Circle is in darkness throughout the 24-hour period of rotation. The North Pole is inclined to its maximum extent (23½ degrees) toward the sun so that all of the area within the Arctic Circle experiences 24 hours of daylight. The sun's rays are tangent to the Arctic Circle on the side farthest from the sun. This is the time that the sun's vertical rays stop migrating toward the North Pole, pause momentarily, and start their journey southward. This theoretical

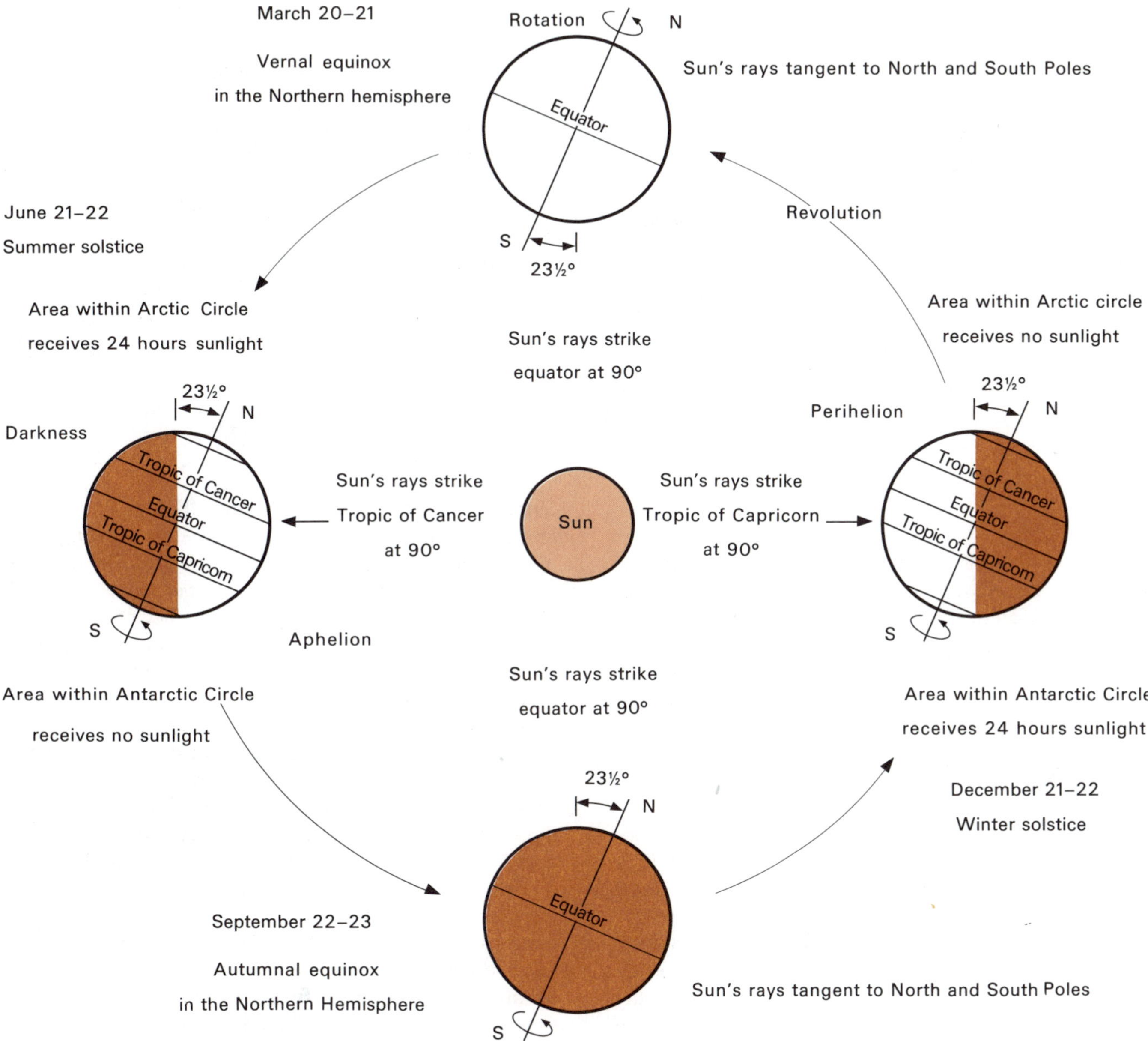


**FIGURE 2.3**
March of the seasons. A diagrammatic sketch of the positions of the earth in relation to the sun during a single year. The circle of illumination illustrates the changes in the length of daylight as the sun strikes the earth at different angles during the course of a year.

"standing still of the sun" is expressed by the word *solstice.* Therefore, this is the *summer solstice* in the Northern Hemisphere and the *winter solstice* in the Southern Hemisphere. In the Northern Hemisphere we experience our "longest" day of the year and the first day of summer. The circle of illumination on June 21 or 22 cuts all the parallels unequally over the earth's surface. In the Northern Hemisphere the greater part of the parallels are in daylight and a smaller portion in darkness. The circle of illumination passes through the Arctic Circle on the side farthest from the sun and through the Antarctic Circle on the side nearest the sun.

The earth completes another quarter of its orbit by September 22 or 23, so that it now occupies a position

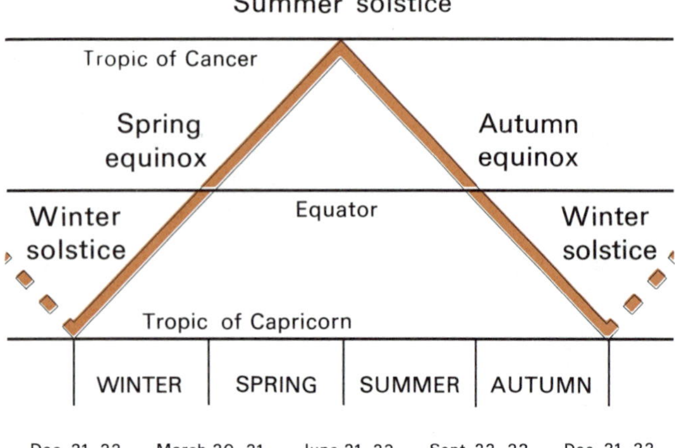


**FIGURE 2.4**
Migration of vertical rays during a single year. The heavy line illustrates where the sun's rays are vertical in the course of a year.

opposite to that of March 20 or 21. This is another equinoctial period, this time the *autumnal equinox* of the Northern Hemisphere, and the *vernal equinox* of the Southern Hemisphere. Conditions on the earth are similar to those experienced on March 20 or 21. The rays of the sun again strike the earth vertically at the equator and tangentially at the poles, the circle of illumination cuts all parallels at all latitudes equally, and day and night are each twelve hours long everywhere on the earth's surface.

On December 21 or 22, the earth moves into a position in its orbit opposite to the one it occupied on June 21 or 22. The vertical rays of the sun fall on the *Tropic of Capricorn,* 23½ degrees south of the equator. The area within the Arctic Circle is in complete darkness, with the sun's rays tangent to the earth's surface at the Arctic Circle on the side closest to the sun. Within the Antarctic Circle, constant daylight occurs because the sun's rays pass over the South Pole and strike the earth's surface tangentially at the Antarctic Circle on the side farthest from the sun. Thus, the South Pole is tilted toward the sun 23½ degrees while the North Pole is tilted away from the sun 23½ degrees. The sun's vertical rays stop momentarily on this date over the Tropic of Capricorn and then reverse direction, migrating once more northward. This date is the *winter solstice* in the Northern Hemisphere and the *summer solstice* in the Southern Hemisphere.

On December 21 or 22, the circle of illumination again cuts all the parallels of latitude unequally. Now the parallels are mostly in darkness in the Northern Hemisphere so the nights are longer than the periods of daylight. The opposite situation occurs in the Southern Hemisphere.

Because of the inclination of the axis 23½ degrees from the perpendicular and the parallelism of the axis, the line of maximum insolation on the earth's surface does not always coincide with the equator. Instead, it shifts through a total of 47 degrees: 23½ degrees to the north and 23½ degrees to the south of the equator. This in turn causes the march of the seasons. Although the amount of solar energy received in the Northern and Southern hemispheres varies with the season, the amount of insolation received annually is the same in each hemisphere.

## MEASUREMENT OF DIRECTION AND LOCATION

Since the dawn of history, human beings have been interested in the problem of accurately locating one place relative to other places on the earth. To create a grid of north-south and east-west lines on a spherical object, we must solve one difficulty. Because the surface has neither beginning nor end, no specific points are available from which to start numbering the lines. However, since the earth rotates, it does possess an axis. The northern end of the axis is the *North Pole,* and the southern end the *South Pole.* Thus direction toward the North Pole is always north, and toward the South Pole, south. These two fixed points form the basis for the construction of an earth grid to determine direction and the location of any specific point (Figure 2.5).

Using the two stationary poles as points, an imaginary line can be drawn around the circumference of the earth midway between them. This line, called the *equator,* is the longest line in the grid because it is the largest circumference on the earth that can be drawn. This is true because the earth is flattened at the poles, making the polar diameter of the earth shorter than the equatorial diameter. The distance around the equator is 40,092 kilometers (24,902 miles).

Other circles parallel to the equator are conveniently drawn at any desired distance between the equator and the poles. Because these lines are parallel to the equator, they are named *parallels* or latitude lines. Each succeeding parallel, farther from the equator and closer to the poles, forms a smaller circle. The pole, represented by a point, is the smallest possible circle.

Parallels thus have an east-west direction but measure distance north and south of the equator. This measurement of distance north and south of the equator is called *latitude* (Figure 2.5). The equator is given the

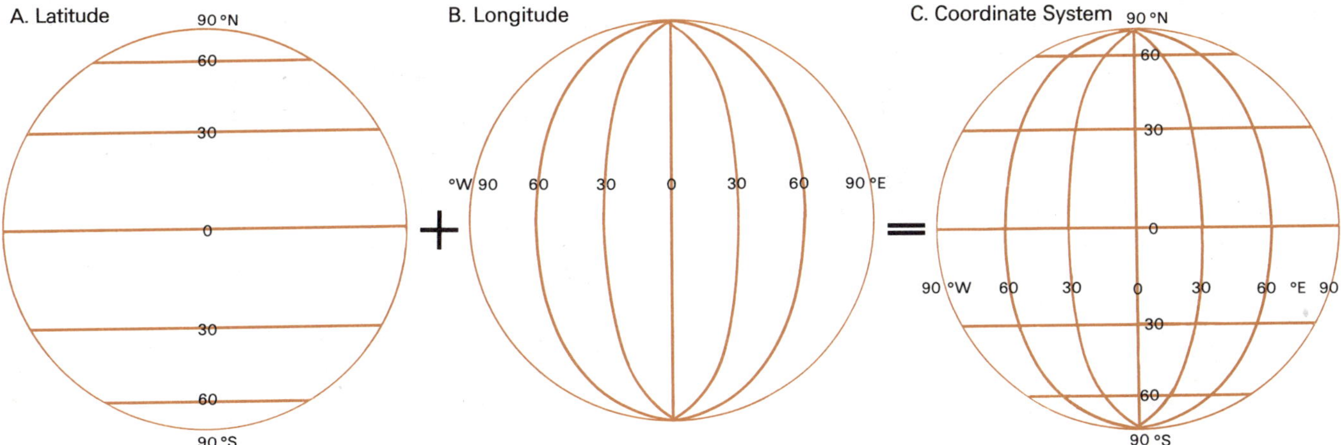


**FIGURE 2.5**
Longitude and latitude. The lines of latitude *(A)* measure distances north and south of the equator. The lines of longitude *(B)* measure distances east and west of the prime meridian to 180° east-west. When latitude and longitude are combined into a coordinate system, the location of any place on the earth can be determined. To define a precise location each degree is divided into 60 minutes, and within each minute are 60 seconds. A precise location, for example, is expressed as 45°18′39″ west longitude and 18°42′58″ north latitude.

value of 0° latitude. Although the distance around the earth forms a complete circle of 360°, the distance from the equator to either pole is a fourth of a circle, or 90°. Therefore the North and South poles are given the value of 90° north and 90° south. The various parallels between the equator and the poles are given values corresponding to their location in degrees between 0° and 90°.

The inclination and parallelism of the axis make certain parallels particularly significant for earth-sun relationships. The most significant parallel is, of course, the equator. As we have seen, the sun's rays are perpendicular to the equator at the equinoxes on March 20 or 21 and September 22 or 23. Because the axis of the earth is inclined 23°30′ from the perpendicular to its orbital plane, several other parallels assume importance. Two of these parallels are designated at 23°30′ north and south latitude. These lines mark the maximum distance from the equator that the sun's rays strike the earth vertically in either hemisphere. In the Northern Hemisphere the 23°30′ parallel is known as the *Tropic of Cancer*, and the corresponding location in the Southern Hemisphere is called the *Tropic of Capricorn*. Two other parallels established at 23°30′ south of the North Pole and 23°30′ north of the South Pole are known as the *Arctic* and *Antarctic circles*. These parallels are also related to the angle of the sun's rays as they strike the earth's surface. On June 21 or 22, when the Northern Hemisphere is inclined toward the sun, the sun's rays strike the North Pole and extend 23°30′ beyond. As a consequence all of the area from 66°30′ north to the North Pole has 24 hours of daylight. On December 21 or 22, the rays of the sun reach a maximum latitude of 66°30′ degrees in the Northern Hemisphere, and the area from 66°30′ to 90° north latitude is in darkness. The reverse situation occurs in the Southern Hemisphere.

The latitude of a given place is determined by an instrument called a sextant. This instrument can measure the angle between the horizon and the highest position of the sun at noon. For example, on March 20 or 21 and September 22 or 23 the sun's rays are perpendicular at the equator, and the latitude of any place on the earth can be determined by subtracting from 90° the angle read on the sextant. At times other than the equinoxes, the sun's rays are perpendicular to the earth north or south of the equator, so tables are available to indicate the perpendicular position of the sun's rays on each day. Latitude can also be obtained for a particular place by instrumental observations upon the North Star.

If the earth were a perfect sphere, each degree of latitude would have the same length. The planet is in fact slightly flattened at the poles, making it an *oblate spheroid*. Therefore, the length of a degree of latitude varies depending upon its location on the earth. For example, the first degree of latitude north or south of the equator has a length of 110.59 kilometers (68.69 miles), while the first degree from either pole is 111.71 kilometers (69.39 miles) long. Each degree of latitude is divided into 60 minutes, and each minute into 60 seconds. On the average each minute of latitude extends 1,853.6 meters (6,080 feet, or 1 nautical mile), and one second is about 30.3 meters (99.3 feet). In the metric system a meter is determined to be precisely one ten-millionth of the meridian distance from the equator to the pole.

To this point, our discussion has centered on measuring locations north and south of the equator. The use of latitude alone does not enable us to pinpoint a location on the earth. For example, the 40th parallel crosses central Illinois, Indiana, and Ohio, but it does not reveal the precise location of any particular place in these areas. In order to completely describe a location, we must be able to locate east-west points as well as north-south points.

In order to measure distances east and west, the grid system uses lines that cross the parallels at right angles, that is, at 90° angles. These lines that circle the earth and converge at the North and South poles are known as *meridians* or *longitude lines* (Figure 2.3). The measuring of distances east and west becomes more complex because there is no natural starting point. Longitude differs from latitude in several other ways:

1. If the lines are drawn from pole to pole, all the circles so formed are the same size. In contrast, the parallels vary in length from the equator to the poles.
2. The north-south trending lines are not parallel to each other, but instead converge at the poles and are farthest apart at the equator.
3. None of the longitude lines exist halfway between two established points, as does the equator in latitudinal measurement.

The problem of establishing a starting line to measure longitudinal distances east-west once caused much confusion. After Europeans began to explore the world in earnest, many countries selected a north-south line that passed through their own country as the initial or primary meridian. The lack of a universal standard for east-west location caused considerable difficulties. Finally, in 1884, through international agreement, the problem was solved by arbitrarily establishing a starting line from which to measure distance east and west. Because of the international importance of the Royal Astronomical Observatory at Greenwich, England, near London, the north-south trending line at this location was selected as the starting point with a value of 0°. This 0° meridian was called the Greenwich meridian or *prime meridian.*

Halfway around the earth from the prime meridian in either direction is 180°. To a westbound traveler it is 180° west; to an eastbound traveler the same line is 180° east. A location is stated as west longitude if it is west of the prime meridian and between 0° and 180° west, and as east longitude if it is east of the prime meridian and between 0° and 180° east. The 180° meridian approximates the *international date line,* which will be discussed in the next section.

To determine the longitude of a given place, we must find the difference in time between that place and the prime meridian. To find this difference an accurate timepiece (chronometer) is set at the time of the prime meridian. When the sun is at its zenith, the local time is exactly 12:00 noon. When the local time is compared with the time at the prime meridian, the difference is then easily translated into degrees, minutes, and seconds of longitude. Today the instantaneous communication by radio satellite signals makes accurate time comparison possible essentially everywhere, improving the exact determination of longitude.

The location of any particular place can be expressed at the intersection of a parallel and a meridian. For example, the location of New York City is 40°42′51″ north latitude and 74°0′23″ west longitude. Thus any place on the earth can be pinpointed by dividing the degrees into minutes and seconds.

## DETERMINATION OF TIME

Measuring the duration of time was an early human need. The basic unit of a day was provided by the uniform rotation of the earth. This rotation caused the sun to make a seemingly westward circuit of the sky each day and produce a succession of periods of daylight and darkness. The division of the day into 24 hours is a convenience chosen because so many fractional parts of that number can be identified in a 360° circle (Figures 2.6 and 2.7).

An old question is, When should the new day begin? The Babylonians began a new day at sunrise; the Athenians at sunset; ancient astronomers preferred noon; but now most of the world begins a new day at midnight. A common practice is to divide the day into two 12-hour periods. The period from midnight to noon is then designated as A.M. (*ante meridiem,* before noon), and the one from noon to midnight as P.M. (*post meridiem,* after noon). However, many foreign countries and transportation systems follow the practice of num-

**FIGURE 2.6**
Time zone map of the United States. There are four time zones in the United States based on the 75°, 90°, 105°, and 120° meridians. The standard meridians are located approximately in the middle of the time zones so that no place deviates more than about 30 minutes from suntime. (Based on data from the Interstate Commerce Commission and the U.S. Department of Transportation)

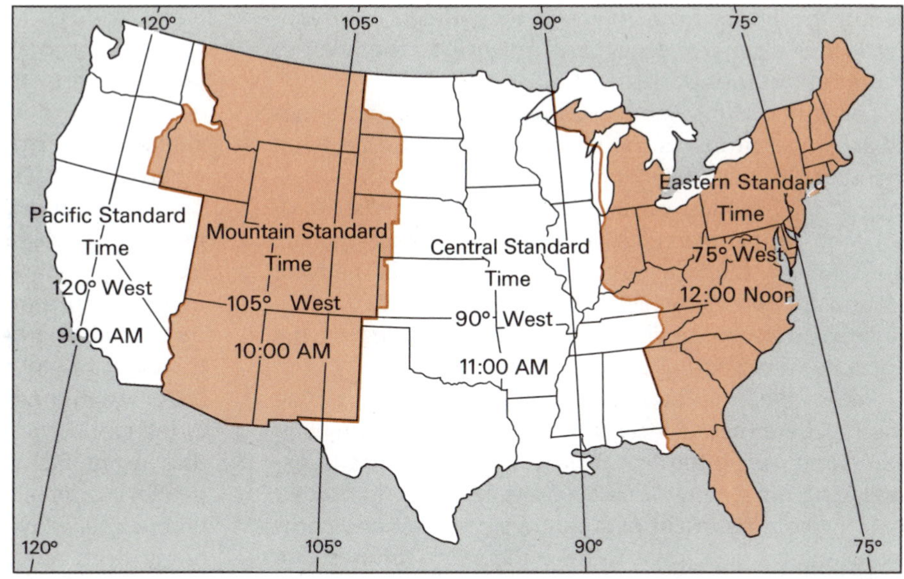


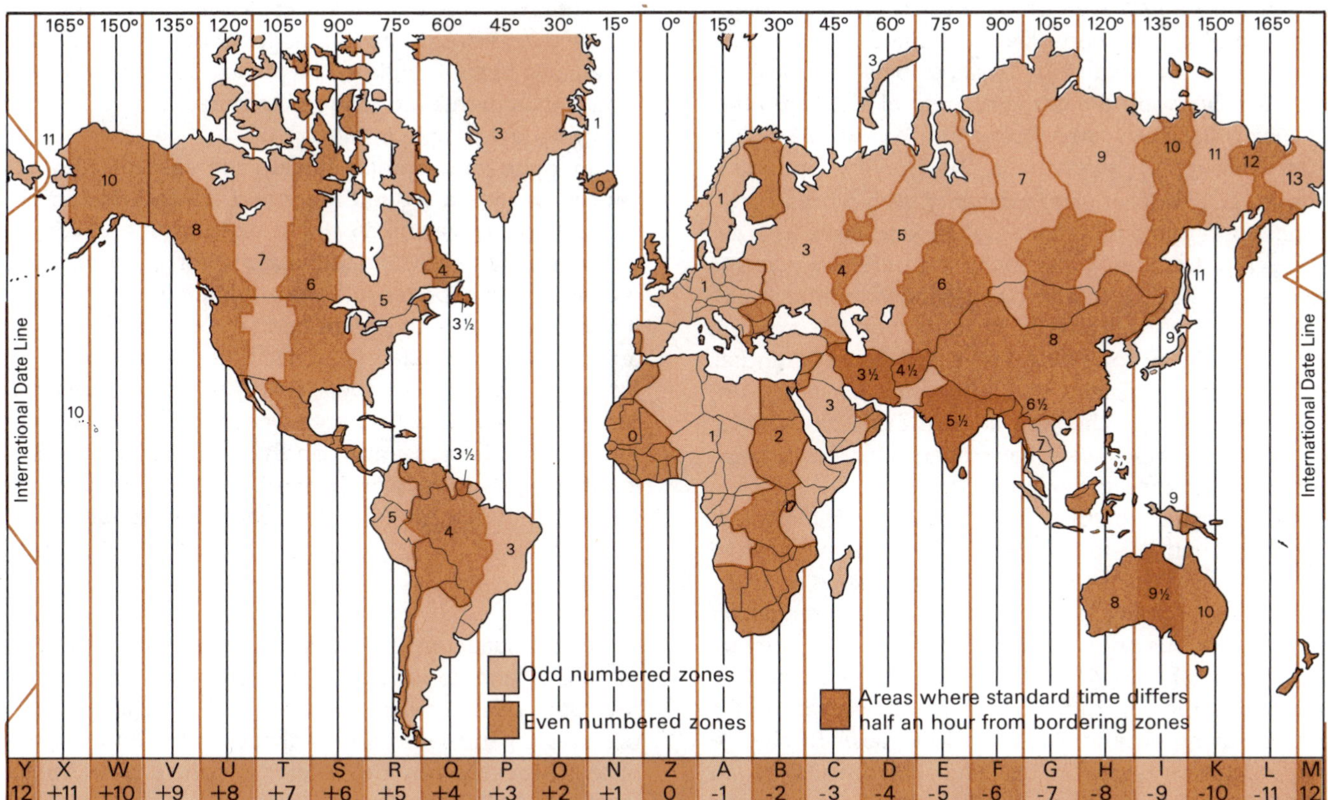


**FIGURE 2.7**
Standard time zones of the world. Each time zone covers approximately 15° of longitude. China deviates from this system and Saudi Arabia does not observe standard time. In all other areas the same time of day is observed within each zone for a distance of approximately 7½° on either side of the standard meridian (0°, 15°, 30°, 45°, 60°, etc.). (Based on data from the U.S. Navy Oceanographic Office)

bering the hours from midnight to midnight consecutively. For example, an airplane might be scheduled to depart at 2100 (9:00 P.M.).

Local time is the same at all places on the same meridian. For example, if it is noon at one point on a given meridian, it is noon at all places on that meridian. Further, it is afternoon on all meridians to the east; forenoon on all meridians to the west; and midnight on the meridian on the opposite side of the earth, halfway around the world. At every moment a new day is beginning on some meridian, and a day is ending on the opposite meridian.

Years ago, the people of different sections of the country determined local time based on the particular meridian passing through their town. This means of establishing time, known as *suntime,* became outmoded with the establishment of rapid transportation and communication. For a town to have the same time as one nearby, it had to lie directly north or south of its neighbor. Because towns were rarely located this way, towns in the same vicinity had different suntimes. The resulting confusion in conducting business between localities led to the development of the concept of *standard time.* Because a meridian turns through 360° every 24 hours, it turns through 15° every hour, and 1° every 4 minutes. Thus each 15° of longitude between two places corresponds to 1 hour's difference in their local time. In order to develop *standard time zones* a central meridian is taken as the basis for determining time within the entire zone. Under this system, the time of even the extreme edges of the time zone differs no more than 30 minutes from suntime. The standard time coincides with suntime in the center of the zone along the bisecting meridian. Standard time zones have been adopted in most countries of the world (Figure 2.7).

The changing length of daylight in the middle latitudes has given rise to a system of *daylight-saving time.* Because most persons have the habit of rising at a certain clock hour, they sleep through one or more daylight hours in the summer morning. In order to make the evening daylight "longer," the clocks are set ahead one hour during the summer months. The basic reason for daylight-saving time is that a clock is easier to change than a person's pattern of thinking. The practice began in World War I when there was an urgent need to conserve coal. The extra hour of light in the evening reduced energy consumption during those peak hours. The longer evening daylight also encouraged home gardening. There are, nevertheless, some disadvantages. When the dark period is extended in the morning, many children must leave their homes for school when it is dark. Also, people who live on the edges of the time zones are more affected by the time differences than those living in the central portions. Despite these difficulties, daylight time is now generally recognized as desirable by a majority of people. In the early 1970s, when energy shortages occurred, President Nixon imposed year-round daylight time for a short period. The period of daylight time in the United States is now controlled by Congress. Current legislation indicates that the nation, with minor exceptions, will have six months of daylight time from the last Sunday in April to the last Sunday in October.

Although a new day is always beginning *somewhere* in the world, we must agree at which meridian the new day begins first. From seafarers' customs the 180° longitude line was gradually established as the meridian where each day would have its start. This line has already been referred to as the *international date line;* it approximates the 180° longitude line, but deviates from it slightly when the meridian bisects an island chain or enters a landmass. The international date line thus falls essentially in the middle of the Pacific Ocean where only small adjustments are required to meet the needs of the relatively few people in the area.

Since the earth rotates toward the east, the day advances westward around the world. Thus, for example, when Monday begins at 180° east longitude, it will remain Sunday at 180° west longitude for 24 hours, until the world has experienced one complete rotation. When a person crosses the international date line, then, an adjustment in the day is needed. If, for example, on January 1, a person travels eastward across the international date line, it becomes December 31 as soon as the date line is crossed. If, on the other hand, a person is traveling westward on December 31 and crosses the international date line, the date becomes January 1.

## CONCLUSION

Time and space on the earth are determined by the tilt of its axis and its fundamental motions of rotation and revolution. Time is a linear concept: The past can never occur again and tomorrow is always in the future. Thus, all earth events can be ordered within a time framework.

The daily, weekly, monthly, and yearly rhythms of the earth are ordered by its relationship to the sun, and to a lesser extent the moon and the stars. The seasons on the earth provide an example of the interrelationship of the earth and the sun. Because the earth is tilted 23½ degrees from the plane of its orbit, the amount of energy received at different places on the earth varies during the year.

Exploration of the earth required people to develop a system to determine precise location. Initially the sun and the stars provided the means for navigation from one place to another. Gradually refinements created a system of coordinates of longitude and latitude so that every place can be precisely located.

## STUDY QUESTIONS

1 Describe the principal earth motions.
2 Define the ellipse of the the earth.
3 Why do the vertical rays of the sun migrate from the Tropic of Cancer to the Tropic of Capricorn between June 21 and December 21 each year?
4 On what dates do all places on the earth receive 12 hours of daylight and 12 hours of darkness? Why?
5 Why do the daylight hours vary from the Arctic Circle to the North Pole during the course of a year?
6 By what means are direction and location measured on the earth?
7 What is the importance of the prime meridian and the international date line in determining time on the earth?

# 3
# THE ATMOSPHERE

## KEY WORDS

aurora australis
aurora borealis
exosphere
interplanetary space
ionosphere
lapse rate
mesopause
mesosphere
nitric oxide
ozone
photochemical smog
photosynthesis
saltation
stratosphere
sublimation
temperature inversion
thermosphere
tropopause
troposphere

The atmosphere is our most basic natural resource. Without it we could not exist for a single moment. Although it is always essential for life on earth, the atmosphere is not static. It is warmed, it is cooled; its moisture content is sometimes high, sometimes low; it experiences periods of high pressure and then low pressure; it can move as a hurricane force, or remain calm for days or even weeks. Measurements of such atmospheric characteristics at a place and time allow us to determine weather conditions.

## COMPOSITION OF THE ATMOSPHERE

The atmosphere is a relatively thin blanket of air surrounding the earth. During the day it shields the earth's surface from the direct heat and ultraviolet rays of the sun; at night it acts as a blanket, preventing excessive loss of warmth to outer space. Without the atmosphere the diurnal range of temperature would be similar to that of the moon, extending from the boiling point of water, or 100°C (212°F), in the daytime to about −120°C (−248°F) at night.

The atmosphere of the earth differs from that of all other planets in the solar system. At sea level it consists largely of nitrogen (78 percent) and oxygen (21 percent), with only traces of such gases as argon (0.93 percent) and carbon dioxide (0.003 percent). Although nitrogen is the most abundant gas in the atmosphere, it is chemically rather inactive and acts as a diluting agent for the oxygen.

Oxygen, in contrast to nitrogen, is an active gas, readily combining with other elements. Although this element is necessary to all life on earth, an atmosphere of pure oxygen would be deadly. Pure oxygen has such a strong affinity for carbon and hydrogen, which are the principal constituents of organic matter, that at the temperature of a lighted match uncontrollable combustion would occur. If the atmosphere were pure oxygen an explosion would sweep the surface of the earth in a blinding flash, destroying all living things. Nitrogen, fortunately, dilutes atmospheric oxygen to a safe level. Oxygen then becomes amazingly suited to meet one of the requirements for life on earth.

Carbon dioxide is as important in sustaining plant life as oxygen is in supporting animal life. Plants extract carbon dioxide and water from the atmosphere in the presence of sunlight to convert green chlorophyll into compounds of carbon, hydrogen, and oxygen that resemble starches and sugars. This process is known as *photosynthesis*. Oxygen is released into the atmosphere during this process.

A growing public concern is that the burning of coal and other fossil fuels is raising the carbon dioxide content of the atmosphere. Investigations have attempted to reveal how the increased carbon dioxide could affect the health of the world's peoples. Fortunately, studies carried out by the Brookhaven National Laboratory on Long Island have revealed that the present concentration of carbon dioxide could be increased many times without affecting human health. Studies show that a concentration of three percent carbon dioxide has no marked effect on a healthy adult, except somewhat increased respiration. A concentration of five to six percent carbon dioxide can be breathed for an extended period, but causes some discomfort, such as headaches and nausea. If the concentration reaches ten percent, nausea, headaches, and unconsciousness result in a few mintues. It thus appears that the present trend of minute increases of carbon dioxide in the atmosphere will have no effect on the health of human beings. The reciprocal use of oxygen by animals and carbon dioxide by plants plays a dominant role in maintaining a favorable ratio between these two gases.

The moisture content of the atmosphere greatly affects weather conditions. The invisible water vapor enters the atmosphere through the endless process of evaporation from moist surfaces, water bodies (particularly the oceans), and plants. The subtropical and tropical oceans are the principal sources of water evaporated into the air. To a much lesser extent the atmosphere receives water vapor by *sublimation,* the process by which snow and ice are converted directly into a gaseous state.

Water vapor acts as a thermal blanket for the earth, making it suitable for life. The presence of moisture in the atmosphere aids in holding the heat in when the earth is cooling and keeping intense heat out when it is warming. For example, on a clear night in autumn, cooling occurs rapidly and frost may result, but when there is a cloud covering, cooling is retarded and the possibility of a frost diminishes.

Water vapor in the atmosphere is the ultimate source of all forms of precipitation: rain, snow, sleet, and hail. The moisture tends to remain relatively close to the earth. It is estimated that half of the atmosphere's moisture is within 1,800 meters (5,900 feet) of the earth; moisture is rarely encountered more than six or seven miles above the surface. Although the amount of water vapor varies from time to time and place to place, it rarely exceeds three percent by volume in even the

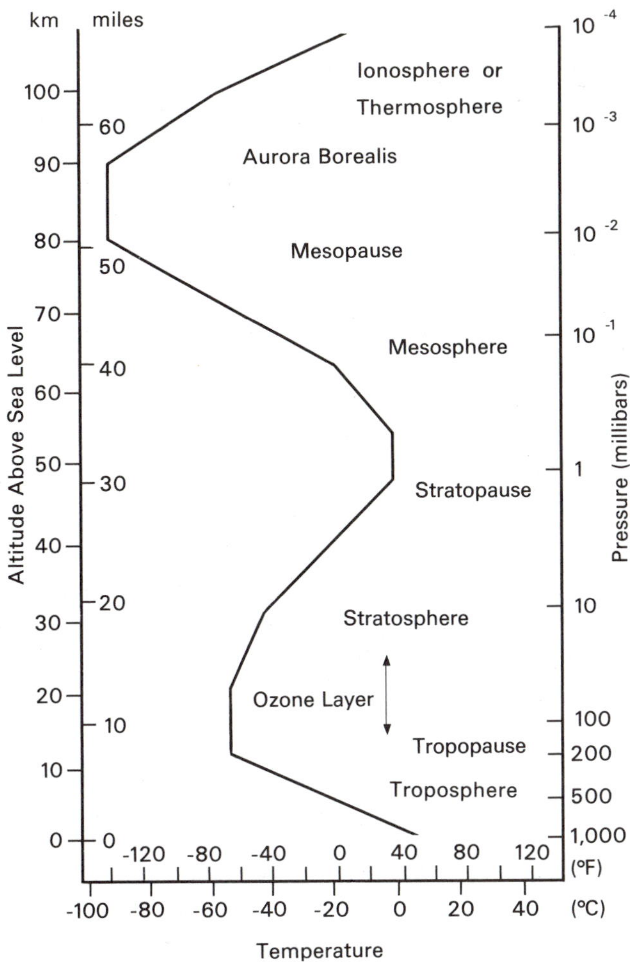


FIGURE 3.1
Layers of the atmosphere. Temperature decreases with elevation in the troposphere, increases with elevation in the stratosphere, decreases again with elevation in the mesosphere, and increases in the ionosphere or thermosphere. Note that the aurora borealis (northern lights) is located at nearly 100 kilometers (60 miles) above the earth, where ionization occurs. The ozone layer lies between 15 and 25 kilometers (10 to 18 miles), immediately above the tropopause. (After U.S. Air Force, 1965)

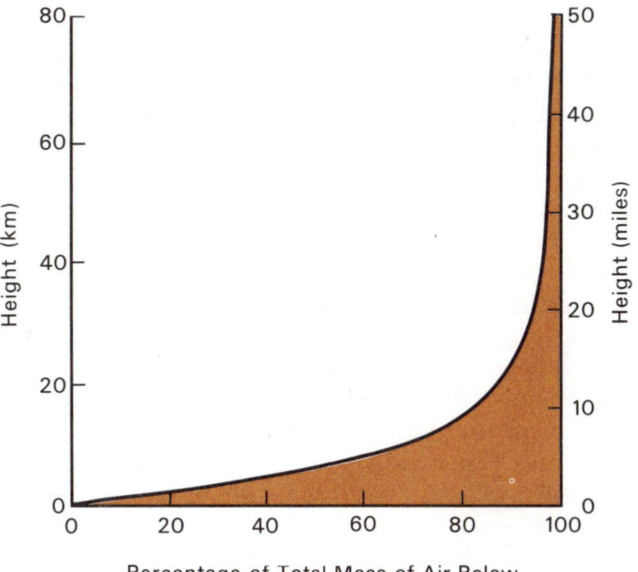


FIGURE 3.2
Mass of the atmosphere as a function of height. About 90 per cent of the atmosphere is concentrated below 20 kilometers (12 miles).

most humid areas of the tropics. This small percentage actually represents an enormous amount of water, however. If all the water vapor in the lower atmosphere were suddenly condensed it would form a layer of water about 2.5 centimeters (one inch) deep over the entire earth's surface.

Moisture in the atmosphere can exist as a liquid, a solid, or a gas, and is constantly changing from one state to another. These characteristics are of major importance in the changing nature of the atmospheric environment.

## LAYERS OF THE ATMOSPHERE

Before the twentieth century, study of the upper atmosphere was limited to observations from mountain tops and experiments using balloons and kites. The coming of the airplane and, later, the space probes increased our understanding of the outer limits of space. In the past, the atmosphere was thought to maintain a fairly uniform composition as its density decreased. This simplistic concept has long been dispelled. It is now recognized that the atmosphere can be divided into five layers that surround the earth at various elevations.

The layer closest to the earth's surface is the *troposphere* (Figure 3.1). The height of this lowest layer varies with latitude. In the vicinity of the equator it reaches a height of about 16 kilometers (10 miles), but its height is only about 9.6 to 12.8 kilometers (6 to 8 miles) at the poles. It contains about 90 percent of the mass of the atmosphere and nearly all of its water vapor (Figure 3.2). The name troposphere means sphere of change, a reference to the fact that this is the layer where weather activity occurs.

Within this layer the temperature normally decreases with increasing altitude, at a rate of approximately 1.8° to 1.9°C (3.3° to 3.5°F) in still air for every rise of 300 meters (1,000 feet). The rate of temperature decrease is called the *lapse rate.* This decrease in temperature stops between 9,000 and 12,000 meters (29,500 and 39,300 feet) at the *tropopause.* Above this zone the temperature rises in the *stratosphere.*

The troposphere is the most important part of the atmospheric environment as far as life on the earth is concerned. Within the troposphere occur most of the air movement, most of the water vapor, dust, and pollutants, and, in general, most of the atmospheric changes that affect us.

Above the tropopause is another layer called the *stratosphere.* This layer extends to about 48 kilometers (30 miles) above the earth's surface. Conditions in the stratosphere are important because they influence conditions in the troposphere. Until high-flying airplanes and rockets began exploring this area, the air in the stratosphere was thought to be still and the temperature was thought to drop with altitude. Both assumptions were wrong. At 30 degrees on either side of the equator, temperature in the stratosphere rises about 3.3°C per kilometer (6°F per mile) in altitude. In the middle latitudes a layer of nearly equal temperatures extends from the tropopause to about 20 kilometers (12 miles), and then temperatures rise steadily to the stratopause.

The heating of the stratosphere is due primarily to the production of *ozone* ($O_3$). Ozone is produced when ultraviolet radiation from the sun reacts with ordinary oxygen ($O_2$). Ozone production proceeds most rapidly at altitudes between 24 and 48 kilometers (15 and 30 miles). Because ozone absorbs incoming ultraviolet rays, it is able to warm the thin atmosphere. Thus the ceiling of the stratosphere is marked by the upper boundary of the warm layer.

Atmospheric motion within the stratosphere consists in general of a very broad, sweeping wind system that varies in strength and reliability (Figure 3.3). World War II pilots discovered a narrow band of winds in the stratosphere above the middle latitudes. These winds vary in velocity from 150 to 500 kilometers (100 to 300 miles) per hour. Because no weather occurs in this zone and the wind velocities improve flying time, the stratosphere became a desirable place for high-altitude flights.

Above the stratopause the temperature again decreases with increasing altitude up to a height of about 100 kilometers (60 miles). This layer, called the *mesosphere,* lies between 48 and 96 kilometers (30 to 60 miles) in altitude. It is thought to be a zone of considerable turbulence. The top of the mesosphere, known as the *mesopause,* has a temperature of about −83°C (−120°F), the lowest in the atmosphere.

The *ionosphere* or *thermosphere,* extending from about 100 to 1,000 kilometers (60 to 600 miles), is the earth's frontier with outer space. The appearance of ionization distinguishes this zone from the stratosphere. In the lower portions of the ionosphere there are several distinctive layers of highly charged particles that make radio and television transmission possible. The impulses from earth transmitters cannot penetrate these

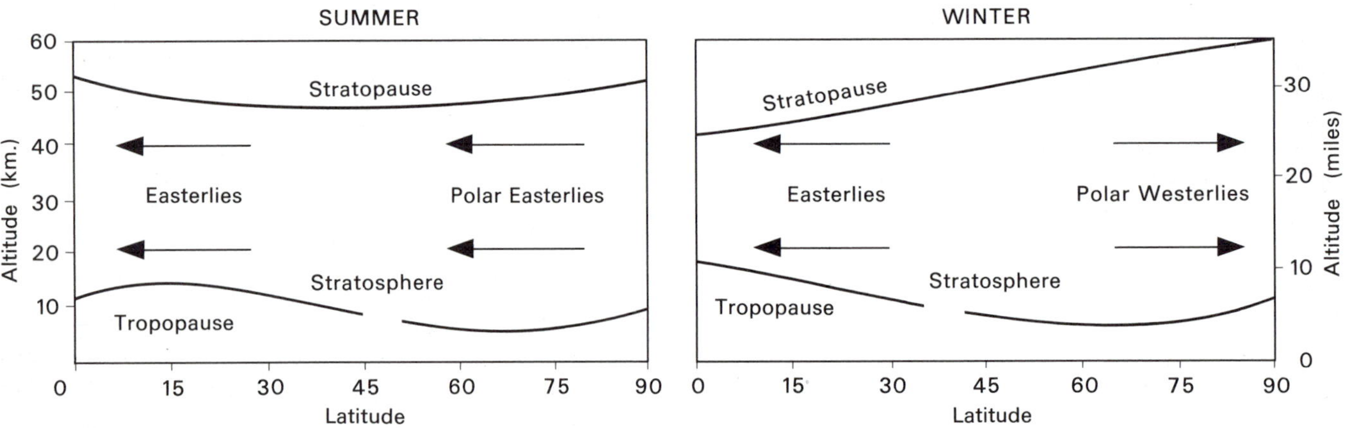


**FIGURE 3.3**
Prevailing winds in the stratosphere. (After Figure 3–13, "The prevailing winds in the stratosphere," from *The Earth in Profile: A Physical Geography* by David Greenland and Harm J. de Blij. Copyright © 1977 by David Greenland and Harm J. de Blij. Reprinted by permission of Harper & Row, Publishers, Inc.)

charged layers, but are reflected back to earth. Reception of distant stations is thus made possible.

Although the ionosphere contains only a tiny portion of the earth's atmosphere, it plays a vital role in conditioning the sun's rays before they reach the earth. If the heat and lethal rays from the sun reached the surface directly, life would likely be impossible. Within the ionosphere the temperature rises rapidly. At an elevation of 500 to 650 kilometers (300 to 400 miles) the temperature is about 1,200 to 1,700°C (2,200 to 3,100°F), exceeding that of molten iron. The heat of this zone is one of the major barriers that had to be overcome before space flights could be successful. The ionosphere is named after the highly ionized gases found there. Oxygen and nitrogen, for example, appear in the troposphere as the neutral molecules $O_2$ and $N_2$. In the ionosphere, however, oxygen appears as free atoms, O, and nitrogen as N.

Within the ionosphere occurs one of nature's most spectacular shows. The *aurora borealis* and *aurora australis* (northern and southern lights) result from the bombardment of the ionosphere by showers of highly charged particles. The auroras are found at about the same height as the radio-reflecting layers. The intensity and form of the auroras vary greatly depending upon the interaction of the ionized particles and the earth's magnetic field.

The *exosphere* extends from about 1,000 kilometers (620 miles) to perhaps 10,000 kilometers (6,000 miles) in altitude. At its outer limit, air molecules disappear, and *interplanetary space* begins. The limit of the exosphere is not a precise line but an undefined layer several hundred kilometers in thickness. In 1957–58 several belts of intense radiation, now known as the Van Allen radiation belts, were discovered 1,600 to 4,800 kilometers (1,000 to 3,000 miles) above the surface of the earth. They are belts of high-energy particles trapped in the earth's magnetic fields. These particles are thought to be high-energy electrons and protons jetted from solar flares. They race from one edge of the belt to the other until they build a critical mass sufficient to escape into the ionosphere. As they encounter the atmosphere in the ionosphere, heat is released, producing the glow known as the auroras.

## POLLUTION OF THE TROPOSPHERE

The pollution of the atmosphere is not a new phenomenon. However, as the human population grows and as industry expands, increasing quantities of solid and gaseous contaminants are released. This increase has created a worldwide concern that the pollution of the atmosphere over considerable areas has reached such a high concentration that it interferes with human comfort, safety, and health.

### SOURCES OF AIR POLLUTION

The air can be polluted by natural causes or by human activities. Of the more than 170 million tons of pollutants emitted into the atmosphere of the United States annually, about 60 percent is attributable to the automobile, 30 percent to industrial activities, and 10 percent to natural causes. Many pollutants may be removed quickly through precipitation or a combination of topographic and meteorological conditions, or they may persist over a long period of time. Pollutants may also be carried great distances by winds. Sulfur pollutants, for example, that originate in western Europe are known to cause acid rain 1,500 kilometers (930 miles) away in Sweden and Finland. In 1968 dust originating in the African Sahara fell over England.

### NATURAL AIR POLLUTANTS

Many natural earth activities cause air pollution. The eruptions of volcanoes frequently hurl tremendous quantities of earth fragments and smoke into the atmosphere. It has been estimated that a single eruption can spew 76 billion cubic meters (100 billion cubic yards) of fine particles into the atmosphere. Because it may take years for the finer particles to be removed from the atmosphere, this phenomenon has an influence on human activities. For example, in 1883 the volcano Krakatoa erupted with such force that fine particles were distributed worldwide, noticeably reducing the amount of solar energy reaching the earth. The particles in the atmosphere caused a small but significant cooling of the earth in the several years following the eruption. As the particles were removed from the atmosphere, the earth temperatures returned to normal.

On May 18, 1980, the eruption of Mount St. Helens spewed volcanic dust particles 20,000 meters (65,000 feet) into the atmosphere. Dark clouds of volcanic ash and dust from the explosion blotted out the sun over eastern Washington, more than 250 kilometers (160 miles) from the volcano. Dust from the volcano was blown more than 800 kilometers (500 miles) downwind from the explosion.

Another source of natural air pollution is the smoke from forest fires. The United States Forest Service estimates that an average of 120,000 forest fires each year burn 600,000 acres of forest. The local smoke pollution effects can be quite serious. A forest fire may burn for many days, shrouding the area downwind in smoke so dense that breathing is difficult. At times the population of such an area must be evacuated.

The air can also be polluted by dust picked up by wind. In humid regions this type of air pollution is minimal, but in dry regions, where there is little vegetation, even moderate winds can cause particles to rise to altitudes of over 3 kilometers (2 miles). A particle of about 1 millimeter (about 0.04 inch) in diameter takes a strong wind to move it. Particles with diameters of 0.2 millimeters (about 0.008 inch) begin moving with winds of 16 to 25 kilometers (10 to 15 miles) per hour. After rolling on the ground they may strike an obstacle and suddenly shoot upward. This process is called *saltation.* Some soil grains are very fine, having diameters of only 0.001 millimeter (about 0.00004 inch). A dust storm may contain tens of millions of dust particles that are so fine that they remain suspended in the atmosphere for weeks. They frequently remain airborne until rain or snow works them out of the atmosphere.

Ocean wave actions release tremendous quantities of minute droplets of seawater into the atmosphere. While the larger droplets will soon fall to the surface, the smallest are transported horizontally. Near the coast, this cloud of sea droplets can have harmful effects on all objects, both living and nonliving, that are not salt-resistant. Certain weather conditions cause sea particles to grow by condensation, leading to fog formation.

## POLLUTANTS OF HUMAN ORIGIN

The motor vehicle constitutes one of the principal sources of air pollution. About 99 percent of motor vehicles burn diesel fuel or gasoline, but they burn it imperfectly, discharging large amounts of partly burned hydrocarbons. Automobiles are by far the nation's largest source of such pollutants as carbon monoxide and other hydrocarbons, as well as nitrogen oxides. This last type of air pollutant is a primary agent for the formation of *photochemical smog.* Standards for carbon monoxide and hydrocarbon emissions from new passenger cars were instituted in 1968. Successively tighter restrictions were imposed with the Clean Air Act of 1970 and later revisions.

Stationary sources of air pollutants include electric generating plants, space heating systems, industrial operations (Photo 1), and refuse incinerators (Photo 2). About 95 percent of the electrical energy generated in the United States is produced by burning coal and oil, which contain elemental sulfur as an impurity. When these fuels are burned, the sulfur combines with oxygen to produce sulfur oxides, which are one of the most serious and prevalent forms of air pollution. Rapidly increasing electrical consumption has increased air pollution. Processes involving the chemical mixing of limestone with the sulfur oxides appear to provide the best

**PHOTO 1**
Dust pollution in the development of a new waste haulage area in copper ore mining. (Courtesy: Kennecott Copper Corporation)

**PHOTO 2**
Air pollution resulting from burning tires at a city garbage dump. (Courtesy: USDA Soil Conservation Service)

**PHOTO 3**
Industrial pollution prior to pollution control. (Courtesy: U.S. Environmental Protection Agency)

solution to this type of pollution problem in the immediate future. Much of the world's oil and coal has a high sulfur content. Cleaning techniques can remove some of the sulfur from coal, but generally not economically enough to produce a sulfur-free coal. Another form of air pollution, nitrogen oxides emissions, are highly dependent on flame temperature and oxygen concentration. To control these emissions, efforts are centered on developing combustion processes that minimize formation of the pollutant, and on devising techniques for removal of the pollutant after it has been formed.

The industrial development of the United States has been successful, but it has generally not been accompanied by concern for the pollution problems that are created (Photos 3, 4, and 5). Industries discharge into the atmosphere more than 20 percent of the nation's emitted sulfur oxides and particulate matter, and more than 10 percent of the carbon monoxide and hydrocarbons. The principal industrial contributors to air pollution include pulp and paper mills, iron and steel plants, smelters, petroleum refineries, and inorganic and organic chemical manufacturers.

The production of solid wastes now exceeds 400 million tons per year in the United States and is increasing at an annual rate of 4 percent. Much of this refuse is burned in incinerators. Many local incinerators are poorly designed and lack emission controls, resulting in a high level of carbon monoxide in the air.

## GEOGRAPHIC ORIGIN OF AIR POLLUTION

There are three geographic sources of air pollution: point source, line source, and regional source.

The point source of pollution is a single origin of emissions into the atmosphere. The pollution may occur as a steady emission in a manufacturing process or

**PHOTO 4**
Atmospheric pollution at a steel plant in Gary, Indiana, prior to compliance with the 1973 Clean Air Act. (Courtesy: U.S. Environmental Protection Agency)

**PHOTO 5**
Air pollution from a sawmill. (Courtesy: U.S. Environmental Protection Agency)

as a single ejection in a short period of time, such as a nuclear or chemical explosion. The distribution of the pollutant will depend on the wind speed and direction at the time of emission. If the air is calm the pollutant will be concentrated in a small area, but wind movement will distribute it over a wider area. The continuous point sources of emissions are the most familiar, the most conspicuous, and most studied.

The line sources of air pollutants are less common than the point sources. A line source might be a heavily traveled highway, or it could be a line of chemical or heavy industrial plants that are strung out along a valley bottom. If the line of pollutants is long enough, the dispersion of pollution will occur both vertically and horizontally. Dispersal of the pollutants along a highway can become a major problem if the wind flows parallel to the highway. In this situation the pollutants may be concentrated at a particular place downwind along the highway.

The regional sources may vary in size. Atmospheric pollution may be limited to a few square kilometers over an industrial park, or it may cover a million square kilometers. Regional sources are made up of many point and line sources that combine to pollute a large area. These sources may include all types of the atmospheric pollutants. The development of regional pollution depends upon stable air conditions that prevent the pollutants from being dispersed by winds. The topography of an area may also concentrate the pollutants in a particular space. Thus the key to regional atmospheric pollution is the total movement of a large volume of air. Anything that reduces the dispersal of air, whether it is a slow-moving body of stable air in a high-pressure cell, or a topographic barrier, is important to understanding regional atmospheric pollution.

## ATMOSPHERIC DIFFUSION OF POLLUTANTS

The atmospheric conditions of temperature, moisture, and wind structure determine how pollutants are dispersed. Both horizontal and vertical movements are possible.

Vertical turbulence occurs when the atmosphere is heated unevenly. The greatest turbulence is associated with a decrease in temperature with height of 10°C per kilometer or greater. If the temperature decreases with altitude at a lesser rate, turbulence tends to be decreased also. If temperature increases with height, an inversion occurs and turbulence is very much reduced. The depth of the overturning of the atmospheric layers depends on the intensity of solar radiation. In the dry air of the desert the vigorous mixing of the cool and warm air may extend well above 3 kilometers (2 miles), while in a densely forested region the turbulence may be limited to several hundred meters above the earth. When a low-level inversion occurs, with cold, dense air lying under warmer air, pollutants such as smoke will spread out horizontally directly under the warm layer. Sometimes, under the stable conditions of early morning when relative humidities are high, smoke and water vapor emitted from a factory may produce dense fog, which will drift slowly downwind.

Pollutants travel with the wind. Forecasting the horizontal movement of pollutants is difficult because winds are constantly changing direction and velocity. For example, within an hour's time wind direction may fluctuate over 30 degrees, dispersing pollutants over a wide area. Predictions are also made less precise by the fact that wind observations are rarely recorded at the source of pollutants. Further, not only does wind vary horizontally from place to place and from time to time, but it also varies vertically. In general, over level terrain, the wind speed is greatest in the lowest few meters, but gradually slows with increasing height. Also, the direction is nearly constant with elevations up to about 100 meters (325 feet), but more significant changes in direction occur at higher altitudes.

## MAJOR AIR POLLUTION INCIDENTS

Excessive concentrations of air pollutants can develop on any geographical scale, thus creating a local or a regional problem.

### Local

A number of local air pollution situations have been devastating. One of these occurred between the 4th and 10th of December, 1952, in London, England. On December 4 a high-pressure atmospheric cell began to center on the city, shrouding it in several layers of clouds. From thousands of chimneys the unburnt remains of coal floated into the atmosphere. The smell of smoke was evident. In the following days the winds were too weak to carry these pollutants away. Smoke and moisture accumulated in the lower layers of the atmosphere. By December 6 people were beginning to complain about the atmospheric conditions. Dense fog blotted out the sky. Visibility was only a few meters. The humidity had risen to 100 percent, with the air completely calm. As the smoke accumulated, coughing could be heard everywhere in the city. On December 7 conditions worsened. Patients with respiratory diseases crowded London hospitals, and many did not survive. On December 9 the high-pressure air cell finally began to move. With winds blowing fairly steadily, the skies began to clear. By December 10 a cold front had passed over the area, bringing fresh, clean air from the North Atlantic. The emergency was over, but during those few days 4,000 Londoners had died.

The United States experienced a major air pollution incident in Donora, Pennsylvania, between October 25 and 31, 1948. Donora, an old heavy-industry town, is located in a deep valley on the Monongahela River. During a period of extremely stable air the industrial pollutants of sulfur dioxide and its oxidation products, along with particulate matter, accumulated in the atmosphere until a dense fog developed. The fog was not dissipated until it rained on October 31. Of a population of 14,000, nearly 6,000 suffered some respiratory problems, 1,500 being seriously ill. In addition, 18 persons died, all of them over 50 years of age. Fourteen of the dead had a previous history of respiratory illness.

In July of 1976, when a stable air mass developed over Milan, Italy, a chemical plant at nearby Seveso released into the atmosphere a cloud of highly toxic dioxin (tetrachlorodibenzo-p-dioxin). The pollutant remained in the area for about 3 weeks, forcing the evacuation of 700 people, at least 500 of whom exhibited symptoms of poisoning. Pregnant women who were affected were advised to have abortions, because the poison causes malformations in fetuses. About 600 animals were poisoned and had to be destroyed, and all contaminated crops were burned. Medical experts recommended that all residents of the area receive periodic medical examinations for the rest of their lives.

### Regional

On a number of occasions excessive pollution concentrations have covered nearly half the area of the United States. One such phenomenon, now known as Episode 104, occurred between August 22 and September 1, 1969 (Figure 3.4). On August 22 the National Meteorological Center forecast a *High Air Pollution Potential* (HAPP) for the upper Midwest. Such a condition occurs when the air near the earth's surface reverses its usual daytime decrease in temperature with altitude. Within the first 400 meters (1,300 feet) or so the temperature will increase with height, creating a *temperature inversion* or *thermal inversion*. In this situation the cooler, pollutant-laden surface air is held near the ground by the warm air above it. If winds during this time are absent or very light, pollutants can move neither upward nor horizontally.

The high-pressure cell that started Episode 104 began to spread rapidly from its source area at the southern tip of Lake Michigan after August 22. On that Friday in Chicago the level of sulfur dioxide pollution was triple that of the previous day. By Saturday a massive high-pressure area (anticyclone) extended from the Great Lakes to the Gulf Coast and eastward to the Atlantic Coast. In this vast region pollutants began to accumulate in the stable air from thousands of home chimneys, factories, and shops; thousands of kilometers of streets; countless sites of refuse burning; and everywhere, the automobile. All cities of the region experienced problems of air pollution. On Thursday, August 28, air pollutants reached their highest levels, ranging from 2 to 8 times greater than under normal conditions. Respiratory ailments increased. On August 29 the high-pressure cell began to move. The sky was clear by September 1, and the air pollutants had moved out over the Atlantic Ocean.

## PHOTOCHEMICAL AIR POLLUTION

Photochemical air pollution—commonly known as smog—has become important since the middle 1940s. This type of pollution is the result of a number of complex chemical reactions. It begins with nitrogen oxide, which is emitted whenever high-temperature combustion occurs. In the presence of sunlight, nitrogen oxide combines with organic compounds, such as hydrocarbons from unburned gasoline, to produce a whitish haze, sometimes tinged with a yellow-brown color. This noxious substance causes eye-smarting and tears in its early stages, and more serious respiratory problems as it accumulates in the atmosphere.

The typical area in the world for photochemical smog is the Los Angeles Basin. An important feature of the weather pattern of this area is a mass of stable high-pressure air that persists for a considerable time over

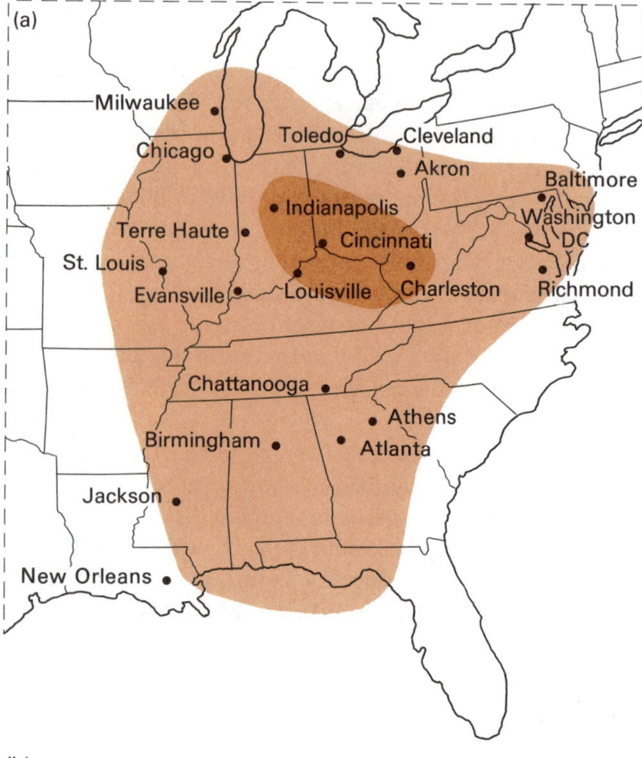


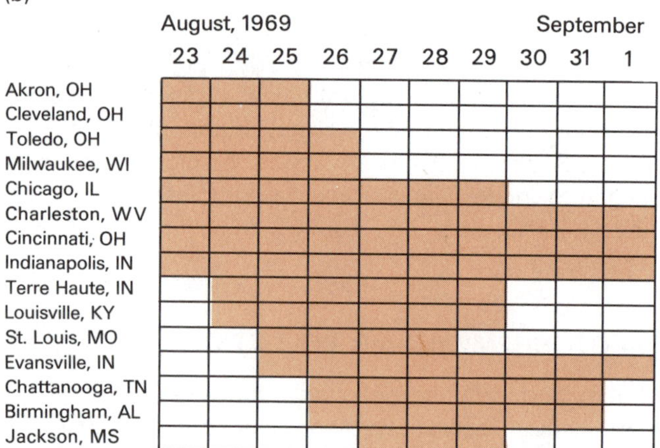


**FIGURE 3.4**
Episode 104. (*a*) Atmospheric pollution in Episode 104 covered most of the eastern United States, with the greatest concentration of pollutants extending from Indianapolis, Indiana, to Charleston, West Virginia. (*b*) Cities for which data were available during Episode 104, showing days each was under the Environmental Science Services Administration's High Air Pollution Potential (HAPP) advisory. In some of these cities, such as Milwaukee and Chicago, weather conditions unfavorable for the dispersion of air pollution began on Friday, August 22, 1969, before the first advisory was issued. (After Environmental Science Services Administration)

the region. The Basin is surrounded by mountains that further restrict air movement. Further, off the California coast is a relatively cold ocean current that is particularly well developed in spring and early summer. Warmer air from over the Pacific Ocean is cooled as it moves over this cold water on its way toward the Basin. The cooling of the air near the ground and the warming of the air aloft leads to the formation of strong and persistent temperature inversions over Los Angeles. Trapped surface air is prevented from rising over the mountain barriers. The smog that develops in the Los Angeles Basin reaches dangerous levels several times each year.

## CLEAN AIR LEGISLATION

The attempt to control air pollution is extremely old. The first abatement law was passed in England in 1273 in the reign of Edward I, in response to a belief that food cooked by burning coal was "prejudicial to health." In 1306 the smoke of London had become so dense that a royal proclamation prohibited the burning of coal. Nevertheless, the smoke problem has persisted through the centuries. In 1847 the London Town Improvement Clauses Act considered the problem of factory smoke, and in 1875 a Public Health Act was passed in the British Parliament relating to smoke abatement. In 1881 the Chicago City Council passed the first smoke ordinance in the United States. Today essentially every industrial nation has passed legislation to control atmospheric pollution.

Modern efforts to control air emissions have met many difficulties. In the 1950s Congress indicated that the control of air pollution should begin at the local and state levels. In keeping with this philosophy, the Federal Air Pollution Control Act of 1955 was limited to providing grants to states. The California state legislature in 1959 passed the first legislation to control emissions from automobiles and to establish some air-quality standards. In 1960 Congress ordered the surgeon general to study the effects of automobile-spawned pollutants on human health. Partly as a response to these studies, Congress in 1967 passed the Federal Air Quality Act. It provided for the development of air quality control regions, and for the establishment of federal auto emission standards effective for all states, except California, which had stricter standards.

Recognizing that more comprehensive emission controls were necessary, Congress enacted the Clean Air Act of 1970. Under this act, the Environmental Protection Agency set national ambient air quality standards for oxides of sulfur, oxides of nitrogen, carbon monoxide, photochemical oxidants, hydrocarbons, particulates, toxic metals, other hazardous substances, odors, and noise. One goal was to reduce auto emissions by 90 percent. Under this act citizens can file suits against polluters to secure enforcement of the act.

This struggle to control air pollution is still not won. Like many environmental issues, air pollution is foremost a political problem. The individuals who attempt to develop solutions are usually not scientists or engineers, but elected officials who lack technical expertise. The process has been slow, arduous, and fraught with uncertainty. Precise reports on the extent of the health problem caused by pollutants are difficult to secure. Adding to the confusion are conflicting reports on the effectiveness of various strategies that are used to combat air pollution. When all of the technical uncertainty is combined with the normal trudging pace of government deliberations, it is not surprising that legislation to control atmospheric emissions has been one of the nation's longest-running legislative endeavors.

### EFFECTS OF AIR POLLUTION

A number of studies that reveal the long-term effects of air pollution on health and the environment have been conducted. For example, epidemiological studies have shown that high air pollution levels have aggravated respiratory problems among persons with chronic pulmonary and cardiac diseases.

Of the gaseous pollutants, sulfur dioxide, nitrogen dioxide, and carbon monoxide are most dangerous to people. Sulfur dioxide interferes with the breathing mechanism and is therefore particularly dangerous. Nitrogen dioxide is a major factor in causing eye irritation, and in sufficient quantities it also stops the function of the lungs. When the concentration of carbon monoxide becomes too high it attacks the hemoglobin in the blood and prevents it from transporting oxygen from the lungs to the tissues of the body. Under normal conditions these air pollutants are so dilute that they do not cause serious health problems. However, in recent years their build-up in certain urban areas has reached a near-critical level.

The effects of air pollution on ecosystems have been studied, but the studies do not provide complete insights into the problems. Evidence does indicate that plant communities suffer serious effects. For example, in a mixed oak-pine forest, sulfur dioxide pollution first causes the elimination of the pine trees; with more severe pollution the oak will be replaced by shrubs; with continued severe pollution the shrubs will be replaced by sedge; and ultimately all vegetation will disappear. Thus the damage ranges from relatively minor to completely devastating. Sulfur dioxide is one of the most destructive gases on vegetation. In many areas where smelters are located sulfur dioxide fumes affect all vegetation. A 10-year study of the forest areas near smelters in Sudbury, Ontario, revealed severe tree damage in an area of 1,870 square kilometers (730 square miles).

Air pollution is a major cause of deterioration in a large variety of materials, including building stone, metals, fabrics, leather, paper, paint, and rubber. Many building stones, notably limestone, deteriorate rapidly when exposed to high concentrations of carbon dioxide. The carbon dioxide combines with water to form carbonic acid, which not only discolors the stone but erodes the surface. Sulfur dioxide combines with water molecules to form sulfuric acid. This acid can do extensive damage to metals such as steel and copper and to such substances as textiles, paper, and leather. A small amount of hydrogen sulfide gas can discolor any surface that has been coated with a lead-base paint. Annually these damages cost the American people over two billion dollars.

Atmospheric pollution is a major factor in determining environmental quality. When the air is clean and dry, visibility in an area can be greatly enhanced. When the air is polluted, fog, haze, and smog conditions are much more likely to develop. For example, fog will develop even when the relative humidity is well below 100 percent if sulfuric or nitric oxide particles are present. A concentration of many types of aerosols will be sufficient to create a haze. Particles in the air reduce visibility by reflecting and absorbing. Pollution thus can not only create hazardous conditions in an area, but it can also damage the natural beauty.

It must be remembered, however, that clean air is not free. In the United States many urban areas are having difficulty reconciling new economic growth with clean air regulations. Under the Clean Air Act, if an area has reached a specified limit of air pollution, no new economic activity that will add additional pollutants to the atmosphere can be established in that area. For example, in 1978 several Oklahoma oil companies agreed to reduce pollution from their oil refineries in order that a new industry could be established in the area. The oil companies had to reduce hydrocarbon emissions by 5,280 tons annually to "offset" the 3,000 tons of emissions expected to come from the new industry.

## POLLUTION OF THE STRATOSPHERE

Until relatively recently, concern about air pollution was focused exclusively on the troposphere. Pollution of the stratosphere is now also considered a potential problem. Nuclear explosions, supersonic transport planes, and aerosol sprays appear to be the principal catalytic agents that may pollute the upper atmosphere. These agents have the potential of decomposing the ozone ($O_3$) that shields the earth's living things from the harmful effects of ultraviolet radiation. The full extent of the environmental hazards associated with the partial destruction of the ozone is still uncertain. It is becoming evident, however, that a wide range of human activities can disrupt the delicate balance of the ozone in the stratosphere. Some scientists even predict that life itself will be endangered if the ozone layer is destroyed.

## OZONE IN THE STRATOSPHERE

Ozone exists in a dynamic equilibrium, the result of a complex array of competing chemical reactions in the stratosphere. Ozone is formed by the destruction of oxygen ($O_2$) by light at wavelengths shorter than 242 nanometers in the stratosphere. (A nanometer is a measure of length, one-billionth of a meter, that is used to measure the wavelength of electromagnetic radiation.) Ozone is a minor constituent in the atmosphere, representing less than 0.0001 percent of the total.

As ozone is being produced, it is also being destroyed through various processes. Naturally occurring nitric oxide destroys 50 to 70 percent of the ozone. Free oxygen also combines with ozone to form $O_2$ molecules, destroying about 18 percent of the total ozone produced. The interaction of ozone with minute particles of chlorine destroys an additional 11 percent, and unknown mechanisms destroy as much as 20 percent of the ozone.

*Nitric oxide* (NO), the major destroyer of ozone, is formed naturally in the stratosphere from nitrous oxide ($N_2O$). The nitrous oxide originates as a product of soil bacteria. Within the troposphere it is an inert gas, but in the stratosphere it is altered chemically to nitric oxide and thus becomes active in destroying the ozone. Nitric acid is also produced by the interaction of cosmic rays with the atmospheric gases.

Under natural conditions the formation and destruction of ozone are in equilibrium, so that over time the concentration of ozone remains constant. Only when these natural processes are interrupted by pollution of the stratosphere is the delicate ozone balance threatened.

## "THREATS" TO OZONE

The pollution of the stratosphere was possibly first recognized when nuclear bombs were tested above ground. Although the effects of nuclear explosions on the stratosphere are not fully understood, they may be catastrophic. Thermonuclear explosions heat the air to very high temperatures so that oxygen and nitrogen combine to produce nitric oxide. Depending upon the latitude and the season, clouds from nuclear explosions may deposit most of their nitric oxide in the lower and middle stratosphere, where the ozone concentration is the highest. Although precise evidence is lacking, there is an indication that this additional nitric oxide will destroy a substantial amount of ozone in the stratosphere. After the intensive nuclear testing in the atmosphere between 1952 and 1962, it was estimated that from 3 to 6 percent of the ozone in the stratosphere over the Northern Hemisphere was depleted. It was also estimated that the ozone regenerating mechanisms would require 2.5 years to restore half of the loss. Between 1963 and 1970, ozone levels in the stratosphere experienced an absolute increase of about 5 percent from the early 1960 levels, indicating that with the cessation of nuclear testing the ozone would regenerate itself.

In the early 1970s the influence of a supersonic air fleet on the ozone in the stratosphere became an issue. The supersonic transport (SST) planes, such as the British- and French-built Concordes, fly at heights greater than 15,000 meters (50,000 feet). During the debate as to whether the United States should build such a plane, one point under consideration was that nitric oxide would be released into the upper atmosphere by the jet engines. A three-dimensional model of the atmosphere constructed at the Massachusetts Institute of Technology revealed that nitric oxide released from a fleet of 500 SSTs flying in the Northern Hemisphere would cause not only a 16 percent reduction of ozone in the Northern Hemisphere but also an 8 percent reduction in the Southern Hemisphere. It was further calculated that the present levels of intensity of the ultraviolet rays reaching the ground would be moved about 15 degrees poleward. In other words, New York State would have the sunburn potential of the Caribbean. Besides the issue of the depletion of the ozone, noise levels and development costs were also considered in the United States. Ultimately the U.S. government withdrew financial support of the SST project, and this move appears to have been fortunate.

Possibly the greatest threat to the ozone is the use of fluorocarbon compounds in aerosol propellants. These compounds appear in a wide variety of such consumer goods as cosmetics, perfumes, deodorants, household products, insect sprays, and automotive sprays. Although their use is worldwide, the United States is the largest producer of aerosol propellants.

The chemical inertness of the fluorocarbons originally led most investigators of atmospheric pollutants to consider them of little interest. They are now receiving some attention because there is no known natural chemical or physical process by which these compounds are removed from the troposphere. Instead, they gradually move upwards into the stratosphere. There the fluorocarbons are altered under the intense ultraviolet radiation, producing free chlorine atoms. Laboratory models predict that the chlorine will react with ozone, causing a substantial net loss of ozone within a few decades. A Harvard University study concluded that if the use of fluorocarbon aerosol propellants continued at the 1975 rate of production, the decrease in stratospheric ozone could be 10 percent by 1994 and as much as 16 percent by the year 2000.

### ULTRAVIOLET RADIATION AND CANCER

Although solar energy is essential to life on earth, excessive ultraviolet radiation would greatly alter or possibly destroy life. Ultraviolet radiation in wavelengths from 280 to 320 nanometers is the range most dangerous to life. The screening of this damaging radiation is done primarily by ozone in the stratosphere.

There is evidence that reducing the ozone concentration will not only increase the intensity of the ultraviolet radiation transmitted to the earth, but may also cause a shift to the shorter and more biologically hazardous wavelengths. Based on laboratory experiments, it has been estimated that a 50 percent reduction of ozone content at 40 degrees latitude would cause a ten-fold increase in the intensity of ultraviolet radiation at the 297-nanometer wavelength.

An increase in ultraviolet radiation reaching the earth is likely to increase the incidence of skin cancer. It is well documented that excessive exposure to sunlight can cause cancer in humans. Wavelengths of radiation between 230 and 320 nanometers induce the growth of skin tumors. Through laboratory models it is predicted that if ozone is reduced by 16 percent by 1990 there will be 100,000 to 300,000 additional skin cancer cases annually in the United States, 500,000 to 1,500,000 more cases in the world, and 20,000 to 60,000 additional deaths each year on a worldwide basis.

Intense ultraviolet rays have a potentially harmful effect on other living organisms as well. Many free-floating microscopic plants, such as algae, and microscopic animal species, such as zooplankton, are susceptible to low wavelength ultraviolet radiation. Several insects, including honeybees and butterflies, are also sensitive to ultraviolet wavelengths. The effects of increased radiation on these organisms are not yet known. One possibility is a higher mutation rate among many species.

The effects of the depletion of ozone in the stratosphere raises many serious questions. Because the answers to many of them are still speculative, or even unknown, the highest priority should be given to continued investigation of these critical issues.

## CONCLUSION

The atmosphere is a system of gases that has evolved over geologic time until today nitrogen and oxygen are its major components. Although the other gases, such as carbon dioxide and water vapor, are a tiny portion of the atmosphere, they are of critical importance to life on earth. As the upper atmosphere has been probed by balloons, airplanes, and in modern time by satellites, it has been revealed that the atmosphere consists of a number of layers, each of which has definite characteristics that affect life on the earth's surface.

Until recently the atmospheric system was considered so vast that it could not be affected by human activities. The pollution of the atmosphere by noxious emissions is now, however, a worldwide phenomenon. Pollution is not limited to the troposphere but has extended into the stratosphere. The effects of pollution are felt in a number of ways. The emissions from factories and motor vehicles provide the basis for the formation of sulphuric and nitric acids in the atmosphere, which in turn fall to the earth as acid rain. When nitric oxide and fluorocarbons move upward into the stratosphere, the destruction of the ozone may occur. Air pollution is recognized as a hazard to life on earth. Scientific studies have begun to document these dangers, and efforts to clean the atmosphere are receiving serious attention.

## STUDY QUESTIONS

1. What is the composition of the atmosphere? What is the importance of nitrogen? Of carbon dioxide?
2. What is sublimation?
3. What is the importance of water vapor in the atmosphere?
4. What are the layers of the atmosphere?
5. Give differences between the troposphere and the stratosphere.
6. Describe the differences in temperature in the layers of the atmosphere.
7. What are the major sources of air pollution in the troposphere?
8. Describe the geographic sources of air pollution.
9. Describe a local air pollution incident. A regional incident.
10. What is photochemical air pollution?
11. Give examples of how air pollution affects health. How does it affect the environment?
12. What is the importance of ozone in the stratosphere? How can ozone be destroyed?

# 4 SOLAR ENERGY AND THE ATMOSPHERE

## KEY WORDS

adiabatic cooling
advection
air drainage
conduction
evapotranspiration
geometric radiation law
heat balance
isotherm
langley
lapse rate
planetary albedo
sensible heat
temperature inversion
transpiration

The sun is the source of energy that shapes the processes of the atmosphere. This energy evaporates the water from the oceans and the earth's surface; it creates the forces that move the winds; it heats the atmosphere; it supplies the fuel for all living creatures. Control of temperature is critical to life. If part of the incoming solar energy were not immediately reflected back into space, the earth's atmosphere would soon become intolerably hot. The balance of heat received and lost maintains a constant temperature and makes the world a livable place. Not all places receive the same amount of energy, however. Average temperatures vary from region to region, contributing to the relative abundance or scarcity of life in particular places. This variation greatly influences human activities.

## SOLAR ENERGY INPUT TO THE EARTH

The sun is virtually the only source of energy to the earth, providing about 99.97 percent of the total. Being a large spherical body, the sun emits radiation in every direction. As the distance from the sun increases, the energy is distributed over a larger and larger area. It has been determined that the energy received per unit area and per unit of time decreases as the square of the radius from the sun. This is known as the *geometric radiation law.*

Although the earth lies about 150,000,000 kilometers (93,000,000 miles) from the sun, it receives a large amount of energy. Each square centimeter at the top of the atmosphere receives 1.94 calories of heat every minute, enough to raise the temperature of water 1 centimeter deep over this square centimeter 2°C every minute. This amount of heat is known as the *solar constant.* The amount of energy received at the top of the atmosphere in one minute is about equivalent to the total world's generation of energy in one year. And yet, it must be remembered that the earth receives only about one two-billionth of the energy released by the sun.

## EFFECTS OF THE ATMOSPHERE UPON THE SOLAR BEAM

When the short-wave solar beam reaches the atmosphere, part of it is reflected back to space, part is scattered or absorbed by the atmosphere, and part reaches the ground (Figure 4.1).

Of every 100 units of solar radiation reaching the atmosphere, about 36 units are returned to space immediately without heating the atmosphere. This short-wave radiation that is reflected back into space is called the *planetary albedo.* Of the planetary albedo about 24 units are reflected back into space from clouds and other particles in the atmosphere. Another 6 units are reflected from the surface of the earth. There is also a scattering of the solar beam in the atmosphere during which 6 units of short-wave energy are lost to space. It is important to remember in studying the heat balance of the earth that no radiation is absorbed from the 36 units lost in the planetary albedo.

The remaining 64 units of short-wave solar energy are converted to long-wave energy to heat the atmosphere and the earth's surface. About 47 of these units reach the earth directly. Of this amount about 30 units are direct radiation and about 17 units are scattered. This proportion will vary somewhat depending primarily on differences in the cloud covering from place to place. For example, the deserts of the southwestern United States receive more than one and one-half times as much direct solar energy than the humid southeastern United States. These two areas lie on the same latitude but differ in the amount of cloud covering. Of the 17 units of energy that are scattered, about 15 units are absorbed by clouds, dust, and gases to heat the troposphere, and 2 units are absorbed by the ozone in the stratosphere.

Because the direct short-wave radiation from the sun is at wavelengths of less than 4 microns, the molecules in the atmosphere do not readily absorb it. Thus most of the energy absorbed by the atmosphere comes from the earth's surface after the short-wave radiation has been changed from short to long waves.

## WORLD ENERGY BALANCE IN THE EARTH'S ATMOSPHERE

If the temperatures at different places on the earth are observed, it appears that they are changing. Certainly there are daily rhythms as well as seasonal rhythms of temperature changes and there are changes in the quantity of heat received as one proceeds from low latitudes to high latitudes. In spite of these thermal cycles and latitudinal contrasts, evidence shows that the earth maintains a uniform thermal environment through time. The earth is neither heating up nor cooling off, but is balancing the energy it receives from the sun and the energy it radiates back into space. The earth thus maintains a *heat balance.* If it did not, it would become too hot or too cold to maintain life.

In the process of losing long-wave heat, 98 units are emitted from the earth's surface into the atmosphere. Of these 98 units, 7 units escape into space immedi-

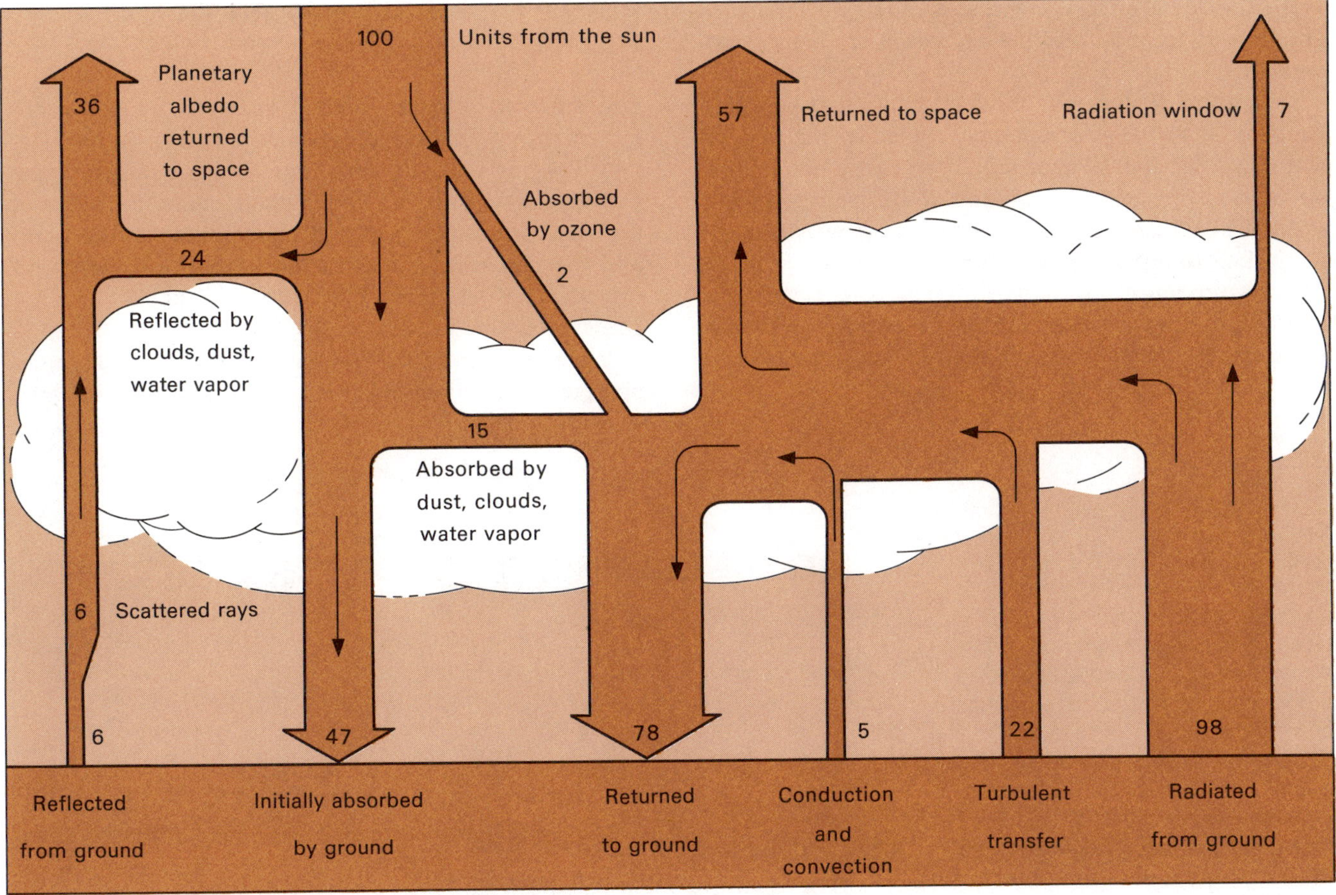


**FIGURE 4.1**
Energy balance of the atmosphere. This diagram traces 100 units of shortwave energy from the time it enters the atmosphere until it is returned to space. The left side of the diagram traces the incoming shortwave energy, while the right side portrays outgoing longwave energy. For each 100 units of solar radiation received 100 units must be returned to space.

ately through what is called the *atmospheric* or *radiation window*. This long-wave radiation escapes because the wavelengths range from 8.5 to 11 microns and the gas molecules in the atmosphere are not efficient absorbers of wavelengths in this range. The remaining 91 units are absorbed by clouds and particles in the atmosphere. The heat transfer mechanisms on the earth also radiate about 22 units by turbulent transfer or evapotranspiration and 5 units by conduction and convection, processes that will be discussed later in this chapter. The atmosphere also contains 15 units that were absorbed as the original short waves passed through it, as well as 2 units of energy from the ozone layer. This makes a total of 135 units of energy in the atmosphere. Of this amount 57 units are radiated into space and 78 units are radiated back to the earth's surface for recycling. This trapping and recycling of terrestrial radiation, which makes the earth warmer than it would otherwise be, is called the *greenhouse effect.*

The way in which incoming solar energy is used is thus determined by the scattering, reflection, and absorption in the atmosphere and on the surface of the earth. These processes together create a complex equilibrium, or energy budget, that determines the mean temperature of the world.

## LOCAL ENERGY BALANCE

On an annual basis the amount of energy received on the earth is precisely matched by the amount of energy lost. On a shorter time basis, however, the amount of energy received and lost at a particular place varies considerably from that received and lost at another place. The local energy balance at any one time depends on its location and the prevailing environmental conditions.

In a period of 24 hours the heat balance at a particular place may vary considerably. At dawn the rate of incoming solar energy rises rapidly so that a net energy gain normally begins. The amount of the incoming solar radiation peaks near the solar noon and returns to zero shortly before sunset. Thus during the day the energy budget is positive.

During the night the long-wave radiation is gradually lost, creating a negative heat balance. The greatest negative balance occurs just before sunrise.

## RECEIPT OF SOLAR RADIATION ON EARTH

The amount of radiant energy received by the atmosphere at any one place depends primarily on two factors: the angle of the sun's rays, and the length of the period of daylight. To a very limited extent, the value of the solar constant and the distance between the earth and the sun can also affect the amount of energy received. These factors differ with the latitude and the season (Figures 4.2 and 4.3).

When the sun's rays are directly overhead at a particular place, and therefore vertical to the surface, that area

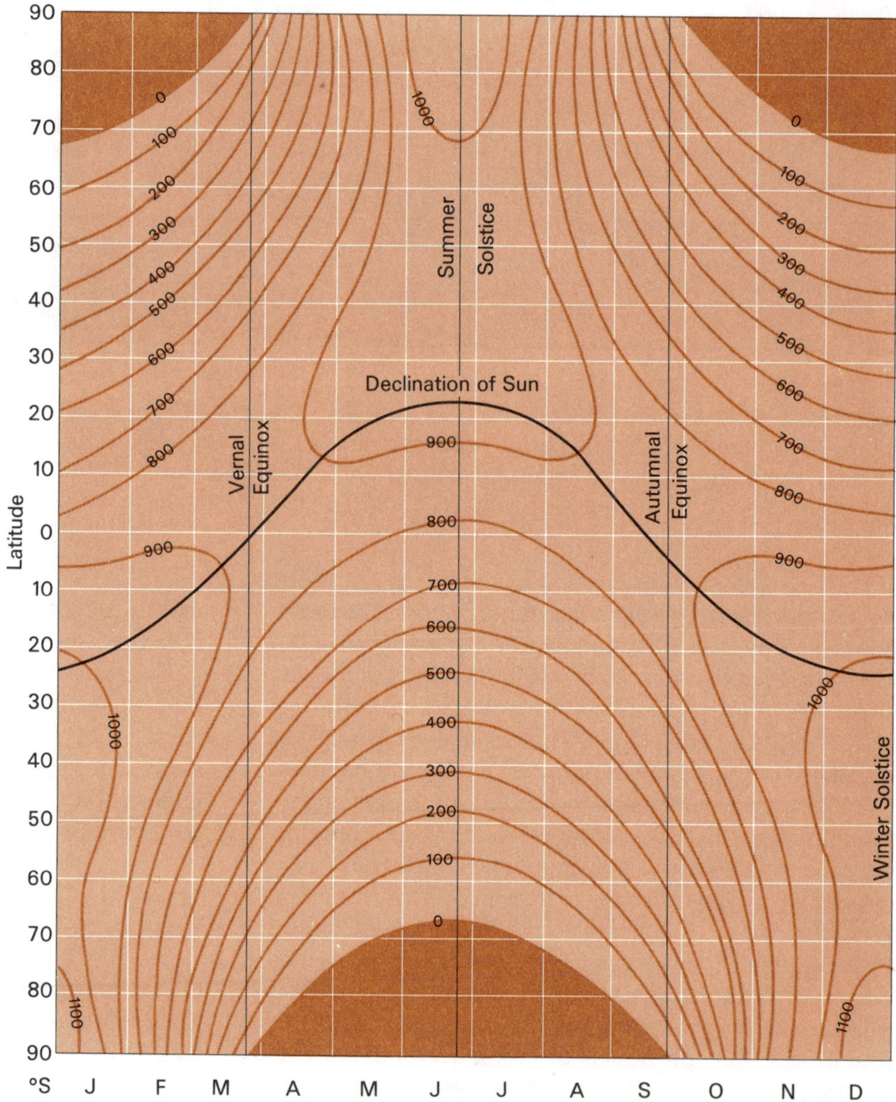


**FIGURE 4.2**
Solar radiation at different latitudes throughout the year. This graph shows the solar radiant energy received (in langleys) at the top of the atmosphere in a 24-hour period. The vertical scale shows latitude north and south of the equator. For example, at the summer solstice on June 21 the equator receives about 800 langleys a day, but areas at about 65 degrees north receive about 1,000 langleys a day. The shaded areas represent periods when there is no solar radiation. The Northern and Southern hemispheres are not symmetrical in their energy receipts because the earth is nearer the sun in January than in July. The energy input to the earth is about 7 percent greater in January than in July. (After Muller and Oberlander, 1978)

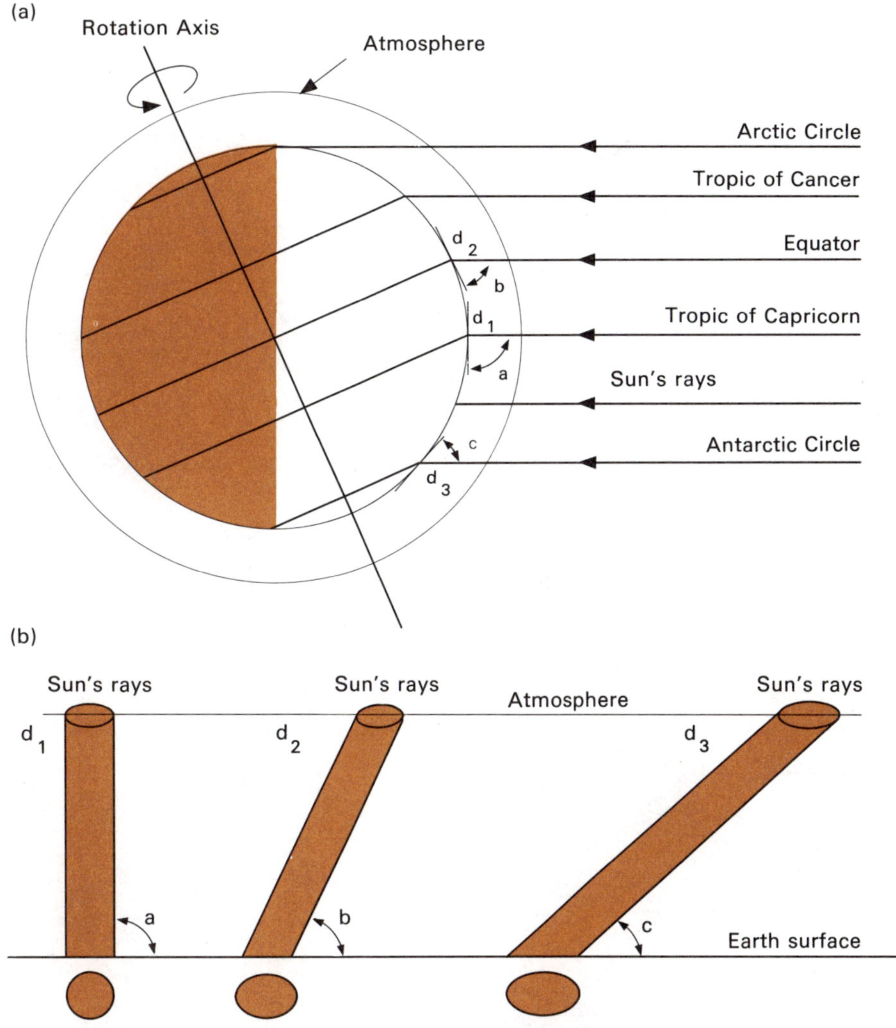


**FIGURE 4.3**
The angle of the sun's rays. The intensity of solar radiation depends upon the angle at which the sun's rays strike the earth's surface. (*a*) Variations in the angle of incidence—*a, b,* and *c*—are shown from the equator to the Antarctic Circle. Variations are shown as $d_1$, $d_2$, and $d_3$. (*b*) Cross sections reveal the variations in areas of the earth's surface struck by the sun's rays. (After Miller, Thompson, Peterson, and Haragan, 1983)

is receiving a maximum intensity of solar radiation. When the sun's rays are farther away from the zenith, the intensity of the solar radiation decreases. At 40 degrees north latitude, for example, the angle of the sun on December 21 or 22 is nearly 64 degrees away from the vertical. As a result a unit surface receives only about 44 percent of the solar energy that would be received if the sun's rays were perpendicular to the earth's surface. In contrast, on June 21 or 22 the noon sun is only about 17 degrees away from the zenith and the comparable figure is 95 percent. This difference occurs largely because the slanted rays are spread over an area twice as large when the sun is 60 degrees from the vertical as when the sun is directly overhead.

The duration of daylight is also a major factor in the insolation received by the atmosphere. Because the sun's rays do not fall perpendicular at the equator at all times of the year, the length of the daylight varies according to latitude. It is significant that during the high-sun season, in either hemisphere, the vertical or nearly vertical rays of the sun are experienced in combination with the longest daylight periods. Figure 4.4 shows the daily input of solar radiation on a horizontal square centimeter at the top of the atmosphere for all latitudes in December and in June. As we have seen, the accepted value of the solar constant is 1.94 calories per square centimeter per minute. A measurement known as the *langley* has been devised to express the solar constant. One langley equals 1 calorie of energy per square centimeter. Thus the solar constant can be expressed as 1.94 langleys per minute.

As Figure 4.4 indicates, the langley units within a 24-hour period at the equator vary only slightly in the course of a year. At the poles, however, the langley

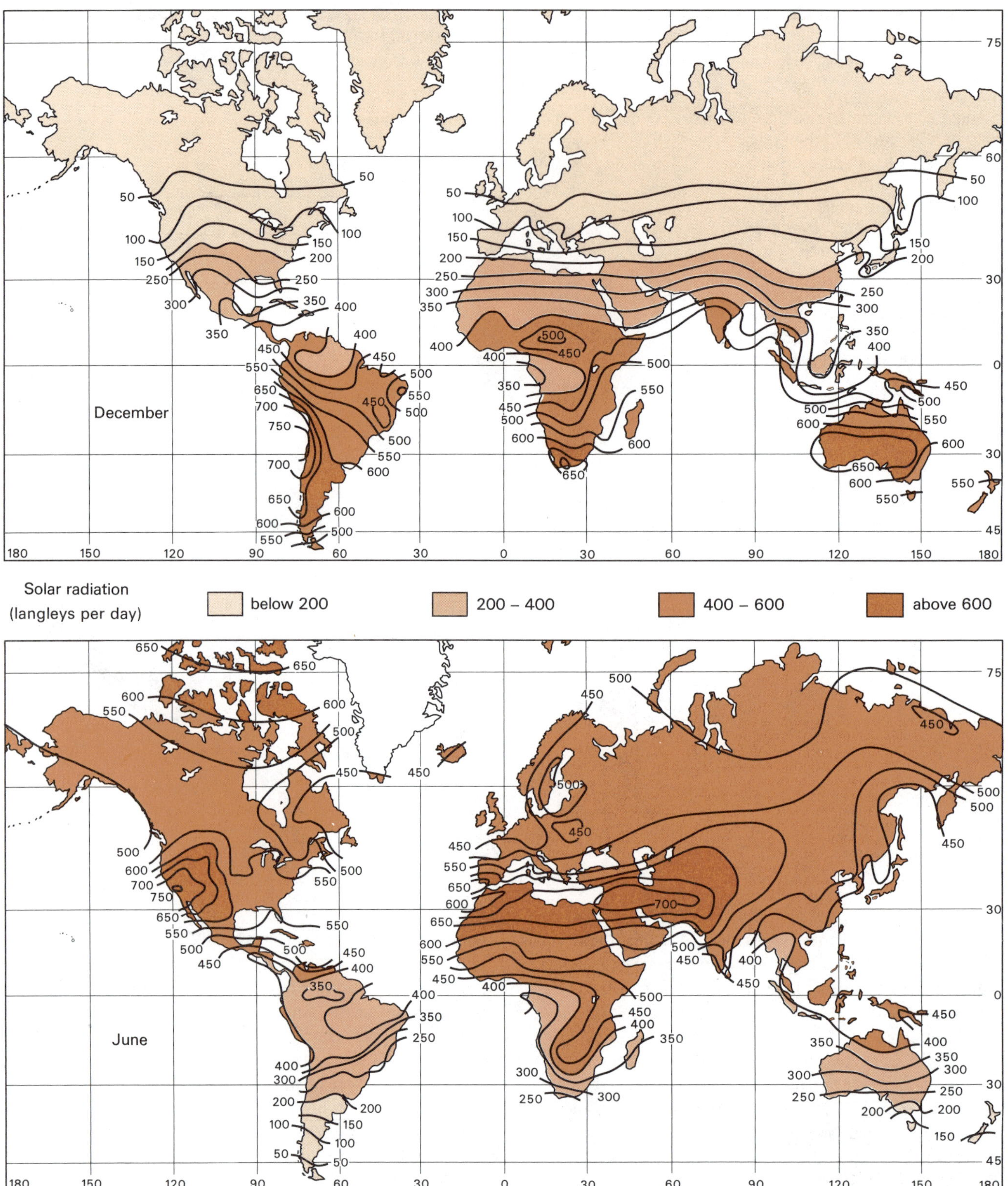


**FIGURE 4.4**
Global solar radiation. The average solar radiation is shown in units of langleys per day received at sea level during December and June. Note that, in June, southern Florida and northern Canada each receive about 550 langleys per day of solar radiation. During the winter, however, latitudinal variations are very great. It is also important to recognize that in both June and December the desert areas of the world receive the most solar radiation. (After Löf, Duffie, and Smith, 1966)

units vary from zero per day in winter to a value or magnitude in summer that is greater than at the equator. The large number of langley units in the polar regions in summer reflects the long duration of the sunlight period. Averaged over the year, however, the areas near the equator receive about two and a half times the amount of energy received by areas near the poles.

The amount of radiation received at the top of the atmosphere depends in a minor way upon some other factors. The energy received from the sun fluctuates up to 3 percent between extremes of 1.88 to 2.01 calories per square centimeter per minute. These variations occur over a period of several years and are thought to be associated with sunspot activity. What effect these variations have on surface earth temperatures is not yet understood.

As we have seen, the earth does not remain the same distance from the sun throughout the year because of its elliptical orbit around the sun. About January 3 the earth is approximately 4.8 million kilometers (3 million miles) closer to the sun than on July 4. However, a difference of 4.8 million kilometers in the earth's distance from the sun is not significant in the amount of solar energy received by the earth. It certainly does not cause the seasons; in fact, the coldest period in the Northern Hemisphere occurs when the earth is nearest to the sun. The difference in the amount of solar energy received at the perihelion and at the aphelion positions of the earth may make the Northern Hemisphere winters slightly warmer and the Southern Hemisphere winters slightly colder.

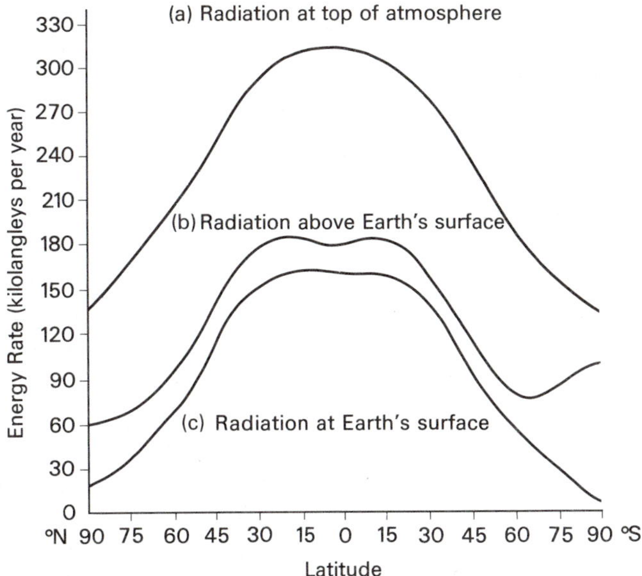


**FIGURE 4.5**
Average annual distribution of solar radiation in the earth's atmosphere. The solar radiation in the earth's atmosphere varies with height at different latitudinal positions. The *a* curve represents incoming solar radiation at the top of the atmosphere; the *b* curve represents the solar radiation just above the earth's surface; and the *c* curve shows the net solar radiation gain at the surface. (After Sellers, 1965. Copyright © 1965 University of Chicago Press.)

## ATMOSPHERIC HEATING PROCESSES

A number of processes influence the heating and cooling of the atmosphere. These processes usually work in some combination.

### RADIATION

When the short-wave solar energy strikes the earth's surface and is converted into longer wavelengths, the heated earth becomes a radiating body. Although the atmosphere is relatively transparent to short waves, it is able to absorb as much as 80 to 90 percent of the outgoing long-wave earth radiation. Of the atmospheric gases, water vapor, and to a lesser extent carbon dioxide, are the major absorbers and emitters of earth radiation. Thus radiation from the earth is much more effective in heating the atmosphere than direct insolation absorbed in the atmosphere (Figure 4.5).

Although terrestrial radiation occurs continuously, it does vary considerably during a 24-hour period. From sunup until about midafternoon more energy is received from the sun than is radiated from the earth. The temperature thus rises until about 4 o'clock in the afternoon. At night, when no energy is received from the sun, radiation of energy results in a cooling of the earth and the atmosphere. Because the earth is a better radiator than the atmosphere, it is usually cooler than the overlying air (Figure 4.6).

The effectiveness of radiation in the heating process depends to a considerable degree on atmospheric conditions. The maximum radiational loss occurs under cloudless skies. Even here, however, the loss varies depending upon the amount of water vapor in the atmosphere. Heat loss is least when the water vapor content is high and concentrated near the surface of the earth. The water vapor not only absorbs the radiation but in turn reradiates it to the atmosphere and to the ground. This recycling process retards the loss of heat to space.

When a cloud covering exists, radiation conditions are quite different than when skies are clear. A cloud covering absorbs and reradiates the long waves in all

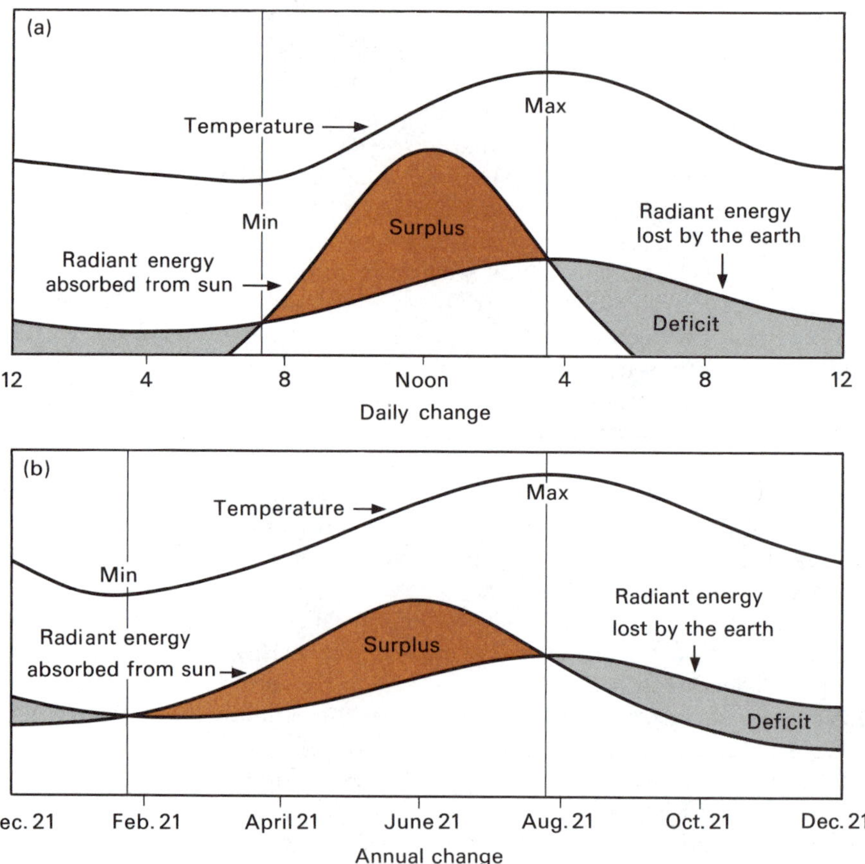


**FIGURE 4.6**
Relationship between energy input and temperature. In both the daily (*a*) and the annual (*b*) cycles, the highest and lowest temperatures occur later than the highest and lowest levels of solar radiation. (After Miller, Thompson, Peterson and Haragan, 1983)

directions. The returning stream of radiation from cloud to earth includes all the wavelengths the cloud received. A cloud covering essentially prevents the escape of energy into space, retarding night cooling not only of the atmosphere but also of the earth's surface.

## CONDUCTION

When two masses of unequal temperature come in contact, such as the atmosphere and the earth's surface, heat flows from the warmer to the colder mass until they both attain the same temperature. The transfer of heat in this manner is called *conduction.* The earth's surface absorbs solar radiation and as a result becomes warmer than the surrounding atmosphere. Since air is a relatively poor conductor of heat, only the lower portion of the atmosphere is warmed by conduction. Commonly, when the land surface is heated rapidly in the daytime during the summer, the layers of air near the earth's surface become warmer than air higher in the atmosphere. This process may trigger the development of convectional heat transfer in the atmosphere. The effect of conduction on a cold winter night is the opposite. The earth's surface is then colder than the overlying atmosphere, so conduction causes the temperature of the atmosphere near the earth to decrease.

## EVAPOTRANSPIRATION

An exchange of energy from the earth's surface to the atmosphere occurs when water or ice becomes water vapor. About 590 calories are required to vaporize one gram of water from the earth's surface. Vaporization occurs in a number of ways. Plants absorb water from the soil through their roots and pass water out through openings in their leaves. This process is called *transpiration.* Water is also evaporated directly from the earth, providing water vapor to the atmosphere. The combined processes of transpiration and evaporation are known as *evapotranspiration.* The energy in the water vapor is stored in the atmosphere in the form of latent heat. This latent heat is changed to *sensible heat,* or heat that can be sensed by our bodies, when the water vapor condenses into water droplets. At this point the energy involved in evapotranspiration becomes effective in heating the atmosphere.

### ADVECTION

One of the most important methods of heat transfer, advection involves horizontal movements of air from one area to another. This movement can be local or it can extend over thousands of miles. For example, if a mass of air originating in the Caribbean Sea in January is transported northward into the eastern United States, a mild period—a January thaw—will occur. In contrast, a polar, continental mass of air from central Canada can create a cold spell in the eastern United States in January. The origin of air masses greatly influences the type of weather experienced in the middle latitudes.

### ADIABATIC COOLING

The convectional process called adiabatic cooling transfers heat through the atmosphere by the upward movement of air itself. As soon as the surface layer of air becomes heated through radiation and conduction from the ground, as well as by absorption of direct and reflected solar radiation, it expands, becoming lighter in weight. This warmer, lighter air rises as cooler and denser air settles from above. The warmer air mass will continue to rise until it reaches an atmospheric environment of its own temperature and density. As it rises its temperature decreases at the rate of about 2.6°C (5.5°F) per 300 meters (1,000 feet), termed the dry adiabatic rate. This process is most effective in the tropics or on hot, sunny summer days in the middle latitudes.

Adiabatic cooling is the only process capable of reducing the temperature of a large mass of air below the dew point. It is the only cooling process capable of producing condensation on such a large scale that abundant precipitation occurs. The frequency of thunderstorms depends largely on the development of such convectional systems of air currents.

### COMPRESSION

When a mass of air settles into the lower atmosphere where air weight is greater, it is compressed into a smaller area. As a result the air molecules are agitated and pushed together so that their points of contact with one another are multiplied. Consequently, temperature rises.

## VERTICAL DISTRIBUTION OF TEMPERATURE

Even in tropical areas, numerous mountain peaks are snow-capped, indicating that temperatures decrease in a stable air mass with increasing elevation. It cannot be assumed that this common phenomenon is due to the cooling of rising air currents. Observations throughout the world have shown that there is a fairly uniform decrease in temperature with increase in altitude. It has been found that the average rate of temperature decrease up to a certain limit is from 1.5° to 1.6°C (3.3° to 3.5°F) for each 300 meters (1,000 feet) of increase in elevation. This is known as the *normal lapse rate* or *vertical temperature gradient* (Figure 4.7).

Under particular atmospheric conditions, temperature may increase with increasing elevations. This situation is known as a *temperature inversion* (Figure 4.8). These are usually local in character. They are most likely to occur on long, clear, calm nights when radiational cooling is most effective. When a temperature inversion occurs, the lowest part of the atmosphere tends to be stable. The coldest, heaviest air is closest to the earth, and the atmosphere tends not to overturn.

If this phenomenon occurs in a hilly or mountainous region, the air lying on the valley walls cools rapidly by both conduction and radiation so that the slopes have a temperature lower than does the valley floor. Because cool air is denser than warm air, the cool air gradually flows down the slopes onto the valley floor. This movement is known as *air drainage.* By early morning the

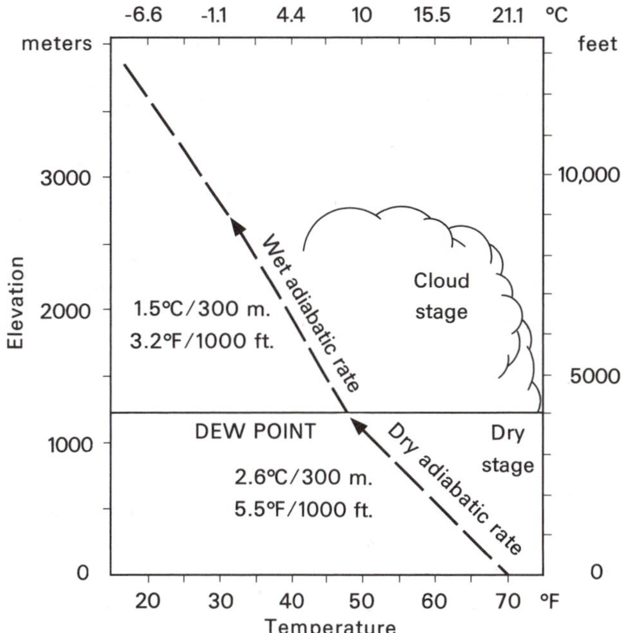


**FIGURE 4.7**
Adiabatic lapse rates. In a rising air current, dry air cools at 2.6°C per 300 meters, while moist air cools at the rate of 1.5°C per 300 meters.

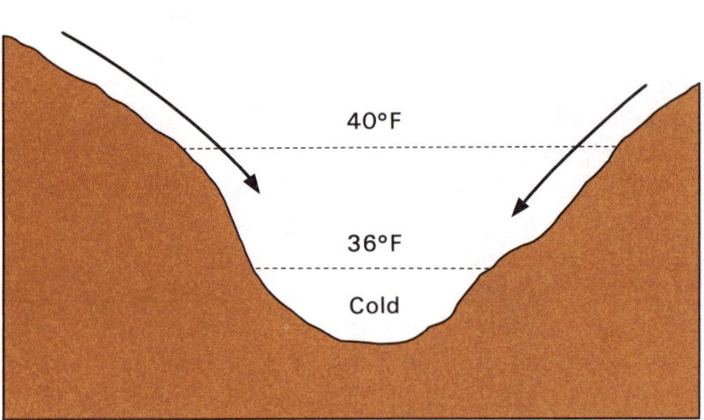


**FIGURE 4.8**
Air drainage. Because colder air is heavier, it slips down slopes and settles in depressions. This process forces warm air upward, producing a temperature inversion.

temperature in the valley bottom will be much cooler than on the upper slopes. The valley bottoms thus may be subject to frost while the higher slopes have temperatures above the freezing point.

Agricultural patterns in regions subject to air drainage reflect these atmospheric conditions. For example, the apple orchards in the Shenandoah Valley of Virginia are situated on the middle to upper slopes, avoiding the lowlands where frost damage is more likely. The coffee plantations of Brazil are located on slopes to take advantage of air drainage conditions. In Florida, smudge pots and oil burners are used in orchards, not so much to heat the air as to create a cloudy smog over the area, thus retarding the loss of heat and preventing the cooler air from draining into the lower areas. Sometimes huge fans are used to alleviate the tendency toward inversion by mixing warmer air from the higher slopes with the colder air below.

## HEATING AND COOLING OF LAND AND WATER

The land and water surfaces of the earth differ greatly in their ability to receive and retain insolation. The nature of the land surface itself affects the amount of insolation retained. Dark-colored soils absorb well while the lighter-colored soils reflect heat and thus retain a smaller amount. A snow-covered area will retain much less heat than will bare ground in the same latitude. Snow not only reflects insolation but acts as a blanket, preventing further accumulation of heat in the ground. On the other hand, a snow that covers the ground before the soil is frozen will frequently prevent the ground from freezing by acting as a blanket, preventing the escape of heat from the covered ground.

Land surfaces heat and cool faster than water surfaces for a number of reasons: (*a*) More heat is required to raise the temperature of water by a given number of degrees than to raise the temperature of dry land. The *specific heat* of a substance is the ratio of heat absorbed by the substance to the increase in its temperature. The specific heat of water is 2 to 5 times that of land, so water surfaces do not warm as quickly as land surfaces. (*b*) Of the insolation that strikes a water body, about one-half is used in evaporating the surface water. This energy is largely lost for heating the water body. (*c*) Water is relatively transparent, so the sun's rays can penetrate under the surface, distributing the solar energy over a larger area than on a land surface. About one-half of the sun's energy penetrates to a modest depth. In contrast, land surfaces are opaque and the insolation is concentrated on the surface. (*d*) Since water is fluid, currents distribute the energy throughout the mass of water, slowing the heating of the surface. Such currents are not present in solid land. The same process slows the cooling of a water body. When a water surface is cooling, the layers of water on top become heavier and denser than those below. The heavy, cool water sinks and is replaced by warm water from below, which in turn is cooled and sinks. Because of these convectional currents, a water body cannot freeze until the entire mass of water is cooled. Deep water freezes only after prolonged cooling. Once frozen, however, it reacts as a land surface.

## WORLD TEMPERATURE REGIMES

The world distribution of temperature is represented on a map by means of *isotherms,* lines that connect points of equal temperature. Variations of temperature on the earth are determined primarily by latitude. Because all places on the same parallel have the same angle of the noonday sun and the same comparative length of daylight, isotherms tend to follow the same east-west trend as the parallels of latitude. This characteristic is apparent in Figures 4.9 and 4.10. The east-west trend is best developed in the Southern Hemisphere where most of the surface is water south of the 25th parallel. In certain areas the general east-west trend of the isotherms is altered. These differences in temperatures are caused by landmasses and water bodies, altitude, and mountain barriers.

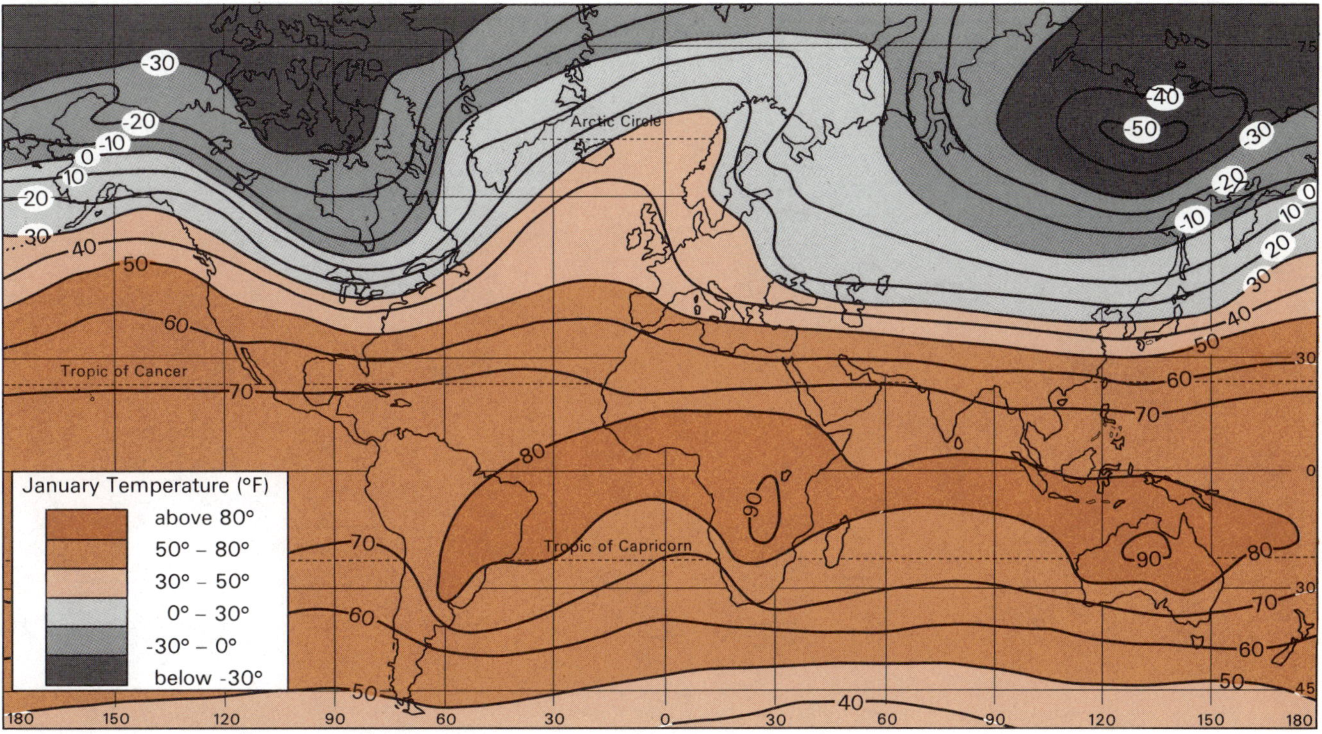


**FIGURE 4.9**
Average temperatures of the world in January (°F), reduced to sea level. The continental areas of the Northern Hemisphere are much colder than oceanic areas in corresponding latitudes. Notice how closely the temperature in the oceanic Southern Hemisphere corresponds to latitude. (After Miller and Langdon, 1964. Copyright © 1964 by Harper & Row, Publishers, Inc. Reprinted by permission of the publisher.)

Three general temperature regions on the earth can be identified: (*a*) continuously warm; (*b*) warm and cold; and (*c*) continuously cold.

## CONTINUOUSLY WARM REGIONS

The continuously warm regions lie on either side of the equator to about 30 degrees north and south latitude (Figure 4.11). Singapore illustrates an equatorial position with an average annual temperature of 26.1°C (79°F) and a range between the warmest and coldest month of only 1.2°C (2.7°F). New Orleans at approximately 30° north latitude is an example of a continuously warm area lying nearest the poles. The average annual temperature of New Orleans is 20.5°C (69°F). July is the warmest month with an average temperature of 27.7°C (82°F) while January is the coldest month, with an average temperature of 12.2°C (54°F). Near the equator the average annual temperature range rarely exceeds 3.2°C (7°F), and at the poleward extremities of the continuously warm regions, the range is usually under 12°C (25°F).

Within the continuously warm regions, altitude and mountain barriers are of major importance in lowering temperatures. In Ecuador, for example, the city of Guayaquil lies at 3° south latitude at an elevation of about 15 meters (50 feet). It has an average annual temperature of 25.5°C (78°F) and an annual range of temperature of 2.3°C (5°F). In contrast, the meteorological station of Quito lies nearly on the equator, but at an altitude of over 1,525 meters (5,000 feet). This station records an average annual temperature of 13.3°C (56°F). The range in temperature is 0.5°C (1°F) from the warmest to the coldest month.

## WARM AND COLD REGIONS

In the middle latitudes, between approximately 30° and 70°, both warm and cold seasons occur. The trend of the isotherms and the ranges of temperature for differ-

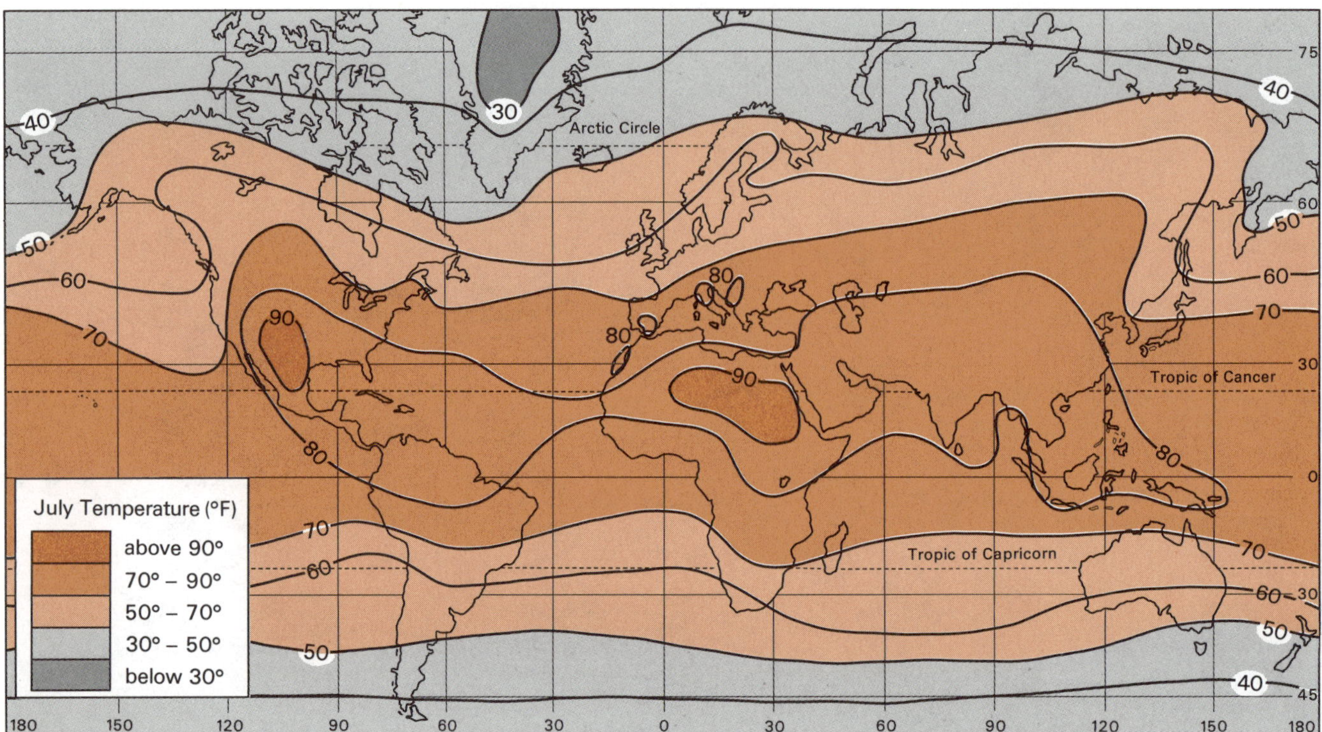


**FIGURE 4.10**
Average temperatures of the world in July (°F), reduced to sea level. The warmest areas of the world are the desert areas of the major landmasses of the Northern Hemisphere. Again, note the gradual decrease in temperature over the oceans in the Southern Hemisphere. (After Miller and Langdon, 1964. Copyright © 1964 by Harper & Row, Publishers, Inc. Reprinted by permission of the publisher.)

ent latitudes are largely dependent upon the distribution of land and water. In the Southern Hemisphere, where oceanic conditions dominate, the isotherms in general follow the east-west trend of the parallels. The 5°C (41°F) isotherm for July, for example, coincides closely with the 50th parallel. The seasonal ranges of temperatures in the Southern Hemisphere are relatively small. Cape Town, a typical oceanic station in South Africa, has an average annual temperature of 16.6°C (62°F). February is the warmest month, with an average temperature of 21.2°C (70°F) and July the coldest month with average temperatures of 12.7°C (55°F).

In contrast, the Northern Hemisphere exhibits wide variations in seasonal temperature because of its large proportion of land. These variations are particularly pronounced over the Asiatic and North American continents (Figure 4.12). Because the continental landmasses heat and cool more rapidly than the surrounding oceans, isotherms, when passing from land to water, bend equatorward in winter and poleward in summer. In addition, ocean currents cause the isotherms to trend away from east-west directions even more. Cold ocean currents flowing toward the equator carry lower temperatures with them, causing an equatorward bending of the isotherms. Warm ocean currents carry warmer temperatures toward the poles, resulting in a poleward bending of the isotherms.

These conditions are illustrated by the 0°C (32°F) isotherm for January and the 15°C (59°F) isotherm for July. As seen in Figure 4.9, the 0°C (32°F) isotherm follows the Aleutian Islands and the panhandle of Alaska, passes southward to Vancouver, Canada, where it enters the continent and continues its southward path. In the interior of North America its most equatorward point lies in the vicinity of St. Louis, Missouri. Thus in January, Juneau, Alaska, and St. Louis have the same average temperatures. The 0°C isotherm leaves the United States at the coastline of southern New Jersey.

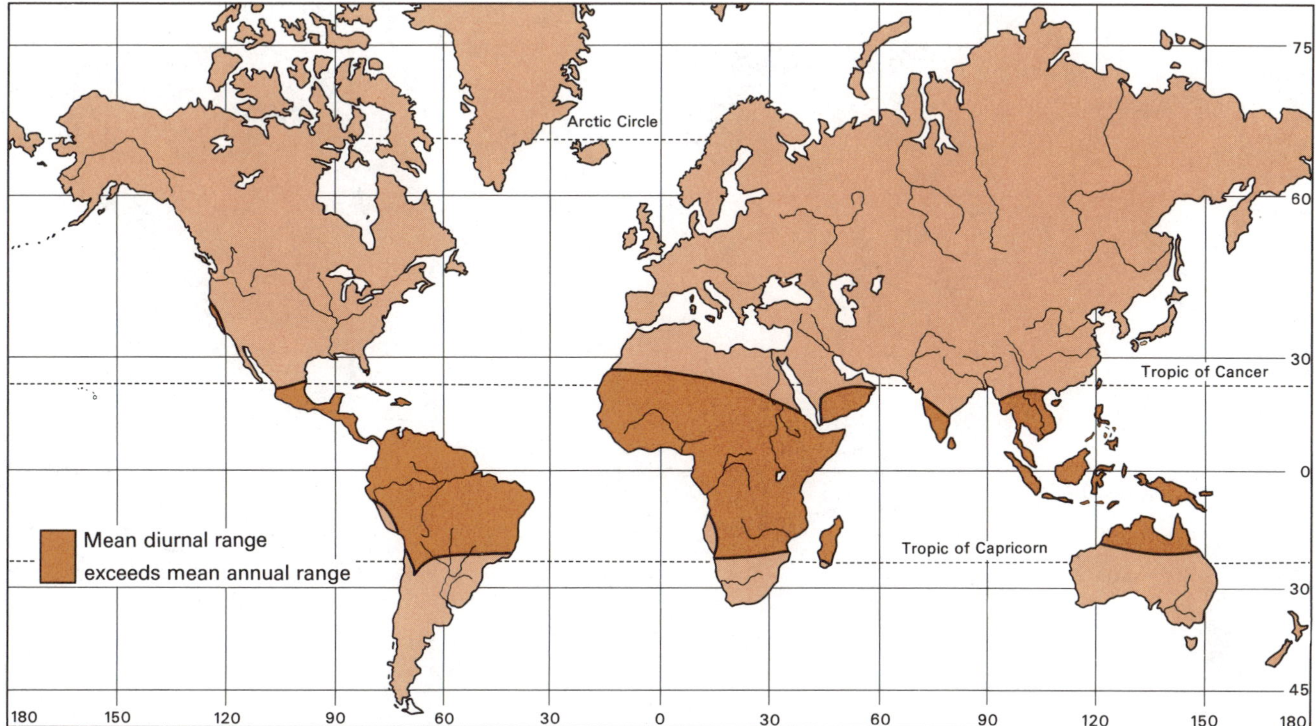


**FIGURE 4.11**
Continuously warm regions. The shaded land areas are those where the mean diurnal range of temperature exceeds the mean annual range. Note that most of these areas are found in the tropics less than 30 degrees on either side of the equator. (After Griffiths and Driscoll, 1982)

As it crosses the Atlantic Ocean it is carried poleward by the warm Atlantic drift, so that it extends to 70° north, on the coast of Lapland. The isotherm then takes a north-south direction, passing through southern Norway, Denmark, eastern Germany, Rumania, and north of the Caspian Sea before again moving in an east-west trend across south central Asia. Because of oceanic and continental influences, Bergen, Norway, at about 5°E and 61°N, has an average January temperature 2.4°C (5°F) higher than Vienna at 16°E and 48°N. Bergen lies about 1,900 kilometers (1,200 miles) north of Vienna.

The 15°C (59°F) isotherm in July illustrates the general trend of summer isotherms in the Northern Hemisphere (Figure 4.10). In contrast to winter, when the isotherms bend equatorward over the continents and poleward over the oceans, the isotherms now bend poleward over the continents and have, relatively speaking, an east-west trend over the oceans.

Although the oceans in the middle latitudes of the Northern Hemisphere tend to have only moderate seasonal ranges in temperature, the landmasses exhibit great extremes (Figure 4.12). Because of its vastness, Asia has the greatest extremes. Verkhoyansk in the eastern portion of the Soviet Union at 68°N has an average annual temperature of −16°C (3°F). This figure gives no indication of the great seasonal variation in temperature. July is the warmest month at Verkhoyansk, with an average temperature of 15.5°C (60°F), and January is the coldest month with an average temperature of −50°C (−58°F); thus the range in average monthly temperature is 65.5°C (118°F). The range in the maximum and minimum temperatures is even more striking. The lowest temperature recorded at Verkhoyansk was −70°C (−94°F), and the absolute maximum 34°C (93°F), giving a range of 104°C (187°F).

## CONTINUOUSLY COLD REGIONS

The higher latitudes north and south of 70° are characterized by their continuous coldness. Most of these places have an average temperature below −6.7°C (20°F). The ice cap areas of Greenland and Antarctica

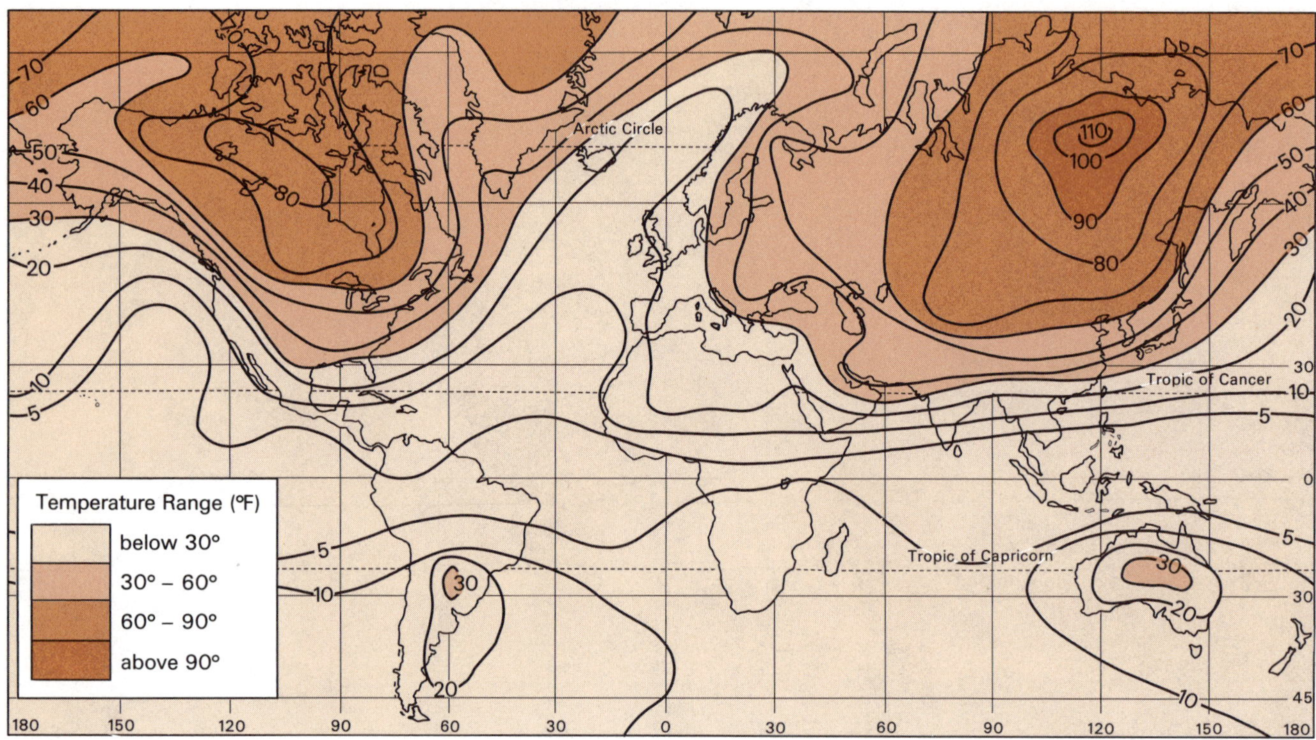


**FIGURE 4.12**
Average annual range of temperatures (°F). The least annual range occurs in the tropics and the largest annual range occurs over the continental masses of the Northern Hemisphere. (After Miller and Langdon, 1964. Copyright © 1964 by Harper & Row, Publishers, Inc. Reprinted by permission of the publisher.)

form the cores of the continuously cold regions. Point Barrow, in Alaska on the Arctic Ocean, is a typical station on the equatorward side of the continuously cold regions. The average annual temperature is −12.2°C (10°F), with January, the coldest month, averaging −28°C (−19°F), and July, the warmest month, having an average temperature of 4.4°C (40°F).

## SOLAR ENERGY

The use of the energy from the sun has intrigued human beings for thousands of years. Socrates (470–399 B.C.) is believed to be the first of the Greek philosophers to have observed and described the importance of locating a home to obtain the greatest benefit from solar radiation. A passage from Xenophon's *Memorabilia* presents the following conclusions:

> **The house should be built high and open toward the south, so that the slanting rays of the sun in winter may enter the portico at the front of the open court in the center of the dwelling. Toward the north it should be low and protected against storms. (*Xenophon Memorabilia*, ed. Josiah Renick Smith [Boston: Ginn, 1903], p. 169)**

There is a legend that Archimedes burned the Roman fleet at Syracuse in 214 B.C. by using the heat of the sun. It is alleged that he constructed on the shoreline a number of focusing metal mirrors so that the reflected rays of the sun were concentrated upon the hulls and riggings of the Roman ships in the harbor. The intense heat beam set the ships on fire, forcing the Romans to abandon the harbor. Until about the 16th century A.D. the only application of sun energy was related to various focusing systems.

Beginning in the 16th century, isolated attempts were made to harness the energy from the sun. The first solar-operated water pump was invented by Salomon de Caus (1576–1626), a French engineer, who described the machine in 1615. An early attempt to produce a solar cooker is recorded by De Saussure (1740–1799), a Swiss philosopher of the late 18th century. As the interest grew, some fundamental aspects of the sun's energy gained attention. Experiments to determine the amount of radiant energy reaching the earth were made by Sir John Herschel early in the 19th century. Herschel's actinometer was based on the principle of exposing a given quantity of water to radiation and measuring the increase in temperature in a given period of time. Late in the 19th century John Ericsson developed a calorimeter to measure solar energy received at a given place. After experimentation he stated on March 7, 1871, that "the dynamic energy developed on one square foot of surface at the boundary of the atmosphere is 7.11 Btu's per minute." This has proved to be a remarkably accurate measurement of the solar constant.

By the late 19th century, as energy became increasingly important to the developing industrial society, attempts were made to use solar energy in a practical way. The earliest U.S. patent relating to focusing radiation in an area was issued to Charles Pope in 1875. One of the earliest space heating attempts was made by E. S. Morse of Salem, Massachussetts, in 1882. In the late 19th and early 20th centuries a number of solar-powered engines were developed.

By 1920, the basic principles of many practical applications were understood, although the applications themselves were restricted. For a short period it appeared that solar energy would gain prominence, particularly in the industrial nations of the world. However, the era of cheap alternative fuels had begun and interest in solar energy declined to insignificance.

After the oil crisis of 1973, when the price of fuels began to soar, interest in solar energy revived. The U.S. Congress soon enacted legislation that established a major demonstration program to show how solar energy could be used in a wide variety of fields. Nevertheless, efforts to prove the feasibility of large-scale use of solar energy have remained minimal.

### SOLAR RESOURCE POTENTIAL

The sun offers a huge amount of energy. Solar energy arrives at the earth's surface at an average rate of 4.76 Kwh per square meter per day, so that in the course of a year, one square kilometer receives about 1.7 billion Kwh. The United States consumes annually a total of about 24 trillion Kwh. Accordingly, 141,000 square kilometers, used for solar energy conversion at about 10 percent efficiency, could meet the United States' energy requirement. Thus the important question is not whether enough solar energy exists but rather how this energy can be harnessed for practical purposes.

### GEOGRAPHICAL DISTRIBUTION

The availability of solar radiation varies over the earth. It depends not only on the angle of the sun's rays and the length of the day, but on the quality of the atmosphere through which it passes. Cloud covering and atmospheric pollution are important factors affecting atmospheric quality. Solar energy potential thus varies from one location to another (Figures 4.13 and 4.14).

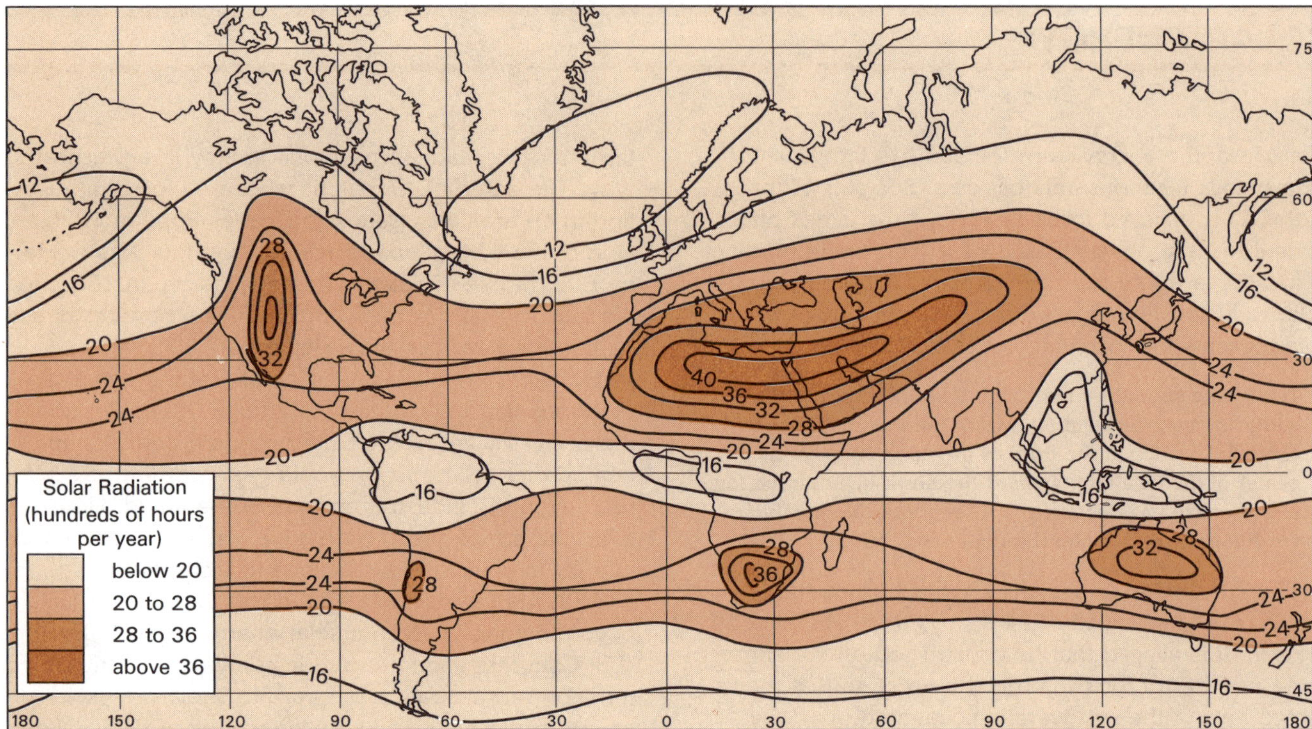


**FIGURE 4.13**
Worldwide distribution of solar energy in hundreds of hours per year. The low latitude deserts receive the greatest amount of solar energy in the course of a year. (From *Solar Energy,* Volume 1, 1957 [cover map])

Areas with the highest potential for harvesting solar energy have a minimum monthly mean radiation of 500 langleys per day and a monthly overall variation of less than 250 langleys per day. These regions are found about 15° to 30° north and south latitude on the equatorial side of the low-latitude deserts. These arid regions have approximately 3,000 hours of sunshine annually with over 90 percent as direct radiation.

The next most favorable region in the world is the equatorial area between 15° north and south latitude. The sunshine there exceeds 2,300 hours per year, but the high percentage of cloud covering scatters much of the radiation. The equatorial regions receive from 300 to 500 langleys per day, and there are few successive days of low radiation.

In the area between 30° and 45° north and south latitude, the greatest solar potential lies in the arid and semiarid regions toward the equator. In these areas the radiation can average 400 langleys per day. Nearer the poles, however, seasonal effects become important, particularly during the winter months of low solar radiation. On the poleward edge of the region the langleys may average only about 200 per day.

The regions poleward of 45° north and south latitude have limited potential for year-round use of solar energy. The seasonal variations are great. Although the direct sunlight varies from a few hours to none at all during winter, the long summer days may provide opportunities for harvesting solar energy. In Antarctica as many as 700 langleys per day have been measured during the high-sun period. Furthermore, the high latitudes are frequently regions of dryness, so that radiation tends to be direct when the sun is shining.

## UTILIZATION OF SOLAR ENERGY

Solar energy is being investigated as a supplement to traditional fuels in the centralized production of electricity. It can also be used as a primary source for isolated applications, such as heating or cooling of homes. Solar energy can be harnessed for the production of electricity in two ways. In one approach, called solar ther-

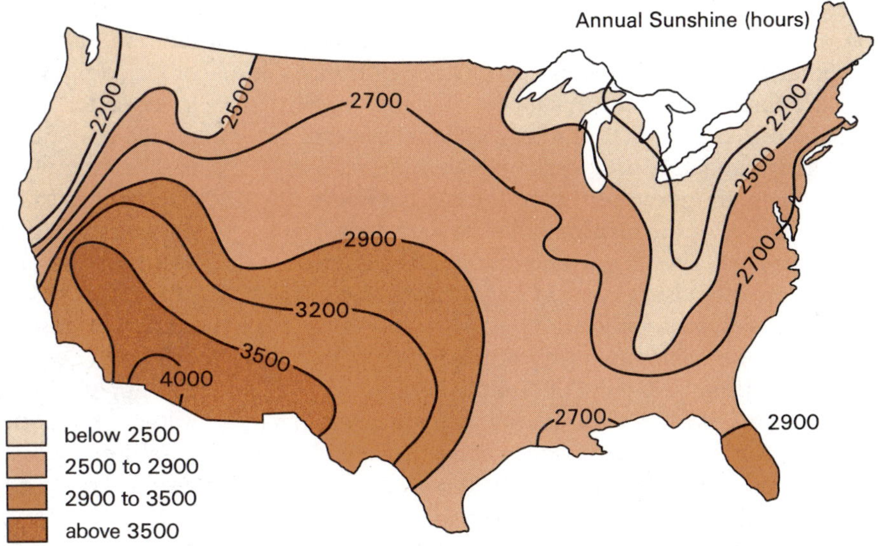


**FIGURE 4.14**
Annual number of sunshine hours in coterminous United States. The southwestern part of the United States receives the largest number of hours of sunshine per year while the northwest and the northeast the least numbers of hours of sunshine. (After Visher, 1954. Reprinted by permission.)

mal power generation, the sun's rays can be focused by mirrors or lenses, as Archimedes did more than 2000 years ago. In modern applications the rays are concentrated on vessels containing fluids. The heated fluids are used to produce steam, which in turn drives turbogenerators to produce electricity. In the second process, called the photovoltaic process, the sun's rays are directed into a structure that converts the sunlight directly into electricity without the use of moving parts. Much emphasis is being placed on the development of a system to produce silicon and other semiconductor photovoltaic cells at a fraction of present cost.

Of all the uses contemplated for solar energy, domestic heating, which includes the heating of houses and household water, appears most feasible. Space heating requires low temperatures, which solar collectors can provide. Housing and solar energy are both widely distributed, eliminating the need to transport electricity. Institutional problems and costs are low because the energy falls directly on the property where it is used.

In the northern half of the United States the average availability of sunshine during the winter is sufficient to meet the heating needs for a home. For example, in Chicago a house having 2,000 feet of floor space will require on the average 1½ to 2 million Btu's per day in January. A collector tilted toward the sun and having an area of about 90 square meters (1,000 square feet) will provide this amount of energy on an average day. Storage systems must take care of the fluctuation in temperature and available solar radiation.

## OBSTACLES TO THE USE OF SOLAR ENERGY

### DOMESTIC HEATING

Many technological, economic, political, and environmental problems must be overcome before solar energy is widely used in domestic heating and cooling systems. Although many solar systems are available, improvements are still needed in their performance, materials, and economy of operations. Most current systems have a low efficiency. Many of the solar converters on the market are difficult to adapt to a particular building. Designing a new system is expensive, and frequently patents prevent its use in a new building. Solar energy collectors currently require about 30 years of service to produce enough heat transfer to warrant their initial capital investment. As a result a long-term investment program must be available and the equipment must be sufficiently durable to last at least 30 years.

Because the sun does not shine all of the time, solar energy must be stored for those times when it cannot be received directly. This is a difficult problem, particularly in areas of moderate cloudiness and in regions where the days are short during the winter period. A solar system is likely to reduce heating costs in such an area, but residents will probably find it necessary to wear heavy clothing, or even close part of the house, during the coldest months. A supplementary heating system using conventional fuels is necessary to assure a comfortable temperature in the house. This will, however, essentially double the cost of the heating system.

Another problem limiting the acceptance of domestic solar heating is that the initial cost of a solar system is usually higher than that of a conventional system. Home financing plans are usually not designed to encourage such an investment even though the lower heating costs over the lifetime of the system may make it feasible. The proponents of solar heating believe that the increasing costs of conventional fuels will alter the present loan policies.

The cost of a solar heating system varies greatly. Eric Farber of the University of Florida, a world-renowned authority on solar energy, has indicated that his sytem of heating and cooling a house in Florida would cost about $5,000 more than a conventional heating and cooling system. However, Howard Hay, a California solar engineer, has indicated that the flat water-bed type collector installed in his house in Atascadero, California, costs no more than a conventional heating and cooling system. Thus more experimentation is needed to analyze costs effectively. House builders traditionally strive to keep heating and cooling costs at the lowest level, a goal that is frequently incompatible with the use of solar energy.

Real estate taxing policies also discourage the use of solar energy. Because real estate taxes are based on property valuation, the high value caused by the expensive solar system results in higher taxes. Legislators are now beginning to recognize that lowering these taxes could encourage the use of solar energy. Indiana, for example, has passed legislation offering a real estate tax incentive for using solar energy in both new and old buildings. Property values are to be determined by subtracting the value of the solar system from the total value of the building.

Making solar houses attractive may be critical to the acceptance of solar energy as a source of heating and cooling. Early solar houses have been so different in appearance that some people feel that solar means ugly or strange. Architects must develop a solar house that will be widely accepted.

Present building codes are not prepared for the installation of solar heating systems. Of these, fire codes are most likely to affect the development of the solar house. Three aspects of these codes pertain to solar energy. Of major importance is the method of storing heat in the system. Paraffin is an excellent material for the storage of heat. As it melts, paraffin collects a large amount of heat, which is released as it solidifies. However, because of paraffin's flammability, it is questioned whether fire codes will permit large quantities of it to be used inside buildings. If paraffin were permitted, fire insurance rates could be raised drastically. Another component affected by fire regulations is the solar collector. It can be made of glass, fiberglass, or plastic material. Fiberglass and plastic collectors are less resistant to smoke and fire than glass. The third component to be considered by fire codes is the material used for insulation in the solar system. All insulation must be able to withstand temperatures of at least 165°C (350°F). Many insulation materials can melt or smoke at these temperatures.

Health codes must also be considered. These codes can apply when ethylene glycol is used as a heat transfer medium. Because this chemical can contaminate drinking water, the solar system must be leakproof.

If solar energy becomes an accepted way of heating buildings, our legal system will have to consider the issue of access to the sun's rays. Legislation must be passed to guarantee that neighboring construction and vegetation does not impede access to solar radiation. California is developing legislation to provide "sun rights" to all users of solar energy.

## ELECTRICITY PRODUCTION

The future of solar energy in the production of electricity will depend on the solution of a number of serious problems. Because the sun's radiation is widely dispersed, a large area of the earth's surface must be covered with solar collectors in order to harvest sufficient energy for the needs of a modern economy. No estimates have been made of the environmental impact of covering several thousand square kilometers with solar collectors. We can assume that the impact would be tremendous on precipitation runoff, temperatures, vegetation cover, animal life, and other aspects of the environment.

Because the sun does not shine all of the time and the demand for electricity varies over time, a system is needed to store energy when it is available and to tap the energy when it is required. The technical problem is easily stated but the solution has eluded scientists and engineers.

Many ways of storing energy have been suggested. For example, thermal energy might be stored in large volumes of molten metal or salt, from which the energy would gradually be extracted. Solar energy could be used to produce hydrogen, which would later be used as a fuel. In yet another scheme, solar energy could power water pumps to fill dams behind hydroelectric power plants, thus converting solar energy into stored energy in water pressure, which would ultimately be converted into electricity by turbogenerators.

Given the present state of the art, the most reliable method of energy storage is still the battery. New types of storage batteries, such as the alkali metal sulfur battery, are being produced, but commercial development is still in the future. As a consequence the traditional lead-acid battery remains the principal type for large-scale storage. However, its cost and durability for storing massive quantities of electricity have not been assessed. It now appears that a massive array of lead-acid batteries would have a maximum storage capacity of 6 to 12 hours, insufficient for continuous service.

## FUTURE

Solar energy will not provide a significant share of the world's energy needs in the near future. However, marketplace factors are encouraging the investigation of alternatives to conventional fossil fuels. The use of solar energy for home heating and cooling appears extremely promising and should be well established by the year 2020.

The commercial use of solar energy may begin by supplying electricity for peak demands, which occur, for example, during summer heat waves when air conditioners are in heavy use. At present, the oldest, least efficient fossil fuel plants are forced into temporary operation to meet these demands. These plants are extremely costly and solar plants could possibly compete with them, particularly as costs rise for the traditional fossil fuels. The Electric Power Research Institute and the U.S. Department of Defense are now considering the feasibility of using solar energy electricity for intermediate and peak demands. It is possible that within the next century solar energy will assume a greater role in supplying the world's energy needs, but even then it will be only one of a number of energy sources.

## CONCLUSION

The solar radiation to the earth creates a giant energy system. Incoming energy heats the earth and outgoing energy cools it. Although seasonal thermal cycles and latitudinal contrasts in temperature occur, strong evidence exists that a global energy balance prevails. The resulting global temperature equilibrium represents the heat balance under the conditions of insolation, albedo, and heat transfer that exist on the earth. Because spatial variations of temperature occur within the system at any one time, regional patterns of temperature can be perceived.

Although solar energy has long been recognized as a source of heat, little thought has been given to harnessing it effectively. As a response to the energy shortages of the 1970s, improvements in technology are now making solar energy a possible energy source for the future.

## STUDY QUESTIONS

1 What is the importance of radiation from the sun to the earth?
2 Explain the geometric radiation law.
3 What is the effect of the atmosphere on the solar beam? What is the planetary albedo?
4 How does the earth maintain a heat balance?
5 What is meant by the "greenhouse effect" of the atmosphere?
6 What factors affect the amount of radiation received from the sun at a particular location? How does the angle of the sun's rays influence the amount of radiation received at a particular place?
7 If the rays of the sun always fell vertically over the equator, what would the temperature of the world be like?
8 What is a langley unit? Why does the amount of langley units received vary from the equator to the poles?
9 Describe each of the processes which influence the heating and cooling of the atmosphere.
10 How does transpiration differ from evapotranspiration?
11 Explain the vertical distribution of temperature.
12 What causes a temperature inversion?

13 Why is there differential heating and cooling of land and water?

14 What is an isotherm?

15 What factors alter the general east-west trend of the isotherms in the world?

16 Why does the Northern Hemisphere have greater contrasts in temperature than the Southern Hemisphere?

17 Describe the location of the 0°C (32°F) isotherm for January in the Northern Hemisphere.

18 What is the potential for the use of solar energy?

19 Where are the favorable regions in the world for the development of solar energy?

20 What are some major obstacles to the use of solar energy?

# 5
# ATMOSPHERIC AND OCEANIC CIRCULATION

## KEY WORDS

anabatic wind
anticyclone
atmospheric pressure
barometer
barometric slope
barometric surface
chinook
Coriolis force
cyclone
Ekman spiral
Ferrel's law
foehn
friction layer
geostrophic wind
gravitational force
Hadley cell
hydrostatic
intertropical convergence
katabatic wind
monsoons
polar easterlies
polar front
pressure gradient
Santa Ana winds
subtropical high pressure belts
trade winds
turbulent friction
westerlies

The circulation systems of the atmosphere and the oceans interconnect to form one of the most fascinating systems on the earth. The manner in which this system operates helps determine the earth's weather and climate on a local, regional, and global scale. The motions of this system are controlled primarily by solar energy. Atmospheric circulation is the major transporter of energy from the lower to the higher latitudes, and is thus a controlling element in the distribution of water over the globe. Much of the moisture originates over the oceans and is distributed, frequently quite unevenly, onto the continents.

## AIR PRESSURE RELATIONSHIPS

Because matter can exist in a gaseous state, the atmosphere has weight. This weight is called *atmospheric pressure.* The pressure that is exerted by the atmosphere at any point on the earth's surface is simply the total weight of a column of air from that point on the surface to the outer limits of the atmosphere.

Standard air pressure can be expressed as 76 centimeters (29.92 inches) of mercury at sea level. This means that a column of air one centimeter square, extending from sea level to the top of the atmosphere, is balanced by a column of mercury 76 centimeters (29.92 inches) tall. Air pressure is measured by the *barometer.*

If temperatures and other conditions were the same for all points at the same elevation, then the atmosphere would be in a state of equilibrium and the air pressure would be constant at all points at the same elevation. Any surface in the atmosphere throughout which all points have the same pressure is called a *barometric surface.* But since atmospheric controls, such as temperature, are not uniform at all places at the same elevation, these barometric surfaces are not parallel to the earth's surface. Instead, they form a series of sloping surfaces or folds, which in turn influence the movement of air in the earth's atmosphere. The changes in the barometric surfaces are called *barometric slopes.* The steepness of such a slope is called the *pressure gradient.*

## THE EQUATION OF CONTINUITY

The equation of continuity states that a given mass of air can be neither created nor destroyed. This means that a given volume, such as a kilogram of air, will always be a kilogram of air. The equation further states, however, that the shape of the kilogram of air can and will change when forces, such as temperature changes, are exerted upon it.

The equation of continuity provides a basic principle for understanding the relationships between horizontal and vertical air movement. For example, when horizontal winds squeeze a parcel of air, the parcel expands vertically to conserve its mass. The equation of continuity is expressed as:

Changes of mass in a volume = Amount of air mass flowing into (or out of) the volume by horizontal motions
+ amount of air mass flowing into (or out of) the volume by vertical motions

This equation relates the horizontal motions of the atmosphere to the vertical motions. One cannot be understood without understanding the other. If in the Northern Hemisphere, for example, the wind spirals outward from a high pressure center, there is horizontal divergence or expansion. To compensate for this movement there must be vertical compression. However, since there is no vertical movement at ground level, the air above the ground must fall, in a motion known as subsidence. The reverse action occurs in a low pressure center.

## LAWS OF AIR MOVEMENT

The horizontal movement of air near the earth's surface is controlled by four forces: the pressure gradient, deflection caused by the earth's rotation (the Coriolis effect), friction, and gravity.

### PRESSURE GRADIENT

The difference in air pressure from place to place is the fundamental cause of air movement. Such differences are normally due to thermal changes, but may be due to physical causes. An air mass always moves from an area of high pressure to an area of low pressure; in other words, air moves down the barometric slope. The pressure gradient thus has both magnitude and direction. The magnitude is inversely proportional to the spacing of the *isobars,* lines that connect points of equal barometric pressure. The closer the spacing of the isobars, the stronger the pressure gradient. When the isobars are closely spaced, a strong wind occurs; if they are widely spaced, a gentle breeze occurs. The pressure gradient force is shown by a line drawn at right angles to the isobars. This line shows the direction of the wind (Figure 5.1).

## CORIOLIS EFFECT

It is a well-known fact that the wind systems of the earth do not follow the north-south course of the meridians, but are deflected by the earth's rotation into an oblique course. This deflection is to the right in the Northern Hemisphere and to the left in the Southern Hemisphere. This statement is known as *Ferrel's law.* The force causing the deflection is known as the *Coriolis force* (Figure 5.2).

The Coriolis force is not a real force but an apparent one. The deflective force on a rotating body was demonstrated with a pendulum by Jean Bernard Léon Foucault in Paris in 1851. The experiment showed that the swinging of a pendulum that was started in a north-south direction gradually assumed a northeast-southwest direction. In reality the pendulum had not changed its course with respect to space, but the earth's rotation altered its apparent position.

Deflection can be easily demonstrated on a rotating globe with a piece of chalk. Rotate the globe in a counterclockwise direction as viewed from the North Pole, that is, from west to east. While the globe is rotating, draw the chalk vertically along a meridian in the Northern Hemisphere. The chalk will make a curved line running from northeast to southwest. Although the chalk did not change from a north-south direction, the turning of the globe under the chalk caused an apparent change in the direction of its movement. Air moves relative to the earth in the same manner. This effect disappears at the equator where the north and south horizons move eastward at the same speed.

The magnitude of the Coriolis force is proportional to

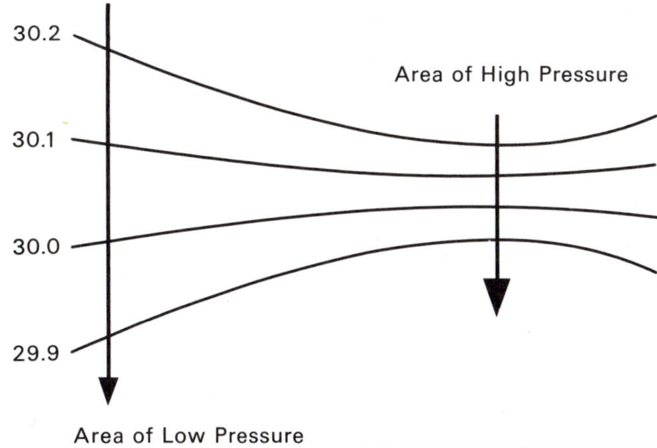


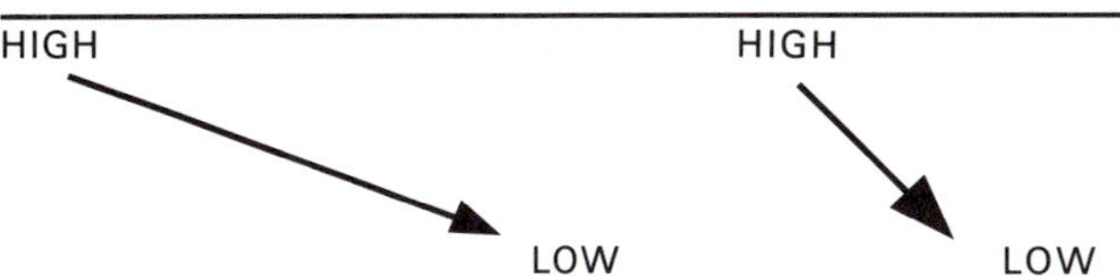


**FIGURE 5.1**
Air pressure gradient. Air moves from areas of high pressure into areas of low pressure. When the isobars are widely spaced, as shown on the left side of the diagram, the slope is gentle and the air movement is moderate. When the isobars are closely spaced, as on the right, the slope is steep and winds are strong.

the latitudinal position. The deflective effects of rotation are most significant in the middle and higher latitudes, where the earth's surface is not parallel to its axis. At 30 degrees latitude, the earth's rotation causes only half as much deflection as at the poles, where the surface is perpendicular to the axis.

Although the Coriolis force is small, it is significant when the pressure gradient is small and a large mass

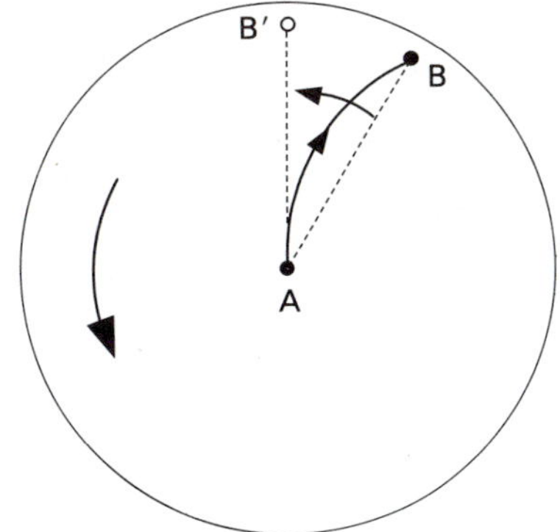


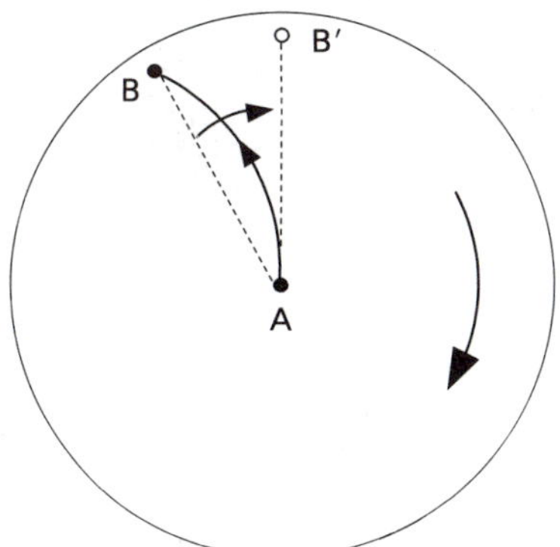


**FIGURE 5.2**
Coriolis force: Effect of rotation on the path of a body. Solid curve *AB* represents the path relative to the rotating body; dashed lines *AB* and *AB′* represent successive positions of the body. (After Miller, Thompson, Peterson, and Haragan, 1983)

of slowly moving air travels a great distance. It is thus important in large-scale air mass movements, but is usually insignificant in local air movements such as land and sea breezes or valley and mountain breezes.

Within the world system the pressure gradient and the Coriolis force eventually balance each other. When they do, the dynamic equilibrium results in a *geostrophic wind.* Such winds normally occur some distance above the earth's surface. Because of the equilibrium of forces, a geostrophic wind always flows parallel to the isobars. The velocity of the geostrophic winds can be determined when the pressure gradient, the air density, and the latitude of the place are known.

## FRICTIONAL FORCES

Whenever a moving air mass comes in contact with the earth or another air mass moving at a different speed, its movement is affected by frictional forces. The effect of friction is important only on the movement of the air nearest the earth, frequently called the *friction layer.* The general effect of friction is to reduce the speed of a moving air mass. This effect occurs when the molecules of a moving air mass collide with the molecules of another mass that is either stationary or moving at a different speed.

Frictional forces are particularly important in changing the momentum of eddies in the atmosphere. These wind currents frequently develop less than one kilometer above the surface of the earth, due to differential heating of the air above the earth. The movement of eddies is opposite that of the solid earth, so that the wind experiences a retarding force, called *eddy friction* or *turbulent friction.* In contrast, the earth's surface experiences an accelerating force. If the surface is water, waves and currents result. If the surface is loose ground, dust will be blown into the atmosphere.

The frictional forces of the atmosphere are best developed when the atmosphere is turbulent. Turbulence is most likely on clear, hot, summer afternoons when

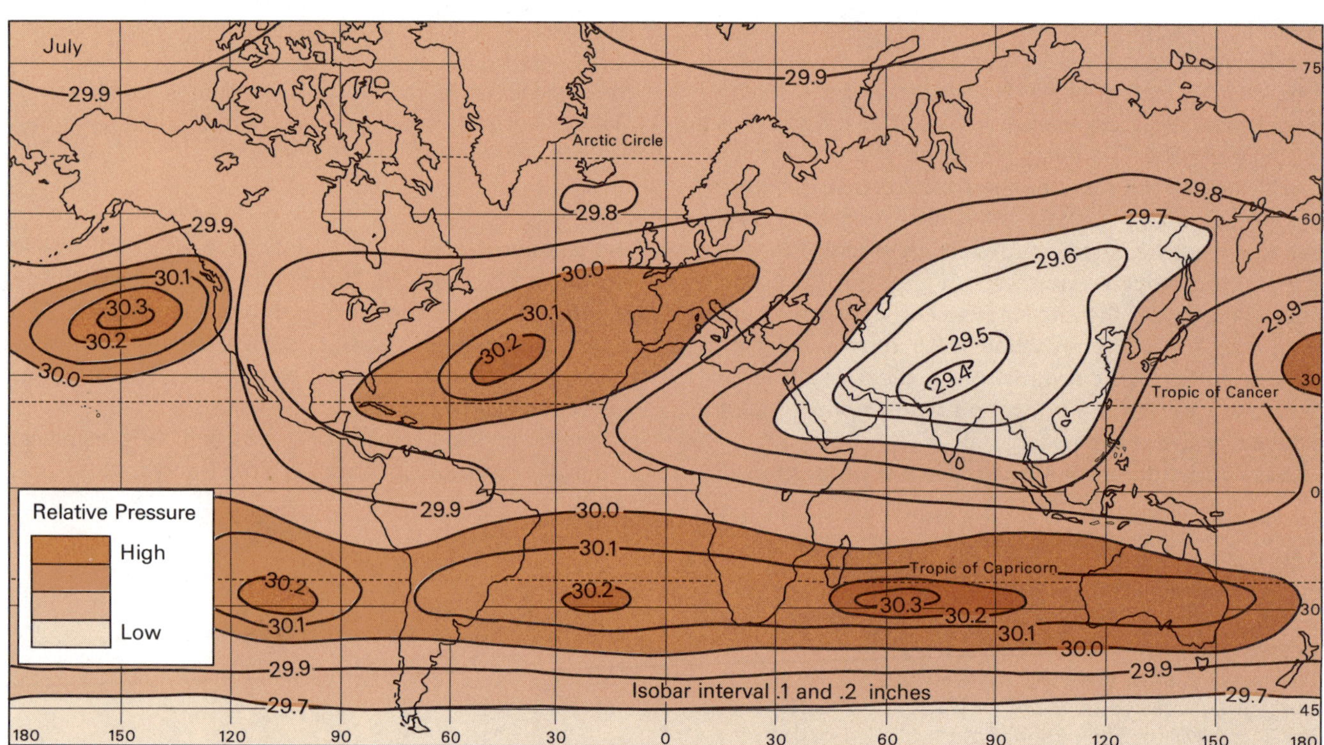


**FIGURE 5.3**
Average July atmospheric pressures of the world, reduced to sea level. The major low pressure cell is over the continent of Asia, and the major high pressure cells exist over the oceans between 20 and 40 degrees latitude. (After Miller and Langdon, 1964. Copyright © 1964 by Harper & Row, Publishers, Inc. Reprinted by permission of the publisher.)

the warm ground heats the overlying cooler atmosphere, causing the atmosphere to begin to overturn. Eddies are least likely to develop on clear, cold nights in winter when the ground is cold. The force of friction thus varies from day to night and from season to season. The thickness of the friction layer also varies, depending upon the heating and cooling processes.

### GRAVITATIONAL FORCES

The gravitational pull of the earth is always downward toward its center. Gravity is almost constant. Although the force of gravity is great, air remains suspended because it is subject to an equal and opposite force away from the earth. This force is provided by the decrease of air pressure with increasing altitude. If air is to be suspended, the upward acceleration due to pressure decrease must exactly balance the downward acceleration due to gravity. Such a balance is called *hydrostatic.*

Although hydrostatic balance prevails over the atmosphere as a whole, local air masses frequently experience rising or falling accelerations. Rarely is more than one percent of such movement caused by gravitational forces. Gravity is thus the least important of the forces that cause an air mass to move.

## WORLD ATMOSPHERIC PRESSURE REGIMES

The outstanding characteristic of the distribution of atmospheric pressure in the world is that the isobars generally follow parallels of latitude (Figures 5.3 and 5.4). This characteristic accounts for the beltlike appearance of pressure areas encircling the globe at various latitudes. The least deviation from the east-west direction occurs in the Southern Hemisphere, where oceanic conditions prevail. Small changes in atmospheric pressure occur from season to season in this area. The large land areas in the Northern Hemisphere interrupt the beltlike course of the pressure areas. The oceanic pressure belts remain permanent, but the landmasses experience seasonal changes. For example, in winter a massive high pressure develops over the Asian conti-

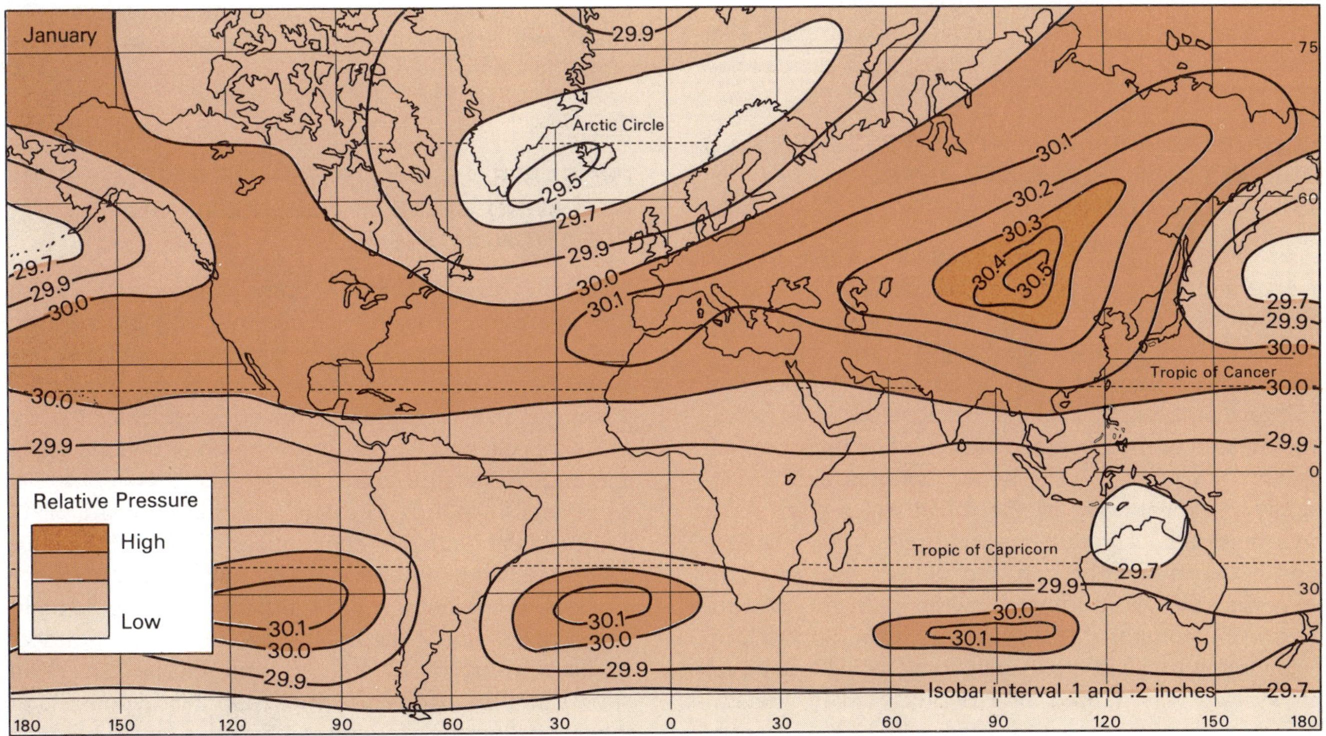


**FIGURE 5.4**
Average January atmospheric pressures of the world, reduced to sea level. In January the pressure is highest in Asia with low pressure cells in the north Atlantic and north Pacific oceans. (After Miller and Langdon, 1964. Copyright © 1964 by Harper & Row, Publishers, Inc. Reprinted by permission of the publisher.)

nent while in summer a low pressure exists in the same area. The North American continent interrupts the pressure belts in the same way, but to a lesser extent because of its smaller land area.

## THEORETICAL ATMOSPHERIC CIRCULATION

The world's atmospheric circulation is influenced by a number of phenomena, including the distribution of insolation, the rotation of the earth, the distribution of land and water surfaces, and inclination and parallelism of the earth's axis. Of these, insolation is most important. Its effect upon atmospheric circulation is often referred to as *thermal control.* The modifications brought about by the earth's rotation are probably next in importance. However, in order to understand the actual world pressure and wind system, all factors must be considered. Because these factors interact to create a complex pressure and wind system, we will begin by using theoretical models to emphasize the two most influential factors, insolation and rotation. Gradually, the modifying influences of the other associated earth phenomena will be introduced to convey the complete evolution of the world patterns of atmospheric circulation.

### PROBABLE ARRANGEMENT OF PRESSURE AND WIND BELTS IF DEPENDING UPON INSOLATION ALONE

Let us assume that the world is totally covered by water, that the sun is always perpendicular to the equator, and that all other modifying influences are excluded (Figure 5.5). On this hypothetical earth, insolation ranges from a maximum in the equatorial regions to a minimum in the polar regions. Because the air is excessively heated in the equatorial areas, a low pressure belt encircles the earth there. The air expands and consequently rises vertically in the equatorial region. As it flows poleward it gradually cools until in the polar regions it becomes very cold and dense, and settles to the earth. The air from this region of high pressure flows to the equatorial low pressure region. Such a loop of circulation is called a *convective cell,* or a *Hadley cell.* This system was named after George Hadley, the English meteorologist who proposed it in 1735. His concept was gradually altered so that the Hadley cell is now restricted to the low latitudes from zero to about 30 degrees north and south, coinciding with the trade wind belts.

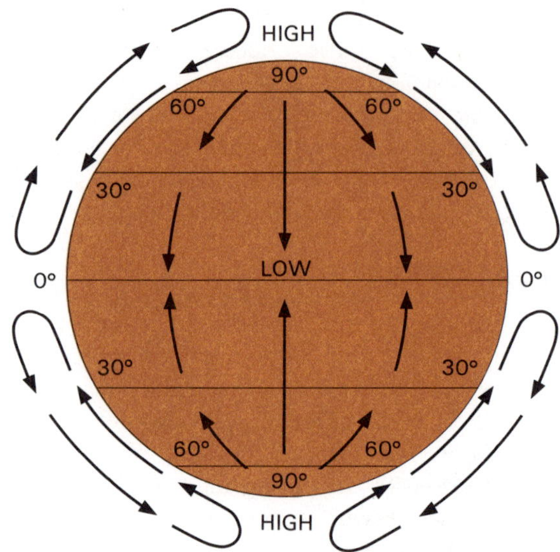


**FIGURE 5.5**
Schematic arrangement of pressure and wind movement on a homogeneous earth where insolation is the single factor involved. Equatorial heating would create a low pressure belt around the equator. The low temperatures near the poles would induce high pressure cells there. Circulation of air would be in a simple pattern from the high at 90° north and south latitudes to the low pressure areas of the equatorial region.

### PROBABLE ARRANGEMENT OF PRESSURE AND WIND BELTS IF DEPENDING ON ROTATION ALONE

Again it is assumed that a homogeneous earth exists, that insolation is evenly distributed, and other associated earth phenomena have no influence (Figure 5.6). In this hypothesis, the rotation of the earth would cause the atmosphere to pile up at the equator, creating a high pressure cell, and thin out over the polar regions so that a reduced pressure zone would exist there. The solid earth itself responds to rotation in this way: the pliable nature of the earth's interior causes a bulge at the equator and a flattening at the poles. Since the atmosphere is a gas, the piling up at the equator and the flattening at the poles would tend to be even more pronounced. A comparison of Figure 5.5 and Figure 5.6 clearly shows that the conditions implied in this hypothesis are the opposite of those induced by the uneven nature of insolation distribution. If rotation is the only factor, a high pressure belt exists at the equator and the air flows from the equator to the poles. The convective cell is thus reversed.

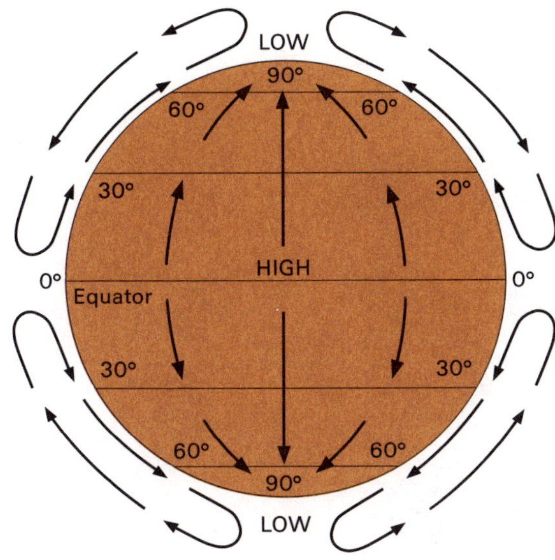


FIGURE 5.6
Schematic arrangement of pressure and wind movement on a homogeneous earth where rotation is the single factor involved. The air movement under this condition would be from the equatorial to the polar regions. Earth rotation, in reality, helps to determine the location of the various pressure belts, but it is not as important as thermal control.

### PROBABLE ARRANGEMENT OF PRESSURE AND WIND BELTS BASED UPON INSOLATION AND ROTATION

Because insolation and rotation exert the greatest influence on the arrangement of pressure belts and the resulting world wind systems, the combination of these two factors approaches conditions as they actually exist on the earth (Figures 5.7 and 5.8). This hypothesis is still simplified, however, because it does not consider the distribution of land and water, the inclination and parallelism of the axis, and other associated earth phenomena.

Because thermal control is dominant over earth rotation in the establishment of the pressure belts, the excessive heating at the equator continues to create a belt of low pressure in the equatorial region. Likewise, the excessive cold in the polar regions continues to produce cells of high pressure in those areas. Thermal control is so influential that the rotationally induced high pressure belt in equatorial regions is split in two and pushed poleward in both hemispheres. The crests of these high pressures are found at approximately 30 degrees north and south latitude. Winds blow both poleward and equatorward from these high pressure belts. Near the poles, the low pressure cells caused by earth rotation are likewise pushed equatorward in both hemispheres by the thermally induced high present there, so that low pressure troughs are located roughly at 60 degrees north and south latitude. A major wind zone blows equatorward from the poles.

## PLANETARY PRESSURE AND WIND SYSTEMS ON A HOMOGENEOUS EARTH

If the earth were completely covered by water, a traveler who followed a meridian from either pole to the equator would encounter first a high pressure, known as a polar high; then a wind belt, the polar easterlies; followed by a low pressure, called the subpolar low; then a wind belt, the westerlies; another high, the subtropical high; followed by the trade winds; and finally the low pressure zone of intertropical convergence. This model of wind and pressure belts was first conceived by George Hadley in 1735. His model was accurate in explaining the origin of the subtropical high and the trade winds by recognizing the heat imbalance of the earth. It was not until 1941 that Carl Gustav Rossby provided a satisfactory explanation for the development of the westerlies. He recognized that the subpolar low could not be thermally induced alone but was a combination of thermal and mechanical actions carrying the flow from the subtropical high to the subpolar low. This succession of pressure and wind belts on a homogeneous earth approaches the actual conditions in the world in the Southern Hemisphere where a water surface predominates. These uniform pressure and wind belts are interrupted by the landmasses of the Northern Hemisphere (Figures 5.9 and 5.10).

### INTERTROPICAL CONVERGENCE

A number of names designate the low pressure zone near the equator. These include doldrums, equatorial low, equatorial trough, intertropical convergence, and intertropical front zone. The last two terms are usually considered most appropriate because they express the actual wind movement in the equatorial latitudes. Most of this belt lies between 5 degrees north and 5 degrees south latitude, although in certain places it extends as much as 20 degrees away from the equator. On the average it varies in width from about 300 to 400 kilometers (180 to 240 miles).

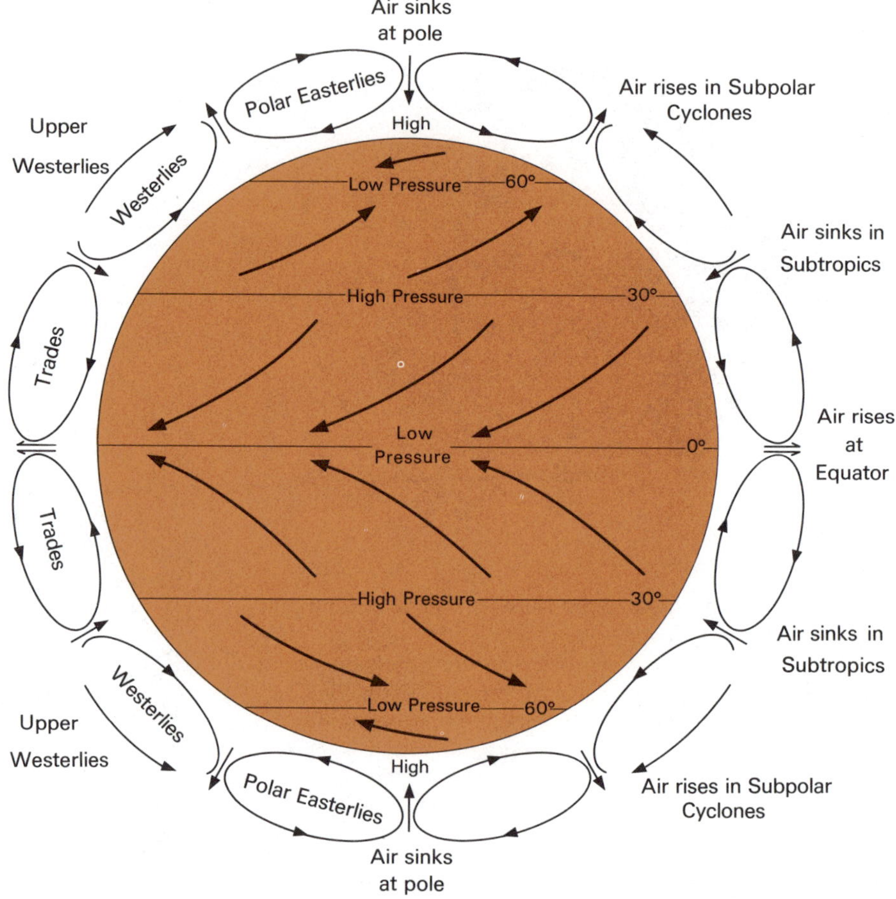


**FIGURE 5.7**
General pattern of planetary pressure and wind systems at sea level on a homogeneous earth taking into consideration rotation and insolation. When rotation and insolation are both present, the earth's pressure and wind patterns become more complicated, with three wind belts in each hemisphere.

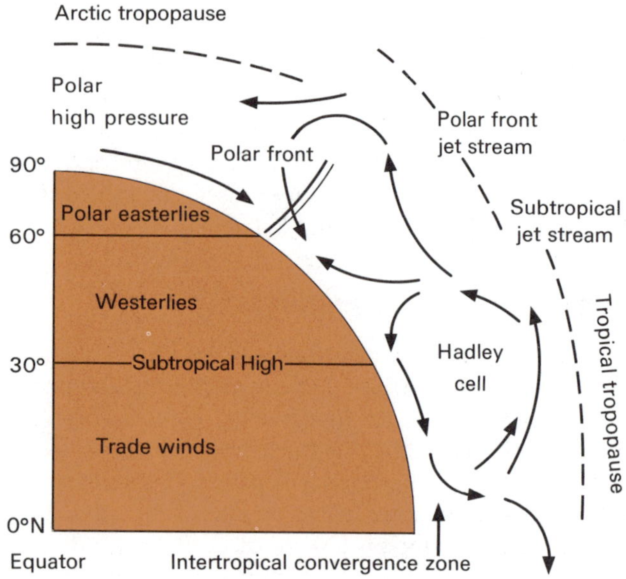


**FIGURE 5.8**
A cross section of the actual circulation of the atmosphere from the equator to the North Pole. (After Palmen, *Quarterly Journal of the Royal Meteorological Society,* 1951)

In this low-latitude region, the trade winds converge and are forced to rise. As a consequence there is no prevailing wind. Instead, light, inconstant breezes blow from all points of the compass with about equal frequency, interspersed with periods of calm.

During its ascent, the heated and humid air cools, and therefore the region of equatorial lows has heavy convectional thunderstorms. Poor circulation exists and the weather is sultry and oppressive. Because of the weakness and irregularity of the winds, this region came to have the common term *doldrums.* The doldrums were avoided in the days of the sailing vessels because of the great danger of becoming becalmed for weeks at a time.

## TRADE WINDS

The trade winds flow down the pressure gradient from the crests of the subtropical highs into the intertropical convergence. They are noted for their persistence and regularity, particularly in the Southern Hemisphere. Because of their reliability they were sought as trade

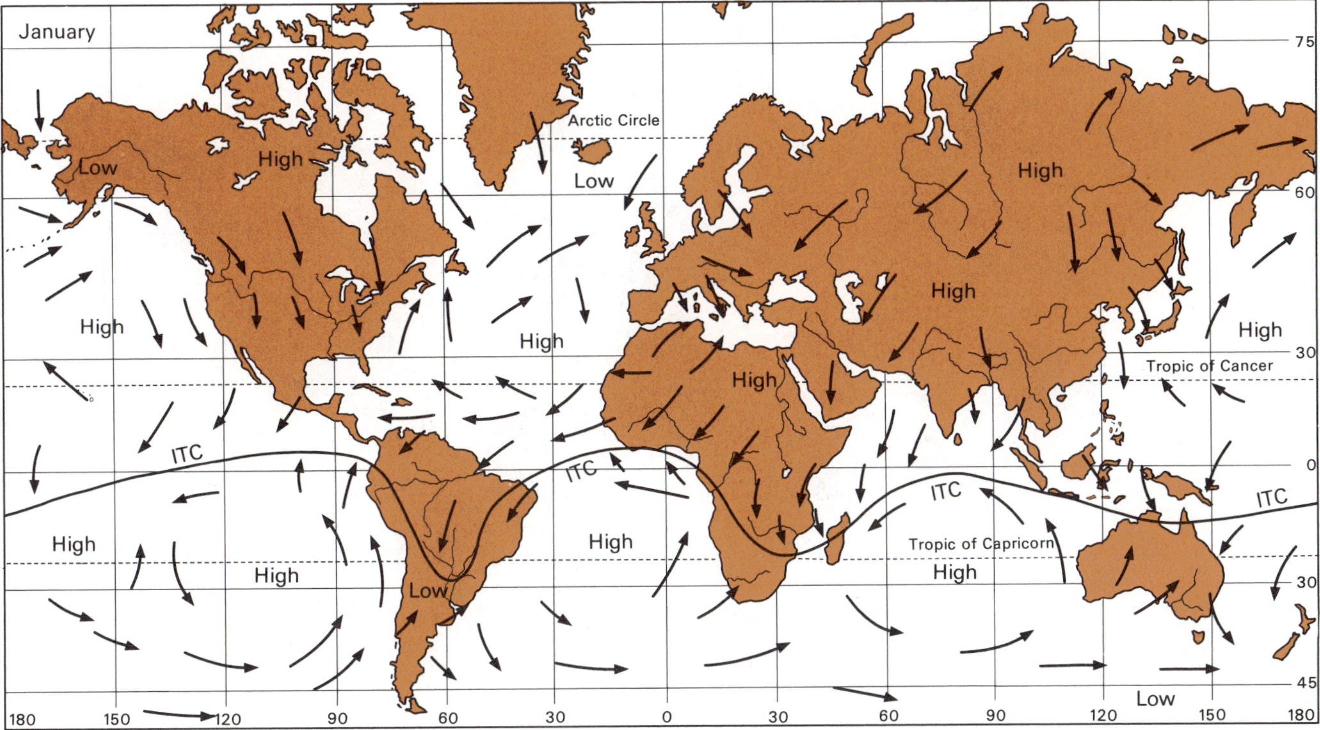


**FIGURE 5.9**
Prevailing winds in January. A well-developed counterclockwise circulation prevails in January over the oceans of the Southern Hemisphere. In the Northern Hemisphere there is a strong clockwise movement of air out of the continental areas. (After Garbell, 1947. Reprinted by permission of Pitman Publishing Ltd., London.)

routes in the days of the sailing vessels. In general they are regions of fine, clear weather with few atmospheric storms. The major exceptions are hurricanes and typhoons, which infest the western and poleward edges of the oceanic trade winds in the autumn.

As the trade winds move out of the crests of the subtropical highs, they are relatively dry, but as they move equatorward, they gather moisture. They pick up moisture not only because they move over water bodies on their journey equatorward, but also because they are getting steadily warmer. As they are warmed, they increase their capacity for holding moisture, so that they remain, relatively speaking, dry winds. The trade winds may be forced to rise if, for example, they encounter a mountainous island. In such a case, they are cooled and precipitation occurs on the windward side of the island. The rainfall pattern of the Hawaiian Islands illustrates this phenomenon very well.

As the trade winds reach the belt of intertropical convergence, they rise and consequently cool. Convectional thunderstorms provide heavy precipitation in these regions. The trade winds are theoretically dry only because they are continually being warmed and are thus capable of increasing their moisture-holding capacity. In essence, the absolute humidity of the wind is high while the relative humidity remains fairly low.

## SUBTROPICAL HIGH PRESSURE BELTS

The subtropical high pressure belts are regions of subsiding winds where two major wind belts originate. The trade winds move out of the equatorward edge and start their journey to the intertropical convergence, while the westerlies originate on the poleward edge and travel in the direction of the subpolar lows. The crests of these high pressure areas are located about 30 degrees north and south of the equator, although the irregularly shaped belts extend anywhere from 20 to 40 degrees latitude.

These belts resemble the intertropical convergence in that they are areas where pressure gradients are weak and light. Variable, shifting winds with long periods of calm are the rule. As the air subsides it is warmed, thus increasing its capacity for holding rather than releasing

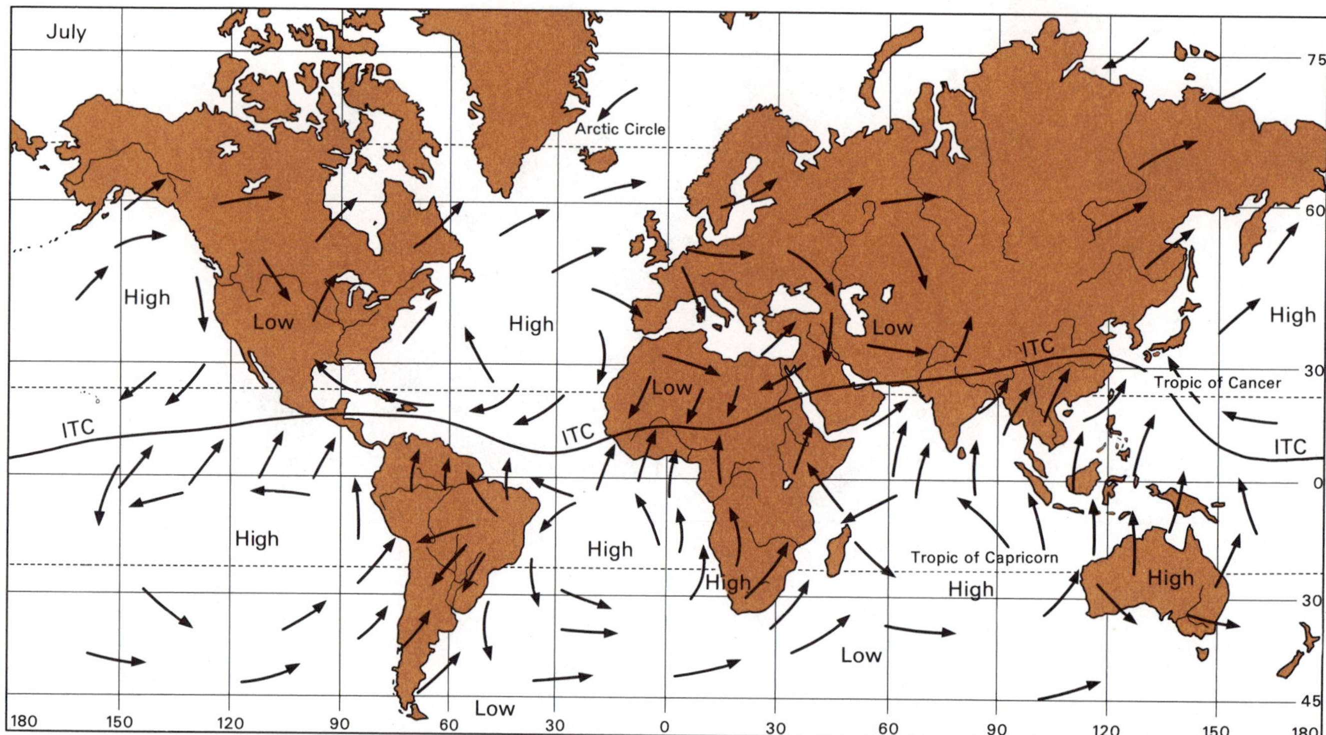


**FIGURE 5.10**
Prevailing winds in July. A well-developed counterclockwise circulation can be seen over the oceans in the Southern Hemisphere; a clockwise circulation prevails in the Northern Hemisphere. In the Northern Hemisphere there is a strong movement of air from the oceans into the continents. (After Garbell, 1947. Reprinted by permission of Pitman Publishing Ltd., London.)

moisture. In many parts of the world the poleward areas of low latitude deserts, such as the Sahara of North Africa and the Great Australian, coincide in location with the subtropical high pressure belts.

Because many Spanish sailing vessels coming to the New World were affected by the pressure and wind belts of the low latitudes, the sailors provided names appropriate to the wind conditions. In the subtropical highs Spanish conquistadors were often becalmed for weeks. As a consequence they sometimes had to throw their horses overboard to save water for the crew. Because of the floating corpses of horses in the water the sailors called this region the horse latitudes, a name that persists to the present.

## WESTERLY WIND BELTS

In the Northern and Southern hemispheres from about 35 to 55 degrees are persistent belts of winds. As they emerge from the subtropical high pressure belts, theoretically, they should blow from the southwest in the Northern Hemisphere and from the northwest in the Southern Hemisphere. Actually, however, there are many deviations from this theoretical direction, although their general movement is from west to east. Within the wind system this movement has come to be known as the Ferrel cell, named after William Ferrel.

The most distinctive feature of the westerly wind belts is their lack of uniformity. At times the winds blow with gale force, and at other times they are merely mild breezes. At times the regions are beset by great storms; at other times they experience superbly fair weather. In no other wind or pressure belt are weather conditions so uncertain or unpredictable. This tendency is largely due to their location in the middle latitudes where polar and tropical air masses meet along the *polar front,* causing great high and low pressure systems to move within the westerlies.

Of these great whirling masses of air, those with high air pressure are called *anticyclones* and those with low air pressure are called *cyclones.* Both travel in an unending procession in a general west-east direction. As they pass over an area they cause changes of pressure, wind, humidity, temperature, and precipitation conditions. Although the basic movement of the winds is from west to east, the winds within the pressure systems actually blow from all points of the compass.

The westerlies are best developed in the Southern Hemisphere where a nearly homogeneous water surface exists. In the days of the sailing vessels these winds were known as the "roaring forties" and the "screeching sixties." Many sailing vessels were wrecked in violent storms as they attempted to move through the Strait of Magellan at Cape Horn on the southern tip of South America. Westward from Cape Horn there are no landmasses, so the westerlies can encircle the globe and attain very high velocities.

### SUBPOLAR LOW PRESSURE BELTS

Troughs of low pressure belts are located at about 60 degrees north and south latitude. In the Southern Hemisphere, the subpolar low pressure areas form one relatively continuous belt, while in the Northern Hemisphere they exist, more or less, in isolated cells of low pressure over the oceans, connected by bridges of slightly higher pressure. The low pressure cells are known as the Aleutian and Icelandic lows. The development of these cells of low pressure is related to the different heating characteristics of land and water. In the Northern Hemisphere the subpolar low pressure belt is interrupted by the large landmasses of North America and Eurasia. The extremes in the heating and cooling of these landmasses interrupt the low pressure system. As a result, the high pressures on land separated by low pressures on the water create an undulating or wavy circulation in these latitudes. This pattern is especially well developed in winter. The amplitude (height and length) of these waves and their location in the circulation pattern relative to the ground are a primary basis of long-range weather forecasting in the middle latitudes.

### POLAR EASTERLIES

Winds called the polar easterlies travel out of the polar highs into the subpolar low pressure area. This wind system is more highly modified and complicated in the Arctic than in the Antarctic area. The result is that the polar easterlies are, for the most part, of little importance in the Northern Hemisphere. The polar easterlies are of moderate velocity most of the time and only occasionally are intensified into galelike winds. It now appears that, at least at the earth's surface, the polar easterlies are a minor wind system.

### POLAR HIGHS

The cells of high pressure found poleward of about 70 degrees in the Northern and Southern hemispheres are thought to be relatively calm areas of subsiding cold air. These are regions of diverging winds, similar to the subtropical highs, but certainly much colder due to their latitude. Unlike the other pressure belts, however, the polar highs are not belts of pressure encircling the earth. Instead they are cells in the polar regions, and out of their equatorward margins emerge the polar easterlies.

## MODIFICATIONS OF THE PLANETARY WIND AND PRESSURE SYSTEMS

Specific conditions on the earth modify the planetary wind and pressure systems just discussed. The modifications vary from those planetary in scope to those local in character. Inclination and parallelism create planetary modifications. The presence of land and water masses creates continental variations, while differences in topography and elevation cause regional and local variations.

### LATITUDINAL SHIFTING OF PRESSURE AND WIND SYSTEMS DUE TO INCLINATION AND PARALLELISM

If the earth's axis were not inclined to the plane of the ecliptic, the pressure belts and prevailing wind systems would remain in the same latitudes. In reality, the pressure and wind systems shift latitudinally in response to inclination and parallelism of the earth's axis. Because the vertical rays of the sun migrate between 23½ degrees north latitude and 23½ degrees south latitude during the course of a year, seasons develop in both hemispheres. Wind and pressure belts may be expected to migrate latitudinally because of thermal control. Thus when the sun's vertical rays are north of the equator, the wind and pressure belts in both hemispheres shift northward. For example, when the sun's rays are vertical at 23½ degrees north latitude, a major portion of the intertropical convergence lies in the Northern Hemisphere. The reverse situation occurs when the sun's rays are vertical south of the equator.

The shifting of the pressure and wind belts is complicated; the extent and rapidity of the shift vary from one place to another. The migrations are not so great over the oceans as over the lands because the thermal contrasts are less over the oceans than over landmasses. Also, the migrations lag a month or so behind the sun's vertical rays, because of the time required for the shifting sun to heat the atmosphere to its maximum degree. In reality, the pressure and wind systems are not truly migrating; instead, changes are occurring in the position and intensity of their centers of action.

The latitudinal shifting of the pressure and wind systems has many important climatic implications. Some latitudes are in intermediate positions between the major pressure and wind systems, and therefore experience contrasting weather conditions in winter and summer. The tropical savanna areas of the world, for example, generally lie about 5 to 10 degrees north and south of the equator. They experience conditions similar to those of the intertropical convergence during their high-sun period and conditions related to the trade winds during their low-sun periods.

## MONSOONS

Because land surfaces heat and cool faster than water surfaces, the temperature change from season to season must be greater over continents than over the oceans. This unequal heating of land and water areas on a continental scale produces large semipermanent high and low pressure systems that govern the flow of air and energy. The monsoon, which comes from the Arabic word for season, *mausim,* is an example of this phenomenon. Although monsoons occur in southeastern Africa, western Africa, southwestern United States, and northeast Australia, they are best developed in southern Asia.

The monsoons of southern Asia are primarily a response to the heating and cooling of the Asiatic landmass (Figure 5.11). This change is reflected in the large movement of the intertropical convergence between winter and summer. Conditions in the upper atmosphere also affect the surface winds and shifting pressure belts, however.

In May and June the westerly wind system over India and Pakistan lessens and disappears. At the same time a warm anticyclone forms over the Tibetan Plateau. As a consequence, during the summer period the intertropical convergence migrates poleward more than 30 degrees from the equator. In June the southwestern monsoon begins with the air flowing from the oceanic areas to the land. A deluge of rain spreads across India, greening the environment and providing water for agriculture. To over 700 million Indians the monsoons provide the moisture for food production.

The southwest monsoons are composed of two main branches. One branch originates in the Bay of Bengal and flows into Burma and northeast India. This area includes some of the wettest places in the world. When the monsoons rise on the Himalayan mountain slopes, orographic precipitation occurs. The mountain town of Cherrapunji receives an average annual rainfall of 1,168 cm (455 inches). About 85 to 90 percent of this rain comes from May to September. The rainiest month recorded was June, 1956, when 570 cm (222 inches) fell.

A second branch of the monsoon originates in the Arabian Sea and flows onto the Konkan and Malabar coasts of western India. The monsoon rains spread inland, affecting the entire subcontinent. The monsoons themselves are not continuous. Rather they depend on low pressure areas within the major system to create convectional currents that increase the amount of rain. Although the monsoon rains are welcomed because they provide water for agriculture, on occasion they cause great floods that not only destroy crops but also take their toll in loss of life and property damage.

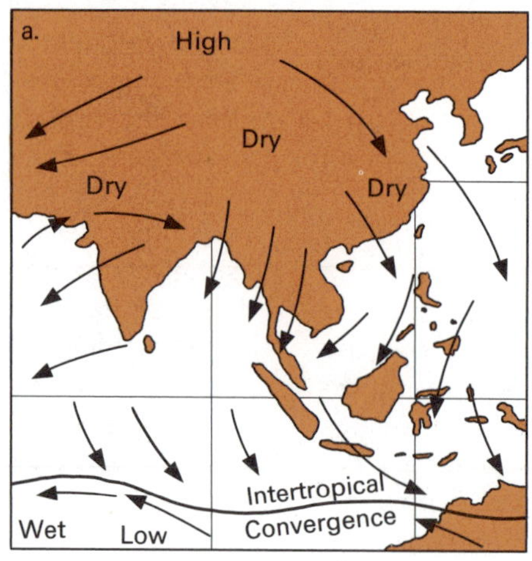


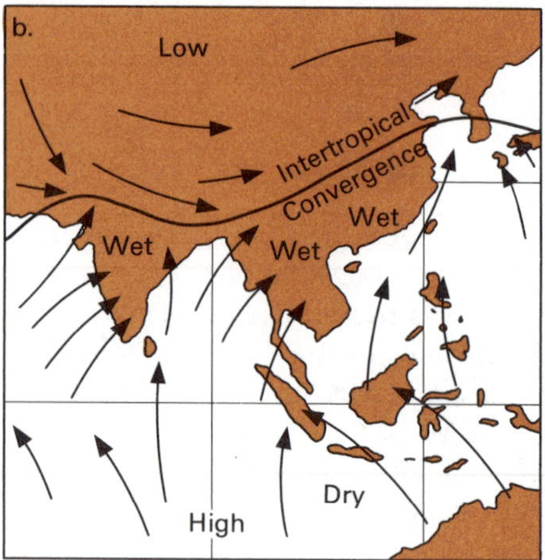


**FIGURE 5.11**
The monsoon system of southern Asia. A dominant feature of the Asian monsoon is a 180-degree reversal of wind direction between the winter (*a*) and summer (*b*) seasons. Note the greater migration of the intertropical convergence between the two seasons.

The summer monsoons, with their southwesterly winds and associated rain, last until September when they begin to retreat and clear skies appear again. The intertropical convergence has now migrated toward the equator. As the northern winter develops, one branch of the subtropical jet stream flows north of the Tibetan Plateau and a second branch south of the plateau over India. Beneath the southern branch of the jet stream, the air subsides, creating dominant northeasterly winds across the Indian subcontinent, a 180-degree reversal of wind direction from the summer monsoons. The season of the dominant northeasterly monsoons extends from January to May. The fine sunny period of January and February extends into the extremely hot, dry periods of April and May. As the land becomes parched, agriculture becomes unproductive, and farmers begin to watch the sky for the coming of the summer monsoon.

## LOCAL WIND SYSTEMS

In a number of places winds develop in response to local differences in atmospheric pressure. Local winds are of short duration, frequently reflecting changes in diurnal pressure regimes.

### CHINOOK, FOEHN, OR SANTA ANA WINDS

The chinook, foehn, or Santa Ana winds are warm, dry downslope winds that normally originate as a response to the passing of a low pressure system (Figure 5.12*a*). When a cyclone is located on the lee side of a mountain range, air is drawn toward the lower pressure down the mountain slopes. As the air descends it is heated adiabatically, bringing much higher temperatures on the lee side of the mountain, especially in winter. Although the air temperature in response to a chinook is rarely above 5°C (41°F), it can be as high as 15° to 20°C (59° to 68°F). These winds typically occur in the High Plains just east of the Rocky Mountains from Colorado northward, where they are called chinooks; in the valleys of the Alps, where the name foehn is used; and in southern California, where they are known as Santa Ana winds.

These winds may have remarkable effects. They frequently occur on the Great Plains after a cold spell. Because the air is warm and the humidity is very low, the snow covering melts within a few hours. High winds are also associated with this phenomenon; chinooks create blinding dust storms on the High Plains of Colorado. While they develop rapidly, chinooks disappear just as quickly. Within as short a period as 48 hours, temperatures may rise 20° to 25°C (40° to 50°F) and fall the same amount. Because a snow cover can disappear in hours, the water from the melting snow may run off the frozen ground rather than slowly penetrating the soil. If a chinook occurs in the spring when the grain fields have sprouted, crops may be seriously damaged.

During the fall, high pressure builds over the mountains of southern California and Nevada, creating winds that sweep through the mountain passes to the low pressure areas along southern California's coast. After a summer of little or no rainfall, the area is almost always dry and a single spark can create a blaze that moves like a giant blowtorch. In late November, 1980, the Santa Ana "devil winds" swept fires with hurricane force for more than 100 miles, from Malibu on the coast to San Bernardino inland. This single wave of fires claimed 4 lives, 323 homes, and 150 other buildings, and

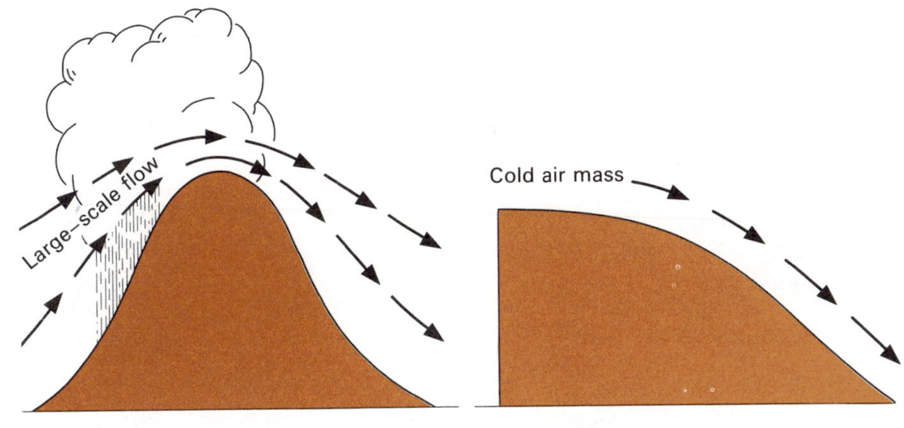


**FIGURE 5.12**
Chinook and katabatic winds.

burned 84,000 acres of land. Officials estimated structural damage at $42 million and watershed damage at another $40 million. Although the fires of 1980 were the most destructive in years, some destruction is practically a seasonal hazard for residents in the region's scenic hills and mountains. President Carter declared 3 counties disaster areas, enabling property owners to qualify for low-interest federal loans, and there was little doubt that most of the residents would rebuild on the same sites. Even after the winds subsided and the fires were controlled, two new dangers existed: disease-carrying wild rats and winter flooding. The starving rats moved down the charred slopes by the thousands to search the wreckages of fire-ravaged homes for food. U.S. Forest Service officials warned of the problems of flooding when the winter rains came. The water runoff from the denuded hills produces the possibility of floods and mudslides that can be as devastating as the fires.

### LAND AND SEA BREEZES

Local winds known as land and sea breezes can occur when temperature variations occur between day and night. On a sunny day the land heats more rapidly than the water. As a consequence the air pressure becomes lower over the land than over the water body. Because of this difference the air begins to flow from the water to the land, creating a *sea breeze.* In this process, energy and air are transferred in the opposite direction above the ground to complete the convectional cell. After sunset the land and the air above it cool more quickly than the water and the air above it. As a result the pressure relationships are reversed from those during the day. The high pressure now exists on the land and the low pressure over the water. Consequently the air movement is from the land, creating a *land breeze* (Figure 5.13).

The use of many beaches is influenced by the effects of the land and sea breezes. Brighton in southern England is noted for its cool sea breezes late in the afternoon and its warm land breezes late in the evening.

### MOUNTAIN AND VALLEY BREEZES

The mountain and valley breezes that occur in rugged terrain are also a response to local differences in temperature and pressure. During hot summer days the laterally restricted but expanding air tends to blow up the valley axis. This movement occurs because the sides of the valley become warmer than the valley floor where a high pressure cell builds up. These valley winds, known as *anabatic winds,* are usually gentle because the pressure gradient is small. At night the reverse situation occurs with the sides of the valley becoming colder than the valley bottoms. The greater loss of heat by radiation at the higher elevations, especially if there is a snow covering, creates a cold mass of air which will flow into the valley bottoms. As a result, dense cold air will gradually collect in the valley bottoms. Air moving down a slope is called a *katabatic wind* (Figure 5.12*b*). These cold winds frequently create frosts in valley bottoms, which are particularly damaging to orchards and vegetable production. Orchards are frequently planted on the valley slope rather than at the bottom to prevent early frost damage in the fall.

## THE OCEANS

The circulation of the atmosphere is closely linked to that of the oceans. As a consequence, ocean currents

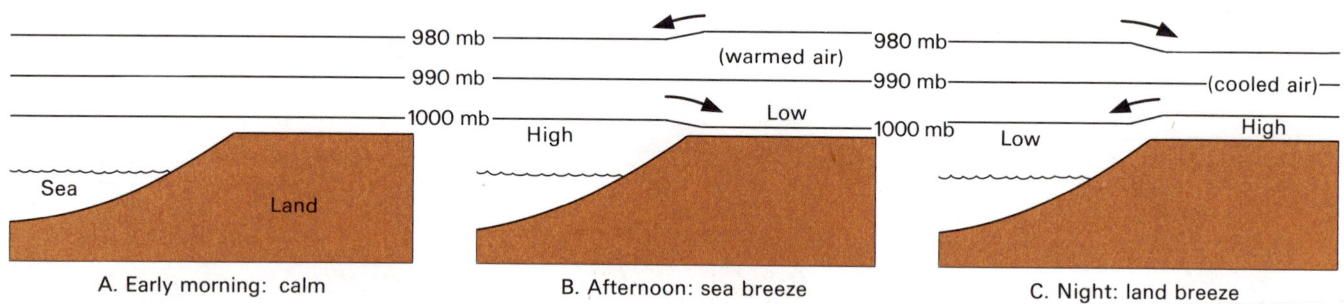


**FIGURE 5.13**
Land and sea breezes. Because temperature changes occur more rapidly on land than at sea, air pressure over land and sea changes on a diurnal basis. The diagram shows the resulting movement of air. (After Petterssen, 1969)

are also major factors in determining weather and climatic patterns.

## OCEAN CURRENTS

In 1856 Matthew Fontaine Maury wrote in his book, *The Physical Geography of the Sea:*

> **There is a river in the ocean. In the severest droughts it never fails, and in the mightiest floods . . . it never overflows. Its banks and its bottoms are of cold water, while its current is of warm. The Gulf of Mexico is its fountain, and its mouth is in the Arctic Seas. It is the Gulf Stream. There is in the world no other such majestic flow of waters. (M.F. Maury, *The Physical Geography of the Sea* [New York: Harper & Bro., 1856], p. 25)**

Although the Gulf Stream has long been recognized, it is only one of the major ocean currents that make up the oceanic circulatory system. The study of the ocean currents began when sailors first started traveling on the oceans. This study is far from complete, but a general understanding of the processes that create these currents now exists.

### Origin of Ocean Currents

The major force moving the ocean currents is the world's wind system (Figure 5.14). Winds blowing across water exert a force that moves the water, but because the friction of the water is much stronger than air, the movement of water is much slower. The fastest speeds are a few kilometers per hour, but more typically water is moved only a few kilometers per day. The ocean currents do not respond to short variations in wind movements, but reflect the average conditions over a long period of time, such as a year or more.

Although the world's wind systems are the major generators of surface currents in the oceans, other factors also influence the movement of ocean currents. The most significant of these is the Coriolis force. Ocean currents are deflected by the earth's rotation in the same way as winds: to the right of their path of motion in the Northern Hemisphere and to the left in the Southern Hemisphere. Because the Coriolis force is greater in the higher latitudes, this deflection is more apparent there. As a consequence of the deflective force, the direction of the surface currents does not coincide with the wind direction. In general the difference between wind direction and the direction of the currents varies from about 15 degrees in shallow ocean depths to a maximum of 45 degrees in the deep oceans. Further, the angle increases with depth so that at depths of about 100 meters (300 feet) the current may flow in the opposite direction to the surface waters. This phenomenon was first discovered by V.W. Ekman and is known as the *Ekman spiral.* The principle of the Ekman spiral is that the moving surface layer of water sets the layer below in motion. This lower layer in turn exerts a frictional drag on the water immediately beneath it, causing it to flow. Each successively deeper layer moves more slowly because of the momentum lost in each transfer between the layers. As each layer moves it is deflected by the Coriolis force. As each layer is deflected to the right or left, depending upon the hemisphere, the direc-

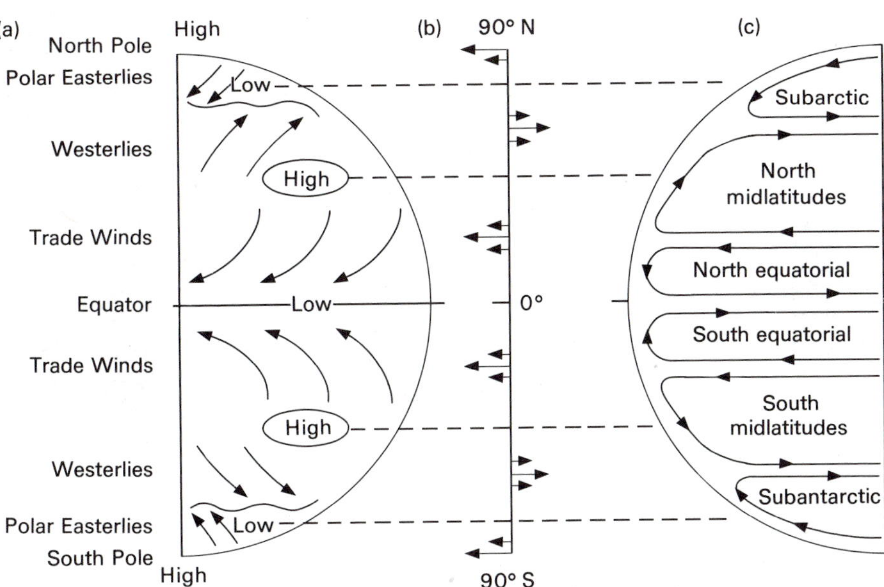


**FIGURE 5.14**
Hypothetical relationship between global wind systems and ocean currents. This schematic diagram illustrates the close relationships between the world wind and pressure systems and the world's ocean currents. (Adapted from *Physical Geography, Principles and Applications* by John E. Oliver. © 1979 by Wadsworth, Inc. Reprinted by permission of Wadsworth Publishing Company, Belmont, California 94002.)

tion of movement shifts with depth until there is a complete 180-degree reversal.

Within the great oceanic circulations there are hills of water that rise as much as 2 meters above the general water levels. The water piles up on these hills until the gravitational force acting on individual particles of water balances the Coriolis force, and the water particles begin to slide down the slope of the rise. This gravitational action plus the influence of the Coriolis force produces *geostrophic currents.*

## Movements within the Oceans

All of the ice-free oceans have developed a system of currents (Figure 5.15). These huge, slow-moving circular whirls are known as *gyre.* Because the gyre are similar in all oceans, the circulation in the North Atlantic will be used as an example.

Beginning at the equator, the north and south Atlantic equatorial currents move westward, deriving their energy from the trade winds. Due to the deflection created by the Coriolis force, these currents have a nearly due west movement. The currents pile up against the eastern shores of South America, and because the trade winds are weak along the equator, some of the water begins to flow eastward, creating the equatorial countercurrent.

As the equatorial current is turned northward by the continent of South America and the Coriolis force, it enters the Caribbean Sea and is known as the Caribbean current. The current that passes east of the Antilles is known as the Antilles current. The Caribbean current moves northwest through the Caribbean to the mouth of the Gulf of Mexico at the Straits of Yucatan. In the Gulf of Mexico the current moves eastward, and at the Straits of Florida, the current known as the Florida current reunites with the Antilles current to form the Gulf Stream.

The Gulf Stream forms a vast river several hundred miles wide flowing within the ocean. As it moves along the east coast of the United States it is strengthened by the prevailing westerly winds and is deflected to the east in the area between 35 and 45 degrees north latitude. As it moves into the Atlantic beyond the Grand Banks it widens and slows until it becomes a vast, slow-moving current called the North Atlantic Drift. Off the coast of Europe this warm but cooling current divides. Part of it moves northward past Great Britain and Norway into the Arctic. To compensate for the penetration of this relatively warm water into the Arctic, there

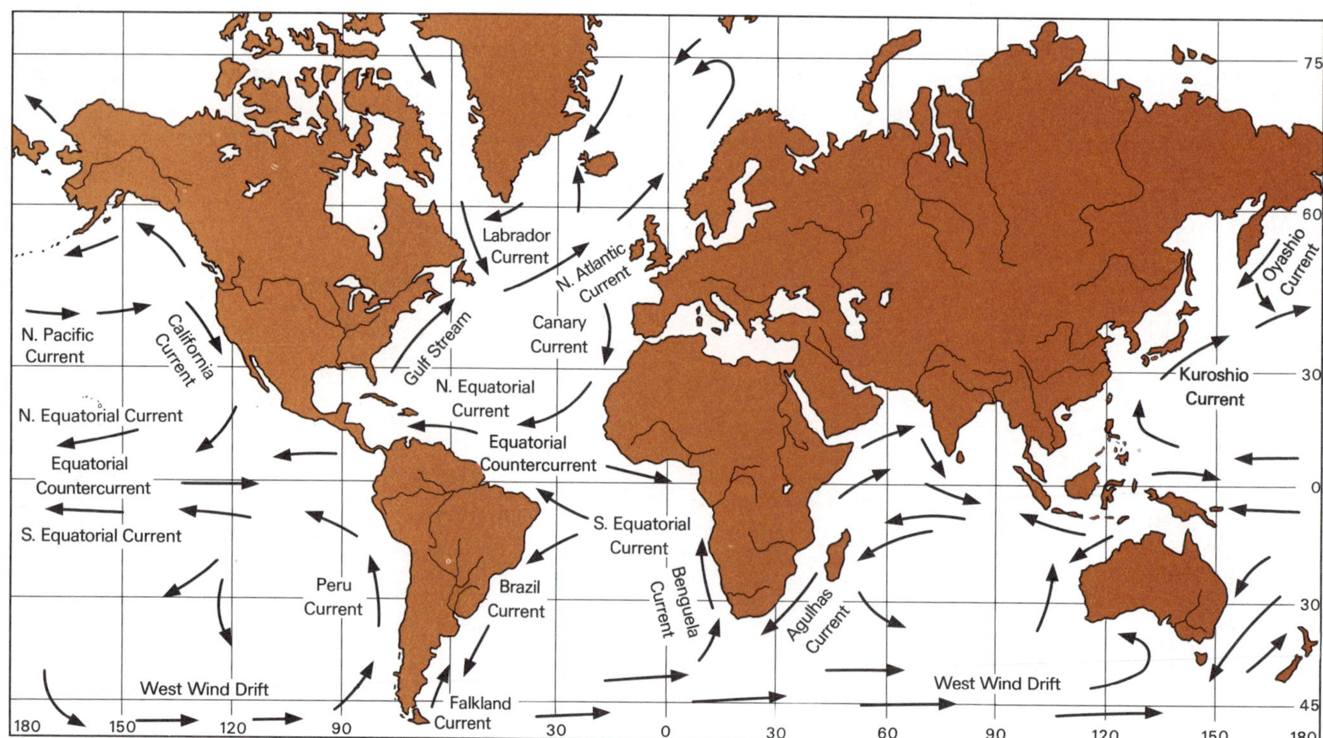


FIGURE 5.15
Surface currents of the oceans. (After U.S. Navy Hydrographic Office)

is a returning cold current flowing east of Greenland known as the East Greenland current and as the Labrador current along eastern Canada. Where these currents encounter the Gulf Stream, the cold air, with its low capacity for holding water, frequently creates a dense fog that has the appearance of smoke rising from the water. The second part of the Atlantic Drift moves southward along the western coast of Europe and continues along the coast of northwestern Africa as a relatively cool current known as the Canaries current. As the Canaries current continues equatorward, it eventually merges with the north equatorial current. The clockwise circulation of the North Atlantic leaves a central zone with no defined currents. This zone of calm water is known as the Sargasso Sea.

## THE OCEANS AS ENERGY STOREHOUSES

The great heat capacity of oceans makes them enormous storage banks of energy (Figure 5.16). A great deal of energy is required to warm the oceans. For example, in the middle latitudes the ocean temperatures during the summer rise less than one degree centigrade each day. A number of factors are responsible for the slow heating. First, water must absorb almost five times as much heat energy to raise its temperature one degree centigrade as does the same volume of dry land. Second, water in the ocean is moving both vertically and horizontally, so that the energy is continually being dispersed. Third, some of the incoming radiation is used to evaporate the water rather than heat it. As a consequence diurnal and seasonal changes in the oceans are gradual and modest.

The difference in the rate of heating and cooling causes continents and oceans to have different temperature regimes. In the Northern Hemisphere, the continents in the middle latitudes are warmest in July and coldest in January, but the oceans in the middle latitudes are warmest in September and coldest in March. Also, the annual range of temperatures is much smaller over oceans than over land.

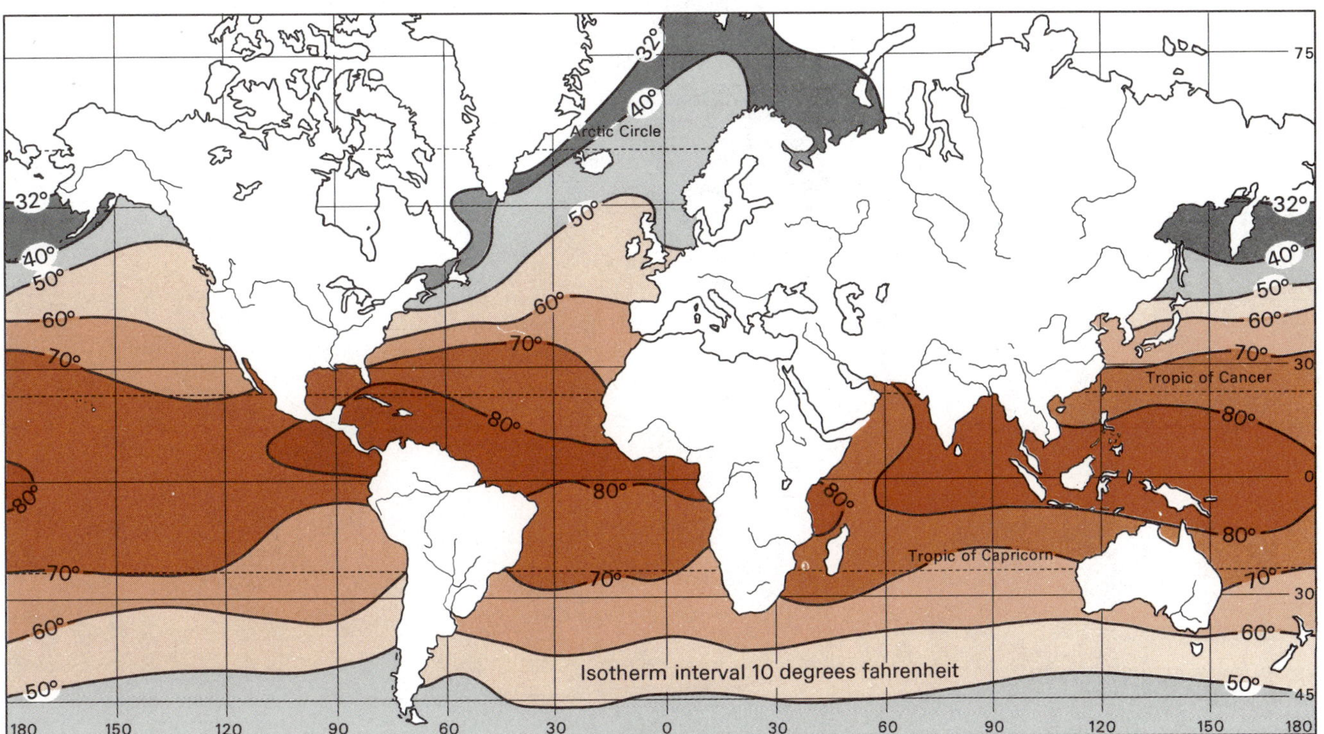


**FIGURE 5.16**

Mean annual temperature of the sea surface (°F). Temperatures of the sea waters in general decrease relatively uniformly from the equator to the poles. Note the warming influence of the North Atlantic Drift on the northern European coast. (Source: Figure 7.9 [after Schott, 1926 and 1935] from Miller and Langdon, 1964. Copyright © 1964 by Harper & Row, Publishers, Inc. Reprinted by permission of the publisher.)

In recent years anomalies of temperature have been found to develop for one or two years in the oceans. Large areas of the oceans have been found where the temperatures may be one or more degrees higher or lower than the water surrounding them (Figure 5.17). These oceanic reservoirs are believed to have a significant effect on the climate over extremely wide areas. In 1971 and 1972, for example, a large mass of warm sea water developed off the east coast of the United States. This warm water may have been responsible for the unusual weather experienced in the areas of the North Atlantic Ocean. During this period the East Coast of the United States experienced precipitation far above average, and the additional energy may have been a factor in energizing Hurricane Agnes, which devastated the East Coast. Further, this warm area may have disrupted the westerly wind system sufficiently to cause droughts and severe frosts in the western Soviet Union during the summer of 1972.

## WIND ENERGY

Because the atmosphere is heated unevenly, a major part of the solar energy reaching the earth is transformed into wind energy. The wind is thus a potential source of energy for human activities.

### WIND ENERGY THROUGH TIME

Moving air was one of the earliest sources of power. Evidence indicates that in Persia more than 2,000 years ago, a simple, vertical-axis wind turbine provided power for the grinding of grain. This simple windmill spread throughout southwestern Asia and the Mediterranean. The simple horizontal-axis windmill was developed somewhat later and is still in existence in the Mediterranean region. For example, on the island of Crete more than 10,000 windmills, which have not advanced in technology for hundreds of years, are used to pump water to irrigate crops.

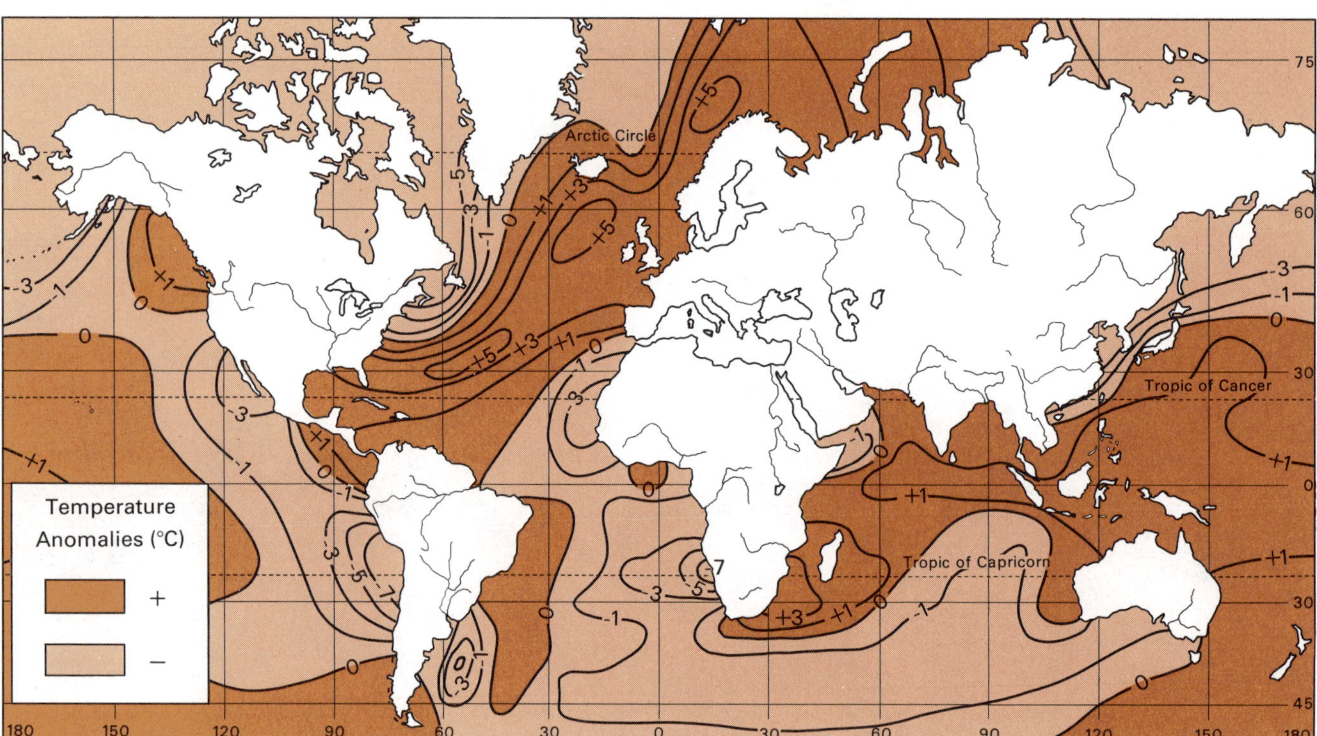


**FIGURE 5.17**

Average annual ocean temperature anomalies (°C). Positive anomalies indicate temperatures that are higher than the average for a particular latitude, and negative anomalies indicate the converse. Compare this map with Figure 15.16 and locate the warm and cold currents of the world. (Source: Figure 7.4 [after James, Markus, and Sokalsky, 1947] from Miller and Langdon, 1964. Copyright © 1964 by Harper & Row, Publishers, Inc. Reprinted by permission of the publisher.)

By the Middle Ages the windmill was found throughout most of Europe. In the 14th century the Dutch made many improvements in its design. As it became more efficient, its power was used not only for milling grain and making paper and lumber, but also for draining marshes and swamplands. By the end of the 19th century there were more than 9,000 wind machines in Holland alone. However, the Danes with over 100,000 windmills in their country were the world leaders in utilizing wind power. By 1890 the Danish government began the installation of a network of wind-powered generators.

The windmill became important as a source of power in the United States about 1870. The most popular model was a multi-vane rotor type that developed about ⅙ hp in a 15 mph wind and could pump 35 gallons of water per minute to a height of about 25 feet. Between 1870 and 1930 about 6 million of these were installed on farms; about 150,000 are still in use. These windmills played a vital role in the settlement of the American plains. Without them beef production would not have evolved, nor would the railroads have been built through the West, because both the cattle ranches and the railroads depended on the multi-vane windmills to supply them with water.

Beginning in the 1890s the windmill was used to generate small quantities of electrical energy. By the 1930s these multi-vane windmills with 14-meter (46-foot) long propellers could produce about 200 watts at 12 volts direct current in a 32 kilometers per hour (20 mph) wind. They were produced by the hundreds of thousands to provide electricity to charge lead-acid batteries for use on farms that were beyond the electric power grid of the day. Without this source of electricity thousands of farm homes would have been denied the use of electricity for lights, refrigeration, and the playing of radios. With the expansion of the power grid into the country by the Rural Electrification Administration most of these windmills disappeared within a few years in the late 1930s. Since then wind power has played essentially no role in the energy economy of the United States.

## WIND POWER POTENTIAL

Only crude estimates are available as to the potential wind power in the world, but we know it is tremendous. In 1961 the World Meteorological Organization selected some 350 sites around the world to measure wind speeds from air currents 50 to 110 meters (160 to 360 feet) above the ground, heights corresponding to those at which windmills might be built. From these observations and others it was estimated that there were some 20 billion kilowatts of wind power available at favorable sites throughout the world.

In the early 1970s William E. Heronemus, professor of engineering at the University of Massachusetts, proposed to build 300,000 wind turbines in the Great Plains at a spacing of about one for each 2.6 square kilometers (one per square mile). It was estimated that the network could provide the equivalent of 189,000 megawatts of power. The power system would actually have a larger installed capacity that would never be achieved because of the variations of the wind velocity in the course of a year. The 189,000 megawatt capacity was significant since the total installed capacity of the United States generating plants was estimated in 1970 at 360,000 megawatts. This proposed system of windmills was never initiated.

## SITING OF WIND TURBINES

The ideal location for a wind machine is one where winds are constant and their speed great. Thus the suitability of a site can be characterized by analyzing wind statistics and topographical data. In the past most of the regions where many windmills were in use were flat areas having little resistance to wind movement, such as the low plains of Denmark and The Netherlands. As wind machines became larger for the production of electricity, location factors became increasingly important. In evaluating the wind power potential of a region it must be remembered that the power produced is proportional to the cube of the wind speed. Reduction of wind velocity has a major effect on the output of electricity. For example, the reduction at a location of average wind velocity from 12.5 to 10 miles per hour represents a lowering of wind power of about 50 percent.

Because the large wind machine has not been used to produce electricity in the United States, data are largely lacking as to its effectiveness in different topographic settings. There is a general principle that wind velocity increases with height since air flow at ground level is retarded by friction. This principle has been found to be reliable on plains, so wind towers several hundred feet high have been proposed. In hilly and mountainous regions, local conditions must be investigated.

In the United States the first modern wind machine was built in 1941 and operated for about three and a half years. From a selection of possibly 50 sites in Vermont, it was located at Grandpa's Knob. It operated in wind speeds up to 185 kilometers (115 miles) per hour and generated as much as 1,500 kilowatts of electrical power. In 1945 the windmill experienced structural problems and the experiment was abandoned.

Although the operation was technically and economically unsuccessful, the information it provided was valuable for future considerations. Meteorological data and theory proved to be faulty in predicting the speed of winds to be expected at Grandpa's Knob. Actual data revealed that the mean annual velocity was only 27 kilometers (17 miles) per hour instead of the 38 kilometers (24 miles) per hour that had been predicted. Further, prevailing wind direction was from the southwest rather than the west as anticipated on the basis of standard tables showing progressive shifts of wind direction according to altitude. Because the level of wind was considerably lower than expected, the electrical output was only about 30 percent of that originally predicted. Subsequent analysis showed that Grandpa's Knob was in the wind shadow of the Green Mountains in Vermont and the air flow was adversely affected. From these observations it became evident that the selection of a site requires wind measurements taken over a period of several years rather than theoretical calculations alone.

On Grandpa's Knob, one of the most accurate indicators of long-term wind velocity was found to be the progressive deformity of trees, particularly balsam fir. At an annual mean wind velocity of 27 kilometers (17 miles) per hour, the firs exhibited flagging, a condition in which the branches extend downward. As the mean annual velocity increases, the vegetation gets lower and lower, so that at an annual mean of 43 kilometers (27 miles) per hour the growth is limited to a living carpet no more than 15 centimeters (6 inches) off the ground. This sensitive ecological indicator defines the change in the path of mountain wind streams, even within distances of 300 meters (100 yards).

## OBSTACLES AND ADVANTAGES

Since the early 1970s about a half dozen modern wind machines have been constructed in such areas as the Hawaiian Islands, Colorado, and Washington, and more than 30 additional sites are planned. However, a number of obstacles must be overcome before wind power can be considered seriously as even a limited source of energy. Because of a lack of interest in wind power in the past half-century, there has been little experimentation to solve major engineering problems. A major obstacle in the turbine design is the need to develop inexpensive gears that can translate the slow rotational speed of the turbine blade into a much faster speed to operate the electrical generator. The small backyard windmill that served farms so well in the 19th century has not provided the prototype for a large wind machine with a 100-foot vane capable of generating electricity. Because tens of thousands of such wind machines would be required to provide a network sufficient to produce a large quantity of electricity, a serious question remains as to the economic feasibility of such an undertaking.

The generation of electricity by wind movement is undependable because wind is not constant. Energy must be stored during periods when electricity is generated so that it can be used when winds are not available. The problem of storing electricity exists for both wind power and solar power. As we have seen, a system has not yet been developed for this tremendous task.

The development of wind power also presents some environmental problems. With its growing awareness of the environment, will the public tolerate thousands of towers 60 to 120 meters (200 to 400 feet) high? Further, if a 30-meter (100-foot) blade should break, persons nearby could be seriously injured.

While there are problems in the development of wind power, there are also some advantages. Wind power is a renewable resource. It will never be depleted and is always free to anyone who can harness it. Wind power is pollution-free as well.

## FUTURE

As the cost of traditional fossil fuels rises, attention will be focused on wind power. The first major thrust is likely to come from small windmills similar to those used to generate small quantities of electricity in farmyards during the 1930s. The technical problems of operating these mills have been solved, making them economically feasible. They will not only supplement the conventional sources of electricity, but when an excess supply of electricity is produced, the electricity can be purchased by the electric companies.

The development of the large wind machine network producing large quantities of electricity is far in the future. Its rate of implementation will depend on its place in the total energy economy.

# POLLUTION IN THE OCEANS

Athelstan F. Spilhaus of the National Oceanographic and Atmospheric Administration has defined oceanic pollution as "anything animate or inanimate that by its excess reduces the quality of living." The key word in this definition is *excess,* for most of the substances called pollutants, such as sediments, salts, metals, and organic materials, are already in the oceans as a response to natural processes. Certain pollutants in the ocean are unquestionably harmful; the difficult problem is to determine what level of concentration is harmful. Research on the effects of pollutants on the oceanic environment is still in its infancy. Only on rare occasions has it been possible to directly link a specific ocean pollutant with permanent biological damage.

## SOURCES OF OCEANIC POLLUTANTS

Pollutants come to the oceans from a wide variety of sources, such as partially treated urban sewage, industrial wastes, intentional discharges from ships that are removing ballast water and cleaning storage tanks, accidental spills from oil wells and tankers, and oil seeps from the sea floor. Another major oceanic pollutant is fecal waste: treated sewage is frequently deposited in the ocean by cities. Industrial wastes enter the oceans from a vast array of manufacturing processes. Power plants and ships dispose of thermal wastes in the ocean. Ships rid themselves of wastes by throwing them overboard. Also entering the oceans are atmospheric pollutants, including such minute particles as crop sprays, exhaust fumes from automobiles, and carbon and metallic oxides from fires.

### OIL POLLUTION

Of all oceanic pollutants, petroleum and its products are most controversial and evoke the greatest emotion. It is estimated that from 2 to 5 million tons of oil enter the oceans annually. Of this amount at least half is from land-based sources, such as refineries, industrial plants, and service stations. However, oil pollution from ships is an equally serious problem. Oil tankers pollute the ocean by three means: (*a*) by accidents, such as collisions or running aground, (*b*) by spills during loading and unloading, and (*c*) by intentional discharge, which includes the purging of bilge water from the oil tanks and the cleaning of the oil tanks. After a tanker unloads its oil, water is pumped into its tanks so that it will not ride so high in the water. Any oil that is left in the tanks mixes with the water and is discharged when the ballast is pumped from the tanks when the vessel reloads with oil.

The problem of oil spills did not receive serious attention until the Torrey Canyon disaster in southern England. This large oil tanker ran aground in March 1967 and for three months leaked oil into the sea. The oil spread on the coasts of southern England and northern France, causing great environmental damage. Oil spills gained further attention when wells drilled on the continental shelf began to leak. The Santa Barbara oil spill was a notable example of this type of spill, and it catalyzed interest in coastal environmentalism. From more than 20,000 wells drilled in the American continental shelf, however, only three wells and one pipeline accident have spilled more than 1,000 tons of oil each since 1953. In contrast, the tanker operations spill about 20 times as much oil annually as does oil production from the world's continental shelves. Nevertheless, the possible consequences of oil spills from offshore production have been the critical issue in debates as to whether the federal government should lease additional offshore areas for drilling.

The controversy centers mainly on the complicated interplay between the oil pollutants and the life forms that inhabit the sea. Proponents of leasing point to the apparent harmony of offshore petroleum production and the abundant marine life of the Gulf of Mexico. In their opinion the economic factors of production are the only ones to be considered for further exploration and drilling. Opponents contend that the low-level but constant pollution may not have a short-term effect but may cause environmental devastation over a long period. Laboratory and field studies indicate that as the pollutants are concentrated at higher and higher levels, the biological food chain may be affected.

Studies indicate that the immediate environmental damage of a spill is related to (*a*) the volume of the spill, (*b*) the rate of release, and (*c*) the physical properties of the oil. Time frequently helps determine the amount of damage a coastline will suffer, because the lighter oils may evaporate before they reach the shore, and the ocean turbulence breaks large oil slicks into smaller patches. In general, weathering processes ameliorate the onshore impact of oil spills that take a long time to reach shore.

### OCEANIC DUMPING

Coastal cities have for many years used the oceans as a place to dispose of a wide variety of wastes. A number of these wastes have generated controversy. Some industries discharge heavy metals and organic compounds into municipal waste-water systems whose effluents ultimately reach the oceans. Some of these metals, such as mercury, chromium, lead, zinc, cadmium, copper, nickel, and silver, are extremely toxic and are subject to stringent regulations. Of the chemical materials, synthetic organic compounds such as DDT are most dangerous. Because these metals and organic compounds are harmful to all living things, the best control is to prevent pollution at its source.

Other waste materials that are considered undesirable in the oceans are those with nutrient values. They are decomposed by bacteria, which consume oxygen in the process. It is possible to overwhelm a local area, such as the New York Bight, where waste from New York City is dumped. The lack of oxygen in the water has created a "dead" area nearly devoid of living creatures. This area illustrates that such waste materials must be dumped in the ocean at the right places and in reasonable amounts. Those areas that are truly ocean must be distinguished from inland waterways, bays, and shallow ocean, where pollution causes more harm. Standards for the type of materials that can be dumped into the oceans are needed, as well as standards for oceanic water quality. Finally, a research program must be developed to provide a better understanding of the waste problem in the oceans.

### THERMAL POLLUTION

Heated water from power plants is discharged into the sea because it is a convenient source of cooling water. The water discharged from a power plant is on the average about 10°C (21°F) higher than it was on intake. This increased temperature is rarely harmful to mature marine animals, but it usually kills eggs, larvae, and young animals. Water discharge pipes would be better placed far offshore in deeper water where there are fewer living organisms.

## CONCLUSION

The global circulation of the atmosphere results from the uneven distribution of energy over the earth. The relationships between temperature and air pressure are fundamental to an understanding of air movements. Differences in air pressure from one place to another cause air to begin to move. After the air is in motion, various other forces affect its movement. Of these, the earth's rotation and the contact with other air masses are most important.

The pressure systems of the world are greatly influenced by the relative proportions of land and water. The world circulation system is least interrupted in the Southern Hemisphere, where a water surface prevails. In the Northern Hemisphere, with its land and water bodies, the circulation system is complex. The thermal differences between continents and oceans cause great pressure cells to evolve, influencing air movements.

Wind was used to power mills more than 2,000 years ago. The use of windmills gradually evolved in areas where wind movement was consistent, but in recent times windmills have largely disappeared as other energy sources have become available. Once again, however, as fossil fuels increase in cost, the potential of wind power is being investigated. While widespread use of wind power is far in the future, local developments could supplement traditional energy sources.

## STUDY QUESTIONS

1 What is air pressure? How is it measured?
2 Distinguish between barometric surface, barometric slope, and pressure gradient. What is the relationship between them?
3 How does the equation of continuity explain the movement of air?
4 What are the four laws of air movement?
5 What is the effect of the Coriolis force on air movement? Why is the Coriolis force most effective in the higher latitudes?
6 What causes a geostrophic wind?
7 How is a turbulent eddy in the air created? What is its importance?
8 What factors influence the development of the world's atmospheric circulation?
9 Describe the atmospheric circulation of the world

if insolation is the single controlling factor.

10 Describe the arrangement of the pressure and wind belts of the world if rotation is the single controlling factor.

11 Why are insolation and rotation the most important factors in establishing the world's pressure and wind belts?

12 How do the continental landmasses affect the world's pressure and wind systems?

13 Describe the major characteristics of the pressure and wind belts of the world.

14 What is the importance of the polar front?

15 Explain the factors that modify the planetary wind and pressure systems.

16 Explain the development of the monsoon over the Asian continent.

17 What is the origin of the chinook winds?

18 Explain the development of land-sea breezes.

19 What is the cause of an anabatic wind? A katabatic wind?

20 What is the origin of ocean currents? What is the Ekman spiral? Explain.

21 Why are oceans storehouses of energy?

22 Why does the temperature of the oceans differ from place to place?

23 Explain the importance of the windmill as a source of energy in the United States.

24 Discuss the potential of wind power in the world.

25 What are the important considerations in the siting of wind turbines?

26 What are some obstacles to the development of wind power? Some advantages?

27 What are the sources of ocean pollution?

# 6

# ATMOSPHERIC MOISTURE AND PRECIPITATION

## KEY WORDS

absolute humidity
acid rain
adiabatic cooling
cirrus cloud
condensation level
convectional precipitation
cumulus cloud
cyclonic precipitation
dew point
humidity
hydrologic cycle
latent heat of condensation
latent heat of vaporization
orographic precipitation
potential evapotranspiration
relative humidity
stratus cloud
sublimation
transpiration
vapor pressure
water budget

Water is one of the earth's most valuable resources. Without moisture, life could not exist. Try to imagine what the weather would be like if the earth's atmosphere had no moisture. Weather would exist, but it would have little resemblance to what we experience. Because temperature differences would exist from the tropics to the poles, cyclones and anticyclones would exist. Without moisture, however, these arid storms would likely produce vast whirlwinds of dust. Without the tempering effects of the oceans, dynamic storms would alternately pull scorching heat from the tropics, then intense cold from the Arctic, into the middle latitudes. A moistureless atmosphere would create a moonlike landscape on the earth.

## ATMOSPHERIC HUMIDITY

The *humidity* of the atmosphere is its content of water vapor. When air is completely dry, which never happens in nature, its humidity is zero. When the atmosphere is holding all the water vapor it is capable of retaining, it is said to be *saturated.* The capacity of an air mass to hold water depends to a great extent upon its temperature (Figure 6.1). The general rule is that the capacity of an air mass to hold water vapor increases as the temperature rises. Further, it increases at a growing rate. For example, if the temperature of 0.028 cubic meters (one cubic foot) of air increases from zero to 10 degrees centigrade (32° to 50°F), its capacity grows by 4.6 grams, but if the temperature rises from 25 to 35 degrees centigrade (77° to 95°F), its capacity increases by 16.6 grams, nearly four times as much moisture. Thus, when the temperature rises on a hot summer day, the air becomes capable of holding much more moisture than when the air temperature on a cold winter day experiences a similar increase.

The total amount of water vapor contained in a given mass of air is called *absolute humidity.* It is expressed in weight of the water vapor per unit volume, as grams per cubic centimeters. Absolute humidity is of limited value for meteorological observations. One of the reasons that it is little used is that the volume of a given weight of air varies with the air pressure.

Of much greater significance is *relative humidity.* Relative humidity designates the proportion of water vapor actually in an air mass in relation to the maximum amount possible at a given temperature. It is always expressed as a comparison, ratio, fraction, or percentage. Thus, if the atmosphere at a given temperature contains half of the water vapor it is capable of holding, its relative humidity is 50 percent. Relative humidity is always altered with a change in the amount of water vapor or with a change in temperature. In contrast, a change in temperature will not alter the absolute humidity or total amount of water vapor in an air mass. It is quite possible for the absolute humidity to be quite large and the relative humidity to be quite low if the temperature is high.

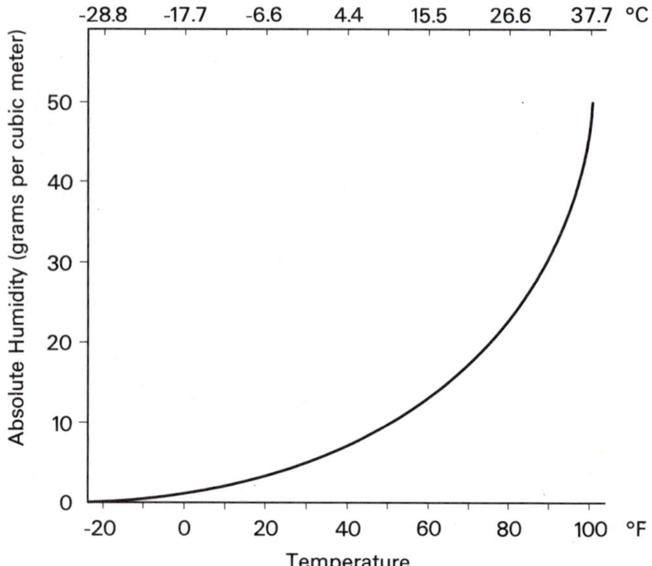


**FIGURE 6.1**
Maximum amount of water vapor in a cubic meter of air at a given temperature. As temperature increases, so does the capacity of the atmosphere to hold moisture. For example, at a temperature of 10°C (50°F) the atmosphere can hold, at saturation, 10 grams of water per cubic meter, but at 20°C (68°F) the atmosphere can hold 20 grams of water per cubic meter. (After List, 1971)

Relative humidity is usually measured by use of a wet-bulb and a dry-bulb thermometer. These two instruments are used simultaneously and the temperatures of both are then compared. If the air has a high relative humidity, little evaporation takes place, and the wet-bulb temperature remains near the dry-bulb temperature. When the air is dry, the water on the wet-bulb thermometer evaporates rapidly and its temperature becomes colder than the air temperature. The difference between the temperatures of the two thermometers, called the *wet-bulb depression,* indicates the relative humidity. Table 6.1 gives the relationship between the relative humidity, temperature, and depression of the wet bulb. For example, if there is an air temperature of 60°F and a wet-bulb depression of 10°F, the relative humidity is 48 percent.

**TABLE 6.1**
Relative humidity (percent). Pressure = 30 in. Hg or 1016 mb.

| Air Temperature (°F) | Depression of Wet-Bulb Thermometer (°F) | | | | | | | | | | | | | | |
|---|---|---|---|---|---|---|---|---|---|---|---|---|---|---|---|
| | 1 | 2 | 3 | 4 | 5 | 6 | 7 | 8 | 9 | 10 | 15 | 20 | 25 | 30 | 35 |
| 20 | 85 | 70 | 55 | 40 | 26 | 12 | | | | | | | | | |
| 25 | 87 | 74 | 62 | 49 | 37 | 25 | 13 | 1 | | | | | | | |
| 30 | 89 | 78 | 67 | 56 | 46 | 36 | 26 | 16 | 6 | | | | | | |
| 35 | 91 | 81 | 72 | 63 | 54 | 45 | 36 | 29 | 19 | 10 | | | | | |
| 40 | 92 | 83 | 75 | 68 | 60 | 52 | 45 | 37 | 29 | 22 | | | | | |
| 45 | 93 | 86 | 78 | 71 | 64 | 57 | 51 | 44 | 38 | 31 | | | | | |
| 50 | 93 | 87 | 80 | 74 | 67 | 61 | 55 | 49 | 43 | 38 | 10 | | | | |
| 55 | 94 | 88 | 82 | 76 | 70 | 65 | 59 | 54 | 49 | 43 | 19 | | | | |
| 60 | 94 | 89 | 84 | 78 | 73 | 68 | 63 | 58 | 53 | 48 | 26 | 5 | | | |
| 65 | 95 | 90 | 85 | 80 | 75 | 70 | 66 | 61 | 56 | 52 | 31 | 12 | | | |
| 70 | 95 | 90 | 86 | 81 | 77 | 72 | 68 | 64 | 59 | 55 | 36 | 19 | 3 | | |
| 75 | 96 | 91 | 86 | 82 | 78 | 74 | 70 | 66 | 62 | 58 | 40 | 24 | 9 | | |
| 80 | 96 | 91 | 87 | 83 | 79 | 75 | 72 | 68 | 64 | 61 | 44 | 29 | 15 | 3 | |
| 85 | 96 | 92 | 88 | 84 | 80 | 76 | 73 | 69 | 66 | 62 | 46 | 32 | 20 | 8 | |
| 90 | 96 | 92 | 89 | 85 | 81 | 78 | 74 | 71 | 68 | 65 | 49 | 36 | 24 | 13 | 3 |
| 95 | 96 | 93 | 89 | 85 | 82 | 79 | 75 | 72 | 69 | 66 | 51 | 38 | 27 | 17 | 7 |
| 100 | 96 | 93 | 89 | 86 | 83 | 80 | 77 | 73 | 70 | 68 | 54 | 41 | 30 | 21 | 12 |
| 105 | 97 | 93 | 90 | 87 | 83 | 80 | 77 | 74 | 71 | 69 | 55 | 43 | 33 | 23 | 15 |
| 110 | 97 | 93 | 90 | 87 | 84 | 81 | 78 | 75 | 73 | 70 | 57 | 46 | 36 | 26 | 18 |
| 115 | 97 | 94 | 91 | 88 | 85 | 82 | 79 | 76 | 74 | 71 | 58 | 47 | 37 | 28 | 21 |

## EVAPORATION

Evaporation is the change of water from the liquid to the gaseous form. Two conditions are necessary for evaporation to occur. First, there must be sufficient heat available at the water surface to change the liquid into a gas. This is called the *latent heat of vaporization* and it amounts to 540 calories for every gram of water. Conversely, when water vapor condenses, it releases 540 calories per gram, known as the *latent heat of condensation.*

The second condition exists when the atmosphere is not able to absorb additional water molecules. In other words, the air must be saturated. Generally the air near the water has the greatest number of water molecules, and the number decreases with height. The pressure created by the water molecules is known as *vapor pressure* and the difference in pressure is known as the *vapor-pressure gradient.* Evaporation is best developed in places such as tropical deserts, where large amounts of heat are present.

On the oceans, evaporation is the only process that changes water into its gaseous state. On land, this process is combined with *transpiration,* which refers to the passage of water through the green tissues of plants. The root systems of plants absorb water from the soil. The water gradually moves through the plants, and most of it is eventually transpired through the stomata, or leaf pores, as vapor.

The term *evapotranspiration* covers both processes by which water is changed into its gaseous form. Evapotranspiration has two distinct aspects. *Potential evapotranspiration* (PE) refers to the maximum amount of water that can be absorbed by the atmosphere from a land surface with a maximum supply of water. *Actual evapotranspiration* (AE) is the amount of moisture absorbed by the atmosphere from a land surface with a particular surface moisture condition. The AE and PE can be the same if the land surface is saturated, but if it is not, the AE is usually less than the PE.

## CONDENSATION

If the atmosphere is not saturated, its water content is in the form of water vapor. As an air mass cools, its capacity to hold water is reduced until it reaches a temperature where its saturation is 100 percent. It is then said to have reached the *saturation point* or simply the *dew point.* If the air continues to be cooled below the dew point, then the excess water vapor is released in the form of water droplets or ice particles. The only way

**PHOTO 6**
Stratus cloud. (Courtesy: National Oceanic and Atmospheric Administration)

**PHOTO 7**
Nimbostratus cloud. (Courtesy: National Oceanic and Atmospheric Administration)

**PHOTO 8**
Cumulus clouds. (Courtesy: Florida State News Bureau)

**PHOTO 9**
Stratocumulus cloud. (Courtesy: National Oceanic and Atmospheric Administration)

**PHOTO 10**
Altostratus cloud. (Courtesy: National Oceanic and Atmospheric Administration)

to release large amounts of water vapor in the atmosphere is to reduce the temperature below the dew point.

The amount of condensation from the atmosphere depends on the amount of cooling and the relative humidity of the air mass. When the relative humidity is high, as it is in the intertropical convergence, a small amount of cooling will reduce the mass of air to the dew point. In contrast, when the relative humidity is low, as it is in the low latitude deserts, a great amount of cooling is required to reach the dew point. If the condensation occurs when the temperature is above freezing, it will be in the form of dew, fog, or clouds. If the temperature is below freezing, frozen condensation may occur. Some clouds exist in the form of supercooled liquid droplets at about −15°C (5°F).

A number of processes can cool the atmosphere sufficiently to produce condensation. When the temperature of the atmosphere is reduced by radiation or condensation cooling, only a small volume of air is cooled and thus only a small amount of water vapor is released. This type of cooling results in dew or fog. It rarely results in precipitation, and when precipitation does occur, the amount is very small. Only when a large air mass is cooled in a rising air current can enough moisture be released to form clouds and ultimately precipitation.

**PHOTO 11**
Altocumulus cloud. (Courtesy: National Oceanic and Atmospheric Administration)

**PHOTO 12**
Cirrostratus cloud. (Courtesy: National Oceanic and Atmospheric Administration)

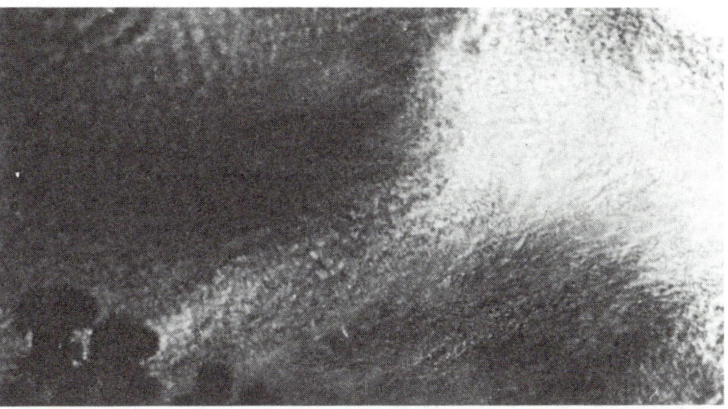

**PHOTO 13**
Cirrocumulus cloud. (Courtesy: National Oceanic and Atmospheric Administration)

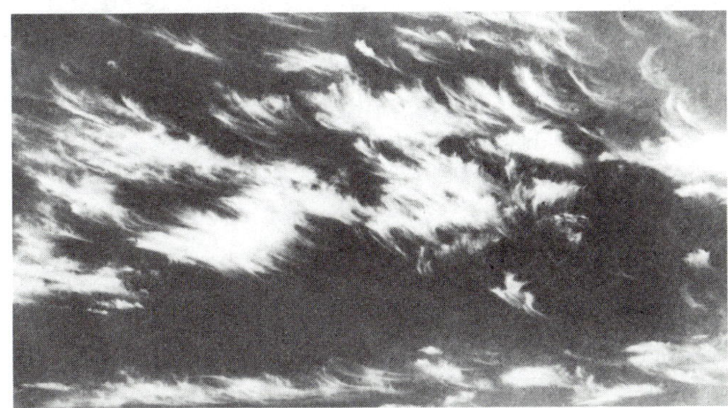

**PHOTO 14**
Cirrus clouds. (Courtesy: National Oceanic and Atmospheric Administration)

**PHOTO 15**
Cumulonimbus cloud. (Courtesy: National Oceanic and Atmospheric Administration)

## CLASSIFICATION OF CLOUDS

Atmospheric phenomena produce a large number of cloud forms. The World Meteorological Organization (WMO) has classified clouds into ten major genera. Differences within a particular genus have led to a subdivision of most of the genera into species. Fourteen species are now recognized. These subdivisions are not included in this discussion, but additional information can be secured from the *International Cloud Atlas,* Volume 1, published by the World Meteorological Organization in 1956. Clouds may be classified according to their altitude into low, middle, and high levels, and the cumulonimbus cloud that extends from the lowest to the highest level.

### LOW ALTITUDE CLOUDS

The clouds that extend upward to about 2,000 meters (6,500 feet) are *cumulus, stratus, nimbostratus,* or *stratocumulus.* Of these, the stratus cloud is the lowest (Photo 6). The stratus cloud covers the sky from horizon to horizon, creating a dull gray overcast sky. When the sun is visible through this cloud, its outline is clearly discernible. Stratus clouds do not produce halo phenomena except at very low temperatures. When precipitation falls from the stratus cloud, it is then known as a nimbostratus cloud (Photo 7, page 80). Low ragged clouds frequently appear below the layer, and may or may not merge with it. The stratus and nimbostratus clouds are common during the winter in the low pressure cyclonic storms of the westerly wind belt. They can persist for days at a time, and are associated with some of the most depressing weather of the year. The nimbostratus cloud often brings precipitation that continues for hours.

Cumulus clouds are also low level phenomena (Photo 8). They are the large fluffy clouds that usually exist singly in the atmosphere and are frequently separated from each other by patches of clear, blue sky. They are formed by an ascending column of air. Characteristically they have flat bases that mark the dew point. Above the condensation level they tower into beautiful, cauliflowerlike forms. In their initial stage they are usually associated with fair weather. At about the 2,000-meter (6,500-foot) level stratocumulus clouds may develop (Photo 9). They are whitish to gray in color and are rough and bumpy in texture. Dark splotches, composed of rounded masses of dense clouds, are almost always evident.

## MIDDLE ALTITUDE CLOUDS

Clouds ranging in altitude from 2,000 to 6,000 meters (6,500 to 20,000 feet) have the prefix *alto* added to their name. The lowest of these clouds are the *altostratus* (Photo 10). They are grayish or bluish cloud sheets that are striated, fibrous, or uniform in appearance. Although they cover the sky, they are thin enough to vaguely reveal the sun or the moon. Altostratus clouds are commonly followed by widespread and rather continuous precipitation.

Above the altostratus are found the *altocumulus* clouds (Photo 11). These are white to gray globular masses of clouds, generally with shading, arranged in lines or waves. The altocumulus differ from the cirrocumulus in that they have a larger mass, often producing shadows. They may or may not be merged in the sky.

## HIGH ALTITUDE CLOUDS

Three genera of high altitude clouds belonging to the *cirrus* group lie at altitudes between 6,000 and 10,000 meters (20,000 to 33,000 feet). The lowest of these are the *cirrostratus* clouds (Photo 12). They appear as a transparent, whitish cloud veil partly or totally covering the sky. Generally they produce a halo around the sun and moon, which is an indication of an approaching storm. Lying above the cirrostratus clouds are the *cirrocumulus* clouds (Photo 13). These are thin white patches, sheets, or layers of clouds without shading. They are composed of small elements in the form of grains, lines, or ripples that may be merged or distinct, forming what is commonly called a mackerel sky. The highest of this genus of clouds are the cirrus (Photo 14). These featherlike clouds appear as a white, delicate filament in the upper sky. They have a fibrous, silky sheen. Atmospheric temperatures at this altitude are well below the freezing point, so cirrus clouds are composed of minute ice crystals. They are normally formed by a direct change from water vapor to ice, known as *sublimation,* without an intermediate water stage. Rarely are they heavy enough to blot out the sun, but they may create a hazy sky. They are associated with fair weather, but when they are systematically arranged, as in bands, or connected with cirrocumulus or cirrostratus clouds, they often foretell the approach of a frontal system in the westerly wind belt of the middle latitudes.

## GREAT VERTICAL DEVELOPMENT CLOUDS

When a local upward air draft creates a fair weather cumulus cloud at low altitude, the air draft may continue, building the cloud to a great height. Such clouds then become localized convectional storm centers and are known as *cumulonimbus* clouds (Photo 15). At this stage they may be thousands of meters thick, extending 9,000 to 12,000 meters (30,000 to 40,000 feet) up into the atmosphere. Because they are so thick they appear as dark, turbulent masses of clouds and are called *thunderheads.* The upper portion usually appears smooth, fibrous, or striated, and it is nearly always spread out in the shape of an anvil or vast plume. Under the base of the cloud, which is often very dark, there are frequently low ragged clouds that sometimes merge with the great mass of clouds above them.

The covering and types of clouds vary greatly over the earth, depending on pressure and wind relationships. In the intertropical convergence, cumulus and cumulonimbus clouds dominate. The heavy precipitation throughout this zone is due to the large number of convectional storms. In the trade wind and subtropical high pressure areas, cloud covering is minimal. In the westerly wind belt, low pressure cyclonic storms bring stratus and nimbostratus clouds. This time of cloudiness and precipitation contrasts with the passage of the high pressure anticyclone, when clear weather prevails. During the summer, convectional heating of the air mass is common in the westerly wind belt. Cumulus clouds develop, and these formations may evolve into cumulonimbus clouds with heavy precipitation in the form of thunderstorms. In the polar regions, the polar high pressure and the polar easterlies are areas of modest cloud covering.

## PRECIPITATION PROCESS MODELS

Precipitation develops in a three-stage process. When a mass of air begins its ascent, the water it contains is in a gaseous state. This is known as the *dry stage.* As the air mass rises, its temperature decreases and its relative humidity increases. The rate of cooling of a vertical current of unsaturated air is about 2.6°C (5.5°F) for each 300 meters (1,000 feet) of increase in elevation. Such cooling is known as *adiabatic cooling.*

Clouds begin to form when the dew point is reached. This level of moisture in the atmosphere is called the *condensation level.* This is the beginning of the *cloud stage* in the precipitation process. As the condensation level is passed, the clouds grow in size, but there may still be no precipitation. The formation of cloud droplets is not sufficient to produce precipitation, because these initial droplets are extremely small and fall through the atmosphere very slowly. For example, a cloud droplet with a radius of 10 micrometers drops at the rate of about 1 centimeter per second. At this rate it would take 84 hours for this tiny droplet to fall about 3 kilometers. Such a tiny speck of moisture would survive for a distance of only a few meters in its fall through a layer of 90 percent humidity. To create precipitation at the surface of the earth, therefore, some process must increase the size of the droplet so that it will be heavy enough to fall through the atmosphere.

Raindrops are created during the third stage, the *precipitation stage.* Two models have been formulated to suggest this process. The most common one, known as the *ice crystal model,* applies most directly to the middle and higher latitudes. This model was identified in the 1930s by Tor Bergeron and Von W. Findeisen. It is based on the principle that the saturation vapor pressure is less over ice than over water. Air that is at 100 percent relative humidity when it is over water has a relative humidity considerably greater than 100 percent when it is over ice. For example, if the temperature is −10°C (14°F) and the relative humidity over supercooled water is 100 percent, it is 110 percent over ice (Figure 6.2).

The difference in saturation vapor pressure creates a physical conflict between the water and ice particles. The air will always "appear" more saturated to the ice crystals than to the liquid droplets. Consequently, the ice crystals will continue to grow while the water droplets will evaporate and yield their moisture to the ice crystals. Because the ice crystals are so supersaturated, they can grow very rapidly. Unless a freezing nucleus exists, however, ice crystals do not form even at temperatures of −20° to −30°C (−4° to −22°F). When the temperature reaches −40°C (−40°F), water freezes without the benefit of freezing nuclei. Once the freezing process starts, it continues itself, with the initial ice crys-

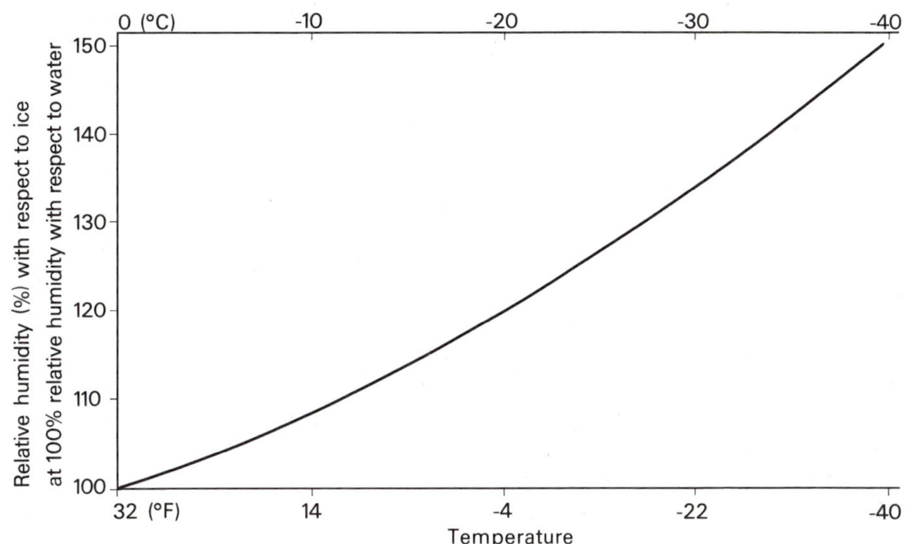


**FIGURE 6.2**
Relative humidity of air over ice when the air is saturated (100 percent relative humidity) over water. (After Anthes, Cahir, Fraser, and Panofsky, 1981)

tals growing, then fracturing and serving as freezing nuclei for future ice crystals.

While the ice crystal model may explain the formation of rain droplets sufficiently heavy to produce precipitation, it is based on the assumption that freezing can begin close enough to the ground to create ice particles. In the lower latitudes, where warm clouds extend into high altitudes, ice crystals do not form. Another explanation must be sought for this situation. It is assumed that the process of collision and coalescence of the droplets can cause them to grow rapidly, resulting ultimately in precipitation. This precipitation process has come to be known as the *coalescence model.*

In this model, cloud droplets are brought together by collision. A number of conditions aid this process. It is best developed when the droplets in the cloud are of different sizes so that they have different *terminal velocities;* that is, they fall at different rates. Thus the big droplets overtake the smaller droplets and coalesce with them. Experiments have also shown that the coalescence of droplets is enhanced if the droplets have opposite electrical charges because opposite charges attract each other. The positive-negative electrical field in natural clouds, therefore, favors the coalescence process. In the low latitude regions where the relative humidity is high and hygroscopic (moisture-absorbing) nuclei are present, the collision and coalescence of rain droplets are thought to be sufficient to produce heavy precipitation.

## TYPES OF PRECIPITATION

Precipitation is a response to the cooling of an air mass as it ascends. Large air masses are caused to rise by three means. The precipitation on the earth can be classified as convectional, frontal, or orographic, depending on which process is forcing the air to rise.

*Convectional* precipitation is commonly known as a thunderstorm. The convectional system occurs when a mass of air is heated on the ground. As it becomes lighter, the column of air begins to rise. This uplift process can be aided in a number of ways, such as by a physical barrier, by mechanical turbulence, or by a cold front of a cyclonic storm.

Because the convectional process is directly related to heating, convectional precipitation is best developed in the areas of the world where there is the greatest heat. It thus has a diurnal and a seasonal pattern of occurrence. During the day, convectional showers are most likely to occur in the hottest part of the afternoon. During the year, convectional precipitation occurs during the warm season and rarely, if ever, during the winter season. Convectional precipitation is common in the low latitudes where there is warmth during the entire year; it rarely occurs in the high latitudes.

A second type of precipitation is known as *frontal* or *cyclonic* precipitation. Its occurrence is associated with the passage of a low pressure system (cyclone), which has converging winds toward its center and which has cold and warm fronts developed within its area. Frontal precipitation is well developed in the middle latitudes. In contrast to convectional precipitation, frontal precipitation typically occurs during the winter season in the middle latitudes.

The third form of precipitation is the *orographic* type (Figure 6.3). It occurs when an air mass is forced to rise over some barrier such as a mountain range or plateau escarpment. This action is called *forced ascent.* As an air mass ascends over the barrier, it is cooled, and the water vapor is condensed into clouds as the first stage in the precipitation process. When the air mass originates over a warm body of water and thus has a high absolute humidity, the resulting precipitation on the windward side of the physical barrier is particularly heavy. Regions of the world that receive abundant orographic precipitation include the southward-facing flanks of the Himalayas in eastern India, the coast of Norway, northwestern United States and western Canada, the east coast of Madagascar, and the west coast of India. The leeward side of these mountains, where the air is descending, warming, and becoming stable, is characteristically drier. Great precipitation contrasts thus exist between the windward and leeward sides of mountains.

## FORMS OF PRECIPITATION

The form of precipitation that reaches the ground depends on atmospheric conditions after the raindrops or ice crystals develop. Of these conditions temperature is most important. If the entire troposphere is below freezing, the ice crystals grow into snow crystals of legendary variety—hexagonal plates, starlike crystals, needles, or granular pellets. The form of snow crystal depends on temperature and relative humidity.

A wide variety of precipitation forms occur when layers of air that are above freezing alternate with layers that are below freezing. When a shallow layer of below-freezing air occurs on the ground and a layer of above-freezing air lies on top of it, rain falling from the warmer upper layer freezes as it passes through the colder air. The accumulation of ice on trees, vines, and buildings under these conditions can be devastating.

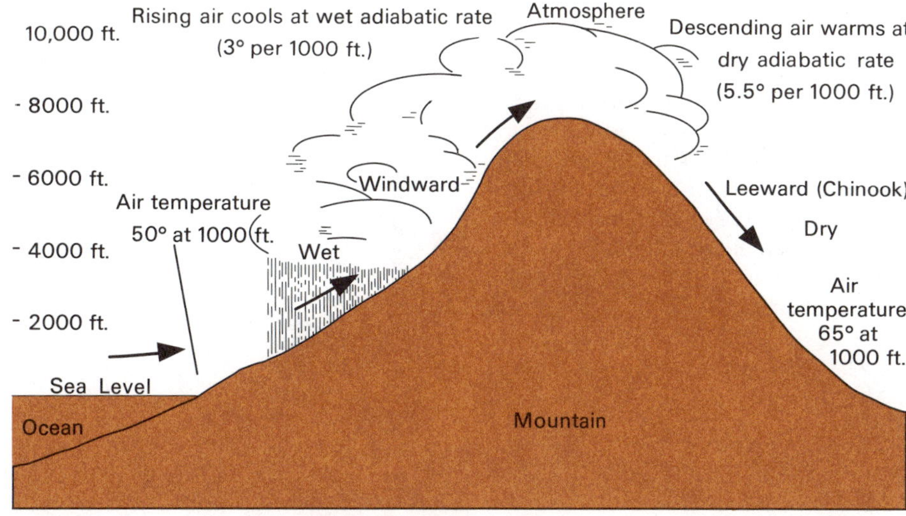


**FIGURE 6.3**
Orographic precipitation on windward slopes of mountain barriers. The adiabatic rate of cooling and heating refers to changes in temperature not involving an addition or withdrawal of heat. These changes are associated with the expansion or compression of air following a decrease or increase in atmospheric pressure.

The occurrence of freezing rains in rugged topography can vary widely. If the coldest air occurs in the valleys, ice will accumulate in the lower elevations. On occasion, the tops of the peaks may penetrate the warm air layers and escape the freezing rain altogether. However, the reverse can also occur. It is even possible for a cold upper layer and a cold layer on the ground to be separated by a warmer, above-freezing layer in the middle. Under these conditions the freezing rain occurs only at the higher elevations and the valleys receive only rain.

Sleet or ice pellets reach the ground when there is a deep layer of below-freezing air near the ground and warmer air aloft. The rain that falls through this layer freezes into ice. As the sleet hits windows or buildings on the ground, it creates a loud clatter.

## HYDROLOGIC CYCLE

Each year about 517,000 cubic kilometers of water are evaporated from the earth and approximately the same amount is precipitated back onto the surface. This closed system of evapotranspiration and precipitation is known as the *hydrologic cycle* (Figure 6.4). This cycle is powered by the energy from the sun, and since the amount of solar energy remains essentially the same from year to year, the total volume of water involved in the cycle is essentially constant.

The hydrologic cycle consists of two subsystems. The first is the precipitation and evaporation that occurs over the oceans, and the second is the precipitation and evapotranspiration that occurs over land surfaces. These two subsystems are connected by horizontal movement in the atmosphere, known as *advection,* and by runoff of water from land surfaces.

Within the hydrologic system the water precipitated into the oceans and the evaporation of water from the oceans is most important. It is estimated that about 79 percent of the world's precipitation occurs over the oceans and that the oceans provide about 84 percent of the earth's total evaporation. Seven percent of the evaporation of the oceans is carried onto the land by advection. Although the oceans cover only about 71 percent of the earth's surface, the large amounts of moisture and energy available in the lower latitudes make the oceans proportionally more significant than land as a source of water vapor.

The land surface of the earth receives about 21 percent of the earth's total precipitation. Of this amount about 58 percent returns to the atmosphere by evapotranspiration and about 42 percent is runoff into the oceans. While land occupies about 29 percent of the earth's surface, it receives proportionally less precipitation, because large areas of the land are semiarid and arid, and because the greatest landmasses are in the middle and higher latitudes where most evaporation is limited to the summer months. Figure 6.5 shows the geographical distribution of annual evaporation. Note the contrasts of evaporation between warm oceans, such as the Atlantic and Indian oceans, and the deserts in the same latitude on the African and Australian continents.

## WATER BUDGET

The amount of water varies greatly from place to place and is not always in sufficient quantity when needed. In

**FIGURE 6.4**
Hydrologic cycle. The oceans are the major source of water in the atmosphere. The moisture is carried onto the continents by the winds, where part of it falls to the earth as precipitation. The water returns to the ocean by running off the land as surface water, by movement in the ground as groundwater, and, indirectly, by evapotranspiration.

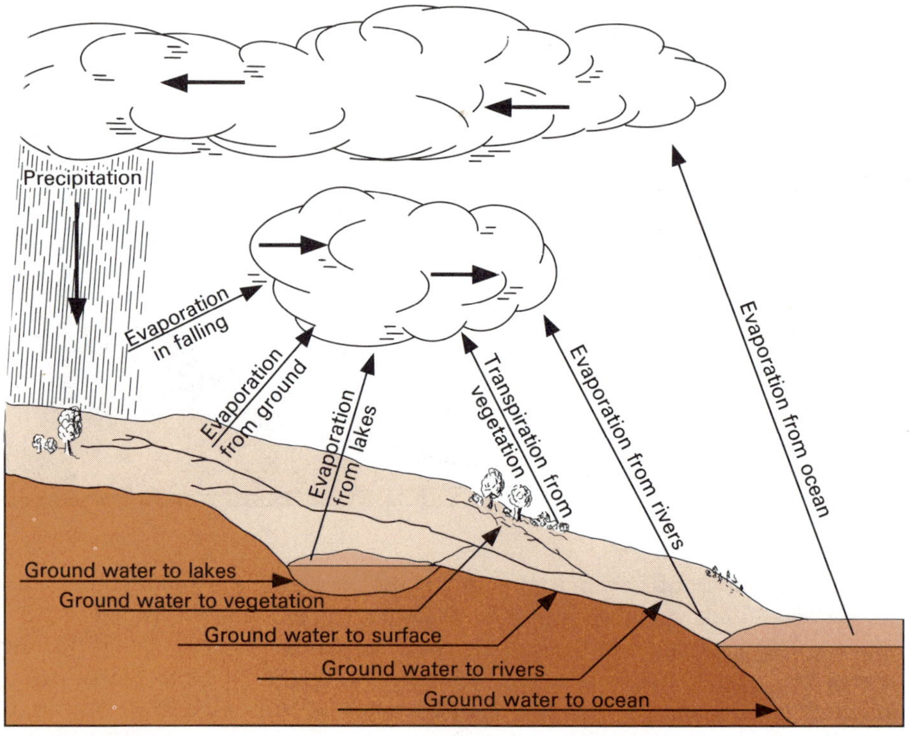


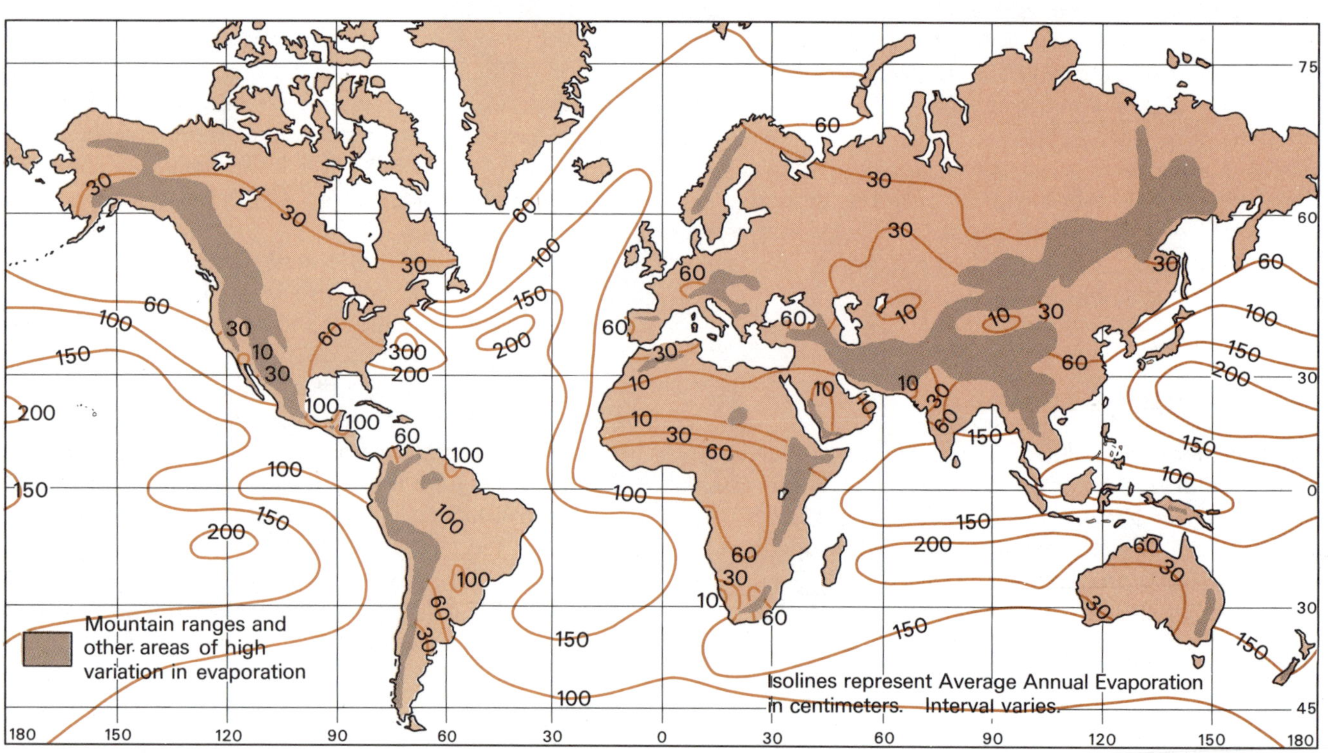


**FIGURE 6.5**
Average annual evaporation from the surface of the earth. The greatest evaporation occurs over the oceans and the equatorial areas; the least evaporation occurs in the major deserts and the polar areas of the Northern Hemisphere. (After Barry, 1969)

order to estimate the availability of moisture, hydrologists make use of the *water budget* (Table 6.2). The water budget is the availability of water at a given place. It has a wide number of practical applications. For example, the water budget will reveal the water content of the soil, and will help determine how much water needs to be supplied to that area in order for crops to grow. The water budget concept also plays a role in calculating evapotranspiration, which greatly affects the agricultural potential of an area. A water budget is also an important indicator of runoff and stream flow from a region.

## WATER BUDGET FACTORS

The water balance of a region depends upon precipitation, evapotranspiration, runoff, and groundwater storage (Figure 6.6). Of these, precipitation and evapotranspiration are the most important. Measuring the water balance of an area is complicated because most areas go through a cycle of water accumulation and depletion. Further, precipitation and evapotranspiration each have different modes of occurrence. Precipitation falls intermittently. For example, in the lower Great Lakes precipitation falls on only about one-third of the days. Further, about one-half of the precipitation comes in 15 days. In contrast to precipitation, evapotranspiration occurs steadily. The rate of evaporation depends upon temperature, with the maximum in the hot season and the minimum in the cold season. Transpiration from plants also changes seasonally. During the summer period it approaches the rate of evaporation, while in winter it is nearly zero. Obviously runoff is directly related to precipitation and evaporation, but it is also influenced by slope, elevation, vegetation cover, and soil saturation. When the soil is saturated, runoff of precipitation increases. Generally level land retards runoff in contrast to areas where there are steep slopes.

## GLOBAL WATER BUDGET

On a global scale, there are latitudinal zones where precipitation exceeds evapotranspiration and others where evapotranspiration exceeds precipitation. As a consequence, an exchange of moisture, with its associated energy, must occur between the zones.

Between 30 and 90 degrees latitude in both hemispheres, precipitation exceeds evapotranspiration, with the greatest moisture excess lying between 30 and 60 degrees. The greatest excess occurs in the westerly wind belt with its dominance of cyclonic storms. Precipitation decreases in the higher latitudes, but because the area is also cooler, evapotranspiration is reduced, resulting in a moisture excess.

Excess precipitation also exists in the intertropical convergence area from 0 to about 10 degrees north and south latitude. Although this is a hot region and evapotranspiration is high, the converging winds bring copious moisture. The precipitation excess is greater here than anywhere else in the world.

**TABLE 6.2**
Global water budget.

The formula for the global water budget is as follows:

$$P = E + R$$

where:

P = Precipitation
E = Evapotranspiration
R = Runoff (positive when out of the continents, negative when into the oceans)

Received from the continents (cubic kilometers):

$$108{,}000 = 62{,}000 + 46{,}000$$

Received from the oceans:

$$409{,}000 = 455{,}000 - 46{,}000$$

When the global water budget is combined for continents and oceans, the runoff is cancelled out. It is stated thus:

$$108{,}000 + 409{,}000 = 62{,}000 + 455{,}000 \quad \text{or}$$
$$517{,}000 = 517{,}000$$

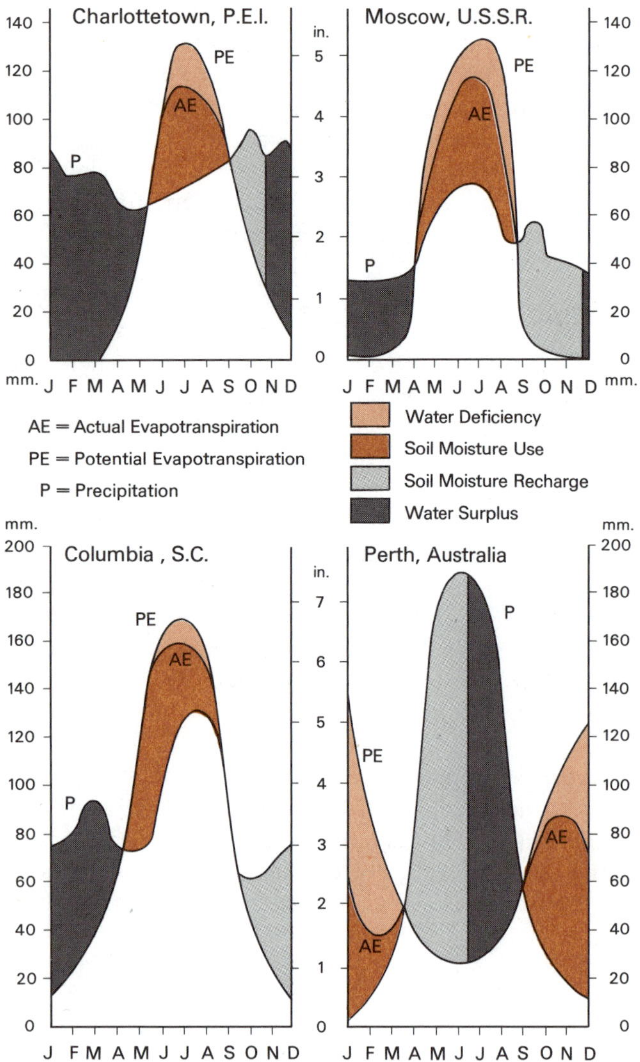


**FIGURE 6.6**
Water balance diagrams. The water budget varies greatly in different regions of the world. (From John R. Mather, University of Delaware)

Between these latitudinal belts of excess precipitation lie two extensive belts of precipitation deficiency, located approximately from 10 to 30 degrees north and south latitude. These are the zones of the subtropical anticyclones and trade winds. In these areas precipitation is low and evapotranspiration is extremely high. Energy, in the form of latent heat in water vapor, is transferred by winds to the equatorial and middle latitudes, when precipitation exceeds evapotranspiration.

## VARIABILITY OF PRECIPITATION

Precipitation data are most frequently given for average annual or average monthly amounts. However, it must be remembered that the actual precipitation received at a place during a given period may vary sharply from the average for that period (Figure 6.7). For a 52-year period, for example, California had an average annual precipitation of 60.7 centimeters (23.9 inches). However, the annual variability extremes ranged from 35.8 centimeters (14.1 inches) for the driest year to 106.9 centimeters (42.1 inches) for the wettest year. When considered on a monthly basis the extremes are even greater.

In general an inverse relationship exists between precipitation amount and precipitation variability. The greatest fluctuations occur in the arid and subarid regions of the world. There are places in the desert that may receive no precipitation for years and then receive as much as 50 centimeters (20 inches) during thunderstorms occurring within a few weeks. The northeastern United States and northwestern Europe have the least annual variability in precipitation with the extremes departing only 10 percent from normal. The areas of intertropical convergence are also regions of low precipitation variability.

## WORLD PRECIPITATION REGIMES

Two outstanding characteristics of precipitation are its uneven distribution over the surface of the earth and its variation from season to season in certain regions. Four types of precipitation regions may be recognized. These are continuously wet, continuously dry, dry summers and humid winters, and dry winters and humid summers (Figures 6.8 and 6.9).

### CONTINUOUSLY WET REGIONS

Three regions in the world are continuously wet. The first area is the intertropical convergence. Typical of this region is Singapore with an average of 235.9 centimeters (92.9 inches) of rainfall annually. February is the driest month with an average of 15.4 centimeters (6.1 inches), and the wettest month is December with an average of 26.4 centimeters (10.4 inches).

The second continuously wet region is situated between 30 and 60 degrees north and south latitude on the western margins of continents. Cyclonic precipitation dominates in these areas throughout the year. Paris, France, has an average annual precipitation of 57.4 centimeters (22.6 inches), and the monthly averages range from 3.0 centimeters (1.2 inches) in February to 5.8 centimeters (2.3 inches) in June. Although the total amount of precipitation is quite small, it is distributed evenly throughout the year, and evaporation is low because of the mild temperatures. Conditions are there-

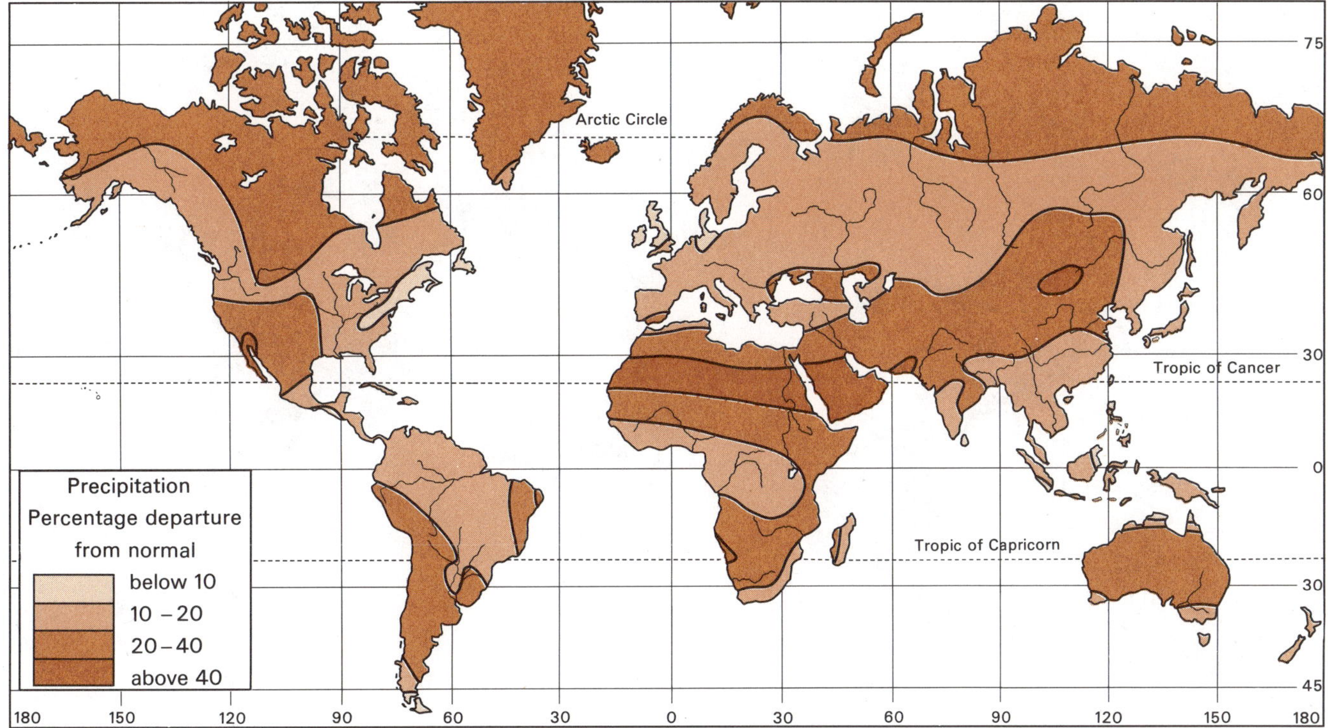


**FIGURE 6.7**
Variability of precipitation. The desert areas of the world have the most variable precipitation. The equatorial and the marine west coast areas of the middle latitudes have the least. (Source: Figure 2.31 [after Trewartha] from Miller and Langdon, 1964. Copyright © 1964 by Harper & Row, Publishers, Inc. Reprinted by permission of the publisher.)

fore humid throughout the year. In the plains areas the precipitation is dominated by cyclonic storms. This cyclonic precipitation is augmented by orographic precipitation in mountainous areas. Bergen, Norway, illustrates this type of location. This city has an average annual precipitation of 214.1 centimeters (84.3 inches), and the monthly averages range from 10.4 centimeters (4.1 inches) in June to 23.6 centimeters (9.3 inches) in October. The extent to which this wet region extends into the interior depends primarily on topography. In northwestern North America and Scandinavia, the wet area is limited to the coastal, windward side of the mountains. In contrast, the wet region on the vast northern European plains extends more than a thousand miles inland, from France to western Soviet Union.

The third continuously wet region is situated on the eastern margin of the continents between 10 and 60 degrees north and south latitude. In the areas from approximately 10 to 30 degrees the moisture is brought by the trade winds to the east coast. The amount of precipitation depends on topography. If the trade winds are forced to rise over mountainous areas, orographic precipitation is usually heavy. In Jamaica, for example, Port Antonio, on the windward northeast coast, has an average annual precipitation of 348.7 centimeters (137.3 inches), and the monthly averages range from 43.6 centimeters (17.2 inches) in December to 11.9 centimeters (4.7 inches) in March. On the east coast from 30 to 60 degrees north latitude, cyclonic precipitation is combined with the monsoonal influences, producing a fairly even distribution of precipitation throughout the year. New York City, for example, receives an average of 106.9 centimeters (42.1 inches) of precipitation annually. August is the wettest month with 10.9 centimeters (4.3 inches) and January, February, April, November, and December are the driest months, with each receiving 8.3 centimeters (3.3 inches) of precipitation.

## CONTINUOUSLY DRY REGIONS

As some areas of the world are continuously wet, others are continuously arid. In the low latitudes, the major dry belts coincide with descending air currents of the

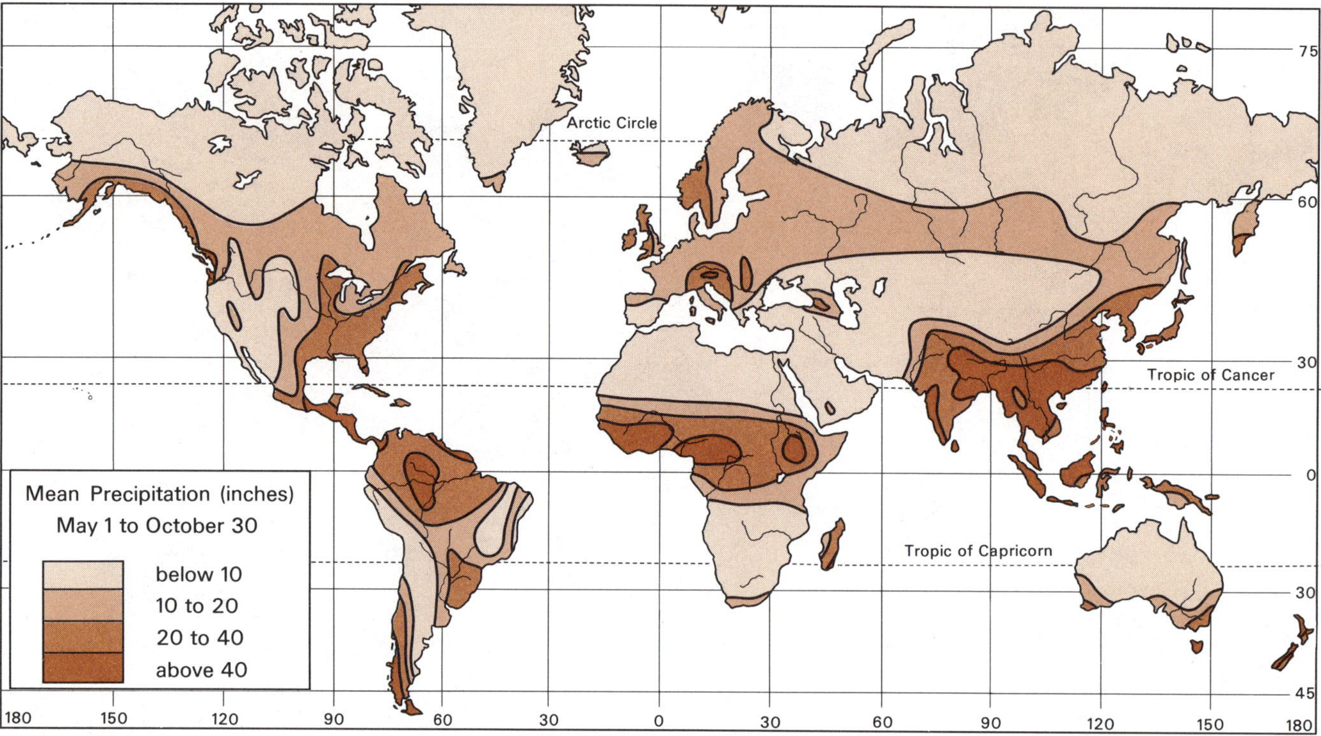


**FIGURE 6.8**
World distribution of precipitation in summer. The heaviest precipitation is received in the equatorial zone north of the equator, and in the monsoonal areas of southeast Asia. (After Miller and Langdon, 1964. Copyright © 1964 by Harper & Row, Publishers, Inc. Reprinted by permission of the publisher.)

subtropical high pressure belt and the moisture-gathering trade winds. The great low latitude dry regions include the Sahara and Kalahari deserts of Africa, the Great Australian Desert, the Thar and Arabian deserts of Asia, the Atacama Desert of South America, and the Sonoran Desert of North America. Cairo in Egypt experiences a typical low latitude precipitation regime with an average of 3.3 centimeters (1.3 inches) of rainfall a year. The months from April to October average less than 0.2 centimeters (0.1 inches) of rainfall. January is the wettest month with only 1.0 centimeter (0.4 inches) of precipitation. Alice Springs, located in the heart of the Australian continent, has an average annual precipitation of 28.1 centimeters (11.1 inches). The wettest month is January, when rainfall averages 4.5 centimeters (1.8 inches), and the driest months are July, August, and September, when rainfall averages 1.0 centimeters (0.4 inches) each month. Almost all precipitation comes as convectional downpours.

The interiors of continents in the middle latitudes are also dry regions, either because they are very far from the oceans or because mountainous barriers prevent the inflow of humid winds from the oceans. Idaho Falls, Idaho, averages but 18.7 centimeters (7.4 inches) of precipitation annually. Precipitation is fairly evenly distributed throughout the year. June, with 2.8 centimeters (1.1 inches), is the wettest month, and November, with 0.7 centimeters (0.3 inches), has the least precipitation. Precipitation in the winter is primarily cyclonic and in the summer convectional.

## REGIONS OF DRY SUMMERS AND HUMID WINTERS

The west coasts of continents between 30 and 40 degrees north and south latitude experience dry summers and humid winters. These regions include southern California, the Mediterranean Basin, central Chile, and southwestern Australia. These are transitional areas lying between the consistently dry areas equatorward and the consistently wet areas poleward. During the summer period the diverging air masses of the subtropical high pressure belt prevail over these regions. In contrast, during the winter months the westerly wind

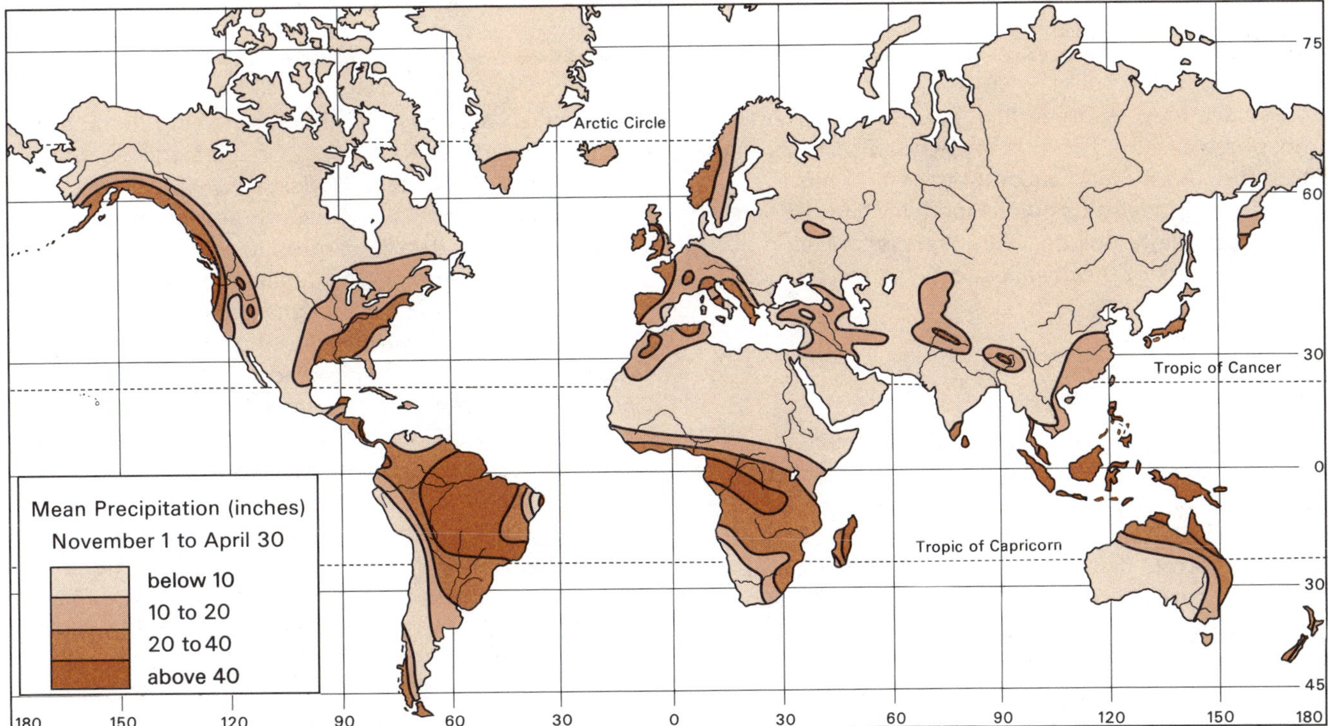


**FIGURE 6.9**
World distribution of precipitation in winter. The heaviest precipitation occurs in the equatorial areas south of the equator. Note the relatively low precipitation in the desert areas, most of Asia, and interior North America. (After Miller and Langdon, 1964, Copyright © 1964 by Harper & Row, Publishers, Inc. Reprinted by permission of the publisher.)

belt with its cyclonic storms shifts equatorward, bringing precipitation. For example, Santa Barbara, California, has an average annual precipitation of 45.2 centimeters (17.8 inches), of which 80 percent comes during the four-month period of December through March. The months June through September have an average rainfall of less than 0.2 centimeters (0.1 inches).

## REGIONS OF DRY WINTERS AND HUMID SUMMERS

There are two major areas that experience dry winters and humid summers. The first is southern Asia where the monsoon influence dominates. The second is the transitional belt between the humid and dry tropics. These areas include the Sudan and Veld in Africa and the Brazilian Campos and Venezuelan Llanos in South America. During the low-sun period the moisture-gathering trade winds prevail in these areas, whereas during the high-sun period the intertropical convergence with associated convectional storms brings precipitation. Mongalla in the African Sudan exhibits a rainfall regime typical of the dry and wet tropics. The total average annual rainfall for this station averages 98.8 centimeters (38.9 inches), ranging from 14.7 centimeters (5.8 inches) in August to only 0.2 centimeter (0.1 inch) in January. About 90 percent of the total rainfall comes during the high-sun period of April to October.

## PRECIPITATION QUALITY

People have long assumed that water falling from the atmosphere is pure. It is now recognized that this may not be true. As the population of the world has increased and industry has developed, the atmosphere has become more polluted. Atmospheric pollution affects the quality of precipitation, causing the problem known as acid rain.

### ACID RAIN

The first warning of acid rain's destructiveness came from Sweden. After years of investigation, a dramatic report was issued in the early 1970s, revealing that massive fish kills had occurred in rivers and lakes, crops and forests had declined in productivity, corrosion had occurred on property, and personal health had been impaired. Only in the mid-1970s was similar destruction recognized in North America. Acid rain pollution is now considered to be possibly the greatest environmental disaster of our time.

#### CAUSES OF ACID RAIN

The level of acidity or alkalinity of a liquid is measured by the pH scale. The scale ranges from 0, which is acid, to 14, which is alkaline. Distilled water, at pH 7.0, is neutral, neither acidic nor alkaline. Because pH values are logarithmic, lemon juice at pH 2.3 is 10 times as acidic as vinegar at pH 3.3. Precipitation is normally slightly acidic, pH 5.6, because rainwater contains carbonic acid formed by the reaction of water with carbon dioxide. Acid rain is defined as having a pH of less than 5.6. In most of the eastern United States, most rainfall today has a pH reading of about 4.5.

A number of factors can increase the acidity of precipitation. Forest fires, sea spray, and volcanoes have contributed through geologic time small quantities of sulfur dioxide to the air masses. This chemical provides the basis for the creation of a weak sulfuric acid. At the same time, however, small quantities of airborne alkaline substances, such as calcium and potassium, tend to neutralize the acidic condition of the atmosphere.

The opportunity exists for the atmosphere to become highly acidic when excessive amounts of sulfur dioxide and nitrogen oxides are emitted into the atmosphere. Sulfur dioxide enters the atmosphere primarily as a response to the burning of coal and oil. It is estimated that from 28 to 30 million tons of sulfur dioxide are emitted annually into the atmosphere in the United States. Canada emits an additional 5.5 million tons. When the sulfur dioxide is dissolved, it becomes sulfuric acid and comes to the earth as acid rain.

In the 1970s data began to indicate that nitrogen oxides had become a substantial and growing contributor to atmospheric acidity. Nitrogen oxides, like sulfur dioxide, can be transformed into a weak acid in the air mass. In certain places nitric acid is the main cause of acid rain. For example, the rainfall in Pasadena, California, had an average pH of 4.0 in 1978. Nitric acid was the dominant component. Pasadena has no ore smelters, its fossil-fueled power plants use low-sulfur western coals, and it is not located downwind from major polluted air masses. It has, therefore, none of the typical sources of sulfur dioxide, but it does have cars and trucks. It is now estimated that nitric acid causes about 30 percent of the acid rain in North America. About half of this acid comes from transportation, while combustion of fossil fuels, coal in particular, provides the remainder.

#### DISTRIBUTION OF ACID RAIN

The problem of acid rain is spreading throughout the world. It was detected in Europe early in the 1950s. At the instigation of Sweden, a network of about 175 meteorological stations was established in northern and western Europe to monitor acid rain conditions. These data have revealed the spread of acid rain over an ever-widening area. In 1956, an area of rain with a pH of 5 was centered over southeastern Britain, northern France, and the Benelux countries. By 1966 this acidic area had expanded to include all of western and northern Europe, and in the original center a pH of 4.0 to 4.5 was common. A secondary center was also forming over western Soviet Union and eastern Europe. By 1970 acid rain was distributed over most of Europe and western Soviet Union.

It is estimated that more than 25 million tons of sulphur dioxide are spewed into the atmosphere in Europe each year. Most of this pollution originates in the industrial areas of central England, the industrial crescent that stretches from central Belgium to the Ruhr Valley, industrial areas of East Germany, and the Silesian area of Poland and Czechoslovakia. It has become clear that the pollution emissions have accumulated in the atmosphere faster than they can be dissipated. As a consequence they have overcome the natural buffering chemicals of air, and are being precipitated out of the atmosphere as acid rain. Hence a permanently acidified mass of air has built up over the European continent.

The distributional pattern of acid rain is not as well documented in North America as in Europe. Records taken before 1930 reveal that rainfall in New York, Virginia, and Tennessee was clean. By 1955 the rainfall from Maine to New Jersey was often 10 times more acidic than normal. By 1966 the New York to New England airborne acidity had dropped to pH 4.4, and the nearest area of regularly clean rain was South Carolina. The area of concentrated acid rain extends into southeastern Canada. It is now estimated that 11 ounces of sulfuric acid fall on every acre of southern Ontario each year. The rainfall of this vast region is usually 10 times more acidic than normal rainfall, and may be as much as 15 to 20 times more acidic.

Current records give evidence that the area of acid rain is spreading into new regions. Like an oil spill in the ocean, acidity of the atmosphere is spread by the prevailing wind system. The acid pall, with a pH of about 4.5, is spreading outward from the northeastern states and southern Canada at a rate of hundreds of miles each 5 to 10 years.

## ACID RAIN IN THE ECOSYSTEM

The impact of acid rain on the ecosystem is becoming apparent from scientific studies carried out throughout the world. Some of the most intensive studies have been prepared in Sweden. A study that tested 4,200 trees found that growth rates began to decline after 1951 in the areas of Sweden receiving acid rain. By 1965 the growth rate was an average of 0.3 percent per year lower in the acid-susceptible areas. The study concluded that the reduction in growth cannot be attributed to any other cause than acidification.

A study of tree growth was conducted between 1968 and 1974 in the Hubbard Brook Forest of the White Mountains of New Hampshire. It was a near-virgin area of sugar maple, yellow birch, beech, red spruce, and mountain maple trees. The study concluded that, until 1950, the forest had grown in a normal fashion. Between 1951 and 1965 the production of wood in the trees decreased by nearly 20 percent. In the previous two centuries this sharp a decline had never occurred. The study concluded that increasing acidity of rainfall may be responsible for the decrease in forest productivity.

When acid rain falls on leaves, it erodes the delicately thin waxy layer that coats and protects the leaves. The acid can directly damage the cells on the surface of the leaf, particularly the "guard cells." These cells control the opening and closing of tiny pores, allowing moisture and gases to breathe in and out. Damaged guard cells result in the suffocation of the leaf material. The leaf's normal metabolism is thus disrupted, resulting in a change of essential photosynthesis. The abnormal growth or premature death of the leaf cells causes a decline or stoppage of the entire tree's growth (Photo 16).

## EFFECT OF ACID RAIN ON RIVERS AND LAKES

The effects of acid rain have been studied in the rivers and lakes of many places. A few examples will docu-

**PHOTO 16**
Dead spruce on Camels Hump in Vermont's Green Mountains. Conifers in high-elevation forests of the northeastern United States are dying in unusual numbers. Mounting evidence suggests acid rain may be the cause. (Courtesy: David Like, University of Vermont, in *Natural History,* November 1982)

ment the widespread devastation that is in progress. A study of the Adirondacks State Park in New York found that 180 of the lakes are acid-dead, bearing no fish of any species. Those 180 are a small sample of the 2,000 lakes to be tested.

Studies of the effects of acid rain began as early as 1957 in Nova Scotia. In that year 16 lakes near Halifax had a pH of 6.5. By the late 1970s, 85 percent of those lakes were 10 to 100 times more acidic, and were worsening quickly. They were essentially dead lakes. Along the southeastern shore of Nova Scotia the 9 major rivers that flow into the Atlantic have lost their Atlantic salmon due to acidity. Most of the trout are also gone. Only eels have survived.

The destructive effect of acidity on fish was shown by an unsuccessful attempt to introduce pink salmon to Lumsden Lake in the Killarney Park area of Ontario. Four thousand young pink salmon were stocked in the lake in 1966. When the lake was checked the following year, all 4,000 fish had disappeared. Tests, however, showed that there was enough food for the fish. Further, the lake trout and perch had also disappeared. Only suckers remained, but these were all mature. The fact that no young suckers were in the lake indicated that the sucker population would also disappear quickly. After investigating all factors it was concluded that the lake's acidity was the only reason that could explain why fish could not survive in it. The pH of Lumsden Lake had fallen from 6.8 in 1961 to 4.4 by August 1971—a highly abnormal 100-fold increase in acidity in a single decade.

Each fish species is vulnerable to a different level of acidity. When the pH level falls below 6.5, brook and rainbow trout begin to disappear. The females lay eggs but these do not hatch in the acid water. When the acidity level reaches pH 5.0, smallmouth bass, walleye, and lake trout have no future. And finally, at about pH 4.0—acidity 1,000 times stronger than neutral water—only chubs, rock bass, pumpkinseed, and lake herring survive.

A fundamental question is, Can the acid lakes be restored? A number of experiments have been attempted in Canada and Scandinavia, usually involving the dumping of lime in lakes. In the Canadian experiment two small lakes, Middle and Lohi, were selected. These lakes are located about 16 kilometers (10 miles) from Sudbury, Ontario. In 1973 and 1974 more than 38 tons of lime were scattered on the lakes. In August 1976, 2,500 small bass were stocked in Middle Lake. While acidity was reduced, by 1977 not one of the fish survived. In Lohi Lake 1,200 brook trout died within 4 months. The liming had failed to reduce the toxic concentration in the lake. Liming lakes is still under investigation by the scientists, but results so far are discouraging. It has been found that the task of liming lakes at the correct moment is almost impossible. Liming in mid-summer is too late to save fish that breed and spawn in the spring. It is generally concluded that liming is only a temporary solution to the problem of acidity in natural ecosystems. As Gene Likens of Cornell University states, "It can be compared to taking morphine before you cut your leg off—it might ease the pain but you still bleed to death." The prospect for recovery of acid lakes appears most bleak at the present time.

## ECONOMIC CONSIDERATIONS

Many regions are beginning to feel an economic impact from acid rain. Recreational areas where fishing is a major activity experience a decline in revenue as fish disappear. For example, in the Adirondacks State Park in New York, it is estimated that nearly $1.5 million in fishing expenditures have been lost annually since 1976 because of the large number of acid-dead lakes. In Ontario the same type of economic decline in recreational fishing exists. Nearly 8,000 kilometers (5,000 miles) away in Sweden it has been calculated that the country is experiencing a $16.5 million annual loss in inland commercial fisheries due to acidified waters.

The impact of acid rain on lumber production has not been thoroughly investigated. Isolated studies indicate it could be devastating, especially for countries such as Canada and Sweden, whose economy is highly dependent upon wood production.

There is also strong evidence that crops are adversely affected by acid rain. Extensive experiments by governmental agencies in the United States and Canada indicate that slight acid rain will damage such crops as radishes, beans, and tobacco. Although the experiments are in an initial stage, evidence is mounting that untold millions of dollars worth of agricultural crops are at risk.

Acid rain also causes enormous damage to property. In Sweden alone it is estimated that acid rain is costing $20 million annually in metal, stone, and wood corrosion. The U.S. President's Council on Environmental Quality has estimated that property damage due to acid rain is $2 billion annually.

Finally, there are the health costs. The U.S. Environmental Protection Agency, by calculating time and productivity lost, and hospital and compensation costs, estimates that air pollution is costing the country more than $10 billion annually. The U.S. Presidential Council on Environmental Quality estimates sulfur dioxide alone costs $1.7 billion for health care each year in the nation. These are conservative estimates that are likely to be too low.

### FUTURE

Legislation or agreements to control acid rain have been slow to develop at all levels: local, national, and international. Solving the problem will require cooperation between geographic regions, because acid rain usually does not occur at the point of the pollutant. Neither Canada nor the United States has laws that relate directly to acid rain. The only control is on sulfur dioxide. The problem is that a small amount of sulfur dioxide from many local sources results in acid rain over a huge region. Acid rain may be a painful example of the old truism: What goes up must come down. Acid rain is thus the stepchild of pollution. It has taken only 30 years of this chemical deluge to jeopardize a basic process of nature that has maintained a stable atmosphere for eons.

In the early 1970s acid rain reports were largely limited to technical and scientific publications. Now they are appearing in newspapers and popular magazines as well. The essential physical facts of acid rain are being established in the minds of everyone. The financial consequences are gaining publicity. Technologies are available to control the pollution, but political commitment to develop effective measures is lagging behind. Canada and the United States now recognize that a serious environmental problem exists. Is it too much to hope that we will develop a solution to acid rain before more environmental damage occurs?

## CONCLUSION

The study of moisture in the atmosphere is fundamental to human welfare. A world without water, as exists on the moon, is a world without life. The elements of the study of moisture conditions are humidity, evapotranspiration, condensation, and precipitation. The exchange of water that occurs in the earth-atmospheric system constitutes the hydrologic cycle.

How precipitation occurs has been studied for decades. Since the earliest civilizations, humans have attempted to change precipitation regimes, sometimes to increase moisture at a place and sometimes to decrease excessive precipitation. Only in recent times, with the development of the Bergeron model that shows that ice crystals grow at the expense of supercooled water, has a scientific explanation been provided for precipitation in the middle latitudes.

The quality of precipitation is now receiving much attention as the damage caused by acid rain becomes more evident. The industrial areas of the world are most affected, but wind movements carry this condition far beyond its original sources. The damage to lakes and forests makes this a critical issue for the peoples of the world to solve.

## STUDY QUESTIONS

1. What is the difference between absolute and relative humidity?
2. Explain the terms *latent heat of vaporization* and *latent heat of condensation.*
3. Explain the terms *transpiration, evapotranspiration,* and *potential evapotranspiration.*
4. Why is the actual evapotranspiration usually less than the potential evapotranspiration when the surface of the land is not saturated?
5. What determines the dew point in the atmosphere? What happens when the atmosphere is cooled below the dew point?
6. Why is a large amount of cooling usually required to reduce the atmosphere below the dew point in low latitude deserts?
7. Why does radiational cooling produce only a small amount of condensation of water vapor when the dew point is reached?
8. Describe the three major types of clouds.
9. What are the three stages in the evolution of the precipitation process? Explain each stage.
10. How does the ice crystal model explain the origin of precipitation?
11. What is the difference between the ice crystal and coalescence models for the origin of precipitation?

12 Explain the three major types of precipitation. How do they differ in origin?

13 Explain the operation of the hydrologic cycle.

14 Why do the oceans receive a proportionally higher amount of precipitation than the earth's landmasses?

15 What factors are important in determining the water balance of a place?

16 Why does the global water balance differ from place to place?

17 Why does the average annual precipitation figure reveal variability in annual precipitation?

18 Describe the types of precipitation regions of the world. Explain why each region exists.

19 What is the cause of acid rain? Where are the major areas where it is found? What are the environmental and economic costs of acid rain?

# 7
# AIR MASSES AND STORMS

## KEY WORDS

air mass
anticyclone
cold front
cyclone
easterly wave
Ferrel's law
hurricane
isobar
jet stream
occluded front
polar front
thunderstorm
tornado
warm front

Weather conditions in the middle latitudes are greatly influenced by air masses originating in tropical and polar regions. An *air mass* is a large body of air that is relatively homogeneous as to temperature, moisture, and other physical characteristics. It develops when air remains in contact with a uniform surface of great extent for some time. During this period of contact, the air mass acquires temperature and moisture properties similar to those of the surface on which it is resting. Air originating over warm water surfaces, for example, will be relatively warm and moist.

Large areas on the earth's surface where air masses originate are called *source regions* (Figures 7.1 and 7.2). Some common source regions are: (*a*) the warm waters of the Gulf of Mexico and the Caribbean Sea; (*b*) the hot lands in summer of the southwestern United States; (*c*) the winter ice- and snow-covered areas of interior Canada and the Arctic Ocean; (*d*) the cool waters of the north Pacific and Atlantic oceans; (*e*) the hot, humid land of the Amazon Basin; and (*f*) the hot, dry land of the Sahara Desert. When these air masses are carried by the world's atmospheric circulation system into other areas, they maintain the temperature and moisture characteristics of their source regions. They often travel thousands of miles and succeed in considerably modifying the weather of the areas they invade. Thus, since tropical air masses basically move poleward and polar air masses move equatorward, great and frequent changes of weather can be expected where they meet in the middle latitudes.

## AIR MASS CLASSIFICATION

Tor Bergeron, a Swedish meteorologist, developed a classification system for identifying air masses (Table 7.1). It is based on temperature and moisture characteristics of the geographic source region of each air mass.

The temperature classification of an air mass indicates the temperature of the air compared to the temperature of the underlying surface. If the air mass is colder than the earth's surface over which it is traveling, for example, the air mass is classified as cold (K). A warm air mass (W) has the reverse characteristic.

Moisture properties of air masses are also directly related to source regions. If the air originates over land, it

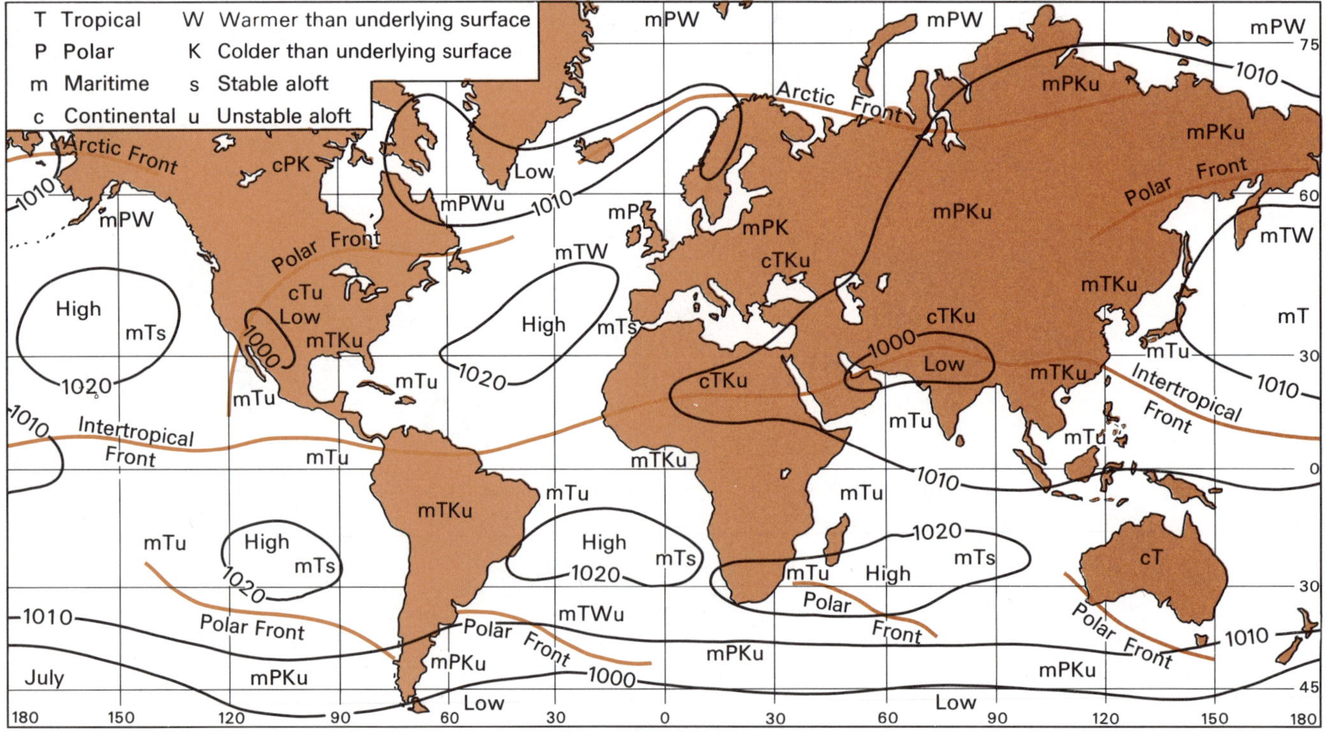


**FIGURE 7.1**
World air mass regions in July. (After Haurwitz and Austin, 1944)

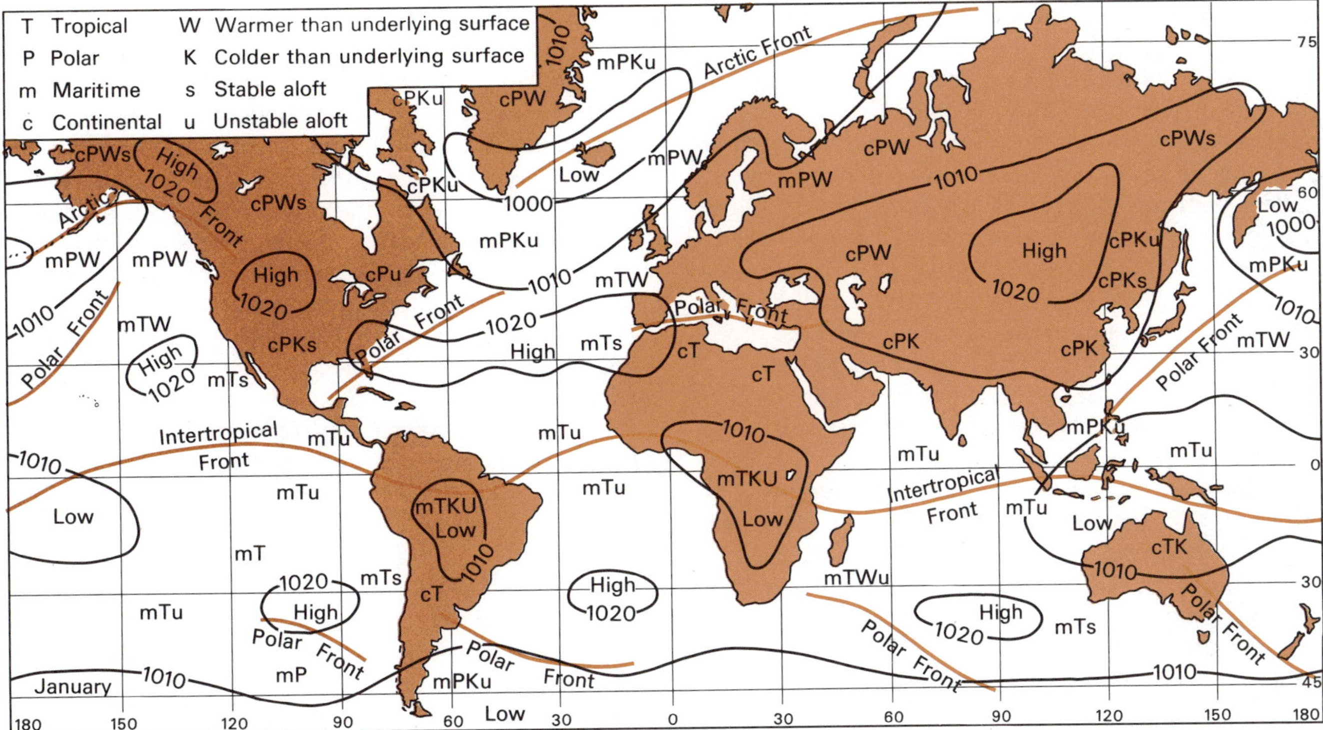


**FIGURE 7.2**
World air mass regions in January. (After Haurwitz and Austin, 1944)

is classified as *continental* (c), or dry, but if it originates over water it is called a *maritime* (m), or moist, air mass.

**TABLE 7.1**
Bergeron air mass classification

| Geographic Location |
|---|
| T—Tropical air mass (0° to 30°N and S) |
| P—Polar air mass (30° to 70° N or S) |
| A—Arctic air mass (70° to 90° N or S) |
| S—Superior air mass (Southwest part of North America) |
| **Temperature** |
| W—Warm air mass (Warmer than underlying surface) |
| K—Cold air mass (Colder than underlying surface) |
| **Moisture** |
| m—Maritime air mass (wet) |
| c—Continental air mass (dry) |
| **Air Stability** |
| s—Stable aloft |
| u—Unstable aloft |

This classification can be used to identify the major features of an air mass moving over an area. The two major types of air masses are tropical and polar. Since air masses can originate over land or water, two other modifiers are used: continental and maritime. Thus, most air masses are tropical continental, tropical maritime, polar continental, or polar maritime. The properties of an oncoming air mass provide meteorologists with fundamental information about the weather in the immediate future.

## NORTH AMERICAN AIR MASSES

The different types of air masses follow certain tracks and create characteristic weather patterns. The continent of North America will serve as an example in the following discussion of air masses and their tracks and weather patterns.

### Polar Continental (cP)

Air masses that originate in winter over the snow- and ice-covered higher latitudes of North America, particularly in the Yukon and Mackenzie basins of Alaska and Canada, are often called polar Canadian air masses. The extremely cold, dry air develops a high pressure cell that ultimately pours into the heartland of the United States.

This polar air mass follows three major wintertime tracks, all of which produce frigid weather in northern United States and southern Canada, and often chilly weather as far south as the Mexican border and Florida. The first path of this polar air mass crosses the Great Lakes, bringing heavy snow showers and gusty winds to the lee side of the lakes. As the air mass moves eastward into the Saint Lawrence lowland, it brings wind and cold temperatures until it moves offshore from northeastern United States and southeastern Canada.

The second path of the cold, dry air comes through the central part of the United States. When this cold air penetrates as far south as the Gulf region, it is known as a *norther.* As this air moves southward, it brings extreme temperature drops, low relative humidity, and clear skies. When this condition occurs, the Florida fruit and vegetable growers prepare to counteract the cold air by using heat and smoke stoves. Such weather occurs several times each winter.

The third path of the cold, dry air from central Canada is to the valleys on the Pacific coast. This movement is not well developed because of the high Rockies and other ranges in western United States. The high pressure must be strong enough to force the air over the high mountain ranges before it appears in such areas as the Central Valley of California. However, the phenomenon does occur occasionally, bringing cold, snowy weather.

In the summer the cP air is much warmer because the area of snow covering is smaller and the land surface is being heated. A summer heat wave in the middle or northeastern part of the continent may be broken by the invasion of a cP air. The cP air rarely extends to southern United States in summer.

## Polar Maritime (mP)

North America has two maritime polar sources of air—one in the Atlantic Ocean, the other in the Pacific Ocean.

The Atlantic mP originates over the cold ocean currents off the coast of Newfoundland and Labrador. Because the prevailing air currents are offshore, the mP air rarely penetrates the continent. However, when there is a strong continental high pressure, this cold, wet air flows onto the shore of eastern Canada and northeastern United States. It brings gale winds, high relative humidity, stratus cloud covering, and wintertime snows. In New England these storms are known as *northeasters* because they come from the northeast.

The Pacific mP originates in the northern Pacific and Alaska. Westerly winds carry the mP air onto the west coast of North America by three distinct routes. The mP air that originates in Alaska travels over the relatively short water route to British Columbia and northwestern United States. In its journey over the north Pacific it gathers moisture, and so brings copious precipitation to the mountainous coastal regions. The second and third mP routes follow Pacific waters for long distances, entering the United States from central California to Mexico. The moisture-laden air brings precipitation to the coastal areas. They are best developed during the winter period when the westerly winds are at their peak. In the summer the mP air, when it moves from the Pacific, brings clear skies and only a few scattered cumulus clouds.

## Tropical Maritime (mT)

The mT air masses originate in the tropical waters of the Atlantic Ocean and Gulf of Mexico. They can originate at any time but have their greatest influence on the eastern United States during the summer period. The mT air is characterized by high temperatures and humidity. As it moves over the warmer land, the air becomes unstable, resulting in convectional storms with heavy precipitation. When mT air penetrates into northeastern United States, it causes a summer heat wave. As it moves off the coast, it overrides the cooler air over the Labrador current, creating an advection fog over such areas as the Grand Banks of Newfoundland.

When a high pressure exists over Bermuda, mT air can move westward through the Gulf of Mexico, entering the continent along the coast of Texas and Mexico. As the air moves over the mountains of eastern Mexico, heavy orographic precipitation results on land that is normally dry.

During the winter months the mT air masses bring warmth and high humidity to the Atlantic and Gulf coasts. A well-developed air mass can penetrate far to the north, bringing a January thaw to the cold northeast. Although this phenomenon may be associated with moving clouds, the afternoons are usually clear with cumulus clouds.

The Pacific mT air affects only the lower coast of California and Mexico, and does so only rarely. When it does penetrate the land, it brings warm, moist air, producing heavy precipitation. This phenomenon occurs only during the winter months when the westerly winds move the air mass from the Pacific. During the summer period the Pacific high pressure areas block the flow of the air mass into the continent.

### Tropical Continent (cT)

The tropical continental air masses have a limited influence on the weather and climate of North America. The source region is small because the North American landmass tapers to a point in the tropical areas of Central America. Nevertheless, a source region does exist in northern Mexico and southwestern United States. This air mass is characterized by dry, extremely hot conditions, and is best developed in summer. Temperatures in this air mass exceed 38°C (100°F) for months, causing severe heat waves.

### Superior (S)

The superior air mass develops in the southwestern United States. It is primarily an upper air mass, but occasionally reaches the surface. This hot, dry air is thought to be associated with the subtropical high pressure belt. Superior air is stable and moves randomly. As a consequence it produces droughtlike conditions wherever it prevails.

## MODIFICATION OF AIR MASSES

As an air mass moves out of its source region, its characteristics slowly change. The changes are primarily a response to the characteristics of the different surfaces, land or water, over which the air mass passes.

The temperature of an air mass gradually assumes the temperature of the surface over which it passes. For example, a polar continental air mass will be warmed when it passes over a surface free from ice and snow. Even in midwinter, the southern United States is seldom affected by frigid polar air. As it crosses the United States, this air is gradually warmed in relation to its source region in central Canada.

The moisture content of an air mass is also changed by the surface over which it passes. For example, if a dry air mass passes over a water body, such as the Great Lakes, it gathers large quantities of moisture. On the lee side of the lakes the air is cooled and snow begins to fall. This phenomenon provides a partial explanation for the heavy snowfalls on the southern side of the Great Lakes.

The topography of a region also influences the character of an air mass, especially in mountainous terrain. Air is forced to rise on the windward side of a mountain and then to subside on the leeward side. This action removes moisture on the windward side as the air mass is cooled and increases the temperature on the leeward side as the air mass descends the mountain slopes.

## MIDDLE LATITUDE CYCLONES AND ANTICYCLONES

In the middle latitudes, where the westerly winds dominate, the atmosphere at the earth's surface is characterized by turbulence and frequent changes in temperature, pressure, humidity, and precipitation conditions. These changes are caused by the passage of great whirling masses of air, called *cells,* of low and high pressure. Those of low pressure are termed *cyclones* and those of high pressure are called *anticyclones.* (The term cyclone as used in this discussion should not be confused with the destructive local storms that are also called by that name.) Pressure cells are, for the most part, systems of gentle winds with normal pressure gradients. They move in a continuous parade toward the east, each cyclone usually separated from the following one by an anticyclone. No two pressure areas have identical conditions. As a result, the weather in the middle latitudes is highly uncertain. Frequent changes occur with the passage of each *cyclonic storm* over a particular area.

### NORWEGIAN CYCLONE MODEL

Before the 1920s there was no acceptable theory as to the origin of cyclonic storms. A satisfactory explanation evolved only after J. Bjerknes and other Norwegian meteorologists presented their polar front theory of the origin of cyclones. Oscillations in the boundary between cold polar air and warm tropical air in the upper middle latitudes were first recognized during World War I. The periodic flareups of weather along this boundary reminded the Norwegian scientists of the long battle line in Europe with its intermittent activity.

According to the Norwegian model, a cyclonic storm develops when a surging mass of polar air moving equatorward comes in contact with a mass of tropical air moving poleward. These two air masses normally meet somewhere over the upper middle latitudes. They do not mix readily; instead, a boundary known as the *polar front* is formed between them, separating the two air masses (Figure 7.3).

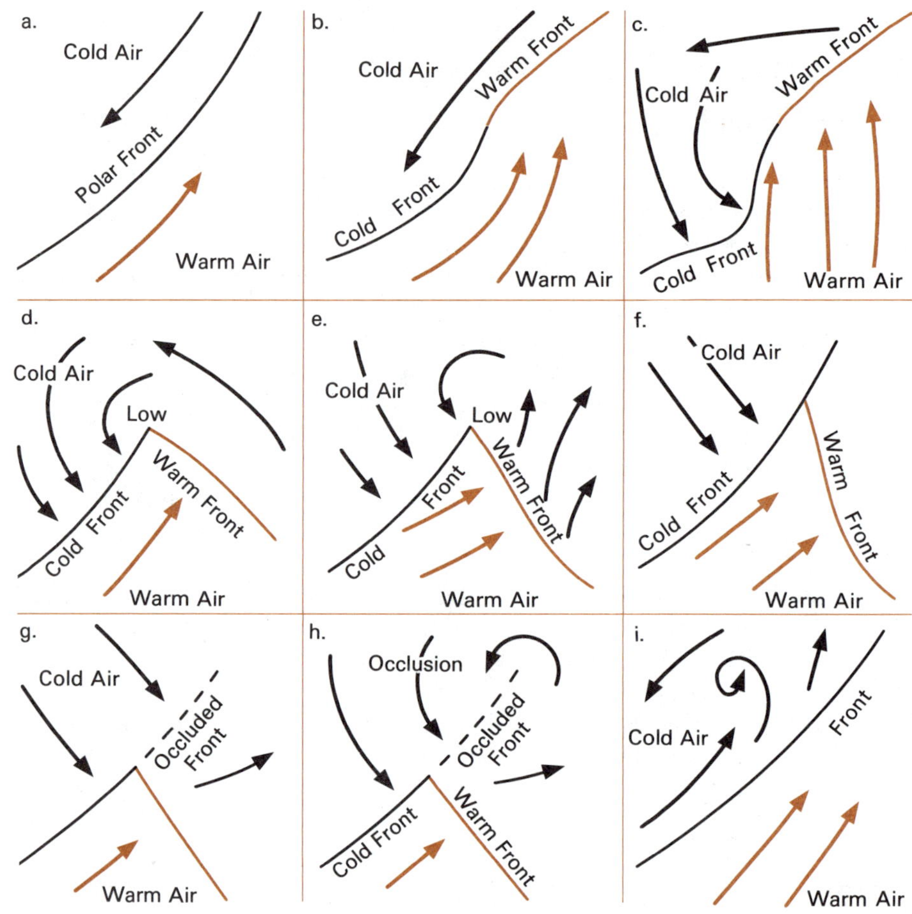


**FIGURE 7.3** Development and occlusion of a cyclonic storm. Development begins when (*a*) cold air surges equatorward while warm air moves poleward. (*b* and *c*) The two air masses deflect each other, causing the front to become indented. (*d, e,* and *f*) A warm front develops in the area where the cold air is the aggressor. By this stage a typical cyclonic storm has developed, with the characteristic counterclockwise swirling air mass. Lowest pressure is near the place where the warm and cold fronts meet. (*g* and *h*) The cyclonic storm is ebbing; an occlusion develops as the cold front overtakes the warm front. (*i*) The occluded front is complete and only a weak front separates the unlike air masses in the area. (After U.S. Weather Bureau)

Along the boundary between the cold and warm air masses the warm air slopes upward over the cold air, because the colder, heavier air mass wedges in and lifts the warm air mass. As a result, the air masses on the polar front, which is 50 to 100 kilometers in width, become deflected, and the front becomes indented. This is the initial stage of a so-called *wave cyclone.*

The polar air mass is deflected to one side, since it now has difficulty in moving closer to the equator, and the poleward-moving tropical air mass is similarly deflected. A bend or wave thus forms in the front. Consequently, the forward portion of the developing cyclone (eastern edge) is penetrated by air from warmer latitudes, and the rear portion of the storm (western edge) receives an influx of air from colder latitudes. The original slight indentation in the front then deepens, and a low pressure forms in its center. The mass of air begins to whirl, as shown in Figure 7.4.

After the typical cyclonic storm of low pressure has developed, a number of *fronts* can be recognized within different sectors of the storm (Figures 7.5 and 7.6). The line to the left of the low pressure center where the cold air is wedging under the restricting warm tropical air is called the *cold front* (Figure 7.5). Here the cold air is the aggressor, and often it lifts the warm air with great force, causing convectional storms to develop. To the right of the low pressure the warm air is the aggressor. Because the warm air is lighter than the cold air, it slips up over the retreating wedge of cold air. This line of contrast is known as the *warm front* (Figure 7.6). In most instances the turbulence on the warm front is not so great as along the cold front, nor is the lifting of the warm air so vigorous. The warm air between the fronts is known as the *warm sector.*

Within the typically developed cyclone, the cold front advances more rapidly than the warm front. As the cold front overtakes the warm front, the cold air masses meet on either side of the warm air mass, forcing the intervening warm air to rise above the surface. When the warm air mass between two fronts is lifted in this manner, an *occlusion* or *occluded front* is formed.

**FIGURE 7.4**
Typical middle latitude cyclone in the Northern Hemisphere. The isobaric arrangement, fronts, wind movements, and areas of precipitation are shown.

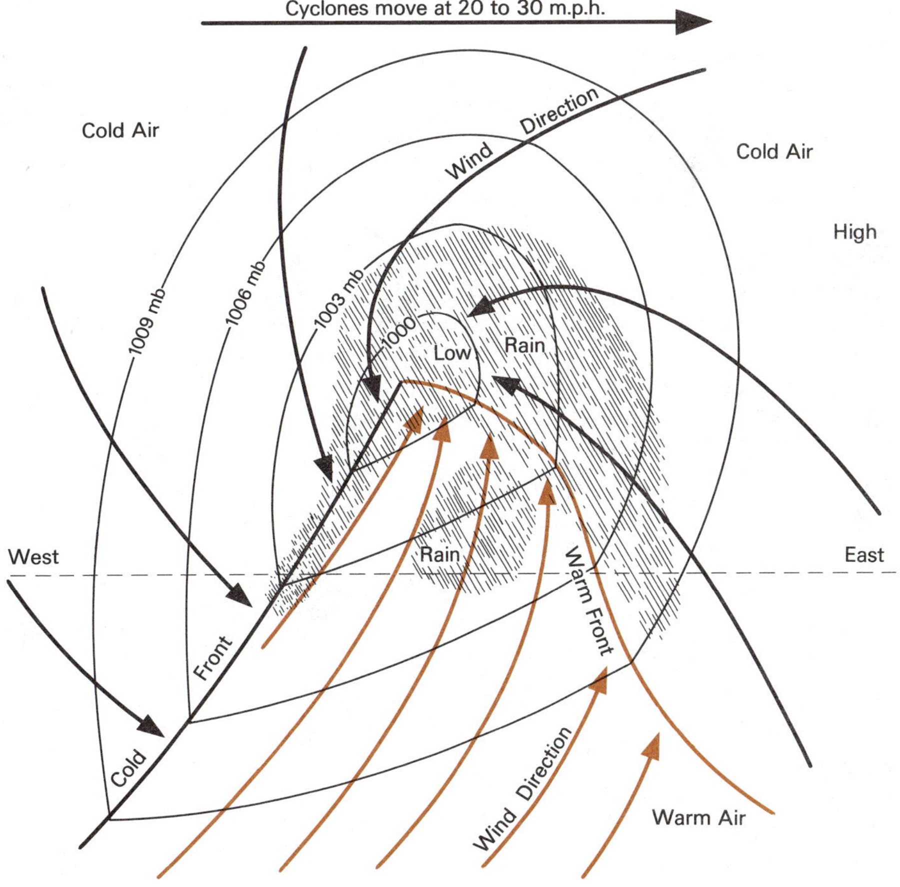


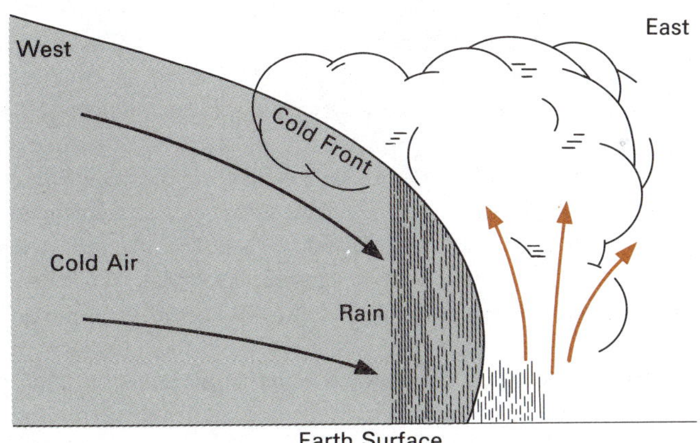


**FIGURE 7.5**
Profile of a cold front. Cold air forces the warm air upward along the cold front, frequently creating a line of violent weather.

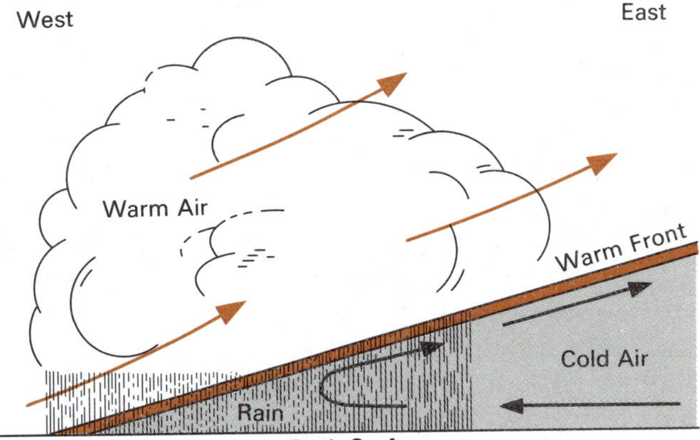


**FIGURE 7.6**
Profile of a warm front. The warm air flows smoothly upward over the cold mass of air on the warm front. This gentle action creates a large area of stratus clouds and an extended period of precipitation.

## GENERAL CHARACTERISTICS OF CYCLONES AND ANTICYCLONES

Cyclones and anticyclones are represented on a weather map by a series of closed, nearly concentric lines of equal pressure called *isobars*. In the cyclone, the pressure is lowest at the center and increases toward the margins; in an anticyclone, the pressure is highest at the center and decreases toward the margins. Thus a cyclone resembles a circular or oval depression, and an anticyclone resembles a dome-shaped hill or elevation. Pressure at the center of cyclones is about 1,000 millibars on the average. For a very strong continental cyclone it averages 970 millibars, and can be as low as 920 millibars for an extreme oceanic storm. A pressure drop of 2 millibars in 3 hours is a warning signal of an impending storm, a drop of 5 millibars is strong, and a drop of 10 millibars is extreme. Pressure at the center of an anticyclone will average about 1,100 millibars. No specific barometric pressure distinguishes a high from a low, however; the distinction is purely relative.

Cyclones and anticyclones vary in size. They sometimes cover areas as extensive as 2.5 million square kilometers (975,000 square miles), or about one-third the area of the continental United States. Because they cover such large areas, the isobars are normally widely spaced and the pressure gradients gentle. Anticyclones sometimes cover larger areas than cyclones. The gentle pressure gradients result in low wind velocities.

Both cyclones and anticyclones are carried along by prevailing westerly winds, and therefore have a general west-to-east movement. However, there are some broad belts over which these storms travel most frequently; these belts are often referred to as *storm tracks* (Figure 7.7). In the United States, for example, a large percentage of the cyclones move northeastward, following a path through the Great Lakes and leaving North America by way of the Saint Lawrence lowlands. Cyclones not only move generally eastward, but also tend to move toward higher latitudes. In contrast, anticyclones usually move equatorward. On the average, cyclones travel about 1,100 kilometers (700 miles) per day, with a range of about 320 to 1,800 kilometers (200 to 1,100 miles) per day. Movement of an individual cyclone may be erratic. It may remain stationary for a while, speed up, slow down, and even reverse its track briefly.

As a general rule, both cyclones and anticyclones are less developed, have weaker pressure gradients, and move more slowly in summer than in winter. The storm tracks they follow shift equatorward in winter and poleward in summer, as does the rest of the world system of pressure and wind belts. Cyclonic storms thus occur most frequently in southern United States in winter, when their track is farther south.

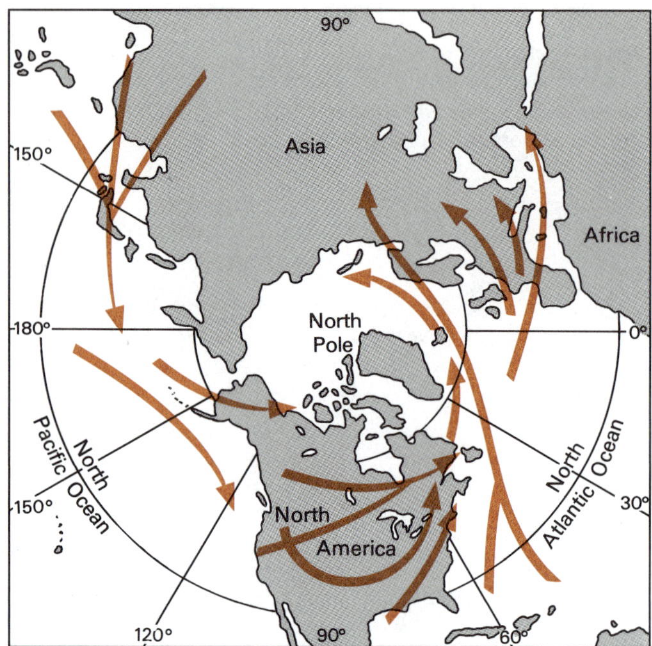


**FIGURE 7.7**
Cyclonic storm tracks in the Northern Hemisphere. Most cyclonic storms originate over the oceans and move across the continents by a number of routes.

Because cyclones are cells of low air pressure and because air moves from high to low pressure, cyclones are regions of *converging* winds. The air flows, in general, from the circumference toward the center of the storm. As the lowest pressure in the center of the storm approaches, a slow, usually gentle, lifting of the air takes place. The converging winds of the cyclone, as well as the prevailing winds, are subject to the effects of *Ferrel's law;* that is, they are deflected by the earth's rotation. The right-handed deflection in the Northern Hemisphere causes the winds to whirl in toward the center of the cyclone in a counterclockwise direction. The reverse motion is found in the Southern Hemisphere.

Anticyclones, in contrast, consist of air masses of *diverging winds.* In the center of the anticyclone is the area of highest pressure and settling air, from which the air flows outward to areas of lower pressure in the cyclones. Deflection due to earth rotation causes the outflowing air to whirl clockwise in the Northern Hemisphere and counterclockwise in the Southern.

As a rule, conditions within certain areas of a cyclone are conducive to condensation and consequent precipitation. In contrast, anticyclones are likely to be fair weather areas. Within a cyclone three general regions of precipitation can be identified (Figure 7.4). To the east of the low pressure center is the warm front, where warm, southerly air meets the cold, usually drier, polar air mass (Photo 17). As the warm air is lifted over the polar air mass, it is cooled by expansion. If the warm air is dry and stable, it will have to be lifted a long distance before precipitation results. Normally, however, the warm air mass is humid and unstable: a stratus cloud covering quickly evolves on the warm front and precipitation results. Because the precipitation falls through the cold polar air, the weather is likely to be chilly and disagreeable. Precipitation is steady and may last 24 hours or more. If the air through which the precipitation falls is below freezing, the rain may be frozen, partly into sleet. The warm front is the major area of precipitation within a cyclone.

The second area of precipitation in a cyclone is associated with the cold front that is located to the south and southwest of the low pressure center. As the cold polar air wedges underneath the warm tropical air, cooling occurs and precipitation results (Photo 18). The upward movement of warm, unstable air is frequently strong. The discontinuity between the warm and cold air masses is usually considerably steeper on a cold front than on a warm front. Cumulonimbus clouds develop in the rapidly rising, warm, humid air, resulting in frontal thunderstorms. The tumultuous weather along a cold front is characterized by heavy downpours of rather short duration. Because the air mass is overturning violently, precipitation can occur in front of as well as behind the cold front.

The third area of precipitation is in the warm southeastern sector of the cyclone. Here there is no driving air mass to lift the air. Instead, southerly winds that are heavily laden with moisture are gently lifted as they converge toward the low pressure center. The converging precipitation is called nonfrontal cyclonic precipitation. Stratus clouds are normal under these conditions, but precipitation is limited because large air masses are not lifted.

Temperature characteristics of cyclones and anticyclones are difficult to generalize, but are in general determined by the origin of the air masses that make up these systems. A well-developed anticyclone advancing rapidly in the middle latitudes will arrive as a mass of cold, dry air with clear skies prevailing. Such is often the case in North America, as a high pressure cell moves from the Yukon or the Mackenzie basins into the central and eastern sections of the United States. The clear, cloudless skies of the anticyclone also promote rapid radiational cooling of the atmosphere in winter. The characteristic winter *cold waves* of the central and eastern part of the United States are caused in this manner. Even in summer, such a well-developed high moving

**PHOTO 17**
Warm front. Warm air is rising over a colder mass of air, causing a cloud to develop. (Courtesy: National Oceanic and Atmospheric Administration)

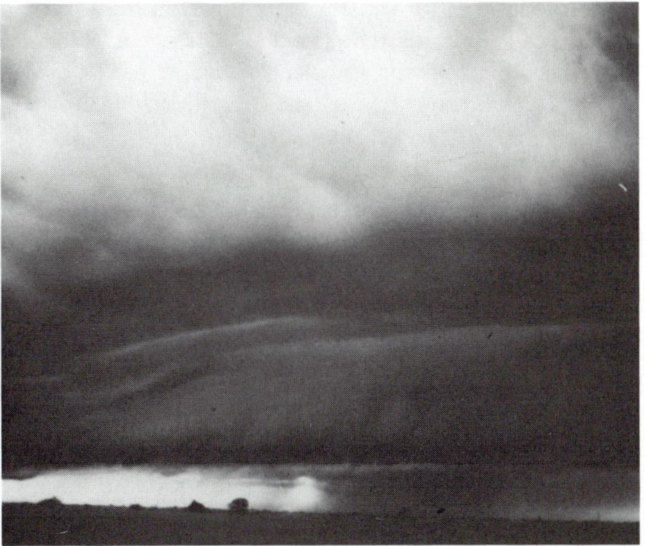

**PHOTO 18**
Cold front. Cold air is pushing under warmer air, forcing it to rise. (Courtesy: National Oceanic and Atmospheric Administration)

rapidly from Canada will result in an abnormally cool spell during an otherwise hot summer.

If a well-developed anticyclone originates in tropical areas, and for some reason stagnates or moves more slowly into the middle latitudes, temperatures become considerably higher than normal. The so-called *heat waves* over central and eastern United States frequently occur in this manner. During the winter, such an anticyclone brings about a mild spell with a midwinter thaw and a rapidly melting snow cover.

Because well-developed cyclones comprise both tropical and polar air masses and are accompanied by cloud covering and precipitation, temperature conditions are more complex than those found in anticyclones. Within the cyclone the different air masses have marked temperature contrasts. Tropical air masses and southerly winds prevail in the south and southeast sections of a cyclone. Temperatures there are considerably warmer than in the northeast, north, and northwest sections, where polar air masses and northerly winds dominate. The importation of these different air masses causes the isotherms in the cyclone to travel from northeast to southwest rather than directly east-west.

The cloud covering associated with a cyclone also influences its temperature. In the winter the cloud cover tends to prevent the rapid loss of heat from the atmosphere. Therefore, temperatures can be expected to be higher than average when an area is under the influence of a cyclone in winter. In contrast, during summer, the cloud cover prevents insolation from effectively heating the atmosphere, for much of it is reflected from the top surface of the clouds. The cloud is once again a blanket, but this time it keeps the heat out. The passage of a cyclone in summer has a tendency to lower temperatures.

### CHANGES IN WIND DIRECTION WITH THE PASSAGE OF A CYCLONIC STORM

We have seen that cyclonic storms move in a general west-to-east direction around the world within the westerly wind belts. A person on the earth's surface, however, will experience a wide variety of wind directions as a cyclonic storm passes. If the low pressure area passes directly over the individual, the following wind directions will be experienced: As the forward edge of the cyclone approaches the observer, easterly winds are flowing into the low pressure center in a direction opposite to the prevailing westerly winds. These easterly winds will persist as long as the center of the low is to the west. As the center of the low pressure passes, the wind direction shifts until it comes directly from the west. These westerly winds are traveling in the same direction as the prevailing winds and indicate the passage of the low pressure center to the east. They herald the approach of an anticyclone, which normally follows a cyclone closely. Easterly winds thus indicate the approach of a low pressure center. They bring increasing cloudiness and probably warm front precipitation. Westerly winds foretell the passage of the cyclonic storm and the coming of an anticyclone with cloudless skies.

If the low pressure passes north or south of the observer, the wind direction will differ accordingly. If the center of the low passes to the south of the observer, then the shift would still be from east to west, but the series of changing directions are from the east, northeast, north, northwest, and west. If the center of the low passes to the north of the observer, the wind directions experienced are easterly, southeasterly, south, southwesterly, and westerly.

## JET STREAMS OF THE UPPER ATMOSPHERE

Although the existence of *jet streams* had long been postulated, they were not observed until 1946, when military planes encountered them while flying above 9,000 meters (30,000 feet) over the Pacific Ocean. These planes had a maximum speed of 320 kilometers (200 miles) per hour. On one occasion they encountered head winds of 320 kilometers and found themselves virtually motionless.

The jet streams have since been found to be circumpolar winds girdling the earth from west to east in both the Northern and Southern hemispheres. Although their courses meander, their average location is between 30° and 50° latitude (Figure 7.8). The jet streams are best defined along the polar front. Because of their relationship to the world's wind and pressure regions, they migrate on a daily as well as a seasonal basis. In summer the jet stream swings poleward (35° to 50° latitude); and in the winter it moves equatorward (25° to 45° latitude).

The intensity of the jet stream varies with the strength of the polar front. Over the United States, the average jet stream speed varies from about 160 kilometers (100 miles) per hour in summer to about 320 kilometers (200 miles) per hour in winter. Winds of over 650 kilometers (400 miles) per hour occur with the strongest fronts. The greatest velocities are obtained at elevations of 9,000 to 12,000 meters (30,000 to 40,000 feet).

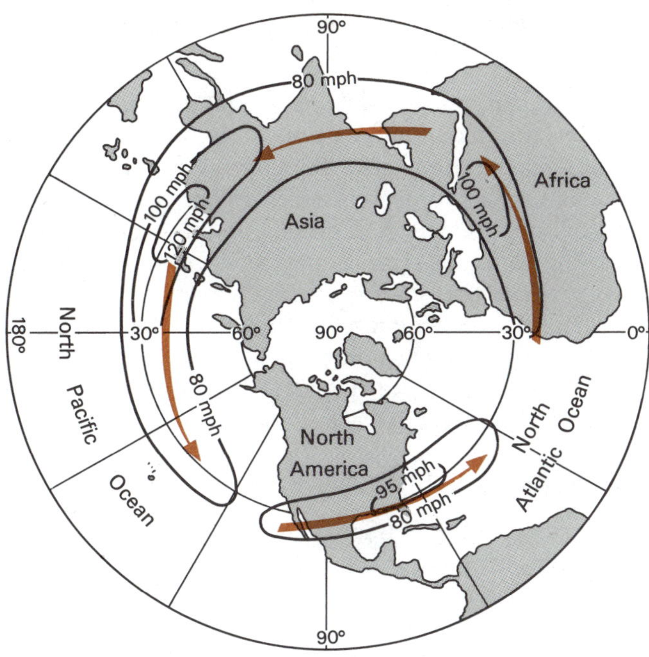


**FIGURE 7.8**
Jet stream in the Northern Hemisphere. The jet stream extends around the world from about 30° to 50° north latitude. The velocity of the jet stream in the upper atmosphere varies from 160 to over 320 kilometers (100 to over 200 miles) per hour. (After Namias, 1952)

Wind speed and direction vary rapidly across the jet stream. (Figure 7.9). A high-flying jet plane crossing the United States may cross the jet stream twice. The first time, the jet stream may have winds from the southwest averaging 320 kilometers (200 miles) per hour. Two hours later the plane could cross the jet stream again, this time encountering winds at a speed of 250 kilometers (155 miles) per hour from the opposite direction. In between the winds would drop to a mild 75 kilometers (45 miles) per hour. Such a strongly curved jet stream flowing across the United States is always associated with strong frontal action in the lower atmosphere.

The development of the jet streams is directly related to world temperature and pressure conditions. If the temperature of the atmosphere decreased uniformly from the equator to the poles, the atmospheric pressure would also decrease uniformly. In reality, however, temperatures tend to remain fairly constant over great distances, and to change abruptly over narrow zones called fronts. These fronts occur when great converging wind currents bring air masses from cold and warm source regions. The major contrasts in temperature from the equator to the poles occur in restricted areas known as *frontal zones.* Significant changes in pressure are also concentrated in these same frontal zones. Because of the direct relationship between pressure gradients and winds, the fastest winds in the upper atmo-

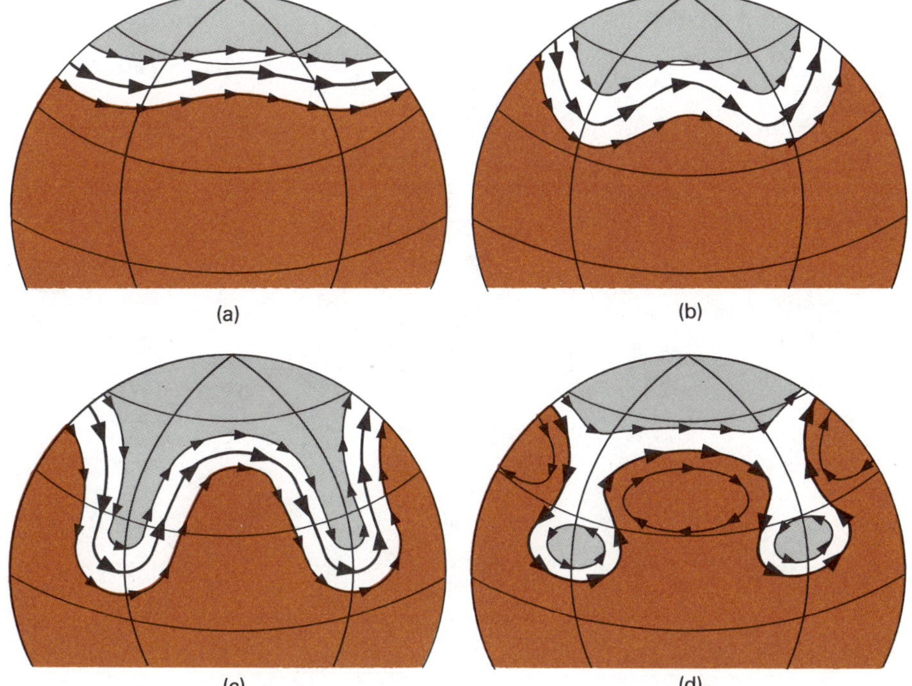


**FIGURE 7.9**
Cycle of the mid-tropospheric jet stream. (*a*) The flow begins with a strong east-west movement. (*b* and *c*) As the amplitude increases, a strong meridional flow results. At this time polar air is carried equatorward and tropical air to the middle and high latitudes. (*d*) In the final stage the warm and cold air masses are cut off, leaving isolated air masses. After this stage, the atmosphere flow reverts to stage *a.* (After Namias, 1952)

sphere occur over fronts. As a general rule, it can be stated that the stronger the polar fronts in terms of temperature differences, the faster the air movement in the jet streams.

At any one time, 3 to 6 jet waves form a complete, but interrupted, pattern around the world. Their oscillations may push cyclones with cold polar air into the lower latitudes. Or, if the jet streams move poleward, the paths of the cyclones also shift poleward, bringing warm tropical air into higher latitudes. The jet stream probably sets in motion the air masses in the middle latitudes, and this motion controls the weather. When a particular jet stream flow persists for several weeks, the area affected may be colder or warmer, or wetter or drier than normal, depending upon the position of the jet stream. For example, precipitation in the middle latitudes appears to be concentrated in areas lying beneath the jet stream. The jet stream phenomenon also helps to explain the transfer of energy from place to place in the middle latitudes.

Jet streams are important not only to meteorologists who are forecasting the weather in the middle latitudes. They also play a major role in modern aviation. Jet liners that fly near or at the top of the troposphere can be aided or handicapped, depending on whether they are flying with or against the high-velocity winds. The jet stream thus influences the consumption of fuel. Navigation of the aircraft is also affected. Turbulence frequently occurs where the wind speed or direction varies greatly with altitude. Also, because jet streams are associated with cyclonic fronts, clouds and storms can make flying difficult.

## ATMOSPHERIC DISTURBANCES IN THE TROPICAL REGIONS

The tropical areas of the world experience two types of atmospheric disturbances. One is the *tropical easterly wave,* which is nonviolent in nature, while the other is the destructive *hurricane,* which is known by several different names. Those originating in the Atlantic Ocean and Caribbean Sea are commonly called *hurricanes.* Over most of the western Pacific, however, these terrifying storms are known as *typhoons.* In other locations they are known by still other names, such as *baguio* in the Philippines. In the Indian Ocean the name commonly used is the *tropical cyclone.*

### TROPICAL EASTERLY WAVE

In the areas of the trade winds, a weak, elongated trough of low pressure occasionally develops and moves from east to west (Figure 7.10). This low pressure moves at a right angle to the movement of the trade winds and usually at a lower speed than the trades themselves. To the west of the easterly wave the weather is clear with possibly a few cumulus clouds, typical of the trade winds. As the wave approaches, the weather changes gradually. The barometer will drop slowly and the surface winds will shift equatorward. The cumulus clouds grow in depth, rising from about 1,500 meters (5,000 feet) to possibly more than 6,000 meters (20,000 feet) as the trade wind inversion rises and the moist surface layer increases in depth. The cumulus clouds gradually develop into cumulonimbus clouds, giving visible evidence of convective currents.

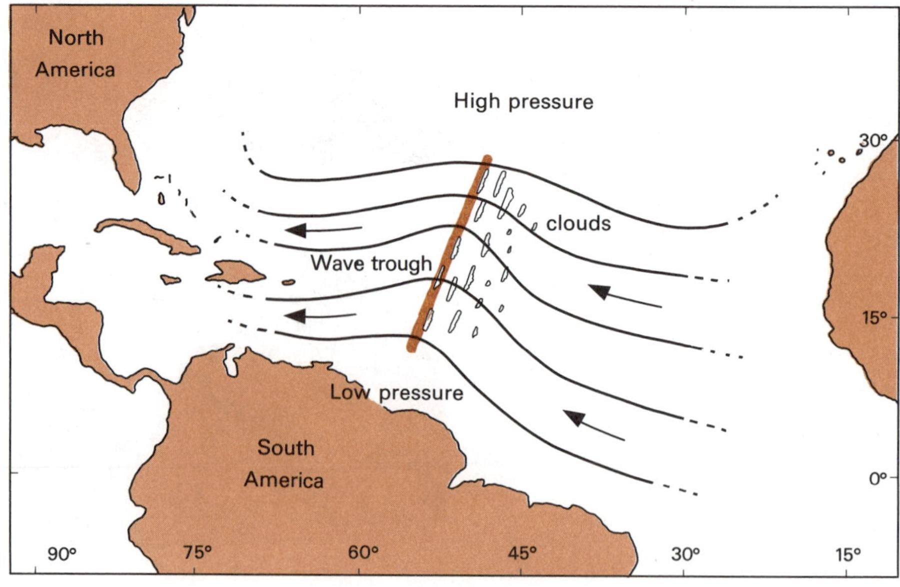


**FIGURE 7.10**
Tropical easterly wave. A low pressure develops in the Atlantic Ocean and is carried westward by the trade winds, bringing high clouds and brief showers. Because temperature differences do not exist in the easterly wave, fronts are not formed.

Frontal activity is absent in the easterly waves because contrasting air masses are not present.

The easterly waves develop most frequently over the ocean. They are usually from 80 to 160 kilometers (50 to 100 miles) wide and advance at 25 to 30 kilometers (15 to 20 miles) per hour. To areas in their path they bring welcome showers that last from 5 to 7 hours. As they pass, the wind inversion subsides and the moist layer becomes shallow, so that fine, clear weather once again prevails.

Easterly waves are most prominently developed north of the equator in the Pacific and Atlantic oceans and in tropical west Africa. They ordinarily pass observation points about once every 4 days. For reasons not yet understood, an easterly wave may become a tropical depression and ultimately develop into a hurricane.

## HURRICANES

Hurricanes are storms that invariably form in the latitudes from 5° to 20° from the equator (Figure 7.11; Photo 19). At first they move westward with the prevailing trade winds. Later, probably because of the Coriolis force and because they encounter high pressure cells, they tend to swing in an arc poleward. This movement brings them into the westerly wind belt of the middle latitudes. They normally then move toward the east, diminishing quickly in intensity and disappearing as a destructive storm. The energy and intensity of a hurricane can span more than 800 kilometers (500 miles), and disturb more than 4 million cubic kilometers of atmosphere (Figure 7.12).

The energy of a hurricane is generated and maintained by the condensation of water vapor within a humid, tropical air mass. Hurricanes are best developed when the ocean waters are their warmest. For example, the temperature of the Atlantic Ocean off the West African coast was relatively cool between 1974 and 1978, and few hurricanes developed. In 1979 the temperature began to warm and by June 1, when the six-month hurricane season began, the temperature of the water around the Cape Verde Islands was 26.6°C (80°F) or more. By late summer 1979 this moist tropical area had spawned 4 hurricanes. One of them, named David, was one of the most destructive storms of this century. It was rated a number 4 on the Saffir-Simpson scale, which is used to classify hurricanes. The scale was devised by consulting engineer Herbert Saffir and Dr. Rob-

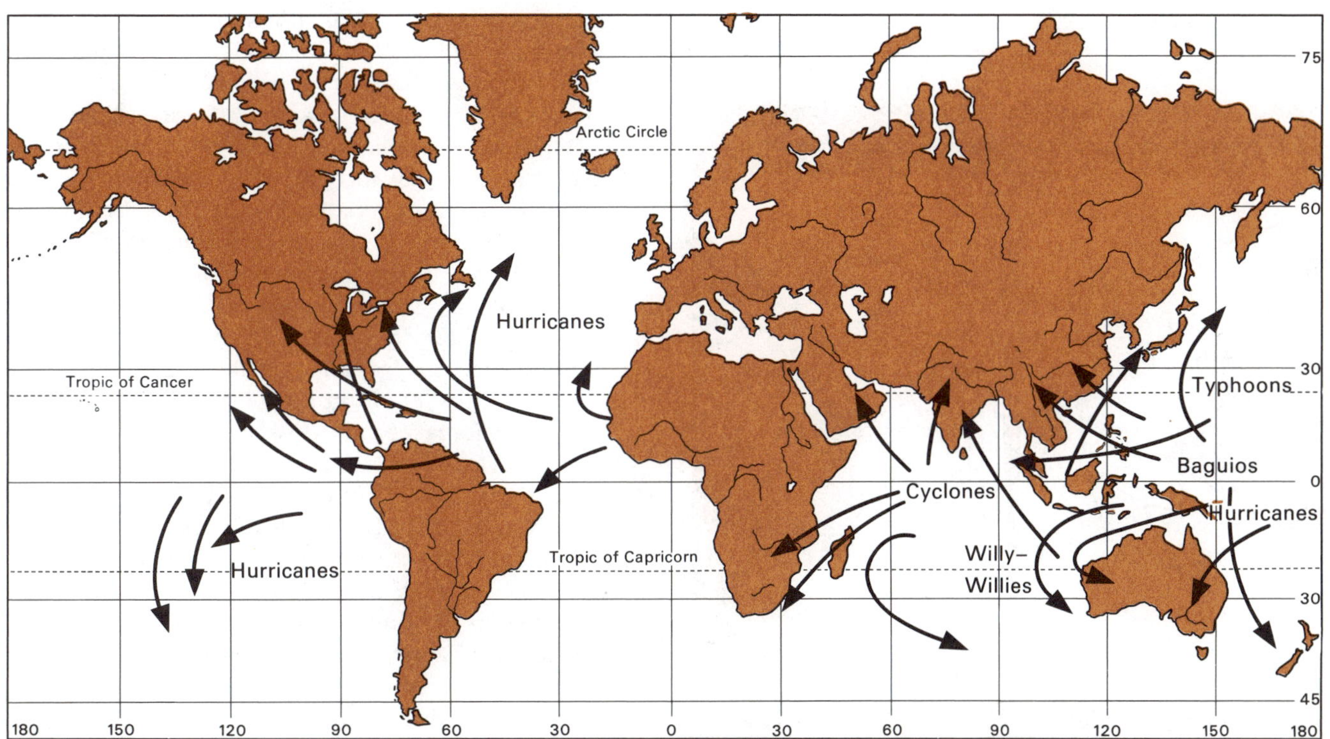


**FIGURE 7.11**
Typical paths of tropical storms.

**PHOTO 19**
Hurricane Frederic, lying off the southern U.S. coast on September 12, 1979. Note a smaller hurricane off the western coast of Mexico. The eye of the storm is visible in both hurricanes. (Courtesy: National Oceanic and Atmospheric Administration)

ert H. Simpson, former director of the National Hurricane Center. A storm ranked 1 is minimal; 2, moderate; 3, extensive; 4, extreme; and 5, catastrophic. Only 3 hurricanes in this century have been classified as number 5: the 1935 Labor Day storm that ravaged the Florida Keys; Camille in 1969 with its devastation in Cuba; and Allen in 1980, the most powerful Caribbean hurricane ever recorded.

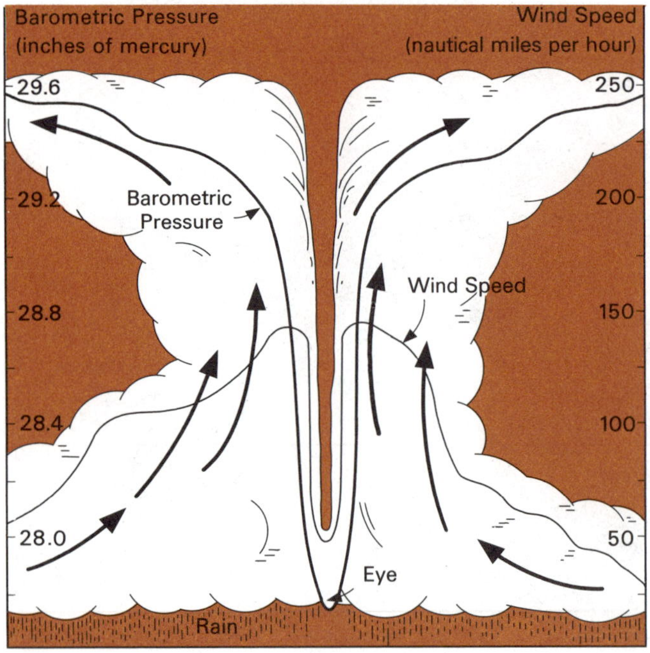

The energy released in a hurricane is enormous. It is estimated that the rate of condensation heating in a typical hurricane is $10^{11}$ kilowatts. Thus in a day a hurricane produces $24 \times 10^{11}$ kilowatt-hours. This far exceeds the daily consumption of electricity in the United States, which is about $15 \times 10^{11}$ kilowatt-hours.

The origin of the hurricane is unique. Although its development is not entirely understood, a strong relationship is generally recognized between two weather systems of different horizontal scale: the large hurricane vortex and the much smaller cumulonimbus clouds of thunderstorms. In the initial stage of hurricane formation, an easterly wave with its high cirrus clouds appears about 500 kilometers (300 miles) in advance of the hurricane. As pressure gradients intensify, warm, moist air is drawn in from the intertropical convergence zone. Wind force begins to exceed the 15 to 30 kilometers (10 to 20 miles) per hour of the normal trade winds. Within 320 kilometers (200 miles) of the center of the hurricane, gale force winds exceeding 65 kilometers (40 miles) per hour develop. The disturbance is now classified as a tropical storm and a name is assigned. When the pressure within 160 kilometers (100 miles) of the center continues to lower and winds of 120 kilometers (75 miles) or greater per hour persist, the storm is upgraded to a hurricane. A cumulonimbus cloud covering now persists and copious rain falls. The circulations associated with the individual clouds and with the hurricane vortex reinforce each other in the condensation of water vapor, providing energy for in-

**FIGURE 7.12**
Profile of a hurricane, showing its strong pressure gradient and extremely high wind velocities.

creasing the pressure gradient and ultimately the force of the winds. Precipitation usually begins 100 to 115 kilometers (60 to 70 miles) from the vortex and increases in intensity toward the center. The air whirling around the calm center may have a steady velocity of 240 kilometers (150 miles) per hour with gusts up to 280 kilometers (175 miles) per hour. The center of the hurricane is called the *eye.* Here the wind stops abruptly, the rains cease, and the sky clears. The clouds may appear as a vertical wall around the eye of the hurricane; their altitude may exceed 12,000 meters (40,000 feet). The eye will soon pass and the observer will experience conditions similar to those during the approach of the hurricane, except in the reverse order. The hurricane is thus an unusually well organized, very large convectional system.

Hurricanes cause much loss of life and tremendous property damage (Photo 20). Since 1900 the hurricanes that have affected the Caribbean, the Gulf of Mexico, and the southern and eastern coasts of North America have killed an estimated 45,000 persons, of whom 13,000 were in the United States. Of the Caribbean nations, Haiti, Cuba, Dominican Republic, and Honduras have experienced the most devastation. In Haiti alone, hurricanes have killed an estimated 8,400 persons, of whom 5,000 died in hurricane Flora in 1963. Nine out of ten victims drowned in *storm tides,* or *storm surges,* which are walls of water swept on shore by the high winds. The extremely low pressure in the eye of the storm causes the ocean surface to rise 0.3 to 0.6 meter (1 to 2 feet). Wind-driven water piles into a huge wave as the hurricane approaches land. When this water is driven against a low shore, the water level can be as high as 7.5 meters (25 feet) above normal tide. The storm surge is frequently augmented by other waves 3 to 4 meters (9 to 12 feet) tall that slam ashore before, during, and after a hurricane. For example, on September 8, 1900, a hurricane roared into Galveston, Texas. A 6-meter (20-foot) high storm tide that followed drowned 6,000 persons. Although the city of 38,000 was warned of the approaching hurricane, many did not heed the danger.

**PHOTO 20**
Hurricane destruction. Rubble is all that remains of a 32-unit apartment building in Gulfport, Mississippi, after the passage of hurricane Camille in August 1969. (Courtesy: National Oceanic and Atmospheric Administration)

Attempts have been made to modify the force of hurricanes to make them less destructive. The procedures involve "seeding" the storm with silver iodide and other hygroscopic chemicals. The principle behind this technique is that seeding releases the latent heat of the storm, expanding the air in the cloud and thus changing its pressure. Under certain circumstances such a variation of pressure will reduce wind velocities within the storm. This technique was first applied to a hurricane off the Florida coast in 1947. After seeding, the storm changed its course and came on land in Georgia, causing extensive damage. Whether the seeding caused this change in course is not known, but the attempt to modify hurricanes was abandoned until 1960. In that year the U.S. Weather Bureau initiated Project Stormfury. This project had two objectives: to obtain more precise data on the weather characteristics of hurricanes, and to develop numerical models for use in planning modification experiments. Strict guidelines were established as to what hurricanes could be seeded. Seeding experiments are limited to hurricanes in which the center is judged to have less than a 10 percent chance of approaching within 80 kilometers (50 miles) of a populated area, either island or mainland, within 18 hours after seeding. Few hurricanes have a course suitable for experimentation. The three hurricanes seeded in the 1960s provided results that could be interpreted as confirming model calculations, but serious uncertainties remained. In 1971 Hurricane Ginger was seeded, but the structure of the storm was so complex that it provided little general information on effectiveness of the seeding technique. Little progress was made in the 1970s, and the National Hurricane Center now believes that attempts to control hurricanes by seeding would be ineffective.

## SEVERE LOCAL STORMS

Two major types of severe local storms are widely distributed in the world: the convectional storm, or *thunderstorm,* and the *tornado.*

## THUNDERSTORMS

Thunderstorms are classified as severe storms because they are often associated with squall winds of high velocity, torrential downpours that sometimes cause local flash flooding, dangerous lightning flashes, and hailstones that can damage crops. Thunderstorms are related to rapid upthrusts of air. This air movement can be caused by (*a*) excessive heating of an air mass, which causes the air to rise in a convectional current; (*b*) orographic action, the movement of air up a mountainside; (*c*) uplift along a cyclonic front; or (*d*) turbulence resulting from friction of moving air along the surface of the earth (Figure 7.13).

The life cycle of the thunderstorm includes three characteristic stages. It begins with the uplift of an air cell to a height where cumulus clouds appear. This is known as the *cumulus stage.* In this stage the cell increases laterally in size from 1.5 to 3 kilometers (1 to 2 miles) to 8 to 10 kilometers (5 to 6 miles). The air mass may reach a height of 10,500 meters (35,000 feet). The updraft is strongest near the top of the cloud, with air coming from all sides.

The *mature stage* begins when the cumulonimbus forms and rain begins to fall from the cloud. In this stage the ice crystals and rain droplets become so large that the updraft can no longer support them and they begin to drop. The precipitation places a frictional drag on the updraft, which stops in time but is replaced by a strong downward motion. When the downdraft meets the ground it spreads out as a cool, gusty surface wind. The mature stage represents the most intense period of the thunderstorm. Heavy rainfall is frequently accompanied by lightning and strong turbulent winds (Photo 21). If the temperature is below freezing in the updraft, the raindrops may become hail. The mature stage normally lasts from 15 to 30 minutes.

The last stage, known as the *dissipating stage,* begins when the downdraft spreads over the entire cell of air. As the updraft diminishes and ultimately disappears, the energy that produces the precipitation is dissipated. Consequently the cloud begins to dissolve, the thunder and lightning lessen, and the storm fades away.

Possibly the most striking aspect of a thunderstorm is the accompanying thunder and lightning. As long ago as 1750 Benjamin Franklin demonstrated that lightning was a giant electrical spark. It has long been known that the cumulonimbus cloud possesses "poles" of concentrations of positively and negatively charged particles.

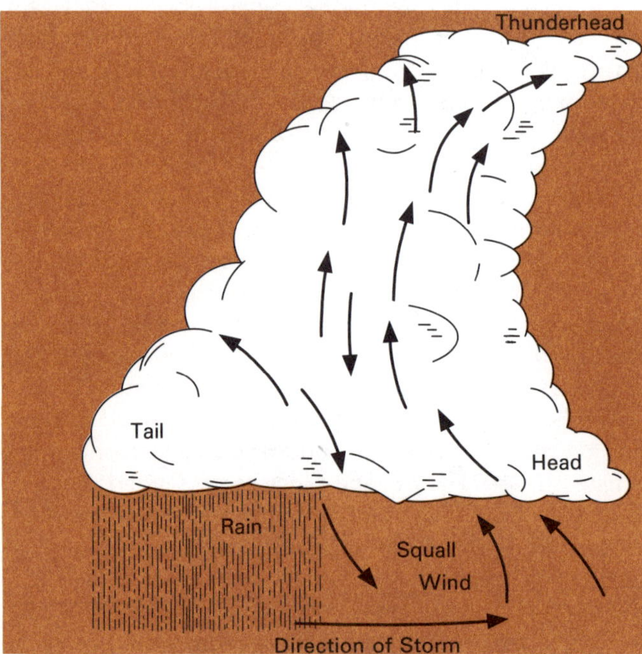


**FIGURE 7.13**
Profile of a typical thunderstorm. Warm, moist air rises in strong updrafts within the storm, creating cumulonimbus clouds. Downdrafts occur behind the updrafts, resulting in squall winds. Electrical exchanges between the positively and negatively charged particles produce lightning and its accompanying thunder.

**PHOTO 21**
Lightning. A bolt of lightning strikes the ground during a violent thunderstorm. (Courtesy: National Oceanic and Atmospheric Administration)

However, it is still not adequately understood how the convective currents within the cloud produce the electrical charge and then separate the positive and negative charges.

The lower portion of the cloud possesses the negative ions, and the upper part the positive ions. A number of hypotheses attempt to explain this phenomenon. Initially, as ice develops at the top of the cloud, friction between the ice crystals results in a negative charge. As the large ice crystals fall, the negative charges will be carried downward. In the rising air currents the positive ions will be captured most readily and pushed upward. The top of the cloud thus becomes positively charged while the negative ions remain at the base of the cloud.

The electrical potential generated within the cloud is enormous. Just before a discharge, the potential electrical charge reaches hundreds of millions of volts. A typical thunderstorm will dissipate electrical energy of more than a million kilowatts. It is estimated that more than 3,000 thunderstorms are occurring on the earth at any one time.

Occasionally hail is associated with a thunderstorm and adds to its severity. Hailstones develop when raindrops are caught in upward thrusts of air currents within the storm and are lifted into air where the temperature is below freezing. An individual hailstone may fall part of the way to the surface, picking up moisture, and then be thrust upward by air currents. This pattern may be repeated a number of times before the hailstone is finally heavy enough to overcome the upward movement of air, or before the force of that thrust diminishes. The number of times a hailstone is lifted into the freezing altitudes determines how many layers of ice it acquires and how large it becomes. Hailstones have been known to grow as large as golf balls or, on rare occasions, as large as a baseball.

Thunderstorms may be dangerous to airplanes in flight. The turbulent air movement in a thunderstorm may force an airplane upward or downward at speeds where control of the plane is lost. Wind speeds as high as 215 kilometers (135 miles) per hour and vertical displacement as much as 3,000 meters (10,000 feet) have been recorded in thunderstorms. If hail is associated with the storm, it can cause structural damage to the airplane. The electrical discharges in the storm can affect the magnetic compass in a plane as well as radio communication. Airplane pilots normally fly around thunderstorms rather than through them. Figure 7.14 shows where thunderstorms occur most frequently in the United States.

## TORNADOES

Tornadoes are the most violent and destructive of all storms (Photo 22). Fortunately the possibility of a tornado affecting a particular area is quite remote. Nevertheless, about 800 to 900 tornadoes occur each year in the United States, mostly in the plains of central and southeastern United States (Figure 7.15). Tornadoes are known to have occurred in every region of the world except the extremely cold regions. They most commonly occur in the spring, but can occur in any season.

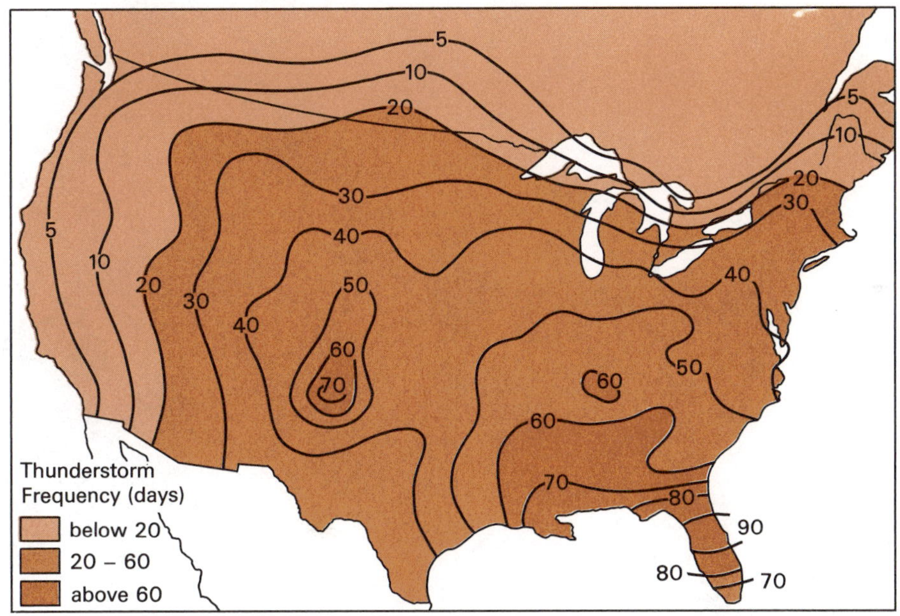


**FIGURE 7.14**
Frequency of thunderstorms in the United States. The greatest number of thunderstorms occur in southeastern United States in the areas of long, hot, humid summers.

**PHOTO 22**
Tornado. General view of a tornado on the Great Plains of Colorado. Note the small area covered by the funnel. (Courtesy: National Archives)

The tornado possesses a number of unique characteristics. Because the pressure in the center of the tornado is abnormally low, the pressure gradient is extremely high (Figure 7.16). The highest velocity winds are too strong for the ordinary *anemometer* to measure, but generally the wind speeds are from 150 to 500 kilometers (100 to 300 miles) per hour. They can exceed 650 kilometers (400 miles) per hour, however. The diameter of a typical tornado is between 100 and 450 meters (300 and 1,500 feet) (Photos 23–26). The paths of tornadoes average only about 6 kilometers (4 miles) in length, but they are extremely erratic. Some will touch the ground along a path of only 200 to 350 meters (650 to 1,150 feet), while others will hop and skip over tracks of several hundred kilometers. Some tornadoes barely move while others travel at speeds up to 200 kilometers (125 miles) per hour.

The tornado is usually heralded by a dark mass of cumulonimbus clouds seemingly in turmoil. From this mass descends a funnel-shaped cloud. Tornadoes are sometimes known as "twisters" because of their wild characteristics. Although the spiraling of air is still not fully understood, in the Northern Hemisphere the air

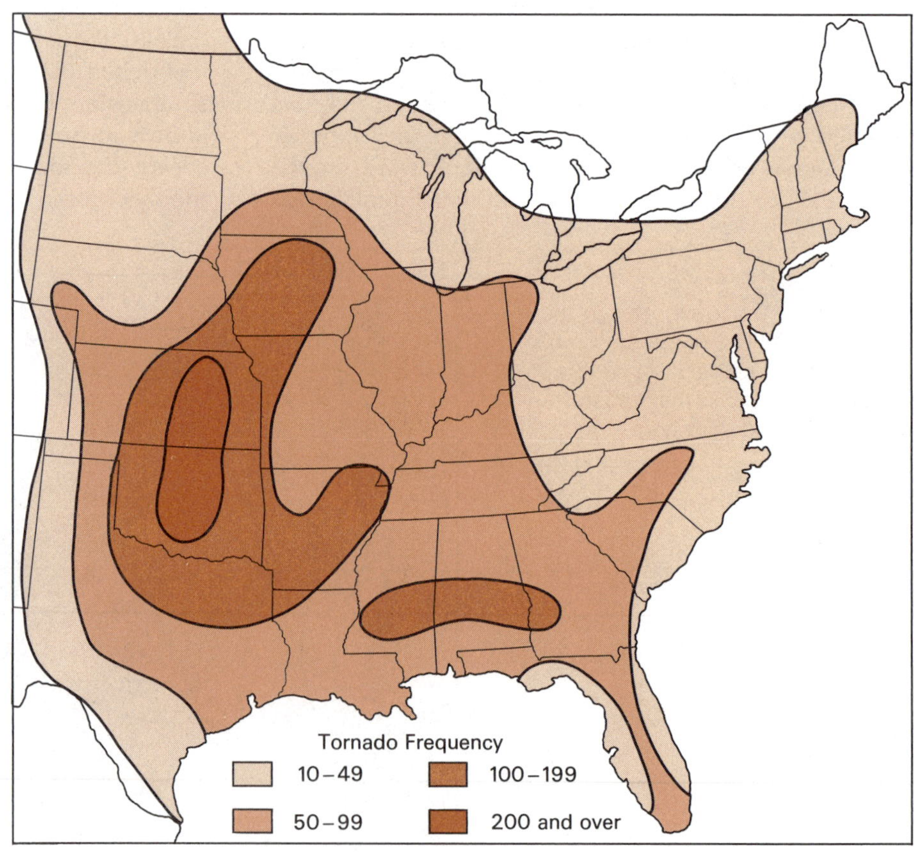


**FIGURE 7.15**
Frequency of tornadoes in the United States. Tornado frequency is in the plains of midwestern United States.

**FIGURE 7.16**
Diagrammatic representation of isobars in a tornado. Because the pressure gradient is so high, winds obtain a velocity of several hundred kilometers per hour.

moves counterclockwise like the common cyclone, with a converging system of winds and rapidly ascending vertical currents near the center. The vertical velocities are thought to be hundreds of miles per hour. Tornadoes have an explosive effect on buildings over which they pass. Because of the extremely high pressure gradient within the storm, the pressure within the building is much greater than the pressure outside (Photo 27). No human structure can survive if a tornado passes directly over it. Trucks and railroad cars have been lifted and carried hundreds of yards. Whole brick houses have been demolished and simply carried away in the funnel of the tornado. This force sometimes causes freakish happenings. The feathers have been stripped from chickens without killing them and roofs have been lifted from houses without touching the contents inside.

23

24

25

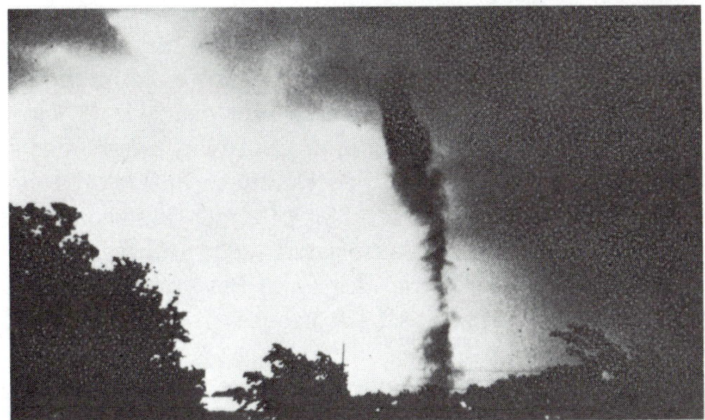

26

**PHOTOS 23–26**
Tornado funnel. The photographs illustrate the evolution of the destructive funnel and its final disintegration. (Courtesy: National Oceanic and Atmospheric Administration)

**PHOTO 27**
Tornado destruction. The destructive path of a tornado in Guin, Alabama. (Courtesy: National Oceanic and Atmospheric Administration)

The atmospheric conditions that spawn tornadoes are frequently the same as those that produce squall lines on fronts and severe thunderstorms. In the United States, these conditions occur most often in the Midwest, and this area has more tornadoes than anywhere else in the world. Tropical maritime air from the south meets polar continental air from the north, which is confined to the central portion of the United States by high mountains. Between 1930 and 1984 the area east of the Rocky Mountains had over 20,000 tornadoes. Although the mechanism that forms a tornado is not fully understood, a violent updraft, as in a thunderstorm, with a concurrent drop in surface pressure, could trigger the creation of a violent tornado. For example, a wind of 65 kilometers (40 miles) per hour with a radius of 5 kilometers (3 miles) could accelerate to 280 kilometers (175 miles) per hour in a radius of about one kilometer. Tornadoes are often associated with hurricanes. In 1967 a hurricane in the vicinity of Brownsville, Texas, spawned 47 tornadoes as it moved from the Gulf of Mexico inland.

Tornadoes are known to form over warm water. Because the air is moisture-laden, the rain from the funnel appears like a stream of water pouring from a cloud base. This phenomenon is called a *waterspout.* These water storms are usually less severe than their counterparts over land. The average waterspout is much smaller than a tornado and rarely has winds over 160 kilometers (100 miles) per hour. Waterspouts are interesting to meteorologists because they originate in the same way as a land tornado. Both are the product of rapid updrafts and associated inflow of low-level air which spins faster and faster as it reaches the low pressure center.

## WEATHER MODIFICATION

Since early civilization people have aspired to modify and control the weather. The Biblical stories of the great flood in the book of Exodus provide dramatic early evidence of human concern about the weather. Throughout history, attempts to control the weather are legend, appearing in all cultures as folklore, Biblical proverbs, and festivals dedicated to weather phenomena, such as the rain dance.

Modern concepts of weather modification are based on scientific and technological principles, with a careful, objective analysis of potentials and limits. In 1933 the Swedish meteorologist, Tor Bergeron, and the German physicist, Walter Findeisen, advanced the hypothesis that clouds would precipitate if they contained the right mixture of ice crystals and supercooled water droplets. In 1946 Irving Langmuir and Vincent Schaefer of General Electric Corporation modified clouds by "seeding" them with dry ice pellets. Shortly afterward, Bernard Vonnegut, a co-worker, demonstrated that silver iodide crystals accomplished the same results. These experiments were the beginning of the American effort to modify weather through cloud seeding.

### MAJOR TYPES OF WEATHER MODIFICATION

Since these early efforts, major projects have been initiated to augment and redistribute precipitation and to reduce hail, lightning, and fog.

#### Precipitation Augmentation and Redistribution

Within the United States a number of areas have been selected as sites for experimental projects. One of the most important of these is the Colorado River Basin Project. Its major goal is to develop effective techniques for increasing winter snowfall in mountain areas. It will also assess downwind effects and economic, social, and ecological impacts. The target area is 5,700 square kilometers (2,200 square miles) in the San Juan Mountains of Colorado. The plan is to seed the clouds when the cloud-top temperatures are between −12°C (10°F) and −23°C (−9°F), the temperature range thought to be most favorable for increasing snowfall. Laboratory experiments have indicated that seeding will increase the snow pack by 30 percent. The value of this additional stored water would be about $100 million, about 30 times the anticipated cost of the program. However, both the benefits and costs are the subjects of controversy and uncertainty. Other benefit-to-cost ratios are much more modest, and little actual development of the project has occurred.

Between 1968 and 1973 the Great Lakes Snow Distribution Project was carried out by the National Oceanic and Atmospheric Administration (NOAA). Its main goal was to shift some of the heavy snowfall along the southern shore of Lake Erie to areas farther inland that receive less snow. During the winter period, winds blowing from the north pick up moisture as they move over the warmer Great Lakes waters. As the air is lifted on the southern shore of the Great Lakes, clouds form and heavy snowfall results. It is theorized that ice nuclei introduced into the clouds containing supercooled droplets should increase the number and decrease the size of ice crystals. The greater number of smaller particles would fall more slowly and reach the ground farther inland than in the normal situation. Although the initial results were encouraging, they provided no firm conclusions before the project was terminated.

A number of projects have attempted to directly modify clouds. One of these is the Cumulus Modification Project developed by NOAA in Miami, Florida. This project seeks to develop means for increasing the buoyancy of cumulus clouds, thus increasing their vertical growth and enhancing their rainfall production. Application of mathematical models to field experimentation has been successful in causing individual cumulus clouds to merge and produce more rain. Although results appear positive, they do not provide adequate statistical data to design an operational program.

The research and field experimentation on increasing precipitation has revealed that the problem is extremely complex. There is great variability in cloud types and in the ways in which precipitation occurs. The techniques of cloud seeding are still quite rudimentary. It is now thought that cloud seeding can increase local precipitation by about 10 percent. These results are, however, obtained in areas where rainfall would have fallen anyway without seeding. There is no evidence that seeding can induce rain to fall when normally there would be none. Thus the present state of technology is not likely to create rain in drought-stricken regions.

### Fog Abatement

The control of supercooled fog is one of the most successful of the weather modification endeavors. By the early 1960s, dissipation techniques were sufficiently advanced to be tested in operation. Seeding with dry ice, propane, or silver iodide from the ground or the atmosphere has proven successful. Efforts are being directed toward making the seeding techniques more effective. Dissipation of supercooled fog is most important for major airports. The cost of flight interruptions is very high in comparison with the cost of dissipating the fogs. Unfortunately, however, supercooled fogs make up only about 5 percent of the fogs occurring in the United States. Warm fogs that are composed of water droplets rather than ice nuclei are difficult to dissipate. A number of techniques have been attempted to control warm fogs, but success is still not assured.

### Lightning Suppression

Research on lightning suppression began in the early 1960s. The objective is to determine how the number and severity of lightning strikes might be reduced, and particularly how to reduce lightning-caused forest fires. Although field tests have indicated some reductions, the results are not clear and the basic mechanisms are still in dispute.

### Hail Research

Because agricultural losses due to hail average more than $300 million annually, hail research has received considerable interest. Researchers are looking for ways to increase the number and thereby decrease the size of hailstones in severe thunderstorms. Although scientists in the Soviet Union have reported considerable success in controlling the size of hail, field testing in the United States is still inconclusive.

### Present Status

Efforts to modify, and even control, the weather have achieved some progress. The techniques that will bring about substantial changes in weather and climate, however, are still far in the future. The development of weather modification techniques must rest on a foundation of fundamental knowledge that can be obtained only through scientific research in all of the physical and chemical processes of the atmosphere.

## HUMAN EFFECTS OF WEATHER MODIFICATION

Like other technological advances, weather and climate modification presents us with many opportunities but also with grave dangers. Because the influences of weather are so pervasive in human minds, modifications may provoke intricate social changes. For example, cloud seeding in a watershed may increase the water supply sufficiently to change the entire economic structure of the region as well as altering the ecological balance of the area. Coastal areas could be changed if hurricanes no longer caused them a quarter of a billion dollars worth of damage annually, and if the loss of life could be reduced. The methods for computing the direct economic benefits are well developed. However, the methods of measuring social changes are still largely conjectural. To the uncertainty of what is within the grasp of the scientist and technician must be added the ignorance of the full consequences of whatever modifications may be achieved.

Weather modification contrasts with the more conventional controls of the environment. It has the possibility of affecting areas far beyond the original site of the proposed change. More than any other technique, it can extend its effects across the borders of states or even nations. Its potential to create conflicts is great. The consequences are felt not only by the physical and biological systems, but by the entire social structure of the area affected. For example, if clouds are seeded in a dry region, such as the southwestern United States, that area will benefit economically. But the removal of moisture from the atmosphere will deprive other regions of precipitation, creating a conflict.

Uncertainty characterizes most current thinking on the effects of weather modification on the physical, biological, and social systems of a region. The uncertainty extends not only to how much weather can be modified but also to how the modification would change the spatial patterns within the area. The common laws evolved before this type of consideration was important. Thus a new set of laws that recognize our ability to alter nature must be developed. If past patterns are followed, human problems will continue to be ignored until they burst into prominence on the heels of a major breakthrough in weather modification technology.

## WEATHER FORECASTING

Weather forecasting developed slowly in the 19th century. Before that time, weather records were gathered sporadically, and there was no systematic approach. The individual collector devised his own procedures. In 1812, however, weather observations were started on a regular basis in the United States. By 1853, ninety-seven army posts were recording the daily weather. The increasing amount of weather data allowed scientists to plot the spatial distributions in temperature, pressure, and winds on a map. Because of slow communications, these data were normally plotted after the storms had occurred and thus were of little or no value for weather forecasting. The maps did summarize in an orderly way many weather observations and became the basis for meteorological research.

In 1849 the first weather observations were transmitted by telegraph. Data were then collected rapidly enough to be used for forecasting purposes. By the 1860s the United States had a network of more than 500 weather stations. The increased data encouraged weather forecasters to improve their techniques. Although weather predicting was only modestly accurate, the field flourished. In 1870 Congress created a national meteorological service under the direction of the Army Signal Corps. By 1872 weather forecasts were being issued daily, with the early forecasters claiming a 75 percent accuracy rate in short-period weather predictions.

### TRADITIONAL WEATHER FORECASTING

Weather forecasting in the late 19th and early 20th centuries was based entirely on surface observations. The data available to the forecaster included temperature, pressure, wind direction and velocity, precipitation, and the speed of movement of the high and low pressures. Forecasters located the weather systems and then predicted their direction and rate of movement for a period of a few days. Although advances have been made, these procedures are still important in modern weather forecasting.

The traditional methods have been aided by a number of technical advances. Prior to 1930 the weather maps did not include the location of fronts. As the concept of air masses originating from different source regions evolved, the location of fronts was made possible. Two other technological advances provided more and better data for weather forecasting. In the late 1930s, balloon-carried instruments called *radiosondes* began making upper air observations. These radiosondes transmitted such data as temperature, pressure, and humidity of the upper atmosphere to ground stations. Thus meteorological conditions not only on the earth's surface but also in the upper atmosphere could be plotted on maps. The three-dimensional structure of the atmosphere could be studied. Although this information made weather forecasting more complicated, it also made it more accurate.

The second technological advance in collecting weather information occurred on April 1, 1960, when the first weather satellite, *Tiros I,* was launched into space. This satellite, at an elevation of 725 kilometers (450 miles), provided television coverage of weather systems on earth from an entirely new perspective. Later satellites have become more sophisticated and reveal the temperature, humidity, and wind movements of the lower atmosphere. One of the problems still perplexing meteorologists is how to mesh these abundant data with those collected on the earth's surface.

## NUMERICAL FORECASTING

As the quantity of weather information has increased, meteorologists have sought to develop mathematical equations to predict the weather. While the equations governing the physical behavior of the atmosphere were developed more than half a century ago, they could not be applied until the 1950s, when the electronic computer evolved. The early applications developed a *barotropic model* in order to forecast the 500-millibar contour patterns. This rather simple model assumed that winds always blow at right angles to the pressure gradient. This early model has evolved into the more complex *baroclinic models* which include frictional and other surface effects. Thus the basic mechanisms of cyclone formation are included. A noteworthy feature is that "fields" of continuous variables such as temperature, pressure, humidity, and winds are evaluated, and fronts are treated as secondary features. These models are based on a continuous flow of data. As a result, millions of calculations are required, and only the fastest electronic computers can handle them. The maps they create are able to keep ahead of changing weather conditions. Numerical forecasting is still in its initial stages and supplements the traditional weather forecasting techniques. Numerical forecasting, however, is the beginning of a new era in weather prediction.

## EXTENDED AND LONG-RANGE FORECASTING

The goal of forecasters has always been to predict the weather long into the future. This type of prediction would have many economic benefits. For example, farmers could know what growing conditions would be like throughout the growing period. A knowledge of weather several months in advance would be most desirable in other long-range endeavors, such as the building industry. Information concerning the amount of snow to fall in northern United States would be of tremendous importance to the state departments of transportation that must keep the roads clear during the winter. Hundreds of other examples could be given. Regrettably, extended and long-range forecasting are still in infancy. The best that can now be accomplished are generalized predictions of the weather for one week, known as *extended forecasts,* and the average deviations of the weather from the normal for up to one month, known as *long-range forecasts.*

Two principal techniques are used in extended and long-range forecasting. One is the *statistical method.* It is based on the principle that many atmospheric features persist over a long period of time. That statistical method has two principal steps. The first step is to prepare a mean millibar contour map for 30 days by extrapolating current weather conditions and attempting to predict changes in the large-scale atmospheric circulation. The statistical records of typical weather conditions for the specific season are considered. The second step is to predict probable anomalies in the weather, such as changes in temperature and precipitation amounts. Thus, from a study of the statistical data of the present and past, a long-range forecast evolves. The United States weather forecasting service has used the statistical method since 1948 to issue 30-day forecasts twice monthly.

The second approach is known as the *analogue method.* This method, developed in Britain, is based on the principle that sequences of weather will be similar if the conditions of origin are similar. Thus the idea is to find a period of past weather that closely resembles the present weather, and to use the past as a guide to the future. These procedures reveal patterns of weather that are known as *weather types.* It has been found, however, that there are no identical sequences of weather. As a result the long-range forecaster is bound to have some failures. A great deal more must be known about the dynamics of the atmosphere before extended, and certainly long-range, forecasts can be made with high accuracy.

# EL NIÑO/SOUTHERN OSCILLATION: MODIFIER OF WEATHER

Every few years normal weather patterns over a wide portion of the earth are replaced by disastrous climatic events of one to two years in duration. Meteorologists believe that many of these drastic weather modifications are a response to a phenomenon known as *El Niño*. The name comes from the Spanish, meaning "The Infant" or "Christ Child." It refers to the fact that each year a weak warm current appears off the coasts of Peru and Ecuador at about Christmastime. About every 4 to 20 years, however, this warm current intensifies and extends across the Pacific nearly a quarter of the way around the world. This phenomenon is now generally referred to as an El Niño/Southern Oscillation (El Niño applying to the vast body of warm Pacific water, and the Southern Oscillation to the associated atmospheric temperature and pressure changes). Major El Niños occurred in 1877, 1891, 1918, 1925, 1940–41, 1957–58, 1965, 1972–73, 1976–77, and, most recently, in 1982–83.

## ORIGIN OF EL NIÑO/SOUTHERN OSCILLATION

The development of the El Niño/Southern Oscillation is preceded by a strong, high pressure in the central Pacific, an intense Indonesian low pressure, and especially vigorous southeast trade winds. Under these conditions the trade winds create a strong ocean current that moves from east to west across the Pacific. This current piles up warm water along the western Pacific continental and island coasts. Sea level in these areas is as much as one-half meter (18 inches) higher than on the eastern Pacific coast of South America. Thus a thick warm layer of water is situated on the western side of the Pacific while on the eastern side the warm water layer remains shallow.

The El Niño/Southern Oscillation is triggered when the atmospheric pressure over Indonesia begins to rise. No satisfactory explanation has been found for this pressure change. In response to this phenomenon, however, the southeast trade winds reverse their movement and now blow from west to east. These winds also reverse the movement of the ocean current so that it flows eastward. As the warm water surges eastward, it not only continues to warm but also deepens and becomes what is known as the Kelvin Wave. The wave sometimes divides into two parts, as it did in 1982–83. The major surge strikes the South American coast from Colombia to Chile. The smaller surge of warm water is reflected northward onto the coasts of northern Mexico and California.

As the deep, warm wave extends across the Pacific, the atmospheric temperatures, pressures, and wind directions are modified, not only in these areas, but also in other parts of the world. These atmospheric changes are extreme, and usually cause a drastic change in the normal weather patterns over a wide region.

## WEATHER MODIFICATION

The El Niño of 1982–83 was probably the strongest of this century. Sea temperatures in the eastern Pacific were as much as 8°C (14°F) above normal. A relationship is evident between this El Niño/Southern Oscillation phenomenon and the adverse weather conditions that extend from the eastern Pacific to Australia and Indonesia and onward to southern Africa. However, there appears to be little or no relationship between the 1982–83 El Niño and such drastic weather conditions as the drought of Ethiopia, the intense summer heat of the American Midwest, or the widespread floods in Europe. The weather modifications that occurred as a response to the 1982–83 El Niño/Southern Oscillation will now be described in some detail.

### EASTERN PACIFIC

Weather patterns in the eastern Pacific in both North and South America were greatly modified during 1982–83. In the coastal areas of Ecuador, Peru, and Chile the cold Peru current was replaced by the warm Pacific waters. As a consequence the normal high pressure was replaced by a low pressure, bringing precipitation. Desert coastal areas that normally receive a few centimeters of rainfall a year received several hundred centimeters. In May 1983 Guayaquil received 20 times its normal rainfall, severely damaging the banana, cacao, and rice crops. In the coastal areas thousands of homes and scores of bridges were destroyed. Foot rot affected cattle that stood in flooded areas too long. Deadly fungus wiped out flocks of chickens. Disease became rampant, with widespread occurrences of typhus, salmonella infection, and typhoid fever. Floods and accompanying disease caused at least 600 deaths, and property damage totaled over $1 billion.

The 1982–83 El Niño appears to be the major cause of the great storms experienced in western and southeastern United States. The jet stream, with winds up to 190 kilometers (120 miles) per hour, swung far to the south, bringing a series of storms with strong winds and torrential rains. The California coast experienced some of its highest tides ever recorded, which devastated many coastal areas. In California alone floods and landslides caused $300 million in property damage, forced 10,000 people to flee from their homes, and killed at least 12 people.

The mountainous western states received one of the heaviest years of precipitation on record. Floods and mudslides battered much of the desert Southwest. Mud and debris poured from Utah's Wasatch range when the snow melted during May 1983. Hundreds of people in such Utah towns as Bountiful, Centerville, and Farmington had to abandon their homes. In Salt Lake City a main street was converted into a canal to channel flood waters through the city.

The jet stream also swung far to the south in eastern United States, bringing storms that created floods in the Gulf states and Cuba. The Pearl River in Mississippi, for example, crested 2 meters (6.5 feet) above flood stage, causing an estimated $21 million in damage. The sugar crop of Cuba was damaged by flood waters.

In contrast to the great storms in parts of the United States and along the South American coasts, sections of Mexico and Central America were experiencing unprecedented drought conditions. A high pressure ridge that existed between the two ocean currents prevented the normal distribution of rainfall. Crop production was greatly reduced and the grazing lands severely damaged. The drought in this region caused an estimated agricultural loss of $600 million.

## CENTRAL PACIFIC

The weather of the trade wind regions of the Pacific, such as the Hawaiian and Polynesian islands, is characterized by an unending succession of warm, bright days. Only on the rarest occasions do they experience adverse weather. Prior to 1983 there had not been a hurricane in French Polynesia for more than 75 years, but in less than 6 months these islands experienced 6 hurricanes. In Tahiti alone 1,500 homes were totally destroyed and another 6,000 lost their roofs. Fortunately, radio broadcasts warned of the approaching hurricanes, and few lives were lost.

North of the equator a rare hurricane struck the western portion of the Hawaiian Islands. Many of the tourist facilities on Kauai were severely damaged and the tourist industry was curtailed for a number of months. Damage due to hurricanes in the central Pacific islands was estimated at $280 million.

## WESTERN PACIFIC

In contrast to eastern Pacific areas, which received heavy precipitation, such western Pacific areas as eastern Australia, the Philippines, and Indonesia experienced an unprecedented drought. A vast high pressure ridge prevailed and the rains disappeared.

Of these areas, none were stricken harder than eastern Australia. Exceptionally high temperatures, dust storms, and bushfires accompanied the drought conditions. On February 8, 1983, a vast dust storm developed in eastern Australia. It extended over 500 kilometers (300 miles) in length and several hundred kilometers in width. It is estimated that within 40 minutes over 11,000 tons of dust were deposited on Melbourne. The dust storms were followed on February 16 by raging bushfires. In all, 75 persons died and 8,000 were left homeless in the fires that extended across the states of Victoria and South Australia.

The agriculture of eastern Australia was seriously affected by the drought. In the wheat lands, the crop withered and died. The loss of cattle and sheep was particularly heavy. On some sheep stations as many as 7,000 to 8,000 sheep died of thirst and starvation.

The drought was broken in eastern Australia by torrential rains that spawned floods that were nearly as devastating as the drought. In many areas sheep weakened by the drought huddled on small islands above flood levels. For nearly two months the Royal Australian Air Force dropped hay to keep these marooned animals alive. In total, the agricultural losses exceeded $1 billion in eastern Australia.

## INDIAN OCEAN

The effects of the 1982–83 El Niño were not limited to the Pacific Ocean areas, but extended across the Indian Ocean. In northern India, Sri Lanka, and southern Africa, a high pressure cell created drought conditions. In southern Africa the drought was most disastrous in the rural regions, particularly in South Africa's national states, the Homelands. In the tribal Homelands, cattle are the symbol of wealth. Consequently, the size of the herds frequently exceeds the capacity of the land to feed them, even during the rainy years. In times of drought there is no surplus feed and the animals perish. In 1983 as many as 90 percent of the cattle died in some regions. Agricultural production, including home vegetable output, declined drastically. Malnutrition, prevalent at all times in the Homelands, increased, and nearly half of the human population was sustained by imported food shipments, mainly from the United States and Canada.

The animals in the wildlife parks also suffered. In the Chobe National Park, for example, the Savuti Channel under normal rain conditions has thousands of buffalo, hundreds of elephants and hippopotamuses, and scores of crocodiles. In summer 1983 the channel was dry and the animals had either died or migrated to other areas, such as the Linyanti swamps, where water still existed. In the Klaserie Reserve, one of the largest of South Africa's private parks, the carcasses of 33,000 animals were counted. It must be recognized, however, that the adverse weather conditions had some beneficial aspects. The drought acted as a natural culling mechanism that weeded out the sick and old animals, thus reducing the wildlife population to a level consistent with the food supply available under normal weather conditions.

## OCEANIC MODIFICATIONS

The El Niño phenomenon not only changes weather patterns but also alters vast areas of the oceans. The South American coastal waters of Ecuador, Peru, and Chile are strikingly changed. Under normal conditions the cold, deep Peru Current persists along the coast. These cold waters are high in nutrients that support plankton, which in turn provide food for fish.

When the Kelvin Wave reaches the coast, the warm water replaces the cold surface current, pushing the cold water deep below the surface. As a consequence the nutrients are not cycled upward, the plankton begin to disappear, and without this necessary food the fish can no longer survive.

In the 1950s Peru began to build a fishing fleet to exploit the coastal fisheries. By 1970 the Peruvian fleet totaled 1,500 modern fishing vessels harvesting 14 million tons of anchovies a year—a fifth of the world's fish catch. In the 1972 El Niño the warm wave herded the anchovies into a narrow band along the coast. Hundreds of thousands of tons of anchovies were harvested in a few weeks, depleting the fish stock to such an extent that the supply never recovered. The anchovy's place was then taken by the less valuable sardine. In the 1982–83 El Niño, the sardines all but vanished. The fishing fleets lay idle and a major question arose: Will a fishing industry exist again in Peruvian waters?

Another concern is that if all fish are depleted, there will be no control over the plankton population when the warm waters of El Niño disappear. Without fish to eat them, the plankton would simply die and sink to the ocean floor. As they decompose, oxygen would be consumed and the ocean floor would become a desert, uninhabitable except for anaerobic worms.

The 1982–83 El Niño was not totally devastating to the fishing industry. The warm water triggered an increase in the shrimp population. While the shrimp industry is small in comparison to the fishing industry, it did provide an income to a small number of the displaced fishermen.

The invading warm water off the California coast also affected the fishing industry there. In the San Diego area, tuna fishing declined greatly. In northern California and the Northwest, the cold-water salmon migrated further northward, leaving the fishing fleets idle. Warm water sea life, such as the barracuda and the red crab, invaded the area. As the oceanic food supply diminished, the mortality among seabirds reached unprecedented levels.

## FUTURE MONITORING

The importance of the El Niño/Southern Oscillation phenomenon as a modifier of weather has been recognized only in recent years. Because of its isolated location in the Pacific Ocean only limited amounts of data were collected in the past. It is now recognized that if a coming El Niño could be identified at an early stage of its development, efforts could be made to lessen the effects of the ensuing storms and droughts.

The 1982–83 El Niño was the first to be monitored in detail. The NOAA ship *Researcher* began to report weather data from the Pacific in October 1982, and 17 drifting buoys transmitted data to satellites. Oceanographers from the Scripps Institution of Oeanography also collected data from field observations.

The origin of the El Niño/Southern Oscillation is still uncertain, but many meteorologists believe this phenomenon is the major force disturbing normal weather patterns. Therefore, the origin and effects of the El Niño/Southern Oscillation will be studied in a 10-year program beginning in January 1985. This investigation, known as the Tropical Ocean and Global Atmospheric (TOGA) program, marshalls the meteorological resources of the nations in the Pacific and Indian ocean basins. It is supported by at least three environmental satellites and a fleet of research vessels, including nine from Colombia, Ecuador, Peru, and Chile. The basic objective is to secure enough data to prepare better models for predicting an approaching El Niño/Southern Oscillation.

## CONCLUSION

The weather and climate conditions of the earth are greatly influenced by relatively homogeneous air masses that originate in tropical and polar regions. In the middle latitudes the jet stream sets these air masses in motion. The meeting of warm and cold air masses provides the mechanism for the development of cyclones and anticyclones. In the frontal areas of the cyclones significant weather changes occur.

In the tropical regions, the tropical easterly wave and the hurricane are major regional storms. The tropical easterly wave is a gentle storm in the trade winds. In contrast, the hurricane is one of the most destructive storms on earth. It originates over water and continues to gain strength as long as sufficient energy exists in the atmosphere.

The convectional or thunderstorm and the tornado are severe local storms. The thunderstorm is best developed in warm, humid regions. The tornado is the most violent of all storms. The atmospheric conditions that produce thunderstorms are similar to those that spawn tornadoes.

Because weather conditions are important to human activities, the ability to forecast, modify, and control weather has long been sought. Modern scientific techniques, such as the weather satellite, have improved short-range forecasts. Regrettably, long-range forecasting is still in its infancy. Modification and control of weather as sound scientific endeavors are also far in the future.

It has long been recognized that normal weather patterns in the world have been disrupted for short periods by disastrous weather conditions. Meteorologists now believe these changes are a response to the phenomenon known as El Niño/Southern Oscillation. Periodically an excessively warm current develops in the central Pacific Ocean that alters the heat balance of the world temporarily. During these periods, certain areas receive excessive precipitation while other areas suffer drought conditions.

## STUDY QUESTIONS

1. What are major source regions for large air masses?
2. What is the basis for the Bergeron classification of air masses?
3. What influence does the polar continental air mass of North America have on the weather of the continent? Polar maritime air mass? Tropical maritime air mass? Tropical continental?
4. How can the characteristics of a large air mass be changed?
5. How does the Norwegian cyclone model explain the origin of middle latitude cyclones?
6. Describe the development of fronts in cyclones. What are their importance?
7. Describe the isobars in a cyclone. Anticyclone.
8. Describe the areas of precipitation in a cyclone.
9. What causes nonfrontal precipitation in a cyclone?
10. Why is an air mass in an anticyclone sometimes cold, causing a cold wave, and sometimes hot, causing a heat wave?
11. When a cyclonic storm approaches and passes in a general west-to-east direction, what wind directions will be experienced?
12. What is the importance of the jet stream to weather?
13. What is an easterly wave? What are its characteristics?
14. Where do hurricanes develop? Give their path in the western Atlantic Ocean.
15. Describe the origin of a hurricane.

16 What are the causes of thunderstorms?
17 What are the stages in the development of a thunderstorm? Give the characteristics of each stage.
18 Explain the theory of the development of lightning in a thunderstorm.
19 Explain the development of hail in a thunderstorm.
20 What are the characteristics of a tornado? Why is it so destructive?
21 What are the major types of weather modification? Explain each.
22 What are some of the human effects of weather modification?
23 What is the basis of traditional weather forecasting? What recent advances have been made?
24 What are the two principal techniques utilized to develop extended and long-range forecasts?
25 Explain the origin of the El Niño/Southern Oscillation.
26 How does the El Niño/Southern Oscillation affect weather patterns in different places in the world? Why do these changes occur?

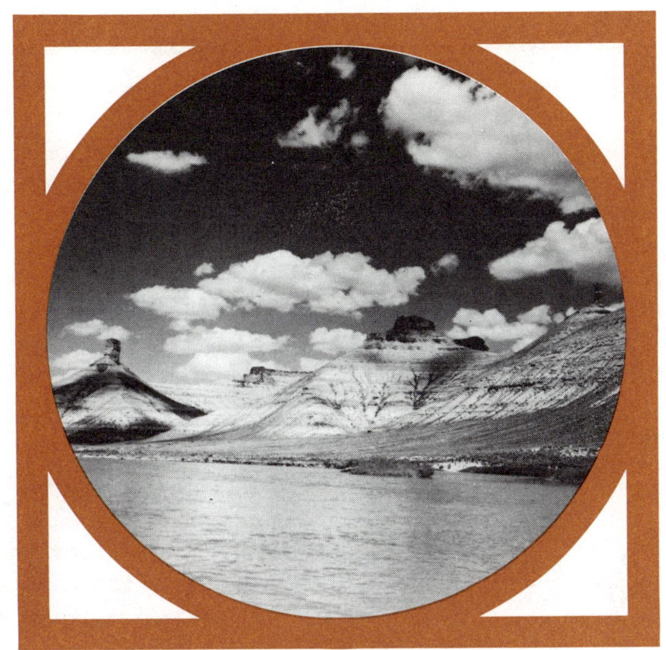

# 8
# WORLD CLIMATIC SYSTEMS

## KEY WORDS

average precipitation
average temperature
climate
hekistotherms
megatherms
mesotherms
microtherms
potential evapotranspiration
precipitation effectiveness
temperature efficiency
weather
xerophytes

Climate is one of the more important geographical phenomena. Its patterns provide a framework into which we try to fit our activities. Climate influences, for example, what foods we eat, how we dress, what crops we can cultivate, what types of vacations we take, and many other aspects of our lives. Climate does more than set the stage for many human activities. Many biological and physical aspects of the earth are related to specific climatic environments. Thus an understanding of the development of natural vegetation and soil regions depends on knowledge of climatic conditions.

## CLIMATIC AVERAGES AND EXTREMES

Climate is normally defined as the *composite of weather for a period of years.* A long weather record minimizes short-term irregularities, so the longer the record, the better the understanding of climate. The long-term averages provide the basis for determining the climatic conditions at a particular place. Within a short period the atmospheric environment can experience wide variations from the average. For example, the average annual temperature at Chicago is 11.1°C (51.9°F), but this figure does not reveal the possible wide fluctuations from the average during the year. Chicago has experienced as high a temperature as 40.6°C (105°F) in the summer and as low as −30°C (−22°F) in winter.

It is frequently more important to understand the extremes of climatic conditions than the averages. The extreme conditions normally set the limits on human use of an area. To understand the climatic environment of a region it is essential to consider not only averages, but also minimum and maximum conditions of such elements as temperature, precipitation, and winds.

Some of the climatic averages included in this discussion of climatology are:

1 *Average daily temperature,* the individual "brick" of which is built the average temperature conditions for a month, season, year, or longer period. It is the average of the temperatures recorded for a 24-hour period.
2 *Average monthly temperature,* the average of the daily average temperatures for any month recorded over a long period of time.
3 *Average annual temperature,* the average of all the average monthly temperatures for a long period of years divided by the number of years represented.
4 *Annual average temperature range,* the difference in the average temperatures for the warmest and coldest months over a period of time.
5 *Average monthly precipitation,* an average of the total daily precipitation for any month recorded over a long period of time.
6 *Average annual precipitation,* an average of the monthly averages.

Other averages of climatic significance include average number of days with a temperature below freezing; average number of days with a temperature above a set figure; average annual snowfall; average number of days with rain, snow, hail, fog, and the like; average percentage of sunshine or cloudiness; average wind velocity; average length of the growing season, and many others.

Some of the climatic statistics that deal with extremes, not averages, are: (*a*) maximum temperatures; (*b*) minimum temperatures; (*c*) maximum precipitation experienced in a given period, such as 24 hours or a month; and (*d*) maximum wind velocity.

## CLIMATIC CLASSIFICATION SYSTEMS

All classifications of climate have three characteristics in common. First, the systems attempt to organize the facts into an orderly arrangement of categories so that generalizations can be made from minute details. Secondly, the systems group together those regions having common characteristics, and thirdly, they provide an analytical description so that boundaries can be identified.

Climatologists have used two approaches to the development of classifications, the empirical and the genetic. The empirical is based on climatic elements that are directly measurable, such as temperature and precipitation. The genetic classifications are based on climatic controls, such as air masses, distribution of land and water, semipermanent high and low pressure cells, ocean currents, mountain barriers, altitude, and others. Of these two approaches, the empirical method is more widely used. The climatic controls used in the genetic method are frequently difficult to measure and to interpret for determining a climatic region.

In the historical development of climatic classification systems, the distribution of natural vegetation has often played a dominant role. Climatologists recognize that natural vegetation integrates the effects of climatic elements better than any other aspect of the environment. Vegetation therefore remains the most important basis for regional climatic classifications, even though climate is not the only factor influencing the distribution of vegetation.

Numerous problems remain to be solved in the development of climatic classifications. The use of a single climatic element or control is inadequate to distinguish a climate's distinctive features. The "best" classification must be a synthesis of all climatic elements and controls. The problem is to express these elements quantitatively in a single system to define a specific climatic region. The most successful attempts have been based upon the relationships between the climatic elements and vegetation.

Other problems hinder the development of classification systems. Worldwide records of long-term weather are lacking. Weather records are improving, however, as satellites are being used to collect data. This problem will thus disappear in the near future. Another problem in defining climatic regions is that climatic boundaries are not sharp; that is, climatic types gradually merge into one another. All boundaries on maps should be interpreted as transition zones. On detailed maps the transition zones may even appear as separate climatic types.

It should be recognized that the definitive climatic classification system will probably never be devised. Possibly the best solution is to devise classification systems for specific uses. For example, a system based on vegetation would serve a botanist's purposes admirably. In contrast, an airline pilot would be far more interested in a classification system based on such climatic elements as temperature, wind velocity, and visibility.

## CLASSIFICATION SYSTEMS BASED ON TEMPERATURE

The ancient Greeks recognized the relationships between latitude and temperature and devised a system of *klima* or zones. Three broad belts of temperature were recognized. The tropical region, in the winterless low latitudes lying between the Tropic of Cancer and the Tropic of Capricorn, was named the *torrid zone.* The areas lying poleward of the Arctic and Antarctic circles, where there is a continuous cold season, was called the *frigid zone.* The two areas that experience seasonal contrasts are between the Tropic of Cancer and the Arctic Circle in the Northern Hemisphere and between the Tropic of Capricorn and the Antarctic Circle in the Southern Hemisphere. The Greeks recognized these areas as the *temperate zones.*

A large number of early classifications were based on temperature. For example, Rubner devised a classification of European climates based on the annual number of warm days. He defined a warm day as one with a mean temperature above 10°C (50°F). Rubner's European zones were:

| Zone | Number of Warm Days |
|---|---|
| Subarctic | 1– 60 |
| Cool | 61–120 |
| Temperate | 121–180 |
| Warm temperate | 181–240 |
| Warm | 241–300 |

## CLASSIFICATION SYSTEMS BASED ON PRECIPITATION

Precipitation, as a major climatic element, is similar to temperature in determining a climatic classification. Such a classification system follows:

| Climatic Type | Mean Annual Precipitation (in inches) |
|---|---|
| Arid | 0–10 |
| Semiarid | 10–20 |
| Subhumid | 20–40 |
| Humid | 40–80 |
| Very wet | over 80 |

A major problem with this system is that the amount of precipitation does not accurately indicate moisture availability in a region. In the low latitudes, where temperatures are high and evaporation excessive, semiarid conditions will prevail with 25 to 50 centimeters (10 to 20 inches) of precipitation. In the higher latitudes, where temperatures are lower and evaporation little, the same amount of precipitation will result in humid conditions.

## CLASSIFICATION SYSTEMS BASED ON VEGETATION

Of the climatic classification systems that use vegetation as the prime criterion, the best known is the one developed by Wladimir Köppen (1846–1940), a German botanist and climatologist. His system was revised by Rudolf Geiger. As a basis for the classification, Köppen developed climatic divisions which were intended to correspond to Augustin de Candolle's five major plant groups. On the basis of temperature, these plant groups are:

1. *Megatherms:* Tropical plants requiring high temperatures and abundant moisture
2. *Mesotherms:* Plants of the middle latitudes that require considerable heat but are tolerant of short winters and also a dry season
3. *Microtherms:* plants of the high latitudes that thrive with short warm summers and long cold winters, but with the mean annual temperature above freezing
4. *Hekistotherms:* the low shrubs and plants of the Arctic that thrive where the average annual temperature is below freezing
5. *Xerophytes:* Vegetation that exists where precipitation is scarce.

In 1900 Köppen devised his first classification system based primarily on vegetation zones, but in 1918 a revised version gave increased importance to temperature, precipitation, and their seasonal characteristics. Köppen's classification is based on the following five major climatic groups:

- **A** Tropical moist climates: hot all seasons
- **B** Dry climates: arid or semiarid where evaporation exceeds precipitation
- **C** Humid mesothermal: mild winters and hot summers
- **D** Humid microthermal: severe winters and mild summers
- **E** Polar climates: no warm season

A sixth differentiation, H, referring to altitude, designates mountain or highland climates. It may be found at any latitude.

These five major divisions are subdivided according to temperature differences and variations in the amount and distribution of precipitation. For the A, C, and D climates the first letter, a capital, refers to a temperature condition. The second letter, *f, s, w* or *m,* a lowercase letter, refers to precipitation. The third letter, *a, b,* or *c,* again a lowercase letter, refines the temperature criteria. (See Appendix C for precise definitions of all temperature and precipitation criteria.) For example, if a climate is characterized as Cfa, the *C* indicates that the average temperature of the warmest month is over 10°C (50°F) and the coldest between 18°C (64.4°F) and 0°C (32°F). The *f* indicates that the average precipitation of the driest month of the year is at least 6.0 centimeters (2.4 inches). The *a* means that the average temperature of the warmest month is 22°C (71.6°F) or above. The descriptive name of this climate is humid subtropical.

The B climates are divided into BW, or the arid, desert type, and the BS, or semiarid, steppe climatic type. The lowercase *h* or *k* attached to either of the B climates refers to hot or cold. The B climates experience a wide range of temperatures and precipitation. As the temperatures increase, the precipitation also increases in the B climates, because they lie between the dry and moist zones where precipitation equals potential evapotranspiration. It must be remembered that potential evapotranspiration increases as temperatures rise.

Köppen subdivided the E climates into the ET, or tundra type, and the EF, or perpetual ice type. The ET climate illustrates the use of vegetation to indicate a climatic type. The ET climate lies in those areas where the temperature of the warmest month averages between 0°C (32°F) and 10°C (50°F). This temperature permits the growth of only shrubs and brush. The 10°C boundary of the warmest month is the poleward limit of forest vegetation.

The Köppen climatic classification system was a major advance in its time, and is still widely used because it is comprehensive and flexible. Its strength lies in its terminology. The use of a second and even a third letter provides more information on the precipitation and temperature of a region.

Köppen has been criticized because many of his boundaries coincide with those of vegetation regions. Regrettably, direct relationships between vegetation and climate cannot be made objectively and independently. Another criticism is that the criteria for selecting the boundaries vary from climatic type to climatic type. For example, the Cs and Cf climatic boundaries are based solely on precipitation, but the boundaries of the B regions are based on both temperature and precipitation.

The Köppen classification's greatest weakness may be its inability to utilize the concept of potential evapotranspiration. For example, the boundary between the dry B climates and the moist A, C, and D climates was assumed to coincide with a forest boundary. This boundary was based on empirical relations of temperature and precipitation. The assumption that the forest boundary occurs where precipitation equals potential evapotranspiration has been shown to be incorrect. Precipitation exceeds potential evapotranspiration at most forest boundaries. As a consequence many of the B boundaries incorrectly indicated the location of the moist and dry regions.

## CLASSIFICATION SYSTEMS BASED ON ENERGY AND MOISTURE INTERACTIONS

The early climatic classification systems neglected the interaction of energy and moisture in the atmospheric system. Many natural systems, such as vegetation, are strongly influenced by the amount of soil moisture available. This moisture may not be directly related to precipitation.

One of the earliest classification systems that recognized the interaction between climate and other systems was that of the German geographer, Albrecht Penck. He conceived of three distinct *realms of climate.* These were based on determining the potential evapotranspiration of a large region. The *moist realm,* where forests prevail, includes all regions where precipitation exceeds potential evapotranspiration. The *dry realm,* characterized by grass and desert vegetation, includes all areas where potential evapotranspiration is greater than precipitation. The *frozen realm* consists of those regions where evapotranspiration equals zero. The temperature of those areas is so low that plants cannot transpire.

In 1931 C. Warren Thornthwaite devised the first classification of climates based upon water budget evaluations of energy and moisture. First applied to North America and in 1933 to the world, it was similar to Köppen's in that it attempted to define boundaries quantitatively, based on vegetation, using a set of symbols. Its chief point of departure from Köppen's was in the development of the concepts of *temperature efficiency* and *precipitation effectiveness.* The effectiveness of precipitation for plant growth depends upon the amount of evaporation in a particular region. Precipitation effectiveness is calculated by dividing the monthly precipitation by the monthly evaporation to obtain the P/E ratio. The sum of the 12 monthly P/E ratios was called the *P/E index.* Because the amount of evaporation is unknown for most climatic stations, Thornthwaite developed a formula to express the P/E index in terms of precipitation and temperature.

The P/E index was the basis for determining major climatic types:

| P/E Index | Humidity Realm | Vegetation |
|---|---|---|
| > 127 | A | Rain forest |
| 64–127 | B | Forest |
| 32–63 | C | Savanna |
| 16–31 | D | Steppe |
| < 16 | E | Desert |

Temperature efficiency (T/E) ratios were determined by using a similar procedure:

| T/E Index | Temperature | Realm |
|---|---|---|
| > 127 | $A^1$ | Tropical |
| 64–127 | $B^1$ | Mesothermal |
| 32–63 | $C^1$ | Microthermal |
| 16–31 | $D^1$ | Taiga |
| 1–15 | $E^1$ | Tundra |
| 0 | $F^1$ | Polar |

In order to show seasonal distribution of precipitation, four further subdivisions are made:

- **r** Rainfall adequate in all seasons
- **s** Rainfall deficient in summer
- **w** Rainfall deficient in winter
- **d** Rainfall deficient in all seasons

In 1948 Thornthwaite refined his classification system by introducing the concept of potential evapotranspiration. This concept recognizes that if water were available in a warm desert, more vegetation would grow and consequently more water would be transpired. Thus the water need is greater in warm climates than in cold climates, and likewise more water is needed in summer than in winter. The P/E index was thus refined to include the amount of precipitation necessary to meet the demand of potential evapotranspiration, compared to the amount of water available through rainfall and stored soil moisture. Temperature efficiency was also related to potential evapotranspiration.

Thornthwaite calculated the mean monthly potential evapotranspiration using tables based on complex equations relating potential evapotranspiration to air temperature. The annual moisture surplus or deficit was calculated by using a moisture index. The value of the moisture index is positive when precipitation is greater than potential evapotranspiration, and negative when precipitation is less than potential evapotranspiration. The moisture index is also positive when the precipitation surplus is greater than the precipitation deficit. Anomalies do occur. Deficits can occur when precipitation is greater than the potential evapotranspiration if precipitation is strongly seasonal.

The difference between the amount of precipitation and the potential evapotranspiration forms the basis of Thornthwaite's moisture index. The moisture index has a value of −100 when precipitation is zero and may exceed +100 when the precipitation exceeds potential evapotranspiration. At the boundary between dry and humid realms the moisture index is 0.

A major difference between the Köppen and Thornthwaite classification systems is the method of determining the boundary between dry and humid regions. While each climatic scheme divides the principal climates into 5 types, each system determines the boundary between the wet and dry regions differently. Thornthwaite's recognition that precipitation must be coupled with potential evapotranspiration results in a different humid/dry boundary. For example, under the Thornthwaite system, the dry grassland region of central United States is so distinct from the drier west and the humid east that it is recognized as a separate climatic region. Under the Köppen system the dry grasslands are not recognized as distinctive.

The great disadvantage of the Thornthwaite system is that it is so complex that it is rarely used to define the world's climatic regions. Thornthwaite prepared maps of the United States showing moisture regions, distribution of average annual thermal efficiency, seasonal variation of effective moisture, and summer concentration of thermal efficiency. Other climatologists have prepared similar maps of other parts of the world, but a single world map presenting a system of climatic regions has not been prepared.

## WORLD CLIMATIC REGIONS

The distribution of the world's climatic regions is created by the interaction of energy and moisture at different places. In a broad sense the major climates can be classified into four groups: tropical, middle latitude, subpolar and polar, and high altitude. Each of these can be further subdivided, based on the variables of temperature and precipitation. This book will define 15 climatic types, based on the Köppen-Geiger classification (Plate 2).

### TROPICAL CLIMATES

All tropical climates are warm; the subdivisions are based on differences in the precipitation regime.

#### Tropical Rainforest (Afi)

The tropical rainforest is located in the intertropical convergence, 10 to 15 degrees north and south of the equator (Photo 28). The diurnal range in temperature is usually greater than the difference between the warmest and coolest months (annual range). Every month has precipitation, and there is normally no season when the rainfall is deficient. Such high amounts of precipitation keep the water balance in a continuous surplus. Evapotranspiration in this area normally occurs at its potential rate; that is, actual evaporation and potential evapotranspiration are equal (Figure 8.1).

**PHOTO 28**
Tropical rainforest. The hot, wet environment produces the luxuriant vegetation of the tropical rainforest (Af).

#### Tropical Savanna (Aw)

North and south of the tropical rainforest (Afi) are areas where the intertropical convergence penetrates during the high-sun period, bringing convectional precipitation. During the low-sun period, the trade winds dominate. Because a distinct dry season exists, moisture deficits frequently exist in the soil. The evapotranspiration is nearly equal to the potential rate on the equatorward side of the tropical savanna (Aw) climate but far exceeds it on the poleward side. The water balance in the region thus varies from a perpetual surplus on the equatorward side to a perpetual deficit on the poleward margins (Figure 8.2).

#### Tropical Monsoon (Am)

The tropical monsoon (Am) climate is similar to the tropical rainforest (Afi) in temperature conditions. It is distinguished from the latter by its rainfall regime. The winter-summer reversal of airflow brings dry and wet seasons to the tropical monsoonal climate. As described in Chapter 5, the monsoonal climate is best developed in South Asia. As the warm, moisture-laden air flows from the Indian Ocean in summer, a wet season prevails. In winter, when the air mass originates over the

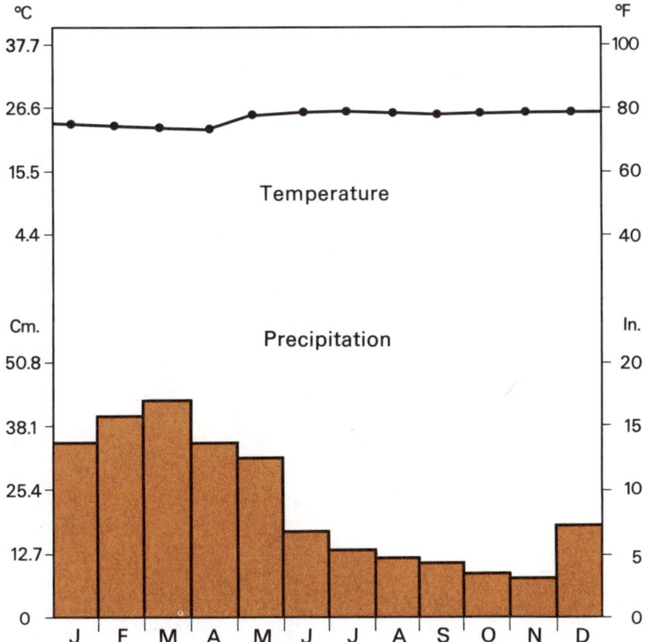


**FIGURE 8.1**
Tropical rainforest (Afi). The tropical rainforest climate is characterized by uniformly high temperatures and rainfall throughout the year. The rainfall comes as convectional storms associated with the intertropical convergence.

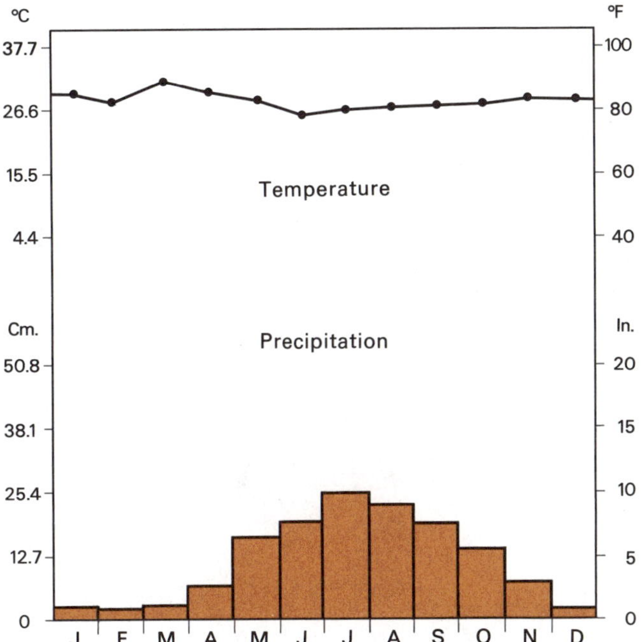


**FIGURE 8.2**
Tropical savanna (Aw). The tropical savanna climate has a uniformly high temperature throughout the year. The region is under the influence of the intertropical convergence during the rainy season and the trade winds during the dry season.

Asian continent, the air is particularly dry. Because the dry season is quite short, and is followed by one with heavy rainfall, there is rarely a soil moisture deficit. The water balance is generally in a surplus state. Evapotranspiration occurs near its potential rate (Figure 8.3).

## Low Latitude Steppes (BSh)

The low latitude steppes (BSh) surround the low latitude deserts (BWh). It is difficult, if not impossible, to distinguish between the BSh and BWh climates by considering temperature data only. Although the precipitation of the low latitude steppe (BSh) is meager, it is greater than the low latitude desert (BWh), and different environmental conditions exist. The typical steppe will have an average of 25 centimeters (10 inches) of rainfall a year, but normally less than 75 centimeters (30 inches). The seasonal distribution of rainfall varies, depending upon whether the steppe is located on the equatorward or poleward side of the low latitude deserts (BWh). For those on the equatorward side, more than 80 percent of the rainfall normally comes in the high-sun period, when the intertropical convergence migrates to the region briefly. In contrast, the steppes on the poleward side of the low latitude deserts experience their maximum precipitation in the low-sun period. They receive precipitation mainly from the cyclonic fronts that occasionally swing far equatorward from the middle latitudes during the period when the sun's vertical rays are in the opposite hemisphere. In most years, precipitation is unreliable and scanty during the steppe dry season.

The water balance in the low latitude steppes (BSh) shows a marked deficiency throughout the year. Poten-

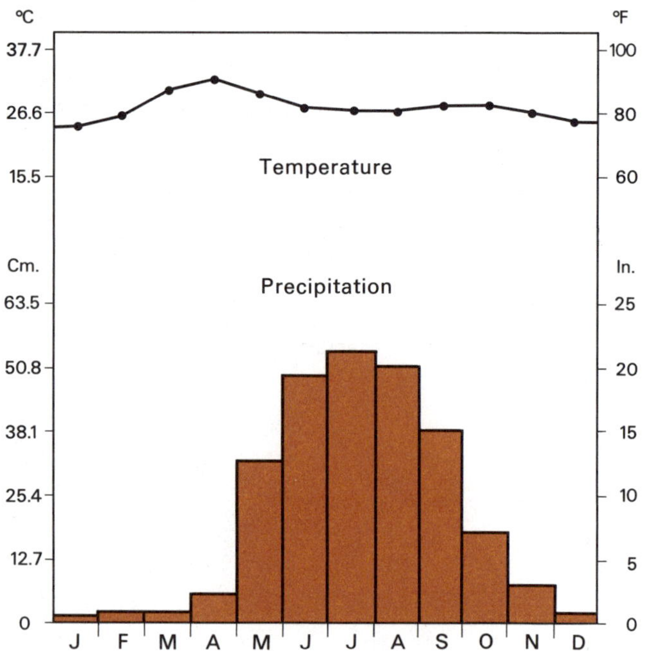


**FIGURE 8.3**
Tropical monsoon (Am). The tropical monsoon climate is associated with the seasonal monsoon winds. During the winter the winds originate over the continents and bring dry conditions; in summer they originate over the oceans, bringing heavy precipitation to the landmasses.

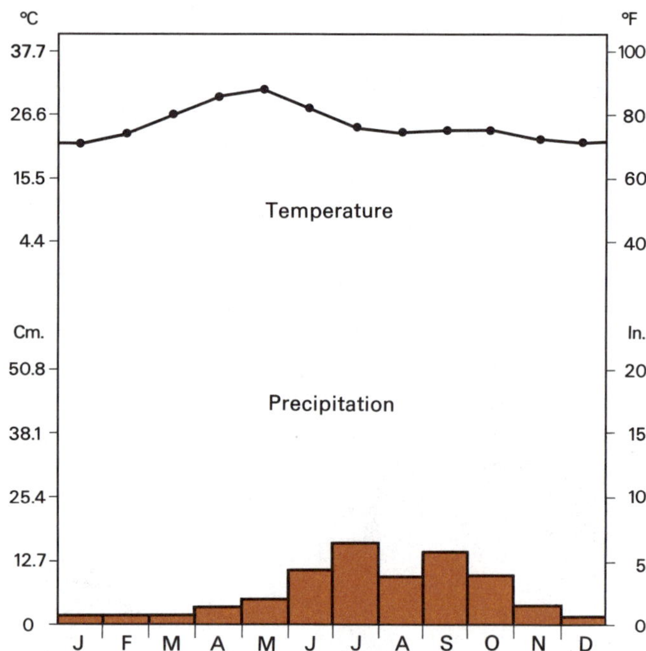


**FIGURE 8.4**
Low latitude steppe (BSh). The low latitude steppes surround the low latitude deserts. Temperatures reflect their latitudinal location on either the poleward or equatorward side of the deserts.

tial evapotranspiration exceeds the precipitation received. The boundary between the steppe and the humid climates is the zone where precipitation and potential evapotranspiration are about equal. The relative humidity is low, primarily because temperatures are high. In contrast, the absolute humidity may be quite high (Figure 8.4).

## Low Latitude Deserts (BWh)

The low latitude deserts (BWh) lie approximately between 18 and 28 degrees in both hemispheres. They coincide with the equatorward edge of the subtropical high pressure cells and the trade winds. The world's great deserts, such as the Sahara, Thar, Great Australian, Sonoran, and Kalahari, are found here. Environmental conditions are harsh; searing heat prevails much of the year. Air flows generally downward and outward, so only rarely do air masses that cause precipitation penetrate these areas. The low latitude desert (BWh) experiences no definite seasonal regime of precipitation. Instead, the climate is characterized by lack of precipitation. The water balance exhibits a marked deficiency for every month of the year. Potential evapotranspiration is far in excess of precipitation. Most water that falls immediately evaporates back into the atmosphere (Figure 8.5).

## MIDDLE LATITUDE CLIMATES

The middle latitude climates are located in the belt of the prevailing westerly winds. They are characterized by

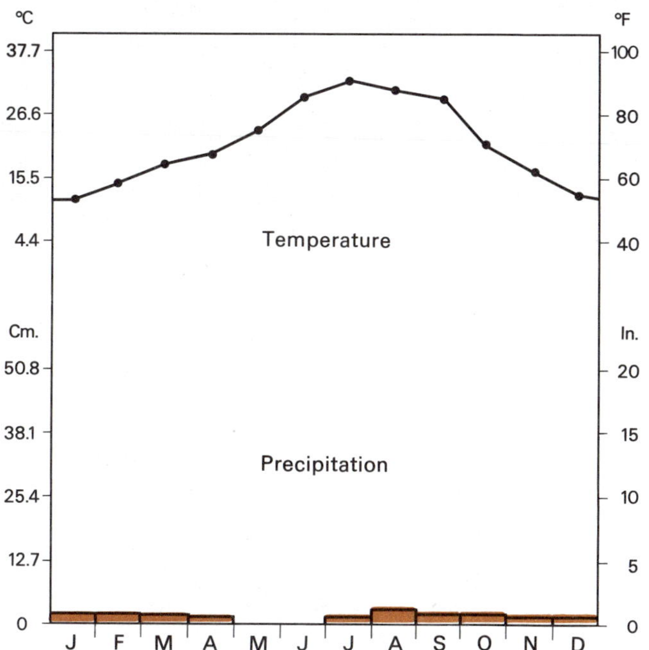


**FIGURE 8.5**
Low latitude desert (BWh). The low latitude deserts occupy the areas of the subtropical high pressure and trade winds.

seasonality in temperatures. Their precipitation regimes depend upon their position in relation to the subtropical high pressure cells and the polar front.

## Dry Subtropical (Csa)

The dry subtropical climate (Csa) is often referred to as the Mediterranean climate, because the Mediterranean Basin contains the largest area of this climate. Such areas are situated on the west coasts of middle latitude continents in, for example, California, Central Chile, South Africa, and western and central Australia. The dry subtropical climate is famous for its long, hot, dry summers and mild, rainy winters (Photo 29). This climate is alternately affected by the subtropical high pressure and the westerlies. Its dry season occurs in the summer when it is under the influence of the subtropical high. The wet winter season occurs when the westerlies with their cyclonic storms prevail. The water balance varies from an excess in winter to a deficit in the long summer. As a consequence, in the winter wet season the actual evapotranspiration reaches the potential, while in summer it falls far short (Figure 8.6).

**PHOTO 29**
Dry subtropical climate. Vineyards are a characteristic feature of the agriculture of the long, hot summers and mild wet winters of the dry subtropical climate (Csa).

## Humid Subtropical (Cfa)

The humid subtropical (Cfa) climate is situated on the southeastern sides of continents, largely between 30 and 40 degrees latitude. This climate is hot and humid during the long summers and cool and humid during the short winter season. It represents a transition between the tropical rainy (A) climates on its equatorward side and the more severe continental (D) climates on its poleward margin (Photo 30). In the United States and China, polar air masses bring cold "spells" in winter. During this season, frontal precipitation from cyclonic storms predominates. This frontal precipitation is largely replaced by convectional precipitation during the summer. Occasionally in the warm season, tropical cyclones will penetrate the coastal areas. The water balance for most Cfa stations is never in deficit, and the deficit at the remaining locations usually occurs for not more than two or three months. Thus the actual evapotranspiration equals or nearly equals the potential evapotranspiration (Figure 8.7).

## Marine West Coast (Cfb)

This climate lies poleward of the dry subtropical (Csa) climate. Its largest area is in Western Europe, but it also lies along the western coasts of North America, southern Chile, New Zealand, and Tasmania (Photo 31). Because it is greatly influenced by oceanic conditions, it

TYPE: DRY SUBTROPICAL (Csa)

Naples, Italy (41°N, 14°E)

| | | |
|---|---|---|
| Average annual temperature | 16.6°C | (62°F) |
| Annual temperature range | 16°C | (29°F) |
| Average annual precipitation | 86 cm. | (34 in.) |

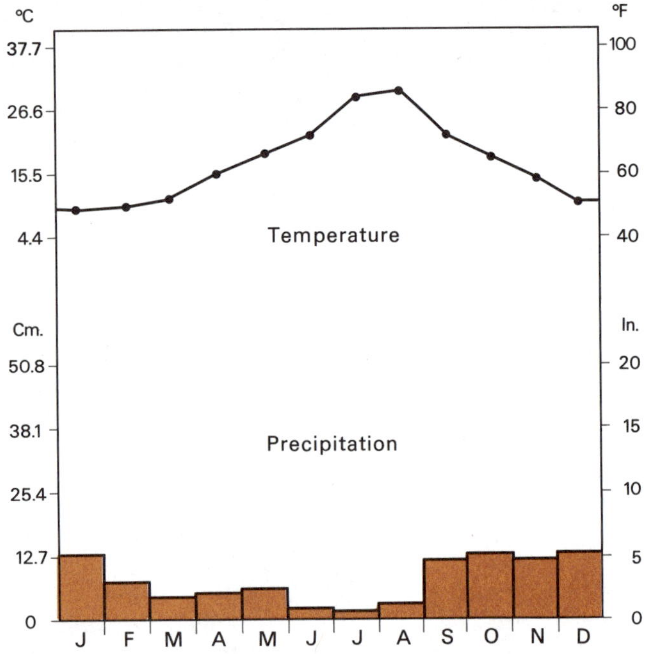


**FIGURE 8.6**
Dry subtropical (Csa). The dry subtropical climates occupy the southwestern portions of continents. This climate is characterized by hot, dry summers and mild, moist winters.

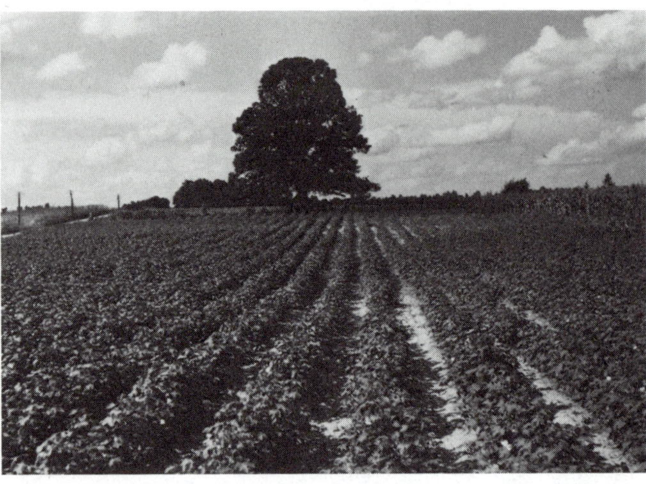

**PHOTO 30**
Humid subtropical climate. In the long, hot, humid summer of the Cfa climate, cotton is a principal crop.

TYPE: HUMID SUBTROPICAL (Cfa)

Charleston, South Carolina (33°N, 80°W)

| | | |
|---|---|---|
| Average annual temperature | 18.8°C | (66°F) |
| Annual temperature range | 17°C | (32°F) |
| Average annual precipitation | 119 cm. | (47 in.) |

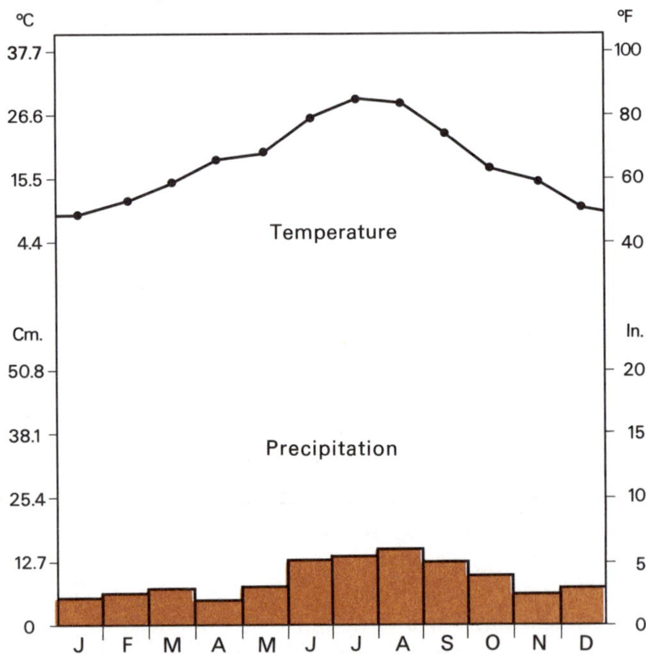


**FIGURE 8.7**
Humid subtropical (Cfa). Precipitation is fairly evenly distributed throughout the year with cyclonic storms dominating in winter and convectional storms in summer.

**PHOTO 31**
Marine west coast. The coniferous forests on the coastal area of Washington reflect the cool, damp conditions of the marine west coast climate (Cfb).

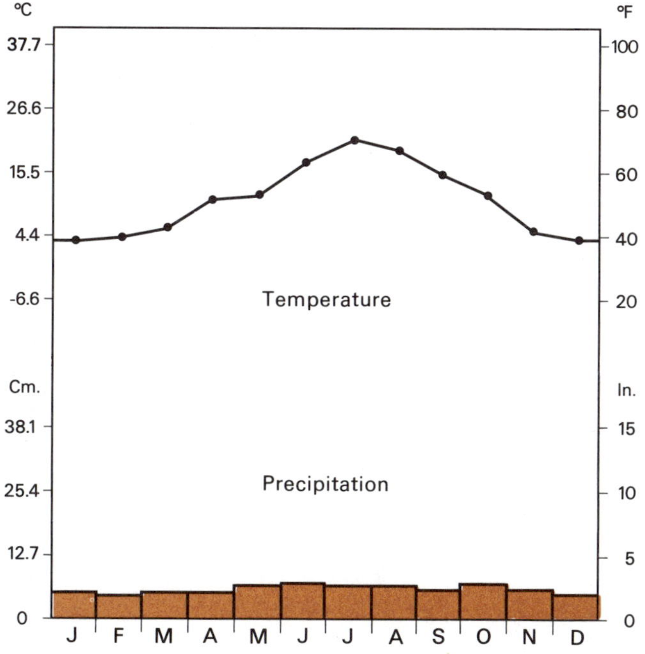


**FIGURE 8.8**
Marine west coast (Cfb). The Cfb climate is characterized by mild weather and cyclonic precipitation throughout the year.

does not experience wide temperature extremes; the summers are mild and the winters cool. These areas lie within the westerly wind belt, so that frontal precipitation dominates throughout the year. The amount of precipitation depends greatly on topographic conditions. Where the coasts are mountainous, as in northwestern United States and Canada, southern Chile, Norway, and New Zealand, the orographic mechanism causes heavy precipitation. The water balance is in excess the entire year, with actual evapotranspiration equaling the potential evapotranspiration (Figure 8.8).

## Humid Continental, Warm Summer (Dfa, Dwa)

Poleward from the humid subtropical (Cfa) climate is the humid continental, warm summer (Dfa) climate, where winters are more severe and temperatures average below freezing for several months (Photo 32). This climate, with its warm to hot summers and cold winters, has a large annual range in temperature. Polar air masses frequently invade during the winter. In contrast, an occasional warm spell in winter occurs when a warm tropical maritime air mass penetrates the area. Frontal precipitation occurs throughout the year, but during the warm season it is supplemented with occasional convectional storms. In Asia, this climatic region receives comparatively little precipitation in winter; it is therefore classified as Dwa rather than Dfa. Because precipitation is adequate throughout the year, the water balance normally has a surplus (Figure 8.9).

## Humid Continental, Cool Summer (Dfb, Dwb)

A more severe phase of the humid continental climates lies poleward of the Dfa type. In general, the humid continental, cool summer climate lies between 50 and 60 degrees north latitude, stretching across the interiors of the North American and Eurasian landmasses. The characteristic that differentiates it from the humid continental, warm summer (Dfa) climate is its cooler summers and shorter growing season. Winter is, by far, the dominant season (Photos 33 and 34). Continentality controls the temperature. Precipitation generally occurs in cyclonic storms, with the major portion coming during the summer. The winters in Asia have little precipitation, so the humid continental, cool summer climate is designated as Dwb there. Because the summers are cool, convectional thunderstorms are relatively rare. Snow falls in greater amounts and lies on the ground longer than in the warm climate (Dfa). The water balance is normally in excess in the region. The potential evapotranspiration usually exceeds the actual evapotranspiration (Figure 8.10).

**PHOTO 32**
Humid continental, warm summer. The long, hot summers (Dfa) in Iowa provide an excellent climate for agriculture. (Courtesy: United States Department of Agriculture, Soil Conservation Service)

**FIGURE 8.9**
Humid continental, warm summer (Dfa). The humid continental, warm summer climate is characterized by a wide temperature range and even distribution of precipitation.

TYPE: HUMID CONTINENTAL, WARM SUMMERS (Dfa)

St. Louis, Missouri (38°N, 90°W)

| | |
|---|---|
| Average annual temperature | 13.6°C (56.5°F) |
| Annual temperature range | 26°C (47.5°F) |
| Average annual precipitation | 99 cm. (39 in.) |

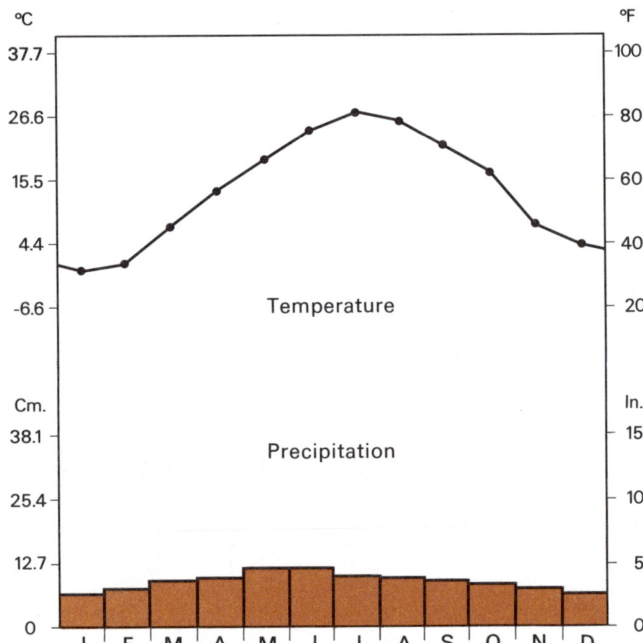

**PHOTOS 33–34**
Humid continental, cool summer. Photo 33 shows the main street of Adams, New York, in summer. Photo 34 of the same street in winter illustrates the heavy snowfall the area receives. (Courtesy: National Oceanic and Atmospheric Administration)

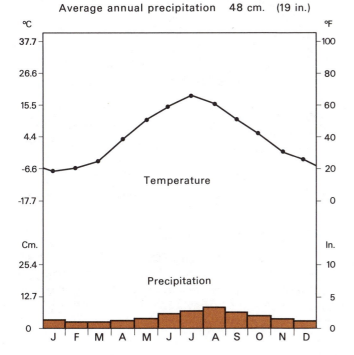

TYPE: HUMID CONTINENTAL, COOL SUMMERS (Dfb)

Leningrad, Soviet Union (59°N, 30°E)

| | |
|---|---|
| Average annual temperature | 4.1°C (39.5°F) |
| Annual temperature range | 25°C (46.5°F) |
| Average annual precipitation | 48 cm. (19 in.) |

°C: 37.7, 26.6, 15.5, 4.4, -6.6, -17.7
°F: 100, 80, 60, 40, 20, 0

Temperature

Cm.: 25.4, 12.7, 0
In.: 10, 5, 0

Precipitation

J F M A M J J A S O N D

**FIGURE 8.10**
Humid continental, cool summer (Dfb). The Dfb climate has long, cold winters and a short, warm summer. Cyclonic precipitation dominates throughout the year.

TYPE: MIDDLE LATITUDE STEPPE (BSk)

Cheyenne, Wyoming (41°N, 104°W)

| | | |
|---|---|---|
| Average annual temperature | 6.9°C | (44.5°F) |
| Annual temperature range | 22.7°C | (41°F) |
| Average annual precipitation | 37.6 cm. | (14.8 in.) |

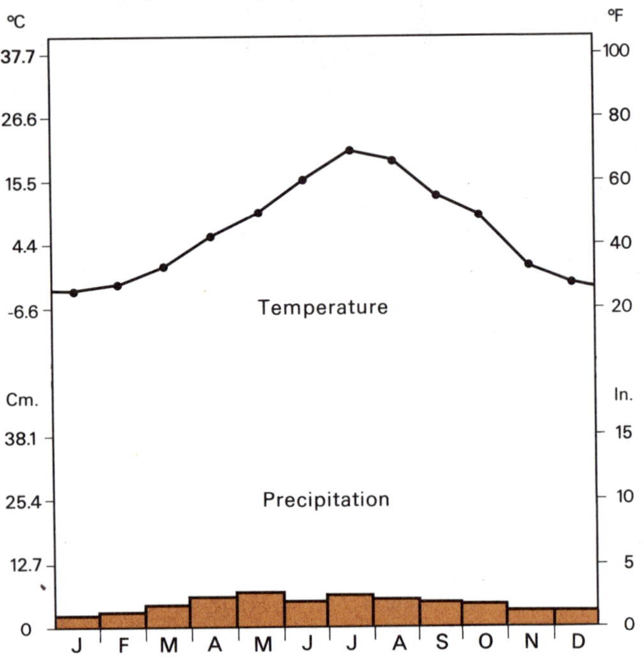


**FIGURE 8.11**
Middle latitude steppe (BSk). The limited precipitation is the major factor differentiating the middle latitude steppe climate from the D climates.

**PHOTO 35**
Middle latitude steppe. The short-grass steppe region (BSk) of the Great Plains reflects the low precipitation. (Courtesy: Kansas Industrial Development Commission)

## Middle Latitude Steppes (BSk)

The middle latitude steppes (BSk) are transitional between the middle latitude deserts (BWk) and the more humid mesothermal (C) and microthermal (D) climates. Precipitation declines on the interior sides of the humid climates, eventually giving way to the steppe (BSk) climate (Photo 35). This climate features distinct summer and winter seasons and, due to its continental location, the annual range of temperature is large. Precipitation reflects the transitional character of the steppe from desert to more humid conditions. As a consequence, in some years the steppe will have desert conditions while in other years humid conditions will prevail. The water balance is in deficit on an annual basis in the middle latitude steppe. For short periods during the humid years, however, there may be a small surplus in the water balance. Potential evapotranspiration thus exceeds precipitation over the long range (Figure 8.11).

## Middle Latitude Deserts (BWk)

The deserts of the middle latitudes are most commonly found in the deep interiors of the larger continental landmasses or on the leeward sides of the mountains. Water sources are not available in these areas (Photo 36). On their more humid margins, the middle latitude

**PHOTO 36**
Middle latitude desert (BWk). Desert scrub in Great American Desert near Ely, Nevada.

TYPE: MIDDLE LATITUDE DESERT (BWk)

Las Vegas, Nevada (36°N, 115°W)

| | |
|---|---|
| Average annual temperature | 18°C (64.5°F) |
| Annual temperature range | 24°C (44°F) |
| Average annual precipitation | 11.1 cm. (4.4 in.) |

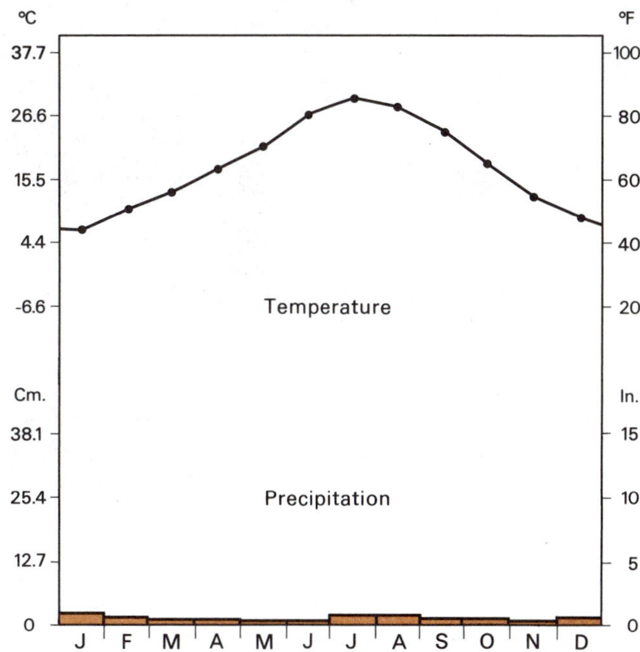


**FIGURE 8.12**
Middle latitude desert (BWk). The BWk climates are situated far from sources of precipitation, either in continental areas of the middle latitudes, or in mountains that prevent the penetration of moisture to these areas.

deserts (BWk) merge into the steppes (BSk). Because of the wide extent of the deserts, temperature conditions vary with such factors as latitude, elevation, and continental location. Average precipitation is always inadequate in the middle latitude deserts (BWk). There is a perpetual deficit in the water balance, and potential evapotranspiration always exceeds precipitation (Figure 8.12).

## SUBPOLAR AND POLAR CLIMATES

Subpolar and polar climates are highly influenced not only by their latitudinal position but by their continental location.

### Subpolar Continental (Dfc, Dfd, Dwc, Dwd)

This climate, found in the higher middle latitudes, at approximately 55 to 68 degrees north latitude, is the most severe of the continental climates (Photo 37). On its poleward side it merges with the treeless tundra (ET), and on its equatorward side with the humid continental, cool summer (Dfb) type. Average temperatures are more misleading than for any other climate, because this climate possesses the greatest range of temperature

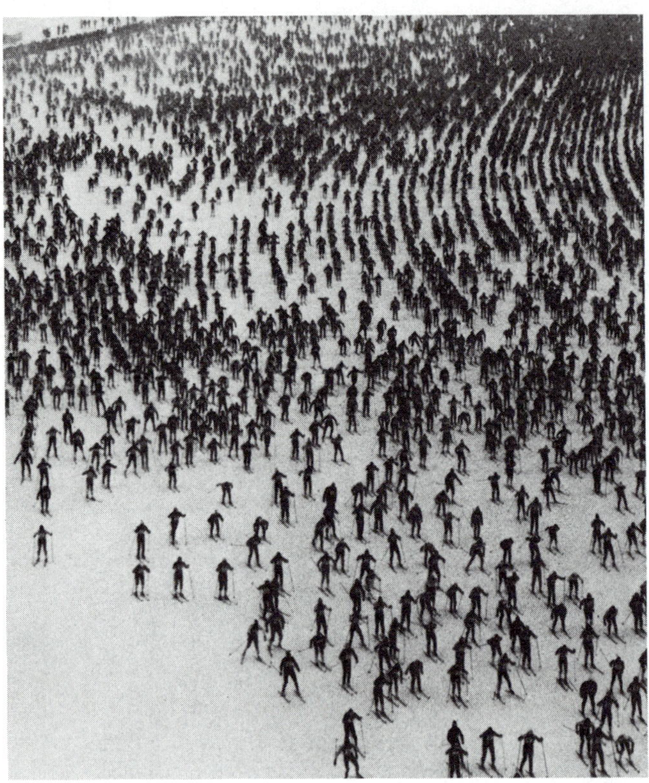

**PHOTO 37**
Subpolar continental climate. The winter season dominates in the Dfc climate. Hämeenlinna, Finland, is the starting point of the 92-kilometer (45-mile) annual Finlandia Ski Race. The 7,000 skiers from over 20 countries begin the race over a frozen lake.

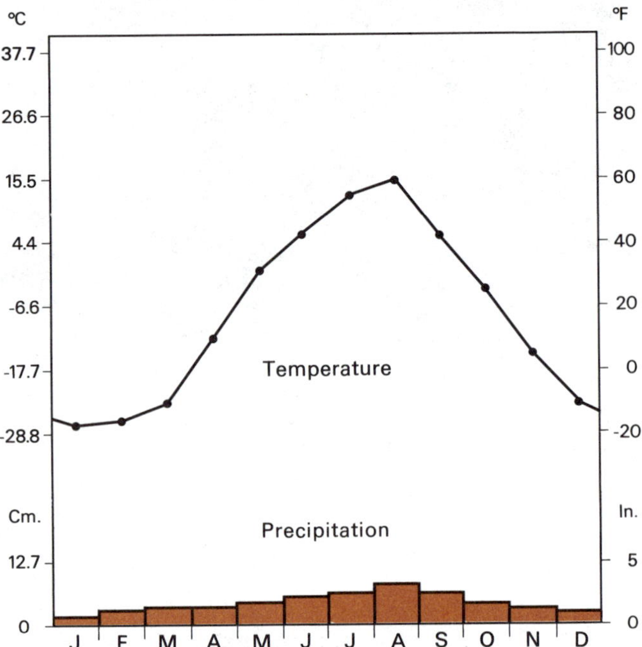


**FIGURE 8.13**
Subpolar continental (Dfc). The Dfc climate exhibits extreme temperature conditions with cool, short summers and long, cold winters. Note the low precipitation of this climatic type.

in the world. Despite the high latitude, the short summers are quite warm, but the long winters are unbelievably cold. Precipitation is meager, coming largely from the passage of cyclonic storms during the summer period. During the winter a continental high pressure cell prevails, and only on rare occasions will a cyclonic storm penetrate the Asian areas (Dwc, Dwd). Because of the low temperatures the water balance normally has a surplus (Figure 8.13).

## Tundra (ET)

The tundra (ET) climate lies between the polar ice caps and the subpolar continental climate (Dfc). Its poleward

**PHOTO 38**
Tundra. The ground is permanently frozen in most of the tundra areas of the world. This photo shows the thawing of permafrost at Nome, Alaska, in order to construct a building.

and equatorward boundaries are delineated by isotherms and vegetation. The 10°C (50°F) average monthly isotherm for the warmest month, which coincides with the tree line, provides the equatorward boundary. The poleward boundary is the 0°C (32°F) isotherm for the average temperature of the warmest month. This line is the limit of most vegetational growth. The tundra (ET) is characterized by long, bitterly cold winters, and very short, cool summers (Photo 38). Average annual precipitation is low with a warm season maximum that is cyclonic in origin. In spite of a popular misconception that the high latitudes have huge snow accumulation, snowfall is considerably lighter than that found in lower latitudes (Figure 8.14).

## Polar (EF)

The polar ice caps (EF) are located poleward of the tundra (ET) climate. They are deserts of permanent ice and snow found in Greenland, Antarctica, and most areas north of 70° latitude. These areas have no warm season. Cyclonic storms occasionally migrate over the icecap, bringing meager precipitation and cloudy weather. Although little snow is precipitated, snow and ice are abundant because there is so little melting.

TYPE: TUNDRA (ET)

Upernavik, Greenland (73°N, 56°W)

| | | |
|---|---|---|
| Average annual temperature | -8.8°C | (16°F) |
| Annual temperature range | 28° C | (51°F) |
| Average annual precipitation | 23.3 cm. | (9.2 in.) |

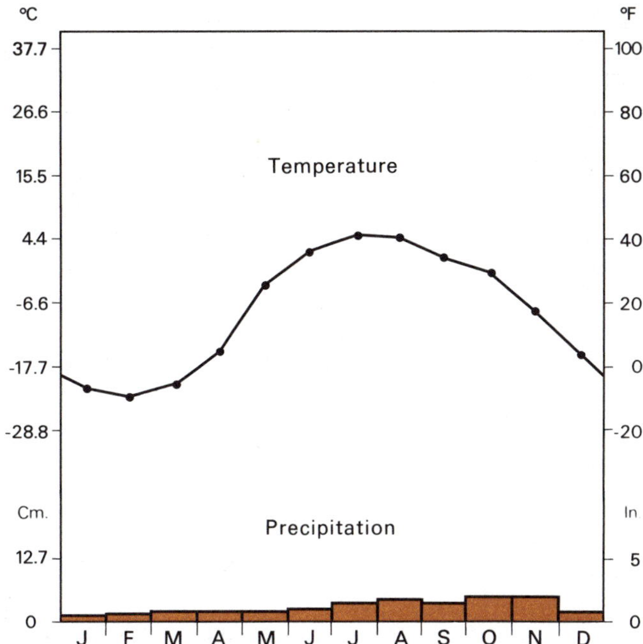


**FIGURE 8.14**
Tundra (ET). The ET climate is noted for its long, cold winters and very short, cool summers. Annual precipitation is low.

### HIGH ALTITUDE CLIMATES

The principal regions of high altitude (H) climates are the main mountain chains and associated highlands in the middle and low latitudes. It is impossible to describe and analyze a typical highland (H) climate because highlands exist in all latitudes and at varying elevations. For example, at the equator the area of permanent snow and ice is found at only the highest elevations, usually at altitudes of more than 4,200 meters (14,000 feet). As latitude increases, the elevation at which permanent ice and snow can exist decreases, until in the polar regions permanent ice and snow are found at sea level. Thus each highland region must be considered individually as to its climatic characteristics. Highlands in the equatorial regions offer particularly rapid changes in climatic environments. In rising from sea level to about 4,500 meters (15,000 feet), one can experience, in a general way, all the various climatic types one would encounter in traveling from the equator to the poles.

## CONCLUSION

The development of climatic classification systems was one of the earliest human efforts to recognize spatial patterns on the earth. These endeavors continue in our time. Each spot on the earth has a distinctive microclimate, and therefore an infinite variety of climatic regions could be devised, but this would not be practical. Climatic classification systems are instead based on dominant atmospheric characteristics that occur over a wide area.

Climatic classification systems have been based on single atmospheric elements such as temperature and precipitation. These classifications are too simplistic to have great value. A number of systems have been based upon the distribution of vegetation as the prime criterion. Of these, the best known is the Köppen-Geiger classification system used in this text. Warren C. Thornthwaite advanced the study of climatic classification by producing a classification system based on the interaction of energy and moisture in the atmosphere.

## STUDY QUESTIONS

1. Why is it important to understand the maximum and minimum climatic conditions of a region as well as the average conditions?
2. List and explain different types of temperature and precipitation data that are important in describing climatic conditions.
3. What is the basis of all climatic classification systems?
4. What is the difference between climatic classification systems based on the empirical approach and those based on the genetic approach?
5. Describe the early climatic classification systems based on temperature. On precipitation. On vegetation.
6. What is the basis of the Köppen-Geiger climatic classification system? What are the advantages and limitations of this system?
7. How does the Thornthwaite climatic classification system differ from the Köppen system?
8. How are the tropical rainforest (Afi) and tropical savanna (Aw) climates differentiated?
9. What are the major characteristics of temperature and precipitation of the tropical rainforest (Afi) climate?
10. How do the rainfall regimes of the tropical rainforest and tropical savanna climates differ? Why?
11. What are the climatic differences between the tropical rainforest and tropical monsoon climates?
12. Why is the night period sometimes known as the winter of the tropics?
13. Why is the rainfall regime of the low latitude steppe (BSh) different on its poleward and equatorward boundaries?
14. Give the principal characteristics of the low latitude steppe (BSh) climate and the low latitude desert (BWh) climate.
15. How do the temperature and precipitation regimes of the dry subtropical (Csa), humid subtropical (Cfa), and marine west coast (Cfb) climates differ?
16. What are the basic differences in location of the dry subtropical (Csa), humid subtropical (Cfa), and marine west coast (Cfb) climates?
17. Why are the summer conditions of the tropical

rainforest (Af) and the humid subtropical (Cfa) climates similar?

18 How do the latitude and oceanic conditions influence the temperature regime of the marine west coast (Cfb) climate?

19 What are the major temperature characteristics of the humid continental, warm summer (Dfa) climate?

20 Explain the precipitation regime of the humid continental, warm summer (Dfa) climate.

21 How is the humid continental, warm summer (Dfa) climate distinguished from the humid continental, cool summer (Dfb) climate?

22 Describe the locations of the middle latitude deserts (BWk) and middle latitude steppes (BWk).

23 Why is the subpolar continental (Dfc) climate the most extreme of the microthermal (D) climates?

24 If you were to travel from the equator to the North Pole along the 75th meridian, through what climatic regions would you pass?

# 9

# CLIMATIC CHANGE

## KEY WORDS

heat island
hygroscopic
isotope
paleoclimatology
sunspots
urban climate

The earth's climates have always been changing. In the geologic past these changes occurred as a response to natural phenomena. Today, however, human activities may be capable of altering the climate of the earth. The causes of climatic changes are complex and are still not completely understood. Many theories have been presented, but few have been proven. Many conflicting predictions of climatic change appear in the news. They range from an approaching ice age on the one hand to the melting of the icecaps on the other, with both natural and human factors postulated as causes. One group of scientists indicates that we are in a very important period of climatic change that will affect the way we occupy the earth, while other scientists of equal stature indicate that such viewpoints at best are without scientific basis and at the worst are apocalyptic nonsense.

## CLIMATES OF THE GEOLOGIC PAST

### METHODOLOGY

The most useful techniques in *paleoclimatology*—the study of climates of geologic eras—are those methods that attempt direct measurements of past temperatures on the earth. To date, oxygen isotopes have proved most useful for this task. Oxygen is one of the elements that has a fixed number of protons in its nucleus but varying numbers of neutrons. Each form, or isotope, of oxygen has the same atomic number but a different atomic weight. These differences in atomic weights in specific geologic time periods give an indication of temperature conditions. A more recent and important technique involves measuring the abundance of deuterium, the hydrogen isotope $H^2$, in rocks. These are the only methods of directly estimating temperatures of the geologic past.

Indirect methods for estimating paleotemperatures are more readily available, but involve greater assumptions. For example, the temperature of ancient sea surfaces has been estimated by mapping the distribution of organic reefs. This method assumes that the ancient reef-building organisms had the same ecological limitations as the modern reef-building organisms. This assumption may or may not be correct.

A further difficulty in determining ancient climates derives from the problem of establishing a mean value for the temperature of the earth. Although isolated determinations of temperature provide some idea of world conditions, they are inadequate. A variety of paleoclimatic indicators is more likely to provide a better understanding of global climates than is a single indicator, such as temperature.

### GEOLOGIC CLIMATES

The thermal state of the earth depends, as we have seen, on the balance of incoming and outgoing radiation. Incontestable evidence indicates that the earth has experienced warm and cold periods that have extended over millions of years. These long periods of cold and warm temperatures have been due to a complex chain of interactions, and precisely which variables were most important is difficult to determine. Nevertheless, the facts of climatic change are recorded in geologic materials (Figure 9.1).

From a geological viewpoint the most obvious climatic changes are the periods of glaciation when ice covered a large portion of the world. During the last approximately 5 billion years, 5 periods of glaciation are known to have occurred. Two periods of glaciation occurred in the Precambrian period, at about 2.3 billion and at about 800 million years ago. In the Paleozoic era glaciation occurred at the end of the Ordovician, 400 million years ago, and in the late Paleozoic during the Carboniferous and Permian periods, about 250 to 300 million years ago. Glaciation did not appear again on the earth until the Pleistocene period of the Cenozoic era, about two million years ago. Paleoclimatological data support the view that glaciation was associated with long periods of earth cooling. There were many periods of earth cooling that did not culminate in glaciation.

The earth has also experienced long periods of warmth. Among these are the long intervals during the Mesozoic and the early Cenozoic eras. Possibly the warmest period of the world came in the Cretaceous. The Devonian Silurian periods as well as much of the Precambrian appears to have been warmer than today.

Geological evidence suggests a strong relationship between glaciation and precipitation conditions. Precipitation appears to increase just prior to a glacial period. It declines during glaciation, however, reaching a low amount by the end of the glacial period. The declining precipitation reflects the cooling of the oceanic bodies. Cooler temperatures reduce evaporation so that less water is carried over the continents to produce precipitation. At the end of glaciation, precipitation appears to gradually increase.

### THEORIES OF PALEOCLIMATIC CHANGE

Numerous theories have attempted to explain climatic change from a geologic perspective. These theories consider the following factors:

1. Variations in solar output, including changes not only in solar radiation but also in ultraviolet radiation.

**FIGURE 9.1**
Generalized temperature and precipitation history of the earth. Dashed lines indicate that data are very sparse. The curves represent postulated departures from present global means, but only relative values are indicated. Note that the time scale is progressively expanded in the more recent eras. Throughout geologic history long periods of warmth have been interrupted by shorter cold periods. (After Frakes, 1979, p. 261)

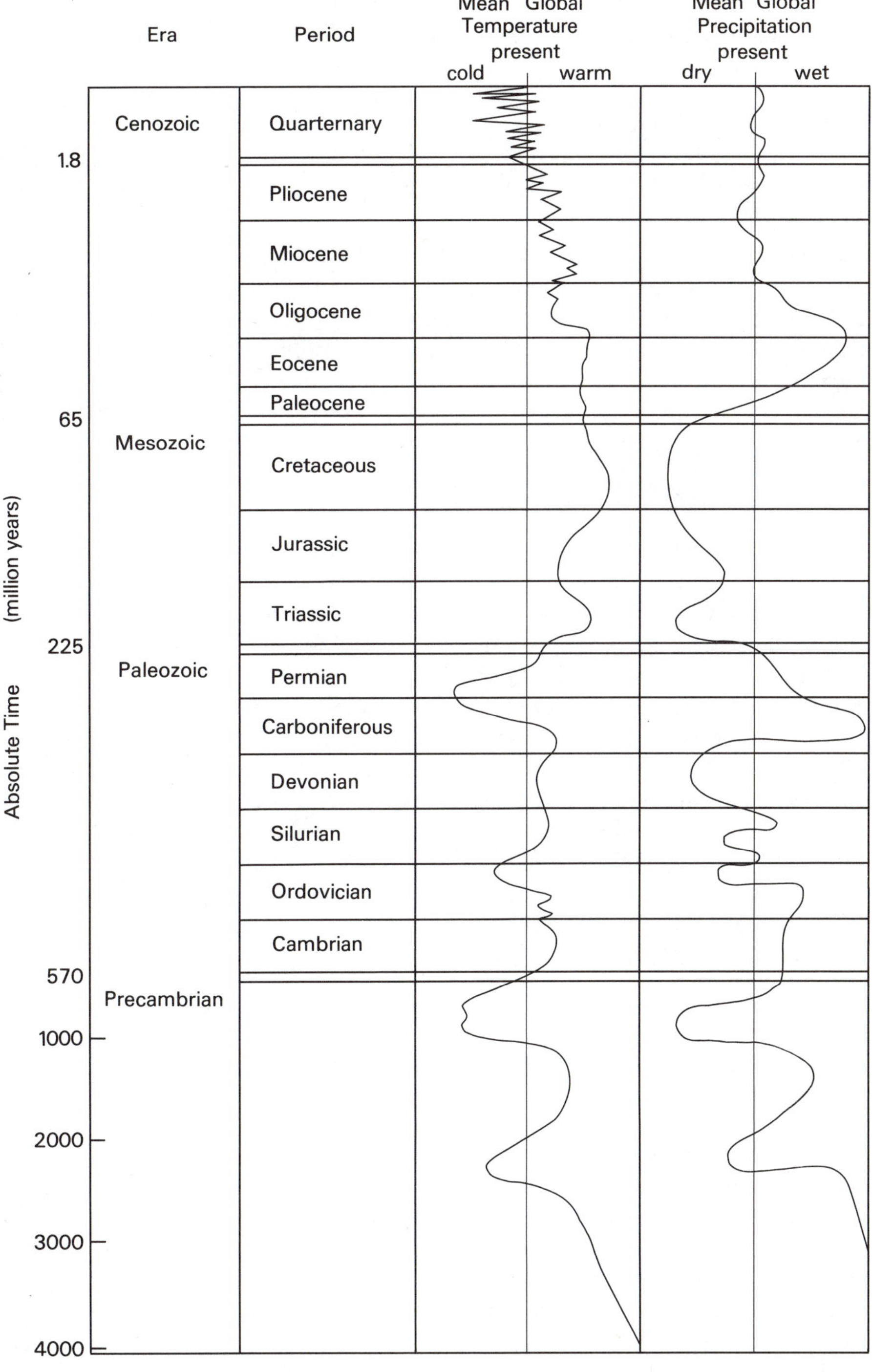


2 Variation of astronomical factors, such as the distance from the earth to the sun and the inclination of the axis.
3 Changes in the atmosphere's ability to transmit and absorb solar radiation, caused by such natural phenomena as carbon dioxide or water vapor.
4 Long-term changes in the distribution of land and water areas on the earth due to plate tectonics, mountain building, or shift of the poles.
5 Variations in the earth's atmospheric albedo.

These theories have not been proved by empirical evidence. It can be suggested, however, that the factors listed above could influence such aspects as the circulation of the atmosphere, the amount of heat stored in the oceans, ocean currents, or the amount of ice stored in glaciers and icecaps.

## CLIMATIC CHANGES IN HISTORIC TIMES

The climate of the earth for the last 10,000 years can be inferred from human artifacts as well as biological and physical evidence. One of the fascinating aspects of such a study is that it reveals the role of climate in influencing the development of human civilization. Several distinct climatic periods can be recognized in Europe and adjacent areas since 8000 B.C.

### DISAPPEARANCE OF THE ICE AGE

The period from 8000 B.C. to 2000 B.C. is characterized by long periods of warmth and much shorter periods of cool temperatures. It has been called the *climatic optimum.* Since then the global climate has been gradually cooling, although irregularly. During the climatic optimum, the ice sheet disappeared from Scandinavia and Britain. It is probably no coincidence that civilization developed in Mesopotamia and the Indus Valley. The climate favored the growth of wild grains, particularly wheat, providing a stable, adequate yield, which is fundamental to an agricultural civilization.

### PERIOD OF DECLINING TEMPERATURES (2000 B.C.–A.D. 800)

After about 2000 B.C. evidence from human activities shows that the world experienced a long period of generally declining temperatures. The average annual temperature may have decreased as much as 2°C. By 500 B.C., a long period of cool, rainy weather prevailed in Europe. Much physical evidence remains of this time, such as the advancement of glaciers in the Alps, the rise of Boden See by about 10 meters, and the flooding of low-lying areas in northern Europe, which caused migrations from these areas. Most of the Alpine mountain passes were filled with ice and could not be traversed for several hundred years.

When the climate became less favorable, the population at that time was not capable of increasing the productivity of the land. Their choice, essentially, was to reduce the population or to migrate to more desirable regions. Although populations in many regions did decline, the common response to adverse changes in climate was to migrate.

Some of history's most important migrations may have been caused by these adverse weather conditions. In Central Asia, for example, a nomadic civilization thrived on the semiarid steppes for over 200 years at about the time of Christ. Although sedentary agriculture existed only at oases, food was plentiful. With a gradual change in the circulation pattern, the principal track of rain-producing cyclones shifted northward, and precipitation decreased. The capacity of the land to support the population declined, and great waves of migrations moved westward into Europe. We may well ask, Did this increasing dryness in Central Asia trigger the Barbarian invasion of Europe that ultimately overran the Roman Empire?

About A.D. 600 the same scenario apparently existed in the Arab lands. Historical records indicate a long, severe drought in the eastern Mediterranean. As a response to declining food resources, the Arabs migrated along the African coast as far as Tunis. The migrations continued under the religious fervor of Mohammed until the Moslem religion reached from Spain to India.

### PERIOD OF OPTIMAL CLIMATES (800–1250)

The next time of increasing warmth in northern Europe and surrounding areas is usually called the *little climatic optimum.* Much evidence of dynamic activities remains in the Scandinavian regions. Most striking were the voyages of the Vikings that culminated in the settlement of Iceland and Greenland. Evidence indicates that these areas were much warmer than they are today. For example, early Norse burials in Greenland were deep in ground that is permanently frozen today. Within Europe warm-weather crops migrated northward. Vineyards flourished in England, and English wine gained a reputation as being nearly as good as that produced in France.

In contrast to the warm conditions in northern Europe, the Mediterranean region experienced variable climatic conditions. Extreme cold prevailed for at least short periods. The Tiber and Nile rivers were frozen over once or twice. In the years 859–60, the northern Adriatic Sea was frozen. Apparently the wind and pressure belts had shifted far to the north, bringing warmth to northern Europe, but causing cold, continental air to invade the Mediterranean on occasion.

### PERIOD OF VARIABLE CLIMATES (1250–1550)

A period of great variability in climatic conditions followed the little climatic optimum. In general, however, severe weather affected much of Europe. As cold weather penetrated farther southward, polar ice was much in evidence in Iceland and Greenland. The voyages of the Vikings in the northern areas virtually ceased, and most settlements in Iceland and Greenland were abandoned.

After 1250 the warm-weather crops of northern Europe again migrated southward. Most of the vineyards of England were abandoned. Agriculture in Iceland experienced a long period of decline. The high cultural aspects of Irish civilization that had flourished for 500 years came to a dramatic halt.

Famines occurred periodically in the 1300s. It is speculated that the harsh weather conditions that caused many crop failures weakened the health of the population. These conditions probably set the stage for the Black Death, which ravaged Europe from 1348 to 1350, killing half of the population. After the Black Death, the plagues disappeared first in the cooler high latitudes that had not experienced weather extremes of such magnitude.

Toward the end of the period the weather ameliorated. Vineyards were replanted in England, and the English orchards once again produced apricots, peaches, and quinces. The reduced storminess further encouraged the great voyages of discovery in the sixteenth century.

## PERIOD OF DECLINING TEMPERATURES (1550–1850)

The average annual temperature declined rapidly after the middle of the 16th century. A long period of coldness prevailed from 1645 to 1715 that is popularly known as the *Little Ice Age.* The remaining physical evidence of this time shows that the alpine glaciers of Europe advanced into the lowlands and that the North Atlantic polar pack ice moved far to the south. Sailing records show that by 1780 the pack ice extended from Greenland to Norway and surrounded Iceland most of the year. The northern European rivers were frozen over on a number of winters. For example, in the 1400s the Thames was frozen over only once, but in the 1700s it was frozen over 6 times. During this period of agricultural uncertainty, crop failure due to late frosts was fairly common. Large areas of cropland were abandoned in Scotland, Scandinavia, and the Alpine countries.

## MODERN PERIOD OF TEMPERATURE VARIABILITIES (1850–PRESENT)

In contrast to the previous period, the time since 1850 has been characterized by a worldwide amelioration of climatic conditions (Figure 9.2). The world average temperature in the middle latitudes rose 1° to 2°C, the highest levels since the climatic optimum about 4000 B.C. This rise in temperature appears to be a response to an intensification of the general atmospheric circulation over widely separated parts of the world. This intensification has increased the maritime influence over continental areas, resulting in milder weather conditions. Regrettably, the cause of this change in atmospheric circulation is unknown.

Since about 1920 world weather records have improved, and regional variations in atmospheric conditions have become better known. A substantial warming trend in the higher middle latitudes began about 1920 and peaked during the late 1930s. Peak temperatures in the lower middle latitudes were reached in the early 1950s, and in the subtropical latitudes in the late 1950s to the early 1970s. In contrast, a substantial cooling trend started in polar and higher middle latitudes in the 1940s, in lower middle latitudes in the late 1950s, and in the subtropical latitudes even later, perhaps extending to the late 1970s. Minimum temperatures in the middle latitudes were reached generally in the early and middle 1960s, followed by a slight warming trend in the late 1960s and early 1970s.

It has been determined that geographical patterns of precipitation departures occur on a much smaller scale

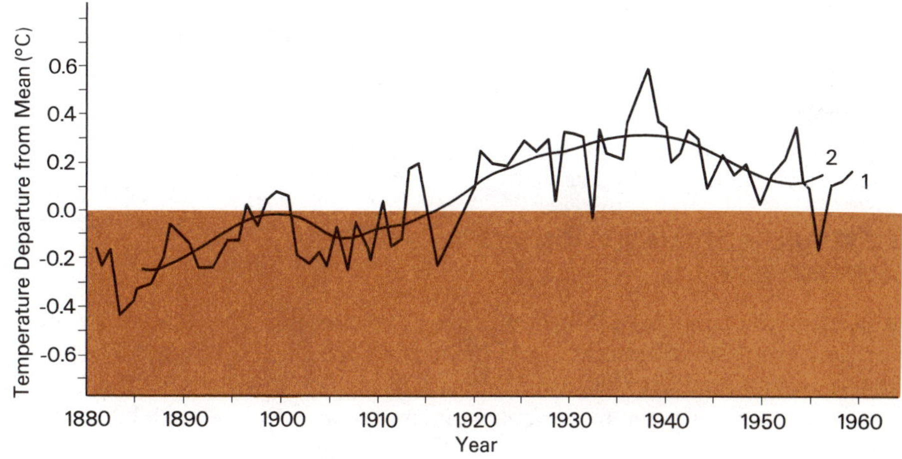


**FIGURE 9.2**
Variations in annual temperature (in °C) from 1880 to 1960. From 1880 to about 1940 a long period of warming occurred in the Northern Hemisphere. After 1940 temperatures declined slightly. Line 1 is the actual temperature, while line 2 averages the temperatures. (After Budyko, 1967)

and are more locally variable than are deviations in temperature. While a worldwide comprehensive analysis of precipitation trends has been somewhat neglected, some major variations of precipitation are evident in recent decades. During the 1930s a severe drought was experienced in many regions lying between 35° and 50° latitude. These areas included the dust bowl of the Great Plains, the Ukraine of the Soviet Union, and the severe drought of southern Australia. In contrast the drought regions of the 1930s experienced significant amounts of precipitation in the 1940s. The early to mid-1950s, like the 1930s, was a markedly dry period on the marginal interior continental regions. Severe drought, however, was restricted to areas equatorward of 40° latitude. The 1960s were like the 1940s in having generous rainfall in the marginal interior continental areas of the middle latitudes, but with some record dry years in extensive east coastal regions. In the 1960s and early 1970s severe drought conditions occurred in the middle and lower subtropics, notably in southern Asia and Africa. In the late 1970s there was again a slight tendency for drought conditions in the southern portions of the marginal interior continental areas.

The weather of the past can be fairly well determined from observations of the physical environments, from written records, and, since about 1680, from instrument readings. Even so, it is impossible to predict the weather at any place even for the immediate future. Without question, we will experience warmer and colder, and drier and wetter periods, but no one can predict when or where these will occur. A bitter cold series of winters or a few stifling hot summers are not an indication of climatic change.

## THEORIES OF CLIMATIC CHANGE

A number of theories have attempted to explain changes of climate. These theories are based on several variables:

1. Natural autovariations of the atmosphere
2. Variation in solar radiation (sunspot cycles)
3. Atmospheric pollutants

### NATURAL AUTOVARIATIONS OF THE ATMOSPHERE

A number of climatologists have theorized that climates can be altered for several hundreds of years by changes in the atmosphere that are not the result of change in the solar output. Crucial to the autovariation theory are a number of positive feedbacks that occur between the atmosphere and the earth over a considerable period of time.

The climatic change may be triggered, for example, by an event that changes the amount of foreign particles in the atmosphere. Such an event might be a series of intense volcanic eruptions over a long period of time. In this process the upper atmosphere is filled with dust. The dust increases condensation nuclei, resulting in greater precipitation. The precipitation, in time, blocks the solar radiation from heating the lower atmospheric layers, and the surface temperature drops. When several winters are colder than normal, the icecaps and snowfields begin to increase.

As this scenario is developed, the ice and snow areas expand, and the north-south temperature gradient increases which in turn strengthens the jet stream. Cyclonic activity is also enhanced and extends farther equatorward. Cold polar continental air masses extend farther equatorward and the ice and snow areas continue to grow. Because of the tremendous amount of ice and snow, spring arrives late. Summer will be cool and cloudy as a response to the more frequent cyclones. If these conditions persist year after year, a mini–ice age gradually evolves.

After the mini–ice age has persisted for perhaps as long as several hundred years, a number of checks and balances begin to slow the expansion of the ice areas. Initially, the cooler temperatures mean that less infrared radiation is lost to space, and the balance of radiation gradually favors an excess of short-wave incoming radiation over outgoing long-wave radiation. Secondly, the general circulation pattern is gradually altered as a response to increasing solar radiation. The high and low pressures are more highly amplified, with strong northerly winds from the west and strong southerly winds from the east. This strong north-south flow gradually increases the heat exchange between the tropics and the poles. Eventually the ice fields and snowfields stop growing and gradually recede. The decreased albedo gradually changes the radiational balance toward the positive side, and the higher latitudes begin to warm. The warming trend is a response to increased atmospheric heating and the poleward transport of warmer air. Finally the climate returns to its warm state and the cycle is complete.

The above scenario is only one of many that could be visualized in which the climate is altered over an extended period without involving a change in solar energy. The atmospheric system that could produce this situation is extremely complex. The change in a single variable could create an unstable condition. This single perturbation may alter the entire system, causing a climatic change of fairly long duration to occur.

## VARIATIONS IN SOLAR RADIATION (SUNSPOT CYCLES)

The first solar feature to be observed was sunspots, a phenomenon recorded by Galileo in 1610. Sunspots appear as dark blotches on the otherwise bright solar surface. These spots are areas of magnetic force and are cooler because heat cannot flow across a magnetic field. Sunspots appear in cycles, and climatologists have identified three types of cycles that may influence weather conditions: the eleven-year sunspot cycle, the double sunspot cycle, and the longer secular cycle of about 80 years (Figure 9.3).

An attempt has been made to measure the variations in radiation caused by sunspots. However, measurements over the past several decades indicate that any variations in the total energy output are probably smaller than ±2 percent, the greatest variation that can be measured. The sunspots do cause intermittent outbursts of charged particles and short-wave ultraviolet radiation that reaches the outer layers of the earth's atmosphere. These outbursts affect the ionosphere and the earth's magnetic field to produce auroras.

The well-defined oscillations of the sunspots appear to coincide with periodicities of about the same lengths for certain weather phenomena, such as changes in air circulation, pressure, and temperature. It is impossible to prove, however, that these weather modifications are linked to sunspots. At this time the relationship between the short-wave radiation received in the upper atmosphere and weather phenomena occurring in the lower atmosphere on a short-term basis has not been proven scientifically.

History provides strong empirical evidence of a significant change in the amount of solar radiation reaching the earth at different levels of sunspot activity. In the period between about 1645 and 1715, there was a pronounced minimum of sunspot activity, which has come to be called the Maunder minimum. The Little Ice Age occurred at the same time, during which the amount of radiation reaching the earth was apparently reduced. In contrast, a period of maximum sunspots occurred between 1100 and 1250, a time of maximum warmth over the Northern Hemisphere. If these two periods represent the extremes in a long-term cycle, then the next major warming of the earth should occur in about 200 years. Sunspot activity has in fact been increasing since about 1700.

## ATMOSPHERIC POLLUTANTS

A number of meteorologists have investigated the possibility that atmospheric pollutants could create world changes in climate. The amount of pollutants in the atmosphere depends upon a number of conditions, including industrial activity, use of motor vehicles, and consumption of fossil fuels by an increasing world population. The principal atmospheric pollutants from human sources are carbon dioxide, sulfur dioxide, nitrogen oxides, and carbon monoxide (Figure 9.4).

Carbon dioxide, which is produced in the burning of fossil fuels, may be a major influence in altering the earth's climates. It is being emitted into the atmosphere

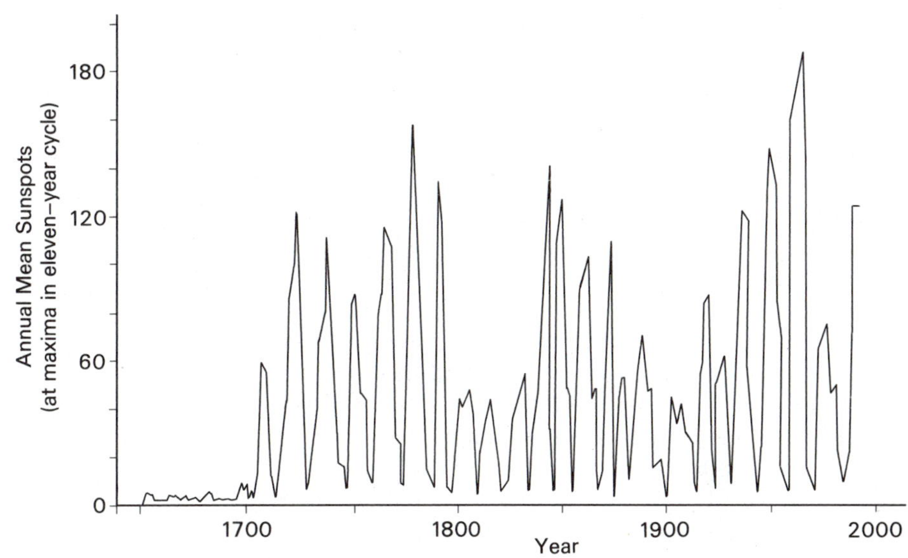


**FIGURE 9.3**
Annual mean sunspot numbers at maxima in the 11-year cycle from 1645 to the present. Note that the number of sunspots in the 11-year cycle has varied greatly from one period to another. (From John A. Eddy, National Center for Atmospheric Research, High Altitude Observatory, Boulder, Colorado)

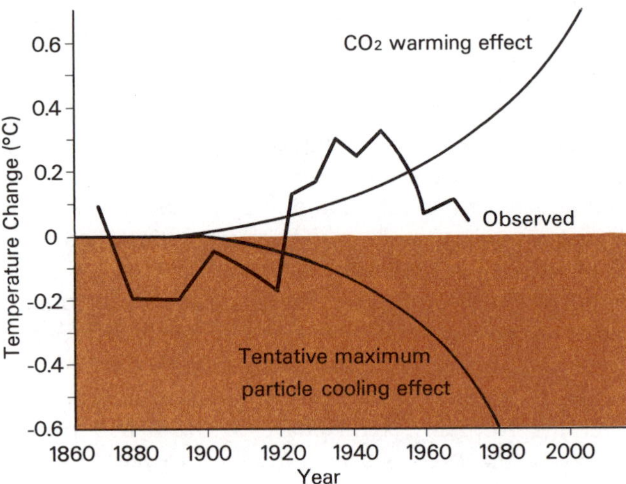


**FIGURE 9.4**
Trends of mean temperature (in °C) from 1860 to 1970, with estimated warming effect due to $CO_2$, and cooling effect due to particles in the atmosphere. Note that one appears to offset the other. (After Mitchell, 1972)

at a rate of about 15 gross tons ($15 \times 10^9$ tons) annually.

At the turn of the century scientists were suggesting that the earth's surface temperatures would increase as the amount of carbon dioxide increased in the atmosphere. The rise in temperature would be a response to the well-known "greenhouse effect," in which the carbon dioxide acts toward the sun's radiation like the glass in a greenhouse. That is, the carbon dioxide is transparent to incoming sunlight but is partially opaque to outgoing long-wave infrared heat rays. Studies have revealed that over a period of time about half of the carbon dioxide provided by the combustion of fossil fuels is retained in the atmosphere.

A study of world mean temperatures from 1880 to 1970 revealed that temperatures rose according to the expectations of the greenhouse effect until about 1940. Since then, however, world mean temperatures have fallen in spite of an accelerating concentration of carbon monoxide in the atmosphere. R. A. Bryson of the University of Wisconsin, a leading authority on climatic change, has suggested that particulate pollution from volcanoes, forest fires, aerosol sprays, and other sources have acted to counteract the carbon dioxide pollutant effect. The theory is that the sunlight-obscuring effect of these particles more than offsets the heat-trapping effect of the carbon dioxide. As a consequence the mean world temperature decreases.

The carbon dioxide question is obscured by many uncertainties. The mathematical models that have been developed contradict each other. Serious doubts are being raised as to whether carbon dioxide in the atmosphere contributes measurably to climatic change. If we assume that carbon dioxide has a negligible heating effect, then the necessity for any balancing cooling effect of particulate pollution disappears. While some evidence indicates that the increase in particulate pollution on recent world-temperature changes has been negative—that is, reflection and scattering of the sun's rays—just as much evidence points to a positive effect—that is, absorption resulting in a greenhouse effect.

The effects of atmospheric pollutants on climate are still not certain. Contradictory studies show that much more investigation is needed. The predictions that a new ice age is coming or that the icecaps will melt cannot be affirmed from present studies. While many mathematical models indicate that increased carbon dioxide will raise the atmospheric temperature, an unambiguous climatic signal has not yet been received.

## HUMAN MODIFICATIONS OF WEATHER AND CLIMATE

Human modification of the natural environment gradually alters the physical conditions of the atmosphere. It is now possible to detect worldwide changes in the atmosphere. For example, we have evidence that enough heat is being added over wide areas to change the heat content of the atmosphere by several degrees. These processes are accelerating as the economic activities of the world expand. A fundamental question is, Will these human activities affect appreciably the climate of the earth? They undoubtedly can do so, but it must be recognized that powerful natural forces are counteracting these changes. The human and the natural forces must be understood sufficiently so that each can be put into a proper perspective.

### URBANIZATION

As the cities of the world have expanded, they have caused fundamental changes to occur in the local natural environments. As a consequence the cities have developed a distinctly different climatic regime than the surrounding countryside. To distinguish the climate of the city from that of the rural area, the term *urban climate* is now widely accepted.

#### Heat Island

One of the most evident differences between the urban atmosphere and its surrounding rural area is the formation of the *heat island.* This phenomenon has been recognized for centuries. The temperature within a city differs from that in the adjoining countryside for a number of reasons. A major cause is the presence of vertical structures, as well as stone, concrete, and asphalt surfaces in the city. These surfaces heat more quickly and store the heat longer than a natural surface of soil and vegetation. Further, the rough surfaces created by the different heights of the buildings reduce the wind speed, and so the heat island is not dissipated by wind movement as rapidly as in the country (Figure 9.5).

Because heat builds up in urban areas, city temperatures can be as much as 10°C higher than in the surrounding rural areas. While this is exceptional, temperatures are normally 2° to 3°C higher in the city than in the country (Table 9.1). In order to reduce the temperature differences from the city to the country, as much open space and vegetation as possible should be provided in the city. Trees and shrubs are better than grass to reduce these temperature contrasts, because grass often dries out in summer, becoming brown and absorbing great quantities of heat.

The temperature contrast between the city and rural areas is a response to a number of factors. Usually as the urban area grows larger, the contrasts become greater. The density of the urban structures is also a major contributing factor. It has been found, however, that the relationship between city size and urban-rural temperature contrasts is not linear. The physical makeup of the city and its natural setting are important factors affecting these temperature differences.

The heat island normally experiences some diurnal variations. During the day the temperature differences are usually considerably smaller than during the night, when the city remains a true heat island. Cooling is thus more rapid in the rural areas.

The average annual temperatures calculated for the city and its environs also reveal the presence of a heat island. In winter the urban areas are somewhat warmer than the surrounding areas, but the summers are also warmer. A heat island offers both advantages and disadvantages to the residents. In winter the fuel bill for heating may be reduced slightly. However, the increased cost of air conditioning in summer offsets the winter saving. Further, the increased heat in summer may have a deleterious effect on the health of certain individuals, particularly those persons with heart and respiratory disorders. It also affects the lower income groups because air conditioning may not be financially feasible for them.

## Radiation

Because of the particulates and pollutants in the atmosphere over cities, less solar energy reaches the ground in urban than in rural areas (Figure 9.6). The longer the radiation passes through the atmosphere, the greater the reduction. When the angle of the sun is low, more solar energy is removed as it passes through the urban atmosphere. Thus, the effect of particulates on solar energy reaching the ground is greatest in high-latitude cities. Hans Landsberg has shown that the average annual total solar radiation received by cities in the higher latitudes is decreased by 15 to 20 percent. Ultraviolet radiation is decreased by 30 percent in winter and by 5 percent in summer. A study by a Dutch meteorologist,

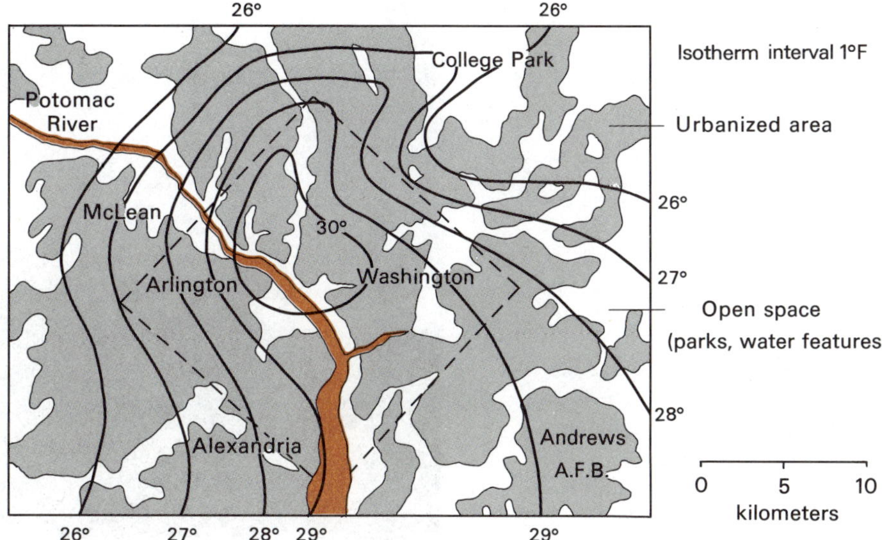


**FIGURE 9.5**
Mean winter temperature over the Washington, D.C., metropolitan area, 1946–1965. The heat island of central Washington is about 4°F warmer than the suburbs. (After Woollum, 1964, from *Weatherwise* 17, no. 6, pp. 263–71, 1964, a publication of the Helen Dwight Reid Educational Foundation)

**TABLE 9.1**
Temperature variations in urban and rural environs of Washington, D.C., and Sheffield, England, on a clear summer day.

| | Washington, D.C. | | Sheffield, England | |
|---|---|---|---|---|
| Land Use | Daytime 1320 EST | Nighttime 2200 EST | Daytime 1459 GMT | Nighttime 2337 GMT |
| Business center | 97°F | 85°F | 69°F | 54°F |
| Industrial | — | — | 71 | 56 |
| Dense residential | 96 | 83 | 70 | 53 |
| Park near city center | 95 | 84 | 66 | 46 |
| Park near city fringe | 94 | 78 | — | — |
| Suburban residential | 95 | 79 | 69 | 51 |
| Rural environs | 95 | 76 | 65 | 42 |
| Temperature contrast | | | | |
| Urban/Rural | 2 | 9 | 6 | 12 |

Sources: H. E. Landsberg, *Physical Climatology* [DuBois, PA.: Gray Publishing Co., 1968], and T. R. Detwyler and M. G. Marcus, eds., *Urbanization and Environment* [Belmont, CA.: Duxbury Press, 1972]

H. J. De Boer, revealed that the city of Rotterdam received 3 to 6 percent less solar energy than the immediate suburbs, and 13 to 17 percent less than the rural areas. When urban areas implement environmental controls, such as smoke abatement, the amount of solar energy reaching the ground increases measurably. Studies in Los Angeles showed that the amount of ultraviolet radiation reaching the ground had a direct correlation with smog. When smog is present, the ground receives 50 percent less ultraviolet radiation than when the atmosphere is clear. On very smoggy days the ultraviolet radiation may be reduced as much as 90 percent.

## Winds

The movement of air in an urban area is extremely complex because of the wide variation in the physical structure of the cities. Winds that are channeled into

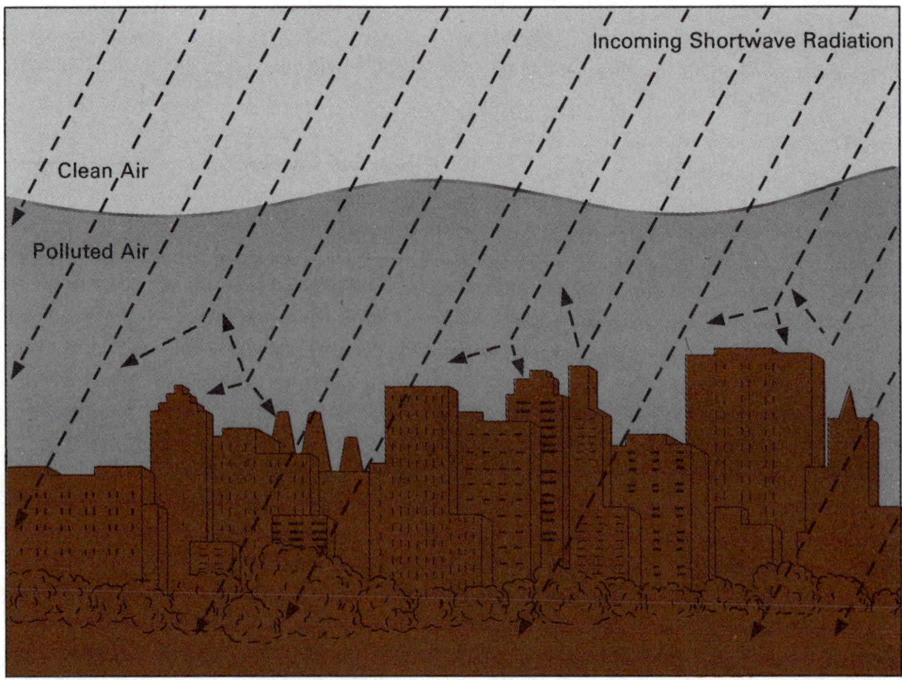


**FIGURE 9.6**
Scattering of incoming radiation by the particles in the atmosphere over an urban area.

streets and buildings of different heights form many eddies. In general, wind movement is lowered from 10 to 40 percent in cities when compared to rural, open areas. As a consequence the air masses over cities are more stable than in the country. This factor encourages the build-up of pollutants, particularly when there are numerous narrow streets flanked by uniform tall buildings. The streets act as a trap for the accumulation of pollutants (Figure 9.7).

When the turbulent eddies are smaller than the city, they are greatly modified or even completely obliterated by the buildings as they move within the city. Air movements larger than the city can also be greatly modified. Regional air movements, such as a land-sea breeze or a mountain-valley breeze, are particularly affected.

Because the city is a heat island, its warm air can be displaced as it rises by cooler, denser rural air. This movement is normally weak, but it can be significant under certain conditions. For example, on clear nights an inflow of air can occur from the cooler rural areas to the warmer city areas (Figure 9.8).

## Precipitation

Many more condensation nuclei are present in the atmosphere over cities. It is therefore reasonable to expect a noticeable increase in cloudiness and even precipitation. Some reasons for this phenomenon may be that the city heat island intensifies thermal convection, combustion of fuels adds water vapor to the atmosphere, the difference in building heights increases mechanical turbulence, and the urban atmosphere contains a higher concentration of particles and possible ice crystals. A few studies have considered urban precipitation, but the importance of each of these factors has not been determined.

The effects of cities on precipitation is difficult to determine for a number of reasons. Rain gauges are rarely located within the metropolitan areas; instead, they are at airports, which are usually far removed from city centers. Many cities are found on water bodies or in hilly terrain, so that it is difficult to separate the natural from the artificial effects. Finally, the natural variability of rainfall, particularly when it occurs as thunderstorms, makes the effect of the city environment difficult or impossible to determine.

Nevertheless, sufficient studies have been made to conclude that cities may influence the frequency and amount of precipitation. S. A. Chagnon has completed a study on the effects of the Chicago urban area on precipitation. He showed that the industrial area between Chicago and La Porte, Indiana, a distance of 30 miles downwind, has greatly increased its cloudy days and the number of days with thunderstorms since 1925. Further, the year-to-year variations correlate directly with the intensity of industrial output. Another study showed that the average rainfall of Paris was 31 percent greater on weekdays than on Saturday and Sunday.

## Humidity

In general the relative humidity of cities is several percentage points lower than that of the surrounding country. The city's atmosphere is warmer and is able to absorb more moisture. While the relative humidity is lower within the city, the absolute humidity may be little different from the city to the country. The relative humidity differences from city to country show some diurnal and seasonal variations. The variations are greatest at night

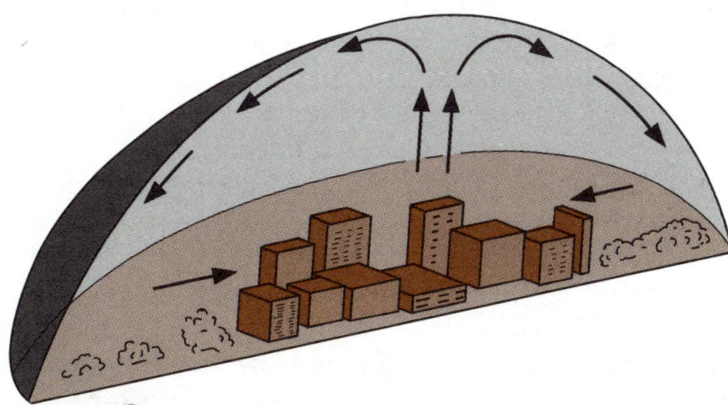

**FIGURE 9.7**
Hypothetical circulation of air in an urban area. Air rises over the city and settles in the suburb, creating a circulation of the air mass. (After Bryson and Ross, "The Climate of the City," in Detwyler and Marcus, 1972, p. 63)

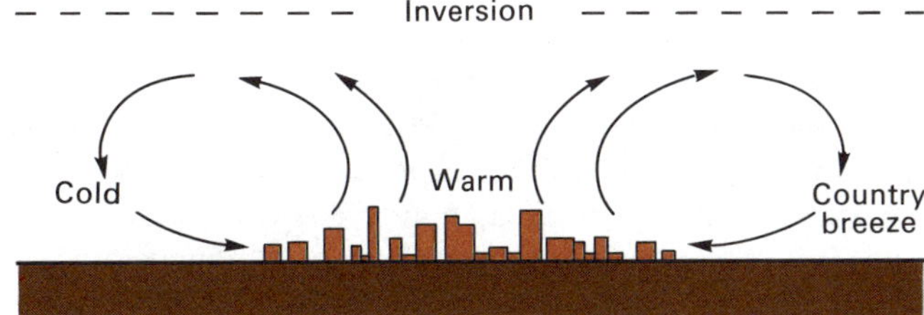


**FIGURE 9.8**
Air flow at night in a metropolitan area. The heat island effect causes cold air from the suburbs to flow into the city, where it rises and spreads outward. (After H. E. Landsberg, *Science* 170, 18 December 1970, pp. 1265–74. Copyright 1970 by the American Association for the Advancement of Science.)

and during the summer, corresponding to the largest differences in temperature.

### Visibility

As a response to air pollution and higher concentrations of particulates, visiblity is restricted and haze is much more likely in cities than in the surrounding country. Many studies show a direct relationship between air pollution and visibility. For example, a study of two German cities revealed that low visibility coincided with periods of stable air conditions and higher concentrations of sulfur dioxide in the atmosphere. It has also been observed that as motor vehicle density increased in New York City, the occurrence of haze grew remarkably.

Fog is created from the particulates in the urban atmosphere through *hygroscopic* action. That is, water vapor condenses on the particles, forming droplets. The densest fogs occur during inversions, when the pollutants are at a maximum. A study of fogs in the Paris region found that, in the period from October through March, Paris mornings are foggy 41 percent of the time. The suburbs experience fog only 28 percent of the time, however, and the country around Paris has foggy mornings only 2 percent of the time. Fog and pollution vary from city to city, depending upon local conditions. Cities have their greatest fog potential when the air is stable.

## LAND USE MODIFICATIONS

The alteration of the physical environment by agricultural practices changes the atmospheric systems. This process began about 8,000 years ago with the conversion of natural vegetation into grazing and arable lands. All types of vegetational regions have been altered in this way. No doubt the earliest changes occurred in the steppe and forested steppe areas of the Middle East. The conversion of the forests of Europe and Asia came somewhat later. In the tropical areas, much of the natural savanna grassland has been burned and replaced by artificial environments. The processes of change continue today in the virgin tropical forests of South America, Africa, and southern Asia. Although precise figures are not available, it has been estimated that 2.5 to $3 \times 10^7$ km$^2$, or 18 to 20 percent of the total area of the continents, has been drastically changed.

Human changes in the use of the land have altered the climatological heat balance and water budget. For example, in southern Tunisia, near Nefta, about 85 percent of the vegetation inside a fenced area remains intact, while outside this fenced area, where animals have grazed unchecked, vegetation covers only 5 percent of the area. The grazed area has turned into a semidesert while the ungrazed area has the vegetational covering of a subhumid region. Both areas receive the same amount of precipitation annually. In many areas of the world, the desert areas are expanding several kilometers per year, depending upon the way the inhabitants use the land.

A number of theories explain why precipitation may decrease as vegetation is removed from a dry region. Dust particles increase in the atmosphere as wind picks them up from the bare soil. Normally dust particles make excellent cloud-seeding nuclei, but in desert areas precipitation may not result from this process. In reality, the clouds may be so overseeded that precipitation is discouraged. With so many particles competing for water vapor, the droplets may be so small and light that they will not fall as rain.

## WATER DISTRIBUTION MODIFICATIONS

Even the earliest civilizations learned to control water discharges in order to irrigate crops, control floods, and drain swamps. When a large body of water has been created or removed, the climate of the nearby areas is changed. An open water body has an albedo substantially lower than that of other land surfaces, creating a distinct environment. In contrast, frozen, snow-covered water has a very high albedo. Thus the amount and the seasonal distribution of absorbed solar energy depend primarily on the type of land surface present.

A water body will influence the temperature of the surrounding area because water is capable of storing large quantities of heat that will be released at a later time. In addition, since the water surface is likely to have a temperature quite different from that of the surrounding land area, the radiation balance will be changed. The sensible heat and evaporation may be significantly altered when a water body is created.

In recent decades a large number of new artificial lakes have been developed by the damming of rivers. Some of these are huge, such as Lake Nasser, which was created by the Aswan Dam on the Nile. Lake Nasser varies from 2 to 5 kilometers in width with a length of about 400 kilometers. The humidity of the hot, dry desert winds increases appreciably as they blow across this massive water body. The humidity affects the radiation balance, and eventually it may influence precipitation.

The climate of an area is also modified by irrigation. It has been estimated that about 1700 km$^3$ of irrigation water evaporates in the world each year. This represents about 5 percent of the total runoff from land areas and approximately 2 percent of the total annual evaporation from land areas. The local effects of irrigation on climate include increased humidity and temperature changes. Irrigation may even cause direct global effects, such as changes in the cloud covering and resulting effects on the radiation balance, but such effects are extremely complex and there is no reliable method for making quantitative calculations. An indirect effect of irrigation has been calculated. The vegetation covering an irrigated area gives the land an albedo significantly lower than that of bare, nonirrigated land. The increased evaporation lowers local temperatures. In contrast, however, global temperatures are raised due to decreased reflection of the incoming solar radiation. A Russian climatologist, M. I. Budyko, has calculated that present irrigation has increased the earth's mean surface temperature by 0.07°C. Estimates indicate that irrigated land will double by A.D. 2000, and the combined demand for water for irrigation, energy, production, industry, and domestic consumption will be 5 times as great on a global scale. Evaporation will at least triple. This increase in evaporation will have a marked effect on solar radiation and ultimately on the hydrologic cycle of the earth.

A number of plans to modify ocean waters are in the conceptual stage. These modifications could have a great influence on global climates. As the world demand for food rises, much thought is being given to increasing the productivity of the oceans. Such vital nutrients as nitrate and phosphate exist in plentiful supply several hundred meters beneath the ocean surface. Ocean waters could be fertilized by pumping these deeper waters to the surface. However, the deeper waters are colder, and a massive exchange of water would lower the surface temperature of the oceanic waters appreciably. The cooler surface water would lower evaporation and could have a marked effect on the available water carried from the oceans onto the world's land surfaces.

Although plans to directly change the character of the earth's waters are only in their initial stages, other human activities have indirectly affected the oceans. In a few places, water is being diverted from one watershed to another, distorting salinity patterns in the oceans. This change produces a number of subtle effects. For example, the increased fresh water lowers salinity in the surface water, increases the stability of the water, and inhibits mixing. As a consequence, a shallow layer of warm water exists on the surface. As this water moves in an ocean current, the heat is transported from one area to another. This action could raise temperatures significantly in areas dependent on warm currents.

## CONCLUSION

There is strong evidence that the world's climate has not been uniform through geologic time, but has experienced long periods of warmth followed by shorter periods of coldness. Nineteenth-century geologists recognized that the most recent ice age began over two million years ago, in the Pleistocene epoch, of which remnants still remain. It is now known that this recent glacial period was only one of a number that the world has experienced in the past 2,000 million years.

Scientific studies have also revealed variations in weather and climate that have occurred within the past several thousand years. At times of optimal climate, warm temperatures have prevailed for several hundred years. At other times, cold conditions have prevailed, creating little ice ages. The reasons for these variations are still not well understood, for data are not available to provide definitive explanations.

Until recently, little attention was given to the possible influence of human activities on the weather and climate of an area. It is now recognized that the metropolitan areas of the world have a distinctly different climatic regime than the surrounding rural areas. Huge river dams have created lakes that have altered the moisture conditions of surrounding regions. Possibly the greatest potential for altering the climate of large areas comes from economic activities that discharge pollutants into the atmosphere. Any small but persistent change in the effectiveness of solar radiation in heating the atmosphere has the potential of changing the climate of the future.

# STUDY QUESTIONS

1. What techniques are used to reveal climatic change in geologic time?
2. How is climatic change revealed in geologic materials?
3. List the theories that attempt to explain paleoclimatic change.
4. What evidence shows that the world's climate has experienced changes in the past 10,000 years?
5. Describe the theories that have attempted to explain present-day climatic change.
6. How does urbanization affect the climatic conditions of an area?
7. What is a heat island?
8. What factors influence temperature variations between urban and rural areas?
9. Why is it difficult to determine the effect of urbanization on precipitation?
10. How can land use modifications affect the amount of precipitation an area receives?
11. How can changes in the distribution of water affect the climate of a region?

# SELECTED REFERENCES

## WEATHER AND CLIMATE

ANTHES, RICHARD A., JOHN J. CAHIR, ALISTAIR B. FRASER, and HANS A. PANOFSKY. *The Atmosphere.* 3d ed. Columbus, OH: Charles E. Merrill, 1981.

BARRY, R. G. "The World Hydrological Cycle." In *Water, Earth and Man,* edited by R. J. Chorley. London: Methuen, 1969.

———, and R. J. CHORLEY. *Atmosphere, Weather and Climate.* 3d ed. London, England: Methuen, 1976.

BATTAN, LOUIS J. *Fundamentals of Meteorology.* Englewood Cliffs, NJ: Prentice-Hall, 1979.

BAUMGARTNER, ALBERT, and EBERHARD REICHEL. *The World Water Balance, Mean Annual Global Continental and Maritime Precipitation, Evaporation and Runoff.* Amsterdam, Netherlands: Elsevier, 1975.

BREUER, GEORG. *Weather Modification: Prospects and Problems.* New York: Cambridge University Press, 1979.

BUCKLEY, SHAWN. *Sun Up to Sun Down.* New York: McGraw-Hill, 1979.

CAMPBELL, IAN M. *Energy and the Atmosphere.* New York: John Wiley, 1977.

CANBY, THOMAS Y. "El Niño's Ill Wind." *National Geographic Magazine* 165 (February 1984): 144–84.

COLE, FRANKLYN W. *Introduction to Meteorology.* 3d ed. New York: John Wiley, 1980.

CRITCHFIELD, HOWARD J. *General Climatology.* 4th ed. Englewood Cliffs, NJ: Prentice-Hall, 1983.

D'ITRI, FRANK M., ed. *Acid Precipitation: Effects on Ecological Systems.* Ann Arbor, MI: Ann Arbor Science, 1982.

DIX, HERBERT M. *Environmental Pollution: Atmosphere, Land, Water and Noise.* New York: John Wiley, 1981.

DOBBINS, R. A. *Atmospheric Motion and Air Pollution.* New York: John Wiley, 1979.

EAGLEMAN, JOE R. *Meteorology: The Atmosphere in Action.* New York: Van Nostrand Reinhold, 1980.

ELDRIDGE, FRANK R. *Wind Machines.* New York: Van Nostrand Reinhold, 1980.

FERRAR, TERRY A., ed. *The Urban Costs of Climate Modification.* New York: John Wiley, 1976.

GARBELL, MAURICE A. *Tropical and Equatorial Meteorology.* London: Pitman, 1947.

GASKELL, T. F., and MARTIN MORRIS. *World Climate: The Weather, the Environment and Man.* New York: Thames and Hudson, 1979.

GEDZELMAN, STANLEY DAVID. *The Science and Wonders of the Atmosphere.* New York: John Wiley, 1980.

GIESE, ARTHUR C. *Living with Our Sun's Ultraviolet Rays.* New York: Plenum Press, 1976.

GREELEY, RICHARD S. et al. *Solar Heating and Cooling of Buildings.* Ann Arbor, MI: Ann Arbor Science, 1981.

GREENLAND, DAVID, and HARM J. DeBLIJ. *The Earth in Profile: A Physical Geography.* San Francisco: Canfield Press, 1977.

GRIBBIN, JOHN, ed. *Climatic Change.* New York: Cambridge University Press, 1978.

GRIFFITHS, JOHN F., and DENNIS M. DRISCOLL. *Survey of Climatology.* Columbus, OH: Charles E. Merrill, 1982.

HARRELL, JOE J., JR. *Solar Heating and Cooling of Buildings.* New York: Van Nostrand Reinhold, 1981.

HAURWITZ, BERNARD, and JAMES M. AUSTIN. *Climatology.* New York: McGraw-Hill, 1944.

HESKETH, H. E. *Air Pollution Control.* Ann Arbor, MI: Ann Arbor Science, 1979.

HESS, W. N., ed. *Weather and Climate Modification.* New York: John Wiley, 1974.

HOBBS, J. E. *Applied Climatology.* Boulder, CO: Westview, 1980.

HUNT, V. DANIEL. *Windpower: A Handbook on Wind Energy Conversion Systems.* New York: Van Nostrand Reinhold, 1981.

INGLIS, D. R. *Wind Power and Other Energy Options.* Ann Arbor, MI: University of Michigan Press, 1978.

LIKENS, GENE E., RICHARD F. WRIGHT, JAMES N. GALLOWAY, and THOMAS J. BUTLER. "Acid Rain." *Scientific American* 241 (October 1979): 43–51.

LIST, ROBERT J., ed. *Smithsonian Meteorological Tables.* 6th ed. Washington, D. C.: Smithsonian Institution, 1971.

LÖF, G. O. G., J. A. DUFFIE, and C. O. SMITH. "World Distribution of Solar Radiation." *Engineering Experiment Station Report,* No. 21. Madison: The University of Wisconsin, 1966.

LUTGENS, FREDERICK K., and EDWARD J. TARBUCK. *The Atmosphere: An Introduction to Meteorology.* 2d ed. Englewood Cliffs, NJ: Prentice-Hall, 1982.

MASON, B. J. *Clouds, Rain and Rainmaking.* 2d ed. New York: Cambridge University Press, 1975.

MILLER, ALBERT, JACK C. THOMPSON, RICHARD E. PETERSON, and DONALD R. HARAGAN. *Elements of Meteorology.* 4th ed. Columbus, OH: Charles E. Merrill, 1983.

MILLER, DAVID H. *Water at the Surface of the Earth* (International Geophysics Series, No. 21). New York: Academic Press, 1977.

MILLER, E. WILLARD, and GEORGE LANGDON. *Exploring Earth Environments: A World Geography.* New York: Thomas Y. Crowell, 1964.

MONEY, D. C. *Climate, Soils and Vegetation.* 3d ed. Sough, UK: University Tutorial Press, 1978.

MONTEITH, J. L., ed. *Vegetation and the Atmosphere.* Vol. 1, *Principles,* 1975. Vol. 2, *Case Studies,* 1976. New York: Academic Press.

MULLER, R. A., and T. M. OBERLANDER. *Physical Geography Today.* New York: Random House, 1978.

NAMIAS, JEROME. "The Jet Stream." *Scientific American* 187 (October 1952): 26–31.

NATIONAL ACADEMY OF SCIENCES. *Severe Storms: Prediction, Detection and Warning.* Washington, D. C.: National Academy of Sciences, 1977.

NAVARRA, JOHN GARBIEL. *Atmosphere, Weather and Climate: An Introduction to Meteorology.* Philadelphia, PA: W. B. Saunders, 1979.

OLIVER, JOHN E. *Physical Geography Principles and Applications.* Belmont, CA: Duxbury Press, 1979.

PALMEN, E. "The Role of Atmospheric Disturbances in the General Circulation." *Quarterly Journal of the Royal Meteorological Society* 77 (July 1951): 337–54.

PERRY, A. H., and J. M. WALKER. *The Ocean-Atmosphere System.* London, England: Longman Group, 1977.

PETTERSSEN, S. *Introduction to Meteorology.* New York: McGraw-Hill, 1969.

PUTNAM, PALMER C. *Putnam's Power from the Wind.* 2d ed. New York: Van Nostrand Reinhold, 1981.

RAPP, DONALD. *Solar Energy.* Englewood Cliffs, NJ: Prentice-Hall, 1981.

RIEHL, HERBERT. *Introduction to the Atmosphere.* 3d ed. New York: McGraw-Hill, 1978.

RYAN, PETER. *Solar System.* New York: Viking Press, 1979.

SCHOTT, GERHARD. *Geographie des Atlantischen Ozeans.* Hamburg: C. Boysen, 1926.

———. *Geographie des Indischen und Stillen Ozeans.* Hamburg: C. Boysen, 1935.

SCRIPPS INSTITUTE OF OCEANOGRAPHY. *World Atlas of Sea Surface Temperatures.* H. O. No. 225. Washington, D.C.: Hydrographic Office, U.S. Navy, 1944.

SELLERS, W. D. *Physical Climatology.* Chicago: University of Chicago Press, 1965.

THORNTHWAITE, C. W. "An Approach Toward a Rational Classification of Climate." *Geographical Review* 38 (1948), 55–94.

THORNTHWAITE, C. W., and JOHN R. MATHER. "Instructions and Tables for Computing Potential Evapotranspiration and the Water Balance." *Publications in Climatology* 10 (1957), 185–311.

———. "The Water Balance." *Publications in Climatology* 8 (1955): 1–86.

TREWARTHA , GLENN T. *The Earth's Problem Climates.* 2d ed. Madison, WI: University of Wisconsin Press, 1981.

———, and LYLE H. HORN. *An Introduction to Climate.* 5th ed. New York: McGraw-Hill, 1980.

VALLEY, SHEA L., ed. *Handbook of Geophysics and Space Environment.* Cambridge, MA: Air Force Cambridge Research Laboratories, U.S. Air Force, 1965.

VISHER, STEPHEN S. *Climatic Atlas of the United States.* Cambridge, MA: Harvard University Press, 1954.

WASHBURN, MARK. *In the Light of the Sun: From Sunspots to Solar Energy.* New York: Harcourt Brace Jovanovich, 1981.

WOLFF, BEN, and H. K. MEYER. *Wind Energy.* Philadelphia, PA: Franklin Institute Press, 1978.

YOKELL, MICHAEL D. *Environmental Benefits and Costs of Solar Energy.* Lexington, MA: Lexington Books, 1980.

## CLIMATIC CHANGE

ANTHES, RICHARD A., JOHN J. CAHIR, ALISTAIR B. FRASER, and HANS A. PANOFSKY. *The Atmosphere.* 3d ed. Columbus, OH: Charles E. Merrill, 1981.

BACH, WILFRID, JURGEN PANKRATH, and WILLIAM KELLOGG, eds. *Man's Impact on Climate.* New York: Elsevier, 1979.

BROECKER, W. S. "Climate Change: Are We on the Brink of a Warning?" *Science* 189 (1976): 460–63.

BROOKS, C. E. P. *Climate Through the Ages.* 2nd ed. New York: Dover, 1970.

BRYSON, R. A., and T. J. MURRAY. *The Climates of Hunger.* Madison: University of Wisconsin Press, 1977.

———. "A Perspective on Climatic Change." *Science* 184 (1974): 753–60.

BUDYKO, M. I. "The Effect of Solar Radiation Variations on the Climate of the Earth." *Tellus* 21, no. 5 (1967): 611–19.

DETWYLER, T. R., and W. G. MARCUS, eds. *Urbanization and Environment.* Belmont, CA: Wadsworth, 1972.

EDDY, JOHN A. "The Maunder Minimum." *Science* 192, no. 4245 (June 1976): 1189–1202.

FRAKES, L. A. *Climates Throughout Geologic Time.* New York: Elsevier Scientific, 1979.

GATES, D. M. *Man and His Environment: Climate.* New York: Harper & Row, 1972.

GRIBBIN, J., ed. *Climatic Change.* New York: Cambridge University Press, 1978.

HAYS, JAMES D. *Our Changing Climate.* New York: Atheneum, 1977.

______. "The Ice Age Cometh." *Saturday Review of the Sciences* 1 (1973): 29–32.

KELLOGG, W. W. "Climate Change and the Influence of Man's Activities on the Global Environment." In *The Changing Global Environment,* edited by S. F. Singer and D. Reidel. Holland: Dordrecht, 1975.

LANDSBERG, H. E. "Man-Made Climatic Changes." *Science* 170 (December 18, 1970): 1265–74.

LEROY LADURIE, E. *Times of Feast, Times of Famine.* London: George Allen and Unwin, 1971.

MANABE, S., and R. T. WETHERALD. "The Effects of Doubling the $CO_2$ Concentration on the Climate of a General Circulation Model." *Journal of Atmospheric Science* 32 (1975): 3–15.

MARSH, WILLIAM M., and JEFF DOZIER. *Landscape: An Introduction to Physical Geography.* Reading, MA: Addison-Wesley, 1981.

MATHEWS, W. H. et al., eds. *Man's Impact on Climate.* Cambridge: MIT Press, 1971.

MITCHELL, J. R., JR. "The National Breakdown of the Present Interglacial and Its Possible Intervention by Human Activities." *Quaternary Research* 2, no. 3 (November 1972): 436–45.

NEWMAN, J. E. "Climate Change, Solar Cycles, and Seasonal Weather Trends." *Agricultural Engineering* 60 (January 1979): 3–16.

WILCOX, H. H. *Hothouse Earth.* New York: Praeger, 1975.

WOOLLUM, CLARENCE A. "Notes from Study of the Microclimatology of the Washington, D. C. Area for Winter and Spring Seasons." *Weatherwise* 17, no. 6 (1964): 263–71.

# II
# SOILS AND NATURAL VEGETATION

# 10
# WORLD SOIL SYSTEMS

## KEY WORDS

aeration
azonal soil
caliche
climax soil
eluviation
ferrallitization
ferricrete
gleization
horizon
illuviation
intrazonal soil
parent material
pedalfers
pedocals
pedogenic processes
peds
soil profile
solifluction
solum
subsoil
zonal soil

Soil forms the basis for the production of food that is necessary for human survival. The importance of soil has long been recognized by soil scientists. As early as 1891, N. S. Shaler of the U.S. Geological Survey wrote, "This slight and superficial and inconstant covering of the earth should receive a measure of care which is rarely devoted to it." Fifty years ago G. N. Coffey of the U.S. Department of Agriculture stated, "It is the one great formation in which the organic and inorganic kingdoms meet and derives its distinctive character from this union."

While soil is found on nearly all land areas, the soil mantle is usually less than one to six feet in thickness. The upper boundary of the soil is usually distinct, but the lower boundary with the bedrock is often obscure. Although soil forms only a veneer on the surface of the earth, if it is to continue its productivity forever, we must gain an understanding of its nature, its types, and their distribution in the world.

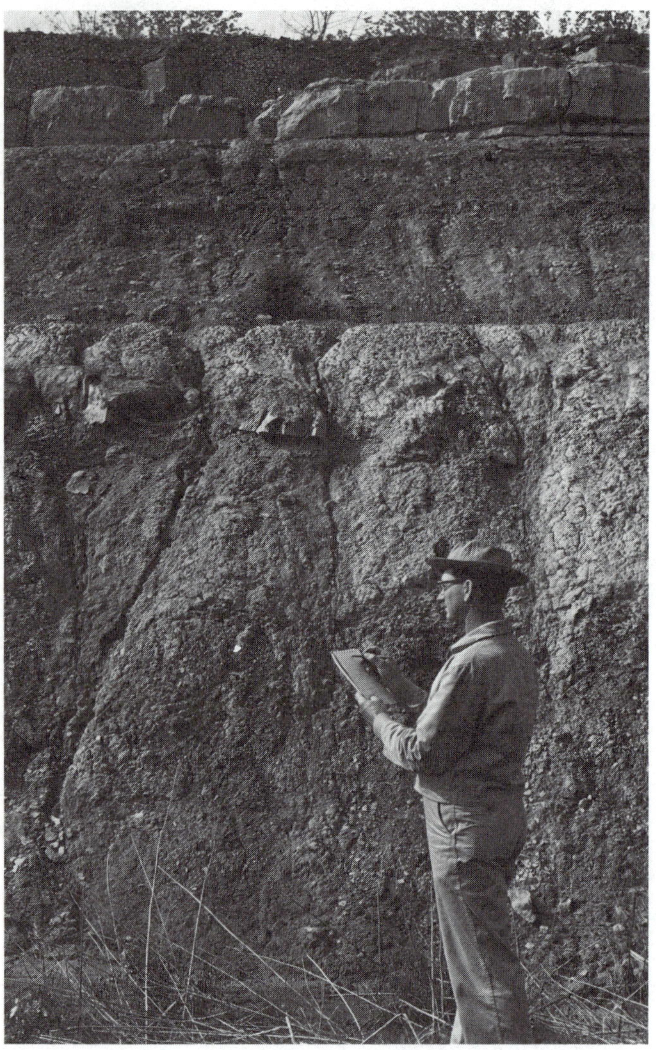

**PHOTO 39**
Soil scientist studying geologic material in relation to soil formation. A deep road cut shows the weathering of interbedded limestone and shale. (Courtesy: U.S. Department of Agriculture, Soil Conservation Service)

## FACTORS OF SOIL FORMATION

The five major environmental factors in soil formation are climate (*c*), vegetation (*v*), organisms (*o*), relief (*r*), and parent material (*p*). Soil (*s*) is the dependent variable relying upon the interaction of five partially independent variables within specified time (*t*) limits. The development of soil at a place can be expressed as

$$s = f(c,v,o,p,r)t^0$$

### PARENT MATERIAL

The original material from which soil is derived may be local bedrock or transported material. Parent material is frequently considered a passive factor in soil formation. The processes of weathering act upon the parent material to form fine *detritus,* which in turn is altered as organic material is incorporated. The change from parent material to true soil requires a considerable length of time, varying from hundreds to thousands of years (Photo 39).

A number of processes are required in the development of a soil. The first process, weathering, causes the disintegration and decomposition of the rock material. The two major types of weathering in soil development are physical weathering, which produces smaller particles from the parent material, and chemical weathering, which changes the chemical composition of the parent material.

Physical and chemical weathering occur simultaneously. The rate is controlled by such factors as temperature and moisture, oxidation state, type of parent material, biological influences, and length of time. In arid regions physical weathering dominates, while in wet regions chemical weathering prevails.

The origin of parent material may be classified into two major groups: residual parent material and transported material moved from one location to another. Soils developing from residual parent material are usually found in stable landscapes when weathering has extended over thousands of years. The rate of weathering, even in the tropics, on residual parent material is usually slow. Only when the parent material is *friable,* or crumbly, is the rate of weathering increased appreciably.

Transported parent material differs in both origin and form from residual materials. Transported material usually occurs in an unconsolidated state, contrasting with consolidated rock. The material may be deposited by running water, or may occur as marine or lacustrine (lake) sediments, glacial deposits, or sediments deposited by wind. Because transported parent materials are unconsolidated, soil development normally occurs at a more rapid rate than for residual parent materials.

## CLIMATE

In early studies of soil formation, climate was considered the dominant soil-forming factor. While climate is still recognized as important, other factors are now also known to be significant. While climate may not dominate, it still remains the most important single factor. All aspects of climate play a role in the *pedogenic*, or soil-forming, processes. Climate influences soil formation in at least three major ways: It is involved in the weathering of parent material, in internal soil processes, and in the transport of parent and weathered materials, causing the erosion of soil bodies (Figure 10.1).

Within the soil body, climate has a marked influence on pedogenic processes. Climate provides water to the soil for the physical removal of soil particles, and for removal of the dissolved chemical compounds. The leaching effectiveness of the local climate is measured by the soluble material removed over a period of time.

Of the climatic factors, the amount, intensity, and distribution of precipitation throughout the year are most critical. These factors directly affect the intensity of erosion. Rainfall is most destructive to soil if it combines volume and velocity to move aggregate soil particles.

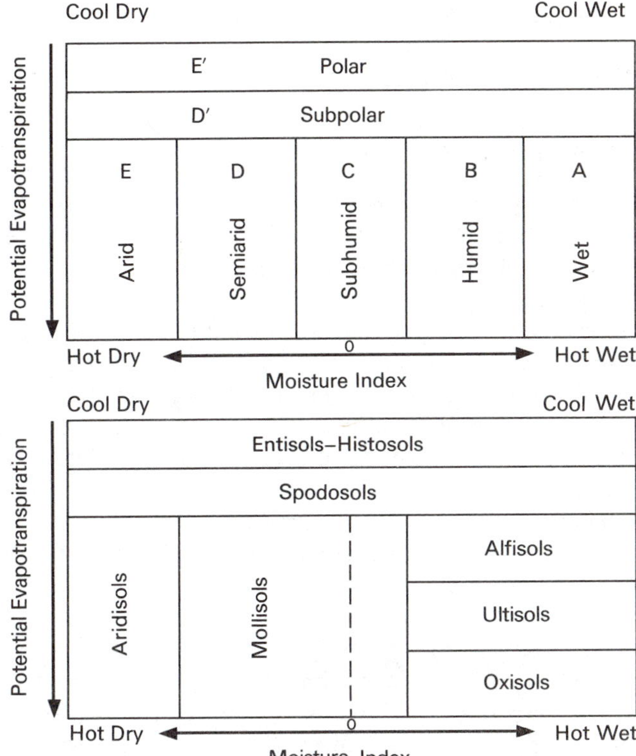


**FIGURE 10.1**
Relationship between soil formation and climate. The top diagram shows the principal climatic types according to the Thornthwaite classification, and the bottom diagram shows the relationship of the soil types to each major climatic type. Note on each diagram that potential evapotranspiration increases as temperature increases, and that the moisture index increases from dry to wet. The diagram reveals that some soils form under a particular climatic type. For example, Aridisols form in an arid environment, while the leached Oxisols form under a hot, wet environment. (After U.S. Department of Agriculture, 1941)

## RELIEF

The topography of an area influences soil formation most strongly by controlling surface runoff and erosion, determining the quantity of precipitation retained in the soil, and by directing the movement of soluble materials from one area to another. In addition, the effectiveness of solar radiation depends upon the direction and degree of slope of the land. By altering soil temperature and water availability, topography influences the effectiveness of weathering.

The availability of water in the soil is greatly influenced by the relief of an area. Low-lying soils in relatively flat areas usually retain a larger proportion of water than soils on adjacent slope areas. Even within a region receiving a uniform amount of water, soil properties may be different due to variations in slope conditions. Some soils have been designated as *upland* or *lowland* to reflect their topographic positions. Lowland soils receive the *alluvium* deposited by running water and are therefore of more recent origin. The classification as upland or lowland often indicates a difference in internal soil drainage. If the parent material is uniform on a slope, a gradual increase in water may develop downslope, with a possibility of water-logged soil at the lower level. This process rarely occurs, but is known as a *hydrologic sequence* in soil moisture.

A mass movement by soil particles may occur in some soils that are at or near the saturation level. This is known as *solifluction*. It most commonly occurs in cold regions such as high latitudes and altitudes. Solifluction is most likely to occur on slopes over a saturated subsoil or on a thawing permafrost surface.

### VEGETATION AND ORGANISMS

The climate of a region influences plant development, which in turn may determine the amount of organic material in the soil. In the tropical rainforest the amount of potential organic matter for the soils is enormous because of the luxuriant vegetational growth, but the vegetation is largely on the surface of the soil. The decaying action of bacteria in the hot, humid climate destroys most of the organic material before it can become part of the soil. Little organic matter thus accumulates in tropical soils. In the *taiga,* or coniferous forest, of the subarctic regions of Canada and the Soviet Union, the cool, moist climate also encourages the formation of organic materials. In contrast to the tropics, however, the decaying action of bacteria is retarded and the raw humus collects as a layer on the surface of the soil.

Unlike forest regions, the grassland areas of the world have major accumulations of organic matter in the soil. This fact results from differences in the growth of the plants and in how the plant residue becomes incorporated into the soil. The roots of grasses are short-lived, and each year the decomposition of the dead roots adds to the organic matter in the soil. The greatest concentration of organic matter is near the surface where the grass roots predominate. A forest ecosystem has a quantity of organic matter similar to that of a grassland. In the forest area, however, the organic matter exists outside the soil, while in a grassland area the organic matter exists predominantly in the soil. The difference in the amount of organic matter in the soil is one of the major reasons that grassland soils are richer than forest soils.

Organic matter in soils is soluble and is continuously being lost. Thus the maintenance of a high organic level in a soil is difficult and expensive. It is estimated that a soil's organic matter decomposes at the rate of about one to four percent annually. Assuming a two percent rate of loss, a grassland soil with 40,000 pounds of organic matter per acre will lose 800 pounds of organic matter per year. For an equilibrium to be maintained, 800 pounds of humus must be added to the soil each year. Part of this additional humus can come from plant life existing in the soil; farmers may also add humus to the soil.

The soil's texture is an important factor in the maintenance of organic matter. The greater the combined supply of water and nutrients, the greater the production and accumulation of organic matter in soils. The finer-textured soils absorb the decomposing organic matter more effectively than coarse soils. Further, organic molecules absorbed on clays are partially protected from decomposition by microorganisms, adding to the organic content of the soils.

### TIME RELATIONSHIPS

Time plays a major role in the soil-forming process. The effect of time is judged by the extent to which the parent material has been changed into a soil. This process of change can be divided into several stages. The initial stage is characterized by accumulations of organic matter in the upper layer of soil and by limited removal of the soluble materials by the weathering processes. At this stage only the upper layer and the bedrock are developed, and the soil properties are those related directly to the parent material. The mature stage occurs when layers develop above the bedrock. When the layers become highly differentiated, the old age stage has been achieved. This soil is frequently known as a *climax soil.*

The length of time required to produce a climax soil depends largely upon the type of parent material and the developmental processes. At the extremes, soil development on hard, siliceous rock may take thousands of years, while on unconsolidated material in a warm and humid region, soil development may occur in less than 100 years.

The soil-forming processes do not occur at the same rate. For example, ion exchange and the loss or accumulation of readily soluble materials can occur rapidly, providing measurable effects on parent materials in a few decades. In contrast, the accumulation of organic matter or changes due to mineral weathering occur very slowly. New humus may darken a soil within a few decades but it may require several hundred years to exert its full effect on soil development.

## SOIL HORIZONS

As soils evolve from parent rock materials to mature soils, distinct layers, known as *soil horizons,* develop (Photo 40). Every mature soil has soil horizons, suggesting that certain processes are common to the development of all soils. A well-developed soil has three distinct horizons. The horizons differ from one another in one or more properties, such as color, texture, structure, and porosity. They may vary in thickness from a

**PHOTO 40**
Soil profile. Profile of Alaska loam soil in Logan County, Colorado. This is a moderately deep, dark colored, well-drained soil with a loam A-horizon of less than 15 inches in thickness. The B-horizon is a calcareous, aeolian deposit, which is underlain by the C-horizon of calcareous sand and gravel. (Courtesy: U.S. Department of Agriculture, Soil Conservation Service)

fraction of an inch to many feet. Generally the horizons merge into one another so that they consist of one or more subdivisions (Figure 10.2).

The A-horizon, the uppermost layer of soil, is usually called the *surface soil.* This is the layer where organic material, such as plants, bacteria, fungi, and small animals, accumulates. These forms of life produce the humus materials of the soil when they die and partially decay. When the humus content in the soil is high, its color is dark brown to black; when the humus content is low, the soil is light-colored.

Leaching occurs to a greater extent in the A-horizon than at deeper horizons. Thus the A-horizon is known as one of *eluviation,* or downward transportation. As a result of leaching, the A-horizon has lost to the B-horizon some of its more soluble minerals such as clay, iron, and aluminum oxides, with the resulting concentrations of quartz and other resistant minerals.

The A-horizon may be further divided. For example, when a soil has developed under a forest cover, the A-horizon has two distinct subdivisions: a thin dark surface layer where humus has collected in large amounts, called the A1-horizon, and a much thicker, lighter colored layer beneath, the A2-horizon, which has less humus. The A1- and A2-horizons rarely are found in grassland and desert soils.

The B-horizon lies directly below the A-horizon and is frequently called the *subsoil.* Together, the A- and B-horizons make up the *solum.* The dominant feature of the B-horizon is the concentration of the oxides and silicate clays and humus materials leached out of the A-horizon. This is known as the zone of *illuviation,* or deposition. The iron oxides make the B-horizon appear redder than the A- or C-horizons. The B-horizon normally has more clay than the A-horizon because this substance is also removed from the overlying horizon. Portions of the clay may be moved downward unaltered by simple physical processes or by biologic agents. Other portions of the material can be resynthesized by chemical means from the soil solution to form secondary minerals. The B-horizon may also have several subdivisions. For example, the top of the B-horizon will have more organic material while the bottom will have larger fragments of parent material.

The C-horizon provides the parent material. It has been little affected by the pedogenic processes. The weathering process is at its initial stage of development in this mineral horizon. Soil is the result of the modification of the parent material so that distinct horizons occur.

## PROPERTIES OF SOIL

The ability of a soil to sustain plant life is to a large degree dependent upon its physical and chemical character. Soils are composed of solid, liquid, and gaseous components. The solid parts constitute the soil proper. The water and air components, which fill the interstices between the solid materials, continuously change, fre-

**FIGURE 10.2**
Contrasting soil profiles. The Mollisols have a thick, black to dark brown A-horizon while the Spodosols have a forest litter on the surface and a thin gray A-horizon, lacking in humus.

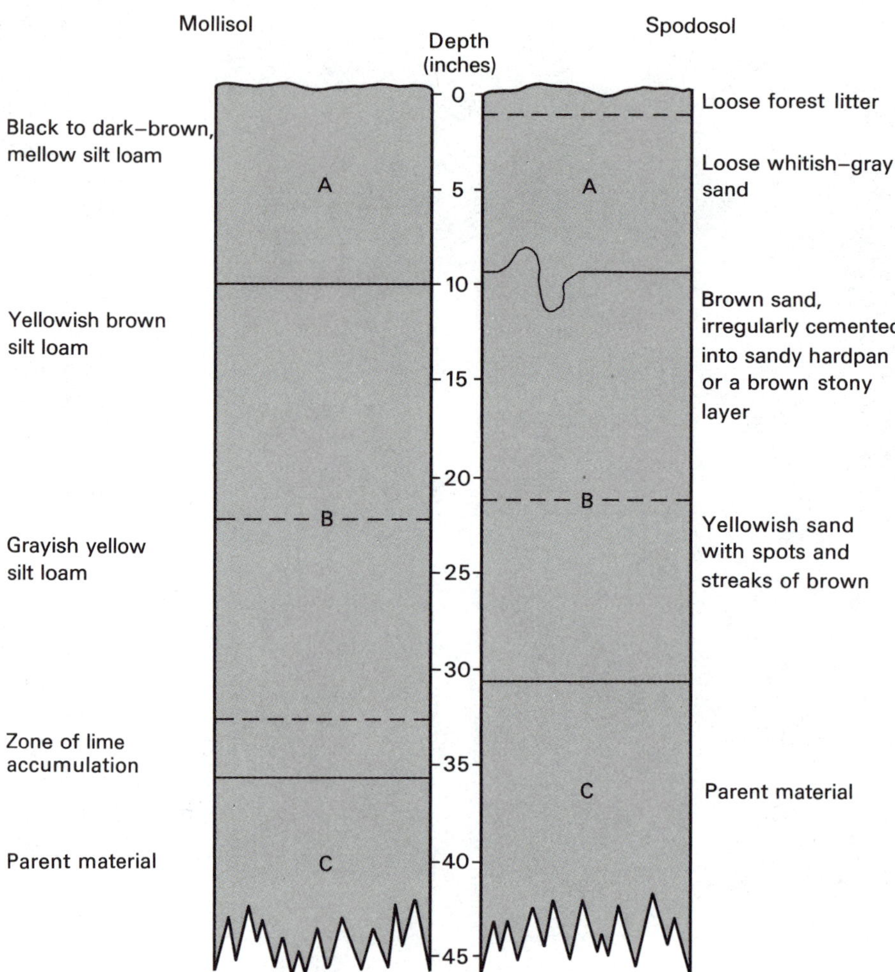


quently depending upon conditions independent of the soil, such as the amount and regime of precipitation. The organic matter varies greatly in amount but is rarely more than five percent of the total volume of the soil.

## STRUCTURE

Of the physical properties of soil, structure is most important. Structure refers to the arrangement of soil particles. The classification of soil structural form is based primarily on the shape of the particles, known as *peds.* These shapes may be spheroidal, platelike, blocklike, or prismlike (Figure 10.3). The spheroidal particles are arranged around a central point bounded by surfaces that may be rounded or irregular. Platelike refers to particles arranged along a plane that is usually horizontal. Blocklike particles are also arranged around a central point and have sharp angular faces. Prismlike peds are grouped around a vertical line in columns with or without rounded caps. Although shape is the main distinguishing characteristic of soil peds, they also differ in size. The spheroidal peds are usually the smallest, varying from 1 to 10 mm, while the platelike structures usually have the largest variation in size and are up to 50 mm long.

There are two major requirements for the development of soil structure. The cohesiveness of a soil is the factor that holds the particles together. For example, a soil rich in clays is much more cohesive than a sandy soil. The second requirement is a mechanism that organizes the particles into an aggregate form.

The soil structure is a response to many factors. These include the chemical nature of the parent material, the amount of weathering, the organic content of the soil, and the moisture and temperature contrasts. Soil structure is also influenced by the burrowing and mixing activities of worms, insects, and other soil animals. Human cultivation of the soil also affects its structure. Soil structure changes greatly with soil depth.

**FIGURE 10.3**
Classification of soil structure. Soil peds provide a basis for classification. There are four major types of peds with subdivisions under each.

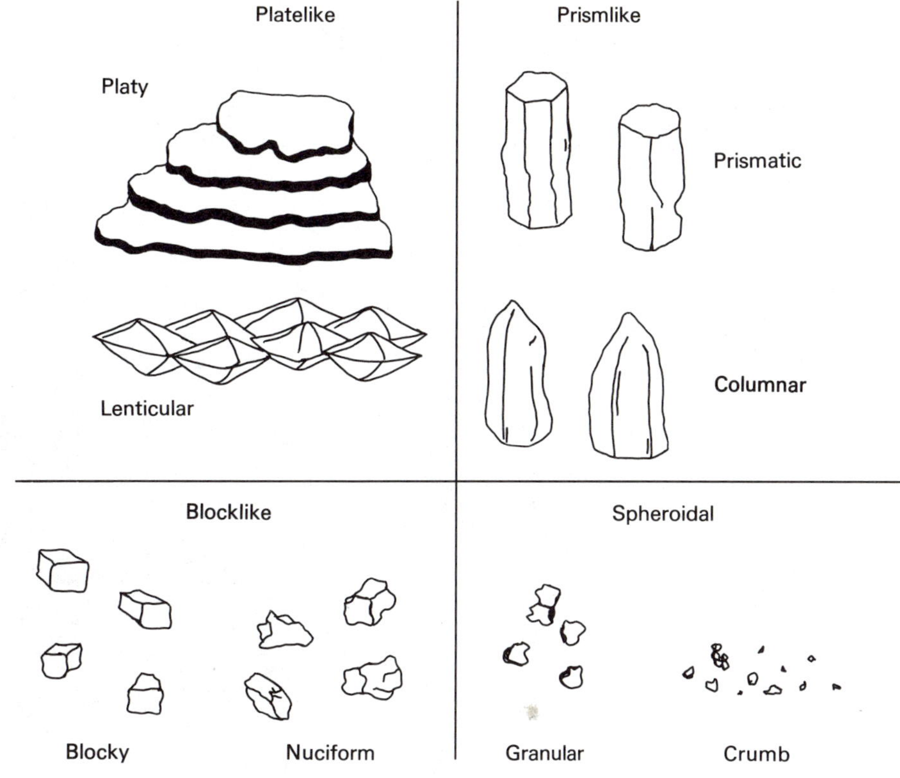


## TEXTURE

Texture refers to the size, shape, arrangement, and distribution of the particles of sand, silt, and clay in the soil. The texture of a soil can be determined in the laboratory by mechanical analysis of the particle sizes. The contents of the sand, silt, and clay are expressed as a percent of the total weight of dry soil. If, for example, a soil sample contains 10 grams of sand, 10 grams of silt, and 20 grams of clay, the percentage of each would be 25 percent sand, 25 percent silt, and 50 percent clay. A soil that has large amounts of all three is called *loam* (Figure 10.4).

It is common practice to group soils into three broadly defined categories—coarse, medium, and fine texture. These are further subdivided depending upon the content of the three main types:

| Coarse Texture | Medium Texture | Fine Texture |
|---|---|---|
| Sandy | Loam | Clay loam |
| Loamy sand | Silt loam | Clay silt |
| Sandy loam | Silt | Clay |

The texture of a soil is closely related to the parent material. If the parent material has a high proportion of quartz, then the soil will have a sandy texture. If there is a high proportion of feldspar, then clay will predominate in the soil. Because the mineral particles are highly permanent, it will take decades to alter the textural composition of a soil.

The texture of a soil is particularly important in determining its water content (Figure 10.5). As texture becomes finer, the size of individual pore spaces decreases but the total pore space increases. This fact can be easily demonstrated when a four-inch cube with a surface area of 96 square inches is divided into one-inch cubes, which will have a total surface of 384 square inches. Thus a given volume of fine clay has 10 times more surface area than the same volume of silt, and 50 times more than that of fine sand. Most soils have a porosity of 35 to 50 percent of total volume. Yet more important than total porosity are the size and distribution of pores. In clay soils the pores are small and tend to hold water by capillary action. In contrast, sandy soils have larger pores, thus promoting the passage of water through them. Porosity is increased in fine-textured soils by proper tillage and addition of organic mat-

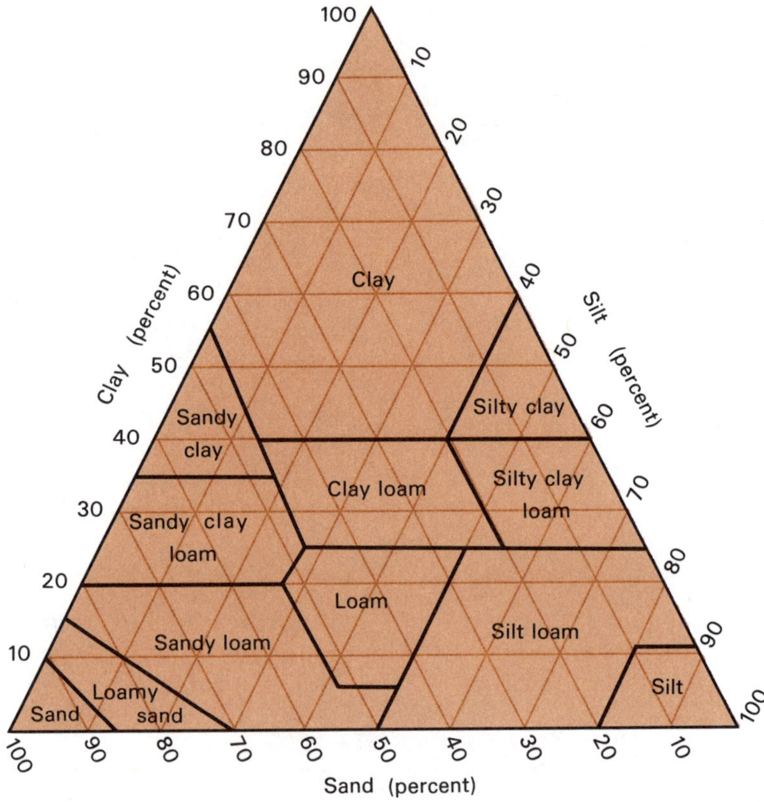


**FIGURE 10.4**
Textural characteristics of soils. The texture of a soil is determined by the proportions of clay, silt, and sand in the inorganic part of the soil. For example, if a soil sample has 40 percent clay, 50 percent sand, and 10 percent silt, it is classified as a sandy clay. (After Bridges, 1978)

ters. Both of these techniques of working the soil favor the development of a granular structure.

Soil pores are occuped by air as well as water. The proportion of air to water decreases rapidly as the particles become smaller. Any increase in soil water decreases the amount of soil air. Thus, poorly drained soils are deficient in air. If air is deficient in a soil, the plants growing there tend to become diseased and give off large amounts of carbon dioxide, which increases further the incapacity of the soil to foster plant life, so that soil ventilation becomes necessary. *Aeration,* the process by which stagnant air is replaced by fresh air, occurs naturally within soil as a result of such processes as changes in temperature and movement of soil water. Tillage may serve either to decrease or to promote aeration. Sandy soils usually possess too much air and need to be compacted; clay soils are usually too dense and need to be loosened to facilitate aeration.

Frequently a relationship exists between soil texture and land use. The yields of many crops are related to texture. For example, corn has its highest yields on loam soils while the yield of potatoes is highest on sandy soils. Texture is frequently important to engineering projects. A clay soil changes greatly in volume from its wet to its dry state. As a result, basement walls may cave in, pipelines may break, and roads may buckle when they are placed in clay soils.

## COLOR

The color of a soil may reveal a number of important characteristics. It is a guide to the extent of mineral weathering and to the amount and decomposition of organic matter. The principal soil colors are gray, red, yellow, brown, and black. Soil colors are now defined objectively by the Munsell Soil Color Chart.

The changes in color of a soil are primarily a response to weathering. The distinct red, yellow, and brown colors are normally due to iron oxides. When the soil colors are a bright red or yellow, evidence of extreme weathering exists. This is a typical condition in a subtropical or tropical soil. When the soil is a dark brown or black, a large amount of partially decomposed organic material is normally present. These soils develop under a number of conditions such as those occurring in semiarid grasslands and bog areas. Unweathered soils with little organic material are usually gray.

The extent to which organic material colors soils depends upon the chemical nature of the material, its texture, and the quantity present. A grassland area where

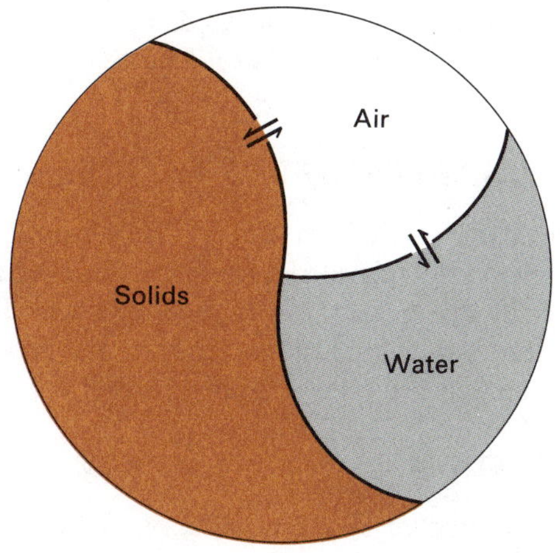


**FIGURE 10.5**
Volume fractions occupied by solids, water, and air are variable and affect soil properties. If, for example, the water content becomes too great, the soil will become waterlogged; if water content decreases too much, the soil becomes compact and plant nutrients will not flow through it. (After U.S. Department of Agriculture, 1941)

the organic material is incorporated into the soil usually has the darkest soil. Under a forest covering the same amount of organic material may be present, but it is located largely on top of the soil, which is much lighter. Thus the important factor is the amount of decomposed humus directly in the soil.

## TEMPERATURE

The temperature of the soil helps determine the rate of chemical weathering (Figure 10.6). The temperature of the soil depends upon the energy balance, but its color also affects the amount of solar radiation that is absorbed. A dark soil can absorb as much as 80 percent of the incoming radiation, while a light-colored soil may not absorb more than 30 percent.

Other factors also affect the temperature condition of a soil, and the water content of the soil is an important one. The heat required to raise the temperature of a gram of mineral particles by 1°C is only about one-fifth as much as is required to warm a gram of water the same amount. The specific heat of dry soil is 0.2. Thus soil with a high water content will heat much more slowly than drier soil. Differences in texture, structure, and organic matter will determine the moisture capacity of a soil, accordingly influencing its ability to absorb and transmit heat.

As air temperature increases, heat generally moves downward in a soil, but as air temperature decreases, heat from the lower soil layers moves upward, heating the surface layer. Soil temperatures normally lag considerably behind atmospheric temperatures. Differences occur in soil temperatures for areas in the same latitudinal location as a result of variations in color, moisture content, direction of exposure, and vegetational covering.

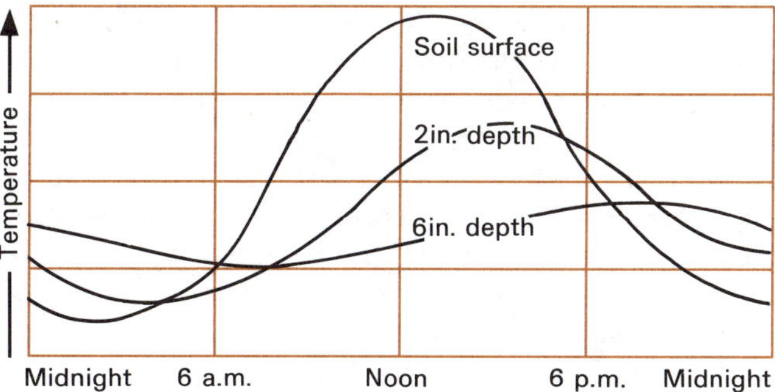


**FIGURE 10.6**
Soil temperature fluctuates widely during a 24-hour period. The variations are greatest on the surface but decrease rapidly within a few inches of the surface. (After U.S. Department of Agriculture, 1941)

Soil temperatures can be altered to a degree by human activities. Dark-colored mulches spread on a soil will increase the absorption of radiation, reduce heat loss, and reduce the evaporation of water from the soil. Soil temperatures can affect crop yields. For example, a higher soil temperature will increase yields in areas of cool summers. Seeds will germinate more quickly in warm soils than in cold soils.

## CHEMISTRY

The chemical characteristics of a soil are particularly important in determining its productivity. As chemical particles dissolve in soil moisture they ionize; that is, they separate into positively and negatively charged ions. The positively charged ions are called *cations,* and the negative ions are known as *anions.*

In a soil containing both clay particles and humus materials, the two combine to form a clay-humus complex. These particles are so small (less than 1 micron in size) that they remain in suspension, in a *colloidal* state, in the soil. The clay-humus particles are negatively charged and attract cations by electrical force. These cations, consisting mostly of calcium (Ca), potassium (K), magnesium (Mg), and sodium (Na), provide food nutrients to plants. If the clay-humus particles were not bound to the nutrients by electrical forces, the food nutrients would soon be leached from the soil, and the soil's fertility would decline.

Not all soils have clay-humus particles to provide the basis for a chemical combination. For example, desert soils contain little or no humus and usually less clay than soils in humid regions. One of the major reasons for the low productivity of desert soils is that soluble plant nutrients are easily leached from them. Irrigating these soils therefore creates a problem.

The acidity of a soil is another important indicator of its productivity. Acidity is measured in terms of the concentration of hydrogen ions, known as the pH of the soil (Figure 10.7). Acidity is then determined by the number of H-ions present. There are many sources of H-ions in nature: rainwater, snow, carbonic acid, mineral acids in the soil, plant roots, and organic and human acids. On the pH scale, 1 indicates a pure acid condition and 14 an alkaline condition. Pure water has a pH value of 7 and contains $10^{-7}$ grams of hydrogen ions per 1,000 cubic centimeters. The lower the pH, the more acidic the soil and the lower its content of plant foods. Soils with a pH value greater than 7 are considered to be basic or alkaline; those less than 7 are acidic. Soil values can extend from pH 3 to 10. On a global scale, soils with a pH less than 6 are common in cool temperature regions. In hot, arid land, many soils have a pH greater than 8 and few, if any, have a pH less than 6. The best agricultural soils have a pH between 5 and 6. The pH of a soil can be altered. For example, lime can be added to a soil to make it less acidic.

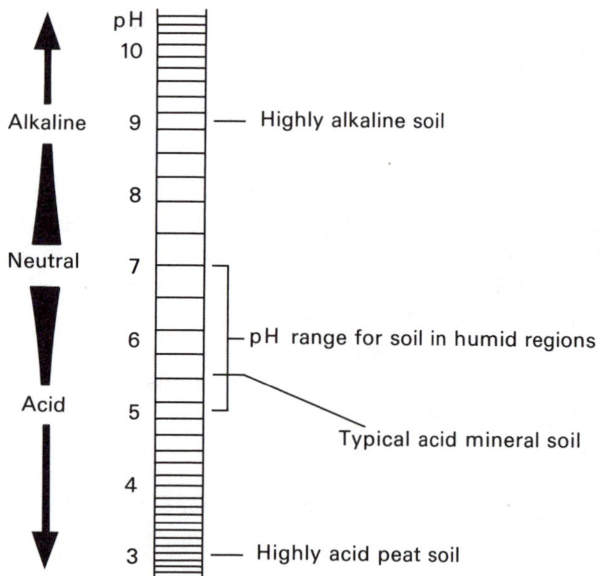


**FIGURE 10.7**
The pH value of a soil. A low pH indicates an acidic soil that may have lost most of its plant nutrients, while a high pH indicates a strong alkaline condition. (After Lyon and Buckman, 1943. © 1943 by MacMillan Publishing Co.)

## PRINCIPAL PEDOGENIC REGIMES

The soils of the earth form under a number of regimes that are related directly to climate. Moisture and temperature conditions in turn affect the vegetational cover. Each of the principal pedogenic systems produces a highly distinctive soil type (Figures 10.8 and 10.9).

### PODZOLIZATION

Podzolization occurs in the cool, moist climates of the world and is best developed under a coniferous forest vegetation. This process is basically the removal of clays and the eluviation of iron and even humus materials by highly acidic soil solutions. The pH content of the soil solution may be as low as 3.5. In the podzolization process of leaching the soils, a white to grayish layer, rich in insoluble silica compounds, forms in the A-horizon. Much of the leached material moves downward into the B-horizon. This produces a heavy-textured B-horizon

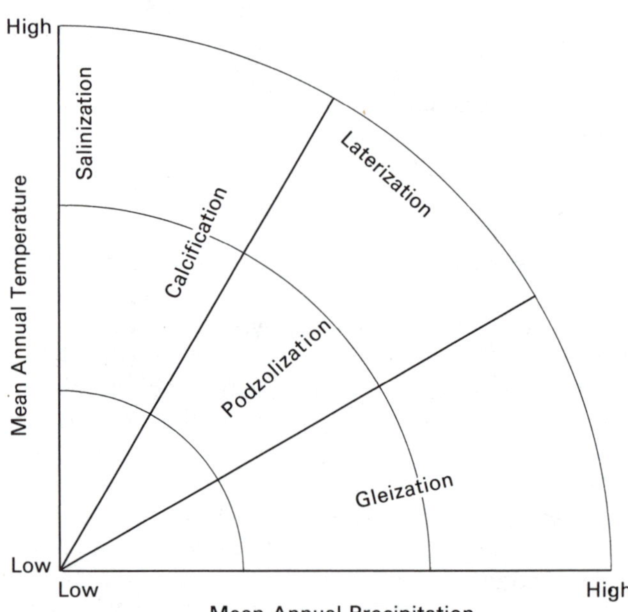


**FIGURE 10.8**
Relationship between soil-forming processes and climate. Salinization, for example, occurs when precipitation is low and temperatures high, while gleization occurs at low temperatures and high precipitation. (After Figure 19–3 [p. 387] in *Physical Geography* by James S. Gardner. Copyright © 1977 by Harper & Row, Publishers, Inc. Reprinted by permission of the publisher.)

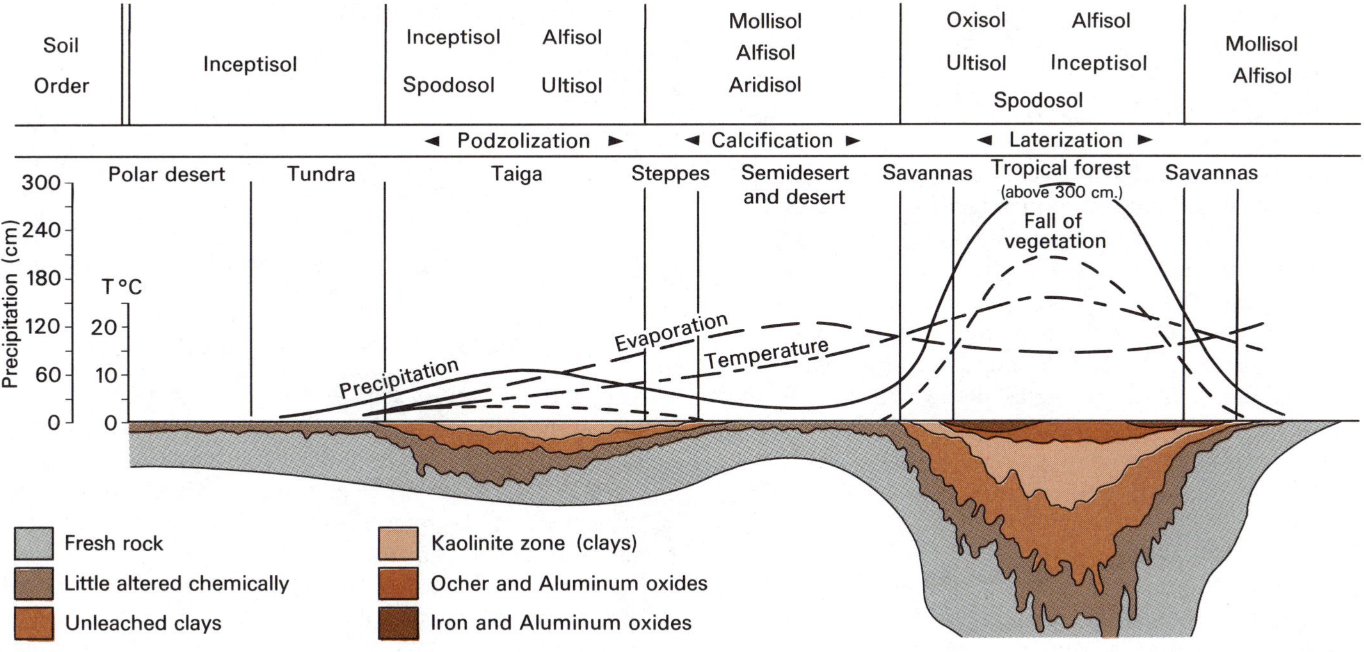


**FIGURE 10.9**
Pedogenic processes from the tropics to the polar regions. This diagram summarizes the influence of precipitation, temperature, evaporation, and vegetation on the weathering of rock and ultimate soil formation. (After Strakhov, 1967, and Birkeland, 1974)

characterized by a fairly high content of organic and inorganic colloids, well-developed structural aggregates, and colors that are bright yellow to red.

## FERRALLITIZATION (LATERIZATION)

Ferrallitization is a soil-forming process producing a red or gray soil that is found in the seasonally or permanently wet regions of the tropics under a forest covering. It involves leaching under mildly acid (pH 5 to 6) to mildly alkaline (pH 8 to 9) conditions. If the leaching process is carried to completion, the soil, known as Oxisol (laterite), may be composed of only iron and aluminum oxides. The organic materials are also largely leached from the soil, a process that is greatly facilitated by the warm, moist climate. If the process of ferrallitization is carried to completion, it decomposes the clays and removes virtually all the postively charged ions, known as cations, in solution, leaving only the quartz sand and the least soluble oxides. Ferrallitization combined with seasonal rainfall causes the water table to fluctuate. The iron and aluminum oxides become concentrated in the zone of water table fluctuation. When exposed to the air, this concentrate hardens to a crust known as *ferricrete* or *laterite.* These crusts can have a thickness of 5 to 6 meters and are common soil features of the tropical savannas.

Numerous contrasts may be observed between soils developed under podzolization and those developed under ferrallitization. The soil horizons developed under ferrallitization are less distinct because no well-developed zone of accumulation exists in either the A- or B-horizons of the Oxisols. In the podzolization process, the highly acidic conditions of the topsoil are partially neutralized by the bases in the B-horizon. As a result, deposition occurs in the B-horizon, making it distinctly different from the A-horizon. Under ferrallitization, the soluble materials removed from the A-horizon are not deposited in the B-horizon, but are completely removed from the soil by the groundwater action.

## CALCIFICATION

The process of calcification occurs in subhumid and arid climates where a grass covering prevails. It is characterized by the leaching of the bases, calcium and magnesium carbonates, from the A-horizon. These alkaline materials are deposited in the B-horizon, where they form the *calcic horizon.* The degree to which horizons develop depends largely on the organic materials available. In the grassland areas a dark organic horizon forms above the B-horizon. In the semidesert areas an organic horizon rarely exists, but the B-horizon is strong textured and usually has veins of carbonates. The precipitation of calcium carbonates results not only from the evaporation of downward-moving water, but also from the evaporation of water brought upward by capillary action. The depth of the calcic horizon depends on the depth to which soil moisture evaporates before the carbonates precipitate. If the deposition process goes to completion, a hard lime crust, known as *caliche,* may develop. The calcium-accumulating soils are collectively known as *pedocals.*

### SALINIZATION

Saline, or halomorphic, soils occur in arid and semiarid regions that do not have enough water to leach the soluble salts from the surface horizons. The salts are brought to the surface by groundwater and are deposited by evaporation and transpiration. There are three main groups of halomorphic soils—saline soils or *solonchaks,* alkaline soils or *solonets,* and the partially leached soils known as *solods.*

The halomorphic soils represent one of the major unused soil resources of the world. In the drier regions, about 40 percent of the soils are subject to some form of salinization. Most halomorphic soils are barren but are potentially productive. They can be reclaimed by removing the soluble salts with irrigation water. If the process is rapid, the water must be impounded on the surface so that it can infiltrate into the soil. In addition to sufficient water, adequate drainage is required to remove the dissolved salts.

### GLEIZATION

Soils that are persistently waterlogged develop particular characteristics. In the fresh water of bay areas, vegetation abounds. As a response, the soils have a dark organic A-horizon. Decomposition of the plant material proceeds slowly in this horizon because the bacterial action is limited by the oxygen-poor environment. Peat may form as the organic matter accumulates.

The decaying vegetation may create an acidic condition. As the acid reacts with iron in the waterlogged soil, it is chemically reduced instead of oxidizing as it normally would. This ferrous iron produces a black to blue-gray color rather than red. These soils are known as *gley* soils and the process is *gleization.*

## SOIL CLASSIFICATION SYSTEMS

The soils of different areas have distinguishing characteristics. Soil classification systems must recognize this fact, and must consider the relationships between soils. A synthesis of knowledge about the different soils is essential, as is an understanding of how soils respond to human cultivation. Through the centuries, general classification systems have been developed for a wide variety of uses.

### DEVELOPMENT OF SOIL CLASSIFICATION

The classification of soils was one of the earliest scientific endeavors. As early as 2300 B.C., the soils of the Kingdom of China were divided into nine classes of productivity. Although other attempts to classify soils may have been made, records are missing. Modern soil classification dates from the late 19th century, when V. V. Dokuchaiev, a Russian geologist, developed a new genetic classification of soils. It was based on the concept that soils were independent natural bodies exhibiting characteristics that resulted from the interaction of such soil-forming factors as parent material, climate, vegetation, topography, and time. Thus soil was considered to be an evolutionary product of a dynamic system; that is, the soil was a result of a number of aspects that changed its character over time. The Russian developments were brought to the world by the publication of K. D. Glinka's volume "Die Typen der Bodenbildung, ihre Klassification und Geographische Verbreitung" in 1914.

In the United States, C. F. Marbut used Glinka's work to develop a classification system based primarily on the genetic origin of soil profiles. Marbut stressed the distributions of such dynamic factors as climate and vegetation and such passive factors as parent material, topography, and time.

Marbut's system was based upon the concept that mature soils have spatial variations that can be mapped. These mature soils were designated as great soil groups. Each group consisted of hundreds of soil series that differed from each other in parent material, topographic setting, and time of development, but maintained a similar soil profile. Soil was thus perceived as an independent natural body with horizons, the equivalent of *solum.* It was recognized that soil changes over time, and in its early stages it may have weakly developed horizons. Thus Marbut's major contribution was in changing the concept of soil from that of a weathered rock to that of an independent natural body.

Until the mid-1930s nearly all soil scientists based their soil classifications on profile analysis. In 1938 a new classification system was devised by Baldwin, Kellogg, and Thorp of the U.S. Department of Agriculture. They developed a system based on soil characteristics. The three main categories, *zonal, intrazonal,* and *azonal,* were defined, in part, in genetic terms. The developers of the classfication system stated:

> **The zonal soils include those great groups having well-developed soil characteristics that reflect the influence of the active factors of soil genesis—climate and living organisms (chiefly vegetation). These characteristics are best developed on the gently undulating (but not perfectly level) upland, with good drainage, from parent material not of extreme texture or chemical composition that has been in place long enough for the biological forces to have expressed their full influence.**

The zonal soils fall into two broad groupings that are related to the pedogenic regimes. Soils subject to laterization and podzolization in humid regions are called *pedalfers,* and those dominated by calcification in the drier areas are known as *pedocals.* The intrazonal soils have fairly well-developed soil characteristics that reflect the dominance of some local factor of relief or parent material over the usual prevailing influence of climate and vegetation. The azonal soils do not possess well-developed characteristics; their soil profiles are not developed.

Each of the soil orders was subdivided into suborders, reflecting the influences of climate, vegetation, and other soil-forming factors in a particular region. The soils were further subdivided into *great soil groups* related to soil morphology. Each of the great soil groups has a specific characteristic that differentiates it from other groups. These differences primarily reflect environmental conditions.

In the 1950s it became apparent that all soil classification systems had one or more serious faults. A major defect was the vague definition of soil classes. For example, the great soil groups were defined in terms of soil properties, but the definitions were brief, and differences of opinion resulted when interpretations were made. Another general defect was that the great soil groups were based primarily on the genesis or properties of virgin soils. Soils that had long been used for cultivation were largely ignored. Finally, the system was based on inferred causes of the present soil characteristics rather than on the characteristics themselves.

### UNITED STATES COMPREHENSIVE SOIL CLASSIFICATION SYSTEM

By the 1950s, more scientific information was becoming available, and the need for a new soil classification was evident. In 1960 the United States Department of Agriculture introduced a new system, called the United States Comprehensive Soil Classification System. It is commonly known as the 7th Approximation because it is the seventh revision of the proposed classification submitted to soil scientists for testing.

The new classification system was based on the current properties of the soil, rather than on the genesis, environment, or virgin conditions. The following assumptions guided the development of the system: Soils were to be classified according to their properties. These properties were to be measurable if at all possible. The properties selected were those affecting or resulting from soil genesis. If more than one property met this requirement, the property with the greater significance to plant growth was selected. Classes were subdivided not according to a common property but according to the properties that gave the best classification. The definition of soil classes was to accommodate all soils that had been studied in some detail. Finally, the classification was to be flexible so that as new scientific information evolved, modifications could be made. Thus the 7th Approximation is an evolutionary classification (Plates 3 and 4).

An entirely new terminology was devised, in which Greek and Roman roots are combined to form precise descriptions of soil properties. The 7th Approximation comprises ten *orders* of soils, each of which is divided into *suborders* reflecting the influence of climate, vegetation, or drainage conditions. Suborders are divided into *great groups* on the basis of horizon development. There are further subdivisions into *subgroups, families,* and finally into *soil series,* each of which is named after a place where that type of soil exists on the earth's surface. As revealed in Table 10.1, some similarity exists between the 1938 classification and the 7th Approximation of 1960. The new classification is, however, much more precise in its description of soils.

## OXISOLS

The Oxisols were originally called laterites in the 1938 classification system. Of all soils, Oxisols have experienced the greatest degree of leaching. They are limited to tropical and subtropical lowland areas where the following conditions exist: intense solar radiation, isothermal or near-isothermal monthly temperatures, relatively uniform diurnal temperatures, a high potential evapotranspiration rate, and high annual precipitation, although there may be some seasonal aridity.

The Oxisols have developed under a forest or savanna vegetation. They are leached to a great depth be-

**TABLE 10.1**
1938 U.S. Soil Classification System and approximate equivalents of the 1960 U.S. Comprehensive Classification

| | | 1938 System | 1960 System |
|---|---|---|---|
| | | Great Soil Groups Order | Order |
| *Zonal* | Pedalfer | Laterite<br>Yellow-red podzolic<br>Latosol | Oxisol<br>Ultisol<br>Alfisol<br>Inceptisol |
| | | Podzol<br>Gray-brown podzolic | Ultisol<br>Spodosol<br>Alfisol<br>Inceptisol |
| | | Prairie<br>Degraded chernozem<br>Noncalcic brown | Alfisol<br>Mollisol<br>Inceptisol |
| | | Tundra<br>Alpine turf<br>Polar desert | Inceptisol |
| | Pedocal | Chernozem<br>Chestnut | Mollisol<br>Alfisol |
| | | Brown<br>Sierozem<br>Desert | Aridisol<br>Mollisol<br>Alfisol |
| *Intrazonal* | | Solonchak<br>Solonetz<br>Soloth | Inceptisol<br>Aridisol<br>Mollisol<br>Alfisol |
| | | Humic gley<br>Bog<br>Planosol | Inceptisol<br>Mollisol<br>Alfisol<br>Spodosol<br>Ultisol<br>Entisol |
| | | Brown forest<br>Rendzina | Inceptisol<br>Mollisol |
| *Azonal* | | Lithosols<br>Regosol<br>Alluvial | Entisol<br>Inceptisol<br>Mollisol |

cause of heavy precipitation. Although these soils are very deep (up to 10 meters), they normally lack distinct A- and B-horizons. Oxisols have a subsurface horizon called an *oxic horizon* in which clay-sized minerals consisting of oxides and silicate clays are concentrated. No deposition of leached organic materials occurs in the B-horizon, for rapid decay reduces surface humus to a minimum. The Oxisols maintain a precarious balance: They must supply the considerable nutrient demand of the tropical forests in the face of the ecological disintegration that follows failure to do so. Although the bright red color of the soil and the lush vegetation of the tropical rain forest give the impression of fertility, these soils are extremely infertile.

## ULTISOLS

The Ultisols are located in the humid tropics and subtropics. They were formerly called red and yellow podzol soils. Their structural characteristics are quite similar to those of the Alfisols, but they are more thoroughly leached of their soluble basic materials. These are the most weathered of all mid-latitude soils. Ultisols commonly have developed over long periods of time, but may occur on young surfaces if the parent material has been thoroughly weathered.

The A-horizon is usually gray or red, depending upon the amount of aluminum or iron oxides in the weathered material. This horizon is highly acidic and poor in humus matter. The small quantity of basic materials present in the A-horizon has normally been deposited there by the deep roots of trees and by the surface vegetational mass. Once the forest cover is removed, the meager store of nutrients is soon consumed and crop yields decline rapidly. In southeastern United States the intensive farming of these soils for the past 200 years has resulted in the erosional loss of nearly the entire A-horizon in many areas. Only when intensive fertilization and soil conservation are practiced can permanent agriculture be accomplished.

## ALFISOLS

In middle latitudes, the Alfisols lie between the Mollisols of the subhumid to semiarid climates and the Spodosols and Ultisols of the humid regions. In the intertropical areas the Alfisols occupy transitional areas between the Aridisols of the desert and the Ultisols and Oxisols of the warm, humid climates. These soils exist in a wide range of temperature regimes and in moisture conditions that vary from humid to seasonally arid. The Alfisols thus exist within a wide range of climates and vegetation types. They have a yellowish to brown A-horizon, indicating that considerable leaching has occurred. The upper soil is thus usually colored by iron and aluminum oxides. These soils appear to have originated on relatively stable landscapes, so that the soil horizons have developed over a long period of time.

Although the Alfisols have experienced some leaching, moderate to high reserves of basic materials are still present. They maintain a fine, platelike to granular structure, but are usually friable and acidic. These soils respond well to fertilization and cultivation. The eastern "Corn Belt" of the midwestern United States, one of the most productive areas of the world, possesses Alfisols.

## SPODOSOLS

The Spodosols are soils that exhibit characteristics of podzolization. The spodic A-horizon is an illuvial accumulation of free oxides with or without organic matter. The typical spodic A-horizon is thus easily recognized by the bright colors in the upper part of the horizon. It is coarse-grained, usually gray to whitish, and is rather highly leached. The parent material is usually siliceous. The Spodosols normally develop under a thin layer of surface humus, which is frequently composed of coniferous forest needles. Commonly the A2-horizon is distinct because of its low humus content. The Spodosols are usually acidic and are low in such minerals as calcium and magnesium carbonates. The available moisture capacity varies with the depth of the soil and the texture of the horizons. As a result of eluviation in the A-horizon, iron and aluminum oxides and organic materials frequently accumulate in the B-horizon.

Spodosols develop only in humid climates, but they are distributed from the subarctic to the tropics. Most of these soils have developed under boreal forests, which are uniform over a wide area of northern North America and the Soviet Union. Bacterial action decomposes the organic material in the surface extremely slowly because of the cool, shaded conditions that prevail during much of the year. The soil is therefore covered with a litter of leaves and partially decomposed materials.

The Spodosols are usually not well suited to agriculture because of their deficiency in organic materials, high acidity, and low mineral fertilizer content. They are, however, responsive to management techniques such as deep plowing, liming, and the addition of fertilizers. The deep plowing mixes the A- and B-horizons, thus increasing the colloidal content, which facilitates the capacity of the soil to retain water and soluble nutrients. The addition of lime reduces the acidity, and fertilizers provide plant foods. Crops such as berries, potatoes, and oats thrive on the Spodosols.

## MOLLISOLS

The Mollisols include a variety of soils previously called Chernozem, Prairie, Chestnut and associated humic gley soils, and Planosols. These soils develop in areas of precipitation deficiency and usually possess a vegetational cover of tall or short grass. A few have developed under a deciduous tree covering. They have a thick, dark A-horizon, the *mollic epipedon,* which is formed by the underground decomposition of organic residues. Part of this decaying residue consists of the small but plentiful roots, and another part is surface organic residues brought underground by animals. The organic material is both living and dead in the soil. The humic material in the soil is replenished rather rapidly; that is, within a period of several hundred years.

The Mollisols normally have A-horizons of great thickness that are reddish, dark brown, or black. Although the more soluble minerals may be leached out of the soil, an abundance of limestone and less soluble alkalines remain. A number of subsurface horizons may develop that are enriched with clay and minerals.

The Mollisols are widely distributed in the world. The climates under which they develop range from boreal to tropical. Large areas of these soils are found in the Great Plains of North America, and in the Soviet Union from the Black Sea to Lake Baikal, a belt from 320 to 480 kilometers (200 to 300 miles) wide and more than 6,400 kilometers (4,000 miles) east-west. In Africa a narrow belt crosses the continent south of the Sahara and then swings in a huge curve southward to the grasslands of Zimbabwe. Other areas of Mollisols are found in the Pampas of Argentina, in the central eastern portion of Australia, and in a large portion of the plateau of India.

The Mollisols of the middle latitudes are the most fertile soils in the world, but they normally do not have the highest crop yields due to the dryness of the climate in which they are found. Production varies from one area to another, depending on the amount of precipitation. Crop failure occurs in both North America and the Soviet Union on these soils. The Mollisols of the tropics are commonly unfavorable for tillage and plant growth. Their high clay content subjects them to great shrinking and swelling when they are cultivated. Because many areas of the tropical Mollisols are tilled without benefit of modern technology, their productivity is low.

## ARIDISOLS

Aridisols develop under arid conditions. Soil horizons are poorly developed or even absent in these soils. They are developed largely by physical weathering; the lack of water retards chemical weathering. Two soil-forming processes are dominant. One is calcification, or deposition of calcium salts, which prevails over wide stretches of the world's arid regions. The other process is salinization, or sodium deposition, which exists in localized areas. The deposits of calcium and sodium salts are usually within 100 centimeters of the soil surface. They form the only distinct horizon in the Aridisols. Most of the soil is composed of large mineral particles and even stones. These arid and semiarid soils are found over nearly one-third of the earth, ranging from the Arctic to tropical deserts.

The Aridisols are generally unsuitable for agricultural development because of moisture and organic matter deficiencies. Crop cultivation may evolve with irrigation and fertilization. The general lack of a vegetational cover encourages wind erosion, sheet wash, and gullying. Many plants will develop deep root systems to seek deep water sources. A major barrier to the agricultural use of Aridisols is frequently their high alkalinity and salinity. When sodium salts exceed 2 percent of the mineral content, a *salic* horizon is produced, which may even appear as a crust on the soil surface. This soil is called a *solonchak*.

## INCEPTISOLS

Inceptisols are young soils with one or more horizons. They have not undergone sufficient weathering to produce mature soils. Although some of the soluble bases have been removed from the A-horizon, these soils do not possess a well-defined illuvial horizon. They are usually moist, with either a light or dark surface horizon. There is normally an appreciable accumulation of organic matter. The native vegetation under which they develop is most often a forest, but it may range from the northern boreal to the tropical rainforest in character. A few of the Inceptisols may develop under a grass covering.

## VERTISOLS

The Vertisols normally develop from limestone or basic igneous parent materials. Clays represent from 40 to 70 percent of their mineral content. These soils are located in subhumid to arid regions from the tropics to the middle latitudes. They have developed under a grassland covering. Because the water supply is irregular, this soil has periods of wetness and dryness. Its most characteristic feature is cracks caused by the swelling and shrinking of the clay. The soil is frequently remoistened by water running into the cracks rather than penetrating downward into the heavy, compact clays. The shrinking, cracking, and shearing, combined with mass movement, make these soils unstable and difficult to use. For example, fences and telephone poles may be thrown out of line by a meter or so when the soil dries out after precipitation. These soils are greatly limited in their distribution.

**PLATE 1**
New York to Norfolk. This image is a composite of six photos taken by the Earth Resources Technology Satellite–1 (ERTS–1) from an altitude of 905 kilometers (562 miles) on two successive days. Three colors—green, red, and infrared—were seen and recorded at NASA's Goddard Space Flight Center, Greenbelt, Md. Healthy crops, trees, and other green plants are shown as varying shades of orange or red. Suburban areas with sparse vegetation can appear as light pink and barren lands as light gray. Cities and industrial areas show as dark gray and clear water is various shades of blue. Some geographical landmarks visible here are: Folded Appalachians, or Valley and Ridge, near Harrisburg, Pa. (upper left); strip-mined surfaces for anthracite coal (extreme upper center); piedmont region, which is geologically old terrain (west of N.Y. City to left center); Fall Line (line west of N.Y. City through Philadelphia, Baltimore, and Washington); offshore bars from Sandy Hook, N.J., to Chincoteague Islands (far right); Blackwater National Wildlife Refuge, typical wetlands area (Eastern shore of Chesapeake Bay); Camp David (Catoctin Mountains, far left, above center); Susquehanna and Delaware rivers emptying into Chesapeake and Delaware bays (upper center); and forested New Jersey Pine Barrens east of Philadelphia. Bright blue water in the Potomac, Rappahannock, and James rivers is sedimentation resulting from runoff after a rainstorm.

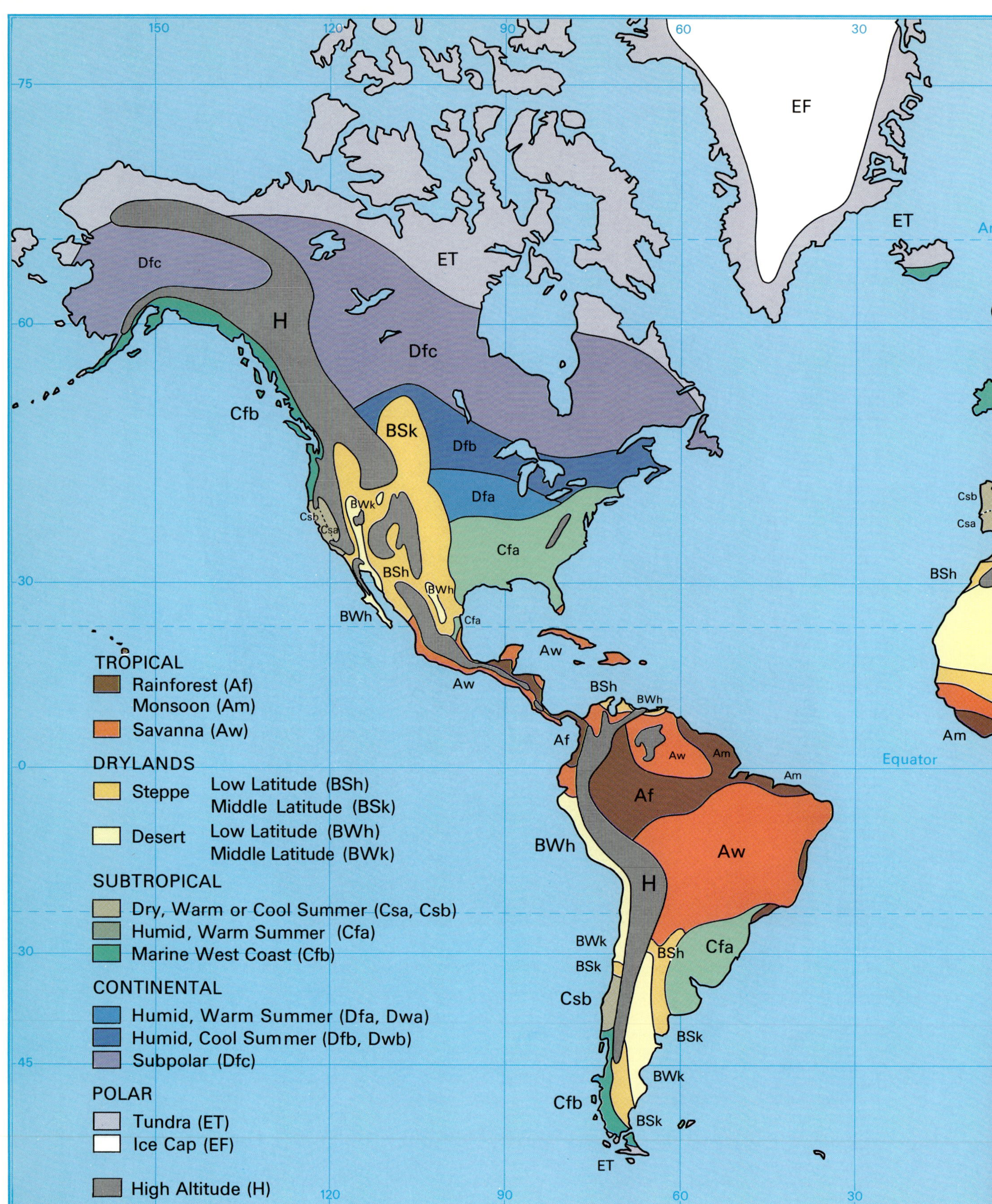


**PLATE 2**
World distribution of climates based on the Köppen-Geiger classification system.

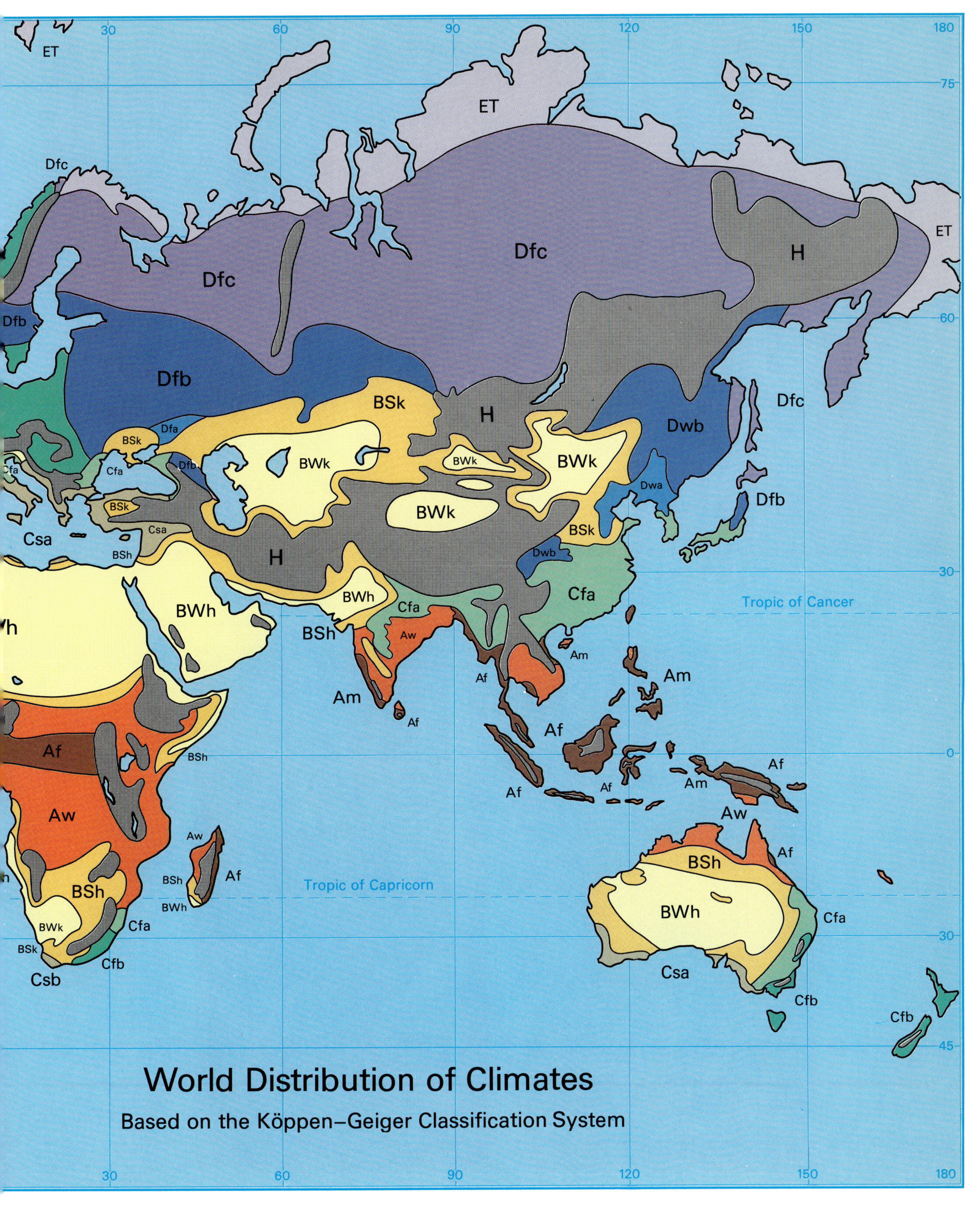
World Distribution of Climates
Based on the Köppen–Geiger Classification System
30
60
90
120
150
180
75
60
30
0
30
45
ET
ET
ET
Dfc
Dfc
Dfc
Dfc
H
H
H
Dfb
Dfb
Dfb
Dfa
Dfb
Dwb
Dwb
Dwa
BSk
BSk
BSk
BSk
BSk
BWk
BWk
BWk
BWk
BWk
Cfa
Cfa
Cfa
Cfa
Cfa
Csa
Csa
Csa
BSh
BSh
BSh
BSh
BSh
BSh
BWh
BWh
BWh
BWh
Am
Am
Am
Am
Aw
Aw
Aw
Aw
Af
Af
Af
Af
Af
Af
Af
Af
Af
Af
Cfb
Cfb
Cfb
Csb
Tropic of Cancer
Tropic of Capricorn
30
60
90
120
150
180

**PLATE 3**

Soil profiles based on the U.S. comprehensive classification (7th approximation). All slides from the Marbut Memorial Slide Collection, 1968, by permission of the Soil Science Society of America.

**PLATE 3.1**
OXISOL
Island of Kauai, Hawaii
Parent material: Residium or alluvium from basic igneous rock

**PLATE 3.2**
ULTISOL
Piedmont of North Carolina
Parent material: Granite gneiss on acid igneous rocks

**PLATE 3.3**
ALFISOL
Southern Michigan
Parent material: Calcareous glacial till

**PLATE 3.4**
SPODOSOL
Northern New York
Parent material: Sandy glacial outwash from granitic rocks

**PLATE 3.5**
MOLLISOL
Central Iowa
Parent material: Loess

**PLATE 3.6**
ARIDISOL
Central Arizona
Parent material: Alluvial fan

**PLATE 3.7**
INCEPTISOL
Coastal tundra of northern Alaska
Parent material: Coastal plain sediments

**PLATE 3.8**
VERTISOL
Lajas Valley, Puerto Rico
Parent material: Limestone and pyroclastic material

**PLATE 3.9**
HISTOSOL
Southern Michigan
Parent material: Highly decomposed muck

**PLATE 3.10**
ENTISOL
Northern Michigan
Parent material: Glacial outwash (sand)

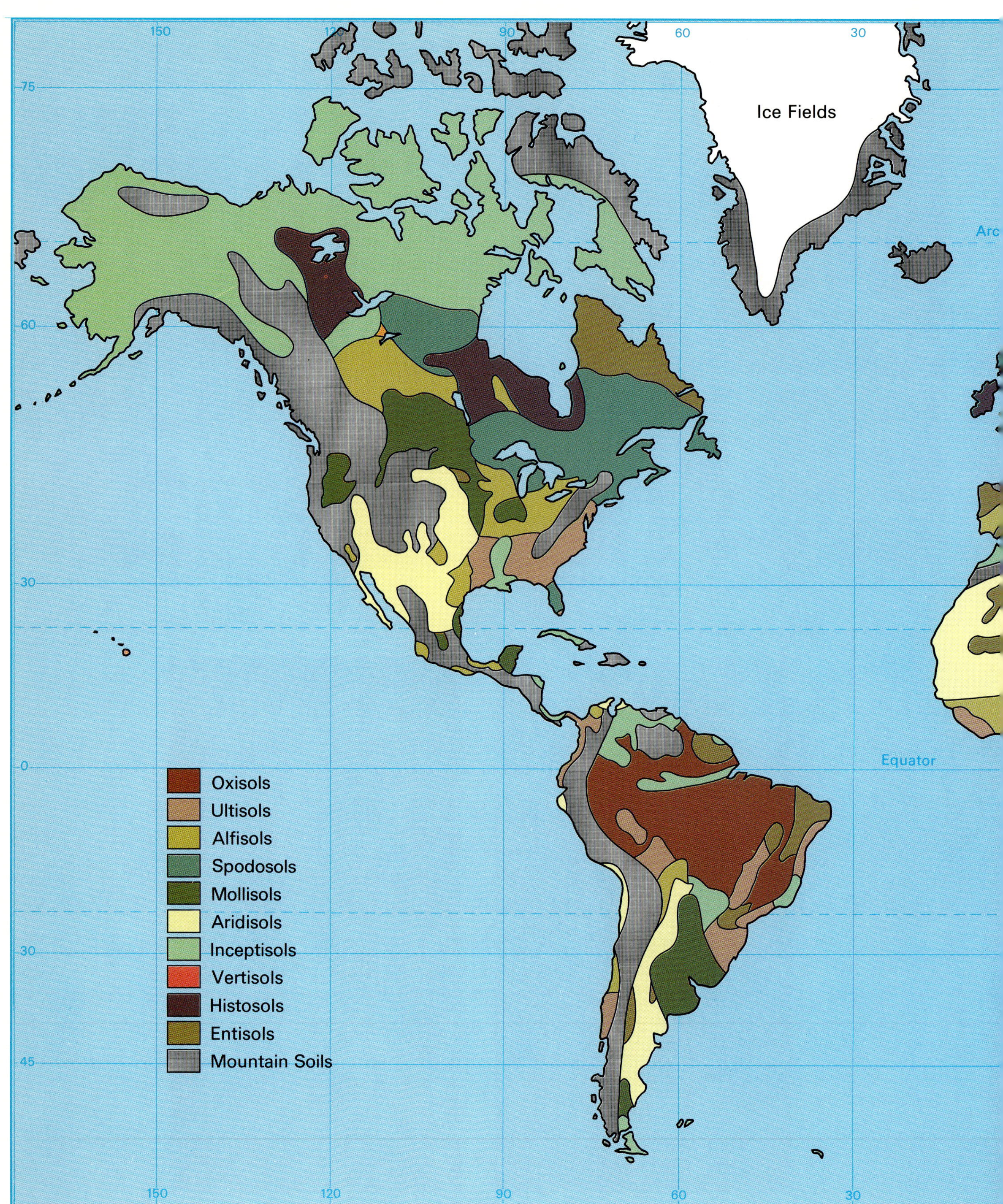


**PLATE 4**
World distribution of soil orders based on the U.S. Comprehensive Soil Classification System.

30
60
90
120
150
180
75
60
30
0
30
45
Tropic of Cancer
Tropic of Capricorn
World Distribution of Soil Orders
Based on the U.S. Comprehensive Soil
Classification System (7th Approximation)

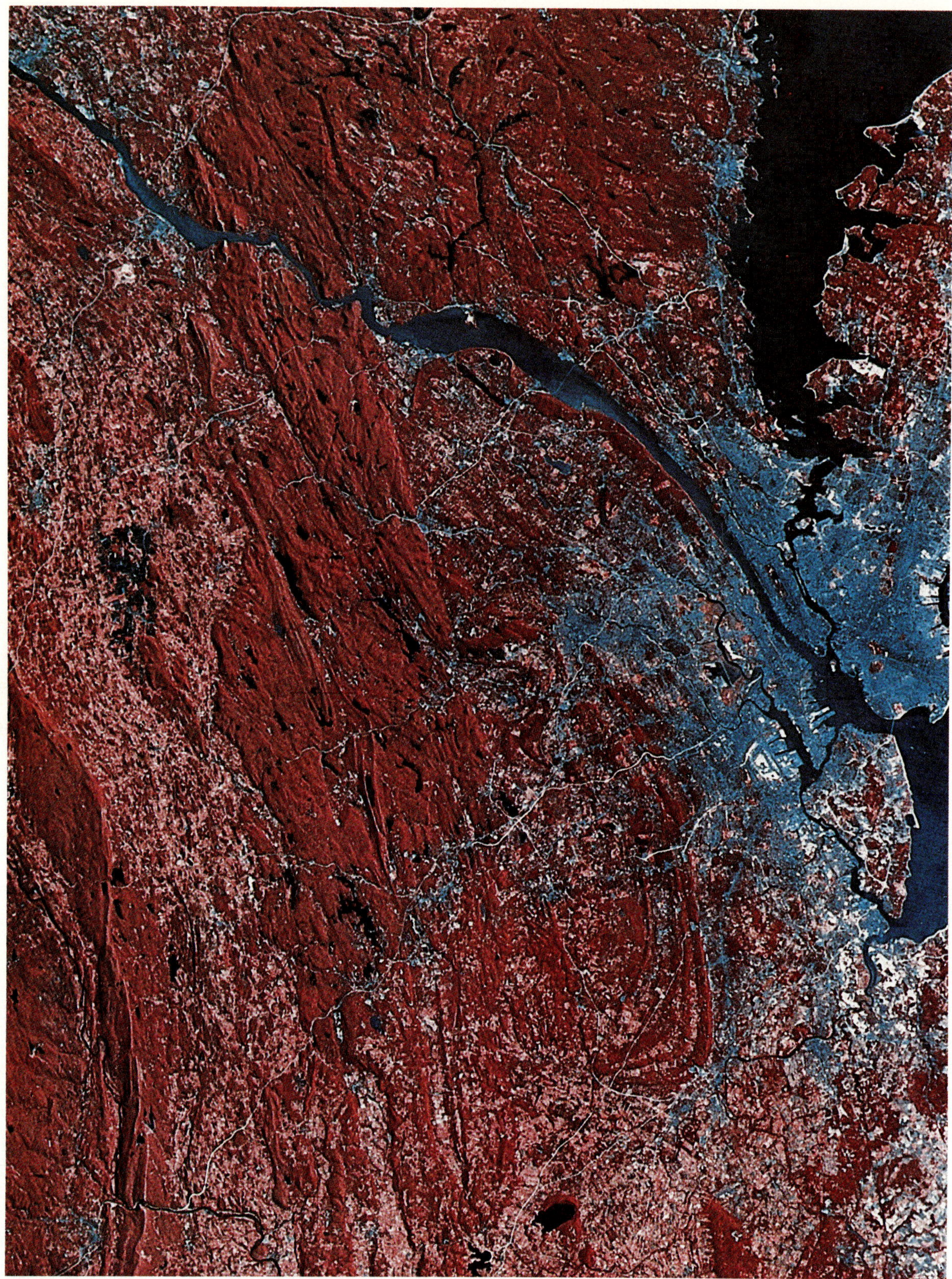

**PLATE 5**
New York–New Jersey area. This composite photo was taken from an altitude of 914 kilometers (568 miles). The Hudson River extends from the upper left down to the middle right. New York City and Staten Island can be seen at the middle right, with Long Island extending from the upper to middle right. Newark, Jersey City, and Elizabeth, N.J., are also visible in the middle right, and the tip of Connecticut is in the upper right of the photograph, to the left of Long Island.

## HISTOSOLS

The Histosols include the soils originally called bog soils or organic soils. They comprise mostly plant material. The soils form in waterlogged environments with little oxygen, causing organic materials to decay slowly. They are found from the arctic to the tropics in all areas except those that are dry. They are most common in high-latitude glaciated regions.

The Histosols have poorly developed horizons. Although they are usually acidic, they can be productive when drained. Because of their high organic content, they compact when they dry and are subject to fire and wind erosion.

## ENTISOLS

The Entisols are youthful soils that have no natural genetic horizons, or only the beginning of horizons. The parent materials of these soils may range from recent alluvial deposits that have been in place only a short time to residual rocks that are geologically ancient. Entisols may be of any color, such as black, bluish-gray, yellow, brown, or red. The quantity of organic material varies from high to low. They include many, but not all, of the soils previously called alluvial soils, regosols, lithosols, tundra, and low-humus gley soils. They also include many of the artificial bog soils of western Europe. These soils are widely distributed in the world.

# SOILS AND HUMAN WELFARE

The world's growing human population demands more intense crop production. As a response, the world's farmers have adopted agricultural production practices that lead to excessive rates of soil erosion (Photos 41–47). At the same time, the growing urban populations with their increased industrialization are creating a demand to convert cropland to nonfarm uses. Although urbanization involves only a relatively small percentage of land, that land is frequently the most productive plains of the world. The processes of erosion and urbanization make the soils of the world less able to supply the food needed by the growing population.

**PHOTO 41**
Dust storm. In the 1930s, the extended drought on the Great Plains caused dust storms to carry off vast quantities of topsoil. (Courtesy: U.S. Department of Agriculture, Soil Conservation Service)

Soil erosion is a natural process that occurs on all land. It occurs at an accelerated rate, however, on land that is cleared and cropped. When the rate of erosion exceeds the natural rate of soil formation, the topsoil is gradually depleted, leaving only the subsoil or bare rock. In the 1930s the U.S. Soil Conservation Service encouraged farmers to practice soil conservation. The government financed contour terracing and the construction of small sediment dams, farm ponds, and shelter belts. Farmers were also persuaded to share in the cost of protecting their own land against erosion. Nevertheless, the Soil Conservation Service has reported that on 94 million acres of cropland, soil loss is too great to sustain crop production indefinitely. The service also warns that if soil erosion in the fertile Corn Belt states of the Midwest continues at current rates for another 50 years, corn and soybean yields could be reduced by 30 percent. Soil scientists have found alarmingly high rates of erosion by water in a number of states (Figure 10.10). Tennessee, for example, loses an average of 14.1 tons of topsoil per acre of cropland; Missouri, 11.4 tons; Mississippi, 10.9 tons; and Iowa, 9.9 tons. In the Great Plains, wind erosion is particularly severe, eroding annually 14.9 tons per acre in Texas and 8.9 tons in Colorado. Water erosion removes about a billion tons of topsoil, more than is formed each year. If one assumes 160 tons per acre-inch of soil with a typical topsoil depth of 8 inches, the loss of one billion tons is equivalent to the loss of 781,800 acres of cropland annually.

**PHOTO 42**
Wind erosion. Wind removed much of the topsoil on this farm during the drought of the 1930s. As a consequence the farm was abandoned. (Courtesy: U.S. Department of Agriculture, Soil Conservation Service)

**PHOTO 44**
Hillside gullying. Landslip on a steep cultivated slope near Colfax, Washington. (Courtesy: U.S. Department of Agriculture, Soil Conservation Service)

**PHOTO 43**
This abandoned farmstead in Colorado stands in ruin from blasting winds, which have shifted topsoil from fields to cover the house. The old turning plow in foreground was abandoned at the end of the furrow in the field. (Courtesy: U.S. Department of Agriculture, Soil Conservation Service)

**PHOTO 45**
Soil erosion that resulted when a ground cover was removed in a citrus grove in Tulare County, California. Previously, a native cover crop was allowed to grow with no observed soil loss. (Courtesy: U.S. Department of Agriculture, Soil Conservation Service)

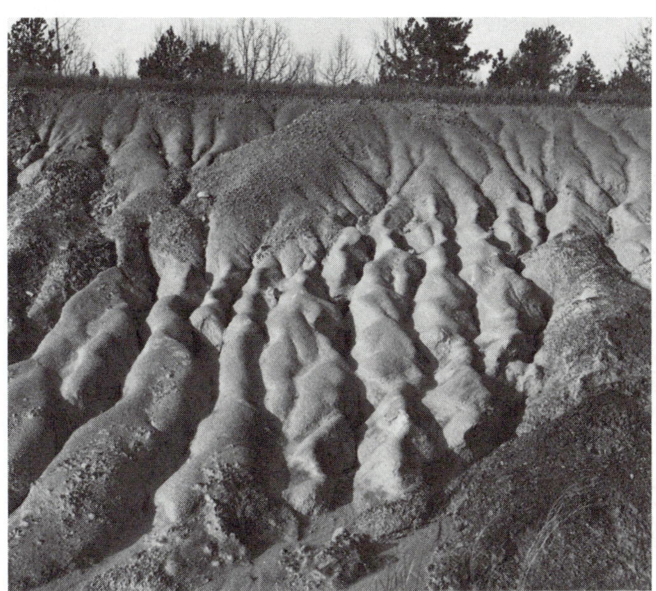

**PHOTO 46**
Gullying on a steep slope in Franklin County, Georgia. Water erosion has removed most of the earth material. (Courtesy: U.S. Department of Agriculture, Soil Conservation Service)

**PHOTO 47**
Soil erosion in Mendocino County, California. Eroded material from the steep slopes in the background has been deposited around the vines in the foreground. In some places the vines are all but completely covered to a depth of 14 or more inches of silt. (Courtesy: U.S. Department of Agriculture, Soil Conservation Service)

Little attention was given to soil erosion until the 1920s, when scientists warned that valuable topsoil was being rapidly depleted. The dust-bowl period of the 1930s added urgency to these warnings. The Civilian Conservation Corps was created to develop large-scale erosion control projects, and the U.S. Soil Conservation Service to work directly with farmers and ranchers. The ensuing years saw impressive progress in controlling erosion (Photos 48–53).

The growing worldwide demand for food, the availability of commercial fertilizers, and the increase in food prices have led to the abandonment of many soil conservation practices. The lure of higher prices plus governmental relaxation of planting restrictions in the 1970s resulted in the cropping of thousands of acres of marginal land, much of it on the steep slopes of hill country. Many of the contour terrains that checked soil loss on hillsides have been plowed because new and much larger farm implements cannot fit over them. In many areas the traditional crop rotation system that included soil-retaining pastures and hay has been abandoned in favor of continuous cropping of corn and other row crops. The resulting gain in crop production has come at a price: loss of topsoil.

The problem of soil erosion is worldwide. In the Soviet Union agriculture has been extended to marginal lands because of food shortages. In many areas these investments have been effective in increasing agricultural productivity, but the soils have lost some of their natural wealth. A recent study by the Soviet Soil Erosion Laboratory has shown that as much as 50 percent of the south-central portion of the USSR could be affected by severe gullying if present practices continue. A similar study in the steppe and forest regions of European Russia revealed that gullying was greatly accelerated as the good agricultural land reserves were depleted and marginal lands began to be cultivated.

In many of the traditional agricultural exporting areas, soil erosion is limiting production and reducing available exports. Australia is a notable example. Many of the best agricultural areas of eastern Australia are experiencing serious soil erosion problems. The same condition is found in Argentina, Canada, the United States, and other countries.

In the Third World countries, soil erosion and depletion become even more critical agricultural problems because in many areas there is little or no excess food supply. Unfortunately the poorest populations are located on the least desirable agricultural lands which

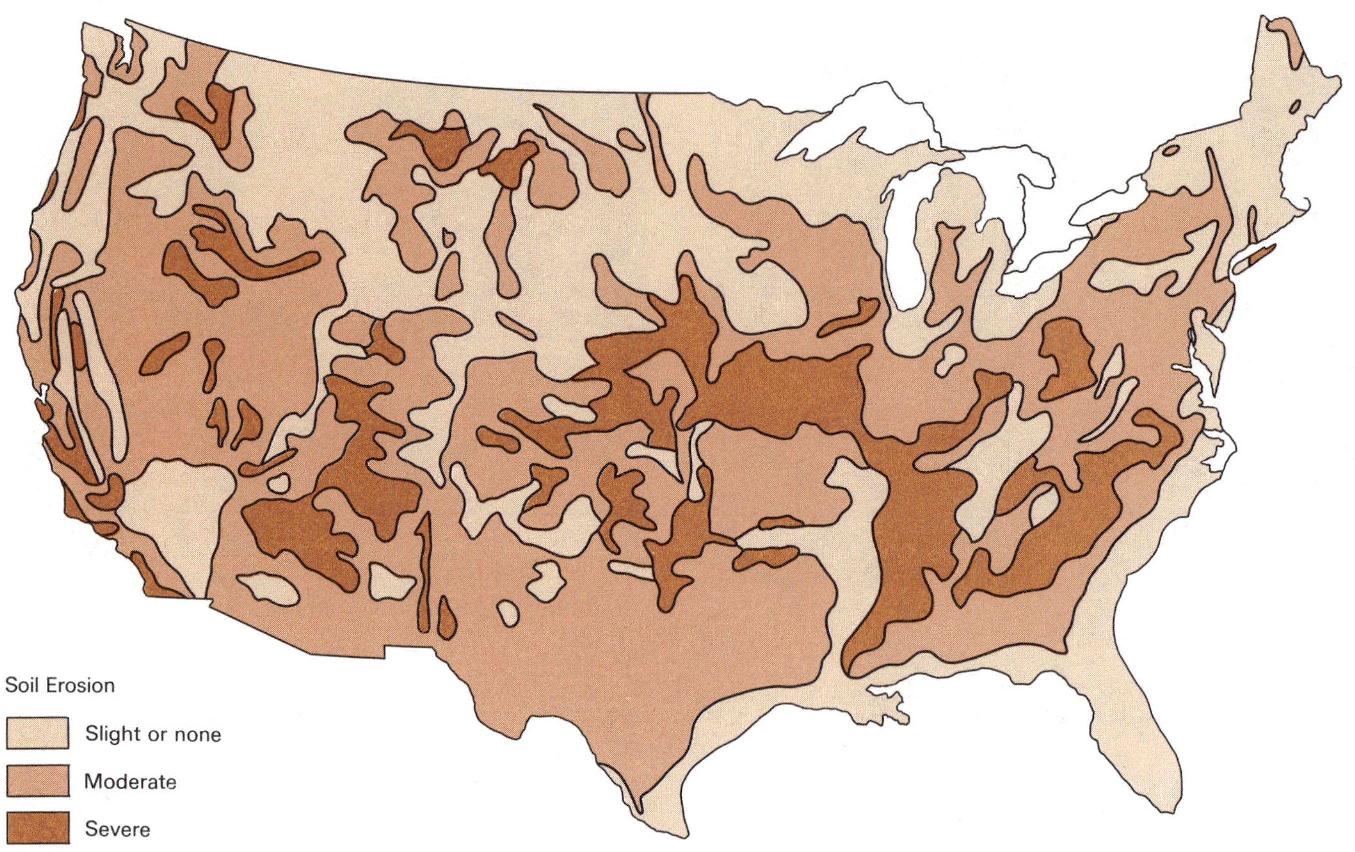


**FIGURE 10.10**
Generalized soil erosion in the United States. The major areas of soil erosion are in the leading agricultural regions of the Southeast and the Midwest. (Data from U.S. Department of Agriculture, Soil Conservation Service)

have the lowest productivity. For example, in the Andean countries of Colombia, Ecuador, Peru, Bolivia, and Chile, the wealthy and potentially powerful ranchers own the valleys where cattle production dominates. Small landowners are forced to cultivate the steep, less fertile slopes. Severe erosion has occurred on these slopes, lowering productivity and the quality of life for some people in these countries.

Reports from many Third World countries reveal the critical nature of the soil conditions and the massive problems that the future holds as population increases. A report from Indonesia indicates that soil erosion is increasing much faster than reclamation programs can restore soil fertility. In Pakistan the same situation exists with several thousand areas being abandoned each year in the Punjab area due to soil degradation caused by erosion. Soil erosion has reached the critical stage in a number of African countries. The reports by the Agency for International Development on Ethiopia indicate:

> **There is an environmental nightmare unfolding before our eyes . . . It is the result of the acts of millions of Ethiopians struggling for survival; scratching the surface of eroded land and eroding it further; cutting down the trees for warmth and fuel and leaving the country denuded . . . Over one billion—one billion—tons of topsoil flow from Ethiopia's highlands each year. (U.S. Agency for International Development, *Fiscal Year 1980 Budget Proposed for Ethiopia* [Washington, D.C.: AID, 1980], 1)**

The quantity and quality of the topsoil lost and the resulting decline in productivity would be difficult to overstate. It is estimated that between one-quarter and one-third of the world's cropland is being steadily degraded as a result of soil erosion. It must further be

**PHOTO 48**
Soil reclamation. Gullied land in Prentiss County, Mississippi, being planted in loblolly pine for erosion control. The small dams in the gullies control the runoff and collect silt to form a planting base. (Courtesy: U.S. Department of Agriculture, Soil Conservation Service)

**PHOTO 50**
Gully control project. The check dam is being constructed in the large gully shown in Photo 49. (Courtesy: U.S. Department of Agriculture, Soil Conservation Service)

**PHOTO 49**
Gully control project. A 15-inch drain pipe is being assembled before construction of a check dam to control a gully 15 meters (50 feet) deep, 30 meters (100 feet) wide, and 300 meters (900 feet) long, that was growing rapidly into good farm land near New Brockton, Alabama. (Courtesy: U.S. Department of Agriculture, Soil Conservation Service)

**PHOTO 51**
Erosion control. Contour strip-cropping on slope land in Wisconsin. (Courtesy: Wisconsin Conservation Department)

**PHOTO 52**
Strip-mined land in Utica County, Illinois, before reclamation. (Courtesy: U.S Department of Agriculture, Soil Conservation Service)

**PHOTO 53**
Reclaimed strip-mined land. Cattle graze on pastures in Illinois where strip-mined spoil banks were seeded in grass and legumes. This was the seventh year of use. Usually lush in the spring, the pasture becomes dry in the fall. It requires careful management to avoid overgrazing. (Courtesy: U.S. Department of Agriculture, Soil Conservation Service)

recognized that the application of erosion-control practices is frequently not cost-effective for the individual farmer. A study in Iowa on land that had experienced severe erosion showed that additional energy and fertilizer would be required to reduce soil erosion to a satisfactory level, and that yields would be reduced. The study concluded that these costs amounted to three times the immediate benefits of reducing erosion. The choices then appear to be to continue the present practices, ultimately abandoning land and facing economic disaster in the future, or to initiate costly erosion controls that may bring about economic disaster more quickly. Neither of these alternatives is satisfactory to the individual farmer, or, possibly even more important, for the welfare of the world's population. It has been forecast that if population increases occur as predicted, then growth in food production could fall below that of population needs by the end of the 1980s. This fundamental problem must be addressed by policymakers, both inside and outside government. Before the problem can be attacked, an effective worldwide understanding of the seriousness of the problem must develop.

Neither average citizens nor politicians appreciate the problem of decreasing soil productivity. For example, in India the land is obviously denuded, but the problem is not being addressed. The Soviet Union's dependence on imported food is not so much a lack of land as it is a problem of low productivity. And yet, in most of the world, governmental support is decreasing rather than growing. In some of the Third World countries, an adequate program to control loss of topsoil will require an expenditure greater than the total national budget. This question remains unsolved: Can the nations of the world stop soil degradation before a catastrophe results?

## CONCLUSION

Soil is a complex system of organic and mineral materials, water, and air that covers parts of the earth's surface. The major factors in soil formation are bedrock (parent material), climate, vegetation, topography, and time. In general, soil formation is related to climatic regimes. For example, laterization or ferrallitization occurs in areas of hot, humid climates, while podzolization is a response to cool, moist climates, and calcification occurs in the wet-dry regimes of the middle latitudes. As a soil weathers, it normally develops different horizons with distinct characteristics.

One of the earliest scientific endeavors was the development of a soil classification system. Because of the many variables in soil formation, the classification process is ongoing. The most recent system, the United States Comprehensive Classification, often labeled the 7th Approximation, describes every soil type and relates each type to a worldwide great soil group.

The maintenance of soil fertility is difficult, for each time a crop is planted the natural soil system is disturbed. Erosion has become a worldwide problem, and many areas have been rendered infertile due to soil mismanagement. The problems are now recognized, and soils can be maintained as a permanent resource when various soil conservation methods are applied. The major question is, Can existing soil knowledge be implemented quickly enough to preserve this precious resource?

## STUDY QUESTIONS

1 What are the principal factors of soil formation?
2 Why are the weathering processes important in soil formation?
3 What is a soil horizon?
4 Characterize each soil horizon.
5 What are the principal soil properties? Describe why each is important.
6 What are the principal pedogenic regimes? Why does each of these produce a highly distinctive soil type?
7 Why has soil classification had a long history of development?
8 Describe the basis of the 1938 soil classification of the U.S. Department of Agriculture.
9 What is the basis of the 1960 United States Comprehensive Soil Classification?
10 What are the 10 major orders of the U.S. Comprehensive Soil Classification? Give two major characteristics of each.
11 What are some of the major problems of maintaining soil productivity in the world?

# 11
# WORLD NATURAL VEGETATION SYSTEMS

## KEY WORDS

biomass
climax vegetation
ecotone
edaphic
ephemeral plants
epiphytes
flagform trees
holocoenotic
hydrophytes
krummholz
megathermal
mesophytes
mesothermal
microthermal
photoperiodism
photosynthesis
plant communities
transpiration
xerophytes

Vegetation makes human life possible on the earth. Through the process of *photosynthesis,* vegetation combines the nutrients of the earth with solar energy to produce oxygen and other matter. Because human activities have altered much of the vegetation of the earth, original or natural vegetation is found only in a few isolated areas. The alteration of vegetation has frequently been deliberate, involving the clearing, cutting, and burning of the original vegetational cover.

Although the world's plant cover has been considerably altered, emphasis in this chapter is on the factors that influence natural vegetational growth and on the patterns of the original vegetative cover. On a world scale, the geographer focuses on the structure, spatial pattern, and distribution of plant species. The largest units considered are known as *plant communities,* which consist of forests, shrubs, tundra, or grasslands. A plant community, for example, would be a tropical rainforest, a broadleaf deciduous forest, or a prairie of the middle latitudes. These communities occur within similar environments of the earth, but the individual species of plants may vary greatly from one region to another.

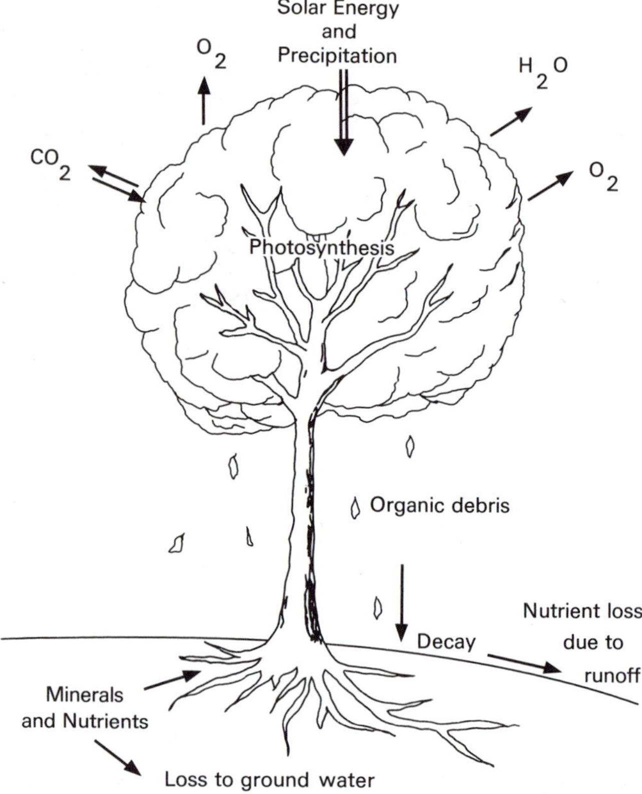


**FIGURE 11.1**
Nutrient cycle in a forest ecosystem. Photosynthesis occurs in the leaves of the tree, and nutrients for growth are obtained from the ground.

## ECOSYSTEMS

In order to understand the evolution of a vegetation region, it is necessary to recognize that nutrients are continuously recycled within a plant community. The concept of the *ecosystem* has gradually evolved to help explain this process. An ecosystem is a basic functional unit in nature. It consists of all plants and animals and their inorganic environment, which are linked by flows of energy and nutrients. A plant community is thus a part of an ecosystem. An ecosystem is not a closed system because external energy flows into the system from solar radiation and because matter in the form of water and nutrients also enters. An ecosystem loses matter as a result of a gaseous exchange and evaporation and drainage of water. Thus a plant community exchanges energy and mass with its surroundings (Figure 11.1).

Any change affecting a single element within an ecosystem causes repercussions throughout the entire system. Materials continually cycle through the plant ecosystem. The nutrients in the soil come from the weathering of the parent materials and from decaying organic matter from plants. In the soil, the nutrients are dissolved in water and are received by the plant from its roots. The nutrients do not move through the system smoothly. The movement depends upon the amounts of soil solution and energy available to the plants, which vary greatly from one season to another.

The second ingredient in the ecosystem that is necessary for photosynthesis to occur is carbon dioxide ($CO_2$) in the atmosphere. Photosynthesis occurs in the leaves of plants, where carbon dioxide, water, and nutrients are acted upon by solar energy to produce carbohydrates and oxygen. The carbohydrate plant material is called *biomass* (Figure 11.2). Because solar energy is a major factor in the output of the biomass, productivity increases from the poles to the equator. It has also been found that the length of the growing season is important in measuring productivity of biomass (Figure 11.3).

Chlorophyll, the green pigment of the leaf, is a fundamental ingredient in photosynthesis. Carbon dioxide from the atmosphere is dissolved in the cell walls of the leaf surface. Small holes in the leaf surface, called *stomata,* permit the water to enter the leaf. The nutrients arrive in the leaf from the stem. The more water that enters the stomata, bringing carbon dioxide and nu-

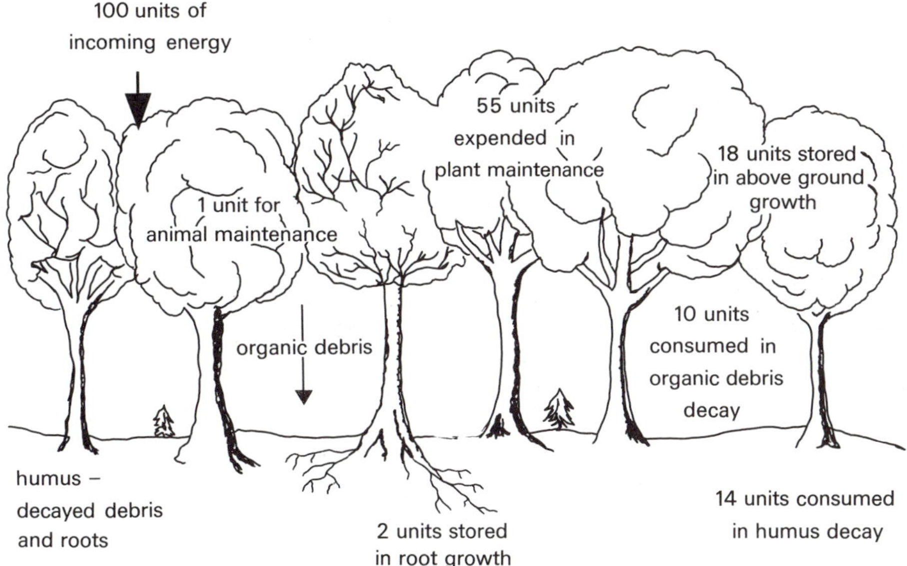


**FIGURE 11.2**
Biomass production. This sketch illustrates the flow of energy through a forest community. The flow lines are simplified. For example, the 55 units expended in plant maintenance come from all the trees but for simplicity are shown coming from a single source. (After Woodwell, 1970)

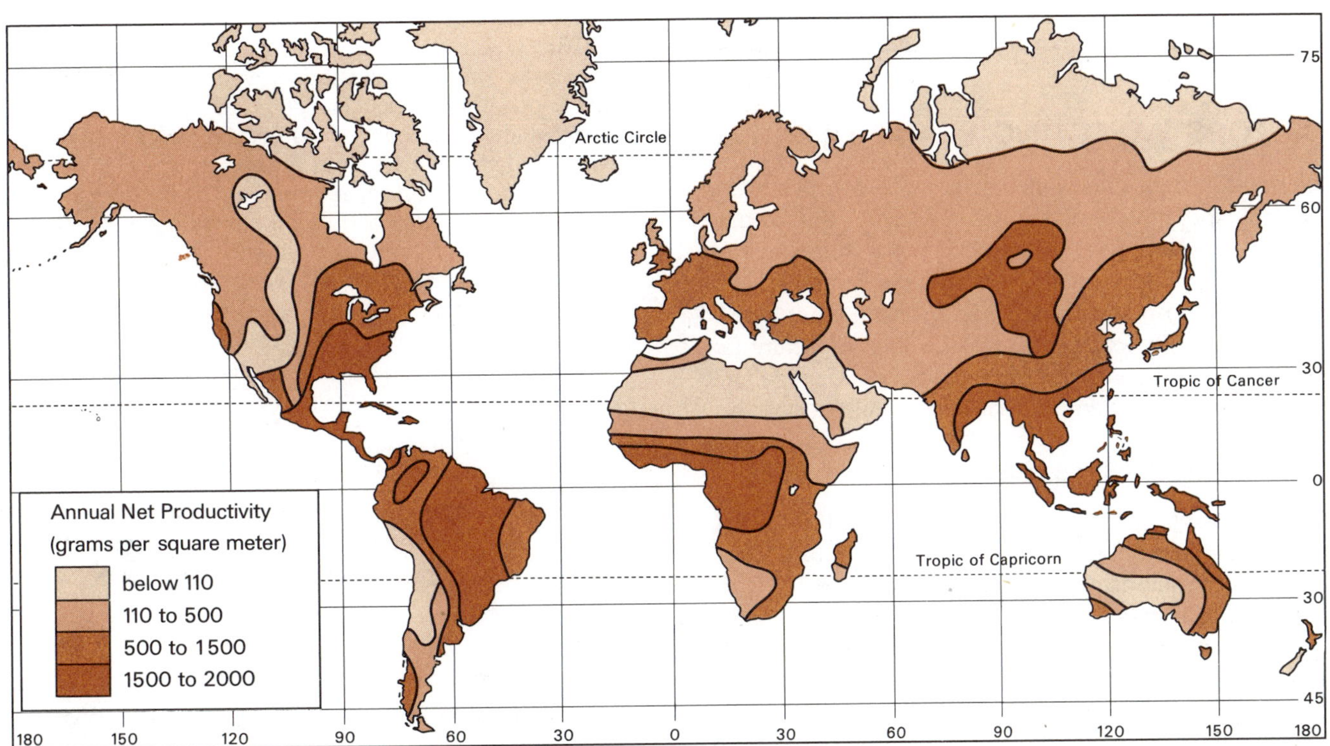


**FIGURE 11.3**
Spatial distribution of annual net production of biomass. The productivity of biomass is directly related to the energy input. The lower latitudes are thus the areas of greatest net production. (After Lieth and Box, 1972)

trients, the greater the amount of biomass produced. The byproduct is oxygen ($O_2$) that is released back into the atmosphere. Of 100 units of energy entering the ecosystem at any one time, about 55 units are used to maintain the biomass already in existence and about 25 units are consumed in the decay of the organic materials present. The remaining 20 units produce new biomass.

It has been estimated that the photosynthetic process requires 688,000 calories of radiant energy to produce one gram of new biomass. If more energy enters the plant community than leaves it, plant growth flourishes. If less energy enters the system than leaves, then the plant community will suffer and ultimately die.

In an ecosystem where the plant community is in equilibrium—that is, where growth is equal to decay—a *climax* condition is said to exist. However, climax conditions rarely exist in nature. Plant communities are subject to continuous changes, such as fluctuations in weather, plant diseases, and interferences by people. Each of these factors affects plant growth. Several years of drought, for example, will greatly retard growth. The introduction of a disease, such as the Dutch Elm blight in northeastern United States, may essentially destroy a single species in the forest. The ecosystem is thus an open system that is in constant change.

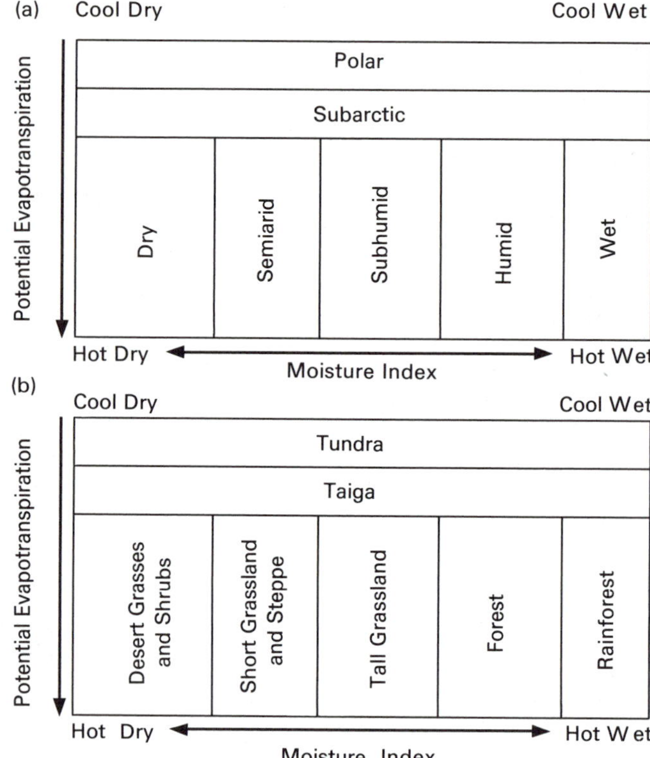


**FIGURE 11.4**
Relationship between climate and vegetation. The top diagram shows the principal climatic types according to the Thornthwaite classification; the bottom diagram shows the relationship of these types to vegetation types. Note on each diagram that potential evapotranspiration increases as temperature increases and that the moisture index increases from dry to wet. The type of vegetational covering is largely a response to energy availability and moisture conditions. For example, the tropical rainforest has developed in a hot, wet environment while the tundra exists under polar conditions. (After U.S. Department of Agriculture, 1941)

## FACTORS AFFECTING PLANT LIFE

The environment of a plant consists of a complex set of physical and biological factors. Of these, the climatic elements of temperature, precipitation, humidity, atmospheric pressure, wind velocity, and length of daylight play an important role in determining what type of plant community exists in a region. Other important factors include soil and geomorphic conditions, prevalence of fires, and animal and human activities.

### CLIMATIC ELEMENTS

While all plants have optimal climatic conditions under which they flourish, growth will normally occur within a range of conditions (Figure 11.4). For example, if the temperature is too hot or too cold, or the precipitation is too heavy or too light, the plant community will experience stress, but only under extreme conditions will the plants be killed. It must also be remembered that the climatic factors affecting plant growth are interrelated and that a change in one element will affect all others. To illustrate, if the temperature increases, the relative humidity is lowered. This in turn increases the *transpiration* of the plant. If additional water is not made available from the soil, the plant will experience desiccation stress. This interrelationship of a series of factors in the environment is known as the *holocoenotic* environment.

#### Temperature

The way a plant controls its temperature involves the most intricate and complicated mechanisms it possesses. Two aspects of temperature are important in the environment of a plant. First, the *absolute temperature* (actual temperature) controls the speed of the biological processes and the physical reactions. Secondly, the *rel-*

*ative temperature* (the effect on plants of a constant temperature with varying humidity) influences the rate at which heat is lost or gained. Plants adapt to a wide variety of temperature conditions throughout the world. Those plants that are tolerant to the high temperatures of the tropics are said to be adapted to *megathermal* conditions; those that are adapted to seasonal change are characterized as *mesothermal;* and those adapted to arctic and alpine conditions are said to tolerate *microthermal* conditions.

All plants have limits of temperature, both high and low, beyond which they cannot survive. Low temperatures are usually most critical. Extended cold temperatures may result in the destruction of cells by freezing. Plants adapt to cold conditions by becoming dormant in the winter and by changes in morphology, such as *dwarfism,* which reduces the exposed leaf surface area. Temperatures in the tropics rarely rise to the point where plant cells are destroyed because plants have the ability to cool themselves through *transpiration* and *evaporation.*

Individual species of plants differ in their biological and physiological response to temperature and in their tolerance to temperature extremes. A considerable difference in temperature tolerance exists not only from species to species, but also within the same plant from season to season. Metabolic activity essentially stops at temperatures below 0°C (32°F) or higher than 45°C (113°F). This factor causes such phenomena as the slow rate of tree growth at the timberline. The trees are unable to produce sufficient food for growth during the short summer season.

## Precipitation

While all plants require water for survival, different plants require different amounts. A single plant's need for water varies depending upon climatic conditions such as solar radiation, temperature, humidity, and wind velocity. Where measurements of these climatic factors are available, the potential water requirements for each plant can be calculated. In the complex relationship among soil, plant, and climate, the vital factor is the evapotranspiration from the plant.

Plants are able to adapt to different water conditions. Some plants avoid water stress by becoming dormant during the dry season. The Mediterranean broadleaf forest is an example of an entire community of vegetation that sustains itself in a hot, dry climate by shedding its leaves in summer. Some plants in dry regions have roots that penetrate deeply to the groundwater table. Such plants are called *phreatophytes* or "well plants." Plants that maintain their leaves during periods of winter stress, such as the boreal coniferous forest of the subarctic, must have a high degree of tolerance for desiccation. Many plants germinate in response to heat and water, and are able to complete their life cycle during a single growing season. These plants are known as *ephemerals.*

Some plants, such as sagebrush, are able to survive through months or even years of drought. These plants, known as *xerophytes,* are the most common form of plant life in severe deserts. They grow only during periods of favorable temperature and water availability. Other plants, such as the mangrove forests, have their roots in standing water. These plants are known as *hydrophytes.* They cannot withstand prolonged droughts. Plants that live in moist, but not wet, conditions are known as *mesophytes.* Some of these plants are able to survive only a short period of drought while others survive somewhat longer. Some plants do not grow on the ground but are found high in the trees of the world's rainforests in both the tropics and temperate climates. These plants are known as *epiphytes.* They rely on rain water falling on the trees.

## Humidity

The relative humidity of an area has a direct effect on transpiration, which in turn plays a major role in determining the character of vegetation. When the relative humidity is high, for example, plants tend to be pulpy and fast-growing. Even at a very high humidity, plants will lose water in transpiration, because the leaf temperature is usually higher than that of the surrounding air due to the influence of radiational heating on the leaf surface. In low relative humidity, plant growth is small and hard. In the desert areas where the lowest relative humidity prevails, the plants develop water storage tissues in order to survive.

The relative humidity is of practical importance in plant life. If, for example, the relative humidity for desert shrubs falls below a certain point for a continuous period, plant disease is more likely. Further, the relative humidity influences the effectiveness of chemical sprays on plants. During periods of low relative humidity, the sprays may not enter leaves and therefore may not control disease.

## Atmospheric Pressure

The density of the atmosphere varies with elevation. In high mountains there is a relative scarcity of oxygen, which affects not only human beings and animals, but also vegetation. Plants that are native to the high altitudes are acclimated to the low amount of oxygen; plants transferred from lowland areas are adversely affected and sometimes die. Some low-altitude plants can become adapted to these conditions if they are slowly acclimated to the low oxygen content of the mountains.

### Wind Velocities

The wind movements of a region affect vegetation both directly and indirectly. They influence the climatic conditions within a region, indirectly affecting plants by changing precipitation regimes and evaporation rates. When air moves through trees, a difference in humidity develops between the leaf surfaces and the surrounding air. This difference thus affects the rate of evaporation and transpiration from the leaves.

Winds of high velocities may alter growth patterns. If a wind blows steadily from a single direction at high velocities, trees will frequently have their leaves and even their trunks stripped on their windward side. This process is enhanced if the wind carries sand, sleet, or snow particles. The stripped trees are known as *flagform trees.* They are found most often in the arctic, in alpine areas, and in semiarid regions.

Wind velocities are also important in controlling tree stands in many parts of the world. Wind is an important factor in toppling weak, old trees, giving young, healthy trees the opportunity to thrive. This process is particularly important in tropical forests. In the subarctic areas, strong winds frequently combine with a thick snow cover to limit the limbs of trees to the heights above the snow cover. The form of these partly denuded trees is called *krummholz.*

### Day Length

The life cycles of many plants are influenced not only by the intensity of light, but also by the length of the light period during the day. In many plants the length of the day controls the date of flower-bud formation and thus the time of flowering. This function is called *photoperiodism.*

Plants that are affected by the length of day can be divided into four groups. First are the long-day plants, which flower when the days are long and cease to flower when the days shorten. This group includes such plants as cineraria, heather, plantain, radish, and spinach. The second group are those plants which require a minimum amount of sunlight and require a dark period of specific length for flower-bud development. These plants include the daisy, poinsettia, ragweed, and strawberry. The third group are plants whose light requirements are intermediate between those of the first two groups. They flower only when the daylight is between 12 and 16 hours. The final group is day-neutral plants, which include the tomato, dandelion, and cucumber. They will flower under all daylight conditions.

## SOIL CONDITIONS

The soil *(edaphic)* factor is as important to vegetation as the climate of an area. Plants and soil are strongly influenced by each other. The type of soil is a major factor in determining which plant species can be grown upon it. Because the roots of most plants are so finely divided, a large portion of the total plant is underground. The plant depends upon soil, not only for anchorage, but also for water and nutrients. Plants also have a major influence on the development of soil, so that an interdependence exists between them.

The chemical properties of the soil affect the growth of all plants. Each plant has an optimum range of acidity or alkalinity, beyond which it is affected adversely. Thus the pH of a soil can be important in determining the type of vegetation found in an area. For example, alkaline soils derived from a limestone bedrock frequently have plant species such as grasses that thrive on calcium-rich soils. The type of vegetation frequently provides a key to the agronomist as to the type of soil found in the area.

The chemical leaching of soils also affects the growth and distribution of vegetation. When a soil is highly leached, many hydrogen ions attach themselves to soil particles, reducing the availability of nutrients to plants. Highly acidic soils, with their high concentration of hydrogen ions, thus have a lower natural fertility than basic soils.

Soil texture is a physical property that is of great importance to the growth of plants. Friable soils, such as sandy soils, permit roots to grow and develop easily. However, sandy soils also present some problems. When the soil is friable, water retention is poor and plants may experience a water deficiency during dry spells. In contrast, if the soil has a high silt and clay content and is compact, roots have difficulty in developing and thus the extent of branching of the roots is decreased. Possibly the most desirable soil for creating a luxuriant vegetational cover is one composed of a mixture of sand and clay. This combination produces a loam soil that allows good root development and also retains sufficient water for plant growth.

## GEOMORPHIC CONDITIONS

Such factors as elevation above sea level, degree of slope, and slope orientation help determine the character and distribution of plant life in a region.

The effect of differences in elevation is easily illustrated in a desert region. In the lowland desert areas the vegetation is sparse, but as elevation increases it is likely to become more luxuriant. The species change as well, frequently forming a succession of plants. Desert shrubs and cacti in the low areas may merge with grassland, and at still higher elevations a forest covering may develop. This change in vegetation is primarily due to increases in precipitation at higher elevations, accompanied by a decrease in temperature and lowered evapotranspiration.

Differences in slope position change the climate and soils of an area, thus affecting vegetation. For example, equatorward-facing slopes receive a great deal more radiation during the course of a year than poleward-facing slopes. In warm regions vegetation is more abundant on the cooler, more humid poleward-facing slopes.

### FIRE

Fire occurs so often in nature that it must be considered an evolutionary force in the development of plant life. Lightning is the major cause of natural fires. It is estimated that the earth receives an average of 100 lightning strikes every second, and it occurs in almost all regions. It is the major cause of natural fires, which may be the dominant factor in the history of many forest, grassland, and desert shrub communities of the world. With the possible exception of the wettest and the coldest regions, fires have ravaged vegetation everywhere for millennia.

Fires are not only the result of natural causes. Even the earliest peoples used fire to clear vegetation from areas. Fires were also used in ancient times in the production of wild seeds, tubers, berries, and nuts. Burning is still a frequently used means of controlling the type of vegetation in an area. In the savanna areas of the tropics, for example, fires can maintain grasslands at the expense of trees. Fires have also been used to preserve wilderness areas, to increase forest production, to enhance the habitat for game, and to increase the productivity of grassland. However, in the burning process the virgin vegetation is altered.

### ANIMALS

Animals alter the vegetation of the earth, both constructively and destructively. Their greatest influence may have come from the great herds that have occupied the grasslands of the world. For example, the bison maintained and altered certain aspects of the North American grasslands. The prairie grasses consist of a number of species. If the taller species, known as *decreasers,* are not grazed, the shorter species, known as *increasers,* will not thrive. As the bison grazed the prairie grasses, they helped develop a balance between the two types of grass so that both thrived.

Animals, including birds, are important in the distribution of seeds of plants. The animals and birds eat the seeds and deposit them in other places in feces. Other seeds are attached to the fur of animals or are carried by birds to distant places, where they sprout.

### HUMANS

Human activities have had a major influence on the growth and distribution of plants. From antiquity fires have been set to burn the grasslands and to clear tracts in forests. This periodic burning has altered the virgin vegetation of vast areas, and the use of fire to clear land continues to the present day.

Humans have eliminated most of the areas of virgin vegetation in the world. Only in the most inaccessible regions, such as the tropical rainforest and the taiga of the subarctic, are there remnants of the original climax vegetation. Forest regions, in particular, have been destroyed. The white pine forests in northeastern United States, for example, were so valuable for lumber that the forest has essentially disappeared.

## WORLD NATURAL VEGETATION REGIONS

Plant communities that have evolved thousands of miles apart may have a very similar appearance, but on close examination these areas are always found to be composed of different species. Thus all world classification systems must be general in nature. Nevertheless, recognizable plant communities do occupy large areas of the world and form the basis of vegetation regions. In essentially all instances vegetation regions merge gradually into one another. These zones of transition are known as *ecotones.* On world-scale maps, the boundary between two vegetation regions is usually drawn, rather arbitrarily, through the middle of the ecotone (Plate 7).

### TROPICAL FORESTS

#### Tropical Rainforest

The tropical rainforest is very widely distributed, generally coinciding with the Afi climate in the Köppen-Geiger classification. Representative areas include the Amazon Basin in South America; large portions of the Congo

Basin, Cameroon, and the southwest coast of Nigeria and Ghana in Africa; and parts of the Indo-Malaysian area of Asia.

The tropical rainforest is a densely forested environment (Photo 54). Three levels of vegetation are frequently recognized in the typical rainforest. The highest level consists of solitary giant trees that reach levels of 50 to 60 meters (165 to 195 feet), extending far above the rest of the forest. The middle layer of trees, at 30 to 40 meters (100 to 130 feet) in height, provides a massive canopy through which sunlight has difficulty penetrating. Beneath this middle layer is the bottom portion of the forest, which has little undergrowth because of lack of sunlight. The tree trunks are usually slender with few branches. The crowns begin at considerable heights where sunlight is available.

About 70 percent of all species growing in the rainforest are trees. Most striking is the large number of species. A single acre of land may contain as many as 50 species, most of them belonging to different families. The species of the tropical rainforest also vary considerably in each of the major areas of the world where this plant community is found.

A number of plants other than trees have adapted themselves to the environment. Lianas are plants that have not developed a rigid stem, but use the trees to support themselves as they reach upward to the sunlight. These twining plants normally have spines or thorns to prevent them from slipping from the trees. Epiphytes germinate in the topmost branches of trees, which then serve as their base for growth.

**PHOTO 54**
Tropical rainforest. This densely forested environment occurs in the upper Amazon Basin in Peru. Note the solitary giant tree and the compact middle layer of trees.

Although the ground may be quite clear from undergrowth, moving about in the rainforest is usually difficult. The soil is perpetually wet, so the roots of the trees do not penetrate deeply into the ground. Plank-buttress roots spread out horizontally to 15 meters (50 feet) or more, and they grow up the trunks of the trees as high as 10 meters (30 feet). As a consequence the ground becomes an impenetrable mass of intertwining roots. Movement is further impeded by the trunks of fallen trees.

The tropical rainforest has developed largely on Oxisols. This soil is extremely poor in nutrients and is highly acid (pH 4.5 to 5.5). The world's most luxuriant vegetation thus grows on an infertile soil. This seemingly contradictory situation exists because the nutrients required by the forest are found in the vegetation that falls on the surface of the ground. Great masses of plant material are deposited on the floor of the rainforest each year. This material decays rapidly in the hot, humid climate and releases its nutrients immediately. The rotting surface material thus provides a plentiful supply of nutrients to the roots of the trees.

If the virgin rainforest is not disturbed, the growth can go on uninterrupted indefinitely. As soon as an area is deforested, however, an intense leaching of the soil begins. Within a few years the existing plant life has absorbed all of the remaining soil nutrients. Cultivation can thus go on only for a few years. If cultivation is discontinued, a secondary forest evolves that requires centuries to reach the luxuriance of the virgin forest.

The rainforest has made many adaptations to the tropical environment. For example, because the radiation is intense, the temperature of the exposed leaves may be as much as 10°C (18°F) higher than the already high air temperature. As a consequence the trees have evolved thick, leathery leaves that resist transpiration losses. The leaves can further reduce water losses by closing their stomata during the daylight hours.

## Tropical Monsoon Forest

The type area of the tropical monsoon forest is the monsoon region of southeast Asia. While it corresponds closely with the monsoon (Am) climate in northeastern India, it is also located in parts of Burma, Thailand, Laos, Cambodia, Vietnam, and northern Australia. These forests are also found on the borders of the tropical rainforest in Africa, Madagascar, Indonesia, South America, and Central America.

The tropical monsoon forest reflects the dry period that prevails in these regions. Not only is the vegetation less luxuriant than in the tropical rainforest, but the trees also shed their leaves during the dry season. As a general rule, the tropical climate is considered to be seasonal if there are fewer than 40 rainy days in the four consecutive driest months.

The three levels of vegetation are not as well developed in the tropical monsoon forest as in the tropical rainforest. The tropical monsoon forest provides a nearly complete canopy, but the great trees that reach the highest levels in the rainforest are poorly developed. Because intense sunlight does not penetrate through the leaf canopy, the floor of the tropical monsoon forest has minimal vegetation.

The tropical monsoon forest has nearly as many species of trees as the rainforest. The lianas and epiphytes are usually well represented. One of the important commercial trees of the monsoon forest is teak, which is found primarily in Burma, Indonesia, and northern Australia. The teak region is sometimes referred to as the moist teak forest. However, teak rarely occupies more than 10 percent of the total stand. The teak forest is largely limited to those areas where rainfall does not exceed 200 centimeters (80 inches). Teak is replaced by other species when the rainfall is less than 150 centimeters (60 inches).

A special feature of the tropical monsoon forest is the flowering of the trees. The flowers tend to be large and conspicuous, appearing during the dry season when the trees stand leafless. The flowering is made possible by the moisture retained in the tree and obtained from the ground after the dry season begins. In places the flowers make the forest a mass of color.

### Savanna Woodlands

The savanna woodlands occur on the equatorward margins of the tropical savanna (Aw) and the poleward margins of the tropical rainforest (Af) climates. The savanna woodlands have a distinct dry season, and they receive less rainfall than the tropical monsoon forest. These forests occupy much of the Brazilian Plateau, large areas of eastern and central Africa, much of the Deccan Plateau of central India, and the margins of the Caribbean.

This woodland looks much like a park, with widely spaced trees and thorny plants dotting the grass mantle. The density of trees varies according to the availability of moisture. The trees, usually 12 to 18 meters (40 to 60 feet) in height, are rarely more than 0.3 meter (1 foot) in diameter, have a thick bark, and normally develop an umbrella-shaped crown. The leaves are small to conserve water, and thus provide little shade. The number of species of trees is much fewer than in the tropical rainforest. They include acacia, mimosa, and members of the legume family. The trees are deciduous in character, losing their leaves during the dry season. They develop leaves and also flower when the rains return. There are few, if any, lianas and epiphytes that are so characteristic of wet tropical forests.

## MIDDLE AND HIGH LATITUDE FORESTS

### Sclerophyll Forest

The sclerophyll forest region has its largest area of development in the Mediterranean Basin. Local names applied to the vegetation include *maquis, garigue, macchia, phrygana, shibliak,* and *tomillares.* Other areas include southern California, where it is known as *chaparral* from the Spanish word *chaparro* meaning scrubby evergreen. In central Chile it is known as *mattaral,* in southwestern Australia as *mallee scrub,* and in southwestern Africa as *fynbosch* or *karroo.*

Because the sclerophyll forest coincides closely with the Mediterranean climate, it would be easy to believe that climate determines the development of vegetation. Plant geographers have in the past accepted the concept of the direct relationship of plant distribution with climatic conditions, which has proved to be an incorrect assumption for many vegetation regions.

The vegetation of the sclerophyll forest is dominated by an evergreen, leathery, drought-resistant foliage that varies in height from 0.5 to 3 meters (18 inches to 10 feet). The woody vegetation varies in structure and appearance, depending largely upon the length of the dry season where it is located. In the wettest areas it consists of small trees such as cork, oak, live oak, pine, and olive. These trees provide an open canopy. In somewhat drier regions, trees tend to disappear, and shrubs form a dense covering over the ground. In the driest regions, the shrub cover is not only discontinuous but also lower, reflecting a lack of moisture. Since the shrubs are hard-wooded and the vegetation dense, passage across these areas is difficult.

Plants have made important adaptations to this fairly rigorous environment. The shrubs' roots go deep to reach sources of water. The species have also adapted to the fires that are common in all sclerophyll forest regions. After a fire, annual grasses dominate for a few years, but the woody plants once again assume dominance by sprouts that come from the roots of old plants or by new germinations. Many species have seeds that will lie dormant for years and will germinate only after their structure has been altered by fire. The plant community of an area is normally completely restored within 30 years after a fire.

### Broadleaf Evergreen Forest

These forests are located on the equatorward borders of the humid subtropical (Cfa, Cwa) climates. Extensive areas of this forest are found along the Gulf coast of the United States, southern Japan, southern China, southwestern South Africa, the eastern Pampas of Argentina, southeastern Australia, and small areas of New Zealand. The extent of these forests is limited by such physical factors as sandy soils, poor drainage, and fire.

These forests resemble the forests of the wet tropics in that they do not have a seasonal leaf fall (Photo 55). The vegetation is not as luxuriant, however, with fewer lianas, epiphytes, and buttressed tree trunks. The number of tree species is quite large, and includes acacia, eucalyptus, cypress, live oak, laurel, and magnolia. The high tree canopy allows sufficient sunshine to penetrate the forest so that a shrub undergrowth develops.

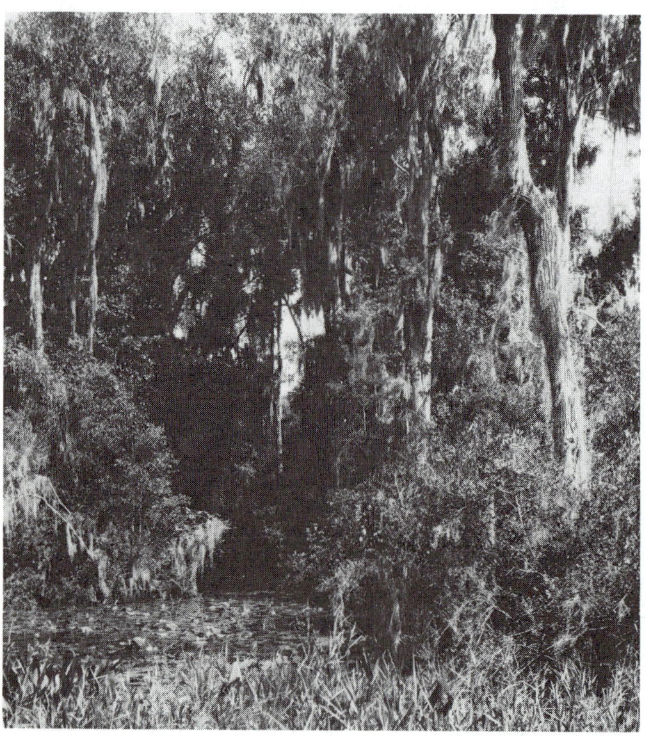

**PHOTO 55**
A cypress and live oak forest in Florida. Note the Spanish moss on the trees. The swampy waters harbor wild ducks, water moccasins, and alligators. (Courtesy: U.S. Forest Service)

### Broadleaf Deciduous Forest

The broadleaf deciduous forests were the virgin forest communities that once covered much of northeastern United States, western and central Europe, and eastern Asia. These forests coincide fairly closely to the humid continental, long summer (Dfa) and the marine west coast (Cfb) climates of the world. These areas thus have cool to cold winters, and mild to hot summers, with adequate year-round precipitation (Photo 56).

The virgin broadleaf deciduous forests have essentially disappeared from the earth. In their places are now some of the most densely populated regions of the world. Nevertheless, the original forest community can be reconstructed from existing remnant forest areas. The number of species of trees in this forest has been greatly influenced by its location in relation to the areas of Pleistocene glaciation. In Europe this forest lay between the continental ice sheet to the north and the area of Alpine glaciation to the south. The forest had nowhere to migrate, so many species perished. In China and the United States, the forest was able to migrate equatorward during the Ice Age, preserving many species. The Chinese and American forests thus have a much greater variety of species. In the United States, for example, such trees as the oak, maple, hickory, beech, ash, birch, walnut, elm, and tulip tree abound.

The broadleaf deciduous forest is normally multilayered. Open canopies of trees about 20 to 35 meters (65 to 115 feet) high exist through which sunlight can penetrate. Beneath the high leaf canopies, rich shrub and

**PHOTO 56**
A broadleaf deciduous forest of maple, oak, beech, hickory, and other species. (Courtesy: Paul A. Moore, Tennessee Conservation Department)

herbaceous strata exist. The weak sunlight on the forest floor discourages the growth of annuals. Moss will develop on the trunks of trees but the leaf covering normally prevents it from growing on the forest floor.

The trees of this forest lose their leaves as an adaptation to the cold season. The change in the color of the leaves from green to yellow and reds in autumn, frequently before the first frost, is likely a response to the decreasing length of daylight. Because the trees are bare in winter, they lose little water, and their water budget has a surplus. In summer, transpiration is great from the broad leaves, so that a tree requires a great deal of water to survive. For short periods during the summer the tree may experience a water budget deficit, retarding its growth.

**PHOTO 57**
White pine stumps. The last major white pine stand was cut in Michigan between 1900 and 1908. These stumps are the remnant of this forest covering. (Courtesy: U.S. Forest Service)

## Middle Latitude Coniferous Forests

The middle latitude coniferous forests occur under a number of climatic regimes, including the humid subtropical, marine west coast, and humid continental, warm and cool summer climates. The largest areas occur in North America, including the coniferous forest of the Pacific Coast states, western Canada, and southern Alaska; the pine forests of the southeastern part of the United States, extending on the Coastal Plain from New Jersey to Florida and westward to Texas; and the remnants of the great pine-hemlock forest that once extended from Minnesota across northern Michigan, northern Pennsylvania, and southeastern Canada to the Atlantic coast. In Europe small areas of coniferous forests occupy the Alps, Carpathians, and other highland areas, as well as sandy areas of a number of coastal plains.

Because of the wide distribution of the forests, each region has developed a distinctive array of species. The middle latitude coniferous forests of North America reveal these differences.

The coniferous forest that extended from Minnesota eastward to the Atlantic was dominated by white pine, red pine, and eastern hemlock. At its climax this forest reached a height of about 70 meters (230 feet). The canopy provided a dense covering so that ground cover was scanty. A mat of needles covered the ground, retarding runoff. Because the trees of this forest were extremely desirable for lumber, nearly all of this virgin forest had been removed by the end of the nineteenth century (Photo 57). The climax forest remains only as small remnants in protected parks such as Cook Forest in northwestern Pennsylvania.

Several coniferous species are localized in southeastern United States (Photos 58, 59, and 60). The loblolly, shortleaf, pitch, longleaf, and slash pines are most common. The pine forests have their best development on sandy, poorly developed soils and in low-lying marshy areas. The climate of southeastern United States is suitable for the development of the same type of broadleaf deciduous forests that developed to the north. Why, then, are only small areas of deciduous trees found in southeastern United States? Ecologists believe that deforestation by Indian tribes occurred over hundreds of years in this region, destroying the deciduous forests. They further believe that if this region were left to reforest itself undisturbed for several hundred years, the pine forests would be ultimately replaced by a deciduous broadleaf forest (Figure 11.5).

The third area of middle latitude coniferous forests in Anglo-America is usually called the Western forest (Photo 61). In contrast to the other two areas, where the virgin forests have essentially disappeared, the Western forest still has vast tracts of virgin timber. Because these forests occupy a large area with changing environmental conditions, the species of trees vary greatly over the region. On the coasts of Alaska and British Columbia, where temperatures are cool and precipitation exceeds 200 centimeters (80 inches) annually, the dominant tree is Sitka spruce (Photo 62). In southern British Columbia and Washington, western cedar and western hemlock assume dominance with extensive tracts of Douglas fir. From Oregon to central Cali-

**PHOTO 58**
Virginia pine forest. A 45- to 50-year-old stand of Virginia pine shows an undergrowth of dogwood, sweet gum, and black oak. (Courtesy: U.S. Forest Service)

**PHOTO 59**
A firelane is being plowed in a pine forest of Mississippi. (Courtesy: U.S. Department of Agriculture, Soil Conservation Service)

**PHOTO 60**
Turpentine production. The tapping of pine trees to produce turpentine in Georgia.

fornia the giant coastal redwood challenges all other species. The redwoods thrive despite a marked summer drought. The high humidity, which is partly due to the dense coastal fogs, provides sufficient moisture for the giant trees. While the redwoods reach a height of over 120 meters (390 feet), the other species are from 50 to 70 meters (160 to 230 feet) tall. Of the species in the Western forest, Douglas fir and the redwoods are most valuable and will soon be depleted by lumbering companies. Because the redwood requires hundreds of years to reach maturity, it must be protected in park areas if it is to survive.

## Boreal Coniferous Forest (Taiga)

The boreal coniferous forest is limited to the Northern Hemisphere, essentially coinciding with the subpolar continental climate (Dfc). In North America it stretches from western Alaska to Newfoundland in eastern Canada. In Eurasia it extends from Norway on the west to the northern Japanese islands on the east (Photo 63). The equatorward boundary of the forest is where the daily average temperature for 120 days is below 10°C (50°F) and where the cold season exceeds 6 months. The polar boundary between the forest and the tundra is where there are only 30 days with a daily mean temperature above 10°C (50°F) and where the cold season is over 8 months.

The typical tree in the boreal coniferous forest is the spruce, but the species composition does vary over the vast areas of this forest. Spruce and pine predominate from Norway to the Ural Mountains, but to the east in Siberia other species of trees appear, such as the Siber-

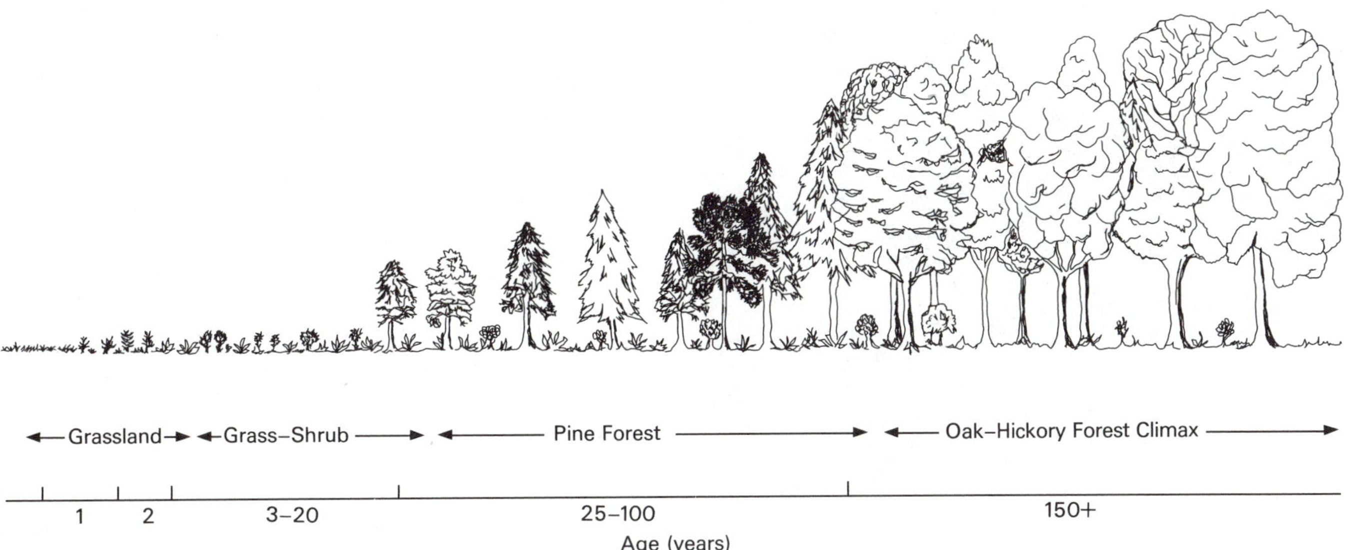


**FIGURE 11.5**
Open-field succession in a middle latitude forest region. This diagram illustrates a typical plant succession from open land to forest in the middle latitudes. The succession goes from grass to shrubs to pine trees, and finally to an oak-hickory forest climax. The succession is likely to require more than 150 years. (From *Fundamentals of Ecology,* 3rd Edition, by Eugene P. Odum. Copyright © 1971 by W. B. Saunders Co. Reprinted by permission of Holt, Rinehart and Winston, CBS College Publishing.)

**PHOTO 61**
Clear-cutting remains a major means of logging in the Western coniferous forests. Logging roads are evident on the steep slopes, where serious erosion has occurred. (Courtesy: U.S. Department of Agriculture, Soil Conservation Service)

**PHOTO 62**
This Sitka spruce cut in British Columbia has a diameter of over 3 meters (9 feet). (Courtesy: Travel Bureau, British Columbia Government)

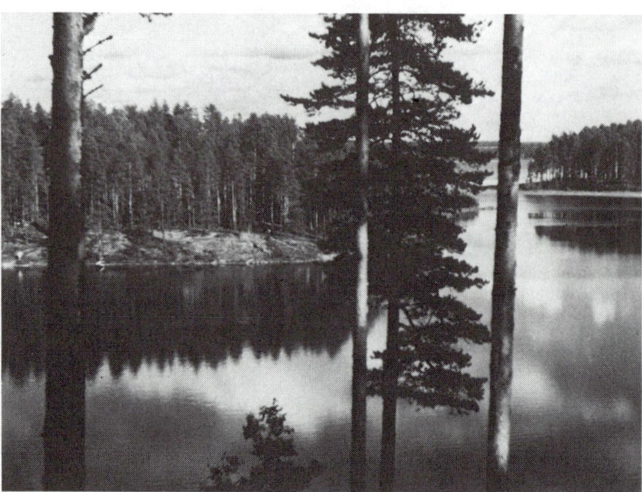

**PHOTO 63**
Boreal coniferous forest. The coniferous taiga in Finland. (Courtesy: Finland National Tourist Office)

ian fir, the Siberian larch, dwarf Siberian pine, and the Siberian spruce. In eastern Siberia and Hokkaido the dominant trees are firs and the Yezo spruce.

This forest has developed largely on Inceptisols, Histosols, and Spodosols that have a raw humus layer, a leached eluvial A-horizon, and a compact B-horizon. Local soil diferrences are important to the type of forest that evolves. In eastern Canada, for example, the white spruce and balsam fir dominate on the better soils, while black spruce and tamarack (larch) are found on the poorly drained areas.

These vast boreal coniferous forests present an impression of monotony. The dense coniferous trees blanket the earth so that the undergrowth is scanty or nonexistent. The ground is covered with a decaying litter of needles and wood. Vast areas also occur where drainage is so poor that trees cannot survive. In these *bogs* or *muskegs,* the dominant plants are bog moss and cotton grass (Photos 64 and 65).

The coniferous trees have adapted well to the cold, hostile environment. Their needles have a small surface area, so the tree loses little water by transpiration during the long winter months when no water is available from the frozen ground. The green needles are also able to begin photosynthesis and other physiological processes as soon as the temperature rises in the spring. The conifers thus have a great advantage over the deciduous trees, which must grow new leaves before the growth processes can begin.

When a forest is cut or destroyed by fire, the area is revegetated very slowly. After the brush stage, the first trees to appear are normally birch and aspen, followed by pine. Spruce appears at the climax stage. The entire process may take one thousand years. In Sweden, a study revealed that the birch stage required 150 years and the pine stage 500 years. Once the virgin forest is removed, it rarely, if ever, achieves a climax stage again.

## GRASSLANDS

### Tropical Grasslands

In the nineteenth century it was usually thought that the low latitude savannas coincided with the tropical savanna (Aw) climate. Recent evidence, however, indi-

**PHOTO 64**
Taiga and muskeg in Alaska. The spruce trees may have 100 years of growth.

**PHOTO 65**
Muskeg on the northern edge of the taiga in Alaska. Brush predominates with isolated spruce trees.

cates that this assumption was incorrect. Studies have revealed that the savanna vegetation has developed in areas that vary from perennially wet to those that are semidesert. Numerous modern researchers have come to the conclusion that frequent fires over a long period are sufficient to replace a forest vegetation with savanna. Some evidence also exists that savannas are a response to local soil conditions and not to a particular climate.

The largest area of tropical savanna is situated in Africa. It lies north, east, and south of the tropical rainforest. In Australia the tropical savanna surrounds the desert region, and in South America the tropical savannas lie north and south of the tropical rainforest in Venezuela and Brazil.

The term *savanna* is used in all tropical areas where grasses and sedges predominate. The tropical savannas are found mostly in the areas where the annual precipitation ranges from 150 centimeters (60 inches) to a low of 60 centimeters (24 inches) and where there is a distinct dry season. Savannas vary widely, from treeless grasslands to sparse woodlands. Trees exist in those areas where the potential evapotranspiration is not excessive. Because of the vegetational differences, the tropical savannas have frequently been divided into three major types.

The most luxuriant savanna is called the high-grass, low-tree savanna. It occupies the area of highest precipitation, and the evapotranspiration is low enough to allow tree growth. This savanna is best developed in Africa where the name elephant-grass savanna is applied. The grasses are never less than 1.8 to 2 meters (6 to 7 feet) high and frequently reach 4 meters (13 feet). The covering is so thick that it is difficult to penetrate. The trees, primarily deciduous, form an open canopy and frequently occur in groves. They rarely stand more than 10 to 15 meters (33 to 50 feet) high.

The tall-grass savanna has a covering that is 0.6 to 1.8 meters (2 to 5 feet) high with a sparse covering of trees. In Africa this region is known as the acacia–tall-grass region, but it has other names in different areas of the world. This savanna reflects the decreasing amount of rainfall and higher evapotranspiration.

The third major type of savanna occurs in the driest areas that border on the low latitude semiarid regions. It is characterized by a discontinuous cover of desert grasses along with a scattering of small thorny trees and brush. In Africa this savanna is called the acacia–desert-grass savanna.

The African savanna supports large herds of grazing and browsing animals such as the elephant, zebra, gazelle, giraffe, and buffalo as well as such predators as lions and cheetahs. These great animals are now endangered in much of the African savanna because the land is increasingly being turned over to agricultural uses.

### Middle Latitude Prairie and Steppe

The middle latitude prairie and steppe occupies extensive areas. In Anglo-America these grasslands extend in a north-south belt from the southern edge of the boreal coniferous forest of Alberta and Saskatchewan to the Gulf coast. They border the foothills of the Rocky Mountains on the west, extending eastward to the Midwest plains of Illinois and western Indiana. Outlying grasslands are found on the intermontane basins and plateaus as well as in the Central Valley of Callifornia, the Kentucky Blue Grass Region, and the Nashville Basin of Tennessee. In the Eurasian continent a belt of grasslands extends eastward from western Ukraine, south of the Ural Mountains. It surrounds the deserts of Central Asia and continues eastward in southern Siberia to Manchuria. In Asia its southern limits are the high mountains, and its northern limits are the boreal coniferous forests. In South America the middle latitude grasslands include the Pampas of Argentina, southeast Brazil, and Uruguay. These grasslands extend from the coast to the foothills of the Andes Mountains. In southern Africa the tropical savanna merges with the middle latitude prairie and steppe.

Because the prairies and steppes occupy vast areas, the grass species vary considerably. The Anglo-American prairies and steppes illustrate these differences in characteristics. Three types of grassland vegetation can be recognized: true prairie or tall-grass prairie, mixed prairie or short-grass steppe, and Pacific prairie or bunch-grass prairie.

The true prairie occupies the area with the highest precipitation, usually averaging between 60 to 100 centimeters (24 to 40 inches). These prairies thus are situated on the eastern side of the Anglo-American grassland. They occur in areas where the depth of the soil moisture is greater than 60 centimeters (24 inches). The luxuriant grasses grow to a height of 1 to 1.2 meters (3 to 4 feet). They are a mixture of sward-forming grasses, bunch grass, and the common stipa grass. These plants form a dense covering of the ground with occasional tussocks standing above the general grass level.

Ecologists have long wondered why trees are generally absent in the true prairie. Experiments have demonstrated that when natural conditions prevail over a sufficient length of time, trees encroach upon the prairie, with a bush zone in the vanguard, at the rate of about one meter (one yard) per three to five years. The lack of trees is likely a response to several factors. First, fire is a common feature of the grasslands. A study of fires in 1965 revealed that one fire caused by lightning occurred for each 5,000 hectares (12,500 acres). Secondly, the prairies at an earlier time were the home of vast herds of bison and antelope. These grazing animals will destroy all small trees and shrubs. Finally, the true prairie region is subject to periods of long droughts, such as the one that occurred between 1934 and 1941. These droughts retard or even destroy trees in the area. These combined factors have provided an environment favoring grass. Because the grasslands have been well-suited to human settlement, little virgin grassland remains.

The true prairie gradually merges with the mixed prairie or short-grass steppe. This area lies eastward of the Rocky Mountains. Because precipitation is less, the depth of the soil moisture is usually less than 60 centimeters (2 feet). As a response two distinct forms of grass appear. Common throughout the area are grasses 0.4 to 0.6 meter (1.5 to 2 feet) in height as well as dwarf grasses, such as buffalo and grama, that provide a dense ground covering.

In the areas west of the Rocky Mountains, particularly in Idaho, Washington, Oregon and California, the Pacific prairie or bunch-grass prairie has evolved on the driest area that still supports a grassland vegetation. In contrast to the true prairie and mixed prairie, which were characterized by a turf or sward, the Pacific prairie is characterized by tussocks of grass. Stipa grass, a common bunch grass, is universally found in these dry grasslands.

## DESERTS AND TUNDRA

### Desert Scrub

The desert vegetation has evolved in the low latitude (BWh) and middle latitude (BWk) desert areas of the world. The largest areas of desert vegetation are located in the great deserts of central and southeastern Asia and northern Africa. Other great desert areas include central Australia, southwest Africa, southwestern United States, and northern Mexico.

Deserts are defined as regions of the world where the potential evapotranspiration is much higher than the annual precipitation. Only rarely are deserts completely without some plant life (Photo 66). Even the most arid regions, which appear without plant life most of the time, contain dormant seeds that spring to life after the rare showers. The rain showers may be years apart.

In the deserts of the world are found two major types of plant life. Some species are nourished directly by rain and may thus be dormant for long periods of time. These rain-dependent plants may be annuals or perennials. They are noted for their ability to complete the life cycle in a short time: Within a few days they will sprout, flower, and produce seeds. The seeds are protected against the long period of dryness by an almost impervious coat of dry plant material.

**PHOTO 66**
Desert scrub. Pricklypear cactus and low brush predominate in this desert scene of southwestern United States. The low grasses have been destroyed by aridity and overgrazing. Most of the rain that strikes bare desert ground is lost by runoff, and that which does penetrate into the Aridisol is used by the brush. Erosion can be a serious problem in such a region. (Courtesy: U.S. Department of Agriculture, Soil Conservation Service)

Other plants live in protected places, such as depressions and valleys, and seek water through their root systems. Two types of root systems have become adapted to the desert environment. Plants such as the sagebrush and creosote bush have roots that penetrate deeply into the earth to the water table. The roots of other plants are shallow but spread out over a wide area. This group of plants includes the saguaro cactus and Joshua tree. Many of these plants store water in their stems or other organs for use during dry spells. In general, the drier the region, the further apart the plant growth.

Although deserts occupy areas of the earth with wide temperature ranges, the structure of desert vegetation from continent to continent is remarkably similar. The vegetation of the Sonoran and Mohave deserts of the United States and Mexico is more spectacular than that of most other desert areas. The Joshua tree, ocotillo, opuntia, and saguaro cacti, which grow 6 to 9 meters (20 to 30 feet) high, give this area the appearance of a colorful, prickly woodland. In the areas of the Great Basin where the precipitation is from 13 to 25 centimeters (5 to 10 inches), the ground may be nearly covered with such bushy plants as sagebrush. Similar stands of aromatic, woody shrubs are found in the deserts of Central Asia.

## Tundra

The tundra is limited to the northern fringes of the North American and Eurasian continents and to high mountain areas where the average temperature does not exceed 10°C (50°F) for the 2- to 3-month growing season. The tundra vegetation consists dominantly of grasses and sedges with a substantial underlayer of dwarf shrubs, mosses, and lichens (Photo 67). On the equatorward side of the tundra a nearly complete covering of these vegetational materials occurs. On the poleward side of the tundra, on the fringes of ice caps, and on exposed sea coasts, the vegetation becomes meager. Exposed areas and stony soils also support little or no vegetation. On the margin between the tundra and the boreal coniferous forest, the tundra vegetation normally occupies the exposed hill crests, and small trees occupy the lower, protected valley bottoms. Over vast areas of the tundra, bogs and moors have evolved that resemble the bogs and muskegs of the taiga. These bogs consist mostly of mosses and cotton grass. In many places they have a luxuriant growth so that, as the vegetation becomes compact, peat develops.

The vegetation of virgin tundra is normally only 10 to 25 centimeters (4 to 10 inches) in height (Photo 68). The tundra does not produce a particularly attractive landscape. The grasses, mosses, and lichens, even when in bloom, appear grayish to yellowish. This color occurs partly because these plants, in order to reduce transpiration, retain the dead remains of the previous year's growth.

The plants of the tundra have adapted to the rigorous environment. The short growing season, strong winds, permafrost, and low temperatures for the extended winter period are major factors influencing tundra development. Many examples can be found to show how plants in the tundra minimize the environmental hazards. On the exposed windward sides of slopes the plants are low growing and cling tightly to the ground, reducing exposure to the winds. Many of the flowering plants bloom at the beginning of the growing season. They use the energy stored from the preceding year to flower, and produce seeds during the remainder of the growing season for the following year. In this way they minimize the danger of the early frosts that are common to the tundra regions.

**PHOTO 67**
A tundra landscape of mosses and lichens in Lapland. (Courtesy: Finland National Tourist Office)

**PHOTO 68**
Tundra. Dwarf shrubs, mosses, and lichens near Nome, Alaska.

# HUMAN MODIFICATION OF THE WORLD'S NATURAL VEGETATION

The modification of natural vegetation began with the appearance of people on the earth. As civilizations evolved, the process accelerated until today only the least accessible areas contain virgin vegetation. Because human beings are now occupying the most inhospitable environments, these areas are undergoing rapid changes that are altering their virgin ecosystems. This process is occurring in two areas: the tropical rainforests and the semiarid and arid desert regions.

## TROPICAL RAINFOREST ECOSYSTEM

It was once thought that the tropical rainforest would never disappear because of its vast extent of possibly 15,000,000 square kilometers, its exuberant growth, and its great number of species. In recent years, however, huge tracts have been cleared, not only to obtain the lumber, but to open areas for agricultural production. New technology and chemicals have helped to advance these endeavors.

It is difficult to balance the benefits against the costs of exploiting the resources of the tropical forests. Balancing positive against negative aspects is rarely an easy task, and it becomes acutely difficult when the effects are unevenly distributed over time. For example, clearing land will bring an immediate return for the lumber sold and will provide the land for permanent agricultural pursuits. However, it may also deprive generations of an irreplaceable genetic resource. If proper conservation methods are not followed, the land may become unproductive in the future. Evaluating short- and long-term costs and benefits is not only an economic matter but also an ethical and moral problem.

### IRREVERSIBLE NATURE OF TROPICAL RAINFOREST DESTRUCTION

If a forest area is cleared, recovery depends upon the persistence of the small seedlings on the spot, the regeneration from dormant seeds, or the possible recolonization from outside. In the temperate forests many of the species can continue to exist as isolated specimens, providing the basis for reforestation. Conditions therefore favor redevelopment. Thus, in spite of mass destruction at a given time, the temperate forests continue to thrive.

The situation in the tropical rainforest is quite different. While the temperate forests have only a few important species—rarely more than 10—the tropical forests have from 100 to 150 species. Many species are represented by a few trees. Dispersal mechanisms are generally inefficient, so the possibilities for recolonization of individual species are small. The life span of the seeds is short, and successful regeneration occurs only under forest conditions. The plants of the tropical rainforest have adapted over millions of years to specific physical conditions; when the land is cleared the tropical plants cannot adjust to the nonforest environment.

When a new vegetational covering develops on cleared tropical forest lands, it is made up of different species, creating a different ecosystem. This process is often called *savannization* or *desertification* of the humid tropical areas. Once the tropical rainforest is removed, it will disappear rather than regenerate itself. The destruction of the virgin tropical rainforest is thus an irreversible process.

### IMPACT OF TROPICAL RAINFOREST DESTRUCTION

The disappearance of the tropical rainforest would have far-reaching consequences. Not only the biological world but also the human society of the tropics would be changed.

#### Climatic Modification

Although precise data are not available, the removal of the tropical rainforest appears to be one of the most powerful mechanisms for altering the planetary climate. Simulation models developed in the Atmospheric Science Division of the Lawrence Livermore Laboratory in California suggest the following conditions will follow deforestation: Initially the surface albedo will be increased, followed by reduced absorption of solar energy. The surface will cool, with less evaporation and sensible heat flux. As a consequence, convective activity and rainfall will decrease, with reduced release of latent heat. These processes will weaken the Hadley circulation and the cooling in the middle and upper tropical troposphere. The tropical lapse rate will increase, resulting in increased precipitation in the latitudinal bands from 5 to 25 degrees north and south of the equator. There will also be a decrease in the equator-pole temperature gradient, causing less heat and moisture to be transported out of the equatorial regions. These changes will result in global cooling and a decrease in precipitation between 45 and 85 degrees north and 40 to 60 degrees south. Thus the temperature and the water budget of the earth would be altered.

It must be remembered that this type of model is speculative. It suggests what would occur to the world's climate, but is not an absolute indicator. Although the forecast of the model cannot yet be proven, it is consistent with physical principles. The basic question demands our attention: Can land use changes in the tropical rainforest irreversibly alter the world's climate?

## Precipitation and Drainage

The forest covering is the principal regulator of the quantity and quality of water available in the tropical rainforest. A study of the Amazon Basin by F. W. Freist found that the soil's capacity to hold moisture declined from 51 percent of the precipitation in the virgin forest to 12 percent on deforested land, but rose after revegetation to 35 percent.

The removal of the forest increases the flooding potential, with consequent rapid soil erosion. As a result, siltation of the flood plains is greatly increased downstream. The erosional phase is frequently followed by drought in the area, because the Oxisols dry out quickly even when the precipitation is heavy.

Land clearing without proper conservation measures produces serious deterioration of the land's fertility. In the tropical rainforest the preservation of a forest covering is likely to be the most effective means of maintaining the productivity of a drainage basin.

## Reduction of Genetic Variety

If the tropical rainforest is destroyed in the near future, millions of years of plant and animal evolution will be lost. Thousands of species will disappear before any aspect of their biology has been investigated, and their value determined. Even today it is known that the range of chemical compounds found in the tropical forests is unmatched anywhere else in the world. This vast forest ecosystem has the potential of providing sources for food, drink, medicines, contraceptives, gums, resins, scents, pesticides, and many other useful items not presently known. A loss of a species is thus a potential loss of a product whose value is unknown today. The loss of species has already occurred in several tropical forest areas, and deforestation continues.

It must be remembered that a great many chemicals now used were not invented but were discovered in plants. It is a frightening prospect that such valuable resources could be lost forever.

## Impact on Indigenous People

In the tropical rainforests are tribes of people whose way of life is adjusted to the forest environment (Photo 69). Although these people hunt, fish, and farm, they coexist with the forest rather than replace it. When development of the forest occurs, these people with their distinctive value systems are ill-equipped to cope with pressures from a new and different society.

When lumbering destroys the forest ecosystem, it also destroys the livelihood of the forest people. Once self-sufficient, they become helpless. They lose their means of subsistence and become demoralized. The most respected and competent individuals in the tribe can no longer cope with everyday life problems. Their skills in hunting, fishing, and gardening are no longer enough when they are confronted with modern economic problems. The newcomers are patronizing; they ridicule the customs and social rituals of the forest people. Traditional institutions are changed if not destroyed. As M. D. Poore of the University of Malaya stated, "This type of demoralization should not be underestimated, for to be deprived of faith in all that a person values can be as devastating as being deprived of a means of subsistence."

**PHOTO 69**
Jivaro Indian tribe. The indigenous Indian tribes of the Amazon Basin have developed a way of life adjusted to the forest environment.

The invasion of their world poses an additional hazard to the forest dwellers. They have no resistance to such diseases as influenza, measles, tuberculosis, and others. Their vulnerability to imported diseases makes these people dependent on modern medicines, and they begin to lose faith in their traditional cures. Regrettably, modern medicine is usually ill-equipped to treat diseases that are prevalent in the forest societies.

### CONSEQUENCES OF TROPICAL RAINFOREST DEFORESTATION

If the tropical rainforest were to be destroyed in the next century, the following scenario might occur: A secondary ecosystem would evolve that would be entirely different from the one that exists today. It would consist of ubiquitous shrubs and grasses, with few trees. Because little humus would be replaced, the soils would soon be leached of their fertility. Agriculture would persist only on a few volcanic soils and on a few floodplains where fertility is continually renewed. Most of the area would consist of barren, deeply eroded soils. The total natural resource of plants and animals would be lost. The indigenous population would at best be absorbed into the dominant culture; at worst, they would die from disease. Much of the area would be abandoned by the exploiters because its economic value would be gone.

While much of the virgin tropical rainforest will disappear, its complete destruction is not likely to occur. Some parts of the forest will be protected from modification, while the use of other parts will be intensified. How large must the protected areas be in order to maintain a satisfactory tropical forest ecosystem? This question remains unanswered, but without doubt the areas must include thousands of square kilometers. If this vast resource is to be preserved, certain fundamental steps must be taken: (*a*) allocation and use of the land must be adequately planned, (*b*) high conservational standards must be established for the conversion from one use to another, and (*c*) a system of continuous management must be maintained. The actions of governmental agencies as well as greater public participation will be required. The outcome will depend largely on the attitude of people and the institutions they create.

## DESERTIFICATION

Desertification is defined as the diminution or destruction of the biological potential of land, ultimately leading to desert conditions on land that was once productive. It is an ancient phenomenon, possibly dating from the earliest civilizations that arose in the semiarid and arid regions of the world. The expansion of dry regions is destructive to civilizations. Grazing lands cease to produce pasture, dry-land farming fails, and irrigated fields are abandoned because of salinization, waterlogging, or other forms of soil deterioration. Desertification is presently occurring in areas that affect about 15 percent of the world's population. It is estimated that 9 million square kilometers of the earth's surface have already been lost to desertification processes, and more than 48 million square kilometers run a moderate to high risk of being encroached upon by desert conditions. On at least 13 million square kilometers the process may be beyond recovery. There is strong evidence that deserts are migrating from their traditional areas and creeping well into subhumid zones (Figure 11.6).

While deserts have always expanded and retreated, never before have the world's deserts increased so alarmingly. During the past half-century the Sahara has lost 1 million square kilometers of land suitable for grazing and farming along its southern margins. In North Africa at least 250,000 acres are lost annually. The Thar Desert in India is extending its boundaries by at least 40,000 acres each year. Desertification of Patagonia has become a hazard in Argentina. It is now estimated that human activities have caused desertification of an area about the size of China.

### CAUSES OF DESERTIFICATION

If people are to use the semiarid and arid regions of the world for extensive periods, they must recognize the great variability of precipitation. During some years, dry regions will support a fairly large number of livestock, but in other years only a much lower number of animals can be supported. During some periods, precipitation may be below the level required for certain economic activities.

An ecological imbalance soon evolves when inhabitants do not recognize the fundamental facts of a variable precipitation regime. Arid land ecosystems are extremely fragile, and if overgrazing persists during dry periods, a rapid and radical change in the vegetational cover occurs. Desert vegetation has evolved over millions of years of adaptation to conditions of low rainfall. The above-ground portion of the plant is usually small. An extensive root system spreads out immediately below the surface to take advantage of the limited rainfall. When the plant is destroyed by aridity, overgrazing, farming, or burning, nothing is left to hold the shallow desert soil in place. Rapid erosion by wind and water then occurs. Soon only bare rock and drift-

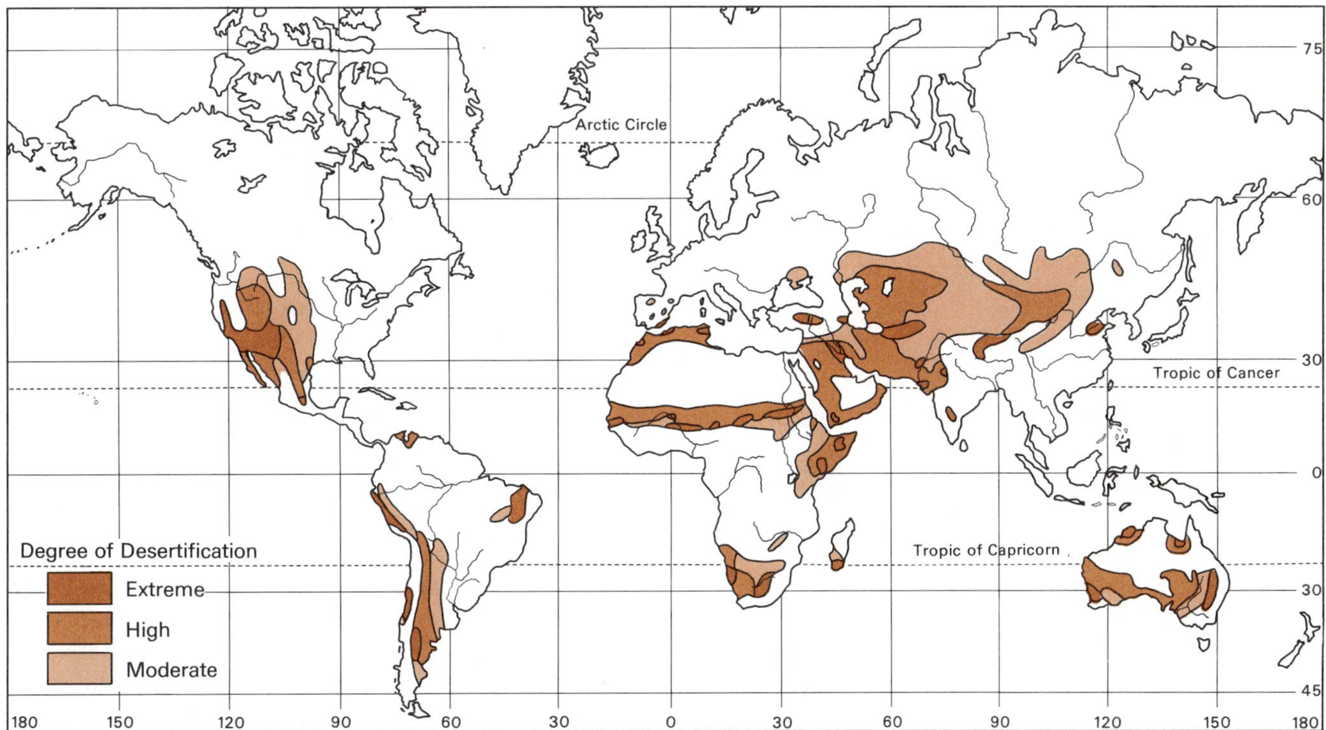


**FIGURE 11.6**
Degree of desertification. Large areas in the world are subject to the desertification process. Particularly vulnerable are western United States, central and southwestern Asia, and the regions around the Sahara and Kalahari of Africa.

ing sand remain. The ecosystem has been destroyed, and the desert invades new areas.

The spread of the desert depends upon two aspects of the arid ecology. First, it has been proven that the reproductive capacity of dry-land vegetation is seriously impaired if the yearly cropping exceeds about one-half of the annual growth. Reproductive potential diminishes even more quickly if the process continues. Secondly, regeneration of vegetation on arid land takes much longer than its destruction. When large areas are destroyed, restoration of a plant cover may require more than 20 years, even on fertile soil. The ecological succession required to restore the area to its original vegetation takes at least a century, and it may never happen.

Desertification is a response not only to physical conditions of aridity but also to the way the land is used. The process is self-perpetuating once it begins. The sequence of destructive events begins with the decrease in the plant cover, allowing wind and water erosion to accelerate. As a consequence the soil loses water-holding capacity and fertility. Vegetational growth is retarded in succeeding years, and if the land-use pattern is not altered, the plant covering is even more severely damaged. Plant cover is further reduced because the soil can no longer support the larger root systems necessary to reach the water table. Annuals can no longer produce sufficient seeds to reproduce themselves. Either a drought or overuse of the land by humans can trigger the initial desertification process. Once it begins, the human response will be fundamental to its control.

## ECONOMIC AND SOCIAL IMPACTS

The loss of the vegetational cover in a semiarid or arid land causes a decline in the economic and social base of the area. This base will ultimately collapse if desertification goes to completion. The initial response to the desertification process is likely to be psychological instability within the local settlements. The inhabitants who see their grazing lands dry up and their water supply diminish become fearful of the future. People begin to migrate to regions better able to support their livestock. These migrations frequently coincide with the dry season. The unstable condition of the economy is reflected in dilapidated housing, lack of services, and limited communication and transportation facilities. The migrants frequently live under the most primitive conditions in temporary quarters. With few or no economic opportunities, the migrants survive on aid from outside the region.

When the migrants return to the arid lands, they face numerous problems. A water supply must be available immediately. If the rains are late, the migrant may have little time to prepare the fields, or the pasture may once again be overgrazed before a vegetational cover develops. Further, it is possible that a rain or two may be missed before the sowing period begins, risking ultimate crop failure. A shortage of water near the end of the growing period may create the need for an early migration with ensuing economic loss. The complete or partial loss of a livestock herd or a crop means the people have little money to purchase basic necessities and certainly nothing for taxes and other social services.

If desertification has reached an advanced stage, the migrants may be unable to return to their original lands. This situation inevitably brings them into areas of permanent settlement where little land is available to newcomers. As a consequence, confrontation occurs for the economic resources of the area. The impact of desertification then extends far beyond the local area.

### CONTROL AND REVERSAL OF DESERTIFICATION

The causes of desertification are known, as are reasons for its recent acceleration. Human actions must be viewed as the principal agent in the deterioration of the arid ecosystems. Although the local peoples cause the problem, they are also the victims of it. The degradation of the land is invariably accompanied by the degradation of human well-being. The efforts to control and reverse the desertification process must thus center on human welfare.

Scientific information and technology are available not only to halt the spread of desertification but to reverse the recent trends. Affluent countries have been able to develop successful plans to control the spread of deserts within their own borders. Since the 1930s when the "dust bowl" devastated the Great Plains, the United States has managed to rehabilitate the area. The plan included a close monitoring of the environment and the education of farmers. When the drought returned in the 1950s, it caused much less damage. The Soviet Union needed only a few years to change cultivation patterns and partially reverse the desertification process in Kazakhstan. Australia has had long experience in preserving its scant rainfall resources and preventing the spread of desert conditions. In the poor countries, however, the reversal of desertification becomes a difficult problem. These nations have neither the funds nor the scientific and technical know-how to proceed. Aid must come from the international community if any plan is to be successful in most of the Third World countries.

Action against desertification can be successful only if governments perceive it as an integral part of their plan for social and economic development. It is gradually being recognized that a firm and self-reliant agricultural base is a prerequisite to national well-being. From this perspective a sound desert ecosystem is a key national resource.

## CONCLUSION

The types of plants, their density and structure, and how they are associated in a region are all responses to such factors as temperature, moisture, light, soil, wind, and time. If vegetation is altered and the area is then abandoned, an orderly and predictable succession of plant communities will take place until a mature, or climax, vegetation is achieved. This process may take several hundred years; in certain cases it may never occur. Once a climax vegetation stage has been reached, the plant community will be in harmony with its environment and will remain unchanged over time.

Scientists have developed world regional classifications of vegetation, similar to the systems used to classify climate and soils. In this chapter, natural vegetation formations have been combined into 12 major regional types. The forest areas are confined to the humid regions, but different types have evolved in response to differences in temperature and moisture conditions. The grasslands and xerophytic vegetation are associated with the drier realms. Forests and grasslands mingle in the transitional areas that lie between humid and dry regions. In the polar areas forests give way to shrubs and other forms of low vegetation, called tundra.

It is increasingly difficult to find areas of natural vegetation that have not been changed by human activities. Most of the grasslands and vast areas of forests have been transformed by agriculture. Forest areas are being depleted by lumbering. The last great natural vegetation expanses, which lie in the tropical rainforest, boreal forest, and deserts, are being developed for economic uses. The ecosystems of the world have been drastically changed by human activities.

## STUDY QUESTIONS

1 Describe the functions of an ecosystem.
2 How do climatic factors affect plant life?
3 Why are soil conditions important in plant growth?
4 How is fire important in altering natural vegetation?
5 How do the tropical forests differ from the middle latitude forests?
6 Why do vegetation regions merge gradually with other regions?
7 In traveling from the equator in Africa to the Mediterranean Sea, through what vegetation regions would you travel? Describe the reasons for the different vegetation regions.
8 Why is the tropical rainforest ecosystem important?
9 Why is it important that the tropical rainforest not be removed?
10 What are the causes of desertification?
11 Why is it difficult to reverse the present desertification trends?

## SELECTED REFERENCES

### SOILS

BASILE, ROBERT M., ed. *Selected Readings in the Geography of Soils.* Las Vegas, NV: University Associates, 1980.

BATTEN, J. W., and J. SULLIVAN. *Soils, Their Nature, Classes, Distribution, Uses and Care.* University, AL: University of Alabama Press, 1977.

BIRKELAND, P. W. *Pedology, Weathering and Geomorphical Research.* New York: Oxford, 1974.

BRADSHAW, A. D., and M. J. CHADWICK. *The Restoration of Land: The Ecology and Reclamation of Derelict and Degraded Land.* Boston: Blackwell Scientific, 1980.

BRIDGES, E. M. "Soil Geography: A Subject Transformed." *Progress in Physical Geography* 5 (September 1981): 398–408.

———. *World Soils.* 2d ed. Cambridge, England: Cambridge University Press, 1978.

BROWN, L. R. "World Population Growth, Soil Erosion, and Food Security." *Science* 214 (November 27, 1981): 995–1002.

BUOL, S. W., F. D. HOLE, and R. J. McCRACKEN. *Soil Genesis and Classification.* 2d ed. Ames, IA: Iowa State University Press, 1980.

BUTLER, B. E. *Soil Classification for Soil Survey.* New York: Oxford University Press, 1980.

CRUICKSHANK, J. G. *Soil Geography.* New York: Halsted Press, John Wiley, 1972.

FINKL, Charles W., ed. *Soil Classification.* Stroudsburg, PA: Hutchinson Ross, 1982.

FITZPATRICK, EWART A. *Soils, Their Formation, Classification and Distribution.* New York: Longman, 1983.

FOTH, H. D., and JOHN W. SCHAFER. *Soil Geography and Land Use.* New York: John Wiley, 1980.

GARDNER, JAMES S. *Physical Geography.* New York: Harper & Row, 1977.

HARPSTEAD, MILO I., and F. D. HOLE. *Soil Science Simplified.* Ames, IA: Iowa State University Press, 1980.

HAUSENBUILLER, ROBERT L. *Soil Science: Principles and Practices.* 2d ed. Dubuque IA: W. C. Brown, 1978.

HOLÝ MILOŠ. *Erosion and Environment.* New York: Pergamon, 1980.

HUDSON, NORMAN. *Soil Conservation.* 2d ed. Ithaca, NY: Cornell University Press, 1981.

JENNY, HANS. *The Soil Resource: Origin and Behavior.* New York: Springer-Verlag, 1980.

KNAPP, BRIAN J. *Soil Processes.* Boston: G. Allen & Unwin, 1979.

LARSON, WILLIAM E. et al. *Soil and Water Resources: Research Priorities for the Nation.* Madison, WI: Soil Science Society of America, 1981.

LYON, T. L., and H. O. BUCKMAN. *The Nature and Properties of Soils.* 4th ed. New York: Macmillan, 1943.

MORGAN, ROYSTON P. C. *Soil Erosion.* New York: Longman, 1979.

PAPADAKIS, JUAN. *Soils of the World.* New York: Elsevier, 1969.

PITTY, A. F. *Geography and Soil Properties.* New York: Methuen, 1979.

SAMPSON, R. NEIL. *Farmland or Wasteland: A Time to Choose.* Emmaus, PA: Rodale Press, 1981.

SIMONSON, R. W. "Soil Classification in the United States." *Science* 137 (1962): 1027–1034.

STEILA, DONALD. *The Geography of Soils.* Englewood Cliffs, NJ: Prentice-Hall, 1976

STRAKHOV, N. M. *Principles of Lithogenesis.* Vol. 1. New York: Plenum, 1967.

TINKER, P. B., ed. *Soils and Agriculture.* New York: John Wiley, 1981.

U.S. DEPARTMENT OF AGRICULTURE. *Climate and Man: 1941 Yearbook of Agriculture.* Washington, D. C.: U.S. Department of Agriculture, 1941.

U.S. SOIL CONSERVATION SERVICE. *Soil Classification: A Comprehensive System.* Washington, D.C.: Soil Survey Staff, 7th Approximation, 1960.

WEBSTER, R. *Quantitative and Numerical Methods in Soil Classification and Survey.* Oxford, England: Clarendon Press, 1977.

WHITE, ROBERT E. *Introduction to the Principles and Practice of Soil Science.* New York: John Wiley, 1979.

ZACHAR, DŬSAN. *Soil Erosion.* New York: Elsevier, 1982.

## VEGETATION

BENNETT, CHARLES F., JR. *Man and Earth's Ecosystems: An Introduction to the Geography of Human Modification of the Earth.* New York: Wiley, 1975.

BILLINGS, W. D. *Plants, Man, and the Ecosystem.* 2d ed. Belmont, CA: Wadsworth, 1970.

BISWAS, MARGARET R., and ASIT K. BISWAS, eds. *Desertification.* New York: Pergamon, 1980.

COLLINSON, A. S. *Introduction to World Vegetation.* London, England: G. Allen & Unwin, 1977.

COUPLAND, R. T., ed. *Grassland Ecosystems of the World.* Cambridge, England: Cambridge University Press, 1979.

DAUBENMIRE, REXFORD. *Plant Geography.* New York: Academic Press, 1978.

DE LAUBENFELS, DAVID J. *Mapping the World's Vegetation: Regionalization of Formations and Flora.* Syracuse. NY: Syracuse University Press, 1975.

———. *Deserts and Grasslands: The World's Open Spaces.* Garden City, NY: Doubleday, 1976.

DUFFEY, ERIC A. G. *The Forest World.* London, England: Orbis, 1980.

EYRE, SAMUEL R. *World Vegetation Types.* New York: Columbia University Press, 1971.

GONZALEZ, NANCIE L. *Social and Technological Management in Dry Lands: Past and Present, Indigenous and Imposed.* Boulder, CO: Westview, 1978.

GUTIERREZ, LUIS T., and W. R. FEY. *Ecosystem Succession: A General Hypothesis and a Test Model of a Grassland.* Cambridge, MA: MIT Press, 1979.

KELLMAN, MARTIN. *Plant Geography.* 2d ed. London, England: Methuen, 1980.

LAMB, ROBERT. *World Without Trees.* London, England: Wildwood House, 1979.

LIETH, H., and E. BOX. "Evapotranspiration and Primary Productivity." *Publications in Climatology* 25 (No. 3, 1972).

MILES, JOHN. *Vegetation Dynamics.* New York: John Wiley, 1979.

MONTEITH, J. L., ed. *Vegetation and the Atmosphere.* 2 vols. New York: Academic Press, 1975–1976.

ODUM, E. P. *Fundamentals of Ecology.* 3d ed. New York: Saunders, 1971.

SEARS, P. B. *Deserts on the March.* 4th ed. Norman, OK: University of Oklahoma Press, 1980.

SEDDON, BRIAN. *Introduction to Biogeography.* New York: Barnes and Noble, 1973.

SPEEDING, C. R. W. *Grassland Ecology.* Oxford, England: Oxford University Press, 1976.

SPURR, STEPHEN H., and B. V. BARNES. *Forest Ecology.* 3d ed. New York: John Wiley, 1980.

———. "Silviculture." *Scientific American* 240 (February 1979): 76–91.

TIVY, Joy. *Biogeography.* New York: Longman, 1971.

TUHKANEN, SAKARI. *Climatic Parameters and Indices in Plant Geography.* Uppsala, Sweden: Svenska Växtgeografiaka Sällskapet, 1980.

U.S. DEPARTMENT OF AGRICULTURE. *Climate and Man: 1941 Yearbook of Agriculture.* Washington, D.C.: U.S. Department of Agriculture, 1941.

VANKAT, JOHN L. *The Natural Vegetation of North America: An Introduction.* New York: John Wiley, 1979.

WALTER, HEINRICH. *Vegetation of the Earth and Ecological Systems of the Geobiosphere.* New York: Springer-Verlag, 1979.

WOODWELL, G. M. "The Energy Cycle of the Biosphere." *Scientific American* 223 (September 1970): 64–74.

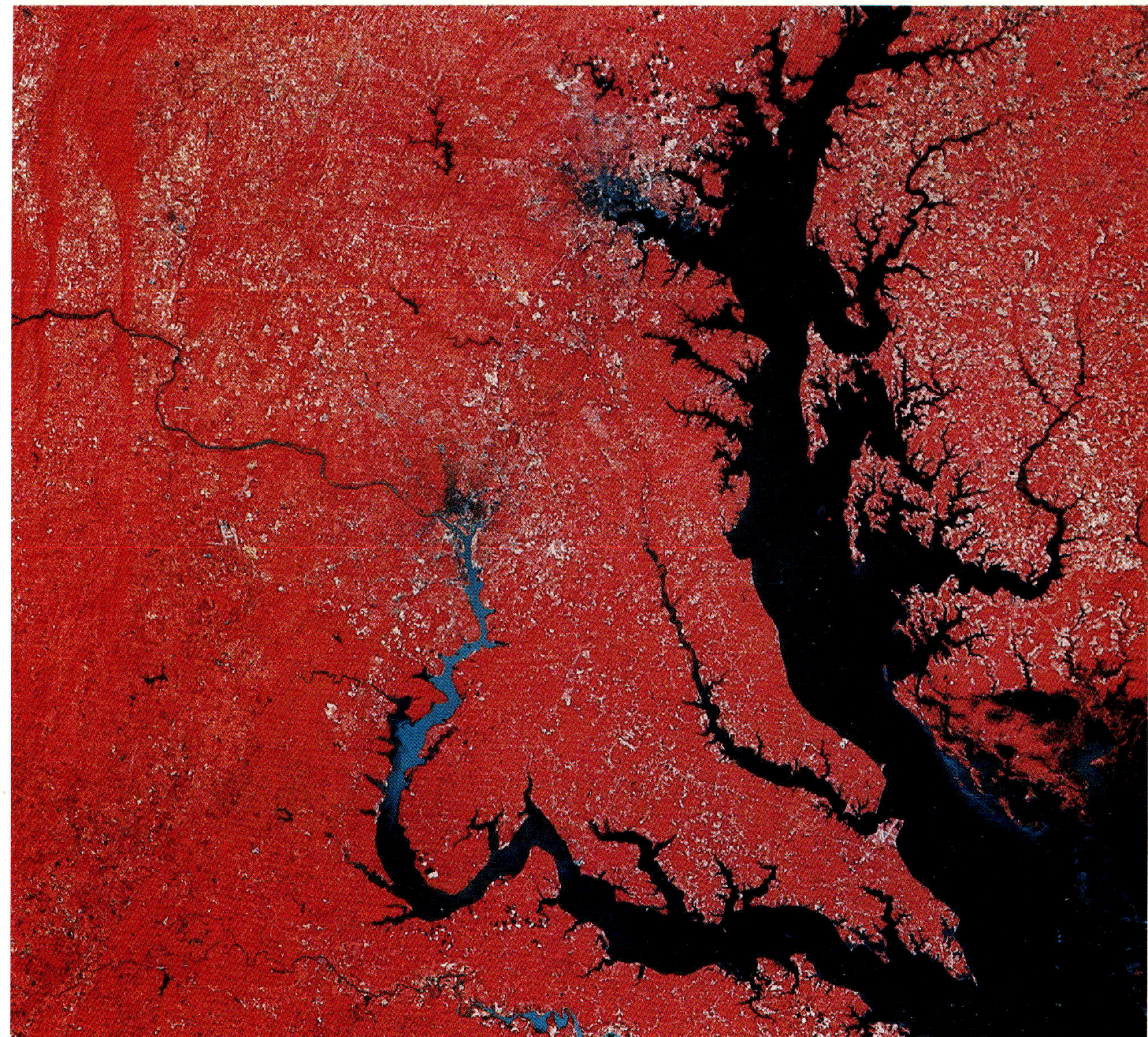

**PLATE 6**
The U.S. capital as seen from space. This satellite photograph shows the Washington, D.C.–Baltimore, Md., area from an altitude of 915 kilometers (569 miles). Some of the geographical landmarks shown here are: Washington, D.C., White House, Capital, RFK Stadium, Mall, Andrews AFB (slightly left of center); Baltimore, Friendship Airport, Liberty and Loch Raven reservoirs (upper center); Chesapeake Bay (top to bottom, right of center); Potomac and Rappahannock rivers (bottom) with light blue indicating silt in the rivers; Patuxent Naval Station (lower right); Fredericksburg, Va. (lower left); Annapolis and Bay Bridge (slightly above and right of center); Highway 70N, Monocacy River, Frederick and Brunswick, Md. (upper left); Dulles Airport (left center); Baltimore Washington Parkway (upper right).

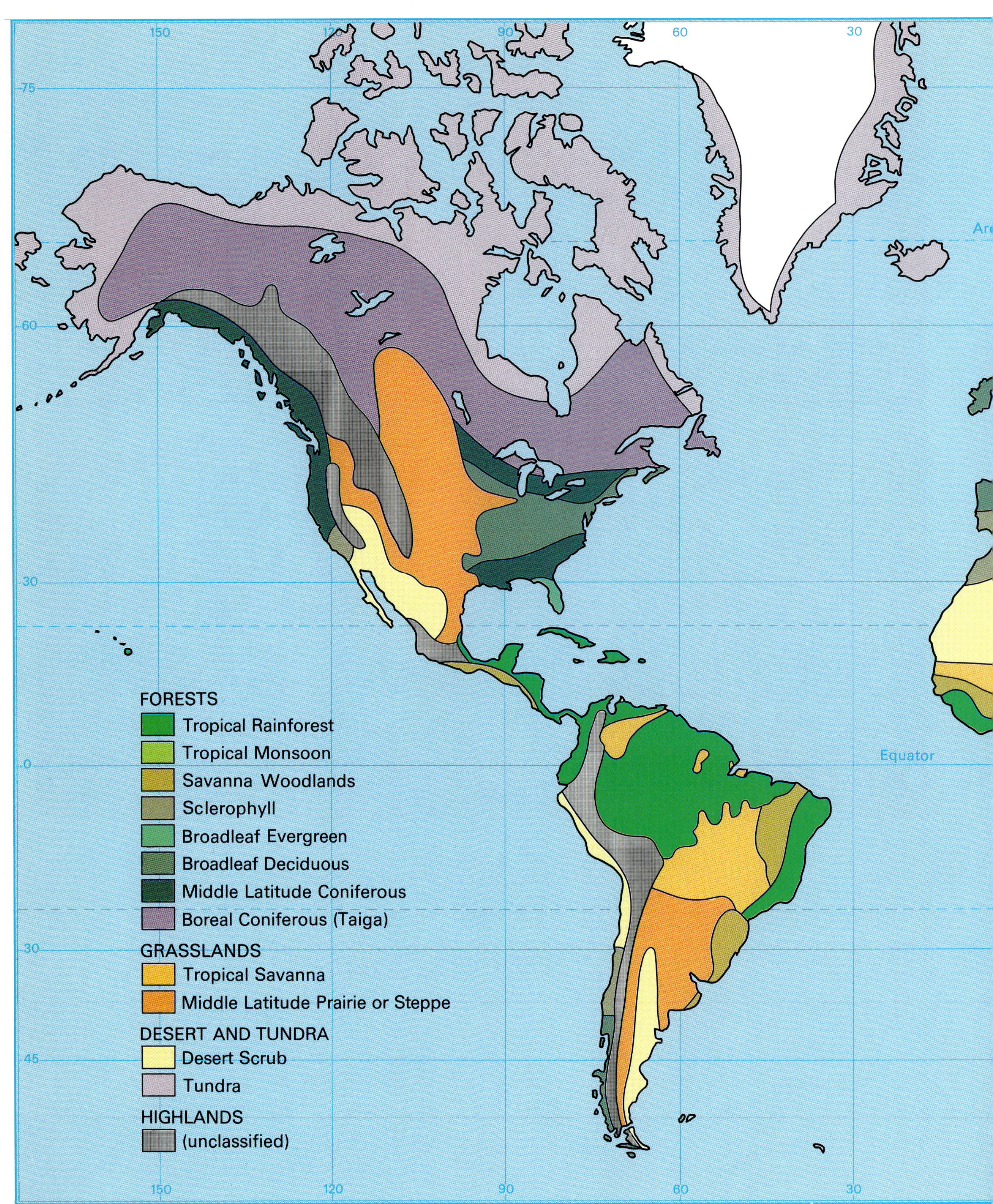


**PLATE 7**
World distribution of natural vegetation.

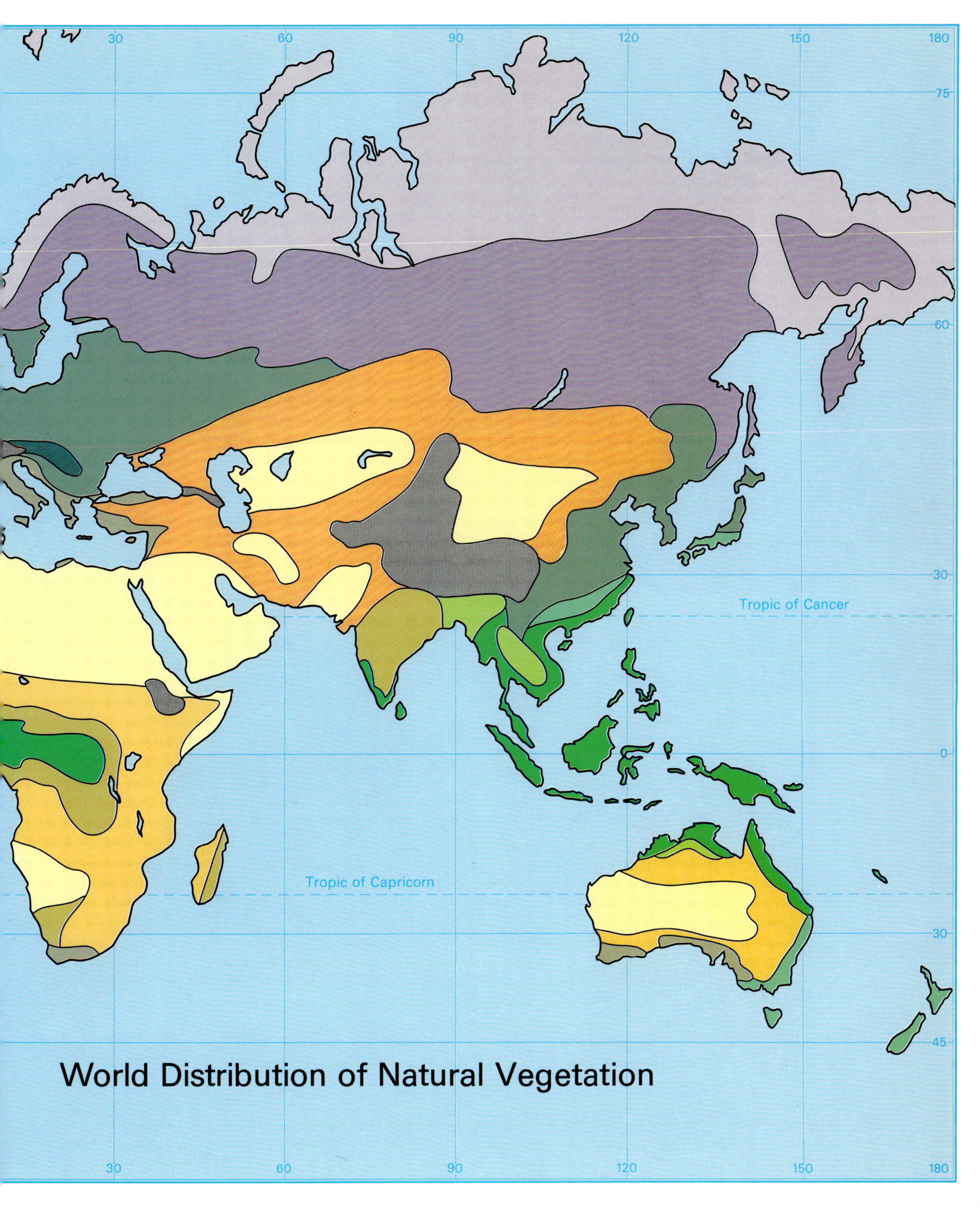


World Distribution of Natural Vegetation

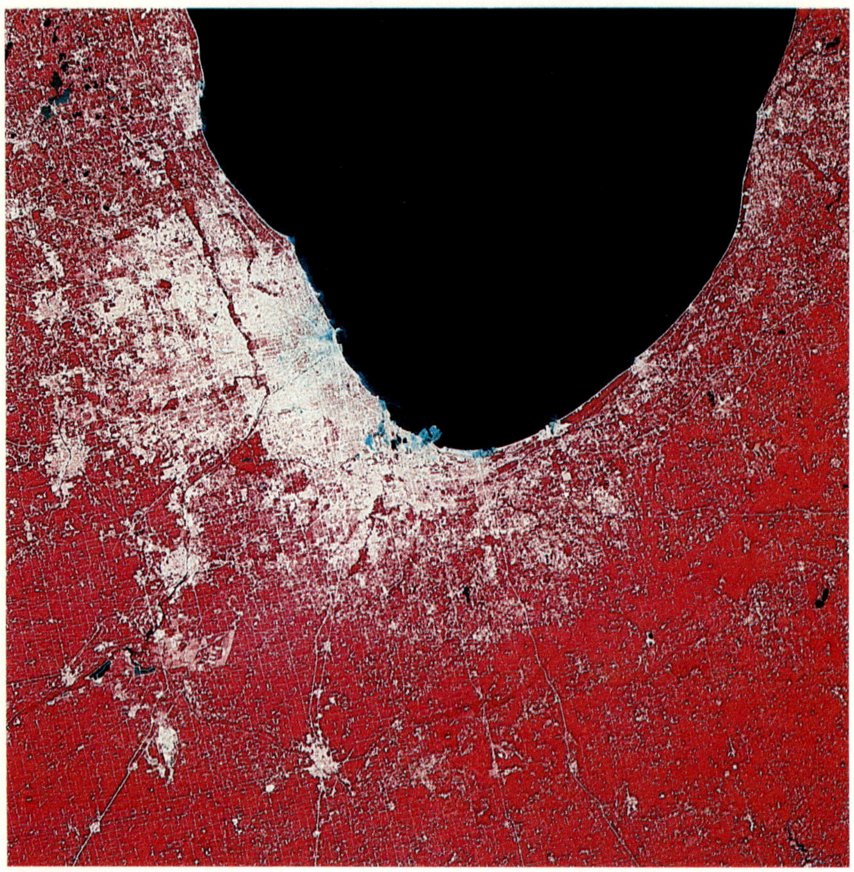

**PLATE 8**
Chicago and Lake Michigan. Landsat 2 took this picture July 22, 1977, from an altitude of 569 miles. The area covers 110 miles by 110 miles. The red color indicates rich green areas during midsummer.

**PLATE 9**
Grand Teton National Park and the Wyoming Mountains. Some of the most spectacular scenery to be seen in the United States is located within the area delineated by this image. The Teton Mountains are seen in the upper center of the image with the Wyoming Mountain Range extending from the base of the Tetons in the center to the lower right corner of the picture. The Snake River enters the scene from the upper left, where irrigated fields can be seen in its plain. The river moves southeast through the Palisades Reservoir (center) and curves northward just to the east of the Teton Range. This latter part of the Snake River flows through Jackson Hole, which appears here as a bluish-gray patch to the right of the Tetons. Jackson Hole is a downfaulted geological area whose floor varies in altitude from 6000 to 7000 feet. From this level, Grand Teton rises to 13,800 feet. The peak of Grand Teton is indistinguishable here because of snow cover over the whole range. Several major geologic faults are shown in this ERTS image. The Snake River Fault is evidenced by the sharp rise in terrain from the low plain of the Snake River where it enters the Palisades Reservoir to the mountains on the southwest shore of the river. Darby Fault and Absaroka Fault run parallel to each other, curving across the center and down to the right of the picture. The two distinct lines of mountain peaks along the Wyoming Range show where the Darby and Absaroka Faults lie.

**PLATE 10**
Northwest Wyoming. A near-vertical view of the snow-covered northwest corner of Wyoming as seen from the Skylab space station in Earth orbit. Approximately 30 percent of the state of Wyoming, as well as small portions of Montana and Idaho, can be seen in this photograph. The dark area is Yellowstone National Park. The largest body of water is Yellowstone Lake. The Absaroka Range is immediately east and northeast of Yellowstone Lake. The elongated range in the eastern part of the picture is the Big Horn Mountains. The Wind River Range is at bottom center. The Grand Teton National Park area is almost straight south of Yellowstone Lake.

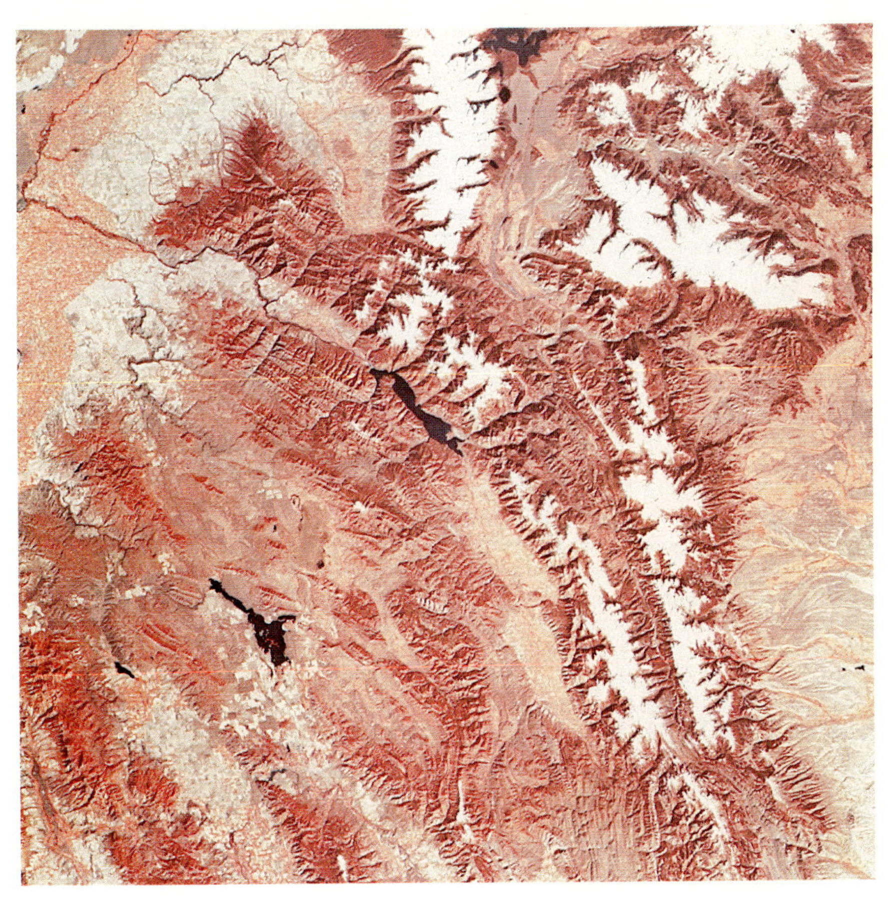

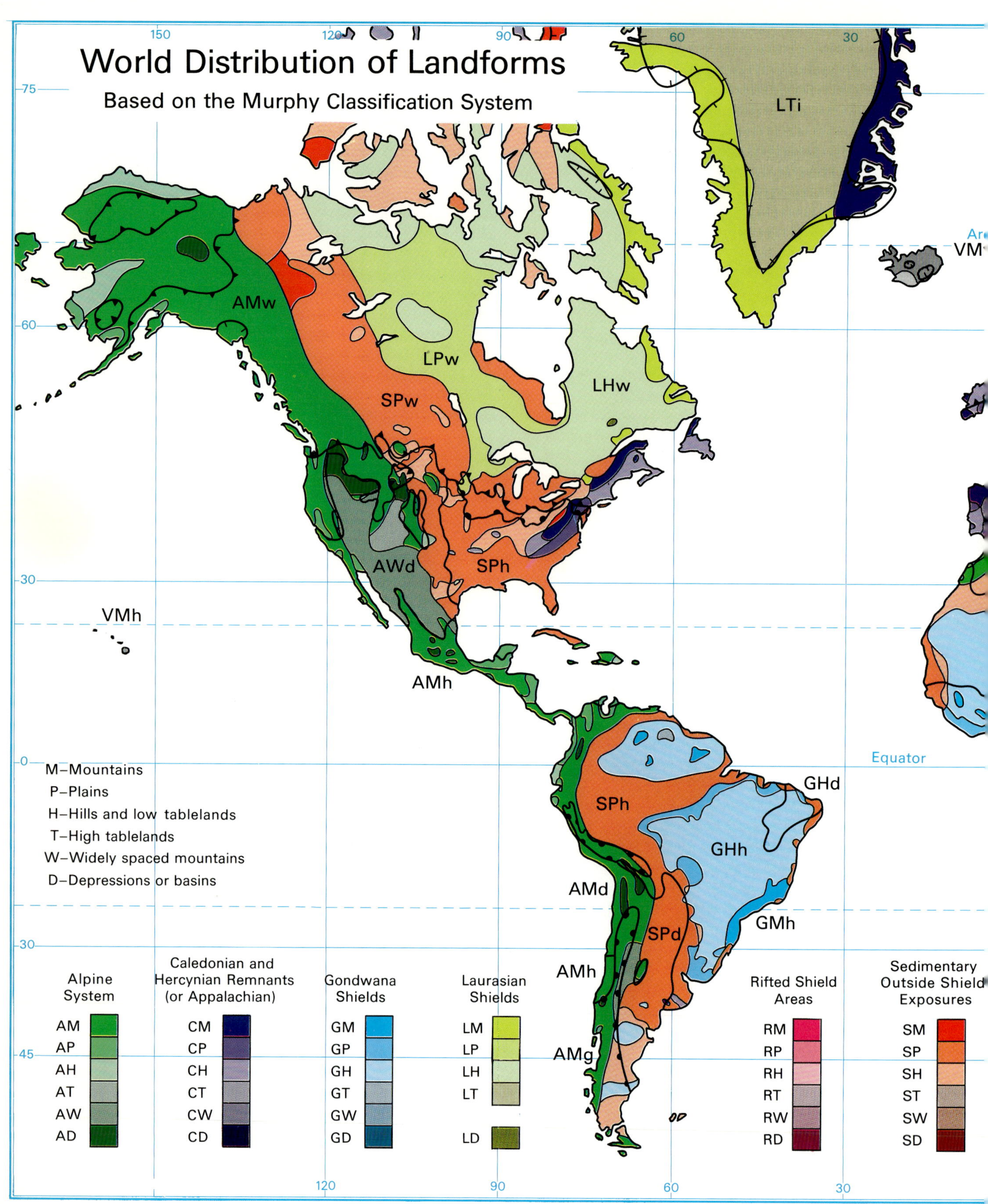


**PLATE 11**
World distribution of landforms based on the Murphy classification system. (After Murphy, 1968)

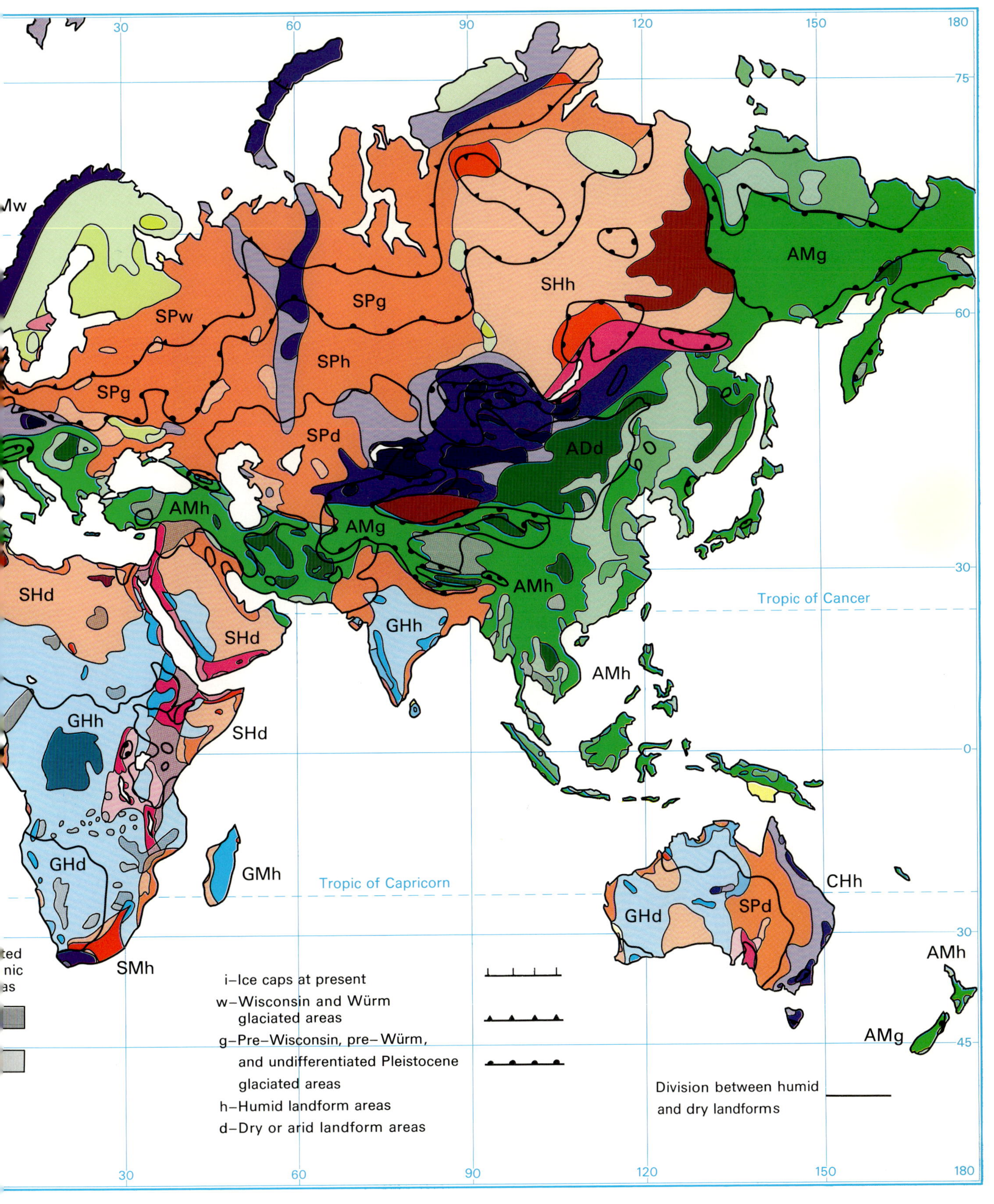

30
60
90
120
150
180
75
60
30
0
30
45
Mw
SPw
SPg
SPh
SPg
SPd
SHh
AMg
ADd
AMh
AMg
AMh
SHd
SHd
GHh
Tropic of Cancer
GHh
AMh
SHd
GMh
GHd
Tropic of Capricorn
CHh
SPd
GHd
AMh
AMg
SMh
ted
nic
as
i–Ice caps at present
w–Wisconsin and Würm glaciated areas
g–Pre–Wisconsin, pre–Würm, and undifferentiated Pleistocene glaciated areas
h–Humid landform areas
d–Dry or arid landform areas
Division between humid and dry landforms

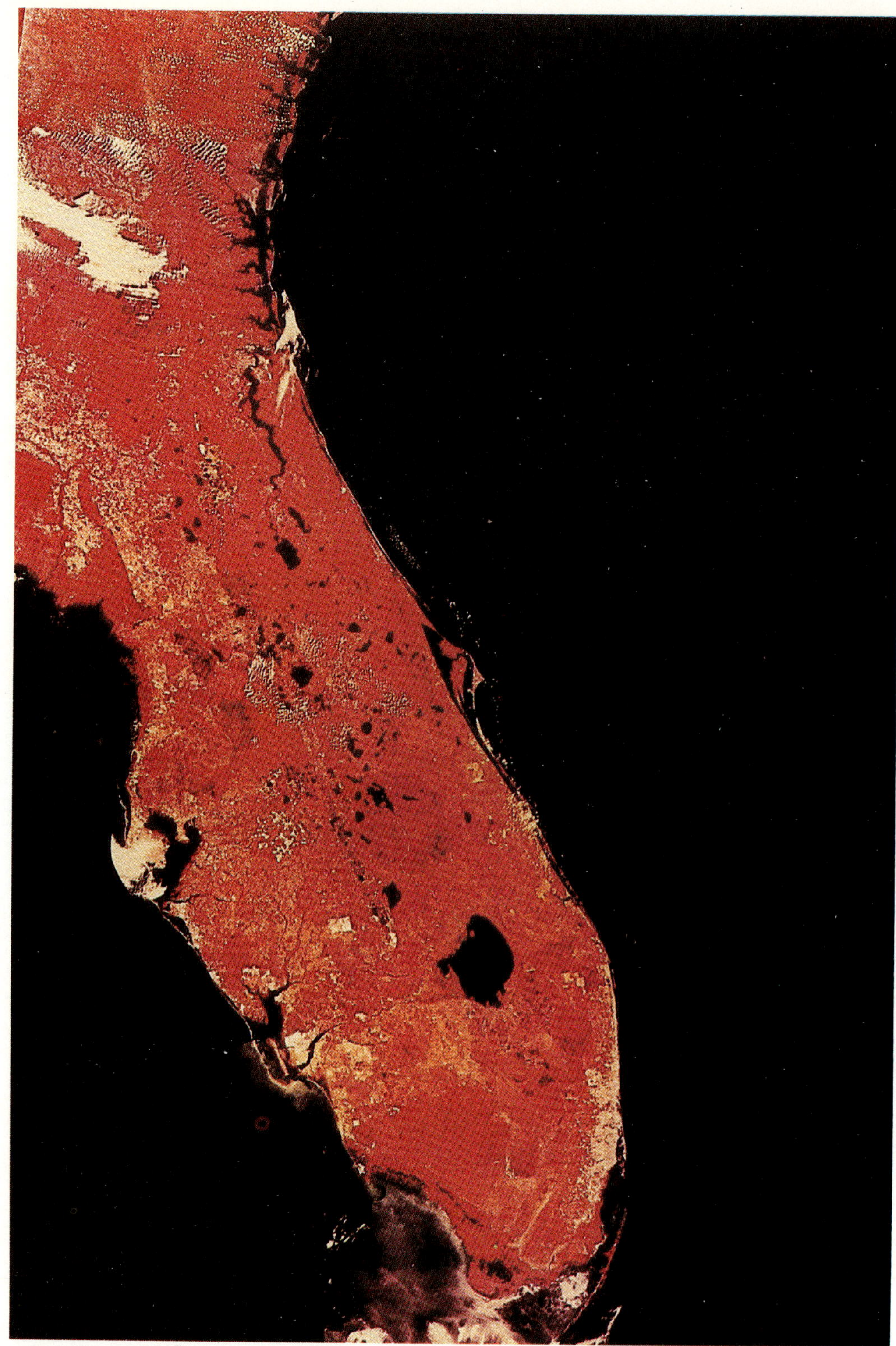

**PLATE 12**
Florida peninsula and southern Georgia. This mosaic of several satellite images covers an area nearly 500 miles from north to south. Although the picture closely simulates the appearance of a single photograph, the photo junction lines are visible in places, especially at upper left and along the coast. Some of the main landmarks visible, from north to south, include: Sea Islands of Georgia; Okefenokee Swamp (just south of cloud patch); the Tampa Bay area (left, partly cloud-covered); Lake Okeechobee (35 miles long, lower center); the Everglades (south of Lake Okeechobee, to the southwest coast); Palm Beach–Miami area (light-colored area along the coast, southwest of Lake Okeechobee); northern Florida Keys (bottom center, partly cloud-covered).

# III

# LANDFORMS

# 12

# NATURE AND ORIGIN OF LANDFORMS

## KEY WORDS

anticline
base level of erosion
caldera
clastic sedimentary rock
cleavage
crustal deformation
cycle of erosion
diastrophism
erosion
extrusive igneous rock
fault
homocline
hot spot
intrusive igneous rock
isochron
joint
lithification
magnetic anomaly
mantle
mature stage
mid-ocean ridge
old age stage
orogeny
paleomagnetism
peneplain
process
rejuvenation
seafloor spreading
stage
stratification
structure
syncline
tectonic plate
uniformitarianism
weathering
youthful stage
zone of convergence
zone of divergence
zone of subduction

Landforms are, to many people, the most distinctive features on the earth. They influence the natural environment in profound ways. A mountain barrier, for example, can alter the climate of an entire continent. It can block the movement of moisture-carrying winds from the oceans, creating a desert on its leeward side. In contrast, when a great plain faces the ocean, the moisture-laden winds penetrate far into the continents, providing water to the land.

Topographic features influence not only the physical landscape, but also the human pattern of occupance of the land. Rugged mountains may limit the number of persons who can occupy a region. A plain, on the other hand, may be densely populated and may have a highly developed economy. The dominant agricultural regions of the world are situated on plains. Because communication and transportation networks are intensively developed on plains, a cultural and political unity frequently evolves over large areas. The type of landforms an area possesses continues to play a crucial role in the evolution of human activities. The way people use a land surface may change greatly over time. Appreciating why people occupy an area in a given way at any moment requires that we understand the nature and distribution of landforms.

## A GEOGRAPHIC APPROACH TO LANDFORM STUDY

Early studies of landforms began with a description of topographic features. Simple descriptions are inadequate for modern purposes; explanations of landform development are also necessary. The present study of landforms is concerned with the processes that created a given landform and with its stage of development. This chapter considers the origin of landforms and some of the historical attempts to explain the natural landscape.

## STRUCTURE OF THE EARTH

The composition of the earth's interior has been inferred from the measurement of shock waves that travel from earthquake centers, and from the measurements of the gravity and magnetic fields of the earth. The velocities at which earthquake waves travel through the earth vary at different depths depending upon the density of the rock. The measurements of these earthquake waves by *seismographs* reveal a layered structure of the earth (Figure 12.1).

Three principal layers have been identified. The outermost shell, or *crust,* is a very thin layer from about 5 to 70 kilometers (3 to 43 miles) in thickness. It is composed of the solid rock materials that form the continents and ocean floors. The major types of rock material in the continents are composed of silicon and aluminum and are collectively known as *sial.* Beneath the ocean floors are denser types of rock consisting primarily of silicon and magnesium, known as *sima.*

The second layer, known as the *mantle,* extends downward to about 2,900 kilometers (1,800 miles). A very sharp break in seismic velocity separates the crust from the mantle. This break occurs at the *Mohorovičić discontinuity,* commonly known as the *M-discontinuity* or *Moho.* The discontinuity appears to be caused by a change in the density of the rocks. The mantle is composed mostly of high-density rocks consisting of iron and magnesium. Although the temperature of the rocks

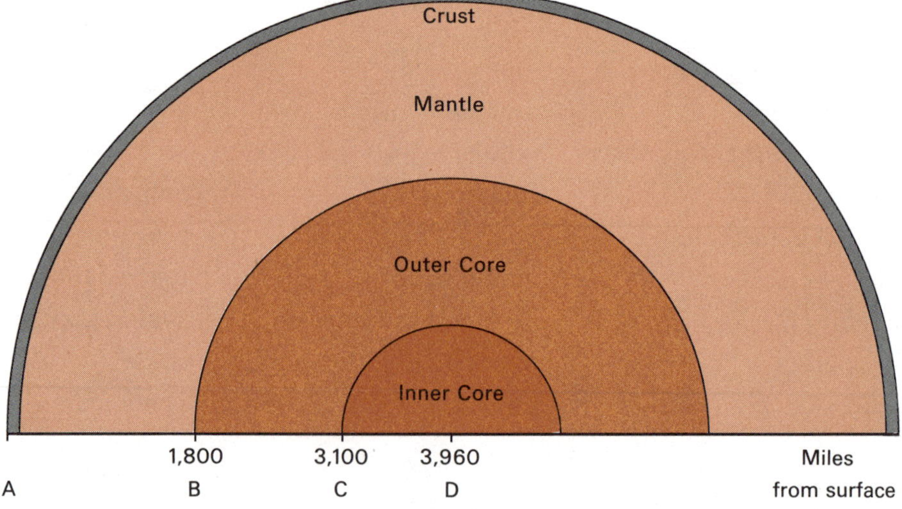


**FIGURE 12.1**
Structure of the earth. The earth is divided into distinct layers through which seismic waves travel at different speeds. Layer A is the thin crust of the earth.

is sufficiently high to melt them, the pressures are so great at these depths that the rocks no doubt remain plastic or even solid.

Molten lava erupting from volcanoes provides evidence that temperatures of the mantle exceed 1,200°C (2,160°F). The disintegration of radioactive materials provides the heat in the mantle rock. Because of density differences between the mantle and the more solid crust, the continents and oceans "float" on the mantle rock.

At the center of the earth is the *core.* This material has a radius of over 3,500 kilometers (2,170 miles), and is presumed to be of iron and nickel. The great density creates extremely high temperatures, so this layer is thought to be divided into a molten outer core and a solid inner core.

## EARTH MATERIALS

The crust and upper portion of the earth's mantle, the *lithosphere* (Greek *lithos* + *sphere*), is the material from which all landforms are developed. The character of rocks—that is, how resistant they are to the weathering and erosional processes—is determined by their origin and composition. A *mineral* consists of a chemical combination of elements, while a *rock* is a physical union of minerals. The character of a rock depends to a great degree on the composition of minerals.

### MINERALS

Most minerals are made up of two or more elements that combine to produce an inorganic solid material. Exceptions do exist: copper, sulfur, carbon, and other substances can appear as elements or as chemical compounds. Minerals have a number of physical properties that give distinctive characteristics: specific gravity, color, hardness, luster, crystal structure, and cleavage and fracture.

#### Specific Gravity

The specific gravity of a mineral is the ratio of its weight to an equal volume of water. For example, graphite is about twice as dense as water: two cubic centimeters of water weigh the same as one cubic centimeter of graphite. The specific gravity of graphite is 2. To compare, the specific gravity of iron is 5.2 and gold, 19.

#### Color

The most obvious property of a mineral is its color, and some minerals, including many gems, can be identified by color alone. Other minerals have a wide range of colors. For example, quartz ranges from absolutely colorless, glass-clear rock crystal to coal-black varieties. The nature and amount of impurities are critical factors in determining the color of a mineral. A considerable amount of experience is required to determine which colors are meaningful in identifying a mineral and which colors are so variable as to be without significance.

#### Hardness

Although hardness is relative rather than absolute, it was one of the first physical properties used to identify minerals. In 1820 Friedrich Mohs of Austria devised a hardness scale based on the concept that a harder mineral will scratch a softer mineral. Because a diamond is harder than most other minerals, Mohs assigned it a 10. Softer minerals were placed in descending order. To illustrate:

| | |
|---|---|
| diamond | 10 |
| corundum | 9 |
| topaz | 8 |
| quartz | 7 |
| feldspar | 6 |
| apatite | 5 |
| fluorite | 4 |
| calcite | 3 |
| gypsum | 2 |
| talc | 1 |

#### Luster

The luster of a mineral is the appearance of its surface in ordinary light. The two most common lusters are metallic and nonmetallic. A metallic luster indicates that the mineral reflects light in the same way as a metal such as gold, silver, or brass. Luster depends on the structure of the surface of the mineral, its transparency, and the way light is reflected from it. Diamonds are minerals having nearly total reflection, giving them a brilliant appearance.

#### Crystal Structure

Except for mercury and a few less familiar minerals, nearly all are crystalline substances. Crystals have fascinated people for centuries. The ancient and medieval literature was filled with stories of the supposed magical and curative powers of minerals. The radiance that excited these writers is caused by the orderly arrangement of the chemical elements that make up the mineral.

### Cleavage and Fracture

Many minerals break along definite planes, so that each fragment has a shape determined by those planes. Minerals that exhibit this characteristic, such as mica, are said to have perfect cleavage. Others such as quartz do not possess cleavage. Some minerals that do not have cleavage nevertheless fracture in a characteristic way. Glass, for example, has a *conchoidal* (shell-like) fracture. Other minerals, such as asbestos, have a fibrous structure and break in minute threads.

## ROCKS

Rocks are natural earth materials that make up most of the earth's crust (Figure 12.2). The form and properties of a rock depend upon the physical and chemical characteristics of the individual minerals from which it originates. Because there are many minerals and many environments in which minerals combine, many types of rocks are formed. Nevertheless, all rocks can be classified into three primary types. These are *igneous rock,* a rock formed from the solidification of molten magma, such as lava; *sedimentary rock,* a rock formed by consolidation and lithification of sediments deposited by water and wind action; and *metamorphic rock,* rocks of igneous or sedimentary origin that have been altered through geologic time by heat, pressure, chemical action, or some combination of these forces.

### Igneous Rocks

At depths of about 70 kilometers (43 miles), temperatures of 900° to 1,200°C (1,620° to 2,160°F) cause rocks to melt. If the molten magma penetrates to the earth's surface before it cools and solidifies, it creates an *extrusive igneous rock.* The lava ejected by a volcano is of this type. Extrusive igneous rocks usually cool so rapidly that the component minerals have little, if any, chance to separate and form crystals. As a consequence they are finely grained or glassy. Some lavas of this type, such as obsidian, are referred to as volcanic glass.

If the molten magma fails to reach the earth's surface before solidifying, it is termed an *intrusive igneous rock* or *plutonic rock.* Intrusive igneous rock that is embedded deep beneath the surface often requires thousands of years to solidify. Such slow cooling provides considerable opportunity for crystallization. The intrusive igneous rocks are therefore often coarse-grained.

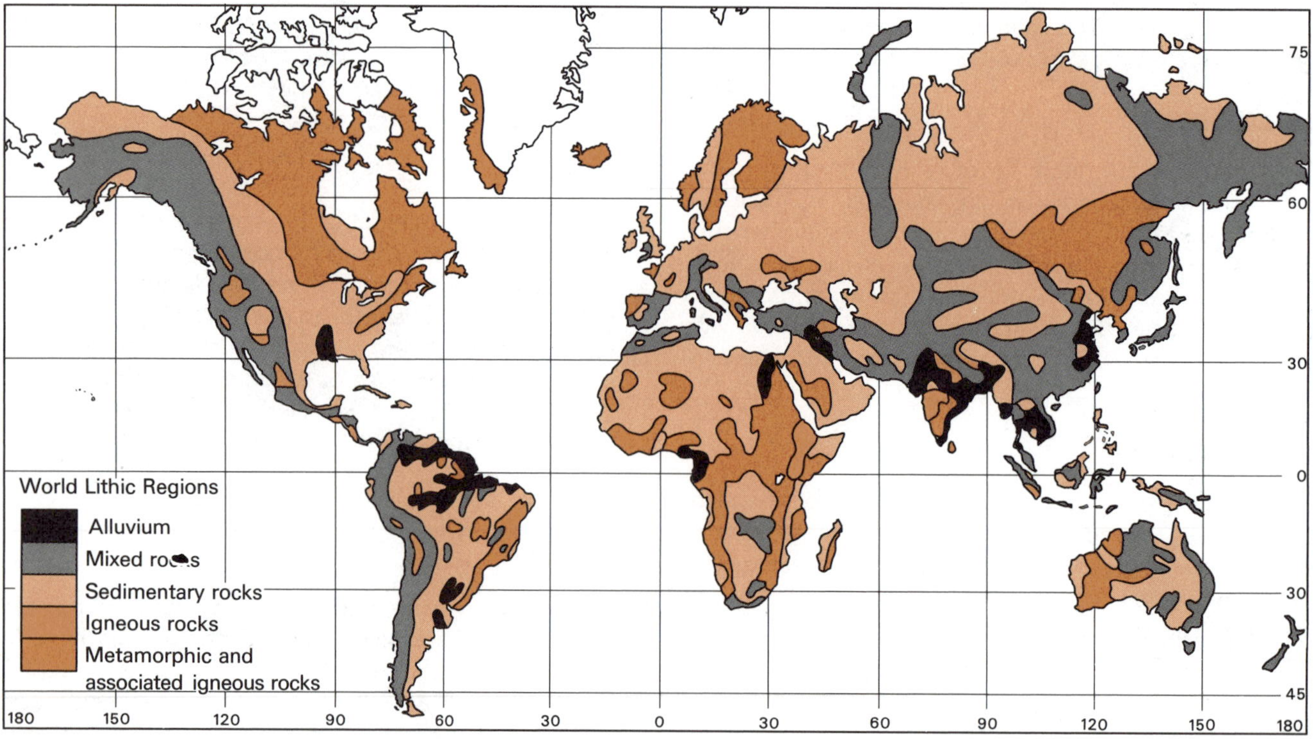


**FIGURE 12.2**
Lithic regions of the world. (After Finch and Trewartha, 1967)

The principal mineral components of igneous rocks are feldspars, quartz, pyroxenes, amphiboles, olivines, and micas. Granite is an example of an igneous rock. Because it contains large quantities of quartz and feldspar, granite is usually light gray to pink, with scattered dark mineral crystals giving it a speckled appearance. In contrast to granite, gabbro is a heavy, dark-colored rock composed almost entirely of ferromagnesian minerals and dark feldspars.

### Sedimentary Rocks

Sediments that are derived from all kinds of rocks combine to form sedimentary rocks. As inorganic sediments are consolidated, they are called *clastic sedimentary rock* and are classified as to their composition and texture (Table 12.1). Sandstones, siltstones, and shales are formed in this manner. Sedimentary rocks may also be derived from chemical reactions that precipitate such rocks as limestone. Others, such as peat and coal, are of organic origin, and a few, including salt and gypsum, are evaporates from salt lakes.

Most sedimentary rocks are transported by streams to a new location and are redeposited in layers. Streams continually wear away the land above sea level and carry these sediments downstream. As the streams enter bodies of water, the sediments are normally sorted and deposited in layers according to size and weight, the heaviest particles being deposited first. This layering, called *stratification,* is the outstanding characteristic in the formation of sedimentary rock.

When sedimentary fragments are deposited on the floor of lakes or oceans, the sediments form nearly horizontal strata. These sediments are gradually compacted and cemented into rock by the weight of the layers resting on top of them. Marine sedimentary rock occurs in successive strata known as *bedding planes.* As the sediments gradually become compacted, deposits of silica, calcium carbonate, and iron oxide enter the spaces between the sediments and cement them into a solid rock. This change from unconsolidated sediments to rock is called *lithification.*

### Metamorphic Rocks

When heat and pressure are applied to rocks of sedimentary or igneous origin, the rocks are eventually transformed so completely that they no longer resemble the original rock. This process is called *metamorphism.* When sandstone, a sedimentary rock, is subjected to great pressure and accompanying heat, the sand grains are fused into a solid mass, producing quartzite. When shale is metamorphosed it becomes slate, and metamorphosed limestone becomes marble. In the same process the minerals in granite are separated into bands, producing gneiss. Metamorphic rocks differ in a number of ways from sedimentary and igneous rocks. While igneous rocks originated from the processes of complete melting, the metamorphic process is transitional to complete melting. Metamorphic rocks are, however, denser and less porous than the rocks from which they originated and are therefore more resistant to weathering and erosion.

The oldest known rocks in the world are of metamorphic origin. These rocks, about 3.8 billion years in age, are exposed on the world's shield areas, where erosion has removed many kilometers of overlying younger rocks. The Laurentian Shield of eastern Canada is an example of such an area. These ancient metamorphic rocks are thought to be the core of mountain ranges that were eroded away hundreds of millions of years ago.

## THE WORLD'S LANDFORM FEATURES

The world's landform features can be classified into three major categories—first, second, and third order—in descending order of magnitude.

### FIRST ORDER LANDFORMS

The continents and the ocean basins constitute the first order landforms. Their positions were once thought to be fixed, but this concept is now rejected by most geologists. The modern view is that the earth's lithosphere

**TABLE 12.1**
Clastic rocks

| Size of Particles (inches) | Size of Particles (mm) | Unconsolidated Sediments | Consolidated Rock |
|---|---|---|---|
| >0.04 | >1.0 | Boulders, cobbles, gravel | Conglomerates |
| 0.004–0.04 | 0.1–1.0 | Sand | Sandstone |
| 0.00008–0.004 | 0.002–0.1 | Silt | Siltstone |
| <0.00008 | <0.002 | Clay | Shale |

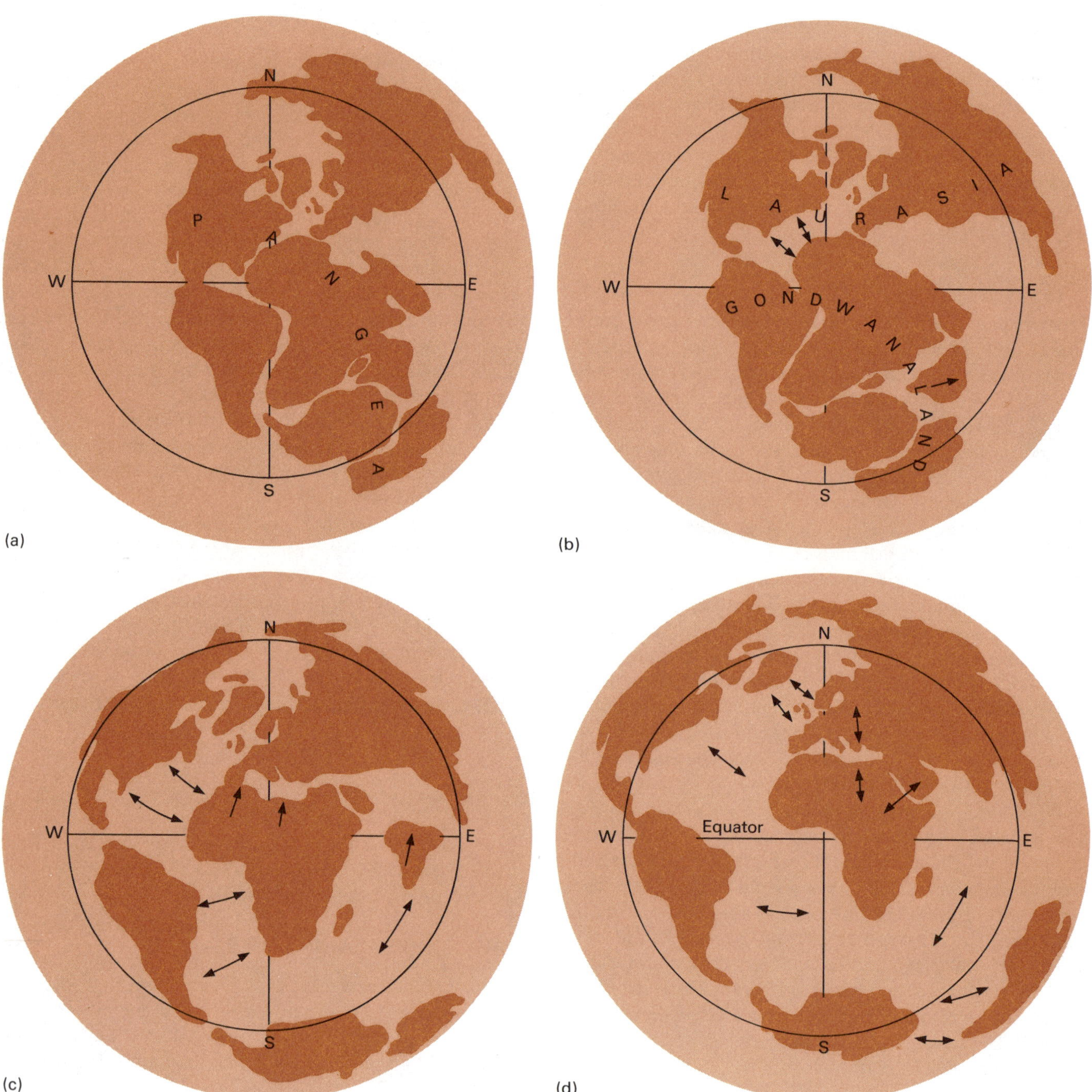


**FIGURE 12.3**
Movement of the tectonic plates. (*a*) About 200 million years ago there was one major continent, called Pangea. (*b*) About 135 million years ago Pangea had divided into two large landmasses, Laurasia and Gondwanaland. This occurred just prior to the opening of the South Atlantic about 120 million years ago. (*c*) About 65 million years ago the present continental configuration was well advanced. The Indian peninsula was not yet connected to Asia, and the North Atlantic was just beginning to open. (*d*) Since then the continents have continued to spread, producing the present configuration. The arrows indicate the present direction of spreading. (After Burchfiel and others, 1982)

is divided into plates that move over the earth. Continents, embedded in the lithosphere, drift along with the moving plates. *Plate tectonics* provides a scientific explanation for the old idea of continental drift.

## Origin of Plate Tectonics

To the average individual the idea that the continents have moved thousands of kilometers over millions of years is inconceivable. And yet, this was a notion that intrigued many early scientists. For example, Francis Bacon, the 16th-century scientist, remarked on his *Novum Organum* that it appeared as if the coasts of South America and Africa could be fitted together.

In the early 20th century the possibility of continental drift was debated by many geologists. In 1915 Alfred Wegener published his hypothesis in his classic volume, *Origin of the Continents and Oceans.* His concept was that the continents were once united into a single supercontinent that he called Pangea (Figure 12.3). This continent existed about 200 million years ago. Although the precise location of Pangea is still vague, its relative location in the world can be estimated considering magnetic patterns, geometric land slopes, fossils, and climatic conditions. From these data the movements of the continental plates were inferred as to distance and relative location.

This theory was known as continental drift. Wegener based his work primarily on the shape of the continental coasts, demonstrating that they could be fitted together as a jigsaw puzzle. He then drew evidence from the similarities of rock structures, fossils, and other geologic events that were found on the different continents.

## Development of Plate Tectonics

The early evidence provided by geologists and paleontologists was not sufficient to convince most scientists that continental drift was a viable theory. Further corroboration was needed to provide the basis for an accepted theory of plate tectonics.

In 1928 Arthur Holmes proposed that the mechanisms of thermal convection in the earth's mantle could move the crust. Holmes stated that the convection forces "dragged the two halves of the original continent apart, with subsequent mountain building in the front where the currents are descending, and ocean floor development on the site of the gap, where the currents are ascending." Holmes was thus providing the modern notions of divergence, subduction, and plates. At the time, however, Holmes wrote, "Purely speculative ideas of this kind, specifically invented to match the requirements, can have no scientific value until they acquire support from independent evidence."

The scientific evidence of plate tectonics began to emerge beginning in the 1940s, when the mapping of the mid-Atlantic region was started. At that time a deep valley, or rift, was found to exist in the middle of the Atlantic Ocean. In 1962 Harry Hess of Princeton University suggested that the seafloors spread along the rifts in *mid-ocean ridges.* He theorized that new seafloor is formed by upwelling of mantle materials in these fissures, followed by lateral spreading, and that at the oceanic trenches the oceanic crust plunges downward into the earth's mantle. Like Holmes, Hess viewed the process as a giant convective system. These ideas created the great concept of *seafloor spreading* from a central axis. The confirmation of these ideas came quickly in the 1960s.

## Scientific Evidence of Seafloor Spreading

In the late 1950s and early 1960s two geologic exploratory studies revealed evidence that became vital to explaining seafloor spreading. The first study indicated that the earth's magnetic field has reversed its polarity several times in the last few million years. The other set of surveys revealed that the oceanic crust of the northeast Pacific Ocean had distinct patterns of magnetic anomalies in parallel stripes. The change of magnetic field was discovered by measuring the direction of magnetism of undersea volcanic mountain ranges. When the new basaltic igneous rock solidified, the polarity of its magnetic minerals was frozen in place. The polarity was essentially consistent with the earth's magnetic field at the time and is known as *paleomagnetism.* Paleomagnetic studies have established magnetic polarity sequences for the last 5 million years. Sequences for about 100 million years are moderately well-established, and work is proceeding to earlier periods. Magnetic surveys revealed that the magnetic direction gradually changed outward from the mid-ocean ridges until the ancient field was reversed with respect to the present-day magnetic field, creating a *magnetic anomaly* (Figure 12.4).

In 1963, Frederick J. Vine and D. H. Mathews developed a hypothesis relating magnetic anomalies of the ocean crust and *magnetic reversals.* In a study of magnetic anomalies of the Mid-Atlantic ridge south of Iceland, they recognized that the anomaly patterns are symmetrical about the central part of the ridge, marked by a median valley. They reasoned that the ocean crust was moving away from the median valley and that molten rock was intruding along the zone of the diverging sections of crust. As the molten rock solidified, it formed new ocean crust and became magnetized in the direction of the earth's magnetic field at that time. As

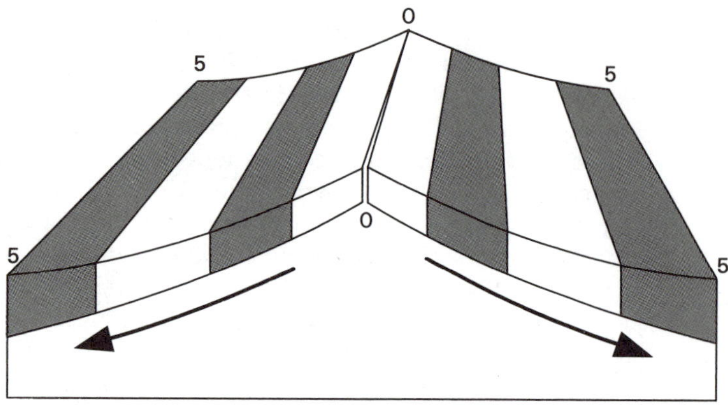


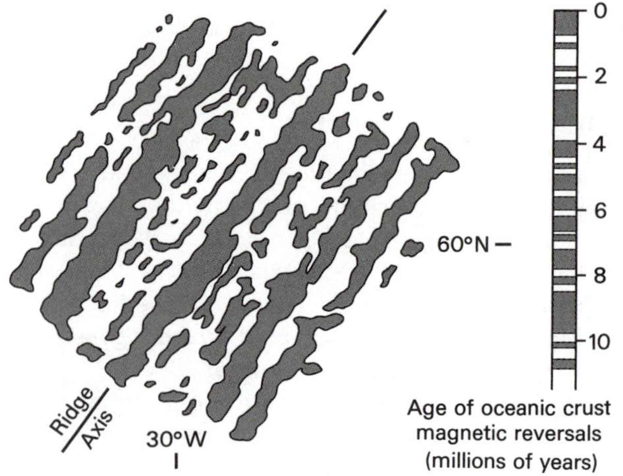


**FIGURE 12.4**
Magnetic anomaly patterns in the ocean basins. (*a*) The hypothesis of Vine and Mathews considered seafloor spreading to be the cause of the patterns. (*b*) The magnetic anomaly of the Reykjanes ridge south of Iceland is an example of the type of pattern found near a spreading ridge. (After Vine, in Robert A. Phinney, ed., *The History of the Earth's Crust*. Copyright © 1968 by Princeton University Press. Fig. 6, p. 82, reprinted by permission of Princeton University Press.)

gradually the earth's magnetic field was reversed, new ocean crust would acquire a magnetization of reversed polarity. The ocean crust that formed would be split apart into equal portions as it moved away from the mid-ocean ridge. Each half of the ocean crust would carry the record of magnetic polarity reversals.

The work of Vine and Mathews spawned further studies, and it was discovered that paired magnetic anomaly patterns, symmetrically aligned about mid-oceanic ridges, occur in all oceans. Further, because the intervals of polar reversals were irregular, magnetic anomalies with definite time intervals were readily identifiable in each ocean. Once the anomaly was dated in one ocean, anomalies in all oceans could be dated. Dating was accomplished by drilling through the overlying sedimentary layer and dating the fossils from the oldest sediments that lay on top of the oceanic crust. The ages of the fossils were then correlated with the absolute time scale, which is calculated in millions of years. From these data a spreading rate can be calculated by dividing the distance from the ridge axis by the absolute age of the magnetic anomaly.

## Rate of Plate Motion

The worldwide pattern of seafloor spreading is being determined by a combination of magnetic, seismic, and bathymetric data. The changes in geographic location are obtained from the position of ocean ridges, deep-sea trenches, earthquake epicenters, and other markers. From these data, *isochrons,* lines that connect points of the same age, are drawn to show the age of the seafloor in millions of years. The distance from a ridge axis, for example, to a 20 million year isochron reveals the extent of a new ocean floor created in that time span (Figure 12.5).

It has been revealed that the spreading rate not only varies from one part of an ocean to another, but also varies from ocean to ocean. The spreading of the seafloor is significantly greater in the Pacific than the Atlantic Ocean. The greatest rate of spreading—18.3 centimeters per year—occurs between two *tectonic plates* named the Pacific and Nazca plates.

The concept of tectonic plate movement is based on sound physical principles, which were developed by the Swiss mathematician Leonard Euler in the 18th century. His theorem stated that a plate moving on a surface of a sphere rotates about its own pole along small circle routes. On the earth a small circle can be of any size. A large tectonic plate will thus move as a unit along many small circle routes, all of which must center on the plane envisioned by Euler. The rate of movement can vary from one part of a plate to another, depending upon the size of the small circles. For example, if a plate extends from the Arctic Circle to the equator, the smaller of the small circles is near the Arctic Circle and

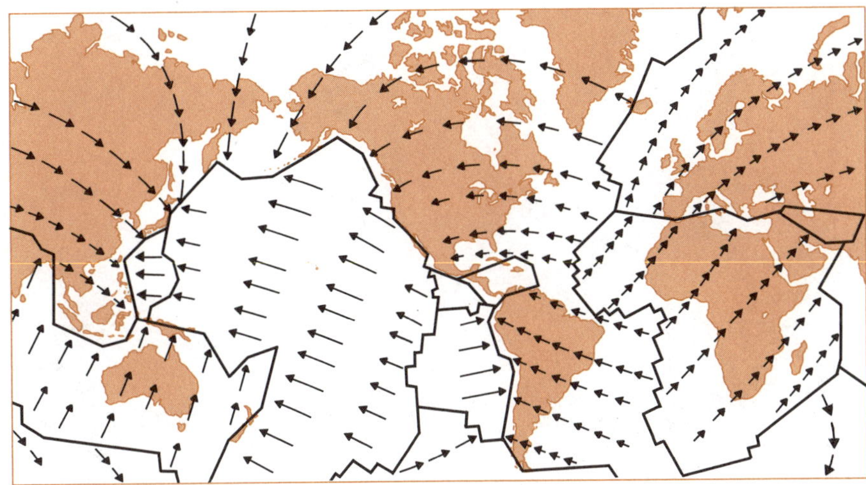

**FIGURE 12.5**
Rate of plate movement. Each arrow represents 20 million years of movement. The length of the arrow indicates the length of movement. For example, the Pacific plates have experienced more rapid movement than the Atlantic plates. (William M. Marsh, Jeff Dozier, *Landscape: An Introduction to Physical Geography,* © 1981, Addison-Wesley Publishing Co. Inc., Reading, MA. Page 63, figure 4.4, and page 363, figure 23.6. Reprinted with permission.)

the larger of the small circles is at the equator. Thus the portion of the plate at the equator must move farther than the polar portion, because a degree on the Arctic Circle is a much smaller distance than a degree at the equator.

## Plate Boundaries

The theory of plate tectonics visualizes that rigid plates move over a partially molten, plastic *asthenosphere.* Evidence revealed by volcanoes and earthquakes suggests that the boundaries between plates can be of three kinds: (*a*) *zones of divergence* where plates are moving apart, (*b*) *zones of convergence* or *subduction* where plates descend into the mantle, and (*c*) *fracture zones* where plates slide past one another (Figure 12.6).

The mid-ocean ridges, which rise from 2,500 to 3,000 meters (8,200 to 9,840 feet) above the general level of the ocean floor, form the zone of crustal spreading between the diverging lithospheric plates (Figure 12.7). New crust is constantly being formed in these areas. As a response to tensional forces, shallow earthquake activity occurs. These tensional forces have a tendency to pull the crust apart rather than push it together. As the lithosphere spreads, the energy released creates molten magma. Basaltic lava erupts from the mantle along the ridges; as it cools, it forms new ocean crust. The mid-ocean ridges are thus areas of accretion where new seafloor develops. Tensional forces also create *joints* and *faults.* When outward-moving tensional forces are applied to a block of earth bounded by joints on either side, a down-faulted block, or *graben,* is created.

The lithosphere is consumed in the zones of crustal convergence or subduction. At this boundary one plate overrides another, with the lower plate being subducted; that is, being thrust into the mantle. Subduction usually occurs when the oceanic plate comes in contact with the continental plate. Because the continental plate is lighter, the oceanic plate is thrust down to the asthenosphere. At the boundary between these plates, the thrusting mechanism tends to produce deep-sea trenches. Because the compressional forces create massive amounts of heat, the subduction zones are the principal volcanic areas of the world. In contrast to the zone of convergence, where the earthquake activity extends downward not more than 10 to 15 kilometers (6 to 9 miles), the earthquake activity in the subduction zone is deep-seated, extending to depths of more than 700 kilometers (430 miles). This massive zone of earthquakes that begins at the ocean trenches and dips at varying angles away from the ocean basins is known as the *Benioff zone,* named for Hugo Benioff, its discoverer (Figures 12.8 and 12.9). Earthquakes in this zone vary greatly in intensity, but some have caused vast destruction.

The third boundary consists of *transform faults* where plates slide past one another, with neither divergence nor subduction of the lithosphere (Figure 12.10). These boundaries are marked by shallow earthquakes. A major transform fault begins at the mouth of the Gulf of California. At this point the boundaries begin to shear, with the Pacific plate sliding northwestward relative to the American plate. A small section of western Mexico and California, once attached to the American Plate, has broken off and is now part of the Pacific plate. Where the plate boundary runs aground it is known as the San Andreas Fault. The shearing action dominates, with the plate on the west moving northward and the plate on the east moving southward. This movement has been in progress for at least 70 million years, cre-

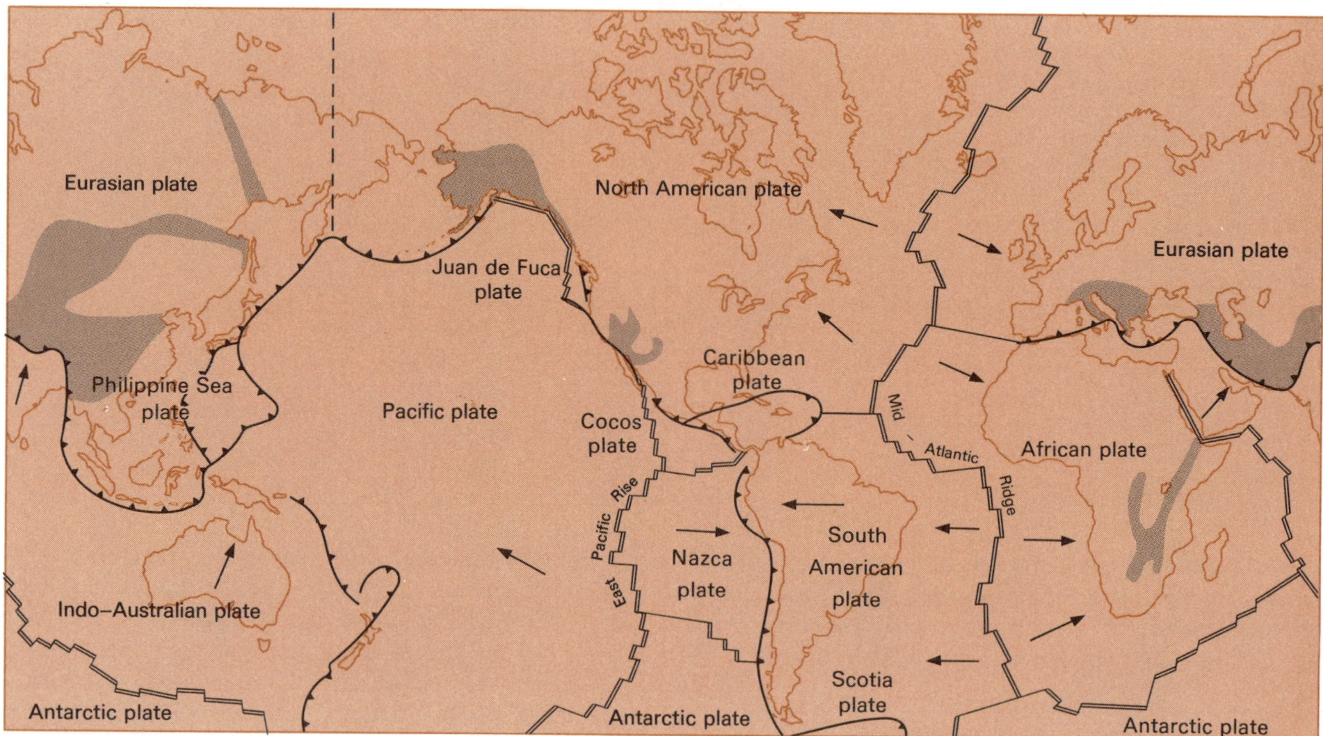


**FIGURE 12.6**
Plate boundaries. The type of movement is shown by different lines: spreading axes (double lines), transform faults (single lines), and convergent or subduction zones (barbed lines on overriding plate). Stippled areas within continents designate regions of active deformation away from the plate boundary. (From "Plate Tectonics" by John F. Dewey. Copyright © 1972 by Scientific American. All rights reserved.)

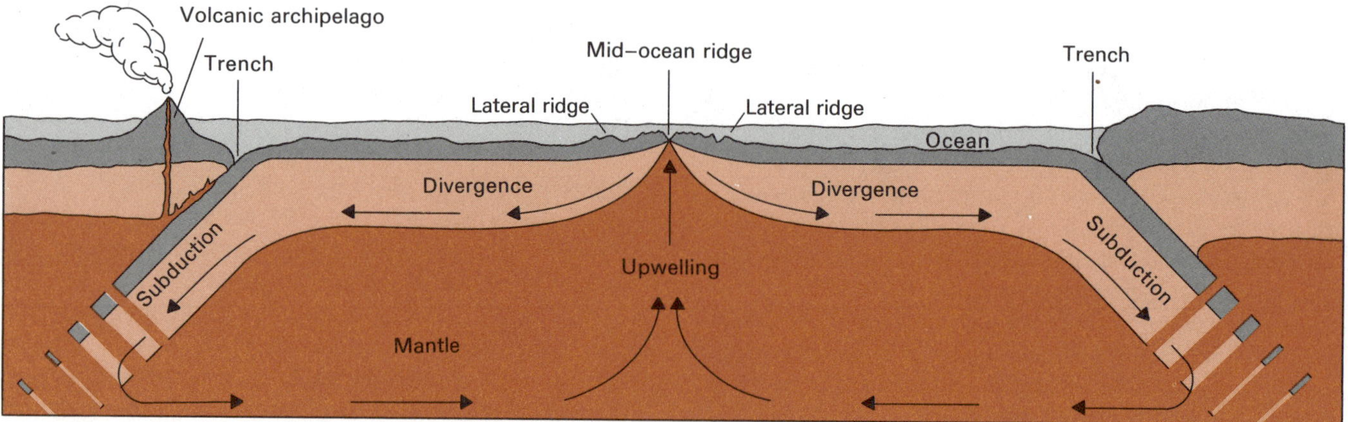


**FIGURE 12.7**
Divergence and subduction. New crust is formed at places of divergence by the pouring out of lava. The continental masses are lighter than the mantle material of the ocean floor, so when contact is made, the continents cannot sink but tend to push over the sinking currents, creating an area of subduction. At these places great oceanic trenches develop.

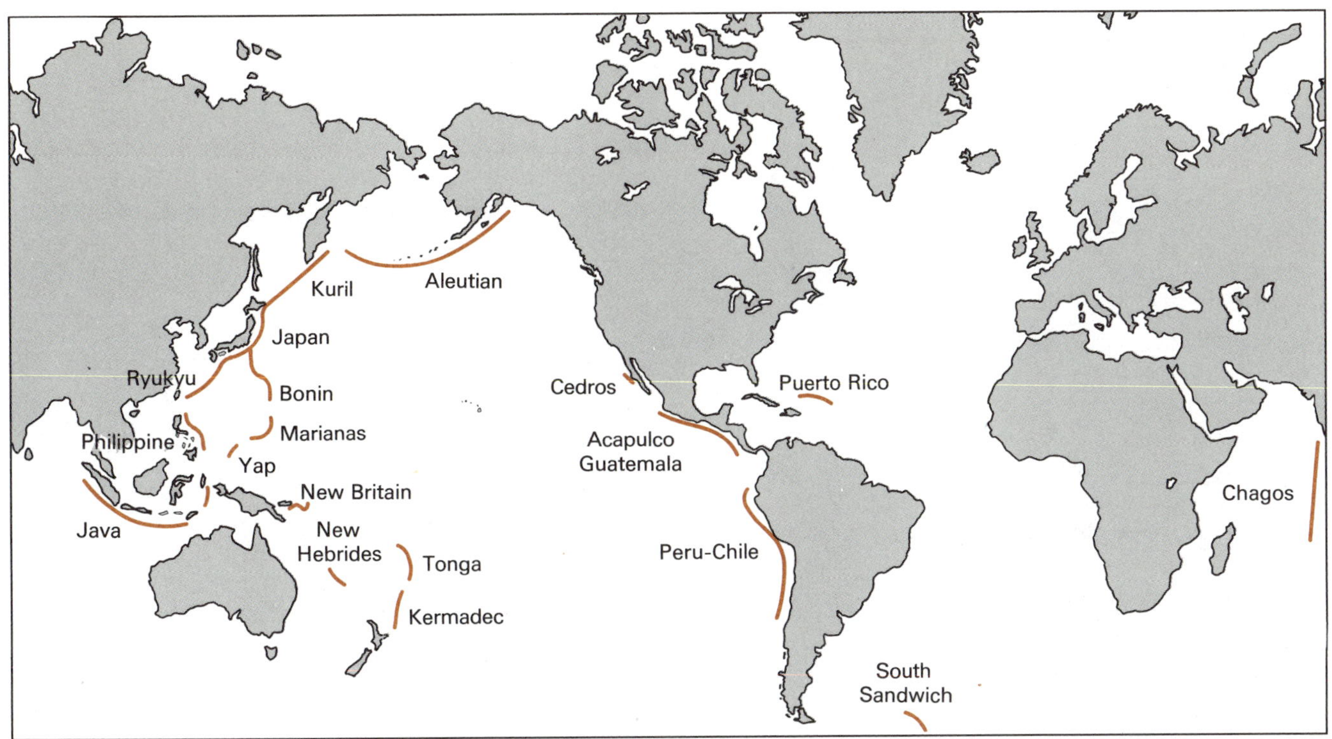


**FIGURE 12.8**
Trenches of the oceans. The trenches are located at the zones where material is being subducted into the earth.

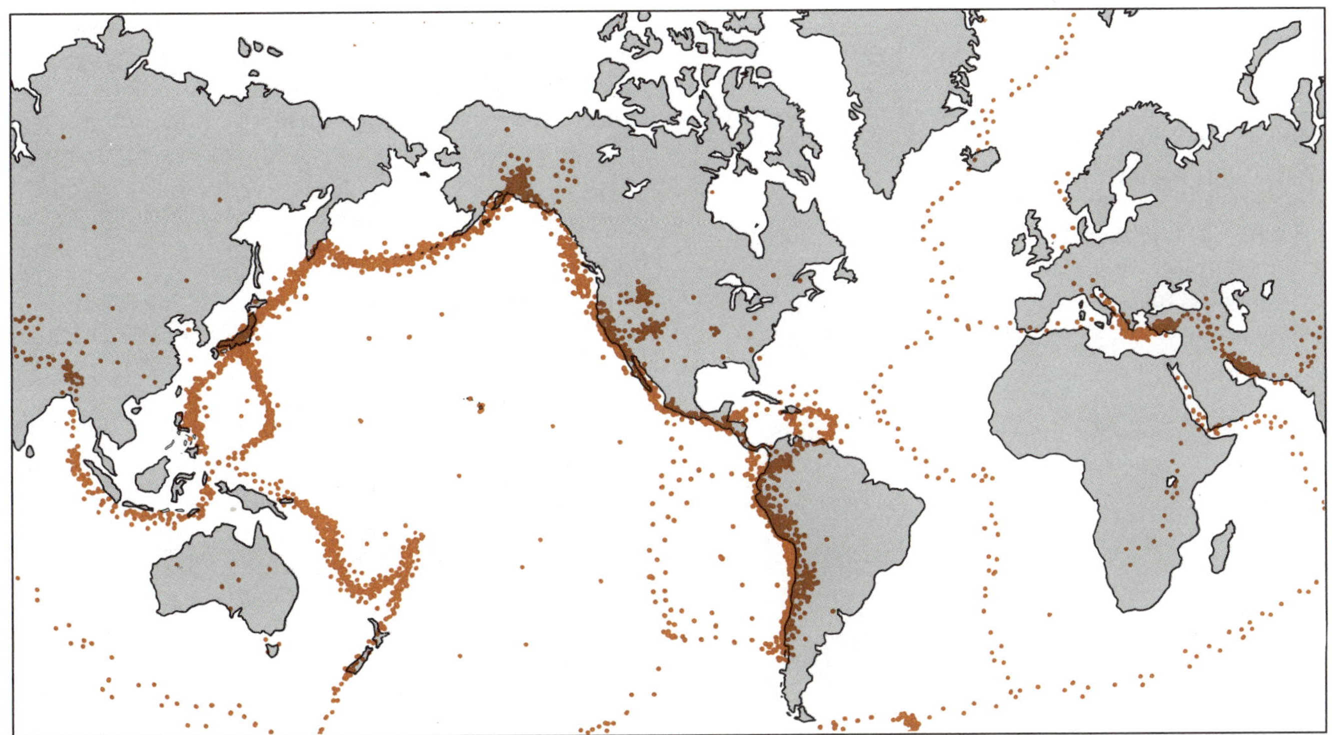

**FIGURE 12.9**
World distribution of earthquake epicenters. The zones of subduction are the principal areas of earthquakes, with the zones of divergence also experiencing activity. Note the relationship of earthquake epicenters to the tectonic plate boundaries (Figure 12.6). (U.S. Coast and Geodetic Survey, 1968; after Burchfiel et al., 1982)

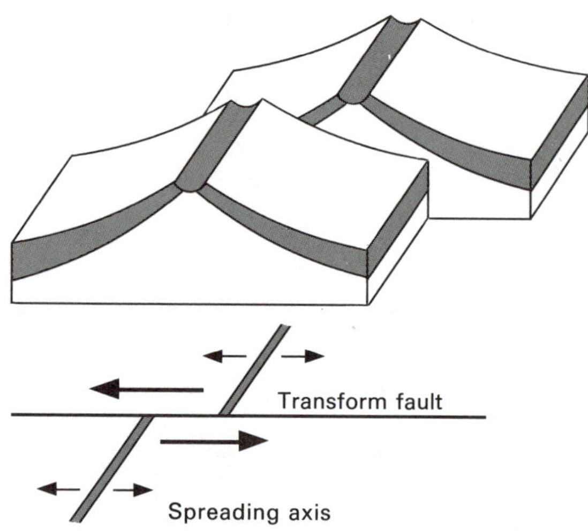


**FIGURE 12.10**
Transform fault. Transform faults are approximately at right angles to spreading ridges.

ating a lateral displacement of more than 100 kilometers (60 miles). The shearing action stops off the Oregon coast and reverts to a spreading motion from the mid-ocean ridges. Farther north, the shearing resumes along a fault that extends nearly to Anchorage, Alaska.

## Location of Tectonic Plates

The tectonic plates are now fairly precisely located. Based on size, three orders of plates are recognized (Figure 12.6). Eight major continental and oceanic basin plates, five second order plates, and nine minor plates are found in the world. The major continental and ocean basin plates each have an area of about 65 million square kilometers (25 million square miles), while the smallest plates, sometimes called platelets, cover only 100,000 to 150,000 square kilometers (40,000 to 58,000 square miles). The platelets are usually located between the major plates in zones of great crustal disturbance.

## Plate Tectonic Convective System

We have seen that plate tectonics involves the creation of lithosphere along a spreading axis at divergence zones, followed by lateral movement, and then the consumption of the mantle at subduction zones. This activity requires some type of convective system to be in operation. It is now conceived that at the subduction zone the lithospheric crust is thrust downward. As it penetrates the asthenosphere it is gradually heated, becoming plastic. From the point of subduction a cold plate will require about 12 million years of heating before it is assimilated into the plastic asthenosphere. This occurs at depths of 400 to 700 kilometers (250 to 430 miles).

The convective system is based on different density relationships. The plastic material in the asthenosphere has a lower density than the overlying material in the lithosphere, creating a density inversion. The movement of the plastic asthenosphere to the surface to form new lithosphere in the mid-oceanic ridges appears to be nature's way of attempting to maintain a density equilibrium. This convective system will exist as long as the earth has sufficient heat to melt the asthenosphere and still has a solid lithosophere in the upper portion.

## Hot Spots and Mantle Plumes

Volcanic activity occurs not only along the boundaries of plates but also in *hot spots* within plates (Figure 12.11). Worldwide more than 100 hot spots have been

**FIGURE 12.11**
World distribution of hot spots. A total of about 110 hot spots are widely distributed in the world.

**PHOTO 70**
Castle Geyser in Yellowstone National Park, a volcanic hot spot.

**PHOTO 71**
Old Faithful Geyser Basin. In Yellowstone National Park there are about 10,000 hydrothermal features, including 200 geysers, bubbling mud volcanoes, and hot springs. (Courtesy: Wyoming Travel Commission)

identified (Photos 70 and 71). Because the hot spots do not appear related to plate movement, it is thought that they originate deep in the mantle, beneath the convective flow associated with plate tectonics. As the heat liquefies the rock, the magma rises through cylindrical ducts, called *plumes.* Volcanoes appear when the magma reaches the surface.

The Hawaiian Islands form a hot spot that has been intensively investigated (Figure 12.12). These volcanic islands lie along the Hawaiian-Emperor ridge. The oldest volcanoes, which are now extinct, lie on the islands of the northwest, and the youngest, active volcanoes lie to the southeast on the island of Hawaii. It is suggested that a stationary hot spot created the Hawaiian Islands. In this hypothesis the plume pushed up magma, creating an initial island. In time the Pacific plate migrated, carrying the island with it. Periodically the hot spot erupts, creating another island, so that each island is progressively older. The island of Hawaii, with its active volcanoes, remains centered over the plume. However, another volcanic island seems to be forming 48 kilometers (30 miles) southeast of Hawaii. In time it may emerge onto the surface to form another island in the chain.

The rate of movement of the Pacific plate may be indicated by the location and age of volcanoes in relation to the hot spots. For example, the age of the volcanic island of Midway has been calculated to be about 25 million years. It lies about 2,400 kilometers (1,500 miles) northwest of Hawaii. If the hot spot that created both Midway and Hawaii has remained stationary, then the Pacific plate has moved about 100 kilometers every million years. About 1,500 kilometers (930 miles) west of Midway, a chain of seamounts, or underwater islands, have an age of 40 million years, which verifies that the Pacific plate's rate of movement is about 100 kilometers per million years.

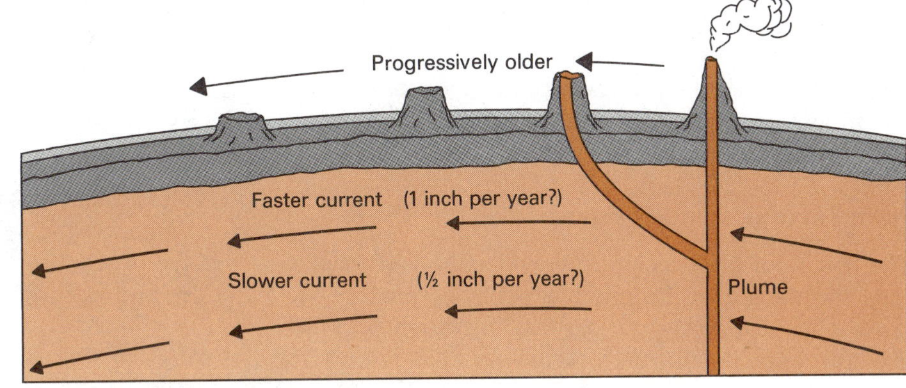


**FIGURE 12.12**
Sketch of a hot-spot volcanic island chain. Chains such as the Hawaiian Islands do not lie on a mid-ocean ridge. It is thought that the lava source lies perhaps 160 kilometers (100 miles) or deeper, in the slow-moving part of the convection currents of the mantle. The differential motion carries old volcanoes away from the lava source, while new volcanoes form over the lava source. The length of the chain depends upon how long the source is active.

Jets of hot air may also escape from hot spots. In 1977 a research vessel investigating the rifts along the Mid–Atlantic Ocean ridge found great formations of warm water jetting into the ocean. These jets had a temperature of about 22°C (72°F). Two years later, off Baja, California, the same research team discovered jets roaring like fire with temperatures around 350°C (662°F). The jets were kept liquid only because of the pressure of an almost two-mile depth of water. The gases were highly mineralized and were called "black smokers." As they cooled they deposited cones and piles of sulfides of iron and other metals. This was a new discovery of how ore deposits can be formed.

Possibly the most interesting discovery of these jets was the strange realm of life associated with them. In the Iceland area there were pink fish swimming in the water and white crabs crawling over the rocks. On the bottom, huge white clams and yellow-brown mussels, as well as tube worms with red plumes, were found. All of this life was occurring in ocean depths where sunlight did not penetrate. Everywhere else on earth advanced life depends on sun for energy and sustenance. In these jet areas, thousands of feet beneath the surface, extraordinary life forms thrive in heated water, depending upon bacteria and organisms synthesized by the bacteria. Chemical reactions rather than sunlight provide the energy to produce nutrients.

## SECOND ORDER LANDFORMS

The second order landforms are the major relief features on the continents and ocean basins. On the continents they include such vast plains as the Central Lowlands of the United States and the North European Plain; such plateaus as the Colorado Plateau, Deccan of India, Patagonia of Argentina, and the African Plateaus; and such mountain ranges as the Rocky Mountains, Andes, Alps, and Himalayas. The ocean basins also possess secondary landform features in the great mid-ocean ridge systems, such as the Emperor Sea Mountain and the Hawaiian Ridge, and in the deep submarine trenches such as the Aleutian, Japan, and the Kuril of the Pacific Ocean. The mid-ocean ridges form undersea mountain chains that rival the greatest of the continental mountain ranges.

### Plate Tectonics and Orogeny

The theory of plate tectonics provides the first satisfactory explanation of the mountain-building process. According to plate tectonics, *orogeny,* or mountain building on the continents, occurs at the zones of subduction. One such location is the circum-Pacific belt, where the subduction zone of the Pacific plate comes in contact with the Indian-Australian, Eurasian, and American plates. The second major subduction zone extends from the Mediterranean area of Europe eastward to the East Indies and lies along the contact zone between the Eurasian, African, and Indian-Australian plates. Mountains also occur along the subduction zones of smaller plates. Mountain building also occurs along the mid-ocean ridges as lithosphere is built in these diverging zones.

The mountains associated with the zones of subduction are narrow in relation to their length. The processes of orogeny in these areas proceed through a number of stages. Initially the interaction of continental and oceanic plates produces a subduction zone with the formation of a deep-sea trench. As the lithosphere is consumed, the descending material is heated, initiating volcanoes. Island arcs of mountains that are composed almost entirely of volcanic rocks then develop. While the mountains are being built, they are also being weathered and eroded, producing sediments that are deposited into basins and the oceans. Thick layers of sediments accumulate in and adjacent to the oceanic trenches. In the next stage, the continuing movement of the plates compresses and deforms the accumulated sediments. As this process proceeds, there may be additional volcanic activity. The sedimentary and volcanic rocks of the area thicken and continue to be deformed. The entire mass is raised by compressional forces that extend deep into the earth's interior. The great heat associated with this process begins to metamorphose the rocks. All of these processes are accompanied by vertical uplift that greatly exceeds the erosional forces, and a mountain belt is formed.

### Tectonic Processes

The processes that deform and rupture the earth's crust are known as tectonic processes. They fall into two classes: *vulcanism* (Photos 72 and 73), which entails the transfer of molten rock (magma) from within the earth into the earth's crust or onto the surface, and *diastrophism,* which includes the folding, breaking, shifting, twisting, bending, or warping of the earth's crust (Photo 74).

**Vulcanism.** Vulcanism is concentrated in the zones of divergence and subduction and at hot spots on the tectonic plates. Vulcanism is divided into two types: intrusive and extrusive.

*Intrusive Vulcanism.* When underground magma solidifies, it cannot be observed until it has been uncovered by erosion. On the basis of the shapes and forms

**PHOTO 72**
Hawaiian volcano. Fountains of molten lava and flame climb to heights of more than 500 meters (1,500 feet) during an eruption of Hawaii's Kilaueaiki volcano. (Courtesy: Hawaii Visitors Bureau)

**PHOTO 74**
Folds. Highly folded rocks in the Ridge and Valley province near Lewistown, Pennsylvania. (Courtesy: Brian Tormey, The Pennsylvania State University)

**PHOTO 73**
Molten lava. A helicopter flies over molten lava on the island of Hawaii. Note the cracked lava crust. (Courtesy: Hawaii Visitors Bureau)

and their relationship to the enclosing rock, these igneous intrusions can then be classified as *dikes, sills, volcanic necks, laccoliths, batholiths,* and *stocks* (Figure 12.13).

Dikes are crudely tabular bodies in which two dimensions are very large compared to the third. Thus dikes are rarely more than a few tens of meters in thickness but some are hundreds of kilometers long. Most dikes of the world are formed when magma is forced into fractures in the rock, pushing the walls apart. Dikes may radiate from volcanic centers and may have a concentric or curved pattern.

Sills, like dikes, are tabular forms, but differ from dikes in that they lie parallel to the *bedding planes* of the enclosing rock (Photo 75). They are sometimes known as intrusive sheets. Frequently sills and dikes are associated. Sills vary greatly in size; they may cover vast areas in the zones of vulcanism or only a few square kilometers.

In places, magma moves through vents to feed volcanoes. When the magma solidifies in a vent, it is called

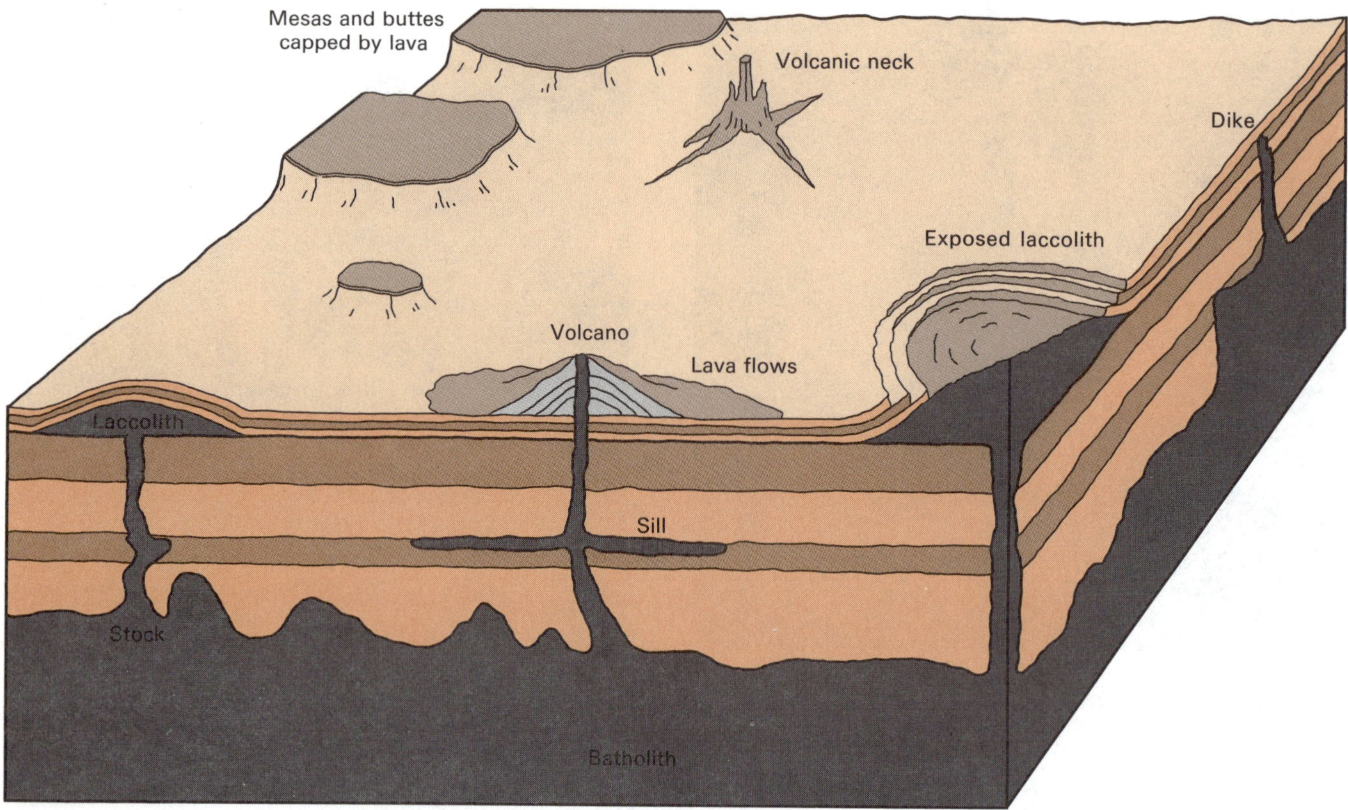


**FIGURE 12.13**
Diagram of structural relations of various intrusive and extrusive igneous masses.

**PHOTO 75**
Palisades of the Hudson. An igneous layer, or sill, was forced between sedimentary rock layers and is now a prominent feature in the Hudson Valley. (Courtesy: J. Goerg, New York State Department of Environmental Conservation)

a neck or plug. Necks may be as large as a thousand meters in diameter, and when uncovered by erosion, they may rise hundreds of meters above the surrounding country. In northwestern New Mexico and adjoining Arizona, more than 150 volcanic necks have been exposed by erosion, producing a variety of striking features on the landscape (Photos 76 and 77).

A laccolith is a large mass that has been forced into a rock, producing a domelike structure. Its origin is similar to that of a sill. The magma is supplied from below through a small fissure, and the domelike intrusion has a flat base. Laccoliths occur in a wide variety of shapes and sizes. One of the world's famous laccolith areas is the Henry Mountains of southern Utah. Individual domes in this group range from one to six kilometers (0.6 to 4 miles) in diameter.

The batholiths are the largest and deepest intrusive bodies of igneous rock. Some of these features measure 80 to 160 kilometers (50 to 100 miles) wide and more than 1,600 kilometers (1,000 miles) long, and many have not been exposed on the surface by ero-

**PHOTO 76**
Volcanic neck. Devils Tower in northern Wyoming is one of the best-known volcanic necks in the world. (Courtesy: N. H. Darton, U.S. Geological Survey)

**PHOTO 77**
Volcanic neck. The volcanic neck at Le Puy in the Central Massif of France. Note the church built at the crest of the neck. (Courtesy: French Government Tourist Office)

sion. They extend downward to great depths and appear to broaden with depth. Most batholiths occur as cores of folded mountain systems, indicating that they were likely formed during the geologic period of crustal deformation. A notable example is the Coast Range batholith of British Columbia, which has a surface area of about 260,000 square kilometers (100,000 square miles). The Idaho batholith, covering 40,500 square kilometers (16,000 square miles), is the largest one in the United States, followed in size by the Sierra Nevada batholith.

The origin of batholiths is still uncertain. One theory suggests that hot magma moved upward and in the process melted large quantities of rock in its path. This process is called *magmatic stoping.* Another theory states that a batholith forms when massive amounts of magma are injected into rocks and push them aside as the magma moves upward in the earth's crust.

*Extrusive Vulcanism.* The volcano is the most striking physical evidence of the process of vulcanism. Three major types of volcanoes occur on the surface of the earth. The first are the great cone volcanoes composed of *lava* or other materials. They are known as *cinder cones, lava cones,* and *stratovolcanoes* or *composite cones* (Photos 78 and 79). The second type of extrusive vulcanism develops when lava wells up from a vent under low pressure and spreads out in thin sheets, forming a gently sloping dome. These domed lava formations are called *shield volcanoes* or *lava domes.* Finally,

**PHOTO 78**
Mt. Shasta, a conical volcano in northern California.

**PHOTO 79**
A volcanic cone at Sunset Crater northeast of Flagstaff, Arizona. (Courtesy: Arizona Office of Tourism)

magma may flow from fissures and spread out in horizontal sheets over vast areas, creating *fissure volcanoes* (Photo 80).

The eruption of a cone volcano, one of nature's spectacular events, is often preceded by earthquakes and loud rumblings like thunder. The nature of the volcanic eruption is determined by the type of material ejected from the vent, which may be gases, molten rock, or solid rock fragments. The intensity of a volcanic eruption depends upon the silica content of the magma. If the pressure is great, a series of violent explosions will occur. Examples of this type of eruption include that of Krakatoa in the East Indies in 1885, Mount Pelée on the island of Martinique in 1902, and Mount St. Helens in 1979. If the gas pressures are less, the volcano usually discharges fluid lava that gradually flows down the slopes into the surrounding lowlands. The eruptions in Hawaii, such as those that occurred on Kilauea in 1984, are usually of this type.

**PHOTO 80**
Fissure volcano. Lava beds on the Columbia Plateau.

The form of the volcanic cone developed depends upon the material ejected. Cinder cones are steep-sided, symmetrical volcanoes composed of angular rock fragments spewed out usually in violent eruptions. If the fragments are large, the cone may have slopes of 30 to 40 degrees. In contrast, if the fragments are small, wind and rain will quickly carry some of the particles away and the slopes may be more gentle. Cinder cone volcanoes include Vesuvius and Mount Pelée.

Some volcanic cones result from a single eruption of lava, but these are quite rare. They are generally developed of composite layers of lava and cinder, with a slope intermediate between that of the cinder and the lava cones. The composite cones are striking features on the landscape. Many are higher than 3,300 meters (10,800 feet). The cinder builds steep slopes while the lava tends to flatten the lower slopes of the cones. Most of the composite cones lie along the margins of the Pacific Ocean. They include Fujiyama in Japan; Majon in the Philippines; and Rainier, Hood, and Shasta in the United States.

At the top of currently or recently active cone volcanoes, a depression known as a *pit* or *crater* usually develops. It is the top of the vent through which material from the volcano is ejected. If the crater is enlarged by the explosive action of the volcano, it is then known as a *caldera* (Photo 81). Most calderas are quite large. Possibly the largest in the world is the Valle Grande in the ancient volcanic field of northern New Mexico. It is about 46 kilometers (28 miles) long and 38 kilometers (23 miles) wide. Sometimes on the floor of a caldera a secondary cone develops as material continues to be ejected by the volcano. Such a cone within a cone is said to be *nested.* Wizard Island in Crater Lake, Oregon, is an example of a nested cone.

The shield volcanoes of the world are composed of lava erupting from a central vent. The low-silica magma builds gentle slopes that resemble shields. Most of the shield volcanoes are associated with the mid-ocean ridges. The Hawaiian Islands are an example of the quiet eruption of lava. Despite the gentle slopes, the Ha-

**PHOTO 81**
Crater Lake in Oregon. The caldera formed when the volcano exploded. Note the secondary cone, Wizard Island, in the central background.

waiian Islands rise 8,540 meters (28,011 feet) from the floor of the ocean to 4,204 meters (13,789 feet) above sea level.

The fissure volcanoes cover possibly the largest areas in the world. The lava flows out from cracks spead over the region, covering thousands of square kilometers. Gradually the prevolcanic terrain is buried. Repeated flows produce a lava plateau. Of these plateaus, the largest are the Columbia Plateau in the U.S. Pacific Northwest, the Deccan Plateau of India, southern Brazil, and much of Ethiopia.

**Diastrophism.** The earth's crust is constantly under stress wherever tectonic plates meet. When the stress goes beyond the resistance of the crusted rocks, motion occurs. These movements over time vary from a few millimeters to thousands of meters. When they exceed the rate of erosion over a long period of time, second order topographic features are formed on the earth.

Although these movements normally occur over geologic time, large-scale movements can occur in a relatively short time. For example, the displacement of the earth's surface during the San Francisco earthquake of 1906 amounted to about 6 meters (20 feet) in a few minutes. During the 1923 earthquake in Japan, the bottom of Sagami Bay moved more than 300 meters (1,000 feet).

*Crustal Deformations.* Compressional or tensional forces create four major types of earth structures: *joints* or *fractures, faults, folds,* and *warps.*

Joints or fractures are breaks in solid rock along which there has been no appreciable movement or displacement. Joints occur when some limited force, either compression or tension, has been applied, usually as part of the weathering process.

If movement or displacement occurs along a joint, then it is said that a fault has occurred (Figure 12.14). Faulting may also take place independent of joints. Faults occur in all types of rocks but are most common

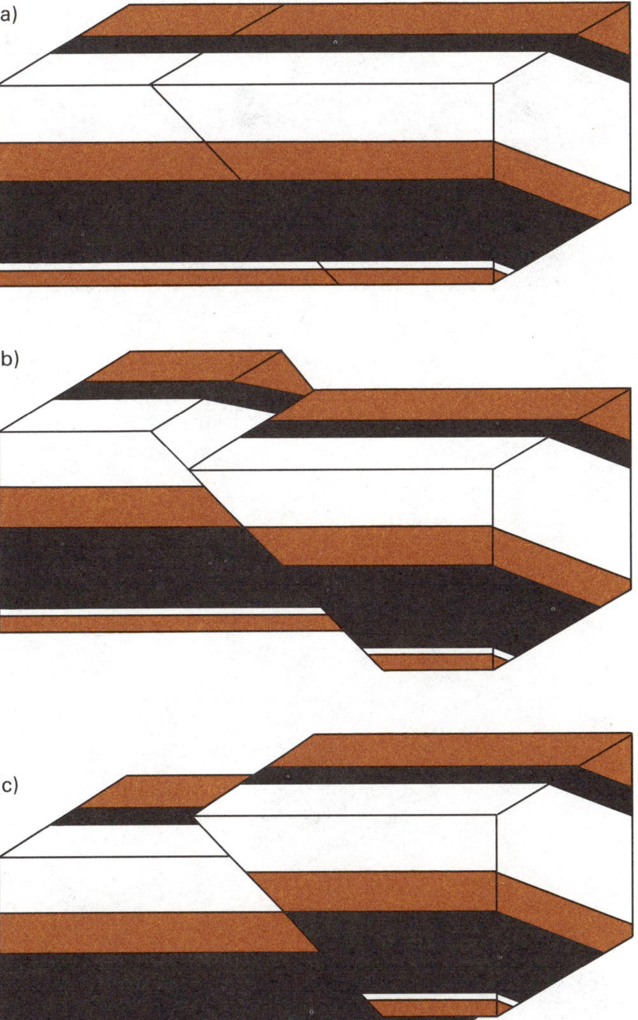


**FIGURE 12.14**
Types of faults. (*a*) Portion of the strata showing joint before faulting; (*b*) normal fault; and (*c*) reverse fault.

**PHOTO 82**
Normal faulting associated with the 1970 Gediz earthquake in Turkey. The fault scarp, in weathered marks, stands almost vertical and in places overhangs. (Courtesy: Earthquake Information Bulletin 340, U.S. Geological Survey)

in sedimentary rocks. The amount of displacement may vary from a few centimeters to thousands of meters. There are a number of different types of faults. A *normal fault* occurs when there is subsidence of one portion of the earth's crust; that is, the hanging wall moves downward in relation to the foot wall (Photo 82). In this process a cliff is produced, called a *fault scarp* (Photo 83). The normal fault rarely occurs alone, but usually creates a series of steep scarps. Many of the mountain ranges of the Great Basin of western United States were formed by a series of normal faults. A *reverse* or *thrust fault* occurs when a portion of the hanging wall is pushed upward in relation to the footwall. This type of fault is a response to compressional forces that cause the crust to shorten.

When pressure is applied to rocks over an extended period, they do not fracture, but bind into a series of folds. The upfolds are known as *anticlines* (Photo 84), and the downfolds as *synclines* (Figure 12.15, Photo 85). A fold can be open and nearly symmetrical, or it can be asymmetrical or even overturned. The degree of folding depends upon the strength of the rock and upon the duration and intensity of the compressional forces. Most of the great mountain ranges are anticlinal folds; that is, the dominant fold is upward in the core area, indicating great upward thrust.

A warp of the earth's crust occurs when a large area of rock has been uplifted uniformly. When a massive magma deposit moves toward the surface, the rocks are usually bent into a gently sloping structure. As a

**PHOTO 83**
A fault scarp in the Humboldt Range of Nevada. The scarp is over 150 feet high as a result of repeated earthquakes over the last several million years. (Courtesy: R. E. Wallace, U.S. Geological Survey)

**PHOTO 84**
Anticline. A small asymmetric anticline formed in Gopher Ridge volcanic rock near the Consumnes River in California. (Courtesy: L. D. Clark, U.S. Geological Survey)

**PHOTO 85**
Syncline. (Courtesy: Pennsylvania Geological Survey)

**PHOTO 86**
Monocline. (Courtesy: Standard Oil Company of New Jersey)

consequence the strata are gently inclined or tilted into a structure called a *monocline* (Photo 86).

## THIRD ORDER LANDFORMS

The sculpting of the second order landforms by the gradational forces of water, ice, wind, and gravity produces the third order landforms, the smallest of the landforms. Third order landforms can be most readily observed and therefore may be most significant to an individual. The local character of an area is important in describing its landforms. For example, an area might be described as having an average elevation of 1,000 meters (3,280 feet). If this area also has great departures from the average, however, with some peaks rising to 3,000 meters (9,840 feet) and some valleys near sea level, then the average elevation is not a useful description. The term *reflief* may describe more accurately the topographic condition of the area. Relief is the difference in elevation between the highest and lowest points within the immediate or local region. If mountains rise to 3,000 meters (9,840 feet) and the valleys are 500 meters (1,640 feet) above sea level, the local relief is 2,500 meters (8,200 feet). Relief describes the topographic character of an area and is frequently used to distinguish major terrain types.

### Gradational Processes

The gradational processes mold and shape the landforms. They occur in two stages. The rocks are changed first, during the *weathering processes.* In this stage, the rocks are disintegrated and decomposed, but remain in essentially the same place where they were formed. In the second stage, the *erosional and gradational processes* pick up and move the weathered materials and deposit them in lower elevations.

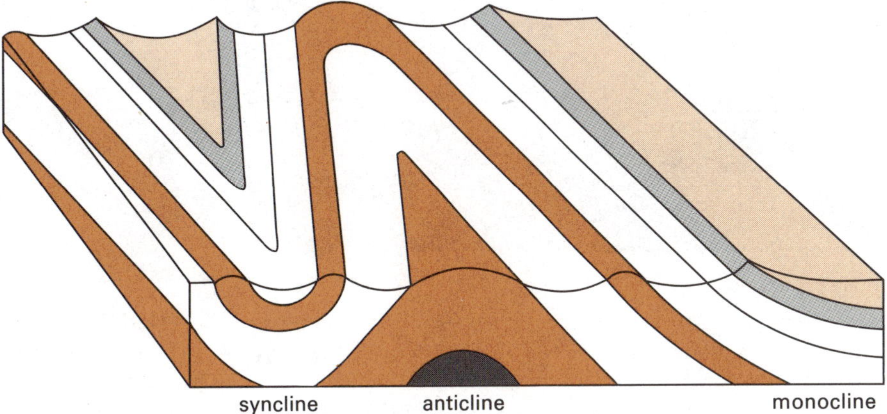


**FIGURE 12.15**
Types of folds.

**Weathering.** The weathering processes break up the rock in two ways: by *mechanical* weathering, which is the physical breaking or *disintegration* of the rock into smaller and smaller fragments; and by *chemical weathering,* in which chemical processes, acting on the small fragments, rearrange the elements into new minerals.

Water in the cooling process is the primary force behind mechanical weathering. When the temperature of water drops from 4° to 0°C (39.2° to 32°F), it expands about 9 percent. When water freezes in a confined space, such as within joints in rocks, it has an enormous outward thrust. At a minimum this thrust is 2,000 pounds per square inch, which is 280,000 pounds per square foot. The outward pressure continues to build below freezing, since a certain amount of expansion continues to take place at subzero temperatures, at least down to −22°C (−7.6°F). The pressure created by freezing water is sufficient to fracture most exposed rocks. Because water in a crevice freezes from the top downward, the freezing water acts as a wedge to spring rocks apart in areas of weakness, such as joints. This is known as *frost wedging* (Photo 87).

Mechanical weathering is most effective when bare rock is exposed in areas where repeated freezing and thawing occurs. It reaches its peak effectiveness on mountains above the timberline outside the permanently frozen Arctic regions. Such summit areas may be covered by a pavement of frost-shattered, angular blocks of rock. In many areas angular blocks will accumulate at the base of steep slopes, creating a *talus* slope (Photo 88).

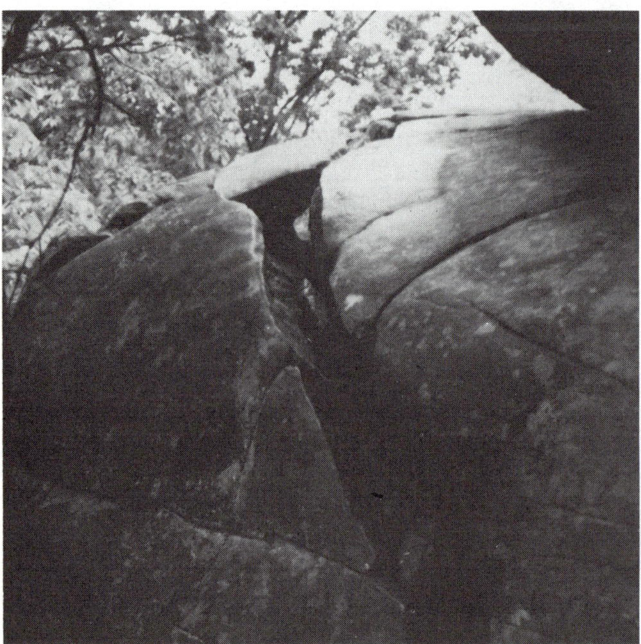

**PHOTO 87**
Frost wedging. This massive rock in Devil's Den of the Gettysburg National Park has been split in two by the freezing and thawing action of water. (Courtesy: Brian Tormey, The Pennsylvania State University)

Mechanical weathering is caused by other agents as well as by the action of freezing water. Roots from plants, primarily trees, will pry rocks apart (Photo 89). The heating and cooling of rocks causes them to expand and contract, and may cause them to break, especially if moisture is present. Mechanical weathering also occurs in rock layers when erosion removes the weight of overlying rocks. The outermost layer of rock may break from the main mass, causing joints to develop.

Decomposition occurs when various substances chemically bond with the rock, resulting in a change in the actual composition of the rock. Chemical weathering is most effective in hot, humid lands where vegetation flourishes. Under these conditions organic acids, which are potent agents of rock decay, are quickly formed and few rocks can resist their effects. Carbonic acid ($H_2CO_3$), formed from the reaction of water and carbon dioxide, is a common acid found in hot, humid regions. Of the many chemical processes involved in weathering, the most important are *oxidation, carbonation, solution,* and *hydration.*

Oxidation is a frequently observed chemical process; the rusting of iron is a familiar example. In the

**PHOTO 88**
Talus slope. Angular blocks of rocks at the base of the mountain in the Lewistown Narrows of the Juniata River. (Courtesy: Pennsylvania Geological Survey)

**PHOTO 89**
Tree wedging. Plants can cause rocks to separate due to the growth of roots. (Courtesy: Pennsylvania Geological Survey)

hot, humid regions of the world all iron products, such as steel bridges, rails, and automobiles, will rust away within a lifetime. Most rocks of the earth contain some iron-bearing minerals. When these are exposed to the atmosphere, oxidation begins to occur. Iron-rich rocks lose their original color and are stained by a wide variety of colors, such as red, yellow, orange, and brown.

Carbonation and hydration are normally combined in nature. Both occur in the following example of chemical weathering.

$$\underset{\text{feldspar}}{KAlSi_3O_8} + \underset{\text{water}}{2H_2O} + \underset{\text{carbon dioxide}}{CO_2} = \underset{\text{clay}}{H_4Al_2Si_2O_9} + \underset{\text{silica}}{4SiO_2} + \underset{\text{potassium carbonate}}{K_2CO_3}$$

This is an important chemical reaction, because feldspar is one of the most common minerals found in nature. The end products, clay and silica, play a vital role in soil formation.

Minerals may also be dissolved in solution. Carbonic acid found in nature is an extremely effective solvent of many minerals, including limestone. The following simple equation illustrates the process.

$$\underset{\text{limestone}}{CaCO_3} + \underset{\text{carbonic acid}}{H_2CO_3} = \underset{\text{calcium bicarbonate}}{Ca(HCO_3)_2}$$

Calcium bicarbonate is soluble and is easily carried away by water either above or below ground. This process creates the great caves found in limestone formations.

**Erosion.** The process of picking up and transporting weathered material is known as *erosion.* The weathered material may be transported as a bed load in *suspension* or in *solution.* It may be picked up and deposited by water, ice, or wind many times in a single day, or it may lie in the same place for thousands of years before it is again moved.

Water is the principal agent of erosion. The amount of material transported by streams is almost beyond the imagination. It is estimated that the Mississippi River alone carries about 2 million tons of sediment each day to the Gulf of Mexico. When the river is in flood stage, the amount of sediment may double. During the last million years or so about 31,200 square kilometers (12,100 square miles) of sand, silt, and clay have been added to the nation's Gulf region. In the central portion of the delta the deposits are at least 1.6 kilometers (one mile) thick.

The rate of movement of the suspended sediments depends upon many factors, including the size and shape of the particles, the specific gravity of the sediment grains, the velocity of the stream, and the degree of turbulence. Fine sediment will remain suspended in the water a very long time. Spherical grains will settle more quickly than flat mineral grains. Specific gravity is also important in that the heavier grains will be deposited far more quickly than lighter grains. This principle is used in gold panning, because gold nuggets with a specific gravity of 16 to 19 will be deposited more rapidly than feldspar grains with a specific gravity of about 2.7. The velocity of a stream is another factor in its carrying capacity. A sluggish stream moving across a meadow has a low carrying capacity compared with a boulder-rolling mountain torrent. As a stream's velocity increases, its carrying capacity increases by a geometric ratio. Turbulence keeps the sediments in suspension. If a particle is about to be deposited, but is caught in an upward swirl of water, it is moved forward by the eddy.

Sediments can be carried not only in suspension, but also in solution. These sediments consist largely of soluble minerals leached out of rocks. Many streams and rivers that are loaded with dissolved minerals have a distinctive taste and color. When this water evaporates it will leave a white residue that blankets the ground. Although the solution load is not visible, it is imposing. It has been estimated that the rivers of the world carry about 2,500 million tons of dissolved material to the oceans each year, or about 62 tons for each square mile of land on the earth. By this means alone the average land surface of the world would be lowered by about one foot in 30,000 years.

## MODELS OF LANDFORM DEVELOPMENT

Late in the nineteenth century, geologists and geographers began to conceive models to explain the development of landscapes. The earliest theories were based on the principle of *uniformitarianism,* an important cornerstone of modern geology. This principle states that the currently occurring processes, given sufficient time, created the existing landforms.

### GEOGRAPHICAL CYCLE OF EROSION

The earliest theory to provide an understanding of the development of a landscape was devised by William Morris Davis early in the twentieth century. The physical processes are so slow that development is not apparent in the space of a human life, and for most landforms even within recorded history. Davis developed a scheme where he classified existing landscapes as to their stage of development. He used the terms youthful, mature, and old age to describe the stages (Figure 12.16). In each of these stages the landforms exhibited particular characteristics. This model fit within the intellectual framework of the period and followed the concept of organic evolution proposed by Charles Darwin in 1859.

In his model, called the geographical *cycle of erosion,* Davis visualized a sudden uplift of a land surface from a lower to a higher elevation. Once the land was uplifted, erosion would begin immediately. Because water is the major erosional agent, Davis concentrated on the action of flowing water from the high ground to the lowlands. He visualized water molding the landscape over time, later extending his model to include the action of other erosional agents, such as wind and ice.

In the *youthful stage* he visualized that the work of the streams has just begun (Photos 90, 91, and 92). The valleys take the form of V-shaped canyons with steep slopes. The valley walls are steep because the streams have not had sufficient time to widen the valleys. Because of the recent uplift the main streams have not developed extensive tributaries. Where the streams are descending over resistant rock layers, rapids and waterfalls are common. Floodplain development is at a minimum. The upland divides between streams are level to gently rolling, and are usually poorly drained, frequently with swamps and lakes. The Grand Canyon of the Colorado River is one of the most spectacular examples of the youthful stage of development. Other examples include the gorge of the Niagara and the canyon of the Yellowstone River in Wyoming.

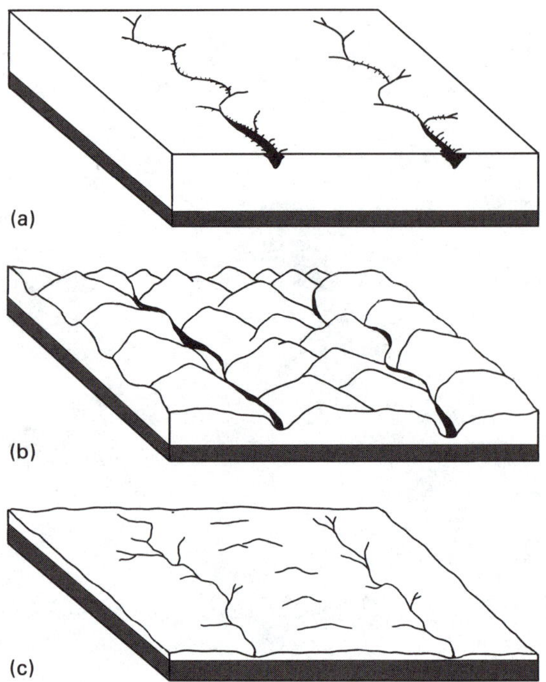


**FIGURE 12.16**
Geographical cycle of erosion. These diagrams represent W. M. Davis's concept of the development of a plain by stream erosion. The erosional surfaces are shown from (*a*) youth, through (*b*) maturity, to (*c*) old age.

As erosion proceeds, the upland interstream areas become smaller as the stream system develops. When no flat interstream areas exist, the landform exhibits *maturity.* In this stage the headwater tributaries have cut headward, the divides are narrow, and the region is highly dissected by a complex network of tributaries. Maturity is the time of maximum relief; that is, the topography is rugged. However, the landscape gradually becomes gently rounded, in contrast to the sharp relief characteristic of the youthful stage. As the tributaries are deepened and the area becomes more rugged, the swamps and lakes of the uplands are drained. The escarpments that produced rapids and falls in the youthful stage are gradually eroded away. At the close of the mature stage the streams have reached the local *base level of erosion:* that is, they can no longer cut downward, and they begin the process of lateral cutting. Typical mature landform regions include the Allegheny and Cumberland plateaus of the Appalachian Mountains. These rugged regions present many obstacles to human utilization. The slope of most of the land limits its agricultural value. Transportation routes are irregular, for they must follow the high ridges or the narrow valley bottoms. These rugged regions of beautiful vistas frequently have a high potential for tourism.

In the final *old age* stage the rugged relief of the topography is gradually reduced and the valleys are broadened with wide floodplains (Photo 93). The gradients of the streams become so gentle that they no longer erode their banks but instead deposit material in the valleys. Gradually the streams begin to meander, cutting laterally rather than downward. The land, which is gradually worn down to a plain, is called a *peneplain.* Occasionally old age plains have a few isolated hills of resistant rock, known as *monadnocks,* rising above the general level of the peneplain.

In the cycle-of-erosion theory, any stage can be interrupted if the area is uplifted or if there is a climatic change. This process is known as *rejuvenation.* When it occurs, the streams begin to cut new valleys in the old surface. If the uplift is uniform, the stream patterns may be rejuvenated without greatly altering the major features of the topography. The Susquehanna River of southern New York and northern Pennsylvania and the New River of the Cumberland Plateau are examples of rejuvenated streams.

The model of the cycle of erosion was a major advancement in understanding the evolution of landforms. The cycle-of-erosion theory was based not on a description of landforms, but on geologic *structure,* geomorphic *process,* and the *stage* of evolution. The length of time for a landscape to advance from one stage to another, according to this theory, depends on the nature of the rock and the vitality of the erosional processes.

While Davis provided a foundation for the understanding of the geomorphological process, many of his original ideas have been disputed as additional studies have been pursued. At the time Davis evolved his theory, little was known about the processes that form slopes. Perhaps the main objection is that Davis's theory visualized rapid uplift and then no further movement while the landscape evolved through the three

90

91

92

**PHOTOS 90–92**
Youthful stage of a stream. Photo 90: Royal Gorge of the Arkansas River in Colorado. Photo 91: Yellowstone Canyon of the Yellowstone River from Inspiration Point in the Yellowstone National Park (Courtesy: Wyoming Travel Commission). Photo 92: Thompson River Canyon in British Columbia as seen from the Trans-Canada Highway (Courtesy: The National Film Board of Canada).

**PHOTO 93**
Old age stage of a stream. The stream now has a wide floodplain and is cutting laterally to broaden its valley. (Courtesy: Mississippi A & I Board)

stages. Further, the Davis model did not consider climatic fluctuations and also fluctuations of the sea. It has also been questioned whether the passage of time is in itself responsible for the succession of the different stages. Finally, more recent geomorphologists have questioned the assumption of Davis that a particular landform characteristic can be produced by a single mechanism. Modern mathematical geomorphological models have, however, not resolved this question.

While most recent models of landform development continue to challenge the process assumptions in the Davis model, it has also been accepted that many of the postulates are quite reasonable. Emphasis has been placed on attempting to restructure the Davis model in the light of more coherent process arguments.

## CRUSTAL DEFORMATION AND SLOPE DEVELOPMENT

By the 1920s a number of geologists and physical geographers were questioning the concepts of Davis's cycle of erosion. Of these, the work of Walther Penck, an Austrian geomorphologist, is noteworthy. He argued that the form of the landscape was directly related not to the passage of time, but to the varying rates of crustal motion that incorporated the effects of uplift, tilting, or warping. Penck visualized that erosion of the land surface began as soon as uplift occurred.

Penck based his model on the concept that the form of the slope was directly related to the local rate of tectonic deformation. As the basis of his model he visualized the evolution of three forms of slopes—straight, concave, and convex (Figure 12.17). The straight slope

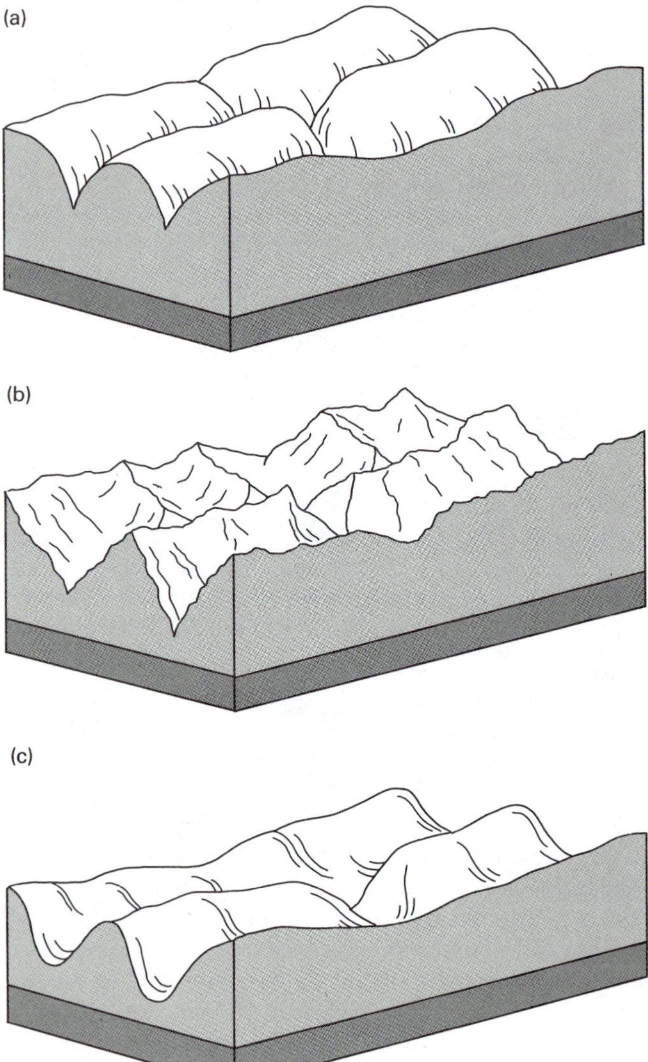


**FIGURE 12.17**
Slope forms according to Walther Penck. The slope form is related to the type of uplift. Convex slopes (*a*) occur during rapid tectonic uplift and downcutting by streams. Straight slopes (*b*) suggest a uniform rate of stream downcutting, either at the maximum rate or due to a steady rate of uplift. Concave slopes (*c*) indicate slow stream erosion. Tectonic uplift has either decreased or ceased. (After Penck, 1953)

is produced by a steady rate of downcutting and erosion of material. This *uniform development* occurs when there is a uniform rate of tectonic uplift. The convex slope becomes progressively steeper, indicating that there has been a sharp tectonic uplift and erosional activity has been accelerated. This process is known as a *waxing development.* The concave slopes appear to indicate a lessening of tectonic uplift and thus a decreasing rate of stream downcutting. Penck called this a *waning development.*

Penck observed slopes and concluded that the angle of the slope did not change through successive stages of development. This concept differs from the Davis model that visualized slopes becoming gentler and more rounded as a landscape evolved. In Penck's view, steep slopes may be present when a landscape exhibits characteristics of old age (Figure 12.18).

Since the 1920s, when Penck presented his model of landscape development, studies have shown that he made some major contributions. Parts of his work are strongly questioned, however. It is now generally agreed that in semiarid and arid regions, where mechanical weathering dominates, the steep upper portions of slopes do maintain constant angles as they retreat, and stream erosion greatly exceeds removal. In humid regions, however, where chemical weathering dominates, observations reveal that the slopes become less steep as the landscape develops.

As the mechanics of erosion become better understood, Penck's concepts may be judged unacceptable. The concave and convex slope forms cannot persist over long periods in rocks that are uniform in resistance to erosional stress. The approaches of Davis and Penck were deductive; modern approaches are based on careful quantitative measurements of slope evolution.

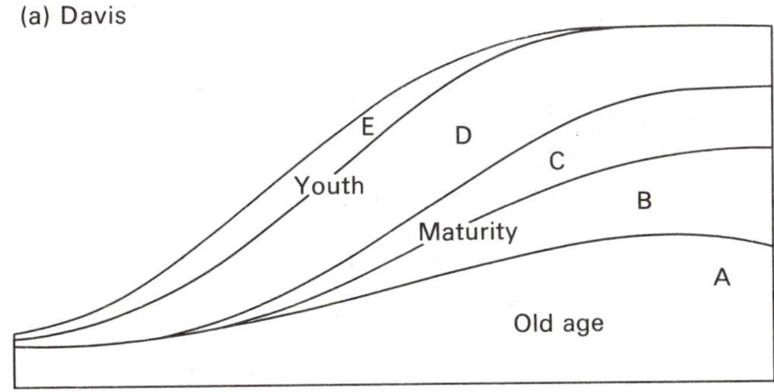


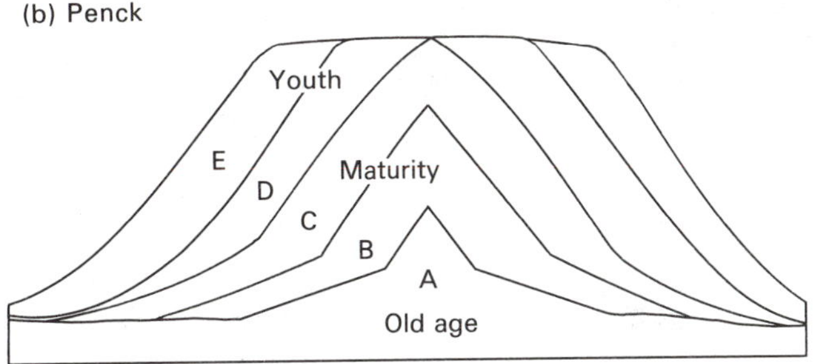


**FIGURE 12.18**
Slope development. William Morris Davis and Walther Penck proposed two varying concepts of slope development. According to Davis (*a*), as a slope retreats it becomes less steep and more rounded. The greater erosion on the steeper portion of the slope removes these areas faster, rounding the slope. According to Penck (*b*), the angle of slope remains essentially constant as erosion occurs. For this type of development to occur, the erosion at the base of the slope must be at about the same rate as the removal of material from the slope face. (After Holmes, 1955)

## EQUILIBRIUM MODEL OF LANDFORM DEVELOPMENT

As geomorphologists developed more sophisticated measurements, they began to question many of the assumptions of the early models. In the 1950s, John T. Hack attempted to develop a model that abandoned the cyclic concept of the evolution of landforms. Hack believed that the Davis theory was predicated on a number of false assumptions. For example, the concept of lateral planation, in which a stream has a tendency to laterally erode the banks from its headwaters to its mouth throughout its history, was considered incorrect.

The Hack model is based on the applied principle of dynamic equilibrium in slope development. This principle implies that any change in the system affects the entire drainage basin so that the whole landscape becomes adjusted to the process of development. Hack applied this principle of equilibrium to his work in the Appalachians, where he was unable to recognize cyclic surfaces or peneplains. As he stated in 1960, his model rests on the principle of dynamic equilibrium because

> **Within a single erosional system all elements of the topography are mutually adjusted so that they are downwasting at the same rate. The forms and processes are in a steady state of balance and may be considered as time independent. Differences and characteristics of form are therefore explainable in terms of spatial relations in which geologic patterns are the primary consideration rather than in terms of a particular theoretical evolutionary development such as Davis envisaged (p. 85).**

> **If the relative rates of erosion and uplift change, however, then the state of the balance or equilibrium constant must change. The topography then undergoes an evolution from one form to another. Such an evolution might occur if diastrophic forces ceased to exert their influence, in which case the relief would gradually lower, it might occur if diastrophic forces become more active, in which case the relief would increase, or it might occur if rocks of different resistance become exposed to erosion. Nevertheless as long as diastrophic forces operate gradually enough so that a balance can be maintained by erosive processes, then the topography will remain in a state of balance even though it may be evolving from one form to another (p. 86).**

In this model it is suggested that once a dynamic equilibrium has been achieved, the landform will remain essentially unchanged in character as long as the conditions which developed it remain constant.

The equilibrium model as developed by Hack and others has been criticized in that the form of a slope does not necessarily indicate the processes that formed it or that still exist. The diversity of slopes within an area hinders the establishment of statistical correlations between slope form and values of climate, rock type and structure, soil parameters, and other factors. Developing a useful model of slope equilibrium and landform development is therefore difficult.

## SLOPE AND DRAINAGE BASIN STUDIES

Since the 1940s the study of slope and drainage basin development has been pursued by a number of geomorphologists. These investigations may be grouped into several categories. A major area of emphasis has been the *analysis of mass movements,* particularly of slope failure characteristics. The processes of *water, sediment, and soluble movement* over a slope have also been studied. These studies are conducted for two purposes: The first is to measure, analyze, and investigate the processes shaping the present landscape. The second, and longer established, objective is to establish the sequence of stages of landscape evolution.

The total drainage basin has also been an area of interest. Recent studies have been concerned with the mathematical topology of stream networks and with the spatial patterns displayed by values of *morphometric parameters.* Studies of *drainage basin processes* have considered how the characteristics of relief, soil, land use, and rock types modify the input of water in drainage basins. A third approach studies *hydraulic geometry* of stream channels. A fourth type of study considers *river channel patterns,* particularly in areas where rapid changes affect land use and human activity. Finally, *drainage basin dynamics* have been considered, with particular emphasis on theoretical models.

The question of how a landscape evolves is still pertinent nearly a century after the first models were conceived. Because landscapes evolve so slowly, we cannot witness the processes directly. Theories must therefore be based on observations of the existing landscapes. Geographers have encountered many false leads in the attempt to solve this puzzle, but modern models provide an improved framework for considering the complex problems. A model does not provide a definitive answer but instead a way of thinking that may advance a field of study.

# VOLCANOES, EARTHQUAKES, AND HUMAN RESPONSES

Volcanoes and earthquakes are unquestionably among the most spectacular and awe-inspiring features of the physical world. Volcanoes have not only brought devastation to human societies, but have also provided great benefits by renewing agricultural soils and by creating geothermal energy. In contrast, earthquakes bring only death and destruction.

## VOLCANIC HAZARDS

The violence of a volcanic eruption has struck terror in humans since the earliest civilizations. History has recorded hundreds of volcanic eruptions, many of them destructive to life and property. It has been estimated that, since 1500 A.D., about 190,000 persons have lost their lives through volcanic eruptions. Impressive as it is, this number is small compared to the deaths caused by earthquakes, floods, and other natural disasters. For example, it is estimated that 650,000 people died in a single earthquake in central China in 1976.

The principal causes of death from volcanic eruptions have been suffocation, drowning, starvation, and disease. In the eruption of Vesuvius in 79 A.D., when Pompeii and Herculaneum were destroyed, a large percentage of the 16,000 deaths were caused by suffocation as ash and sulfuric gases poured over the area.

The eruption of Laki in 1783 in Iceland was responsible for many deaths from starvation and disease. This eruption destroyed so much of the pasture land of Iceland that 80 percent of the sheep and horses and half of the cattle were lost. As a result, about 20 percent of the human population died of disease and hunger the following year. This type of tragedy is now prevented by modern means of disaster relief. In the eruption of Paricutín in Mexico from 1934 to 1952, and Irazú in Costa Rica from 1963 to 1965, the destruction of livestock from ash-falls was large, but human deaths were prevented.

Molten lava from volcanoes has caused great property damage, and, on a few occasions, great loss of life as well. In the eruptions of Saint Pierre, Martinique, in 1902 and on the island of Bali in 1963, lava raced down the slopes of the volcanic cone, destroying everything in its path. Most of the flows, however, are of the type that occur in the Hawaiian Islands: The lava moves slowly and, while property may be destroyed, life is not greatly endangered. Most of the deaths in this type of eruption come from burns and inhalation of hot gases and ash.

The destruction of property depends to a large degree on the direction of the volcanic explosion. If the major force is vertical, the ash will be carried high into the atmosphere and may be spread over millions of square kilometers. If, in contrast, the major explosive force is horizontal, the destruction of property and possibly life will be far greater. The Mount St. Helens eruption in Washington on March 26, 1980, not only spewed ash and gases into the atmosphere to a height of about 4,600 meters (15,000 feet), but also created a tremendous horizontal blast (Photos 94–98).

The eruption of Mount St. Helens was preceded by a week-long series of earthquakes registering an average of 4.0 on the Richter scale. The initial eruption created dark clouds of volcanic ash and dust that blotted out the sun more than 260 kilometers (160 miles) away and created problems of fallout in areas 800 kilometers (500 miles) downwind. The eruption triggered flows of superheated rock and gas that swept down the volcano's slopes, toppling every tree in a 310-square-kilometer (120-square-mile) area. The wa-

**PHOTO 94**
The volcanic cone of Mount St. Helens prior to the eruption on March 26, 1980. (Courtesy: Roland V. Emetez, United States Department of Agriculture, Forest Service)

**PHOTO 95**
Aerial view of Mount St. Helens during the initial eruption activity. (Courtesy: U.S. Geological Survey)

**PHOTO 96**
The crater of Mount St. Helens after the major eruption. A small secondary volcano of ashes is still erupting. (Courtesy: Jim Hughes, United States Department of Agriculture, Forest Service)

ter temperature in the nearby streams reportedly rose to about 40°C (100°F), killing all fish. Dead deer and elk were seen on the mountainside.

Although most people were evacuated from the sparsely populated Mount St. Helens area, more than 60 persons lost their lives in the eruption. Economic damage was set at $2.7 billion. Losses in felled and seared timber on federal lands alone were reported at $500 million. The cost of reforestation and estimated loss of wildlife and fish added another $300 million. Agricultural losses in wheat and other crops totaled $250 million, and the repair and replacement costs of bridges, roads, sewer systems, and dredging were estimated at $270 million. Some 370,000 persons were temporarily unemployed, costing Washington an additional $250 million in unemployment compensation. Other economic losses in the area included lost tourism and the temporary loss of transportation on the Columbia River due to volcanic debris.

## ATMOSPHERIC AND CLIMATIC EFFECT

Volcanic dust spewed into the atmosphere may affect the weather and climate both locally and worldwide. This phenomenon has been known for many years. In 1784 Benjamin Franklin wrote

> **During several of the summer months of the year 1783, when the effects of the sun's rays to heat the earth in these northern regions should have been greatest, there existed a constant fog over all Europe, and parts of North America. This fog was of a permanent nature; it was dry and the rays of the sun seemed to have little effect in dissipating it as they easily do a moist fog rising from water . . . . Of course their summer effect in heating the earth was exceedingly diminished . . . perhaps the winter of 1783–84 was more severe than any that happened for many years.**
>
> **The cause of this universal fog is not yet ascertained . . . whether it was the vast quantity of smoke, long continuing to issue during the summer from Hecla [volcano] in Iceland, and that other volcano [Skaptar Jökul] which rose out of the sea near the island, which smoke might be spread by various winds is yet uncertain. (Cleveland Abbe, "Benjamin Franklin as a Meteorologist,"** ***Proceedings of the American Philosophical Society*** **45 [1906]: 127.)**

Although the Icelandic volcanoes were a major source of volcanic dust in 1783, the massive eruption

**PHOTO 97**
Mount St. Helens. This view shows the destruction of the forests caused by the horizontal blast in the eruption. (Courtesy: Jim Hughes, United States Department of Agriculture, Forest Service)

**PHOTO 98**
Overall view of the devastated area around Mount St. Helens. (Courtesy: Jim Hughes, United States Department of Agriculture, Forest Service)

in the same year of the volcano Asama in Japan was possibly the greatest source of atmospheric ash.

Since then the relationship of volcanic eruptions to the lowering of the atmospheric temperatures over wide areas has been well documented. The year 1816, known as "the year without a summer," followed the explosion of the volcano Tambora on the island of Sumbawa, Indonesia. The eruption sent dust over 4,000 meters (over 12,000 feet) into the atmosphere. At a distance of 500 kilometers (300 miles), the ash was so dense that it caused total darkness for three days. For months, the dust in the upper atmosphere caused lengthy twilights and brilliant sunsets all over the world. The world temperature fell about 1.1° C below normal. Cyclonic activity was concentrated from Newfoundland to northern Europe, resulting in almost continuous rain from May to October 1816. The average temperature of London was 2° to 3°C below normal. In New England a heavy snow occurred between June 6 and 11, and frost occurred every month of 1816. Some crops did not ripen, other crops rotted in the fields, and widespread food shortages occurred.

The eruption of Krakatoa in the East Indies in 1883 also appears to have had a worldwide climatic effect. The volcano shot ash into the atmosphere at least 30 kilometers (18 miles) high. A third of this dust fell within a radius of 50 kilometers (30 miles), another third within 3,000 kilometers (1,860 miles), and the remainder was spread worldwide. Even a year after the explosion, much of the dust was still suspended at heights of about 15 kilometers (9 miles), and it was three years before most of the dust settled to the level of the highest clouds. The worldwide temperature during this period was lowered.

The two most recent massive volcanic eruptions were Mount St. Helens in Washington in 1980 and El Chichon in Mexico in 1982. The materials ejected from these two volcanoes have been compared. The ash from both eruptions, after being compacted by rainfall, had an estimated bulk of about half a cubic kilometer. This material would equal a football field piled 100 kilometers (60 miles) high.

The eruption of material from the two volcanoes differed significantly. The total volume ejected at Mount St. Helens was probably six to seven times greater than at El Chichon. However, the El Chichon eruption had a far greater effect on atmospheric pollution than that of Mount St. Helens. Three factors help to explain the difference. The eruption of material was almost entirely upward at El Chichon, whereas at Mount St. Helens the energy was expanded horizontally more than vertically. At El Chichon the atmospheric conditions were more favorable to stratospheric penetration and transport of the aerosols, and finally, the El Chichon magma had an unusually high content of sulfur dioxide. At the National Oceanic and Atmospheric Administration's Mauna Loa Observatory in Hawaii, the lasar radar indicated that the El Chichon cloud was more than one hundred times denser than that from Mount St. Helens. A satellite called the *Solar Mesosphere Explorer* indicated that the ash from El Chichon spread an uneven veil over much of the earth, extending from about 18 kilometers (11 miles) to 35 kilometers (21 miles) in altitude.

Scientists have raised a question: Has the ejection of volcanic ash into the atmosphere really affected the weather, or have the climatic changes been simply coincidental? Until the past century, solar radiation could not be directly measured, and so the effects of volcanic eruptions could not be verified. Since 1880, however, an instrument called the pyrheliometer has been used to measure the energy received on the earth. This energy shows marked fluctuations from year to year. The periods when less energy reaches the earth coincide with the great volcanic eruptions. The marked decrease in solar radiation in 1884–85 occurred after the 1883 eruption of Krakatoa. The low in 1890–91 was preceded by the eruptions of Bandai-san in 1888, Vulcano in 1888–90, and Bogoslof in 1883. The low in 1902–1903 coincided with the eruptions of Mount Pelée and Santa Maria, and the 1912 low coincided with the eruption of Mount Katmai. Evidence from more recent eruptions confirms the earlier findings that volcanic dust in the upper atmosphere does decrease the direct solar radiation on the earth.

The dust particles in the atmosphere affect the radiation in a number of ways. Dust not only absorbs some of the solar radiation, but it also reflects and scatters the sun's rays. Since dust particles can absorb terrestrial radiation more readily than solar radiation, it would appear that more earth-radiated than sun-radiated heat would be absorbed. The net effect of the dust, so far as absorbed heat is concerned, would be to increase the world's temperatures slightly. However, reflection and scattering are also important and function in different ways. If the wavelengths are small compared to the size of the particles, more reflection and scattering will occur. It has been calculated that the wavelength of terrestrial radiation is six to seven times the diameter of the ash particles and would pass through the dusty air with little loss. Thus the dust particles not only prevent heat from reaching the earth's surface but permit it to escape freely into space. As a result volcanic activity has a cooling effect on the earth.

The ash from volcanoes could affect the climate of the world in other ways. For example, dust clouds could reduce the temperature in a particular region, and since differences in temperature between the tropics and the higher latitudes are responsible for the prevailing wind systems, areas outside the direct influence of the volcanic dust cloud may be affected. It has also been found that the dust particles can act as nuclei to form ice crystals in the upper atmosphere, increasing not only rainfall, but the potential for snow.

Long records indicate that the major portion of dust from a volcanic eruption remains in the atmosphere only about a year, and the effect of the largest eruption is about a decade. Carbon dioxide as well as dust is ejected by volcanoes. This gas may contribute to the "greenhouse effect" that tends to raise temperatures slightly. However, the volcanic sources of carbon dioxide are extremely small compared to the amount produced by the earth's biological processes. It appears that the effect of volcanic eruptions is limited to a few years unless major eruptions continue over a long period.

## VULCANISM AND AGRICULTURE

Although volcanic eruptions create temporary havoc on the landscape, they may ultimately produce local agricultural prosperity. Rainy tropical regions benefit especially. Warm temperatures and heavy precipitation lead to rapid depletion of soil fertility. Unless fertilizer is applied, tropical lands can be farmed profitably only for a few years because productivity declines rapidly.

In many tropical places in the world, the high agricultural productivity is dependent upon volcanic soils. The island of Java is a notable example. Volcanoes dominate the landscape, with 58 of the cones stretching across the island. Javanese volcanoes erupt more frequently with ash than with lava, and when lava is ejected it is generally basic, so that the volcanic soils contain high proportions of calcium, nitrogen, magnesium, and phosphorus, which provide plant nutrients to the soil. In Java a few areas possess acid igneous rock. If leaching is at an advanced stage so that the soluble minerals have been removed, poor acidic soils are found. These differences account for the agricultural potential in Java. On the acid soils the population is sparse and agricultural yields low, while on the basic volcanic soils the population pressure is great and the agricultural yields high. Periodic ash-falls from volcanoes can turn low-productivity lands into highly productive agricultural areas. This situation prevails in many places. For example, most of the sugar, cotton, and other large-scale plantings in Central America and the Philippines, as well as Indonesia, are located near recently active volcanoes.

The time required to develop volcanic ash and lavas into a productive soil depends upon the texture and composition of the material and the climatic conditions. In general, the time required in soil development varies directly with the silica content of the original material. The basaltic ash from some Central American volcanoes is cultivated within a year after its deposition. Ash with an intermediate amount of silica takes 10 to 20 years to develop a soil under humid conditions. In contrast to these rapidly developed soils, the siliceous rhyolite that covers much of Guatemala and El Salvador has shown only slight alterations in 2,000 years and requires about 5,000 years to develop a soil sufficiently deep to encourage agriculture. The type of climate can be of major importance in the time required to develop a soil. It has been observed on the Hawaiian Islands that the rate of weathering is 10 to 20 times greater on the humid windward side of the islands than on the drier leeward sides.

The best way to keep the soil fertile is to have a new blanket of basic ash deposited every decade or so. The value of the ash material in soil renewal is now recognized, and in some places it is being transported from the volcanic areas and spread on depleted soils. This process increases the value of marginal farmlands without the use of costly commercial fertilizers.

## GEOTHERMAL ENERGY FROM MAGMA

Even thousands of years after eruptions have ceased, the magma remains hot in volcanic areas. This energy heats adjacent water to at least 180°C (356°F) and sometimes to 200°C (392°F). Although volcanic activity is widely distributed throughout the world, these high geothermal temperatures are on or near the surface only in limited areas. The geothermal heat of the earth, therefore, has been utilized in just four areas—California, Iceland, New Zealand, and Italy—where geysers, hot springs, fumaroles, and related phenomena occur.

In the United States the only geothermal power facilities are located in The Geysers area about 120 kilometers (75 miles) north of San Francisco and at Salton Sea in southern California. The Geysers area has been producing electric power since 1960 and, with an output of 1,137 megawatts, is one of the world's largest geothermal power developments. The project produces sufficient power to satisfy the energy needs of more than one million people, or the population of San Francisco and Oakland combined. The Geysers are in a zone of faulting where deep-seated magma provides the heat for the steam vents and hot springs.

Because Italy is poor in mineral fuels, the nation has pioneered the use of geothermal energy. Although volcanic activities are widespread in Italy, geothermal energy sources have been developed only in the Larderello and nearby Monte Amiata areas in Tuscany, south of Florence. The natural steam vents and hot water pools have been known for centuries but were long regarded as places of evil by the peasants. Only at the end of the nineteenth century was the natural steam used to operate engines. In 1931 the first major well was drilled to tap the underground steam to produce electricity. The area covers about 250 square kilometers (100 square miles) and is now covered with a network of wells spaced about 600 feet apart. The power plant produces over 2,000 million kilowatt hours of electricity, or about four percent of the total Italian power production.

The hot springs and geysers of Iceland have been utilized by its population since the earliest settlements. Settlers cooked their food either in the hot ground or in the hot springs. Since 1928 hot water has been pumped to Reykjavik and used in hospitals, schools, and since 1943 to heat buildings. Now more than 90 percent of the homes in the capital city are heated by the municipally owned hot water system. The hot water is also used to produce electricity, providing Iceland with sufficient power to develop an aluminum smelting industry.

The geothermal energy resources of New Zealand are confined to the volcanic zone of the North Island. Like the Icelandic settlers, the Maori people have used the hot water for cooking and washing since ancient times. In the 1950s a small electric power plant was based on geothermal energy, but development stopped after the discovery of natural gas. Municipal and industrial use of the hot-water resources is still encouraged.

Although geothermal energy originating from volcanic activity has long been used, its development as a modern energy source has lagged. As demand for energy increases and the costs for traditional fuels rise, geothermal energy becomes more attractive as a potential energy source. The engineering problems of utilizing steam and hot water from shallow depths in the earth have largely been solved by the application of oil-field technology. Huge reserves of geothermal energy are stored in the earth, and research is urgently needed to determine whether it is economically feasible to take greater advantage of this energy source.

## EARTHQUAKE DISASTERS

An earthquake is one of the earth's most devastating geophysical activities. When the internal pressure of a limited portion of the earth is altered, waves are created that travel in all directions. These waves produce an earth movement that is known as an earthquake. All earthquakes, great or small, are a response to a change in the volume of rock. The volume of rock involved will vary depending upon the energy released in the earthquake. In the largest shocks as much as 2 million cubic miles of rock may be involved. The displacement of the rock—that is, the slippage along two fault surfaces—may vary from a few centimeters to nearly 15 meters (50 feet). After an earthquake occurs, the fault surfaces again become locked by friction and cementation. Pressure may build again and in time another earthquake occurs. As we have seen, the great earthquake zones coincide with the areas of subduction, spreading mid-ocean ridge, or transform faults.

Annually there are about 50,000 earthquakes that are sufficiently strong to be noticed without the aid of the seismograph. Of these, about 100 are large enough to produce substantial damage. Disastrous earthquakes occur on the average of about one per year (Photos 99–104).

Among the great earthquakes in historic times was the one that struck Lisbon, Portugal, in 1755. Twelve thousand buildings were destroyed and the death toll was at least 60,000. Some damage from this quake was reported in Algiers, 1,120 kilometers (700 miles) to the east.

In New Madrid, Missouri, three great shocks occurred in 1811 and 1812, and at least 1,874 aftershocks were felt more than 320 kilometers (200 miles) away. The areas of greatest shocks covered about 104,000 square kilometers (40,000 square miles). In one area, 240 kilometers (150 miles) long and 64 kilometers (40 miles) wide, the ground sank one to three meters (3 to 10 feet).

**PHOTO 99**
Earthquake landslide in Turnagain Heights, Anchorage, Alaska. A view of damage to the land and houses caused by the Alaska earthquake of March 27, 1964. (Courtesy: Robert A. Page, U.S. Geological Survey)

On April 18, 1906, the San Andreas Fault in California slipped in a segment over 430 kilometers (270 miles) long. The slip was felt from Los Angeles in the south to Coos Bay, Oregon, in the north. Devastation was greatest in San Francisco. About 700 people were killed, and fires started when gas mains were broken, causing about $400 million damage. Many insurance companies could not meet their obligations and defaulted.

A great earthquake destroyed a large portion of Tokyo, Japan, on September 1, 1923, causing about 74,000 deaths. Fifty-four percent of the brick buildings and 10 percent of the reinforced concrete structures collapsed. The shock started a tsunami that reached a wave height of 10 meters (32 feet) in Sagami Bay, where it caused many deaths and great destruction.

**PHOTO 100**
Earthquake faulting. Bent rails caused by faulting in the Guatemala earthquake of February 4, 1976. (Courtesy: A. F. Espinosa, U.S. Geological Survey)

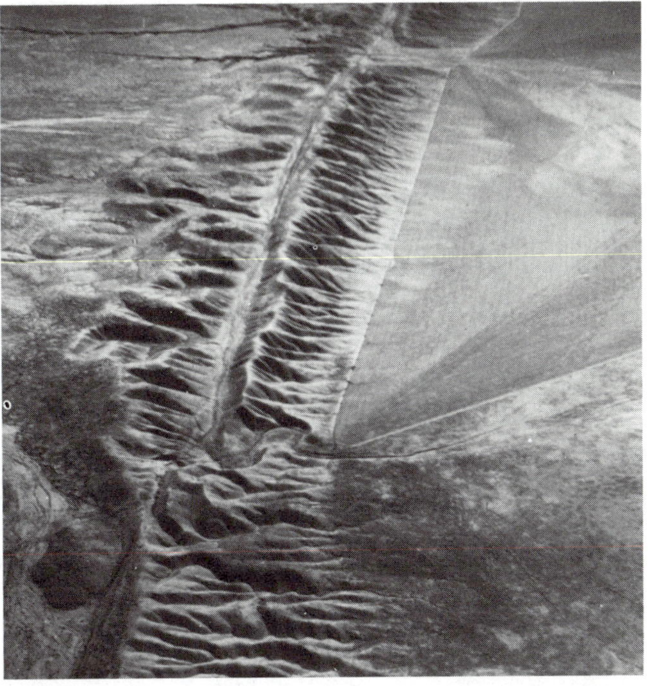

**PHOTO 102**
San Andreas Fault. An aerial view of the fault in central California. (Courtesy: J. R. Balsley, U.S. Geological Survey)

**PHOTO 101**
Earthquake damage. A view of the overpass connecting Foothill Boulevard and Golden State Freeway, which collapsed during the San Fernando earthquake in California on February 9, 1971. (Courtesy: Earthquake Information Bulletin 230, U.S. Geological Survey)

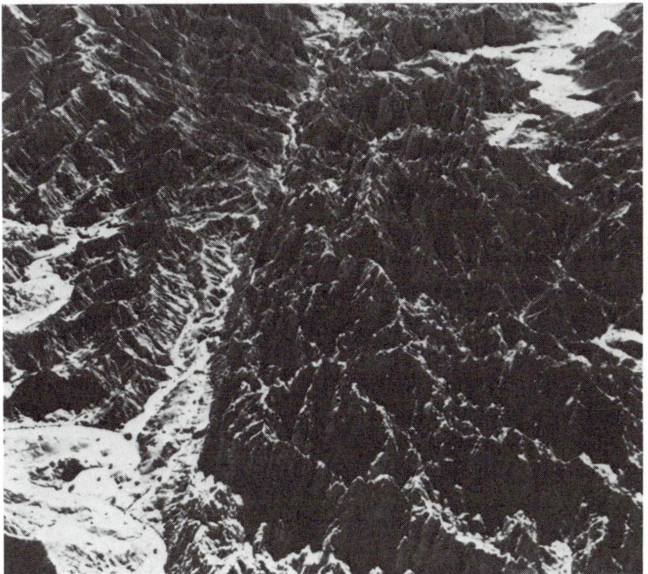

**PHOTO 103**
Borrego Mountain earthquake. Aerial view of linear valley eroded along the San Andreas Fault in the Mecca Hills of Riverside County, California. (Courtesy: Borrego Mountain Earthquake 39, U.S. Geological Survey)

**PHOTO 104**
Borrego Mountain earthquake. A band of complex earth fractures about one meter (three feet) wide across a hardened silty sand crust at the eastern end of the Borrego Mountain in San Diego County, California. (Courtesy: Borrego Mountain Earthquake 4, U.S. Geological Survey)

One of the large recent earthquakes occurred in southern Italy on November 23, 1981. The most devastating earthquake in Italy in 70 years, it measured 6.8 on the Richter scale. The major earthquake was followed by 32 aftershocks felt from the island of Sicily to Trieste on the Yugoslav border. About 4,500 persons were killed and more than 7,500 injured. Property damage occurred over 26,000 square kilometers (10,000 square miles). The quake devastated at least 97 villages and towns, crumbled bridges and roads, and toppled high buildings. Rescue efforts in the mountain area east of Naples were hampered by blocked roads, downed telephone lines, and winter weather. More than 50,000 people were initially without shelter. Many thousands lived in temporary shelters for months after the earthquake.

The earthquake zones of the world support some of the densest populations. At the present time the occurrence of an earthquake cannot be predicted. Because the shock of an earthquake is expended within a few minutes, there is no possibility of evacuating people from an area. Attempts to produce buildings that are "earthquake proof" have been only partially successful. As long as people live in areas where earthquakes occur, they will be subject to these unpredictable violent earth movements.

## CONCLUSION

The earth's landforms can be divided into several categories. The first order features consist of the continents and ocean basins. The second order features are the major landforms, such as mountains and plains, that exist on the first order landforms. Third order features are the sculptured details, such as hills and valleys, of the second order landforms.

In the last several decades, scientific thought regarding the origin of landforms has undergone a revolution with the development of the theory of plate tectonics. This theory visualizes that the earth's surface is composed of a number of plates that move over geologic time. In certain areas the plates spread apart and in other areas they collide. In the area where the plates diverge, vulcanism creates earth crust. In the areas where the plates collide, one plate plunges beneath another, re-entering the mantle. In these subduction zones, deep trenches are created. The zone of subduction is characterized by mountain building with active volcanoes and earthquakes. The theory of plate tectonics provides the first scientific explanation for the origin of the world's mountains and uplands.

As soon as a landform is created, the processes of gradation begin to change it. The tremendous diversity of landform features is a response to the structure of the rock, the type of gradational process, and the length of time of development. The study of slope development is fundamental to understanding the origin of landforms, for slopes are the basic element of a landform.

Relief features are normally formed too slowly for us to observe them. Models have therefore been developed to explain their origin. One of the earliest models was devised by William Morris Davis when he recognized the importance of structure, process, and stage in the development of landforms. Walther Penck's contribution, the theory that slopes retreat at constant angles rather than gradually as in the Davis model, appears to be valid under certain developmental conditions. The equilibrium model of slope development stresses the adjustment of slope to geomorphic processes.

## STUDY QUESTIONS

1. Explain a geographic approach to the study of landforms.
2. What are the three principal layers of the earth? How do they differ?
3. How does a rock differ from a mineral?
4. Describe each of the three classifications of rocks. What is the origin of each?
5. Describe the development of the theory of plate tectonics.
6. What is the scientific evidence that the seafloor is spreading?
7. How is the motion of plates measured?
8. What are the types of plate boundaries? Describe the activity at each plate boundary.
9. Why is the plate tectonic convective system important?
10. Explain the origin of hot spots.
11. How do second order landforms differ from first order landforms?
12. How does the theory of plate tectonics explain the mountain-building process?
13. What are the major types of tectonic processes? Describe each.
14. What are the principal classifications of intrusive volcanic forms? How does each differ?
15. What is the evidence of extrusive vulcanism?
16. What are the principal types of crustal deformations? How does each differ?
17. How do the gradational processes occur? Describe each of them.
18. What are the principal chemical processes in weathering? Describe each.
19. Describe the geographical cycle of erosion.
20. How does the Penck explanation of slope development differ from the Davis explanation?
21. What is the basis of the equilibrium model of landform development?

# 13 FLUVIAL PROCESSES AND LANDFORMS

## KEY WORDS

antecedent stream
base level
consequent stream
cut bank
dendritic stream
distributaries
drainage basin
drainage net
ephemeral stream
exotic stream
floodplain
graded stream
gradient
intermittent stream
knickpoint
laminar flow
longitudinal profile
meander
oxbow
perennial stream
rill
rivulet
slip-off slope
stream order
subsequent stream
suspension
trellis drainage
water gap
wind gap

Of all the geomorphic processes, running water may have had the greatest influence on history. The availability of water has always shaped the way we view the world. One of the earliest human endeavors was the development of irrigation to improve crop yields in the Middle East. In 3200 B.C. the Egyptians built a long dike on the west bank of the Nile. The dike was the basis for a system of canals to carry flood waters into fields adjacent to the river. For such projects to be successful, skills in mathematics, surveying, and hydraulics had to be developed.

Streams have always provided transportation routes, and even today, many major routes follow low-level valleys in the rugged regions of the world. Streams can provide access to the interiors of continents. In Asia today the Yangtze serves as a major transportation route from Shanghai to Chungking, a distance of more than 1,200 kilometers. The same is true of the Mississippi River system, as barges move, for example, from Pittsburgh to New Orleans, a distance of more than 1,500 kilometers.

Rivers have not always linked different societies, however; they have frequently acted as barriers. The Rhine River has from the earliest times established the boundary between France and Germany. Two distinct cultures developed on the east and west sides of this river. In Roman times the Danube River was long an obstacle to the invading barbarians. Their crossing of the Danube was heralded as one of the major events leading to the fall of the Roman Empire.

## DRAINAGE BASIN HYDROLOGICAL CYCLE

The principles that apply to the atmospheric hydrological cycle also apply to the *drainage basin,* the total area drained by a stream. To illustrate, let us follow the path of water from a single rainfall through a drainage basin. As rain begins to fall, a portion of it will be *intercepted* by vegetation. In the early stages of a rainstorm this can be as much as 30 to 40 percent of the total, but vegetation is soon saturated and then only a small amount is intercepted for the duration of the storm. A considerable amount of *surface storage* of the water also occurs in the early stages of a rainstorm. This can be as much as one-half of the total rainfall in the early stages, but, like vegetation interception, surface storage soon diminishes to a small percentage of the falling water. A small percentage of the rain will fall directly into streams as *channel precipitation.*

After these processes have been satisfied, infiltration begins with *soil-moisture storage* and later *groundwater storage.* When the upper soil becomes saturated, the water gradually penetrates the groundwater zone. When all of the surface is filled and when the ground is saturated, *runoff* begins. The water moves by *throughflow* in the soil moisture zone, by *interflow* in the *capillary or aeration zone,* and by *baseflow* in the groundwater zone.

The rate of infiltration depends upon the type of vegetation covering, the permeability of the soil, and the water content of the soil. If infiltration is as rapid as the amount of precipitation falling, there will be no runoff. Infiltration occurs most effectively on friable, sandy soils and least effectively on heavy, clayey soils.

## DRAINAGE BASIN SYSTEMS

When rain falls on an area, a part of it will penetrate the soil and rock strata and become known as *groundwater.* However, when the ground becomes saturated, the rainfall has then exceeded the rate of infiltration, and the water begins to flow along the surface in a thin layer, creating small channels known as *rills.* As the process continues, the rills develop into larger *rivulets* and then into *gullies.* The gullies can become so well developed that they intersect the groundwater table and become permanent streams. This small stream is the primary unit, a first-order stream, in the growth of a drainage system. As each stream joins with another stream, the system develops into a drainage network. The collecting area is called a *watershed,* and the size of the watershed is determined by the drainage area of the river and its tributaries. A drainage system consists of many small basins, each determined by the size and shape of the streams it serves. The size of the basins, and ultimately of the watershed, is dynamic, gradually expanding as the headwaters of streams are enlarged.

A drainage basin is one of the best examples of a system on the earth's surface. It is an open system, with both materials and energy flowing through it. Water enters the system through precipitation in all parts of the basin and leaves the system by evaporation and when the river enters the ocean. The movement of the water in the system carries with it energy. The movement of water in a river represents the transformation of *potential energy* into *kinetic energy,* the energy of movement. The water uses kinetic energy to move itself and to carry its load of sediment. The potential energy is consumed by a stream to reach its base level. At this point there is no potential energy remaining to create kinetic energy, and the river can no longer perform any work. *Entropy* measures the inability to perform work. Thus entropy is at its maximum when a river system reaches base level.

The river system is a steady-state system; physical laws determine that a river will act in an established way. First, a river system will always expend the least possible energy from its origin at its highest point to its lowest level, where it enters the sea. In other words, it will seek to flow in the most direct course. Theoretically, this course would consist of a waterfall from the highest to the lowest point. A second axiom in a steady-state river system is that the work is distributed evenly. In reality, the headwater of the system usually has the steepest slope, and the mouth of the drainage basin reaches a nearly horizontal level. The variation in grade of a river from its headwaters to its mouth provides a compromise between the principles of least work and uniform distribution of work.

## STREAM RUNOFF

It is estimated that about three-eighths of the total precipitation that falls on the earth is carried seaward by streams as *runoff.* Runoff is the principal degrading agent on the land surface, and it is therefore the most important factor in the erosional process. The amount of runoff varies considerably from area to area, even in areas with equal amounts of precipitation. Besides total amount and regime of precipitation, runoff depends upon such factors as relief of the area, type of bedrock and soil, and vegetational cover. The greater the relief, the greater the runoff. Unconsolidated sediments and soil absorb more water than consolidated rock. Most vegetation holds water, delaying runoff. In climates where the humidity is low and wind movements are high, a high evaporation rate reduces the amount of water available for surface runoff.

Streams can cause great disasters during flood periods. These events are sometimes sudden and catastrophic. For example, in 1889 and again in 1977, after many days of heavy rain, dams on the Conemaugh River suddenly collapsed, causing flooding in Johnstown, Pennsylvania. In both instances, torrents of water devastated the city, causing great loss of life. The 1889 flood, with a loss of 2,200 lives, is known as the nation's worst flood disaster. However, this disaster pales to insignificance when it is remembered that one million Chinese lost their lives in the Hwang Ho flood of 1887, and 100,000 were drowned in the Yangtze River flood of 1911. It is estimated that more than a billion people have lost their lives in floods, and that property damage, in terms of present-day currency, amounts to trillions of dollars.

The discharge of rivers varies so greatly from one region to another that developing a general classification is difficult. As a rule of thumb, however, in areas with an annual precipitation of 125 centimeters (50 inches) or more, about 50 percent is discharged directly into rivers. As precipitation decreases, a smaller percentage is discharged by runoff. In areas where precipitation totals 55 centimeters (20 inches), only about 15 percent is discharged by runoff. To illustrate, the Ohio River discharges about 30 percent of the rainfall of its basin while the Missouri River carries away only about 15 percent.

## VELOCITY OF A STREAM

A stream's velocity is likely to change throughout its course. Such changes are important because the velocity of a stream is directly related to its ability to carry sediments and thus erode. The factors that determine velocity or rate of flow are *slope or gradient, channel shape* and *size, load,* and *volume* or *discharge.*

The slope or gradient, which refers to the drop per unit distance, varies greatly not only from stream to stream but also in the length of a single stream. Gradient can be stated in meters per kilometer or feet per mile. Thus a slope of two meters per kilometer means that the stream's surface has a vertical drop of two meters for each kilometer of horizontal distance downstream.

At the headwaters of a mountain stream the gradient is usually steep and may drop several meters within a very short distance. When that same stream enters the sea hundreds of kilometers from its origin, the gradient may be only a few centimeters in many kilometers. For example, the Amazon River drops only 6 meters (20 feet) in its last 800 kilometers (500 miles) before it enters the Atlantic Ocean. A portrayal of the gradient of a stream from its source to the place it enters another river or the ocean is known as its *longitudinal profile.* Because the gradient varies along the length of the stream, its profile is normally concave with the upward curve at its source (Figure 13.1).

The shape of the channel determines the amount of water in contact with the stream's bottom and sides. Precise terms have been developed by hydraulic engineers to describe the shape and size of a channel. The *depth* of a channel refers to the vertical distance from the surface of the stream to its bottom or bed. The

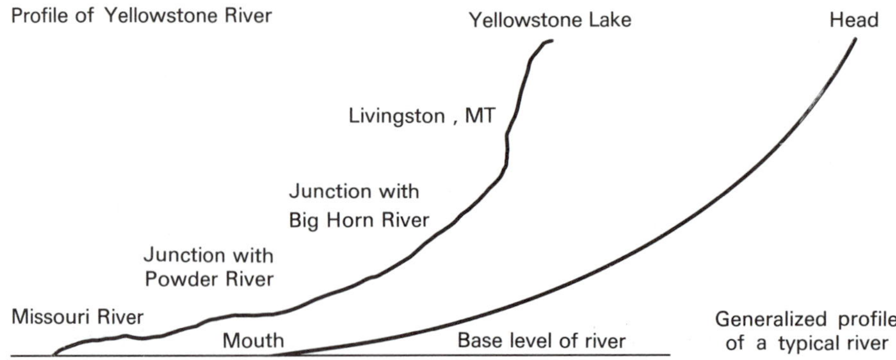


**FIGURE 13.1**
Longitudinal stream profile. This diagram illustrates the change in slope of a stream from its headwaters to its mouth. (After U.S. Geological Survey, Water Supply Paper 41, 1901)

*width* is the distance from one edge of the water to another edge. The *cross-sectional area,* designated as *A,* is the area in square meters (or square feet) of a vertical slice across a stream at any specified place. The *wetted perimeter, P,* is the length of the line of contact between the water and the bed of the stream. The *hydraulic radius, R,* of a stream, which is an important element in determining velocity, is defined as the cross-sectional area, *A,* divided by the wetted perimeter, *P,* or $R = A/P$.

The stream's load refers to the dissolved materials as well as the solid earth particles it can transport. For example, when a stream has a steep gradient, it can carry fairly large boulders. When the gradient is reduced to a few centimeters per kilometer, the load will consist of fine-grained sand and silt. The flow will range from extreme speed on high slopes, where the water cascades down the channel, to very slow movement through a channel with a low slope. Thus the flow varies from high *turbulence* to a *laminar* flow. A laminar flow, which moves as if it were made up of very fine layers that slip smoothly over one another, rarely occurs in streams. In all streams, except the most sluggish, turbulence occurs throughout the course.

Finally, the *volume* or *discharge, D,* of a stream is the amount of water flowing past a given point in a given unit of time. Discharge is usually measured in cubic meters or feet per second. In order to determine discharge, the mean velocity, *V,* must first be known. Mean velocity is obtained by measuring the velocity of the stream at several places along a cross section. The mean velocity is multiplied by the stream's cross-sectional area, *A,* to determine discharge: $D = VA$. This equation is known as the equation of continuity of flow. For a river to possess a great volume of water it must have a large drainage basin in a humid region. Rarely does a stream flowing through a desert have a large discharge. The Amazon River, to illustrate, has a discharge 50 times greater than that of the Nile River, although the Nile River is longer.

The discharge of a river varies over time. During floodstage the amount of water in a river basin is significantly increased. In order to accommodate the increased amount of water, a river will change its width, depth, cross-sectional area, and wetted perimeter, and correspondingly its hydraulic radius. In this way the volume of the stream is increased. When the volume increases, the velocity usually does also. Thus the eroding power of a stream will vary from time to time, depending upon its velocity. During low-water periods, sediments will accumulate in the channel, while during high-water periods, the channel will be cleaned of its deposits and the stream will erode towards base level.

## KNICKPOINT

At any sharp break in the longitudinal profile of a stream, the stream gradient increases abruptly, creating cataracts, rapids, and waterfalls. Such a change in a stream's gradient is called a *knickpoint* (Figure 13.2, Photos 105–107).

A number of conditions can cause a rapid change in the gradient of a stream. A change in the resistance of the bedrock frequently creates a change in the gradient. For example, Niagara Falls are created by a resistant sandy limestone, the Lockport dolomite, on the surface, and less resistant sedimentary rocks beneath the dolomite. As the water falls from the dolomite ledge, it erodes the less resistant material more rapidly. The dolomite ledge is gradually retreating, however, and the falls will eventually disappear.

Knickpoints can also be created by differential erosion, such as that produced by glacial action. A glacier will frequently erode its main valley to a greater depth than its tributary valleys. The valleys that lie high above

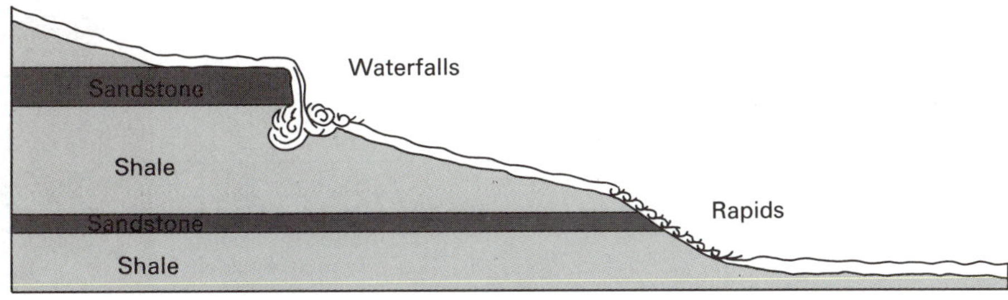


**FIGURE 13.2**
Knickpoints in a stream profile. Resistant rocks retard erosion and cause falls and rapids in a stream's course.

the main valley are known as hanging valleys. Waterfalls occur at the points where the tributaries enter the main valley. Because glacial erosion is differential, offsets will be created in the main valleys. In these areas rapids and falls will occur along the streams.

Crustal movement is another cause of knickpoints. This situation is frequently evident in coastal areas where the sea level has dropped or the land has been raised in a short period of time. This action creates a change in the gradient near the original mouth of the river, and rapids and falls will result at that location.

105

106

**PHOTOS 105–106**
Niagara Falls. Photo 105 shows the American Falls; Photo 106 shows the Canadian Falls. The Niagara limestone, a resistant formation that is underlain by soft shales and sandstone, is responsible for the escarpment.

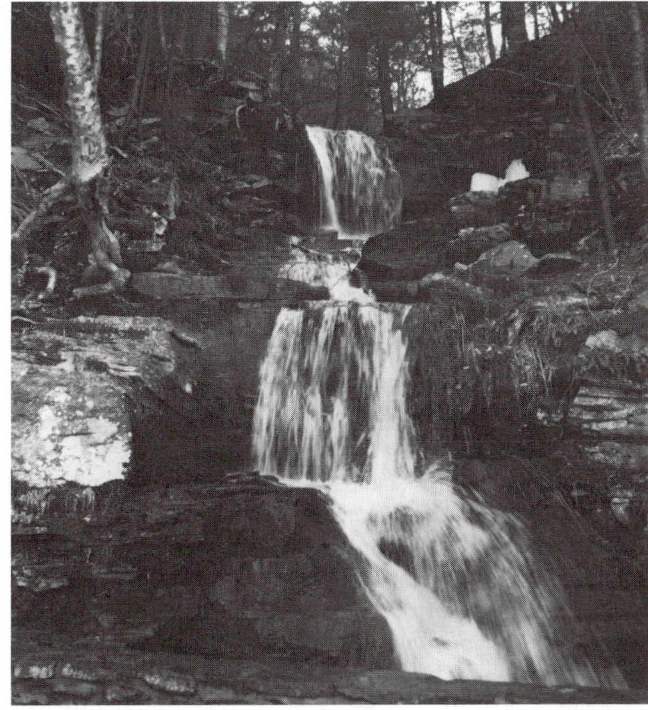

**PHOTO 107**
Knickpoints. A series of knickpoints create cataracts on the Neversink River in the Catskill Mountains of New York. (Courtesy: New York State Department of Environmental Conservation)

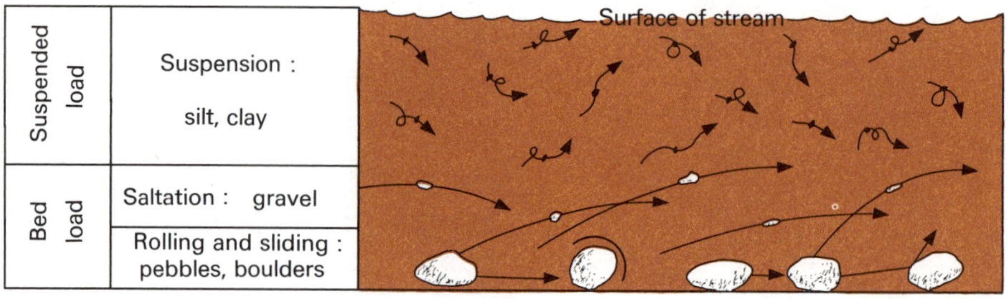

**FIGURE 13.3**
Transportation of a stream's load. The diagram shows the movement of materials by rolling and sliding, by saltation, and by suspension. (After Tarbuck and Lutgens, 1979)

## STREAM SEDIMENT TRANSPORTATION

The load of a stream is transported by three means: *suspension, bed load,* and *solution* (Figure 13.3). A muddy stream reveals that it is carrying suspended material, and the amount of this material may be immense. The Mississippi River carries an estimated 2 million tons of sediment to the Gulf of Mexico each day, and this amount may double when the river is in flood stage.

Most of the sediments in a drainage basin are carried in suspension. The amount of material that can be suspended in a stream of water depends upon such factors as size and shape of the sediments, the specific gravity of the particles, the velocity of the current, and the degree of turbulence. A spherical object will be transported more readily than one with protruding edges. An object with a low specific gravity, such as sand and silt, will be carried more readily than one with a high specific gravity, such as gold, and a rapidly flowing stream will more easily transport suspended material than a slow-moving stream. Turbulence is one of the more important factors in keeping particles in suspension. Typically, suspended material in a stream is not uniformly distributed. The larger grains are likely to be concentrated near the bottom. Turbulence must occur in order to keep the large grains, such as sand and pebbles, suspended.

Part of the material is carried by streams by rolling and sliding the individual particles along the bottom of the stream, or by a jumping motion, a process termed *saltation.* The material carried in these ways is called the *bed load.* The sediments that roll along the stream bed are largely responsible for the scouring and widening of the channel. This abrasive action is highly effective as an erosional agent. Most of the bed load in streams is moved during flood stages when the velocity of the stream is sufficient to carry the earth material along the channel bottom.

When some minerals, such as limestone or mineral salts, are dissolved by chemical weathering, they are carried in solution in streams. A significant part of the soluble load in streams in humid regions comes from minerals that have been dissolved in groundwater. Desert streams frequently have large quantities in solution when they flow across regions where soluble minerals exist on the surface. In most streams, however, the minerals in solution make up but a small part of the total load.

## STREAM CHANNELS

The channel of a stream is determined by such factors as the original slope of the land and subsequent differential erosion, and by such structural features as jointing, faulting, and folding.

Streams forming on the original slope of a landform are known as *consequent streams.* Examples of these streams are found on the coastal plains of the Atlantic and Gulf coasts of the United States. Other consequent streams flow from the sides of newly developed volcanic cones and form on the rolling plains of recent glacial deposition.

After erosion has molded the topography of a region, the softer rocks are gone and the more resistant rocks stand out as prominent features. In such areas the streams tend to follow the valleys where the soft material has been eroded away. In the course of the history of the stream, its location may be changed as differential erosion occurs. Rivers having such a history of development are known as *subsequent streams* (Figure 13.4).

The development of a valley is often controlled by fissures or joints, because erosion is accelerated along these weaknesses in the rocks. Valleys that develop along joints may have angular drainage courses, as joints are frequently at right angles to each other. Such patterns occur on the Colorado Plateau, and in Connecticut and Ontario.

Rivers typically follow fault zones, and when the faults create grabens, these downfaulted areas often become river valleys. Examples include the Jordan River in Israel and the lower Rhine River of Germany.

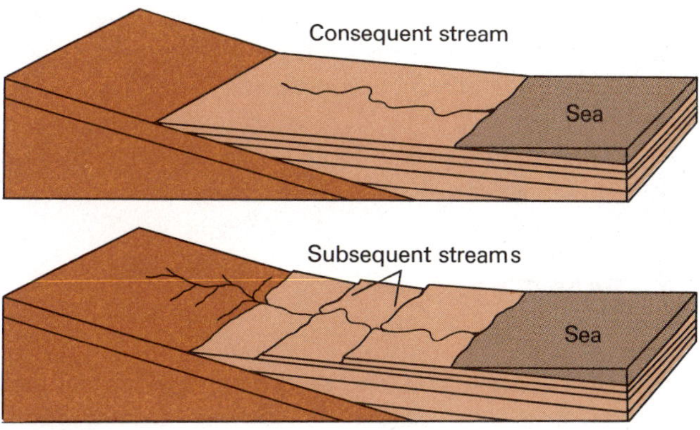


**FIGURE 13.4**
Development of a subsequent stream tributary to an initial consequent stream.

When an area is folded, *structural valleys* and *structural ridges* are formed. These folds govern the direction of the consequent streams, which follow the troughs of the folds. Subsequent valleys are also influenced by the trend of the folding. Such folded areas of the world as the Ridge and Valley Province of the Appalachians have stream courses that are influenced by the rock structures.

Some streams follow their original channels regardless of later folding of the surface. These streams have been able to adjust their course, or to deepen their valleys, as rejuvenation by uplift has occurred. These streams are called *antecedent streams.* The Columbia River is a classic example of an antecedent stream.

## STREAM PATTERNS

The three major types of drainage patterns are *dendritic, radial,* and *trellis* (Figure 13.5).

The dendritic stream pattern develops in areas underlain by horizontal sedimentary rocks or on massive crystalline rocks of uniform hardness. This pattern is characterized as treelike (Photo 108). These streams develop on all types of topography from lowlands to mountains. Most of the major streams of the world, such as the Mississippi and Amazon rivers, have a dendritic pattern.

A radial pattern of streams develops when water flows down the slopes of cone volcanoes or domelike uplifts. The course of these streams is determined by the original slope of the land. Examples of this drainage pattern are found in the structural dome of the Black Hills in South Dakota and on the volcanoes of the circum-Pacific volcanic zone.

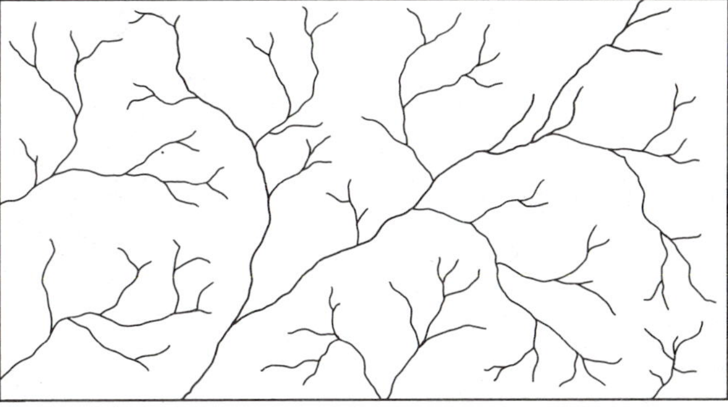
(a) Dendritic

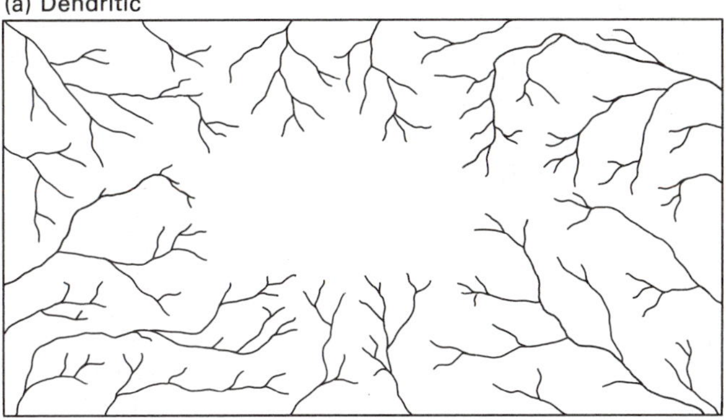
(b) Radial

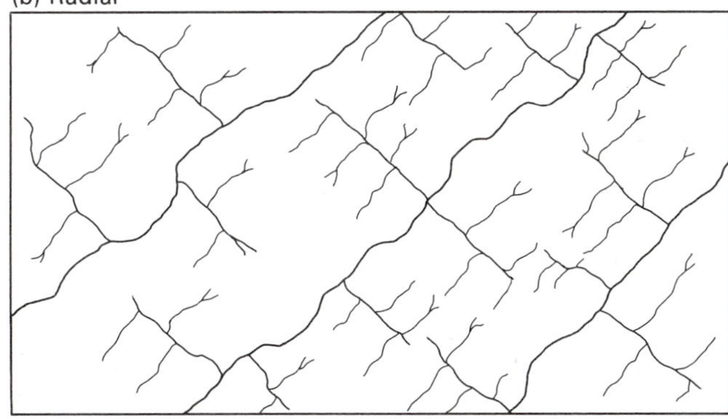
(c) Trellis

**FIGURE 13.5**
Stream patterns. (*a*) Dendritic stream patterns develop on uniform rock structure; (*b*) radial stream patterns develop on conical structures such as volcanoes; and (*c*) the trellis stream pattern develops in ridge and valley regions.

In the folded regions of the world many of the streams first follow valleys and then cut abruptly through the ridges. These narrow notches with streams are called *water gaps* (Photo 109). Other notches were begun by streams but were abandoned when the streams changed their courses due to uplifting or the presence of harder rock. These notches are called *wind gaps.* The streams in these regions have adjusted their

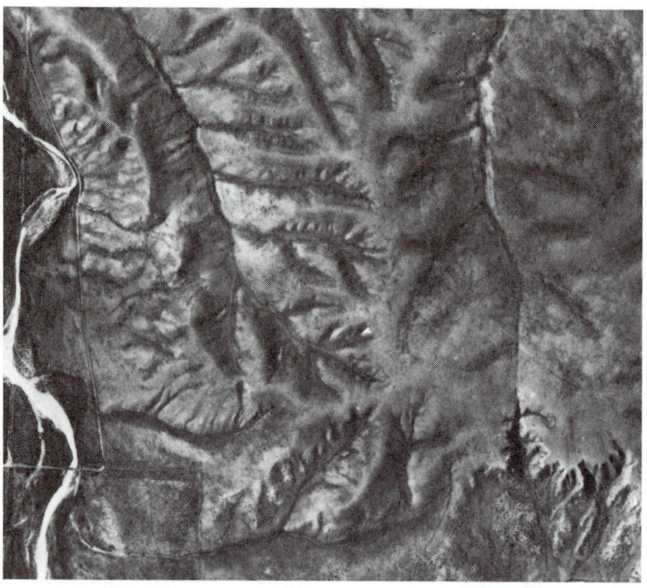

**PHOTO 108**
Dendritic drainage. This well-developed pattern has developed on the soft rock of the Ogallala formation, where stream gradients are steep, in Baca County, Colorado. (Courtesy: T. G. McLaughlin, U.S. Geological Survey)

courses to the folded rock structure. They flow in the valleys and then cut at right angles through the ridges. This pattern has come to be known as *trellis* drainage. Excellent examples of trellis drainage patterns are found in the Ridge and Valley Province of the Appalachian Highlands in eastern United States.

## STREAM TYPES

The availability of water in a stream depends upon a number of factors, including amount and regime of precipitation in the drainage basin, availability of groundwater in the water table, character of the soil and vegetation, proportion of the area that is urbanized, type of land use, and nature of the stream channel.

Streams can be classified according to their source of water. If the water table lies above the stream bottom for the entire year, and the stream is always supplied with water, it is called a *perennial* stream. If during the year the water table drops below the stream bed, the flow of water will cease and the stream is said to be *intermittent* (Photo 110).

Some streams, known as *ephemeral,* are not dependent upon water from the water table but rely entirely on surface runoff from rainfall or snowmelt. In desert areas ephemeral streams may be dry for years and have water in them for a short period only after precipitation occurs.

Some streams actually provide water to the groundwater rather than depending on it for their water supply. This is a common phenomenon among streams that

**PHOTO 109**
Water gap. The Delaware Water Gap has cut through resistant layers of rock. (Courtesy: Pennsylvania Bureau of Travel Development)

**PHOTO 110**
Arroyo. Water flows in this intermittent stream only after precipitation.

originate in humid areas and then flow through semiarid or arid regions. While flowing across the dry regions, the stream is continuously losing water to the local groundwater. Only large rivers are able to sustain continuous loss of water and maintain their existence. Rivers of this type are known as *exotic,* and include the Colorado, Tigris, and Indus. The best example is the Nile, which has no tributaries in the last 2,000 kilometers (1,240 miles) of its journey to the Mediterranean.

## STREAM-ORDERING SYSTEM

Most streams are part of a complex *drainage basin,* the area drained by a stream and its tributaries. A drainage basin may be very small or occupy most of a continent. The pattern of streams in a drainage basin is known as the *drainage net.* Robert Horton in 1945 devised a system for classifying streams according to their location in the drainage net. His system uses the concept of *stream order* (Figure 13.6).

The stream-ordering system is based upon the size of the stream and the drainage basin in which it flows. The first-order streams are unbranched headwater streams that lack tributaries but flow in a defined channel. These streams are usually small and may be dry a portion of the year. At the junction of any two first-order streams, a second-order stream is formed. As the second-order stream descends the valley, a third-order stream is formed when it meets another second-order stream. However, if a first-order stream joins a second-, third-, or higher-order stream, no increase in order occurs. The main stream in the system has the highest order.

When a stream system has been ordered, some generalizations can be made about the form and physical size of the drainage network of a particular region. Fundamental to this concept is that as each higher-order stream is drained, at least a doubling of the drainage area occurs. For example, a second-order basin is at least twice as large as a first-order basin, and a third-order basin is at least twice as large as a second-order basin, and so on. From the number of streams in each order a *bifurcation ratio* can be determined. This is the ratio between the number of stream segments at any given order to the number of segments of the next higher order. In Figure 13.6 there are 25 first-order streams, 11 second-order streams, 5 third-order streams, 2 fourth-order streams, and one fifth-order stream. The corresponding bifurcation ratios are 2.27, 2.20, 2.50, and 2.00, respectively. The mean is 2.24, quite close to the minimum value of 2.0.

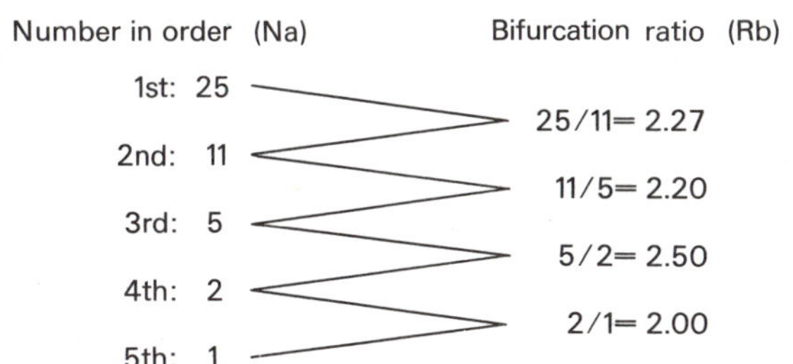


**FIGURE 13.6**
Stream-ordering system. The smallest headwater streams are numbered one. When two number-one streams unite, they form a second-order stream; at the junction of two second-order streams a third-order stream is formed, and so on. (Adaptation of Fig. 5.2 of *Fluid Processes in Geomorphology* by L. B. Leopold, M. Gordon Wolman, and J. P. Miller. W. H. Freeman and Company. Copyright © 1964.)

## VALLEY DEVELOPMENT

On a newly uplifted land surface, runoff of rain begins the process of valley development. Slight topographic irregularities begin to direct the water into definite channels. The process begins with the formation of a tiny *rill* which erodes small furrows on the land surface. The rills unite to form *rivulets,* which in turn unite to form streams and rivers. The valley is developed by *lengthening, deepening,* and *widening.*

**PHOTO 111**
Colorado River canyon. The Colorado River, with an elevation exceeding 2,000 meters (6,000 feet), has carved deep canyons.

A stream is normally lengthened by *headwater erosion*. That is, the stream lengthens by cutting headward into the slopes. In this process it increases its number of tributaries so that the river system becomes more complex. When the backward cutting reaches a point that it meets the tributary from another stream, a *divide* or *interfluve* separates the streams. If erosion is about equal on either side of the divide, a *fixed divide* is established, even though erosion continues to lower the general altitude of the area.

As the valley lengthens, it also deepens. More and more water enters the main channels, increasing the erosional potential. The valley deepens faster in areas where the gradient is steep, and the deeper valleys occur in areas of high elevation. High plateaus, such as the Colorado Plateau with its Grand Canyon, and high mountains, such as the Rocky Mountains with its Royal Gorge, normally have the deepest valleys (Photo 111). In contrast, many of the great rivers of the world, such as the Mississippi, lie only a few meters above sea level for hundreds of kilometers above their mouth. Their valleys are extremely shallow but wide.

A stream eventually deepens its valley to a level where it can no longer cut downward. The stream has then reached its *base level* and is said to be a *graded stream* (Figure 13.7). The stream has achieved a state of equilibrium, with a slope and velocity adequate to carry the sediments it contains. The equilibrium can be altered by increasing the volume and velocity of water. Because the stream cannot cut downward, it begins to erode the sides of its valley. If this lateral erosion did not occur, all valleys would remain V-shaped canyons. A stream approaching a graded condition experiences times of deposition and times of erosion. That is, during periods of normal flow the stream will deposit sedi-

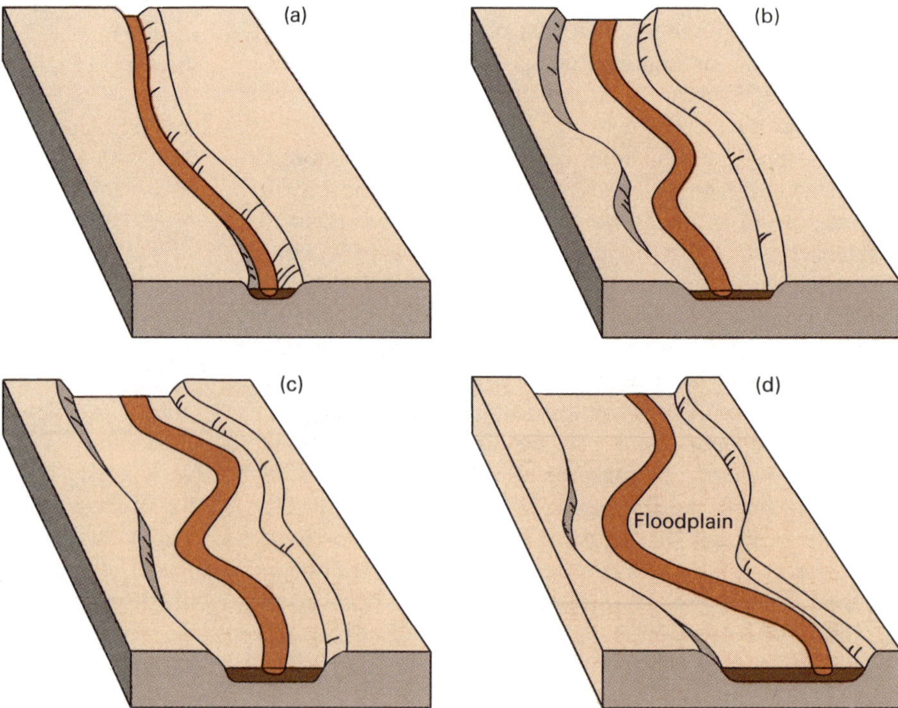


**FIGURE 13.7**
Valley development. Initially a stream cuts downward (*a*) until it reaches base level. The stream then begins to erode laterally (b, c, and *d*), gradually developing a meandering course as it erodes into the uplands. A floodplain is created where sediments are deposited during flood stages when the stream overflows its normal channel.

ments, but during high waters it will erode its valley. A dynamic equilibrium with continuous adjustments of erosion and deposition is necessary to achieve the base level state of stability.

## ALLUVIAL LANDFORMS

A number of depositional landforms develop in a stream valley. These include *floodplains* and associated features, *alluvial terraces, deltas,* and *alluvial fans.*

### FLOODPLAINS

Streams on low and moderate slopes cannot be confined to precise channels during high-water stages. When the water spills out of a channel, the area that it covers is known as the *floodplain* (Figure 13.8). Thus the floodplain becomes the river channel during high-water stages. The current during such a stage is strongest along the axis of the river channel, where the water is deepest. At the margin of the rapidly flowing current, where it contacts the slow-moving water of the floodplain, the velocity suddenly declines. The floodplain is the area of greatest deposition of sediments. The greatest deposits are built up at the immediate border of the swiftly moving channel. They then slope gradually across the floodplain to the valley side. These embankments of alluvial materials tend to confine the stream to its low-water channel, and are known as *natural levees.* Higher artificial levees are frequently constructed on top of the natural levees in order to help control floods in populated areas.

Natural levees are low ridges, many no more than a few feet high, on the edge of the main channel. The slope in back of them is usually so slight that the land appears level to an observer. However, along major streams exceptions do occur. The levees may be so high that during a flood stage they will stand out as islands in the flood waters. During moderately high floods the levees protect the river flats from the flood waters. However, during great floods the river may break through the embankment and flood the lowlands behind the levees.

The floodplains may vary greatly in width from a few meters along small streams to many kilometers along the major rivers of the world. For example, the floodplain along the Mississippi River from Cairo, Illinois, to the delta varies from 50 to 100 kilometers (about 30 to 60 miles) in width and is 1,000 kilometers (600 miles) long. In places, the natural and artificial levees are so high that tributary streams must flow parallel to the main river for considerable distances before they can enter the main channel. The Yazoo River, which parallels the Mississippi River for about 320 kilometers (200 miles), is an example.

As a stream approaches base level, it rarely has a straight course. The currents of a slow-moving stream are deflected by obstacles on the floor of the channel, such as a projection of a more resistant rock, or by the entrance of a swifter tributary stream. The deflected current moves from side to side as it proceeds downstream, creating *meanders.* This word comes from the Latin word, *Maeander,* meaning *to wander* (Photos 112 and 113).

As the stream develops meanders, the velocity increases in one portion, but decreases in another. The water tends to "pile up" on the bends, with the outsides receiving the greater volume of water. As a consequence, the concave side of the stream is the steeper, for it is continuously being undermined. It is commonly called the *cut* or *undercut bank.* The opposite, more gently convex bank is the site of deposition of alluvial sediments of sand and silt and is known as the *slip-off slope.*

Once the river begins to meander, the successive meanders tend to be about the same size. The strip they occupy is known as the *meander belt.* While it is difficult to measure, the width of this belt is about 18 times that of the stream. However, the meander belt itself meanders, causing it to appear quite wide.

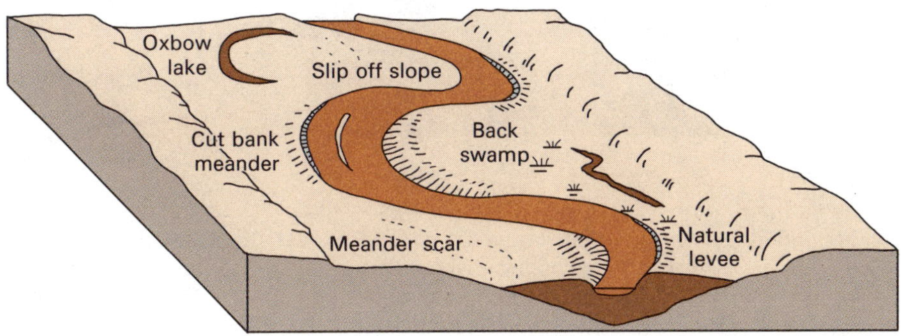


**FIGURE 13.8**
Floodplain. The activity of the stream creates a number of landforms on the developing floodplain.

**PHOTO 112**
Meanders in the Laramie River, Wyoming. Note the oxbow lakes, meander scars, and the edge of the floodplain. (Courtesy: J. R. Balsley, U.S. Geological Survey)

Meanders become more and more pronounced as they develop. Ultimately they appear as a river of loops separated by narrow necks of land. If the velocity of the stream is increased, as during a flood, the water cuts across the narrow neck of land, producing a cutoff between the two loops, filling in the two ends with sediments, and isolating the meander as a long, curved *oxbow lake.* These shallow lakes are rapidly filled and become stagnant pools and swamp areas.

**PHOTO 113**
Braided stream. High-altitude, oblique aerial photograph of the braided stream valley at the junction of the Yukon and Koyukuk rivers in Alaska. The floodplain shows the linear, coalescent, and scalloped deposits from sediment-laden streams. (Courtesy: T. L. Pewe, U.S. Geological Survey)

## ALLUVIAL TERRACES

When a river has deposited alluvial materials to a considerable depth, it may erode a portion of these deposits. The remaining sediments stand out as one or more terrace levels above the present floodplain. These terraces are the remnants of former floodplains (Figure 13.9).

Terraces may develop as a response to changes in the stream channel and floodplain. These changes can include the uplift, or rejuvenation, of the stream; a partial loss of sediment with accompanying renewed erosion by the stream; a differential erosion in which coarse sediments are exchanged for finer materials; the elimination of meanders, increasing the velocity and the erosive power of the stream; and an increase in the volume of water so that the erosion force is also increased.

Most streams have developed one or more terraces. They normally form along the lower, or older, portions of the stream first. Farther upstream the terraces grade into the floodplains. Terraces, like floodplains, are constantly being eroded by the action of the stream changes.

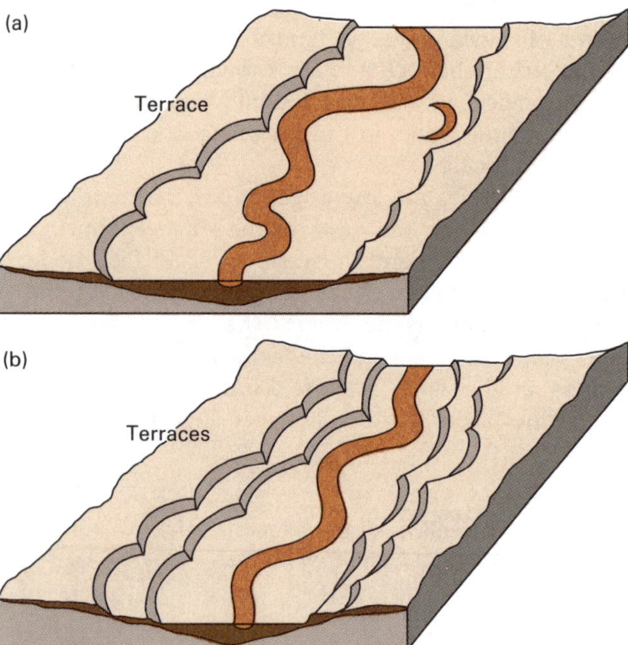


**FIGURE 13.9**
Alluvial terraces. A number of terraces are formed when a stream erodes the alluvial fill of its valley. This occurs when the eroding power of the stream is increased, or when the area is uplifted.

## DELTAS

When a stream flows into a quiet body, such as a lake or an ocean, its velocity is immediately decreased and the sediments it carries are deposited. If the shore currents are not strong enough to carry these sediments away, a *delta* develops (Figure 13.10). The largest deltas of the world, such as those of the Ganges-Brahmaputra and the Mississippi rivers, are formed in oceans where the largest rivers discharge their sediments. The Ganges-Brahmaputra delta has an area of about 155,000 square kilometers (60,000 square meters), and the Mississippi delta's area exceeds 78,000 square kilometers (over 30,000 square miles).

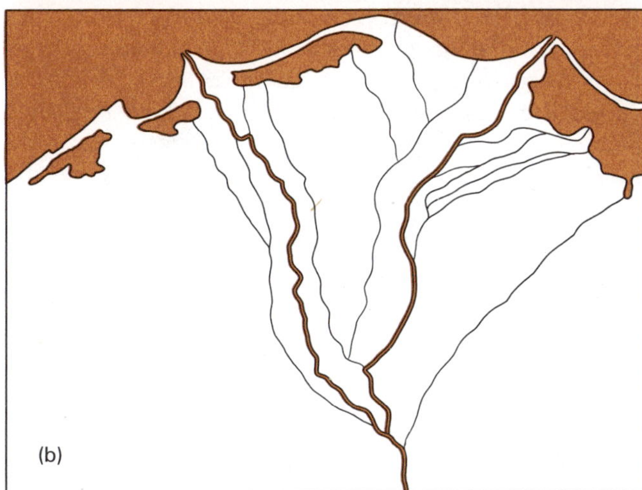


**FIGURE 13.10**
Delta. Sediments are deposited at the mouth of a stream. The form of the sediments may resemble that of the Mississippi delta (*a*) or the Nile delta (*b*).

The delta is built up of successive layers of sediments spread out over a fan-shaped area. The bulk of the coarse materials is deposited near the mouth of the river, and the finer sediments are carried farther into the still water. The rate of deposition depends upon the stream's velocity, the amount of water, and the character of the drainage basin. Because the Mississippi River is highly sediment-laden, its delta is growing at a rate of about 1.6 kilometers (1 mile) each 16 years.

The delta is very near or at base level. As a consequence the streams fill rapidly with sediments, and soon form sub-branches known as *distributaries.* The newly formed channels will wind to and fro across the delta deposits. Sediments will build up in the channels until they are choked and new ones form. Swamps and shallow lakes are thus common features on the delta.

Because the sediments are unconsolidated, large deltas sometimes subside. In most deltas, new deposits keep pace with the sinking, but in some, marine deposits of limestone and shales are interbedded with freshwater sediments. Delta deposits have been found to extend to great depths. In the geologic past, deltas have been built to depths of more than 3,000 meters (10,000 feet). Deltas with 150 to 250 meters (500 to 800 feet) of sediments are commonly found today.

## ALLUVIAL FANS

An alluvial fan may develop at the foot of a mountain (Figure 13.11). At the point where the gradient changes from a steep to a gentle slope, sediments will be de-

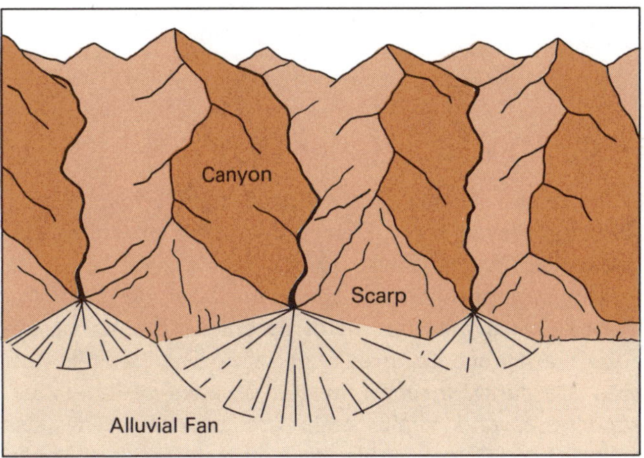


**FIGURE 13.11**
Alluvial fan. When a rapidly flowing, sediment-laden stream emerges from an upland area onto a plain, its velocity and carrying capacity are reduced. Sediments are deposited in a fan-shaped pattern.

**PHOTO 114**
South Dakota Badlands. Torrential downpours and intermittent streams are carving the soft rock formations into fantastic shapes.

**PHOTO 115**
Cuestas. Ridges formed by hard sandstone outcrops in Sante Fe County, New Mexico. (Courtesy: W. T. Lee, U.S. Geological Survey)

posited. A fan-shaped deposit of stratified stream sediments develops in a pattern similar to that of delta formation. The coarse materials are deposited first, and the finer sediments later. As the stream loses velocity, it is usually not confined to a particular channel but separates into a large number of distributaries, producing a braided pattern.

A stream may be able to cross the fan during flood stages, but under normal conditions the water sinks into the loose alluvial sediments. Sometimes the water percolates downward through the fan and emerges as a spring at the end of the fan. The alluvial fan has its best development in the dry regions of the world, where water flows from wetter uplands to dry, level lowlands.

## DEGRADATIONAL LANDFORMS

Softer rocks are eroded away more rapidly than harder, resistant rocks. This differential erosion produces distinctive landforms (Photo 114).

The inner portions of the Gulf Coast plains of the United States are formed of recent sediments of unequal resistance to stream erosion. The beds in this area are gently inclined so that a series of limestone, sandstone, and shale strata are exposed. The less resistant rocks of shale and limestone have been eroded more rapidly than the resistant sandstones. The shale and limestone bands appear as lowlands, and the sandstones stand out as low hills known as *cuestas* (Photo 115). They have a relief of 30 to 60 meters (100 to 200 feet) above the valleys. These lowland and hill areas appear as bands that are several kilometers wide and extend for many kilometers parallel to the coast. A region with such a landform development has come to be known as a *belted coastal* or *cuestiform* plain. The steeper slopes that face inland are known as *escarpments*, and the gentler slopes are called *dip slopes* (Figure 13.12).

A distinctive land use pattern has evolved on the cuestiform plains. On the limestone lowlands a rich agricultural economy exists with such distinctive names as the Alabama Black Belt and the Texas Black Prairie. In contrast, the sandstones have evolved into a poor acidic soil. These areas are frequently known for their pine barrens.

Stream-eroded plains are not limited to coastal areas but are also found in the interior of continents. These plains develop features that resemble those of coastal plains. The less resistant rocks become lowlands, and the resistant rocks stand out as eroded cuestas, forming hills. The older strata of the interior may have been subjected to tectonic movement, changing their inclination or even forming broad structural domes or basins. As a consequence the local relief is frequently greater than in the coastal plains.

## KARST LANDSCAPE

A karst landscape begins to develop when water is able to sink rapidly into the ground in regions of soluble rocks such as limestone, dolomite, or gypsum. As the water percolates through the ground, the rock is gradually dissolved. The specific type of development depends upon the location of the soluble rock layers

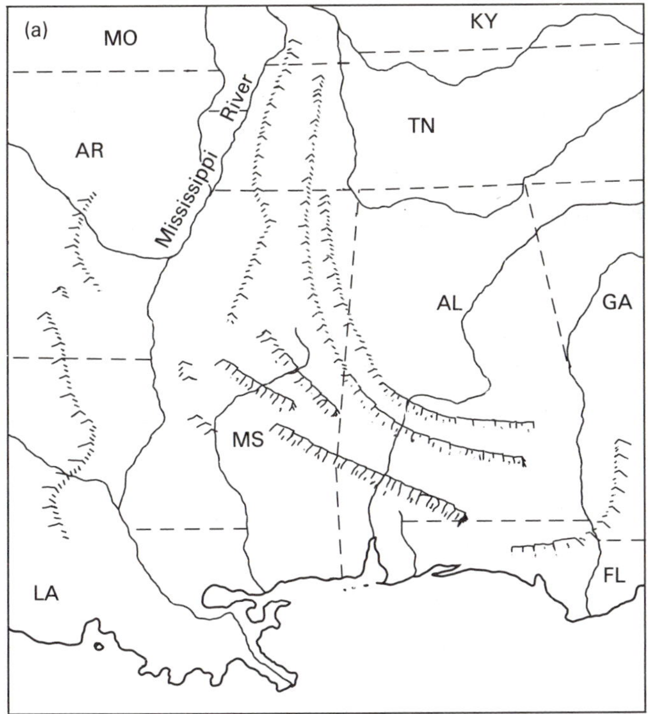


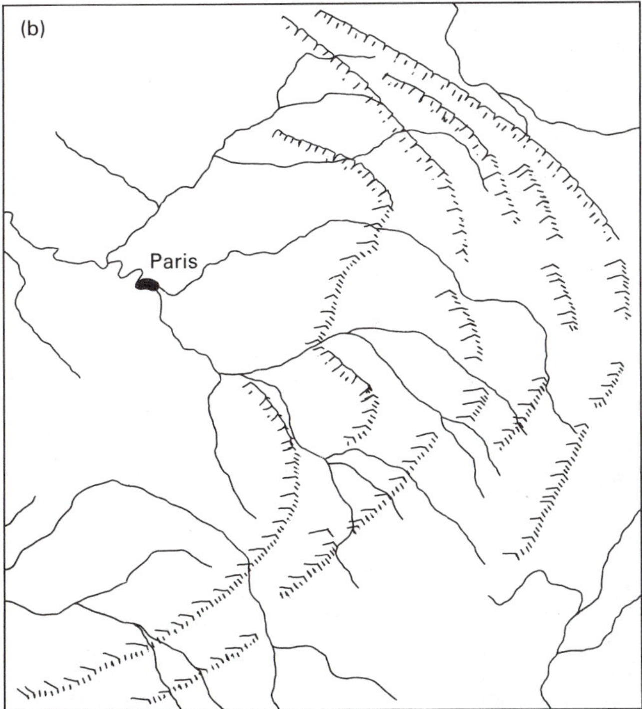


**FIGURE 13.12**
Cuestiform plain. These plains form when rocks of an area have different resistance to erosion. The resistant rocks, such as sandstones, stand out as ridges, while the less resistant rocks, such as limestones or shales, appear as lowlands.

**PHOTO 116**
Karst landscape of Kweilin, China.

(Photo 116). For example, the Ocala limestone of the Florida peninsula covers a large region, and the many karst features, such as sinkholes, are evident on the surface (Figure 13.13). In contrast, around the Mammoth Cave area of Kentucky a resistant sandstone covers the soluble limestone. In this area the karst features, such as caves, are largely underground.

If water percolates through pure limestone or gypsum, the entire rock is dissolved (Figure 13.14). An elaborate system of tunnels and open chambers

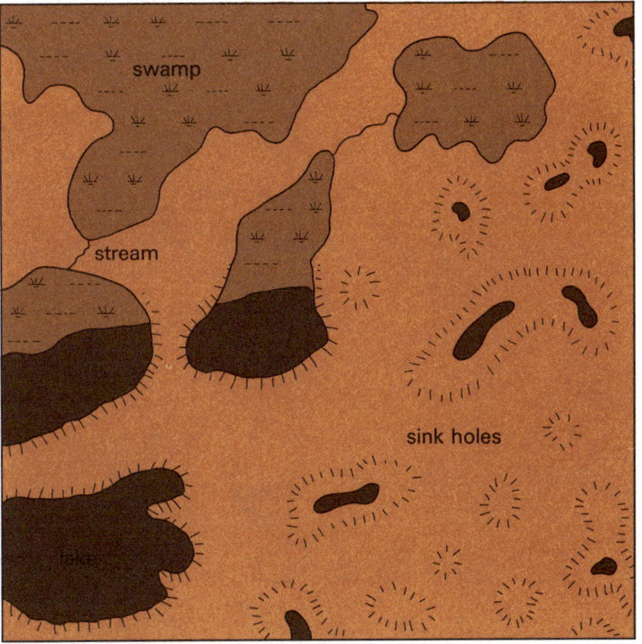


**FIGURE 13.13**
Karst plain. A karst plain is characterized by numerous sinks, swamps, and lakes.

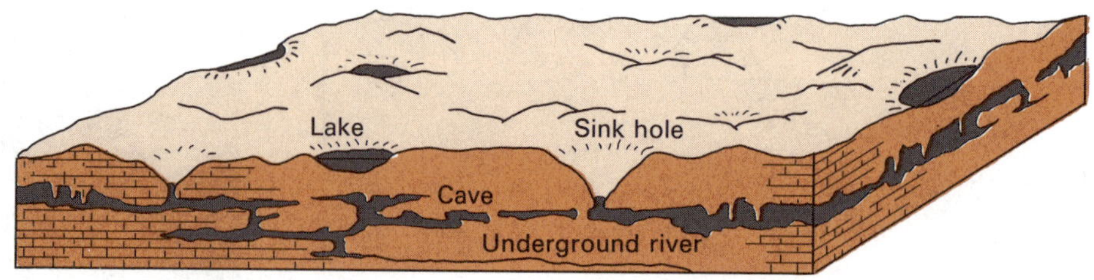


FIGURE 13.14
A karst plain and underground features of limestone solution. Karst plains develop on rocks that are soluble, such as limestone. These plains develop not only surface features, but also underground features, such as caves and underground rivers.

evolves, and major cave systems are created. In the United States a large number of limestone regions have caves. One of the largest of these is the Carlsbad Caverns in New Mexico. One gallery, the Big Room, is about 1,230 meters (4,000 feet) long, has a maximum width of 190 meters (625 feet), and a maximum ceiling height of about 90 meters (300 feet). Another well-known cave is Mammoth Cave, Kentucky, where a labyrinth of channels consists of several hundred miles of connecting galleries, with underground rivers, waterfalls, and lakes. The galleries vary from a third of a meter to over 120 feet in height; Mammoth Dome is the largest. Other well-known caves in the United States include Penns Cave in Pennsylvania, Luray Caverns in Virginia, Wyandotte and Marengo Caves in Indiana, Wind Cave in South Dakota, and Marble Cave in Missouri.

When caves develop in a region where the water table is lowered below the cave level, deposits may precipitate from water entering the cave from above (Photos 117 and 118). Most of these mineral deposits are calcium carbonate. When they project from the roof, they are known as *stalactites.* When the deposit builds up on the floor of the cave, the resulting mounds or cones are known as *stalagmites.* The stalactites assume many beautiful forms, appearing as icicles with shining crystals of calcite or resembling draperies hanging from a ceiling.

The stalactites begin when a drop of water on the roof of the cave begins to evaporate and loses carbon dioxide. The drop then becomes saturated with calcium carbonate, and a small deposit occurs in a ring form. Drop after drop lengthens the ring into a long pendant with a small hole in the middle. The stalactite is lengthened at its lower end and thickened from the center of the structure. If the stalactite reaches the floor, it may form a column or pillar. Many pillars are formed when a stalactite and a stalagmite meet.

The first surface evidence in the development of a karst topography may be small sinks on the ground

PHOTO 117
Limestone cave. A view of stalactites and stalagmites in Wayima Lodge, Carlsbad Caverns National Park. (Courtesy: W. T. Lee, U.S. Geological Survey)

PHOTO 118
Limestone cave. Colossal Cave located in the Rincon Mountain Range of Arizona. (Courtesy: Arizona Office of Tourism)

**PHOTO 119**
Natural bridge. The Natural Bridge of Virginia is a rock span 30 meters (90 feet) long, 15 to 50 meters (50 to 150 feet) wide, and about 13 meters (40 feet) thick. It stands about 65 meters (200 feet) above the narrow gorge of Cedar Creek. It is thought to be the roof of a limestone subterranean passageway that has been eroded away. It is so strong that it supports a major highway. (Courtesy: C. D. Walcott, U.S. Geological Survey)

surface, called *dolines.* As development progresses, solution creates large cavities underground. If they are near the surface, the roof may collapse or subsidence may occur, forming *sinkholes.* While only a few dolines and sinkholes may be present in the initial stages, the region may be dotted with these features as it develops.

Surface drainage is greatly affected by dolines and sinkholes. The small tributary streams gradually disappear as the water originally carried by them is diverted to underground flows. When karst topography reaches maturity, surface drainage is limited to short streams that soon disappear into the ground. At this stage the streams flow for long distances through underground tunnels. Occasionally there are *natural bridges,* remnants of limestone formations that have partially collapsed (Photo 119).

When a karst region advances to the old age stage, the dolines, sinkholes, natural bridges, and underground tunnels disappear because all limestone rock has been removed in solution. The area is near the regional base level, so that it is relatively level with possibly a few isolated rises.

## HUMAN IMPACT ON STREAMS

Human societies have always had a vital interest in stream regimen and river quality. They have directly influenced streams by physically manipulating river channels, building dams and reservoirs (Photo 120), channelizing (Photo 121), manipulating banks (Photos 122 and 123), and constructing levees. People have indirectly influenced streams by altering the land use in drainage basins, and particularly by expanding urban areas, which affect the entire hydrologic system.

### HUMAN MODIFICATIONS OF RIVERS

An uncontrolled river normally widens and deepens its channel during flood periods. The size of a river's channel over an extended period is thus a function of maximum discharge, all other hydrologic and geomorphologic factors being equal.

*Channelizing* is the straightening and shortening of the stream channel. It has the effect of increasing the gradient and, at the same time, the velocity of the discharge. Large quantities of water are normally stored on the floodplain, but when the water is confined to the channel by artificial levees or dikes, upstream floodplain storage is reduced. The effect of channelization may be to increase the flood peak downstream.

The Mississippi River provides an excellent example of an attempt to control a river. Under natural conditions the Mississippi deepened its channel during flood stages, making room for some flood water. The remaining water filled the floodplain area. Because of artificial restrictions, the channel of the Mississippi is no longer being eroded effectively. The first effort to control the river took place in 1837, when Lieutenant Robert E. Lee built confinement dikes to remove sand bars threatening St. Louis harbor. Since then the river has lost about one-third of its volume. As a consequence, when a flood occurs the water stages are higher for a given discharge. In some sections of the river, deposition of sediments occurs, causing a further rise in the water levels. In these sections the excess channel water is contained by levees, so that the flood crests are even higher. As flood stages rise, the influence of channel confinement is reduced by the increased stream velocity. The stream is in disequilibrium.

The massive 1973 flood on the Mississippi River illustrates the effect of human mismanagement of the river. The crest of the flood at St. Louis occurred on April 28, 1973, when the waters reached a height of 13.18 meters, 4.03 meters above flood stage. The flood topped the 189-year record by 0.3 meter. The 1973 flood was 0.61 meter higher than the one in

**PHOTO 120**
Check dams. Small check dams control the flow of water and silt. This wire mesh dam is backed up with asphalt-soaked sacking to help control silting. In the background are two rock-type check dams. (Courtesy: United States Department of Agriculture, Soil Conservation Service)

**PHOTO 121**
Channelization. A stream in Monmouth County, New Jersey, is channeled by using jute matting and trap rock. (Courtesy: United States Department of Agriculture, Soil Conservation Service)

**PHOTO 122**
Bank manipulation. Sticks are driven into the stream bank to control erosion. (Courtesy: Wisconsin Conservation Department)

1844, but it was estimated that the flow was about 35 percent less. The 1908 flood had the same flow as the 1973 flood but the flood crest was 2.51 meters lower. The higher-cresting flood in 1973 was attributed to the artificial levees, which confined the water to the river channel and prevented it from occupying the floodplain. As a result of river confinement, the channel at St. Louis was narrowed from 1,300 meters in 1849 to 610 meters in 1907 and finally to 580 meters in 1969. This striking evidence confirms that the construction of river channels makes flood crests higher.

## DAM AND RESERVOIR EFFECTS

Humans can alter the channel of a river in many ways, but none is more important than the construction of a dam on a river (Photo 124). It completely alters the regimen of the stream. The first recorded dam was built about 3000 B.C. along the Nile in Egypt. Since then, thousands of dams have been built on the world's rivers in an attempt to control stream flow, improve agriculture, prevent floods, generate power, or provide a reliable water supply.

Many more dams have been constructed in recent decades to satisfy the demands for more effective water use. Further, the dams have increased in size so that the amount of water impounded behind them has reached enormous proportions. For example, Lake Nasser, created by the Aswan Dam on the Nile, is now estimated to possess 157 billion cubic meters of water. The larger the dam, the greater the regulation of stream flow.

Besides regulating stream flow, a dam and its reservoir play an important role in controlling the character of a river, both upstream and downstream. Of primary importance is the fact that the reservoir traps sediments. The water released from a dam is therefore sediment-free, so that erosional changes have to take place within the stream channel in order to develop a new equilibrium. These changes are felt not only in the physical aspects of the stream but also in its aquatic ecosystem.

Dams also affect the quality of the stream's water. Because evaporation is increased in the reservoir's water, salinity can increase correspondingly in the water downstream. In arid regions of the world the loss of water by evaporation may be of great importance. To reduce evaporation, the surface of some reservoirs has been sprayed with monomolecular films. Studies have revealed that this procedure has reduced evaporation by 12 to 25 percent.

**PHOTO 123**
Bank manipulation. Riprapping streambanks with old car bodies can be an effective control of erosion. This technique is not generally recommended except when other methods cannot be used. The old bodies make streams look like junkyards, and this type of riprap is only temporary, since the bodies will eventually rust out. (Courtesy: United States Department of Agriculture, Soil Conservation Service)

The temperature of a stream's water is also altered by the construction of a dam and its accompanying reservoir. Two different types of heat budgets can exist in a reservoir, depending on whether the water is released from the top or the bottom of the dam. If water is released from the top, the reservoir is a heat exporter; if from the bottom, it is a heat trap.

**PHOTO 124**
Grand Coulee Dam on the Columbia River.

## URBANIZATION AND ITS EFFECT ON RIVERS

Urbanization has affected the flow of streams in a number of ways. Fundamentally, the pavement and buildings greatly increase the percentage of land area that is impervious to water. A high proportion of precipitation, instead of seeping into the underground reservoirs, runs off into streams. In addition, the installation of sewers and storm drains accelerates runoff. Because peak discharges are higher and occur sooner in urbanized areas, the potential for flooding along streams is greatly enhanced.

The disposal of effluent from sewage plants decreases the quality of water in streams flowing through urban areas. Even more damaging is the ejection of raw sewage into the streams. The minerals in the discharged material provide nutrients and promote growth of algae and plankton in a stream. This growth alters the biological balance, affecting all organic life within the stream.

Urbanization is also likely to affect the amenities provided by a stream because of the increased flood potential. Luna Leopold, formerly hydrologist for the U.S. Geological Survey, has stated that urbanization has affected the hydrologic environment in three ways. First, the increase in flooding causes the stream channel to become unstable. Vegetation on the banks is disturbed, and the channel bed becomes muddy or scoured, decreasing the stream's usefulness for recreation. Second, floods increase the accumulation of debris such as cans, rotting lumber, and other items in the expanded floodplain. The floodplain becomes an unsightly area. Finally, the disruption of the biological life of the stream changes it from a clear stream to one where the rocks may be covered with slime and the odor repels any recreational use. As the oxygen content of the water is reduced, the game fish are gradually replaced by less desirable species.

## FLOODS AND FLOOD CONTROL

The flooding of the land is a common occurrence in all areas of the world. A flood is said to occur when the discharge of a stream or river cannot be contained within its established channel. As a consequence the water spreads out over the adjoining floodplain. In some rivers, floods are a periodic occurrence, in others they occur at irregular intervals, and in still others floods rarely occur.

Floods have many causes. They are often a response to excessive rainfall within a short period of time. Damage to property and loss of life can be prevented under such natural circumstances only if it is recognized beforehand that having property and living on a floodplain are hazardous. An overwhelming number of people live on floodplains throughout the world and are thus subject to flooding.

Many floods are caused by a combination of natural conditions and human interference with the environment. For example, the deforestation of vast areas in Appalachia has resulted in rapid runoff of the rainfall, increasing the probability of floods. In urban areas the placement of concrete and asphalt on the surface has also accelerated runoff. Along some of the largest rivers of the world, notably the Mississippi River in the United States, artificial levees have been built on top of natural levees. As the levees are built higher and higher, the sediments that the river would have deposited on the floodplain during floods are deposited within the river channel, raising the river grade. When the high levees finally break at the times of high water, the succeeding floods are more devastating, for the river channel may be many feet higher than the floodplain lying behind the levees.

Because floods have such disastrous effects on a region, the attempts to predict them have increased. The National Oceanic and Atmospheric Administration operates a River and Flood Forecasting Service at 85 selected offices located at strategic points on the nation's major river systems. These offices issue reports that cover the flood conditions in large watersheds. Flood reports are publicized immediately over radio and television networks. The service also cooperates closely with allied agencies, such as the American Red Cross and the U.S. Army Corps of Engineers, in order to aid stricken individuals and plan evacuations if necessary. As part of the flood warning system, NOAA has designated a particular stage or gauge height at critical places along rivers as the *flood stage.* Flooding occurs if water rises above this level.

Vast amounts of money have been spent to control floods. Two basic forms of control have been developed: the first attempts to delay runoff, and the second to modify the lower reaches of the river, where flooding is common.

Two techniques are commonly used to delay runoff. One is to build dams in the headwaters of the river catchment basin to impound the excess water and then release it gradually. This system is usually designed not only to control floods but also to provide recreational facilities. A major problem associated with this method of control has been the failure of some of the dams. When these dams break, they release a torrent of water in the valley downstream, causing massive property damage and sometimes loss of life.

For example, the Teton Dam, located in a deep, narrow canyon of the Teton River, a tributary of the Snake River, failed on June 5, 1976. As the dam burst, a tremendous wall of water poured through the dam. In the flood that ensued, nine people were killed, more than 1,000 were injured, over 400,000 acres of land were inundated, and several agricultural communities were flooded.

The dam was constructed largely of material that was obtained from the bed of the reservoir area and compacted to form a solid barrier. The rock on either side of the dam was fairly porous and not very strong, but it had been cemented to prevent leaks. The reason for the dam's collapse has been difficult to determine because most of the dam has been washed away. This situation emphasizes the problem that can arise when the natural flow of water is altered in a stream course. No satisfactory procedures have been developed to assess how safe a dam is.

Runoff has also been controlled by reforestation or planting of other vegetation so as to increase the infiltration of water and reduce the rate of runoff. This process has been effective in many areas.

Two quite different methods are used to modify the lower reaches of the river. The oldest of these methods is to build levees and dikes parallel to the river channel in order to contain the high waters. Since they must contain the highest water levels, they must be designed to withstand the greatest water pressures under flood conditions. The largest levee system in the United States is along the Mississippi River. It was begun in 1879 and is now more the 2,500 miles in length and in places as high as 30 feet.

Because levees are sometimes breached, a new technique has been developed by the U.S. Army Corps of Engineers to control floods. The river's channel is straightened by cutting across the great meander loops in order to produce a more direct river flow. The slope and the velocity of the stream are thus increased. Greater velocity means that the water discharge is greater which in turn lowers the height of the water in the channel. Channel improvement has had a noticeable effect on reducing the flood levels of the Mississippi River.

## CONCLUSION

The action of running water is of major importance in the development of landforms. The ability of a stream to transport materials, in suspension or as a bed load, depends upon the volume of water and the width, depth, and gradient of a stream. In general, the greater the velocity of flow, the higher the amount of material it can carry. The down-cutting power of a stream and its lateral adjustments are the means by which a stream balances its energy and erosional capabilities.

The fluvial processes have created both degradational and aggradational landforms. The degradational landforms have been formed by erosional processes. Cuestas, created by differential erosion, are one example. The aggradational landforms are depositions of sediment. Natural levees, terraces, alluvial fans, and deltas are the principal forms of floodplain deposits. All of these landforms are a response to the tendency of streams to maintain an equilibrium in the fluvial processes.

Human beings have attempted to control the work of streams and rivers in many ways. Stream channels have been narrowed, widened, or deepened. Dams have been constructed across streams, changing their pattern of flow. These endeavors focus on a particular aspect of a stream or river, such as flooding, but they have an impact on total stream regime. When one change is made in the stream system, the entire system is altered. Additional studies are needed to evaluate the human modifications of streams.

## STUDY QUESTIONS

1 What factors determine the velocity of a stream?
2 What creates a knickpoint in a stream?
3 How is material transported in a stream?
4 What factors determine stream channels?
5 Describe the three major types of drainage patterns.
6 How may a stream pattern be ordered?
7 What are the processes of valley development?
8 How are the principal alluvial landforms developed?
9 How is a cuestiform plain formed?
10 How is a karst landscape developed? What unique features are formed?
11 Explain how human modifications of a river can increase the flood potential.
12 Give some examples that show how the damming of a river can alter the environment.

# 14
# GLACIERS AND GLACIAL LANDFORMS

## KEY WORDS

| | | | |
|---|---|---|---|
| ablation | firn | kame | recessional moraine |
| alpine glacier | glacial spillway | kettle moraine | roche moutonnée |
| arête | glacial trough | lateral moraine | rock glacier |
| cirque | glaciofluvial deposits | medial moraine | striation |
| drumlin | ground moraine | muskeg | tarn |
| end moraine | hanging valley | outwash plain | terminal moraine |
| erratic | horn | Pleistocene | till |
| esker | interglacial stage | plucking | |

An astronaut looking at the earth from outer space could get the impression that we live in an ice world. During the winter in the Northern Hemisphere over half of the world's land surface and more than 30 percent of the oceans are covered by a blanket of snow and ice. As part of this present-day covering of snow and ice, glaciers make up about 10 percent of the earth's surface. In the recent geologic past, during the *Pleistocene* era, about one-third of the world's surface was covered by glaciers.

The ice world has a significant influence on our lives. Some of the most densely populated areas of the earth, in northern United States and northern Europe, have been drastically affected by glacial processes. As the earth's human population increases and seeks additional living space, the role of glaciers will become even more significant. Especially important will be the worldwide influence of the Greenland and Antarctic ice caps on weather and climate.

About 75 percent of the fresh water of the world is now locked up in glaciers. If the continental glaciers of Greenland and Antarctica were to melt, the oceans' waters would rise and inundate the coastal cities of the world. The expansion or melting of the world's glaciers can thus have a profound effect on the availability of water and on land use.

Glaciers hold the secrets of many human endeavors. It is known that about 1,000 years ago Erik the Red established a flourishing society on the coast of Greenland. It thrived for hundreds of years and then disappeared, no doubt succumbing to an advancement of the glaciers. Some of the sites of these ancient Norse settlements are now emerging from beneath the retreating ice. Study of these sites is revealing how glacial activities influenced the rise and fall of a once prospering economy.

## FORMATION AND MASS BALANCE OF GLACIERS

A glacier begins when more snow accumulates in winter than melts during the summer. In this manner, a *snowpack* and eventually a *perennial snowfield* evolve. A snowfield, however, will not become a glacier unless the mass is large enough to change the snow into *glacial ice* (Figure 14.1). The snow is transformed when a critical thickness of 60 to 75 meters (200 to 245 feet) is achieved. The change of snow to glacial ice requires (*a*) an increase in density and in grain size, (*b*) a decrease in porosity, (*c*) the development of interlocking ice crystals, and (*d*) a decrease in the amount of air contained in the original snow. The increase in density is quite marked. The first ice, known as *firn,* has a density in relation to water of about 0.55, but by the time it becomes glacial ice the density has increased to about 0.90. To illustrate, when an *iceberg* floats in a body of water, about 90 percent of its mass is submerged. The process of creating glacial ice requires many years.

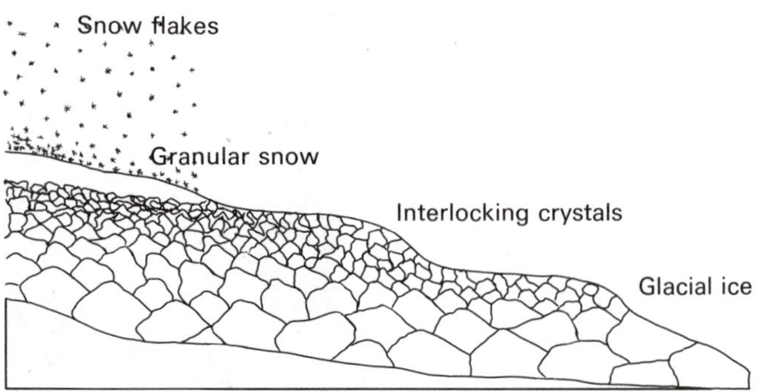


**FIGURE 14.1**
Stages in the transformation of snow to glacial ice. Snow is gradually compacted until the crystals interlock. Glacial ice crystals may be several inches in diameter. (After Foster, 1979)

The *mass balance* of a glacial ice mass is the difference between the amount accumulated and the amount lost by *ablation;* that is, the water lost by sublimation or by direct melting (Figure 14.2). When about 30 meters (100 feet) of glacial ice have accumulated, the great weight forces the lower layers to begin to flow. For alpine (mountain) glaciers, the line between the *zone of accumulation,* where the ice mass accumulates, and the zone of *ablation,* where the glaciers are moving, is known as the *firn line.* Above the firn line the glacier is snowy, but below the firn line it has the blue-gray color of glacial ice.

## GLACIAL MOVEMENT

A glacier's rate of movement is determined by the weight of the accumulated glacial ice, the shape of the landforms over which it passes, and its location. A glacier will move most rapidly if the terrain slopes downward and its progress is not impeded by terrain features. Glaciers also generally move more rapidly at lower latitudes than at higher latitudes. In warm areas ice movement is accelerated by the melting and refreezing processes.

Measurement of ice movement in alpine valleys has revealed that the ice does not move uniformly. The

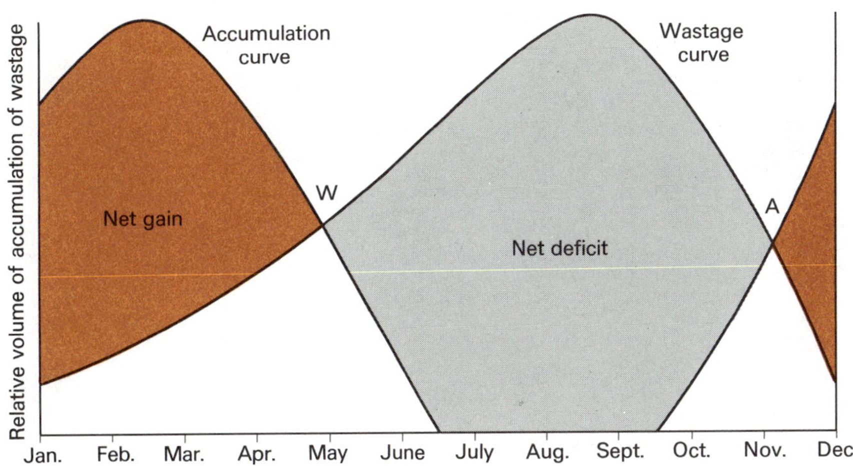


**FIGURE 14.2**
Annual snow and ice mass balance during the formation of a glacier. Between late October and mid-April, more snow and ice accumulates than is lost, and the budget is positive. Mid-April to late October is the time of the negative budget, when more is lost than is accumulated. The intersection at *A* marks the start of the budget year and *W* defines the start of the melting season. If the areas between the curves are equal, there is neither accumulation nor loss in that year. (After Burchfiel and others, 1982)

most rapid movement is at the glacier's highest level and in its center. Movement is slower at the margins and terminus. These variations in ice movement, however, are affected by the valley profile and the melt rate of the glacier.

The rate of movement depends upon the situation of each glacier. It is estimated that most alpine valley glaciers move at an average speed of not more than 0.3 to 0.6 meter (1 to 2 feet) per day. For steep-sloped glaciers, movements of 3 to 6 meters (10 to 20 feet) have been recorded on a seasonal basis. For shorter periods of time an abnormal accumulation of ice may cause the glacier to move rapidly. This movement, known as a *surge,* may be from two to six times the normal mean velocity of the ice.

## GLACIAL EPOCHS

The last great glacial period occurred in the Pleistocene epoch that began more than 2 million years ago and ended about 10,000 years ago in North America and Europe. The glacial period continues in Greenland, the Arctic islands, and Antarctica. At the peak of Pleistocene glaciation, glaciers covered more than 26 million square kilometers (10 million square miles) (Figure 14.3). In North America, the southern boundary of the continental glaciers is marked by the present Missouri and Ohio rivers. Their eastward extension included all of New England and Long Island. This ice sheet had its center on the Laurentian Shield of Canada. Another sheet originated in the Canadian Rockies and moved eastward, meeting the eastern continental glacier. At its maximum extent glacial ice extended completely across North America. In Europe, the ice sheet centered on Scandinavia and extended as far west as the United Kingdom and southward into northern Germany, Poland, and eastern Soviet Union. Glaciers also occupied the high mountains around the world during the Pleistocene, changing the physical appearance of many of them. Pleistocene glaciation has left a legacy, not only on the vast plains of the world, but also on its picturesque mountain scenery.

Vast areas of the northern continents are covered by sediments deposited by continental ice or by meltwaters flowing from the ice. After this fact was recognized, it also became evident that a series of distinct and different *tills,* or unconsolidated glacial deposits, were laid down at different times. To illustrate, more recent deposits of till were found on top of weathered till, on which a landscape possessing plant growth and animal life had developed (Photo 125). This documentation revealed that Pleistocene continental glaciation was not a single event but actually consisted of several advances and retreats of the continental glacial ice (Figure 14.4). This long period included at least four, and perhaps as many as eighteen, *glacial stages* separated by warmer *interglacial stages.* From this evidence the concept of *multiple glaciation* has evolved.

It is estimated that the Pleistocene continental ice sheet was between 1 and 2 kilometers (0.6 to 1.2 miles) thick, with a maximum thickness of about 4 kilometers (2.5 miles). The weight of this ice mass averaged about 900,000 kilograms (1,000 tons) for each square meter of area it covered. The tremendous weight of the ice depressed the earth's crust as much as 1,200 meters (4,000 feet) where the ice was thickest and had lasted the longest. This subsidence is known as *isostatic depression.* This depression was, however, not permanent. As the glaciers diminished in size and finally disappeared, a slow re-elevation, or *isostatic rebound,* occurred. This rebound, averaging several cen-

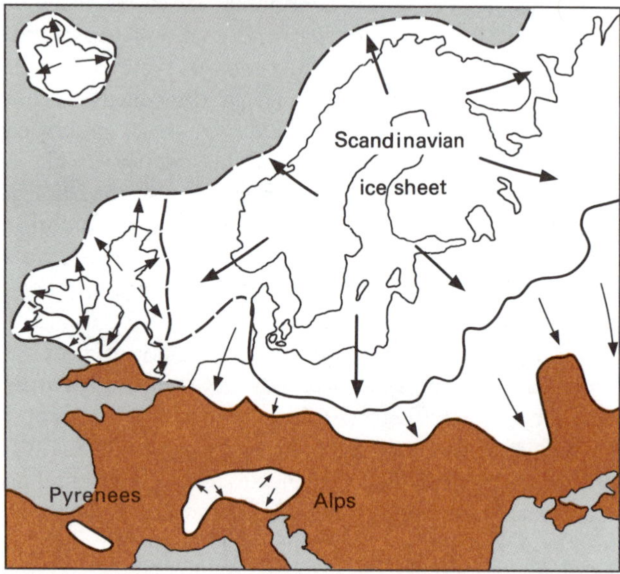


**FIGURE 14.3**
Continental glaciation during the Pleistocene. In North America, the ice sheet covered all of Canada and spread south as far as the Ohio and Missouri rivers. In Europe, the Scandinavian ice sheet spread southward to northern Europe. Secondary centers of ice developed in the European mountains. (After Flint, 1971)

**PHOTO 125**
Glacial epochs. Buried forest humus layer between glacial till deposits in Kewanee County, Wisconsin. Note tree limbs in buried forest humus. (Courtesy: Francis D. Hole, Wisconsin Geological and Natural History Survey)

timeters per year, is still in progress in the area of the Great Lakes north to the Hudson Bay. The best evidence of this change in elevation is found in the ancestral shorelines of the Great Lakes. When the ancient Great Lakes shorelines are traced from south to north, it is found that the north shorelines are lower than those farther south. This indicates that the northern portions of the Great Lakes are still undergoing an isostatic rebound, while at the southern boundaries the rebound is completed and elevations are stable. Since the shoreline of any water body is formed at a uniform elevation, the tilting of the Great Lakes shoreline is solid evidence of regional variations in the isostatic rebound.

Continental glaciation locked up a tremendous quantity of the earth's water. During the Pleistocene period sea level was between 100 and 150 meters (330 to 500 feet) lower. Evidence of this change appears in the river valleys that now extend into the submerged coastal shelves. Most, if not all, of the Atlantic continental shelf was above sea level during the Pleistocene period, for water on its outer edge today is only about 130 meters (430 feet) deep.

While the vast glaciers of the Pleistocene epoch have disappeared, glaciers have not disappeared from the world. It is estimated that about 14.9 million square kilometers (6 million square miles), about 10 percent of the world's land surface, is still covered with ice. Antarctica with 12.5 million square kilometers (5 million

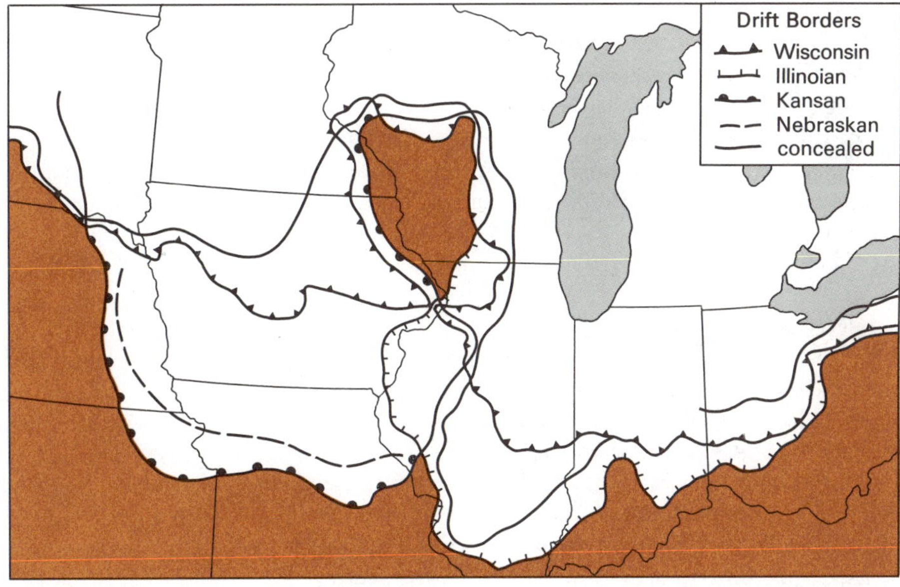


**FIGURE 14.4**
Glacial stages are marked by different boundaries of rock deposits. The outer boundaries of four major stages of Pleistocene glaciation are shown. (After Flint, 1971)

square miles) and Greenland with 1.7 million square kilometers (660 thousand square miles) have the largest glaciers. This leaves about 700,000 square kilometers (270,000 square miles) of glacial ice that is widely distributed in small glaciers in the upland areas of the world and on small polar ice caps.

## THEORIES OF THE ORIGIN OF CONTINENTAL GLACIATION

In the last hundred years a number of theories have been proposed to explain the origin of continental glaciation. One of the early theories was based upon variations in the amount of carbon dioxide or dust in the atmosphere. Because carbon dioxide prevents the escape of radiation from the earth, a decrease in the amount of this gas in the atmosphere would cool the earth. However, it is questioned whether any possible change in the amount of carbon dioxide could be sufficient to trigger the development of glaciers on the earth.

Large quantities of dust in the atmosphere can also alter the heating of the earth. Dust in the atmosphere from volcanic eruptions has changed the climate of a region, and perhaps even the world, for a short period of time, but whether this effect could continue over a sufficient period of time to cause glacial development is to be questioned.

Theories suggest that changes in the location of the earth's rotational poles could alter the climate of certain areas. No evidence exists to confirm that the rotational poles have shifted toward the cold poles. However, the regular periodic movements of the poles are well documented. Whether these movements are sufficient to create great continental glaciers is questionable. Further, all the known glacial periods do not coincide with these movements. Nevertheless, larger movements of the direction of the poles could have occurred in the geologic past, and these movements might have triggered glacial epochs.

Another theory suggests a relationship between lowered amounts of solar energy and high elevation. If a sufficiently long period of lower-than-average solar heating is combined with the low temperature of high and vast continents, then perennial snow may gradually evolve into an ice sheet. One model suggests that a decrease in solar energy of 6 percent or more would create a glacial epoch. However, there is no evidence that such variations have occurred.

Possibly the most promising theory postulates changes in ice conditions over the oceans as a cause of Pleistocene glaciation. The theory begins with an ice-free Arctic Ocean, which would initiate an increase in precipitation and a cooling effect sufficient to freeze the ocean. The warm ocean currents would be pushed equatorward, and snow would accumulate on the land, gradually turning into glacial ice. The glacial epoch would continue until it became too cold to provide enough moisture to sustain itself. Melting would then begin, causing the continental glaciers to retreat, and ultimately the Arctic Ocean would again be ice-free. This theory could account for the more recent glacial advances. However, new studies suggest that the present Arctic ice may be much older than the Pleistocene epoch, a finding that raises questions about the validity of this theory.

No theory explaining the origin of the Ice Ages has been accepted by the scientific community. The search continues for a satisfactory theory that can explain such major climatic changes.

## TYPES OF GLACIERS

Glaciers may be classified according to their place of origin. When a glacier covers a vast area, such as Antarctica, it is called a *continental* or *ice sheet glacier.* Those that originate in mountains and descend the valleys are known as *alpine* or *valley glaciers.* If the mountain glacier is confined to its high basin of origin—that is, its cirque basin—it is known as a *cirque glacier.* In the United States there are many cirque glaciers that are the remnants of former alpine glaciers. If the alpine glacier flows out from its valley onto the adjacent lowlands in a deltalike form, it becomes a *piedmont glacier.* An alpine glacier that discharges its ice directly into the ocean is named a *tidewater glacier.* Such glaciers occur in Alaska and other areas.

## GLACIAL MODIFICATION OF LANDSCAPES

### CONTINENTAL GLACIATION

Continental glaciers have left an indelible imprint wherever they have occurred. The vast ice-scoured landscapes, as well as areas dominated by glacial depositional deposits, possess distinctive landforms.

#### Erosional Landforms of Continental Glaciation

Glaciers erode landscapes by the processes of *plucking* and *abrasion.* At the bedrock surface there are many pieces of rock that are loosened by the action of freezing and thawing. When a glacier passes over such a surface, the rocks are *plucked* from the ground and become part of the ice mass. As the glacier moves these rock fragments along, it acts as a giant piece of sandpaper on the underlying soil and rock, creating an abrasive action.

These processes of continental glaciation create a unique type of landscape. The largest ice-scoured plains of the world are found near the centers of origin of the Pleistocene glaciers. The principal regions are the Laurentian plains of Canada and the Scandinavian Peninsula. Although the glaciers disappeared several thousand years ago from these areas of crystalline rock, the weathering of the resistant rock has not been sufficient to greatly change the ice-carved landforms.

The glacially eroded plains thus have a scoured appearance. The moving ice mass removed the mantle soil and weathered rock. The landscape is characterized by rounded rock hills and broad open valleys with comparatively low local relief. The rock surface may have grooves and scratches known as *striations.* In a few places ice-scoured rock projections rise above the surface. On the side of the glacial advance the slopes are gently polished, but on the opposite side, where abrasion and plucking have been less effective, the slopes are often steep and rough. These glacially shaped hillocks are known as *roches moutonnées* or sheep rocks, for at a distance they appear as sheep lying on a plain (Photo 126).

When the ice flow was parallel to zones of easily erodable bedrock, the continental ice sheets scoured deep linear troughs that became valleys with the melting of the ice. The Great Lakes and the Finger Lakes of New York originated in this manner. The erosional fea-

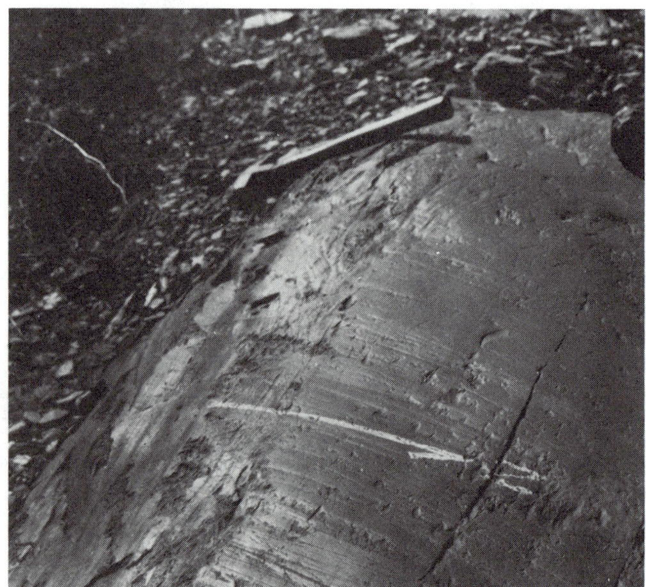

**PHOTO 126**

Roche moutonnée. A polished and striated roche moutonnée exposed by stripping of glacial drift in Crow Wing County, Minnesota. (Courtesy: R. G. Schmidt, U.S. Geological Survey)

**TABLE 14.1**
Erosional features of continental and valley glaciers

| Erosional Feature | Continental Glacier | Valley Glacier |
|---|---|---|
| Grooves | Abundant | Abundant |
| Scratches | Abundant | Abundant |
| Polishing | Abundant | Abundant |
| Roches moutonnées | Abundant | Rare |
| Cirques | ——— | Abundant |
| Arêtes | ——— | Abundant |
| U-shaped valleys | Rare | Abundant |
| Hanging valleys | Rare | Abundant |
| Fiords | ——— | Abundant |

tures common to continental and valley glaciation are summarized in Table 14.1.

Glacial scouring normally changes the pre-existing drainage pattern. The present drainage system on the ice-scoured plains is characterized by its indefinite pattern and its lack of relationship to rock structures. It exhibits characteristics of the stage of youth, including many falls and rapids.

Because the abrasive action produced fine sediments that are eroded by the streams, the glacial meltwater often has a light, cloudy appearance, and is known as *glacial milk.* Lakes are particularly numerous. Many of them lie in the shallow rock basins eroded by the ice. Some of the shallow lakes have been filled with vegetation such as sphagnum moss. These bog areas in Canada are known as *muskegs.*

## Depositional Landforms of Continental Glaciation

Earth materials eroded from the ice-scoured areas are ultimately deposited, creating a number of different types of landforms. The depositional areas are more extensive and of greater human significance than the ice-scoured areas. They occupy the outer margins of the glaciated areas of North America and Europe (Figure 14.5).

The rock materials that are spread over depositional plains originated not only from the ice-scoured regions, but also from the local earth materials. All glacial deposits are collectively known as *glacial drift.* The drift varies in thickness from less than a meter to as much as 175 meters (575 feet). The drift is commonly deep in preglacial valleys and shallow in higher areas.

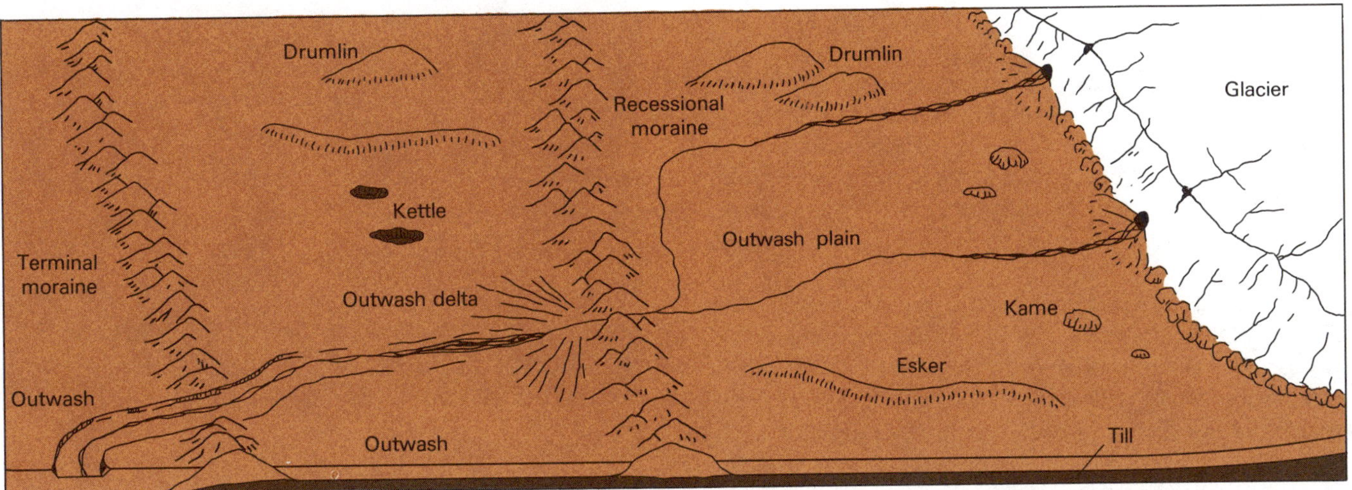


**FIGURE 14.5**
Landforms of continental glaciers.

**PHOTO 127**
Ground moraine. A close-up of ground moraine in Langlade County, Wisconsin. (Courtesy: Francis D. Hole, Wisconsin Geological and Natural History Survey)

**PHOTO 128**
Erratic. The Enos Rock is the largest erratic on Cape Cod, measuring about 5 by 7 meters (15 by 20 feet) at its base. It consists of crystalline rock. (Courtesy: Brian Tormey, The Pennsylvania State University)

A mantle of unstratified drift is known as *ground moraine* or a *till plain* (Photo 127). Ground moraine is deposited not only under the glacier but also on the margin of the glacier. It contains rock materials of all sizes and shapes.

The rocks carried by a glacier may have originated hundreds of kilometers from the place where they were deposited. These foreign rocks, known as *erratics,* vary in weight from a few ounces to as much as 18,000 tons, providing evidence of the tremendous carrying power of the glacier (Photo 128). If the rocks have a distinctive composition, such as an igneous rock found lying on top of bedrocks of sedimentary origin, the exact location of the origin of the erratic can sometimes be determined.

A number of landform features are associated with the till plain. Moraines are the most prominent and widespread features that have developed on till plains due to the direct action of ice (Photo 129). When the margin of the glacier oscillated in a small area for a period of time, the moving ice continued to pile up material at its outermost border, providing an area of drift 15 to 50 meters (50 to 165 feet) higher than that of the surrounding till plain. The farthest advance of a glacier is commonly marked by a high, irregular ridge of heterogeneous rock debris, called the *terminal moraine* (Photo 130). A receding glacier makes minor readvances, building a series of *recessional moraines.* These belts are from 2 to 8 kilometers (1 to 5 miles) wide and as much as several hundred kilometers long (Figure 14.6).

**PHOTO 129**
Moraine. A boulder-strewn end moraine in Langlade County, Wisconsin. It extends several miles and lies from 10 to 20 feet above the level of the till plain. (Courtesy: Francis D. Hole, Wisconsin Geological and Natural History Survey)

**PHOTO 130**
Pitted terminal moraine. A pitted terminal moraine two miles northeast of Prairie du Sac, Columbia County, Wisconsin. (Courtesy: W. C. Alden, U.S. Geological Survey)

**PHOTO 131**
Kettle moraine. This photograph illustrates the hummocky topography of a pitted kettle moraine. (Courtesy: Francis D. Hole, Wisconsin Geological and National History Survey)

**FIGURE 14.6**
Moraine belts in the Midwest of the United States. (After Flint, 1945)

A special type of moraine is characterized by an internal structure of abundant small, parallel ridges and troughs. This structure suggests that the moraine was built when the ice front experienced a series of minor advances and retreats extending over a number of years. The most spectacular of these moraines is known as a *kettle moraine*, characterized by deep pits, depressions, or "kettles" (Photo 131). Many of these depressions are now filled with water and so are called *kettle lakes*. These depressions are the result of the melting of blocks of ice that were buried in the moraines.

Another striking glacial landform is the *drumlin* (Photo 132). These linear, streamlined ridges on the till

**PHOTO 132**
Drumlin. Drumlins strewn with boulders, near West Plains, southwest Saskatchewan Province, Canada. (Courtesy: W. G. Pierce, U.S. Geological Survey)

plain occur in clusters that may number in the hundreds. When this happens, the area is designated as a *drumlin field.* Although the origin of drumlins is not completely understood, their shape suggests that they were formed by longitudinal shearing where rapidly advancing ice moved across previously deposited ground moraine. They are commonly half-egg-shaped, with their higher and steeper ends facing in the direction from which the ice advanced. They are rarely more than 0.8 kilometer (one-half mile) long and 30 meters (100 feet) high. The best examples of drumlins in the United States are found in central New York, Michigan, Wisconsin, and Minnesota; they are also found in southern Ontario and Poland (Figure 14.7).

As a glacier melted, huge quantities of water flowed from many temporary and shifting streams. They were normally laden with sediment, so they formed *glaciofluvial deposits* that resemble floodplains and alluvial fans. Meltwater flowing from the continental ice deposited *outwash plains* that covered many square kilometers (Photo 133). These outwash plains may be dotted with ice-block depressions called *pits,* whose origin is similar to kettles in moraines. Many of these pits filled with water and became lakes. In other places ice formed a dam between the end of the ice and the higher land, creating temporary or *proglacial lakes.* When the ice melted, the dam disappeared and the lake vanished. However, during the years the lake existed, sediments accumulated in its bed. The existence of these lakes is revealed from the seasonal deposits of laminated or layered lake silts or clays, called *varves.*

**PHOTO 133**
Glacial outwash plain. This massive outwash plain of sand and gravel in Waukesha County, Wisconsin, is now being mined for construction materials. (Courtesy: Francis D. Hole, Wisconsin Geological and Natural History Survey)

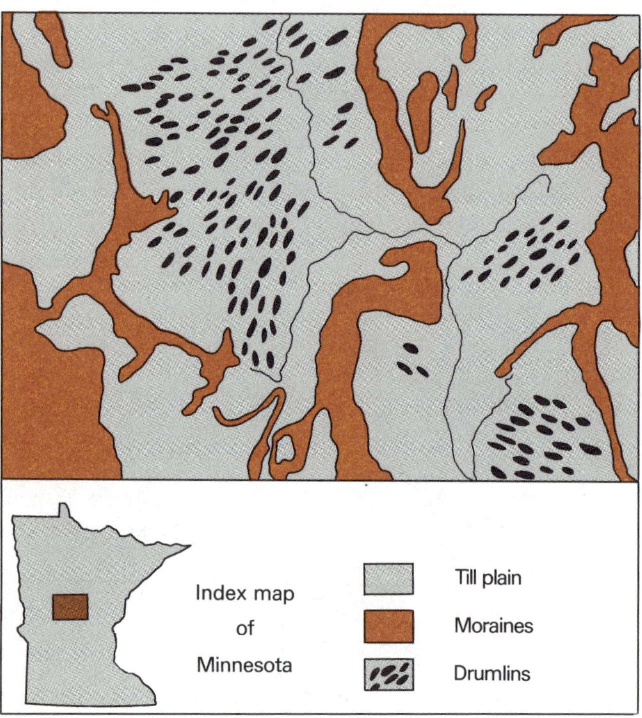


**FIGURE 14.7**
Drumlin fields in central Minnesota. (After Emmons and others, 1960)

A number of special landforms are associated with the glaciofluvial deposits. At times joints and cracks developed on the surface of the continental glaciers due to movements of the ice. As meltwater poured into these openings, the sediments it carried built up in the fractures. When the ice melted, deposits, known as *kames,* were left as small hills on top of the ground moraines. Sometimes the kames are linked together as beads on a string, with the high mounds connected by lower ridges marking the line of the old fracture. These are known as *kame ridges.* When water flowed through subterranean passages of the glacier, sediments were deposited in the channel. When the glacier melted, these sediments remained as long, sinuous ridges known as *eskers,* generally 3 to 5 meters (10 to 16 feet) high, and extending from less than a kilometer to many kilometers in length (Photo 134).

**PHOTO 134**
An esker in Oswego County, New York. (Courtesy: C. R. Tuttle, U.S. Geological Survey)

## ALPINE GLACIATION

Like continental glaciation, alpine glaciation produces both erosional and depositional landforms.

### Erosional Landforms of Alpine Glaciation

Alpine glaciers normally occupy valleys. Initially these valleys are usually formed by the action of running water. However, a glacier immediately changes the area it occupies (Figure 14.8). The erosional characteristics of glaciers are so distinct that a glacial valley is readily identifiable even though the glacier has disappeared. The alpine erosion is accomplished not only by the action of the moving ice, but also by the abrasive action of the sand, gravel, and boulders within the ice body (Photo 135). A tremendous force is exerted by the moving ice mass: a single cubic meter of ice weighs about 550 pounds, and a glacier 300 meters thick exerts a pressure of approximately 250 tons on each square meter of earth it passes over.

The floors and walls of valleys show striking evidence of the passage of an alpine glacier. They are gouged, scraped, and smoothed on the side of the glacial advancement and exhibit sharp angular projections on the leeward side, where plucking rather than abrasion occurred. The grinding of the rock produces much fine silt, known as *rock flour,* that gives a milky appearance to glacier meltwater streams. Reflection of light from these fine rock particles suspended in the water creates the lovely shades of light blue and turquoise of the lakes into which these waters drain. No one can look into such a lake as Lake Louise in Banff National Park in Alberta, Canada, without enjoying the beautiful touch of color that glaciers have added to a magnificent mountain scene.

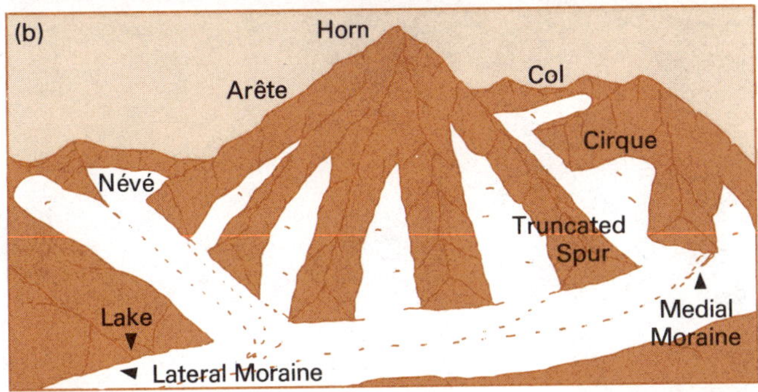


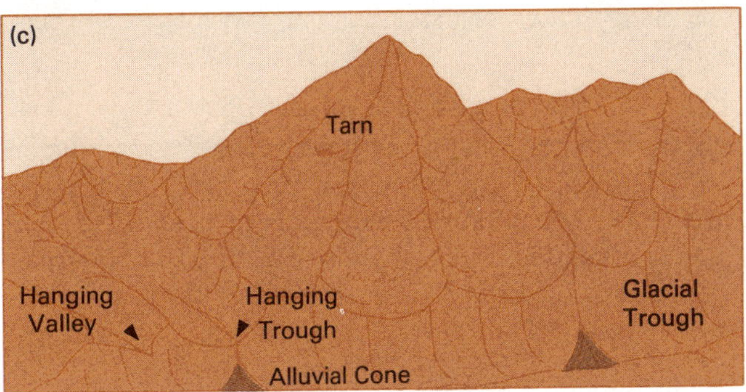


**FIGURE 14.8**
Sculpturing of mountains by glaciers. (*a*) The landforms are molded by water erosion before glaciation occurs. (*b*) After several thousand years of glaciation, new landforms are created. (*c*) The new glacial landforms dominate after the ice disappears.

Alpine glaciers begin at the head of their valleys, where the greatest ice erosion occurs. They remain there for a long time before moving down the valley, and they disappear last in this area as they wane. Most of the valley heads have therefore been eroded into deep recesses. These amphitheaters, closed by steep

**PHOTO 135**
Glacial ice. The Pers glacier, located in the Bernina Mountain range of Switzerland. (Courtesy: Swiss National Tourist Office)

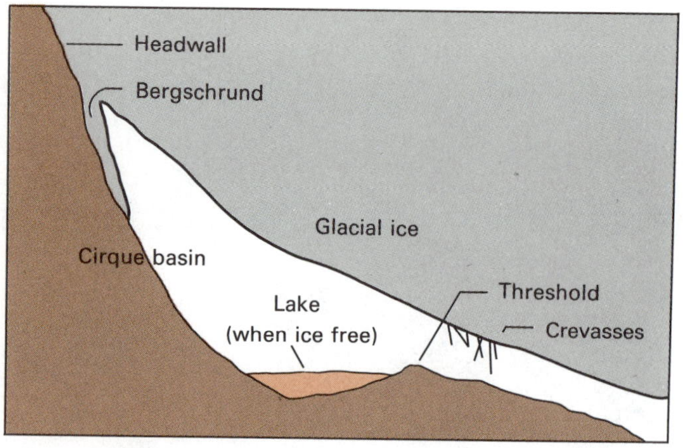

**FIGURE 14.9**
Formation of a cirque. In the *bergschrund* area, frost action on the headwall frees fragments of bedrock, which drop to the base of the ice. The rock fragments are incorporated into the ice mass, and as the ice moves, it abrades the bottom and sides of the cirque. Gradually a basin is formed. When the ice melts, the cirque basin becomes the site of a tarn, or cirque lake, that exists in the scoured-out area. (After Burchfiel, 1982)

slopes on three sides, are known as *cirques* (Figure 14.9). If cirques are formed on both sides of a mountain, they will ultimately reduce it to a sharp-crested, jagged ridge, known as an *arête* (Photo 136). The meeting of two opposing cirques makes a notch in the arête, known as a *col.*

In the highest portion of a mountain range, glaciers normally radiate in all directions (Photos 137–140). As the cirques surround the highest point, they eventually create a sharp-pointed pyramidal peak, called a *horn.* Each face of the horn is the headwall of the encroaching cirque. The most famous horn in the world is probably the Matterhorn in the Swiss-Italian Alps, but there are thousands more in the once-glaciated mountains of the

**PHOTO 136**
The jagged arête of the Finsteraarhorn (14,026 feet high) in the Bernese Alps of Switzerland. Note the cirque basin in the center of the photo. (Courtesy: Swiss National Tourist Office)

**PHOTO 137**
Alpine glaciation. Aerial view of the Obergabelhorn from the north with the Wellenkuppe and the Matterhorn to the left. To the right is the Durand glacier. (Courtesy: Swiss National Tourist Office)

world. The steep slopes of horns make them a challenge to mountain climbers. Many of the highest unclimbed peaks are horns.

Valleys occupied by glaciers for an extended period of time develop a number of ice-sculptured topographic

**PHOTO 139**
Aerial view of the Morteratsch glacier of the Bernina mountain range in the Grisons, forming as two flows of ice from cirque basins unite. (Courtesy: Swiss National Tourist Office)

**PHOTO 138**
Alpine glaciation. Merger of the Gorner and Grenz glaciers in the Monte Rosa area of Switzerland. (Courtesy: Swiss National Tourist Office)

**PHOTO 140**
Valley glacier. The Mer de Glace glacier near Chamonix, France, flows through the mountain valley. (Courtesy: French Government Tourist Office)

features. One of the most striking changes affects the shape of the valley. Most mountain valleys prior to glaciation exhibit the characteristics of a youthful river valley; they have a V-shape in cross section. When a glacier has scoured and shaped the valley sides, as well as the bottom, a broad, flat-bottomed U-shaped valley results, called a *glacial trough* (Photo 141). High on the valley side there is usually a break in slope, known as the *trimline,* that divides the ice-scoured from the water-eroded portion. From the height of the trimline the thickness of the alpine glacial ice can be determined. Some glaciated valleys have rock strata with different resistance to erosion. As a consequence, a stair-step profile, or *glacial stairway,* may develop on the sides of the valley.

In the valley floor, a glacier is able to gouge more easily into the land, producing deep depressions. When the ice disappears, these basins immediately fill with water, becoming *tarns* or *paternoster lakes.* Other lakes may be dammed behind the terminal moraines deposited across the valley by the glacier. Practically all lakes in the Alps, Rockies, and other mountains where glaciers once existed were formed in one of these two ways.

One of the spectacular valleys carved out by glaciers is the Yosemite Valley of California. Although the glacier scoured this valley to a depth of more than 1,000 meters (3,280 feet), it also filled the valley with deposits as the glacier retreated. For example, in the vicinity of Camp Curry and the Ahwahnee Hotel, the bedrock floor lies at a depth of about 600 meters (2,000 feet) below the surface. Further down the valley near El Capitan the fill is 400 meters (1,300 feet) thick. A visitor thus sees only about half the height of the imposing walls. If all the sediments were removed from the valley, a great lake would form in the scoured basin, and the granite cliffs of El Capitan and Glacier Point would tower almost 300 meters (1,000 feet) higher above its waters than they do above the valley floor today.

In some areas of the world alpine glaciers scour valleys that open directly on the ocean. Usually the glacier deepens the valley so that it lies below sea level. When the glacier melts, the flooded valleys are called *fiords* (Photo 142). These are among the most scenic of glacial valleys. The best-known ones are along the Alaskan and Norwegian coasts, but the entire perimeter of Greenland is notched by fiords, as are many other places, including Chile, New Zealand, British Columbia, Iceland, Scotland, Labrador, and the islands of Arctic Canada. Many of the Norwegian fiords are more than 80 kilometers (50 miles) in length. The longest, Sogne Fiord near Bergen, is 190 kilometers (120 miles) long and has a depth of about 1,210 meters (4,000 feet) below sea level.

When the glacier cuts the main valley deeper, its tributary glaciers do not deepen their valleys to the same extent. Being smaller and thinner, the tributary glaciers do not possess the erosional power of the main glacier.

**PHOTO 141**
Red Mountain Pass, a U-shaped valley south of Ouray, Colorado. (Courtesy: L.C. Huff, U.S. Geological Survey)

**PHOTO 142**
Fiord. Milford Sound in the South Island of New Zealand. Note the ice-scoured walls of the cliff.

**PHOTO 143**
Hanging valley. Yosemite Falls in Yosemite National Park plunges over a hanging valley. (Courtesy: United Air Lines)

**PHOTO 144**
Rhone glacier. The Rhone glacier in the Valais of Switzerland has deposited a vast amount of morainal material in its valley. (Courtesy: Swiss National Tourist Office)

As a result the tributary valleys are left hanging, once the ice is gone, far above the main valley. These distinctive landforms are known as *hanging valleys* (Photo 143). As streams flow into the main valley, they form spectacular falls along the hanging valleys. One of the most beautiful of these is the Upper Yosemite Fall, one of the highest free-leaping waterfalls in the world. From the point where the water leaps into space, it drops about 433 meters (1,420 feet) in a sheer fall before crashing onto the rock below.

## Depositional Landforms of Alpine Glaciation

Although the erosional features created by alpine glaciation may appear most spectacular, some noteworthy depositional landforms also exist (Photo 144). Like a continental glacier, an alpine glacier marks its farthest advance by a *terminal moraine,* and if the recessive stages of the glacier are marked by minor readvances, a number of *recessional* or *end moraines* will develop across the valley floor. These moraines may dam the flow of water down the valley, creating *tarn* lakes. On the sides of the valley, rock falls may accumulate into *lateral moraines.* On occasion two or more tributary valley glaciers may merge in their descent to the main valley. The rock materials carried by each glacier may become trapped between the ice masses, producing *medial moraines* paralleling the valley floor. The medial moraines are frequently covered with sediments from fluvial activity in the valley and rarely are found as prominent features in the landscape.

As alpine valley glaciers retreat, the melting ice produces a large discharge of water. Sediments carried by this discharge are deposited some distance downstream from the ice margin as *outwash fans.* If confined to the course of the stream channel, the sediments are identified as *valley train.*

In the mountains of western United States, *rock glaciers* are a common landform remnant of former glaciation. These masses of rocks contain ice in the spaces between the rock blocks. When these rock glaciers are found high in the mountain, gravity may gradually force the rock mass downslope. The surface of these rock masses is rough and hummocky, with occasional depressions which may represent local rock collapse as interstitial ice melts. These areas may become an important water supply in the future, because they contain a large quantity of fresh water in the semiarid West.

# GLACIATION AND HUMAN ACTIVITY

## AGRICULTURE AND GLACIATION

Glaciers have created some of the most fertile land on the earth; they have also ruined some land for virtually any agricultural use. The ice-scoured areas have been glaciated so recently that little, if any, soil covering has developed. These areas are largely devoid of agriculture except for small lowland pockets where glacial scouring did not occur.

The depositional areas are strikingly diverse in their agricultural potential. For example, New England and the Midwest have surface deposits of glacial materials, but farming has nearly disappeared from New England while the Midwest is one of the richest farming areas in the world. The type of glacial till in the two regions is a major factor in the human use of the land.

When the continental ice sheet spread southward from Canada, it gouged the weak shales and limestones in the lowlands now occupied by the Great Lakes. The glacier ground these rocks into clay, then pushed and spread the tremendous load hundreds of miles southward. This great mass of drift blanketed the landscape, burying the original preglacial surface and protecting it from further gouging and scraping. The original surface is thus hidden, but its presence is revealed by thousands of wells that have been drilled through the drift sheet above it. The agricultural heartland of the nation has developed on this gently rolling plain of youthful glacial soils that have developed in the past 10,000 years. Today one can drive for hours through fertile farmlands on the glacially derived surface.

The granite and other crystalline bedrock of New England's hills and mountains did not provide the same type of material to the glaciers as did the Great Lakes region. However, constant scraping of this hard bedrock for thousands of years by glacial action did loosen some rock materials. Because the rock fragments were resistant, they were not pulverized as in the Midwest. As the glacier receded, these rock fragments were deposited as a thin layer of stony drift on the surface. Thus, in New England the drift may be only 3 to 5 meters (10 to 16 feet) thick, in contrast to 100 or more meters (330 feet) in the Midwest. New England farmland is a sea of stones. Every small field is outlined by a fence of stone. These fences grew slowly through the years as each spring farmers added to them the stones brought to the surface during the winter's freezing and thawing. In the colonial period farmers attempted to work these stony fields, but they were gradually abandoned as more productive lands were brought into cultivation to the west. Today the fields are reverting to their natural state of a forest covering.

Land use is affected not only by the scouring and depositional activities of the glaciers. During the Ice Age the glaciers created vast lakes when the ice mass acted as a dam. Where the natural flow of the water was blocked by the ice mass, great lakes formed between the glacier and the crest of the drainage basin. Water from the ice front during this period was forced to rise until it could escape at a higher outlet. Sediments, primarily from the glacier, have created some of the flattest and most fertile plains in the world. Notable among these plains is the one created by Lake Agassiz. This lake existed when the glacial drainage was impounded in a large lake between the wasting ice mass in central Canada and the higher continental divide of southern Minnesota. A broad and shallow lake, created on the northward sloping land, found its outlet to the south through the Mississippi River system. Today, Lakes Winnipeg and Winnipegosis are remnants of greater Lake Agassiz. The plains of the Red River basin of the United States and Canada have become a major region of spring wheat production. The lake sediments are the basis for one of the most productive soils in the world.

## GLACIATION'S EFFECT ON TRANSPORTATION ROUTES

Glaciers have influenced the development of waterways in a number of areas of the world. At the places where a glacier pauses in its retreat, tremendous quantities of water pour from the ice and flow along the ice edge, creating *glacial spillways.* These spillways were especially well developed on the north European plain in Germany and Poland. As the ice retreated, the waterways were gradually re-established along the natural slope of the land. Thus on the north European plain the present rivers drain the land dominantly from south to north while the glacial spillways extend east-west. The east-west graded channels now have a system of canals that provide links to the natural waterways of the area.

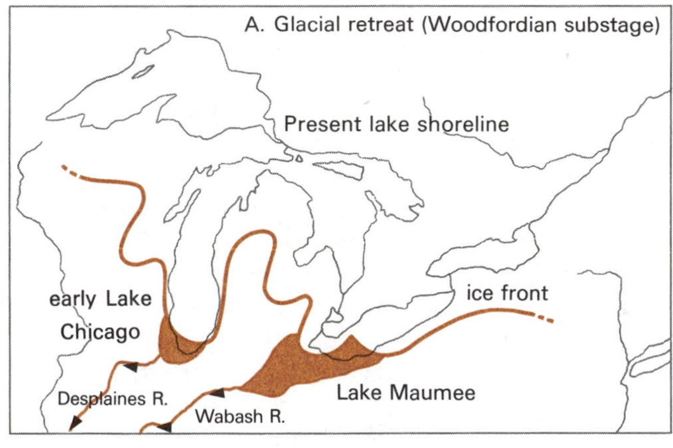


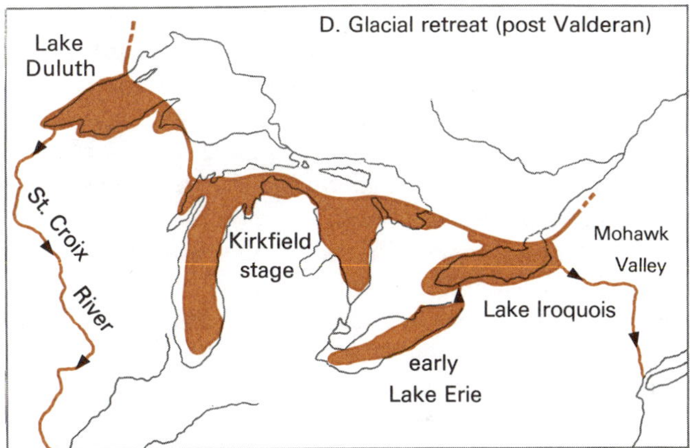


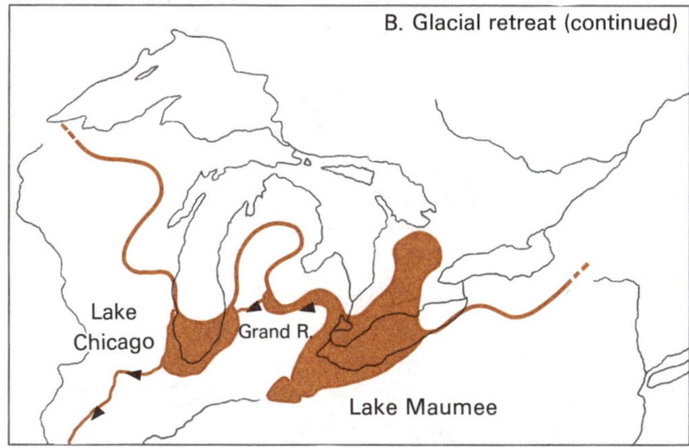


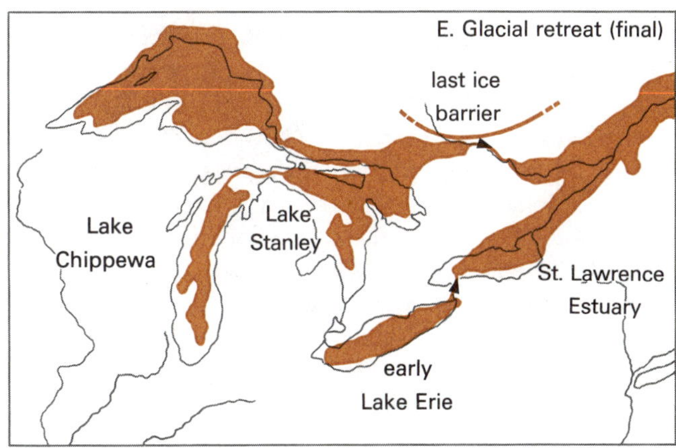


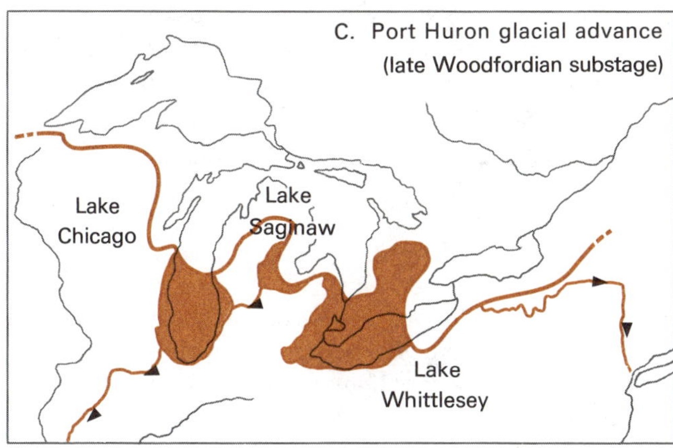


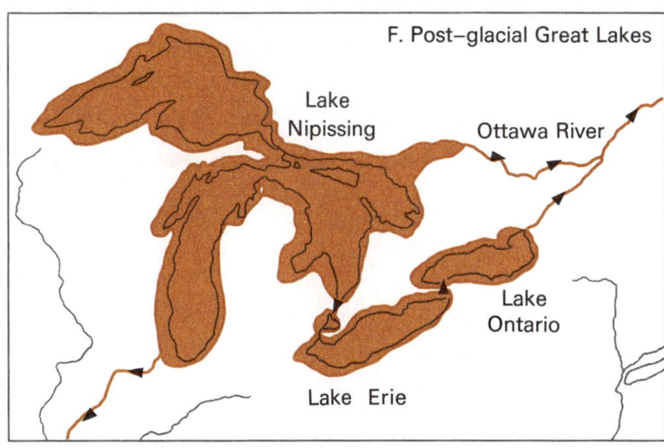


**FIGURE 14.10**
Evolution of the Great Lakes. The Great Lakes were formed by the action of the continental glaciers. (After Hough, 1958. Copyright © 1958 The University of Illinois Press)

The Pleistocene glacial epoch created the greatest inland waterway in the world in the American and Canadian Great Lakes (Figure 14.10). In preglacial times, lowlands existed where the Great Lakes now stand. These lowlands were occupied by a great system of rivers. Repeated ice invasions during the glacial eras eroded the rocky material from the river basins, creating deep depressions. When the glaciers finally disappeared, water filled these depressions, which became an inland lake system. The Great Lakes occupy 246,000 square kilometers (95,000 square miles), a much greater area than any other single freshwater lake in the world. The Great Lakes have enabled oceangoing vessels to penetrate more than a thousand miles into the interior of the continent.

Immediately after the glacial period, the Great Lakes were larger than they are now. Sediments were deposited in portions of the lakes that have become flat plains. These marginal plains are some of the best agricultural lands of the world, and they also possess—in Chicago, Milwaukee, Detroit, Toledo, Cleveland, Erie, Buffalo, and Toronto—some of the continent's largest urban agglomerations. Not only have the Great Lakes created a major water route, but also bordering lowlands have become the leading corridor to the interior of the continent.

## GLACIATION AND RECREATION

Glaciers have carved some of the most spectacular mountain scenery in the world. Because of their wild beauty many of these areas have been set aside as national or state parks so that they can be preserved in their natural state forever. Notable areas of natural beauty created by glacial action in the United States and Canada are Yosemite National Park, Grand Teton National Park, Glacier National Park, and Banff National Park.

The Teton Mountains are often referred to as the "American Alps." Besides obvious active glaciers and snowfields and all of the striking features of glacial carving, the park contains 6 glacial lakes and many smaller bodies of water. The Teton Mountains contain one of the most jagged skylines of arêtes in North America. The highest peak, Grand Teton, stands at 4,124 meters (13,747 feet), but more than 20 other peaks rise above 3,300 meters (10,000 feet). While the park has a number of splendid trails, possibly the most dramatic is the Teton Glacier Trail, which climbs the steep east side of the Grand Teton and leads to a small glacier above the 3,300 meter (10,800 feet) level. During the Ice Age every large canyon in the Tetons contained a glacier. The rolling area of depositional landforms, called Jackson Hole, was once a huge field of ice.

The Grand Teton National Park attracts visitors not only because of its unique natural beauty but because the steep peaks test the ability of mountain climbers. No one is allowed to climb alone because of the danger involved. The timberline in the Tetons is at about 3,500 meters (11,480 feet), and much of the park area lies above this level in the land of everlasting snow. Mountain climbers are told to be prepared for any kind of weather. Snowfalls have been reported in every month of the year.

## CONCLUSION

Alpine and continental glaciers today cover about 10 percent of the earth's surface, but in the Pleistocene epoch they may have covered nearly a third. Glaciers are formed when snow accumulates and is gradually changed into firn ice, which in turn becomes glacial ice. Once glacial ice is formed, internal pressure and gravitational forces cause it to move.

Glaciers produce many characteristic features by both erosional and depositional action. The alpine glaciers have produced such features as cirques, towering horns, knife-edged arêtes, and U-shaped valleys, as well as moraines and fluvial deposits.

The continental glaciers have eroded vast areas, producing ice-scoured plains, and have also deposited rock debris over equally vast areas. Meltwater from glaciers has produced glaciofluvial plains far beyond the glaciers' outer extent. While moraines are the principal landform features of continental glaciation, a number of unique landforms such as drumlins and eskers have also been formed. Glaciers are also responsible for such major features as the North American Great Lakes, the fiords of the world, and the vast till plains of the American Midwest and northern Europe.

The continental glaciers have influenced human use of the land. In most ice-scoured areas little soil remains to support agriculture. In contrast, the high agricultural productivity of the American Midwest is related directly to the soils developed on glacial till.

## STUDY QUESTIONS

1 Explain the formation of a glacier.
2 What is meant by the *mass balance* of a glacier?
3 Explain how a glacier moves. What is the rate of movement of a glacier?
4 What is the evidence of glaciation during the Pleistocene epoch?
5 Give a number of theories that have been developed to explain Pleistocene glaciation. Why are many of these questioned?
6 What are the major types of glaciers? How do they differ?
7 Describe an ice-scoured landscape of continental glaciation.
8 Describe the development of moraines of a continental glacier. How do moraines differ from glacial till?
9 Describe glaciofluvial deposits. Why do they occur?
10 What are the differences between drumlins, eskers, and kames?
11 Describe the principal erosional landforms of alpine glaciation.
12 List several characteristics that distinguish an alpine glacial valley from a valley formed in a mountain by water erosion.
13 How do lateral moraines produced by an alpine glacier differ from end moraines built by a continental glacier?
14 How has continental glaciation influenced patterns of land use?

# 15
# LANDFORMS OF ARID LANDS

## KEY WORDS

abrasion
alluvial fan
arroyo
barchan
deflation
desert varnish
erg
hamada
loess
pediment
reg
rock island
saltation
surface creep
suspension
ventifact

To most people, the semiarid and arid regions are among the least familiar landscapes in the world. Nevertheless, the desert regions cover vast areas and have distinct physical features. An estimated 31.4 million square kilometers (12.2 million square miles) of the earth's surface are semiarid and arid (Table 15.1). The longest stretch of desert extends from Central Asia across North Africa to the Atlantic Ocean, a distance of nearly 11,000 kilometers (6,800 miles) (Figure 15.1).

The desert areas of the world are not fixed; evidence indicates that they have varied considerably in size in recent centuries. For example, during the period of the Roman Empire much of the southern shore of the Mediterranean Sea was the granary of Rome, with flourishing cities such as Leptis Magna in Libya. These areas are now stark deserts, and the relics of the cities are half-buried in sand.

Desert landscapes vary tremendously from place to place. Those people living in the humid world commonly have a misconception that deserts are vast areas of sand dunes and shifting, simmering sands. Although many deserts are sand covered, the majority are not. Most desert areas are likely to be broad expanses of barren rock and stony ground. Soil covering is either lacking or poorly developed. The color of the desert landscape is normally derived from the original bedrock rather than from chemical weathering processes.

## WIND EROSION PROCESSES

Wind is a major erosional agent in arid regions, lifting, transporting, and depositing earth materials. This erosional action involves two major processes: *deflation* (from Latin *deflatus,* or blown off) and *abrasion* (from Latin *abrasus,* or scraped off).

### DEFLATION

Deflation is the picking up and moving of earth particles by wind movement (Figure 15.2). This action is quite similar to a turbulent stream of water picking up and moving materials. The power of wind to erode is determined by two factors: velocity of the air mass and air density. It can be expressed as

$$E = V^3 p$$

where $E$ equals erosive power, $V$ equals velocity, and $p$ equals air density. Of the two factors, velocity is by far the more significant. The force of moving air varies with the third power of its velocity. To illustrate, if the velocity of moving air increases from 2 km/sec to 4 km/sec, the erosive force increases 8-fold. An increase from 2 to 10 km/sec produces a 125-fold increase in erosional power.

**TABLE 15.1**
Desert areas of the world

| Continent | Area (square kilometers) |
|---|---|
| Eurasia | 14,700,000 |
| Africa | 10,000,000 |
| Australia | 3,400,000 |
| North America | 1,900,000 |
| South America | 1,800,000 |

Experiments have shown that earth materials respond to wind action differently. Fine- and medium-grained sand is most easily moved by air turbulence. When air reaches a speed of about 16 kilometers per hour (about 15 feet per second), sand grains will be lifted by the currents. Fine clay and silt particles are extended above the still air layer that is on the ground. Winds can move coarse material, such as gravel, but only when velocities exceed 55 to 60 kilometers (34 to 38 miles) per hour.

Earth materials are transported in the atmosphere by *surface creep, saltation,* and *suspension.* The movement of particles begins when wind action is sufficient to cause a surface rolling motion, or surface creep. The particles are not lifted above the surface, but are simply moved across it. This action may account, however, for one-quarter of the particles moved in a single windstorm.

As the wind velocity rises to about 10 to 15 kilometers (6 to 9 miles) per hour, particles of about 1 millimeter (about 0.04 inch) are lifted and begin to bounce along the surface. Those with diameters of 2 millimeters (about 0.08 inch) begin moving with winds of 16 to 25 kilometers (10 to 15 miles) per hour. After rolling on the ground they may strike an object and suddenly shoot skyward. This process is called saltation (from the Latin *saltatus* for jump or leap). After the particle is airborne, it spins as rapidly as 1,000 revolutions per second. This tremendous driving force accounts for most of the particles transported in a windstorm. Saltation is an effective erosional agent because (*a*) the air immediately above the surface offers little resistance to the erosional force of the airborne particles, and (*b*) the turbulence above the ground has a strong force to lift the eroded particles.

Once the clay and silt particles are lifted into the atmosphere, strong turbulent currents will carry them up-

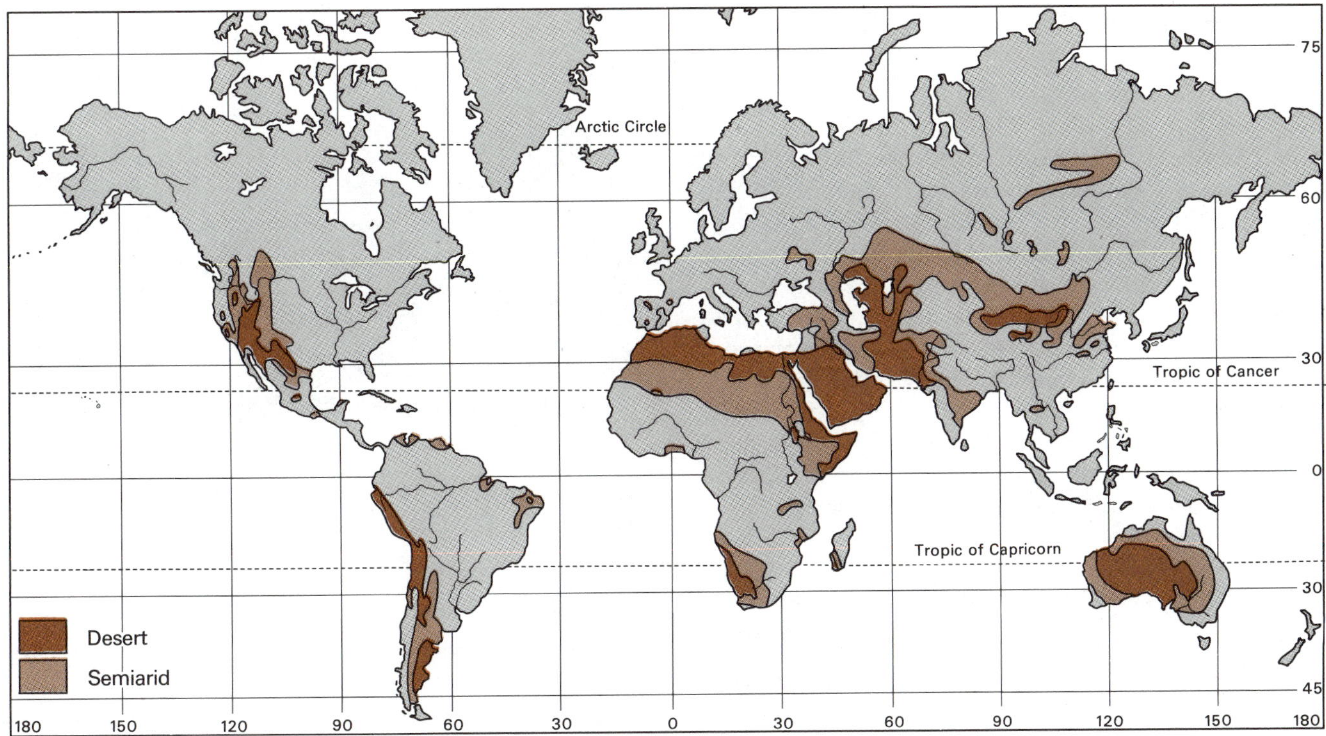


**FIGURE 15.1**

Major arid regions of the world. These regions occur in the subtropics and middle latitudes, in the areas of high pressure cells, in deep continental interiors, to the lee of high mountain ranges, and along cold-water coasts where moisture-laden cold air is transported to the warmer land. (After Meigs, 1956)

ward in suspension for thousands of meters. The suspended materials then enter the great wind systems of the world, where they may be transported thousands of kilometers. For example, in 1973 meteorologists determined that dust particles settling over the Caribbean Sea had their origin in the Sahara of North Africa. The amount of material in suspension may amount to as much as 875 metric tons of dust in a cubic kilometer of air (3,600 metric tons per cubic mile). This dust is usually, however, only a small percentage of the particles

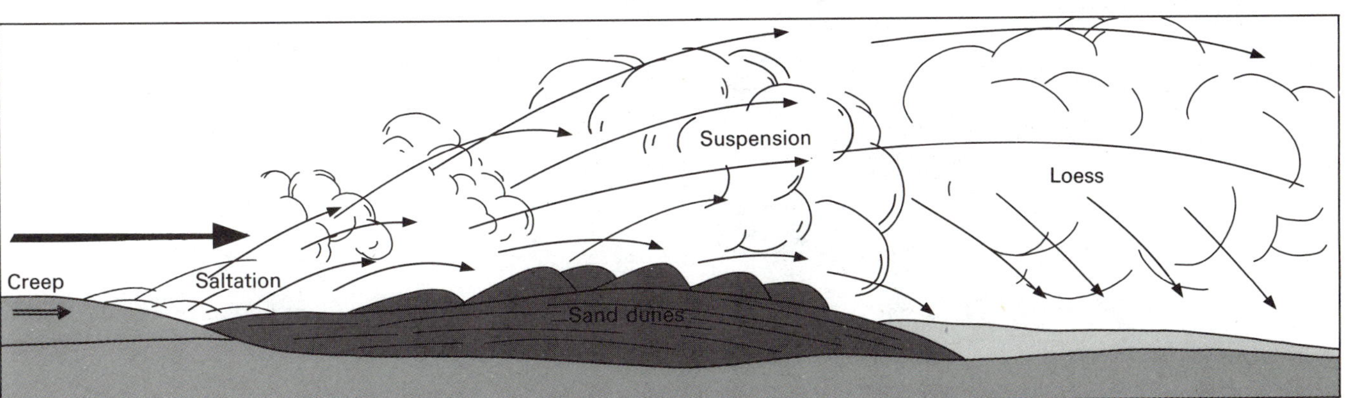


**FIGURE 15.2**

Wind erosion processes. Air movement transports earth materials by creep, saltation, and suspension. This movement is similar to stream action.

transported by wind action in a single strong windstorm.

### ABRASION

Wind abrasion occurs because the particles carried in the atmosphere act as a cutting tool (Photos 145 and 146). Sand particles will gradually mold a surface, wearing away the earth material by mechanical impact in a process similar to stream abrasion. Abrasion, or sandblasting, can produce some interestingly shaped pebbles called *ventifacts* or *dreikanter* (a German word meaning *three edges*). Sand hitting a pebble produces, on the side facing the wind, a flat surface that may be polished and slightly pitted. Most ventifacts have three or possibly more sides, produced by different wind directions or perhaps by the turning of the pebble in the deflation process.

### CONDITIONS FOR WIND EROSION

Wind erosion occurs everywhere on the earth, but its rate and magnitude vary greatly from place to place. Factors most important in determining the intensity of wind erosion are climate (primarily precipitation), vegetation cover, and type of landform.

Wind erosion is usually most effective in dry regions. In humid areas, water and vegetation bind the earth materials together so that the wind cannot easily move the earth particles. As the climate becomes drier, the binding action of surface tension decreases, and eventually the water film becomes too thin to act as a binding agent. The loose particles are then more susceptible to wind erosion.

**PHOTO 145**
Wind erosion. Monument Valley on the Navajo Indian Reservation in northeastern Arizona is a wind-worn land of awesome pinnacles, arches, monoliths, and spires. (Courtesy: Arizona Office of Tourism)

**PHOTO 146**
Wind erosion. Wind sculpturing aided in producing these angular masses of rock in the Arches National Monument.

A vegetational cover acts as a shield, decreasing the force of the wind on the surface. If the vegetational cover is diminished, as in the great drought of the 1930s on the Great Plains of the United States, the soil is exposed and the wind picks up the particles. Sometimes great dust storms carry suspended particles for hundreds of kilometers.

The type of landforms in an area also influences wind action. A rolling and hilly terrain reduces wind speeds and retards erosion. Special types of landforms, such as wind gaps, may channel the flow of wind currents, thus accelerating them and increasing the potential for erosion.

## LANDFORMS OF WIND DEPOSITION

The two major types of wind deposits are *loess* and *dunes.* Loess consists of layers of silt that cover large areas of the world. Dunes are hills or ridges of sand that may assume a number of shapes.

### LOESS

Loess is a fine-grained silt that has been transported by wind. A loess deposit is relatively unstratified because of its uniform grain size (Photo 147). A major characteristic is its vertical cleavage, a result of the small angular particles derived from a variety of rock types. The angular particles also make loess cliffs stable, and roads cut into it or streams flowing through it often have

**PHOTO 147**
Loess deposits. Excavation in loess near Council Bluffs, Iowa. (Courtesy: R. D. Miller, U.S. Geological Survey)

vertical sides. The material is usually pale yellow or buff-colored. The mineral composition of loess varies, depending upon its region of origin. The particles are typically rich in calcium carbonates.

Loess deposits cover vast areas of the world (Figure 15.3). Those in the United States extend from western Indiana to Colorado, and from Minnesota and South Dakota to Mississippi. Loess deposits are also found in southeastern Washington and western Idaho. The thickness of the loess in these areas will vary from a few centimeters to over 30 meters (100 feet). Other extensive loess deposits exist on the pampas of Argentina, the deserts of central Asia, northern China, and central Europe. In China some loess deposits are over 90 meters (300 feet) thick.

A number of theories attempt to explain the origin of loess. In the dry areas of the world, such as central Asia and northern China, the *aeolian,* or wind-borne, origin of the loess cannot be questioned. These large loess areas have formed on the downwind side of vast dry lands where great dust storms carried silt from the arid to the subhumid areas. Although brief dust storms prevail today, there is little evidence that significant quantities of loess are still being deposited.

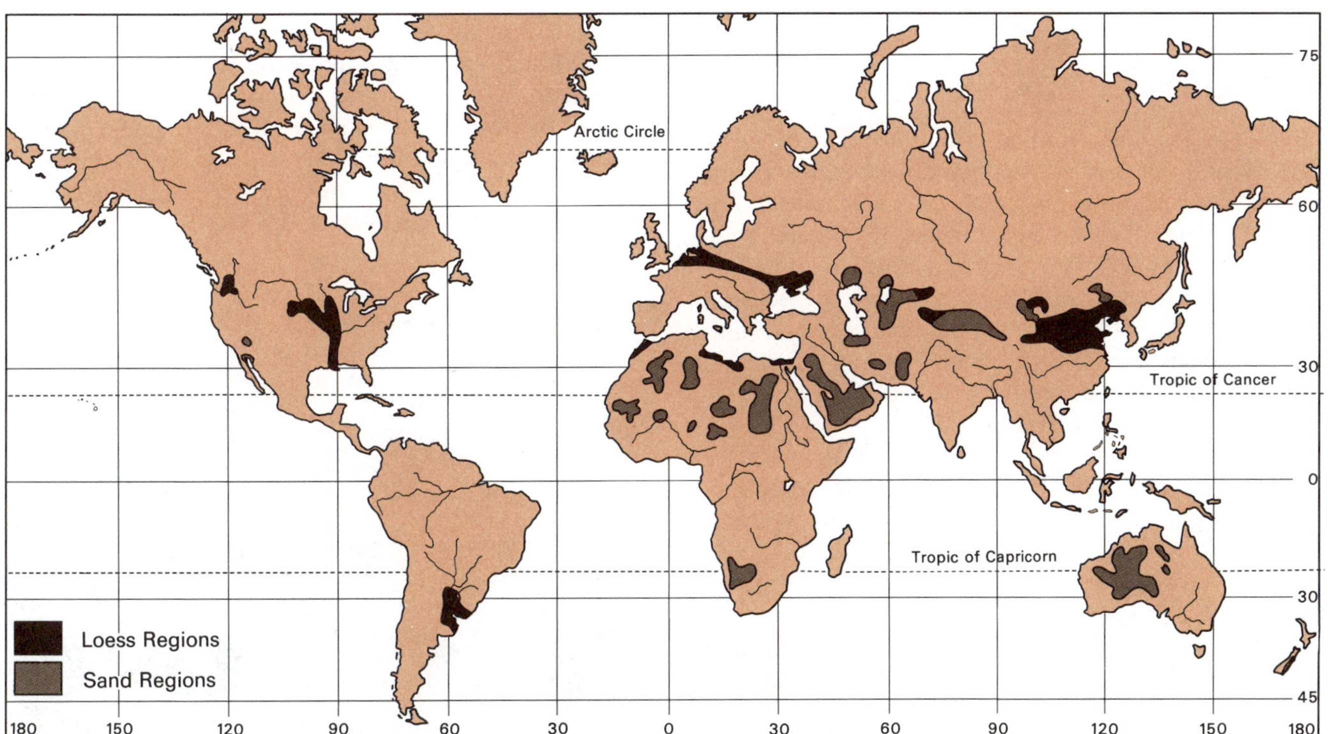


**FIGURE 15.3**
Major loess and sand dune deposits of the world. Many of the loess areas lie downwind of the deserts that provide the silt particles.

In other areas of the world, loess deposits are far removed from deserts. Those found in the Mississippi-Missouri River Basin of the United States and in central Europe are examples. In these areas a different theory of origin postulates that the loess was deposited at the end of the Pleistocene epoch. At that time, as the ice receded, large areas of glacial till and alluvial deposits were exposed. The wind blew from the high pressure cell over the cool ice to the lower pressure around the edges of the glacier. In doing so, the wind picked up the fine, unconsolidated particles and carried them in suspension until the wind force subsided. The wind-blown material was then deposited, forming loess plains. The loess deposits are particularly thick along the eastern edge of the glaciated areas due to the carrying action of the prevailing westerly winds.

When loess weathers, it produces one of the finest agricultural soils in the world. These soils have developed deep, rich horizons and have become part of the granary of the United States. They are components of the Mollisols and Alfisols of the Midwest. The highly productive soils of the Argentine pampas, southern Soviet Union, and northern China have their origin on loess deposits. Because these soils are friable but possess vertical walls, they are easily excavated to produce dwellings, particularly in China and central Europe.

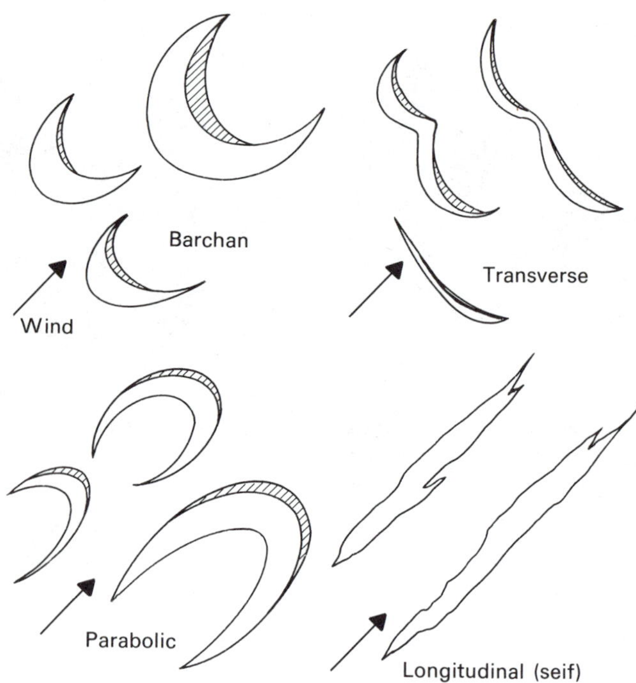


**FIGURE 15.4**
Types of sand dunes. (After Foster, 1979)

## SAND DUNES

Dunes are naturally formed accumulations of sand. Sand dunes are found in most desert and semiarid areas of the world and frequently on sandy coasts (Figure 15.3). They may be active, changing positions under the force of winds, or they may be fixed when an obstruction prevents the sand from shifting. Because wind action forms the sand into different shapes, dunes may be classified as to their origin. The most important types are *barchan, transverse, parabolic,* and *longitudinal* dunes (Figure 15.4; Photos 148–150).

The barchans (from Russian *barkhan,* from a Kirghiz word meaning "moving sand dune") are crescent-shaped dunes that are distinct features on the landscape. They are formed when the wind blows dominantly from a single direction, pushing the sand forward (Figure 15.5). The maximum length from point to point is from 300 to 400 meters (1,000 to 1,300 feet), and its maximum height is about 30 meters (100 feet).

Barchans may originate when sand begins to collect around some object, such as a clump of vegetation or a protruding rock. The greatest force of the wind will be felt on the windward slope of the mound of sand, and there is a pronounced movement of sand grains to the crest. At the crest of the dune, where the force of wind diminishes, the sand grains tend to accumulate. Accumulation of the sand grains at the top of the dune produces the asymmetrical shape with the gentle slope toward the wind and the steep slope on the lee side. This steepening of the lee slope by accumulation of sand proceeds until the angle of the rest of the material is

**PHOTO 148**
Longitudinal dunes. (Courtesy: Arabian American Oil Company)

**PHOTO 149**
Parabolic dunes. (Courtesy: Arabian American Oil Company)

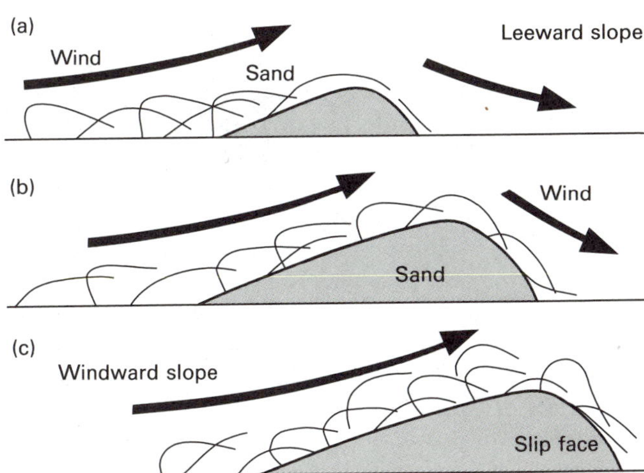


**FIGURE 15.5**
Formation and migration of a sand dune. A dune begins (*a*) when wind is impeded by some object, such as a stone or vegetation, and sand begins to pile up. The wind blows up the windward slope of the evolving dune, moving sand particles toward the crest. (*b*) As the dune develops, the sand particles tumble down the leeward slope. (*c*) By losing sand on the windward side and adding it on the leeward side, a dune migrates across the earth's surface.

exceeded. The material then begins to slip down the concave slope, or *slip face.* The barchan advances by a process of oversteepening and then shearing at the crest. The flanks of the original mound of sand advance more rapidly than the center, for the rate of advance is inversely proportional to the height of the sand dune. This process forms the crescent shape of the barchan.

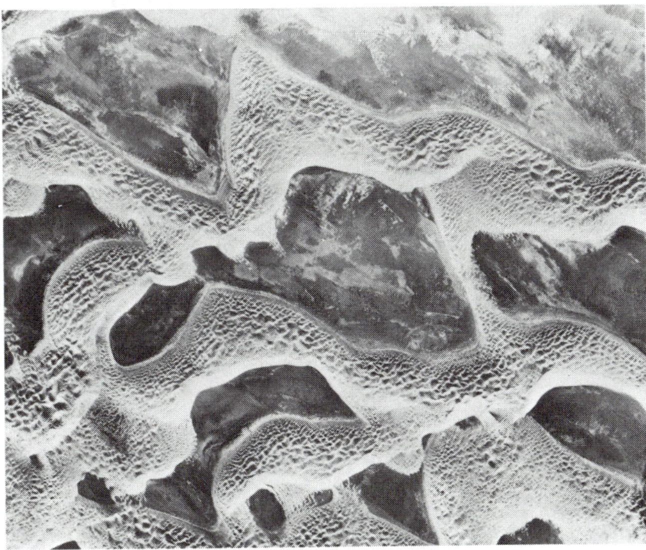

**PHOTO 150**
Barchans. Aerial view of compound and complex barchan dunes in the eastern Rub' al Khali, Saudi Arabia. Segments of these ridges average 2.76 kilometers (about 1.75 miles) from horn to horn and are about 3.1 kilometers (1.8 miles) long, from the base of the gentle slope to the base of the main slip face. (Courtesy: E. D. McKee, U.S. Geological Survey)

The transverse dune does not possess a crescent form as does the barchan. It appears as a steep-faced wave with the general alignment of its crest at a right angle to the prevailing winds. In order to form the transverse dune, massive sand deposits must completely cover the ground. These dunes are usually found in areas where the bedrock is a soft sandstone, or on beaches where there are strong onshore winds and abundant sand. These dunes shift slowly with the wind in a manner similar to the movement of barchans. Their maximum length is about 200 to 250 meters (650 to 820 feet) and their height is 15 to 20 meters (50 to 65 feet). An entire area may be covered by transverse dunes; such regions have come to be known as *sand seas.* In the Sahara these vast expanses of dunes and sand plains have been given the name of *erg* by the nomads of the desert.

The parabolic dune is formed when the wind creates a saucerlike depression. The name *blowout dune* is sometimes given to it. This wind action contrasts with the formation of the barchan, in which the wind piles up the sand. Flowing back from the crest of the parabolic dunes are sweeping ridges of sand, called *hairpins.* The hairpins develop because the forward movement of the sand is inhibited by some obstruction, usually a clump of vegetation. These dunes are rarely more than 300 meters (1,000 feet) wide and 30 meters (100 feet) high, but the hairpins may be 500 meters (1,600 feet) long. Parabolic dunes form where there are great masses of sand and wind from a single direction. They are common in coastal areas where the sand is blown inland by the prevailing winds. As these dunes advance landward, they cover the vegetation, including small trees, killing everything in their path. A remarkable example of this type of dune development is found in the Indiana Dunes State Park on the southern and eastern shores of Lake Michigan.

Longitudinal dunes appear as great sand ridges that may extend for many kilometers, even up to a hundred kilometers. They have uneven crests, and the slip slope appears on both sides of the dune. They are formed by high variable winds. The dominant wind produces the ridge while periodic crosswinds of shorter duration remove the sand from between the ridges. Longitudinal dunes form when the supply of sand is sparse and vegetation is virtually absent. They are especially well developed in the deserts of southwestern Asia and northern Africa and the Australian desert.

## LANDFORMS OF WIND EROSION

Landforms produced by wind deflation or abrasion are relatively insignificant. The major features of deflation occur in areas of loosely consolidated, fine earth particles. The material is blown out of these areas, forming a shallow depression known as a *deflation hollow* or *blowout*. These depressions are usually a few feet deep and may be from one to two kilometers in width. Deflation hollows can develop under a number of conditions. They frequently occur in semiarid regions where the vegetational cover has been removed during a dry period. The exposed soil becomes dry and friable and amenable to wind erosion. They also occur on sandy beaches, where the sand is easily shifted by wind action. In exposed places deflation gradually forms depressions with crests of moving sand on the downwind side.

Wind erosion will also carve rocks into interesting shapes called *mushroom, table,* or *pedestal rocks* (Photos 151 and 152). The bases of these isolated rocks have been partially removed by undercutting by windblown sand. Often the top of the pedestal is a resistant rock, while the bottom portion has been more susceptible to wind erosion. This process creates some fantastic forms, such as the balanced rocks and arches in deserts (Photo 153).

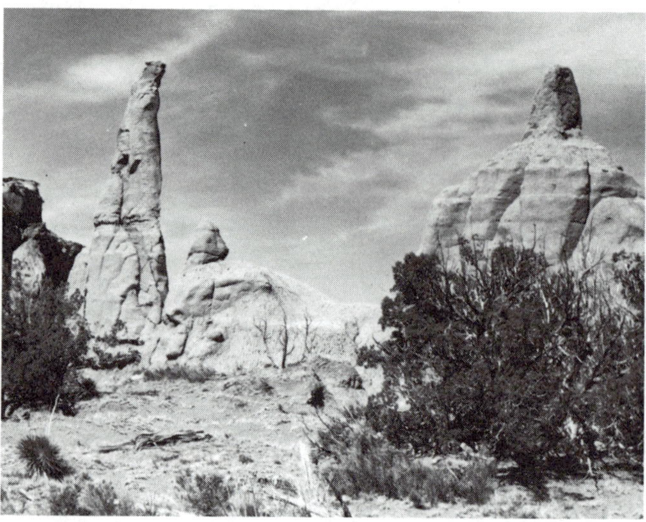

**PHOTO 151**
Pedestal rocks. Isolated rocks in Kodachrome Basin State Park, Utah, from which the base has been partially removed by undercutting by windblown sand. (Courtesy: Utah Department of Natural Resources and Energy)

The deflation process removes the lighter material and leaves the heavier fragments. Pebbles and rock fragments may cover considerable areas, called *desert pavements* in southwestern United States and *hamadas* in the Sahara (Photo 154). If they contain a sparse vegetational cover, they are known as *regs*. When the surface of these rocky plains is colored by iron oxide or other chemicals, it is frequently polished by wind abrasion and is called *desert varnish*. In many areas the groundwater moves upward and evaporates in the arid environment, depositing limestone, gypsum, and other salts on the surface. These salts cement the pebbles so that further deflation is retarded or even stopped.

## WATER EROSION IN ARID ENVIRONMENTS

Although water is generally scarce or even absent during much of the year, water erosion is of major importance in the desert (Figure 15.6). Much of the precipitation in the arid regions of the middle and low latitudes comes as convectional thunderstorms. Tremendous quantities of water pour down within a short time.

In arid regions, stream beds that are dry most of the time fill with torrents of water after heavy thunder-

**PHOTO 152**
Pedestal rocks in Goblin Valley State Park, Utah. (Courtesy: Utah Department of Natural Resources and Energy)

storms. Because ground covering is sparse, the desert streams quickly acquire a load of sediments. These intermittent streams are known as *arroyos* in southwestern United States and *wadis* in north Africa (Photo 155).

Erosional action in these streams is limited to short periods of downward erosion. Lateral cutting is slight, so the streams have steep walls and flat bottoms. They are also little dissected by gullies. Any tributary valleys that exist show the same profile. As a consequence, a desert plain may appear flat even though it contains many arroyos.

**PHOTO 153**
Skyline Arch in the Arches National Monument.

**PHOTO 154**
Desert pavement. The closely spaced, angular stones are fragments of large, rounded ones that originally composed the gravel deposit in Death Valley National Monument, California. (Courtesy: C. B. Hunt, U.S. Geological Survey)

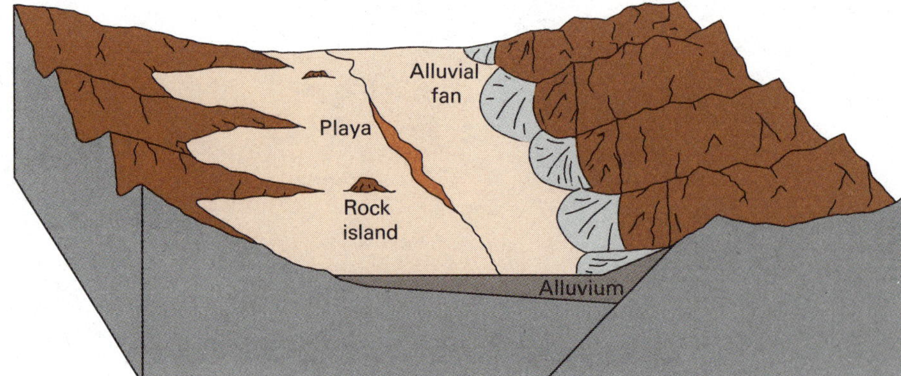


FIGURE 15.6
Landform features created by the action of water in an arid region.

The dry stream channels have frequently been used as routes of transportation and as havens of shelter from sandstorms. Unfortunately, sudden downpours cause flooding, and a person can easily become trapped by the steep valley walls and drown. At one time a strict order prohibited the French Foreign Legion from camping in the bottom of a wadi in North Africa.

While waters do not flow in arroyos most of the time, the channels normally have enough moisture from storage and seepage to support some vegetation that desert animals use for forage. In some desert valleys, water holes and springs provide small oases.

PHOTO 155
Arroyo. Note the steep banks of the stream and the lack of tributaries.

Many desert areas contain hills and uplands that receive higher amounts of precipitation and are source regions for streams. As these streams flow into the lowland areas, the water evaporates and sediments are deposited. If they are deposited at the foot of the uplands as the water spreads out, *alluvial fans* are produced. On occasion, *rock islands* made of the bedrock will protrude through the alluvial plain.

Another feature of stream erosion in arid lands is the rock floor, known as a *pediment*, which is usually covered by a thin veneer of gravel. Pediments are found in belts around the margins of many desert mountain ranges. They are especially well developed about the mountain ranges of the southwestern American desert. In the Sahara they are rocky expanses of desert plain, sometimes 200 to 300 kilometers (120 to 180 miles) across. They are bordered on their upper margins by the steeper slope of the mountains, and on their lower slopes they disappear beneath thicker alluvial deposits.

Only the major streams have sufficient water to cross desert areas. When water from streams is contained within the desert area, an *interior drainage basin* is formed. Although the water cannot drain out of the area, at times the quantity is too great to evaporate immediately. The water then collects in basin areas and forms temporary lakes called *playas*. In some places the water entering these lakes is essentially equal to the evaporation from the lakes. As the dissolved salts are precipitated, salt lakes are created, such as the Caspian and Aral seas in the Soviet Union and the Great Salt Lake of Utah.

## HUMAN USE OF ARID LANDS

Although the deserts cover about one-third of the world's land area, they support only about four percent of the world's population. Less than three percent of the deserts is cultivated with the aid of irrigation. Nevertheless, with the world's population expanding rapidly, attention is being focused on how these areas can be made more productive. Development of the natural resources of deserts involves two approaches. The first improves traditional techniques of such activities as animal husbandry. The second approach applies the latest advances in science and technology to the development of the dryland resources. Because most of the desert areas have not been surveyed, an initial step in economic development is the preparation of potential land-use maps. The techniques of remote sensing will reveal the areas of such features as sand dunes and desert pavements, where the potential is very low, as well as the areas where animal husbandry and agriculture can be developed.

### AGRICULTURE

Nomadic and seminomadic animal husbandry and primitive irrigation have been practiced in arid lands from the dawn of history to the present day. The maximum possible cattle production in a particular desert has now been roughly estimated. This figure, however, will fluctuate greatly, depending upon moisture and vegetation conditions. One of the major means of increasing productivity of livestock raising in deserts is to improve the vegetational covering as well as the species composition and the veterinary services.

The development of agriculture in arid lands is limited by the lack of soil covering and water. Irrigation systems, however, can bring water to large tracts of almost all deserts. The new trickling method of irrigation, whereby plant roots receive water directly through underground pipes, is of great interest for future plant cultivation in dry areas, because this system reduces evaporation.

A new economic endeavor in deserts is called an agroindustrial complex. It is based on large multipurpose industrial organizations. A prototype of this system has been developed by the universities of Arizona and Sonora. They have built a special type of hotbed farm to use a closed integrated system for the production of energy and food products.

### MINERAL WEALTH

The salt deposits of deserts have been mined since antiquity. Salt lakes contain huge amounts of solid salt deposits, such as halite. Within the brine are sodium chloride, sodium and magnesium sulfates, and compounds of bromine, potassium, and other elements. These salts may serve as raw materials for industry. Only a small part of these salt deposits is currently being exploited.

The arid lands of the world are storehouses of other important mineral resources that are not directly related to the desert environment. The deserts contain oil and gas, coal, iron ore, copper, manganese, lead, and uranium. Some of the largest settlements in deserts have been built to exploit these mineral resources. These settlements are likely to be temporary, however, for when the minerals are exhausted, no other economic base exists to maintain them.

### ENERGY

The arid lands have the greatest potential for the development of solar energy. These areas receive the maximum amount of sunlight for their latitudinal position. The development of solar energy in deserts is in its initial stage, but in the future it will be used to generate electric power. Because low and even middle latitude deserts are extremely hot at least part of the year, settlements with an artificial climate cooled by solar power may be built. Many environmental problems must be solved before such ideas can be realized. For example, no one yet fully understands the effect on the environment of the large land area that must be covered by solar reflectors. Solar energy projects have the potential to significantly alter the desert environment.

### RECREATION

Recreation facilities have been developed in many of the desert lands. Notable examples include Palm Springs in California and Phoenix and Tucson in Arizona. The physical and biological environment of the desert provides an attractive landscape for tourists. Possibly most important for recreational purposes is the large amount of sunshine that prevails in arid climates. Many retired people have been attracted to the desert environment because of the abundance of sunshine, dry air, and the unique nature of the desert. People gather there not only to relax but also to treat arthritis, rheumatism, and nervous complaints. Anyone who has lived in the desert is aware of its tranquility and serene beauty.

## AEOLIAN THREAT TO DESERT USES

Blowing sand is a continuous threat in desert regions. It can bury agricultural areas, irrigation canals, highways, industrial facilities, houses, and even settlements (Photo 156). The aeolian danger is greatest at the edge of the desert where human activities are normally greatest. Sandstorms originating in the heart of the desert deposit huge masses of sand over these areas.

Desert dwellers have attempted to cope with this problem. Centuries ago in North Africa it was realized that palm fronds planted around an oasis provided some protection. The sand built up around this breastwork of fronds, leaving a saucer-shaped hollow for the date palms and other agricultural activities. Eventually the fronds were smothered with sand and the oasis disappeared, but not before many crops of dates had been taken.

Migrating dunes have invaded many agricultural areas in the desert. Because the amount of sand is so great, the only temporary solution is to abandon such an area. The dunes move onward, however, and often after a few years the fields are once again free of sand and cultivation resumes.

In a number of deserts, notably the Sahel of Africa, the increased human use of the area has seriously damaged the sparse vegetational covering. This problem becomes acute during periods of drought, such as that of 1968 to 1973. Without vegetation, the deep sand mantle is exposed to wind action. To minimize this damage, researchers must discover wind directions, and then study the type of dunes present, the degree of desertification they can cause, and any possible means of control and protection of the area.

**PHOTO 156**
Aeolian threat to agriculture. Sand dunes on formerly cultivated land near Dalbart, Texas. (Courtesy: United States Department of Agriculture, Soil Conservation Service)

To exploit the wealth of the desert, modern industrial structures are required. Migrating sand can seriously damage these facilities. For example, when the iron ore port of Port Étienne (now Nouadhibou) was constructed on the Atlantic coast of Mauritania, it was attacked by sand transported by strong coastal winds. Geologists estimate that up to 1.6 million cubic meters of sand are blown along the desert coastal shore each year. In order to protect the port facilities, the buildings were aerodynamically shaped so that the blowing sands continued their journey down the coast.

Blowing sands have long hampered the construction and maintenance of transportation facilities. An airport built in the 1970s at Dubai, on the Trucial Coast of Saudi Arabia, was located in one of the largest sand seas in the world. It was feared that blowing sand from the nearby dunes would force runways and other facilities to close. Studies of wind direction and velocity showed that the dominant winds prevailed from the southwest to the northeast, meaning that the dunes lying southwest of the airport needed to be stabilized or removed. Millions of tons of sand were removed in order to protect the airport.

## CONCLUSION

Wind action creates depositional features, such as dunes, as well as erosional features, such as desert pavement and pedestals. Wind erosion removes and transports earth material in much the same manner as water, but the particles are distributed over a much larger area. The landforms created by wind action are usually small. Sand dunes are the most widely distributed of these landforms. In deserts they may form great sand seas. The shape of the dune depends upon the quantity of sand transported as well as the direction and velocity of the wind movement.

The dry lands of the world present a great challenge to those who wish to develop their natural resources. As the population pressures of the world increase, migration into the drier and more rigorous landscapes will continue. If this movement is to be successful, a greater understanding of the economic potential of the deserts must develop. Deserts remain one of the world's great frontiers.

## STUDY QUESTIONS

1. Describe the two major wind erosion processes.
2. What are the differences among surface creep, saltation, and suspension of wind-transported material?
3. Explain the origin of loess deposits in different areas of the world.
4. Why are loess deposits important in agricultural development?
5. What are the major types of sand dunes? What is the origin of each?
6. What is a blowout? How is it formed?
7. Describe the landforms created by wind erosion.
8. How does a reg differ from a hamada?
9. What are some of the important economic activities in arid regions?

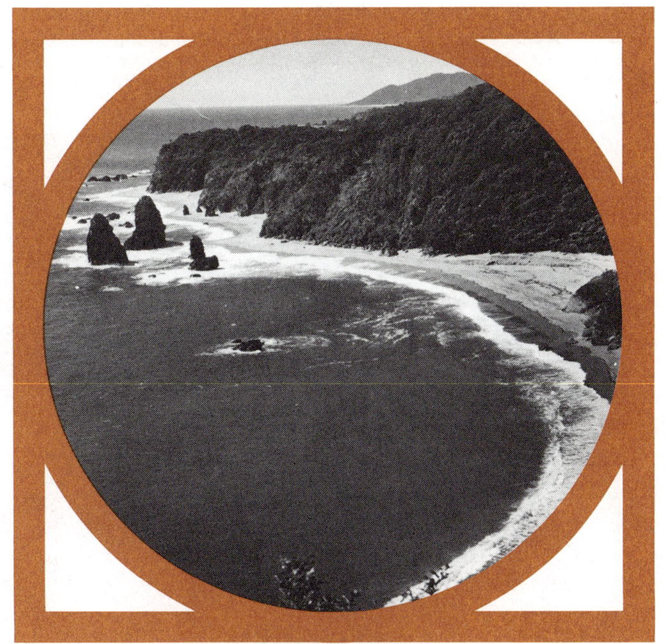

# 16

# MARINE PROCESSES AND COASTAL LANDFORMS

## KEY WORDS

atoll
barrier reef
bay bar
blowhole
breakwater
continental rise
continental shelf
continental slope
coral reef
cuspate spit
emergence coast
groin
headlands
hook
jetty
lagoon
littoral drift
longshore currents
neutral coast
ria shoreline
rip current
sandbar
sea stack
spit
submergence coast
swash
turbidity current
wave of oscillation
wave of translation
wave-cut cliffs

The continental margins are the boundary between land and seawater. The precise extent of this coastal zone, although difficult to define, has been described as a variable band of dry land and adjacent ocean space which is affected by both land and ocean ecology. Physical processes occur there at an intense rate, and ecologically it is also a dynamic area of activity.

The coastal zone may extend inland from a few meters to several kilometers. The seaward boundary is easier to define, and is usually placed at the edge of the continental shelf. The discharge of the major rivers extends well beyond this demarcation, however. The coastal waters differ chemically from those of the open sea, even in areas where human activity has a limited impact.

The coastal zone is a unique environment. Because a large portion of the world's people live near coasts, controversy arises concerning their use of these areas. Waves and tides dissipate enormous amounts of energy in coastal zones, subjecting the complex physical systems and ecosystems to constant change. Development programs for rational use of these zones must include an understanding of the physical processes that shape the land as well as an understanding of the changes that are constantly occurring in the complex ecosystems. A balance must be struck between utilization and preservation.

## WAVE ENERGY

Wave movements not only are scientifically interesting, but can be almost hypnotically fascinating. Each wave is distinctly different. A person standing on the shore and watching the endless procession of waves has difficulty visualizing that it is the *form* of the wave that moves forward through the water and that the water moves only when the waves break. To understand this concept, watch a bottle bobbing on the surface of the ocean. Waves pass under it, and unless there is a current, the bottle will remain in the same position. An analogy for waves in the sea are the waves the wind makes when it blows across a field of grain. This basic principle of wave motion was discovered in 1802 and has come to be known as the *wave of oscillation* (Photo 157).

**PHOTO 157**
Wave energy. Waves breaking in Waialua Bay on Oahu, Hawaiian Islands.

A wave develops as a response to the friction between moving air and the water body. At low wind speeds the air flow is parallel to the surface, and therefore nonturbulent, so that the water remains undisturbed. As the air speed increases, the turbulence grows and small disturbances are set up in the water. This friction between the wind and the water sets up a rotating action near the surface. As the wave form passes, the water moves forward in the crest, then down to form a trough, and then upward as the next crest forms (Figure 16.1). Each water particle at the end of a complete rotation is moved horizontally only a very slight distance, if at all.

Waves become important in the study of landforms when they strike the shoreline. At that point the *waves of oscillation* are changed into surf or *waves of translation.* As the depth of the water decreases, the waves become smaller. This action changes the structure of the waves so that they steepen on the landward side. The crest of the wave then breaks and spills forward. This occurs when the speed of the crest exceeds the speed of the water movement in the trough of the wave. Thus the break of the wave occurs when the depth of the water is less than the wave height.

As the wave crest breaks, the energy of the water released can erode, transport, and deposit coastal materials. The action of waves is not uniformly distributed over the year. The stormier the weather, the greater the wave action. In the middle latitudes the seasonal contrast in storminess and the accompanying coastal erosion may be significant. In winter the frequency of the steep-crested waves increases so that erosion is accelerated. Under these conditions the backflow or *rip current* is stronger than the *surge* or *swash* of the wave, resulting in erosion. In summer the long, relatively flat

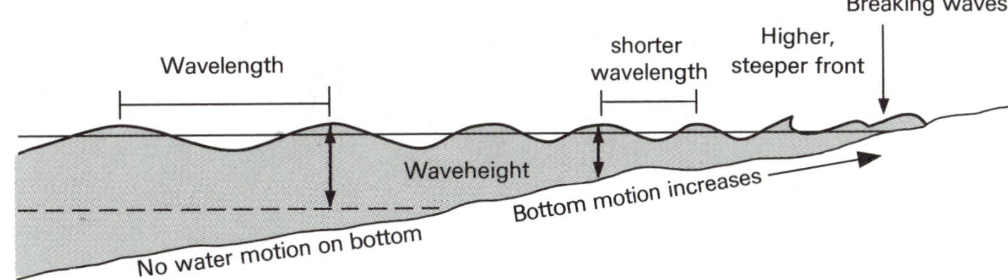


**FIGURE 16.1**
The energy of a wave as it moves onto the shore. The wave length decreases and bottom motion increases until the water breaks on the beach.

waves dominate so that the surge of the wave is stronger than the rip current. This action tends to move sand onto the beach rather than eroding it.

## BEACH DRIFTING AND LONGSHORE CURRENTS

When waves break on a beach, a mass of turbulent water surges forward as *swash*. Fine sediments in the swirling water are carried onto the beach. When the forward surge of the wave stops, much of the water sinks into the beach sand, but a portion, pulled by gravity, flows back down the beach as *backwash*, carrying part of the sediments with it. The sediments are moved not only forward and backward in the wave action, but also along the shore, in a movement known as *beach drifting*. This motion occurs because the waves approach the shoreline at a slight angle rather than perpendicularly. The water flows at an angle up the beach, but after the wave energy is spent, the water is pulled by gravitational force directly to the ocean. The sediments in the water are thus transported back to the sea, but to a position slightly different from their starting point. Because consistent winds will move waves in the same direction for a considerable period of time, sediments gradually drift along the shore.

Associated with the wave action is the development of the *longshore current*. As the backwash flows into the ocean, the excess water cannot build up vertically at the shoreline. In order for the water to escape, a current develops that flows along the shoreline. This sediment-laden current deposits materials in a process called *longshore drifting*. Beach and longshore drifting thus act in conjunction with each other in moving and depositing sediments along a coast. The amount of sediment carried by the longshore current will vary with wave and wind conditions. The greatest movement of sediments occurs during storms. Beaches will thus be enlarged or decreased, depending upon the amount of deposition or erosion that takes place in these coastal geomorphic processes.

## FACTORS IN COASTAL EROSION

A number of factors influence coastal erosion. The movement of water in waves and currents can be a powerful erosional agent, particularly if the water carries sediments. Ocean waves are a major force (Photo 158). If evidence of erosional action is apparent after a strong storm, the greatest degradation was likely caused by pebbles and rock fragments carried by the rampaging waves.

Topography also influences the amount of erosion on a coast. When the beach has a gentle slope, the amount of erosion is usually limited. If the shoreline is a cliff, however, the erosional effect is much enhanced.

The third factor that influences the amount of coastal erosion is the resistance of the rock at the ocean's edge. A soft sandstone or shale will erode rapidly, as will a

**PHOTO 158**
Coastal erosion. The 15 meters (50 feet) of sandstone bluffs are constantly being attacked by the surging sea at Shore Acres State Park in southern Oregon. (Courtesy: Oregon State Highway, Travel Section)

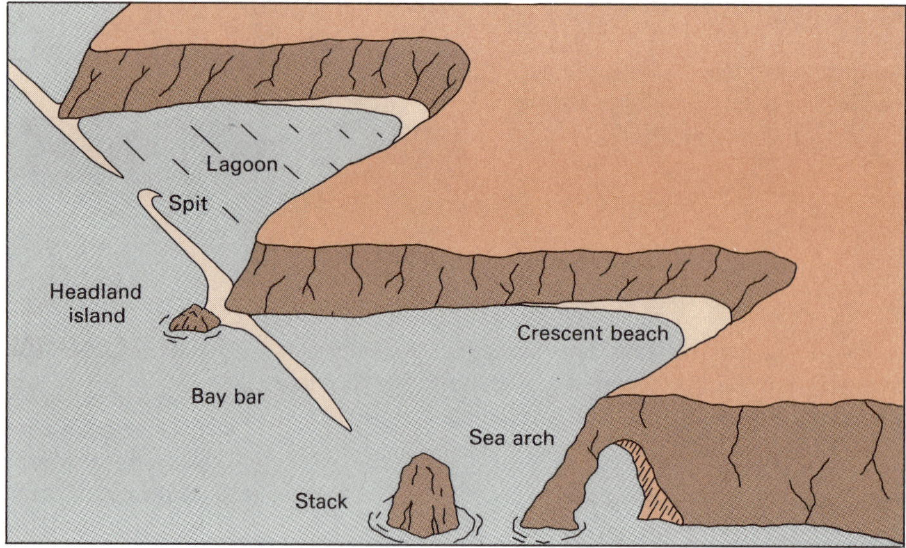


**FIGURE 16.2**
Erosional and depositional landforms along a rugged coast.

shoreline of fragmented glacial till. A resistant crystalline rock on the coast will erode slowly.

## WAVE DEPOSITION LANDFORMS

Beaches and sandbars, either offshore or attached to the shore, are the principal types of wave deposits (Figure 16.2). They are formed of sediments that are distributed along the shore by wave and current movements. Streams and rivers provide more than 90 percent of these coastal sediments. The erosion of land areas provides about 15 billion cubic meters of sediments to the coastlines each year. The movement of sediments along a coast is termed *littoral transport* and the total material transported is known as *littoral drift.*

### BEACHES

Beaches are the most common type of wave-deposited features (Photo 159). The beach includes the area covered by the highest tides and by the maximum storm waves. Along lowland shores, the beaches are usually wide and may extend for many kilometers without interruption. Where the shoreline is hilly or mountainous, beaches are usually narrow or may even be absent.

Beaches may be composed of a variety of materials. Commonly they consist of sand (Photo 160). If waves erode shoreline cliffs, where coarse materials are available, a beach may consist of rock debris and pebbles (Photo 161). In some places the pebbles are flattened and overlap, forming a pavement or *shingle beach.* Because most beach deposits are composed of unconsolidated materials, they may be altered greatly when storms redistribute the sands and clays. Small beaches are often destroyed. At other times active deposition occurs and the beaches are rebuilt or expanded.

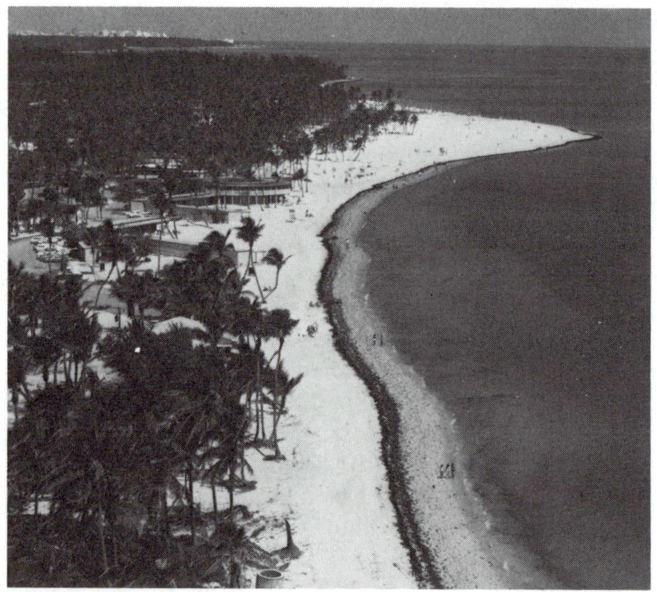

**PHOTO 159**
Miami Crandon Park Beach. (Courtesy: Florida Division of Tourism)

Beaches may assume a number of different forms, depending on wave and current action. Sand and pebbles may fill the inland portion of bays, smoothing the

**PHOTO 160**
A sandy beach on the Gulf of Mexico near Panama City, Florida. (Courtesy: Florida Division of Tourism)

**PHOTO 162**
Spit. Presque Isle is a sand and gravel spit on the south shore of Lake Erie. The current from the southwest has built the spit, which provides a harbor for Erie, Pennsylvania. (Courtesy: Pennsylvania Bureau of Travel Development)

contour of the ocean fronts. The deposits assume the shape of the bays to form *crescent beaches.*

Transported material may be blocked at some point along the shore by the angle of the shoreline or by deeper water which slows the current, reducing the energy available to transport the sediments. The material builds into a ridge connected to the shoreline that eventually projects above the level of the water. Such landforms are known as *spits* or *hooks* (Photo 162). Examples of these features on the Atlantic coast are Sandy Hook at the entrance to New York Bay and the curved tip of Cape Cod. If a spit extends entirely across the entrance of a bay and encloses it, it is known as a *bay bar.* At times a bay bar may connect a coastal island with the mainland. Such bars are numerous along the New England coast, where several islands have become connected and the string of islands is tied to the coast. The Rock of Gibraltar is tied to the mainland by a bay bar.

**PHOTO 161**
Pebble beach of glaciated material on South Manitou Island in Lake Michigan. (Courtesy: Michigan Department of Natural Resources)

When sediment-laden longshore currents are deflected seaward on both sides of a point of land, a spit is formed with cusped or curved sides. This formation is called a *cuspate spit* or *cuspate foreland.* Cape Canaveral, Florida, is an outstanding example of a cuspate foreland.

## SANDBARS

Some shallow coasts exhibit long, narrow sandbars—some very near the coast, others situated far offshore. A number of theories attempt to explain the origin of these low-lying sandbars. One theory suggests that they originate at about the depth where the larger waves break. The waves at their plunge point begin to pile up sand in low ridges. Eventually so much sand accumulates that the bar reaches the surface.

Initially a body of shallow water called a *lagoon* exists between a sandbar and the shore (Photo 163). As waves continue to erode the seaward portion of these sand islands, and as wind transports sand landward, the entire structure migrates toward the shore. Finally, the offshore bar reaches the mainland, and the lagoon, partly filled with sediment eroded from the land, disappears. Much of the sand may then be transported by winds to form a belt of coastal dunes.

**PHOTO 163**
Lagoon. Ocracoke Island, on the Outer Banks of North Carolina, lies between the lagoon of Pamlico Sound on one side and the Atlantic Ocean on the other side. (Courtesy: North Carolina Travel and Tourism)

The east coast of the United States has a string of sandbars. Possibly the most striking example is the continuous sandbar forming Capes Hatteras, Lookout, and Fear. This bar is located as far as 48 kilometers (30 miles) off the Carolina coast. Other sandbars extend along Long Island, and around Florida and the Gulf of Mexico to Texas (Photo 164).

These sandbars have been important in the development of the coastal areas. The ill-fated first English colony was established on Roanoke Island—an island in the sound behind a barrier bar off the Carolina coast. During the Civil War sandbars were the locale of scores of amphibious landings and minor naval operations. In recent years a number of major resort centers have been built on sandbars.

**PHOTO 164**
Sandbar. The luxury hotels of Miami's beach are built on a sandbar. A small lagoon lies between the hotels and the mainland. (Courtesy: Florida Division of Tourism)

## WAVE EROSION

Waves not only deposit materials on shorelines, but under certain conditions they are also an erosional force. Waves will undercut a cliff at the water's edge to form a *sea cliff* (Photo 165). For example, on the south shore of Nantucket Island, waves cut into the sea cliff as much as 2 meters (6 feet) annually. At the base of the sea cliff are horizontal *notches* or *nips* carved by the waves.

As the erosional process proceeds, the sea cliff is gradually worn away and becomes a rock bench called a *wave-cut terrace, strand flat,* or *wave-cut platform.* These rock benches frequently show such effects of abrasion as grooves and furrows. The most resistant rocks may be left standing as *rock reefs.*

In areas where the cliff is highly jointed or faulted, the waves may quarry out a *sea cave* (Figure 16.3). If the roof of the sea cave has a small hole, the waves may force water through the opening, creating a *blowhole* or *spouting hole* (Photo 166). These blowholes occur along many coasts, notably in New England and the Hawaiian Islands. When the roof of the cave collapses, the seaward portion may become a small island or *sea*

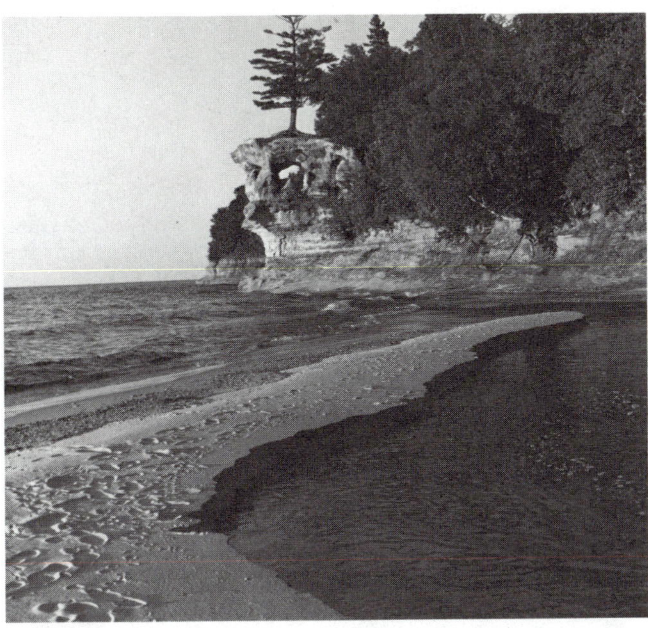

**PHOTO 165**
Sea cliff. The wave action of Lake Superior has undercut the rock, creating this sea cliff. (Courtesy: Michigan Department of Natural Resources)

**PHOTO 166**
Sea cave and blowhole. The waves have undercut the coastal lava formations on Oahu, forming a blowhole.

*stack.* Most stacks form not in this way, however, but develop where a resistant rock is not eroded by the waves. These resistant rocks frequently jut out into the ocean as *headlands.* When a shore has many caves and headlands, it appears irregular or *crenulated.* In contrast, a cliffed area of unconsolidated sediments, such as glacial till, may have a nearly straight shoreline.

## PLATE TECTONICS AND SHORELINES

The development of shorelines can be directly related to tectonic processes. To illustrate, the Atlantic coast shorelines have developed in a zone of divergence while the shorelines of the Pacific coast have evolved primarily in a fracture area and a zone of subduction.

Submergence has been proceeding on the North Atlantic coast for about 150 million years. During this time sediments eroded from the continent have accumulated to a maximum depth of 15 kilometers (9 miles). This vast accumulation of sediments is made possible by the plastic asthenosphere, which allows the lithosphere to flex downward as the sediment burden increases. Once this process begins, it is never reversed, although the rate of subsidence will vary with the sediment supply.

In contrast to the submergence of the Atlantic coast, the Pacific coast is characterized by its emergence. The deposits of sediments on the Pacific coast are poorly developed. The Pacific coast is thus generally an area of lithospheric uplift rather than submergence.

## CLASSIFICATION OF SHORELINES

Geographers and geologists have long sought to classify shorelines. One of the earliest genetic classifications was devised by William Morris Davis and later modified by

**FIGURE 16.3**
Coastal erosional features.

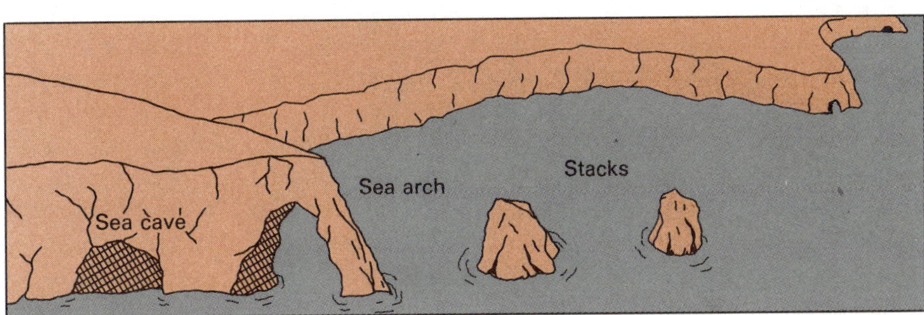

Douglas Johnson. This classification system was based on evidence that shorelines have not been stable in recent geologic time. Along some coasts are stranded marine platforms backed by sea cliffs, isolated beach deposits, and other evidence of marine activity many meters above the present ocean level. These landforms have been produced by an uplift of the continent, a lowering of sea level, or both.

In other areas, relics of beaches and shoreline erosional features lie submerged beneath the water, overlying the continental shelf. These features, along with drowned river mouths, are evidence of submergence. This submergence must have been caused by a subsidence of the continent, a rise in sea level, or both.

Based on these geologic activities, the shorelines of the world can be classified as *submergence, emergence,* or, if neither submergence nor emergence has occurred, *neutral* shorelines. The present landform development on each of these shorelines is determined by its geologic structure, topographic configuration, and modification by waves and currents.

The genetic shoreline classification discussed here is extremely simple. Other classification systems have been developed that do not emphasize land movement. Francis Shepard (1937) prepared a system that recognizes that shores are primary or secondary, depending upon whether the agencies shaping them are nonmarine or marine. The primary, nonmarine coasts include those shaped by erosion on land and subsequently drowned; those shaped by deposits originating on land, including river-deposition, glacial-deposition, and wind-deposition coasts; coasts shaped by volcanic activity; and coasts shaped by diastrophism, such as fault-scarp and folded rock coasts. The secondary, marine coasts include shorelines shaped by marine erosion and marine deposition.

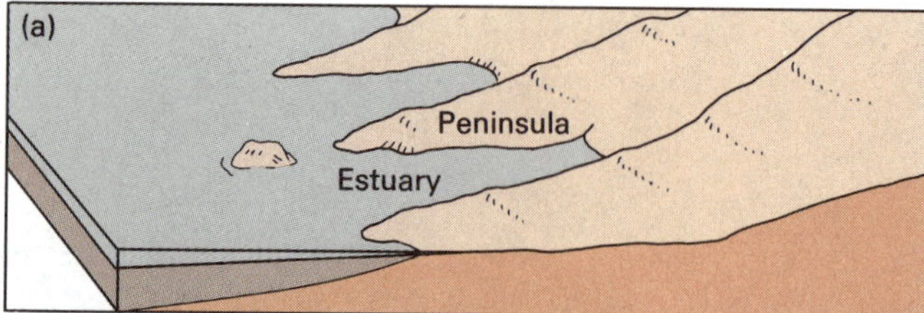


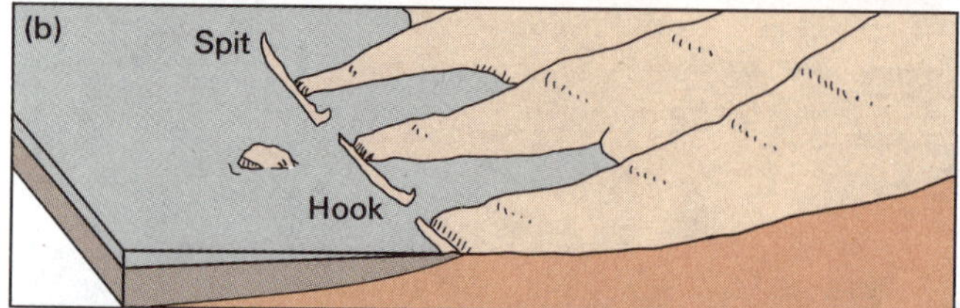


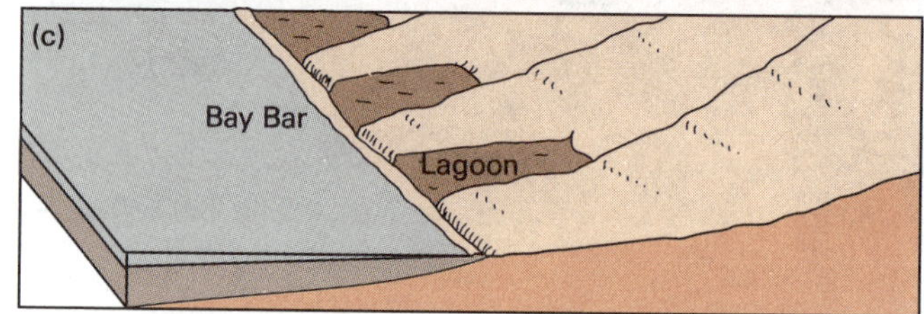


**FIGURE 16.4**
Development of a shoreline of submergence. Drowned valleys and jutting peninsulas (*a*) characterize a recently submerged coast. When the tips of the peninsulas are eroded (*b*), hooks and spits are created. Further erosion (*c*) fills the estuaries with sediments, and bay bars develop.

## SHORELINES OF SUBMERGENCE

Whenever the earth's crust is lowered at a shoreline, or the water level rises because of melting glacial ice, part of the original coastal area is drowned and a new shoreline evolves.

The shorelines of submergence have developed distinct topographic features (Figure 16.4). When numerous stream valleys are drowned, a highly irregular, embayed shoreline, termed a *ria shoreline,* is produced. The embayments at the mouths of river valleys are separated by the higher *headlands* or promontories. In the drowned valleys the higher lands stand out as islands in the bays. In the youthful stages of development the headlands are quickly attacked by wave action, producing *wave-cut cliffs, sea stacks,* and other wave erosional features. Examples of shorelines of submergence occur on the Atlantic coast of the United States from New Jersey to Cape Hatteras. This coast features such major embayments as the Delaware and Chesapeake bays. Other submerged shorelines include the eastern half of the northern Mediterranean, especially Greece and Turkey; the northwest part of Europe; most of Japan; the Malay peninsula; and parts of Australia.

## SHORELINES OF EMERGENCE

When the shoreline rises at the edge of a continent, a portion of the continental shelf is raised above sea level (Figure 16.5). Thus the edge of the water is located in the area that was originally submerged, and above this line a new coastal plain exists. These areas are nearly featureless, flat, and covered with unconsolidated marine sediments. Because the gentle slope of the coastal plain extends beyond the shoreline, one of the first features to develop on these coasts are submerged bars, which form initially on the landward side of the zone of

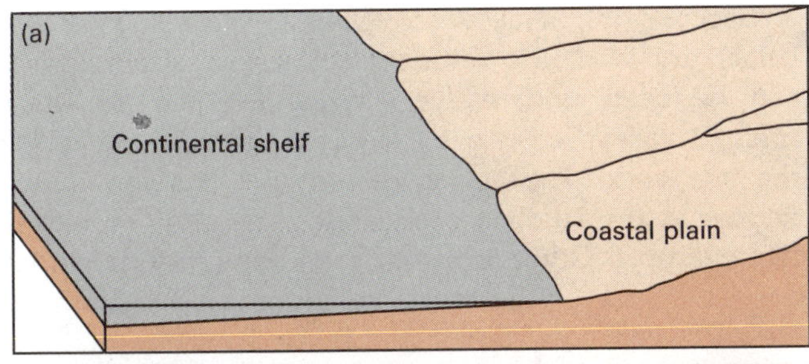

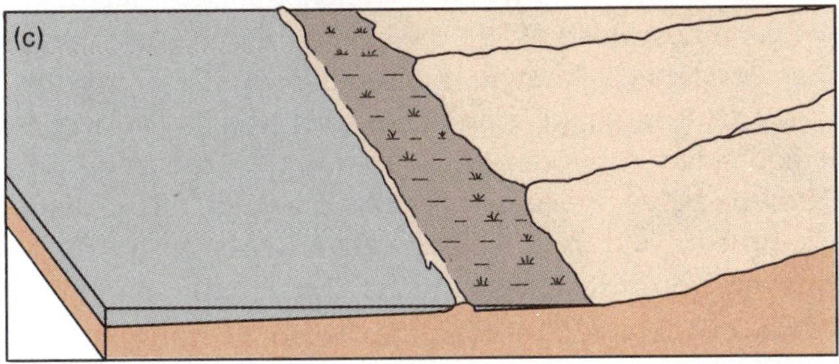


**FIGURE 16.5**
Development of a shoreline of emergence. As part of the continental shelf, the shoreline (*a*) is smooth at first. As it matures an offshore bar or barrier beach develops (*b*). The lagoon between the bar and the shore gradually fills with sediments (*c*), and a tidal marsh evolves.

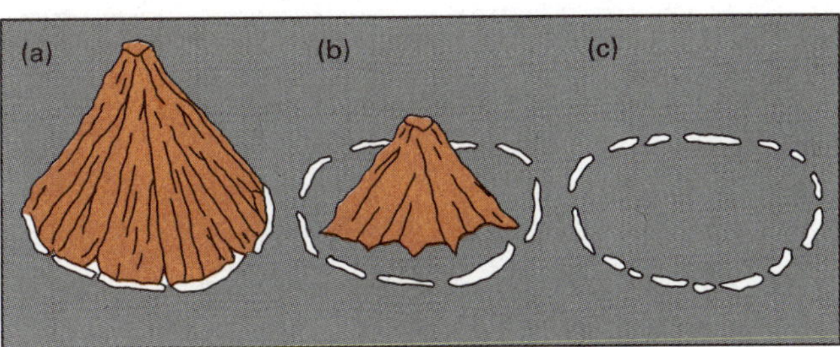


**FIGURE 16.6**
Formation of an atoll. (*a*) In its initial stage organisms build a fringing reef close to a volcanic island. (*b*) The island gradually sinks but the organisms continue to build the reef, which stays above the water. (*c*) Finally the volcanic island is completely submerged, leaving an atoll which encloses a lagoon.

breakers. As they develop, they emerge above the surface as sand bars. The almost continuous bars on the Atlantic coast from Cape Hatteras southward are of this origin.

### NEUTRAL SHORELINES

The coastal areas that show no effects of either submergence or emergence include *deltas, volcanic shorelines, coral reefs,* and *fault scarp shorelines.* The delta, volcanic, and fault scarp shorelines are found throughout the world, but reef shorelines are confined to tropical waters.

Of the neutral shorelines, the reef areas are perhaps the most interesting. They are produced in tropical waters by calcareous marine algae and lime-secreting marine animals that live in colonies. Coral skeletons are conspicuous in the structures produced by these colonies, giving rise to the name *coral reefs.* Modern reef-building corals live in water that does not fall below 18°C (68°F) and at depths of less than about 50 meters (150 feet) below mean sea level. The total area covered by present-day coral reefs is estimated at 1,300,000 square kilometers (500,000 square miles).

As the coral grows in the shallow water, its deposits form a *barrier reef.* A lagoon develops between the reef and the mainland. The reef grows most vigorously toward the ocean, which is the principal source of calcium-rich food required by the coral. The Barrier Reef, extending for about 1,600 kilometers (1,000 miles) off the northeast coast of Australia, is the best known of the world's reefs.

In the open ocean, fringing reefs have developed around some islands, particularly volcanic islands. These more or less circular reefs are called *atolls* (Figure 16.6). If the island sinks slowly enough, the corals will build up the reef so that they remain near the surface, where the food supply is concentrated. Submergence may continue until the island is completely submerged and only the coral atoll remains. Eniwetok in the western Pacific is an atoll where the coral is 1,872 meters (6,140 feet) thick.

## CONTINENTAL MARGINS

The edges of the continents can be classified into three parts: *continental shelf, continental slope,* and *continental rise* (Figure 16.7).

The continental shelf, the submerged portion of the coastal plain, can be very narrow or very wide. On the west coast of South America, in parts of Indonesia and parts of the Mediterranean Sea, it is very limited. Off the

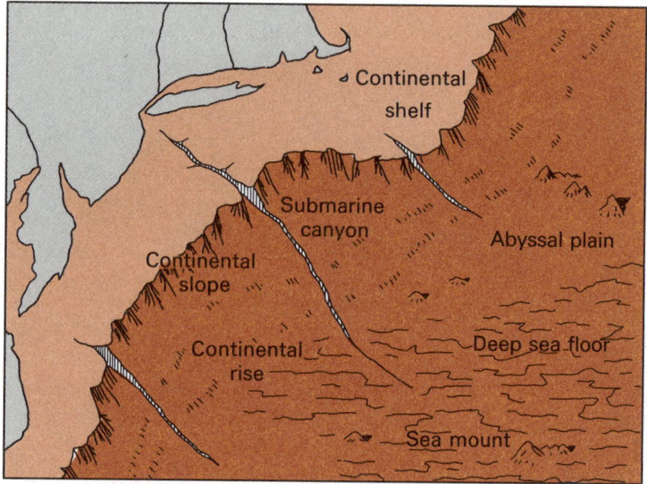


**FIGURE 16.7**
The continental margin. This diagram shows the continental shelf, slope, and rise that leads into the deep-sea areas. (Based upon bathymetric studies by Bruce C. Heezen and Marie Tharp on the Physiographic Diagram of the North Atlantic—1968. Redrawn by Abby Curtis by permission of Marie Tharp and the Geological Society of America.)

coast of northern Siberia, however, it extends 1,200 kilometers (750 miles) offshore. The continental shelf is a shallow, gently sloping surface. The overall slope does not exceed one-tenth of one degree, although locally the slope may be greater. This slope is so slight that it cannot normally be perceived. As a consequence, wave erosion and deposition can occur on the inner margins of the continental shelf. During stormy periods, when waves reach their maximum size, this action can be quite vigorous. The outer margin of the continental shelf is usually at a depth between 150 and 200 meters (490 to 650 feet).

Since the mean sea level has risen from 75 to 90 meters (250 to 300 feet) with the melting of the Pleistocene continental glaciers, the shallower portions of the continental shelves have been submerged. These areas once served as land bridges between some islands and continental areas. They were important routes for the movement of both humans and animals. It is theorized that pre-Colombian Indians migrated from the Asian continent to North America by way of the Bering Straits, which was then a land bridge, and then fanned out across the two continents of North America and South America. Land bridges also served as migration routes between India and Sri Lanka as well as between many of the islands of Indonesia.

Because the shallow continental shelves were recently dry land, the remnants of terrestrial landforms can be seen underwater. Typical features are submerged valleys eroded by streams before the level of the sea rose. The lower part of the Hudson River, known as the Hudson submarine canyon, is an excellent example. Other terrestrial landforms include glacial deposits, such as the moraines found off the southern New England coast and in the North Sea.

At the outer edge of the continental shelf, the slope becomes steeper in the zone known as the *continental slope.* The slope averages between 4 and 5 degrees, descending to some 3,000 to 4,000 meters (9,800 to 13,100 feet), marking the margin of a number of the continental tectonic plates. The continental slope is not abrupt but is normally about 160 kilometers (100 miles) wide. It is irregular, and along many coasts it is furrowed by deep, canyonlike trenches incised far below its general surface. While the existence of these canyons has long been known, their origin is still a mystery. They vary in shape from U-shaped troughs to narrow, steep-sided canyons. While many are associated with drowned river valleys, such as those of the Hudson, Columbia, and Zaire, other canyons are found far removed from present-day rivers. Those with the highest walls are found between the islands of Cuba and the Bahamas. Many of the canyons extend to the depths of the seafloor at nearly 5,000 meters (16,400 feet); these are far too deep to be drowned river valleys. A major characteristic of these canyons is that they appear to channel great quantities of sediments from the continental shelf to the deep ocean basins.

It appears logical that some of the canyons are the submerged portions of river valleys. Where river valleys do not exist, it appears reasonable that the canyons were formed by *turbidity currents.* A turbidity current is one that contains suspended sand and silt and is sufficiently dense that it will flow down the continental slope. These currents will gradually erode a canyon in the continental slope. At the exits of these canyons, fanlike delta deposits of sand and silt have been found. The turbidity currents are sometimes sufficiently strong to break the marine cables that cross the continental slopes.

Beyond the continental slope is the *continental rise.* This zone appears to consist of sediments that originate on land and are deposited beyond the continental slopes. These sediments are frequently crumpled and folded by compression resulting from the collisions of the great crustal plates. Stretching out from the continental rises are the deep ocean floors. Some of these areas are featureless plains known as *abyssal plains.*

# HUMAN MODIFICATION OF SHORELINES

The shorelines of the world are increasingly being developed as residential, industrial, and recreational sites, particularly in densely populated areas. Coastal areas are thus being modified, both physically and biologically, wherever people have access to the sea.

## CONTROL OF COASTAL EROSION

As use of the coastal areas has expanded, so have attempts to control the natural wave and current actions.

### BEACH AND HARBOR PROTECTION

A number of structures have been devised to protect beaches. These include *groins, jetties,* and *breakwaters.*

Groins are favored in the attempt to reduce the loss of beach sand. A groin is a wall constructed nearly perpendicular to the shore. These structures are usually built in groups known as groin fields. Major examples of groin fields exist between Palm Beach and Miami and between Clearwater and Sarasota on the east and west coasts of Florida. In these areas beaches were receding as much as 10 meters (32 feet) annually. The groin field is designed to trap a portion of the sand behind each groin as it is carried by coastal currents. Sand will accumulate updrift—that is, on the current side—of each groin, thus building a scalloped but wider beach. The problem is that, as the current swings around the groin, erosion occurs in the downdrift direction. Sand will accumulate in one area, giving a wider, protected beach, while in another area erosion will remove the beach sand. Erosion may be reduced by trucking sand to the area and filling each groin. With artificial nourishment the groin will take less sand from the natural coastal currents, and the downdrift erosion is reduced. If the beach is large, the groin field may have to be greatly extended. Local conditions will dictate the solution to the problem. However, because groins may cause undesirable erosion, their use in many coastal areas must be questioned.

A breakwater is usually constructed at the mouth of a harbor to provide protection for boat moorings (Photo 167). The breakwater may be attached to the beach or constructed in open water. Because breakwaters alter the energy available to move sediments in the coastal currents, they change the patterns of deposition and erosion. Like groins, the breakwater traps sand in the updrift direction. As the sand is trapped at the entrance to the harbor, a sandbar or spit may form. The sand may need to be removed by dredging in order to keep the entrance to the harbor open. The dredged sand is normally hauled to the downdrift side of the harbor, where the currents remove it naturally.

**PHOTO 167**
This breakwater provides a haven for boats, protecting the harbor from wave action.

Jetties are constructed, usually in pairs, at the mouths of rivers, bays, or estuaries in order to stabilize channels and minimize the deposition of sediments in the channels. Like other structures that change the coastal currents, jetties block the movement of sediments. As the current hits the jetty, its speed is reduced and sediments are built up on the updrift side. Erosion occurs on the downdrift beaches. The deposition of sediments may eventually fill the channels so that dredging will be required to keep them open.

The building of groins, breakwaters, or jetties on coastal areas does not provide a permanent solution to the problem of protecting the coasts. No structure has yet been devised that does not interfere with the normal longshore movement of sediments. Careful planning will minimize some of the least desirable aspects of both deposition and erosion. Helpful measures may include installation of a dredging and artificial sediment-bypass system, a beach nourishment system and seawalls, or some combination of these.

### PROTECTION OF COASTS

On rugged coasts a narrow shoreline lies between the water and the land. Coastal erosion during stormy pe-

**PHOTO 168**
Coastal erosion. These buildings were undercut during a storm on the Lake Michigan coast. (Courtesy: National Oceanic and Atmospheric Administration)

**PHOTO 169**
A seawall has been constructed on Cape Cod Bay to reduce winter storm damage. (Courtesy: Brian Tormey, The Pennsylvania State University)

riods endangers the structures, particularly roads and adjacent buildings, that have been built there (Photo 168). For example, on the California coast, cliffs have been so eroded that structures have tumbled into the ocean, and roadways have been undercut to the extent that they have had to be closed.

Measures to protect the cliffs from eroding include: constructing seawalls at the base of the cliff (Photo 169); planting the surface of the cliff with grasses (Photo 170), shrubs, or trees; placing sand and gravel at the base of the cliffs; coating the surface of the cliff with plastic; and building groins offshore. Of these measures, the construction of a seawall to control erosion appears most satisfactory. This is, however, a costly undertaking and the economic factor has limited its use.

Because no direct approach has been totally successful in solving the problem of coastal erosion, alternative approaches must be considered. Land-use patterns could be changed, for example, from intensive to extensive utilization. Zoning restrictions could prevent the development of hazardous areas. With controls, buildings and roads could not be built in coastal cliff zones. There would be no attempts to eliminate erosion; rather, it would be recognized that erosion is a natural process and that the recession of the cliff will occur. A second alternative is to develop public lands, such as parks and open space, in the hazard zone. The natural recession of the cliff would occur and damages would be minimal to low-cost recreational facilities. The cost of acquiring such land for public use would depend on whether or not it has already been developed.

## MINING AND DREDGING OF SAND

The mining and dredging of beach sand have become important activities in areas of dense population. In or-

**PHOTO 170**
Coastal planting. The sand dunes of Lake Michigan are stabilized by special grass plantings. (Courtesy: National Oceanic and Atmospheric Administration)

der to supply the demands of industry and construction, millions of tons are removed each year. At one time it was thought that the sand would be replaced by natural processes. These processes, however, do not always prevail. Many beaches are denuded, and the sand that protected the coastline from wave erosion no longer exists. Further, it can be expected that as the sand is removed, local changes in water depth may alter the erosional and depositional patterns of the shoreline currents.

The biological balance of a dredged area will obviously be disrupted. The level of dissolved oxygen will be temporarily lowered and the nutrients available in the water will be changed. If a silt is deposited on the new sand bottom, the marine life, such as flounder and other flatfish, that require a sandy seafloor will disappear. When old oyster reefs are dredged, oysters are frequently unable to reappear because the shell patches that are necessary for the oysters to survive have been removed.

## POLLUTION OF COASTAL WATERS

Because most of the sewage produced on land is ultimately discharged into the oceans, coastal waters receive the bulk of human wastes. These pollutants are of both a biological and a chemical nature. Wave and current actions may distribute the pollutants for great distances along the coast. For example, the plume of the Columbia River can be traced for nearly 400 kilometers (250 miles) along the Oregon coast.

Another major pollutant in coastal waters is plastic containers. This material does not decompose readily in the saltwater of the oceans. The containers are carried by currents and ultimately deposited on the world's beaches. Some beaches are now covered with plastic bottles that started their journey thousands of kilometers away.

The increased use of petroleum products has led to more oil spills of various types. The large modern oil tankers with thousands of barrels of oil possess the potential for disastrous spills. When oil is deposited by wave and current actions on a beach, it mixes with the sand, destroying the beach for recreational use until the oil is physically or chemically removed. The destruction of marine organisms and birds is associated with oil spills.

Power plants and industries use coastal waters and streams that flow into the ocean as coolants for heat exchangers, condensers, and extraction processes. Water used for these purposes is heated, particularly in protected bays and inlets. The inflow of warmer water changes the ecological balance in the coastal waters, destroying much marine life.

## COASTAL PLANNING

The understanding of shoreline processes is still in an early stage. Only in recent years have sufficient field observation and research been completed to formulate general planning programs to control shoreline processes. Any guidelines must be based upon an understanding of the natural physical processes that shape shorelines.

Three steps are fundamental in effective planning. First, phenomena vital to coastal processes must be specifically studied. Second, data systems must be developed so that shoreline conditions can be continuously monitored. Third, laws must be passed to implement effective controls of shoreline problems.

Coastlines should be managed under a set of stated objectives. A well-conceived program must maintain and in many areas improve the coastal zone's usefulness by improving the quality and extent of the existing natural system. Such a program must be consistent with economic, social, and environmental goals.

The steps in the development of such a management program include: (*a*) determining the desired use of the coastal area, (*b*) studying whether the coast is suited to this use, (*c*) weighing the desired use against the feasible use of the coastal area, (*d*) communicating what is needed to the public, and finally, (*e*) implementing a plan that is compatible with the natural and human conditions of the area.

## CONCLUSION

The ocean's movements—waves, currents, and tides—are important agents in geomorphic change. Waves and currents erode shores as well as transport and deposit sediments. The action of waves depends upon the wind velocity and its duration. The most intensive waves are produced in storms or by underwater disturbances such as earthquakes or volcanoes. The waves have their greatest erosional force along irregular coasts, where they erode headlands. Wave action has a tendency to make coasts more regular. The movement of sediments along the shore follows the movement of waves and currents.

Coastal landforms are related to whether the coast is submerging, emerging, or neutral. The type of coast is determined by oceanic and continental tectonic plates. Coasts that exhibit submergence characteristics are low-lying with broad coastal indentations. Emergence coasts slope gently from the shoreline.

The coastal areas are among the world's most densely populated. Human modifications of the coast are extensive. The problems of coastal erosion and pollution are now recognized in many areas. The solutions to the problems are not easy to find; greater planning of coastal resources is needed in the future.

## STUDY QUESTIONS

1 Describe a wave of oscillation and a wave of translation. Why does a wave erode a shoreline?
2 What is the importance of currents in transporting material?
3 What factors influence coastal erosion?
4 Explain the origin of a spit. In what coastal areas do spits develop?
5 How does a spit differ from a sandbar?
6 Describe how wave erosion occurs.
7 What landforms are created by coastal wave action? Explain the origin of each landform.
8 What are the characteristics of submergence shorelines, emergence shorelines, and neutral shorelines?
9 What is the difference between the continental shelf, continental slope, and continental rise?
10 What is a turbidity current?
11 Describe attempts to control coastal erosion.
12 What are the sources of coastal water pollution?
13 What does coastal planning entail?

# 17 WORLD LANDFORM SYSTEMS

## KEY WORDS

- differential erosion
- erosional and depositional regions
- Fall Line
- geologic time scale
- geosyncline
- local relief
- plateau
- structural regions
- topographical regions

A major characteristic of any place on the earth is its topography—the configuration of the land surface. Some areas of the world are nearly flat while other areas exhibit extremely rugged mountainous conditions. The world offers a fascinating variety of topographic features. Like all physical systems, landforms undergo constant change. While tectonic forces require hundreds of thousands or even millions of years to create a great mountain range, some changes can be readily observed in a brief period. A severe thunderstorm will alter the channel of a stream or river, and a landslide can remove a mountainside. It is sometimes difficult for human beings, with our short life spans, to believe that once-great mountains have been worn away by erosion and that only their igneous core remains as a low peneplain. All landforms are being degraded and will disappear in time.

Even a casual observer notices differences in the landforms from one region to another. At first it appears that all landforms are unique. However, a more careful observer will soon note similarities of landforms, such as the form of the valleys, the shape of the hills, the types of bedrock, and the patterns of the hills and ridges. Landforms can thus be categorized and classified according to a system that becomes the basis for determining geomorphological regions. World landform regions are not determined by the distribution of solar energy and are therefore not as clearly defined as the climate, soil, or vegetation regions. The basic determinant of a landform region is the bedrock. The type of landform that develops depends upon the degradational processes and the length of time it has evolved. Thus the fundamental controls in landform development are rock structure, process of development, and stage of development.

## GEOLOGIC TIME SCALE

Because the earth is extremely old and has experienced great events in its evolution, a *geologic time scale* has been devised. Until the early twentieth century no accurate way of measuring geologic time existed. A person cannot easily conceive the length of geologic time, because a human life span is infinitesimally short in relation to the history of the earth. If we consider the history of the earth as a span of 24 hours, the life span of a human being is less than one second.

The scientific measurement of geologic time began in 1902 when Lord Rutherford in New Zealand discovered that radioactivity could be used to measure geologic time. This method is based on the assumption that each radioactive substance disintegrates at its own rate, and for many the rate is extremely slow. Uranium is a radioactive substance that disintegrates slowly enough to measure vast time spans. As it disintegrates, it changes into lead with the release of helium and energy. In 4,500 million years half of the original radioactivity is left. Thus, in theory, if the ratio of unchanged uranium to lead can be calculated, and the rate of disintegration is known, then the age of the host mineral or rock can be determined. Other isotypes do not take as long a time to disintegrate, so that it is possible to date more recent geologic features more precisely.

In Table 17.1 the four major divisions of the geologic time scale are called *eras*. The oldest, Precambrian, is the period before 600 million years ago, extending to the beginning of the earth, possibly 4.5 to 5 billion years ago. Since 600 million years ago, three eras have occurred: the earliest, Paleozoic, followed by the Mesozoic, and the present era, Cenozoic. Each new era is marked by a major change in the form of life on the earth.

Each of the eras is subdivided into time units called *periods*. The Paleozoic has seven, the Mesozoic three, and the Cenozoic two. Since the Cenozoic is the present era, more than two periods may occur before it ends. Each period is characterized by a somewhat less profound change in life form compared with that of an era. Each of the twelve periods is further divided into smaller units called *epochs*. Only the epochs in the Cenozoic are named.

The geologic time scale reveals that the earth has undergone a long evolution. To understand the present landforms it must be remembered that the structures that influence present-day topography may have had their origin hundreds of millions of years ago. For example, the surface of the great Laurentian Shield of eastern Canada dates from the Precambrian era and thus is more than 600 million years old.

## LANDFORM CLASSIFICATION SYSTEM

Classification of the world's climate, vegetation, and soils has had a long history of development. In contrast, world classifications of landforms are rather recent. In 1968 Richard E. Murphy developed a geomorphic classification system combining the genetic and empirical components of earlier systems. As the author stated, "The genetic factors used are those which are not mere speculations or hypotheses but rather the generally accepted geological record. The empirical factors have been chosen with an eye to simplicity." (p. 198)

**TABLE 17.1**
Geologic time scale

| Era | Period | Epoch | Estimated Age (in millions of years) |
|---|---|---|---|
| Cenozoic (Age of Mammals) | Quaternary | Recent (Holocene) | 2 |
| | | Pleistocene | |
| | Tertiary | Pliocene | 13 |
| | | Miocene | |
| | | Oligocene | |
| | | Eocene | |
| | | Paleocene | 70 |
| Mesozoic (Age of Reptiles; first appearance of birds) | Cretaceous | | 135 |
| | Jurassic | | 180 |
| | Triassic | | 225 |
| Paleozoic (Invertebrate forms abundant and varied; first appearance of fish, amphibians, and land plants) | Permian | | 280 |
| | Pennsylvanian | | 330 |
| | Mississippian | | 350 |
| | Devonian | | 400 |
| | Silurian | | 440 |
| | Ordovician | | 500 |
| | Cambrian | | 600 |
| Precambrian (First multicelled organisms) | | | 5000 |

The system developed by Murphy uses structure, topography, and erosional or depositional features to prepare three world maps that are fundamental to the final world landform map (Plate 11). The map of the structural regions of the world is based on the geologic origin and rock composition of each major area. The topographic map relies on local relief and elevation to present the configuration of the surface of the earth, and the final map presents the geomorphic processes, either erosional or depositional, that have shaped the landscape. The first and third maps provide the genetic basis for the final landform map of the world, while the topographic map provides the empirical information on the process. The three maps are reproduced in this chapter in Figures 17.1, 17.2, and 17.3.

## STRUCTURAL REGIONS

The Murphy classification system defines seven *structural regions.* They are designated by the capital letters *A, C, G, L, R, S,* and *V* (Figure 17.1).

- Alpine System (A)—The world-girdling system of mountain chains and ranges formed since the Jurassic period. Faulted areas, plateaus, basins, and coastal plains enclosed by such ranges are included in the system.
- Caledonian and Hercynian (or Appalachian) Remnants (C)—Remains of mountain chains and ranges formed during the Paleozoic and Mesozoic eras prior to the Cretaceous period and experiencing no orogenesis since then. Faulted areas, plateaus, basins, and coastal plains enclosed by these remnants are included with them.
- Gondwana Shields (G)—South of the great east-west portion of the Alpine System.
- Laurasian Shield (L)—North of the great east-west portion of the Alpine System. The Gondwana and Laurasian shields are areas of stable, massive blocks of the earth's sial crust. Precambrian rocks form either the entire surface rock

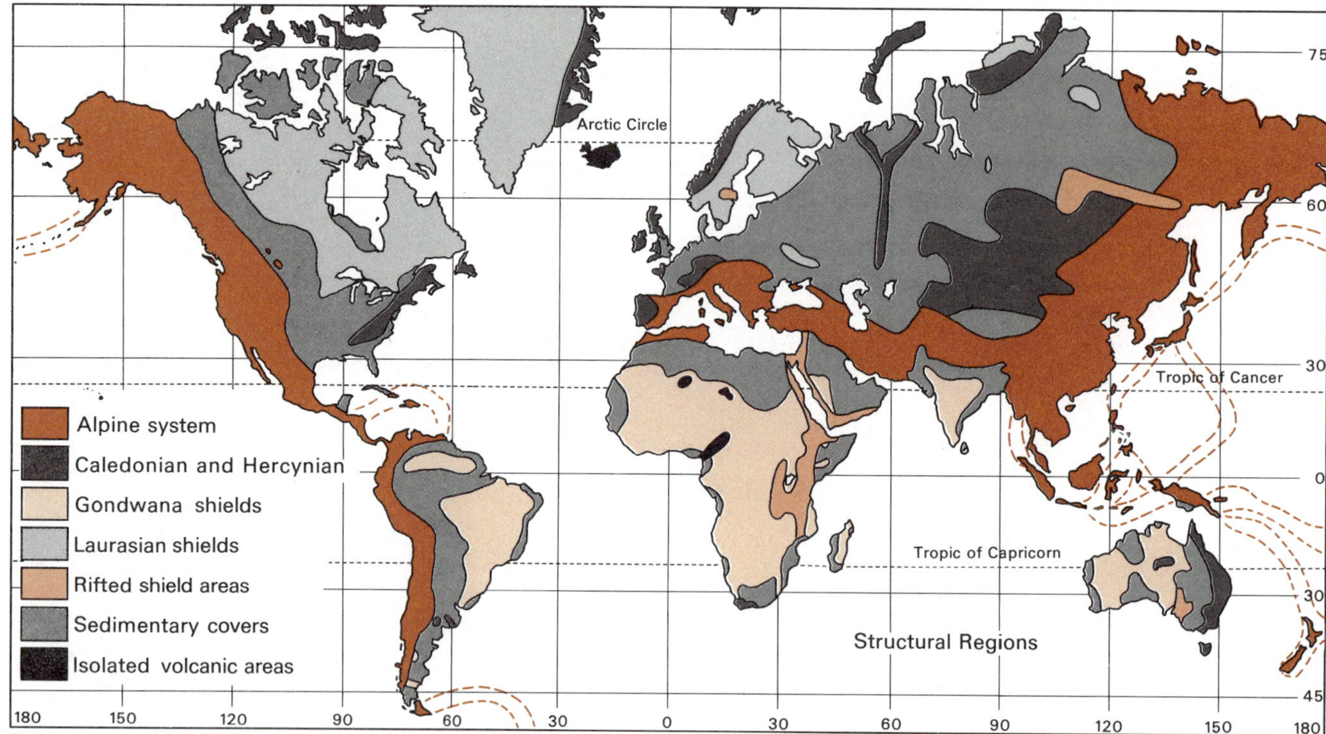


**FIGURE 17.1**
Structural regions of the world. (After Murphy, 1968)

material of the shield or an encircling enclosure with no gap of more than 320 kilometers (200 miles) between outcroppings or covering extrusives. Within the shield, crystalline rocks form more than 50 percent of the surface rock material.

- Rifted Shield Areas (R)—Block-faulted areas of shields, forming grabens together with associated horsts and volcanic features.
- Sedimentary Covers (S)—Areas of sedimentary layers which have not been subjected to orogenesis and which lie outside either the crystalline rock enclosures of the shields or the enclosing mountains and hills of the Alpine or other orogenic systems. These areas of sedimentary rock form continuous covers over underlying structures.
- Isolated Volcanic Areas (V)—Areas of volcanoes, active or extinct, with associated volcanic features, lying outside the Alpine or older mountain system and outside the rifted shield areas.

## TOPOGRAPHICAL REGIONS

The six types of *topographical regions* are designated by the capital letters *P, T, H, M, W,* and *D* (Figure 17.2).

- Plains (P)—*Local relief* (difference between highest and lowest points) less than 100 meters (325 feet). At the ocean edge, the surface slopes gently to the sea. Plains rising continuously inland may attain the elevations of high plains, over 600 meters (approximately 2,000 feet).
- High Tablelands (T)—Elevation over 1,500 meters (4,900 feet) with local relief less than about 300 meters (1,000 feet) except where cut by occasional canyons.
- Hills and Low Tablelands (H)—*Hills:* Local relief approximately 100 meters (325 feet) or more, but less than 600 meters (2,000 feet). At the edge of the sea, however, the local relief may be as low as 60 meters (200 feet). *Low Tablelands:* Elevation less than 1,500 meters (approximately 5,000 feet) with local relief less than 100 meters (325 feet). Unlike plains, a low tableland either does not reach the sea or, if it does, a bluff at least 60 meters (approximately 200 feet) high delimits the edge, where the tableland overlooks the sea or a coastal plain.
- Mountains (M)—Local relief more than 600 meters (approximately 2,000 feet).
- Widely Spaced Mountains (W)—Mountains are

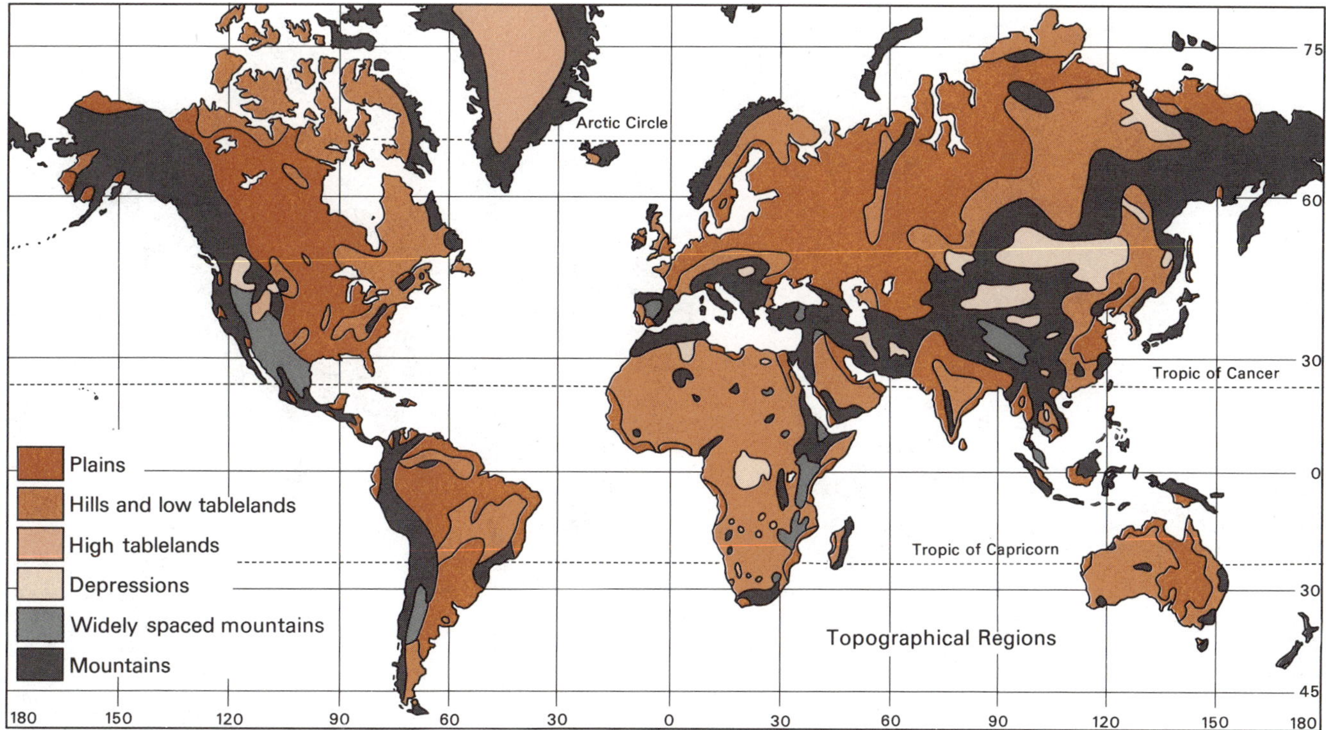


**FIGURE 17.2**
Topographical regions of the world. (After Murphy, 1968)

discontinuous and stand in isolation with intervening areas having a local relief of less than 150 meters (approximately 500 feet).

- Depressions or Basins (D)—Basins surrounded by mountains, hills, or tablelands, which abruptly delimit the basins.

## EROSIONAL AND DEPOSITIONAL REGIONS

There are five classes of *erosional and depositional regions* designated by the lower-case letters *h, d, g, w,* and *i* (Figure 17.3). These areas are based on the geomorphic processes that have occurred recently on the geologic time scale or are currently shaping the landscape.

- Humid Landform Areas (h)—Permanent stream density of at least one stream every 16 kilometers (approximately 10 miles). These areas are not subject to Pleistocene glaciation.
- Dry Landform Areas (d)—Permanent stream density more sparse than one stream every 16 kilometers (approximately 10 miles). These areas are not subject to Pleistocene glaciation.
- Glaciated Areas (g)—Areas subject to Pleistocene glaciation earlier than the Wisconsin (Würm) glaciation, or areas of undifferentiated Pleistocene glaciation.
- Wisconsin or Würm Glaciated Areas (w)—Areas of Wisconsin (Würm) glaciation, but now clear of ice cap.
- Ice Caps (i)—Areas presently covered by ice caps.

## WORLD CLASSIFICATION OF LANDFORMS

The landform classification of the world is a composite of the three basic categories just presented. The symbols from the three maps may be used to designate any area on the landform map. For example, the Atlantic and Gulf Coastal Plains are designated SPh, indicating that structurally they consist of sedimentary rock (S), that they are plains (P), and that they are humid (h). The Colorado Plateau is symbolized as ATd, meaning that it is enclosed within an Alpine system (A) consisting of high tablelands (T) and has a landscape formed under arid conditions (d). (See Plate 11.)

As in the world classification systems for climates, soils, and vegetation, this scheme is a synthesis that provides unity and organization. As Murphy (1968) states:

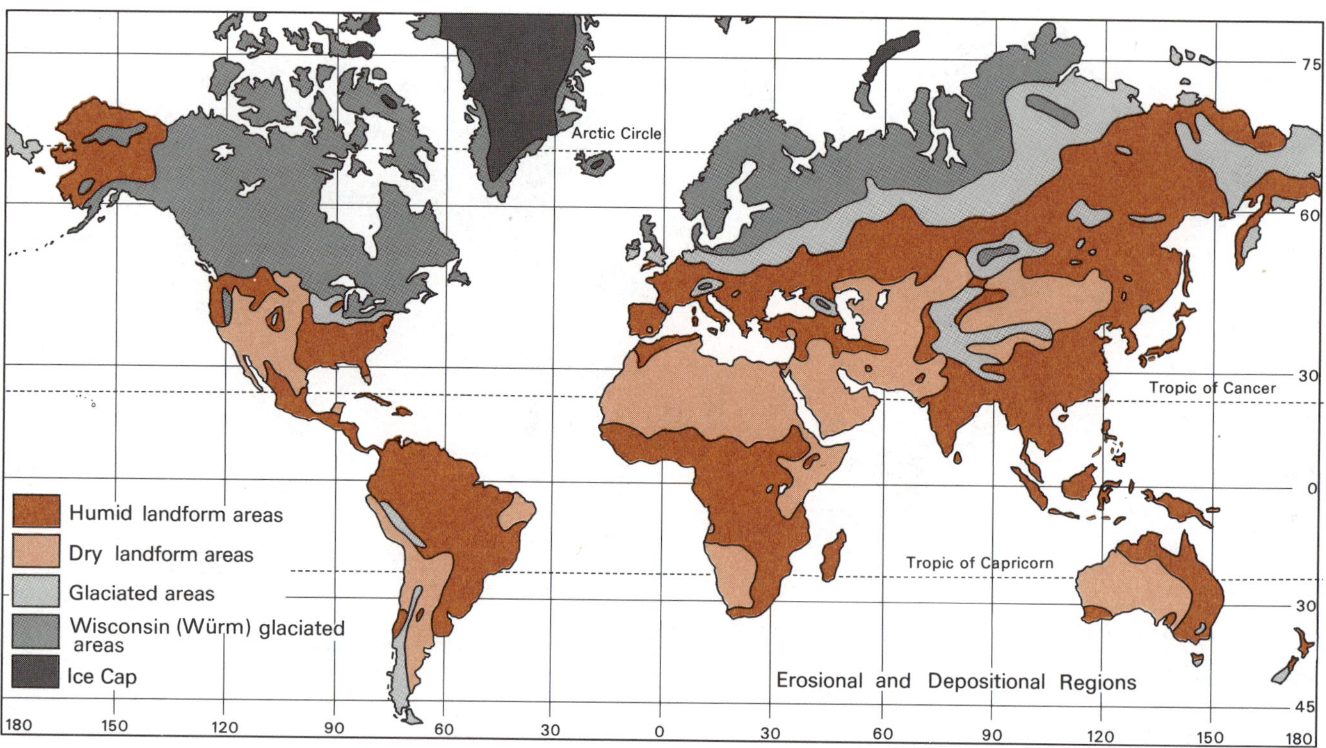


**FIGURE 17.3**
Erosional and depositional regions of the world. (After Murphy, 1968)

The location of the Gondwana and Laurasian shields and the enveloping Alpine system are immediately evident as are the vast sedimentary plains of the Americas, Europe, the Soviet Union, and Australia. The rifted areas of eastern Siberia, southern Australia, and the Great African Rift are readily seen. Here and there are Caledonian or Hercynian or Appalachian remnants such as much of Scotland, the Appalachians, the Urals, and the Great Dividing Range. Isolated volcanic areas are seen as characterizing such far-flung places as Iceland and Hawaii.

An effort has been made throughout to have the categories reflect the more significant aspects of landforms consistent with scale in a logical hierarchy of organization. The author [Murphy] is acutely aware, nevertheless, of the pitfalls in any attempt at a spatial classification of landforms. Classification is severely inhibited by the lack of adequate topographic maps for huge areas and by the virtual absence of reliable information about basic structure in many places. Arbitrary decisions of necessity, sometimes have been rendered. Additional work may suggest better terminology or more accurate delimitation, although it is doubtful, considering the level of generalization of the map, if such delimitation should alter the pattern appreciably.

Anyone who has worked with landform categorization or classification cannot help being aware of the difficulties. The precision of statistics which we have for climate are lacking for landforms. Landforms, furthermore, are a product not only of forces acting today but of processes dating back to the early history of the planet. Spatial organization and system are difficult to determine. Yet the need for such organization is there, and this map and the classification upon which it is based are offered in the hope that they will provide a rational simplicity and order out of the confusing complexity of landforms.(p.199)

## REGIONAL GEOMORPHOLOGY OF THE UNITED STATES

Like climate, soils, and natural vegetation, the world's landforms can be classified into regions. Because of the complexity and great number of landform regions in the world, this section gives examples drawn from the United States. The Murphy classification system provides the basic framework for this discussion. Four major geomorphic regions of the United States are defined—Plains, Hill Lands, and Mountains with Sedimentary Cover; Appalachian Highlands; Laurasian Shield; and the Alpine System. These basic regions are then subdivided to reveal more precise regional differences.

## PLAINS, HILL LANDS, AND MOUNTAINS WITH SEDIMENTARY COVER

The large area of sedimentary cover in the United States consists of the Atlantic and Gulf Coastal Plains (SPh), the Central Lowlands (SPhgw), and the Great Plains (SPhdw), and the following hill lands and mountains: Appalachian Plateaus (SHhwSMh), Interior Low Plateaus (SHh), and Interior Highlands (SHh). These areas are characterized by their nearly horizontal sedimentary rocks. All of the subdivisions have been developed in a humid environment except the western Great Plains, where dry conditions prevail. The Central Lowlands, the northern portion of the Appalachian Plateaus, and the area north of the Missouri River on the Great Plains have been modified by Pleistocene glaciation. The local relief of the sedimentary areas varies greatly, from less than about 100 meters (325 feet) in the plains to more than 600 meters (2,000 feet) in the mountains. To illustrate these regions, the Atlantic and Gulf Coastal Plains and the Appalachian Plateaus are described in some detail.

### Atlantic and Gulf Coastal Plains (SPh)

The Atlantic and Gulf Coastal Plains, from 160 to 800 kilometers (100 to 500 miles) wide, extend for 3,500 kilometers (2,200 miles) from Cape Cod to the Mexican border and then an additional 1,600 kilometers (1,000 miles) along the east coast of Mexico. On its landward side it is bounded by the Piedmont and the Ouachita Mountains, and in Texas it blends into the Interior Plains with only a fault scarp marking the boundary. When the softer sedimentary rock of the Coastal Plain meets the harder igneous rock of the Piedmont, the boundary is marked by rapids and falls. This boundary has come to be known as the *Fall Line*. Because the Fall Line marks the head of navigation and a source of water power, such cities as Philadelphia, Pennsylvania; Richmond, Virginia; and Columbia, South Carolina, developed on the Fall Line. On its seaward side the Coastal Plain continues as the Continental Shelf for 160 to 320 kilometers (100 to 200 miles) offshore.

The Coastal Plain is an elevated sea bottom of sedimentary rock deposits. The sediments are of Cretaceous, Tertiary, and Quaternary origin. The topography of the area is characterized by low relief, rarely exceeding 30 meters (100 feet) and usually considerably less (Photo 171). The sediments dip gently toward the sea. Differential erosion has degraded the various deposits at different rates, so the harder sandstones and gravels stand out as low cuestas, and the softer rock areas, such as limestones and chalks, appear as shallow valleys. Because the outcrops are essentially parallel to the coast, the erosional features produce a belted Coastal Plain. When the soils of the valleys are weathered from limestone, they are dark and fertile, producing such rich agricultural regions as the Black Belt of Alabama and the Black Prairie of Texas. Much of central and northern Florida is underlain with limestone, producing a karst topography with many sinkholes which contain lakes.

**PHOTO 171**
The low-lying Coastal Plain of southeastern Pennsylvania. (Courtesy: Pennsylvania Geological Survey)

The shoreline of this region reflects both submergence and emergence. Because the surface of the plain slopes down to the north, the shoreline north of North Carolina has been drowned, producing such bays as Chesapeake and Delaware and Long Island Sound. In the areas of emergence from Cape Hatteras to Texas long stretches are marked by offshore bars and accompanying lagoons as well as wide, sandy beaches.

A major subdivision of the Coastal Plain is the Mississippi Alluvial Plain that extends from Cairo, Illinois, to the delta south of New Orleans. This valley, varying from 40 kilometers (25 miles) near Natchez to 210 kilometers (130 miles) near Helena, Arkansas, has river sediments covering all bedrock. The river flows across its wide floodplain, constantly shifting its course as its meanders change their position. The floodplain exhibits such features as oxbow lakes, abandoned channels, and wide, marshy flats. The valley sides are marked by prominent bluffs that rise from 30 to 60 meters (100 to 200 feet) above the valley floor.

## Appalachian Plateaus (SHh)

The Appalachian Plateaus consist of nearly horizontal or gently folded strata of sandstones, limestones, and shales. Their eastern edge marks the boundary between the horizontal rocks of the plateaus and folded rocks of the Ridge and Valley. This escarpment, extending from Alabama to the Catskill Mountains in New York, stands from 160 to over 1,000 meters (500 to 3,200 feet) high (Photo 172). On the western edge of the plateaus a highly dissected, low escarpment marks the boundary with the Central Lowlands and Interior Low Plateaus.

Topographically the Appalachian Plateaus are highly dissected (Photo 173). The dendritic stream pattern has produced a mature landscape with most of the land in steep slopes. Elevations vary from about 300 meters (1,000 feet) to over 1,500 meters (4,800 feet), and local relief varies from 150 to 300 meters (500 to 1,000 feet) or more. The highest elevations are on the eastern margins of the plateaus.

The northern portion of the plateau was glaciated during the Pleistocene epoch, and many glacial deposits, such as drift, moraines, drumlins, and kames, are found there. The drainage of the region has been highly altered by glacial actions. As the ice melted, it created a network of streams that were later abandoned when the streams were adjusted to the natural slope conditions. These glacial valleys have come to be known as *through valleys.* Many of the present streams cross them, indicating that they had a different origin.

The Finger Lakes of New York State are striking examples of how effective glacial erosion can be (Photo 174). These lakes occupy preglacial stream valleys that have been overdeepened by the work of ice scouring. In many ways they resemble fiords.

**PHOTO 173**
California Overlook of the Monongahela River. The river lies about 200 meters (600 feet) below the upland surfaces. (Courtesy: Pennsylvania Geological Survey)

**PHOTO 172**
The Allegheny Front marks the boundary between the Appalachian Plateau to the west and the Ridge and Valley Province to the east. This high escarpment extends from southeastern New York to central Alabama.

**PHOTO 174**
Finger Lakes. Long, narrow Keuka Lake was produced by glacial erosion in central New York State.

## APPALACHIAN HIGHLANDS

Between the Atlantic Coastal Plain and the Appalachian Plateaus are four landform regions: Piedmont (CPh), Blue Ridge (CMh), Ridge and Valley (CHh), and New England (CHhw and CMhw), with the Ouachita Province (CHh) as an outlier to the west. On the east, in the Piedmont and Blue Ridge, the rocks are mostly Precambrian granite and gneiss, but to the west, in the Ridge and Valley and Ouachita provinces, the rocks are sedimentary and many of them have been metamorphosed. The local relief varies from 100 to 600 meters (325 to 2,000 feet). All of the regions have been developed under humid conditions. Pleistocene glaciation has modified the landforms in New England. The Blue Ridge and Ridge and Valley provinces illustrate the structural and topographic diversity of the Appalachian Highlands.

### Blue Ridge (CMh)

The Blue Ridge is a mountain chain that extends from southern Pennsylvania about 960 kilometers (600 miles) to northern Georgia with a maximum width of 130 kilometers (80 miles) in North Carolina. Elevations range from a low of about 390 meters (1,300 feet) at Harpers Ferry to a maximum of 2,005 meters (6,576 feet) at Mount Mitchell in North Carolina.

The boundary with the Piedmont is sharp. In the southern Blue Ridge it is marked by an eastward-facing scarp varying from 750 meters (2,500 feet) near Roanoke to over 1,200 meters (4,000 feet) near Blowing Rock in North Carolina. The western boundary with the Great Valley is equally distinct, as the Precambrian rocks abut against the folded and faulted Paleozoic rocks.

The rocks of the Blue Ridge are largely Precambrian granite and gneiss that formed the basement of the Appalachian geosyncline. These rocks form the highest peaks in the Appalachian Highlands. Besides the crystalline rocks, the southern Blue Ridge contains some Precambrian sedimentary rocks that have been highly metamorphosed.

The local relief of the Blue Ridge varies greatly from 150 meters (500 feet) to over 450 meters (1,500 feet). In general the valleys are narrow and most of the land surface is in slope, leading to narrow ridge summits (Photo 175). The area is thus highly dissected, with deep valleys separating the ridges. Rugged mountains isolate the southern Blue Ridge region. In the north a few low-level water gaps are provided by the Potomac, James, and Manassas rivers. Natural lakes are essentially absent from the region, but dammed rivers now provide some artificial water bodies.

The region has become one of the principal outdoor recreation areas of eastern United States. The Great Smoky Mountains National Park, which contains Mount Mitchell, is visited by hundreds of thousands of people each year. The Skyline Parkway in Virginia and the Blue Ridge Parkway in North Carolina follow the crests of the ridges, providing one of the most attractive mountain highways in the world.

**PHOTO 175**
The Blue Ridge Mountains of Virginia. Note the low-lying fog in the valleys. (Courtesy: Standard Oil Company of New Jersey)

### Ridge and Valley (CHh)

The Ridge and Valley Province extends 1,930 kilometers (1,200 miles), the entire length of the Appalachian Highlands from the St. Lawrence Lowlands to Alabama. The topography of this region is distinctive, consisting of folded structures that have produced parallel ridges and valleys that trend northeast to southwest (Photo 176). The province is normally divided into three sections. The first, lying in the Hudson Valley, consists largely of shale deposits. The second, extending from Pennsylvania to northern Virginia, has a bedrock of sandstones, limestones, and shales. The third area, stretching from Virginia south to Alabama, also consists of limestones, sandstones, and shales, but is highly faulted.

The rocks of the Ridge and Valley Province represent the entire Paleozoic era from Cambrian to Permian. The sediments, in places 12,000 meters (39,360 feet) thick, originated from high mountains to the east that have

**PHOTO 176**
Penns Valley from Nittany Mountain in the Ridge and Valley Province of central Pennsylvania.

**PHOTO 177**
The Great Valley of the Ridge and Valley Province has low relief and is one of the richest agricultural regions in the world.

now been completely eroded away. At the end of the Paleozoic era, the earth's crust to the east, now represented by the Piedmont and Blue Ridge, was pushed westward against these deposits in the *geosyncline* or large downwarped area. The rocks were gradually folded into anticlines and synclines, and in the southern section, faulting occurred. The original uplifted folds were then eroded away, creating what has come to be known as the Schooley peneplain. Later the Schooley peneplain was lifted and erosion began once again on the uplifted, folded structures. Because the structures were highly tilted, the streams removed the less resistant rocks, such as shales and limestones, creating valleys. The more resistant rocks, such as the sandstones and the quartzites, were left standing as ridges. As a result of differential erosion, some of the ridges have synclinal structures, and some of the valleys are anticlines. It is believed that three cycles of erosion followed by uplift have created the present landscape of the region.

Of the topographic features, the Great Valley or Appalachian Valley is remarkable for its length. It extends from Lake Champlain in the north to the Coosa River in the south (Photo 177). Throughout its length it is a continuous lowland. Regional names include the Lehigh, Lebanon, and Cumberland valleys in Pennsylvania and the Shenandoah Valley in Virginia. The width of the valley, which separates the first major ridge of the province from the Blue Ridge on the east, varies from 3 to 50 kilometers (1.5 to 30 miles).

Because of the folded topography, the region has developed a distinctive drainage pattern. It is characterized by a few major transverse streams with notable development of subsequent streams, giving the area a trellis drainage pattern. In many places the streams cut directly across the ridges in water gaps, such as the Delaware Water Gap, the six gaps in the Susquehanna above Harrisburg, and in the Potomac at Harpers Ferry. Some streams eroding resistant layers were captured by pirate streams eroding rocks of less resistance, so that the water gaps were abandoned, becoming wind gaps.

## LAURENTIAN SHIELD

Only a small area of the huge Precambrian Canadian Laurentian Shield extends into the United States as two outliers—the Adirondack Mountains (LMhw) and the Superior Uplands (LHhw and LPhw).

### Adirondack Mountains (LMhw)

The Adirondack Mountains in northern New York State, with an area of about 26,000 square kilometers (10,000 square miles), form a nearly circular, domed structure. The core rocks are igneous and metamorphic of Precambrian age, surrounded by early Paleozoic sediments that dip away from the dome in all directions. The oldest formations are thus near the center of the dome with progressively younger rocks extending outward. As a consequence, a series of inward-facing cuestas surround the mountains.

The Adirondacks are a rugged region with local relief exceeding 600 meters (2,000 feet) (Photo 178). At the

PHOTO 178
Whiteface Mountain from the Ausable River near Lake Placid, part of the rugged Adirondack Mountains. (Courtesy: J. Goerg, New York State Department of Environmental Conservation)

center of the dome there are 14 peaks exceeding 1,200 meters (4,000 feet), with the highest peak, Mount Marcy, at an altitude of 1,603 meters (5,257 feet). The region was affected by the continental glacier, which left numerous lakes and swamps, kames, eskers, and other glacial features. Many of the lake basins were scoured out of bedrock by the glaciers or are a response to the damming of preglacial stream valleys by glacial deposits.

The present drainage of the region has a roughly radial pattern. On close examination, the stream pattern appears as a well-developed rectangle, which suggests a basic structure controlled by jointing and faulting.

Because of the natural beauty of the landscape, the Adirondacks have become a major resort region. Lakes Saranac, Placid, and George are famous resort lakes. The high mountain slopes are ideal for outdoor sports such as skiing and camping.

## ALPINE SYSTEM

The western third of the United States is a part of the world's Alpine System. On the east are the Rocky Mountains (AMh), with three subdivisions: the Southern (AMh), Middle (AMh), and Northern (AMh) Rockies. On the western border the Pacific Ranges and Troughs (AMh, AMd) are made up of the Sierra Nevada–Cascade Mountains (AMh), the Pacific Border Mountains (AMh, AMd), and the associated Pacific Coast Troughs (APh). Between the mountains are the Intermontane Provinces of the Colorado Plateau (ATd), the Basin and Range Province (AWd), and the Columbia and Snake River plateaus (ADd).

The Alpine area is an extremely complex region of mountains, plateaus, and basins. The region is structurally complex, ranging from nearly horizontal sedimentary rocks in the Colorado Plateau, to volcanic deposits on the Columbia Plateau, and highly folded and faulted structures in the mountains. Elevations extend from sea level to over 4,200 meters (14,000 feet), the highest peaks of the Rocky Mountains. Local relief is from zero to over 600 meters (2,000 feet). The mountain topography was developed under mostly humid conditions, but much of the region has a dry-land environment. The Rocky Mountains and Colorado Plateau are described in some detail.

### Rocky Mountains (AMh)

The Rocky Mountains are a part of the great chain of mountains extending from Alaska to southern Chile. In the United States the Great Plains provide the eastern boundary, and the western boundary consists of the Intermontane Plateaus and Pacific Mountain System. The Rockies are extremely rugged, with local relief of 1,500 to 2,100 meters (5,000 to 6,800 feet), the highest in the United States. The Rocky Mountains consist of igneous, metamorphic, and sedimentary rocks that exist in various structural uplifts and basins that began forming at the beginning of the Cenozoic era. Differences in origins and topography provide sufficient contrasts to divide these mountains into three parts.

**Southern Rocky Mountains (AMh).** The Southern Rocky Mountains extend as a major barrier across central Colorado. The passes through the mountains are all higher than 2,700 meters (8,900 feet). The Southern Rockies consist of a series of ranges, such as the Front, Laramie, and the Sangre de Cristo ranges, each with distinctive topography. The continental divide follows the crest of the Park Range.

Since the Cretaceous period, the mountains have experienced a complex geologic history. The present mountains were uplifted early in the Cenozoic period. The major ranges, all trending north-south, are anticlinal in structure and separated from each other by large intermontane down-folded or down-faulted basins. These high basins include North, Middle, and South park, and Wet and San Luis valleys. Erosion has exposed the Precambrian core of the anticlinal mountains, and the up-

**PHOTO 179**
Hogbacks. Upturned monoclinal ridges along the foothills of the Front Range in Colorado. (Courtesy: T. S. Lovering, U.S. Geological Survey)

turned resistant monoclinal ridges have produced hogbacks on the flanks of the mountain core (Photo 179).

A number of the mountain ranges are spectacular in appearance. Of these, the Colorado Front Range extends for 300 kilometers (185 miles) north-south without a major pass, and rises about 900 meters (2,900 feet) abruptly from the level of the Great Plains (Photo 180). With Longs Peak at 4,276 meters (14,025 feet), and Pikes Peak at 4,232 meters (13,880 feet), the Front Range has some of the highest peaks in the Rocky Mountains.

At the southern end of the Southern Rockies, the San Juan Mountains are composed primarily of Tertiary volcanic rocks (Photos 181 and 182). They thus contrast in origin and structure to most of the ranges of the Southern Rockies. The area is known for its lava formations, ash deposits, and mud flows. One ash formation is estimated to contain over 4,000 cubic kilometers (1,000 cubic miles) of ash.

During the Pleistocene period, alpine glaciers produced a distinctive topography through scouring and deposition. In the highest area, cirques and arêtes have been carved in the mountain face. At lower elevations, glacier deposition, consisting of moraines and other features, predominates.

**Middle Rocky Mountains (AMh).** The Middle Rocky Mountains are located primarily in Wyoming with extensions into northern Utah and Idaho. These mountains exhibit a wide variety of rock types and structure. On the eastern side a group of ranges, including the Bighorn, Owl Creek, Wind River, and Beartooth mountains, are anticlinal uplifts and resemble many of the ranges of the Southern Rockies. On the western side such mountains as the Wasatch Range and the Grand Tetons are block faults and resemble the Basin and Range Province. A third type, represented by the Absarokas, are of volcanic origin.

The topography is varied, reflecting the diversity of origin of the individual ranges. The Middle Rockies possess some of the most impressive ranges in western United States. Most of the peaks of the ranges, how-

**PHOTO 180**
The Front Range is a massive mountain range in central Colorado.

**PHOTO 181**
The San Juan Mountains with Telluride in the valley.

ever, lie at elevations below 3,300 meters (11,000 feet).

Of the ranges in the Middle Rockies, the Grant Tetons are among the highest. The Grand Tetons rise dramatically along a fault line. The highest peak, Grand Teton, is 4,140 meters (13,579 feet) above sea level. The ice sculpturing of the mountains has produced a classic display of glacial features, such as cirques, arêtes, horns, tarns, and hanging valleys, as well as various depositional landforms at lower elevations.

In contrast to the structure of the Grand Tetons, the Bighorn Mountains are a classic example of an anticlinal mountain range. They consist of a Precambrian granite core flanked by steeply dipping sedimentary rock of the Paleozoic and Mesozoic eras. The remnants of the uplifted, eroded surface appear as an extensive area of low relief at the highest elevations. The slopes are rugged due to erosion of the steeply dipping strata. As in other ranges, the highest areas have experienced glacial erosion.

Within the Middle Rockies is a small area of volcanic activity represented by the Yellowstone Plateau and Absaroka Mountains (Photo 183). Vulcanism began in this

**PHOTO 182**
The volcanic San Juan Mountains from the dry plateaus of southwest Colorado. (Courtesy: U.S. Department of Agriculture, Soil Conservation Service)

**PHOTO 183**
Upper Geyser Basin in Yellowstone Park. Old Faithful Geyser is one of the major geysers in the world.

region in the Cretaceous period, and the evidence still exists in the thousands of hot springs and geysers. The subsurface water is heated by hot shallow lavas. Gases escaping from the rocks provide the pressure on the subterranean waters that create the geysers.

**Northern Rocky Mountains (AMh).** The Northern Rocky Mountains consist of a large number of ranges that are topographically and structurally not very different from those found in the Middle and Southern Rockies. The mountains include anticlinal groups that have developed on extensive granite batholiths. Others are fault-block mountains, and still others have a linear pattern, reflecting thrust faulting.

A few notable mountain ranges are found in the Northern Rockies. The massive Idaho Batholith covers 41,000 square kilometers (16,000 square miles). From it has been carved such individual ranges as the Coeur d'Alene, Clearwater, Sawtooth, and Salmon River. This is one of the most rugged regions in the Rockies. Although altitudes range only from 900 to 2,100 meters (3,000 to 7,000 feet), most of the mountain valleys are narrow and gorgelike.

A notable feature within the Northern Rockies is the Rocky Mountain Trench—a graben or rift valley—that begins in Montana and extends several hundred kilometers into Canada. Because of its great length, it has a number of regional names, such as Bitterroot and Flathead valleys. The structural origin of the trench has been obscured because it has been gouged by glaciers and then mantled with glacial drift.

As the Middle and Southern Rockies were glaciated during the Pleistocene epoch, so were the Northern Rocky Mountains. Glacial erosional and depositional features can be found throughout the region. The remnants of glaciation still exist in Glacier National Park in Montana. Because of the northern location, the alpine glaciers extended out of the mountains into the surrounding areas (Photos 184 and 185).

**PHOTO 184**
Northern Rocky Mountains. The glacially molded landscape of Glacier National Park. Note the arêtes on the crests of the ridges. (Courtesy: Montana Department of Highways)

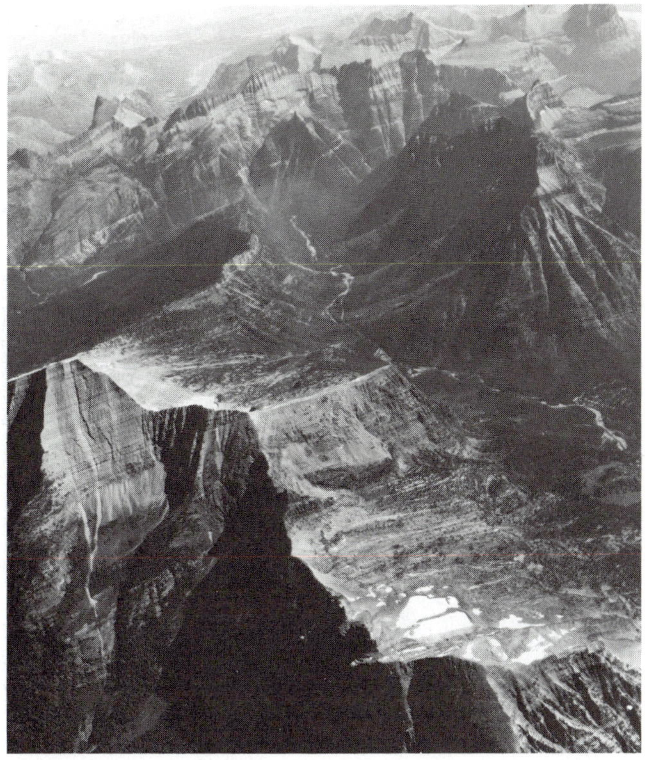

**PHOTO 185**
Northern Rocky Mountains. The Glacial Wall Fire Area in Glacier National Park. (Courtesy: Montana Travel Promotion)

## Colorado Plateau (ATd)

The Colorado Plateau, covering approximately 340,000 square kilometers (130,000 square miles), is situated west of the Southern Rockies and is separated from the Basin and Range Province by a lengthy fault scarp. It is one of the most distinctive and colorful topographic areas in the United States, possessing many canyons. Its average elevation is about 1,500 meters (5,000 feet), with small portions reaching over 3,480 meters (11,600 feet) and its canyon floors at nearly sea level.

This is a structurally upwarped area of nearly horizontal Mesozoic and Paleozoic sedimentary formations. Within the sedimentary rocks, covering about 10 percent of the plateau, are some igneous structures, including volcanoes with cinder cones and high, lava-capped plateaus and mesas. There are also some dome mountains created by intrusions of stocks and laccoliths.

The characteristic upland topography consists of broad, flat-topped surfaces. A number of levels occur because of faulting or because the broad tilting of the rock has created monoclines. As these areas have eroded, hogback ridges have evolved where the bedrock dips steeply, and cuestas have formed where the dip has been more gentle. This is an arid region with little vegetation; the colorful rock layers stand out in picturesque fashion.

The topography of the area reflects its youthful stage of development, with the flat-topped uplands cut by deep canyons (Photo 186). Because the sedimentary horizontal layers consist of sandstones, limestones, and shales, there has been differential erosion on the can-

**PHOTO 186**
Colorado Plateau. The Canyon de Chelly has been eroded into the horizontal rock strata.

yon sides. The canyons thus have steplike slopes with the sandstones and limestones forming cliffs and the shales forming gentler slopes.

Within the Colorado Plateau the Grand Canyon of the Colorado River is the most distinctive feature (Photo 187). The river has eroded a mile-deep canyon, through Paleozoic sediments of sandstones, limestones, and shales, into the Precambrian granite and schists. The rocks at the rim of the canyon are of Permian age; the age increases to the bottom of the canyon. The canyon from rim to rim averages about 20 kilometers (12 miles) wide. The walls are steplike through the sedimentary rock, and gorgelike in the Precambrian crystalline rock. The beauty of the canyon is not limited to its magnificent topography, but also includes the colorful walls.

**PHOTO 187**
Colorado Plateau. The upstream canyon of the Colorado River from the Navajo Bridge on U.S. Highway 89. The vertical cliffs expose rocks of the Lower Permian overlying Kaibob limestone. (Courtesy: R. M. Turner, U.S. Geological Survey)

## CONCLUSION

The Murphy spatial classification system of the world's landforms is based on genetic as well as empirical factors. Other attempts to classify global landforms have tended toward systems that were either genetic or empirical. The genetic classification systems lacked precision for regional studies, while the empirical systems lacked unity for genetic explanation. One of the major advantages of the Murphy classification is that, similar to the Köppen climatic classification, the world landform map reconciles genetic and empirical factors into a single system that can be used readily for genetic explanation. The genetic and empirical factors are those available from accepted geological records. The world landform classification system is thus a composite of the world maps on structure, topography, and erosional or depositional landscapes.

# STUDY QUESTIONS

1. What is meant by a geologic time scale?
2. What is the basis of the Murphy landform classification system?
3. What is meant by a structural region? A topographic region? A depositional or erosional landscape?
4. What are the major geomorphic regions of the United States?
5. Describe the topography of each of the subdivisions of the major geomorphic regions.

# SELECTED REFERENCES

## LANDFORMS

BAGNOLD, R. A. *Blown Sand and Desert Dunes.* London, England: Chapman and Hall, 1973.

BARROW, JOHN D., and JOSEPH SILK. "The Structure of the Earth Universe." *Scientific American* 242 (April 1980): 118–29.

BASCOM, WILLARD. *Waves and Beaches.* Rev. ed. New York: Doubleday, 1979.
BIRD, JOHN M., ed. *Plate Tectonics.* 2d ed. Washington, D.C.: American Geophysical Union, 1980.
BOORE, D. M. "The Motion of the Ground in Earthquakes." *Scientific American* 237 (December 1977): 68–78.
BULLARD, FRED M. *Volcanoes of the Earth.* Austin, TX: University of Texas Press, 1976.
BURCHFIEL, B. CLARK et al. *Physical Geology.* Columbus, OH: Charles E. Merrill, 1982.
BUTZER, KARL W. *Geomorphology from the Earth.* New York: Harper & Row, 1976.
CONDIE, K. C. *Plate Tectonics and Crustal Evolution.* 2d ed. New York: Pergamon, 1982.
COOKE, R. U., and A. WARREN. *Geomorphology in Deserts.* Berkeley, CA: University of California Press, 1973.
DAVIES, P. A., and S. K. RUNCORN, eds. *Mechanisms of Continental Drift and Plate Tectonics.* New York: Academic Press, 1980.
DAVIS, W. M. *Geographical Essays.* New York: Dover, 1954.
DECKER, ROBERT, and BARBARA DECKER. "The Eruptions of Mount St. Helens." *Scientific American* 244 (March 1981): 68–91.
DENTON, GEORGE H., and TERENCE J. HUGHES, eds. *The Last Great Ice Sheets.* New York: John Wiley, 1980.
DERBYSHIRE, E., K. J. GREGORY, and J. R. HAILS. *Geomorphological Processes: Studies in Physical Geography.* Boulder, CO: Westview, 1979.
DEWEY, JOHN F. "Plate Tectonics." *Scientific American* 226 (May 1972): 56–68.
DYSON, JAMES L. *The World of Ice.* New York: Knopf, 1963.
ELBY, G. A. *Earthquakes.* New York: Van Nostrand Reinhold, 1980.
EMMONS, WILLIAM H. et al. *Geology: Principles and Processes.* 5th ed. New York: McGraw-Hill, 1960.
FINCH, VERNOR C., and GLENN T. TREWARTHA. *Physical Elements of Geography.* 5th ed. New York: McGraw-Hill, 1967.
FLINT, R. F. *Glacial and Quaternary Geology.* New York: John Wiley, 1971.
FLINT, R. F. et al. "Glacial Map of North America." Special Paper 60, Part I. Boulder, CO: Geological Society of America, 1945.
FOSTER, ROBERT J. *Physical Geology.* 3d ed. Columbus, OH: Charles E. Merrill, 1979; 4th ed., 1983.
FREEZE, R. A., and J. A. CHERRY. *Groundwater.* Englewood Cliffs, NJ: Prentice-Hall, 1979.
FRYBERGER, S., and A. S. GOUDIE. "Arid Geomorphology." *Progress in Physical Geography* 5 (September 1981): 420–28.
GOREAU, THOMAS F., NORA I. GOREAU, and THOMAS J. GOREAU. "Corals and Coral Reefs." *Scientific American* 241 (August 1979): 124–37.
GOUDIE, ANDREW. "Arid Geomorphology." *Progress in Physical Geography* 4 (June 1980): 276–82.
GREGORY, K. J. "Fluvial Geomorphology." *Progress in Physical Geography* 5 (September 1981):409–19.
———, and D. E. WALLING, eds. *Man and Environmental Processes.*Boulder, CO: Westview, 1979.
HACK, J. T. "Interpretation of Erosional Topography in Humid Temperate Regions." *American Journal of Science* 258A (1960): 80–97.
HEATHER, D. C. *Plate Tectonics.* London: Edward Arnold, 1980.
HEEZEN, BRUCE C., and CHARLES D. HOLLISTER. *The Face of the Deep.* New York: Oxford University Press, 1971.
HOLMES, C. D. "Geomorphic Development in Humid and Arid Regions: A Synthesis." *American Journal of Science* 253 (No. 7, 1955): 377–90.
HORIKAWA, K. *Coastal Engineering.* New York: John Wiley, 1978.
HOUGH, J. L. *Geology of the Great Lakes.* Urbana, IL: University of Illinois Press, 1958.
HUNT, C. B. *Natural Regions of the United States and Canada.* San Francisco, CA: W. H. Freeman, 1974.
HUTCHINSON, PETER, and PAUL BARNETT, eds. *Planet Earth: An Encyclopedia of Geology.* Oxford, England: Elsevier Phaidon, 1977.
JOHN, B. S. *The World of Ice.* London, England: Orbis, 1979.
JORDAN, THOMAS H., "The Deep Structure of the Continents." *Scientific American* 240 (January 1979): 92–107.
KAUFMAN, WALLACE, and ORRIN PILKEY. *The Beaches Are Moving: The Drowning of America's Shoreline.* Garden City, NY: Anchor Press, 1979.
KING, C. A. M. *Beaches and Coasts.* 2d ed. London, England: Edward Arnold, 1972.
KOMAR, PAUL D. *Beach Processes and Sedimentation.* Englewood Cliffs, NJ: Prentice-Hall, 1976.
KRAUSKOPF, KONRAD B. *The Third Planet: An Invitation to Geology.*San Francisco, CA: Freeman, Cooper, 1974.
LEOPOLD, L. B., M. G. WOLMAN, and J. P. MILLER. *Fluvial Processes in Geomorphology.* San Francisco, CA: W. H. Freeman, 1964.
MARSH, WILLIAM M., and JEFF DOZIER. *Landscape: An Introduction to Physical Geography.* Reading, MA: Addison-Wesley, 1981.
McCANN, S. B. "Coastal Landforms." *Progress in Physical Geography* 5 (June 1981), 286–291.
McCORMICK, MICHAEL E. *Ocean Wave Energy Conversion.* New York: John Wiley, 1981.
McELHINNY, M. W. *The Earth, Its Origin, Structure, and Evolution.* New York: Academic Press, 1979.
McPHEE, JOHN. *In Suspect Terrain.* New York: Farrar, Straus and Giroux, 1983.
MEIGS, P. "Map of Deserts and Semiarid Regions." In *Future of Arid Lands,* edited by G. F. White. Pub. No. 43. Washington, D.C.: American Association for the Advancement of Science, 1956.
MURPHY, RICHARD E., "Annals Map Supplement Number Nine: Landforms of the World." *Annals of the Association of American Geographers* 58 (March 1968): 198–200.
PARK, C. C. "Man, River Systems and Environmental Impacts." *Progress in Physical Geography* 5 (March 1981): 1–31.

PENCK, WALTHER. *Morphological Analysis of Landforms.* London, England: Macmillan, 1953.

PETROV, M. V. *Deserts of the World.* New York: John Wiley, 1976.

PRICE, R. J. *Glacial and Fluvioglacial Landforms.* New York: Longman, 1976.

RHODES, FRANK H. T., ed. *Language of the Earth.* New York: Pergamon Press, 1981.

RITCHIE, D. *The Ring of Fire.* New York: Atheneum, 1981.

RITTER, D. F. *Process Geomorphology.* Dubuque, IA: William C. Brown, 1978.

SCHUMM, S. A. *The Fluvial System.* New York: John Wiley, 1977.

SEYFERT, C. K., and L. A. SIRKIN. *Earth History and Plate Tectonics.* 2d ed. New York: Harper & Row, 1979.

SHELTON, JOHN S. *Geology Illustrated.* San Francisco, CA: W. H. Freeman, 1966.

SHEPARD, FRANCIS P. "Revised Classification of Marine Shorelines." *Journal of Geology* 45 (1937): 602–24.

SKINNER, BRIAN J., ed. *Earth's History, Structure, and Materials: Readings from* American Scientist. Los Altos, CA: W. Kaufmann, 1980.

SMITH, ROBERT B., and ROBERT L. CHRISTIANSEN. "Yellowstone Park As a Window on the Earth's Interior." *Scientific American* 242 (February 1980): 104–117.

SUGDEN, D. E., and B. S. JOHN. *Glaciers and Landscape.* London, England: Edward Arnold, 1976.

SWEETING, MAJORIE M. *Karst Landforms.* New York: Columbia University Press, 1973.

TARBUCK, EDWARD J., and FREDERICK K. LUTGENS. *Earth Science.* 3d ed. Columbus, OH: Charles E. Merrill, 1982.

THEAKSTONE, WILFRED H. "Glacial Geomorphology." *Progress in Physical Geography* 5 (June 1981): 257–66; 4 (June 1980): 241–53.

THORNBURY, W. D. *Regional Geomorphology of the United States.* New York: John Wiley, 1965.

TRIBUTSCH, HELMUT. *When the Snakes Awake: Animals and Earthquake Prediction.* Cambridge, MA: MIT Press, 1982.

VINE, F. J. "Magnetic Anomalies Associated with Mid-Ocean Ridges." In *The History of the Earth's Crust,* edited by Robert A. Phinney. Princeton, NJ: Princeton University Press, 1968.

WALTHAM, A. C. "Origin and Development of Limestone Caves." *Progress in Physical Geography* 5 (June 1981): 242–56.

YOUNG, KEITH. *Geology, the Paradox of Earth and Man.* Boston, MA: Houghton Mifflin, 1975.

# APPENDICES

A METRIC AND ENGLISH MEASUREMENT CONVERSIONS
B TOOLS FOR GEOGRAPHIC ANALYSIS
C KÖPPEN CLIMATIC CLASSIFICATION SYSTEM
D CLIMATIC DATA FOR SELECTED STATIONS
E GLOSSARY

# A METRIC AND ENGLISH MEASUREMENT CONVERSIONS

### UNITS

| | |
|---|---|
| 1 kilometer (km) | = 1000 meters (m) |
| 1 meter (m) | = 100 centimeters (cm) |
| 1 centimeter (cm) | = 0.39 inch (in) |
| 1 mile (mi) | = 5280 feet (ft) |
| 1 foot (ft) | = 12 inches (in) |
| 1 inch (in) | = 2.54 centimeters (cm) |

### CONVERSIONS

| When you know | multiply by | to find |
|---|---|---|
| *Length* | | |
| inches (in) | 2.54 | centimeters (cm) |
| centimeters (cm) | 0.39 | inches (in) |
| feet (ft) | 0.30 | meters (m) |
| meters (m) | 3.28 | feet (ft) |
| yards (yd) | 0.91 | meters (m) |
| meters (m) | 1.09 | yards (yd) |
| miles (mi) | 1.61 | kilometers (km) |
| kilometers (km) | 0.62 | miles (mi) |
| *Area* | | |
| square inches ($in^2$) | 6.45 | square centimeters ($cm^2$) |
| square centimeters ($cm^2$) | 0.15 | square inches ($in^2$) |
| square feet ($ft^2$) | 0.09 | square meters ($m^2$) |
| square miles ($mi^2$) | 2.59 | square kilometers ($km^2$) |
| square kilometers ($km^2$) | 0.39 | square miles ($mi^2$) |

*Temperature*

To convert degrees Fahrenheit (°F) to degrees Celsius (°C), subtract 32 degrees and divide by 1.8.

To convert degrees Celsius (°C) to degrees Fahrenheit (°F), multiply by 1.8 and add 32 degrees.

# B TOOLS FOR GEOGRAPHIC ANALYSIS

Maps are the most important traditional tools used by geographers to record, describe, and analyze spatial problems. Maps are now supplemented by some important modern tools. Of these, aerial photography and remote sensing techniques offer new ways of viewing the earth.

## MAP PROJECTIONS: NATURE AND CONSTRUCTION

Many systems have been devised to portray the surface of the earth. The method of representing a spherical surface on a flat plane is known as a *map projection* or *map transformation*. Because transferring the distributions on the earth's curved surface to a flat surface is geometrically impossible, each projection has characteristic advantages and disadvantages. The projection chosen by a cartographer is one that serves best for what is to be portrayed.

Although hundreds of map projections have been devised, only a few are widely used. In transferring the earth's grid to a map, the cylinder, the cone, and the plane provide the basic concepts of projection.

### CYLINDRICAL PROJECTIONS

One of the oldest and simplest of the world projections is the central cylindrical projection (Figure B.1). It is produced by having a cylinder tangent to the equator and projecting the grid onto the cylinder from light originating at the earth's center. The meridians are thus correctly spaced along the equator. The parallels are drawn parallel to the equator and the same length as the equator. The parallels and meridians intersect at right angles as they do on the earth. However, because the parallels do not decrease in length but are represented by lines as long as the equator, the greatest distortion, both east-west and north-south, occurs at the poles. The only place where true shape and area are preserved is at the equator. In all other areas neither shape nor area is preserved.

Although the cylindrical projection is of little value, it has been modified to develop more satisfactory projections. Of these, the projection devised by Mercator in the 16th century is most familiar. On the Mercator projection the meridians remain parallel to each other, and the parallels are represented by lines as long as the equator; but to balance the distortion between the parallels and meridians, the spacing of the parallels is computed mathematically so that the north-south expansion occurs at the same rate as the east-west expansion.

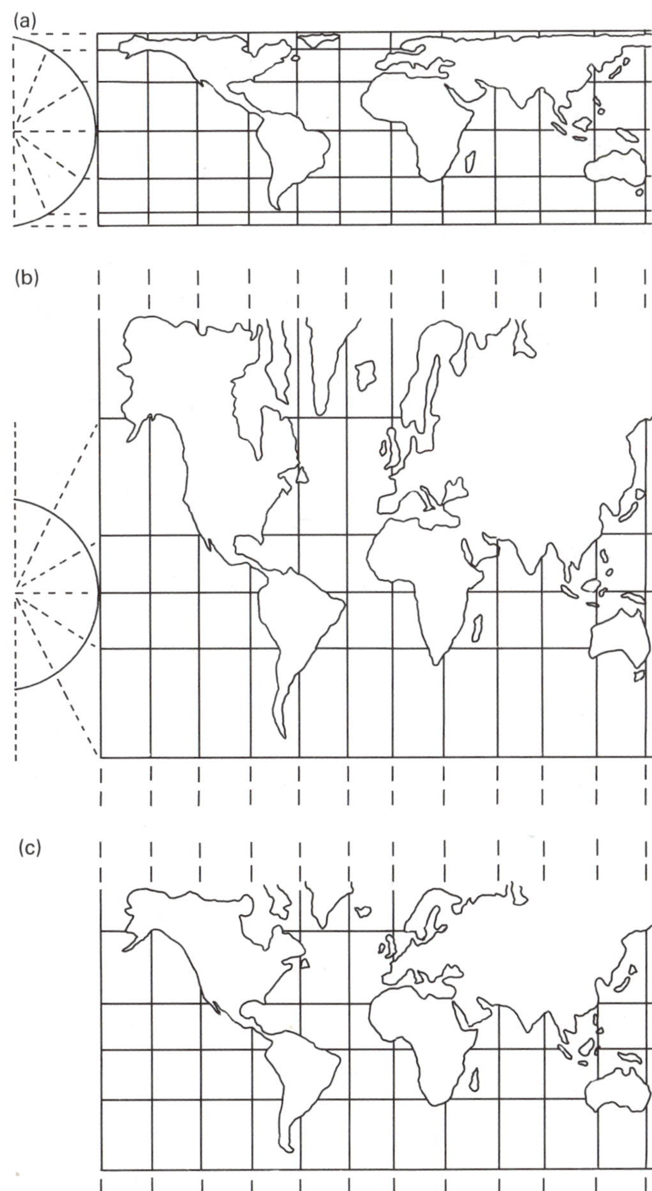


**FIGURE B.1**
Cylindrical projections: (*a*) cylindrical equal-area projection, (*b*) central perspective cylindrical projection, (*c*) Mercator projection.

The major value of the Mercator projection is that although the scale is constantly changing along the meridian, any straight line cuts all parallels and meridians at the same angle. This is known as a *rhumb line* or *loxodrome,* a line of *true compass direction.* Because true direction can be easily determined, this projection is of particular value for use in navigational and meterorological charts.

Further, the Mercator projection has the advantage of being a *conformal projection,* showing small areas with practically true shape. Larger areas, nevertheless, are distorted in size and shape because of the constant change of scale from place to place on the map. The areal distortion is small near the equator but is exceptionally great in polar areas. On such a map, for example, Greenland appears as large as South America, although Greenland covers only 2,072,000 square kilometers (800,000 square miles) while South America has an area of about 18,130,000 square kilometers (7,000,000 square miles). Thus, the Mercator projection portrays shapes rather well, but greatly distorts the size of most areas.

Because the Mercator projection is widely used to produce world maps for the general public, many misconceptions have resulted as to the size of the countries of the world. The problem is greatest in the Northern Hemisphere, where a large number of the countries lie in the middle or higher latitudes where the areal distortion is the greatest. In contrast, the lower latitude countries are frequently thought of as being smaller than they actually are.

## ELLIPTICAL PROJECTIONS

While the cylindrical projections portray the world on a rectangular grid, other projections show the world in an oval or elliptical form (Figure B.2). These include the *homolographic* and *homolosine* projections. These projections have a number of common characteristics. The meridians converge on the poles, in contrast to the cylindrical projections where the poles appear as lines. All are developed on polar axes that are one-half the length of the equatorial axis, which is the correct ratio of the length of the equator to the meridian dis-

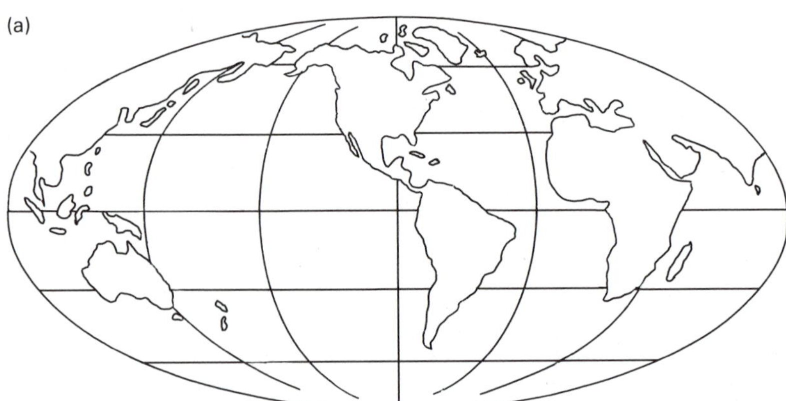


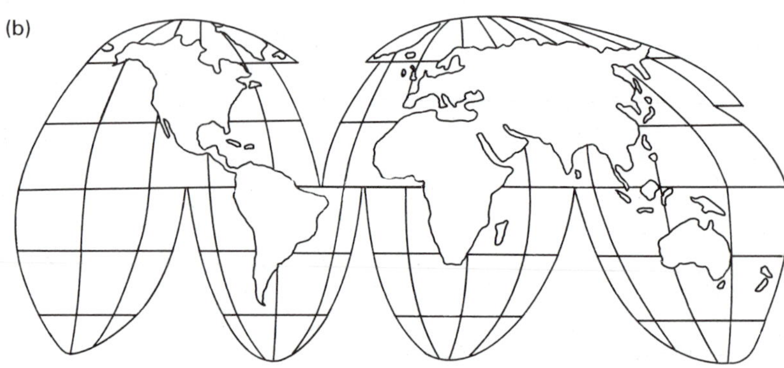


**FIGURE B.2**
Elliptical projections: (*a*) Mollweide's equal-area projection, (*b*) Goode's homolosine equal-area projection.

tance to the poles. Possibly most important, each region shown has the same area as it would have on the globe of the same scale. These projections are thus known as equal-area projections.

*Mollweide's homolographic projection* is one of the oldest of the elliptical projections. The parallels are straight lines but are not equally spaced along the central meridian. The meridians are all ellipses except the central meridian, which is a straight line, and the 90th meridian (reckoning from the center of the map), which becomes a circle. The main problem in constructing this projection is to obtain the correct spacing of the parallels along the central meridian. While it is an equal-area map, it does distort shape, especially near the borders of the map and in the higher latitudes.

Several modifications of the elliptical projections are characterized by spatial interruptions that make it possible to have more than one central meridian. One of the most widely used of these is *Goode's interrupted homolosine projection.* This projection retains the equal-area principle and shows the entire world without greatly distorting its shape. By balancing each continent on its own central meridian, this projection shows the shape and area of the world better, in many ways, than a globe can, since the entire world can be seen at a glance on a flat surface. The homolosine projection is a contrived projection produced by combining a sinusoidal projection between the equator and 40° with a homolographic projection from 40° to the poles. The parallels are straight lines. The equator is drawn as a continuous line, but all other parallels are interrupted. Because the central meridian is repeated, it appears as if each continent were devised on a separate projection and therefore the shape is very good. Thus, if continents are being shown, they are centered on meridians. If the oceans are to be emphasized, the central meridians are located over the oceans instead. The principal objection to the map is its use of spatial interruptions. When the map portrays world patterns, these interruptions must be bridged. However, since distortions are concentrated in the interruptions, the intact part of the map allows for a rather faithful representation of both shapes and area. The homolosine projection has come to be one of the most widely used.

## AZIMUTHAL PROJECTIONS

Another group of projections visualizes the earth's grid as projected onto a plane tangent to a given point on the globe (Figure B.3). These projections can show no more than half of the globe. All of these are *azimuthal,* for true direction is shown from the tangent point on the plane. Three common azimuthal projections—*orthographic, stereographic,* and *gnomonic*—are used. Each of these terms defines where the source of the light would be located in projecting the grid of the globe onto the tangent plane.

To construct the *orthographic* projection, it is assumed that the projecting light is located at an infinite distance from the earth so that the light rays passing through the earth will be parallel to one another. If the plane is tangent at the equator, the parallels appear as straight lines, but are closer to each other approaching the poles. Despite the inequality in spacing, they remain parallel on the projection. The meridians appear as arcs, but crowd together toward the outer margins of the map. If the plane is tangent at the poles, the parallels are unequally spaced circles and the meridians are straight lines that converge at the pole. On this projection the shape and the area are well presented in

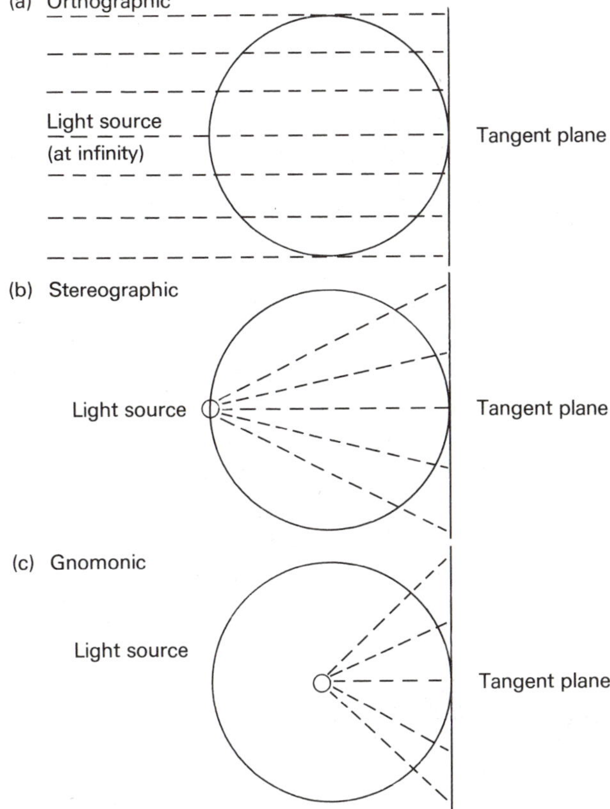


**FIGURE B.3**
Azimuthal projections: (*a*) orthographic, (*b*) stereographic, (*c*) gnomonic.

a limited area near the center of the map. Distances are increasingly shortened and sizes of areas are reduced toward the margins of the map, so that distortion in shape of areas results. With the plane tangent at the poles, this projection has frequently been used to plot the stars in each hemisphere.

The *stereographic* projection shows a portion or an entire hemisphere as if the source of light that projects the grid system onto the tangent plane were located on the opposite side of the hemisphere. If the plane is tangent at a point on the equator, the parallels and meridians will appear as arcs of circles which become progressively farther apart toward the margins of the map. Only the center meridian and the equator appear as straight lines. If the plane is tangent at the poles, the parallels are unequally spaced areas that are extended farther apart away from the pole, and meridians are straight lines converging on the pole. Because the parallels and meridians are arcs of circles that cross at right angles, this projection renders the shapes of limited areas accurately. In contrast to the orthographic projection, the sterographic projection has a tendency to compress the areas nearest the tangent point. Toward the margins of the map, however, distances and areas are greatly increased.

A projection can also be constructed when it is assumed that the projecting light originates at the center of the earth and that the grid is projected onto a plane tangent at any point on the earth. This is the *gnomonic* projection. If the plane is tangent at a pole, the parallels are arcs that widen toward the edges of the projection, and the meridians are straight lines that converge at the pole. If the plane is tangent at a point on the equator, the parallels are diverging arcs and the meridians are straight lines. The outstanding feature of the gnomonic projection is that all straight lines represent arcs of *great circles,* the shortest distance between two points on the earth's surface. It is thus used in navigation, along with the Mercator projection, for plotting great circle courses. The great disadvantage of this projection is that it is neither equal-area nor conformal. Distortion of shape and area increases rapidly with distance from the point of tangency.

## CONIC PROJECTIONS

The conic projections are commonly used to show areas that are less than continental in size. The *simple conic projection* is constructed as if a huge cone were placed over the earth tangent along a single parallel, with the parallels and meridians projected upon it from a light at the center of the globe. The parallel upon which the cone is tangent is called the *standard parallel.* The meridians appear as straight lines radiating from the pole as a center, and the parallels are represented as concentric areas around the pole. The simple conic projection is rarely, if ever, used in mapmaking, but it serves as a basis for other conic projections. Shape and area are true only at the point of tangency, and distortion increases with distance from the standard parallel (Figure B.4).

More precise conic projections are developed when the cone is *secant* to two standard parallels on the globe rather than tangent to a single parallel. By mathematically adjusting the meridians and parallels, equal-area or conformal types of projections can be devised. An example of the latter is *Lambert's conformal conic projection.* In this projection the meridians are converging straight lines, and the parallels are increasingly wider apart beyond the standard parallels. Areal distortion increases slowly with increasing distance from the standard parallels. The scale is thus slightly too small along meridians between the standard parallels and slightly too large outside of them. Lambert's projection has been used to produce air navigation charts, because all straight lines represent great circles. In *Alber's equal-area conic projection,* the meridians are also converging straight lines and the parallels are arcs of concentric circles, but, in contrast to Lambert's projection, the scale is slightly too large between the standard parallels and somewhat too small outside them. This is an excellent projection for countries, such as the United States, that extend primarily in an east-west direction, for it is equal-area, and also has little distortion of shape. It is the projection used in the National Atlas of the United States.

In order to secure the least distortion in shape and area, a *polyconic projection* has been devised in which there are a series of tangent cones placed so that their axis is coincident with the axis of the globe. Each imagined cone is tangent to the earth at a different latitude, dividing the earth's surface into narrow belts of latitude. Thus all values of shape and area are true on the tangent parallels and on the central meridian. Although the map is neither equal-area nor conformal, the distortions are more evenly distributed than on the simple polyconic projection. Both parallels and meridians appear as curved lines with the meridians converging on the pole, just as in the conic projections. The polyconic, in contrast to the conic projection, is best for showing areas with a wider latitude and narrow longitude, such as the continent of South America.

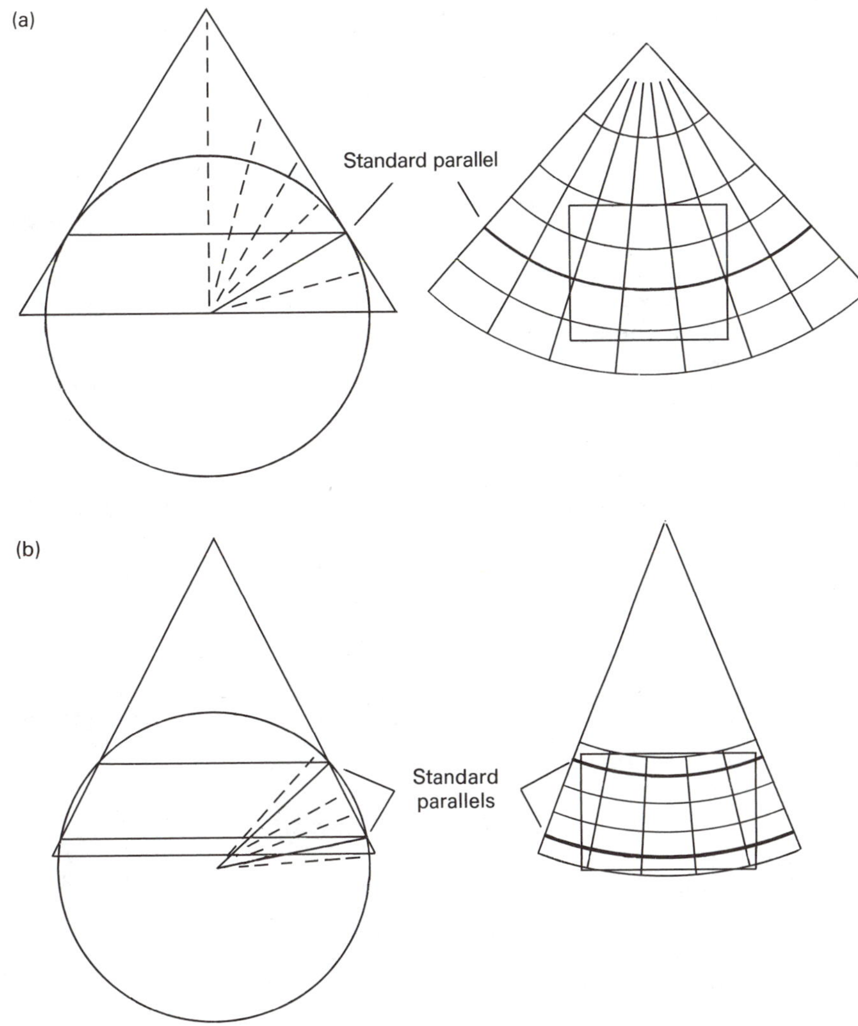


**FIGURE B.4**
Conic projections: *(a)* simple conic projection, *(b)* Lambert's conformal conic projection.

## MAPS OF THE EARTH

### NATURE OF A MAP

The problem of how to represent a spherical surface on a plane surface has long intrigued scholars. The difficulty arises from the fact that the geometric relationships must be modified in some manner. A small area, such as a town or a farm, may be shown on a flat surface without distortion of shape or area, because the curvature of the earth is so small over short distances that the earth appears to be flat. As the distances and consequently the size of areas increase, the importance of the curvature of the earth increases also, and a map cannot be made without some distortion. Some maps attempt to show true shape, other maps will attempt to show true area, and, of course, still others will try to compromise these two and thus portray neither true area nor true shape. The only true representation of the earth is, thus, the globe.

Any phenomenon on the earth can be mapped. Maps may be extremely simple, such as the outline of a country, or extremely complex, such as those portraying an intricate land-use pattern. If a map shows a single distribution, such as glacial landforms, the interrelations with other aspects of the physical environment are not revealed. If, however, two distributions—for example, glaciation and soils—are mapped on a single sheet, a synthesis of information begins to appear. To prepare a map, the scientist must carry out research that provides information to the cartographer pertinent to the purpose that the map is to serve. The map is thus a graphic form of information.

## FUNDAMENTAL INFORMATION FOR INTERPRETING MAPS

A map must contain a number of items—title, scale, orientation, and key or legend—if it is to provide basic information to the user.

### Title

Because a map presents information, it must be labeled properly. The title must state precisely what information the map conveys, for example, the world's climatic patterns, or the soil regions of the United States.

### Scale

A map *scale* is the relationship between a given distance as represented on the map and the same distance on the earth's surface. It may be expressed verbally; that is, we may say that one inch on the map equals one mile on the earth's surface. It may also be expressed by means of a measured line known as a *graphic or linear scale.* More often it is expressed as a ratio or fraction, such as 1:10,000,000 or 1/10,000,000, which means that one unit on the map is equal to 10,000,000 units on the earth's surface. This scale is called the *representative ratio* or *fraction.* A unit can be any measurement of distance.

On a globe, the scale is applicable to all areas. On maps, however, because a round surface has been transferred to a flat surface, the scale may change from one part of the map to another. This consideration applies particularly to small-scale maps. For example, a scale of one inch to 100,000,000 inches on the earth produces a small-scale map that will portray the world on a 10 x 15 inch sheet of paper. In contrast, one inch to 100,000 inches is a large-scale map frequently used to portray small areas such as a state or part of a state. A ratio of 1 to 1 would indicate that the map is as large as the area represented. Small-scale maps are thus used to portray the world, continents, and portions of continents, while large-scale maps show cities and small regions.

### Orientation

Because a map portrays an area with a north-south and east-west orientation, direction should be easily identified. Parallels and meridians are usually drawn to provide a grid system from which precise locations can be determined. Direction on the map may also be given by means of a north-pointing arrow. North may be marked by *true north* or *magnetic north.* The true north arrow is aligned with the meridian and points to the North Pole. An arrow showing magnetic north is aligned with the flow of magnetic force which affects the earth.

### Key or Legend

The *key* or *legend* provides an explanation of the symbols that are shown on the map. The colors, symbols, and like information must be understood in order to correctly interpret a map. The United States Geological Survey has prepared a chart of generally accepted symbols that are used to portray physical features on selected maps.

## TYPES OF MAPS

Spatial information may be portrayed on maps in a number of different ways. These earth features are represented by numerous devices and symbols. When a map shows one or more types of information, such as rainfall, temperature, pressure, vegetation, climate, or topography, it is known as a *thematic map.* These maps may be classified as either qualitative or quantitative.

Qualitative maps are used to show areal extent and shape of an earth phenomenon. For example, pictorial *relief maps* show the topography of an area by using hachures or shading to convey a three-dimensional picture of terrain. Further a qualitative map may show some classification scheme by using a particular color or pattern of shading. Thus the use of lines and color becomes paramount to portray concepts on these maps. In order to understand the purpose and information shown on the map, the user should always refer to the symbols in the legend. Many qualitative maps attempt to emphasize patterns of arrangements such as stream patterns or glacial features found in a region.

The quantitative map is based on statistical information. The *isarithm* maps, which are constructed of lines connecting points of equal value, are based on quantitative data. Of these maps, the topographic map, which is of the utmost importance to the study of geomorphology, is constructed by using *contours,* lines of equal elevation. The *contour interval,* the vertical distance between contours, varies with the type of terrain mapped. Commonly a 20-foot interval is used, although some maps may have an interval of 1 foot, and others as much as 1,000 feet, depending upon the slope of the land. It is logical that on a steep slope the contours are closely spaced, while on a gentle slope or on a relatively flat area, they are widely separated. Elevations at a particular place can be determined by counting the contour lines above or below a labelled base contour and multiplying this number by the value of the contour interval.

Besides contour maps there are many other types of isarithmic maps. In the realm of climatic data *isotherms* show areal differences in temperature, *isohyets* areal differences in precipitation, and *isobars* areal differences in atmospheric pressure. All of these items and others can be measured from a regional to a world scale and shown on maps by isarithmic lines. One of the major difficulties in interpreting maps using isarithmic lines is that the beginning map reader gets the impression that the value changes where the line is drawn. This is usually not so. The zone of contact on either side of the value is really a transitional belt where the value passes from slightly below a given level to one slightly above that level. This impression of gradation is sometimes enhanced by the use of shading as well as value lines on a map.

There are also maps, based on statistical data, that portray an earth phenomenon by use of shading or color. Classes or categories are identified by aggregating data, and are shown by distinctive patterns or colors. For example, maps showing rainfall or landform regions are known as *choropleth maps.* This type of map may be used for many kinds of ratios and when the statistical units are small may reveal sufficient areal differentiation so that it appears as an *isometric map.*

## AERIAL PHOTOGRAPHY AND REMOTE SENSING

New techniques for obtaining a more comprehensive understanding of the earth are always being sought. In the past the map was one of the most effective ways to visualize large areas. Mapping the complexity of the earth's environments by traditional methods is difficult, if not impossible. The survey of the earth's resources has thus been greatly enhanced with the development of photography and the ability to take pictures from above the earth's surface, first using balloons, later airplanes, and most recently satellites.

The chief value of an aerial photograph is that it is an extremely detailed pictorial map. Data can be extracted from the photo to prepare other maps. For example, the techniques of photogrammetry have been so perfected that topographic maps are now made in the laboratory from aerial photographs rather than from ground surveys in the field.

With the development of satellites, imagery of the earth could be obtained from outer space. This process is known as *remote sensing.* The pictures from space cover a much greater physical area than the lower-elevation aerial photographs. They thus provide a new dimension in interpreting the earth's features.

When aerial photographs are interpreted from near the earth or from images from space, five properties are to be considered: (*a*) the relative size of objects, (*b*) the shape of earth features, (*c*) the degree of tone due to shading, (*d*) the distinctive pattern of each feature, and (*e*) the texture of the feature.

### TECHNIQUES OF IMAGERY

The most familiar sensor, the conventional camera, uses wavelengths to which the eye is sensitive. Images of the earth can be recorded on film by the ordinary camera. Although new techniques have been developed in recent years, conventional photography is not likely to be replaced by nonphotographic remote sensing techniques in the foreseeable future. Rather, they complement each other. Aerial photographs have a number of advantages over earth images made by other techniques. The conventional photo is superior in quality to that obtained by other sensors. Further, it provides a more familiar view and is usually less expensive.

Remote sensing depends on the development of instruments that can measure radiant energy that is either reflected or emitted by the object or landscape being viewed. Radiant energy, called *electromagnetic energy,* is given off by all earth objects, biological or physical, and has both electric and magnetic properties. The wavelengths emitted vary from long wavelengths of several meters down to unimaginably short wavelengths. The total array is called the *electromagnetic spectrum.* Remote-sensing instruments have been devised that catch not only the visible rays that humans can see, but also the longer wavelengths, such as infrared and microwave rays, as well as the shorter ultraviolet rays. These wavelengths can be detected and converted into images of objects on the earth, such as terrain, trees, or buildings. There is a fundamental relationship between the temperature of a radiating body and the wavelength of its radiant energy.

A number of new sensor techniques have been developed to photograph the electromagnetic energy released by earth objects that are beyond the visibility of the eye and thus the traditional camera. The energy used to take infrared photographs is reflected solar radiation, the same as for conventional photographs, except only the infrared rays are recorded in the image. When infrared film is used, most features of the earth do not appear in their normal colors. For example, green vegetation is shown in red and bare soil in greenish blue. Each earth object reflects different amounts of infrared radiation. These objects are then identifiable by the shades of red produced. The advantage of the red tones is that they appear in greater variety than the shades of gray provided by the traditional aerial photograph, so that the identification of earth objects is enhanced.

## IMAGERY TECHNOLOGY

Aerial photography began when photos were taken from balloons. The field was greatly advanced by the use of the airplane. Although large areas of the globe, such as the United States, were photographed from airplanes, the photographing of the total world had to wait until satellites could be placed in space. In 1966, the National Aeronautics and Space Administration (NASA) established an Earth Resources Survey Program (ERSP) that had as its specific objective the development of satellites to survey the earth's resources. In July, 1972, the first Earth Resources Technology Satellite, *ERTS 1*, later renamed *Landsat 1*, began to acquire images of the earth's surface. Since then, other Landsats have been launched. The initial satellite was somewhat similar to weather satellites of the early 1960s. The basic objective of the Landsats is to survey the earth's land surface on a systematic and continuing basis. Each new satellite has an improved ability to acquire, analyze, and utilize earth resources information.

The Landsat system has a number of unique capabilities. By selecting the appropriate orbital parameters and employing specialized sensor systems, the present Landsats can acquire images of very large areas anywhere in the world, except at the poles. Moreover, the resultant images can be from a single spectral band, such as infrared, or from several spectral bands, producing multi-spectral imagery. Repetitive coverage not only increases the probability of cloud-free images of a given area, but also permits the detection of ground surface changes over time intervals.

In order to cover a wide area, the Landsat satellites are placed in a near-polar, circular earth orbit at an altitude of 920 km (570 miles). They circle the earth in 103 minutes and complete 14 orbits a day. Because the earth rotates under the orbiting satellite, each pass has a ground trace that is displaced 2,875 km (1,785 miles) west of the previous one, measured at the equator. Every day the spacecraft begins a new cycle of passes, which are displaced 160 km (99 miles) from the previous day's cycle. These coverage gaps caused by the earth's rotation are filled in progressively, day by day, by the 185-km (115-mile) ground swath of the sensors. By this procedure Landsat views the entire earth every 18 days, except for the polar regions (Plates 1, 5, 6, 8, 9, 10, and 12).

## APPLICATION OF LANDSAT AND OTHER SYSTEMS OF REMOTE SENSING

Remote sensing has many uses. Its applications can be grouped into seven major categories: agriculture, forestry, and range resources; land-use mapping; geology; atmosphere; water resources; oceanography and marine resources; and environment. Examples of the specific applications within each of these categories are shown in Table B.1. While Landsat monitors the earth's resources, the atmosphere has been monitored since 1960 by a series of weather satellites.

### Agriculture, Forestry, and Range Resources

The population of the world is estimated by the United Nations to be over 4 billion persons and is increasing at a rate of 250,000 persons each day. Meeting this growing population's demand for food requires not only an ever-increasing productivity from the land, but also additional acreage. Even in the most advanced countries, accurate surveys of total acreage of crops, anticipated yields, conditions of production, and other factors affecting production are often incomplete or delayed with respect to the needs of agricultural managers. Decisions on planting, fertilizing, watering, control of pests and diseases, harvesting, storage, crop quality, and adding or decreasing acreage can be made on a timely basis with the help of Landsat imagery. This type of information is also important to predict marketing conditions, evaluate effects of crop failure, and assess damage from natural disasters.

Landsat remote sensing has been effectively applied to agricultural land-use assessment. Land in agricultural crops can be identified in a Landsat image because it normally has regular boundaries, forming such well-defined shapes as rectangles, polygons, and circles. It is now possible to recognize many crop types with an accuracy of 90 percent or greater in fields as small as five acres. The identification is made by distinctive color characteristics. For example, fallow or unplanted fields appear as blues, tans, or brown—the specific color being selected by the computer. Growing crops usually appear in various shades of pink or red; young

**TABLE B.1**
Applications of Landsat and Weather Satellites

| Atmosphere | Agriculture, Forestry, and Range Resources | Cartography and Land Use/Cover | Geology | Water Resources | Oceanography and Marine Resources | Environment |
|---|---|---|---|---|---|---|
| Weather data | Discrimination of vegetative types: Crop types, Timber types, Range vegetation | Classification of land uses/cover | Identification of rock types | Determination of water boundaries and surface water area and volume | Determination of turbidity patterns and circulation | Monitoring surface mining and reclamation |
| Pollution mapping | Measurement of crop acreage by species | Mapping and map updating | Mapping of major geologic units | Mapping of floods and floodplains | Mapping shoreline changes | Mapping and monitoring of water pollution |
| Cloud types | Measurement of timber acreage and volume by species | Categorization of land capability | Revising geologic maps | Determination of areal extent of snow and snow boundaries | Mapping of shoals and shallow areas | Determining effects of natural disasters |
| Water vapor content | Determination of range readiness and biomass | Separation of urban and rural categories | Delineation of unconsolidated rock and soils | Measurement of glacial features | Mapping of ice for shipping | Monitoring environmental effects of human activities (lake eutrophication, defoliation, etc.) |
| Fog | Determination of vegetation stress | Preparation of regional plans | Mapping igneous intrusions | Measurement of sediment and turbidity patterns | Study of eddies and waves | |
| Haze conditions | Determination of soil associations | Mapping of transportation networks | Mapping recent volcanic surface deposits | Determination of water depth | | |
| | Assessment of grass and forest fire damage | Mapping of land-water boundaries | Mapping landforms | Delineation of irrigated fields | | |
| | | Mapping of wetlands | Search for surface guides to mineralization | Inventory of lakes and water impoundments | | |
| | | | Determination of regional structures | | | |
| | | | Mapping lineaments (fractures) | | | |

Source: *The Landsat Story* (Washington, D.C.: Earth Resources Satellite Data Application Series, Module U-2, 1980), p. 14.

plants tend to appear pink while mature crops are bright red.

Crop patterns can be best interpreted from computer-processed digital data that reveal quantitative measures of radiance. In general, all leafy vegetation has a similar reflectance spectrum regardless of plant or crop species. Interpretation can be precise only if the radiance level can be measured from the degree of maturity, percent of canopy cover, and differences in soil type and moisture. In practice, the crops are differentiated in the satellite image by using training sets; that is, the spectral signature or reflective response of specific known crop types is determined in several individual fields in the image, and similar conditions are looked for elsewhere in the image or from computer data.

## Land-Use Mapping

The term *land use* refers to the present land surface, whether it is directly used for human purposes or remains in its natural state. Land-use planning is concerned with how to use the land in the most beneficial way. To the present, land-use planning has been severely handicapped not only by lack of up-to-date maps but also by the inadequate means to analyze and interpret the large quantities of data involved. This situation applies not only to the less developed countries of the world, but also to most of the highly industrialized nations.

This problem can now be largely remedied by using Landsat imagery. Human use of the land can be deduced or inferred directly by identifying distribution patterns of vegetation, surface materials, and cultural features as revealed by images or computer-processed data.

In 1974 the U.S. Geological Survey prepared a Land-Use Classification Scheme for the preparation of land-use maps. As part of this scheme, the world is being mapped at scales of 1:1,000,000 to 1:250,000. The use of Landsat has greatly reduced the cost of mapping. For example, the relative cost of land-use mapping for the three southern states of New England, using ground survey, high altitude aircrafts, and Landsat, is estimated to be approximately $20, $6, and $0.40 per square kilometer ($50, $15, and $1 per square mile), respectively.

## Geology

Geologic maps, which aid in interpreting the composition, structure, processes of development, and history of rock materials, have traditionally been prepared by ground surveys. Mapping of large regions by this method may require years of field work. In recent years this process has been aided by the use of aerial photographs, but these have some disadvantages in geologic mapping. Variations in the background tone, known as *vignetting,* occur from the center to the edge of the photograph and may present problems of interpretation. Further, geometric distortion, depending upon the angle of the aerial camera, makes joining adjacent photographs difficult.

The major value of Landsat imagery for geological applications is that mosaics can be constructed over vast areas, covering an entire geological province. For example, the glacial features on a continental scale can be examined as a unified surface. Remote sensors have revealed much about rock type and structure. The microwave radiometer and the thermal scanners have identified fault zones and other cracks in bedrock by detecting differences in emitted radiation. Thus Landsat imagery appears to have the ability to single out linear features of structural significance.

Landsat imagery still poses some serious problems for geologic interpretation. Most layered rocks cannot be identified because of limitations in spatial resolution and the inherent lack of unique characteristics in color and brightness of different rocks. Also, it is not possible to determine the stratigraphic age of recognizable surface units. Vegetation or a covering of soil may also mask the geologic features.

Research to develop sensors to determine rock types is progressing. This is a difficult task. For example, in using thermal imagery, the same rock will change in appearance at different times of the day. However, when the capabilities for mapping lithology, form, or structure, by day or night, in good or inclement weather, are perfected, our entire perception of the lithosphere could change.

## Atmosphere

The atmosphere is one of the earth's most precious resources. The task of monitoring this vast ocean of air is, however, monumental. Nevertheless, the growing problem of air pollution and the diminishing gap between water supply and water needs are requiring that we understand how the atmosphere functions. Until 1960, weather data were collected mostly from stations on the earth, and sparsely augmented by aircraft and balloon observations. Beginning in 1960, weather satellites were launched into space to transmit data back to earth. Like the Landsat system, this group of satellites uses remote sensors to return imagery of reflected and emitted infrared radiation.

The weather satellites provide a variety of data from such systems as the Television Infra Red Observation System (TIROS), the Environmental Science Service Administration (ESSA), and the Advanced Vidicon Camera System (AVCS). For example, the infrared data are especially important for determining cloud types. Cloud-top temperatures are related to cloud heights, which aid in identifying types. Cloud types are particularly important as indicators of atmospheric characteristics, and monitoring cloud development propvides information relating to potential weather changes. In addition to monitoring clouds, sensors provide data about the water vapor content of the atmosphere and about temperature conditions at different levels.

## Water Resources

The freshwater resources of the world are gradually becoming scarce as consumption increases. However, there are also periods when flood control is of major importance. The greater the understanding of the hydrologic cycle, the easier it becomes to make decisions on the utilization of the world's water resources.

The data collected by Landsat imagery of the earth's water add the areal dimension to the conventional data collected at water measurement points. Satellite sensors make it possible to estimate the amount and distribution of water on the earth. Further, the repetitive coverage reveals the rapid changes associated with the continuous regional-scale processes of the hydrologic cycle.

Water is one of the easiest features to identify in Landsat imagery because it strongly absorbs the near-infrared bands. Standing water appears very dark on Landsat imagery in contrast to soil, rock, or vegetation, which appear bright and lighter. Further, snow and ice are extremely reflective and contrast sharply with land surfaces. Thus, the liquid and solid forms of water are readily identifiable. This will result in improved snow and ice mapping, surface water inventories, flood assessment, and water quality monitoring.

## Oceanography and Marine Resources

Landsat imagery is also providing information on the oceans and coastal zones. Particular emphasis is being placed on the natural conditions and on human activities that directly or indirectly alter, destroy, or preserve these resources. There is also interest in increasing the information on such physical properties as depth, temperature, and physical state of the world's oceans.

The specific goals in the remote sensing program are to develop efficient management plans of the living marine resources, to develop better management techniques for activities within the coastal zone regions, to increase the effectiveness of the oceans as transportation routes, and to contribute toward the advancement of marine biology and oceanography. Achieving these goals requires the identification, measurement, and analysis of a number of processes that function together in a highly dynamic environment. The physical, chemical, geometrical, and optical properties of the coastal areas and the open oceans must be measured, including such specific features as temperature, currents, salinity, sea ice, coastal topography, biological features, bathymetry, and other aspects.

Remote sensing systems can be developed to provide information on these features. The techniques to provide these data from Landsat imagery have been identified. More advanced sensor systems must, however, be developed to achieve all goals of this program.

## Environment

Remote sensing is being widely used to gather information concerning the quality, protection, and improvement of land, water, and air resources. Of particular importance is the detection of changes in the environment as a response to human activities. Landsat imagery is especially adaptable to providing a synoptic overview of the total environment as an integrated system, and further, it can monitor changes in the environment over a continuous time span.

Landsat imagery has been applied to strip mining and reclamation problems, changes in urban quality, measurement of damage by pipeline construction, classification of vegetation in different ecosystems, delineation of permafrost zones, and changes in the coastal environment. In the area of water quality problems, remote sensing techniques have been used to detect acid and iron wastes and oil spills, to define surface circulation patterns, to monitor lake eutrophication, and to determine dispersal patterns in turbid waters.

Landsat imagery has also provided data for managing wildlife, assisting with such problems as the delineation and assessment of wildlife habitats, management of waterfowl, measurement of available water and food supplies, determining the carrying capacity of the ecosystem, and assessment of damage from logging operations. Landsat imagery is also contributing knowledge about the atmosphere. It reveals sources and dispersion of smoke plumes, and the influence of air pollution on weather and climate. It helps detect urban haze, and monitors the regional and global effects of atmospheric aerosols. Because it operates continuously, Landsat is capable of monitoring such short-lived events in the natural environment as volcanic eruptions, earthquakes, hurricanes and tornadoes, and forest fires.

## SELECTED REFERENCES

FREDEN, STANLEY C. *Survey of the Landsat Program.* Washington, D.C.: National Aeronautics and Space Administration, 1978.

LINTZ, JOSEPH, and DAVID SIMONETT, eds. *Remote Sensing of Environment.* Reading, MA: Addison-Wesley, 1976.

SHORT, NICHOLAS M., PAUL D. LOWMAN, JR., STANLEY C. FREDEN, and WILLIAM A. FINCH. *Mission to Earth: Landsat Views the World.* Washington, D.C.: National Aeronautics and Space Administration, 1976.

WILLIAMS, RICHARD S., and WILLIAM D. CARTER. *ERTS-1: A New Window on Our Planet.* U.S. Geological Survey Professional Paper 929. Washington, D.C.: Superintendent of Documents, 1976.

# C KÖPPEN CLIMATIC CLASSIFICATION SYSTEM

**Relationship between Major Categories of Climate and the Subdivisons**

| Principal Climatic Categories | Precipitation Subdivisons | Temperature Subdivisions |
|---|---|---|
| A (always hot) | f (always moist)<br>m (seasonal excessive moisture)<br>w (seasonal drought) | |
| B (dry) | S (semiarid) | h (hot)<br>k (cool or cold) |
| | W (arid) | h (hot)<br>k (cool or cold) |
| C (mild winter) | f (always moist) | a (long, hot summer)<br>b (short, warm summer)<br>c (short, cool summer) |
| | w (summer rainy, winter dry) | a (long, hot summer)<br>b (short, warm summer) |
| | s (winter rainy, summer dry) | a (long, hot summer)<br>b (short, warm summer) |
| D (severe winter) | f (always moist)<br>w (summer rainy, winter dry) | a (long, hot summer)<br>b (short, warm summer)<br>c (short, cool summer)<br>d (very cold winter) |
| E (always cold) | T (short growing season)<br>F (no growing season) | |
| H (highland) | | |

## DEFINITION OF SYMBOLS

**A Climates**

Primary Category

**A** No month with mean temperature below 64.4°F (18°C).

Precipitation Subdivisions

**f** at least 2.4 inches (60 millimeters) of rain in every month.

**w** precipitation of driest month of the year less than the amount listed in Table C.1.

**m** precipitation of the driest month of the year less than 2.4 inches, but more than amount shown in Table C.1.

**B Climates**

Primary Categories

**BS** Precipitation less in inches than the amount 0.44 (t − 19.5) when it is evenly distributed throughout the year; or less than the amount 0.44 (t − 32) when it is concentrated in winter (70 percent in winter six months); or less than the amount 0.44 (t − 7) when it is concentrated in summer (70 percent in summer six months). See Table C.2.

**BW** The BW–BS boundary is exactly one-half the figure for the BS-humid boundary, as determined by the above formulas or from Table C.1.

Temperature Subdivisions

**h** Mean average annual temperature above 64.4°.

**k** Mean average annual temperature below 64.4°.

**C Climates**

Principal Category

**C** Average temperature of the warmest month over 50°F (10°C) and of the coldest month between 64.4°F (18°C) and 26.6°F (− 3°C).

Precipitation Subdivisions

**f** No definite dry season. Precipitation in driest month of summer more than 1.2 inches. Difference between wettest and driest months less than required for s or w.

**s** Summer dry season; at least three times as much precipitation in the wettest month of the year as in the driest month of summer; precipitation in the driest month of summer less than 1.2 inches.

**w** Winter dry season; at least ten times as much rain in the wettest month of summer as in the driest month of winter.

Temperature Subdivisions

**a** Hot summer; temperature of the warmest month above 71.6°F (22°C).

**b** Cool summer; temperature of the warmest month below 71.6°F (22°C), but at least 4 months above 50°F (10°C).

**c** Short, cool summer; one to three months above 50°F (10°C).

**D Climates**

Principal Category

**D** Coldest month below 26.6°F (−3°C); warmest month above 50°F (10°C).

Precipitation Subdivisions

f, s, and w defined as in C climates.

Temperature Subdivisions

a, b, and c defined as in C climates.

d Average temperature of the coldest month below −36.4°F.

**E Climates**

Primary Categories

**ET** Average temperature of the warmest month of the year between 50°F and 32°F.

**EF** Average temperature of the warmest month of the year 32°F or below.

**TABLE C.1**
Determination of Aw and Am Boundary

| Annual Rainfall (inches) | Rainfall of Driest Month (inches) | Annual Rainfall (inches) | Rainfall of Driest Month (inches) |
|---|---|---|---|
| 40 | 2.34 | 68 | 1.22 |
| 41 | 2.30 | 69 | 1.18 |
| 42 | 2.26 | 70 | 1.13 |
| 43 | 2.22 | 71 | 1.10 |
| 44 | 2.18 | 72 | 1.06 |
| 45 | 2.14 | 73 | 1.02 |
| 46 | 2.10 | 74 | 0.98 |
| 47 | 2.07 | 75 | 0.94 |
| 48 | 2.02 | 76 | 0.90 |
| 49 | 1.98 | 77 | 0.86 |
| 50 | 1.94 | 78 | 0.81 |
| 51 | 1.90 | 79 | 0.78 |
| 52 | 1.86 | 80 | 0.74 |
| 53 | 1.82 | 81 | 0.70 |
| 54 | 1.78 | 82 | 0.66 |
| 55 | 1.75 | 83 | 0.61 |
| 56 | 1.70 | 84 | 0.58 |
| 57 | 1.66 | 85 | 0.54 |
| 58 | 1.63 | 86 | 0.50 |
| 59 | 1.58 | 87 | 0.46 |
| 60 | 1.55 | 88 | 0.42 |
| 61 | 1.51 | 89 | 0.37 |
| 62 | 1.47 | 90 | 0.34 |
| 63 | 1.42 | 91 | 0.29 |
| 64 | 1.38 | 92 | 0.26 |
| 65 | 1.34 | 93 | 0.22 |
| 66 | 1.30 | 94 | 0.18 |
| 67 | 1.26 | 95 | 0.14 |

Table C.1 gives the amount of precipitation in inches during the driest month of the year along the boundary between Am and Aw climates for varying amounts of yearly precipitation. If the average monthly precipitation is more than 2.4 inches, f designates the precipitation characteristic of the A climate; if the amount in the driest month is between 2.4 and the amount shown in this table, the symbol m is used; and if the amount in the driest month is less than that shown in this table, the symbol w is used.

**TABLE C.2**
Average annual precipitation marking the BS-humid boundary

| Average Annual Temperature | Even Distribution | 70 Percent of Rain in Winter | 70 Percent of Rain in Summer | Average Annual Temperature | Even Distribution | 70 Percent of Rain in Winter | 70 Percent of Rain in Summer |
|---|---|---|---|---|---|---|---|
| 32 | 5.5 | 0.0 | 11.0 | 59 | 17.3 | 11.8 | 22.8 |
| 33 | 6.0 | 0.4 | 11.5 | 60 | 17.8 | 12.3 | 23.3 |
| 34 | 6.4 | 0.9 | 11.9 | 61 | 18.2 | 12.7 | 23.7 |
| 35 | 6.9 | 1.3 | 12.3 | 62 | 18.6 | 13.1 | 24.1 |
| 36 | 7.3 | 1.7 | 12.8 | 63 | 19.1 | 13.6 | 24.6 |
| 37 | 7.7 | 2.2 | 13.2 | 64 | 19.5 | 14.0 | 25.0 |
| 38 | 8.1 | 2.6 | 13.6 | 65 | 20.0 | 14.4 | 25.5 |
| 39 | 8.6 | 3.1 | 14.1 | 66 | 20.4 | 14.9 | 25.9 |
| 40 | 9.0 | 3.5 | 14.5 | 67 | 20.8 | 15.3 | 26.3 |
| 41 | 9.5 | 3.9 | 15.0 | 68 | 21.3 | 15.7 | 26.8 |
| 42 | 9.9 | 4.4 | 15.4 | 69 | 21.7 | 16.2 | 27.2 |
| 43 | 10.3 | 4.8 | 15.8 | 70 | 22.1 | 16.6 | 27.6 |
| 44 | 10.8 | 5.3 | 16.3 | 71 | 22.6 | 17.1 | 28.1 |
| 45 | 11.2 | 5.7 | 16.7 | 72 | 23.0 | 17.5 | 28.5 |
| 46 | 11.6 | 6.1 | 17.1 | 73 | 23.5 | 17.9 | 29.0 |
| 47 | 12.1 | 6.6 | 17.6 | 74 | 23.9 | 18.4 | 29.4 |
| 48 | 12.5 | 7.0 | 18.0 | 75 | 24.3 | 18.8 | 29.8 |
| 49 | 13.0 | 7.4 | 18.5 | 76 | 24.8 | 19.2 | 30.3 |
| 50 | 13.4 | 7.9 | 18.9 | 77 | 25.2 | 19.7 | 30.7 |
| 51 | 13.8 | 8.3 | 19.3 | 78 | 25.6 | 20.1 | 31.1 |
| 52 | 14.3 | 8.7 | 19.8 | 79 | 26.1 | 20.6 | 31.6 |
| 53 | 14.7 | 9.2 | 20.2 | 80 | 26.5 | 21.0 | 32.0 |
| 54 | 15.1 | 9.6 | 20.6 | 81 | 27.0 | 21.4 | 32.5 |
| 55 | 15.6 | 10.1 | 21.1 | 82 | 27.4 | 21.9 | 32.9 |
| 56 | 16.0 | 10.5 | 21.5 | 83 | 27.8 | 22.3 | 33.3 |
| 57 | 16.5 | 10.9 | 22.0 | 84 | 28.3 | 22.7 | 33.8 |
| 58 | 16.9 | 11.4 | 22.4 | 85 | 28.7 | 23.2 | 34.2 |

Table C.2 gives the amount of precipitation in inches between the BS semiarid and humid climates for each annual temperature from 32° to 85°F, and for the three possible distributions of precipitation through the year. The BS–humid climatic boundary corresponds to the following formulas:

1. Precipitation evenly distributed:
   $R = 0.44\ (t - 19.5)$
2. Seventy percent of precipitation in winter 6 months:
   $R = 0.44\ (t - 32)$
3. Seventy percent of precipitation in summer 6 months:
   $R = 0.44\ (t - 7)$

In the above formulas, $R$ = mean annual precipitation in inches, and $t$ = mean annual temperature in degrees Fahrenheit.

BW refers to arid. The BW–BS boundary is exactly one-half the figure for the BS–humid boundary as determined from the formulas above or from Table C.2.

# D CLIMATIC DATA FOR SELECTED STATIONS

## TROPICAL RAINFOREST (Af)

| | | Jan. | Feb. | Mar. | Apr. | May | June | July | Aug. | Sept. | Oct. | Nov. | Dec. | Year |
|---|---|---|---|---|---|---|---|---|---|---|---|---|---|---|
| Singapore, | T | 78 | 78 | 79 | 80 | 81 | 80 | 80 | 80 | 79 | 80 | 79 | 78 | 79 |
| Malaysia | R | 9.7 | 7.1 | 7.3 | 7.8 | 6.5 | 7.0 | 6.7 | 7.8 | 6.9 | 7.9 | 10.1 | 10.4 | 95.1 |
| Padang, | T | 79 | 80 | 79 | 80 | 80 | 79 | 79 | 79 | 79 | 79 | 79 | 79 | 79 |
| Sumatra | R | 13.5 | 9.9 | 11.9 | 14.0 | 12.6 | 13.0 | 11.8 | 13.7 | 16.1 | 20.0 | 20.7 | 19.4 | 176.6 |
| Akassa, | T | 78 | 79 | 80 | 80 | 79 | 77 | 76 | 76 | 76 | 77 | 78 | 79 | 78 |
| Nigeria | R | 2.6 | 6.5 | 10.0 | 8.6 | 17.0 | 18.6 | 10.1 | 9.3 | 19.3 | 24.7 | 10.6 | 6.5 | 143.8 |
| Stanleyville, | T | 77 | 77 | 77 | 77 | 76 | 75 | 74 | 74 | 75 | 76 | 76 | 76 | 76 |
| Congo | R | 3.2 | 4.0 | 6.9 | 5.6 | 6.0 | 3.5 | 4.4 | 8.9 | 7.5 | 9.7 | 6.7 | 2.8 | 69.4 |
| Georgetown, | | | | | | | | | | | | | | |
| British | T | 79 | 79 | 80 | 81 | 81 | 80 | 81 | 81 | 82 | 82 | 81 | 80 | 81 |
| Guyana | R | 7.9 | 4.6 | 7.2 | 6.0 | 11.1 | 11.7 | 9.9 | 6.5 | 3.1 | 2.9 | 6.7 | 11.1 | 88.7 |
| Iquitos, | T | 78 | 78 | 76 | 77 | 76 | 74 | 74 | 76 | 76 | 77 | 78 | 78 | 77 |
| Peru | R | 9.1 | 10.4 | 9.4 | 13.6 | 10.7 | 5.7 | 6.4 | 5.2 | 10.5 | 7.3 | 9.1 | 10.3 | 107.7 |

T = average monthly temperature in °F
R = rainfall in inches

## TROPICAL MONSOON (Am)

| | | Jan. | Feb. | Mar. | Apr. | May | June | July | Aug. | Sept. | Oct. | Nov. | Dec. | Year |
|---|---|---|---|---|---|---|---|---|---|---|---|---|---|---|
| Rangoon, | T | 77 | 79 | 84 | 87 | 84 | 81 | 80 | 80 | 81 | 82 | 80 | 77 | 81 |
| Burma | R | 0.2 | 0.2 | 0.3 | 1.4 | 12.1 | 18.4 | 21.5 | 19.7 | 15.4 | 7.3 | 2.8 | 0.3 | 99.6 |
| Cochin, | T | 81 | 82 | 84 | 85 | 84 | 80 | 79 | 79 | 80 | 80 | 81 | 81 | 81 |
| India | R | 0.8 | 0.8 | 1.7 | 3.7 | 11.4 | 27.8 | 25.3 | 12.5 | 9.2 | 12.9 | 6.7 | 1.9 | 114.7 |

T = average monthly temperature in °F
R = rainfall in inches

## TROPICAL SAVANNA (Aw)

| | | Jan. | Feb. | Mar. | Apr. | May | June | July | Aug. | Sept. | Oct. | Nov. | Dec. | Year |
|---|---|---|---|---|---|---|---|---|---|---|---|---|---|---|
| Saigon, | T | 79 | 81 | 84 | 86 | 84 | 82 | 82 | 82 | 82 | 81 | 80 | 79 | 82 |
| Vietnam | R | 0.9 | 0.1 | 0.3 | 1.7 | 8.3 | 12.6 | 11.1 | 11.0 | 13.3 | 11.1 | 3.7 | 3.1 | 77.2 |
| Madras, | T | 76 | 78 | 81 | 85 | 90 | 90 | 88 | 86 | 85 | 82 | 79 | 77 | 83 |
| India | R | 1.1 | 0.3 | 0.3 | 0.6 | 1.8 | 2.0 | 3.8 | 4.5 | 4.8 | 11.1 | 13.6 | 5.3 | 49.2 |
| Darwin, | T | 84 | 83 | 84 | 84 | 82 | 79 | 77 | 79 | 83 | 85 | 86 | 85 | 83 |
| Australia | R | 15.9 | 12.9 | 10.1 | 4.1 | 0.7 | 0.1 | 0.1 | 0.1 | 0.5 | 2.2 | 4.8 | 10.3 | 61.8 |
| Mongalla, | T | 80 | 82 | 83 | 81 | 79 | 77 | 76 | 76 | 77 | 78 | 79 | 79 | 79 |
| Sudan | R | 0.1 | 0.8 | 1.5 | 4.2 | 5.4 | 4.6 | 5.2 | 5.8 | 4.9 | 4.3 | 1.8 | 0.3 | 38.9 |
| Caracas, | T | 69 | 69 | 69 | 73 | 74 | 73 | 72 | 73 | 73 | 71 | 71 | 69 | 71 |
| Venezuela | R | 0.9 | 0.3 | 0.6 | 1.2 | 2.8 | 4.0 | 4.8 | 3.8 | 4.2 | 4.4 | 3.3 | 1.6 | 31.9 |
| Miami, | T | 66 | 68 | 72 | 74 | 79 | 81 | 82 | 82 | 81 | 77 | 73 | 69 | 76 |
| Florida | R | 2.4 | 2.0 | 2.4 | 3.4 | 7.1 | 7.4 | 5.3 | 6.4 | 8.9 | 9.0 | 3.3 | 1.7 | 59.2 |

T = average monthly temperature in °F
R = rainfall in inches

## LOW LATITUDE STEPPE (BSh)

| | | Jan. | Feb. | Mar. | Apr. | May | June | July | Aug. | Sept. | Oct. | Nov. | Dec. | Year |
|---|---|---|---|---|---|---|---|---|---|---|---|---|---|---|
| Lahore, | T | 53 | 57 | 69 | 81 | 89 | 93 | 89 | 87 | 85 | 76 | 63 | 55 | 75 |
| Pakistan | R | 0.9 | 1.0 | 0.8 | 0.5 | 0.7 | 1.4 | 5.1 | 4.7 | 2.3 | 0.3 | 0.1 | 0.4 | 18.1 |
| Broome, | T | 86 | 85 | 85 | 83 | 76 | 71 | 70 | 73 | 77 | 81 | 85 | 86 | 80 |
| Australia | R | 6.2 | 6.1 | 3.8 | 1.4 | 0.6 | 1.0 | 0.2 | 0.2 | 0.1 | 0.0 | 0.9 | 3.7 | 24.2 |
| Kimberley, | T | 76 | 75 | 72 | 64 | 56 | 50 | 51 | 56 | 62 | 68 | 73 | 76 | 65 |
| South Africa | R | 2.8 | 3.0 | 2.8 | 2.0 | 0.7 | 0.5 | 0.1 | 0.3 | 0.2 | 0.8 | 2.1 | 2.9 | 18.2 |
| Maracaibo, | T | 81 | 81 | 83 | 83 | 84 | 84 | 84 | 84 | 84 | 82 | 81 | 81 | 82 |
| Venezuela | R | 0.0 | 0.0 | 0.3 | 0.5 | 2.4 | 1.6 | 1.4 | 1.3 | 3.3 | 4.3 | 2.5 | 0.4 | 18.0 |
| Monterrey, | T | 58 | 62 | 68 | 73 | 79 | 82 | 82 | 83 | 78 | 71 | 64 | 57 | 71 |
| Mexico | R | 0.5 | 0.5 | 0.7 | 1.1 | 1.2 | 2.3 | 2.1 | 2.0 | 4.4 | 2.4 | 1.3 | 1.0 | 19.5 |

T = average monthly temperature in °F
R = rainfall in inches

## LOW LATITUDE DESERT (BWh)

| | | Jan. | Feb. | Mar. | Apr. | May | June | July | Aug. | Sept. | Oct. | Nov. | Dec. | Year |
|---|---|---|---|---|---|---|---|---|---|---|---|---|---|---|
| Cairo, | T | 55 | 57 | 63 | 70 | 76 | 80 | 82 | 82 | 78 | 74 | 65 | 58 | 70 |
| Egypt | R | 0.4 | 0.2 | 0.2 | 0.2 | 0.0 | 0.0 | 0.0 | 0.0 | 0.0 | 0.0 | 0.1 | 0.2 | 1.3 |
| Karachi, | T | 65 | 68 | 75 | 81 | 85 | 87 | 84 | 82 | 82 | 80 | 74 | 67 | 78 |
| Pakistan | R | 0.5 | 0.5 | 0.4 | 0.2 | 0.1 | 0.9 | 2.9 | 1.5 | 0.5 | 0.0 | 0.1 | 0.1 | 7.6 |
| Alice Springs, | T | 83 | 82 | 77 | 73 | 60 | 54 | 53 | 58 | 66 | 74 | 79 | 82 | 70 |
| Australia | R | 1.7 | 1.7 | 1.2 | 0.7 | 0.6 | 0.6 | 0.4 | 0.4 | 0.4 | 0.7 | 1.0 | 1.5 | 10.9 |

T = average montly temperature in °F
R = rainfall in inches

## HUMID SUBTROPICAL (Cfa, Cwa)

| | | Jan. | Feb. | Mar. | Apr. | May | June | July | Aug. | Sept. | Oct. | Nov. | Dec. | Year |
|---|---|---|---|---|---|---|---|---|---|---|---|---|---|---|
| Macon, | T | 50 | 52 | 57 | 64 | 72 | 79 | 81 | 81 | 75 | 68 | 55 | 50 | 66 |
| Georgia | R | 3.4 | 4.3 | 4.9 | 3.7 | 3.3 | 3.3 | 5.6 | 4.2 | 2.8 | 2.0 | 2.4 | 4.0 | 43.9 |
| Washington, | T | 34 | 35 | 43 | 54 | 64 | 72 | 77 | 74 | 68 | 57 | 46 | 36 | 55 |
| D.C. | R | 3.2 | 3.0 | 3.5 | 3.3 | 3.6 | 3.9 | 4.4 | 4.0 | 3.1 | 3.1 | 2.5 | 3.1 | 40.7 |
| Buenos Aires, | T | 74 | 73 | 69 | 61 | 55 | 50 | 49 | 51 | 55 | 60 | 66 | 71 | 61 |
| Argentina | R | 3.1 | 2.7 | 4.4 | 3.5 | 2.9 | 2.5 | 2.2 | 2.5 | 3.0 | 3.5 | 3.1 | 3.9 | 37.3 |
| Hong Kong | T | 60 | 59 | 63 | 70 | 77 | 81 | 82 | 82 | 81 | 76 | 69 | 63 | 72 |
| | R | 1.3 | 1.8 | 2.7 | 5.3 | 12.0 | 15.8 | 14.0 | 14.6 | 9.7 | 5.1 | 1.7 | 1.1 | 85.1 |
| Tokyo, | T | 37 | 39 | 44 | 54 | 62 | 69 | 76 | 78 | 71 | 60 | 50 | 41 | 57 |
| Japan | R | 2.2 | 2.8 | 4.4 | 4.9 | 5.7 | 6.5 | 5.3 | 5.7 | 8.7 | 7.4 | 4.2 | 2.1 | 59.9 |
| Allahabad, | T | 61 | 66 | 77 | 87 | 93 | 93 | 86 | 84 | 84 | 79 | 69 | 62 | 78 |
| India | R | 0.7 | 0.5 | 0.4 | 0.1 | 0.3 | 4.7 | 12.0 | 11.0 | 6.3 | 2.3 | 0.3 | 0.2 | 38.8 |

T = average monthly temperature in °F
R = rainfall in inches

## DRY SUBTROPICAL (Csa)

| | | Jan. | Feb. | Mar. | Apr. | May | June | July | Aug. | Sept. | Oct. | Nov. | Dec. | Year |
|---|---|---|---|---|---|---|---|---|---|---|---|---|---|---|
| San Francisco, | T | 49 | 51 | 53 | 54 | 56 | 57 | 57 | 58 | 60 | 59 | 56 | 51 | 55 |
| California | R | 4.8 | 3.6 | 3.1 | 1.0 | 0.7 | 0.1 | 0.0 | 0.0 | 0.3 | 1.0 | 2.4 | 4.6 | 22.2 |
| Valparaiso, | T | 64 | 63 | 61 | 58 | 56 | 52 | 52 | 53 | 54 | 57 | 60 | 62 | 58 |
| Chile | R | 0.0 | 0.0 | 0.9 | 0.1 | 2.7 | 6.0 | 5.3 | 3.4 | 0.4 | 0.5 | 0.3 | 0.0 | 19.6 |
| Adelaide, | T | 74 | 74 | 70 | 64 | 58 | 53 | 51 | 54 | 57 | 62 | 67 | 71 | 63 |
| Australia | R | 0.7 | 0.7 | 1.0 | 1.8 | 2.8 | 3.1 | 2.7 | 2.5 | 2.0 | 1.7 | 1.2 | 1.0 | 21.2 |
| Rome, | T | 45 | 47 | 51 | 57 | 64 | 71 | 76 | 75 | 70 | 62 | 53 | 46 | 60 |
| Italy | R | 3.2 | 2.7 | 2.9 | 2.6 | 2.2 | 1.5 | 0.7 | 1.0 | 2.5 | 5.0 | 4.4 | 3.9 | 32.7 |
| Athens, | T | 48 | 50 | 53 | 58 | 66 | 74 | 80 | 80 | 73 | 66 | 57 | 52 | 63 |
| Greece | R | 2.1 | 1.8 | 1.3 | 0.9 | 0.8 | 0.6 | 0.3 | 0.6 | 0.7 | 1.4 | 2.9 | 2.5 | 15.9 |
| Algiers, | T | 49 | 50 | 52 | 56 | 61 | 68 | 73 | 75 | 70 | 64 | 57 | 52 | 61 |
| Algeria | R | 4.0 | 2.6 | 3.3 | 2.0 | 1.7 | 0.7 | 0.1 | 0.1 | 1.2 | 3.4 | 4.1 | 4.0 | 27.4 |
| Cape Town, | T | 70 | 70 | 68 | 63 | 59 | 56 | 55 | 56 | 58 | 61 | 64 | 68 | 62 |
| South Africa | R | 0.7 | 0.6 | 0.9 | 1.9 | 3.8 | 4.5 | 3.7 | 3.4 | 2.3 | 1.6 | 1.1 | 0.8 | 25.3 |

T = average monthly temperature in °F
R = rainfall in inches

## MARINE WEST COAST (Cfb)

| | | Jan. | Feb. | Mar. | Apr. | May | June | July | Aug. | Sept. | Oct. | Nov. | Dec. | Year |
|---|---|---|---|---|---|---|---|---|---|---|---|---|---|---|
| Bergen, | T | 34 | 34 | 36 | 42 | 49 | 55 | 58 | 57 | 52 | 45 | 39 | 36 | 45 |
| Norway | R | 9.0 | 6.6 | 6.2 | 4.3 | 4.7 | 4.1 | 5.7 | 7.8 | 9.2 | 9.3 | 8.5 | 8.9 | 84.3 |
| London, | T | 39 | 40 | 42 | 42 | 53 | 59 | 63 | 62 | 59 | 50 | 44 | 40 | 50 |
| England | R | 1.9 | 1.7 | 1.8 | 1.5 | 1.8 | 2.0 | 2.4 | 2.2 | 1.8 | 2.6 | 2.4 | 2.4 | 24.5 |
| Vancouver, | | | | | | | | | | | | | | |
| British | T | 36 | 38 | 42 | 47 | 54 | 59 | 63 | 62 | 56 | 49 | 43 | 48 | 48 |
| Columbia | R | 8.6 | 6.1 | 5.3 | 3.3 | 3.0 | 2.7 | 1.3 | 1.7 | 4.1 | 5.9 | 10.0 | 7.8 | 59.8 |
| Valdivia, | T | 62 | 60 | 58 | 53 | 50 | 45 | 46 | 46 | 48 | 52 | 55 | 59 | 53 |
| Chile | R | 2.6 | 2.9 | 5.5 | 9.3 | 15.7 | 17.2 | 16.3 | 13.7 | 8.4 | 5.5 | 5.0 | 4.4 | 106.3 |
| Dunedin, | T | 58 | 58 | 55 | 52 | 47 | 44 | 42 | 44 | 48 | 51 | 53 | 56 | 51 |
| New Zealand | R | 3.4 | 2.7 | 3.0 | 2.7 | 3.2 | 3.2 | 3.0 | 3.1 | 2.8 | 3.0 | 3.3 | 3.5 | 36.9 |

T = average monthly temperature in °F
R = rainfall in inches

## HUMID CONTINENTAL, WARM SUMMER (Dfa, Dwa)

| | | Jan. | Feb. | Mar. | Apr. | May | June | July | Aug. | Sept. | Oct. | Nov. | Dec. | Year |
|---|---|---|---|---|---|---|---|---|---|---|---|---|---|---|
| Chicago, | T | 25 | 27 | 36 | 47 | 57 | 67 | 73 | 72 | 65 | 54 | 40 | 29 | 49 |
| Illinois | R | 1.9 | 1.8 | 2.7 | 2.8 | 3.6 | 3.5 | 3.1 | 3.1 | 3.2 | 2.6 | 2.4 | 2.0 | 32.9 |
| New York City, | T | 33 | 33 | 41 | 50 | 61 | 70 | 75 | 73 | 67 | 57 | 40 | 36 | 54 |
| New York | R | 3.4 | 3.6 | 3.4 | 3.1 | 3.6 | 4.2 | 4.2 | 4.2 | 3.7 | 3.5 | 2.5 | 3.3 | 41.6 |
| Mukden, | T | 8 | 14 | 30 | 47 | 60 | 70 | 76 | 74 | 61 | 48 | 29 | 14 | 44 |
| China | R | 0.2 | 0.3 | 0.7 | 1.1 | 2.2 | 3.4 | 5.8 | 5.3 | 3.3 | 1.5 | 0.9 | 0.2 | 24.9 |
| Bucharest, | T | 26 | 31 | 41 | 52 | 62 | 70 | 72 | 72 | 63 | 53 | 40 | 31 | 51 |
| Rumania | R | 1.3 | 1.1 | 1.6 | 1.7 | 2.5 | 3.5 | 2.7 | 2.0 | 1.6 | 1.7 | 1.9 | 1.6 | 23.1 |
| Milan, | T | 32 | 38 | 46 | 55 | 63 | 70 | 75 | 73 | 66 | 56 | 44 | 36 | 55 |
| Italy | R | 2.4 | 2.3 | 2.7 | 3.4 | 4.1 | 3.3 | 2.8 | 3.2 | 3.5 | 4.7 | 4.3 | 3.0 | 39.8 |

T = average monthly temperature in °F
R = rainfall in inches

## HUMID CONTINENTAL, COOL SUMMER (Dfb, Dwb)

| | | Jan. | Feb. | Mar. | Apr. | May | June | July | Aug. | Sept. | Oct. | Nov. | Dec. | Year |
|---|---|---|---|---|---|---|---|---|---|---|---|---|---|---|
| Bismarck, | T | 8 | 12 | 25 | 43 | 55 | 64 | 71 | 68 | 58 | 45 | 28 | 15 | 41 |
| North Dakota | R | 0.4 | 0.5 | 0.9 | 1.5 | 2.2 | 3.4 | 2.3 | 1.8 | 1.3 | 1.0 | 0.6 | 0.5 | 16.4 |
| Calgary, | T | 12 | 15 | 25 | 40 | 49 | 56 | 61 | 59 | 51 | 42 | 28 | 19 | 38 |
| Alberta | R | 0.5 | 0.6 | 0.7 | 0.8 | 2.3 | 2.9 | 2.6 | 2.5 | 1.3 | 0.7 | 0.7 | 0.5 | 16.1 |
| Moscow, | T | 13 | 16 | 24 | 39 | 55 | 61 | 66 | 62 | 51 | 40 | 28 | 18 | 39 |
| Soviet Union | R | 1.1 | 0.9 | 1.2 | 1.5 | 1.9 | 2.0 | 2.5 | 2.9 | 2.2 | 1.4 | 1.6 | 1.5 | 21.0 |
| Uppsala, | T | 24 | 23 | 27 | 38 | 49 | 57 | 62 | 59 | 50 | 41 | 32 | 25 | 41 |
| Sweden | R | 1.3 | 1.1 | 1.2 | 1.2 | 1.7 | 2.0 | 2.7 | 2.8 | 2.0 | 2.1 | 1.7 | 1.6 | 21.4 |
| Nemuro, | T | 23 | 22 | 32 | 37 | 44 | 50 | 58 | 63 | 59 | 50 | 39 | 29 | 42 |
| Japan | R | 1.3 | 1.0 | 2.2 | 2.9 | 3.7 | 3.7 | 3.8 | 4.3 | 5.6 | 3.8 | 3.3 | 2.3 | 37.9 |

T = average monthly temperature in °F
R = rainfall in inches

## SUBARCTIC (Dfc, Dfd, Dwc, Dwd)

| | | Jan. | Feb. | Mar. | Apr. | May | June | July | Aug. | Sept. | Oct. | Nov. | Dec. | Year |
|---|---|---|---|---|---|---|---|---|---|---|---|---|---|---|
| Dawson, | T | −23 | −11 | 4 | 29 | 46 | 57 | 59 | 54 | 42 | 25 | 1 | −13 | 22 |
| Yukon | R | 0.8 | 0.8 | 0.5 | 0.7 | 0.9 | 1.3 | 1.6 | 1.6 | 1.7 | 1.3 | 1.3 | 1.1 | 13.6 |
| Churchill, | T | −20 | −15 | −3 | 22 | 32 | 43 | 56 | 53 | 42 | 27 | 8 | −9 | 19 |
| Manitoba | R | 0.6 | 1.1 | 1.1 | 1.0 | 0.9 | 2.0 | 1.8 | 2.4 | 2.6 | 1.3 | 1.2 | 0.8 | 16.8 |
| Nome, | T | 1 | 6 | 8 | 17 | 34 | 45 | 50 | 50 | 41 | 29 | 14 | 6 | 25 |
| Alaska | R | 1.0 | 1.1 | 0.9 | 0.6 | 0.9 | 1.2 | 2.9 | 3.0 | 2.3 | 1.5 | 1.0 | 1.1 | 17.5 |
| Verkhoyansk, | T | −58 | −48 | −24 | 9 | 36 | 56 | 60 | 52 | 36 | 6 | −34 | −51 | 3 |
| Soviet Union | R | 0.2 | 0.1 | 0.1 | 0.2 | 0.3 | 0.9 | 1.0 | 1.0 | 0.5 | 0.4 | 0.3 | 0.1 | 5.0 |
| Okhotsk, | T | −11 | −7 | 7 | 21 | 35 | 45 | 55 | 55 | 46 | 27 | 6 | −8 | 22 |
| Soviet Union | R | 0.1 | 0.1 | 0.1 | 0.2 | 0.5 | 1.1 | 0.5 | 1.8 | 2.1 | 0.7 | 0.2 | 0.2 | 7.5 |

T = average monthly temperature in °F
R = rainfall in inches

## MIDDLE LATITUDE STEPPE (BSk)

| | | Jan. | Feb. | Mar. | Apr. | May | June | July | Aug. | Sept. | Oct. | Nov. | Dec. | Year |
|---|---|---|---|---|---|---|---|---|---|---|---|---|---|---|
| Denver, | T | 30 | 32 | 39 | 47 | 57 | 67 | 72 | 71 | 62 | 51 | 39 | 32 | 50 |
| Colorado | R | 0.4 | 0.5 | 1.0 | 2.1 | 2.4 | 1.4 | 1.8 | 1.4 | 1.0 | 1.0 | 0.6 | 0.7 | 14.3 |
| Tashkent, | T | 30 | 34 | 46 | 58 | 68 | 76 | 80 | 76 | 66 | 54 | 45 | 36 | 56 |
| Soviet Union | R | 1.8 | 1.4 | 2.6 | 2.6 | 1.1 | 0.5 | 0.1 | 0.1 | 0.2 | 1.1 | 1.4 | 1.7 | 14.6 |
| Ankara, | T | 31 | 31 | 41 | 52 | 62 | 68 | 72 | 74 | 65 | 57 | 47 | 36 | 53 |
| Turkey | R | 0.9 | 1.1 | 1.2 | 1.3 | 2.0 | 1.0 | 0.5 | 0.3 | 0.5 | 0.6 | 0.9 | 1.5 | 11.8 |

T = average monthly temperature in °F
R = rainfall in inches

## MIDDLE LATITUDE DESERT (BWk)

| | | Jan. | Feb. | Mar. | Apr. | May | June | July | Aug. | Sept. | Oct. | Nov. | Dec. | Year |
|---|---|---|---|---|---|---|---|---|---|---|---|---|---|---|
| Astrakhan, | T | 19 | 21 | 32 | 48 | 64 | 73 | 77 | 74 | 63 | 50 | 37 | 26 | 49 |
| Soviet Union | R | 0.5 | 0.3 | 0.4 | 0.5 | 0.7 | 0.7 | 0.7 | 0.5 | 0.5 | 0.4 | 0.4 | 0.5 | 5.9 |
| Ely, | T | 23 | 27 | 34 | 43 | 50 | 59 | 68 | 66 | 59 | 46 | 34 | 27 | 45 |
| Nevada | R | 0.8 | 0.7 | 0.9 | 0.9 | 0.9 | 0.5 | 0.7 | 0.5 | 0.6 | 0.7 | 0.6 | 0.7 | 8.5 |
| Port Nolloth, | T | 60 | 60 | 59 | 58 | 57 | 55 | 55 | 54 | 55 | 58 | 59 | 60 | 58 |
| South Africa | R | 0.0 | 0.1 | 0.2 | 0.2 | 0.4 | 0.3 | 0.2 | 0.3 | 0.3 | 0.0 | 0.2 | 0.1 | 2.3 |
| Santa Cruz, | T | 59 | 58 | 54 | 48 | 41 | 35 | 35 | 38 | 43 | 49 | 53 | 56 | 47 |
| Bolivia | R | 0.6 | 0.4 | 0.3 | 0.6 | 0.6 | 0.5 | 0.7 | 0.4 | 0.2 | 0.4 | 0.5 | 0.8 | 5.9 |

T = average monthly temperature in °F
R = rainfall in inches

**TUNDRA (ET)**

| | | Jan. | Feb. | Mar. | Apr. | May | June | July | Aug. | Sept. | Oct. | Nov. | Dec. | Year |
|---|---|---|---|---|---|---|---|---|---|---|---|---|---|---|
| Barrow, | T | −19 | −13 | −14 | −2 | 21 | 35 | 40 | 39 | 31 | 16 | 0 | −15 | 10 |
| Alaska | R | 0.3 | 0.2 | 0.2 | 0.3 | 0.3 | 0.3 | 1.1 | 0.8 | 0.5 | 0.8 | 0.4 | 0.4 | 5.6 |
| Spitsbergen, | T | 4 | −2 | −2 | 8 | 23 | 35 | 42 | 40 | 32 | 22 | 11 | 6 | 18 |
| Norway | R | 1.4 | 1.3 | 1.1 | 0.9 | 0.5 | 0.4 | 0.6 | 0.9 | 1.0 | 1.2 | 1.0 | 1.5 | 11.8 |
| Ivigtut, | T | 19 | 19 | 24 | 31 | 40 | 47 | 50 | 47 | 41 | 34 | 26 | 21 | 33 |
| Greenland | R | 3.3 | 2.7 | 3.4 | 2.4 | 3.6 | 3.0 | 3.3 | 3.8 | 6.0 | 5.9 | 4.4 | 3.1 | 44.9 |

T = average monthly temperature in °F
R = rainfall in inches

# E GLOSSARY

**Ablation** Loss of glacial ice and snow by melting, evaporation, and sublimation.

**Absolute humidity** Weight of water vapor present per unit volume of air, usually expressed as grams of water per cubic meter of air.

**Abyssal plain** Low-relief portion of the deep ocean floors that are covered with a deposit of marine sediments over older volcanic rocks.

**Acid rain** Precipitation having a pH less than 5.6.

**Adiabatic cooling and heating** Change of temperature within an air mass because of compression (resulting in heating) or expansion (resulting in cooling). The air mass does not receive or lose energy.

**Advection** Horizontal heat transfer within the atmosphere by wind movement.

**Advection fog** Fog formed when warm, moist air moves over a cool surface and is cooled to its dew point.

**Air drainage** Flow of cold, heavy air down slopes into lowland areas.

**Air mass** A large uniform body of air that moves as a unit.

**Albedo** Proportion of solar radiation reflected by a surface.

**Alluvial fan** Fan-shaped deposit of alluvium at the point where a stream emerges from a steep mountain channel to a gentle gradient of a plain.

**Alluvium** Deposits of earth materials by a stream or river.

**Alpine glacier** Glacial ice confined by valley walls as it moves from a high mountain crest to lower elevations; also called a valley glacier.

**Anabatic wind** A wind blowing up a slope, usually warm.

**Angle of inclination** Tilting of the axis of the earth, so that it lies at an angle of 23½ degrees to the vertical of the plane of the ecliptic.

**Antarctic Circle** Parallel at 66½ degrees south latitude.

**Antecedent stream** A stream that maintains, during and after uplift, the course it had established prior to uplift.

**Anticline** Rock fold that dips upward toward its center.

**Anticyclone** An area of high atmospheric pressure characterized by diverging, rotating winds, clear skies, and lack of precipitation.

**Aphelion** Position of the earth's orbit that is farthest from the sun.

**Aquiclude** Impermeable and nonporous rock layer that restricts flow of groundwater.

**Arctic Circle** Parallel of latitude at 66½ degrees north.

**Arête** Jagged, sawtooth ridge formed by erosion where two neighboring cirque basins are separated.

**Arroyo** Stream channel which, although carved by water, is usually dry; also known as a wadi.

**Artesian well** Well bored into the earth reaching water which, due to internal pressure, flows spontaneously like a fountain.

**Asthenosphere** A zone within the earth below the lithosphere where the rocks are weaker and slow flowage of rocks takes place.

**Atmospheric pressure** Mass weight of a column of air above a given elevation.

**Atoll** Circular coral reefs and islands enclosing a lagoon.

**Aurora borealis and aurora australis** Bright lights occurring in the skies of the Northern and Southern hemispheres, respectively, caused by the penetration of ionized particles through the thermosphere.

**Azimuthal projection** Map projection that shows direction correctly from a given point on the map.

**Azonal soils** Soils that do not possess developed profiles, such as new alluvial soils.

**Bar** A sand embankment built on the floor of the ocean by waves and currents. May also occur on stream beds.

**Barchan** Sand dune shaped like a crescent in which the cusps face downwind.

**Barometer** Instrument to measure atmospheric pressure.
**Barometric slope** Changes in the barometric surfaces to higher or lower air pressure.
**Barometric surface** Any surface in the atmosphere throughout which the same pressure prevails.
**Barrier reef** Coral reef that is separated from an island or mainland by a lagoon.
**Base level** Lowest elevation to which a stream can erode a land surface.
**Batholith** Very large intrusive igneous rock.
**Bay bar** A spit that encloses the entrance of a bay.
**Bed load** Material transported by a stream along its bed by saltation and traction.
**Bedding plane** Plane dividing sedimentary beds, or layers, of the same or different kind of rock.
**Bedrock** Solid rock of the lithosphere.
**Biomass** Total weight of dry organic matter occupying a unit area; also, the total weight of organic matter in the ecosystem.
**Blowhole** A hole in a sea cave through which waves force water, creating an intermittent fountain.
**Blowouts** Hollows caused by wind erosion.
**Butte** Isolated erosional, flat-summit remnant of a tableland, often bordered with steep-sided escarpments.

**Caldera** A crater of a volcano enlarged by an explosive action.
**Caliche** Hardened layer of limestone deposited on the surface of soil by evaporating capillary water.
**Celestial sphere** The spherical array of planets and stars visible from a given point on the earth.
**Chemical weathering** Reactions that occur between a rock and its surroundings; water, oxygen, and carbon dioxide are normally involved.
**Chinook** Dry, warm wind blowing down the leeward slopes of the Rocky Mountains. The wind is warmed by compression as it descends.
**Chlorophyll** An organic molecule that is a catalyst in photosynthesis.
**Circle of illumination** Boundary line between the daylight and night halves of the earth.
**Cirque** A steep-sided amphitheater high in a mountain, formed by the erosive action of a glacier.
**Cirrus clouds** Feathery, high-altitude clouds composed of ice crystals.
**Classification** Systematic arrangement of phenomena into groups or categories according to established criteria.
**Clastic sedimentary rock** Inorganic sediments that are consolidated into a rock, such as sandstone.
**Cleavage** The property of some rocks of breaking more readily in one or more directions than in others.
**Climate** Average conditions of weather in a particular locality or region.
**Climax soil** The ultimate, stabilized pattern of soil to develop in a region.
**Climax vegetation** Final stage of natural vegetation to develop in a region.
**Col** Notch formed when two cirques meet, producing a high saddle in the mountains.
**Cold front** Steep frontal surface between a confrontation of two masses of air in which the cold air is displacing the warmer air.
**Condensation** Conversion of water vapor to liquid during which process energy is released in the form of latent heat.
**Conduction** Transfer of heat by direct contact from a warmer to a colder body by means of collisions between atomic particles.
**Conformal projection** Map projection on which the shape of any area on the earth is rendered exactly.
**Conic projection** Projection of a portion of the earth on a tangent cone.
**Connate water** Original water trapped in the pores of rocks.
**Consequent stream** A stream whose course was determined by the original slope of the surface on which it developed.
**Continental drift** A general term for the concept originally proposed by Wegener that continents can move relative to one another.
**Continental glacier** A large, thick glacier caused by a buildup of ice on a continent.
**Continental rise** Transition between the continental slope and the deep ocean floor.
**Continental shelf** Shallow ocean area between the shoreline and the continental slope.
**Continental slope** Relatively steep slope between the continental shelf and the continental rise.
**Contour interval** Vertical distance between contour lines.
**Contour line** A line on a map connecting points of equal elevation.
**Convectional precipitation** Precipitation caused by the condensation of water vapor in an updraft of heated air.
**Convergence, zone of** Areas where tectonic plates descend into the mantle, such as in the western Pacific Ocean.
**Coral reef** Ridge of limestone built up by the skeletal remains of tiny marine animals.
**Core** The earth's interior, divided into a molten outer core and a solid inner core.
**Coriolis force** Effect of the earth's rotation in the apparent deflection of moving objects to the right in the Northern Hemisphere and to the left in the Southern Hemisphere.
**Crust** Outermost layer of the lithosphere, ranging from 8 to 65 kilometers (5 to 40 miles) in thickness.
**Crustal deformation** The altering of the earth's crust by volcanic and earthquake actions.
**Cuesta** Resistant layer of rock with a steep slope on one side and a gently dipping back slope.
**Cumulus cloud** Cloud that is formed locally by an updraft of an air mass.
**Cuspate bar** A crescent-shaped bar, or spit, attached to the shore at one end.

**Cuspate foreland** Coastal projection where spits or barrier islands are linked.
**Cut bank** Side of a stream where erosional actions occur.
**Cycle of erosion** Classification of landscapes according to their stage of erosional development.
**Cyclone** A low pressure storm in the middle latitudes, frequently 2,400 kilometers (1,500 miles) in diameter, characterized by converging, rotating winds and frontal precipitation.
**Cyclonic precipitation** Precipitation associated with the passage of a large low pressure system, which has converging winds toward its center and cold and warm fronts developed within its area.
**Cylindrical projection** Map projection based on a cylinder tangent to the earth at the equator.

**Deciduous** Pertaining to plants that shed their leaves at a particular time or season.
**Deflation** Removal of loose materials from a surface by wind.
**Degradation** Lowering of a stream channel by action of water.
**Delta** Alluvial deposit at the mouth of a stream in a lake or ocean.
**Dendritic stream pattern** Treelike drainage pattern in which tributaries enter the main stream at acute angles.
**Denudation** Lowering of land surface by erosional processes.
**Desert pavement** Mantle of wind-sorted pebbles and stones that covers an arid surface.
**Desert varnish** Wind-polished, rocky plain in a dry region.
**Dew point** Temperature at which relative humidity reaches 100 percent.
**Diastrophism** Processes that have disturbed the earth's crust by bending, folding, warping, or faulting.
**Differential weathering and erosion** Processes in which bedrock is weathered and eroded at different rates due to differing resistance.
**Dike** Tabular intrusive, igneous body that bisects older rock.
**Discharge** Volume of water transported by a stream past a given point within a specified time.
**Dissolved load** Material carried in solution by a river.
**Distributaries** Many smaller channels into which the main channel of a stream is divided.
**Divergence, Zone of** The area where tectonic plates are moving apart.
**Divide** Bridge or section of high ground between two drainage basins.
**Doldrums** Area of low pressure bordering the equator in the intertropical convergence.
**Dome** Large uplift of sedimentary rock produced by tectonic forces such as a volcano.
**Drainage basin** Total area drained by a stream system.
**Drainage network** System of stream channels.
**Drift** Collective term for all deposits derived from a glacier.
**Drumlin** Elongated mound of glacial till that has its long axis in the direction of the movement of the ice.
**Dry adiabatic rate** Rate of cooling of a rising air mass by expansion when no condensation occurs (10.2°C/1,000 meters, or 5.6°F/1,000 feet).
**Dynamic equilibrium** Action of a system, such as a river network, to achieve a state of equilibrium that is rarely attained. The equilibrium is altered by a change in the available energy that moves the system.

**Earth grid** Imaginary scheme of lines over the surface of the earth by which location and direction may be determined.
**Earth's axis** Imaginary line extending through the earth from pole to pole.
**Easterly wave** Weak, low pressure trough that moves east to west in the trade winds.
**Ecotone** Transition zone between neighboring plant communities, such as grassland and forest, in which plants of both communities compete for dominance.
**Edaphic** Pertaining to the soil and soil factors; affected by soil rather than climate.
**Ekman spiral** The pattern of change in water and wind direction and velocity with depth or height.
**Electromagnetic spectrum** Complete range of wavelengths and frequencies of electromagnetic radiation, from gamma rays to the longest radio and light waves.
**Elevation** Height above the level of the sea.
**Eluviation** Downward movement of suspended or dissolved material from the A-horizon to the B-horizon of a soil.
**Emergent coast** Coast that has risen relative to the sea so that submarine features are exposed.
**End moraine** Terminal moraine. An accumulation of glacial drift at the end or margin of a glacier.
**Entrophy** Degree of uniformity in an earth system.
**Ephemeral plant** Short-lived plant.
**Ephemeral stream** Stream that flows only during or after precipitation.
**Epiphytes** Plants that extract water from the air and nutrients from plant matter found on tree branches.
**Equal-area projection** Map projection on which the size of areas on the earth is accurately shown.
**Equator** Great circle around the earth equidistant from the two poles.
**Equinox** Time when the sun crosses the equator and day and night are of equal length all over the world. The vernal equinox occurs on about March 21; the autumnal equinox on about September 23.
**Erg** Large area of sand and dunes in a desert region.
**Erosion** Picking up and transporting of weathered material from a higher to a lower elevation.
**Erratic** A large rock fragment transported by glacial ice, so that it is different from the bedrock on which it lies.
**Escarpment** Precipitous face of a region of high local relief.
**Esker** Long, narrow ridge of stratified alluvium, deposited by a flowing stream in or under a stagnant glacier.
**Evapotranspiration** Process by which the earth's surface

loses moisture by evaporation of water and by transpiration from plants.

**Exosphere** Thin outer layer of the atmosphere that extends from about 1,000 kilometers (620 miles) to perhaps 10,000 kilometers (6,200 miles) in altitude. At its outer limits, air molecules disappear.

**Exotic stream** Stream originating in a humid region that has sufficient water to carry it through an arid region.

**Extrusive igneous rocks** Molten magma that penetrated to the earth's surface before it cooled and solidified.

**Fault** Fracture in the earth's crust along which relative displacement has occurred.

**Fault block** A mass of rock that moves as a unit during fault movement; it is bounded by faults on at least two sides.

**Fault scarp** Exposed face of a fault along which one crustal block has been displaced vertically relative to another.

**Ferrallitization** Process of soil leaching that produces the red iron or aluminum-rich soils of the rainy tropics.

**Ferrel's law** Tendency of all moving bodies of water or air to deflect to the right in the Northern Hemisphere and to the left in the Southern Hemisphere as a result of the earth's rotation.

**Ferricrete** Hard crust on tropical soil formed by concentrates of iron and aluminum oxides.

**Fetch** Open stretches of water across which winds blow in a nearly constant direction, influencing wave height.

**Fiord** A steep-walled, glacial, U-shaped mountain valley opening onto the sea.

**Firn ice** Compacted granular snow formed by partial freezing and refreezing due to compaction of overlying snow cover; intermediate form of glacial ice; also known as *névé.*

**Firn line** Boundary between accumulated firn and glacial ice.

**First order relief** The largest relief features on the earth—continents and ocean basins.

**Flagform trees** Trees stripped of their leaves, and even their bark, by winds carrying sand, sleet, or snow particles.

**Floodplain** A plain that has been formed by deposits of sediments carried by the stream which it borders.

**Flood stage** Level of water when a stream is flooding.

**Flood tides** Period of rising sea level along a coast caused by tides.

**Fluvial processes** Processes associated with the work of streams and rivers in the shaping of landforms.

**Foehn** A dry, warm wind blowing down the leeward slope of a mountain caused by adiabatic heating of descending air.

**Folding** Bending of rock strata.

**Fossil dunes** Relic dunes that developed in response to severe drought conditions during the Pleistocene.

**Friction** Forces that retard movement of any object on the earth or in the atmosphere.

**Fringing reef** A coral reef built laterally from the shore.

**Front** Surface boundary between two types of air masses.

**Frontal precipitation** Precipitation that occurs when an air mass rises over another air mass along a front.

**Frost wedging** Fracturing of bedrock by the expansive power of water freezing, melting, and refreezing in joints and cracks.

**Full moon** Phase of the moon when it is aligned, or nearly so, with the sun and earth during opposition.

**Galaxy** A mammoth number of stars held together by gravitational attraction.

**General atmospheric circulation** Planetary circulation of winds that are persistent features of the atmosphere.

**Genetic classification** Classification based on the causes, theory, or origins of phenomena.

**Geoanticline** A large, gentle, elongated upwarping of an area, commonly many square kilometers in area.

**Geometric radiation law** The law stating that the energy received per unit of area and per unit of time decreases as the square of the radius from the sun.

**Geomorphic surfaces** Landform surfaces produced by either erosion or depositional processes.

**Geostrophic wind** Wind blowing at right angles to the pressure gradient and parallel to isobars; also ocean currents.

**Geosyncline** A large, gentle, elongated downwarping of an area in which many thousands of meters of sediments are deposited.

**Geyser** A spring that throws forth intermittent jets of heated water and steam.

**Glacial budget** Balance between the accumulation and ablation of snow and ice in a glacier.

**Glacial epoch** A subdivision of a period in the geologic time scale when an ice age prevailed.

**Glacial ice** Any ice that forms in or was part of a glacier; recrystallized snow forming large ice crystals.

**Glacial milk** Finely ground sediments that appear whitish in water flowing from a glacier.

**Glacial spillway** Channel created by tremendous quantities of water pouring from a continental glacier at a time of pause in its retreat.

**Glacial stairway** A glacial valley whose side is shaped like a broad stairway caused by the uneven erosion of the underlying rock by glacial action.

**Glacial till** Unstratified and unsorted rock materials that are transported and deposited by glaciers.

**Glacial trough** A deep, steep-sided, U-shaped, glacially eroded valley originating at a cirque.

**Glacier** A mass of moving ice.

**Glaciofluvial deposit** Sorted glacial drift deposited by meltwater.

**Glaciolacustrine deposit** Sorted glacial drift deposited in lakes associated with the margins of glaciers.

**Gleization** Pedogenic regime developed where soil is waterlogged.

**Gley soils** Soils developed under wet conditions; blue-gray to black in color due to availability of iron compounds.

**Gnomonic projection** Only projection where all great circles are straight lines; used in navigation.

**Gondwanaland** An ancient supercontinent of the Paleozoic and early Mesozoic eras, consisting of Africa, Antarctica, Australia, India, South America, and several smaller areas.

**Graben** A portion of the earth's crust that has sunk downward in relation to adjacent areas. It is bounded on at least two sides by faults.

**Gradational processes** Processes by which the landforms are worn down and depressions filled in by water, ice, and wind in the movement of earth materials from high to low elevations.

**Graded stream** A river in equilibrium that has just the slope and velocity to transport the load provided by the drainage basin.

**Gradient** Degree of slope of a stream.

**Gravitational water** Water which moves freely through the soil due to gravitational forces.

**Gravity** Force of attraction exerted by the earth.

**Gravity spring** A stream of water that flows by the pull of gravity.

**Great circle** Largest circumference of the earth that can be drawn.

**Greenhouse effect** The warming of the atmosphere that occurs because the atmosphere is nearly transparent to short-wave solar radiation, but nearly opaque to long-wave terrestrial radiation. As a result the surface of the earth receives not only solar radiation but also the longer wave radiation absorbed by the atmosphere and reradiated. Also known as the *atmospheric effect.*

**Greenwich mean time** Time at zero degrees longitude; provides the base for the earth's 24 time zones.

**Groin** Jetty extending from the shore to control the flow of longshore currents.

**Ground moraine** An accumulation of till released from a glacier during ablation.

**Groundwater** Water within the earth; especially in the zone of accumulation.

**Guyot** A steep, isolated pinnacle rising from the ocean floor, formed by the slow subsidence of a volcanic island. Also known as a *sea mount.*

**Hadley cell** A thermal circulation between the tropics and the subtropics. The trade winds are a manifestation of the Hadley cell.

**Hailstones** Precipitation that consists of pellets or balls of ice that have concentric layers formed by repeated cycling due to strong convectional currents.

**Hamada** A desert area of pebbles and rock fragments remaining after deflation removes the lighter material. Also known as *desert pavement.*

**Hanging valley** A tributary valley whose floor is higher than that of the main stream valley at its junction. Commonly caused by glaciation.

**Hardpan** Dense, compacted, clay-rich layer developed in subsoils as an end product of excessive illuviation.

**Headlands** Cape or promontory that extends into the ocean; usually prominent.

**Heat** A form of energy associated with the rate of vibration of molecules.

**Heat balance** Relationship between the amount of solar radiation entering the atmosphere and the loss of energy from the atmosphere.

**Heat island** An area that is warmer than the surrounding area, for example, a city versus the surrounding rural area.

**Hekistotherms** Low shrubs and plants of the arctic that thrive when the average annual temperature is below freezing.

**High** An area of high pressure; an anticyclone.

**Histosol** Soils composed largely of plant material; usually developed in a waterlogged environment.

**Hogback ridge** Narrow, sharp-crested ridge with steep slopes on its sides; formed by resistant, sharply tilted rock.

**Holocoenotic environment** An environment that acts as a single unit or system due to lack of barriers. A single change in the environment will affect the total system.

**Homocline** An earth structure in which the strata dip uniformly in one direction; for example, one limb of an anticline or syncline, or part of a monocline.

**Homolographic projection** An equal-area projection on which the parallels are straight lines and all meridians except the central one are ellipses.

**Homolosine projection** An equal-area projection combining the features of the sinusoidal and homolographic projections.

**Horizon** The circle that bounds the part of the earth's surface visible from a given point.

**Horizon, soil** Distinctive horizontal layers in soil, produced by pedogenic processes.

**Horn** A sharp, pyramidal peak formed by headward erosion of glacial cirques.

**Horst** Vertically uplifted block of the earth bounded by faults on either side.

**Hot spot** A volcanic center persisting for millions of years thought to exist above a rising plume of mantle material.

**Hot spring** A flow of water that is heated in the interior of the earth.

**Humidity** Any one of a number of measures of the water vapor content of the atmosphere.

**Humus** Organic material found on the surface and within soil horizons in various stages of decomposition.

**Hurricane** A severe tropical cyclone with a low pressure center of 80 to 800 kilometers (50 to 500 miles) and wind movement over 65 knots.

**Hydration** The attachment of water molecules to molecules of other elements or compounds without chemical change.

**Hydrologic cycle** The flow and exchange of water throughout the atmosphere, ground, and oceans; complete circulation of water in the earth system.

**Hydrolysis** The union of water with other substances, involving chemical change and formation of new compounds.
**Hydrophytes** Plants that survive in water.
**Hydrosphere** The major subsystem consisting of all water on the earth.
**Hydrostatic equilibrium** Balance between the vertical pressure gradient force and the force of gravity acting on the atmosphere.
**Hygroscopic** Having an affinity for water.

**Ice age** Age when large portions of the earth were covered by continental glaciers. The most recent ice age was known as the Pleistocene epoch.
**Ice cap** Small ice sheets located at high elevations in mountains.
**Ice sheet** Mass of glacial ice that is continental in size, as in Antarctica.
**Iceberg** Free-floating mass of glacial ice detached from a glacier into a body of water.
**Ice-scoured plain** A plain formed by the erosional action of glaciers.
**Igneous rock** Rock formed when molten magma cools and crystallizes.
**Illuviation** Deposition of soil components in the subsoil (B-horizon) by gravitational water.
**Inceptisols** Poorly developed soils with weak profiles developed in humid regions of recent deposits, such as alluvial, glacial, aeolian, or volcanic materials.
**Inclination of the earth** The tilting of the axis of the earth, so that it lies at an angle of 23½ degrees to the vertical from the plane of the ecliptic.
**Insolation** Radiation received from the sun.
**Interfaces** Boundary between systems where the interchange of energy occurs.
**Interfluve** Higher land that separates two river valleys.
**Interglacial stage** Period of warmth during an ice age when the glaciers recede temporarily.
**Intermittent stream** A stream that has water only during and after periods of precipitation.
**International date line** The meridian at approximately 180 degrees longitude; internationally accepted as the line where the new day begins first.
**Intertropical convergence** Zone of low pressure between approximately 5° north and 5° south latitude, where the trade winds from both sides of the equator converge and are forced to rise.
**Intertropical front** The front that may develop between the trade winds at the intertropical convergence.
**Intrazonal soils** Major soil order of the 1938 American classification system. These soils have well-developed profiles, reflecting local environmental conditions of parent material, drainage, and slope.
**Intrusive igneous rock** Molten magma that solidified beneath the surface.
**Inversion, temperature** A situation where air at lower altitudes is cooler than air immediately above it.
**Ion** Electrically charged atom that has an excess or a deficiency of electrons.
**Ionosphere** A region of the atmosphere above about 70 kilometers (40 miles) that is dense in ions.
**Island arc** A chain of islands, generally volcanic in origin, rising from the deep sea floor and located close to continents.
**Isobar** A line on a map connecting points of equal barometric pressure.
**Isochron** Line that connects points of the same geologic age.
**Isohyet** A line connecting points of equal precipitation.
**Isorithm** A line on a map connecting points of the same numerical value, such as an isotherm or isobar.
**Isostasy** Theory that the earth's crust floats in hydrostatic equilibrium in the denser material of the mantle.
**Isotherm** A line on a map connecting points of equal temperature.
**Isotope** An element that has an identical number of protons in its nuclei but varying numbers of neutrons.

**Jet stream** Narrow bands of high velocity winds traveling at 120 to 640 kilometers per hour (75 to 250 miles per hour) in the upper atmosphere.
**Jetty** A structure built from the shore into the ocean to protect a harbor or navigable passage from being closed by deposits from longshore currents.
**Joint** A fracture in a rock not accompanied by dislocation.
**Jointing** A system of fractures in a rock mass.
**Juvenile water** Water derived from the interior of the earth in rock-forming or tectonic processes that has not existed previously as meteoric water.

**Kame** A low mound, knob, or short irregular ridge composed of stratified sand and gravel deposited by glacial meltwater in ice pits, crevasses, and deltas at the ice margin.
**Kame terrace** Landform developed along the margin of a glacier from accumulation of glaciofluvial deposits of sand and gravel in a valley in an area of high relief.
**Karst topography** Landforms developed by the dissolving of limestone bedrock by groundwater.
**Katabatic wind** A wind blowing down a slope, usually cold; the opposite of *anabatic.*
**Kettle** Depression formed by melting of an ice mass embedded in a glacial till plain.
**Kettle moraine** A terminal or recessional moraine whose surface is marked by steep-sided, bowl-shaped depressions called kettles that form when a block of glacial ice is stranded, becomes covered with till, and subsequently melts.
**Kinetic energy** Energy formed from moving objects; sometimes called energy of motion.

**Knickpoint** A sharp vertical break that creates a fall in the longitudinal profile of a stream.

**Krummholz** Limiting of the limbs of trees in the subarctic to the height above the snow cover.

**Laccolith** Massive igneous intrusion that bends overlying rock upward, creating a domal structure.

**Lagoon** A shallow water body that is protected from the ocean by a depositional feature, such as a barrier beach.

**Laminar flow** Streamline flow in which the water moves smoothly; speed and direction are generally steady.

**Land breeze** Local wind blowing from land toward the water during the night in a coastal region.

**Langley** Unit of energy defined as one calorie received per square centimeter of area.

**Lapse rate** Temperature decrease from 1.55° to 1.65°C (3.3° to 3.5°F) for each 300-meter (1,000-foot) rise in elevation in the troposphere.

**Latent heat of condensation** Energy released when one gram of gaseous vapor condenses to a liquid at the same temperature; equal to the latent heat of vaporization at the same temperature.

**Latent heat of vaporization** Energy required to change one gram of water from a liquid to a gaseous state at the same temperature.

**Lateral moraine** Ridge of till deposited along the sides of an alpine glacier composed mostly of material that fell from the valley walls.

**Lateral planation** Process of valley-floor widening by the action of streams that erode valley walls on the outside of each meander.

**Laterite** A highly leached soil that is found in the humid tropics, rich in iron and aluminum oxides and low in humus.

**Laterization** The pedogenic process that produces iron-rich soils in the wet tropics.

**Latitude** Measurement of distance in degrees north and south of the equator.

**Lava** Molten magma expelled from a volcano; material from which igneous rock is formed.

**Lava cone** A conical mountain produced by lava.

**Leaching** Removal of soluble materials from the surface layers of the soil by the action of percolating water.

**Leeward** Located on the side facing away from the wind movement.

**Lithification** Processes of compaction and cementation that transform elastic sediments into solid sedimentary rock.

**Lithosphere** The rigid outer layer of the earth, including the crust and upper mantle.

**Littoral transport** The movement of sediments along the shore.

**Local water budget** The system to determine the components of water distribution in a local area. Precipitation, runoff, evapotranspiration, and soil moisture are included.

**Loess** Deposits of wind-blown silt derived from arid or glacial regions. It lacks visible layers and is capable of maintaining nearly vertical cliffs.

**Longitude** The measurement of distance in degrees east and west of the prime meridian.

**Longitudinal profile** Plot of the vertical elevation of a stream bed versus its horizontal distance from its source to its mouth.

**Longshore current** A near-shore current that flows parallel to the shore.

**Long-wave radiation** Electromagnetic radiation emitted by the earth; waves more than 4.0 microns in amplitude; also infrared radiation.

**Low** An area of low pressure.

**Magma** Molten material originating in the earth's interior that may reach the earth's surface as lava during volcanic eruptions.

**Magmatic water** Water formed when hydrogen and oxygen unite during volcanic activity.

**Magnetic anomaly** Evidence that the earth's ancient magnetic field was reversed with respect to the present-day field, seen in rocks originating from mid-ocean ridges.

**Magnetic declination** The deviation of the magnetic compass from true north.

**Magnetic north** North direction determined by magnetic compass.

**Magnetic reversal** A change in the earth's magnetic field between normal and reversed polarity.

**Mantle** The interior of the earth lying between the crust and the core. It is composed of high-density rocks that are molten near the outer margin.

**Mantle plume** A long, narrow neck through which hot mantle material is extruded. Plumes are thought to cause many volcanic islands, including the Hawaiian Islands.

**Map** A representation of a portion of the curved earth on a plane surface.

**Map scale** The ratio between the actual size of an area and its size on a map.

**Maquis** Sclerophyllous woodland and plant community adapted to periodic droughts and found in the Mediterranean area; known as *chaparral* in California.

**Marine terrace** An ancient wave-cut cliff and wave-cut bench that lie above the present shoreline. It is developed by uplift or by falling sea level.

**Mass wasting** Movement of surface material down a slope due to the earth's gravitational forces.

**Mature landscape** A term used by W. M. Davis to describe a landscape that is all in slope and thoroughly dissected by streams, with no original surface preserved and no new surface developed.

**Meander** A series of loops and curves in a stream course.

**Meander scar** A meander that has been abandoned by a stream and filled in with sediments.

**Medial moraine** A moraine in or carried upon the middle of a glacier and parallel to its side. It is usually formed by the merging of a tributary and a main glacier in alpine glaciation.

**Megathermal** Climates characterized by warm, humid conditions throughout the year.

**Mercator projection** Conformal map, mathematically produced, with parallels and meridians at right angles so that all straight lines have true compass bearings.

**Meridian** An imaginary line that connects points of the same longitude.

**Mesa** A broad, flat-topped erosional remnant flanked on at least one side by a steep cliff.

**Mesopause** Top of the mesosphere layer of the atmosphere, at about 100 kilometers (60 miles).

**Mesophyte** A plant that requires average amounts of water and cannot adapt to drought or excessive moisture.

**Mesosphere** Layer of the atmosphere above the stratosphere, characterized by temperatures that decrease with altitude. It is located 400 to 1,000 kilometers (240 to 650 miles) above the earth's surface.

**Mesothermal** Climates characterized by seasonal changes.

**Mesquite** A spiny, drought-adapted shrub found in the desert areas of southwestern United States and northern Mexico.

**Metamorphic rock** Rocks, either igneous or sedimentary, that have been altered in texture, mineralogy, or composition through heat and pressure.

**Meteoric water** Water that originated in or is derived from the atmosphere.

**Microclimate** Climate associated with a small area at or near the surface of the earth.

**Microthermal** Climates characterized by cold conditions throughout the year.

**Mid-ocean ridge** A long, broad ridge that lies approximately in the middle of most ocean basins, except north Pacific Ocean. Commonly it rises 1 to 3 kilometers (0.6 to 1.8 miles) above the ocean floor, is 2,000 to 4,000 kilometers (1,200 to 2,800 miles) long, and is completely submerged.

**Mineral** A naturally occurring inorganic substance with a definite chemical composition.

**Moho** Boundary marked by rapid change in seismic velocity that separates the earth's crust from the underlying mantle; also known as the *Mohorovičić discontinuity* or *M-discontinuity.*

**Monadnock** An isolated, low hill that is an erosional remnant on a plain.

**Monsoon** A wind that reverses direction between summer and winter. A classic monsoon area is southeast Asia.

**Moraine** Unsorted till deposited by a glacier; forms include *terminal moraine, ground moraine, recessional moraine,* and *lateral moraine.*

**Morphology** The shape and dimensions of any object.

**Mountain breeze** Cool, dense air flowing down the slope of a mountain toward a valley during the night.

**Mountain glacier** Any glacier in a mountain range except an ice cap or ice sheet; also known as an *alpine glacier.*

**Multiple glaciation** Concept that repeated periods of glaciation advanced and retreated during the Pleistocene.

**Muskeg** Poorly drained, vegetation-rich marshes and swamps overlying permafrost areas in the polar climatic regions.

**Natural arch** An opening through a narrow wall of rock.

**Natural levees** An elevated embankment that parallels some streams and acts to contain their waters.

**Natural vegetation** Climax vegetation in a region where there has been little or no human modification.

**Neap tide** The two periods during the month when tides are lowest. It occurs when the sun and moon are at a 90-degree angle with the earth.

**Nebula** A flattened, rotating disk of interstellar matter.

**Negative feedback** Processes that trigger a system that is in equilibrium to changes that restore its original state.

**Net (glacial) budget** The difference between the amount of snow or ice accumulated and the amount lost by ablation in a glacier during one year, or averaged over a longer time period.

**Neutral coast** A coast that has experienced neither emergence nor submergence.

**Neutron** A fundamental particle with no electrical charge found in the nuclei of atoms.

**Névé** See *firn ice.*

**Nimbostratus cloud** A dark, thick layer of clouds that covers the entire sky, and from which prolonged precipitation occurs.

**Nimbus cloud** A cloud description to indicate precipitation; for example, a cumulonimbus cloud is a cumulus cloud from which precipitation is falling.

**Normal fault** A fault in which the hanging wall, or block above the fault plane, has moved downward relative to the footwall.

**Nutrient cycle** Cycling of nutrients between organisms and their environment.

**Oasis** A fertile spot in a desert.

**Oblate spheroid** A sphere that is flattened or depressed at the poles; for example, the earth.

**Occluded front** The front formed by the process of occlusion, when a cold front overtakes a warm front. The warm air mass is lifted, cutting off its contact with the earth's surface.

**Ocean current** Horizontal movement of ocean water that is usually a response to major atmospheric circulation.

**Oceanic ridge** High ridge on the ocean floor where new crustal material is being formed by volcanic activity.

**Oceanic trench** Long, narrow zone on the ocean floor that has great depth; the place where one crustal plate is descending beneath another in the process of subduction.

**Offshore bar** Beach material that is deposited in the zone of wave break.

**Old age landscape** Term used by W. M. Davis to describe a landscape reduced to a plain of low relief with broad river valleys and low, isolated hills.

**Orbit** The path described by a celestial body, such as the earth, in its revolution around another body.

**Orders of relief** Classification of relief features of the earth's surface into different orders of magnitude.

**Orogeny** Period in geologic history associated with major tectonic or mountain-building activity.

**Orographic precipitation** Precipitation resulting from the condensation of water vapor in an air mass that is forced to rise to a higher elevation.

**Outcrop** Bedrock exposed at the earth's surface.

**Outwash plain** Plain created of sediments carried out of a glacier and deposited by meltwater streams.

**Overthrust fault** Nearly horizontal fault in which rock layers are sheared off and thrust on top of adjacent rock masses.

**Oxbow lake** The lake created by an abandoned river channel on a floodplain.

**Oxidation** Chemical union of oxygen with other elements to form new chemical compounds.

**Oxisols** Thoroughly leached soils of the wet tropics, characterized by an oxic horizon of clay and iron and aluminum oxides and hydroxides with virtually all bases removed by leaching.

**Ozone** Gas with a molecule consisting of three atoms of oxygen ($O_3$). It forms a layer in the atmosphere that absorbs much of the ultraviolet radiation before it reaches the earth.

**Paleoclimatology** The study of the climates of geologic eras.

**Paleomagnetism** The record of ancient magnetism in volcanic rocks.

**Pangea** A hypothetical supercontinent that existed about 200 million years ago.

**Parabolic sand dune** A dune with its concave side facing the wind and its peaks pointed into the wind.

**Parallel** An imaginary line connecting points of the same latitude.

**Parallelism of axis** The parallel position of the axis of the earth, at any time in its orbit around the sun, to its position at any other time. This parallelism is due to the fixed inclination of the earth.

**Parent material** The original material from which soil is derived. Either bedrock or transported material may provide the basis for soil formation.

**PE index** Precipitation effectiveness is calculated by dividing the monthly precipitation by the monthly evaporation to obtain the PE ratio. The sum of the 12 monthly PE ratios is called the PE index.

**Pedalfers** A class of soil rich in iron and aluminum compounds due to leaching of the basic materials. It is found in humid regions.

**Pediment** A gently sloping surface located at the foot of a mountain range in an arid region, usually covered with fluvial deposits from streams originating in the higher elevations. The pediment is formed when erosion causes the mountain front to retreat.

**Pedocals** Soil developed in drier regions and characterized by an accumulation of calcium carbonate in the upper horizons.

**Pedogenic regimes** The soil-forming processes, each of which produces distinct soil types as a response to variations in temperature, moisture, and biotic activities.

**Peds** Soil aggregate or mass of individual mineral particles that have a distinctive shape that characterizes a soil structure.

**Peneplain** A theoretical plain characterized by "old age" in W. M. Davis's cycle of erosion. The land mass has been reduced to nearly base level by stream erosion in a humid region.

**Perennial stream** A stream in which water flows continuously.

**Perihelion** The point in the earth's orbit that is closest to the sun.

**Permafrost** Perennially frozen layer of soil and underlying rock at depths of a few feet in cold, moist regions.

**Permeability** The measure of a material's ability to transmit a fluid, such as water.

**pH** Measure of soil acidity or alkalinity; a measurement of the concentration of hydrogen ions in soil moisture.

**Photochemical reaction** A chemical reaction in the atmosphere triggered by sunlight on such pollutants as nitric oxide and carbons, often creating a secondary pollutant, smog.

**Photoperiodism** A response of an organism, such as a plant, to the length of the day.

**Photosphere** The luminous envelope of the sun.

**Photosynthesis** The process by which green plants utilize carbon dioxide, water, and sunlight to produce plant-forming tissue.

**Piedmont glacier** The coalescing of valley glaciers at the base of a mountain range, forming a thick, continuous sheet of ice.

**Pitted outwash plain** A plain with depressions that are occupied by lakes or marshes. It is formed by the deposition of glaciofluvial materials around isolated masses of glacial ice that subsequently melted.

**Plane of the ecliptic** An imaginary plane that passes through the sun and extends outward to all points on the earth's orbit.

**Planetary albedo** The shortwave radiation reflected by the earth's surface.

**Plant community** Association of vegetation types that exist through time and are in harmony with their environment.

**Plate tectonics** A theory of global tectonics in which the lithosphere is divided into a number of segments of *plates* whose pattern of motion is that of rigid bodies that move about various poles of rotation. At the boundaries of the plates, deformation and earthquakes generally occur.

**Plateau** A surface of low local relief occurring at a high elevation.

**Playa** A lake bed in an arid region that is dry most of the time; a basin where water accumulates after precipitation but soon evaporates.

**Pleistocene** The epoch from 2.5 million years ago to about 10,000 years ago; this epoch is best known for its continental glaciation.

**Plucking** Process by which active glaciers carry away fractured and weathered bedrock.

**Plutonic rock** Mass of igneous rock formed by cooling magma deep within the earth.

**Podzolization** Soil-forming process in humid climates with long, cold winters, involving the breakdown of clays, the eluviation of iron, cations, and humus, leaving a residue of silica.

**Polar easterlies** Easterly blowing winds that move from the polar high toward the subpolar lows and are deflected westward by the Coriolis force.

**Polar front** A line of demarcation at the surface of the earth between air masses of polar and tropical origin.

**Polar high** High pressure area centered over the poles where the atmosphere is settling and diverging.

**Pore space** Spaces between the particles that make up rocks and soils; place of storage and movement of water.

**Porosity** The amount of pore space between individual soil or rock particles, which determines the storage capacity for liquids of the earth material.

**Potential evapotranspiration** Hypothetical rate at which water would be lost to the atmosphere from the earth and vegetation where there is always an available supply of water.

**Precipitation effectiveness** Effectiveness of precipitation in supporting plant growth. It is calculated by dividing the monthly precipitation by the monthly evaporation to obtain the PE ratio.

**Pressure** A force exerted per unit area by collision of molecules; measured in inches or millibars of mercury.

**Pressure belts** Zones of high or low pressure that encircle the earth parallel to the equator.

**Pressure gradient** Rate of change of pressure occurring over a horizontal distance.

**Prime meridian** An arbitrary meridian selected as the base line in order to measure longitude.

**Projection** Any method that transfers the position of places on the earth's surface to a flat map.

**Radial drainage pattern** Streams that extend in all directions from a central elevated landform, such as a volcano.

**Radiation** Transmission of heat through space by electromagnetic waves.

**Radiation fog** Fog that forms when moist air is cooled to its dew point by contact with the ground, which has been cooled by radiation heat loss.

**Rain shadow** Leeward side of a mountain range, where the air mass is descending and heating, resulting in dry conditions.

**Recessional moraine** Glacial deposit behind the terminal moraine, marking pauses in the retreat of a continental or alpine glacier.

**Reef** A chain of rocks or ridge of sand lying at or near the surface of the water.

**Reg** Desert surface of gravel and pebbles when the finer material has been removed by wind erosion.

**Regolith** A covering of loose stones laid upon the solid bedrock.

**Rejuvenation** Interruption of the cycle of erosion when an area is uplifted or when a climatic change occurs. The cycle is thus renewed.

**Relative humidity** The ratio of the air's water vapor content in relation to its water vapor capacity at that temperature if it were saturated; usually expressed as a percentage.

**Relief** Difference in elevation between the highest and lowest points within a local area.

**Remote sensing** Study of the earth's surface from space by using forms of electromagnetic radiation.

**Representative fraction** A means of measuring distance on a map in terms of the ratio of distance on the map to the corresponding distance on the earth.

**Reverse fault** A fault in which the hanging wall moves upward in relation to the footwall; also known as a *thrust fault.*

**Revolution** The annual movement of the earth in its orbit around the sun.

**Rhumb line** A line on the surface of a sphere which makes equal oblique angles with all meridians.

**Ria shoreline** A shoreline that is drowned by submergence of the coast, forming long bays and inlets.

**Richter scale** A scale of earthquake magnitude based on the motions of a seismograph.

**Rift valley** A valley formed by a down-faulted block of the earth's surface; an area where divergence occurs.

**Rill** A tiny surface channel where runoff may first collect; usually only a few centimeters deep.

**Rip current** A strong, narrow jet of water flowing away from the shore, formed by return of water piled up at the shore by incoming waves.

**Rivulet** A small stream or brook.

**Roche moutonnée** A bedrock hill that has been subjected to intensive glacial abrasion on its upstream side and some plucking on its downstream side.

**Rock** Solid mineral matter of any kind occurring naturally in large quantities; forms a considerable part of the earth's mass.

**Rock flour** Ground-up rock produced by the grinding action of a glacier.

**Rock glacier** Masses of rock that contain ice in the spaces between the rock blocks.

**Rossby waves** Undulations in the flow of upper-level westerly winds in the middle latitudes.

**Rotation** The daily turning of the earth on its polar axis.

**Runoff** Flow of water from the surface of the land.

**Salinization** Pedogenic regime in which salt is found in the soil or on its surface due to the evaporation of saline water.

**Saltation** Leaping or jumping motion of earth particles driven by wind or flowing water.

**Sand dune** Mounds of loose, windblown sand, usually with gentle slopes on the windward side and steeper slopes on the leeward side.

**Sandbar** Long, narrow band of sand that forms an island offshore.

**Sandstone** A common sedimentary rock formed by the cementing of sand into a solid form.

**Santa Ana wind** A warm wind that blows down the mountain slopes in southern California.

**Saturation** The condition in which the water-vapor pressure is equal to the maximum vapor pressure that can occur at that temperature.

**Savanna** Tropical grassland with scattered trees, located between the tropical rainforest and low-latitude steppes.

**Scale** Relationship between distance measured on the earth and that shown on a map.

**Scouring** A mechanism of erosion by which particles carried in ice and water abrade the underlying rock.

**Sea arch** An arch formed by wave action when sea caves on opposite sides of a headland unite.

**Sea breeze** A wind blowing from the water during the afternoon in coastal regions.

**Sea level pressure** Atmospheric pressure at sea level.

**Sea stack** A small rocky island or pillar formed by wave erosion and separated from the coast.

**Seafloor spreading** Extrusion of molten material at oceanic ridges, creating new crust, combined with the lateral motion of the seafloor away from the ridges.

**Seamount** A volcanic mountain in an ocean basin not associated with the mid-ocean ridge or zone of subduction.

**Secant** A line that cuts another, especially a straight line cutting a curve in two or more points.

**Second order relief** Global relief features on the continents and ocean basins, such as mountain ranges, ocean ridges and trenches, and interior plains.

**Secondary circulation** Daily pressure and wind systems that control weather, such as cyclonic storms, tropical easterly waves, and tropical hurricanes.

**Sedimentary rock** A rock formed by sediments that have been transported, deposited, and solidified.

**Seismic sea waves** Sea waves of massive dimensions created by submarine earthquakes or volcanic eruptions.

**Semiarid region** A transition zone between humid and arid regions in either the tropics or the middle latitudes.

**Sensible temperature** Temperature that the human body feels.

**Seventh approximation** The modern soil classification system developed by the U.S. Department of Agriculture.

**Sextant** An instrument for measuring angular distances, especially the altitude of the sun, which is necessary for determining latitude.

**Shield volcano** A broad, gently sloping volcano derived from fluid lavas.

**Sial** Rock types that form continental crusts, consisting primarily of compounds of silica and aluminum.

**Sill** A tabular intrusion of lava between parallel layers of rock strata.

**Sima** Rock constituting the oceanic crust, consisting predominantly of compounds of silicon and magnesium.

**Sinkhole** A pitlike depression in areas of karst topography, caused by solution of limestone or dolomite by underground drainage.

**Slip-off slope** Convex bank of a stream, opposite the cut bank, where alluvial sediments of sand and silt are deposited.

**Slump** Downward slipping of unconsolidated material moving as a unit along a sloping surface.

**Smog** A combination of chemical pollutants and particulate matter in the lower atmosphere.

**Soil** The upper layer or layers of the earth in which fine rock particles and organic material provide the basis for plant growth.

**Soil moisture** Water in soil that is available for absorption by plant roots.

**Soil profile** Organization of a soil into A-, B-, and C-horizons by vertical and horizontal movement of materials.

**Soil texture** Soil characteristic according to the size of particles in its mineral content.

**Solar constant** Rate at which solar radiation is received at the top of the earth's atmosphere in a unit area perpendicular to the sun's rays; approximately 1.94 langleys per minute per square centimeter.

**Solar radiation** Incoming energy received from the sun.

**Solifluction** Process by which wet soil moves down a slope in a series of distinct lobes.

**Solstice** June 21 and December 22, when the vertical rays of the midday sun strike the earth at 23½ degrees north and south, respectively; the farthest positions of the vertical rays from the equator.

**Solum** Soil generated by the pedogenic processes; the A- and B-horizons combined.

**Source region** A large area of land or water over which an air mass acquires uniform characteristics of temperature and humidity.

**Species** Subdivision of the plant and animal kingdoms below the genus category.

**Specific heat** The ratio of the heat absorbed by a unit mass of a substance to the resulting change in temperature.

**Spit** Accumulation of marine sediment that is attached to the shore at one or both ends.

**Spodosols** Soils in which the light-colored A-horizon is eluviated and leached and overlies a B-horizon that is illuviated and is colored by iron and aluminum compounds.

**Spreading center** Zone of diverging crustal plates where new crust is forming due to upwelling of molten lava.

**Squall line** A line of atmospheric turbulence, frequently associated with a rapidly advancing cold front.

**Standard time** Time based on zones of 15 degrees of longitude. The central meridian in each zone is taken as the basis for determining time within the entire zone.

**Stationary front** Frontal system in which tropical and polar air masses meet and remain stationary for a period of time.

**Steppe** Semiarid middle latitude grasslands; the grass is short and is concentrated in bunches.

**Storm tracks** The paths that cyclonic storms tend to follow in their passage from west to east.

**Strata** Distinct layers or beds of sedimentary rock.

**Stratification** Deposition of sediments in layers according to size and weight.
**Stratopause** The upper limits of the stratosphere; zone of separation with the mesophere.
**Stratosphere** The layer of the atmosphere immediately above the troposphere, lying between 20 to 100 kilometers (12 to 60 miles) in altitude, in which temperature increases with altitude due to concentration of ozone.
**Stratovolcano** A volcano formed by alternating layers of lava expelled from a vent.
**Stratus clouds** Low clouds that form a uniform gray covering from horizon to horizon.
**Stream order** The rank of a stream in a drainage basin. The smallest streams without tributaries are first order, streams with two first-order tributaries are second order, and so on.
**Striations** Grooves or scratches produced in bedrock as a response to rock fragments and boulders imbedded in a glacier.
**Structure** Nature, arrangement, and relationship of the bedrock layers of the earth.
**Subarctic climate** Climatic region lying between the humid continental and arctic climates, characterized by long, cold winters and short, warm summers.
**Subduction, zone of** Area of descent of the lithospheric plate into the earth's mantle, producing earthquakes and volcanoes.
**Sublimation** Conversion of a solid directly to a gas without passing through the liquid state, or vice versa.
**Submarine canyon** A valley that has been eroded into the continental shelf or continental slope.
**Submergent coast** A coastline that has been drowned, either by a rise in the level of the ocean or by subsidence of the land below sea level.
**Subpolar lows** East-west trending cells or belts of low pressure located at the poleward margins of the westerly wind belts.
**Subsequent stream** A stream with a course that has been changed by differential erosion.
**Subsoil** B-horizon of a soil profile.
**Subtropical highs** High pressure east-west trending cells or belts at 25 to 35 degrees north and south latitudes; source of the westerlies that flow poleward and the trade winds that flow equatorward.
**Succession** Progression of natural vegetation from one plant community to another until a final stage of equilibrium has been reached.
**Sunspot** A dark spot on the sun that is cool in contrast to the surrounding photosphere.
**Suntime** Time determined by the movement of the sun.
**Superimposed stream** A stream that originally flowed on rocks overlying older geologic structures and that has maintained its course and cut into the older rocks as uplift subsequently occurred.
**Surf zone** The area where the waves of the sea break upon the shore, as upon a sloping beach.
**Surface runoff** Precipitation that neither soaks into the ground nor evaporates back into the atmosphere.
**Surge** Temporary rapid advance of the margin of a glacier.
**Suspension** Earth particles that are mixed in the atmosphere or water due to turbulent movement.
**Swash** Water that flows up a beach after a wave breaks on the shore.
**Swell** Regular pattern of waves on the ocean, generally caused by prevailing winds.
**Syncline** A rock fold that dips downward toward its center.
**System** Any group of interacting processes and units that together form an organized whole: *open* systems receive energy and material from outside; *closed* systems do not.

**Taiga** Northern Hemisphere coniferous forest of the subarctic climatic region.
**Talus slope** An accumulation of rock debris caused by gravitational movement at the foot of a slope.
**Tarn** A small lake in a cirque.
**Tectonic processes** Processes that derive their energy from within the earth, such as earthquakes and volcanoes.
**Temperature gradient** The horizontal rate of change of temperature in any direction from a given point.
**Temperature inversion** An increase in temperature with height occurring in the troposphere, where temperature normally decreases with height.
**Terminal moraine** The end moraine, marking the farthest advance of the glacier.
**Thematic map** A map portraying a single element, such as temperature, precipitation, or landforms.
**Thermal gradient** The increase in temperature with depth in the earth's crust; it averages 1°C per 30 meters (1° to 2°F per 100 feet).
**Thermosphere** Highest layer of the atmosphere, extending from the mesopause to outer space.
**Third order relief** Small, observable relief features, such as a river terrace, hill, beach, or cliff.
**Thrust fault** Fault in which the hanging wall is above the fault plane; upward movement in relation to the footwall.
**Thunderstorm** Intense storm induced by vertical movement of a local air mass, characterized by thunder and lightning and a heavy downpour of short duration.
**Till plain** Unsorted glacial drift that is deposited beneath an ice sheet. The size of the material varies from clay particles to boulders.
**Tombolo** A deposit of sand by waves that connects an island to the mainland.
**Topographic map** Large-scale map showing physical and cultural features of the earth's surface.
**Tornado** A small, funnel-shaped destructive storm with wind velocities from 160 to 800 kilometers (100 to 500 miles) per hour, but with a diameter of only 100 to 500 meters (300 to 1,500 feet).
**Trade winds** Consistent northeasterly and southeasterly surface winds blowing equatorward from the subtropical highs toward the intertropical convergence zone.

**Transform faults** Faults that occur when seafloor spreading is transformed to strike-slip faulting by a series of fractures.

**Transpiration** Transfer of water vapor from the surface of green tissues in plants.

**Trellis drainage pattern** A system of streams in which nearly parallel tributaries occupy valleys in folded strata.

**Trench** A long depression in the seafloor produced by oceanic crustal bending during subduction.

**Tropic of Cancer** The parallel 23½ degrees north of the equator which is the northernmost distance that the sun's rays strike vertically in the Northern Hemisphere.

**Tropic of Capricorn** The parallel 23½ degrees south of the equator which is the southernmost distance that the sun's rays strike vertically in the Southern Hemisphere.

**Tropical cyclone** An intense storm in which wind velocity exceeds 120 kilometers (75 miles) per hour; known by different names throughout the world, such as *hurricane, typhoon,* and others.

**Tropopause** The level in the atmosphere between the troposphere and the stratosphere, where temperature ceases to decline with increase in altitude.

**Troposphere** The lowest layer of the atmosphere and the site of weather phenomena. It is characterized by a decrease in temperature with increasing altitude.

**True north** The direction from any point on earth to the North Pole.

**Tsunami** Ocean waves produced by submarine earthquakes or volcanic eruptions; they rise to great heights in shallow waters along coastal areas.

**Tundra** Vegetation of the high latitudes, consisting of grasses, low shrubs, mosses, and lichens.

**Turbidity current** The flow of a suspension of sand and silt down submarine slopes. It may be an erosional force sufficient to create submarine canyons.

**Turbulence** The state of violent agitation.

**Ultisols** Soils highly leached of their basic materials, found in warm, wet climates. In their A-horizons they normally have large quantities of iron and aluminum oxides and are poor in humus.

**Ultraviolet radiation** Electromagnetic radiation with a wavelength shorter than that of light but longer than X rays; range of wavelengths from 0.4 to 0.01 micron.

**Unconformity** A surface that represents a break in the rock record caused by erosion or no new deposition of materials.

**Unconsolidated sediment** Sediment in which the individual particles are not bound together by some cementing agent.

**Undertow** Water returning to the sea beneath the incoming waves or breakers.

**Uniformitarianism** The theory that the processes that shaped the landforms in the geologic past are essentially the same as those existing today.

**Upwelling** Upward movement of deep, cool ocean waters, replacing warmer surface water that has been carried away.

**Valley breeze** Air flow upslope from a valley toward the mountains during the day; also known as a *valley wind.*

**Valley glacier** A flow of glacial ice in a preexisting valley; also known as an *alpine glacier.*

**Valley train** Outwash material from a glacier that is confined to the valley floor.

**Vapor pressure** Pressure exerted by molecules of water vapor; used as a measure of the moisture content of the air.

**Vaporization** Change in the physical state from a liquid to a gaseous vapor; for example, water to steam.

**Varve** A sedimentary layer or layers deposited in a still body of water within a single year. Glacial varves often consist of a summer layer of coarse sediments and a winter layer of fine sediments.

**Ventifact** A rock fashioned by wind abrasion.

**Vernal equinox** Time when the sun is directly overhead at noon at the equator on March 21 or 22.

**Vertisols** Soils with poorly developed horizons due to alternate dry and wet periods.

**Volcanic dust theory** A climatic change theory that suggests that the injection of dust and ash into the atmosphere during periods of volcanic eruptions causes global cooling.

**Volcanic neck** Column composed of igneous rocks orginally found in the vents through which magma passed from a volcano.

**Vulcanism** The movement of molten magma, either within or at the surface of the earth's crust.

**Warm front** Forward edge of a relatively warmer air mass advancing upon a cooler, denser air mass.

**Warping** Broad and gentle uplift or settling that extends over a wide area.

**Water budget** Relationship between evapotranspiration, condensation, and water storage within the earth system.

**Water gap** Erosional gap in a ridge of resistant rock through which streams pass.

**Wave-built terrace** A submarine deposit of sediments that borders an abrasion platform and extends further seaward.

**Wave crest** The highest point on a wave.

**Wave-cut cliff** A cliff produced by the landward cutting of wave erosion.

**Wave height** Height of wave between crest and trough.

**Wave of oscillation** A wave in which there is no mass transport of water; the movement of the wave is circular.

**Wave of translation** A wave that produces a mass transport of water and material; often a breaking wave.

**Wave period** Time required for successive wave crests to pass a given point.

**Wave refraction** Change in direction of wave movement, caused by friction with the ocean bottom or shoreline.

**Wave trough** Lowest part of a wave lying between successive crests.

**Wavelength** Distance between successive crests or successive troughs of waves

**Weather** Atmospheric conditions at a given time and specific location.

**Weathering** Physical disintegration and chemical decomposition of rock at or near the surface.

**Westerlies** The prevailing eastward flow of air over land and water in the mid-latitudes of both hemispheres; often called the *prevailing westerlies.* They carry fronts and storms, providing variable weather conditions.

**Wind gap** A notch in a ridge, indicating the position of a former stream channel opposite to the ridge.

**Wind power** Power generated by moving air.

**Windward** Location on the side facing the prevailing wind movement.

**Winter solstice** Dates when the sun's rays are vertical at 23½ degrees north latitude (Tropic of Cancer) and 23½ degrees south latitude (Tropic of Capricorn): June 21–22 and December 21–22, respectively.

**Xerophyte** Vegetation that has genetically evolved so that it can withstand long periods of drought.

**Youthful stage** Initial stage in the cycle of erosion in the theory of landform development proposed by William Morris Davis; streams are in deeply incised valleys or canyons, and uplands are areas of low relief.

**Zenith** Point in the sky directly overhead.

**Zonal soil** Major soil order of the Russian-American classification system. The soils have well-developed horizons that are strongly influenced by climate and vegetation types.

# INDEX